Handbook of Cognition
and Emotion

Handbook of Cognition and Emotion

Edited by
Tim Dalgleish
MRC Cognition and Brain Sciences, Cambridge, UK
and
Mick J. Power
Department of Psychiatry, University of Edinburgh, UK

JOHN WILEY & SONS
Chichester · New York · Weinheim · Brisbane · Singapore · Toronto

Copyright © 1999 by John Wiley & Sons Ltd,
Baffins Lane, Chichester,
West Sussex PO19 IUD, England

National   01243 779777
International   (+44) 1243 779777
e-mail (for orders and customer service enquiries): cs-books@wiley.co.uk
Visit our Home Page on http://www.wiley.co.uk
or http://www.wiley.com

Reprinted December 1999, November 2000

Other Wiley Editorial Offices

John Wiley & Sons, Inc., 605 Third Avenue,
New York, NY 10158-0012, USA

WILEY-VCH Verlag GmbH, Pappelallee 3,
D-69469 Weinheim, Germany

Jacaranda Wiley Ltd, 33 Park Road, Milton,
Queensland 4064, Australia

John Wiley & Sons (Asia) Pte Ltd, 2 Clementi Loop #02-01,
Jin Xing Distripark, Singapore 129809

John Wiley & Sons (Canada) Ltd, 22 Worcester Road,
Rexdale, Ontario M9W IL1, Canada

British Library Cataloguing in Publication Data

A catalogue record for this book is available from the British Library

ISBN 0-471-97836-1

Typeset in 10/12 pt Times by Best-set Typesetter Ltd., Hong Kong
Printed and bound in Great Britain by Bookcraft (Bath) Ltd, Midsomer Norton, Somerset
This book is printed on acid-free paper responsibly manufactured from sustainable forestry,
in which at least two trees are planted for each one used for paper production.

Contents

About the Editors   ix

List of Contributors   xi

Foreword—Keith Oatley   xvii

Preface   xix

PART I   **GENERAL ASPECTS**

Chapter 1   The cognition–emotion debate: a bit of history
Richard S. Lazarus   3

Chapter 2   The philosophy of cognition and emotion
William Lyons   21

Chapter 3   Basic emotions
Paul Ekman   45

Chapter 4   Research methods in cognition and emotion
W. Gerrod Parrott and Paula Hertel   61

Chapter 5   Cognition, emotion, conscious experience
and the brain
Jeffrey A. Gray   83

Chapter 6   Neuropsychological perspectives on affective styles
and their cognitive consequences
Richard J. Davidson   103

Chapter 7   The role of the self in cognition and emotion
Michael Lewis   125

PART II   **COGNITIVE PROCESSES**

Chapter 8   Selective attention and anxiety: a cognitive–motivational
                   perspective
                   Karin Mogg and Brendan P. Bradley   145

Chapter 9   The cognitive science of attention and emotion
                   Gerald Matthews and Adrian Wells   171

Chapter 10   Mood and memory
                   Henry C. Ellis and Brent A. Moore   193

Chapter 11   Organization of emotional memories
                   Sven-Åke Christianson and Elisabeth Engelberg   211

Chapter 12   Autobiographical memory
                   Helen Healy and J. Mark G. Williams   229

Chapter 13   Inhibition processes in cognition and emotion:
                   a special case
                   Tim Dalgleish, Andrew Mathews and Jacqueline Wood   243

Chapter 14   Prospective cognitions
                   Andrew K. MacLeod   267

Chapter 15   Unintended thoughts and images
                   Frank Tallis   281

Chapter 16   Facial expressions
                   Paul Ekman   301

Chapter 17   Distinguishing unconscious from conscious emotional
                   processes: methodological considerations and
                   theoretical implications
                   Arne Öhman   321

Chapter 18   Self-regulation, affect and psychosis: the role of social
                   cognition in paranoia and mania
                   Richard P. Bentall and Peter Kinderman   353

Chapter 19   The early emergence of emotional understanding and
                   appraisal: implications for theories of development
                   Nancy L. Stein and Linda J. Levine   383

PART III   **EMOTIONS**

Chapter 20   Anger
                   Leonard Berkowitz   411

Chapter 21   Disgust: the body and soul emotion
                   Paul Rozin, Jonathan Haidt and Clark R. McCauley   429

Chapter 22   Anxiety and anxiety disorders
              Colin MacLeod   447

Chapter 23   Panic and phobias
              Richard J. McNally   479

Chapter 24   Sadness and its disorders
              Mick J. Power   497

Chapter 25   Positive affect
              Alice M. Isen   521

Chapter 26   The self-conscious emotions: shame, guilt,
              embarrassment and pride
              June Price Tangney   541

Chapter 27   Jealousy and envy
              Martin P. East and Fraser N. Watts   569

PART IV   **THEORIES IN COGNITION AND EMOTION**

Chapter 28   Network theories and beyond
              Joseph P. Forgas   591

Chapter 29   Attributional theories of emotion
              Ian H. Gotlib and Lynn Y. Abramson   613

Chapter 30   Appraisal theory
              Klaus R. Scherer   637

Chapter 31   Multi-level theories of cognition–emotion relations
              John D. Teasdale   665

Chapter 32   Self-organization of cognition–emotion interactions
              Marc D. Lewis and Isabela Granic   683

PART V   **APPLIED ISSUES**

Chapter 33   Cognition and emotion research and the practice of
              cognitive–behavioural therapy
              Zindel V. Segal, Mark A. Lau and Paul D. Rokke   705

Chapter 34   Psychodynamic theory and technique in relation to
              research on cognition and emotion: mutual implications
              Drew Westen   727

Chapter 35   Mechanisms of change in exposure therapy for anxiety
              disorders
              Susan Mineka and Cannon Thomas   747

Chapter 36   Creativity in the domain of emotion
              James R. Averill   765

Chapter 37   Forensic applications of theories of cognition and
                emotion
                Debra A. Bekerian and Susan J. Goodrich   783

Chapter 38   Cognition and emotion: future directions
                Tim Dalgleish and Mick J. Power   799

Author index   807

Subject index   831

About the Editors

Tim Dalgleish is a Research Scientist at the MRC Cognition and Brain Sciences Unit in Cambridge, UK and a practising Clinical Psychologist at Addenbrooke's Hospital, Cambridge. He carried out his doctoral thesis at the Institute of Psychiatry in London and also completed his clinical training there, before moving to Cambridge. His research interests include psychological reactions to trauma and cognition–emotion relations in emotional disorders in general. He has co-authored a book, *Cognition and Emotion: From Order to Disorder*, with Mick Power.

Mick J. Power is currently Professor of Clinical Psychology at the University of Edinburgh and a practising clinical psychologist in the Royal Edinburgh Hospital. In the past he has been a Senior Lecturer at the University of London and has worked as a clinical psychologist at Guy's Hospital, and the Bethlem and Maudsley Hospitals. He has worked for the Medical Research Council and currently acts as a Research Advisor to the World Health Organization. He has carried out research on emotion and on emotional disorders for many years and is the co-author, with Tim Dalgleish, of *Cognition and Emotion: From Order to Disorder*.

Contributors

Lynn Y. Abramson, *Department of Psychology, University of Wisconsin-Madison, 1202 W. Johnson Street, Madison, WI 53706, USA*

James R. Averill, *Department of Psychology, University of Massachusetts at Amherst, Tobin Hall, Amherst, MA 01003, USA*

Debra A. Bekerian, *Department of Psychology, University of East London, Romford Road, London E15 4LZ, UK*

Richard P. Bentall, *Department of Clinical Psychology, University of Liverpool, Ground Floor, The Whelan Building, Liverpool L69 3BX, UK*

Leonard Berkowitz, *Department of Psychology, University of Wisconsin-Madison, 1202 W. Johnson Street, Madison, WI 53706, USA*

Brendan P. Bradley, *Department of Experimental Psychology, Downing Street, Cambridge CB2 3EB, UK*

Sven-Åke Christianson, *Department of Psychology, University of Stockholm, S-106 91 Stockholm, Sweden*

Tim Dalgleish, *MRC Applied Psychology Unit, 15 Chaucer Road, Cambridge CB2 2EF, UK*

Richard J. Davidson, *Department of Psychology, University of Wisconsin-Madison, 1202 W. Johnson Street, Madison, WI 53706, USA*

Martin P. East, *Department of Experimental Psychology, University of Cambridge, Downing Street, Cambridge CB2 3EB, UK*

Paul Ekman, *Human Interaction Laboratory, University of California at San Francisco, School of Medicine, Psychiatry Department, Langley Porter Institute, 401 Parnassus Avenue, Box HIL, San Francisco, CA 94143-0984, USA*

Henry C. Ellis, *University of New Mexico, Department of Psychology, Albuquerque, NM 87131-0001, USA*

Elisabeth Engelberg, *Department of Psychology, University of Stockholm, S-106 91 Stockholm, Sweden*

Joseph P. Forgas, *Professor of Psychology, School of Psychology, University of New South Wales, Sydney 2052, Australia*

Susan J. Goodrich, *Department of Psychology, University of East London, Romford Road, London, E15 4LZ, UK*

Ian H. Gotlib, *Department of Psychology, Building 420, Jordan Hall, Stanford University, Stanford, CA 94305, USA*

Isabela Granic, *Centre for Applied Cognitive Science, OISE, 252 Bloor Street W., Toronto, Ontario M5S IV6, Canada*

Jeffrey A. Gray, *Professor of Psychology, Department of Psychology, Institute of Psychiatry, De Crespigny Park, London SE5 8AF, UK*

Jonathan Haidt, Assistant Professor of Psychology, Giler Hall, University of *Virginia, Charlottesville, VA 22901, USA*

Helen Healy, *School of Psychology, University of Wales, Bangor LL57 2DG, UK*

Paula Hertel, *Department of Psychology, Trinity University, 715 Stadium Drive, San Antonio, TX 78284-0001, USA*

Alice M. Isen, *Johnson Graduate School of Management, Cornell University, Ithaca, New York 14853, USA*

Peter Kinderman, *School of Psychiatry and Behavioural Sciences, University of Manchester, Rawnsley Building, Oxford Road, Manchester M13 9LW, UK*

Richard S. Lazarus, *Professor Emeritus, 1824 Stanley Dollar Drive, Walnut Creek, California 94595, USA*

Linda J. Levine, *Department of Psychology and Social Behaviour, School of Social Ecology, 3340 Social Ecology II, Irvine, CA 92697-7085, USA*

Marc D. Lewis, *Centre for Applied Cognitive Science, OISE, 252 Bloor Street W., Toronto, Ontario M5S IV6, Canada*

Michael Lewis, *Institute for the Study of Child Development, Robert Wood Johnson Medical School, University of Medicine and Dentistry, 97 Paterson Street, CN19, New Brunswick, NJ 08903, USA*

William Lyons, *Professor of Moral Philosophy, Department of Philosophy, Trinity College, Dublin 2, Ireland*

Andrew MacLeod, *Royal Holloway College, University of London, Egham, Surrey TW20 0EX, UK*

Colin MacLeod, *Department of Psychology, University of Western Australia, Perth, WA, Australia*

Andrew Mathews, *MRC Cognition and Brain Sciences Unit, 15 Chaucer Road, Cambridge CB2 2EF, UK*

Gerald Matthews, *Department of Psychology, University of Dundee, Dundee DD1 4HN, UK*

Clark R. McCauley, *Professor of Psychology, Dalton Hall, Bryn Mawr College, Bryn Mawr, PA 19010, USA*

Richard J. McNally, *Department of Psychology, Harvard University, 33 Kirkland Street, Cambridge, MA 02138, USA*

Susan Mineka, *Department of Psychology, Northwestern University, Evanston, IL 60208, USA*

Karin Mogg, *Department of Experimental Psychology, Downing Street, Cambridge CB2 3EB, UK*

Brent A. Moore, *University of New Mexico, Department of Psychology, Albuquerque, NM, 87131-0001, USA*

Arne Öhman, *Department of Clinical Neuroscience and Psychiatry, Karolinska Hospital, S-17176 Stockholm, Sweden*

Gerrod Parrot, *Department of Psychology, Georgetown University, Box 571001,Washington, DC 20057-1001, USA*

Mick J. Power, *Department of Psychiatry, University of Edinburgh, Kennedy Tower, Royal Edinburgh Hospital, Morningside Park, Edinburgh, UK*

Paul D. Rokke, *Department of Psychology, North Dakota State University, Fargo, ND 58105-5075, USA*

Paul Rozin, *Department of Psychology, University of Pennsylvania, 3815 Walnut Street, Philadelphia, PA 19104-3604, USA*

Klaus R. Scherer, *Section of Psychology, University of Geneva, 9 Rte de Drize, CH-1227 Carouge-Geneva, Switzerland*

Zindel V. Segal, *Clarke Institute of Psychiatry, University of Toronto, 250 College Street, Toronto, Ontario MST IR8, Canada*

Nancy L. Stein, *Department of Psychology, University of Chicago, 5848 University Avenue, Chicago, IL 60637, USA*

Frank Tallis, *Edward House, 7 Lisson Grove, Charter Nightingale Hospital, London NW1 6SH, UK*

June Price Tangney, *Associate Professor of Psychology, George Mason University, Mail Step 3F5, Fairfax, Virginia 220030-4444, USA*

John D. Teasdale, *MRC Cognition and Brain Sciences Unit, 15 Chaucer Road, Cambridge CB2 2EF, UK*

Cannon Thomas, *Department of Psychology, University of Virginia, 102 Gilmer Hall, Charlottesville, VA 22906, USA*

Fraser N. Watts, *Queens College, University of Cambridge, Cambridge CB3 9ET, UK*

Adrian Wells, *Clinical Psychology Department, Rawnsley Building, Manchester Royal Infirmary, Oxford Road, Manchester M13 9WL, UK*

Drew Westen, *Department of Psychiatry, Cambridge Hospital, Harvard Medical School, 1493 Cambridge Street, Cambridge, MA 02139, USA*

J. Mark G. Williams, *School of Psychology, University of Wales, Bangor LL57 2DG, UK*

Jacqueline Wood, *MRC Cognition and Brain Sciences Unit, 15 Chaucer Road, Cambridge CB2 2EF, UK*

Foreword

Keith Oatley

Cognition and emotion—this phrase connects two concepts, but it is ambiguous. For some people it means the cognitive approach to emotion. For others it means the joining of two domains, cognition and affect, that were previously thought to be disparate. Understandings of cognition and emotion, under both meanings of the phrase, now occupy a prominent place in psychology and psychiatry, and this useful book is a result.

In their excellent textbook, *Cognition and Emotion: From Order to Disorder*, Mick Power and Tim Dalgleish offered, for the first time, a cognitive treatment that was systematically applied all the way from normal emotions through to emotional disorders. Fresh from that success, Dalgleish and Power have now assembled this impressive handbook which, again, is a first. With a transparent organization, it offers a broad coverage of cognition and emotion by a set of distinguished contributors, many of whom have been instrumental in establishing the field.

Books such as this are important in any science: they mark the phase in which enough is understood to define a field. Research on emotion generally has progressed from a state in which there were scattered publications, infrequent conferences and occasional edited books, to one in which there are journals devoted to emotions, an international society, textbooks, and handbooks such as this one.

After a lull during the first half of the century after it came to be dominated, at least in America, by the theory of William James and by opposition to it from his son-in-law Walter Cannon, research on emotion branched into new directions. In 1951, John Bowlby published his first book on attachment, the theory of which came to be based on the cognitive idea of mental models. From that time, emotions and their functions came to be of interest to developmental psychologists. Emotional development, which turns out also to be social development, has now achieved an importance at least equal to intellectual development. In this volume, developmental research—with a cognitive emphasis—is represented in a chapter by Michael Lewis, and one by Nancy Stein and Linda Levine.

At almost the same time, in 1954, Sylvan Tomkins began his work on emotion. He, too, had cognitive interests. Inspired by his new approach, there was a renewal of research on facial expression and restatements of the idea of a small number of basic emotions, each with distinctive cognitive and experiential properties. Here, this line of research is represented in two chapters by Paul Ekman. Also in 1954, Magda Arnold began developing her approach to appraisal of events as the principal means by which emotions are elicited. Appraisal has come to be central to almost all cognitive theories of emotion—discussions in this book are offered by Richard Lazarus and by Klaus Scherer. By now, a distinctive family of cognitive theories of emotion has grown up (see Part IV of this book).

The field of cognition and emotion is important in psychology and psychiatry, because it has finally established emotion as essential to the understanding of mind. A current cognitive conception, for which there is a broad consensus, is that emotions are central to mental and social life because they are our fundamental mediators between inner and outer worlds. They relate what is personally important (goals, concerns, aspirations) to the world (events, people, things). If we humans merely worked from what was important to us, we would be bundles of drives and species-typical action patterns. If we merely responded to events, we would be reflex machines. Instead, because of mediation by emotions, some aspects of our lives are given meaningful urgency, some people we know become uniquely important, and our many goals are prioritized.

From cognitive reformulations of psychology of the 1960s and 1970s, emotions were at first excluded, perhaps because they seemed too amorphous. Now, however, a growing understanding of effects of emotions on memory, reasoning, and attention (see Part II) and cognitive analyses of the elicitation and functions of specific emotions (see Part III) have established the field.

Understanding emotions has distinctive areas of application, notably the psychological therapies. These are modern descendents of those pioneered by the Hellenistic ethical philosophers, the Epicureans and Stoics, who were the first in the West to study systematically the relations between cognition and emotion, as ways of understanding their implications for self and society, and among the first to show how unwanted passions might be controlled. Such applications are represented in Part V.

This book shows how research on emotions has thrived in the social sciences and in philosophy in recent years. It demonstrates how our understanding of emotions has been influenced by cognitive approaches and, if we take cognition and emotion as separable domains, it shows also how fundamentally important these domains are in their influence on each other.

Keith Oatley is Professor of Psychology in the Centre for Applied Cognitive Science, Ontario Institute for Studies in Education, University of Toronto.

Preface

Any historical analysis of the evolution of ideas about emotions, both in philosophy and more recently in psychology, shows us that the publication of a *Handbook of Cognition and Emotion*, implying as it does a productive marriage between the two research areas in its title, is something of an achievement. Cognition and emotion have by no means always been such comfortable bedfellows. The Platonic notion, as outlined in the *Republic,* that feelings were the enemy of reason and that true "citizens" would do all they could to banish emotion from their day-to-day "cognitive" decisions, has had far-reaching implications for the way Western society has dealt with the subtleties and vagaries of emotional life, and has dominated psychological and philosophical thinking until relatively recently.

Perhaps outside of the discussion and exchange of ideas in the academic and clinical traditions, this Platonic view of emotions prevails. There is clearly a degree of folk psychological suspicion of emotions and what they can do, with relatively little emphasis on how useful or functional they might be. However, within psychology and philosophy, there has been a sea change in our approach to emotions over the last 50 years. The Aristotelian view that cognition is an integral part of emotion, an approach that has faired so badly for two millennia, is now probably the dominant paradigm. Furthermore, the perhaps more radical suggestion that emotions are integral to adaptive cognitive processing, as evidenced by recent work in neuropsychology, is enticing many cognitive psychologists to take a closer look at the issue of cognition–emotion interactions. Many of these changes have of course gone hand-in-hand with the subtle shaping and extension of what we mean when we use terms like "cognition" or "emotion"; for example, few now think of cognition solely in terms of conscious, rational information handling. However, debates concerning such semantic controversies have evolved into highly productive discussions about the nature of cognition–emotion interactions, regardless of whether we can all agree on what to label them.

There are many such debates in cognition and emotion, some heated; in putting together this volume we have endeavoured not to take any stances, methodological or theoretical, as to its contents. As Fraser Watts noted in his editorial to the first issue of *Cognition and Emotion* in 1987, which addressed the nature of the area and the policy of the new journal:

> There may come a time when there is a consensus on how to frame the questions and how to seek answers to them, but that time has not yet come. Until it does, the prudent policy for a journal is to be catholic and to publish good work of all kinds.

A lot has happened in cognition and emotion since 1987: Fraser, for example, is now a lecturer in theology![1] Nevertheless, his words still apply, there remains little consensus in the area about the exact questions that need answering or indeed how to answer them. However, as in much of psychology, there is increasing acceptance that the pursuit of such consensus may be a red herring. What we need to do is approach the same broad issues from a multiplicity of directions: from neuroscience, from a developmental perspective, from the socio-cultural domain, from philosophy, in the clinic, and in the experimental psychology laboratory. If anything, it may be that emotions are the perfect test case for such multiple levels of analysis and integration because they do not fit readily into any one approach. Indeed, this reason may be why emotions have proved so compelling a research focus for some of us, but have at the same time been so readily overlooked by the mainstream research community.

Our first aim, then, in putting together the *Handbook of Cognition and Emotion*, was to try to gather together for the first time in one volume contributions from the leading researchers in the field, across the range of theoretical perspectives and methodologies. We are not suggesting that we have succeeded in sampling the whole gamut of cognition and emotion research. There are inevitably some gaps but, nevertheless, the diversity of content in the 38 chapters represents most theoretical and empirical persuasions within the area.

Our second aim was to try to provide a balance across a number of dichotomies in the literature; in particular, work on "normal" emotional experiences and research on emotional disorders, on pure theory and empirical data, and on relatively more abstruse as well as more applied issues. It is to the credit of all of the contributors that the volume delivers the variety and depth that we were hoping for.

Finally, we would like to acknowledge some of those whose patience and wisdom have been significant in the development of the project. In particular, Michael Coombs, Wendy Hudlass and Lesley Valerio at Wiley, the Cognition

---

[1] Although we are pleased that he came out of retirement to co-author something for this volume; see Chapter 27.

and Emotion Research Group at the Cognition and Brain Sciences Unit in Cambridge, especially John Teasdale, Andrew Mathews, Phil Barnard and Jenny Yiend, our secretarial support, Jane Bartolozzi, and not least our partners, Lorna Champion and Nicola Morant, for their patience and support as we grappled with the delights of book editing!

Tim Dalgleish
Mick Power
Cambridge and Edinburgh, March 1998

Part I

General Aspects

Chapter 1

The Cognition–Emotion Debate: A Bit of History

Richard S. Lazarus
University of California, Berkeley, CA, USA

The purpose of this essay is not to renew the cognition–emotion debate, but to interpret it in the context of history and my emotion theory. I shall be cool yet partisan in my analysis.

The role of cognition in emotion has long been the subject of intense psychological interest and controversy. Somewhat less attention has been given to the role of cognition in motivation, an issue that covers much the same ground. This was the topic of a much earlier volume edited by Bernard Weiner (1974), based on a conference at which a number of cognitivists presented papers, including me (Lazarus, 1974). Tetlock & Levi (1982) later noted the similarity of the two issues and expressed doubts about the conclusiveness of what has been and, indeed, can be said about these functional relationships.

We need to recognize that to speak of a relationship implies the independent identities of three concepts of mind—namely, cognition, emotion and motivation, which are more or less fictions of scientific analysis, whose independence doesn't truly exist in nature. Thus, in my monograph on emotion and adaptation (Lazarus, 1991a), I referred to the theory I presented as cognitive, motivational and relational to emphasize that emotion does not occur in the absence of meaning, which an individual constructs out of an ongoing person–environment relationship, and a goal that creates a stake in that relationship. To do justice to the broader issues inherent in the nature of adaptation, the debate must be broadened considerably and contribute to a theory of mind.

Handbook of Cognition and Emotion. Edited by T. Dalgleish and M. Power.
© 1999 John Wiley & Sons Ltd.

CLASSICAL ORIGINS OF THE DEBATE

From a historical perspective, speculation about these three psychological functions is part of a philosophical tradition of the Ancient Greeks and Romans. Bolles (1974) has made the stunning claim that psychology has always emphasized the cognitive mediation of emotion and motivation. He wrote, for example (1974, p. 14), that:

> Originally, before psychology became an autonomous discipline [when, in the 1940s, it finally split off from philosophy in the university], cognitive views of man prevailed. The early philosophers as well as the man of letters and the thoughtful layman all stressed man's rationality and explained his behavior in terms of ideas, perceptions and other intellectual activities. Then psychologists suffered that curious passion to be scientific. Thinking was merely a physical process going on in the brain; perception was merely the result of certain neural inputs; man was reduced to a mass of S–R connections; and behavior was explained by a vast matrix containing nothing but S–R units. This was an appealingly simple system but it was soon found to be inadequate even for the explanation of animal behavior.

In effect, academic psychology in the USA after the 1960s and 1970s was beginning to abandon radical behaviorism and logical positivism. Seen from the perspective of the long history of cognitivism, behaviorism was a historical aberration whose guiding epistemological force was greatly weakened, if not lost, when psychology returned some decades later to its original cognitivist tradition in what has been called, in a fit of over-sanguinity, "the cognitive revolution".

When the history of behaviorism is recounted, we tend to forget that this movement was strong mainly in academic rather than applied circles, and by no means universal, even in academe. We tend to ignore the extensive influence of a number of outstanding cognitivists, many of whom could also be called phenomenologists, such as Lewin (1935), Murray (1938) and Tolman (1932), and a later group that includes, among others, Asch (1952), Harlow (1953), Heider (1958), Kelly (1955), McClelland (1951), Murphy (1947), Rotter (1954) and White (1959). We should include Freud and other psychoanalytic writers of the day, especially the ego psychologists, as having given substantial attention to cognition as the executive of the mind.

Some of these theorists, such as Harlow, McClelland and White, contributed to the demise of the simple drive concept by adding cognitive drives or, later on, by showing that goals involve directional or cognitive underpinnings as well as energetic ones. Bolles (1974) views Tolman—a deviant from the behaviorist–mechanist scientific oversimplification—as an early father of the value-expectancy approach to human motivation and action, which now dominates the treatment of motivation in social science circles, and which he considers to be the basic framework for all modern cognitive models of behavior. Nor should we forget the "New Look" movement in the late 1940s and 1950s, which gave perception a more cognitive and phenomenological look, emphasizing as it did individual differences and the role of motives and ego-defenses in the way we perceive the world.

Other theorists, such as Schachter (1966) and Mandler (1984) sought to preserve the behaviorist concept of drive while giving more importance than previously to the role of cognition in emotion. The Zeitgeist in recent years seems to have favored abandonment of the drive concept, which seems too close to tissue tension or arousal, in favor of an emphasis on·goals, which are directed by and suffused with thought. I view these two-factor theories as a cautious step—a delay *en route*—on the way to a strong and affirmative cognitive position.

It is remarkable that psychology regards the emphasis on cognition as modern when, in reality, Plato was a cognitivist, and so was Aristotle. The ecclesiastical philosophers of the medieval Catholic Church, such as Thomas Aquinas, who drew heavily on Aristotle, also emphasized what we call today "cognitive mediation". However, the Church was mainly preoccupied with helping people make moral choices in which animal instincts would be subordinated to reason and controlled by acts of will (or will-power).

The cognition–emotion and cognition–motivation debates were necessitated by the ancient Greek tendency to separate—indeed, to put it more strongly, to presume the inevitability of conflict between—desire, reason and passion. This idea of separation and conflict created the modern need in philosophy and psychology to specify the functional relationships between what are now called cognition, motivation and emotion.

Plato (1961) appears to be the first to have divided the soul (or mind) into these three different parts or functions. This tripartite formula has dominated psychology ever since. For Plato, each operates as a kind of homunculus, guiding human choices in action and feeling. He regarded reason as the highest of the three functions, and as the moral agency holding destructive animal passions in check.

I note in passing that conflict, and the concern of classical writers and the medieval Church about the role of reason in the control of the passions, implicate the concept of *coping* in the emotion process. Space limitations prevent me from discussing coping here. Suffice it to say, however, that it is an integral feature of emotion. It, and the thoughts on which it rests, appears in all stages of the emotion process and depends on both cognition and motivation. Coping has been under-emphasized in most emotion theories.

Anyway, all is not conflict, however, which becomes clear in Aristotle's treatment of the functions of mind. For Aristotle, emotion and action were said to depend on reason. In "Rhetoric" (1941, p. 1380), he wrote: "Anger may be defined as a belief that we, or our friends, have been unfairly slighted, which causes in us both painful feelings and a desire or impulse for revenge". He was, in effect, saying that anger is the result of particular thoughts (cognitive causation) which, in turn, motivate aggressive actions.

Even before Christianity, Roman scholars adopted and expanded on many of Plato's and Aristotle's views, and of these, Seneca stands out most clearly. During the cognition–emotion debate of the 1980s, the readership of the *American Psychologist* was treated to an informative comment by Hans Toch (1969, 1983) about Seneca's views on anger and violence. Long concerned with violence and its control, and as part of the cognition–emotion debate, Toch (1969) wrote a brief but useful account of Seneca's approach to anger, which was as cognitive as it could be. For Seneca, the instigation to violence is a perceived injury, hurt or affront (I would use the word "appraised", which is more evaluative than a cold perception).

Thus, as Aristotle opined, although reason must control emotion, the arousal of an emotion also depends on reason. Like Aristotle, Seneca also drew on the concept of motivation, writing that the goal of anger is usually retribution for an injury. However, he distinguished between the desire to avenge an injury and sadistic aggression, in which cruel people delight in the suffering of others. He believed that the proneness to react with anger and violence was the result of a vulnerable self-esteem, which disposes a person to feel hurt. In this respect, Seneca anticipated the modern personality-centered concern with individual differences. (Although they deal with aggression rather than anger, for a somewhat different view about the role of self-esteem, see Baumeister, Smart & Boden, 1996.)

Seneca also focused attention on efforts to inhibit the urge to retaliate in anger, and viewed this as the most promising way to control the runaway feelings leading to angry violence. The interventions Seneca suggested mounting against the tendency to react with anger and violence, writes Toch, can be viewed as versions of the modern concept of cognitive restructuring. They consist of efforts to persuade violence-prone persons to abandon their aggressive actions, and enjoinders to hold themselves above the foolishness inherent in an angry attack.

One should not assume from this brief history that cognitive approaches to motivation and emotion are to be found only in classical thinking and the medieval Church, or that in the nineteenth century the dominant cognitive–mediational outlook had waned. For example, in Lazarus (1991a), I quoted a Rashomon-like statement by Robertson, a late nineteenth century British philosopher at University College London, which shows the continuing prominence of the cognitive outlook. Notice in the quote below (Robertson, 1877, p. 413) the use of the concepts of motivation and emotion, and the emphasis on individual differences and physiological arousal:

> Four persons of much the same age and temperament are travelling in the same vehicle. At a particular stopping-place it is intimated to them that a certain person has just died suddenly and unexpectedly. One of the company looks perfectly stolid. A second comprehends what has taken place, but is in no way affected. The third looks and evidently feels sad. The fourth is overwhelmed with grief, which finds expression in tears, sobs, and exclamations. Whence the difference of the four individuals before us? In one respect they are all alike: an announcement has been made to them. The first is a foreigner, and has not understood the communication. The second has never met with the deceased, and could have no special regard for

him. The third had often met with him in social intercourse and business transactions, and been led to cherish a great esteem for him. The fourth was the brother of the departed, and was bound to him by native affection and a thousand ties earlier and later. From such a case we may notice that [in order to experience an emotion] there is need first of some understanding or apprehension; the foreigner had no feeling because he had no idea or belief. We may observe further that there must secondly be an affection of some kind; for the stranger was not interested in the occurrence. The emotion flows forth from a well, and is strong in proportion to the waters; is stronger in the brother than in the friend. It is evident, thirdly, that the persons affected are in a moved or excited state. A fourth peculiarity has appeared in the sadness of the countenance and the agitations of the bodily frame. Four elements have thus come forth to view.

ISSUES RAISED BY THE 1980S DEBATE

The modern argument about cognition and emotion began with an article by Zajonc (1980) in the *American Psychologist* about feeling and thinking, which was delivered on the occasion of his Distinguished Scientific Contribution Award from the American Psychological Association. In it he took exception to contemporary treatments of affect as post-cognitive, maintaining that a considerable number of experimental findings on preferences, attitudes, impression formation and decision making, strongly suggest "that affective judgments may be fairly independent of, and precede in time, the sorts of perceptual and cognitive operations commonly assumed to be the basis of these affective judgments" (1980, p. 151).

Two key issues are expressed in Zajonc's quoted summary of his position. First, emotion (Zajonc speaks of affect) can, to some extent, be independent of thought; and second, emotion can precede thought. Following Zajonc's article, there ensued a remarkable series of comments and articles over the next 6 years, including my rebuttal (Lazarus, 1982). They were remarkable because of their verve, thoughtfulness, diversity and number. Zajonc had touched a nerve and uncovered an unresolved set of modern issues that apparently had lain dormant in the minds of many psychologists.

The list of contributions to this debate, ordered by date, is as follows: Zajonc (1980), Baars (1981), Slife (1981), Lazarus (1982), Zajonc (1984), Lazarus (1984), Ellis (1985), Kleinginna & Kleinginna (1985), Scheff (1985) and Leventhal & Scherer (1987). Although seemingly not directly motivated by the debate, the list should include a relevant article by LeDoux (1986), who focused on the neurophysiology of cognition and emotion, and a comment about it by me (Lazarus, 1986) in the same journal issue. The chapters of an edited book by Bearison & Zimiles (1986), which address the relationship from the standpoint of development, should also be added to the list.

Rather than discussing the points made in each comment or article sequentially, the best tack is to center discussion of the substance of the debate on what seem to me to be the most important issues. I shall first address the issue— or non-issue, as I would prefer to say—of primacy, then discuss the problem of definitions of emotion and cognition, and finally, the role of metatheory in how the earlier-stated issues are cast.

The Primacy of Emotion or Cognition

After the smoke had settled I could see that there were many mistakes in the way some of the issues had originally been cast, for example, primacy. So, in an article based on my own American Psychological Association Distinguished Scientific Contribution Award address (Lazarus, 1991b), I tried to clarify some of the misstated and misunderstood points.

For example, in our 1984 interchanges (Zajonc, 1984; Lazarus, 1984), it might have been clever for each of us to entitle our articles, respectively, "The Primacy of Affect" and "The Primacy of Cognition". As one might say, however, too clever by half! Many readers were misled by this language about whether we meant by primacy the relative importance of emotion and cognition or which came first. I certainly didn't mean the former and, as you will see below, not the latter either; the question of which is temporally first is an epistemological error.

I tried to overcome this confusion about primacy by denying that either emotion or cognition was more important, or for that matter, that motivation was any less important than either of the other two functions. I emphasized the position that emotion could not occur without *both* cognition and motivation. Emotion is always a response to meaning, which includes the implications of a transaction for one's personal goals, regardless of how that meaning was achieved. And in creating meaning out of the person–environment relationship, personal motives play a fundamental role, since without a goal at stake there would be no emotion. I also argued that, although thought can occur without significant emotion, the opposite is not true—that is, emotion is never completely divorced from meaning.

Does this suggest that cognition always comes first in the cognition–emotion relationship? Not at all. Part of the confusion about this is metatheoretical. In accordance with the principle of reciprocal causality (e.g. Bandura, 1978), which applies to a systems view of emotion and adaptation, mental states and behavior occur in a continuous flow. Depending on where one begins one's entry into the flow, which is arbitrary, any response can also be a stimulus, but not at the same instant (see also Lazarus, 1991a). In a comment after the Zajonc article, Scheff (1985) made a similar point. Slife (1981) also adopted this view, predicated on Rychlak's (1977) teleological position.

In other words, although emotion is a response to meaning, it can also occur prior to the next thought, which is, in its turn, a response to the experienced emotion and its perceived impact on oneself and others. Thus, if we feel ashamed of what we have done, we may try to deny blameworthiness, with the consequence that we experience defensive anger rather than shame. In any complex and continuing transaction, an emotion can certainly come before a subsequent cognition or emotion in the continuous flow of cognitive, motivational and emotional processes. But this emotion also includes within it the thoughts and goals that aroused it in the first place. To see this clearly, it helps to use the metaphor of a motion picture rather than a still photo in thinking about human behavior, since the still photo captures only a single response to a given stimulus.

I was and am still firm in holding to the basic thesis that cognition, in the form of an evaluation (technically an appraisal that involves meaning), is always involved in emotion, regardless of what mental states and acts flow from that emotion. Motivation is also always involved in an emotion, both as an antecedent that creates the personal stake in the emotional transaction, and as a consequence of the emotion itself, in the form of new situational goals and intentions generated by the emotional person–environment relationship.

The issue is not the time sequence, but rather that the key role in emotion is played by a cognitive appraisal, an evaluation that depends on motivation and yields personal meaning. To focus on sequence is to miss the point that cognition (and motivation) are always necessary features of an emotion, and that any change in the emotion is a consequence of a new appraisal, perhaps provoked by subsequent events or a defensive reappraisal. I think the best view is that all three functions are always conjoined and interdependent, but this anticipates the discussion of separation and interdependence with which I close this essay.

I have been criticized for taking the strong position that cognition is a necessary condition of emotion, to which I later (Lazarus, 1991b) added motivation. Actually, this is the most parsimonious stance, but for some psychologists it weakens the credibility of my approach, since they want to treat neural processes reductively as causal agents of emotion, without the mediating role of cognition. Why be extreme? say my friends.

To these psychologists, I reply, okay, if there are good reasons for accepting non-cognitive causal determinents in emotion. For example, it could be argued reasonably that many stimuli, such as a mother's vocal, facial and gestural approval or disapproval, have inherent meaning even without an opportunity for an infant to have learned it. Although it is dangerous to dichotomize biological givens and learning, I could accept the idea of alternative mechanisms for the arousal of emotions comfortably under limited circumstances, especially if the role of appraisal was unconfounded empirically from such mechanisms. However, I am still convinced that, in the most common instances of adult anger, learned meaning is essential, and that appraisal theory (a version of cognitive mediation) is fundamentally correct and, in the main, a sufficient explanation for most adult emotions. It may well be necessary too.

Even if they were right, however, it is still the case that in most garden-varieties of emotion-arousing processes, symbols and meanings—the products of cognitive appraisals—are deeply involved, so my analysis fits well the most common instances of the emotion process, and stands on its own without reference to the brain. Nor do we need to make reference to material (neural) causes, since psychology should search for causes at its own level of analysis, in addition to building bridges to physiology.

Definitional Issues

One of the issues identified by some who entered the debate has to do with what is meant by cognition and emotion. Writing about the cognition–emotion relationship as a chicken-and-egg problem, Plutchik (1985) pointed out that neither Zajonc nor I explicitly defined cognition or emotion, concepts that have a long history of ambiguity. Leventhal & Scherer (1987) even suggested that the dispute was not substantive but largely a matter of semantics.

Some, myself included (Lazarus, 1984), saw Zajonc's implicit definition of emotion as too broad, since preferences and statements about attitudes are not necessarily emotional. What Zajonc took to be an aesthetic emotional response may be nothing more than a pro forma statement about preferences, indicative more of labeling than emotion. Others regarded my treatment of cognition as too broad and vague (e.g., Kleinginna & Kleinginna, 1985), especially when I included automatic, built-in forms of discrimination. Later on (Lazarus, 1991a,b), I tried to correct this by limiting cognition to learned judgments.

On the other hand, along with others (e.g. Baars, 1981; Kleinginna & Kleinginna, 1985), I continue to regard Zajonc's treatment of cognition as too narrow. He seemed constantly, though implicitly, to identify cognition with deliberate, seriatim information processing and consciousness. Even in a very recent and interesting series of psychophysiological experiments, which studied unconscious affect (Murphy, Monahan & Zajonc, 1995), I believe that Zajonc still tends implicitly to contrast cognition with affect and to equate cognition with consciousness.

I should note too that in the trilogy of mind, there is a real difference between emotion and the two other functions, cognition and motivation. Thought without motivation is emotionless. Motivation without thought is drive or energy, without the direction that cognition provides. The three constructs are also not parallel in that emotion is an amalgam of the other two. That emotion should be a superordinate concept containing both cognition and motivation is a complication that has not been sufficiently recognized.

Metatheory: Can Cognition and Emotion Be Separated?

The metatheoretical issue that most divides psychologists about the nature of the mind concerns the independence of cognition, motivation and emotion. It has great ontological and epistemological significance and underlies most other issues addressed in the debate. I saved it for last even though it came up early in the debate, because I would like my main contribution here to be its clarification and the presentation of a workable resolution.

In the course of my long professional life I have learned that findings rarely alter the way we think about theoretical and metatheoretical issues. Seldom does research settle such matters or conform perfectly or even well to the working assumptions, often implicit, drawn on by researchers with different theories and metatheories.

A substantial number of those addressing the issue of the cognition–emotion relationship have taken the position that cognition and emotion are seamlessly conjoined or fused in nature. Scheff (1985) is a case in point. In addition to emphasizing a cybernetic, non-linear view of causation, in which stimulus and response can be both cause and effect, Scheff cited John Dewey's (1896) wonderful essay on the reflex arc as the appropriate epistemological stance (see also Dewey & Bentley, 1989).

Several participants in a recent conference on cognition and emotion, who had not expressed themselves previously in the debate, adopted a similar position about the fusion of cognition and emotion. Jerome Bruner (1986), for example, used the second portion of the title of his essay—"Can Humpty Dumpty be put back together again?"—as a rhetorical reminder that dividing mind into cognition, motivation, and emotion violated the unity of these psychological functions. My colleagues and I (Lazarus, Coyne & Folkman, 1982) had earlier used the same colonic metaphor, "the Doctoring of Humpty-Dumpty", in an attempt to convey a similar message—namely, that cognition, emotion, and motivation are interdependent.

Bruner (1986) suggested that, rather than being neutral, every way of experiencing and structuring the world involves a *stance* that is emotional, a view similar to the one Judy Dunn (1988) adopted on the role of motivation and emotion in young children's transactions. Bruner wrote:

> The issue is not whether emotion (or stance) affects the selectivity of knowledge and its elaboration in thought, but rather *which* stance is taken. One [stance] is always taken in facing the world. We require some sort of stance-switching principle, some executive-routine to deal with the *which*. And with no further ado, I want to give the switch a simple, if cantankerous name: Self. . . .
>
> Children, it seems, do not simply master syntax for its own sake or learn how to mean simply as an intellectual exercise—like little scholars or lexicographers. They acquire these skills in the interest of getting things done in the world: requesting, indicating, affiliating, protesting, asserting, possessing, and the rest (1986, p. 13).

And a bit later in that essay, Bruner said:

> Eventually, as the child comes to use the language and to participate in the culture, the affective element becomes so locked in with the knowledge that it requires such major institutions as schooling, science, and a written language to create a new set of rational concepts that can be operated upon by those famous (but non-natural) rules of right reasoning" (1986, p. 15).

I quote one further statement from Bruner about *negotiation* with the environment, perhaps because I said something similar, but less well in Lazarus (1991a), and also because it expresses so clearly a relational view of mind and behavior, which is still missing from much of psychology:

I conceive of the detachment of Self as requiring mastery of the possibilities of getting things done in a manner congruent with constraints of the culture and with one's own perceived requirements—getting things done both with words and with acts. But getting things done with words is the essence of negotiation, of going from the culturally explicit to the situationally explicit (Bruner, 1986, p. 19).

The idea that cognition, motivation and emotion are always intertwined, to use Bruner's term, needs some qualification. Both Bruner and Dunn (1988) were speaking of the context of adaptation, that is, when there are important stakes that children and adults have in their negotiations with their social environment. Having a stake in an encounter creates what Bruner called a "stance".

But a stance, like Zajonc's preferences and attitudes, is not always active in every encounter—that is, it can be dispositional rather than expressed. Nor does it have to reflect a strong emotion. To put it differently, although emotion always contains cognitive activity, cognitive activity, and even having a goal, does not always involve emotion. There are plenty of occasions when nothing of importance is at stake, and cognition can be cool or cold, rather than warm or hot. Besides, hot and cold are relative concepts and our mental life slides easily from that which is uninvolving to that which is intensely involving.

In the same volume (Bearison and Zimiles), Santostefano (1986) adopted a position similar to Bruner's about the interdependence of cognition and emotion, arguing intelligently that interdependence does not mean mere interaction. He wrote:

When cognition and emotion are conceived as separate but interacting systems, investigators frequently are cornered into taking a position that either cognition (e.g. Arnold, 1960) or emotion (e.g. Bower & Cohen, 1982) is more important in this interaction. Related, Izard (1977) argued that models that see emotion as arising from cognition tend to evaluate reason and rationality as good and emotion as bad and thus view reasoning as a control and substitute for emotion. The debate over the relative dominance of cognition and emotion becomes meaningless and dissolves when the two systems are conceived as one (Santostefano, 1986, pp. 204–205)

Finally, in this selective review of writers who have challenged the separateness of cognition, motivation and emotion, in the same volume Sigel (1986) makes the following point:

My argument is that one reason we perpetuate the problem is that we insist on the cognition–affect dichotomy, where affect or emotions refer to non-rational feelings, whereas cognition refers to the thought, the rational human functions (p. 212).

Although Sigel cites me favorably as one of those who has spoken of cognition and emotion as usually fused, he suggests that my position that they may also be dissociated has a logical problem. Fusion and separation appear to be contradictory. Perhaps fusion is a stronger analogy than interdependence, which is the word I tend to use. Still, as I shall argue shortly, even if the ideal mental state is integration and harmony, dissociation also occurs under certain conditions. In this connection, Sigel also notes that, although Piaget viewed cognition and affect as indissociable, he also states that, "In none of his writings does Piaget concern himself with the affective features inherent in the child's performance on the various tasks, nor does he incorporate 'affect' in his interpretation of findings" (Sigel, 1986, p. 214). Sigel adds the following epistemological point:

> There are no categories in nature. We construct the categories, define their parameters, and strive to discover legitimate instances representing the categories. Is there a pure affective category—that is, a category with no indication of cognitive awareness? Is there a category of pure cognition? It all depends on whom one asks and what criteria and definitions are used as bases for seeking answers (1986, p. 214).

RESOLVING THE DILEMMA

How can we deal with these opposing epistemologies and metatheories? My solution is to say that the way we think about cognition, motivation and emotion depends on whether we view them from the point of view of reductive causal analysis or from the perspective of complex but integrated systems operating in part-whole relationships.

Sigel, Bruner, Santostefano and others suggest that cognition and emotion are fused, to which I add motivation in order to complete the trilogy. To separate them is to create arbitrary scientific categories that don't exist in nature. The two points of view, that of analytic reduction and that of holistism, are *both* credible.

There has long been a widespread failure to realize that reduction distorts the way phenomena operate naturally. Every animal is comprised of a complex system of variables and processes organized into a composite whole in which the separate causal agents lose their identities. Reduction artificially separates the cognitive, motivational and emotional functions. In making a commitment to understand via the analytic search for elemental causal variables, no effort is usually made to return to the way biological and psychological systems exist in nature.

The distortions of nature engendered by reductive analysis must be compensated for by an opposing strategy—namely, *synthesis*, which is the effort to put the variables back together into a living whole. That almost forgotten man in psychology, John Dewey, said this, but his views are all but ignored by psychology today. Dewey illustrated this theme by making a vivid contrast between the cell *in vitro*—that is, in the test tube—and the cell *in vivo*—that is, as it operates in living tissues. When the cell is part of an organ which, in turn, functions within a still more complex but organized system of tissues, such as a stomach, heart or brain in a living body, its characteristics are different from the way it works *in vitro*.

A knowledge of old embryological experiments by Weiss (1939; and others in the 1930s; see Murphy, 1947/1966) can help us here. Weiss sought, for example, to transplant embryo cells of the newt. If these cells had remained in their original location, they would have grown into skin or hair cells, because they originated in a particular part of the body and were destined to be skin and hair. However, if the cells were grafted very early in the embryo's development onto a part of the body destined to become an eye, they grew into eye cells rather than skin or hair cells. And if they were grafted later, they grew into skin or hair cells—in effect, resisting the new environmental pressure to be eye cells, which came too late to change their original local destiny. On the basis of these experiments, we are forced to conclude that the younger a cell is in the development of an organism, the more plastic is its identity. In other words, we cannot regard the cell as the building block for all tissues. Rather, it derives its specific biological characteristics from its location in the body—that is, the tissues in which it develops, as well as from the species in which it is found.

By failing to consider the *context* or environmental field in which a phenomenon occurs, reductive analysis and an overemphasis on the idea of universal mechanisms lead us to ignore the dependency of all biological phenomena on its functional position in a larger, integrated system, which calls the tune with respect to its individual part in the system.

Expanding a bit further on this problem, reductive analysis leads us to speak of separate afferent and efferent nerves, a separate brain without a body, and separate stimuli and responses (or perception and action). We treat them as if they operated independently when, in reality, their characteristics operate interdependently with each other.

In contrast with such a view, when I began my career at Johns Hopkins in 1948 I remember being told that the most important modern neurophysiological discovery was the existence of separate pathways for afferent and efferent nerves (the Bell and Magendi law). This was viewed as the biological basis for separate stimuli and responses. Although such pathways do exist, afferent and efferent nerves operate interdependently as parts of an organized system. We constantly forget that a stimulus always implies a response and action is always inherent in perception. This holistic theme has also been stated by a number of thoughtful writers in Frese and Sabini (1985; for example, in chapters by Gallistel, von Hofsten, and Neisser).

I don't wish to suggest that reductive analysis *per se* is the enemy of truth. Quite the contrary. But what distorts our understanding is the failure to put the parts back together again as they are and work in nature. *Both* analysis and synthesis are essential to a complete science.

The above statement argues against those, such as Leventhal & Scherer (1987), and Santostefano (1986), who say that the issues of cause-and-effect relationships between cognition and emotion, and between cognition and motivation, are really moot. There is nothing wrong with asking how the functions of mind influence each other. It also argues against those who say that we should not disturb the whole in efforts at analytic reduction. Both ways of thinking are important—indeed, necessary for proper understanding—and to adopt one perspective or the other alone is unwise.

The problem of different levels of abstraction also applies to the role of appraisal and meaning in emotion. Separate appraisal components do not produce an emotion. It is, rather, the combined *meaning* these components make possible that is the proximal cause of an emotion. This meaning, which refers to the significance of a transaction between person and environment for well-being (Lazarus, 1991b, 1998a,b), can often be sensed in an instant without serial processing of the individual appraisal components that have contributed to that meaning. I refer to the personal meaning underlying each emotion as the *core relational theme*.

An increasing number of psychologists, worldwide, resonate to the epistemological and metatheoretical outlook I have been espousing. One recent and striking example is a book by Guiseppe Mantovani (1966) of Padua University in Italy. He draws on some of these ideas—for example, about the importance of relational meaning and contextualism, which he refers to as "situated actions"— in examining virtual reality. He finds the status of virtual reality wanting because its focus has been limited to perceptual–motor patterns rather than relational meanings. I am encouraged that more psychologists than ever before, and social scientists in general, are unhappy about the stultifying state of our field and its methodological narrowness, and are thinking more favorably about a narrative approach, holism, and relational meaning as essential to the study of the mental life.

In my view the relational meaning of each of the emotions is pan-cultural (Lazarus, with commentaries, 1995). Loss is a universal human meaning and emotional experience regardless of the way it is labeled and interpreted. So is being dealt with treacherously, or in a manner likely to be demeaning. And so on with each of the other emotions. If we want to understand the garden variety of human emotions, we need to understand universal relational meanings, as well as the cultural variations in the conditions that influence them (see Lazarus, 1991a, 1998a,b).

It is widely accepted that emotion is a consequence of a transaction in which thought and motivation play essential causal roles. However, I argue that emotion contains causal thoughts and motivations, a position that has been criticized as circular because the cause is contained in the effect. I liken my analysis to the germ theory of disease in which the effect, disease, disappears if the germ is killed or goes dormant and, therefore, is no longer actively present. We don't think it odd or circular to say that germs cause disease and yet are an integral aspect of the effect, the disease itself. Why do we resist the same kind of reasoning about emotion? Perhaps this epistemological foolishness stems from a discredited linear view of behavior, or a residual form of radical behaviorism and logical positivism in which mechanism is everything and context is of little or no importance. We should be moving full speed ahead to a systems view, and cease evading the concept of meaning, on which most of what we do and feel depends.

While we are considering causation, an additional point should be made— namely, that there are two different meanings to the concept of causality, each of which offers a very different epistemological stance when we consider in what sense cognition causes emotion (the same argument could apply to motivation; see, for example, White, 1990). One meaning is captured in the term "*synthetic* causality", which states that particular patterns of appraisal result in particular emotions, just as particular germs cause particular diseases. The other meaning, termed "*logical*" or "*analytic* causality", is that given appraisals imply specific emotions, without there being any causal ascription in that statement (see the interchanges between Lazarus, 1993, and Shweder, 1993).

Despite my penchant for holism and logical causation, I am reluctant to abandon synthetic causality, for two reasons. First, this approach has greatly advanced the fortunes of science in respect to the degree of prediction and control it made possible over our lives. Second, it also makes it possible to test our understanding by manipulating antecedents and examining their consequences. Always a fan of flexibility, maybe we can have it both ways.

FINAL COMMENT

Given the absence of suitable research paradigms, and the difficulties of measuring the variables, which are hypothetical constructs, there is little current prospect of the final word being said about how best to view the relationships among cognition, motivation and emotion. I am doubtful that the debate can be resolved solely by research data. Therefore, we are forced to rely largely on logic and theory, while keeping an eye out for observations that could help us evaluate the tenability of our assumptions, propositions and hypotheses.

I have a friend who is an engineer who, after reading this essay, asked me what possible difference what I have said could make in an effort to improve the well-being of humanity. I had difficulty answering him. To practical people, the arguments I have raised here sound uncomfortably like the proverbial ecclesiastical debates during the Middle Ages about how many angels could fit on the head of a pin. I tried to give him the standard academic scholar's response, that in the long run getting it right could make an important difference in what we learn about the world. Many empirical discoveries and philosophical positions may presently have no immediate utilty, but later make a major difference in the understanding and control over our lives. We need to get our thinking right, even though it is difficult now to anticipate in what ways this will matter in the future.

While we were discussing this in a Chinese restaurant, I received the following Confucian-style message in my fortune cookie, which sets the stage for trying to get it right. It said, "Discontent is the first step in the progress of a man or a nation". After thousands of years of thought, this statement justifies today's continuing and contentious exploration of how to view cognitive, motivational and emotional relationships.

REFERENCES

Aristotle (1941).   Rhetoric. In R. McKeon (ed.), *The Basic Works of Aristotle*. New York: Random House.

Arnold, M. B. (1960).   *Emotion and Personality. Vol. I, Psychological Aspects*. New York: Columbia University Press.

Asch, S. E. (1952).   *Social Psychology*. Englewood Cliffs, NJ: Prentice-Hall.

Baars, B. J. (1981).   Cognitive versus inference. *American Psychologist*, **36**, 223–224.

Bandura, A. (1978).   The self system in reciprocal determinism. *American Psychologist*, **33**, 244–358.

Baumeister, R. F., Smart, L. & Boden, J. M. (1996).   Relation of threatened egotism to violence and aggression: the dark side of high self-esteem. *Psychological Review*, **103**, 5–33.

Bearison, D. J. & Zimiles, H. (1986).   *Thought and Emotion: Developmental Perspectives*. Hillsdale, NJ: Erlbaum.

Bolles, R. C. (1974).   Cognition and motivation: some historical trends. In B. Weiner (ed.), *Cognitive Views of Human Motivation*. New York: Academic Press, pp. 1–20.

Bower, G. H. & Cohen, P. R. (1982).   Emotional influences in memory and thinking. In M. S. Clark & S. T. Fiske (eds), *Affect and Cognition*. Hillsdale, NJ: Erlbaum, pp. 291–332.

Bruner, J. (1986).   Thought and emotion: can Humpty Dumpty be put together again? In D. J. Bearison & H. Zimiles (eds), *Thought and Emotion: Developmental Perspectives*. Hillsdale, NJ: Erlbaum, pp. 11–20.

Dewey, J. (1896).   The reflex arc concept in psychology. *Psychological Review*, **3**, 357–370.

Dewey, J. & Bentley, A. F. (1989).   Knowing and the known. In J. A. Boydston (ed.), *The Later Works of John Dewey, 1925–1953*, Vol. 16. Carbondale, IL: Southern Illinois University Press (original work published in 1949).

Dunn, J. (1988).   *The Beginnings of Social Understanding*. Cambridge, MA: Harvard University Press.

Ellis, A. (1985).   Cognition and affect in emotional disturbance. *American Psychologist*, **40**, 471–472.

Frese, M. & Sabini, J. (1985).   *Goal Directed Behavior: The Concept of Action in Psychology*. Hillsdale, NJ: Erlbaum.

Gallistel, C. R. (1985).   Motivation, intention, and emotion: goal directed behavior from a cognitive–neuroethological perspective. In M. Frese & J. Sabini (eds), *Goal Directed Behavior*. Hillsdale, NJ: Erlbaum, pp. 48–65.

Harlow, H. F. (1953).   Mice, monkeys, men and motives. *Psycyhological Review*, **60**, 23–32.

Heider, F. (1958).   *The Psychology of Interpersonal Relations*. New York: Wiley.

von Hofsten, C. (1985).   Perception and action. In M. Frese & J. Sabini (eds), *Goal Directed Behavior*. Hillsdale, NJ: Erlbaum, pp. 80–96.

Izard, C. E. (1977).   *Human Emotions*. New York: Plenum.

Kelly, G. A. (1955).   *The Psychology of Personal Constructs*. New York: Norton.

Kleinginna, P. A. & Kleinginna, A. M. (1985).   Cognition and affect: a reply to Lazarus and Zajonc. *American Psychologist*, **40**, 470–471.

Lazarus, R. S. (1974).   Cognitive and coping processes in emotion. In B. Weiner (ed.), *Cognitive Views of Human Motivation*. New York: Academic Press, pp. 21–32.

Lazarus, R. S. (1982).   Thoughts on the relations between emotion and cognition. *American Psychologist*, **37**, 1019–1024.

Lazarus, R. S. (1984).   On the primacy of cognition. *American Psychologist*, **39**, 124–129.

Lazarus, R. S. (1986).   Commentary on LeDoux. *Integrative Psychiatry*, **4**, 245–247.

Lazarus, R. S. (1991a).   *Emotion and Adaptation*. New York: Oxford University Press.

Lazarus, R. S. (1991b).   Cognition and motivation in emotion. *American Psychologist*, **46**, 352–367.
Lazarus, R. S. (1993).   Lazarus rise. *Psychological Inquiry*, **4**, 343–357.
Lazarus, R. S. (1995).   With commentaries. Vexing research problems inherent in cognitive–mediational theories of emotion, and some solutions. *Psychological Inquiry*, **6**, 183–265.
Lazarus, R. S. (1998a).   *Fifty Years of the Research and Theory of R. S. Lazarus: An Analysis of Historical and Perennial Issues.* Mahway, NJ: Erlbaum.
Lazarus, R. S. (1998b).   *The Life and Work of an Eminent Psychologist: Autobiography of Richard S. Lazarus.* New York: Springer.
Lazarus, R. S., Coyne, J. C. & Folkman, S. (1982).   Cognition, emotion and motivation: The doctoring of Humpty-Dumpty. In R. W. J. Neufeld (ed.), *Psychological Stress and Psychopathology.* New York: McGraw-Hill, pp. 218–239.
LeDoux, J. E. (1986).   Sensory systems and emotion: a model of affective processing. *Integrative Psychiatry*, **4**, 237–248.
Leventhal, H. & Scherer, K. (1987).   The relationship of emotion to cognition: a functional approach to a semantic controversy. *Cognition and Emotion*, **1**, 3–28.
Lewin, K. A. (1935).   *A Dynamic Theory of Personality* (trans. K. E. Zener & D. K. Adams). New York: McGraw-Hill.
Mandler, G. (1984).   *Mind and Body: Psychology of Emotion and Stress.* New York: Norton.
Mantovani, G. (1996).   *New Communication Environments: From Everday to Virtual.* London: Taylor & Francis.
McClelland, D. C. (1951).   *Personality.* New York: Sloane.
Murphy, G. (1947/1966).   *Personality: A Biosocial Approach to Origins and Structure.* New York: Basic Books.
Murphy, S. T., Monahan, J. L. & Zajonc, R. B. (1995).   *Journal of Personality and Social Psychology*, **69**, 589–602.
Murray, H. A. (1938).   *Explorations in Personality.* New York: Oxford University Press.
Neisser, U. (1985).   The role of invariant structures in the control of movement. In M. Frese & J. Sabini (eds), *Goal Directed Behavior.* Hillsdale, NJ: Erlbaum, pp. 97–108.
Plato (1961).   E. Hamilton & H. Cairns (eds), *The Collected Dialogues.* Princeton, NJ: Princeton University Press.
Plutchik, R. (1985).   On emotion: the chicken-and-egg problem revisited. *Motivation and Emotion*, **9**, 197–200.
Robertson, G. C. (1877).   Notes. *Mind: A Quarterly Review*, **2**, 413–415.
Rotter, J. B. (1954).   *Social Learning and Clinical Psychology.* Englewood Cliffs, NJ: Prentice-Hall.
Rychlak, J. F. (1977).   *The Psychology of Rigorous Humanism.* New York: Wiley-Interscience.
Santostefano, S. (1986).   Cognitive controls, metaphors, and contexts: an approach to cognition and emotion. In D. J. Bearison & H. Zimiles (eds), *Thought and Emotion: Developmental Perspectives.* Hillsdale, NJ: Erlbaum, pp. 175–210.
Schachter, S. (1966).   The interaction of cognitive and physiological determinants of emotional state. In C. D. Spielberger (ed.), *Anxiety and Behavior.* New York: Academic Press, pp. 193–224.
Scheff, T. J. (1985).   The primacy of affect. *American Psychologist*, **40**, 849–850.
Shweder, R. A. (1993).   Everything you ever wanted to know about cognitive appraisal theory without being conscious of it. *Psychological Inquiry*, **4**, 322–342.
Sigel, I. E. (1986).   Cognition-affect: a psychological riddle. In D. J. Bearison & H. Zimiles (eds), *Thought and Emotion: Developmental Perspectives.* Hillsdale, NJ: Erlbaum, pp. 211–229.
Slife, B. D. (1981).   The primacy of affective judgments from a teleological perspective. *American Psychologist*, **36**, 221–222.

Tetlock, P. E. & Levi, A. (1982).   Attribution bias: On the conclusiveness of the cognition–emotion debate. *Journal of Experimental Social Psychology*, **18**, 68–88.

Toch, H. (1969).   *Violent Men*. Chicago: Aldine.

Toch, H. (1983).   The management of hostile aggression: Seneca as applied social psychologist. *American Psychologist*, **38**, 1022–1025.

Tolman, E. C. (1932).   *Purposive Behavior in Animals and Men*. New York: Century.

Weiner, B. (1974) (ed.).   *Cognitive Views of Human Motivation*. New York: Academic Press.

Weiss, P. A. (1939).   *Principles of Development: A Text in Experimental Embryology*. New York: Holt.

White, R. W. (1959).   Motivation reconsidered: the concept of competence. *Psychological Review*, **66**, 297–333.

White, P. A. (1990).   Ideas about causation in philosophy and psychology. *American Psychologist*, **108**, 3–18.

Zajonc, R. B. (1980).   Feeling and thinking: preferences need no inferences. *American Psychologist*, **35**, 151–175.

Zajonc, R. B. (1984).   On the primacy of affect. *American Psychologist*, **39**, 117–123.

Chapter 2

The Philosophy of Cognition and Emotion

William Lyons
Trinity College, Dublin, Ireland

FOREWORD

Very recently I acquired a shiny new textbook on the psychology of the emotions. In the chapter entitled, "What is an emotion?", I was astonished, in the way that one might be astonished to be served mackerel described as salmon, to find that the definition of an emotion, which began with the words, "An emotion is usually caused by a person consciously or unconsciously evaluating an event as relevant to a concern (a goal) that is important...", was held to be a recent major breakthrough in the psychology of emotion and given a reassuringly recent date of 1986 (Oatley & Jenkins, 1996, Chapter 4). In this essay I will endeavour to point out that causal–evaluative theories of emotion are arguably as old as Aristotle and the Stoics, and in our own time have been much discussed by philosophers and psychologists well before 1986. But I suppose that I should not be astonished by strange claims about the history of ideas in modern textbooks of psychology. Part of psychology's laudable aim to be accepted as a science means, for many practitioners unfortunately, that it must ape the physical sciences in all ways, including by becoming more or less uninterested in the provenance of the problems they currently discuss and in the history of their own subject.[1] So, be

---

[1] When recently I received the latest edition of the esteemed *Hilgard's Introduction to Psychology* (Atkinson et al., 1996), I was pained to find that the section entitled, "Brief History of Psychology", was now consigned to an Appendix. Yet that, I suppose, is better than the previous edition, where the history of psychology was summed up in three paragraphs. Somewhat ironically, in his most scholarly book on emotions, *Best Laid Schemes*, Keith Oatley does take the trouble to sketch in the provenance

---

Handbook of Cognition and Emotion. Edited by T. Dalgleish and M. Power.
© 1999 John Wiley & Sons Ltd.

warned, in what follows I will lead the reader into that by now quite unfamiliar territory, the history of theorizing about emotion. In particular I will endeavour to relate the current revival of cognitive theories of emotion to past events. Frequently my story will refer to debates and theories in both philosophy of mind and psychology, for it would be historically inaccurate to do otherwise. In the last 100 years, indeed until very recently, especially in the matter of theorizing about the nature of emotion, philosophy of mind and psychology have quite openly drawn upon one another's resources.

THE ANCIENT GREEKS

Like so much in the ancient subject of philosophy, in Western culture at any rate, discussions about the nature of emotion began with the Greeks. However—and this is a matter of some curiosity to students of philosophy—detailed discussion about the nature of emotion begins with Aristotle, rather than Plato. Plato (Plato, 1982, Section 47 ff.; 1955, Sections 440, 576–577, 603–607) had comparatively little to say about the emotions and seemed to look upon them with deep suspicion and even outright contempt at times. Like so many of the ancient Greeks, and for that matter so many of us after Freud, Plato saw the human personality as an ever-lasting battle to maintain an equilibrium between warring components. Plato saw both human moral perfection and mental health in terms of the triumph of cool reason over hot passion and desire. In consequence, Plato looked upon the emotions or passions as a wild, not easily controlled and potentially danger-ous aspect of human psychology. The emotions were like wild horses which constantly threatened to escape the control of the charioteer, who represented reason.

Plato had a dualist or quasi-dualist account of human nature which depicted humans more or less as comprised of a soul inhabiting a body. The body was the soul's local runabout during the lifetime of the person whose soul it was. Death was the breakdown of the body and the ensuing flight of the soul to some shadowy other world. Somewhat surprisingly, Plato located the emotions in the soul, as special non-bodily feelings or perceptions, and not in the body, as one might naturally expect. Hence, for Plato, the battle between reason and passion, as to who would be master and who slave, was constantly being fought in the immaterial arena of the human soul (or, in the Greek, *psuche*, from which comes our modern term "psyche" and our word "psychology"). Like Mao Tse Tung many centuries later, Plato believed that certain sorts of music and drama were dangerous and corrupting. Unlike Mao Tse Tung, Plato believed this for psychological rather than political reasons. Certain sorts of music and drama— and if he were alive today I imagine that Plato would list the performances of The

---

of current cognitive theories of emotion and mentions their source in Aristotle (Oatley, 1992, e.g. p. 3—in fact, there are 30 references to Aristotle). In that work he is also keen to stress "the case for pluralism" or the need to draw on a variety of sources besides those in psychology.

Sex Pistols and Madonna among his *opera damnata*—appealed above all to the emotions, thereby encouraging them to be unruly, so that reason lost control over both them and the desires stemming from them, and so the subtle and fragile performance of balancing these three parts of the soul was upset.

Aristotle (see Aristotle, 1941a, Book II, and 1941b, Book I, Chapter 1) looked far more favourably on the emotions, as he had a far richer view of them and saw very clearly both their power and their use in politics. Unlike his esteemed teacher, Plato, Aristotle was not a dualist. For him there was no ghostly soul lurking inside the body. There was merely non-living and living matter. Among the latter were numbered the animals, including the human animal. Psychology was the study of the higher functions of the human animal, namely the cognitive, appetitive and affective functions of humans. Emotions, or the affective life of humans, were explained by Aristotle as a combination of this higher cognitive and appetitive life of humans, together with their lower, purely sensual life. Many bodily feelings in humans, Aristotle was suggesting, were caused by the way humans view the world around about them. Of course, some bodily feelings do not arise in this way. We might, for example, suffer a pain in the stomach from eating prawns which were "off". Or you can feel a pain in your foot because you dropped a hammer on it. But unique to humans (and possibly the "higher" animals) were the feelings caused by our beliefs and desires about the world and about the people around about us. Thus, Aristotle defined anger "as an impulse, accompanied by pain, to a conspicuous revenge for a conspicuous slight directed without justification towards what concerns oneself or towards what concerns one's friends" (Aristotle, 1941a, p. 1380.) In more contemporary prose, Aristotle is telling us that anger is that desire for revenge, accompanied by negative feelings which arise when we feel that we (or those close to us) have been the victim of a gratuitous insult. Indeed, for Aristotle, what distinguishes one emotion from another is not a difference of feeling or bodily upset (although emotions might happen to differ also in this respect), but a difference in belief. This bodily upset of yours is to be labelled "anger" because it results from your belief that you or your friends have been unjustly slighted. This bodily upset is shame, because it results from your belief that you are responsible for some regrettable action which, in turn, you believe has belittled you in front of others.

However the most detailed, yet most neglected, of all the ancient Greek accounts of emotion are those of the Stoics and Epicureans, who were the most original philosophers of the Hellenistic period.[2] The Stoics and Epicureans were often less interested in a theory of emotion, as such, than with learning about the genesis of our emotions, which in turn could teach us how to control them. So one might think of them as the first psychotherapists. Both were "modern" in their view of the mind, in that both were resolutely materialist. Minds were neither

---

[2] The best single work to refer to here is Julia Annas's splendid *Hellenistic Philosophy of Mind*, University of California Press, 1992.

god-delivered souls nor even Platonic free-floating "Forms".[3] Minds were nothing more than humans viewed from the point of view of their function and the organization of those functions. If they could have read Charles Darwin, I imagine they would very readily have embraced the theory of evolution. What is clear is that both the Stoics and the Epicureans were, if I might again ruminate anachronistically, decidedly un-Cartesian.

Stoicism was founded in Cyprus by Zeno of Citium around the turn of the fourth and third centuries BC, but the Stoic view of emotion is associated especially with the extant fragmentary works of Arius Didymus, Posidonius and, especially, Chrysippus, the third head of the Stoic school in the third century BC and the systematizer of its doctrines. For the Stoics, emotion was a cognitively-induced impulse to act or plan for emergency action, caused by the subject making a judgement or forming a belief about the current state of affairs and what one should do about it. Thus, fear was an impulse to run away or fight one's way out of trouble, resulting from the subject's negative judgement that he/she was caught in a dangerous situation and must do something about it, quickly.

It is probably because of a related thesis about the emotions that the Stoic account of emotion has been neglected in comparison, say, to the Aristotelian view. For the Stoics embedded their discussions of emotion in discussions of ethics.[4] While the Stoics held that emotions were not merely complex states involving cognition, impulse and behaviour, they also held that the cognitive processes[5] that gave rise to emotion were morally subversive. The reasoning involved in emotion must have been faulty, they argued, because the reasoning bypassed the "higher rationality" of other-regarding moral reasoning and the ensuing virtuous behaviour. For "emotional thinking" is often self-interested. It often involves thinking about one's own situation—as, say, of being in grave danger (fear) or, say, of having been insulted (anger) or, say, of having lost face (shame)—and thereby being involved in purely self-centred reflection.

The Stoics did not condemn the emotions, as it is sometimes alleged; rather they looked askance and suspiciously at an emotional person. This is the true connection between Stoicism and our current use of the term "stoical" to mean "the acceptance of adversity without complaint". For, if your mind is truly

---

[3] For Plato, the "Form" (the usual translation of the Greek word *eidos* in the works of Plato) of something was its intelligible essence or nature, which in turn was separable from (could live a separate existence from) anything which incarnated this essence or nature. Thus the "Form" of a human was separable from any human but was normally the organizing principle of an individual human's life.

[4] One of Chrysippus's books on the emotions was called *Therapy and Ethics* (see Long & Sedley, 1987).

[5] The word "cognitive" is derived from the Latin word *cognoscere*, which means "to know" and so, strictly, should only be used in connection with epistemological concepts like knowing, believing, surmising and so on. Unfortunately, especially in the contemporary psychological literature, the term "cognitive" has come to be used, so that it embraces not merely genuinely cognitive concepts, such as knowledge and belief, but also evaluative ones, such as evaluation or appraisal, and appetitive ones, such as wanting, wishing and desiring.

imbued with the Stoic point of view, then you will not be self-centred and so will take little account of your emotions. In short, you will be a dispassionate, stoical sort of person.

The Epicureans approached their study of emotion from a quite different point of view, one which was much more uncompromisingly materialist than that of the Stoics. For the Epicureans held that the universe was composed of nothing more than atoms in a void. These atoms combined in various ways to form compounds, some of which are humans. But humans and their emotions and actions are not privileged parts of the universe, they are simply wholly mortal parts of it, much the same as anything else.

The founder of Epicureanism, Epicurus himself, of whose work only fragments remain, flourished around the turn of the third and fourth centuries BC. But our best knowledge of Epicurean philosophy comes from the *magnum opus* of the great Latin poet Lucretius, his poem in six books entitled *De Rerum Natura* (On the Nature of Things). While, strictly speaking, this is a later synthesis of Epicureanism from the first century BC, it is often pointed out that, somewhat in the manner of a religion, its doctrines changed little over the centuries.

Rather than a cognitively-guided impulse, as the Stoics suggested, the Epicureans saw emotion more passively, as a cognitively-induced and directed feeling or set of feelings which may or may not result in behaviour. Unfortunately they were less formal and rigorous in their approach and left us no clear account of the components of emotional states and the causal interplay between them. What is clear is that they were allied with the Stoics in treating the emotions with some suspicion. Where the Stoics saw display of emotion as a sign of lack of virtue, the Epicureans saw it as indicating a lack of knowledge (i.e. as being in the grip of false beliefs). This attitude should be understood against the background of the more fundamental Epicurean view that most of our fundamental beliefs—such as that death was to be feared and that the gods controlled our fate—were simply mistaken. Thus, fear of what is dangerous, which very often stems in turn from a fear of death, is a bad thing. We should be indifferent to such things. Sometimes, of course, on the spur of the moment, we will be startled and so afraid, or deeply offended and so very angry, but these are more or less reflex and natural responses. As long as we then bring them under control and do not wallow in them, they will do us no harm. In general, Epicurus advised, we should learn a sort of personal quietude whereby we are more or less indifferent to the perturbations of the world. He might be said to have advocated a sort of Hellenistic Buddhism.

THE MEDIEVALS, THE NEW SCIENCE AND DESCARTES

As I will make clear later on, it is this Aristotelian–Stoic view that, wittingly or unwittingly, has been championed by both contemporary philosophy and psychology in recent times, although, of course, with some modifications. Why, then, did this view of emotion drop out, more or less completely, between the time of the Stoics and our own day?

There were two main reasons. The first was that, in the medieval period, the Stoics were not a major influence on theology or philosophical theology, probably because their resolutely physicalist stance would not have been congenial to a Christian philosophy of mind as soul. So, when the medieval theologians looked back to the Greeks, it was first to Plato and then, in the late medieval period, to a suitably Christianized Aristotle. However, ironically, in the process of Christianizing Aristotle, the theologians could be said to have turned Aristotle back into Plato. Aristotle's account of human nature as matter and form, that is, as matter "informed" or structured and organized so as to function as a rational cognitive animal, was changed back into an account of a body inhabited by an immaterial soul which housed all the "higher" cognitive and evaluative functions of humans. In part, this transformation was an unwitting one, for the only Aristotelian texts available to the Christian world were those with neo-Platonic and Islamic nuances, for these texts came to Europe via the commentaries of the Hellenistic and Islamic Middle East (see, for example, Kretzmann, Kenny & Pinborg, 1982, Section II.) In part, however, this Platonizing of Aristotle was done with open eyes, at least in the sense that an un-Platonized unreformed Aristotle would not have been acceptable. For there were, of course, strong theological reasons for preferring a Platonized Aristotle to Aristotle. A Platonic Form was a separable immaterial substance, and so rather like the soul in Christian theology, and so helped make theoretical sense of the Christian eschatology of death, judgement, hell or heaven. For such a Form was immortal and so perfectly suited to life after death.

In counterbalance to these theological gains, there were a number of philosophical losses resulting from sanitizing Aristotle in this way. One of these was that the resulting account of emotion was far less convincing than Aristotle's own account. Or more accurately, the possibilities for giving a subtle and complex account of emotion seemed to have been drastically reduced. Theoretically speaking, emotions could no longer be seamlessly psychosomatic. A mediaeval philosopher–theologian had to choose whether to place emotions in the soul or in the body. Contrary to my expectations, at least, Aquinas (1967), for example, placed emotions primarily in the body. This will be more understandable when we realize that Aquinas made emotions into what, in modern terminology, we would call drives or impulses. Emotions were primarily passions, things we suffered or things that suddenly came upon us, rather than things generated by how we viewed the world and ourselves, and ourselves in relation to the world. Emotions were viewed as felt bodily tendencies or desires, and only impinged upon the soul and its cognitive, evaluative and volitional life in so far as these bodily desires were reflected upon by humans. Sometimes our emotions remained wholly bodily or sensory. Thus, pleasure or pain resulting immediately and spontaneously from some perception of the environment, and an accompanying tendency to be attracted to the source of pleasure or to avoid the source of pain, was said to comprise the first level of basic emotions. All other emotions were, in effect, basic ones "sicklied o'er by the pale cast of thought". Thus, fear was an aversion in cognitive clothing, or the body's desire taken over and directed by the soul's powers of thought. Fear was our impulse or desire to run away from something we came to realize was threatening and difficult to avoid.

In terms of such an account, emotions are more unreasoning than reasonable, and their cognitive aspects have been given second place, and so they become more difficult to explain in rational psychological terms. Why was Fred afraid of the dog, while Mary was not? All that can be said, on this account, is that Fred is so "wired up" physiologically that he generated the bodily drive or tendency which is at the core of fear and, although this is less central, also generated the appropriate accompanying "thoughts", but that Mary is "wired up" differently. Alternatively, while both Fred and Mary reacted impulsively in the same way to the sight of the Alsatian, only Fred was the sort of person who would think about it in such a way as to be said to fear it. All you can say, ultimately, is, "That's the way it is". Aristotle has not merely been Platonized but, in the area of emotion, more or less de-cognitivized as well. Such a reduced account of emotion makes nonsense of our ordinary commonsense tendency to think of emotions as appropriate or inappropriate, justified or unjustified, reasonable or unreasonable. For bodily impulses, like volcanic eruptions or outbreaks of measles, just occur.

The second main reason why the Aristotelian cum Stoic cognitivist account of emotions was out of favour, more or less until the revival in modified form in the twentieth century, was the rise of the new approach to science. For the widespread adoption, in the seventeenth century, of the new and strikingly successful approach to science, based on observation and experiment, and bolstered by new instruments such as the telescope, led to the abandonment of the old Aristotelian–Scholastic view of scientific method. This long-embedded orthodoxy of church and university was suddenly being described as ignorant and retrograde, and so much that was worth preserving in Aristotle, such as his cognitive account of emotion, was jettisoned along with his natural philosophy. The ideas of the new natural philosophers, Galileo, Bacon and Descartes, became the focus of both scientific and philosophical discussion.

For better or for worse, and with few notable exceptions,[6] Descartes' account of emotion was to hold sway in philosophy and with its new nineteenth century offspring, psychology, till the onslaught of behaviorism in our own time. Despite his radical mould-breaking work in many areas, including that of philosophical methodology, Descartes was sometimes surprisingly orthodox and Scholastic. In philosophy of mind, this seems especially to be true. He not merely adopted the dualism or quasi-dualism of the Scholastic Platonized Aristotle, he made it

---

[6] Notable exceptions were Descartes' contemporaries, Hobbes and Spinoza, and, in the late nineteenth and early twentieth century, the Scottish psychologists Shand and McDougall.

hard-edged. He saw the human body in the uncompromisingly "matter of fact" manner of the new physiology, but described the human mind as an immaterial immortal soul whose essence was consciousness. A human's mental life, on his account, was so ethereal and non-physiological that it became a problem for him to account for how we are often conscious of what is happening in and to our bodies, and often able to issue conscious "commands" which set our bodily machinery in motion. Notoriously, Descartes surmised that the point where the immaterial conscious soul met the non-conscious material body was the pineal gland.

Unlike Aquinas, Descartes (1911–12) located emotions primarily in the human soul. Animals could act and react as if under the stress of emotion but they could not in reality experience any emotion because they lacked the immaterial organ, the human soul, with which to have such experiences. Although Descartes had a subtle and complex account of the genesis of emotions—as involving perception, memory, belief, physiological changes, and behaviour—only the soul's conscious perception or feeling of what was occurring in the body was the emotion proper. Thus, for Descartes, the beginning of fear is our being confronted by a suitably fearful object, say by the approach of "some strange and frightful animal". This sighting of the "strange and frightful" animal is then transmitted, via the pineal gland, and by means of the body's message carriers (which Descartes, along with the physiologists of his day, believed were extremely subtle bodily fluids), to the soul. Once in the soul, this perception is compared in memory with previous similar ones and there is a realization of some sort that this animal is liable to prove as harmful as previously experienced "strange and frightful" animals did. In turn the soul, once again via the pineal gland, instructs the body "to turn the back and dispose the legs for flight", and to speed up the lung's respiration rates and the heart's rate of pumping blood around the arteries and veins. Finally, and only now, with everything organized, does the soul produce a final mirror-image in consciousness of all these physiological events. This mirror-image is the feeling which *is* the emotion.

Because, for mainly pious reasons I expect, Descartes had already committed himself to the view that anything important to humans must be found wholly in the immortal soul, and must thereby be simple,[7] he had to maintain that only the final, culminating, reactive, simple and unitary mirror-feeling in the soul of all that was going on in the body, could be called "the emotion". Even so, this view contained the seeds of what was to be the attempt, the first attempt, to turn the study of emotion into a scientific enterprise. For Descartes stressed that it was our body's actions and reactions, resulting from perceptions of our environment and guided in part by the soul's cognitive powers of memory, imagination and deliberation, that produced what was distinctive in each emotion. It was the qualitative differences in the patterns of the body's actions and reactions

---

[7] For only if it were simple, would the soul, possessing no parts, be impervious to death or destruction, for any such perishing was thought of as involving the break-down or break-up of something complex into its constituent parts.

that produced the qualitative differences in the mirror-image feelings, of those patterns, in the soul.

SPINOZA AGAINST THE ORTHODOXY

It was this Cartesian view of emotion which was to dominate psychology and philosophy of mind until almost our own time. However, before seeing how and why this came to be, I want to mention, if only briefly, a dissenting voice from the seventeenth century. Benedict (or Baruch) de Spinoza was born of Jewish parentage in Amsterdam and spent his life in Holland. His parents had fled from Portugal to escape Catholic persecution, and he himself was both expelled from the Jewish community in Holland and had some of his writings condemned by the Catholic Church. Thus, the book which among other things contained his theory of emotion, *The Ethics*, was not published in his lifetime. Like Descartes, whose work he studied closely, Spinoza was greatly impressed by the new science of the seventeenth century. In particular, he was impressed by how the new physics had become hardened and disciplined by mathematics such that, if one could form mathematically rigorous general laws or axioms about, say, the motion of a certain class of bodies or objects, then one could explain and predict the motion of any newly discovered body that could be classified as a member of that class. Indeed, he surmised, all genuine explanation was of this kind. In *The Ethics* (Spinoza, 1883), whose title is somewhat confusing for a modern reader, he set out to produce an axiomatic and deductively rigorous system of metaphysics which would include an account of human action and motivation. To accomplish this latter part of his project, he realized that part of his task was to work out what was the ultimate good for humans. This, in turn, led Spinoza to investigate the nature of humans and their emotions (see also Hampshire, 1962, especially Chapter 4.)

His views about human nature might be best understood in contrast to those of Descartes. Spinoza denied that humans were made up of two substances, a soul and a body. He was a monist who saw mind (or thought) and body (or extension) as merely two different ways or "conceptual schemes" in which events of the one infinite primal substance might be recognized and discussed by humans. To the confusion of the religiously orthodox, he also equated this infinite primal and wholly deterministic substance with God (or, rather, an impersonal god-stuff).

Spinoza was also resolutely anti-Cartesian about the emotions, for he described them as essentially cognitive although, certainly, he also put desire (or at least a sort of *libido*) and feeling at the heart of emotion. Arguably, his account could be construed as a materialistic and deterministic version of Aquinas's impulse account. Emotions, for Spinoza, were "modifications of the body, whereby the active power [of the inbuilt, in modern terminology "genetically inherited", unconscious natural impetus to survive, or *conatus*] of the said body is increased or diminished, aided or constrained, and also the ideas of such modifications" (Spinoza, 1883, p. 130). These basic "modifications of the body" plus thought are Spinoza's way of referring to the manifestations of the interplay of the three basic emotional building blocks. For pleasure is the result of the fundamental impulse to survive giving rise to a general contentment when being aided by events in the environment, and pain the result of its giving rise to feelings of discomfort or discontent when hindered by them. For Spinoza, the emotions as we know and refer to them, emotions such as anger, fear, love, jealousy and so on, are the latter two of these basic emotional building blocks, namely pleasure and pain, modified by thought. Thus, Spinoza tells us that:

> *Love* is nothing else but *pleasure accompanied by the idea of an external cause: hate* is nothing else but *pain accompanied by the idea of an external cause* (Spinoza, 1883, p. 140).

That is, undergoing the emotion love is experiencing pleasure and at the same time, believing, rightly or wrongly, that something, in this case presumably some person or quasi-person, is the cause of the pleasure. Conversely with hate. Essential to love and hate, on this account, are the beliefs about what is the cause of the pleasure and pain ingredients (in modern terminology, of the cause of the physiological changes and feeling ingredients) of occurrent states of love and hate. Thus, Spinoza's account of emotion is a classical example of a cognitive theory of emotion. Where his account differs from most modern cognitive theories is his view that the beliefs in question do not have any causal role (certainly any core causal role). For Spinoza, the beliefs or thoughts associated with emotions *accompany* the "bodily modifications", and so give the latter a role in our mental life, rather than *cause* them. The beliefs give a cognitive colouring to certain types of bodily events that are occurring, rather than give rise to these events themselves. Nevertheless, for Spinoza, these bodily events would not amount to what we call "emotions" unless and until they entered our cognitive life in the way described.

Given the priority Spinoza gives to the bodily events, his view of emotions might be described as more somatopsychic than psychosomatic. What is more, the chief source of motivation and emotion is the unconscious inbuilt *conatus*, which clearly bears comparison with Freud's *libido* in being the fundamental source of our emotional life. Like Freud, he also seems to have held the view that, because of their subterranean source in the *conatus*, our emotions are not in themselves blameworthy and so puritanism and asceticism are foolish attitudes to adopt. Our emotions manifest our psychical stability or lack of it, and knowledge about our emotions can only help us to come to terms with our complex psychical structure and organization.

One can only speculate why it was that philosophy of mind, and in the late nineteenth century, the new experimental science of psychology, followed Descartes rather than Spinoza on the matter of emotion. One reason, possibly, was that Spinoza's texts are not easy reading. Much of what he has to say could have been put more clearly. Certainly his writings do not have the clarity and the impact of Descartes's works. A more likely cause of Spinoza's neglect might be that it would have been dangerous for anyone to champion his view of anything in any Christian era or Christian region, for Spinoza denied the existence of a personal God, of the soul and of free will, and in consequence made the Christian message and its eschatology look like a pious myth. However, when the time was ripe to give Spinoza a fair hearing, it was too late, for the Cartesian account of emotion was by then the entrenched orthodoxy. While every now and again a contemporary philosopher does champion Spinoza's account of emotion (e.g. Neu, 1977), it is generally accepted that nowadays there are better cognitive views around which have rendered it obsolete.

NEO-CARTESIANISM AND THEN BEHAVIOURISM

It could be said that William James's account of emotion is export quality Cartesianism[8] machined to high standard by means of nineteenth century positivism. James (1950), at least when he wrote his masterpiece, *The Principles of Psychology*, was more or less a regular subscriber to the nineteenth century version of Cartesian dualism. In *The Principles* he wrote, famously, that:

> *bodily changes follow directly the perception of the exciting fact, and that our feeling of the same changes as they occur is the emotion.* Common-sense says, we lose our fortune, are sorry and weep ... The hypothesis here to be defended says ... that we feel sorry because we cry"(James, 1950, Vol. 2, pp. 449–450; see also James, 1884).

That is, our feeling of sadness, which is the emotion, is our conscious experience of our weeping. More generally speaking, we act and react automatically after the perception of something, at least sometimes. If these actions and reactions involve physiological arousal (say increased heart beat, increased respiration rate, sweating, pallor, etc.), then it is very likely that we will be conscious of this bodily upset. The Gestalt feeling of this complex upset or pattern of arousal is the emotion. In short, James whole-heartedly concurred with Descartes in holding that it was the qualitative differences in the patterns of the body's actions and reactions that produced the qualitative differences in the mirror-image feelings, of those patterns, in (although not any longer "the soul") the subject's stream of consciousness.

James, and his colleague in this area of research, the Danish physiologist Carl Lange (1922), believed that they had improved on Descartes' account by showing how the study of emotion could become scientific. Since each emotion was nothing but the mirror-feeling of some complex of bodily arousal (some pattern of physiological changes), then all you needed to know in order to distinguish and describe the various emotions was to study the physiological details of each

---

[8] Of course, between Descartes and James there were a number of other Cartesian or quasi-Cartesian views, most notably (in regard to the emotions) that of Hume (1969), Book II, "Of the Passions". Hume held that emotions were feelings or sensations in the soul but he added to this, as causal precursor, a complicated choreography of associations and relations of impressions and ideas rather than, as did Descartes, a complicated pattern of bodily actions and reactions. So Hume was more of a cognitivist than Descartes ever was.

pattern of arousal. The psychology of emotion was, in effect, now a part of physiology, and so as "hard-nosed" and "tough-minded" and as scientific an enterprise as you like.

Of course matters were not really as simple as this, they never are. When investigated with the ever-increasing skills of the new science of psychology, brought about by the ever-increasing subtlety of instrumentation and experiment, it was discovered that the physiological patterns associated with emotion were not sufficiently diverse and distinct to give us any clear and distinct listing of emotions (see Cannon, 1927; Munn, 1961; Mandler, 1975). Furthermore, there were some gaps in the theory as well. How could we be sure that the emotion (that is, the feeling in the soul or at least in the privacy of one's own stream of consciousness) which you have when you are running away from a Rottweiler, is the same as the one I have when I am in the same situation? How can a comparison be made, if only you have access to your feeling and only I have access to mine? If, in the final analysis, love, for example, becomes just a "lovey-dovey feeling", then no-one could ever be quite sure whether it was love or anxiety or indigestion that was keeping him/her awake at night.

In that disturbed decade from 1910 to 1920, there was a permanent sea-change in the subject of psychology, to be followed not long afterwards by a similar one in philosophy. In psychology, the old Cartesian experimental method, of subjects introspecting their stream of consciousness with their "mental eye" and reporting on their discoveries about the mind and mental events, albeit under strict laboratory conditions, was being castigated for having produced little or nothing of value. No "discoveries" were being made. Besides, the whole enterprise seemed altogether too subjective and uncheckable, that is altogether too dubious, to be the mainspring of a scientific psychology. For, while agreement might sometimes be reached about some claim about human psychology within the confines of one school or one particular laboratory, it was notorious that it was more or less impossible to reach any agreement across schools and in a number of laboratories. If one school of introspectionists said that you could have thoughts that were not mediated by one of the senses (that is, that you could have thoughts which were not in the form of visual images or heard speech or some such), another school would claim that the evidence from their introspectionist laboratory told a different story. With their morale sapped by such controversies and by a lack of any incontrovertible gains in the accumulation of facts about human psychology, the introspectionists fell easy victim to the invading behaviourist army.

In effect, J.B. Watson produced the behaviourist manifesto when he wrote his exciting and combative paper, "Psychology as a behaviourist views it" (Watson, 1913).[9] At a stroke, from being "the science of mind", psychology had been

---

[9] Compare also the following: "Behaviorism as I tried to develop it in my lectures at Columbia in 1912 and in my earliest writings, was an attempt to do one thing—to apply to the experimental study of man the same kind of procedure and the same language of description that many research men had found useful for so many years in the study of animals lower than man. We believed then, as we do now, that man is an animal different from other animals only in the types of behavior he displays" (Watson, 1930, p. v).

redefined by Watson as "the science of behaviour". The way to study humans, including human psychology, is to employ just the same methods as you would use to study non-human animals, that is by means of scientifically controlled, objective observation and experiment, and by taking no account of any alleged introspective access to a mind or soul.

As regards the investigation of human emotions, somewhat surprisingly, Watson did not produce an account in terms of human behaviour (as did later behaviourists; see, for example, Skinner, 1953, Chapter 10) but in terms of patterns of physiological changes. Indeed, his account of emotion is really William James's account shorn of any reference to feelings or any other sort of conscious state. Whereas James had said that an emotion is the feeling-record in consciousness of a distinguishing pattern of physiological reactions or changes in the body, Watson held that the emotion is *nothing but the pattern* of physiological reactions or changes. Furthermore, since infants are the obvious bridge between humans and other primates and, at least when their mothers are not within earshot, can be described as animal-like humans, the best research strategy is to study the emotions of the newborn (Watson, 1930, 187).

Psychological behaviourism was one of the major sources of philosophical behaviourism, but there were other sources. The most important of these latter sources was logical positivism, which amounted to nineteeth century positivism retooled with the modern logic of Frege, Russell and Wittgenstein, and fashioned into a philosophical methodology. Nineteenth century positivism was a hymn to natural science, extolling it as the sole repository of real, factual or positive knowledge. Logical positivism reorchestrated this hymn in logico-linguistic terms.

One of the central figures in the logical positivist movement was the German philosopher, Rudolf Carnap. One of his most famous papers, first published in *Erkenntnis*, the house journal of the Vienna Circle (the best known group of logical positivists, who met regularly for discussion in Vienna before the Second World War), was entitled "Psychology in the Language of Physics", (Carnap, 1995). In this paper Carnap wrote that, "all the sentences of psychology are about physical processes, namely about the physical behaviour of humans and other animals"(Carnap, 1995, p. 43.) The "sentences" referred to are not the sentences psychologists themselves may employ, for they may be unredeemed introspectionists or whatever, but the sentences into which, Carnap believed, any meaningful sentences employed by psychologists could and should be translated. In due course these sentences describing the physical behaviour of humans would be retranslated into statements in the language of physics, the fundamental science. Thus, said Carnap, "Now psychology, which has hitherto enjoyed a certain elevated position as the theory of psychic or mental processes, is to be degraded into a part of physics" (Carnap, 1995, p. 46.)

When he came to the task of delineating the details, Carnap admitted that at present one could not go much further than a translation of, say, "He is excited", into something like, "His body (especially his central nervous system) is charac-terized by a high pulse rate and respiration rate, by the occurrence of agitated movements, by vehement and factually unsatisfactory answers to questions, etc."[10] In short, Carnap was under no illusion about what sort of "translation" work was possible. In regard to psychology, including the psychology of the emotions, he realized that his "translations" had advanced no further than those of the psychological behaviourists. What he believed was important in his way of getting to this point was in seeing the task as one of translating one language (strictly speaking, one vocabulary) into another.

There was yet another source of behaviourist analyses in the philosophy of emotion. This source was linguistic analysis, which in turn was markedly anti-Cartesian in spirit. One of the central figures in mid-twentieth century British philosophy was Gilbert Ryle, and he is often considered to be the most notable member of the philosophical movement called linguistic analysis. One of the sources of this movement was logical positivism. Another was the tandem of Cambridge philosophers, Moore and Wittgenstein. Wittgenstein, in particular, saw philosophy as the task of untying knots in our thinking, where the knots resulted chiefly from philosophers' own misuse of ordinary language when they employed it in the more exacting tasks of philosophy. In the 1930s, Ryle wrote a paper entitled, "Systematically misleading expressions" (Ryle, 1971, p. 39 ff.), which has sometimes been called "the manifesto of linguistic analysis". In that paper, Ryle argued that philosophical achievement lay in correcting the category mistakes (or mistakes in our understanding of concepts), which philosophers perpetrated when they mishandled ordinary language in the course of propounding and defending philosophical theories or theses, and of substituting a correct understanding of the concepts under scrutiny.

Ryle described his analytic masterpiece, *The Concept of Mind* (Ryle, 1949), as a sustained piece of hatchet work on the Cartesian doctrine of mind, that is on Cartesian dualism. Cartesian dualism, he said, was one big category mistake because the Cartesian dogma explained the meaning of mental terms and expounded mental concepts in terms of inner mental faculties, such as the intellect and the will, each of which allegedly produced its own proprietary acts. Ryle argued that the real analysis of the meaning and reference of our mental terms and concepts was in terms of dispositions. To be intelligent, for example, is not to possess a special faculty in the mind or soul which is able to do clever calculations in a private mental arena and occasionally publish its findings in speech and behaviour. To be intelligent is to be disposed to do certain specifiable actions in certain circumscribable environmental conditions, and to do them successfully. It is to be good at intellectual tasks. In general, then, said the philosophical behaviourist, whether it be to animals or humans, we attribute mental terms on the basis of the ordinary observation of ordinary behaviour, over time, and in observable and circumscribable circumstances, not on the basis of some single person's alleged inner introspective observation of some of his/her alleged inner private mental events.

Ryle had also read his Watson and his Carnap, and his account of emotion

---

[10] This is an adaptation of material from Carnap, 1995, 48–53.

is a product of the triad of influences: psychological behaviourism, logical positivism, and anti-Cartesianism. Thus, in Chapter 4 of *The Concept of Mind*, Ryle puts forward an account of emotions as being behavioural dispositions. To be afraid is not to undergo a private Cartesian experience such as a feeling, but it is to be disposed to act and react in a certain way in certain circumstances, and here and now to have that disposition activated. To be in love is not to harbour a private feeling of a special sort in one's mental parlour, but to be prone to doing quite ordinary and observable things, such as talking about someone to the exclusion of other topics, overpraising that person, defending him/her against any criticism, seeking out that person's company in an overweening way, and so on. In short, Ryle produced an account of emotion which was not very different from the account which the psychological behaviourists gave, although for very different reasons. Where behaviourists in psychology were behaviourist for reasons of methodology, those in philosophy were so for logico-linguistic reasons.

Ryle also added to his account of emotion something which was peculiar to linguistic analysis. He set about exposing the ambiguity in our ordinary use of the term "emotion", explaining that, depending on the context, it meant inclinations (or motives), moods, agitations (or commotions), or feelings. The first three usages should be analysed as referrring to dispositions; the latter (feelings) in terms of ordinary bodily sensations such as itches, twinges and tickles.

How, then, did cognitive theories of emotion make the overwhelming comeback that they have made? Without hindsight it is hard to imagine that cognitive theories could ever have made a comeback. For behaviourism seemed, both to philosophical and psychological behaviourists, to rule out any reference to any inner (or "inside the head") events because these must be strictly unobservable events. Besides, such reference would be backsliding once again into Cartesianism. By a further inference, this prohibition seemed to rule out any mention of cognitive (or evaluative or appetitive) events, such as beliefs, surmises, evaluations, desires, wishes, wants and so on, for these were all clearly "inside the head" events. Thus, one could say that the manner of the demise of Cartesianism, especially in psychology, ruled out of order any place for cognition and so for cognitive theories of emotion.

The answer, we now know, is that the shiny new science of behaviourist psychology and the new positivistic philosophy of mind were hardly more successful than the old Cartesian philosophy of mind or the neo-Cartesian introspectionist psychology. Explanations of human actions and emotions, without reference to cognitive processes, simply did not work. But let us see this crucial turning point in more detail.

THE REAPPEARANCE OF COGNITION IN PHILOSOPHY AND PSYCHOLOGY

Generally speaking, behaviourism and behaviourist accounts of emotion, appeared in philosophy much later than they appeared in psychology. On the other hand, behaviourism and behaviourist accounts of emotion were jettisoned in philosophy much earlier than they were in psychology. Ryle himself admitted that there was a permanent gap in behaviouristic analyses in general, mainly in their inability to give any account, as he memorably put it, of what "Le Penseur" ("The Thinker" as depicted in Rodin's statue) was doing. For here we have a person to whom we readily apply the paradigm mental (and cognitive) predicate, "thinking", yet no behaviour is taking place, no noticeable physiological changes of an abnormal kind are occurring, and no notice is being taken of what is going on in the immediate environment. All the usual ingredients for a behaviouristic analysis are simply not available.

Another very basic problem for behaviouristic analyses, which shows up all too clearly in the context of the emotions, is what might be called "The problem of diffuseness". Any account of an emotion which states that "emotion X" is to be analysed as "a disposition to behave in manner a, b and c in context p" will encounter an intractable problem. For the behaviour which, in fact, we associate with any particular emotion cannot be circumscribed in a neat, definitive and packaged way. For example, one person might display anger by banging the table, shouting, and slamming the door. Another might display it by being unusually quiet and undemonstrative, and by closing the door with studied carefulness as he left the room with exaggerated courtesy. What an angry person will do will depend on what sort of temperament he has, what culture he is part of, what context he finds himself in, and so on. What an angry person might do, then, is "open-ended" rather than "neatly parcelled".

The very diffuseness and unpredictability of emotional behaviour, unless we know a great deal about the subject of the emotion in question, is an indication that we consider behaviour to be a quite variable *manifestation* of an emotion, rather than all that an emotion is. Indeed, unless we considered it thus, how could we decide that slamming the door and shouting, or tightening the muscles of the face and narrowing the eyes, or speaking in an unnaturally even tone of voice, or going red in the face and weeping, or some other pattern of behaviour, is angry behaviour, while picking your nose or scratching your neck is not? Behaviour does not come hallmarked with the name of some emotion. We need to link behaviour to some emotion or to learn that this behaviour is a sympton or sign or manifestation of that emotion. We have to learn that giggling is a sign of nervousness in Japanese people and not a sign of frivolity. We have to learn that sobbing can be a sign of relief as well as grief.

If behaviouristic accounts can be described as "peripheralist" ones, in that they emphasise and make reference only to the periphery, that is, to human behaviour and its context, then the reaction to behaviourism in both philosophy and psychology might be called "centralist". For the main theories of mind and emotion, which superseded behaviourist ones, gave accounts which emphasized what they believed was going on inside human heads and so was central to the human organism. This reaction was not a return to Cartesian substance dualism, and I doubt if there ever will be a reaction of that sort, for contemporary philosophers and psychologists tend to be uncompromising materialists, but the adoption of a different sort of dualism, namely that between function and structure. For a time, from roughly 1960 to 1980, the guiding metaphor in philosophy of mind was the computer. The mind is to the body, so the slogan went, as a computer's program or software (its functioning) is to its electronics or hardware (its structure). The study of a human's mental life or psychology amounts to the investigation of the human program (or functioning). Evolution is both the programmer of the software and the designer of the hardware. It is up to humans to unravel what evolution has knitted.

The pendulum had swung back. Psychology and philosophy of mind were seen once again as mental science, but with the "mentalism" removed. Human psychology was first and foremost about what went on inside human heads. The core of psychology, as a discipline, became the scientific account of human cognition and appetition, or "cognitive science", for short. In philosophy of mind and philosophical psychology—and this latter term was increasingly being substituted for the former as, once again, if briefly, philosophers and psychologists found common cause—this "centralism" took the form of making it legitimate once again to talk about beliefs and desires and hopes and wants. On the other hand, there arose soon enough an uncompromising and unrelenting debate about the correct account of such terms as "belief", "desire", "want", "hope" and so on. Do these terms refer ultimately and literally to neuronal states of the brain, it was asked? Or do they refer rather to functional tasks which are performed by the brain? Or are such terms really just a useful "folk" way of talking about what goes on inside human heads but which must not be taken literally?

These mainstream core debates in philosophy of mind are not our concern here. What is our concern is that the reaction against the behaviouristic accounts of emotion produced what came to be known as cognitive accounts. The core of emotions, as Aristotle had claimed long ago, were beliefs and desires or, in modern jargon, "cognitions" of various sorts. Emotions were viewed once again as complexly psychosomatic; that is, emotions were analysed in terms of physiological changes, feelings, behavioural actions and reactions caused by beliefs, desires, wants and wishes. Indeed, the latter were held to be the core of emotional states. What differentiated one emotion from another, and an emotional state from an non-emotional state, was a cognitive "something". Which sort of *cognitive* state was the essential one was itself a matter of considerable debate, and still is to some extent. Some saw the essential cognitive state or item to be beliefs, others argued that it was judgements, others desires, and still others appraisals or evaluations.

In my attempt to get to the essentials when describing the demise of behaviourism and the rise of cognitivism in philosophy and psychology, no doubt I have tidied up the story a little too much. Certainly, the move away from behaviouristic accounts of emotion to cognitive accounts was a slow and unspectacular affair. The beginnings are probably to be found in a series of careful but undramatic papers in philosophy[11] which drew attention to the shortcomings of non-cognitive accounts of emotion and to the attractions of bringing reference to beliefs, evaluations and desires into the analysis of emotional states.

At this point, somewhat immodestly, I will discuss the cognitive view I myself put forward in *Emotion* (Lyons, 1980) because, besides being the account I know best, it sets out in considerable detail the philosophical reasons why philosophers have jettisoned Cartesian and behaviourist theories of emotion and revived cognitive theories.[12] For this book was, in effect, a long, historically-introduced, theoretical argument, drawing not merely upon philosophical debate but also on empirical work in psychology and neuroscience, as to why a cognitive theory is best placed to answer our most fundamental queries about the nature of emotion. In *Emotion*, I first pointed out that emotion terms are sometimes used dispositionally and sometimes occurrently. "Rage", for example, is always used occurrently, that is, it is always used to refer to an actual here-and-now bout or state of extreme anger in some person. The term "irascible", on the other hand, is a purely dispositional term, for it means that the person to whom it is applied is disposed or liable to fits or bouts of anger at the drop of a hat. "Love", in contrast to the phrase "in love", is another term that is used almost always in a dispositional sense, while the term "excited" is used almost always in an occurrent sense. I suggested that, since an emotional disposition amounts to being disposed to be in an occurrent emotional state of some sort in certain circumstances, then the focus of investigation and theoretical discussion should be occurrent emotional states. For they are "the full case". Whatever it is that is latent in an irascible person, which makes him/her irascible, will still be there, although now activated, in a person who is now angry. In addition, the other "parts" of emotional states—the feelings, behaviour, physiological changes, expressions—will now be present.

I then argued for a causal-evaluative (cognitive) account of emotional states; namely that a subject is in an emotional state if and only if he is in an abnormal physiological state caused by his evaluation of the context in relation to himself. "Abnormal", in relation to physiological changes, was defined as departing significantly from a human's normal physiological states in either direction, that is, in the direction of arousal or perturbation, or in the direction of unusual dampening down or depression. "Evaluation" was defined as a grading of the situation according to a wide spectrum of possible gradings or values. Thus, the subject is afraid if he evaluates the situation as dangerous and this evaluation affects him physiologically, that is, if it makes his heart beat faster, his respiration rate increase dramatically, his hands sweat, and his jaw tighten. This realization of danger, if the danger in question is the appearance of a Rottweiler from around the corner, will also make him want to avoid or escape the danger, which

---

[11] See, for example, Bedford (1956–57), Penelhum (1956–57), R. S. Peters (1960 and 1961–62), Kenny (1963), Pitcher (1965) and Alston (1967).
[12] In fact, this book is predated by a number of papers beginning in the early to mid-1970s; see e.g. Lyons (1973, 1974, 1976).

in turn will make him want to run away or call for help. But it might not. He might be knowledgeable about dogs and know that if he stands stock still, does not gesticulate and speaks to the dog in a soft and even voice, with lots of phrases like, "Nice doggy" and "Aren't you a handsome fellow", the dog will eventually lope off.

The evaluation, which is at the heart of each emotion, it was argued, is also what differentiates one emotion from another. Your agitation is to be labelled "anger" rather than "fear" if you believe he has insulted you rather than that he is about to attack you. In fact your evaluation of the situation may be wrong. He *is* about to attack you and he was *not* the person who insulted you. Nevertheless, your emotional state is still one of anger rather than fear, for your emotion is caused by what you "cognize" about the situation and its relevance to you, not what some objective observer guesses or even knows about the situation.

A cognitive approach to the explanation of the nature of emotion clearly makes emotions out to be part of the deliberative, thoughtful and rational side of humans rather than, as Plato claimed, the animal-like foe of reason. Our evaluations of particular situations express our personal values, which in turn will very often be influenced by our culture. Our values are, usually, things we hold dear for good reasons, and the things by which we order our life at its deepest level. Emotions, indeed, are probably a better guide to what we really approve and disapprove of than are our words and actions, for we can readily simulate the latter but not the former. When we speak of our fearlessness, our physiology and gesture and behaviour may contradict us. When we say "No matter", our flushing or blushing may say that it matters very much.

A cognitive account of emotion solves the behaviourist's problem of diffuseness. We call this behaviour emotional and that not, and this behaviour angry behaviour rather than anxious behaviour, because we know or guess that the subject of the behaviour considers that he himself, or someone dear to him (his quasi-self), has been insulted or the victim of some outrage. It is the emotional person's "cognitions" that we employ as a sieve to sift out and label the behaviour under scrutiny, for a cognitive theory holds that the behaviour stems rationally and appropriately from those "cognitions". It is this link which enables us to label this behaviour as typically angry behaviour, or as a symptom of anxiety or a sign of embarrassment, but to decide that this reaction is fatigue or stomach upset. No non-cognitivist account can explain why both running for a bus and dieting can be a sign of fear. For only a cognitivist can explain how humans can have both a fear of missing an appointment and a fear of getting fat.

A cognitive account of emotions also explains best how emotions are motives and how emotional behaviour is most often rational and appropriate behaviour. If the core of the emotion of anger is an evaluation, an evaluative belief, that one has been insulted or is in some sense a victim of outrage, then it makes sense that an angry person will lash out vengefully, verbally or otherwise, at the author of the insult or outrage. Contrariwise, if the core of the emotion in question is an evaluation of someone as possessing special personal characteristics, such as beauty or charm or goodness, or all three, then it makes sense to say that the appropriate, and so likely, response of someone who is in the grip of that emotion will be the opposite of vengeful lashing out.

Put more generally, only a cognitive account of emotion seems to make sense of emotions as not merely motives behind our actions but as subtle, rational, finely-tuned motives. For a cognitive account can make the factual belief–evaluation–desire "cognitive core" of any particular emotional state as complex and "thick" as you like. "She cried because she was sad" can be thickened to, "she cried because she was sad that Mary had died", to "she cried because she was sad that Mary had died because Mary was her friend" and so on. Thus, the person's reaction can be revealed, at least very often, as the result of more than one emotion (as, for example, the result of sadness, affection, loneliness, all mixed in). Sometimes these emotions can clash. Sometimes we are ambivalent in our emotional responses. Sometimes we are emotional about our emotions. Only a cognitive account seems able to make sense of such complexities and subtleties.

Of course, feelings and physiological changes are an integral part of emotions. Rather, the point is that they must not be seen in isolation. They are "produced by and so impregnated with cognition". However, there are rare but theoretically interesting cases when feelings can be absent from emotional states. As William James pointed out, feelings are *consciously experienced* happenings in our bodies and so part of our conscious attention. When a person's attention is wholly taken up by something else, say something very important, then there can be no "attention room" left over for anything else. On the other hand the "something important" will often generate an emotional state but, *ex hypothesi*, one with no "attention room" left over for feelings. For example, during a philosophical discussion about politics, I might become very angry at someone claiming that I am a crypto-something-or-other but, because my attention is wholly taken up by the discussion, my being aroused (physiologically aroused) will escape my attention. My arousal will not enter my consciousness as feelings. I am emotional but, owing to the circumstances, do not in fact feel anything. Of course feelings are most often a part of emotional states. Indeed, it would be very odd if someone claimed that they were overcome by love or anger or anxiety or hate but felt nothing at all. We would doubt the sincerity of their claim.

More generally speaking, the lack of emphasis upon feelings in the cognitive account of emotion is another sign of the long retreat from a Cartesian subjectivist view of emotions. Feelings are subjective experiences, while evaluations and physiological changes are not. While a cognitivist account of emotion is a centralist account, and thereby in conflict with any behaviourist or peripheralist account, it is not a return to subjectivism. Evaluations are objective items. It may be possible in the future, given advances in neurophysiology, to identify them with neurophysiological events (see, for an interesting attempt, Gray, 1981.) Then again, it may be a mistake to reify evaluations in such a crude one-to-one way. The word "slippery", for example, as applied to roads, is not a simple perceptual term on a par with "wet", although it may appear to be so, for "slippery" means "the level of wetness which in the past has been found to make the tyres of vehicles, which travel on such a surface, lack adhesion and so to slide across the surface". Similarly, "evaluating" may not be a comparatively straight-forward term like "perceiving", but a highly relational theory-laden, multi-layered one. "Evaluating" may be a term which is properly employed only at a higher, macro, "whole person", functional level of description and which is attributed not merely by reference to "central" neurophysiological and conscious events but also to "peripheral" ones, such as the perceived environment and a person's reaction to his perceived environment, and finally attributed not merely by reference to present events but across a considerable slab of time. Thus, there may be no single area in the brain or easily circumscribed pattern of brain activity which could be labelled "evaluative centre" or "evaluative cortex", in the way that there is a visual cortex. However, this does not mean that evaluations are any the less objective. It just means that their explanation will not be simple and straightforward.

It is probably fair to say that cognitivism is still the orthodoxy in philosophy of the emotions today. However, the cognitive theory of emotion is being and will probably continue to be modified in the future, perhaps quite radically, when philosophers and psychologists settle the current debates about the status of beliefs and desires. If it is found, as some philosophers advocate, that the terms "belief" and "desire" (and presumably "evaluative belief" would be grouped with them) are not the labels of real biological or even psychological realities at all but just a useful "folk" way of talking, then cognitive theories of emotion will either look very different from our current ones or disappear altogether.

Even now, some philosophical cognitivists in regard to emotions are suggest-ing that the belief and evaluation aspects have been overemphasized and that emotions are much more like perceptions or judgements or Gestalts (see, for example, Solomon, 1978; Gordon, 1986; de Sousa, 1987) or, in neo-Spinozistic fashion, that some emotions at any rate are associated especially with imagina-tion and are sometimes more like affects smeared with thought or imagination than affects that result from thought (see e.g. Greenspan, 1988.) Some psycholo-gists have also been engaged in work that suggests that we should consider the term "cognitive" as referring not to one single process but to a large integrated set of subsystems which operate in parallel. In turn, this would mean that the "cognitions" associated with emotional states will almost always involve not merely "propositional knowledge" but also sensory information. These findings will, I suspect, also cause further changes in the construal of philosophical cognitive accounts of emotion.[13]

There is also a wealth of research in philosophy into particular aspects of

---

[13] Barnard & Teasdale (1991) and Barnard (1985) outline a very sophisticated model of human cognition that involves a large number of interacting cognitive subsystems, which in turn are divided into peripheral ones (such as acoustic, visual, body state ones, etc.) and central ones (such as morphonolexical, propositional ones, etc.). As a corollary, these authors suggest that the cognitional aspect of emotional states should be seen as involving, in an integrated way, both "sensory and propositional meaning contributions" or, in less technical language, as involving both the head and the heart.

emotion, such as emotions as justifying motives for actions, the semantics of emotion vocabulary, the causes, objects, targets, and forms of emotions, appropriate and inappropriate expressions of emotion, the intentionality of emotion, true and false emotions, the rational and irrational aspects of emotion, emotions and personal relations, emotions and personal identity, emotions and character, self-deceptive emotions, emotions and choice, emotions and culture, the axiological and ethical dimensions of emotion, ambivalence in emotions, the expressions of emotion, emotions and ideology, and so on and so forth (see e.g. in the philosophical literature, Rorty, 1980; Irani & Myers, 1983; Schoeman, 1987.)

In the space of this short review article, I have only been able to depict the course of philosophy's reinstatement of cognitive theories of emotion with broad brushstrokes. What I have signally neglected in this article is any real indication of the immense harvest of papers, in the philosophy journals over the last 50 years, which investigate in meticulous fashion particular aspects of emotion or the "logic" of particular emotions. To do this, even superficially, I would need several volumes, not a few dozen pages.[14] On the other hand it should be clear that I believe that the cognitive account of emotions is here to stay, although I can imagine that future cognitive accounts may look very different from current ones.

ACKNOWLEDGEMENTS

I would like to thank the editor and publishers of the volume in which Lyons (1992) appeared for permission to reprint certain parts of that article, and Tim Dalgleish and Michael Power for their advice and constructive criticism in preparing this article.

REFERENCES

Atkinson, R. L., Atkinson, R. C., Smith, E. E., Bem, D. J. & Nolen-Hoeksema, S. (1996). *Hilgard's Introduction to Psychology*. Fort Worth, TX: Harcourt Brace.
Alston, W. (1967). Emotion and feeling. In P. Edwards (ed.), *The Encyclopedia of Philosophy*, Vol. 2. New York: Collier Macmillan—The Free Press.
Annas, J. (1992). *Hellenistic Philosophy of Mind*, Berkeley, CA: University of California Press.

---

[14] The collections in Rorty (1980), Irani & Myers (1983) and Schoeman (1987) will be a good start for anyone wanting to begin on a survey of the vast accumulation of journal papers on emotion by philosophers. The bibliographies in Lyons (1980), de Sousa (1987), Greenspan (1988), Armon-Jones (1991), Oakley (1992) and Stocker & Hegeman (1996) would also be of help. However, the best source is *The Philosopher's Index*, produced by the Philosophy Documentation Center at Bowling Green State University. It is an international index to all the major philosophical periodicals (as well as a source of information about books published in philosophy). *The Philosopher's Index* is published quarterly and there is also an annual cumulative edition. Articles are indexed according to both author and subject matter—thus, each issue contains a considerable number of entries under the title "emotion(s)" (see also Acknowledgements).

Aquinas, Thomas (1967).   In E. D'Arcy, (ed. & trans.) *Summa Theologiae* (c. 1265–73), Vol. 19, *The Emotions*. London: Blackfriars and Eyre and Spottiswoode.

Aristotle (1941a).   Rhetoric. (c. 335 BC). In R. McKeon (ed.), *The Basic Works of Aristotle*. New York: Random House.

Aristotle (1941b).   De Anima (c. 330 BC). In R. McKeon (ed.), *The Basic Works of Aristotle*. New York: Random House.

Armon-Jones, C. (1991).   *Varieties of Affect*. New York: Harvester Wheatsheaf/Simon and Schuster.

Barnard, P. (1985).   Interacting cognitive subsystems: a psycholinguistic approach to short-term memory. In A. Ellis (ed.), *Progress in the Psychology of Language*, Vol. 2. London: Erlbaum.

Barnard, P. J. & Teasdale, J. D. (1991).   Interacting cognitive subsystems: a systemic approach to cognitive-affective interaction and change. *Cognition and Emotion*, **5**(1).

Bedford, E. (1956–57).   Emotions. *Proceedings of the Aristotelian Society*, **57**.

Cannon, W. B. (1927).   The James–Lange theory of emotions: a critical examination and an alternative theory. *American Journal of Psychology*, **39**.

Carnap, R. (1995).   Psychology in the language of physics (1931). In W. Lyons (ed.), *Modern Philosophy of Mind*. London: J.M. Dent.

Descartes, R. (1911–12).   The Passions of the Soul (1649). In E. L. Haldane & G. R. Ross (eds & trans.), *The Philosophical Works of Descartes*. Cambridge: Cambridge University Press.

de Sousa, R. (1987).   *The Rationality of Emotion*. Cambridge, MA: MIT Press.

Gordon, R. M. (1986).   The passivity of emotions. *Philosophical Review*, **95**.

Gray, J. (1981).   *The Neuropsychology of Anxiety: An Enquiry into the Functions of the Septo-Hippocampal System*. Oxford: Oxford University Press.

Greenspan, P. (1988).   *Emotions and Reasons: An Inquiry into Emotional Justification*. London: Routledge.

Hampshire, S. (1962).   *Spinoza* (1951). Harmondsworth: Penguin.

Hume, D. (1969).   In E. C. Mossner (ed.), *A Treatise of Human Nature* (1739–40). Harmondsworth: Penguin.

Irani, K. D. & Myers, G. E. (eds) (1983).   *Emotion: Philosophical Studies*. New York: Haven.

James, W. (1884).   What is emotion? *Mind*, **9**.

James, W. (1950).   *The Principles of Psychology*, 1890. Vol. 2. New York: Dover.

Kretzmann, N., Kenny, A. & Pinborg, J. (eds) (1982).   *Cambridge History of Later Medieval Philosophy: from the Rediscovery of Aristotle to the Disintegration of Scholasticism, 1100–1600*. Cambridge: Cambridge University Press.

Kenny, A. (1963).   *Action, Emotion and Will*. London: Routledge & Kegan Paul.

Lange, C. (1922).   Om Sindsbevaegelser (1885). English trans. in Knight Dunlap (ed.), *The Emotions*. Baltimore, MD: Williams and Wilkins.

Long, A. A. & Sedley, D. N. (eds) (1987).   *The Hellenistic Philosophers*. Cambridge: Cambridge University Press.

Lyons, W. (1973).   A note on emotion statements. *Ratio*, **15**.

Lyons, W. (1974).   Physiological changes and the emotions. *Canadian Journal of Philosophy*, **3**.

Lyons, W. (1976).   Emotions and motives. *Canadian Journal of Philosophy*, **6**.

Lyons, W. (1980).   *Emotion*. Cambridge: Cambridge University Press.

Lyons, W. (1992).   An introduction to the philosophy of the emotions. In K. T. Strongman (ed.), *International Review of Studies on Emotion*, Vol. 2. Chichester: Wiley.

Lyons, W. (ed.) (1995).   *Modern Philosophy of Mind*. London: J.M. Dent.

Mandler, G. (1975).   *Mind and Emotion*. New York: Wiley.

Munn, N. L. (1961).   *Psychology: The Fundamentals of Human Adjustment*. London: Harrap.

Neu, J. (1977). *Emotion, Thought and Therapy*. London: Routledge & Kegan Paul.

Oakley, J. (1992). *Morality and the Emotions*. London: Routledge.

Oatley, K. (1992). *Best Laid Schemes: The Psychology of Emotions*. Cambridge: Cambridge University Press.

Oatley, K. & Jenkins, J. M. (1996). *Understanding Emotions*. Oxford: Blackwell.

Penelhum, T. (1956–57). The logic of pleasure. *Philosophy and Phenomenological Research*, **17**.

Peters, R. S. (1960). *The Concept of Motivation*. London: Routledge & Kegan Paul.

Peters, R. S. (1961–62). Emotions and the category of passivity. *Proceedings of the Aristotelian Society*, **62**.

Pitcher, G. (1965). Emotion. *Mind*, **74**.

Plato (1955). In H. D. P. Lee (ed. & trans.), *The Republic* (c. 355 BC). Harmondsworth: Penguin.

Plato (1982). In R. A. H. Waterfield (ed. & trans.), *Philebus* (c. 350 BC). Harwondsworth: Penguin.

Rorty, A. (ed.) (1980). *Explaining Emotions*. Berkeley, CA: University of California Press.

Ryle, G. (1971). Systematically misleading expressions (1932). In G. Ryle, *Collected Papers Vol. 2, Collected Essays 1929–1968*. London: Hutchinson.

Ryle, G. (1949). *The Concept of Mind*. London: Hutchinson.

Schoeman, F. (ed.) (1987). *Responsibility, Character, and the Emotions: New Essays in Moral Psychology*. Cambridge: Cambridge University Press.

Skinner, B. F. (1953). *Science and Human Behaviour*. New York: Macmillan—The Free Press.

Solomon, R. (1978). *The Passions: The Myth and Nature of Human Emotion*. New York: Anchor.

Spinoza, B. de. (1883). In R. H. M. Elwes (trans.) *The Chief Works of Benedict de Spinoza. Vol. II, The Ethics* (1677). London: George Bell & Sons.

Stocker, M. & Hegeman, E. (1996). *Valuing Emotions*. Cambridge: Cambridge University Press.

Strongman, K. T. (ed.) (1992). *International Review of Studies on Emotion*, Vol. 2. Chichester: Wiley.

Watson, J. B. (1913). Psychology as the behaviorist views it. *Psychological Review*, **20** (reprinted in Lyons, 1995).

Watson, J. B. (1919). *Psychology from the Standpoint of a Behaviorist*. Philadelphia, PA: Lippincott.

Watson, J. B. (1930). *Behaviorism* (revised edn). Chicago, IL: Phoenix Books/University of Chicago Press.

Chapter 3

Basic Emotions

Paul Ekman
University of California, San Francisco, CA, USA

INTRODUCTION

In this chapter I consolidate my previous writings about basic emotions (Ekman, 1984, 1992a, 1992b) and introduce a few changes in my thinking. My views over the past 40 years have changed radically from my initial view (Ekman, 1957) that: (a) a pleasant–unpleasant and active–passive scale were sufficient to capture the differences among emotions; and (b) the relationship between a facial configuration and what it signified is socially learned and culturally variable. I was forced to adopt the opposite view by findings from my own and others' cross-cultural studies of facial expressions. There are some who have challenged this by now quite large body of evidence; I describe those challenges and the answers to them in Chapter 16.

The framework I describe below is most influenced by Darwin (1872/1997) and Tomkins (1962), although I do not accept in total what either said. There are three meanings of the term "basic" (see also Ortony & Turner, 1990). First, it distinguishes those who maintain that there are a number of separate emotions, that differ one from another in important ways. From this perspective, fear, anger, disgust, sadness and contempt, all negative emotions, differ in their appraisal, antecedent events, probable behavioral response, physiology and other characteristics described below. So, too, amusement, pride in achievement, satisfaction, relief and contentment, all positive emotions, differ from each other. This basic emotions perspective is in contrast to those who treat emotions as fundamentally the same, differing only in terms of intensity or pleasantness.

To identify separate discrete emotions does not necessarily require that one also take an evolutionary view of emotions. A social constructionist could allow

---

Handbook of Cognition and Emotion. Edited by T. Dalgleish and M. Power.

for separate emotions without embracing the second meaning of the adjective "basic". Even the discovery of universals in expression or in antecedent events does not require giving a major role to evolution. Instead, one can attribute universals to species-constant learning—social learning which will usually occur for all members of the species, regardless of culture (cf. Allport, 1924). In this view it is ontogeny, not phylogeny, which is responsible for any commonalities in emotion; universals in expression are due to what ethologists call "conventionalization", not "ritualization" (see Ekman, 1979 for a discussion of these distinctions as applied to emotion).

The second meaning of the adjective "basic" is to indicate instead the view that emotions evolved for their adaptive value in dealing with *fundamental life tasks*. Innate factors play a role in accounting for the characteristics they share, not species-constant or species-variable learning. There are a number of ways to describe these fundamental life tasks. Johnson-Laird & Oatley (1992) say they are universal human predicaments, such as achievements, losses, frustrations, etc. Each emotion thus prompts us in a direction which, in the course of evolution, has done better than other solutions in recurring circumstances that are relevant to goals. Lazarus (1991) talks of "common adaptational tasks as these are appraised and configured into core relational themes" (p. 202) and gives examples of facing an immediate danger, experiencing an irrevocable loss, progressing towards the realization of a goal, etc. Stein & Trabasso (1992) say that in happiness a goal is attained or maintained, in sadness there is a failure to attain or maintain a goal, in anger an agent causes a loss of a goal, and in fear there is an expectation of failure to achieve a goal. Tooby & Cosmides (1990) tell us that emotions impose ". . . on the present world an interpretative landscape derived from the covariant structure of the past . . .". Emotions, they say, deal with recurrent ". . . adaptive situations . . . fighting, falling in love, escaping predators, confronting sexual infidelity, and so on, each [of which] recurred innumerable times in evolutionary history . . ." (pp. 407–408). Tooby & Cosmides emphasize what I consider the crucial element which distinguishes the emotions: our appraisal of a current event is influenced by our ancestral past.

These different descriptions are quite compatible, each emphasizing another aspect of the phenomenon. Common to all these views is the presumption that emotions are designed to deal with inter-organismic encounters, between people or between people and other animals. Nevertheless, it is important to note that emotions can and do occur when we are not in the presence of others, and are not imagining other people. We can have emotional reactions to thunder, music, loss of physical support, auto-erotic activity, etc. Yet I believe the primary function of emotion is to mobilize the organism to deal quickly with important interpersonal encounters, prepared to do so by what types of activity have been adaptive in the past. The past refers in part to what has been adaptive in the past history of our species, and the past refers also to what has been adaptive in our own individual life history.

The term "basic" has been used also to describe elements that combine to form more complex or compound emotions. So, for example, smugness might be considered to be a blend of the two elemental emotions, happiness and contempt. Earlier we (Ekman & Friesen, 1975) made just such a proposal about facial expressions. I am less certain now about whether or not two basic emotions can occur simultaneously, although that may well depend upon what aspect of emotion is considered. In any case, I will not consider further this meaning of the term "basic", since no-one (other than Plutchik, 1962), who currently works from a basic emotion framework, has been much concerned with this meaning.

THE CHARACTERISTICS THAT DISTINGUISH BASIC EMOTIONS

I will describe a number of characteristics which are useful in distinguishing one emotion from another. I will also describe other characteristics shared by all emotions, but which are helpful in distinguishing emotions from other affective phenomena, such as moods or emotional traits.

Distinctive Universal Signals

I have gone back and forth on the question of whether or not a universal signal is the *sine qua non* for emotion (Ekman, 1984; 1992a, 1992b). Once again I will set out that claim, as a challenge for someone to identify states which have all the other characteristics I describe below but which have no signal. To date there is no such evidence, and I doubt it will be found. I believe it was central to the evolution of emotions that they inform conspecifics, without choice or consideration, about what is occurring: inside the person (plans, memories, physiological changes), what most likely occurred before to bring about that expression (antecedents), and what is most likely to occur next (immediate consequences, regulatory attempts, coping). For example, when we see a person with a disgust expression, we know that the person is responding to something offensive to taste or smell, literally or metaphorically, that the person is likely to make sounds such as "yuck" rather than "yum", and is likely to turn away from the source of stimulation. Elsewhere (Ekman, 1993; 1997) I have described seven classes of information that emotional signals may provide, and the research necessary to establish that this is so.

Emotional expressions are crucial to the development and regulation of interpersonal relationships. To mention just three examples, facial expressions should be involved in the formation of attachments (in infancy as well as in courtship), and in the regulation, acceleration or deceleration of aggression. People I have studied who have congenital facial paralysis (Mobius syndrome) report great difficulty in developing and maintaining even casual relationships, since they have no capability for facial expressiveness. Ross (1981) also found that stroke patients who can not properly identify the prosody that accompanies speech, or who cannot generate the prosody that accompanies emotion utterances, have severe interpersonal difficulties.

Moods and emotional traits do not own their own distinctive signals, but instead we infer these affective phenomena, in part at least, from the fact that they are saturated with the signals of one or another emotion. A high incidence of anger-related signals can suggest an irritable mood or a hostile trait, for example.

To say that it was crucial to the evolution of emotions that they inform conspecifics about matters of import, does not mean that in each and every instance in which emotions occur a signal will be present. Emotions obviously do occur without any evident signal, because we can, to a very large extent, inhibit the appearance of a signal. Also, a threshold may need to be crossed to bring about an expressive signal, and that threshold may vary across individuals. If we could measure the brain areas which send information to the facial nucleus during spontaneous emotional experience, I expect we would find that there is some distinctive activity, even in low threshold states or when an individual is attempting to inhibit emotion. This remains an empirical question.

Not only can there be emotion without expression, there can be what appears to be expression without emotion. Humans can deliberately or habitually fabricate a facsimile of an emotional expression, facially and vocally. This may happen for many reasons; for example, to mislead or to refer to an emotion that is not currently experienced. There is quite robust evidence (for a summmary, see Ekman & Davidson, 1990) that facial expressions differ in subtle ways when a smile occurs involuntarily as part of one or another enjoyment experiences, as compared to either social smiling or deliberately made false smiles. If the research was done I expect it would also be possible to distinguish fabricated signs of emotion from actual emotional expressions for other emotions, and in the voice as well as the face (for a further discussion of when there is emotion without expression and expression without emotion, see Ekman 1993; 1997).

Emotion-specific Physiology

If basic emotions evolved to deal with fundamental life tasks, they should not only provide information through expressions to conspecifics about what is occurring, but there should also be physiological changes preparing the organism to respond differently in different emotional states.

There is evidence (Ekman, Levenson & Friesen, 1983; Levenson, Ekman & Friesen, 1990) for distinctive patterns of autonomic nervous system (ANS) activity for anger, fear and disgust, and it appears that there may also be a distinctive pattern for sadness (Levenson et al., 1991). These findings have now been replicated in four separate experiments, in two different age groups. Although there are some inconsistencies between the ANS patterns they found and the findings of other investigators, there are many consistencies with the results of Schwartz,

Weinberger & Singer (1981), Ax (1953), Roberts & Weerts (1982) and Graham (1962).

The only recent challenge to our findings was Stemmler's (1989) report that ANS patterning was specific to how the emotion was elicited. However, this may be due to a number of methodological problems, including measuring physiology a considerable period after the induction was over, studying very low emotional intensities, and including a substantial number of subjects who reported not experiencing the emotion. We have preliminary evidence in two different studies (Levenson et al., 1991; Ekman & Davidson, 1991) of the same emotion-specific pattern when emotion was elicited in very different ways.

Boiten (1996) also claims to have disproved our findings of emotion-specific ANS changes as a result of assembling different patterns of facial muscular movement. We (Levenson & Ekman, in preparation) believe he did not produce such evidence, but instead that his data further supports our findings. However, we acknowledge that the matter is far from being completely settled. Noting that qualification, I will further consider what the implications are if further research strengthens and supports our findings to date of emotion-specific physiology.

Such evidence would be a challenge to those who view emotion as a social construction with no important biological contribution. Social constructionists might dismiss our findings by claiming that these different patterns of ANS activity were socially learned, not the product of evolution. Their argument would be that people are taught to engage in different types of behavior when experiencing different emotions. Over time this will establish different patterns of ANS activity, subserving these different actions patterns. If people show the same emotion-specific ANS activity, that may simply reflect common, culturally-based socialization practices. Presumably those who advocate such a view should expect different behavioral patterns to be taught for each emotion, and therefore different patterns of ANS activity should come to be established with each emotion in cultures which are known to differ in their attitudes about emotion.

Most simply put, the social constructionist emphasizes the past history of the individual, while the evolutionary theorist emphasizes the past history of the species in explaining why there is emotion-specific ANS activity. If it is only ontogeny, then to the extent to which different people learn different ways of behaving when experiencing one or another emotion, there should be different patterns of ANS activity observed for the emotions we have studied. Levenson et al. (1992) recently repeated their experiments in a non-Western culture. They studied the Minangkabau of Western Sumatra, a fundamentalist Moslem, matrilineal society. They replicated Ekman, Levenson & Friesen's (1983) original findings of emotion-specific ANS activity in this very different culture. This provides important support consistent with an evolutionary view that these are basic emotions.

Does the failure to find emotion-specific ANS activity for enjoyment and surprise mean that these are not basic emotions? Kemper (1978) would make that argument, for he views differentiated ANS activity as the *sine qua non* for basic emotions. But consider why we expect emotion-specific ANS activity in the first place. Our presumption is that these ANS patterns evolved because they subserve patterns of motor behavior which were adaptive for each of these emotions, preparing the organism for quite different actions. For example, fighting might well have been the adaptive action in anger, which is consistent with the finding that blood goes to the hands in anger. Fleeing from a predator might well have been the adaptive action in fear, which is consistent with the finding that blood goes to large skeletal muscles (for a more elaborate discussion of this reasoning, see Levenson, Ekman & Friesen, 1990).

Freezing in fear might seem to create a problem for this line of reasoning, but not if freezing is interpreted as a fearful state in which the organism is nevertheless still prepared, autonomically, for fast flight if the freezing action does not provide concealment. Not every fearful experience involves a threat from which one can flee. The doctor's report, that more tests are necessary to confirm whether the preliminary results are correct in indicating a terminal illness, arouses fear but the event is not one the person can flee from. The ANS pattern of activity which subserves flight might still occur in this example, if the evolved motor program for this emotion is flight. It is a question which awaits research.

Öhman's (1986) analysis of fear is relevant to these complexities. He distinguishes fear of animals, fear of people, and fear of inanimate objects, suggesting that different actions may have evolved for fear of a predator as compared to social fears. It is not clear whether he views predator fear as including fear of other aggressive humans, or whether it is strictly limited to fear of other animals. Neither is it certain from his writings whether he would consider the fear of the doctor's news about terminal illness to be a predator or social fear.

If no specific pattern of motor activity had survival value for an emotion, then there would be no reason to expect a specific pattern of ANS activity to have been established for that emotion. That is why I think we have not found an emotion-specific pattern, a pattern which differs from each of the other emotions, for either surprise or enjoyment.

However, it is necessary to posit emotion-specific central nervous system (CNS) activity in my account of basic emotions. The distinctive features of each emotion, including the changes not just in expression but in memories, imagery, expectations and other cognitive activities, could not occur without central nervous system organization and direction. There must be *unique* physiological patterns for each emotion, and these CNS patterns should be specific to these emotions not found in other mental activity. Here I am reaching far beyond the data, but not far beyond what the new techniques for measuring brain activity may allow us to discover in this decade of the brain.

My contention is consistent with the findings of those who have used EEG measures of regional brain activity to study emotion (for reviews of this literature, see Davidson, 1984, 1987). Davidson et al.'s (1990) recent findings of different patterns of regional brain activity coincident with enjoyment and disgust facial expressions can be explained as reflecting *either* differences in approach vs.

withdrawal, or positive vs. negative emotions. More critical for my argument are new findings of LeDoux (1992).

Automatic Appraisal Mechanism

Many years ago I (Ekman, 1977) proposed two appraisal mechanisms, one automatic and the other extended:

> There must be an appraiser mechanism which selectively attends to those stimuli (external or internal) which are the occasion for . . . [one or another emotion]. Since the interval between stimulus and emotional response is sometimes extraordinarily short, the appraisal mechanism must be capable of operating with great speed. Often the appraisal is not only quick but it happens without awareness, so I must postulate that the appraisal mechanism is able to operate automatically. It must be constructed so that it quickly attends to some stimuli, determining not only that they pertain to emotion, but to which emotion . . . Appraisal is not always automatic. Sometimes the evaluation of what is happening is slow, deliberate and conscious. With such a more extended appraisal there may be some autonomic arousal, but perhaps not of a kind which is differentiated. The person could be said to be aroused or alerted, but no specific emotion is operative. Cognition plays the important role in determining what will transpire. During such extended appraisal the evaluation may match to the selective filters of the automatic appraiser. . . . It need not be, however; the experience may be diffuse rather than specific to one emotion" (pp. 58–59).

Similar views have since been described by Zajonc (1985), Öhman (1986), Leventhal & Scherer (1987) and Buck (1985). LeDoux's (1991) study of the anatomy of emotion has led him also to a take a view nearly identical to what I proposed:

> Emotional processing systems . . . tend to use the minimal stimulus representation possible to activate emotional response control systems, which characteristically involve relatively hard-wired, species-typical behaviors and physiological reactions. Emotional reactions . . . need to be executed with speed, and the use of the highest level of stimulus processing is maladaptive when a lower level will do . . . However, not all emotional reactions can be mediated by primitive sensory events and subcortical neural circuits (p. 50).

In a major shift in his own position to incorporate the evidence on basic emotions, Lazarus (1991) recently adopted my position on this issue: "I distinguish between two modes of appraisal: one automatic, unreflective, and unconscious or preconscious, the other deliberate and conscious" (p. 3, Chapter 5). Lazarus succinctly described what he called a "psychobiological principle" which, he said, "provides for universals in the emotion process. Once the appraisals have been made, the emotional response is a foregone conclusion, a consequence of biology" (pp. 191–192). Lazarus here goes further than I do, as I believe that the responses reflect not just biology but social learning as well. Stein & Trabasso's

(1992) analysis of appraisal, while based on very different data, is very similar, as they point out, to Lazarus's position.

It is not known exactly how a biological contribution to appraisal operates; what it is that is given, which is then operated on automatically. It seems reasonable to presume that that which is biologically given must be related to the universal antecedents of emotion described below. How does this occur, by what mechanism?

Automatic appraisal does not simply and solely operate on what is given biologically, dealing only with stimulus events that exactly fit what is given. In all likelihood, not enough is given for automatic appraisal to ever operate without considerable amplification and detailing through social learning (see, especially, Öhman, 1986 on this point). An exception might be the appraisal which occurs to a sudden loss of support, or when an object is perceived to be moving very quickly directly into one's visual field. But such examples are probably rare. Perhaps they act as metaphors for many other events to become associated through experience with emotion.

Automatic appraisal operates also on a variety of stimulus events that we have repeatedly encountered or with events which though rare were extraordinarily intense. Lazarus notes how differences in our experience allows for enormous variations in the specifics of what calls forth emotion which are attributable to personality, family and culture. And yet it is not totally malleable. There are some commonalities in what calls forth an emotion for anyone:

> The ancestrally recurrent structured situation that the organism categorizes itself as being in is the "meaning" of the situation for that organism. It "sees", i.e. is organized to respond to, previous fitness contingencies, not present ones . . . Emotions . . . lead organisms to act as if certain things were true about the present circumstances, whether or not they are, because they were true of past circumstances . . . In this lies their strength and their weakness . . . [The automatic appraisal] cannot detect when the invariances that held true ancestrally no longer obtain (Tooby & Cosmides, 1990, pp. 418–419).

Often in civilized life, our emotions occur in response to words, not actions, to events which are complex and indirect, and it is an extended appraisal process which operates with consciousness and deliberation. Then the person is quite aware of what Lazarus calls the "meaning analysis" which occurs. Here is another entry place for social learning to generate large differences between cultural groups, and major individual differences within a culture.

A number of theorists (see reviews by Ellsworth, 1991; Scherer, 1991) have developed models of how appraisal processes may operate. Reading their descriptions and considering most of their data sources, it appears that they are considering only extended appraisal, but I think that they believe their models to characterize automatic appraisal as well. Their models are not contradictory with a basic emotions position, but they apparently do see a contradiction. Lazarus, I believe, is the only appraisal theorist who also incorporates basic emotions in his framework. Lazarus differs from the other appraisal theorists in not offering a model of how the appraisal process works. Instead, he more abstractly describes the relevant principal and the prototypic events (core relational themes) for each emotion.

Universal Antecedent Events

If emotions are viewed as having evolved to deal with fundamental life tasks in ways which have been adaptive phylogenetically, then it is logically consistent to expect that there will be some common elements in the contexts in which emotions are found to occur. This is not to presume that every social context which calls forth an emotion will be the same for all people within or across cultures. Clearly, there must be major differences attributable to social learning experiences. Öhman (1986) describes how both evolution and social learning contribute to the establishment of those events which call forth one or another emotion.

> . . . evolutionary economy has left to environmental influences to inscribe the exact characteristics of dangerous predators . . . learning is critically involved in selecting which stimuli activate the predatory defense system. But this learning is likely to be biologically primed or constrained in the sense that the responses are much more easily attached to some types of stimuli than to others. In other words, it is appropriate to speak about biologically prepared learning. Thus it is likely to require only minimal input in terms of training, and to result in very persistent responses that are not easily extinguished (pp. 128–129).

Öhman cites research by Mineka et al. (1984) showing that limited exposure is sufficient for establishing snake fears in monkeys which are very difficult to extinguish. Lazarus (1991) cites this same study to argue his rather similar view. Although he emphasizes what he calls "meaning analysis", Lazarus also describes common antecedent events. Johnson-Laird & Oatley's (1992) view is also similar.

My view on this matter, which is in agreement with Öhman, Lazarus, Johnson-Laird & Oatley, and Stein and her colleagues, developed in the 1970s when I learned of the findings of Boucher & Brant, which they did not publish until some years later (1981). They found commonalities in emotion antecedents in the many non-Western cultures they examined. It was not in the specific details but on a more abstract level that universality in antecedent events was found. The loss of a significant other, they found, is ". . . an antecedent to sadness in many, perhaps all, cultures. But who a significant other is or can be will differ from culture to culture" (Boucher, 1983, p. 407).

On the basis of Boucher & Brant's findings, Ekman & Friesen (1975) formulated prototypic interpersonal events which would universally call forth each of this set of emotions. For example, the antecedent event for fear is physical or psychological harm. Lazarus (1991), has a similar but in some ways different account, describing what he calls the "core relational theme" unique to the appraisal of each emotion. Neither of us has evidence, but what we each have proposed is consistent with Boucher & Brant's findings, and with those of Scherer and his group (Scherer, Summerfield & Wallbott, 1983) in their study of the antecedents of emotion in Western cultures.

Unfortunately there is little ethological description of the commonalities in the naturally occurring antecedent events for emotions within and across cultures. There is questionnaire and also interview data in which subjects are asked to describe emotional events. However, we do not yet know the extent to which such data resembles what actually occurs during emotion, how much idealization, and stereotyping may occur when subjects coldly describe what they think about their emotional experience.

So far I have discussed a number of characteristics which distinguish one emotion from another—universal signals, distinctive physiology, automatic appraisal influenced by both ontogenetic and phylogenetic past, and commonalities in the antecedents events which call forth the emotion. Now I will much more briefly describe a number of other characteristics.

I do *not* maintain that if biology has played an important role in emotion, then emotions must appear, fully differentiated, at birth or early in life before much opportunity for learning has occurred. Izard (1977) disagrees and has reported evidence which he believes shows the early appearance of each emotion. His position and evidence has been convincingly challenged by Camras (1992) and also by Oster, Hegley & Nagel (1992). When this matter is settled, regularities in the first appearance of each emotion may be useful in differentiating one emotion from another.

Emotions are likely to be observable in other primates. Darwin considered that to be crucial, and it was the chief focus of his book *The Expression of the Emotions in Man and Animals* (1872/1998). In modern times, Plutchik was the first (1962) to make this a defining characteristic of emotions. A number of those studying animal behavior have resisted emotion terminology, much like the Skinnerians of times past, but some (Chevalier-Skolnikoff, 1973; Redican, 1982) have pointed to similarities in expression between humans and other primates. It is possible that there might be some emotions which are unique to humans, but there is no convincing evidence that is so. Of course, the capacity to represent emotional experience in words changes many aspects of emotional experience in ways which I can not describe here.

Emotions can have a very fast onset, beginning so quickly that they can happen before one is aware that they have begun. Quick onset is central to the adaptive value of emotions, mobilizing us quickly to respond to important events. It is also adaptive for the response changes which can occur so quickly not to last very long unless the emotion is evoked again. Here is not the place to argue about just how long an emotion typically lasts, but certainly it is not hours or days, but more in the realm of minutes and seconds. I believe those who claim that emotions endure for much longer time periods are summating what is actually a series of briefer emotion episodes. Because emotions can occur with a very rapid onset, through automatic appraisal, with little awareness, and with involuntary changes in expression and physiology, we often experience emotions as happening to us. Emotions are unbidden, not chosen by us.

I expect that specific emotions regulate the way in which we think, and that this will be evident in memories, imagery and expectations. I suspect that the relationship between emotions and thoughts is not solely a function of social learning because of biological constraints put on the cognitive system as well as the emotion system.

The subjective experience of emotion, how each emotion feels, is for some at the center of what an emotion is. This presumably includes physical sensations, and other feelings which are the consequence of feedback from the various response changes which occur uniquely for each emotion. Regrettably, most of what we know about subjective experience comes from questionnaires, filled out by people who are not having an emotion, trying to remember what it feels like. It is no easy matter to assess subjective experience, especially if what is wanted is something more than simply the amount of positive or negative emotion (see Rosenberg & Ekman, 1994).

Before turning to the question of how many emotions there are, let me mention the concept of emotion families, which may help to clear away some of the confusion and argument about this matter. Each emotion is not a single affective state but a family of related states. Each member of an emotion family shares the characteristics I have described. These shared characteristics within a family differ between emotion families, distinguishing one family from another. Put in other terms, each emotion family can be considered to constitute a theme and variations. The theme is composed of the characteristics unique to that family, the variations on that theme are the product of individual differences, and differences in the specific occasion in which an emotion occurs. The themes are the product of evolution, while the variations reflect learning.

Although the evidence is certainly not available now, I propose that the following list of emotions will be found to share the characteristics listed in Table 3.1, and to be distinguishable one from another: amusement, anger, contempt, contentment, disgust, embarrassment, excitement, fear, guilt, pride in achievement, relief, sadness/distress, satisfaction, sensory pleasure, and shame. When it is remembered that each of these words denotes a family of related emotions, then this list of 15 emotions is quite expanded. Clearly, it omits some affective phenomena which others have considered to be emotions. Guilt is a likely candidate, and I have no reason to make a guess one way or another. Interest, which Tomkins & Izard considered an emotion, I think may be better regarded as a cognitive state rather than an emotion, but see Reeve's (1993) relevant study. The decisions are not mine; they instead should be resolved by research, which will establish whether or not these candidates evidence the characteristics listed in Table 3.1.

More irksome to some may be my omission of romantic or parental love and hate, which are clearly affective, as is grief, and jealousy. Elsewhere (Ekman, 1984; 1992a, 1992b) I have more fully explained my view that these are emotional *plots*, more specific, more enduring than the basic emotions, specific contexts in which a number but not all of the basic emotions can be expected to occur. There is another set of affective phenomena, the moods, which have different causes and last much longer, and are highly saturated with emotions. And still

Table 3.1 Characteristics which distinguish basic emotions from one another and from other affective phenomena

1. Distinctive universal signals
2. Distinctive physiology
3. Automatic appraisal, tuned to:
4. Distinctive universals in antecedent events
5. Distinctive appearance developmentally
6. Presence in other primates
7. Quick onset
8. Brief duration
9. Unbidden occurrence
10. Distinctive thoughts, memories images
11. Distinctive subjective experience

another set of affective phenomena are the affective personality traits, such as hostility.

Before leaving the struggle over the question as to how many emotions there are, it is worth considering the possibility that there are probably more emotional words than there are emotions, terms which refer not only to the emotion but features of the eliciting situation, of differential response to that situation, etc. Oatley & Johnson-Laird (1987) and Stein & Trabasso (1992) elaborate how this occurs, and how such variations in emotion terms can be dealt with from a basic emotions viewpoint.

DOES ANY ONE CHARACTERISTIC DISTINGUISH THE BASIC EMOTIONS?

I do not think any of the characteristics should be regarded as the *sine qua non* for emotions, the hallmark which distinguishes emotions from other affective phenomena. What is unique is that when an emotion occurs we are dealing with current fundamental life tasks in ways which were adaptive in our evolutionary past. This is not to deny that our own individual past experience will also influence how we deal with these fundamental life tasks, but that is not what is unique to emotions. It is our past as a species in dealing with fundamental life tasks and how that organizes and at least initially influences how we appraise and respond to a current event which marks the emotions. I would add also the high probability that at least some of the time the occurrence of that emotion is signaled to others involuntarily.

THE VALUE OF THE BASIC EMOTIONS POSITION

The basic emotions position which I have described does not dismiss the variety of affective phenomena, it attempts to organize those phenomena, highlighting possible differences between basic emotions and other affective phenomena which can only be determined by further research. It should be clear by now that I do not allow for "non-basic" emotions. All the emotions which share the characteristics I have described are basic.

If all emotions are basic, what then is the value of using that term? It underlines the differences between this and other viewpoints and approaches to emotion, which do not consider emotions to be separate one from another and/or do not take an evolutionary viewpoint. It captures what is unique about emotion, and what emotions have in common which distinguish them from other phenomena. The basic emotions framework allows us to distinguish emotions from other affective phenomena in terms of the characteristics I have described. This framework serves us well in raising for empirical study a number of questions about other affective states which further research might show are also basic emotions. The adjective "basic" should not be the issue, however, but instead what questions this stance raises for research about emotion. The characteristics I have described are meant as challenges for more research. They point us to what we still need to learn about the emotions. They highlight the gaps in our knowledge. The utility of this approach will be evident 10 years from now by what research it generates to confirm or disconfirm the possibilities I have suggested, and new possibilities I have not conceived of.

ACKNOWLEDGEMENTS

I thank Richard Davidson, Phoebe Ellsworth, Wallace V. Friesen, Dacher Keltner, Richard Lazarus, Robert Levenson, Nancy Stein, Keith Oatley, Harriet Oster and Erika Rosenberg for their helpful criticisms and suggestions on earlier versions of this paper. Preparation was supported by a Research Scientist Award from the National Institute of Mental Health (MH06091).

REFERENCES

Allport, F. H. (1924). *Social Psychology*. Boston: Houghton Mifflin.

Ax, A. F. (1953). The physiological differentiation between fear and anger in humans. *Psychosomatic Medicine*, **15**, 433–442.

Boiten, F. (1996). Autonomic response patterns during voluntary facial actions *Psychophysiology*, **33**, 123–131.

Boucher, J. D. (1983). Antecedents to emotions across cultures. In S. H. Irvine & J. W. Berry (eds), *Human Assessment and Cultural Factors*. New York: Plenum, pp. 407–420.

Boucher, J. D. & Brant, M. E. (1981). Judgment of emotion: American and Maylay antecedents. *Journal of Cross-cultural Psychology*, **12**, 272–283.

Buck, R. (1985). Prime theory: an integrated theory of motivation and emotion. *Psychological Review*, **92**, 389–413.

Camras, L. A. (1992). Expressive development and basic emotions. *Cognition and Emotion*, **6**, 269–283.

Chevalier-Skolnikoff, S. (1973). Facial expression of emotion in nonhuman primates. In P. Ekman (ed.), *Darwin and Facial Expression*. New York: Academic Press, pp. 11–83.

Darwin, C. (1872/1998). *The Expression of the Emotions in Man and Animals* (1872). New York: Philosophical Library. 3rd edn (1998) with Introduction, Afterword and Commentary by Paul Ekman: London: Harper Collins New York: Oxford University Press.

Davidson, R. J. (1984). Affect, cognition and hemispheric specialization. In C. E. Izard, J. Kagan and R. Zajonc (eds), *Emotion, Cognition and Behavior.* New York: Cambridge University Press, pp. 320–365.

Davidson, R. J. (1987). Cerebral asymmetry and the nature of emotion: implications for the study of individual differences and psychopathology. In R. Takahashi, P. Flor-Henry, J. Gruzelier & S. Niwa (eds), *Cerebral Dynamics, Laterality and Psychopathology.* New York: Elsevier.

Davidson, R. J., Ekman, P., Saron, C., Senulis, J. & Friesen, W. V. (1990). Emotional expression and brain physiology. I: Approach/withdrawal and cerebral asymmetry. *Journal of Personality and Social Psychology,* **58**, 330–341.

Ekman, P. (1957). A methodological discussion of nonverbal behavior. *Journal of Psychology,* **43**, 141–149.

Ekman, P. (1977). Biological and cultural contributions to body and facial movement. In J. Blacking (ed.), *Anthropology of the Body,* London: Academic Press, pp. 34–84.

Ekman, P. (1979). About brows: emotional and conversational signals. In M. von Cranach, K. Foppa, W. Lepenies & D. Ploog (eds), *Human Ethology,* Cambridge: Cambridge University Press, pp. 169–248.

Ekman, P. (1984). Expression and the nature of emotion. In K. Scherer & P. Ekman (eds), *Approaches to Emotion.* Hillsdale, NJ: Erlbaum, pp. 319–344.

Ekman, P. (1992a). An argument for basic emotions. *Cognition and Emotion,* **6**, 169–200.

Ekman P. (1992b). Are there basic emotions? *Psychological Review,* **99**, 550–553.

Ekman, P. (1993). Facial expression of emotion. *American Psychologist,* **48**, 384–392.

Ekman, P. (1997). Expression or communication about emotion. In N. Segal, G. E. Weisfeld & C. C. Weisfeld (eds), *Genetic, Ethological and Evolutionary Perspectives on Human Development: Essays in Honor of Dr Daniel G. Freedman.* Washington, DC: American Psychological Association.

Ekman, P. & Davidson, R. J. (1991). Hemispheric activation in different types of smiles. Unpublished manuscript.

Ekman, P., Davidson, R. J. & Friesen, W. V. (1990). Emotional expression and brain physiology II: The Duchenne smile. *Journal of Personality and Social Psychology,* **58**, 342–353.

Ekman, P. & Friesen, W. V. (1975). *Unmasking the Face: A Guide to Recognizing Emotions from Facial Clues.* Englewood Cliffs, NJ: Prentice-Hall. Reprint edn, Palo Alto, CA: Consulting Psychologists Press, 1984.

Ekman, P., Levenson, R. W. & Friesen, W. V. (1983). Autonomic nervous system activity distinguishes between emotions. *Science,* **221**, 1208–1210.

Ellsworth, P. (1991). Some implications of cognitive appraisal theories of emotion. In K. T. Strongman (ed.), *International Review of Research on Emotion.* New York: Wiley, pp. 143–161.

Graham, D. T. (1962). Some research on psychophysiologic specificity and its relation to psychosomatic disease. In R. Roessler & N. S. Greenfield (eds), *Physiological Correlates of Psychological Disorder.* Madison WI: University of Wisconsin Press, pp. 221–238.

Izard, C. E. (1977). *Human Emotions.* New York: Plenum Press.

Johnson-Laird, P. N. & Oatley, K. (1992). Basic emotions: a cognitive science approach to function, folk theory and empirical study. *Cognition and Emotion,* **6**, 201–223.

Kemper, T. D. (1978). *A Social Interactional Theory of Emotions.* New York: Wiley.

Lazarus, R. S. (1991). *Emotion and Adaptation.* New York: Oxford University Press.

LeDoux, J. E. (1991).   Emotion and the brain. *Journal of NIH Research*, **3**, 49–51.

LeDoux, J. E. (1992).   Emotion in the amygdala. In J. P. Aggleton (ed.), *The Amygdala: Neurobiological Aspects of Emotion, Memory and Mental Dysfunction*. New York: Wiley-Liss, pp. 339–351.

Levenson, R. W., Carstensen, L. L., Friesen, W. V. & Ekman, P. (1991).   Emotion, physiology, and expression in old age. *Psychology and Aging*, **6**, 28–35.

Levenson, R. W. & Ekman, P. (in preparation).   Emotion specific ANS patterns are supported, not refuted by Boiten.

Levenson, R. W., Ekman, P. & Friesen, W. V. (1990).   Voluntary facial expression generates emotion-specific nervous system activity. *Psychophysiology*, **27**, 363–384.

Levenson, R. W., Ekman, P., Heider, K. & Friesen, W. V. (1992).   Emotion and autonomic nervous system activity in the Minangkabau of West Sumatra. *Journal of Personality and Social Psychology*, **62**, 972–288.

Leventhal, H. & Scherer, K. R. (1987).   The relationship of emotion to cognition: a functional approach to a semantic controversy. *Cognition and Emotion*, **1**, 3–28.

Mineka, S., Davidson, M., Cook, M. & Keir, R. (1984).   Observational conditioning of snake fear in Rhesus monkeys. *Journal of Abnormal Psychology*, **93**, 355–372.

Oatley, K. & Johnson-Laird, P. N. (1987).   Towards a cognitive theory of the emotions. *Cognition and Emotion*, **1**, 29–50.

Öhman, A. (1986).   Face the beast and fear the face: animal and social fears as prototypes for evolutionary analyses of emotion. *Psychophysiology*, **23**, 123–145.

Ortony, A. & Turner, T. J. (1990).   What's basic about basic emotions? *Psychological Review*, **97**, 315–331.

Oster, H., Hegley, D. & Nagel, L. (1992).   Adult judgment and fine-grained analysis of infant facial expression: testing the validity of *a priori* coding formulas. *Developmental Psychology*, **28**, 1115–1131.

Plutchik, R. (1962).   *The Emotions: Facts, Theories and a New Model*. New York: Random House.

Redican, W. K. (1982).   An evolutionary perspective on human facial displays. In P. Ekman (ed.), *Emotion in the Human Face*, 2nd edn, pp. 212–280. Elmsford, NY: Pergamon.

Reeve, J. (1993).   The face of interest. *Motivation and Emotion*, **17**, 353–376.

Roberts, R. J. & Weerts, T. C. (1982).   Cardiovascular responding during anger and fear imagery. *Psychological Reports*, **50**, 219–230.

Rosenberg, E. L. & Ekman, P. (1994).   Coherence between expressive and experiential systems in emotion. *Cognition and Emotion*, **8**, 201–229.

Ross, E. D. (1981).   The aprosodias: functional–anatomical organization of the affective components of language in the right hemisphere. *Archives of Neurology*, 38, 561–569.

Scherer, K. R. (1991).   Criteria for emotion-antecedent appraisal: a review. In V. Hamilton, G. H. Bower & N. H. Fridja (eds), *Cognitive Perspective on Motivation and Emotion*. Dordrecht: Nijhoff, pp. 89–126.

Scherer, K. R., Summerfield, W. B. & Wallbott, H. G. (1983).   Cross-national research on antecedents and components of emotion: a progress report. *Social Science Information*, **22**, 355–385.

Schwartz, G. E., Weinberger, D. A. & Singer, J. A. (1981).   Cardiovascular differentiation of happiness, sadness, anger and fear following imagery and exercise. *Psychosomatic Medicine*, **43**, 343–364.

Stein, N. L. & Trabasso, T. (1992).   The organization of emotional experience: creating links among emotion, thinking and intentional action. *Cognition and Emotion*, **6**, 225–244.

Stemmler, G. (1989).   The autonomic differentiation of emotions revisited: convergent and discriminant validation. *Psychophysiology*, **26**, 617–632.

Tomkins, S. S. (1962).   *Affect, Imagery, Consciousness. Vol. 1, The positive affects*. New
    York: Springer.
Tooby, J. & Cosmides, L. (1990).   The past explains the present: emotional adaptations
    and the structure of ancestral environment. *Ethology and Sociobiology*, **11**, 375–424.
Zajonc, R. B. (1985).   Emotion and facial efference: a theory reclaimed. *Science*, **228**,
    15–21.

Chapter 4

Research Methods in Cognition and Emotion

W. Gerrod Parrott
Georgetown University, Washington, DC, USA
and
Paula Hertel
Trinity University, San Antonio, TX, USA

INTRODUCTION

In this chapter we critically survey research methods used in the field of cognition and emotion. Research on cognition and emotion addresses a great variety of topics, which include the ways in which emotional states influence cognitive processes, the role of cognition in producing emotion, and folk categories and knowledge of emotion. So great is this variety that a brief chapter cannot address all the research methods that have contributed to the expansion of knowledge that has occurred in recent years; there are too many methods, and many are relevant only to particular specialized topics. Specialized research methods are discussed throughout this volume in the chapters devoted to the relevant topics. In this chapter we restrict our attention to methodological issues that span the field of cognition and emotion, yet are in some way unique to it. Not surprisingly, these are the issues and methods that have to do with emotion itself.

What is common to most research on cognition and emotion is the inclusion of emotional states as an element of the research design. Emotions are sometimes treated as independent (or quasi-independent) variables, as categories or dimensions that may be associated with changes in other variables. At other times, emotions are treated as dependent variables, as states whose quality or intensity may be influenced by other variables. There is a noteworthy parallel between research designs in which emotional state is an independent variable and those in

Handbook of Cognition and Emotion. Edited by T. Dalgleish and M. Power.
© 1999 John Wiley & Sons Ltd.

which emotional state is a dependent variable. Research on emotions' effects on cognition uses mood or emotion as an independent variable, and an important methodological issue for such research is how to produce different emotional states that then can be compared in their effects. A typical solution is to employ a "mood induction"—showing a film or playing music, for example—so that participants can be randomly assigned to one of the emotional states of interest. In such research, the techniques of inducing emotional states are prerequisite to studying the effects of the emotional states. Compare this research design to one that investigates the circumstances that give rise to moods or emotions: here, the independent variable will be a manipulation of factors hypothesized to influence the quality or intensity of emotional states, and the dependent variable will be the emotional state itself. In such research the independent variable will be analogous to what in the previous design was the mood induction, and the dependent variable will be analogous to what in the previous design was the independent variable. When the quality and intensity of moods and emotion are measured, they have the status of "manipulation checks" if emotional states are an independent variable and of "dependent variables" if emotional states are a dependent variable.

Because of these parallels we organize this chapter into three sections: the first on the ways that emotional states are incorporated into research, whether as independent, quasi-independent, or dependent variables; the second on the manner in which emotion is measured, whether as manipulation check or as dependent variable; and the third on general issues regarding the design of research on cognition and emotion.

WAYS THAT EMOTIONAL STATES ARE INCORPORATED INTO RESEARCH

When emotional states define one of the independent variables, the research methods associated with them play a foundational role in the research, for they define (and sometimes literally produce) the phenomena to be studied. The selection of method is therefore crucial and yet often complex, for all methods carry disadvantages as well as advantages, and successful research often requires matching these to the research question as well as demonstrating convergence of several methods. When emotional states serve as one of the dependent variables, the focus of the research is usually on the causes or concomitants of the emotion, and the manner in which emotion is assessed can powerfully affect the types of conclusions that can be drawn.

There are four basic approaches to incorporating emotional states into research. First, the states may be induced by circumstances imposed by the researcher. Alternatively, naturally occurring circumstances (outside the researcher's control) may be taken advantage of for purposes of creating temporary emotional reactions. Third, longer-lasting emotional tendencies, such as emotional traits or affective disorders, may be employed as quasi-independent variables or as correlational variables to study cognition and emotion. Finally, one may consider a fourth approach to consist of methods that do not attempt to induce emotional states at all: participants may be asked only to imagine a certain emotional state, to read a vignette describing one, or to recall an occasion in which they experienced a certain emotional state. Each of these methods has its place in research on emotion and cognition, as well as its limitations, so each is discussed separately below.

Manipulations that Induce Emotional States

Induced Emotional States as an Independent Variable

Because researchers want to be able to infer a causal relationship between emotional states and performance on cognitive tasks, they have developed a variety of experimental techniques for inducing emotional or neutral states in randomly assigned participants. The success of each technique is then assessed by one or more measures. Techniques have been developed for eliciting a variety of emotional states under randomized laboratory conditions. These include such emotions as anger, anxiety, pride, envy, guilt, and embarrassment; however, by far the most attention has been devoted to moods rather than to emotions, and most of that to elation and sadness.

The earliest of the modern techniques is the Velten Mood Induction Procedure (Velten, 1968). Participants are randomly assigned to read a series of statements that gradually increase in the degree of affectivity or, in the neutral induction, describe mundane facts. A multitude of other techniques exists, including hypnosis (Bower, 1981; Friswell & McConkey, 1989), auto-biographical recall (Goodwin & Williams, 1982), guided imagery (Miller et al., 1987), and experiences of success or failure (Isen et al., 1978); participants may be exposed to films (Gross & Levenson, 1995; Philippot, 1993), to photographs (Fox, 1996), to odors (Ehrlichman & Halpern, 1988), or to music (Clark, 1983); there are mood inductions that use posed emotional facial expressions (Laird et al., 1991), symmetric facial contractions (Larsen, Kasimatis & Frey, 1992), and unilateral facial contractions (Schiff, Esses & Lamon, 1992). Some researchers have developed hybrid inductions, including two or more techniques at once, which may produce greater intensity (Mayer, Allen & Beauregard, 1995).

Researchers face a variety of issues when selecting a mood induction. One concern is the duration of the resulting mood, because moods can be relatively brief under some conditions (Chartier & Ranieri, 1989). Another concern is the intensity of the resulting mood, which can affect the generalizability of the findings if it is either greater or lesser than the corresponding everyday phenomena of interest (see e.g. Ellis & Ashbrook, 1988).

In selecting a method it is important to avoid producing confounds with the

dependent measures—one certainly should not induce mood using autobiographical recall when studying the effect of mood on autobiographical recall, and
more subtle confounds must be avoided as well. It is crucial to keep in mind that
either the induction itself or the measure of its effectiveness may invite participants to perform cognitive tasks in particular ways. For example, Velten's statements included some that suggest impaired cognitive processes, so Seibert &
Ellis (1991) modified his technique by removing such statements and by introducing a new procedure of asking participants to free associate to each statement.
The latter modification may have introduced a different source of demand,
however, because the subsequent cognitive procedures in their research assessed
mind wandering (Hertel, 1997). Other induction procedures can establish other
forms of demand, depending on their cover stories. Musical procedures, for
example, might establish changes in arousal that are subsequently perceived
as alterations of emotional state only when participants are asked to make
mood ratings. In this regard, the manipulation check becomes part of the manipulation, and its use as a verification of mood misses the mark of independence.
More generally, a mood manipulation can increase the likelihood that certain
subsequent materials will be better attended to, or that certain thoughts and
memories will come to mind, merely on the basis of within-session cueing,
regardless of effects on mood. Such changes could be an intentional strategy
adopted by participants trying to act as if they were sad or happy (Perrig &
Perrig, 1988) or they could also be due to recruitment of mood-related material
by a conceptual context that has been established. Whatever the mechanism,
researchers need to be wary of such confounds between mood inductions and
dependent variables.

Two issues that figure importantly in such considerations are whether
research participants are to be informed that mood alteration is the goal of the
procedure, and whether participants are to be asked to try to alter their own
moods. Some mood inductions quite explicitly inform the participants that the
topic of the research involves the effects of emotional states and that an emotional state will likely be induced; some inductions also explicitly request that the
participants cooperate in this effort by trying to achieve and sustain the desired
emotional state. Other mood inductions attempt to alter participants' emotional
states more surreptitiously with success/failure, odor, background music, autobiographical recall, or narratives, and often disguise the induction with a cover
story (such as the device of the "prior unrelated experiment"). Whether enlisting
the participants' cooperation in altering mood makes the induction more effective seems to depend on the type of induction: it appears to help with autobiographical recall (Lanterman & Otto, 1996) but to be unnecessary for music
(Kenealy, 1988).

Most important is the implication of these issues for demand characteristics
and thus for interpretation of the results. There are many types of demand,
and their consequences for internal and external validity depend on the controllability of the cognitive process being studied and on the relevance of self-
regulation and generalizability to the topic of the research. There is some

evidence that cover stories are generally effective and that participants' responses are probably not faked in any straightforward sense (Berkowitz & Tróccoli, 1986), but more subtle demand characteristics remain a concern. For example, one particular form of demand characteristic has been termed the *subject compliance hypothesis* of mood-congruent memory (Blaney, 1986). According to this hypothesis, mood inductions that explicitly encourage subjects' efforts to sustain their induced moods may cause participants to direct their thinking in ways that produce mood-congruent biases; the observed effects would therefore be due to participants' efforts at maintaining their moods, rather than to the moods themselves. The hypothesis has credibility given that, in the absence of any mood induction, instructions to cooperate in establishing the target mood can have effects similar to those produced by music or the Velten technique (Slyker & McNally, 1991) and that participants who are told to act as if they are in a particular mood show mood congruent recall (Perrig & Perrig, 1988). In fact, when cooperation instructions were omitted from a musical mood induction, Parrott & Sabini (1990) found evidence of mood incongruence in autobiographical recall. In a different study, however, Parrott (1991) instructed participants to cease their mood maintenance, and their performance nevertheless demonstrated a mood-congruent effect in autobiographical recall. It may be that the subject compliance hypothesis holds true while participants seek to maintain their moods, but that once the moods are well established they resist self-regulation for a time without continued efforts at mood maintenance. Thus, when the procedures allow, mood maintenance or role playing might underlie effects from experimental inductions, whereas attempts at mood regulation more likely typify participants in naturally dysphoric states (Hertel & Rude, 1991; Parrott, 1993).

Because the effects of mood inductions can include cognitive and demand effects, it is advisable to include control conditions to test for their effects (or to employ an induction that has already been so tested). A good example is the series of experiments conducted by Snyder & White (1982), who introduced control conditions to differentiate the cognitive and demand effects of the Velten induction from its emotional effects. In addition to the standard Velten procedure, they included conditions in which participants only anticipated an elated or depressed induction (Experiment 2) as well as conditions in which participants received an ineffective mood induction (Experiment 3), and they showed that only participants receiving the actual Velten mood induction showed cognitive bias.

Given the difficulties in eliminating demand effects, it is generally safer to use one of the more surreptitious mood inductions. However, it should be noted that participants may glean the purpose of even these inductions. The simple presence of numerous emotion-related questions asked before and after the procedure may make the point of the procedure rather obvious. This problem can sometimes be solved by placing the manipulation check after the cognitive task (Parrott & Sabini, 1990), but this solution may not always work because the effects of inductions are not always evident after the distraction and delay of the experimental task. It is good practice, whenever participants' awareness of the experimental hypotheses may be an issue, to question participants about this issue during a post-experimental debriefing session.

In reaching some tentative conclusion about the utility of experimental inductions, we make the following suggestions. First, induction procedures should be chosen on the basis of their freedom from demand characteristics for the specific topic being researched. If the topic of research concerns how people normally react to emotional states, then surreptitious mood inductions are preferred; more obvious inductions may be acceptable if the implications of the research do not include people's reactions to and regulation of their emotional states. Second, it should be acknowledged that the effects of the induction might result from changes unrelated to mood *per se*; solutions to this problem include running control conditions to check for effects of demand or contextual priming, as well as looking for convergence of findings in multiple experiments that use a variety of inductions and tasks. Third, most research using mood inductions should evaluate the influence of demand characteristics by debriefing participants, asking for their beliefs and suspicions about the experimental hypotheses while also realizing that some sources of demand can occur outside of awareness.

Induced Emotional States as a Dependent Variable

Induced emotional states serve as a dependent variable when the purpose of research is to discover the causes of emotion or the emotional consequences of an independent variable. Just as random assignment of participants to mood inductions provides the best evidence of the effects of emotional states, so too does randomized manipulation of emotional precursors provide the best evidence of emotions' causes. The power of this type of research stems from the use of actual emotional states to assess the effects of factors that are experimentally manipulated. Experimental manipulation of the degree and legitimacy of frustration, for example, has yielded insight into the causes of anger (Kulik & Brown, 1979), and systematic variation of the outcome and self-relevance of bogus personality tests has yielded insight into the effects of upward social comparisons on envy (Salovey & Rodin, 1984). Research on the emotional consequences of artistic and scientific problem solving (Feist, 1994), or of rumination and distraction (Nolen-Hoeksema & Morrow, 1993) are further examples of this type of research design.

This approach is subject to several limitations, however. Foremost are the ethics of subjecting participants to conditions producing intense emotions, or of deceiving them about the presence of such conditions. It is unethical to randomly assign participants to conditions eliciting profound emotional states such as grief or depression, and other research methods must be used to study these emotions. Pragmatic limitations also exist: some emotional elicitors are difficult to produce even when it is ethical to do so. One difficulty stems from the brevity of experiments, which makes it difficult to simulate the goals and interpersonal relationships that typically influence emotions. One solution is to personalize the manipulation, tailoring it to the individual participant's self-concepts and concerns so that long-term concerns may be addressed even within short-term experiments. Another difficulty stems from the subtlety of appraisals needing to be tested as compared with the relative clumsiness of experimental manipulations. Here the only solution rests with researchers' cleverness and skill, as exemplified in the research cited in the previous paragraph. The advantages of employing induced emotional states as the dependent variable make it ideal for research on antecedents of emotional states, including appraisals, but for other topics the difficulties we have described have led researchers to opt for other methods.

Naturally Occurring Temporary Emotional Reactions

A variety of techniques take advantage of emotions and temporary moods that occur naturally in the context of the participant's daily life; these states can serve either as quasi-independent variables or as dependent variables. One motivation for adopting such techniques is to avoid threats to internal validity caused by the experimental context serving as a framework for the participants' behavior. And even if one grants the internal validity of a laboratory method, a researcher nevertheless may wish to adopt more naturalistic methods to ensure the ecological validity and generalizability of the findings. Furthermore, some effects are not captured well in the laboratory: long emotional episodes, long-lasting effects, and emotion's consequences for ongoing social relationships are generally not available in laboratory research. Some aspects of emotional states simply must be studied naturalistically: The epidemiology of emotions, the rates of occurrence of emotions, or the actual features of emotion that appear in everyday life are all examples.

The principal drawback of this approach is that it cannot ensure that participants are randomly assigned to conditions. Research designs using naturally occurring states are quasi-experimental or correlational. If issues of causality are to be addressed, it is therefore necessary to try to test plausible alternative explanations of the findings by examining the data (Cook & Campbell, 1979). The extra difficulty of establishing causality is often worth the trouble, because research on cognition and emotion in field settings permits use of situations that have strong personal significance and are enmeshed in the context of real life.

Because of the decrease in experimental control, the distinction between emotional states as independent and dependent variable is less sharp; still, one can contrast research that emphasizes the consequences of emotional states with research that emphasizes the precursors of emotional states. Examples of the former would be research in which participants are approached as they leave a movie theater, still in an emotional state, and asked to make social judgments (Forgas & Moylan, 1987); or research on flashbulb memory, in which emotional reactions to a public event are considered as possible factors in later memory reports (Conway et al., 1994). An example of research focusing on the precursors of emotional states might be research on the effect of expectations and attributions on emotion, in which participants are queried shortly after receiving an important grade in a course (Van Overwalle, Mervielde & De Schuyter, 1995).

Another advantage of naturalistic methods is that they enable researchers to take advantage of exceptional circumstances to test emotions that are more profound than can be produced in the laboratory and are unusual even in everyday life. For example, the withdrawal of a political candidate from an election allowed a test of laboratory findings about appraisal (Levine, 1996), and the occurrence of an earthquake after the administration of a questionnaire to a large sample permitted a test of the effects of certain cognitive styles on depression and distress (Nolen-Hoeksema & Morrow, 1991)

A number of research methods have been developed specifically for working with naturally produced emotional states. Some researchers supply participants with questionnaires or structured diaries in which data can be recorded as soon as possible after emotional states occur in everyday life (Oatley & Duncan, 1994; Planalp, DeFrancisco & Rutherford, 1996; Rimé et al., 1991). Other researchers, interested in sampling time rather than sampling emotions, have supplied participants with alarm-equipped wrist watches or radio-activated beepers to signal the time for data gathering.

Emotional Traits and Affective Disorders

Some research on cognition and emotion investigates longer-lasting emotional tendencies, such as emotional traits or affective disorders, rather than (or in addition to) momentary emotional states. These longer-lasting dispositions enter research designs in several ways. Sometimes researchers are interested in these stable emotional dispositions themselves, comparing the performance on a cognitive task of participants who score high and low on some individual difference measure such as trait anxiety (Dalgleish, 1995). At other times researchers are interested in distinguishing the effects of these stable emotional dispositions from those of temporary emotional states, using an individual difference measure of the former in combination with a mood induction of the latter (Byrne & Eysenck, 1995; Fox, 1996).

Because traits or disorders are pre-existing at the time of research in all but longitudinal research, studies most often focus on the concomitants or consequences of these longer-lasting tendencies. Yet there is nothing in principle to prevent researchers from investigating the precursors of traits or disorders; researchers simply must adopt the same quasi-experimental and correlational methods that are necessary for studying naturally occurring temporary emotional states, with similar difficulties in establishing causality. But, whereas non-experimental approaches are optional for research on temporary emotional states, they are virtually the only option for research on affective disorders and emotional traits. There is now a large literature on the precursors of emotional disorders, which employs correlational, quasi-experimental and longitudinal research methods (see the chapters in this volume on affective disorders). It is less common to see research on the precursors of emotional traits, but similar methods may be used. A good example would be recent research investigating how adult emotional traits are related to early attachment experiences and parental rearing styles (Magai, Distel & Liker, 1995).

The use of clinically derived categories of affective disorders (e.g. generalized anxiety disorders, phobias, major depression or dysthymia) and categories based on self-report measures of enduring mood states and traits (e.g. test anxiety or depressed states) introduces a host of methodological issues, but we must limit our discussion to only two: generalizability and specificity. Other relevant issues, including the validity of diagnostic instruments and methods for establishing the etiology of affective disorders, are beyond the scope of this chapter.

Generalizing from self-reports on inventories such as the Beck Depression Inventory (BDI; Beck et al., 1961) to emotionally disordered samples cannot be justified. In this regard, the literature contains several useful sets of guidelines for research with student samples (e.g. Deardorff & Funabiki, 1985; Kendall et al., 1987). In particular, Kendall et al. recommended multiple method assessment, including a clinical interview if the researcher intends to use the term "depressed" as a nosologic category. Without multiple measures, the use of cut-off scores, such as 10 or greater on the BDI, should be accompanied by references to "dysphoria", a term that denotes non-specific negative affectivity. Yet, in spite of these and other guidelines for the use of the BDI, published reports of experiments on "depression" and cognition often still include one-session, one-method assessments and refer to their participants as "depressed" if their scores exceed a low cut-off (see Haaga & Solomon, 1993).

Even less well-justified is the tendency to generalize from induced moods to natural long-term states and dispositions, yet many researchers use terms like "depressed" to refer to the participants who have undergone an induction procedure (e.g. Ellis & Ashbrook, 1988; Snyder & White, 1982). Such usage seems imprecise without systematic comparisons of experimental inductions and naturally occurring states (see Gotlib, Roberts & Gilboa, 1996). Consider that in one of few such comparisons, Hertel & Rude (1991) found a lack of correspondence in free recall between experimentally induced participants and dysphoric participants; the different patterns were interpreted in terms of differing motivation and demand in the two samples.

A second issue concerns the specificity of the findings to particular disorders, compared to their applicability to psychological distress more generally. For example, it has long been acknowledged that scores on the BDI are moderately correlated with scores on anxiety inventories and other measures of negative states (Clark & Watson, 1991; Gotlib, 1984); both college students and patient samples show such correlations (Vrendenburg, Flett & Krames, 1993). Indeed, anxiety may characterize depressed states (Alloy et al., 1990).

Therefore, the issue of specificity—to "depressed" mood apart from anxious mood—extends to studies with participants diagnosed with depressive disorders (e.g. major depression or dysthymia) via a structured clinical interview. Consider, for example, that memory impairments are not unique to depressed samples but characterize other psychopathological syndromes (Burt, Zembar & Niederehe, 1995).

Although comorbidity is an ongoing concern in the clinical literature, building a literature on cognitive correlates of dysphoria or depression does not necessarily entail claims that the phenomena are unique to those states or syndromes. Clearly, when the research hypothesis concerns the cognitive components of a particular theory of depression (e.g. Beck's theory), we must contrast findings from a carefully diagnosed sample of depressed participants to those obtained from other diagnosed groups. However, if the research is guided by theories in cognitive psychology, it should be sufficient to show that performance differs according to the presence or absence of dysphoria or depression, and other studies might examine similar patterns in anxiety. When cognition–emotion interactions take the same form across diagnostic groups or mood categories, this outcome is no less interesting to the researcher than if the pattern had been constrained to one category alone. As the field has matured in recent years, interest in the interaction of emotion and cognition is motivated not merely by the goal to distinguish among nosological categories (Ingram, 1984) but also by the goal to examine the adequacy of mainstream cognitive theories in accommodating individual differences in emotional states (Williams et al., 1988).

In summary, we recommend that researchers who examine the correlates of any classification scheme: (a) carefully describe the research as correlative and not indirectly imply causal status to the category; (b) distinguish between essentially self-reported and diagnostic categories fully throughout their discourse; (c) resist the temptation to generalize from data on temporary mood state to more stable syndromes or disorders; and (d) attend to whether their concerns are primarily diagnostic (leading to differentiation among disorders, traits and states) or descriptive of particular disorders, traits and states in ways that might also apply to others.

Remembered and Hypothetical Emotional States

In some research there is no attempt to incorporate ongoing emotional states at all. Instead, the research relies on participants' memories of past emotional states, or on their intuitions about the nature of emotional reactions to scenarios that are depicted via text or film. There are various reasons for adopting such methods. For some research, actual emotional states are beside the point; for example, research on conceptions of emotion and on emotion knowledge quite properly addresses participants' conceptions rather than their emotions. In other cases the choice of remembered or imagined emotions is one of necessity or convenience rather than of preference. In research on appraisal, for example, most research has emphasized recollections or intuitions, not because real-time appraisals are not of interest but because these cognitive events are fleeting and subtle and thus difficult to capture with existing methods. Such research has been subject to various criticisms. Recollections may be more prone to schematic distortion than ongoing events, and imagined vignettes may lack the immediacy, personal importance, and gradual temporal development of real-life events (Levine, 1996; Parkinson & Manstead, 1993).

One way to overcome some of these criticisms is to sample memories of emotions that are very recent, such as by scheduling frequent visits to the laboratory to report on recent emotional experiences (Sonnemans & Frijda, 1995). In fact, the distinction between naturally occurring emotional states and remembered emotional states blurs as the interval between the end of the emotional state and collection of data shortens. The questionnaire and diary methods described in the section on naturally occurring emotions may well be more properly considered to be studies of remembered emotional states than of ongoing naturally produced ones.

Another way to blunt these criticisms is to ensure that participants recall or imagine the emotional state in such detail as to re-experience it prior to answering questions about it. This procedure may help to overcome the tendency toward schematic recall (Parrott & Smith, 1991). Interestingly, it may work by actually reinstating (or inducing) an emotional state to some extent. It should be recalled that autobiographical memory is sometimes used as a mood induction, and that there is evidence that asking participants to re-experience a remembered emotional event makes the reinstated emotion more intense (Lantermann & Otto, 1996). Procedures employing remembered or hypothetical emotional states may, therefore, actually induce real emotional states, at least under some circumstances. Nevertheless, the limitations of memory and intuition cannot be eliminated completely and, ideally, other methods should be used to complement them.

MEASURING EMOTIONAL STATES

Research that incorporates emotional states into the design requires that the quality and intensity of the emotional state be assessed in some way. The issues surrounding the measurement of emotional states are often complex and technical; all but the most basic overview is beyond the scope of this chapter. We try to supply that overview below, and include references that will guide the interested reader to more complete discussions. Our presentation is organized according to the three aspects of emotion that are commonly measured: self-report, behavior and physiology. It is important to note that these aspects are not components of a coherent emotion construct and correlate only imperfectly. They are often conceptualized as being separate processing levels or response systems that are not closely linked (Lang, 1988; Leventhal & Scherer, 1987).

Self-report

If one begins with the belief that emotional states are conscious, the primary way to assess their presence is self-report. But not all researchers believe that emotional states need be conscious, and even those that do usually also believe that there are interesting concomitants of these conscious states that occur outside of awareness (Ekman & Davidson, 1994). Thus, for most researchers, self-reports of emotional states tap an important aspect of emotion, but not the only one. Self-report is recommended when a person's conscious experience of emotional states is what needs to be assessed. An obvious advantage of self-report is that it is simple and convenient to use.

The assessment of conscious states can be problematic, however. There is little consensus about how conscious states arise; contemporary working hypotheses include direct causation by neural activity, perception-like inferences based on behavior or physiology, and perception of emotional meaning in objects and events (Parrott, 1995). All of these admit to a variety of distortions and biases due to expectations, social norms, attributions, allocation of attention and the like, and researchers must be mindful of these influences. Certainly, when an actual emotional state is not present at the time of self-report these influences would seem likely to be especially threatening (Parkinson & Manstead, 1993; Smith & Lazarus, 1993). One recent study found some cause for reassurance by demonstrating that, although self-reports of hedonic tone may be influenced by the social desirability of the state, such bias cannot adequately account for the pattern of responses (Barrett, 1996). One possible disadvantage of self-report is that participants in research may infer that their emotional states are of interest to the researcher, which may lead to self-consciousness that may alter behavior. If this possibility is deemed a problem, solutions include disguising the self-report items by embedding them in another questionnaire, delaying measurement of emotional state until other critical variables are assessed, or assessing emotion with a method other than self-report.

For whatever reasons, self-report is overwhelmingly the most common method of measuring emotional states. The most common technique is the administration of a series of Likert or analog rating scales, although other formats may be used (e.g. Eich, 1995). These measures are often devised especially for each study, but it is also common to administer a published standardized inventory of ratings scales or a checklist. Among the most commonly used are the Positive and Negative Affect Scale (Watson, Clark & Tellegen, 1988), the Discrete Emotions Scale (Izard, 1972), the Multiple Affective Adjective Checklist—Revised (Zuckerman & Lublin, 1985), and the Spielberger State–Trait Anxiety Inventory (Spielberger et al., 1983). Different methods of scoring such measures introduce different forms of bias, and these must be taken into account when planning research (Green, Goldman & Salovey, 1993).

Behavioral and Cognitive Indices

An alternative means of measuring emotional states is to detect behavioral and cognitive patterns that are associated with them. The most common behavior used in research on cognition and emotion is the psychomotor retardation associated with sadness. Psychomotor retardation can be indexed via writing speed (Clark, 1983) or letter cancellation (Mayer & Bremer, 1985). Other emotional states are associated with discrete behaviors, such as gaze aversion and blushing in the case of embarrassment (Asendorpf, 1990), and these can be very useful in detecting elements of emotional states not accessible to consciousness, as well as in detecting emotional states without making participants aware of researchers' interest in these states.

Facial expressions are one type of behavior often associated with emotional states. Research suggests that their occurrence is sensitive to the presence of actual or imagined social contexts, but when these are of interest or are controlled for, facial expressions may have some use as evidence for the presence and intensity of certain emotions (Ekman, Friesen & Ancoli, 1980; Keltner & Ekman, 1996).

The cognitive aspects of emotion that are the topic of much of this volume are understood well enough to be used as measures of emotion. Although it has been rare to date, alterations in attention, memory or judgment could serve as an index of particular emotional states, just as psychomotor retardation has been. When such tasks have been used as indexes of mood they have proven as effective as behavioral tasks (Kuykendall, Keating & Wagaman, 1988; Mayer & Bremer, 1985).

Psychophysiological Indices

Measurements of the physiological concomitants of emotional states may be used for all the reasons cited in favor of behavioral and cognitive indices. Researchers have creatively employed such measures to avoid the drawbacks of self-report measures, as when Pecchinenda & Smith (1996) used measures of skin conductance activity to supplement possibly untrustworthy verbal reports of appraisal.

A variety of psychophysiological measures are commonly employed. They include heart rate, blood pressure, skin conductance, finger temperature, respiration and eye movement variability. Description of these methods is beyond the scope of this article, and readers are referred to such standard references as Cacioppo & Petty (1983) and Wagner & Manstead (1989). An interesting combination of psychophysiological and behavioral methods is employed when electromyographic (EMG) methods are used to detect activity of the muscles responsible for emotional facial expressions (Fridlund & Cacioppo, 1986). EMG signals can be detected for movements too slight to be visible on the face, and the combined activity of different facial muscles can discriminate among emotions (Sinha & Parsons, 1996).

More generally, as cognitive psychology moves in a neuroscience direction, interactions of cognition and emotion are increasingly assessed with neuro-psychological techniques. For example, Henriques & Davidson (1991) have linked depression-related difficulties in sustained attention to hypoactivation in the prefrontal cortex via EEG recordings. Dynamic neuroimaging techniques offer great promise as well, as illustrated by evidence from positron emission tomography suggesting changes in blood flow to various brain areas during emotional and non-emotional states (Drevets & Raichle, in press). It is important to be aware that evidence concerning where in the brain such convergence occurs is correlational evidence, and therefore the usual warnings about causal inference apply (Sarter, Berntson & Cacioppo, 1996).

GENERAL ISSUES AND CONCLUSION

Control Conditions

In designing experiments on cognition and emotion, the selection of appropriate control conditions is frequently necessary for two aspects of the experiment: first, if emotional state is an independent variable, there will usually need to be a control condition that establishes some sort of emotional baseline; and, second, if emotional stimulus materials are presented there will usually need to be materials that serve a non-emotional control. The selection of either type of control is less clear-cut than is often appreciated.

When emotional state serves as an independent variable, it is desirable to include a non-emotional control condition to clarify whether observed differences between emotional states are due to the effects of both states or only to those of one. For example, an experiment that compares the effects of elation to that of sadness will be unable to determine whether differences are due to changes caused by elation, by sadness or by both. If a non-emotional control condition is included, the two emotional conditions can be compared with it. The additional condition requires additional participants, and may have the effect of requiring smaller standard errors to detect a significant difference, but the benefits are often worth these costs.

The question that arises is how to construct the control. What is the proper control: no emotion at all? A random sample of everyday emotions? A random sample of everyday emotions that have been "toned down" so that there are no intense emotions? These conceptions imply different techniques and procedures. Some researchers do indeed try to eliminate emotional states in any participants experiencing them at the onset of the experiment. The opposite approach is to do nothing at all to the participants in the control condition and have them completely bypass the mood induction portion of the procedure. An intermediate approach is to provide control participants with an activity similar to that of the mood induction, but without the mood-altering qualities.

The three approaches are best clarified with an example. A study that uses comedy and tragedy films to induce happy and sad moods might attempt the first control strategy by showing a film that has a calming effect; the second control strategy would entail showing no film at all; and the third strategy would entail showing a brief film on a non-emotional subject, but only for the purpose of providing a film-watching experience, not with any attempt at altering the participants' emotional states. In general, the second strategy of bypassing the induction will have the problem of confounding emotional state with unknown effects of participating in film-watching, and is therefore usually not the best choice if only one control condition is to be used but can be informative in conjunction with other control conditions. The first strategy of inducing a "neutral" mood is conceptually problematic because of a lack of agreement about whether such a state exists, but the procedures may nevertheless have the effect of reducing the average intensity and thereby decreasing variability within the control group. The third strategy accepts a diverse sample of emotional states as the proper control, but probably alters them somewhat by imposing the task of watching a film. Either of these latter two controls has something to recommend it.

When an experiment exposes participants to emotional stimulus materials, another problem of control arises. Most frequently the problem arises when verbal materials are used, but pictures or photographs invite similar concerns (e.g. research on memory for central vs. peripheral details in emotional vs. non-emotional slides; see Heuer & Reisberg, 1992). As an illustration, consider any finding of differential memory for materials that vary according to valence. Are emotional materials perceived or remembered better because they are emotional or because they differ in a number of characteristics from typically chosen neutral materials? The problem is obviously one of not being able to control, concomitantly, all the non-emotional characteristics of the materials. If we select within certain ranges of word frequency, length, linguistic function and concreteness, for example, we might find that the neutral words are more unrelated to one another than are the emotional words. Some researchers have approached this problem by using categorized neutral words, such as musical instruments or household items (Dalgleish, 1995; Mogg et al., 1991), but perhaps there are process-specific differences between these kinds of categorical relations and relations among words that are organized primarily in terms of the emotions they denote or evoke. "Materials effects", therefore, are difficult to interpret, although they tend to be suspected primarily when they are revealed as main effects (e.g. Hertel & Milan, 1994). Moreover, they are suspected typically in experiments that use lists of words, instead of more ecologically valid scenes or descriptions, where they also might arise. Word-list experiments, however, typify mainstream cognitive paradigms, not because researchers lack imagination or concern with ecological validity, but because some measures of cognition require multi-trial formats and because characteristics of words have been normed. In short, problems arising from the use of emotionally valenced materials cannot be avoided merely by eschewing word lists. When the emotionality of the event is central to the issue under investigation, the researcher should consider explicitly the possibility that other co-varying characteristics of the event contribute to the outcome. This prescription is equally applicable to the study of naturally occurring events.

Ecological Validity

The challenge of ecological validity, increasingly raised by cognitive researchers more generally (Herrmann et al., 1996), is particularly sharp when events are infused with emotion, due to the methodological and ethical difficulties inherent in simulating emotional meaning or arousal in the laboratory (see Yuille & Tollestrup, 1992). These difficulties have encouraged research paradigms that abandon traditional goals of experimental control. For example, assessments of autobiographical memories compounds the problems of lack of appropriate "materials" control with other potential confounds (e.g. practice in retrieval). When alternative explanations are thoroughly acknowledged or addressed, however, the study of autobiographical memory in emotional states or disorders reveals phenomena previously ignored or even obscured by traditional methods, such as the tendency of depressed people to produce overly general memories (Williams, 1992), or the phenomenon of mood-incongruent recall (Parrott & Sabini, 1990). As a result, several researchers have advocated the two-pronged approach of complementary laboratory and naturalistic studies (e.g. Kihlstrom, 1996; Williams, 1992), and we concur. Few research programs to date actually incorporate both techniques, however. Although this research strategy has difficulty in addressing the issue of the causal status of the emotional valence of events, it does invite generality through diverse operational definitions of emotional value.

Conclusion

The issue of ecological validity in research on cognition and emotion is reminiscent of the debate about laboratory vs. "real-world" approaches to the study of memory (see Banaji & Crowder, 1989, and the replies following Loftus, 1991). The themes that emerged from that debate stress the advantages of multiple methods for investigations of memory. The value of conducting memory research in everyday settings is not only that it builds confidence in the external validity of laboratory findings, but also that it permits study of important phenomena that are difficult to produce or to address under more controlled conditions. Our survey of research methods suggests that the same point holds true for research on cognition and emotion. While adhering to the values of controlled experimentation, we have emphasized the advantages to naturalistic investigation of cognition and emotion, and suggested that there is a natural complementarity between the two styles of research.

As the field of cognition and emotion matures, there is a more general need for a two-pronged approach combining laboratory and more naturalistic studies. This recommendation emerges from the difficulties associated with the use of any one method alone. For example, the causal status of emotional states can best be established by experimental inductions of mood, but to gain this advantage one must pay the price of concern about demand characteristics, contextual priming and generalizability to natural states. Those costs can often be reduced through recruiting participants who experience such states "naturally" or by studying emotions produced under natural conditions. But these states may be accompanied by other characteristics that affect performance. The obvious solution is to use both methods—to manipulate and to measure emotional differences—while taking pains to acknowledge the methodological challenges of each method and to base conclusions on the consistencies or inconsistencies in the patterns obtained. Such comparisons can be made across studies rather than within if other aspects of the methods are similar, but they should be made.

With a few exceptions, however, this approach has been taken haphazardly or reconstructed in hindsight by writers of literature reviews. Greater systematic combination of multiple methods in laboratory and real-world settings would be a notable advance in the research methods in cognition and emotion. Such advances are necessary to continue the progress in understanding the causes and consequences of emotion from a cognitive perspective.

REFERENCES

Alloy, L. B., Kelly, K. A., Mineka, S. & Clements, C. M. (1990). Comorbidity in anxiety and depressive disorders: a helplessness/hopelessness perspective. In J. D. Maser & C. R. Cloninger (eds), *Comorbitity in Anxiety and Mood Disorders*. Washington, DC: American Psychiatric Press, pp. 499–543.

Asendorpf, J. (1990). The expression of shyness and embarrassment. In W. R. Crozier (ed.), *Shyness and Embarrassment: Perspectives from Social Psychology*. Cambridge: Cambridge University Press, pp. 87–118.

Banaji, M. R. & Crowder, R. G. (1989). The bankruptcy of everyday memory. *American Psychologist*, **44**, 1185–1193.

Barrett, L. F. (1996). Hedonic tone, perceived arousal, and item desirability: three components of self-reported mood. *Cognition and Emotion*, **10**, 47–68.

Beck, A. T., Ward, C., Mendelson, M., Mock, J. & Erbaugh, J. (1961). An inventory for measuring depression. *Archives of General Psychiatry*, **4**, 561–571.

Berkowitz, L. & Tróccoli, T. (1986). An examination of the assumption in the demand characteristics thesis: with special reference to the Velten mood induction procedure. *Motivation and Emotion*, **10**, 337–349.

Blaney, P. H. (1986). Affect and memory: a review. *Psychological Bulletin*, **99**, 229–246.

Bower, G. H. (1981). Mood and memory. *American Psychologist*, **36**, 129–148.

Burt, D. B., Zembar, M. J. & Niederehe, G. (1995). Depression and memory impairment: a meta-analysis of the association, its pattern, and specificity. *Psychological Bulletin*, **117**, 285–305.

Byrne, A. & Eysenck, M. W. (1995). Trait anxiety, anxious mood, and threat detection. *Cognition and Emotion*, **9**, 549–562.

Cacioppo, J. T. & Petty, R. E. (1983). *Social Psychophysiology: A Sourcebook*. New York: Guilford.

Chartier, G. M. & Ranieri, D. J. (1989). Comparison of two mood induction procedures. *Cognitive Therapy and Research*, **13**, 275–282.

Clark, D. M. (1983). On induction of depressed mood in the laboratory: evaluation and comparison of the Velten and musical procedures. *Advances in Behavior Research and Therapy*, **5**, 27–49.

Clark, L. A. & Watson, D. (1991). Tripartite model of anxiety and depression: psychometric evidence and taxonomic implications. *Journal of Abnormal Psychology*, **100**, 316–336.

Conway, M. A., Anderson, S. J., Larsen, S. F., Donnelly, C. M., McDaniel, M. A., McClelland, A. G. R., Rawles, R. E. & Logie, R. H. (1994). The formation of flashbulb memories. *Memory & Cognition*, **22**, 326–343.

Cook, T. D. & Campbell, D. T. (1979). *Quasi-experimentation: Design and Analysis Issues for Field Settings*. Boston, MA: Houghton Mifflin.

Dalgleish, T. (1995). Performance on the emotional stroop task in groups of anxious, expert, and control subjects: a comparison of computer and card presentation formats. *Cognition and Emotion*, **9**, 341–362.

Deardorff, W. W. & Funabiki, D. (1985). A diagnostic caution in screening for depressed college students. *Cognitive Therapy and Research*, **9**, 277–284.

Drevets, W. C. & Raichle, M. E. (in press). Reciprocal suppression of regional cerebral blood flow during emotional versus higher cognitive processes: implications for interactions between emotion and cognition. *Cognition and Emotion*.

Ehrlichmann, H. & Halpern, J. N. (1988). Affect and memory: effects of pleasant and unpleasant odors on retrieval of happy and unhappy memories. *Journal of Personality and Social Psychology*, **55**, 769–779.

Eich, E. (1995). Searching for mood-dependent memory. *Psychological Science*, **6**, 67–75.

Ekman, P. & Davidson, R. J. (eds) (1994). *The Nature of Emotion: Fundamental Questions*. New York: Oxford University Press.

Ekman, P., Friesen, W. V. & Ancoli, S. (1980). Facial signs of emotional experience. *Journal of Personality and Social Psychology*, **39**, 1125–1134.

Ellis, H. C. & Ashbrook, P. W. (1988). Resource allocation model of the effects of depressed mood states on memory. In K. Fiedler & J. Forgas (eds), *Affect, Cognition and Social Behavior*. Toronto: Hogrefe, pp. 25–43.

Feist, G. J. (1994). The affective consequences of artistic and scientific problem solving. *Cognition and Emotion*, **8**, 489–502.

Forgas, J. P. & Moylan, S. (1987). After the movies: transient mood and social judgments. *Personality and Social Psychology Bulletin*, **13**, 467–477.

Fox, E. (1996). Selective processing of threatening words in anxiety: the role of awareness. *Cognition and Emotion*, **10**, 449–480.

Fridlund, A. J. & Cacioppo, J. T. (1986). Guidelines for human electromyographic research. *Psychophysiology*, **23**, 567–589.

Friswell, R. & McConkey, K. M. (1989). Hypnotically induced mood. *Cognition and Emotion*, **3**, 1–26.

Goodwin, A. M. & Williams, J. M. G. (1982). Mood-induction research—its implications for clinical depression. *Behavior Research and Therapy*, **20**, 373–382.

Gotlib, I. H. (1984). Depression and general psychopathology in university students. *Journal of Abnormal Psychology*, **93**, 19–30.

Gotlib, I. H., Roberts, J. E. & Gilboa, E. (1996). Cognitive interference in depression. In I. G. Sarason, G. R. Pierce & B. R. Sarason (eds), *Cognitive Interference: Theories, Methods, and Findings*. Mahwah, NJ: Erlbaum, pp. 347–377.

Green, D. P., Goldman, S. L. & Salovey, P. (1993). Measurement error masks bipolarity in affect ratings. *Journal of Personality and Social Psychology*, **64**, 1029–1041.

Gross, J. J. & Levenson, R. W. (1995). Emotion elicitation using films. *Cognition and Emotion*, **9**, 87–108.

Haaga, D. A. F. & Solomon, A. (1993). Impact of Kendall, Hollon, Beck, Hammen, and Ingram (1987) on treatment of the continuity issue in "depression" research. *Cognitive Therapy and Research*, **17**, 313–324.

Henriques, J. B. & Davidson, R. J. (1991). Left frontal hypoactivation in depression. *Journal of Abnormal Psychology*, **100**, 535–545.

Herrmann, D., McEvoy, C., Hertzog, C., Hertel, P. & Johnson, M. K. (1996). *Basic and Applied Memory Research: Theory in Context*. Mahwah, NJ: Erlbaum.

Hertel, P. T. (1997). On the contributions of deficient cognitive control to memory impairments in depression. *Cognition and Emotion*, **11**, 569–583.

Hertel, P. T. & Milan, S. (1994). Depressive deficits in recognition: dissociation of recollection and familiarity. *Journal of Abnormal Psychology*, **103**, 736–742.

Hertel, P. T. & Rude, S. R. (1991). Recalling in a state of natural or induced depression. *Cognitive Therapy and Research*, **15**, 103–127.

Heuer, F. & Reisberg, D. (1992). Emotion, arousal, and memory for detail. In S. Christianson (ed.), *The Handbook of Emotion and Memory*. Hillsdale, NJ: Erlbaum, pp. 151–180.

Ingram, R. E. (1984). Toward an information processing analysis of depression. *Cognitive Therapy and Research*, **8**, 443–478.

Isen, A. M., Shalker, T. E., Clark, M. & Karp, L. (1978). Affect, accessibility of material in memory, and behavior: a cognitive loop? *Journal of Personality and Social Psychology*, **36**, 1–12.

Izard, C. E. (1972). *Patterns of Emotions: A New Analysis of Anxiety and Depression*. New York: Academic Press.

Keltner, D. & Ekman, P. (1996). Affective intensity and emotional responses. *Cognition and Emotion*, **10**, 323–328.

Kendall, P. C., Hollon, S. D., Beck, A. T., Hammen, C. L. & Ingram, R. E. (1987). Issues and recommendations regarding use of the Beck Depression Inventory. *Cognitive Therapy and Research*, **11**, 289–299.

Kenealy, P. (1988). Validation of a music mood induction procedure: some preliminary findings. *Cognition and Emotion*, **2**, 41–48.

Kihlstrom, J. F. (1996). Memory research: the convergence of theory and practice. In D. Herrmann, C. McEvoy, C. Hertzog, P. Hertel & M. K. Johnson (eds), *Basic and Applied Memory Research: Theory in Context*. Mahwah, NJ: Erlbaum, pp. 5–25.

Kulik, J. A. & Brown, R. (1979). Frustration, attribution of blame, and aggression. *Journal of Experimental Social Psychology*, **15**, 183–194.

Kuykendall, D., Keating, J. P. & Wagaman, J. (1988). Assessing affective states: a new methodology for some old problems. *Cognitive Therapy and Research*, **12**, 279–294.

Laird, J. D., Cuniff, M., Sheehan, K., Shulman, D. & Strum, G. (1991). Emotion specific effects of facial expressions on memory for life events. In D. Kuiken (ed.), *Mood and Memory: Theory, Research, and Applications*. Newbury Park, CA: Sage, pp. 87–98.

Lang, P. J. (1988). What are the data of emotion. In V. Hamilton, G. H. Bower & N. Frijda (eds), *Cognitive Perspectives on Emotion and Motivation*, NATO ASI, Series D, Vol. 44. Dordrecht: Kluwer, pp. 173–191.

Lanterman, E. D. & Otto, J. H. (1996). Correction of effects of memory valence and emotionality on content and style of judgments. *Cognition and Emotion*, **10**, 505–527.

Larsen, R. J., Kasimatis, M. & Frey, K. (1992). Facilitating the furrowed brow: an unobtrusive test of the facial feedback hypothesis applied to unpleasant affect. *Cognition and Emotion*, **6**, 321–338.

Leventhal, H. & Scherer, K. (1987). The relationship of emotion to cognition: a functional approach to a semantic controversy. *Cognition and Emotion*, **1**, 3–28.

Levine, L. J. (1996). The anatomy of disappointment: a naturalistic test of appraisal models of sadness, anger, and hope. *Cognition and Emotion*, **10**, 337–359.

Loftus, E. F. (1991). The glitter of everyday memory . . . and the gold. *American Psychologist*, **46**, 16–18.

Magai, C., Distel, N. & Liker, R. (1995). Emotion socialisation, attachment, and patterns of adult emotional traits. *Cognition and Emotion*, **9**, 461–481.

Mayer, J. D., Allen, J. P. & Beauregard, K. (1995). Mood inductions for four specific moods: a procedure employing guided imagery vignettes with music. *Journal of Mental Imagery*, **19**, 133–150.

Mayer, J. D. & Bremer, D. (1985). Assessing mood with affect-sensitive tasks. *Journal of Personality Assessment*, **49**, 95–99.

Miller, G. A., Levin, D. N., Kozak, M. J., Cook, E. W. III, McLean, J. A. & Lang, P. J. (1987). Individual differences in imagery and the psychophysiology of emotion. *Cognition and Emotion*, **1**, 367–390.

Mogg, K., Mathews, A., May, J., Grove, M., Eysenck, M. & Weinman, J. (1991). Assessment of cognitive bias in anxiety and depression using a colour perception task. *Cognition and Emotion*, **5**, 221–238.

Nolen-Hoeksema, S. & Morrow, J. (1991). A prospective study of depression and distress following a natural disaster: the 1989 Loma Prieta earthquake. *Journal of Personality and Social Psychology*, **61**, 105–121.

Nolen-Hoeksema, S. & Morrow, J. (1993). Effects of rumination and distraction on naturally occurring depressed mood. *Cognition and Emotion*, **7**, 561–570.

Oatley, K. & Duncan, E. (1994). The experience of emotions in everyday life. *Cognition and Emotion*, **9**, 369–381.

Overwalle, F. Van, Mervielde, I. & De Schuyter, J. (1995). Structural modelling of the relationships between attributional dimensions, emotions, and performance of college freshmen. *Cognition and Emotion*, **9**, 59–85.

Parkinson, B. & Manstead, A. S. R. (1993). Making sense of emotion in stories and social life. *Cognition and Emotion*, **7**, 295–323.

Parrott, W. G. (1991). Mood induction and instructions to sustain moods: a test of the subject compliance hypothesis of mood congruent memory. *Cognition and Emotion*, **5**, 41–52.

Parrott, W. G. (1993). Beyond hedonism: motives for inhibiting good moods and for maintaining bad moods. In D. M. Wegner & J. W. Pennebaker (eds), *Handbook of Mental Control*. Englewood Cliffs, NJ: Prentice-Hall, pp. 278–305.

Parrott, W. G. (1995). Emotional experience. In A. S. R. Manstead & M. Hewstone (eds), *The Blackwell Encyclopedia of Social Psychology*. Oxford: Basil Blackwell, pp. 198–203.

Parrott, W. G. & Sabini, J. (1990). Mood and memory under natural conditions: evidence for mood incongruent recall. *Journal of Personality and Social Psychology*, **59**, 321–336.

Parrott, W. G. & Smith, S. F. (1991). Embarrassment: actual vs. typical cases, classical vs. prototypical representations. *Cognition and Emotion*, **5**, 467–488.

Pecchinenda, A. & Smith, C. A. (1996). The affective significance of skin conductance activity during a difficult problem-solving task. *Cognition and Emotion*, **10**, 481–503.

Perrig, W. J. & Perrig, P. (1988). Mood and memory: mood-congruity effects in absence of mood. *Memory & Cognition*, **16**, 102–109.

Philippot, P. (1993). Inducing and assessing differentiated emotion-feeling states in the laboratory. *Cognition and Emotion*, **7**, 171–193.

Planalp, S., DeFrancisco, V. L. & Rutherford, D. (1996). Varieties of cues to emotion in naturally occurring situations. *Cognition and Emotion*, **10**, 137–153.

Rimé, B., Mesquita, B., Philippot, P. & Boca, S. (1991). Beyond the emotional event: six studies on the social sharing of emotion. *Cognition and Emotion*, **5**, 434–465.

Salovey, P. & Rodin, J. (1984). Some antecedents and consequences of social-comparison jealousy. *Journal of Personality and Social Psychology*, **47**, 780–792.

Sarter, M., Berntson, G. G. & Cacioppo, J. T. (1996). Brain imaging and cognitive neuroscience. *American Psychologist*, **51**, 13–21.

Schiff, B. B., Esses, V. M. & Lamon, M. (1992). Unilateral facial contractions produce mood effects on social cognitive judgements. *Cognition and Emotion*, **6**, 357–368.

Seibert, P. S. & Ellis, H. C. (1991). A convenient self-referencing mood induction procedure. *Bulletin of the Psychonomic Society*, **29**, 121–124.

Sinha, R. & Parsons, O. A. (1996). Multivariate response patterning of fear and anger. *Cognition and Emotion*, **10**, 173–198.

Slyker, J. P. & McNally, R. J. (1991). Experimental induction of anxious and depressed moods: are Velten and musical procedures necessary? *Cognitive Therapy and Research*, **15**, 33–45.

Smith, C. A. & Lazarus, R. S. (1993). Appraisal components, core relational themes, and the emotions. *Cognition and Emotion*, **7**, 233–269.

Snyder, M. & White, P. (1982). Moods and memories: elation, depression, and the remembering of the events of one's life. *Journal of Personality*, **50**, 149–167.

Sonnemans, J. & Frijda, N. H. (1995). The determinants of subjective emotional intensity. *Cognition and Emotion*, **9**, 483–506.

Spielberger, C. D., Gorsuch, R. L., Lushene, R., Vagg, P. R. & Jacobs, G. A. (1983). *Manual for the State-Trait Anxiety Inventory (Form Y)*. Palo Alto, CA: Consulting Psychologists Press.

Velten, E. (1968). A laboratory task for induction of mood states. *Behavior Research and Therapy*, **6**, 473–482.

Vredenburg, K., Flett, G. L. & Krames, L. (1993). Analogue versus clinical depression: a critical reappraisal. *Psychological Bulletin*, **113**, 327–344.

Wagner, H. L. & Manstead, A. (eds) (1989). *Handbook of Social Psychophysiology*. Chichester: Wiley.

Watson, D., Clark, L. A. & Tellegen, A. (1988). Development and validation of brief measures of positive and negative affect: the PANAS scales. *Journal of Personality and Social Psychology*, **54**, 1063–1070.

Williams, J. M. G. (1992). Autobiographical memory and emotional disorders. In S. Christianson (ed.), *The Handbook of Emotion and Memory*. Hillsdale, NJ: Erlbaum, pp. 451–477.

Williams, J. M. G., Watts, F. N., MacLeod, C. & Mathews, A. (1988). *Cognitive Psychology and Emotional Disorders*. New York: Wiley.

Yuille, J. C. & Tollestrup, P. A. (1992). A model of the diverse effects of emotion on eyewitness memory. In S. Christianson (ed.), *The Handbook of Emotion and Memory*. Hillsdale, NJ: Erlbaum, pp. 201–215.

Zuckerman, M. & Lubin, B. (1985). *Manual for the Multiple Affect Adjective Checklist— Revised*. San Diego, CA: Edits.

Chapter 5

Cognition, Emotion, Conscious Experience and the Brain

Jeffrey A. Gray
Institute of Psychiatry, London, UK

Cartesian dualism is today sufficiently moribund that almost no-one denies that cognition, emotion and conscious experience are all products of the brain. Yet there has for long been a common, if usually unspoken, tendency to believe that, somehow, discussions of the brain and these other enitities belong to different, even opposing, realms of discourse. Fortunately, this barrier is beginning to break down, especially as cognitive scientists encounter the enormous opportunities for directly visualizing human brain function opened up by modern neuroimaging techniques. The time has perhaps come, therefore, for proper consideration of the relations that exist, or should exist, between these different types of discourse. Such consideration is made more complex, however, by the fact that, within cognitive science itself, the relations between cognition, emotion and conscious experience remain, to say the least, obscure. It is necessary, therefore, to examine the relationships between all four of the terms that figure in the title of this chapter. Here I shall explore what these relations might be, using as an example the development of a neuropsychological model that was applied, first, to anxiety (a prototypical emotion; Gray, 1982a, b, c), then to the cognitive aberrations that present as positive psychotic symptoms in schizophrenia (Gray et al., 1991a,b), and finally to the contents of consiousness (Gray, 1995a,b).

Handbook of Cognition and Emotion. Edited by T. Dalgleish and M. Power.
© 1999 John Wiley & Sons Ltd.

COGNITIVE PSYCHOLOGY AND COGNITIVE THERAPY

As one surveys from this point of view the now very broad landscape covered by the rubric, "cognition and emotion", it is striking how different it looks from the perspectives of cognitive psychology (roughly, the branch of psychology that flows from Broadbent's seminal 1958 text on *Perception and Communication*) and cognitive therapy (roughly, the branch of psychology that flows from Beck's equally seminal therapy for depression; Beck et al., 1979). This difference affects the links between, on the one hand, "cognition", as this is understood within each of these perspectives, and both emotion and consciousness on the other.

Within cognitive psychology, for the most part, neither conscious experiences nor emotion have played significant roles; indeed, they have both been somewhat of an embarrassment. The processes (often neatly encapsulated in little boxes connected by arrows) of cognitive psychology are not usually specified as being conscious or unconscious. This ambiguity has the great advantage that the theorist can have things both ways (Gray, 1993). If he wishes to build a computer model of his theory, he can treat all the terms in the model (e.g. "working memory") as function words that can be modelled by a symbolic computer programme or a neural network. But it is quite useful to have the conscious overtones of the terms in order to explain to others (who will be sure to draw upon the relevant introspections) what the theory is all about. For the most part, if pushed to the wall, the theorist will claim that only the unconscious version of the model is truly intended. To be sure, some theorists have explicitly indicated that parts of their models apply to unconsious events, others to conscious events, and others even to the transitions between consciousness and unconsciousness (e.g. Schneider & Shiffrin, 1977; Shallice, 1988). But it is noteworthy that, even in such cases, these identifications are apparently without effect on how the model is to be simulated or empirically evaluated. All that happens is that the theorist points to some of the boxes and says, "conscious experience here", or words to that effect. The true allegiance of the boxology of cognitive psychology is to the putatively fully unconscious processing that can readily be simulated on a computer without worrying whether the computer might suddenly have an experience (Searle, 1992) (Let's hope the boxologists have got this right!) When there is explicit reference to consciousness, this is always to what Block (1995) calls "access consciousness", never to the "hard" problem of consciousness (Chalmers, 1996) posed by subjective experiences (or "qualia") as such.

Emotion has also usually been left out in the cold by cognitive psychology, although this situation is rapidly changing (e.g. Oatley & Johnson-Laird, 1987). The frequently used synonym for cognitive function, "information processing", indicates why. It is easy to think of cognitive functions like learning, memory, attention and perception as the processing of information pure and simple; and equally easy, therefore, to think in terms of programming computers to process information in similar ways. But emotions seem to call for something more than just the processing of information; and that "something more" is much harder to imagine as being instantiated in a computer program. This tension between the concept of information processing and the reality of emotional experience becomes particularly apparent in the attempts actually to construct theories of emotion within the normal framework of cognitive psychology; the resulting analyses of, for example, "anger" or "resentment" (Ortony, Clore & Collins, 1988) feel empty of real substance in a way that contrasts strongly with the equivalent analyses of, say, the "central executive" or "working memory".

Within the tradition of cognitive therapy the situation is exactly the reverse. The central manoeuvre of this therapy is to bring internal cognitions fully into consciousness, so that the patient can be trained in ways of challenging them, altering them, etc. And the whole point of doing this is to use the altered cognitions so as to gain control over the emotional reactions (depression, panic, etc.) that bring the patient into the clinic in the first place. Thus, cognitive therapy deals directly with just those two elements—explicitly conscious cognitions and emotions—that cognitive psychology has most trouble handling.

To some extent, to be sure, I have exaggerated these contrasts (although I believe that, historically, they are accurate); and the contents of this *Handbook* are eloquent testimony to the fact that they are being rapidly eroded from both directions. But it is worth bringing them out clearly, for the same kind of reason that it is helpful to bring out fleeting and largely unconscious cognitions into the full glare of conscious scrutiny: left unexpressed, they constitute a hidden barrier to further progress. They also set the stage for the rest of the argument to be deployed here. This consists of an attempt to sketch out a unified approach to information processing in relation to both cognition and emotion and in relation to both conscious and unconscious processing. It may come as something of a surprise that the path to this approach has gone via the brain.

THE NEUROPSYCHOLOGY OF ANXIETY

The theory of anxiety advanced by Gray (1982a) is complex in detail, both psychologically and in terms of brain function. This is not the place to enter into those details, or to consider how well the theory has fared since it was first developed (see, however, Gray & McNaughton, 1996). Rather, I shall pick out just certain aspects which will be important for the rest of the argument followed here. These aspects relate to the psychology, the information processing and the neurology of the theory.

Psychologically, the theory postulated a behavioural inhibition system (BIS), defined behaviouristically in terms of the relations between its inputs and outputs. The inputs consist of stimuli associated (by Pavlovian conditioning) with unconditioned punishment or with unconditioned frustrative non-reward

(Amsel, 1962), or of novel stimuli. In response to these inputs, the BIS produces outputs of behavioural inhibition (interruption of any ongoing motor programmes, whether conditioned or innate), an increased level of arousal (energizing subsequent behaviour) and increased attention to the environment, especially to novel or threatening elements in the environment (the latter aspect of the theory has received strong support in the intervening years from experiments on attention to threat in anxious human subjects, using paradigms from cognitive psychology; e.g. Mathews & MacLeod, 1994; McNally, 1996). Anxiety was then defined as the state that arises from activity in the BIS. In neurological terms, a widely distributed brain system was postulated as discharging the functions of the BIS, centering upon the hippocampal formation and related structures in the temporal and frontal cortex, thalamus and hypothalamus, as well as ascending monoaminergic pathways innervating these structures. Finally, the overall system was considered in terms of its information processing functions. Central to this analysis was the concept of a comparator function: the system was seen as comparing upon a moment-to-moment basis (where a moment lasts of the order of 100 ms) the current state of the world (as analysed by thalamo-cortical perceptual systems) with a predicted state of the world (the prediction being derived by taking account of previous regularities of experience in similar circumstances together with the current motor programme). The concept of the comparator was encapsulated in a fairly typical, if rudimentary, box-and-arrow diagram (Figure 5.1) of the kind familiar within cognitive psychology and computer models of information processing. However, it was directly linked to brain function, by a series of postulated equivalences between boxes and arrows, on the one hand, and structures and pathways within the brain, on the other (Figure 5.2). In this way, a consideration of brain function led directly to the territory staked out by cognitive psychology. This progression should hardly come as a surprise,

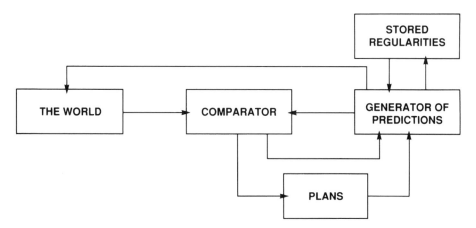

Figure 5.1 Information processing required for the comparator function of the septohippocampal system. Reproduced from Gray (1982a), with permission

since it is widely agreed that the central function of the brain consists precisely in the processing of information; yet similar progressions have been remarkably rare in the development of theories of how brain function relates to emotion. Within this overall theory, anxiety was identified (in input–output terms) with a high level of activity in the BIS; and (in information-processing terms) as a state in which the comparator detects either mismatch (an unpredicted event or the failure to occur of a predicted event) or threat (predicted punishment or non-reward).

Overall, then, this model of the neuropsychology of anxiety encompassed a behavioural level (the initial concept of the BIS; Gray, 1976), a neurological level (Figure 5.2) and an information processing level (Figure 5.1), with defined relations between each. What was missing was any attempt to grapple with the subjective emotional experience of anxiety: the conscious level. Clearly, this gap has at some time to be filled, since the theory was an attempt to account for

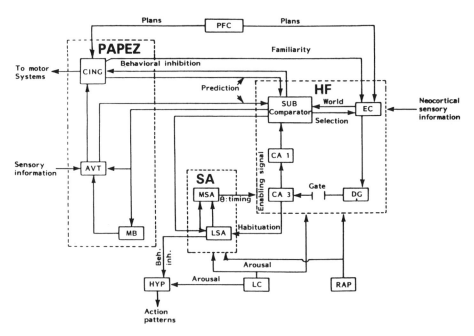

Figure 5.2 The septohippocampal system: the three major building blocks are shown in heavy print: HF, the hippocampal formation, made up of the entorhinal cortex, EC, the dentate gyrus, DG, CA 1 and the subicular area, SUB: SA, the septal area, containing the medial and lateral septal areas, MSA and LSA; and the Papez circuit, which receives projections from and returns them to the subicular area via the mammillary bodies, MB; anteroventral thalamus, AVT; and cingulate cortex, CING. Other structures shown are the hypothalamus, HYP; the locus coeruleus, LC; the raphe nuclei, RAP; and the prefrontal cortex, PFC. Arrows show direction of projection; the projection from SUB to MSA lacks anatomical confirmation. Words in lower case show postulated functions; beh. inhib. = behavioural inhibition. Reproduced from Gray (1982a), with permission

clinical data on anxiety and anxiety disorders, and these include a number of explicitly subjective features (feelings of tension, apprehension, and so on). Both the gap and the failure even to consider how to fill it are, of course, characteristic of theories in this field.

THE NEUROPSYCHOLOGY OF SCHIZOPHRENIA

The gap where conscious experience ought to lie became more acutely evident when we attempted to expand the model to the positive psychotic symptoms of schizophrenia (Gray et al., 1991a,b). For these, virtually in their entirety, are defined in terms of subjective experience, available to people other than the patient only by his self-report (e.g. auditory hallucinations, fragmentation or "grabbing" of attention, delusional beliefs; see Table 5.1). Development of the model so as to apply it to schizophrenia also forced us to expand the neurology, as we shall now see. As before, I shall recount only those features of the expanded model that are directly relevant to the argument pursued here.

The central additional hypothesis, in psychological terms, was proposed by Hemsley (1987, 1994). This is that positive psychotic symptoms (Crow, 1980) arise from a failure to integrate current information processing (as this affects virtually all psychological functions, perception, action, learning, memory, etc.) with past regularities of similar experience. Put simply, such a failure has the consequence that events which ought to be predicted and appear familiar (because under similar circumstances and given similar action programmes similar events have taken place in the past) are, in the schizophrenic, under-predicted and appear novel. Hemsley (1987, 1994) has shown how in principle such a failure of integration of past with current information processing can plausibly give rise to the positive symptoms of psychosis. Two experimental examples may help to understand the general argument. In the first, latent inhibition, a stimulus that has previously been presented a number of times without other consequence, normally undergoes a loss of associability (when subsequently used as a conditioned stimulus, CS, in a Pavlovian conditioning experiment). This is a phenomenon of wide cross-species generality which we have recently (Schmajuk, Lam & Gray, 1996) incorporated into a neural-network model able to simulate most of

Table 5.1 Positive psychotic symptoms

Auditory hallucinations
Delusional beliefs
Enhanced sensory awareness
"Over-attention"
Visual illusions
Racing thoughts

the data in Lubow's (1989) book-length account of it. In the second example, the Kamin (1969) blocking effect, a subject first learns one association between a CS1 and an unconditioned stimulus (UCS) and then a second association between a compound stimulus, CS1 + CS2, and the same UCS. The prior learning of the CS1–UCS association retards learning of the second association. These phenomena appear to serve the function of preventing the formation of what, given past experience, may be spurious (latent inhibition) or redundant (Kamin blocking effect) associations, so allowing the concentration of attention upon current stimuli that are more likely to be genuinely informative. In acute schizophrenia, both latent inhibition (Baruch, Hemsley & Gray, 1988; N. S. Gray, Hemsley & Gray, 1992a; N. S. Gray et al., 1995) and the Kamin effect (Jones, Gray & Hemsley, 1992) are disrupted, but normalized by neuroleptic medication (Baruch, Hemsley & Gray, 1988); in addition, latent inhibition is blocked by the psychotomimetic indirect dopamine agonist, amphetamine, in human volunteers (N. S. Gray et al., 1992b; Thornton et al., 1996) as in rats (for review, see Gray et al., 1995). In terms of Hemsley's (1987) hypothesis, these observations reflect a failure in the schizophrenic of integration of past experience (prior unreinforced CS presentation in latent inhibition; the CS1–UCS association in the Kamin effect) with current associative learning. Symptomatically speaking, loss of latent inhibition and the Kamin effect would be likely to lead to increased attentional salience for stimuli that are in fact familiar and of no significance but seem novel and potentially important; and to the formation of spurious or "clang" associations.

Hemsley (1987) proposed that the failure of the schizophrenic to integrate past and current experience might be due to malfunction in Gray's (1982a) comparator system (Figure 5.1). Developments in neuroanatomy made it possible to put this proposal on a reasonably firm structural basis. First, it had become clear from post-mortem studies of schizophrenic brains that there is neuropathology in just those regions that Gray (1982a) had implicated in the comparator function, specifically, the hippocampal formation and overlying temporal lobe structures that send to (entorhinal cortex) and receive from (the subicular area) the hippocampal formation. Second, work in experimental animals (Kelley & Domesick, 1982; Yee, Feldon & Rawlins, 1995) had shown that the subicular and entorhinal regions project to the nucleus accumbens (Figure 5.3), a structure already believed to be involved in psychotic behaviour. The grounds for the latter belief were largely neuropharmacological. It has been known for many years that indirect dopamine agonists, such as amphetamine, can cause or exacerbate positive psychotic symptoms, and that the efficacy of medication in controlling these symptoms is well correlated with a drug's capacity to block dopamine receptors, especially of the D2 type (Carlsson, 1988). These findings have led to the "dopamine" hypothesis of schizophrenia, i.e. that positive symptoms reflect overactivity in dopaminergic systems. The most prominent such system is the nigrostriatal pathway, projecting from the substantia nigra to the caudate putamen. However, this is mainly concerned with motor behaviour (its degeneration underlies the symptoms of Parkinson's disease), so it is unlikely to be

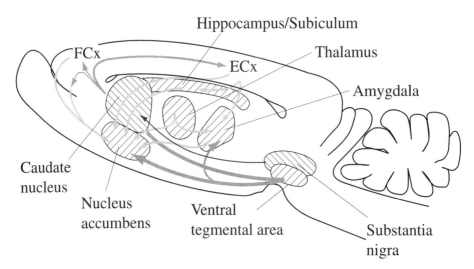

Figure 5.3 Schematic representation of the ascending dopaminergic projections (solid arrows) from nucleus A 10 in the ventral tegmental area to the nucleus accumbens, amygdala, frontal (FCx) and entorhinal (ECx) cortex; together with the descending glutamatergic projections (outline arrows) from the subiculum (carrying hippocampal output), FCx, ECx and the thalamus to the nucleus accumbens. Also shown (shaded arrow), the ascending dopaminergic projection from the substantia nigra to the caudate nucleus. Figure by Dr A. Young

involved in schizophrenia. The other major ascending dopaminergic pathways originate in nucleus A 10 in the ventral tegmental area (Figure 5.3); the "mesolimbic" branch of this pathway has a prominent projection to the nucleus accumbens, which (given the neuropharmacological evidence) thus constitutes a likely candidate for involvement in schizophrenia. However, studies of post-mortem schizophrenic brain do not reveal particular neuropathology in this region.

So as to fit these two pieces of the puzzle together, we (Gray et al., 1991a, b) proposed that the positive symptoms of schizophrenia arise from a failure in the normal communication between the hippocampal system (owing to the observed structural abnormalities in this part of the brain) and the nucleus accumbens, to which the hippocampal system projects via both the subicular and the entorhinal regions; and that this failure of normal communication results in dopaminergic overactivity (either directly or as the result of imbalance), as postulated in the dopamine hypothesis of schizophrenia. In information-processing terms, we proposed that the normal function of these projections from the hippocampal system to the nucleus accumbens is to convey the output of the comparator system (Figure 5.1) to the brain's major motor programming systems in the basal ganglia (for which the nucleus accumbens acts as a gateway; Mogenson & Nielsen, 1984; see Figure 5.4). These postulates are summarized in Figure 5.5 as a series of equivalences between structural and psychological disconnections. The resulting

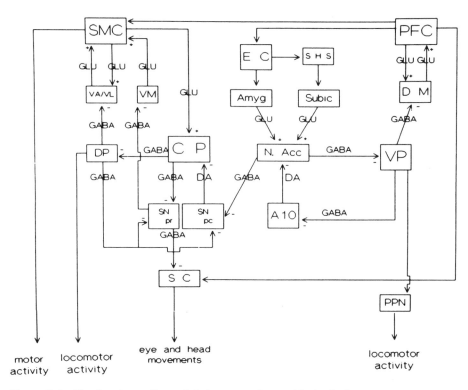

Figure 5.4 The basal ganglia and their connections with the limbic system. Structures: SMC = sensorimotor cortex; PFC = prefrontal cortex; EC = entorhinal cortex; SHS = septohippocampal system; Subic = subicular area; Amyg = amygdala; VA/VL = nucleus ventralis anterior and ventralis lateralis thalami; VM = nucleus ventralis medialis thalami; DM = dorsalis medialis thalami; DP = dorsal pallidum; VP = ventral pallidum; CP = caudate-putamen; N. Acc = nucleus accumbens; SNpr = substantia nigra, pars compacta; A 10 = nucleus. A 10 in ventral tegmental area; SC = superior colliculus; PPN = pedunculopontine nucleus. Transmitters: GLU = glutamate; DA = dopamine; GABA = γ-aminobutyric acid. Reproduced from Gray et al. (1991a), with permission

theory is eminently testable and has provided the impetus for a steady stream of empirical investigations in both our own laboratory and elsewhere. But this is not the place to review the results of these studies (see Weiner, 1990; Gray, 1998; Gray et al., 1995, 1997; Hemsley, 1987, 1994).

THE CONTENTS OF CONSCIOUSNESS

It is clear from Table 5.1 that any theory of the positive symptoms of schizophrenia, however it wishes to present itself, must ultimately be a theory about conscious experiences (Gray, 1993); but this issue was ducked when we proposed the model outlined in Figure 5.4 (Gray et al., 1991a,b). Given the hardness of the

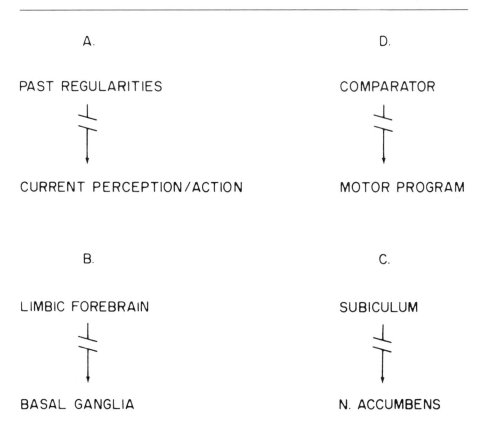

A.

PAST REGULARITIES

CURRENT PERCEPTION/ACTION

D.

COMPARATOR

MOTOR PROGRAM

B.

LIMBIC FOREBRAIN

BASAL GANGLIA

C.

SUBICULUM

N. ACCUMBENS

Figure 5.5   An illustration of the theory of schizophrenia proposed by Gray et al. (1991a). (A) The abnormality of cognitive processing consists of a failure to integrate past regularities of experience with the current control of perception and action. (B) This reflects a dysfunctional connection between the limbic forebrain and the basal ganglia. (C) The specific pathway carrying the dysfunctional connection is from the subiculum (in the limbic forebrain) to the nucleus accumbens (in the basal ganglia). (D) The computing functions thus disrupted are the passage of information from a comparator system utilizing stored traces of past regularities (limbic forebrain) to a motor programming system (located in the basal ganglia) controlling perception and action. Reproduced from Gray (1993), with permission

"hard" problem of consciousness (Gray, 1971; Chalmers, 1996), this is an entirely respectable act of cowardice: it is at present unknown how the brain gives rise to conscious experiences of any kind; neither is there yet on the horizon any remotely adequate theory of how the trick is done (Gray, 1995a,b). However, while not presuming to offer such a theory, I have recently advanced a conjecture about why the *contents* of consciousness take the form they do (Gray, 1995a,b); and this speculation may have some bearing on what goes wrong in the conscious experiences of schizophrenics.

It is useful to approach Gray's (1995a) conjecture in the context of the "binding" problem, that is, the problem of how the brain manages to put together

Table 5.2 Conscious awareness is not necessary for

Analysis of sensory input
Analysis of speech input
Learning
Memory
Selection of response
Control of action
Production of speech output

After Velmans (1991)

the various disparate bits of information, spread out in both time and (brain) space, that constitute the integrated contents of a perceptual scene. In a recent electronic seminar devoted to consciousness, Newman (1996) discussed various hypotheses aimed at dealing with this problem. All implicitly deal with the putting together of a "neuronal Gestalt" in the immediate period of time (approximately, the first 100–200 ms; let this be $t1$) after sense organs first receive stimuli from the environment; but in this period, as is well documented (Velmans, 1991), the brain is capable of a high degree of perceptual analysis, extraction of meaning, cognitive processing and organization of action, all of which remain entirely unconscious, at least by all normal tests (Table 5.2). This initial solution of the binding problem is the one which, for example the hypotheses of Crick (1984), Crick & Koch (1990) and Llinas et al. (1994) all appear to address. But, for this initial solution then to lead on to the conscious experience of a complex, multimodally specified, coherent scene of some kind, something further has to happen in a following period of time (approximately, the next 100–200 ms, $t2$); for it takes a period of about $t1 + t2$ after initial stimulation begins for the appropriate experience to enter consciousness (Velmans, 1991). To dramatize this part of the hard problem of consciousness, consider world-class tennis: Becker has completed his return of Borg's service before he has consciously seen the ball reach the net (McCrone, 1993). Thus, all the binding required for Becker's detection of the ball and organization of the return stroke must have been successfully completed without yet leading to conscious perception of the events that guide this "on-line" behaviour.

It was to address this problem that I conjectured that the contents of consciousness might consist in outputs from the comparator depicted in Figure 5.1 (Gray, 1995a). More specifically, according to the hypothesis, they consist of the successive outputs of the comparator system, tagged according to the degree to which the different elements making up these outputs are variously expected (i.e. predicted by the comparator circuitry) or unexpected. In neural terms, it is proposed that the outputs of the comparator system are determined by its feedback to the cortical sensory systems whose inputs to the comparator system have just (i.e. in the preceding "instant", with a duration of approximately 100 ms) entered into the process of comparison (for details, see Gray 1995a,b; and, for a more detailed treatment of the timing involved, see below). Thus, the contents of consciousness necessarily arise after completion of on-line processing that has fully analysed the perceptual world prior to presenting the results of this analysis to the comparator for matching with the current predicted state of the perceptual world. In this way, the lateness of conscious experience with respect to on-line processing is given a plausible explanation.

What, however, is the function served by this late, conscious processing? As summarized in Table 5.2, there are many functions which, on the experimental evidence reviewed by Velmans (1991), we can exclude. My conjecture is that the contents of consciousness (i.e. the outputs of the comparator) serve the general function of an error-detection system: if something goes wrong with on-line processing, the system can detect the error and, if necessary, interrupt the motor plan which has given rise to the error. This, indeed, is the very same function that was attributed to the comparator system when it was first proposed as an account of the information processing that underlies the emotion of anxiety (Gray, 1982a,b). If this hypothesis is correct, there should be a particularly close link between conscious experience and that emotion. Introspectively, this appears to be the case: anxious cognitions have a particularly demanding hold upon consciousness.

Elsewhere (Gray, 1995a), I have summarized a number of other features of conscious experience for which the conjecture provides a natural account, e.g. the fact that we are conscious only of the outputs of motor programmes (suitable for the evaluation of error), not of motor programming itself, as well as a few that do not fit so well. However, even supposing that the conjecture is on the right lines to provide an account of a number of features of the contents of consciousness, it would still leave the central mystery of consciousness untouched. In the present context, this mystery can be phrased in two equivalent ways: (a) since the brain can do so many clever things unconsciously, why, when it came to this late error detection requirement, did it need to use a conscious medium to meet it?; (b) how does brain activity, which does not generate conscious experiences in relation to all the on-line processing summarized in Table 5.2, perform the trick when it comes to late error detection? I have no way of answering these questions; but then neither does anyone else (Chalmers, 1996).

THE TRANSITION FROM AUTOMATIC TO CONTROLLED PROCESSING

Let us again suppose that Gray's (1995a) conjecture about the contents of consciousness is on the right lines. While I have no handle on *how* the brain might do the trick of bringing these contents into consciousness, there is scope for reasonable speculation about *where* it does it. This speculation takes off from existing knowledge about how amphetamine blocks latent inhibition, thus mimicking a cognitive abnormality that is present in acute schizophrenics (see above).

The results of a number of recent experiments, both from our group and other laboratories, make a very convincing case that the key site of action of this compound is in the nucleus accumbens: enhancement of dopaminergic transmission in this structure blocks latent inhibition (increases the spread of selective associability); conversely, blockade of dopaminergic transmission augments latent inhibition (narrows this spread) (Gray, 1998; Gray et al., 1995, 1997). In this section, therefore, I try to relate these effects to the outputs from the nucleus accumbens.

Following common practice (e.g. Mogenson & Nielsen 1984; Swerdlow & Koob 1987), I have so far treated the nucleus accumbens as the gateway to a basal ganglia motor programming system. But latent inhibition does not readily fit into this framework. Blockade of latent inhibition, e.g. by amphetamine, suggests a change, not in motor programming but rather in sensory analysis, one that allows a stimulus that would otherwise be ignored to re-enter current information processing. The symptoms of schizophrenia that Gray et al. (1991a,b) attempted to relate to blockade of latent inhibition similarly suggest changes in perceptual experience rather than motor programming. However, a solution to this problem has recently become apparent from work in Grace's laboratory.

Lavin & Grace (1994) have studied what happens to the outputs from the nucleus accumbens further downstream. Using electrophysiological and tract-tracing techniques, these workers have demonstrated that the inhibitory γ-aminobutyrate (GABA) output from the nucleus accumbens synapses, in the ventral pallidum, upon further GABA-ergic inhibitory neurons that project to the nucleus reticularis thalami (NRT). The NRT is unusual among thalamic nuclei in that it consists mainly of inhibitory GABA-ergic neurons; these project to a number of the surrounding thalamic nuclei whose job is to relay impulses originating in peripheral sense organs to the appropriate sensory regions of the cerebral cortex (Jones, 1975). The possible role of the NRT in the selection of stimuli for attention and conscious processing was first pointed out by Crick (1984), and has been incorporated into a neural-network model by Taylor & Alavi (1992). Note that, since the pallidal output to these neurons is itself inhibitory, its activation has the effect of disinhibiting these sensory relay pathways, i.e. increasing the entry to the cerebral cortex of those stimuli that are currently engaging the thalamocortical sensory processing loops (see Figure 5.6).

Let us consider how the circuitry of Fig. 5.6 would be likely to work under the conditions of an experiment in which an indirect dopamine agonist, such as amphetamine, is used to block latent inhibition by causing dopamine release in the nucleus accumbens. As indicated above, the basic phenomenon of latent inhibition consists in the fact that a pre-exposed CS is slow to enter into an association with a Pavlovian UCS. One way to interpret this (see Gray, 1995a, b) is as reflecting a lack of access to conscious processing by the pre-exposed CS. If, however, presentation of this CS is accompanied by enhanced dopamine release in the nucleus accumbens, as induced pharmacologically or during acute psychosis, latent inhibition is overcome, indicating that the pre-exposed CS has regained the capacity to engage conscious processing. The circuitry of Figure 5.6 consti-

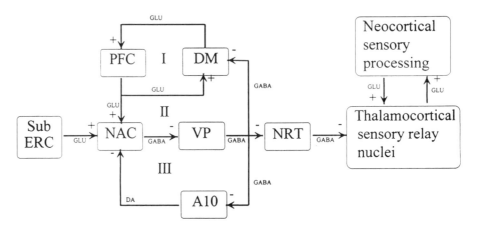

Figure 5.6 Connections from the subiculum (Sub) and entorhinal cortex (ERC) to the nucleus accumbens (NAC) component of the motor system, and from that system to the nucleus reticularis thalami (NRT) and thalamocortical sensory pathways. LCX = limbic cortex, including prefrontal and cingulate areas; DM = dorsomedial thalamic nucleus; NAC = nucleus accumbens (ventral striatum); VP = ventral pallidum. A 10 = dopaminergic nucleus A 10 in the ventral tegmental area; GLU, GABA and DA = the neurotransmitters, glutamate, γ-aminobutyric acid and dopamine; +, − = excitation and inhibition; I, II, III-feedback loops, the first two positive, the third negative. Reproduced from Gray (1995b), with permission

tutes a mechanism by which this effect can be produced. Dopamine release within the nucleus accumbens inhibits (by acting on dopamine D2 receptors; Robertson & Jian, 1995) the GABA-ergic pathway to the ventral pallidum, thus disinhibiting the pallidal GABA-ergic pathway to NRT, which in turn inhibits the GABA-ergic projections from NRT to the ascending thalamocortical sensory relay projections, so disinhibiting the latter. In this way, accumbal DA release should lead to an intensification of processing in whichever thalamocortical sensory relay projections were already operative in the prior instant of time (as defined by the basic comparator circuitry briefly outlined above and described in detail in Gray, 1982a,b, and Gray et al., 1991a). In the latent inhibition experiment, this intensification of sensory processing will allow the pre-exposed CS (which otherwise would not have been fully processed) to enter more readily into association with the UCS.

Taking this approach further, we may suppose that there are two passes through the thalamocortical system on which the formation of a perceptual description of the world depends (Figure 5.6). The first pass solves the initial binding problem, but leaves the solution still at an unconscious level (although one still capable of providing highly processed guidance for the current step in an on-line action programme). Only at a second pass, when the outcome of that step in the programme is compared to the expected outcome (predicted by reference to memory stores of previous regularities of past experience, as described in detail by Gray, 1995a, b, and Gray et al., 1991a), does consciousness come into play. As proposed above, a critical role is played in the initiation of that second pass by the pathway that links the output from the hippocampal formation (via the subiculum) to the nucleus accumbens and its dopaminergic afferents from nucleus A 10 in the ventral tegmental area; and thence via the NRT to the thalamocortical systems (see Figures 5.2, 5.3 and 5.6). What enters consciousness at the second pass is a mixture of elements that are surprising (i.e. mismatched within the comparator system) and not surprising, but with priority given to the former. According to the theory, stimuli are more easily tagged as surprising in the state of acute, positively symptomatic schizophrenia (due to dopaminergic overactivity, whether direct or indirect, in the mesolimbic system; Gray et al., 1991a,b), so leading to an excess of conscious processing in such patients relative to normal individuals.

As we have seen, Gray's (1995a,b) conjecture as to the nature of the contents of consciousness springs in part from the previous model of the neuropsychology of schizophrenia (Gray et al., 1991a,b). Applying the hypothesis back again to schizophrenia, we are able to make contact—but, I believe, in a more fully specified and testable manner—with an older tradition (e.g. Frith, 1979, p. 233; Venables, 1984, p. 75; Knight, 1984, p. 120) in understanding this disorder. According to this tradition, schizophrenic symptoms reflect (using Schneider & Shiffrin's, 1977, widely accepted terminology) a failure in "automatic processing", with a consequent breaking into "conscious processing" of material that would not normally figure there (see Gray et al., 1991b, pp. 65–66, for further discussion). In terms of the model outlined here, this transition to conscious processing would, in neural terms, be due to abnormalities in the functioning of the limbic–basal ganglia interface constituted by the projection from the hippocampal formation and the retrohippocampal region to the nucleus accumbens. The consequent overactivity in the dopaminergic projection to the nucleus accumbens (whether direct, or due to imbalance between this input and that from the retrohippocampal region) would then, via the NRT and the thalamocortical sensory relays (Figure 5.6), boost back into conscious processing parts of the perceptual world that would otherwise receive only automatic processing. (It bears saying yet once more that it remains totally mysterious that one, but not the other, of these types of processing is associated with subjective, conscious experience. That is the "hard problem" of consciousness, for which, as yet, no solution is to hand; see Chalmers, 1996; Gray, 1995a,b.)

CONSCIOUSNESS AND EMOTION

The conjunction of several of the previous arguments implies a close association between conscious experience and emotion. If the outputs of the comparator system constitute the contents of consciousness, and if the comparator system lies at the information-processing core of the neuropsychology of anxiety, then it follows that conscious experience is an essential concomitant of anxious behaviour. The same arguments, together with the treatment of positive psychotic symptoms as reflecting a failure of the comparator system correctly to predict what, given the patient's previous experience, ought to be expected events, imply that positive psychotic symptoms (themselves essentially elements of conscious experience; see Table 5.1) should be accompanied by heightened anxiety; and this appears indeed to be the case (Chapman, 1966; Hemsley, 1994). These inferences are sharply at variance with a number of other views, ranging from the psychodynamic (stemming from Freud's emphasis on unconscious mental processes) to the neurobiological (e.g. LeDoux, 1987; Panksepp, 1990), which place a sharp boundary between the realms of emotion and conscious experience, respectively. Like so many other issues in this field, this may be no more than a question of terminology: all may turn on whether one wishes to attribute the term "emotion" to the fast, unconscious neural processes which organize the immediate behavioural response to an emotional (e.g. threatening) stimulus, or to the conscious experience of both the stimulus and the ensuing behaviour, which, as noted above, takes place after this immediate response has been organized and emitted. If so, we can all have prizes; although an agreed definition of what to describe as "emotion" would be a still greater collective prize.

It is possible, however, that there is a deeper link between emotion and consciousness. The combination of the role attributed to the comparator system in the neuropsychology of anxiety (Gray, 1982a,b) with the conjecture (Gray, 1995a,b) that this system generates the contents of consciousness leads to a view in which it functions as a late (i.e. in the terminology of the previous section, at the "second pass") error detector. The neurology of the system, with its emphasis on the hippocampal formation, coupled with other knowledge of the cognitive functions of the hippocampal formation (O'Keefe & Nadel, 1978; Eichenbaum, Otto & Cohen, 1994), suggest that error detection is accomplished by the analysis of associations between a background context and foreground focal stimuli (cf. Gaffan's, 1994, recent studies of the role of the hippocampal formation in the analysis of "scenes"). Now, the most important type of context for mammals is typically spatial, consistent with O'Keefe & Nadel's (1978) well-known and well-supported hypothesis that the hippocampus plays a key role in the analysis of the spatial environment. The close link between this type of context–stimulus associative analysis, on the one hand, and anxiety, on the other, has been demonstrated in a detailed ethological and psychopharmacological analysis of defensive behaviour in the rat by Blanchard & Blanchard (1990a,b). The results of this analysis are largely consistent with the view of anxiety expressed by Gray (1982a), provided that one replaces "stimuli associated with punishment" in his formulation of the adequate stimuli for anxiety by "stimuli indicative of a potential (as distinct from actually present) predator" (Gray & McNaughton, 1996). In particular, the Blanchards' analysis emphasizes the necessity for an animal faced with possible threat from a potential predator to analyse its environment in order to determine whether there is any sign that, and if so where, such a predator might be located in it: hence the balanced transitions between silence-plus-immobility and cautious exploration that characterize behaviour under such circumstances. This behaviour turns out to be sensitive to the action of compounds that human beings find to be anxiolytic and so, by inference, reflects the emotion of anxiety.

In the light of these observations and their theoretical background, it seems possible that the evolutionary development of consciousness was intimately related to the necessity for an error-detection system that would permit the interruption of on-line motor programmes under just these conditions of potential threat to survival. If so, anxiety may have been the first consciously experienced emotion to emerge during evolution (consistent with its great potency still to dominate consciousness today). For what they are worth, my own introspections (and they are probably no different in relevant respects from those of others) are in line with a view of this kind. I often find that I have reacted behaviourally to a threat of some kind (a potential traffic hazard is the most common example) and only then experience a detectable emotional reaction, i.e. after the threat has already passed (all of this on a time-scale of fractions of a second). It seems (again, speaking introspectively) that the function of this late emotional reaction is to cause one to replay the events that have just taken place, cogitate upon them and, if possible, draw lessons from them with regard to future conduct. It is just at this stage that cognitive therapy attempts to intervene. Its demonstrated effectiveness in changing maladaptive emotional reactions may, in the light of the present analysis, be due to its acting upon a natural pivot: one that links behaviour, feeling and thought so as to improve future adaptation to an always hazardous environment.

REFERENCES

Amsel, A. (1962). Frustrative nonreward in partial reinforcement and discrimination learning: some recent history and a theoretical extension. *Psychological Review*, **69**, 306–328.

Baruch, I., Hemsley, D. R. & Gray, J. A. (1988). Differential performance of acute and chronic schizophrenics in a latent inhibition task. *Journal of Nervous & Mental Disease*, **176**, 598–606.

Beck, A. T., Rush, A. J., Shaw, B. F. & Emory, G. (1979). *Cognitive Theory of Depression*. New York: The Guilford Press.

Blanchard, R. J. & Blanchard, D. C. (1990a). An ethoexperimental analysis of defense, fear and anxiety. In N. McNaughton & G. Andrews (eds), *Anxiety*. Dunedin: University of Otago Press, pp. 124–133.

Blanchard, D. C. & Blanchard, R. J. (1990b). Effects of ethanol, benzodiazepines and serotonin compounds on ethopharmacological models of anxiety. In N. McNaughton & G. Andrews (eds), *Anxiety*. Dunedin: University of Otago Press, pp. 188–199.

Block, N. (1995). On a confusion about a function of consciousness. *Behavioral and Brain Sciences*, **18**, 227–287.

Broadbent, D. E. (1958). *Perception and Communication*. London: Pergamon.

Carlsson, A. (1988). The current status of the dopamine hypothesis of schizophrenia. *Neuropsychopharmacology*, **1**, 179–203.

Chalmers, D. J. (1996). *The Conscious Mind: In Search of a Fundamental Theory*. New York: Oxford University Press.

Chapman, J. (1966). The early symptoms of schizophrenia. *British Journal of Psychiatry*, **112**, 225–251.

Crick, F. (1984). The function of the thalamic reticular complex: the searchlight hypothesis. *Proceedings of the National Academy of Science USA*, **81**, 4586–4590.

Crick, F. & Koch, C. (1990). Towards a neurobiological theory of consciousness. *Seminars in Neuroscience*, **2**, 263–275.

Crow, T. J. (1980). Positive and negative schizophrenic symptoms and the role of dopamine. *British Journal of Psychiatry*, **137**, 383–386.

Eichenbaum, H., Otto, T. & Cohen, N. J. (1994). The functional components of the hippocampal memory system. *Behavioral and Brain Sciences*, **17**, 449–518.

Frith, C. D. (1979). Consciousness, information processing and schizophrenia. *British Journal of Psychiatry*, **134**, 225–235.

Gaffan, D. (1994). Scene specific memory for objects: a model of episodic memory impairment in monkeys with fornix transection. *Journal of Cognitive Neuroscience*, **6**, 305–320.

Gray, J. A. (1971). The mind–brain identity theory as a scientific hypothesis. *Philosophical Quarterly*, **21**, 247–253.

Gray, J. A. (1976). The behavioural inhibition system: a possible substrate for anxiety. In M. P. Feldman & A. M. Broadhurst (eds), *Theoretical and Experimental Bases of Behaviour Modification*. Chichester: Wiley, pp. 3–41.

Gray, J. A. (1982a). *The Neuropsychology of Anxiety: An Enquiry into the Functions of the Septohippocampal System*. Oxford: Oxford University Press.

Gray, J. A. (1982b). Précis of "The neuropsychology of anxiety: an enquiry into the functions of the septohippocampal system". *Behavioral and Brain Sciences*, **5**, 469–484.

Gray, J. A. (1982c). On mapping anxiety. *Behavioral and Brain Sciences*, **5**, 506–525.

Gray, J. A. (1993). Consciousness, schizophrenia and scientific theory. In J. Marsh & G. Bock (eds), *Experimental and Theoretical Studies of Consciousness*. Ciba Foundation Symposium Series, No. 174. Chichester: Wiley, pp. 263–281.

Gray, J. A. (1995a). The contents of consciousness: a neuropsychological conjecture. *Behavioral and Brain Sciences*, **18**, 659–676.

Gray, J. A. (1995b). Consciouness and its (dis)contents. *Behavioral and Brain Sciences*, **18**, 703–722.

Gray, J. A. (1998). Integrating schizophrenia. *Schizophrenia Bulletin*, **24**, 249–266.

Gray, J. A., Feldon, J., Rawlins, J. N. P., Hemsley, D. R. & Smith, A. D. (1991a). The neuropsychology of schizophrenia. *Behavioral and Brain Sciences*, **14**, 1–20.

Gray, J. A., Hemsley, D. R., Feldon, J., Gray, N. S. & Rawlins, J. N. P. (1991b). Schiz bits: misses, mysteries and hits. *Behavioral and Brain Sciences*, **14**, 56–84.

Gray, J. A., Joseph, M. H., Hemsley, D. R., Young, A. M. J., Warburton, E. C., Boulenguez, P., Grigoryan, G. A., Peters, S. L., Rawlins, J. N. P., Taib, C-T., Yee, B. K., Cassaday, H., Weiner, I., Gal, G., Gusak, O., Joel, D., Shadach, E., Shalev, U., Tarrasch, R. & Feldon, J. (1995). The role of mesolimbic dopaminergic and retrohippocampal afferents to the nucleus accumbens in latent inhibition: implications for schizophrenia. *Behavioural Brain Research*, **71**, 19–31.

Gray, J. A. & McNaughton, N. (1996). The neuropsychology of anxiety: reprise. In D. A. Hope (ed.), *Perspectives on Anxiety, Panic and Fear*. Nebraska Symposium on Motivation, Vol. 43. Lincoln NE: University of Nebraska Press, pp. 61–134.

Gray, J. A., Moran, P. M., Grigoryan, G. A., Peters, S. R., Young, A. M. J. & Joseph, M. H. (1997). Latent inhibition: the nucleus accumbens connection revisited. *Behavioural Brain Research*, **88**, 27–34.

Gray, N. S., Hemsley, D. R. & Gray, J. A. (1992a). Abolition of latent inhibition in acute, but not chronic schizophrenics. *Neurology, Psychiatry and Brain Research*, **1**, 83–89.

Gray, N. S., Pickering, A. D., Hemsley, D. R., Dawling, S. & Gray, J. A. (1992b). Abolition of latent inhibition by a single 5 mg dose of *d*-amphetamine in man. *Psychopharmacology*, **107**, 425–430.

Gray, N. S., Pilowsky, L. S., Gray, J. A. & Kerwin, R. W. (1995). Latent inhibition in drug naive schizophrenics: relationship to duration of illness and dopamine D2 binding using SPET. *Schizophrenia Research*, **17**, 95–107.

Hemsley, D. R. (1987). An experimental psychological model for schizophrenia. In H. Hafner, W. F. Fattaz & W. Janzavik (eds), *Search for the Causes of Schizophrenia*. Stuttgart: Springer Verlag.

Hemsley, D. R. (1994). Perceptual and cognitive abnormalities as the bases for schizophrenic symptoms. In A. S. David & J. C. Cutting (eds), *The Neuropsychology of Schizophrenia*. Hove: Erlbaum, pp. 97–116.

Jones, E. G. (1975). Some aspects of the organisation of the thalamic reticular complex. *Journal of Comparative Neurobiology*, **162**, 285–308.

Jones, S. H., Gray, J. A. & Hemsley, D. R. (1992). Loss of the Kamin blocking effect in acute but not chronic schizophrenics. *Biological Psychiatry*, **32**, 739–755.

Kamin, L. J. (1969). Predictability, surprise, attention and conditioning. In B. A. Campbell & R. M. Church (eds), *Punishment and Aversive Behavior*. New York: Appleton Century Crofts, pp. 279–296.

Kelley, A. E. & Domesick, V. B. (1982). The distribution of the projection from the hippocampal formation to the nucleus accumbens in the rat: an anterograde and retrograde horseradish peroxidase study, *Neuroscience*, **7**, 2321–2335.

Knight, R. A. (1984). Converging models of cognitive deficit in schizophrenia. In W. Spaulding & J. K. Cole (eds), *Theories of Schizophrenia and Psychosis*. Lincoln, NE: University of Nebraska Press.

Lavin A. & Grace, A. A. (1994). Modulation of dorsal thalamic cell activity by the ventral pallidum: its role in the regulation of thalamocortical activity by the basal ganglia. *Synapse*, **18**, 104–127.

LeDoux, J. E. (1987). Emotion. In V. Mountcastle (ed.), *Handbook of Physiology: The Nervous System. Vol. 5, Higher Functions of the Brain*. Bethesda, MD: American Physiological Society, pp. 419–459.

Llinas, R., Ribary, U., Joliot, M. & Wang, C. (1994). Content and context in temporal thalamocortical binding. In G. Buzsaki (ed.), *Temporal Coding in the Brain*. Berlin: Springer Verlag.

Lubow, R. E. (1989). *Latent Inhibition and Conditioned Attention Theory*. Cambridge: Cambridge University Press.

Mathews, A. & MacLeod, C. (1994). Cognitive approaches to emotion and emotional disorders. *Annual Review of Psychology*, **45**, 25–50.

McCrone, J. (1993). Good timing. *New Scientist Supplement*, 9 October, 10–12.

McNally, R. J. (1996). Cognitive bias in the anxiety disorders. In D. A. Hope (ed.), *Perspectives on Anxiety, Panic and Fear*. Nebraska Symposium on Motivation, Vol. 43. Lincoln, NE: University of Nebraska Press, pp. 211–250.

Mogenson, G. J. & Nielsen, M. (1984). A study of the contribution of hippocampal–accumbens–subpallidal projections to locomotor activity. *Behavioral and Neural Biology*, **42**, 52–60.

Newman, J. (1996). Commentary on commentaries. In J. Newman (conductor), *Thalamocortical Foundations of Conscious Experience*, electronic seminar of the Association for the Scientific Study of Consciousness, July 1–30.

Oatley, K. & Johnson-Laird, P. (1987). Towards a cognitive theory of emotions. *Cognition and Emotion*, **1**, 29–50.

O'Keefe, J. & Nadel, L. (1978). *The Hippocampus as a Cognitive Map*. Oxford: Clarendon.

Ortony, A., Clore, G. L. & Collins, A. (1988). *The Cognitive Structure of Emotions*. Cambridge: Cambridge University Press.

Panksepp, J. (1990). Gray zones at the cognition/emotion interface: a commentary. In J. A. Gray (ed.), *Cognition and Emotion*. Special issue: Psychobiological Aspects of Relationships between Cognition and Emotion. Hove: Lawrence Erlbaum Associates, pp. 289–302.

Robertson, G. S. & Jian, M. (1995). D_1 and D_2 dopamine receptors differentially increase fos-like immunoreactivity in accumbal projections to the ventral pallidum and midbrain. *Neuroscience*, **64**, 1019–1034.

Schmajuk, N. A., Lam, Y.-W. & Gray, J. A. (1996). Latent inhibition: a neural network approach. *Journal of Experimental Psychology: Animal Behaviour Processes*, **22**, 321–349.

Schneider, W. & Shiffrin, R. M. (1977). Controlled and automatic human information processing: 1. Detection, search and attention. *Psychological Review*, **84**, 1–66.

Searle, J. R. (1992). *The Rediscovery of the Mind*. Cambridge, MA: MIT.

Shallice, T. (1988). *From Neuropsychology to Mental Structure*. Cambridge: Cambridge University Press.

Swerdlow, N. R. & Koob, G. F. (1987). Dopamine, schizophrenia, mania and depression: toward a unified hypothesis of cortico-striato-pallidothalamic function. *Behavioral and Brain Sciences*, **10**, 197–245.

Taylor, J. G. & Alavi, F. N. (1992). Mathematical analysis of a competitive network for attention. In J. G. Taylor (ed.), *Mathematical Approaches to Neural Networks*. Amsterdam: Elsevier, pp. 341–382.

Thornton, J. C., Dawe, S., Lee, C., Capstick, C., Corr, P. J., Cotter, P., Frangou, S., Gray N. S., Russell, M. A. H. & Gray, J. A. (1996). Effects of nicotine and amphetamine on latent inhibition in human subjects. *Psychopharmacology*, **127**, 164–173.

Velmans, M. (1991). Is human information processing conscious? *Behavioral and Brain Sciences*, **14**, 651–726.

Venables, P. H. (1984). Cerebral mechanisms, automatic responsiveness and attention in schizophrenia. In W. D. Spaulding & J. K. Cole (eds), *Theories of Schizophrenia and Psychosis*. Lincoln, NE: University of Nebraska Press.

Weiner, I. (1990). Neural substrates of latent inhibition: the switching model. *Psychological Bulletin*, **108**, 442–461.

Yee, B., Feldon, J. & Rawlins, J. N. P. (1995). Latent inhibition in rats is abolished by NMDA-induced neuronal loss in the retrohippocampal region but this lesion effect can be prevented by systemic haloperidol treatment. *Behavioural Neuroscience*, **54**, 5–9.

Chapter 6

Neuropsychological Perspectives on Affective Styles and Their Cognitive Consequences

Richard J. Davidson
University of Wisconsin-Madison, Madison, WI, USA

INTRODUCTION

Among the most striking features of human emotion is the variability that is apparent across individuals in the quality and intensity of dispositional mood and emotional reactions to similar incentives and challenges. Some people appear very resilient in the face of life's slings and arrows, while others decompensate quickly. Certain individuals show a dispositional tendency toward positive affect and success, while others are more prone to negative affect and failure. The broad range of differences in these varied affective phenomena has been referred to as "affective style" (Davidson, 1992; 1998). Differences among people in affective style appear to be associated with temperament (Kagan, Reznick & Snidman, 1988), personality (Gross, Sutton & Ketelaar, in press) and vulnerability to psychopathology (Meehl, 1975). Moreover, such differences are not a unique human attribute, but appear to be present in a number of different species (e.g. Davidson, Kalin & Shelton, 1993; Kalin 1993; Kalin, et al., 1998).

In the next section of this chapter, conceptual distinctions among the various components of affective style will be introduced and methodological challenges to their study will be highlighted. The third section will present a brief overview of the anatomy of two basic motivational/emotional systems—the approach and

Handbook of Cognition and Emotion. Edited by T. Dalgleish and M. Power.
© 1999 John Wiley & Sons Ltd.

withdrawal systems. The fourth section will consider individual differences in these basic systems, indicate how such differences might be studied and discuss the behavioral consequences of such individual differences. Finally, the last section will consider some of the implications of this perspective for the assessment and treatment of disorders of affect, and for plasticity.

THE CONSTITUENTS OF AFFECTIVE STYLE

Many phenomena are subsumed under the rubric of affective style. A concept featured in many discussions of affective development, affective disorders and personality is "emotion regulation" (Thompson, 1994). Emotion regulation refers to a broad constellation of processes that serve to either amplify, attenuate or maintain the strength of emotional reactions. Included among these processes are certain features of attention which regulate the extent to which an organism can be distracted from a potentially aversive stimulus (Derryberry & Reed, 1996) and the capacity for self-generated imagery to replace emotions that are unwanted with more desirable imagery scripts. Emotion regulation can be both automatic and controlled. Automatic emotion regulation may result from the progressive automization of processes that initially were voluntary and controlled and have evolved to become more automatic with practice. We hold the view that regulatory processes are an intrinsic part of emotional behavior, and rarely does an emotion get generated in the absence of recruiting associated regulatory processes. For this reason, it is often conceptually difficult to distinguish sharply between where an emotion ends and regulation begins. Even more problematic is the methodological challenge of operationalizing these different components in the stream of affective behavior.

When considering the question of individual differences in affective behavior, one must specify the particular response systems in which the individual differences are being explored. It is not necessarily the case that the same pattern of individual differences would be found across response systems. Thus, for example, an individual may have a low threshold for the elicitation of the subjective experience (as reflected in self-reports) of a particular emotion but a relatively high threshold for the elicitation of a particular physiological change. It is important not to assume that individual differences in any parameter of affective responding will necessarily generalize across response systems, within the same emotion. Equally important is the question of whether individual differences associated with the generation of a particular specific emotion will necessarily generalize to other emotions. For example, are those individuals who are behaviorally expressive in response to a fear challenge also likely to show comparably high levels of expressivity in response to positive incentives? While systematic research on this question is still required, initial evidence suggests that at least certain aspects of affective style may be emotion-specific, or at least valence specific (e.g. Wheeler, Davidson & Tomarken, 1993).

In addition to emotion regulation, there are likely also intrinsic differences in certain components of emotional responding. There are likely individual differences in the *threshold* for eliciting components of a particular emotion, given a stimulus of a certain intensity. Thus, some individuals are likely to produce facial signs of disgust upon presentation of a particular intensity of noxious stimulus, whereas other individuals may require a more intense stimulus for the elicitation of the same response at a comparable intensity. This suggestion implies that dose–response functions may reliably differ across individuals. Unfortunately, systematic studies of this kind have not been performed, in part because of the difficulty of creating stimuli that are graded in intensity and designed to elicit the same emotion. In the olfactory and gustatory modalities, there are possibilities of creating stimuli that differ systematically in the concentration of a disgust-producing component and then obtaining psychophysical threshold functions that would reveal such individual differences. However, the production of such intensity-graded stimuli in other modalities will likely be more complicated, although with the development of large, normatively rated complex stimulus sets, this may be possible. An example is the *International Affective Picture System* (Lang, Bradley & Cuthbert, 1995) developed by Peter Lang and his colleagues. This set includes a large number of visual stimuli that have been rated on valance and arousal dimensions and that comprise locations throughout this two-dimensional space. The density of stimulus exemplars at all levels within this space allow for the possibility of selecting stimuli that are graded in intensity for the sort of dose–response studies described above.

There are also likely to be individual differences in the *peak* or *amplitude* of the response. Upon presentation of a series of graded stimuli that differ in intensity, the maximum amplitude in a certain system (e.g. intensity of a facial contraction; change in heart rate, etc.) is likely to differ systematically across subjects. Some individuals will respond with a larger amplitude peak compared with others. Again, such individual differences may well be quite specific to particular systems and will not necessarily generalize across systems, even within the same emotion. Thus, the individual who is in the tail of the distribution in her heart rate response to a fearful stimulus will not necessarily be in the tail of the distribution in her facial response.

Another parameter that is likely to differ systematically across individuals is the *rise time to peak*. Some individuals will rise quickly in a certain response system, while others will rise more slowly. There may be an association between the peak of the response and the rise time to the peak within certain systems for particular emotions. Thus, it may be the case that, for anger-related emotion, those individuals with higher peak vocal responses also show a faster rise time, but to the best of my knowledge, there are no systematic data related to such differences.

Finally, another component of intrinsic differences across individuals is the *recovery time*. Following perturbation in a particular system, some individuals recover quickly and others recover slowly. For example, following a fear-provoking encounter, some individuals show a persisting heart rate elevation that might last for minutes, while other individuals show a comparable peak and rise time but recover much more quickly. Of course, as with other parameters, there are likely to be differences in recovery time across different response systems. Some individuals may recover rapidly in their expressive behavior, while recovering slowly in certain autonomic channels. The potential significance of such dissociations has not been systematically examined.

The specific parameters of individual differences that are delineated above describe *affective chronometry*—the temporal dynamics of affective responding. Very little is known about the factors that govern these individual differences and the extent to which such differences are specific to particular emotion response systems or generalize across emotions (e.g. is the heart rate recovery following fear similar to that following sadness?). Moreover, the general issue of the extent to which these different parameters that have been identified are orthogonal or correlated features of emotional responding is an empirical question that has yet to be answered. For reasons that I hope to make clear below, affective chronometry is a particularly important feature of affective style and is likely to play a key role in determining vulnerability and resilience. It is also a feature of affective style that is methodologically tractable and can yield to experimental study of its neural substrates.

We also hold that affective style is critical in understanding the continuity between normal and abnormal functioning and in the prediction of psychopathology and the delineation of vulnerability. On the opposite side of the spectrum, such individual differences in affective style will also feature centrally in any comprehensive theory of resilience. The fact that some individuals reside "off the diagonal" and appear to maintain very high levels of psychological well-being despite their exposure to objective life adversity is likely related to their affective style (Ryff & Singer, 1998). Some of these implications will be discussed at the end of this article.

We first consider some of the neural substrates of two fundamental emotion systems. This provides the foundation for a consideration of individual differences in these systems and the neural circuitry responsible for such differences.

THE ANATOMY OF APPROACH AND WITHDRAWAL

Although the focus of my empirical research has been on measures of prefrontal brain activity, it must be emphasized at the outset that the circuit instantiating emotion in the human brain is complex and involves a number of interrelated structures. Preciously few empirical studies using modern neuroimaging procedures that afford a high degree of spatial resolution have yet been performed (see George et al., 1995; Paradiso et al., 1997, for examples). Therefore, hypotheses about the set of structures that participate in the production of emotion must necessarily be speculative and based to a large extent on the information available from the animal literature (e.g. LeDoux, 1987) and from theoretical accounts of the processes involved in human emotion.

Based upon the available strands of theory and evidence, numerous scientists have proposed two basic circuits, each mediating different forms of motivation and emotion (see e.g. Gray, in press; Lang, Bradley & Cuthbert, 1990; Davidson, 1995). The approach system facilitates appetitive behavior and generates certain types of positive affect that are approach-related, e.g. enthusiasm, pride, etc. (for review, see Depue & Collins, in press). This form of positive affect is usually generated in the context of moving toward a desired goal (for theoretical accounts of emotion that place a premium on goal states, see Lazarus, 1991; Stein & Trabasso, 1992). The representation of a goal state in working memory is hypothesized to be implemented in dorsolateral prefrontal cortex. The medial prefrontal cortex seems to play an important role in maintaining representations of behavioral-reinforcement contingencies in working memory (Thorpe, Rolls & Maddison, 1983). In addition, output from the medial prefrontal cortex to nucleus accumbens (NA) neurons modulates the transfer of motivationally-relevant information through the NA (Kalivas, Churchill & Klitenick, 1993). The basal ganglia are hypothesized to be involved in the expression of the abstract goal in action plans and in the anticipation of reward (Schultz et al., 1995a,b). The NA, particularly the caudomedial shell region of the NA, is a major convergence zone for motivationally relevant information from a myriad of limbic structures. Cells in this region of the NA increase their firing rate during reward expectation (see Schultz et al., 1995a). There are likely other structures involved in this circuit which depend upon a number of factors, including the nature of the stimuli signaling appetitive information, the extent to which the behavioral-reinforcement contingency is novel or over-learned, and the nature of the anticipated behavioral response.

In a very recent study using PET with ^{18}F-labeled deoxyglucose (FDG), we (Sutton et al., 1997) presented aversive or appetitive pictures during the FDG uptake procedure in separate sessions. We found significant left-sided metabolic increases during the appetitive condition in inferior prefrontal cortex, nucleus accumbens and superior prefrontal, premotor and motor regions. The significant left-sided focus of these metabolic increases was confirmed by formally testing the condition × hemisphere interactions for these regions. Similar findings have recently been reported by Thut et al. (1997) in response to monetary reward. These data imply that, at least in humans, the circuitry for appetitive (and aversive) emotion is lateralized. Such a functional neuroanatomical arrangement may be advantageous in helping the brain to compute affective value (for additional discussion of this issue, see Davidson, 1998).

It should be noted that the activation of this approach system is hypothesized to be associated with one particular form of positive affect and not all forms of such emotion. It is specifically predicted to be associated with *pre-goal attainment positive affect*, that form of positive affect that is elicited as an organism moves closer toward an appetitive goal. *Post-goal attainment positive affect* represents another form of positive emotion that is not expected to be associated with activation of this circuit (for a more extended discussion of this distinction, see Davidson, 1994). This latter type of positive affect may be phenomenologically experienced as contentment or joy (although conventional emotional terms appear inadequate in capturing these hypothesized differences) and is expected to occur when the prefrontal cortex goes off-line after a desired goal has been achieved. Cells in the NA have also been shown to decrease their firing rate during post-goal consummatory behavior (e.g. Henriksen & Giacchino, 1993).

Lawful individual differences can enter into many different stages of the approach system. Such individual differences and their role in modulating vulnerability to psychopathology will be considered in detail below. For the moment, it is important to underscore two issues. One is that there are individual differences in the tonic level of activation of the approach system which alters an individual's propensity to experience approach-related positive affect. Second, there are likely to be individual differences in the capacity to shift between pre- and post-goal attainment positive affect and in the ratio between these two forms of positive affect. Upon reaching a desired goal, some individuals will immediately replace the just-achieved goal with a new desired goal, and so will have little opportunity to experience post-goal attainment positive affect, or contentment. There may be an optimal balance between these two forms of positive affect, although this issue has never been studied.

There appears to be a second system concerned with the neural implementation of withdrawal. This system facilitates the withdrawal of an individual from sources of aversive stimulation and generates certain forms of negative affect that are withdrawal-related. Both fear and disgust are associated with increasing the distance between the organism and a source of aversive stimulation. From invasive animal studies and human neuroimaging studies, it appears that the amygdala is critically involved in this system (e.g. LeDoux, 1987). Using functional magnetic resonance imaging (fMRI), we have recently demonstrated for the first time activation in the human amygdala in response to aversive pictures, compared with neutral control pictures (Irwin et al., 1996). In addition, the temporal polar region also appears to be activated during withdrawal-related emotion (e.g. Reiman et al., 1989; but see Drevets et al., 1992). These effects, at least in humans, appear to be more pronounced on the right side of the brain (for reviews, see Davidson, 1992, 1993). In the human PET and electrophysiological studies, the right frontal region is also activated during withdrawal-related negative affective states (e.g. Davidson et al., 1990b). In the recent FDG–PET study from our laboratory mentioned above (Sutton et al., 1997), we observed increased glucose metabolism in response to aversive pictures (compared with appetitive pictures) in the right prefrontal cortex (Brodmann's area 9) and amygdala. In addition to the prefrontal and temporal polar cortical regions and the amygdala, it is also likely that the basal ganglia and hypothalamus are involved in the motor and autonomic components, respectively, of withdrawal-related negative affect (see Smith, De Vita & Astley, 1990).

The nature of the relation between these two hypothesized affect systems also remains to be delineated. The emotion literature is replete with different proposals regarding the interrelations among different forms of positive and negative affect. Some theorists have proposed a single bivalent dimension that ranges from unpleasant to pleasant affect, with a second dimension that reflects arousal (e.g. Russell, 1980). Other theorists have suggested that affect space is best described by two orthogonal positive and negative dimensions (e.g. Watson & Tellegen, 1985; Cacioppo & Bernston, 1994). Still other workers have suggested that the degree of orthogonality between positive and negative affect depends upon the temporal frame of analysis (Diener & Emmons, 1984). This formulation holds that when assessed in the moment, positive and negative affect are reciprocally related, but when examined over a longer time frame (e.g. dispositional affect), they are orthogonal. It must be emphasized that these analyses of the relation between positive and negative affect are all based exclusively upon measures of self-report, and therefore their generalizability to other measures of affect are uncertain. However, based upon new data from our laboratory showing reciprocal relations between metabolic activity in the left prefrontal cortex and the amygdala (Davidson et al., in preparation), we believe that one function of positive affect is to inhibit concurrent negative affect. It seems likely that the presence of negative affect would interfere with the generation of pre-goal attainment positive affect and with the production of approach behavior. It would therefore be adaptive for negative affect to be inhibited during the generation of certain forms of positive affect. Of course, the time course of this hypothesized inhibition and the boundary conditions for its presence remain to be elucidated in future research.

INDIVIDUAL DIFFERENCES IN ASYMMETRIC PREFRONTAL ACTIVATION: WHAT DO THEY REFLECT?

This section will present a brief overview of recent work from my laboratory that was designed to examine individual differences in measures of prefrontal activation and their relation to different aspects of emotion, affective style and related biological constructs. These findings will be used to address the question of what underlying constituents of affective style such individual differences in prefrontal activation actually reflect.

In both infants (Davidson & Fox, 1989) and adults (Davidson & Tomarken, 1989), we noticed that there were large individual differences in baseline electrophysiological measures of prefrontal activation and that such individual variation was associated with differences in aspects of affective reactivity. In infants, Davidson and Fox (1989) reported that 10 month-old babies who cried in response to maternal separation were more likely to have less left and greater right-sided prefrontal activation during a preceding resting baseline, compared with those infants who did not cry in response to this challenge. In adults, we first noted that the phasic influence of positive and negative emotion elicitors (e.g. film clips) on measures of prefrontal activation asymmetry appeared to be superimposed upon more tonic individual differences in the direction and absolute magnitude of asymmetry (Davidson & Tomarken, 1989).

During our initial explorations of this phenomenon, we needed to determine whether baseline electrophysiological measures of prefrontal asymmetry were reliable and stable over time and thus could be used as a trait-like measure. Tomarken et al. (1992) recorded baseline brain electrical activity from 90 normal subjects on two occasions, separated by approximately 3 weeks. At each testing session, brain activity was recorded during eight 1-minute trials, four eyes open and four eyes closed, presented in counterbalanced order. The data were visually scored to remove artifacts and then Fourier-transformed. Our focus was on power in the alpha band (8–13 Hz), although we extracted power in all frequency bands (for a discussion of power in different frequency bands and their relation to activation, see Davidson et al., 1990a). Using the asymmetry measures derived from each of the eight 1-minute trials as the data, we computed coefficient alpha as a measure of internal consistency reliability, separately for each session. The coefficient alphas were quite high, with all values exceeding 0.85, indicating that the electrophysiological measures of asymmetric activation indeed showed excellent internal consistency reliability. The test–retest reliability was adequate, with intraclass correlations ranging from 0.65 to 0.75, depending upon the specific sites and methods of analysis. The major finding of import from this study was the demonstration that measures of activation asymmetry based upon power in the alpha band from prefrontal scalp electrodes showed both high internal consistency reliability and acceptable test–retest reliability to be considered a trait-like index.

The large sample size in the reliability study discussed above enabled us to select a small group of extreme left and extreme right-frontally activated subjects for MR scans to determine whether there existed any gross morphometric differences in anatomical structure between these subgroups. None of our measures of regional volumetric asymmetry revealed any difference between the groups (unpublished observations). These findings suggest that, whatever differences exist between subjects with extreme left vs. right prefrontal activation, such differences are likely functional and not structural.

On the basis of our prior data and theory, we reasoned that extreme left and extreme right frontally activated subjects would show systematic differences in dispositional positive and negative affect. We administered the trait version of the Positive and Negative Affect Scales (PANAS; Watson, Clark & Tellegen, 1988) to examine this question and found that the left-frontally activated subjects reported more positive and less negative dispositional affect than their right-frontally activated counterparts (Tomarken et al., 1992; see Figure 6.1). More recently, with Sutton (Sutton & Davidson, 1997), we showed that scores on a self-report measure designed to operationalize Gray's concepts of Behavioral Inhibition and Behavioral Activation (the BIS–BAS scales; Carver & White, 1994) were even more strongly predicted by electrophysiological measures of prefrontal asymmetry than were scores on the PANAS scales (see Figure 6.2). Subjects with greater left-sided prefrontal activation reported more relative BAS

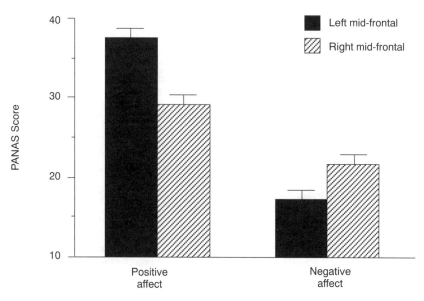

Figure 6.1 Dispositional positive affect (from scores on the PANAS-General Positive Affect Scale) in subjects who were classified as extreme and stable left-frontally active ($n = 14$) and extreme and stable right-frontally active ($n = 13$) on the basis of electrophysiological measures of baseline activation asymmetries on two occasions separated by three weeks. Reproduced from Tomarken et al. (1992), with permission

to BIS activity, compared with subjects exhibiting more right-sided prefrontal activation. Importantly, in each of these studies, measures of asymmetry from posterior scalp regions derived from the identical points in time showed no relation with the affect variables. In the Sutton & Davidson (1997) study, where we had a sufficiently large sample size, we tested the significance of the difference in the magnitude of correlation between measures of activation asymmetry in anterior and posterior regions and the BAS–BIS scores. We found that the prefrontal asymmetry measures were significantly more highly correlated with the affect measures than the measures of posterior asymmetry from the identical periods, underscoring the specificity of this relation to the anterior scalp region.

We also hypothesized that our measures of prefrontal asymmetry would predict reactivity to experimental elicitors of emotion. The model that we have developed over the past several years (see Davidson, 1992; 1994; 1995 for background) features individual differences in prefrontal activation asymmetry as a reflection of a diathesis which modulates reactivity to emotionally significant events. According to this model, individuals who differ in prefrontal asymmetry should respond differently to an elicitor of positive or negative emotion, even when baseline mood is partialled out. We (Wheeler, Davidson & Tomarken, 1993) performed an experiment to examine this question. We presented short film clips designed to elicit positive or negative emotion. Brain electrical activity

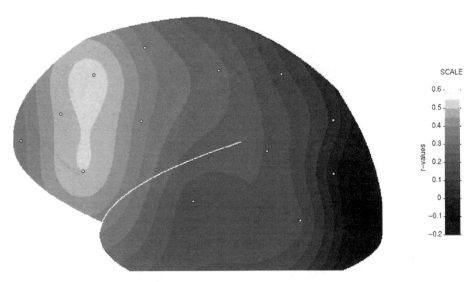

Figure 6.2   Relations between electrophysiological measures of asymmetry and the difference between the standardized score on the Behavioral Activation and Behavioral Inhibition Scales (BIS/BAS scales; Carver & White, 1994), n = 46. Electrophysiological data was recorded from each subject on two separate occasions separated by 6 weeks. The BIS/BAS scales were also administered on these two occasions. Data were averaged across the two time periods prior to performing correlations. The topographic map displays the correlations between alpha power asymmetry (log right minus log left alpha power; higher values denote greater relative left-sided activation) and the difference score between the standardized BAS minus BIS scales. After correlations were performed for each homologous region, a spline-interpolated map was created. The top end of the scale denotes positive correlations. The figure indicates that the correlation between the BAS–BIS difference score and the electrophysiology asymmetry score is highly positive in prefrontal scalp regions, denoting that subjects with greater relative left-sided activation report more relative behavioral activation compared with behavioral inhibition tendencies. The relation between asymmetric activation and the BAS–BIS difference is highly specific to the anterior scalp regions, as the correlation drops off rapidly more posteriorly. The correlation in the prefrontal region is significantly larger than the correlation in the parieto-occipital region. Reproduced from Sutton & Davidson (1997), with permission

was recorded prior to the presentation of the film clips. Just after the clips were presented, subjects were asked to rate their emotional experience during the preceding film clip. In addition, subjects completed scales that were designed to reflect their mood at baseline. We found that individual differences in prefrontal asymmetry predicted the emotional response to the films even after measures of baseline mood were statistically removed. Those individuals with more left-sided prefrontal activation at baseline reported more positive affect to the positive film clips and those with more right-sided prefrontal activation reported more negative affect to the negative film clips. These findings support the idea that individual differences in electrophysiological measures of prefrontal activation asymmetry mark some aspect of vulnerability to positive and negative emotion elicitors. The fact that such relations were obtained following the statistical removal of baseline mood indicates that any difference between left and right frontally activated subjects in baseline mood cannot account for the prediction of film-elicited emotion effects that were observed.

In a very recent study, we (Davidson et al., in preparation) examined relations between individual differences in prefrontal activation asymmetry and the emotion-modulated startle. In this study, we presented pictures from the *International Affective Picture System* (Lang, Bradley & Cuthbert, 1995) while acoustic startle probes were presented and the EMG-measured blink response from the orbicularis oculi muscle region was recorded (see Sutton et al., 1997 for basic methods). Startle probes were presented both during the 6-second slide exposure as well as 500 ms following the offset of the pictures, on separate trials.[1] We interpreted startle magnitude during picture exposure as providing an index related to the peak of emotional response, while startle magnitude following the *offset* of the pictures was taken to reflect the recovery from emotional challenge. Used in this way, startle probe methods can potentially provide new information on the time course of emotional responding. We expected that individual differences during actual picture presentation would be less pronounced than individual differences following picture presentation, since an acute emotional stimulus is likely to pull for a normative response across subjects, yet individuals are likely to differ dramatically in the time to recover. Similarly, we predicted that individual differences in prefrontal asymmetry would account for more variance in predicting magnitude of recovery (i.e. startle magnitude post-stimulus) than in predicting startle magnitude during the stimulus. Our findings were consistent with our predictions and indicated that subjects with greater left-sided prefrontal activation show a smaller blink magnitude following the offset of the negative stimuli, after the variance in blink magnitude *during* the negative stimulus was partialled out. Measures of prefrontal asymmetry did not reliably predict startle magnitude during picture presentation. The findings from this study are consistent with our hypothesis and indicate that individual differences in prefrontal asymmetry are associated with the time course of affective responding, particularly the recovery following emotional challenge.

In addition to the studies described above using self-report and psycho-physiological measures of emotion, we have also examined relations between individual differences in electrophysiological measures of prefrontal asymmetry

---

[1] In this initial study on the recovery function assessed with startle probe measures, we had only a single post-stimulus probe at 500 ms following the offset of the picture. Readers may be surprised that the interval between the offset of the picture and the presentation of the probe was so short. However, it should be noted that these emotional pictures are not particularly intense and so the lingering effects of emotion following the presentation of such pictures is likely not to last very long in most individuals. Future studies will probe further out following the offset of the picture. Since at most only a single probe can be presented for each picture, so that habituation effects are minimized, each new probe position requires a substantial increase in the overall number of pictures presented. There is a finite limit to the number of pictures contained in the IAPS. Even more importantly, we have found that it is critical to keep the picture viewing period to well under 1 hour to minimize fatigue and boredom.

and other biological indices, which in turn have been related to differential reactivity to stressful events. Two recent examples from our laboratory include measures of immune function and cortisol. In the case of the former, we examined differences between left and right prefrontally activated subjects in natural killer (NK) cell activity, since declines in NK activity have been reported in response to stressful, negative events (Kiecolt-Glaser & Glaser, 1991). We predicted that subjects with increased right prefrontal activation would exhibit lower NK activity compared with their left-activated counterparts, because the former type of subject has been found to report more dispositional negative affect, to show higher relative BIS activity and to respond more intensely to negative emotional stimuli. We found that right-frontally activated subjects indeed had lower levels of NK activity compared to their left frontally-activated counterparts (Kang et al., 1991).

Recently, in collaboration with Kalin, our laboratory has been studying similar individual differences in scalp-recorded measures of prefrontal activation asymmetry in rhesus monkeys (Davidson, Kalin & Shelton, 1992, 1993). Recently, we (Kalin et al., 1998) acquired measures of brain electrical activity from a large sample of rhesus monkeys ($n = 50$). EEG measures were obtained during periods of manual restraint. A sub-sample of 15 of these monkeys were tested on two occasions four months apart. We found that the test–retest correlation for measures of prefrontal asymmetry was 0.62, suggesting similar stability of this metric in monkey and man. In the group of 50 animals, we also obtained measures of plasma cortisol during the early morning. We hypothesized that if individual differences in prefrontal asymmetry were associated with dispositional affective style, such differences should be correlated with cortisol, since individual differences in baseline cortisol have been related to various aspects of trait-related stressful behavior and psychopathology (see e.g. Gold, Goodwin, & Chrousos, 1988; Tomarken et al., 1996). We found that animals with right-sided prefrontal activation had higher levels of baseline cortisol than their left-frontally activated counterparts (see Figure 6.3). Moreover, when blood samples were collected 2 years following our initial testing, animals classified as showing extreme right-sided prefrontal activation at age 1 year had significantly higher baseline cortisol levels when they were 3 years of age compared with animals who were classified at age 1 year as displaying extreme left-sided prefrontal activation. These findings indicate that individual differences in prefrontal asymmetry are present in non-human primates and that such differences predict biological measures that are related to affective style.

AFFECT–COGNITION INTERACTION: TOP-DOWN INFLUENCES OF PREFRONTAL CORTEX

The prefrontal cortex is uniquely situated, with extensive cortico-cortical connections to posterior perceptual processing regions (e.g. Goldman-Rakic, 1987) and

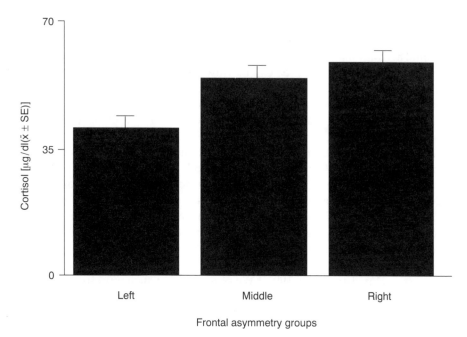

Figure 6.3 Basal morning plasma cortisol from 1 year-old rhesus monkeys classified as left (n = 12), middle (n = 16) or right (n = 11) frontally activated, based upon electrophysiological measurements. Reproduced from Kalin et al. (1998), with permission

extensive connections to limbic structures such as the amygdala (e.g. Amaral et al., 1992). By virtue of its unique pattern of anatomical connectivity, the prefrontal cortex is likely to play an important role in top-down influences on brain regions that are critical components of circuitry required for many complex emotional and cognitive functions. The role of the prefrontal cortex in three aspects of cognition–emotion interaction will be featured in this section. First, the influence of the prefrontal cortex on posterior cortical regions, and the cognitive consequences of such influence, will be described. Second, the role of the prefrontal cortex in biasing preattentive processes will be illustrated with data from a new study. Third, the role of the prefrontal cortex in emotion regulation will be briefly discussed. These three functions of the prefrontal cortex under-score the importance of this structure for both emotion and cognition and high-light its role in understanding the interaction between certain key aspects of thought and feeling.

One function of the cortico–cortical connections from the dorsolateral prefrontal cortex to posterior cortical regions is inhibitory. For example, Knight (1991) reviewed data from his laboratory and others showing sensory gating deficits following damage to the dorsolateral prefrontal cortex. Evoked potentials elicited in response to sensory stimuli are enhanced in patients with prefrontal damage, implying that the prefrontal cortex is exerting top-down inhibitory control over posterior processing regions. One important implication of this prefrontal inhibitory influence over posterior processing regions is that prefrontal activation asymmetries may be reciprocally related to posterior activation asymmetries (for review, see e.g. Davidson, 1995). A number of studies that have used either electrophysiological or hemodynamic imaging methods have reported findings consistent with this notion (e.g. Davidson, Schaffer & Saron, 1985; Wood, Flowers & Naylor, 1991). For example, in a study examining patterns of EEG activation in response to the presentation of lateralized faces, we observed a reciprocal relation between frontal and parietal activation asymmetry, particularly among depressed subjects. Wood, Flowers & Naylor (1991) have reported a similar pattern of inverse relations between blood flow asymmetry measures derived from anterior and posterior cortical regions.

What are the cognitive consequences of such reciprocal relations between anterior and posterior cortical asymmetry? In several previous studies, we have found that depressed subjects show a pattern of relative right-sided prefrontal activation (caused primarily by decreased left-sided prefrontal activation; Henriques & Davidson, 1990, 1991). We reasoned that such a prefrontal pattern should be associated with less relative right-sided posterior activation. This hypothesis leads to the prediction of performance decrements on cognitive tasks known to require right posterior activation, such as certain measures of visuospatial cognition. Some studies have reported such performance decrements in depressed subjects (e.g. Bruder, 1995; Heller, Etienne & Miller, 1995; Jaeger, Borod & Peselow, 1987). In a recent study, Henriques & Davidson (1997) administered psychometrically-matched verbal (word finding) and spatial (dot localization) tasks known to differentially elicit relative left vs. right-sided posterior EEG activation (Davidson, Chapman, Chapman & Henriques, 1990a) to depressed and non-depressed subjects. As predicted, based upon the model described, depressed subjects showed a specific differential performance deficit, with impairment in the dot localization task compared with controls. Importantly, the groups did not differ in response to the verbal task. Non-depressed subjects showed the expected pattern of EEG changes with task—greater right-sided central and parietal activation during the spatial compared with the verbal task. In contrast, the depressed subjects failed to show any difference in posterior EEG asymmetry between the two tasks. These findings are consistent with the idea that relative left-sided prefrontal hypoactivation among the depressed subjects is associated with relative right-sided posterior hypoactivation, thus resulting in a failure among the depressed subjects to activate the right posterior region in response to the dot localization task.

A variety of evidence implicates the prefrontal cortex in attentional control and vigilance (e.g. Pardo et al., 1990; Posner & Petersen, 1990). Based on the view that the prefrontal cortex plays an important role in directing attention, we recently examined whether individual differences in electrophysiological measures of prefrontal asymmetry predict attentional biases to positive or negative stimuli (Sutton, Davidson & Rogers, 1996). In this study, subjects were first assessed for baseline electrophysiological measures of activation asymmetry on two occasions separated by 6 weeks. In a third session, held between 4 and 28 months following the EEG sessions, subjects were tested on a simple choice task where two word-pairs were presented simultaneously, with one word pair on the left and the other on the right of a computer monitor. The subject was instructed to choose the word-pair that "went together best". Word-pairs were previously categorized as either negative (e.g. "hurt-cry"), neutral (e.g. "mail-box") or positive (e.g. "happy-glad") on the basis of prior ratings. Word-pairs were matched on the degree of similarity in meaning, as rated in a prior study. One-third of the trials consisted of negative–neutral pairs, one-third of positive–neutral pairs and one-third of negative–positive pairs. We predicted that subjects with greater relative left-sided activation would be biased toward processing the positive word pairs and would therefore select more of the positive word pairs as going together best. Particularly among subjects whose prefrontal EEG asymmetry was stable across testing occasions, those with greater relative left-sided activation selected more of the positive word pairs ($r = 0.40$). These findings suggest that individual differences in prefrontal activation asymmetry bias attention selectively toward positive or negative stimuli in our environment. Such selective attentional biases might act to maintain and preserve the dispositional affective characteristics of individuals who differ in their trait-levels of prefrontal activation asymmetry.

The prefrontal cortex also appears to play an important role in emotion regulation. The component of emotion regulation subserved by the prefrontal cortex that is probably the most well characterized is the inhibition of negative affect. As noted earlier, there are extensive descending connections from the prefrontal cortex to the amygdala (Amaral et al., 1992). The glutamatergic efferents from the prefrontal cortex likely synapse on GABA neurons (Amaral et al., 1992), and thus provide an important inhibitory input to the amygdala. LeDoux and his colleagues (Morgan, Romanski & LeDoux, 1993; but see Gewirtz, Falls & Davis, 1997) demonstrated in rats that lesions of the medial prefrontal cortex dramatically prolong the maintenance of a conditioned aversive response. In other words, animals with medial prefrontal lesions retain aversive associations for a much longer duration of time than normal animals. These findings imply that the prefrontal cortex normally inhibits the amygdala as an active component of extinction. In the absence of this normal inhibition, the amygdala remains unchecked and continues to maintain the learned aversive response.

As noted in Section IV above, we (Davidson et al., in preparation) have recently observed that subjects with greater left-sided prefrontal activation show increased inhibition of startle magnitude following the offset of a negative emotional stimulus. These findings imply that subjects with this pattern of prefrontal activation are able to more rapidly terminate a negative emotional response once it is elicited. New findings using PET from my laboratory indicate that in normal subjects, glucose metabolism in the left medial and the lateral prefrontal cortex is strongly reciprocally associated with glucose metabolic rate in the amygdala (Abercrombie et al., 1996). Thus, subjects with greater left-sided prefrontal metabolism have lower metabolic activity in their amygdala. These findings are consistent with the lesion study of LeDoux and colleagues and imply that the prefrontal cortex plays an important role in modulating activity in the amygdala. At the same time, the left prefrontal cortex is also likely to play a role in the maintenance of reinforcement-related behavioral approach. Perhaps the damping of negative affect and shortening of its time course facilitates the maintenance of approach-related positive affect.

IMPLICATIONS AND CONCLUSIONS

Earlier in this chapter, the constituents of affective style were described. We considered individual differences in threshold, peak amplitude, rise time to peak, and recovery time. Together, these constitute parameters of affective chronometry and dictate important features of the time course of affective responding. Following a description of the functional neuroanatomy of the approach and withdrawal systems, individual differences in prefrontal activation asymmetry were discussed and their relation to affective style described. The final section considered the role of the prefrontal cortex in the top-down control of affect–cognition interactions. Three aspects of prefrontal involvement in affect–cognition interaction were described: (a) prefrontal inhibition of posterior cortical zones; (b) prefrontal control of affect-relevant attentional processes; and (c) prefrontal inhibition of the amygdala and its role in regulation of negative affect.

The questions that are featured in this chapter are more tractable now than ever before. With the advent of echoplanar methods for rapid functional MR imaging, sufficient data can be collected within individuals to examine functional connections among regions hypothesized to constitute important elements of the approach and withdrawal circuits discussed above. Individual differences in different aspects of these systems can then be studied with greater precision. fMRI methods also lend themselves to address questions related to affective chronometry. In particular, we can calculate the slope of MR signal intensity declines following the offset of an aversive stimulus to provide an index of the rapidity of recovery from activation in select brain regions. PET methods using new radioligands that permit quantification of receptor density for specific neurotransmitters in different brain regions is yielding new insights directly relevant to questions about affective style (see e.g. Farde, Gustavsson & Jönsson, 1997). Trait-like differences in affective style are likely reflected in relatively stable differences in characteristics of the underlying neurochemical systems. Using PET to examine such individual differences promises to provide important syntheses between neurochemical and neuroanatomical approaches to understanding the biological bases of affective style.

Affective neuroscience seeks to understand the underlying proximal neural substrates of elementary constituents of emotional processing (Davidson & Sutton, 1995). In this chapter, I have provided a model of the functional neuroanatomy of approach and withdrawal motivational/emotional systems and illustrated the many varieties of individual differences that might occur in these systems. Research on prefrontal asymmetries associated with affective style and their cognitive consequences was used to illustrate the potential promise of some initial approaches to the study of these questions. Modern neuroimaging methods used in conjunction with theoretically sophisticated models of emotion and cognition offer great promise in advancing our understanding of the basic mechanisms giving rise to affective style and its cognitive consequences.

ACKNOWLEDGEMENTS

The research reported in this chapter was supported by NIMH grants MH43454, MH40747, Research Scientist Award K05-MH00875 and P50-MH52354 to the Wisconsin Center for Affective Science (R. J. Davidson, Director), by a NARSAD Established Investigator Award and by a grant from the John D. and Catherine T. MacArthur Foundation. I thank the many individuals in my laboratory who have contributed substantially to this research over the years, including Andy Tomarken, Steve Sutton, Wil Irwin, Heather Abercrombie, Jeff Henriques, Chris Larson, Daren Jackson, Stacey Schaeffer, Terry Ward, Darren Dottl, Isa Dolski, as well as the many collaborators outside my laboratory too numerous to name. Portions of this chapter were extracted from Davidson (in press).

REFERENCES

Abercrombie, H. C., Larson, C. L., Ward, R. T., Schaefer, S. M., Holden, J. E., Perlman, S. B., Turski, P. A., Krahn, D. D. & Davidson, R. J. (1998). Metabolic rate in the amygdala predicts negative affect and depression severity in depressed patients: a FDG–PET Study. *Neuro Report*, **9**, 3801–3807.

Amaral, D. G., Price, J. L., Pitkanen, A. & Carmichael, S. T. (1992). Anatomical organization of the primate amygdaloid complex. In J. P. Aggleton (ed.), *The Amygdala: Neurobiological Aspects of Emotion, Memory and Mental Dysfunction* New York: Wiley-Liss, pp. 1–66.

Bruder, G. E. (1995). Cerebral laterality and psychopathology: perceptual and event-related potential asymmetries in affective and schizophrenic disorders. In R. J. Davidson & K. Hugdahl (eds), *Brain Asymmetry*. Cambridge, MA: MIT Press, pp. 661–691.

Cacioppo, J. T. & Bernston, G. G. (1994). Relationship between attitudes and evaluative space: a critical review, with emphasis on the separability of positive and negative substrates. *Psychological Bulletin*, **115**, 401–423.

Carver, C. S. & White, T. L. (1994). Behavioral inhibition, behavioral activation and affective responses to impending reward and punishment: the BIS/BAS scales. *Journal of Personality and Social Psychology*, **67**, 319–333.

Davidson, R. J. (1992). Emotion and affective style: hemispheric substrates. *Psychological Science*, **3**, 39–43.

Davidson, R. J. (1993). Cerebral asymmetry and emotion: conceptual and methodological conundrums. *Cognition and Emotion*, **7**, 115–138.

Davidson, R. J. (1994). Asymmetric brain function, affective style and psychopathology: the role of early experience and plasticity. *Development and Psychopathology*, **6**, 741–758.

Davidson, R. J. (1995). Cerebral asymmetry, emotion and affective style. In R. J. Davidson and K. Hugdahl (eds), *Brain Asymmetry*. Cambridge, MA: MIT Press. pp. 361–387.

Davidson, R. J. (1998). Affective style and affective disorders: perspectives from affective neuroscience. *Cognition and Emotion*, **12**, 307–330.

Davidson, R. J. & Fox, N. A. (1989). Frontal brain asymmetry predicts infants' response to maternal separation. *Journal of Abnormal Psychology*, **98**, 127–131.

Davidson, R. J. & Sutton, S. K. (1995). Affective neuroscience: the emergence of a discipline. *Current Opinion in Neurobiology*, **5**, 217–224.

Davidson, R. J. & Tomarken, A. J. (1989). Laterality and emotion: an electrophysiological approach. In F. Boller & J. Grafman (eds), *Handbook of Neuropsychology*. Amsterdam: Elsevier.

Davidson, R. J., Chapman, J. P., Chapman, L. P. & Henriques, J. B. (1990a). Asymmetrical brain electrical activity discriminates between psychometrically-matched verbal and spatial cognitive tasks. *Psychophysiology*, **27**, 528–543.

Davidson, R. J., Dolski, I., Laron, C. & Sutton, S. K. (in preparation). Electrophysiological measures of prefrontal asymmetry predict recovery of emotion-modulated startle.

Davidson, R. J., Ekman, P., Saron, C., Senulis, J. & Friesen, W. V. (1990b). Approach/withdrawal and cerebral asymmetry: emotional expression and brain physiology, I. *Journal of Personality and Social Psychology*, **58**, 330–341.

Davidson, R. J., Kalin, N. H. & Shelton, S. E. (1992). Lateralized effects of diazepam on frontal brain electrical asymmetries in rhesus monkeys. *Biological Psychiatry*, **32**, 438–451.

Davidson, R. J., Kalin, N. H. & Shelton, S. E. (1993). Lateralized response to diazepam predicts temperamental style in rhesus monkeys. *Behavioral Neuroscience*, **107**, 1106–1110

Davidson, R. J., Schaffer, C. E. & Saron, C. (1985). Effects of lateralized presentations of faces on self-reports of emotion and EEG asymmetry in depressed and non-depressed subjects. *Psychophysiology*, **22**, 353–364.

Depue, R. A. & Collins, P. F. (in press). Neurobiology of the structure of personality: I. Dopamine, behavioral facilitation and positive emotionality. *Behavioral & Brain Sciences*.

Derryberry, D. & Reed, M. A. (1996). Regulatory processes and the development of cognitive representations. *Development and Psychopathology*, **8**, 215–234.

Diener, V. E. & Emmons, R. A. (1984). The independence of positive and negative affect. *Journal of Personality and Social Psychology*, **47**, 1105–1117.

Drevets, W. C., Videen T. O., MacLeod A. K., Haller J. W. & Raichle M. E. (1992). PET images of blood changes during anxiety: correction. *Science*, **256**, 1696.

Farde, L. Gustavsson, J. P. & Jönsson, E. (1997). D2 dopamine receptors and personality. *Nature*, **385**, 590.

George, M. S., Ketter, T. A., Parekh, P. I., Horwitz, B., Hersovitch, P. & Post, R. M. (1995). Brain activity during transient sadness and happiness in healthy women. *American Journal of Psychiatry*, **152**, 341–351.

Gewirtz, J. C., Falls, W. A. & Davis, M. (1997). Normal conditioned inhibition and extinction of freezing and fear-potentiated startle following electrolytic lesions of medial prefrontal cortex. *Behavioral Neuroscience*, **111**, 712–726.

Gold, P. W., Goodwin, F. K. & Chrousos, G. P. (1988). Clinical and biochemical manifestations of depression: relation to the neurobiology of stress. *New England Journal of Medicine*, **314**, 348–353.

Goldman-Rakic, P. S. (1987). Circuitry of primate prefrontal cortex and regulation of behavior by representational memory. In V. B. Mountcastle (ed.), *Handbook of Physiology*, Vol. V. Bethesda, MD: American Physiological Society, pp. 373–417.

Gray, J. A. (1994). Three fundamental emotion systems. In P. Ekman & R. J. Davidson (eds), *The Nature of Emotion: Fundamental Questions*. New York: Oxford University Press, pp. 243–247.

Gross, J. J., Sutton, S. K. & Ketelaar, T. V. (in press). Relations between affect and personality: support for the affect-level and affective-reactivity views. *Personality and Social Psychology Bulletin*.

Heller, W., Etienne, M. A. & Miller, G. A. (1995). Patterns of perceptual asymmetry in depression and anxiety: implications for neuropsychological models of emotion and psychopathology. *Journal of Abnormal Psychology*, **104**, 327–333.

Henriksen, S. J. & Giacchino, J. (1993). Functional characteristics of nucleus accumbens neurons: evidence obtained from *in vivo* electrophysiological recordings. In P. W. Kalivas & C. D. Barnes (eds), *Limbic Motor Circuits and Neuropsychiatry*. Boca Raton, FL: CRC Press, pp. 101–124.

Henriques, J. B. & Davidson, R. J. (1990). Regional brain electrical asymmetries discriminate between previously depressed and healthy control subjects. *Journal of Abnormal Psychology*, **99**, 22–31.

Henriques, J. B & Davidson, R. J. (1991). Left frontal hypoactivation in depression. *Journal of Abnormal Psychology*, **100**, 535–545.

Henriques, J. B. & Davidson, R. J. (1997). Brain electrical asymmetries during cognitive task performance in depressed and non-depressed subjects. *Biological Psychiatry*, **42**, 1039–1050.

Irwin, W., Davidson, R. J., Lowe, M. J., Mock, B. J., Sorenson, J. A. & Turski, P. A. (1996). Human amygdala activation detected with echo-planar functional magnetic resonance imaging. *NeuroReport*, **7**, 1765–1769.

Jaeger, J., Borod, J. C. & Peselow, E. (1987). Depressed patients have atypical biases in perception of emotional faces. *Journal of Abnormal Psychology*, **96**, 321–324.

Kagan, J., Reznick, J. S. & Snidman, N. (1988). Biological bases of childhood shyness *Science*, **240**, 167–171.

Kalin, N. H. (1993). The neurobiology of fear. *Scientific American*, **268**, 94–101.

Kalin, N. H., Larson, C., Shelton, S. E. & Davidson, R. J. (1997). Asymmetric frontal brain activity, cortisol, and behavior associated with fearful temperament in Rhesus monkeys. *Behavioral Neuroscience*.

Kalivas, P. W., Churchill, L. & Klitenick, M. A. (1993). The circuitry mediating the translation of motivational stimuli into adaptive motor responses. In P. W. Kalivas & C. D. Barnes (eds), *Limbic Motor Circuits and Neuropsychiatry*. Boca Raton, FL: CRC Press, pp. 237–287.

Kang, D. H., Davidson, R. J., Coe, C. L., Wheeler, R. W., Tomarken, A. J. & Ershler, W. B. (1991). Frontal brain asymmetry and immune function. *Behavioral Neuroscience*, **105**, 860–869.

Kiecolt-Glaser, J. K. & Glaser, R. (1991). Stress and immune function in humans. In R. Ader, D. L. Felten & N. Cohen (eds), *Psychoneuroimmunology*, 2nd edn. San Diego, CA: Academic Press, pp. 849–868.

Knight, R. T. (1991). Evoked potential studies of attention capacity in human frontal lobe lesions. In H. S. Levin, H. M. Eisenberg & A. L. Benton (eds), *Frontal lobe Function and Dysfunction*. New York: Oxford University Press, pp. 139–153.

Lang, P. J., Bradley, M. M. & Cuthbert, B. N. (1990). Emotion, attention and the startle reflex. *Psychological Review*, **97**, 377–398.

Lang, P. J., Bradley, M. & Cuthbert, B. (1995). *International Affective Picture System: Technical Manual and Affective Ratings*. Gainesville FL: Center for Research in Psychophysiology, University of Florida.

Lazarus, R. S. (1991). *Emotion and Adaptation*. New York: Oxford University Press.

LeDoux, J. E. (1987). Emotion. In V. B. Mountcastle (ed.), *Handbook of Physiology, Section 1: The Nervous System, Vol. V: Higher Functions of the Brain*. Bethesda, MD: American Physiological Society.

Meehl, P. E. (1975). Hedonic capacity: some conjectures. *Bulletin of the Menninger Clinic*, **39**, 295–307.

Morgan, M. A., Romanski, L. & LeDoux, J. E. (1993). Extinction of emotional learning: contribution of medial prefrontal cortex. *Neuroscience Letters*, **163**, 109–113.

Paradiso, S., Robinson, R. G., Andreasen, N. C., Downhill, J. E., Davidson, R. J., Kirchner, P. T., Watkins, G. L., Boles, L. L. & Hichwa, R. D. (1997). Emotional activation of limbic circuitry in elderly and normal subjects in a PET study. *American Journal of Psychiatry*, **154**, 382–389.

Pardo, J. V., Pardo, P., Janer, K. & Raichle, M. E. (1990). The anterior cingulate cortex mediates processing selection in the Stroop attention conflict paradigm. *Proceedings of the National Academy of Science, USA*, **87**, 256–259.

Posner, M. I. & Petersen, S. E. (1990). The attention system of the human brain. *Annual Review of Neuroscience*, **13**, 25–42.

Reiman, E. M., Fusselman M. J. L., Fox B. J. & Raichle, M. E. (1989). Neuroanatomical correlates of anticipatory anxiety. *Science*, **243**, 1071–1074.

Russell, J. A. (1980). A circumplex model of emotion. *Journal of Personality and Social Psychology*, **39**, 1161–1178.

Ryff, C. D. & Singer, B. (1998). The contours of positive human health. *Psychological Inquiry*, **9**, 1–28.

Schultz, W., Apicella, P., Romo, R. & Scarnati, E. (1995a). Context-dependent activity in primate striatum reflecting past and future behavioral events. In J. C. Houk, J. L. Davis & D. G. Beiser (eds), *Models of Information Processing in the Basal Ganglia*. Cambridge, MA: MIT Press, pp. 11–28.

Schultz, W., Romo, R., Ljungberg, T., Mirenowicz, J., Hollerman, J. R. & Dickinson, A. (1995b). Reward-related signals carried by dopamine neurons. In J. C. Houk, J. L. Davis & D. G. Beiser (eds), *Models of Information Processing in the Basal Ganglia*. Cambridge, MA: MIT Press, pp. 233–248.

Smith, O. A., DeVita J. L. & Astley, C. A. (1990). Neurons controlling cardiovascular responses to emotion are located in lateral hypothalamus-perifornical region. *American Journal of Physiology*, **259**, R943–R954.

Stein, N. L. & Trabasso, T. (1992). The organization of emotional experience: creating links among emotion, thinking, language and intentional action. *Cognition and Emotion*, **6**, 225–244.

Sutton, S. K. & Davidson, R. J. (1997). Prefrontal brain asymmetry: a biological substrate of the behavioral approach and inhibition systems. *Psychological Science*, **8**, 204–210

Sutton, S. K., Davidson, R. J. & Rogers, G. M. (1996). Resting anterior EEG asymmetry predicts affect-related information processing. *Psychophysiology*, **33**, S81.

Sutton, S. K., Davidson, R. J., Donzella, B., Irwin, W. & Dottl, D. A. (1997). Manipulating affective state using extended picture presentation. *Psychophysiology*, **34**, 217–226.

Sutton, S. K., Ward, R. T., Larson, C. L., Holden, J. E., Perlman, S. B. & Davidson, R. J. (1997). Asymmetry in prefrontal glucose metabolism during appetitive and aversive emotional above states: An FDG-PET study. *Psychophysiology*, **34**, S89.

Thompson, R. A. (1994). Emotion regulation: a theme in search of definition. In N. A. Fox (ed.), *The Development of Emotion Regulation: Biological and Behavioral Aspects*. Monographs of the Society for Research in Child Development, Vol. 59 (Serial No. 240), pp. 25–52.

Thorpe, S., Rolls, E. & Maddison, S. (1983). The orbitofrontal cortex: neuronal activity in the behaving monkey. *Experimental Brain Research*, **49**, 93–113.

Thut, G., Schultz, W., Roelcke, U., Nienhusmeier, M., Missimer, J., Maguire, R. P. & Leenders, K. L. (1997). Activation of the human brain by monetary reward, *NeuroReport*, **8**, 1225–1228.

Tomarken, A. J., Brown, L. L., Orth, D. N., Loosen, P. T., Kalin, N. H. & Davidson, R. J.

(1996). Individual differences in repressive-defensiveness predict basal salivary cortisol levels. *Journal of Personality and Social Psychology*, **70**, 362–371.

Tomarken, A. J., Davidson, R. J., Wheeler, R. E. & Doss, R. C. (1992). Individual differences in anterior brain asymmetry and fundamental dimensions of emotion. *Journal of Personality and Social Psychology*, **62**, 676–687.

Watson, D. & Tellegen, A. (1985). Toward a consensual structure of mood. *Psychological Bulletin*, **98**, 219–235.

Watson, D., Clark, L. A. & Tellegen, A. (1988). Developmental and validation of brief measures of positive and negative affect: the PANAS scales. *Journal of Personality and Social Psychology*, **54**, 1063–1070.

Wheeler, R. E., Davidson, R. J. & Tomarken, A. J. (1993). Frontal brain asymmetry and emotional reactivity: a biological substrate of affective style. *Psychophysiology*, **30**, 82–89.

Wood, F. B., Flowers, D. L. & Naylor, C. E. (1991). Cerebral laterality in functional neuroimaging. In F. L. Kitterle (ed.), *Cerebral Laterality: Theory and Research*. Hillsdale, NJ: Erlbaum, pp. 103–115.

Chapter 7

The Role of the Self in Cognition and Emotion

Michael Lewis
Robert Wood Johnson Medical School, New Brunswick, NJ, USA

This chapter has as its central theme the idea that emotional life requires cognitions. While some have argued for a one-to-one correspondence between stimulus elicitors and emotional responses (e.g. Zajonc, 1980), such an analysis is difficult to understand, especially in regard to the class of emotions called *self-conscious emotions*. Darwin (1965/1872), for one, argued that these self-conscious emotions were produced by people's ideas that they were the focus of the attention of others. The cognitions underlining these emotions mean that there are no elicitors of these emotions which do not involve ideas, especially ideas or cognitions about the self.

In the model of emotional development that is schematized in Figure 7.1, I have suggested (Lewis, 1992a; Lewis & Michalson, 1983a) that cognitions and emotions follow a fugue-like pattern, where emotions lead to cognitions, which in turn lead to new emotions. In this model of emotional development, the earliest emotions, called at times "primary" or "basic" emotions, those that can be seen in the facial expressions, emerge at birth and may require little cognition. Even here it is difficult to think of the elicitors–expression connection without invoking some cognition—if nothing more than the cognition necessary for perception. At around 15–18 months, a critical cognition, that involving the idea of "me" (Lewis, 1995a), or what I have called self-awareness or consciousness, emerges (Lewis, 1992b; Lewis & Brooks-Gunn, 1979; Lewis & Michalson, 1983a). The emergence of this cognition gives rise to a set of self-conscious emotions which *at this time do not have* evaluation of self as their basis (Lewis, 1992a). Rather, they are based on the use of the self; embarrassment as the result of the self being observed (Lewis, 1995b) and empathy or the ability to place the self in the place of the other in order to gather information about how the other thinks or feels. These self-

---

Handbook of Cognition and Emotion. Edited by T. Dalgleish and M. Power.

self and self-conscious emotions   **age at acquisition**

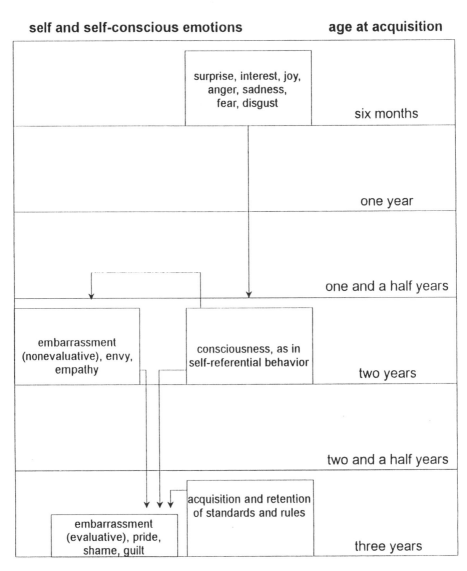

Figure 7.1   A model of emotional development. Reproduced from M. Lewis (1995c), with permission

conscious non-evaluative emotions emerge in the second half of the second year, at the same time that the cognition of self-awareness emerges.

Somewhere around the third birthday, a second set of cognitions emerges. These include standards, rules and goals, the ability to evaluate one's behavior against those standards, the rise of attributions about the self, and the ability to focus on the self or on the task requirements (Stipek, Recchia & McClintic, 1992).

These cognitions involving the self give rise to a new set of emotions, self-conscious evaluative emotions, which now do require the child to have these evaluative capacities. Such a developmental sequence of emotional development, therefore, has as its center the development of cognitions, especially those involving the self. In this chapter, I will address this connection between cognition and emotion. In the first section, The Elephant's Tail, the meaning of the term "feeling" is considered, since much confusion results from the use of this term. Following this, I will focus on the self-conscious emotions, for these provide an important case study on the interconnection between thinking and feeling. The role of the self is considered next, since cognitions about the self appear to be those most relevant for understanding emotional development after the first year of life. Given the importance of self-cognitions, the importance of the self's divided attention needs to be addressed, since this divided attention gives rise to particular individual differences in cognitions and self-attributions. The chapter concludes with a description of the role of these cognitions in the development of psychopathology in children and adults.

THE ELEPHANT'S TAIL

The focus of this chapter derives from our broad interest in the relation between thinking and feeling. The Western mind, at least since pre-Socratic times, has been comfortable in separating thinking and feeling and in giving each a reality of its own. Perhaps they are separate; however, it is reasonable to consider the proposition that these two actions constitute in reality a single action viewed from two perspectives. Consider two examples. In the first, the infant exhibits an action (a set of behaviors, including facial expression and autonomic and central nervous system changes) when a novel event follows a familiar one. We use the term "surprise" to capture this set of behaviors. Surprise is used by the observer (and by the child when old enough) to reference a cognitive as well as an affective action, yet all we observe is a set of co-occurring behaviors. The second example utilizes Jaynes' (1977) notion that the pre-Greeks considered the action of their right hemisphere to be the gods' communication to them, whereas we now consider this same hemispheric action to be our own thinking. What we (as others) choose to call "thinking" or "feeling" may be no closer to reality than what Jaynes' primitives called their action.

Such concerns give rise to the possibility that in examining the actions we call "thinking" and "feeling" we are behaving as the blind men in their examination of an elephant. Recall that their blindness led them to conclude that each limb and tail of the elephant was a separate and accurate description of what they experienced. The error of reification of these terms, even when we substitute for them the terms "cognition" and "emotion", is an error that must concern us, especially because our common language is all that we have when we set about to study these problems. As becomes evident, these terms cause trouble enough. Although we are aware of this problem of reification, we do not avoid it;

rather, we seek to articulate our meanings more carefully and thus sharpen the argument.

Here, our specific interest in this broad question assumes a more limited perspective, focusing on the relation of consciousness as the interface between cognitive and emotional actions (see also Piaget, 1976). Elsewhere (Lewis, 1990; Lewis & Michalson, 1983b; Lewis & Rosenblum, 1978) I have attempted to disassemble emotional life into five components—emotional stimuli, receptors, expressions, states, and experiences—in order to clarify what we mean when we use the term "emotion". Moreover, I have tried to show how each emotional component has cognitive features. This approach continues with a focus on self-conscious emotions, a class of emotions that can only exist as a consequence of complex cognitive ability.

In order to pursue this inquiry, it will be necessary for us first to consider what we mean when we use the term "feeling". Feeling has at least two meanings, referring to both emotional and thinking actions. We pursue our interest in thinking by next focusing on the thinking aspect of feeling in order to argue that thinking about one's feeling (like thinking about one's thinking) requires a consideration of self-awareness or self-consciousness. This feature of the self-system can be shown to evolve around the last half of the second year of life (Lewis & Brooks-Gunn, 1979) and once self-awareness occurs, it gives rise to an entirely new set of feelings (Lewis, 1992a). Thus, our developmental model links thinking and feeling (Lewis, 1992b; Lewis & Michalson, 1983a).

Feeling without Thinking

Some have argued for a restricted meaning of feeling and have suggested that feeling refers only to the first definition, namely, that "I am in a state of happiness". This restricted meaning implies that feeling is something real, much like an internal state, which, given the proper observational techniques, could be measured and described. Indeed, such a view of feeling as an internal emotional state has preoccupied theorists since the earliest writings on emotion (see Cannon, 1927). Several different locations for this state have been proposed and it is not possible in this discussion to elaborate extensively on them (see Lewis & Michalson, 1983a, Chapter 3, for a more complete discussion). Some have located this state in the soma (see e.g. James, 1890), some in the autonomic nervous system (Wegern, Jones & Jones, 1956), some in the central nervous system (Cannon, 1929; Olds & Forbes, 1981), some in the endocrine hormonal system (Watson, 1924), and some in all three (Izard, 1977). Following Darwin (1965/1872), who observed external manifestations of these presumed internal emotional states in the facial, vocal and postural behavior of men and beasts, more recent theorists have looked specifically at facial expressions as a direct measure of these states (see Ekman, Friesen, & Ellsworth, 1972; Izard, 1977; Tomkins, 1962). Such a view of the term "feeling" as an internal emotional state, that is, physically real and measurable, allows for the conceptualization of feelings or internal emotional states independent of cognition (see e.g. Zajonc, 1980). In theories such as the one proposed by Zajonc, Murphy and McIntosh (1993) and others, eliciting stimulus events act in some manner so as to produce an emotional state or feeling. Although some types of cognition may be necessary to link these eliciting stimulus events to feeling, cognition is not involved in the feeling (or state) itself. Support for such specificity can be found, for example, in the perception literature. Gross, Rocha-Miranda and Bender (1972) report that in monkeys some cells in the visual cortex are so finely tuned that they respond only to specific shapes and objects. In other words, specific features or locations have been reserved for specific eliciting events. Because of this one-to-one correspondence, little or no cognitive function is necessary.[1] Examples of elicitors that are commonly used to characterize such immediate processes are: fear, triggered by loss of balance, falling, or visual looming; startle, by a loud noise; and joy, by seeing the face of a beloved person, whether it is the mother, in the case of an infant, or the significant other, in the case of an adult. Hochschild (1979) has called theories of one-to-one correspondence between elicitor and emotion "hiccup-like theories".

One needs the cognitions necessary for perceptual discrimination or the cognitions associated with the meaning of an emotional elicitor, but one does not need cognition for the feeling itself. For example, cognition is needed to discriminate a doctor's white coat from another color and is also needed for the association between the white coat and past pain, but cognition is not needed for the emotional response of fear. In other words, once the elicitor does its job, cognition gives rise to feeling but is not the feeling state. This view of the term feeling appears perfectly reasonable, although the measurement of feeling of these internal emotional states has been somewhat elusive. Facial expression, which has been argued to have a one-to-one correspondence with feeling (see e.g. Eibl-Eibesfeldt, 1970; and Ekman's 1973 work on universal facial expression) must be perturbated by socialization factors (Ekman, 1972; Lewis & Michalson, 1984b).

Feeling and Thinking

The second meaning of the term "feeling" has more to do with thinking. Here feeling has to do with the conceptualization that, while emotional states may exist independently of cognition, our awareness of them is a very important factor in emotional life. Such awareness is itself cognition, a cognition about a feeling state or about the experience of certain behavior. Analogous to knowing about knowing, it is knowing about feeling, a counterpart to meta-cognition. Thus, it might be the case that I am in a state of happiness yet I do not feel happy; that is to say, I

---

[1] To the degree to which sensory mechanisms have a cognitive component, this argument is made difficult. Nevertheless, excluding the cognitive processes involved in sensory processing, information from eliciting events may act directly in eliciting emotion (Zajonc, 1980).

do not have awareness of my happiness. Although it is presumed that there is a self-awareness of happiness most of the time, there are many emotional states occurring at many different times of which we are not aware. Three classes of such happenings follow as examples of potentially different processes at work in associating or disassociating the thinking or attending aspect of feeling from the state aspect of feeling.

Unnoticed Feeling

While driving my car at 60 miles per hour, the front left tire has a blowout. For the next 15 seconds I struggle with the steering wheel to try to bring the car safely to a halt on the side of the road. After having succeeded in bringing the car to a stop, I observe that I am fearful. I further observe that my fearfulness started at the point that I noticed my hands were shaking and when I began reflecting on the last 15 seconds of events.

The question here to be asked is: was I, from the point of the blowout until I noticed that I was fearful, feeling fear? It seems reasonable to assume that had we the proper measurement system (for example, the measurement of facial expression or various body behaviors) and if we knew what the correct constellation of fear behaviors was, we might have determined that I was in a fearful state during that time period. However, because I was attending to stimuli other than those emanating from my "emotional centers"—perceptions of the road, the direction of the car, etc.—I was not attending to these states and therefore not feeling the emotion of fear. In this situation, the entire array of proprioceptive feedback from the wheels and visual information around me was so intense, and the situation so grave, that it forced or required me to focus attention on those external events rather than on myself. The degree to which I was attending to other events was the degree to which I was unaware of my state.

Disassociated Feeling

John recently received the news that a very dear relative, an aunt, had just died and John reports at first experiencing great sadness at her loss. During the last few weeks, he found himself rather agitated and had some trouble eating and sleeping. When John was asked how he felt, he replied that he was feeling rather tired lately. If you asked him whether he was depressed, he would say to you that he did not feel depressed.

In this example, John reports that he feels, that is, he is aware of a particular emotional state. In this case, the emotional state that he is aware of and the state he reports is that of fatigue. Here, rather than distraction, another mechanism may be at work that can dissociate the feeling as self-awareness from the feeling as state. In this example, John engages in an active attempt to pay attention to and focus on one feature or aspect of his feeling, rather than another. What might be the mechanism(s) that might cause him to focus on one aspect of his feelings (his emotional state) as opposed to another, or, in some cases, might cause him to state that he is feeling fine rather than feeling sad or depressed?

Two possible causes for such a disassociation of awareness from emotional state might account for these findings. In the first, the notion of an active and perhaps unconscious mechanism called *intrapsychic censorship* (see Freud, 1949) might seek to prevent one's conscious self-awareness from engaging the "true" emotional state of sadness. Such a proposition takes the form: "I am unaware that I am aware of a feeling or internal state". For some intrapsychic reason, one aspect of myself prevents another aspect of myself from being aware of a particular emotional state. Such a system requires both a cognitive self-awareness and a cognitive unconsciousness endowed with the same or similar cognitive structures that may occupy my conscious self. In this system, these unconscious cognitive structures, called unconscious self-awareness, act on one's self-conscious self-awareness as it pertains to "feeling" or emotional state. Although such a model has been articulated by others, I am not sure how one would go about empirically putting such a conception to the test. Nevertheless, the notion of unconscious mental processes has great appeal and has been widely used as an explanatory device because it accounts for a wide range of phenomena.

Unconscious or Unlearned Feeling

John is informed by a therapist that, in her view, his awareness of being tired is an incomplete self-awareness; in fact, he is sad or depressed at his aunt's death. The therapist's understanding in some fashion acts to alter John's attention and he suddenly discovers that the other's observation is correct. John realizes that he is more than just tired, he is depressed.

Whether or not this change in attention represents (a) bringing into consciousness that of which his unconscious was already aware, or (b) simply John's succumbing to the suggestions of another, remains an important distinction. If it were the former, we would have evidence of divided attention, whereas in the latter, it would simply be a change in his conscious awareness. The issue of divided attention and the possible brain modularity that might support it is discussed in more detail below.

The second mechanism that has been invoked to explain why John focused on fatigue rather than sadness has to do less with a conflicting topology of self-features, or the mechanisms of repression or suppression, and more with simple learning processes. Lewis & Michalson (1984a) suggest that during socialization children are given specific verbal labels and are sometimes responded to in a unique fashion when they exhibit certain emotional behaviors. Ideally, parental responses to emotional states and their associated behaviors should result in children learning to think about and having self-awareness about their emotional states. However, when parents teach children their unique and inappropriate label for an emotion, children may come to have an awareness not in agreement with their internal states. For example, John as a child may have exhibited the same sad behaviors (both externally and internally) to a situation of loss; however, his social environment informed him that those behaviors in those situations meant he was tired, not sad. In other words, using simple learning processes we can argue that past experience may be capable of shaping people's self-awareness about an emotion, even producing an awareness that is idiosyncratic *vis-à-vis* the emotional state that actually exists. This type of learning is likely to account not only for differences termed pathological, but perhaps also for familial, group and cultural differences in emotional experience.

SELF-CONSCIOUS EMOTIONS—A CASE STUDY IN THINKING AND FEELING

The term "feeling" is most often used when talking about emotional behavior. "Feelings" appear to denote two meanings which affect our understanding of the relation of thinking and feeling. When we say, "I am feeling happy", we mean, first, that "I am in a state of happiness" and second, that "I am aware that I am in this state" (see James, 1884). When we consider the early emerging emotions, those called "primary" or "basic", it is not uncommon to attribute to these emotions little cognition (Zajonc, 1980). This idea is supported by the belief that there may be some direct one-to-one correspondence between certain stimuli and a particular emotional state.

While such a theoretical approach, one that does not invoke cognitive processes, may be possible for some classes of emotion, the difficulty with such an analysis becomes apparent when we consider more complex emotions. The problem of deciding which emotions are primary and which are complex and, therefore, may require more cognition, is not easily solved (see Oatley & Johnson-Laird, 1987; Ortony & Turner, 1990). Darwin (1965/1872) suggested that self-conscious emotions (he made little distinction between them) were elicited by thoughts about the self. Later, Plutchik (1980) offered several decision rules to separate the emotions, one of which is relevant for the current discussion. He suggested that the basic emotions are *not* dependent on introspection; in other words, they are not dependent on cognitions. The other class is dependent on cognitions. Elsewhere (Lewis, 1992a; Lewis et al., 1989) I have proposed a division of emotions based on the concept of self-conscious vs. non-self-conscious emotions. I argue that those emotions often considered to be primary—such as fear, interest, anger, disgust, sadness and joy—do not involve introspection or self-consciousness and, therefore, do not involve elaborate cognitive processes. However, the more complex emotions do.

In the case of jealousy, envy, empathy, embarrassment, shame, pride and guilt, it is very difficult to think of some one-to-one correspondence between specific environmental elicitors and the production of such emotions. These emotions generally require that the organism make a comparison or evaluate its behavior *vis-à-vis* some standard, rule or goal. Thus, for example, pride occurs when one's evaluation of one's behavior is compared to a standard and indicates that one has succeeded, whereas shame or guilt follows when such evaluation leads to the conclusion that one has failed. The cognitions which give rise to this class of emotions involve elaborate cognitive processes, and these elaborate cognitive processes have, at their heart, the notion of self. While some authors, for example the psychoanalytic theorists Freud (1936) and Erikson (1950), have argued for some universal elicitors of shame, such as failure at toilet training or exposure of the backside, the idea of an automatic non-cognitive elicitor does not seem to make much sense. Cognitive processes must be the elicitors of these complex emotions (Darwin, 1965/1872; Lewis, 1995a). It is the way we think or what we think about that becomes the elicitor. There may still be a one-to-one correspondence between thinking certain thoughts and particular emotions; however, the elicitor remains a cognition. Cognitive processes, therefore, play a vital role in eliciting these types of emotions.

THE ROLE OF SELF

There exists a wide range of emotions that, by definition, involve the concept of self (see Lewis, 1992a). Those specific aspects of self that are involved in the self-conscious emotions can be highlighted by considering the specific emotions of shame, guilt and pride. To begin with, the self-evaluative emotions involve a set of standards, rules and goals (SRGs) that are inventions of the culture and that are transmitted to the child. As Stipek and her colleagues (1992) have shown, by 2 years of age children are able to demonstrate that they have incorporated, in some fashion, the SRGs of their parents. By "incorporation" we mean simply that the child knows these SRGs and, at the same time, does not need the support of the actual presence of another in order to react to them. Although the reaction may at first anticipate what parents might say or do, it is still the case that the child is able to build a representation that he/she alone possesses about these SRGs and about what will happen if they are violated or successfully fulfilled. Incorporation is nothing more than the ability of the organism to take the eye of the other into the self and make it the eye of the self. What is intriguing is that this process appears to start at extremely early ages (see Stipek, Recchia & McClintic, 1992).

The second point to stress is that the child must be capable of "owning" his/her behavior; if children are unable to perceive that they are the actors or the producers of a particular set of behaviors, then, in fact, there would be no basis for evaluation. Self-evaluation, therefore, implies not only a standard, rule or goal but also the realization that it is one's own action. This ability emerges at this time (Kagan, 1981). The self also enters into the comparison between one's action and one's standard in terms of responsibility. I can, for example, evaluate my behavior against my SRG and conclude that I have succeeded or failed. However, this will not lead me to either pride or shame unless I am prepared to believe that I am responsible for that success or failure. In the attributional literature, this has been considered as the distinction between an internal and an external attribution (Weiner, 1986). Consider the following example. I take an examination and do not perform well, but I believe that my failure was due to the fact that I was kept awake all night by construction next door. If this was my attribution, then it is unlikely that I would feel shame. The same holds for pride. Thus, only when I attribute a responsible self in the comparison between my action and the SRG does my comparison result in specific emotions.

Still another cognition to consider has to do with the evaluation of one's self in terms of specific or global attribution. "Global" refers to the focus on the self and refers to the stable features of "me". "Specific" refers to a focus on my action (see Dweck & Leggett, 1988; Weiner, 1986). This distinction has been described in various ways; of particular usefulness is Dweck's distinction between task and self-focus. If one internalizes (i.e. accepts) the fact that one has failed a particular standard, rule or goal and makes a global attribution or self-focus, one is likely to feel shame. However, if the attribution, or focus, is about the task, one is apt to feel guilt or regret (Lewis, 1992b; Tangney, 1995).

Let me give an example of this difference. Imagine that you have written a research paper and submitted it for publication. It is returned rejected. You can assume that the reviewers did not know what they were talking about and, thus, refuse to accept the rejection as a failure having to do with you. Alternatively, you can accept it as a failure for which you are responsible. If you do not accept the rejection as failure on your part, you may simply send the paper off to another journal. If you do accept it as failure, you still have a second attribution to make, namely, to determine whether this reflects a global or self-focus, or a specific or task-focus, about your failure. If you made a global/self-evaluation, such as, "I am not a good scientist", you are much more likely to feel shame than if you make a specific/task attribution, such as, "I should have conducted an analysis of co-variance rather than what I did". The response of global/self-attribution and, therefore, shame is likely to lead to the cessation of activity—that is, the body collapse (H. B. Lewis, 1971), as well as a lack of repair and reparation (see Barrett & Zahn-Waxler, 1987).

In the case of our hypothetical colleague, under a global/self internal attribution of failure, he/she is likely to take the manuscript and put it in a drawer, not to be looked at again, or at least not for a long time. In contrast, failure that is internalized and specific (task focus) is likely to lead to reparation, since a specific feature in need of repair has been identified. In such a case, our hypothetical scientist is likely to revise the article and send it off again.

We can see, therefore, that the role of self-cognitions in this class of emotions is quite elaborate, involving; (a) knowledge of standards, rules, and goals; (b) incorporation of these SRGs; (c) evaluation of one's behavior vis-à-vis the SRG; (d) distribution of the blame to oneself or to others; and (e) attribution and focus, either global/self-focus or specific/task-focus. In each one of these processes, a concept of the self and self-processes needs to be considered.

SELF- VS. TASK-FOCUS: THE ISSUE OF DIVIDED ATTENTION

It seems obvious that self- vs. task-focus refers to our attention toward our selves. In self-focus the attention is drawn toward our global selves and the stable attributes by which we define ourselves. Task focus, on the other hand, refers to attention drawn toward our task; it may refer to our selves through our actions *vis-à-vis* a specific task, but not to the stable attributes by which we define ourselves.

Adults have the capacity to direct our attention inward toward ourselves or outward toward the task. Even without directing our attention inward toward ourselves (e.g. our actions and emotional states), we are capable of performing highly complex and demanding tasks. In fact, the example of solving complex mental problems without focusing on them directly is well known. Solutions to mental problems often "come to us" as if someone inside our heads has been working on it while we go about attending to other problems.

While the term "consciousness" could be used to talk about attention directed inward toward the self as well as outward to the world, it is important that we try and specify some difference between them. Hilgard (1977) and, before him, Janet (1929), for example, talked about divided consciousness; others have talked about subconsciousness or unconsciousness (Freud, 1960). More recently, work on the modularity of brain function has demonstrated that areas of the brain are quite capable of carrying out complex tasks or learning complex problems without other areas having knowledge of them. Gazzaniga (1985), for example, has shown that patients with their corpus callosum ablated (usually to reduce epileptic seizures) are capable of haptically having knowledge in their right hands while being unable to report (to know) what that knowledge is. More recent work by LeDoux (1989), working with animals, and Bechara et al. (1995) with humans, has demonstrated that both perceptual processes as well as complex learning can take place in the amygdala and hippocampus without cortical involvement or without knowledge of that learning.

Such findings lend support to the idea of modularity of brain function—that is, for the involvement of some brain areas without the involvement of others—as well as the idea that complex mental operations can take place without the subject's own knowledge or self-attention (what I wish to call consciousness) of these operations. These new findings of brain function fit with our own well-known experiences of sudden insight or spontaneous solution to complex mental problems, as well as a set of common phenomena which require intra-psychic differentiation and even conflict. I list, in no particular order, some of these well-known phenomena: hypnotism, perceptual defenses, self-deception, active forgetting, acts of loss of will or akraxia, and multiple personality. These processes, although receiving some attention, have not been given the study they need.

Hilgard (1977), for one, has called the underlying processes involved in each of them "disassociation", a term once in favor but now not used. This is because Freud (1960) argued for an active process of repression rather than splitting off of consciousness, a concept favored by Charcot (1889) and Janet (1929). Each of these phenomena appears to rest on a process involving the idea of our ability of divided consciousness, which may be supported by the modularity of brain functions.

The ability to direct attention both toward ourselves and toward the outer world is an adaptive strategy. Divided consciousness's adaptive significance is that it allows us to check on our own internal responses in addition to our behavior in the world (self-focus) and quite separately to act in the world (outer or task focus). It is obvious from observations of animals, or even cells, that it is possible to behave in a highly complex fashion in the world as a function of internally generated plans and programs. This action-in-the-world does not re-quire that we pay attention to ourselves. Paying attention to ourselves allows us to modify action-in-the-world and allows us to modify this action by thinking about our actions, rather than by the use of trial and error. Thus, when I want to cross a busy street, it is probably adaptive not to be thinking about how well I am doing but rather coordinating action in context. On the other hand, if I have almost had an accident, then thinking about myself and my fear at being almost hit allows me to modify my plan for the future. Both directions of focus are important.

It is clear that adult humans possess the capacity of directed self-focus or attention. The question, then, is raised: does this capacity develop? My col-leagues and I have been addressing this problem for over 20 years (Lewis, 1992a, 1995a; Lewis & Brooks, 1974; Lewis & Brooks-Gunn, 1979; Lewis, Goldberg & Campbell, 1969; Lewis & Michalson, 1983b). Recently, Lewis (1995a) has sug-gested that there may be some advantage in considering that the self is made up of two systems; the first called the "machinery of the self". This consists of complex capacities that are part of the operating rules of the species. One possible such capacity has recently been studied. Although more data are needed, the evidence points to the fact that the amygdala is capable of learning through environmental interaction and that this learning may not involve other areas of the brain, such as the cortex (LeDoux, 1989). This machinery is made up of many features, including built-in, but open to learning, sensory and perceptual capacities. This "machinery of the self" itself develops through the interaction with the environment.

The second system is that of ideas, and in particular the "idea of me". This aspect is what I have referred to as consciousness. While people use the idea of consciousness in a broader sense, often to include the "machinery of the self" system, I wish to restrict my usage of the term consciousness to include *only* this "idea of me".

This aspect, the "idea of me", is a meta-cognition. It is like the memory of a memory, as in "I remember that as I get older I am likely to forget a person's name"[2]. It is also like R.D. Laing's *Knots* (1970); "I know that you know that I know that today is Saturday". This "idea of me" develops, and some have suggested regions of the brain that may be involved in this cognition and which themselves develop. Elsewhere, I have argued that the development of the cognition "the idea of me" (or what I call self-consciousness or self-focus) occurs in the middle of the second year of life (Lewis, 1995a). Such a conclusion is supported from a variety of data, notably the emergence of personal pronoun "me", self-recognition, and pretend play (Lewis & Ramsay, in press), as well as the relation between self-recognition and the onset of empathy and embarrassment (see Bischof-Kohler, 1991; Lewis et al., 1989).

This problem of focused attention on the self or on the self's action in the world has been addressed most noticeably with children by Dweck (1991; Dweck, Hong & Chiu, 1993). Dweck's data indicate that children, at least by 6–8 years, differentially use task- or self/performance-focus (Smiley & Dweck, 1994). Moreover, their differential use is related to achievement motivation. Thus, for example, children who are performance-oriented (self-focus) show poor social and academic achievement (Dweck & Leggett, 1988), as well as low persistence at academic tasks (Dweck, 1991).

There has been little work looking at these strategies in younger children, in part because younger children do not have the verbal abilities necessary to demonstrate these strategies. Recently, my colleague Margaret Sullivan and I have begun to explore whether it is possible to obtain data on attentional focus in children who are 3–6 years of age. Children of this age might well possess such focus of attention differences, since there is now sufficient data to indicate that 3 year-old children's response to success and failure on tasks is dependent on their perceptions of whether the tasks are easy or difficult to complete (Lewis, Alessandri & Sullivan, 1992; Stipek et al., 1992).

In order to measure attentional orientation, children were given four tasks, two easy and two difficult. On one easy and one difficult task, they succeeded, and on the other easy and difficult tasks they failed. In this way, four conditions were created for each child: easy-fail easy-succeed, difficult-fail and difficult-succeed. In the first phase of the study, we measured children's emotional responses to these four conditions. The findings are quite consistent across age and studies; children show shame when they fail, especially when they fail easy tasks, and show pride when they succeed, especially when they succeed in difficult tasks.

After each of the four tasks, the children were asked a series of questions about the task and about why they succeeded or failed. The responses to one of our questions on one of the four tasks caught our attention. Each child was asked if the task was easy or difficult. The responses to the "easy-fail" task present the possibility to look at attentional focus. The task itself was easy; however,

---

[2] As we age, we naturally increasingly forget things. Pathology of brain function (e.g. senility) is when we forget that we forget—a higher order process involving self-focus.

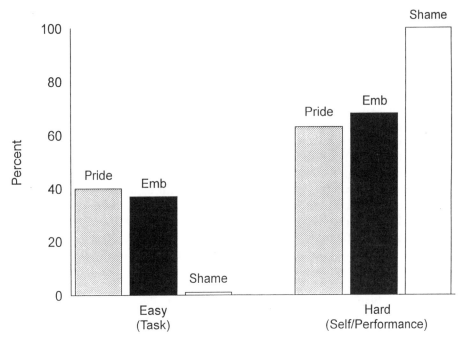

Figure 7.2 Self-conscious emotional expression as a function of task-vs.-self/performance-focus. Emb = embarrassment

all children failed it. We reasoned that if they focused on the task itself, they would say the task was easy; if they focused on their performance, they would say hard.

Data on over 100 children's responses on the easy-fail task revealed a significant relation to the children's emotion behavior, including facial and bodily actions. Figure 7.2 presents the percentage of children showing shame, embarrassment and pride as a function of individual differences in self/performance-focus vs. task-focus. Across studies, the findings remain quite consistent. For the self-conscious evaluative emotions, self/performance-focused children showed more embarrassment and shame when they failed and more pride when they succeeded than children who were task-focused. There are no group differences in either sadness or joy, suggesting that self-focus does not lead to a general increase in emotional behavior but rather only affects those emotions which are elicited by thinking about the self (Lewis, 1992a).

CONSCIOUSNESS, SELF-FOCUS AND PATHOLOGY

As adults we are capable of directing our attention both inward toward ourselves and outward toward our action-in-the-world, what might be called contextualism

(Lewis, 1997). This ability to focus attention differentially is a human capacity. Moreover, it is apparent that adults differ in their focus, some showing too great a self-focus and some too little. Too great a focus toward the outside world results in the loss of self-evaluation and therefore the ability to correct a problem; too great a self-focus also results in problems. One of the major difficulties is the increase in the self-conscious evaluative emotions, especially the negative ones of shame, guilt and embarrassment (Lewis, 1992a). The increase in these emotions has been linked to many of the major disassociative disorders (H.B. Lewis, 1987; Lewis, 1992a).

Recently, we have begun to explore the relation between children's trauma, self-cognition and emotional well-being. Alessandri & Lewis (1996) looked at young children's emotional responses as a function of whether or not they were maltreated. Using the paradigm we have described above, we were interested in seeing whether maltreated children were more likely to make self-cognitions that led to shame and embarrassment when they failed a task and less likely to lead to pride when they succeeded. While we have not collected data on their attributions, our first study revealed that the trauma of maltreatment, at least for 3–5 year-olds, has important consequences on their self-conscious evaluative emotions. For example, maltreated girls showed more shame when they failed and less pride when they succeeded than non-maltreated girls. Maltreated boys, on the other hand, showed less emotional responses of all kinds than did non-maltreated boys, suggesting that girls' attributions are thrown toward internal blame and global/self-focus, while boys' attributions are thrown toward external blame and emotional suppression. Such an example indicates that early emotional trauma impacts on self-cognitions, which in turn impact on their emotional responses. Recently, we have been working on the problem of sexual abuse and symptom formation (Feiring, Taska & Lewis, 1998). Our model of self-cognitions and shame suggests that shame mediates between the sexual abuse and symptom formation (Lewis, 1992b). In a sample of children aged 6–12 years known to be sexually abused, we have found that while severity of abuse is related to shame, it is shame and the changes in shame which predict such symptoms as depression or hyper-eroticism. This approach also is relevant for other forms of psychopathology, including acting out disorders in children (Dodge & Frame, 1982), depression (Beck, 1979), and post-traumatic stress disorder (Foa, Zinbarg & Rothbaum, 1992). Such findings as these indicate that the relation between self-cognitions and emotion are useful for our understanding of development as well as developmental psychopathology (Lewis & Miller, 1990).

The role of cognitions, especially those that involve the self, is critical in the generation of emotions; more, they are a central part of these emotions! While these cognitions are readily identified, I do not mean to imply that the emotional experiences of shame or embarrassment or even of the earlier emerging emotions, such as joy or fear, are just cognitions. Rather, I prefer to consider these cognitions as elicitors of a set of internal processes. While we have been as yet unable to identify these internal processes or states, there is no reason yet to believe they do not exist, for it is difficult to imagine that we learn fear or shame. While we may learn about the elicitors of these emotions or about what responses are culturally appropriate, these experiences themselves are not learned. Because of this, our dilemma remains; cognitions and emotions remain as separate entities of human life.

REFERENCES

Alessandri, S. M. & Lewis, M. (1996). Differences in pride and shame in maltreated and non-maltreated preschoolers. *Child Development*, **67**, 1857–1869.
Barrett, K. C. & Zahn-Waxler, C. (1987). Do toddlers express guilt? Paper presented at the meeting of the Society for Research in Child Development, Toronto, April.
Bechara, A., Tranel, D., Damasio, H., Adolphs, R., Rockland, C. & Damasio, A. R. (1995). Double dissociation of conditioning and declarative knowledge relative to the amygdala and hippocampus in humans. *Science*, **269**, 1115–1118.
Beck, A. T. (1979). *Cognitive therapy and emotional disorders*. New York: Times Mirror.
Bischof-Kohler, D. (1991). The development of empathy in infants. In M. E. Lamb & H. Keller (eds), *Infant Development: Perspectives from German-speaking Countries*. Hillsdale, NJ: Erlbaum, pp. 245–273.
Cannon, W. B. (1927). The James–Lange theory of emotion: a critical examination and an alternative theory. *American Journal of Psychology*, **39**, 106–124.
Cannon, W. B. (1929). *Bodily Changes in Pain, Hunger, Fear, and Rage*. New York: Appleton.
Charcot, J. M. (1889). *Clinical Lectures on Diseases of Nervous System*. London: New Sydenham Society.
Darwin, C. (1965/1872). *The Expression of the Emotions in Animals and Man*. Chicago: University of Chicago Press (original edition, 1872).
Dodge, K. A. & Frame, C. L. (1982). Social cognitive biases and deficits in aggressive boys. *Child Development*, **53**, 630–635.
Dweck, C. S. (1991). Self-theories and goals: their role in motivation, personality and development. In R. A. Dienstbier (ed.), *Nebraska Symposium on Motivation, 1990: Perspectives on Motivation*. New York: Wiley, pp. 643–691.
Dweck, C. S., Hong, Y. & Chiu, C. (1993). Implicit theories: individual differences in the likelihood and meaning of dispositional inference. *Personality and Social Psychology Bulletin*, **19**, 644–656.
Dweck, C. S. & Leggett, E. L. (1988). A social-cognitive approach to motivation and personality. *Psychological Review*, **95**, 256–273.
Eibl-Eibesfeldt, I. (1970). *Ethology: The Biology of Behavior*. New York: Holt, Rinehart & Winston.
Ekman, P. (1972). Universal and cultural differences in facial expression of emotion. In J. R. Cole (ed.), *Nebraska Symposium on Motivation*. Lincoln, NE: University of Nebraska Press.
Ekman, P. (1973). Cross-cultural studies of facial expression. In P. Ekman (ed.), *Darwin and Facial Expression*. New York: Academic Press.
Ekman, P., Friesen, W. V. & Ellsworth, P. (1972). *Emotion in the Human Face: Guidelines for Research and an Integration of Findings*. New York: Pergamon.
Erikson, E. H. (1950). *Childhood and Society*. New York: Norton.
Feiring, C., Taska, L. & Lewis, M. (1998). The role of shame and attribution style in children's and adolescents' adaptation to sexual abuse. *Child Maltreatment*, **3**(2), 129–142.
Foa, E. B., Zinbarg, R. & Rothbaum, B. O. (1992). Uncontrollability and

unpredictability in post-traumatic stress disorder: an animal model. *Psychological Bulletin*, **112**(2), 218–238.

Freud, S. (1936).   *The Problem of Anxiety*. New York: Norton.

Freud, S. (1949).   Repression. In S. Freud (ed.), *Collected Papers*, Vol. 3. London: Hogarth (originally published in 1915).

Freud, S. (1960).   In A. Tyson (trans.), *The Psychopathology of Everyday Life*. New York: Norton.

Gazzaniga, M. S. (1985).   *The Social Brain: Discovering the Networks of the Mind*. New York: Basic Books.

Gross, C. J., Rocha-Miranda, C. E. & Bender, D. B. (1972).   Visual properties of neurons in the inferotemporal cortex of the macaque. *Journal of Neurophysiology*, **35**, 96–111.

Hilgard, E. R. (1977).   *Divided Consciousness*. New York: Wiley.

Hochschild, A. R. (1979).   Emotion work, feeling rules, and social structure. *American Journal of Sociology*, **85**, 551–575.

Izard, C. E. (1977).   *Human Emotions*. New York: Plenum.

James, W. (1884).   What is emotion? *Mind*, **19**, 188–205.

James, W. (1890).   *The Principle of Psychology*. New York: Holt.

Janet, P. (1929).   *Major Symptoms of Hysteria*. New York: Hafner.

Jaynes, J. (1977).   *The Origin of Consciousness in the Breakdown of the Bicameral Mind*. Boston: Houghton-Mifflin.

Kagan, J. (1981).   *The Second Year: The Emergence of Self-Awareness*. Cambridge, MA: Harvard University Press.

Laing, R. D. (1970).   *Knots*. New York: Pantheon.

LeDoux, J. (1989).   Cognitive and emotional interactions in the brain. *Cognition and Emotion*, **3**, 265–289.

Lewis, H. B. (1971).   *Shame and Guilt in Neurosis*. New York: International Universities Press.

Lewis, H. B. (1987).   *The Role of Shame in Symptom Formation*. Hillsdale, NJ: Erlbaum.

Lewis, M., Goldberg, S. & Campbell, H. (1969).   A developmental study of information processing within the first three years of life: response decrement to a redundant signal. *Monographs of the Society for Research in Child Development*, **34**(9), Serial No. 133.

Lewis, M. (1990).   Development, time, and catastrophe: an alternate view of discontinuity. In P. Baltes, D. L. Featherman & R. Lerner (eds), *Life Span Development and Behavior Series*, Vol. 10. Hillsdale, NJ: Erlbaum, pp. 325–350.

Lewis, M. (1992a).   *Shame, the Exposed Self*. New York: Free Press.

Lewis, M. (1992b).   The self in self-conscious emotions. A commentary. In D. Stipek, S. Recchia & S. McClintic (eds), *Self-evaluation in young children*. Monographs of the Society for Research in Child Development, Vol. **57**(1), Serial No. 226.

Lewis, M. (1995a).   Aspects of self: from systems to ideas. In P. Rochat (ed.), *The Self in Early Infancy: Theory and Research*. Advances in Psychology Series. North Holland: Elsevier Science Publishers, pp. 95–115.

Lewis, M. (1995b).   Embarrassment: the emotion of self exposure and embarrassment. In J. P. Tangney & K. W. Fischer (eds), *Self-conscious Emotions: The Psychology of Shame, Guilt, Embarrassment and Pride*. New York: Guilford, pp. 198–218.

Lewis, M. (1995c).   Self-conscious emotions. *American Scientist*, **83**, 68–78.

Lewis, M. (1997).   *Altering Fate: Why the Past Does Not Predict the Future*. New York: Guilford.

Lewis, M., Alessandri, S. & Sullivan, M. W. (1992).   Differences in shame and pride as a function of children's gender and task difficulty. *Child Development*, **63**, 630–638.

Lewis, M. & Brooks, J. (1974).   Self, others and fear: infants' reactions to people. Presented at a conference on the Origins of Behavior: Fear. Princeton, NJ, October 1973. Also in M. Lewis & L. Rosenblum (eds), *The Origins of Fear: The Origins of Behavior*. New York: Wiley, pp. 195–227.

Lewis, M. & Brooks-Gunn, J. (1979).   *Social Cognition and the Acquisition of Self*. New York: Plenum.

Lewis, M. & Michalson, L. (1983a).   *Children's Emotions and Moods: Developmental Theory and Measurement*. New York: Plenum.

Lewis, M. & Michalson, L. (1983b).   From emotional state to emotional expression: emotional development from a person–environment interaction perspective. In D. Magnusson & V. L. Allen (eds), *Human Development: An Interactional Perspective*. New York: Academic Press.

Lewis, M. & Michalson, L. (1984a).   Emotion without feeling? Feeling without thinking? *Contemporary Psychology*, **29**, 457–459.

Lewis, M. & Michalson, L. (1984b).   The socialization of emotional pathology in infancy. *Infant Mental Health Journal*, **5**, 121–134.

Lewis, M. & Miller, S. M. (eds). (1990).   *Handbook of Developmental Psychopathology*. New York: Plenum.

Lewis, M. & Ramsay, D. S. (in press).   Onset of self-recognition and the emergence of self-awareness. *Developmental Psychology*.

Lewis, M. & Rosenblum, L. (1978).   Issues in affect development. In M. Lewis & L. Rosenblum (eds), *The Development of Affect: The Genesis of Behavior*, Vol. 1. New York: Plenum, pp. 1–10.

Lewis, M., Sullivan, M. W., Stanger, C. & Weiss, M. (1989).   Self-development and self-conscious emotions. *Child Development*, **60**, 146–156.

Oatley, K. & Johnson-Laird, P. N. (1987).   Toward a cognitive theory of emotions. *Cognition and Emotion*, **1**, 29–30.

Olds, M. E. & Forbes, J. L. (1981).   The central basis of motivation: intracranial self-stimulation studies. *Annual Review of Psychology*, **32**, 523–576.

Ortony, A. & Turner, T. J. (1990).   What's basic about basic emotions? *Psychological Review*, **97**, 315–331.

Piaget, J. (1976).   *The Grasp of Consciousness*. Cambridge, MA: Harvard University Press.

Plutchik, R. (1980).   *Emotion: A Psychoevolutionary Synthesis*. New York: Harper & Row.

Smiley, P. A. & Dweck, C. S. (1994).   Individual differences in achievement goals among young children. *Child Development*, **65**, 1723–1743.

Stipek, D., Recchia, S. & McClintic, S. (1992).   *Self-evaluation in Young Children*. Monographs of the Society for Research in Child Development, Vol. **57**(1), Serial No. 226.

Tangney, J. P. (1995).   Shame and guilt in interpersonal relationships. In J. P. Tangney & K. W. Fischer (eds), *Self-conscious Emotions: The Psychology of Shame, Guilt, Embarrassment, and Pride*. New York: Guilford, pp. 114–142.

Tomkins, S. (1962).   *Affect, Imagery, and Consciousness, Vol. 1. The Positive Affects*. New York: Springer.

Watson, J. B. (1924).   *Psychology from the Standpoint of a Behaviorist*, 2nd edn. Philadelphia, PA: Lippincott.

Wegern, M. A., Jones, F. N. & Jones, M. H. (1956).   *Physiological Psychology*. New York: Holt.

Weiner, B. (1986).   *An Attributional Theory of Motivation and Emotion*. New York: Springer-Verlag.

Zajonc, R. B. (1980).   Feeling and thinking: preferences need no inferences. *American Psychologist*, **35**, 151–175.

Zajonc, R. B., Murphy, S. T. & McIntosh, D. N. (1993).   Brain temperature and subjective emotional experience. In M. Lewis & J. M. Haviland (eds), *Handbook of Emotions*. New York: Guilford, pp. 209–220.

Part II

Cognitive Processes

Chapter 8

Selective Attention and Anxiety: A Cognitive–Motivational Perspective

Karin Mogg *and* **Brendan P. Bradley**
University of Cambridge, Cambridge, UK

INTRODUCTION

Both selective attention and emotions have important evolution-driven functions. The main functions of attention are to facilitate fast and accurate perceptual judgements and actions, and to sustain processing resources on selected stimulus inputs (LaBerge, 1995). The attentional system underlies the detection and monitoring of stimuli that are relevant to the organism's drives and goals. Depending on these goals certain stimuli will be favoured in attention at the expense of others. The evolutionary function of emotions depends on the type of emotion (e.g. Oatley & Johnson-Laird, 1987). For example, the main function of the mechanisms underlying fear is to facilitate the detection of danger in the environment and to help the organism respond promptly and effectively to threatening situations. Following this perspective, this chapter will be concerned with biases, rather than overall deficits, in information processing associated with emotional states. In particular, we will focus on how anxiety is associated with enhanced selective attention to threat information, since several recent theories have attributed a primary role to attentional process in explaining anxiety states (e.g. Mathews, 1990; Eysenck, 1992; see also MacLeod, this volume; Öhman, this volume). Attentional processes are generally given less prominence in theoretical accounts of other emotions, such as joy or sadness. We will briefly review theories linking anxiety and attention, describe relevant research findings, identify some limitations, and consider from a cognitive-motivational perspective the mechanisms that may underlie attentional biases in anxiety; an

Handbook of Cognition and Emotion. Edited by T. Dalgleish and M. Power.

analysis which we have introduced in more detail elsewhere (Mogg & Bradley, 1998a).

We will also focus primarily on trait anxiety (rather than phobia or panic) and on generalized anxiety disorder (GAD), given that the latter reflects the far end of the spectrum of individual differences in anxiety-proneness (Rapee, 1991). GAD is a relatively common anxiety disorder that tends to be chronic, with the following main symptom clusters: apprehensive expectation (unrealistic or excessive anxiety or worry focused on more than one life circumstance), muscle tension, autonomic hyperactivity, and vigilance or scanning (Barlow, 1988).

COGNITIVE FORMULATIONS OF PREATTENTIVE AND ATTENTIONAL BIASES IN ANXIETY

A key proposal of cognitive models is that biases in information processing play an important role in the aetiology and/or maintenance of emotional disorders, such as GAD and depression (e.g. Beck, 1976; Eysenck, 1992; Mathews & MacLeod, 1994). Beck's cognitive theories of emotional disorders (Beck, 1976; Beck, Emery & Greenberg, 1986; Beck, et al., 1979) have been influential in leading to effective treatments of depression and anxiety, namely cognitive-behavioural therapy (e.g. Simons et al., 1986; Butler et al., 1991). Beck proposed that, in depression, there are dysfunctional *schemata* which are concerned with information about loss or failure, whereas, in anxiety, the schemata are concerned with information relevant to threat or danger. The activation of such schemata is presumed to result in the selective processing of schema-congruent information.

Bower (1981) proposed an alternative model of the relation between emotion and cognition. Each emotion was represented as a node in an *associative network* in which it was linked with other representations within the network, such as memories of happy or sad events. Activation of the emotion node would lead to increased accessibility of mood-congruent material and hence to mood-congruent information processing biases. Both Beck's and Bower's models predict that in anxiety and depression there will be similar mood-congruent biases in all aspects of information processing, including selective attention, memory and reasoning. According to these views the primary cognitive difference between the emotions pertains to the specific content of each emotion, with anxiety being associated with themes of danger, and depression being associated with loss or failure.

A variety of tasks has been used to examine anxiety-related biases in selective attention. In the modified Stroop colour-naming task, subjects are shown words printed in different colours, and are asked to name the colour as quickly as possible and to ignore the word meaning. Colour-naming latency is assumed to reflect the extent to which processing resources are allocated to the word content. Generally anxious patients take longer to name the colours of threatening words (e.g. cancer, collapse) than neutral words (e.g. carpet), compared to normal controls (e.g. Mathews & MacLeod, 1985; Mogg, Mathews & Weinman, 1989; see review by Williams, Mathews & MacLeod, 1996), which is consistent with an attentional bias to threat. However, the interpretation of Stroop results is not clear-cut because the interference effect could arise not only in selective attention, but also in other aspects of processing, such as response selection.

The probe detection task provides a more direct measure of the allocation of visual attention. This task was adapted by MacLeod, Mathews & Tata (1986) from paradigms in experimental cognitive psychology which indicated that spatial attention can be assessed from the speed of manual responses to visual probes (e.g. Posner, Snyder & Davidson, 1980; Navon & Margalit, 1983). That is, subjects tend to be faster to respond to a probe stimulus (e.g. a small dot) that is presented in an attended, rather than unattended, region of a visual display. For example, in a typical version of this task assessing attentional responses to emotional stimuli, a series of word pairs is presented on a computer screen, with one member of the word pair above the other. On critical trials, one word of each pair is threat-related and the other neutral. Each word pair is presented relatively briefly (e.g. 500 ms), and when it disappears, a dot is presented in the position just occupied by one of the words. Subjects are required to respond as quickly as possible to the dot probe. Individuals with GAD are faster to respond to probes that replace threat words than neutral words, in comparison with normal control subjects, indicating an attentional bias for threat stimuli (e.g. MacLeod, Mathews & Tata, 1986; Mogg, Mathews & Eysenck, 1992; Mogg, Bradley & Williams, 1995b).

By the late 1980s, there was a considerable amount of evidence consistent with predictions from the schema and network theories, such as anxiety-congruent biases in attentional tasks (e.g. MacLeod, Mathews & Tata, 1986) and depression-congruent biases in self-referent recall tasks (e.g. Bradley & Mathews, 1983; see Blaney, 1986 for a review). But not all findings supported these theories, such as failures to find an attentional bias in depression (e.g. MacLeod, Mathews & Tata, 1986) and an anxiety-congruent bias in explicit memory (Mogg, Mathews & Weinman, 1987). Thus, contrary to expectation, cognitive biases do not appear to operate in all aspects of processing. Instead, anxiety seems mainly associated with a bias in selective attention, and depression with a negative recall bias, particularly for self-relevant material.

In the light of such findings, a revised cognitive formulation of anxiety and depression was advanced by Williams et al. (1988). They proposed that different emotional disorders are associated with different patterns of cognitive bias. That is, anxiety is primarily characterized by a bias which favours threat stimuli in *preattentive* processes (i.e. prior to awareness) and in *selective attention*. Specifically, they suggested that preattentive vigilance for threat reflects a cognitive vulnerability factor for clinical anxiety. That is, individuals who have a permanent tendency to show automatic vigilance for threat are more susceptible to the development of anxiety disorders when under stress. By contrast, depression is associated mainly with a bias in postattentive elaborative processes, which facilitates recall of negative material. The underlying mechanism responsible for these biases was described in terms of Graf & Mandler's (1984) model of memory, whereby anxiety was associated with a bias in automatic activation, and depression with a bias in strategic elaboration. Cognitive-behavioural therapy was assumed to be effective by correcting the underlying cognitive biases; the removal of these biases should alleviate anxious and depressed mood and reduce vulnerability to future emotional disorder.

According to this model, two mechanisms are responsible for the preattentive and attentional biases to threat in anxiety (see top panel of Figure 8.1). An Affective Decision Mechanism (ADM) assesses the threat value of environmental stimuli, and its output feeds into a Resource Allocation Mechanism (RAM) which determines the allocation of processing resources. The operation of the RAM is influenced by trait anxiety, i.e. high trait anxious individuals have a permanent tendency to orient attention to threat, whereas low trait individuals are avoidant of threat. This difference in attentional bias between high and low trait anxious individuals becomes more apparent as output from the Affective Decision Mechanism increases (e.g. due to increased state anxiety or stimulus threat value). Thus, under stress, high trait anxious individuals become more vigilant, whereas low trait anxious become more avoidant of threat. So, this *interaction hypothesis* proposes that preattentive and attentional biases are an interactive function of state and trait anxiety.

Williams et al. (1997) have updated their 1988 model within a connectionist framework. The Parallel Distributed Processing (PDP) model of Cohen, Dunbar & McClelland (1990) is used to account for findings from the emotional Stroop task. Within this PDP framework, the operation of the Affective Decision Mechanism may be conceptualized instead as activation of *input units* which are associatively "tagged" with a threat value and which are subject to neuromodulatory control. The latter is responsible for mediating the effect of state anxiety. The Resource Allocation Mechanism is re-conceptualized as a Task Demand Unit in PDP terms. Nevertheless, several core assumptions remain unchanged between the 1988 and 1997 models. That is, "high trait anxiety reflects a permanent tendency to react to increased activation of threat units at the preattentive stage by switching resources towards the source of threat" (Williams et al., 1997, p. 309), whereas low trait anxious individuals have a permanent tendency to direct processing resources away from an item that has been judged to be threatening at the preattentive stage. The *interaction hypothesis* also remains a key feature of the reformulated theory. That is, when the activation level of threat input units is low, these attentional differences between high and low trait anxious individuals may not be apparent. But, as the activation of the threat units increases (e.g. as state anxiety increases), their predisposition to allocate processing resources towards and away from threat becomes more evident (i.e. increased vigilance in high trait and increased avoidance of threat in low trait anxiety). Thus, the direction of these preattentive and attentional biases provides an index of vulnerability to generalized anxiety. A notable strength of Williams et al.'s analyses is not only their scholarly review of the research area, but also

Cognitive mechanisms underlying biases in initial orienting to threat in anxiety:

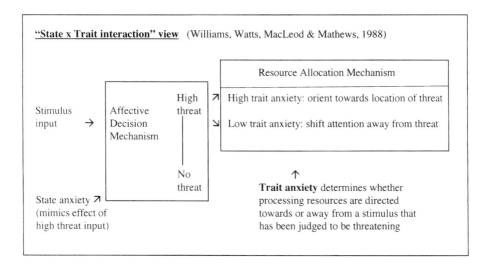

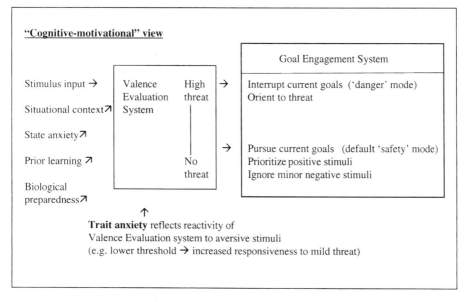

Figure 8.1 Cognitive mechanisms underlying biases in initial orienting to threat in anxiety. Upper figure adapted from Williams et al. (1988), with permission. Lower figure reproduced from Mogg & Bradley (1998a), with permission from Elsevier Science

their detailed analysis of the cognitive mechanisms that may underlie the relative effects of state vs. trait emotions, and of anxiety vs. depression, on specific aspects of information processing such as preattentive and attentional processes.

Other theoretical formulations have been advanced in recent years that are complementary to Williams et al.'s (1988, 1997) views. Following Oatley & Johnson-Laird (1987), who stressed the adaptive value of emotion in its evolutionary context, Mathews (1990, 1993) suggested that each primary emotion imposes a specific mode of operation within the cognitive system that serves to determine *processing priorities*. Specifically, anxiety represents a shift into a mode of hypervigilance, such that the person scans the environment for threatening stimuli. In this mode the cognitive system prioritizes the initial automatic encoding of threat, but not more detailed elaborate processing of threat that would aid recall. Individuals differ in their readiness to adopt a vigilant processing mode for threat, and this mode is most likely to be found in vulnerable individuals experiencing stressful life events (i.e. the bias is an interactive function of trait vulnerability and stressors).

The proposal that preattentive and attentional biases for threat reflect a latent cognitive vulnerability factor for GAD is also the "central ingredient" of Eysenck's (1992) *hypervigilance theory*. According to this view, such biases should be evident primarily in anxiety-prone individuals under conditions of stress and/or high state anxiety, such as in individuals suffering from GAD or in non-clinical individuals with high trait anxiety who are experiencing a stressful life event. An additional feature of Eysenck's theory is its concern with the non-biasing effects of anxiety on attention. For example, he proposed that high trait anxious individuals not only exhibit specific hypervigilance (a propensity to attend selectively to threat stimuli), but also general hypervigilance (a propensity to attend to any task-irrelevant stimuli, i.e. distractibility), a high rate of environmental scanning, a broadening of attention prior to the detection of a salient (e.g. threat) stimulus, and a narrowing of attention when a salient stimulus is being processed.

From a different research perspective, Öhman (1993; Öhman & Soares 1993, 1994) proposed that vulnerability to phobias is also mediated by automatic, preattentive processes. That is, fear responses are initiated by automatic, stimulus analysis mechanisms, which operate prior to awareness and which are sensitive to biologically-prepared aversive stimuli (e.g. spiders, angry faces). Preattentive analysis of such stimuli elicits autonomic anxiety responses independently of awareness of the fear-provoking stimulus. Moreover, once a threat stimulus is detected by this preattentive mechanism, there is an automatic shift of attention to its location. Öhman has proposed that such automatic elicitation of fear responses outside awareness may underlie their resistance to change, as this preconscious mechanism may be relatively immune to conscious influences (e.g. verbally-mediated attempts to modify fear responses).

So a common theme across these different research approaches is emphasis on the role of *preattentive processes* which are involved in stimulus appraisal and directing the focus of selective attention, and which mediate anxiety responses to potential threats in the environment. Several theories have proposed that individual differences in the response of these preattentive and orienting mechanisms to threat stimuli may underlie vulnerability to anxiety disorders. Moreover, therapy that modifies the operation of such preattentive and attentional mechanisms may be particularly effective in reducing anxiety and preventing relapse (see also McNally, 1995, for further discussion of automatic processing biases in anxiety).

PREATTENTIVE BIAS FOR THREAT IN CLINICAL ANXIETY

Several studies have investigated whether clinical anxiety is associated with a preconscious[1] processing bias for threat stimuli presented outside awareness. One method is the dichotic listening task, which involves presenting two different channels of information simultaneously, one to each ear. Mathews & MacLeod (1986) required subjects to shadow a message on one channel, while a list of threatening and neutral words was presented on the other, unattended channel. Subjects also monitored a visual display for the occasional appearance of a dot probe. In comparison with normal controls, anxious patients were slower to respond to the probe when the words on the unattended channel were threatening, rather than neutral, which was consistent with a processing bias for threat outside awareness. However, on this task, subjects may have fleeting awareness of information on the unattended channel due to attentional switching, and Holender (1986) argued that paradigms using visual masking are likely to be more effective in restricting awareness.

Masked versions have been developed of both the emotional Stroop (e.g. MacLeod & Rutherford, 1992; Mogg, Kentish & Bradley, 1993b) and dot probe task (e.g. Mogg, Bradley & Hallowell, 1994; Mogg, Bradley & Williams, 1995b; Mathews, Ridgeway & Williamson, 1996). In the masked version of the emotional Stroop task used by Mogg et al. (1993a), each word was presented on a computer screen very briefly (14 ms), in white letters superimposed on a background patch of colour (e.g. red, green or blue). The word was replaced immediately by a string of random white letters on a black background. The letter string effectively masked the preceding word but not the background patch of colour, and subjects were required to name the colour as quickly as possible. Half the trials were presented in this subthreshold condition, and half in a suprathreshold condition which was similar except that the word remained displayed on the screen (instead of a mask), thereby allowing awareness. Individuals with GAD

---

[1] In this chapter we have followed the common convention of using the terms "*preconscious*" and "*preattentive*" interchangeably to refer to processes occurring outside awareness. However, we share Bargh's (1989) reservation about the latter term as it might be misleading by implying that preconscious processes are not involved in the selection of stimulus inputs for orienting and further processing.

showed greater interference in colour-naming performance on trials with threat, rather than neutral, words in comparison with normal controls, irrespective of whether the words were masked or unmasked (Mogg et al., 1993a; Bradley et al., 1995a).

To evaluate awareness of the masked stimuli, two separate checks were used to assess each subject's ability to discriminate (a) whether a word was present or absent before the mask, and (b) whether a word or non-word was displayed before the mask. These tasks reflect *objective* thresholds of awareness, as indexed by forced choice discrimination performance (as opposed to a *subjective* threshold measure of awareness, which reflects subjective experience; Cheesman & Merikle, 1985, 1986). Subjects showed no evidence of awareness of either the presence or lexical content of the masked stimuli (i.e. performance on each awareness check did not significantly differ from chance level).[2] Thus, the results from the masked condition of the Stroop task are indeed consistent with a preconscious bias in clinical anxiety.

Converging evidence of a preconscious bias in GAD has been obtained from a masked version of the dot probe task (Mogg, Bradley & Williams, 1995b). In the subthreshold exposure condition, a word pair was presented for 14 ms, followed by a pair of masks (random letter strings) for 14 ms. A dot probe then appeared in the position of one of the masks, immediately after its presentation, and subjects indicated the position of the probe with a button-press response. The task also included a suprathreshold condition, where the word pairs were presented for 1000 ms without a mask. On critical trials, one word was negative and the other neutral, and response times to the probes reflected the extent to which attentional resources were directed towards the spatial location of negative rather than neutral words. Individuals with GAD showed greater vigilance for negative words than normal controls, irrespective of whether the word stimuli were masked or unmasked. On the subsequent awareness check, each subject's ability to discriminate the presence of the masked word stimuli was within chance level of performance. These findings further suggest that the bias in anxiety operates at an early stage of information processing, prior to awareness.

Results from these tasks also suggest that the content specificity of the processing bias in anxiety depends on the level of analysis of the stimulus. So, with presentation conditions that allow awareness and post-conscious processing, there is evidence that individuals with GAD preferentially attend to stimuli that are congruent with their predominant concerns. For example, results from suprathreshold versions of the emotional Stroop and dot probe tasks indicated that patients with predominant social worries selectively attend to social threat (e.g. incompetent, stupid), rather than physical threat words (e.g. illness, attack) (e.g. Mathews & MacLeod, 1985; Mogg, Mathews & Weinman, 1989; Mogg,

---

[2] The use of such awareness checks also allows exclusion of any individual whose performance on the discrimination tasks is significantly outside chance limits (using similar criteria to those used in individualized threshold setting procedures, such as performance outside 95% confidence limits of chance level; e.g. Mogg, Bradley & Williams, 1995b; Kemp-Wheeler & Hill, 1988).

Mathews & Eysenck, 1992). However, when the stimuli are presented briefly and masked, individuals with GAD exhibit a bias for negative information in general, including both anxiety- and depression-relevant words (e.g. Mogg et al., 1993a; Mogg, Bradley & Williams, 1995b; Bradley et al., 1995a). These results suggest that, prior to awareness, stimuli undergo a relatively superficial level of semantic analysis, e.g. along a basic positive–negative dimension (Pratto, 1994), while more detailed analyses, such as evaluating relevance to specific self-relevant concerns, depend on post-conscious processes.

DOES THE PREATTENTIVE BIAS FOR THREAT REFLECT A VULNERABILITY FACTOR FOR ANXIETY?

MacLeod & Hagan (1992) conducted a prospective study to investigate whether the preattentive bias for threat is a predictor of emotional distress. Using the emotional Stroop task with both sub- and supra-threshold exposure conditions, they tested a group of women who attended a clinic for cervical smear tests, and two months later followed up those with abnormal cell results. Women who initially showed a processing bias for subthreshold threat stimuli subsequently reported more distress following their diagnosis. This did not seem to be due simply to an association between the bias and current mood state, because, when the effect of this was controlled statistically, the predictive relationship between preconscious bias and subsequent emotional distress still remained. The results suggested that the preconscious bias for threat words reflects a vulnerability factor; i.e. individuals who have an enduring tendency to be vigilant for threat may be more susceptible to developing emotional disorders when under stress. Further evidence of a relationship between the preconscious bias on the masked Stroop and self-report measures of vulnerability to life stress and trait anxiety was found in a cross-sectional study of healthy volunteers by van den Hout et al. (1995), which was consistent with MacLeod & Hagan's findings. The latter are of potential theoretical importance, and there is a need for additional convergent research using prospective studies.

EFFECT OF TREATMENT ON PREATTENTIVE AND ATTENTIONAL BIASES

Longitudinal studies of anxious individuals indicate that attentional biases commonly disappear following treatment, as in spider phobia (e.g. Lavy, van den Hout & Arntz, 1993), social phobia (Mattia, Heimberg & Hope, 1993), obsessive-compulsive disorder (e.g. Foa & McNally, 1986), and GAD (e.g. Mathews et al., 1995). In the latter study, the colour-naming interference effect of threat words in GAD patients disappeared after cognitive-behavioural therapy (CBT). However, this study used only suprathreshold stimuli, so it was uncertain whether the reduction in bias in GAD patients following treatment reflected a change in controlled strategies, or in automatic preconscious processes. To address this issue, we used the emotional Stroop task with both sub- and supra-threshold exposure conditions to examine the effect of CBT on processing biases in GAD patients (Mogg et al., 1995a). Before treatment, GAD patients without concurrent depressive disorder showed greater interference in colour-naming negative words in both supra- and sub-threshold exposure conditions, compared with controls. However, after treatment, there was no difference in bias between the groups. This suggested that the preconscious bias in GAD was altered by psychological treatment. Furthermore, the reduction in preconscious bias correlated with reduction in anxious thoughts. This relationship between the change in the interference effect of masked anxiety words and change in anxious thoughts was significant not only over two months, but also over 20 months. Our findings suggested that the preconscious bias and anxious thoughts may reflect a common underlying mechanism that operates automatically outside awareness, diverting processing resources away from on-going activities in favour of negative information. Thus, the preconscious bias for verbal material may contribute to clinical anxiety, given that anxious thoughts are a defining feature of GAD.

INFLUENCES OF STATE AND TRAIT VARIABLES ON PREATTENTIVE AND ATTENTIONAL BIASES

The interaction hypothesis, described earlier, can be separated into two distinct components. First, in the absence of stress, there may be little difference between high and low trait anxious individuals in their preattentive and attentional biases for threat. But, when state anxiety or stress levels are elevated, high trait anxious individuals will exhibit vigilance for threat. This first part of the interaction hypothesis mainly concerns the attentional responses of high trait anxious individuals, and it implies that the vigilant attentional style is a latent vulnerability factor for anxiety (e.g. Eysenck, 1992). The second part of the interaction hypothesis concerns the attentional responses of low trait anxious individuals. That is, as the activation of cognitive representations of threat increases (e.g. as state anxiety and/or stimulus threat value increases), low trait anxious individuals should become more avoidant of threat (Williams et al., 1988, 1997).

Several studies have directly tested the interaction hypothesis by examining the relative effects of stressors and trait anxiety on attentional bias in non-clinical subject samples (see also Williams et al., 1997, for a review of state and trait influences on attentional biases). Using the dot probe task, MacLeod & Mathews (1988) found no difference between high and low trait anxious students in their attentional bias for threat stimuli, when tested several months prior to their examinations, when state anxiety levels were low. However, when tested one week before their end-of-year examinations, when state anxiety levels were elevated, high trait anxious students showed increased vigilance for threat, whereas low trait anxious students did not. This supports the first aspect of the interaction hypothesis (i.e. stress increases vigilance only in vulnerable individuals). With regard to the second aspect of the hypothesis, there was a non-significant trend for low trait anxious to become more avoidant of threat under examination stress. These results were confirmed by Mogg, Bradley & Hallowell (1994), i.e. high trait anxious students became significantly more vigilant for threat under examination stress, while there was a non-significant trend for low trait students to become more avoidant.

Using the modified Stroop task with both sub- and supra-threshold exposure conditions, MacLeod & Rutherford (1992) found that, in comparison with low trait anxious students, high trait anxious students under examination stress showed greater interference in colour-naming performance on trials with threat words than neutral words, but only when awareness of the word stimuli was restricted. Their results appeared to be consistent with the first part of the interaction hypothesis, i.e. the vigilant processing mode operates in preconscious processes in anxiety-prone subjects under stress. With regard to the second part of the hypothesis, there was a trend for low trait anxious individuals to show reduced interference for masked threat words as a result of increased examination stress.

So these studies suggest that there may be little difference in attentional responses to threat words between high and low trait anxious individuals in the absence of stressors, but as stress and/or state anxiety levels increase, high trait anxious individuals show increased vigilance for such threat in preattentive and attentional processes. Thus, the first part of the interaction hypothesis seems to be supported, although conclusions should be guarded given that this bias for threat was found in the subthreshold, but not suprathreshold, condition of the Stroop task, but vice versa in the dot probe task (MacLeod & Rutherford, 1992; Mogg, Bradley & Hallowell, 1994). The evidence for the second part of the interaction hypothesis is not conclusive, given that three studies showed non-significant trends (two in the suprathreshold condition of the dot probe task; and one in the subthreshold condition of the Stroop task) for low trait anxious individuals to become more avoidant of threat words under examination stress.

Moreover, different types of stressors may exert different influences on attentional bias. Short-term acute stressors (e.g. mock IQ test in medical students) sometimes elicit attentional biases towards threat in both high and low trait anxious individuals, although this effect is not invariably found (e.g. Mogg, Bradley & Hallowell, 1994; Mogg et al., 1990). By contrast, longer-term, naturalistic stressors (e.g. impending exams) seem to elicit vigilance for threat more selectively in high trait anxious individuals. Such differences between stressors are difficult to explain solely in terms of the effects of state and trait anxiety. However, long-term stressors are likely to be associated with increased rehearsal of threat-related material (e.g. examination-related worries) in high trait anxious students, and so this selective priming and/or subjective word frequency effect might contribute to their attentional bias for threat words.

The distinction between the two components of the interaction hypothesis has important implications regarding the potential mechanisms underlying attentional biases. For example, if only the first part is confirmed (i.e. increased vigilance in high trait anxious individuals under stress), then this could be explained by some simple threshold effect of state and trait anxiety on eliciting an attentional bias for threat, in which state and trait variables might contribute in an additive manner. However, if the second part of the interaction hypothesis is also confirmed (i.e. increased avoidance of threat in low trait anxious individuals under stress), this would support the view that vulnerability to anxiety is mediated by the mechanism determining the *direction* of the attentional bias, and that an individual's enduring predisposition to be either vigilant or avoidant for threat is revealed by increasing threat inputs (e.g. by increasing state anxiety). However, it may also be consistent with another interpretation, such as a curvilinear relationship between the attentional bias and stimulus threat value. Several months before examinations, examination-relevant words may have minimal threat value, and so elicit no bias. However, just before examinations, they may have moderate threat value for low trait anxious, but higher threat value for high trait anxious students. Thus, the results may also be consistent with a general tendency to avoid mild threat, but to orient to more severe threat stimuli.

So far, we have only considered studies using words as stimuli. However, these findings may provide an incomplete picture of preattentive and attentional biases for emotional information. Such stimuli introduce a potential confound of subjective word frequency effects (e.g. threat words are likely to have a higher subjective frequency of usage in high rather than low trait anxious individuals). Single words also have a limited range of threat value (e.g. individually presented words such as "illness" and "stupid" have relatively mild threat value). Consequently, we shall now turn to studies using a wider range of stimuli.

PREATTENTIVE AND ATTENTIONAL BIASES FOR EMOTIONAL FACIAL EXPRESSIONS

We have conducted a series of studies examining anxiety-related biases for emotional facial expressions because these are particularly salient stimuli for humans. An angry or threatening face, staring directly at the subject, is a clear sign of hostility towards the individual, whereas a threat-related word is an arbitrary symbol. Indeed, recent theories of anxiety suggest that the automatic appraisal and detection of environmental threat and consequent anxiety responses are mediated by a basic cross-species biologically-prepared mechanism, and that this mechanism should be particularly sensitive to innate stimuli (e.g. LeDoux, 1995), such as threatening faces in humans (e.g. Öhman, 1993). Thus, angry faces not only represent a potent and ecologically valid type of threat, but also avoid the potential confounds associated with subjective word frequency effects.

We have modified the dot probe task to assess attentional biases for emotional faces (Bradley et al., 1997a). The facial expressions were either threatening, happy or neutral. Each emotional face was paired with a neutral face of the same person. Following presentation of the face pair for 500 ms, a dot probe appeared in the location of one of the faces and subjects were required to indicate the position of the probe. Our first two non-clinical studies provided evidence of emotion-congruent attentional biases, as non-dysphoric individuals (i.e. those with low levels of depression and anxiety) showed a greater bias to shift attention away from threatening faces, relative to happy or neutral faces, in comparison with dysphoric individuals (Bradley et al., 1997a). It was not clear from these results whether avoidance of threat faces was primarily associated with the absence of either depression, anxiety or some common underlying emotional factor, such as negative affect (Watson & Clark, 1984). However, two subsequent non-clinical studies using the dot-probe task with face stimuli have suggested that increased vigilance for threatening faces is associated with "high" levels of trait anxiety (Bradley et al., 1998b; Mogg & Bradley, 1998b).

We subsequently investigated the validity of the dot probe task in providing a measure of *initial orienting* to threat. A limitation of the task is that it presents only a snapshot picture of attentional biases. For example, when stimuli are shown for 500 ms, this might be long enough to allow more than one shift of attention between the members of the stimulus pair. If so, an individual might initially orient towards the neutral stimulus (of a threat—neutral face pair, or word pair) but then shift attention to the threat stimulus and show an apparent bias to threat (due to faster RTs to probes in the currently attended location). Thus, the bias measure obtained at 500 ms might not necessarily reflect the direction of initial orienting.

Consequently, we assessed, within the same experiment, biases for emotional stimuli in both *overt* and *covert orienting*, by monitoring the direction of gaze while subjects performed the dot probe task with face stimuli (Bradley, Mogg & Millar, 1998a). The stimuli were threatening, sad, happy and neutral facial expressions, and the stimulus pairs shown for 500 ms. Two main measures of attentional bias were derived from (a) the manual RTs to probes (covert orienting), and (b) the direction of the initial eye movement (EM) towards or away from the emotional face (overt orienting). The results provided further evidence of anxiety-related biases in orienting to face stimuli. The manual RT data indicated that greater vigilance for negative than positive facial expressions was associated with higher state anxiety in this non-clinical sample. This bias could not be explained solely in terms of overt orienting mechanisms, because it was also evident in a subsample of subjects who made relatively few eye movements to the faces (e.g. by maintaining centrally fixated gaze). Nevertheless, there was evidence of concordance between the two attentional bias measures from the manual RT and EM data. That is, where subjects made eye movements to the faces, vigilance for negative faces relative to positive faces, as reflected by the EM data, was consistent with corresponding vigilance reflected by the manual RT data. Thus, manual RT bias measures taken at 500 ms on this particular task do indeed seem to reflect the direction of *initial orienting* to emotional face stimuli.

We have also examined biases in gaze towards emotional faces in clinical anxiety (Mogg, Bradley & Millar, in preparation). Results showed that individuals with GAD were more likely to shift their gaze towards threat faces rather than neutral faces, in comparison with depressed and normal control subjects. The GAD group were also faster in looking towards threat faces than away from them, in comparison with the other groups.

We have also investigated preattentive biases for face stimuli in a series of studies using a masked version of the dot probe task (Mogg & Bradley, 1998c). In the first study, each face pair was presented for 14 ms, immediately followed by a pair of masks for 14 ms. The masks were photographs of faces that had been cut up and randomly reassembled. A dot probe was presented in the location of one of the masks, immediately after their offset. The main awareness check was a gender discrimination task, and each subject's ability to discriminate whether the masked faces were male or female was within chance limits. Subjects were faster to detect probes occurring in the same location of masked threat faces, in particular, when the threat face and probe were presented in the left visual field. Thus, the results suggested not only a preattentive bias for threat, but also a possible underlying hemispheric asymmetry, consistent with related research indicating right hemisphere dominance in processing of threat (e.g. Christianson, Saisa & Silfvenius, 1995). In a subsequent study in this series, we not only replicated these findings (i.e. a preattentive bias favouring threat rather than happy faces, particularly for threat faces in the left visual field), but also found that the preattentive bias for threat faces was more evident in high rather than low trait anxious individuals, whereas our first study had not revealed such anxiety-related effects.

Another paradigm that has been used to investigate attentional biases for threat faces is the popout task. Subjects are presented with an array of faces, in which one facial expression differs from the others in emotional valence (e.g. a angry face in a "crowd" of happy faces, or vice versa), and they are required to detect the "odd face out" as quickly as possible. Hansen & Hansen (1988) found that an angry face in a happy crowd was detected significantly faster than a happy face in an angry crowd. This "threat superiority effect" seems consistent with our findings of a preattentive bias favouring threat rather than happy faces on the masked version of the dot probe task. Early studies using the popout task did not examine the effect of individual differences in anxiety level, but more recently Byrne & Eysenck (1995) reported that this threat superiority effect was greater in high rather than low trait anxious individuals. They included a state anxiety mood induction procedure before the popout task, but found no effects due either to state anxiety, or to an interaction of state and trait anxiety. We have also conducted a similar popout task, but without a mood induction procedure, and found that the threat superiority effect depended on subjects' anxiety levels. However, in our study this effect was associated with state rather than trait anxiety.

A striking feature emerging from these studies using pictorial stimuli is the robust nature of the findings. In summary, in our laboratory, we have used a variety of tasks to investigate attentional biases for emotional faces (including dot probe, eye movement and popout tasks), and the vast majority of studies revealed emotion-congruent effects in both non-clinical and clinical samples. There is some variability in results, as some implicated state anxiety, others trait anxiety, or negative emotional valence in general, as primarily influencing attentional biases. Such variability might stem from methodological variables, such as sampling differences (e.g. trait anxiety effects may be more evident when extreme trait scorers are pre-selected) or self-report measures not being sufficiently sensitive in discriminating anxiety and general negative affect (Watson et al., 1995). Nevertheless, the results from studies using face stimuli stand in contrast to those using word stimuli, because anxiety-related biases are not often found for suprathreshold word stimuli in non-clinical studies unless some stressor is used (e.g. MacLeod & Mathews, 1988; Mogg, Bradley & Hallowell, 1994; although there are exceptions, e.g. Fox, 1993). Thus, the hypothesis that attentional biases for threat are mainly a feature of high trait anxious individuals under stress may only pertain to weak threat stimuli. Thus, it is helpful to examine further the effect of stimulus threat value on attentional biases.

ATTENTIONAL BIASES FOR PICTORIAL SCENES

Cognitive formulations of anxiety, such as Williams et al.'s (1988, 1997), may apply primarily to mild threat stimuli, as they may not account for attentional responses for severe threat stimuli. According to the *interaction hypothesis*, as activation of cognitive representations of threat increases (e.g. due to increased state anxiety and/or stimulus threat value), high trait anxious individuals become more vigilant, whereas low trait anxious individuals become more avoidant of threat. However, it is clearly important from an evolutionary perspective that an effective threat detection system would have to ensure that attention is directed to real or severe threats (e.g. an attacking animal). Thus, even low trait anxious individuals should attend to threat stimuli that exceed some threshold of severity, otherwise the system would be dysfunctional. This issue has been somewhat overlooked in recent theoretical accounts, and the *interaction hypothesis* may need revision to take account of attentional biases across a wider range of threat stimuli.

We developed a pictorial version of the dot probe task to test the prediction that both high and low trait anxious individuals should show increased vigilance for threat, as stimulus threat value increases (Mogg et al., 1998d). In our first study, which we carried out with Rawlinson and Seiffer, the stimuli were monochrome photographs depicting severe threat (e.g. mutilated bodies, victim of assault) and moderate threat scenes (e.g. soldiers, man behind bars), selected on the basis of judges' ratings of threat value. Each threat scene was paired with a neutral scene and presented for 500 ms within the dot probe task. Results from an unselected non-clinical sample showed greater vigilance for severe threat than for milder threat scenes. Moreover, individuals who scored below the median in trait anxiety also showed this enhanced vigilance for stimuli with higher threat value.

In a subsequent study, which we carried out with MacNamara and Powys, the pictorial scenes were taken from the International Affective Picture System (IAPS; Lang, Bradley & Cuthbert, 1995). The severe threat and milder threat pictures were selected on the basis of the normative valence data, and each was paired with a neutral scene (also from the IAPS) and presented for 500 ms within the dot probe task. The subjects were pre-selected on the basis of having extreme high or low trait anxiety scores. The results confirmed those of our previous study, i.e. generally greater vigilance for severe than milder threat scenes. The low trait anxious group showed avoidance of the milder threat scenes, but their avoidance of threat reduced as threat value increased. In addition, the high trait anxious group showed greater vigilance for threat scenes (irrespective of their threat severity) than did low trait anxious individuals. Our results suggested that the effects of trait anxiety and stimulus threat value on vigilance were additive, rather than interactive. These findings are not predicted from the interaction hypothesis, but appear to be more consistent with a cognitive-motivational view of anxiety, which suggests that the direction of the attentional bias for threat may primarily be a function of the subjective threat value of the stimulus, which we will return to later.

TIME COURSE OF ATTENTIONAL BIASES

So far we have focused on biases in preattentive and attentional processes; particularly those involved in the initial orienting of processing resources towards threat. However, it is unclear whether anxiety exerts a consistent influence on all aspects of selective attention. Recent research indicates that the attentional system is not unitary; in particular, there is a distinction between shifting and maintenance of attention (e.g. Allport, 1989; LaBerge, 1995), and separate subsystems may underlie various aspects of orienting, such as shifting, engagement and disengagement (Posner & Petersen, 1990). Thus, anxious individuals may initially shift their attention towards threat stimuli (as a result of automatic preattentive capture), but not necessarily maintain their attention on such stimuli.

As noted above, there is evidence of an anxiety-related bias in initial orienting towards threat stimuli presented for 500 ms or less (e.g. MacLeod, Mathews & Tata, 1986; Bradley, Mogg & Millar, 1998), although it is less clear what subsequently occurs. One possibility is a "vigilance–avoidance" pattern of bias (e.g. Mogg, Mathews & Weinman, 1987; Mathews, 1990) where anxious individuals initially direct their attention to threat, but then try to avoid detailed processing of it in an attempt to minimize their discomfort. This pattern of bias could maintain anxiety states, because anxious individuals would be more likely to identify potentially threatening events, whereas subsequent cognitive avoidance would interfere with habituation or objective evaluation of them; which in turn would contribute to a failure of emotional processing (Rachman, 1980). Another possibility is that anxious individuals have greater difficulty in disengaging their attention from threat stimuli, and so there may be a pervasive bias throughout attentional processes, as suggested by the cognitive models of Beck (1976) and Bower (1981). A third possibility is that anxiety only influences initial orienting to threat, and that there are no systematic anxiety-related biases in the maintenance of attention.

To examine the time course of attentional biases we have used the dot probe task with a variety of stimulus exposure durations. In one study, a non-clinical sample of individuals who scored above the median on state anxiety showed greater vigilance for threat words shown for 100 ms, with similar non-significant trends at 500 and 1500 ms, in comparison with those with lower state anxiety scores (Mogg, Bradley, de Bono & Painter, 1997). In another study, high trait anxious individuals showed greater vigilance for threat faces relative to happy faces at both 500 and 1250 ms durations (Bradley et al., 1998b). Thus, these non-clinical studies using relatively mild threat stimuli, such as words and photographs of faces, suggested that the bias in initial orienting to threat was not significantly counteracted by subsequent avoidance strategies (at least for the durations observed here). However, it would be unwise to generalize from these results to clinical anxiety disorders. That is, attentional avoidance strategies might be associated with more extreme levels of anxiety, or with stimuli of greater threat value.

To investigate this issue, we recently carried out a study with Ellory and Smith (in preparation) examining the time course of attentional responses to fear-provoking stimuli in simple phobia (for related studies of vigilance for phobic stimuli, see van den Hout et al., 1997; Lavy, van den Hout & Arntz, 1993; Kindt & Brosschot, 1997). The stimuli were photographs of spiders presented in the dot probe task, with three stimulus durations: 200, 500 and 2000 ms. Individuals with spider phobia showed significantly more vigilance for fear-provoking stimuli at 200 ms, compared with non-phobic controls, while neither group showed a bias for the phobic stimuli at the longer stimulus exposure durations. These results suggest that anxiety-related biases towards threat are not found across all attentional processes, but that they are most reliably evident at short durations that are more likely to reflect automatic initial orienting to external stimuli (see also Bradley, Mogg & Lee, 1997b). The extent to which attention is maintained on aversive stimuli does not necessarily co-vary with this bias in initial orienting (although they may be more likely to co-vary when anxiety and/or threat levels are relatively low). Sustained attention to threat may also be determined by the anxiety level of the individual and/or stimulus threat value, but the underlying mechanisms may be partially independent of those responsible for preattentive orienting. It would seem useful to investigate further the interplay between the mechanisms involved in initial orienting vs. sustained attention to threat, given that these might play an important role in the maintenance of clinical anxiety states.

PREATTENTIVE AND ATTENTIONAL BIASES IN CLINICAL ANXIETY VS. DEPRESSION

There has been considerable debate about whether depression is associated with an attentional bias for negative information. With regard to preattentive biases for negative word stimuli in clinical depression, several studies have failed to find such biases on masked versions of the emotional Stroop and dot probe tasks (e.g. Mogg et al., 1993a; Bradley et al., 1995a; Mogg, Bradley & Williams, 1995b; Mathews, Ridgeway & Williamson, 1996). These null findings do not seem to be due to insensitive tasks because each study included a group who had clinical anxiety without depressive disorder, who indeed showed evidence of a preattentive bias for negative information. A similar pattern of results emerged from our eye movement study as individuals with depressive disorder (the majority of whom also had high levels of generalized anxiety) showed no bias in their initial shift of gaze for either angry or sad faces, whereas individuals with GAD in the absence of depressive disorder showed a bias to look towards angry rather than neutral faces (Mogg, Bradley & Millar, in preparation).

Studies of attentional biases for suprathreshold word stimuli in clinical depression have produced more mixed results. Several studies failed to find such biases on the Stroop and dot probe task (e.g. Bradley et al., 1995a; Mogg et al., 1993a; MacLeod, Mathews & Tata, 1986). But other studies have found such biases in clinical depression, although these have tended to use stimulus exposure conditions that have relatively long durations and/or have encouraged priming (e.g. Gotlib & Cane, 1987; Mogg, Bradley & Williams, 1995b; Segal et al., 1995; see also Mathews, Ridgeway & Williamson, 1996, for further discussion of discrepant results).

These findings suggest that depressed individuals do not automatically orient their attention towards negative information in the environment. However, once such material has come into the focus of their attention, they may have greater difficulty in disengaging their attention from it. In other words, depression may be primarily associated with a bias in the maintenance of attention (rather than initial shifting) to negative information. This would be consistent with the view that an increased tendency to ruminate on negative information, together with difficulty in distracting oneself from such material, may play an important role in maintaining depressed mood (Nolen-Hoeksemsa, 1991).

Consequently, we examined the time course of depression-congruent attentional biases in two non-clinical studies using the dot probe task with three exposure conditions: 14 ms (+ mask), 500 ms and 1000 ms (Bradley, Mogg & Lee, 1997). The first study showed that induced depressed mood was associated with greater vigilance for depression-related words at 500 ms, with a similar trend at 1000 ms. In the second study, measures of naturally occurring dysphoria and depression-proneness correlated positively with vigilance for negative words in the 1000 ms condition. There was no evidence from the masked condition of either study that depressed mood *per se* was associated with a preconscious bias for negative information, although we did find that this bias was associated with trait anxiety. These results further support the view that depression and anxiety are associated with biases in different aspects of attentional processes. Anxiety appears to be linked mainly with a bias in preconscious processes involved in initial orienting to negative stimuli, whereas depression may be more closely associated with a bias in other aspects of processing, such as those involved in sustained attention.[3]

A COGNITIVE-MOTIVATIONAL VIEW OF ANXIETY

It seems likely that two mechanisms underlie preattentive and attentional biases in anxiety: Valence Evaluation and Goal Engagement Systems. The distinction between these mechanisms is consistent with a body of research suggesting that at least two primary factors underlie emotions. These factors have been variously labelled, such as the personality traits of Neuroticism and Extraversion (Eysenck & Eysenck, 1969), and Anxiety and Impulsivity (Gray, 1990); and the emotional states of Valence and Arousal (Lang, Bradley & Cuthbert, 1990), and Negative and Positive Affect (Watson & Tellegen, 1985). Despite some critical differences between these theoretical views, there is considerable conceptual overlap, as they may be mapped on to a common underlying two-dimensional framework reflecting *emotional valence* and *goal engagement* (Tellegen, 1985; Lang, Bradley & Cuthbert, 1990). This commonality may be explained by a motivational analysis, which assumes that fundamental underlying motivational systems mediate cognitive and behavioural responses to aversive and appetitive stimuli (e.g. Fowles, 1994).

According to this cognitive-motivational view, the Valence Evaluation System is responsible for assessing stimulus threat value (see bottom panel of Figure 8.1). Its functions correspond largely to the stimulus appraisal processes elucidated in LeDoux's (1995, 1996) neural model of anxiety, and include not only the automatic, rapid analysis of crude stimulus features (e.g. dark, looming objects) but also the integration of more detailed contextual and memorial information. According to LeDoux, the amygdala plays a central role in the appraisal of danger because it directly receives not only the "quick-and-dirty" sensory inputs via the thalamus that allow rapid responses on the basis of limited stimulus

---

[3] It should be noted that we have only considered above evidence of preattentive biases on tasks involving *selection* between different stimuli (e.g. dot probe, eye movement tasks) or between different stimulus features (Stroop task). While these tasks have failed to show depression-congruent preattentive biases, it would be wrong to conclude that depression is not associated with any biases in preconscious processes. In fact, several studies have indicated such biases in depression on implicit memory tasks, such as priming by masked word stimuli (e.g. Bradley, Mogg & Williams, 1994, 1995b; Bradley, Mogg & Millar, 1996; Scott, Mogg & Bradley, 1998), suggesting that high levels of depression are associated with biases in both automatic and strategic aspects of memory. On the other hand, depression does not seem to be associated with a bias in those preconscious processes specifically involved in the *selection* of stimulus information from the visual scene and in automatic initial orienting, as assessed on attentional tasks.

information, but also the more detailed stimulus information via inputs from longer and slower neural pathways from hippocampal and cortical regions. Thus, the appraisal of stimulus threat value depends on the integration of various sources of information from both subcortical and cortical levels of analyses. Once the amygdala has been activated by a threat stimulus, LeDoux suggests that it may influence in turn a range of cognitive processes, including perception, selective attention and explicit memory, for example, via projections to sensory processing areas, the nucleus basalis and hippocampus. LeDoux's theory provides a clear and detailed account of the stimulus processing and neural mechanisms that may underlie threat appraisal.

Thus, several variables may influence the output of the Valence Evaluation System—not only the nature of the stimulus (including the degree of biological preparedness), but also its situational context, possibly interoceptive information about current arousal level, as well as previous learning experiences. In addition, trait anxiety reflects the reactivity of the Valence Evaluation System to aversive stimuli. That is, the system is more sensitive in anxiety-prone individuals; so trivial negative stimuli are tagged as having a disproportionately high threat value.

Output from the Valence Evaluation System feeds into a Goal Engagement System, which in turn determines the allocation of processing resources to external goals and stimuli. So if a stimulus is tagged as having a high threat value, this mechanism automatically interrupts ongoing activities and allocates processing resources towards the threat (cf. Gray, 1985). However, if the stimulus is tagged as having little or no threat value, then the organism will disregard it, inhibit any further processing of it, and maintain processing resources on current goals. The operation of these two motivational systems would have evolutionary adaptive value, in being sensitive to stimuli that may endanger the well-being of the organism, and in automatically and rapidly eliciting a coordinated set of response tendencies (cognitive, behavioural and physiological) that interrupt ongoing goals and activities to deal with the potential threat.

The functions of the Valence Evaluation and Goal Engagement Systems share some common features with those of the Affective Decision and Resource Allocation Mechanisms, respectively, in Williams et al.'s (1988) model.[4] However, the models differ in their accounts of the roles of these mechanisms in mediating vulnerability to anxiety (see Figure 8.1). A key aspect of our cognitive-motivational view is that anxiety-prone individuals have a lower threshold for appraising threat. Thus, a high trait anxious individual would evaluate a relatively innocuous stimulus as being more threatening, compared with a low trait anxious individual. The subjective threat value of a stimulus is influenced largely by stimulus features (e.g. real-life threatening situation vs. photograph or word), but

---

[4] In their updated model, Williams et al. (1997, p. 308) suggest that there is no need to assume that the Affective Decision Mechanism is a separate mechanism, but that it may be viewed instead as input units to the Resource Allocation Mechanism (the Task Demand Unit, in PDP terms) being "tagged" with a threat value.

also by individual differences in anxiety (e.g. studies showing that high anxiety is associated with a bias in interpreting ambiguous stimuli as threatening; e.g. Eysenck et al., 1991).

It is further assumed that everyone orients to stimuli that have been subjectively judged as having significant threat value. However, the relationship between subjective stimulus threat value and the direction of the orienting bias does not appear to be linear. Specifically, when stimuli have no threat value, there would be no attentional bias. However, when stimuli are evaluated as having low subjective threat value, then the focus of attention appears to be directed away from the threat. Such avoidance of trivial threat stimuli in the environment would presumably not only be helpful in maintaining attention on current goals, but may also serve as a mood regulation mechanism, i.e. to help preserve a positive mood state. This view seems consistent with findings that low anxious individuals tend to show attentional avoidance of single threat words, photographs of angry facial expressions, and milder threat scenes (e.g. MacLeod, Mathews & Tata, 1986; Bradley et al., 1997a; our unpublished study with MacNamara and Powys). However, as subjective appraisal of threat increases—for example, as a function of increasing objective stimulus threat value and/or individual differences in trait anxiety—then attention is increasingly more likely to be allocated to the salient stimulus. The enhanced subjective appraisal of threat by anxiety-prone individuals would explain why they automatically orient towards objectively low threat stimuli (i.e. such stimuli are appraised as having relatively high threat value which then elicits automatic attentional capture).

This analysis may also account for cognitive differences between anxiety and depression. Thus, an anxious individual would show a preattentive bias for external threat cues (i.e. negative valence + engagement → vigilance for environmental threat). However, when external goal engagement is low or impaired, as in the case of depression or mixed anxiety–depression, the preattentive bias for external threat cues will be absent (i.e. negative valence + disengagement → no orienting bias for environmental threat). Such an explanation is consistent with depression being viewed as an amotivational state associated with increased apathy and reduced interest in external goals and activities.

A preattentive or attentional bias for threat is not necessarily a sign of anxiety-proneness, because it is found in low trait anxious individuals when external stimuli have high threat value. However, the presence of such biases for *mild* threat stimuli, such as words, may be a sign of anxiety vulnerability, without necessarily being a determinant. The primary factor underlying anxiety-proneness may instead be a bias in the appraisal of stimulus threat value. This analysis has clinical implications, for example, in suggesting that anti-anxiety treatments may be more usefully focused at biases in valence evaluation processes (i.e. re-appraisal of threat stimuli and their situational context), rather than directly targeting preattentive or attentional biases.

Nevertheless, preattentive and attentional biases may be important in the *maintenance* of anxiety states. For example, as a result of such biases, minor threat stimuli in the environment may be more likely to enter the focus of attention of anxiety-prone individuals, which would reinforce their perception of the world as being an aversive and unsafe place, and enhance their anxious mood. Moreover, if anxiety-prone individuals automatically orient their attention to minor threats in the environment, but do not maintain their attentional focus on such stimuli sufficiently to allow objective evaluation of them, this might potentiate sensitization and interfere with habituation, and so maintain anxiety in the long-term.

Our discussion has been primarily concerned with the mechanisms involved in preattentive processing of, and initial orienting, to threat stimuli, and their potential role in the development and maintenance of anxiety states. This analysis is clearly not intended to provide a comprehensive account of all cognitive and behavioural phenomena associated with non-clinical and clinical anxiety. Other researchers have focused more on the roles of "meta-cognitive" and controlled verbal processes in mediating anxiety and worry (e.g. Matthews & Wells, this volume) and it is beyond the scope of this chapter to review such approaches. However, the brain systems mediating anxiety and fear responses reflect a basic cross-species motivational mechanism that has evolutionary adaptive value. Given that there are individual differences in anxiety-proneness in other species, it is unlikely that a complete explanation will be provided by cognitive theories that emphasize the role of self-knowledge and controlled verbal processes (for example, see Mineka's, 1985 and Mineka & Zinberg's, 1996, reviews of the contribution of animal models of anxiety disorders). In the long term, an integrated model of anxiety will need to take account of developments from cognitive, motivational and neurobiological perspectives.

ACKNOWLEDGEMENTS

Our research has been supported in part by the Wellcome Trust, Medical Research Council, Pinsent-Darwin Fund and the Meres Trust of St John's College. Karin Mogg holds a Wellcome Senior Research Fellowship in Basic Biomedical Science.

REFERENCES

Allport, A. (1989). Visual attention. In M. I. Posner (ed.), *Foundations of Cognitive Science*. Cambridge, MA: MIT Press.

Bargh, J. A. (1989). Conditional automaticity: vatreties of automatic influence in social perception and cognition. In J. A. Bargh & J. S. Uleman (eds), *Unintended Thought*. New York: Guilford.

Barlow D. H. (1988). *Anxiety and Its Disorders: The Nature and Treatment of Anxiety and Panic*. New York: Guilford.

Beck, A. T. (1976). *Cognitive Therapy and the Emotional Disorders*. New York: International Universities Press.

Beck, A. T., Emery, G. & Greenberg, R. C. (1986). *Anxiety Disorders and Phobias: A Cognitive Perspective*. New York: Basic Books.

Beck, A. T., Rush, A. J., Shaw, B. F. & Emery, G. (1979). *Cognitive Therapy of Depression: A Treatment Manual.* New York: Guilford.

Blaney, P. H. (1986). Affect and memory: a review. *Psychological Bulletin*, **99**, 229–246.

Bower, G. H. (1981). Mood and memory. *American Psychologist*, **36**, 129–148.

Bradley, B. P. & Mathews, A. (1983). Negative self-schemata in clinical depression. *British Journal of Clinical Psychology*, **22**, 173–181.

Bradley, B. P., Mogg, K. & Lee, S. (1997b). Attentional biases for negative information in induced and naturally occurring dysphoria. *Behaviour Research and Therapy*, **35**, 911–927.

Bradley, B. P., Mogg, K. & Millar, N. (1996). Implicit memory bias in clinical and non-clinical depression. *Behaviour Research and Therapy*, **34**, 865–879.

Bradley, B. P., Mogg, K. & Millar, N. (1998a). Overt and covert orienting of attention to emotional faces in anxiety (unpublished manuscript).

Bradley, B. P., Mogg, K. & Williams, R. (1994). Implicit and explicit memory for emotional information in non-clinical subjects. *Behaviour Research and Therapy*, **32**, 65–78.

Bradley, B. P., Mogg, K. & Williams, R. (1995b). Implicit and explicit memory for emotion-congruent information in depression and anxiety. *Behaviour Research and Therapy*, **33**, 755–770.

Bradley, B. P., Mogg, K., Falla, S. J. & Hamilton, L. R. (1998b). Attentional bias for threatening facial expressions in anxiety: manipulation of stimulus duration. *Cognition & Emotion*, **12**, 737–753.

Bradley, B. P., Mogg, K., Millar, N. & White, J. (1995a). Selective processing of negative information: effects of clinical anxiety, concurrent depression, and awareness. *Journal of Abnormal Psychology*, **104**(3), 532–536.

Bradley, B. P., Mogg, K., Millar, N., Bonham-Carter, C., Fergusson, E., Jenkins, J. & Parr, M. (1997a). Attentional biases for emotional faces. *Cognition and Emotion*, **11**, 25–42.

Butler, G., Fennell, M., Robson, P. & Gelder, M. (1991). Comparison of behaviour therapy and cognitive behaviour therapy in the treatment of generalised anxiety disorder. *Journal of Consulting and Clinical Psychology*, **59**, 167–175.

Byrne, A. & Eysenck, M. W. (1995). Trait anxiety, anxious mood and threat detection. *Cognition & Emotion*, **9**, 549–562.

Cheesman, J. & Merikle, P. M. (1985). Word recognition and consciousness. In D. Besner, T. G. Waller & G. E. MacKinnon (eds), *Reading Research: Advances in Theory and Practice* (pp. 311–352). Orlando, FL: Academic Press.

Cheesman, J. & Merickle, P. M. (1986). Distinguishing conscious from unconscious perceptual processes. *Canadian Journal of Psychology*, **40**, 343–367.

Christianson, S. A., Saisa, J. & Silfvenius, H. (1995). The right hemisphere recognises the bad guys. *Cognition & Emotion*, **9**, 309–324.

Cohen, J. D., Dunbar, K. & McClelland, J. L. (1990). On the control of automatic processes: a parallel distributed processing account of the Stroop effect. *Psychological Review*, **97**, 332–361.

Eysenck, H. J. & Eysenck, S. B. G. (1969). *Personality Structure and Measurement.* London: Routledge.

Eysenck, M. W. (1992). *Anxiety: The Cognitive Perspective.* Hove: Erlbaum.

Eysenck, M., Mogg, K., May, J., Richards, A. & Mathews, A. (1991). Bias in the interpretation of sentences related to threat in anxiety. *Journal of Abnormal Psychology*, **100**, 144–150.

Foa, E. B. & McNally, R. J. (1986). Sensitivity to feared stimuli in obsessive-compulsives: a dichotic listening analysis. *Cognitive Therapy and Research*, **10**, 477–486.

Fowles, D. C. (1994). A motivational theory of psychopathology. In W. D. Spaulding (ed.), *Integrative Views of Motivation, Cognition and Emotion.* Vol. 41, Nebraska Symposium on Motivation. Lincoln, NE: Lincoln Press.

Fox, E. (1993). Allocation of visual attention and anxiety. *Cognition and Emotion*, **7**, 207–215.

Gotlib, I. H. & Cane, D. B. (1987). Construct accessibility and clinical depression: a longitudinal investigation. *Journal of Abnormal Psychology*, **96**, 199–204.

Graf, P. & Mandler, G. (1984). Activation makes words more accessible, but not necessarily more retrievable. *Journal of Verbal Learning and Verbal Behaviour*, **23**, 553–568.

Gray, J. A. (1985). Issues in the neuropsychology of anxiety. In A. H. Tuma & J. D. Maser (eds), *Anxiety and the Anxiety Disorders*. Hillsdale, NJ: Erlbaum.

Gray, J. A. (1990). Brain systems that mediate both emotion and cognition. *Cognition & Emotion*, **4**, 269–288.

Hansen, C. H. & Hansen, R. D. (1988). Finding the face in the crowd: an anger superiority effect. *Journal of Personality and Social Psychology*, **54**, 917–924.

Holender, D. (1986). Semantic activation without conscious identification in dichotic listening, parafoveal vision, and visual masking: a survey and appraisal. *Behavioral and Brain Sciences*, **9**, 1–66.

Kemp-Wheeler, S. M. & Hill, A. B. (1988). Semantic priming without awareness: Some methodological considerations and replications. *Quarterly Journal of Experimental Psychology*, **40A**, 671–692.

Kindt, M. & Brosschot, J. F. (1997). Phobia-related cognitive bias for pictorial and linguistic stimuli. *Journal of Abnormal Psychology*, **106**, 644–648.

LaBerge, D. (1995). *Attentional Processing*. Cambridge, MA: Harvard University Press.

Lang, P. J., Bradley, M. M. & Cuthbert, B. N. (1990). Emotion, attention and the startle reflex. *Psychological Review*, **97**, 377–398.

Lang, P. J., Bradley, M. M. & Cuthbert, B. N. (1995). *International Affective Picture System: Technical Manual and Affective Ratings*. Florida State University.

Lavy, E., van den Hout, M. & Arntz, A. (1993). Attentional bias and spider phobia: conceptual and clinical issues. *Behaviour Research and Therapy*, **31**, 17–24.

LeDoux, J. E. (1995). Emotion: clues from the brain. *Annual Review of Psychology*, **46**, 209–235.

LeDoux, J. E. (1996). *The Emotional Brain*. New York: Simon & Schuster.

MacLeod, C. & Hagan, R. (1992). Individual differences in the selective processing of threatening information, and emotional responses to a stressful life event. *Behaviour Research and Therapy*, **30**, 151–161.

MacLeod C. & Mathews, A. (1988). Anxiety and the allocation of attention to threat. *Quarterly Journal of Experimental Psychology*, **40**, 653–670.

MacLeod C., Mathews, A. & Tata, P. (1986). Attentional bias in emotional disorders. *Journal of Abnormal Psychology*, **95**, 15–20.

MacLeod, C. & Rutherford, E. M. (1992). Anxiety and the selective processing of emotional information: mediating roles of awareness, trait and state variables, and personal relevance of stimulus materials. *Behaviour Research and Therapy*, **30**, 479–491.

Mathews, A. (1990). Why worry? The cognitive function of anxiety. *Behaviour Research and Therapy*, **28**, 455–468.

Mathews, A. (1993). Biases in processing emotional information. *The Psychologist*, **6**, 493–499.

Mathews, A. & MacLeod, C. (1985). Selective processing of threat cues in anxiety states. *Behaviour Research and Therapy*, **23**, 563–569.

Mathews, A. & MacLeod, C. (1986). Discrimination of threat cues without awareness in anxiety states. *Journal of Abnormal Psychology*, **95**, 131–138.

Mathews, A. & MacLeod, C. (1994). Cognitive approaches to emotion and emotional disorders. *Annual Review of Psychology*, **45**, 25–50.

Mathews, A., Mogg, K., Kentish, J. & Eysenck, M. (1995). Effects of psychological treatment on cognitive bias in generalised anxiety disorder. *Behaviour Research and Therapy*, **33**, 293–303.

Mathews, A., Ridgeway, V. & Williamson, D. A. (1996). Evidence for attention to threatening stimuli in depression. *Behaviour Research and Therapy*, **34**, 695–705.

Mattia, J. I., Heimberg, R. G. & Hope, D. A. (1993). The revised Stroop color-naming task in social phobics. *Behaviour Research and Therapy*, **31**, 305–314.

McNally, R. (1995). Automaticity and the anxiety disorders. *Behaviour Research & Therapy*, **33**, 747–754.

Mineka, S. (1985). Animal models of anxiety-based disorders: their usefulness and limitations. In A. H. Tuma & J. D. Maser (eds), *Anxiety and the Anxiety Disorders*. Hillsdale, NJ: Erlbaum.

Mineka, S. & Zinberg, R. (1996). Conditioning and ethological models of anxiety disorders: stress-in-dynamic-*con*text anxiety models. In D. A. Hope (ed.), *Perspectives on Anxiety, Panic and Fear*. Nebraska Symposium on Motivation, Vol. 43. Lincoln, NE: University of Nebraska Press.

Mogg, K. & Bradley, B. P. (1998a). A cognitive-motivational analysis of anxiety. *Behaviour Research & Therapy*, **36**, 809–848.

Mogg, K. & Bradley, B. P. (1998b). Some methodological issues in assessing atttentional biases for threat faces in anxiety: a replication study using a modified version of the probe detection task. *Behaviour Research & Therapy* (in press).

Mogg, K. & Bradley, B. P. (1998c). Orienting of attention to threatening facial expressions presented under conditions of restricted awareness (unpublished manuscript).

Mogg, K., Bradley, B. P. & Hallowell, N. (1994). Attentional bias to threat: roles of trait anxiety, stressful events, and awareness. *Quarterly Journal of Experimental Psychology*, **47A**, 841–864.

Mogg, K., Bradley, B. P., MacNamara, J., Powys, M., Rawlinson, H. & Seiffer, A. (1998d). Selective attention to threat: a test of two cognitive models of anxiety (unpublished manuscript).

Mogg, K., Bradley, B. P. & Millar, N. (in preparation). Direction of gaze to threatening facial expressions in generalized anxiety disorder and depression.

Mogg, K., Bradley, B. P., de Bono, J. & Painter, M. (1997). Time course of attentional bias for threat information in non-clinical anxiety. *Behaviour Research and Therapy*, **35**, 297–303.

Mogg, K., Bradley, B. P., Millar, N. & White, J. (1995a). Cognitive bias in generalized anxiety disorder: a follow-up study. *Behaviour Research and Therapy*, **33**, 927–935.

Mogg, K., Bradley, B. P., Williams, R. & Mathews, A. (1993a). Subliminal processing of emotional information in anxiety and depression. *Journal of Abnormal Psychology*, **102**, 304–311.

Mogg, K., Bradley, B. P. & Williams, R. (1995b). Attentional bias in anxiety and depression: the role of awareness. *British Journal of Clinical Psychology*, **34**, 17–36.

Mogg, K., Kentish, J. & Bradley, B. P. (1993b). Effects of anxiety and awareness on colour-identification latencies for emotional words. *Behaviour Research & Therapy*, **31**, 559–567.

Mogg, K., Mathews, A. & Eysenck, M. (1992). Attentional bias in clinical anxiety states. *Cognition and Emotion*, **6**, 149–159.

Mogg, K., Mathews, A. & Weinman, J. (1987). Memory bias in clinical anxiety. *Journal of Abnormal Psychology*, **96**, 94–98.

Mogg, K., Mathews, A. & Weinman, J. (1989). Selective processing of threat cues in clinical anxiety states: a replication. *Behaviour Research and Therapy*, **27**, 317–323.

Mogg, K., Mathews, A., Bird, C. & Macgregor-Morris, R. (1990). Effects of stress and anxiety on the processing of threat stimuli. *Journal of Personality and Social Psychology*, **59**, 1230–1237.

Navon, D. & Margalit, B. (1983). Allocation of attention according to informativeness in visual recognition, *Quarterly Journal of Experimental Psychology*, **35A**, 497–512.

Nolen-Hoeksema, S. (1991). Responses to depression and their effects on the duration of depressed mood. *Journal of Abnormal Psychology*, **100**, 569–582.

Oatley, K. & Johnson-Laird, P. (1987).   Towards a cognitive theory of emotions. *Cognition & Emotion*, **1**, 29–50.

Öhman, A. (1993).   Fear and anxiety as emotional phenomena: clinical phenomenology, evolutionary perspectives, and information processing mechanisms. In M. Lewis & J. M. Haviland (eds), *Handbook of Emotions*, New York: Guilford.

Öhman, A. & Soares, J. J. F. (1993).   On the automaticity of phobic fear: conditioned skin conductance responses to masked phobic stimuli. *Journal of Abnormal Psychology*, **102**, 121–132.

Öhman, A. & Soares, J. J. F. (1994).   "Unconscious anxiety": phobic responses to masked stimuli. *Journal of Abnormal Psychology*, **103**, 231–240.

Posner, M. I. & Petersen, S. E. (1990).   The attention system of the human brain. *Annual Review of Neuroscience*, **13**, 25–42.

Posner, M. I., Snyder, C. R. & Davidson, B. J. (1980).   Attention and the detection of signals. *Journal of Experimental Psychology: General*, **109**, 160–174.

Pratto, F. (1994).   Consciousness and automatic evaluation. In Niedenthal. P. M. & Kitayama, S. (eds), *The Heart's Eye*. San Diego, CA: Academic Press.

Rachman, S. (1980).   Emotional processing. *Behaviour Research and Therapy*, **18**, 51–60.

Rapee, R. M. (1991).   Generalised anxiety disorder: a review of clinical features and theoretical concepts. *Clinical Psychology Review*, **11**, 419–440.

Scott, K. M., Mogg, K. & Bradley, B. P. (1998).   Masked Semantic priming of emotional information in subclinical depression (unpublished manuscript).

Segal, Z. V., Truchon, C., Gemar, M., Guirguis, M. & Horowitz, L. M. (1995).   A priming methodology for studying self-representation in major depressive disorder. *Journal of Abnormal Psychology*, **104**, 205–213.

Simons, A. D., Murphy, G. E., Levine, J. L. & Wetzel, R. D. (1986).   Cognitive therapy and pharmacotherapy for depression. *Archives of General Psychiatry*, **43**, 43–50.

Tellegen, A. (1985).   Structures of mood and personality and their relevance to assessing anxiety, with an emphasis on self-report. In A. H. Tuma & J. D. Maser (eds), *Anxiety and the Anxiety Disorders*. Hillsdale, NJ: Erlbaum.

van den Hout, M., Tenney, N., Huygens, K. & de Jong, P. (1997).   Preconscious processing bias in specific phobia. *Behaviour Research & Therapy*, **35**, 29–34.

van den Hout, M., Tenney, N., Huygens, K., Merkelbach, H. & Kindt, M. (1995).   Responding to subliminal threat cues is related to trait anxiety and emotional vulnerability: a successful replication of MacLeod and Hagan (1992). *Behaviour Research and Therapy*, **33**, 451–454.

Watson, D. & Clark, L. A. (1984).   Negative affectivity: the disposition to experience aversive emotional states. *Psychological Bulletin*, **96**, 465–490.

Watson, D. & Tellegen A. (1985).   Toward a consensual structure of mood. *Psychological Bulletin*, **98**, 219–235.

Watson, D., Weber, K., Assenheimer, J. S., Clark, L. A., Strauss, M. E. & McCormick, R. A. (1995).   Testing a tripartite model: I. Evaluating the convergent and discriminant validity of anxiety and depression scales. *Journal of Abnormal Psychology*, **104**, 3–14.

Williams, J. M. G., Mathews, A. & MacLeod, C. (1996).   The emotional Stroop task and psychopathology. *Psychological Bulletin*, **120**, 3–24.

Williams, J. M. G., Watts, F. N., MacLeod, C. & Mathews, A. (1988).   *Cognitive Psychology and Emotional Disorders*. Chichester: Wiley.

Williams, J. M. G., Watts, F. N., MacLeod, C. & Mathews, A. (1997).   *Cognitive Psychology and Emotional Disorders*, 2nd edn. Chichester: Wiley.

Chapter 9

The Cognitive Science of Attention and Emotion

Gerald Matthews*
University of Dundee, Dundee, UK
and
Adrian Wells
University of Manchester, Manchester, UK

INTRODUCTION

Emotion and attention are intimately linked. States of emotion influence both the contents of consciousness and performance on tasks requiring selection of stimuli or intensive concentration. In reviewing the relationship between emotion and attention, this chapter has three principal aims. First, we provide a brief overview of the cognitive science of attention and emotion, which focuses on both processing mechanisms and strategies for regulation of processing. We identify issues relating to automaticity and executive control as being of critical importance in theory development. We focus mainly on negative emotions, which have two distinct types of effect: *impairment* effects associated with reduced quality or efficiency of performance, and *bias* effects associated with prioritization of processing of stimuli of negative valence. Second, we consider how attentional disturbance and emotion may be interrelated within a comprehensive multi-level model, Wells & Matthews's (1994b, 1996) Self-Regulatory Executive Function (S-REF) model. Third, we review clinical applications of the model.

Various definitions of attention have been provided (e.g. Posner, 1975), but central to the concept is the *prioritization* of some aspects of processing, possibly

---

* To whom correspondence should be addressed.

Handbook of Cognition and Emotion. Edited by T. Dalgleish and M. Power.
© 1999 John Wiley & Sons Ltd.

at the expense of other aspects. Prioritization may be necessitated by capacity limits of the processing system, although the extent of limits on stimulus analysis remains controversial (Van der Heijden, 1992). *Selective attention* refers to the prioritization of one or more concurrently presented stimuli or categories of stimuli. Paradigms for investigating selection typically involve multiple information channels, such that the person must select a single channel on the basis of stimulus properties, or switch between channels in searching for target stimuli (e.g. Broadbent, 1971). It is useful to distinguish selective attention from the *intensive* attention seen when a person concentrates and applies effort to a task. At one level, intensive attention is a general prioritization of task-related processing. More subtly, it might be seen as a prioritization of processing at certain time periods, balanced by reduced performance efficiency at other times.

Emotion may be related to both selective and intensive aspects of attention. Conscious distress is often accompanied by bias in selective attention towards threat or other negative stimuli. Studies such as those of Watts et al. (1986) and Mathews & MacLeod (1985) pioneered a highly productive decade of research on performance-based measures of attentional bias. There is also a longer-established literature showing that anxiety and depression tend to impair performance on tasks without overt affective content, especially attentionally or cognitively demanding tasks (Eysenck, 1992; Hartlage et al., 1993). Such effects are intensive to the extent that negative emotion reduces total processing capacity or effort. However, when deficits reflect diversion of attention from the task to internal worries, they reflect a change in selective attention and prioritization of internally-sourced stimuli. Both degradation of attentional efficiency and bias in selection may contribute to the disturbances of conscious awareness central to everyday emotional distress and to emotional disorders.

The view we shall take in this chapter is that there may be multiple attentional mechanisms whose functioning is linked to emotional states. Even "attentional bias" may be an excessively monolithic construct; the biases seen on different selective attention tasks do not necessarily derive from a common processing mechanism. Similarly, various discrete mechanisms are likely to contribute to attentional efficiency, such as the multiple resources distinguished by Revelle (1993). This perspective is compatible with contemporary views of attention, which emphasise its modularity (Allport, 1989; Pashler, 1994), and with "cognitive patterning" models of stress research (Hockey, 1984), which describe effects of "stressors", such as anxiety, in terms of patterns of performance change across several independent indicators of cognitive functioning.

PROCESSING MODELS AND LEVELS OF EXPLANATION

There is a basic difficulty in interpreting experimental findings linking emotion to attention: any given finding is open to radically different types of explanation.

Suppose that we find that spider phobics are slow to name the colours of spider-related words like WEB (an emotional Stroop effect). Classical cognitive science theory (Pylyshyn, 1984) distinguishes three levels of explanation, which we shall call the biological, the architectural and the knowledge levels. First, the bias may be explained in terms of properties of the neural hardware. For example, in spider phobics, the neurones of an innate spider-detection circuit might be particularly prone to fire. Second, the formal properties of the internal "programming language" of the brain might explain the bias. Perhaps computations on internal codes representing spider words execute more quickly in spider phobics, increasing the probability of interference with response to the colour stimulus. Third, bias might be attributed to the person's goals; a spider phobic might choose to monitor for spider stimuli. These distinctions are critical for any cognitive explanation of empirical phenomena, but have been rather neglected in studies of emotion and attention. People may differ in attentional functions either because the processing routines supporting attention differ, or because attention serves differing goals.

In this chapter, we are concerned especially with differentiating architectural and knowledge-based explanations. Biological explanations for bias or abnormality in attentional functioning have some promise, as articulated in most detail by Gray's (1982) theory of anxiety and septo-hippocampal function. There is also good evidence for an inherited component to negative affectivity (Loehlin, 1992), buttressed by the recent finding of an association between a serotonin transporter gene and anxious personality (Lesch et al., 1996). However, so far, the biological approach has made only a limited contribution to understanding the performance correlates of negative emotion in human subjects (Wells & Matthews, 1994b, 1996). Next, we look in more detail at explanations for relationships between emotion and cognition.

Experimental studies of emotion and cognition support inferences about component processes and the flow of information between them: the *cognitive architecture* which supports processing of emotional stimuli (Newell, Rosenbloom & Laird, 1989). Newell et al. and Pylyshyn (1984) require the architecture to be symbolic in nature, but, given the successes of connectionist models using distributed representations, and other evidence for non-propositional coding of affective information (e.g. Matthews & Harley, 1996), it may be unwise to impose this constraint. The architecture may contain processing components which are sensitive to the emotional content of stimuli. There is convincing evidence for a general tendency, across all individuals, for emotional stimuli to be prioritized at early, "pre-attentive" stages of processing (Kitayama, 1991). One of the properties of the architecture is that the computations supporting stimulus analysis are affected by stimulus valence. Furthermore, trait and/or state emotion may influence system parameters, and hence the outputs of computation. Williams et al. (1988) describe a cognitive architecture comprising a series of processing stages. Observable bias in response is generated by variation with emotion of the sensitivity of discrete processes, such as allocating a threat value to a stimulus. Alternatively, the architecture may be modelled by a network, within which nodes representing emotion-related constructs vary in activation level (Bower, 1981; Ingram, 1984). The normal methods of cognitive psychology may be used to generate and test competing predictions from such models, typically by testing for moderating effects of task parameters. There is now a considerable literature in this area, based on tasks such as the emotional Stroop.

The knowledge level raises rather different questions, relating to intentionality, meaning and the design of the processing system for handling adaptive challenges. First, we may ask whether people's goals and self-knowledge relate to attentional functioning. In general, the answer is affirmative. As Neisser (1976) pointed out, attention is governed by a *perception–action cycle* within which attention is directed by a schema, which is modified by subsequent perception. In the clinical context too, Beck (1967) emphasized the importance of goals and beliefs about personal goal attainment. Emotional disorder is closely linked to people's appraisals of themselves as failing in their attempts to meet significant goals such as forming relationships, preserving personal security and maintaining self-worth (e.g. Oatley, 1992). Further questions then arise concerning the origins of knowledge: how has the system been engineered by genes and learning to pursue specific goals? In part, at least, attentional bias may be a consequence of the person's self-knowledge and beliefs about his/her place in the world, constructs requiring analysis at the knowledge level.

The knowledge level explanation contrasts with the assumption of architectural explanations, that attentional bias is something of a computational accident, which feeds into the person's self-knowledge, but is not affected by it. People unfortunate enough to have sensitive threat-detection processes show attentional bias, and, in consequence, are more prone to anxiety. In this chapter, we will argue against this view, emphasizing instead the role of self-knowledge in guiding attention in pursuit of personal goals (see Wells & Matthews, 1994b, 1996, for a more detailed exposition).

AUTOMATICITY AND EXECUTIVE CONTROL

This review is especially concerned with explanations for performance on attentional tasks, and so we must start from a description of the relevant cognitive architecture. One of the key distinctions in the psychology of attention is that between automatic and controlled processing (see Schneider & Detweiler, 1987, for a computational account). Automatic processing is reflexively triggered by incoming stimuli, whereas controlled processing is effected by a discrete supervisory system (e.g. Norman & Shallice, 1985). These *levels of control* of attention appear to be involuntary and voluntary, respectively. Additional assumptions are often made that controlled processing requires a greater allocation of attentional resources and is more accessible to conscious awareness (Schneider, Dumais & Shiffrin, 1984). Recent work on control architectures, such as Cohen, Dunbar & McClelland's (1990) connectionist analysis, envisages a continuum of automaticity, depending on the strength of interventions of the supervisory executive.

The criteria for automaticity permit experimental studies which are informative about effects of emotion on automatic and controlled processing. For example, Schneider, Dumais & Shiffrin's (1984) search paradigm has been used to demonstrated controlled processing deficits in depressives (Brand & Jolles, 1987) and in normal individuals low in energetic arousal (Matthews, Davies & Lees, 1990). However, studies of this kind provide only a partial explanation for empirical phenomena. It is necessary, of course, to describe the architecture which supports controlled processing, as Shallice (1988) does for the various specific executive routines which implement voluntary control. To understand why the person has chosen to use a particular controlled processing routine, we must also investigate the person's goals and beliefs about the task. In this chapter, we will emphasize especially the self-knowledge and self-regulatory goals (e.g. Carver & Scheier, 1990) that influence controlled processing and attentional functioning.

Demonstrations that emotions influence automatic processing are similarly limited in explanatory content. It is often overlooked that there are several routes to automaticity of processing of affective stimuli. First, there may be biologically-based and possibly inherited individual differences in the functioning of brain systems concerned with processing affective stimuli, such as Gray's (1982) septo-hippocampal system, or the cortico-amygdalar circuits described by LeDoux (1995). Second, automatic processing of specific stimuli may be learnt through repeated exposure to consistent S–R contingencies (Schneider, Dumais & Shiffrin, 1984). Furthermore, learned automaticity may result from a personal choice to seek out specific situations characterized by consistency, so, again, we cannot afford to neglect the knowledge level. In the clinical context, these distinctions have treatment implications. If anxiety is attributed to an automatic prioritization of threat stimuli, should it be treated with drugs, or with attempts at counter-conditioning, or through discussing with patients why they choose to expose themselves to damaging life experiences?

Levels of Control of Attentional Efficiency

In this section, we discuss evidence on the level of control of emotion effects on attention. The problem of control may be seen initially as one of cognitive architecture: are processes sensitive to emotional state located within involuntary or voluntary processing components? In the case of interference effects, there is a reasonable consensus that the worry associated with negative emotions such as anxiety and depression impairs controlled processing, which is diverted from the task at hand to processing the content of worries (e.g. Hartlage et al., 1993). The deficit has been variously characterized as one of attentional resources (Sarason, 1988), working memory (Eysenck, 1992) or task-directed effort (Humphreys & Revelle, 1984). It is demonstrated within a variety of specifically attentional paradigms, including visual search (Mathews et al., 1990), reaction time to secondary task stimuli (Eysenck, 1992) and vigilance (Geen, 1985). Negative emotion may also impair complex tasks such as problem-solving (Hartlage et al., 1993), which presumably tap a variety of specific processes. The generality of detrimental effects of anxiety and depression across a range of qualitatively different tasks is suggestive of a resource mechanism (e.g. Humphreys & Revelle, 1984). So, too, is the tendency for anxiety effects to become more detrimental as task demands increase (Eysenck, 1982). However, there have been few attempts to test resource explanations against alternative hypotheses using the rigorous dual-task methods necessary to demonstrate resource limitation (see Wickens, 1992).

As discussed in the previous section, deficits in controlled processing are open to alternative explanations. One type of explanation for impairment of performance in negative emotion states refers to fundamental properties of the architecture. In non-clinical samples, dual-task studies suggest that states of low energy and tiredness are associated with impairment of controlled processing on demanding attentional and working memory tasks (Matthews & Westerman, 1994). High energy subjects may simply have more resources available for this type of task, irrespective of strategy (Matthews, 1992). In other cases, knowledge level explanation seems more appropriate. Several studies show that, somewhat paradoxically, performance impairment in states of negative emotion may be reduced by increasing task demands (Matthews, Sparkes & Bygrave, 1996). For example, depressives have particular difficulties in effortful performance (Johnson & Magaro, 1987), but show improved intelligence test performance when a secondary digit-repetition task is added (Foulds, 1952). These findings are instances of more general "challenge effects", in which, paradoxically, perform-ance improves with increased task demands (e.g. Bakan, 1959). It is difficult to envisage plausible formal properties of the architecture which might account for accentuation of such effects in states of negative emotion. In fact, a key factor seems to be *self-focus of attention*, the diversion of attention from the external world to internal stimuli (Ingram, 1990). Self-focus tends to accentuate perform-ance deficits associated with negative emotion. Carver et al. (1983) manipulated self-focus experimentally, and then had subjects perform an anagram task. The self-focus induction impaired performance only in subjects high in test anxiety. Such individuals are prone not just to anxious emotion, but also to diversion of attention from the task to processing personal concerns and worries, leading to performance impairment (Wine, 1981). Deficit may result from a conflict between task goals and self-regulatory goals which drive worry and rumination. In other words, an apparent loss of efficiency of intensive attention is actually due to changes in selection which must be explained at the knowledge level. For example, changing task goals may sometimes enhance performance, even if the task becomes more demanding.

Levels of Control of Attentional Bias

The level of control of attentional bias effects is much less clear. Many empirical studies are concerned simply with demonstrating bias effects, but do not test the

moderation of bias by task parameters relevant to attentional theory. Performance on tasks such as the emotional Stroop probably reflects both automatic and
controlled processing. Delayed response on Stroop-like tasks may reflect both
the strength of involuntary response tendencies competing with the correct
response, and the level of voluntary effort applied to suppress the competing
response. There is a case that attentional bias is automatic in nature (e.g.
McNally, 1995), for which the strongest evidence is demonstrations of emotional
Stroop effects with "subliminal" stimuli (see Mogg & Bradley, this volume).
We will not repeat here criticisms of subliminal Stroop studies we have made
elsewhere, which focus on the methodological difficulties and limited implications for processing models of demonstrations of "unconscious" processing
(Matthews & Wells, in press; Wells & Matthews, 1994b).

In addition, the nature and extent of attentional bias may differ across
different types of processing. MacLeod & Mathews (1991) claimed that simple
detection and recognition tasks with a single source of stimuli were insensitive to
emotion. Demonstrations of mood-related bias in tasks such as near-threshold
word recognition (Small & Robins, 1988) and lexical decision (Matthews &
Southall, 1991; Matthews, Pitcaithly & Mann, 1995) suggest that this view is
somewhat overstated. As previously discussed, early, pre-attentive processing is
primarily sensitive to stimulus valence, but individual differences are sometimes
observed. Matthews, Pitcaithly & Mann (1995) investigated priming for word
pairs of differing valence using a lexical decision task. The study suggested a
general enhancement of automatic priming of negative word pairs, compared
with neutral and positive stimuli. In addition, an "extreme groups" analysis of
subjects selected on the basis of state mood scores showed a mood-congruent bias
in priming, such that unhappy subjects showed greater priming on negative word
pairs. Matthews et al. suggest that mood state "fine-tunes" the extent of the
general processing advantage for negative stimuli.

Nevertheless, we agree with MacLeod & Mathews (1991) that attentional bias
on tasks with an explicit selection component may well be more reliable than bias
in single stimulus detection. It may also differ in level of control. Next,
we consider evidence for bias in selective attention operating at the upper rather
than the lower level of control. Evidence of this kind requires the use of
paradigms within which the two levels of control may be clearly distinguished.
Studies of lexical decision suggest that priming at stimulus onset asynchronies
(SOAs) of less than 200–300 ms is involuntary, but priming at longer SOAs is
voluntarily controlled on the basis of expectancies, although a third mechanism,
post-access checking, may also contribute to priming effects (Neely, 1991).
Richards & French (1992) ran a lexical decision study in which trials included
presentation of ambiguous words as primes (threat/non-threat homographs),
followed by target words associated with the threatening meaning of the homo-
graph. Trait anxious subjects showed enhanced priming by the threat meaning
only at the longer SOAs used in this study (750 and 1250 ms), and not at the
shortest SOA of 500 ms. Studies of primed word naming (Calvo & Castillo, 1997)
and of the emotional Stroop (Segal & Vella, 1990) also show biasing of priming
only at the longer SOAs characteristic of an upper level of mechanism.

Other studies show that attentional bias varies with contextual factors other than priming stimuli. Bargh (1992) reports briefly that the context provided by pre-task administration of a depression scale influences subsequent emotional Stroop effects. Richards et al. (1992) compared emotional Stroop effects across blocked trials, with words grouped into blocks by meaning, and mixed trials, in which word order was quasi-random. If bias depends on the short-duration automatic activation processes demonstrated in lexical decision studies, bias should be found irrespective of trial blocking. However, they obtained the normal trait anxiety bias only when trials were blocked by word type, affording the subject the opportunity to form an expectancy concerning subsequent stimuli. Development over time of the attentional bias found with visuospatial attention tasks is also suggestive of an expectancy-based effect (Broadbent & Broadbent, 1988). Fox (1996) reports three studies requiring subjects to discriminate digit stimuli, presented concurrently with potentially distracting threat words. When stimuli were masked to prevent conscious awareness, attentional bias was sensitive to various contextual factors. Bias was found only when distractors were within focal attention, masked and unmasked distractors were randomly intermixed, and masked trials were presented following unmasked trials. Anxious subjects were not "eternally vigilant" for threat, in that bias appeared to be contingent upon prior conscious identification of threat stimuli. More subtle strategic effects may also operate: anxious individuals tend to use linguistic rather than image-based strategies for processing threat-related sentences (Richards, French & Randall, 1995). Fine-grained analysis of the time-course of reading ambiguous sentences shows that anxiety-related bias in interpreting ambiguous words is associated with strategic processing following initial lexical access (Calvo, Eysenck & Castillo, 1997).

An alternative approach is to simulate computational models of attentional bias generated by different mechanisms. A recent simulation study of the emotional Stroop (Matthews & Harley, 1996) compared different connectionist models for bias, using standard three-level back-propagation networks based on an earlier study of the standard Stroop effect (Cohen, Dunbar & McClelland, 1990). Three fundamentally different types of model were compared with an unbiased baseline model. The first model was an automatic processing model of bias in which the activation induced in input units by threat stimuli was amplified, rather as in the Williams et al. (1988) stage model of bias. This model might also serve as an analogue to biologically-based individual differences in threat sensitivity. In fact, although this mechanism disrupted colour-naming of threatening stimuli, it also disrupted reading of emotional words. Anxiety does not seem to affect speed of reading threat words (Martin, Williams & Clark, 1991), so the model is inadequate. The second model was concerned with the introduction of bias through exposure to threat stimuli: learned as opposed to innate automatic bias. The network was given extra training on emotional stimuli, but this manipulation failed to influence emotional Stroop interference. The third model investigated upper level control. It was supposed that people may choose to monitor for threats as a task distinct from word-reading and colour-naming. The architecture of the model, as in Cohen, Dunbar & McClelland's (1990) study, included network "task demand" units implementing top-down voluntary control of each task through modulation of activation responses to input. Activation of the task demand unit for threat monitoring during colour-naming generated an emotional Stroop effect, but there was no interference between threat monitoring and reading emotional words. Hence, the simulation, although highly simplified with respect to reality, suggested that the emotional Stroop effect may result from anxious individuals voluntarily monitoring for threat while concurrently performing the laboratory task. Although response to Stroop stimuli is a direct outcome of lower-level activation processes, these processes are biased by upper-level control.

BEYOND THE COGNITIVE ARCHITECTURE: BIAS AT THE KNOWLEDGE LEVEL

So far, we have argued that effects of negative emotion on both intensive and selective aspects of attention are primarily associated with the processing routines which implement voluntary control. Such an explanation is incomplete: we must also address the knowledge level problem of why emotion influences voluntary control. The basic claim made here is that the cognitive architecture is used to meet somewhat different adaptive goals, depending on emotional state and personality. In other words, bias to threat derives from a configuration of processing, which has adaptive benefits in at least some environments. Matthews & Dorn (1995) propose that the bundle of processing functions associated with trait anxiety and neuroticism is adaptive in environments in which threats are subtle or disguised. Such environments require both active monitoring for threat, and at least a certain amount of "worry" in analysing and reflecting on ambiguous stimuli. As Eysenck (1992) has argued, the system may have the overall goal of hypervigilance for threat, supported by a variety of processing functions independent at the information-processing level. In many cases, pursuit of threat-monitoring goals may be maladaptive. When threats are obvious or absent, threat-monitoring may distract from other, more adaptive processing activities.

To explore the adaptive basis for attentional bias further, we must consider the anxious person's motivations and goals. Several authors, notably Carver & Scheier (1981, 1990), have identified self-regulatory goals as being of critical importance in stress and anxiety. People are motivated to reduce discrepancies between their current status and personal and social standards (Higgins, 1990). Negative emotion may derive both from unrealistic goals, as shown by the association between perfectionism and depression (Hewitt & Flett, 1993), and, perhaps more generally, from appraisals of failure to meet goals. Oatley & Johnson-Laird (1987) propose that emotional states may derive from evaluation of current goal status: anxiety reflects a threat to a self-preservation goal, for example. Stable predispositions to negative emotion may derive from self-beliefs pertaining to goal failure. Affective disorder patients are characterized by beliefs of personal inefficacy, from which lack of self-worth may be inferred, and beliefs that their self-efficacy will not improve in the future (e.g. Beck, 1967). Stability of personality may derive to some degree from stability of self-knowledge held in long-term memory.

Cognitive theories of negative emotion, such as Beck's (1967) schema theory, are limited in that they do not specify computationally how the behaviours driven by self-regulatory goals are expressed as objective performance measures. The interface between self-knowledge and architecture is not explicit. The key bridging construct is that of *strategy*: voluntary choice of controlled processing routines to meet a particular goal. Strategy selection drives the use of the architecture to support specific processing sequences. Strategies implemented when self-regulatory goals are threatened may be described as coping strategies. As specified by the transactional model of stress (Lazarus & Folkman, 1984), it is useful to distinguish emotion-focused coping, directed towards re-appraisal of the source of stress, and problem- or task-focused coping, directed towards altering external reality. Both classes of strategy have implications for attention (Matthews & Wells, 1996). Task-focused coping may directly influence the efficiency or style of performance as the person voluntarily alters his/her behaviour. Task-focused coping may affect the intensive aspect of attention, as the person mobilizes more resources. It may also influence selective aspects if the person changes strategy to perform more effectively: "working smarter" rather than working harder (Kluger & DeNisi, 1996). In negative emotion states, task-focused coping may or may not be adaptive. As Eysenck (1992) has argued, anxiety may be associated with compensatory, task-directed effort which tends to reduce performance impairment. However, Matthews & Wells (1996) suggest that most clinical conditions related to negative affect are characterized by a task-focused strategy of threat monitoring, with the nature of the threat varying with the particular condition, and the idiosyncratic concerns of the individual. Attentional bias may be a consequence of this threat monitoring strategy, implemented through biasing task demand units in a connectionist network, as described previously (Matthews & Harley, 1996).

The distressed person is often prone to use emotion-focused coping strategies, such as rumination on problems. Such strategies tend to focus attention on the self, and may divert processing effort away from the task at hand, as described by Sarason's (1988) "cognitive interference" theory of test anxiety. There is some controversy over which specific processing functions are impaired, such as resources or working memory (e.g. Eysenck, 1992). The present analysis emphasizes the origins of cognitive interference in conflict between task-related and self-regulatory goals, rather than any specific processing-level construct. Wells & Matthews (1994b) also emphasize the importance of meta-cognition in influencing strategy. Generalized anxiety disorder (GAD) patients may worry because they believe it to be an effective strategy for dealing with their problems (Wells, 1995, 1997b).

In general, prediction of performance on attentional tasks requires both a specification of how self-beliefs and goals influence formulation of a coping strategy, and a computational specification of the implementation of the strategy. Processing may perhaps be characterized as an outflow from strategy selection to performance in the context of a brief laboratory study, but not in real life. As Neisser's (1976) concept of the perception–action cycle indicates, feedback from performing tasks or activities modifies the "schema" which initiates further behaviours. The transactional model of stress (Lazarus & Folkman, 1984) emphasizes the dynamic nature of stressful encounters, such that the person's appraisals of his/her coping efforts modify his/her beliefs about the encounter, and perhaps also more general self-knowledge. One of the critical features which distinguishes everyday stress reactions from clinical disorder is the tendency for pathology to be associated with "vicious circles" of appraisal and action which serve to perpetuate the disorder. For example, depressed patients generate negative interpersonal cycles, which confirm their sense of lack of self-worth (Coyne, 1976). Similarly, panic disorder patients, by monitoring for signs of ill-health, progressively increase their sensitivity to somatic anxieties. A more subtle instance derives from the "rebound" of unpleasant thoughts which the person has attempted actively to suppress (McNally & Ricciardi, 1996). Continued efforts at thought suppression may serve to perpetuate the thoughts and contribute to pathological conditions, such as obsessive-compulsive disorder (Wells & Matthews, 1994b, 1996).

INTEGRATING LEVELS OF EXPLANATION: THE S-REF MODEL

Thus far, we have seen that computational models of processing are necessary but not sufficient to understand the interrelationship of emotion and attention. Theory must also address the role of self-knowledge in guiding coping strategies and the modification of self-knowledge over time as stressful encounters unfold dynamically. In this section, we describe a multi-level model of attention and emotion which attempts to tackle these issues, the Self-Regulatory Executive Function (S-REF) model (Wells & Matthews, 1994b, 1996). It aims to accommodate the following key features of the interrelationship between emotion and cognition:

- Interaction between levels of control of the cognitive architecture.
- The importance of self-regulatory goals and self-knowledge.
- The implementation of self-regulation through voluntary selection of coping strategies.
- Attentional impairment and bias as consequences of strategy choice.
- The central role of dynamic disturbance in chronic maladaption.

The architecture of the model is shown in Figure 9.1. It comprises three interacting levels: a stimulus-driven lower-level network of interconnected network

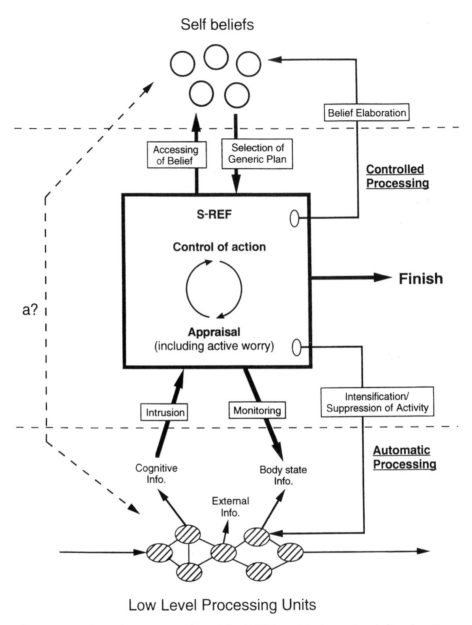

Figure 9.1 Schematic representation of the S-REF model of emotional disorder. Reproduced from Wells & Matthews (1994a, p. 268), with permission

units, a supervisory executive system implementing voluntary control, and stored self-knowledge in long-term memory. Much self-knowledge is stored in generic and procedural form, as described by Anderson's (1982) skill theory, which we refer to as "plans". For example, the person's preferred coping strategies are represented as incompletely-specified production systems for response to threat. In the face of some specific threat, the plan is retrieved from long-term memory, and tailored to the needs of the immediate situation by the executive system, using controlled processing. Plans are distinguished from automatic processing routines in that no fixed response or processing sequence is specified. Threats encountered in everyday life are typically variable across occasions (e.g. social threats) or rare (e.g. physical attack), so that response to threat is normally controlled by plans rather than by automatic processing. However, especially when the person endures prolonged exposure to threatening environments, there may be some capacity for automatic control of response. For example, military training and experience may automatize some responses to perceived physical threat, which may be responsible for the seemingly irrational violent behaviours of veterans with PTSD.

The system as a whole may operate in different configurations. The one most relevant to negative emotion is the self-regulatory executive function (S-REF), in which processing is driven by self-regulatory goals derived from discrepancies between actual and preferred self-status. Self-regulation focuses attention on the self, and appraisal of the personal significance of external stimuli, somatic stimuli and internal cognitions. Broadly, the person is inclined to ruminate and worry perseveratively about problems while concurrently experiencing negative emotions such as anxiety and depression.

Operation of the S-REF may be stated in more detail by considering the system's inputs, processing activities and outputs. S-REF activity is initiated by various external and internal threat stimuli. Criticism by others is a particularly potent source of S-REF activation, for example. Incoming stimuli activate self-regulatory goals and plans for self-knowledge, which guide the executive system in implementing controlled processing routines, which perform stimulus analysis and select coping strategies. The S-REF remains activated until the self-discrepancy is resolved. Often, episodes of S-REF activity are brief and inconsequential. However, various factors dispose the person to more prolonged bouts of S-REF activity, including, of course, threats which are genuinely difficult to bring under personal control. A further type of factor comprises personality traits, such as dispositional self-focus of attention (Fenigstein, Scheier & Buss, 1976), which relates to dysfunctional coping, especially when the situation is potentially controllable (Wells & Matthews, 1994b; Matthews, Mohamed & Lochrie, 1998). Another important trait is neuroticism, which may relate to negative biases in the availability and accessibility of the contents of long-term memory (e.g. Mayo, 1989), and to a preference for coping through emotion-focus (Deary et al., 1996; Morgan, Matthews & Winton, 1995). A second type of factor influencing maintenance of S-REF activity is the person's meta-cognitive beliefs, in the utility of worry, for example, which may be represented as plans specifying the use of rumination or thought control as coping strategies (Wells, 1995, 1997b).

Once activated, the S-REF performs two types of operation: initiation and monitoring of coping strategies, and modification of self-knowledge. Both types of activity require controlled processing and attentional resources. Coping strategies include monitoring for external and internal threat stimuli, rumination and attempts at suppressing or intensifying internal stimuli. Depending on the exact demands of the processing implementing coping, the person is vulnerable to overload of attention. As indicated previously, the person in the S-REF state is liable to show impaired performance on attentionally demanding tasks due to self-regulatory goals overriding task goals and diverting resources from the task at hand. The facilitation of performance by additional task goals, which distract from self-regulation (Matthews, Sparkes & Bygrave, 1996), are incompatible with naive resource models which neglect the knowledge level of analysis. In addition, resource shortfalls may also lead to impairment of core S-REF operations. Wells & Matthews (1994b) argue that attempts to cope may be disrupted by lack of resources, with task-focused coping and the more active forms of emotion-focus particularly vulnerable. Lack of resources may also impair modification and restructuring of self-knowledge, hindering the replacement of maladaptive self-beliefs with more successful routines for dealing with problems.

The S-REF model develops the strategic hypothesis for attentional bias discussed above. Wells & Matthews (1994b) propose that common to most affective and anxiety disorders is a plan for monitoring sources of threat, which specifies maintenance of the focus of attention on channels associated with threats congruent with the individual's affective condition. Consistent with this hypothesis, emotional Stroop effects generalize across disorders, but the stimuli sensitive to the effect vary across conditions and individuals (Matthews & Harley, 1996). At a computational level, threat-monitoring may operate through top-down activation of low-level processing units, as in the Matthews & Harley (1996) simulation. Threat-monitoring contributes not just to attentional bias, but also to the dynamics of affective reactions. As Wells & Matthews (1994b) discuss, this strategy serves to sensitize the system to threats, and the development of self-perpetuating cycles of threat-detection and further monitoring. For example, panic disorder patients become progressively more aware of minor somatic symptoms because of their strategy of actively monitoring for such systems. The acute panic attack derives from a combination of somatic awareness and the self-beliefs that the threat stimuli indicate an impending catastrophe, such as cardiac arrest (Clark, 1986). Bias in selective attention is embedded within the system as a whole, and cannot be understood without reference to both executive functions, specified computationally, and the person's goals and self-knowledge.

IMPLICATIONS FOR THERAPY

In this section we discuss some of the clinical implications of the S-REF model. Space does not permit a detailed discussion but the interested reader may refer to other sources for further details (Wells & Matthews, 1994b; 1996; Wells, 1997a). We confine the present discussion to briefly considering the dynamic interplay between self–knowledge and processing within the S-REF cognitive–attentional syndrome.

The model distinguishes between declarative knowledge, which may be verbally expressed (e.g. "I'm inadequate"; "I'm seriously ill") and the procedural knowledge represented by plans, which is not consciously accessible. The present account emphasizes maladaptive plans as a source of pathology, as opposed to specific declarative beliefs, which may merely be the outcomes of running particular plans for processing and behaviour. Plans are dysfunctional to the extent that they promote counter-productive processing operations and behaviours that maintain emotional disorder through various cyclical relationships. Meta-cognitive plans, which lead to changes in belief or modifications in low-level processing, may be particularly important. Although the plan itself is not verbally expressible, it may direct on-line meta-cognitive processing activities, which can be expressed verbally. For example, some patients with GAD believe that worrying is a means of coping with future threat (Wells, 1995; 1997b). Plans can also be associated with unrealistic goals for self-regulation so that the S-REF is in a chronic state of readiness, but in the following discussion, we focus on processing operations.

It follows that maladaptive plans should be modified in treatment to produce stable improvement in emotional disorder. If plans remain unmodified the individual will be prone to generate familiar patterns of maladaptive processing that generate and maintain a distorted impression of the self and the world. Earlier approaches in cognitive therapy have focused on 'interrogating' the content of thought at the on-line appraisal level in order to produce changes in declarative belief, with little specification of how this strategy could work. The S-REF model emphasizes that it is necessary to understand the processing configuration that supports emotional dysfunction, since the configuration offers a direct link to the nature of plans. By a procedure of meta-cognitive profiling (Wells & Matthews, 1994a) it is possible to determine the nature of attentional, ideational, memory and behavioural processes operating during acute phases of emotional disorder.

Dysfunctional plans may be overwritten by reversing elements of the processing configuration in a way that maximizes belief change. To illustrate this principle, consider the problem of social phobia. Assessment of the direction and content of attention during anxiety-provoking social situations shows that social phobics focus on an impression of themselves as a social object. More specifically, attention is focused on interoceptive information, which social phobics use to construct a negative impression of how they appear to others (Wells, Clark & Ahmad, 1995; Wells & Papageorgiou, 1998). The self-impression is used to infer what other people will see and what they will think about the self (e.g. Clark & Wells, 1995; Wells, 1997a). The configuration is maladaptive in several respects. First, it diminishes attention focused on the social environment, so that disconfirmatory information concerning other people's true reaction to the self is not processed. Second, self-focus intensifies the subjective experience of symptoms and increases the probability of impairment in social performance.

Individuals with social phobia also engage in behaviours that set up other vicious cycles of problem maintenance. In particular, avoidance and in-situation safety behaviours remove the opportunity to practise alternative attentional and behavioural strategies that are capable of disconfirming negative appraisals and beliefs (Wells et al, 1995). In formulating the nature of the S-REF component in social phobia, the emphasis for understanding the problem shifts away from earlier concepts of social skills deficits and fear of negative evaluation as central causal agents. Treatment should consist of attentional and behavioural manipulations that enhance external disconfirmatory processing, and provide a plan for self-processing that is capable of generating and sustaining an accurate and positive public self-perception.

The S-REF performs a meta-cognitive function of modifying beliefs and low-level processing. Cognitive modification in cognitive therapy is achieved by manipulating the processing which alters self-knowledge. Attempts in treatment to modify self-knowledge are likely to fail if the S-REF cannot be configured and used in a way that enhances meta-cognitive recalibration processes. Active worry or the recycling of information in the limited capacity S-REF system may deplete attentional resources necessary for belief modification under meta-cognitive control. Here, failure to change dysfunctional processing is not the result of failure to detect disconfirmatory data (as in social phobia), but results from failures to access appropriate beliefs and to change self-knowledge, due to perseverative rumination. Brief worry following exposure to a stressful film also appears to incubate intrusive images associated with the film over a subsequent 3-day period (Wells & Papageorgiou, 1995). If, as these data suggest, some forms of processing exacerbate intrusions, individuals who have plans specifying the use of ruminative worry-based strategies may be prone to distress and a diminished sense of mental control. These examples serve to illustrate the dynamic nature of processing in emotional disorder, and emphasize the involvement of plans and cognitive processes apart from declarative beliefs in the genesis of emotional problems.

In summary, the S-REF model advocates exploring the dynamics of processing in emotional disorder, with the aim of elucidating the role of existing plans and implementing new plans that can modify maladaptive appraisals and coping strategies and sustain new beliefs. This requires patients to develop a heightened *meta-cognitive awareness*, so that the nature of dysfunctional processing configurations can be identified. Patients should be trained to suspend ruminative engagement with intrusive mental experience. Such *detached mindfulness* is not intended to suppress awareness of thoughts, but to introduce new strategies for dealing with intrusions that liberate resources for cognitive change. Attentional strategies should be introduced that re-configure attention in a way that promotes disconfirmatory processing and overwrites dysfunctional plans. The deployment of new behavioural strategies that promote belief change are equally important. *Meta-cognitive profiling* offers a means of determining the nature of plans. Some patients may lack executive control over cognitive–attentional processes. For example, self-focus may be inflexible and adhesive. New strategies such as *Attention Training* (Wells, 1990; Wells, White & Carter, 1997) offer a means of increasing executive control over processing and a means of short-circuiting the perseverative S-REF syndrome. The S-REF model, like schema theory of emotional disorder, implies that it is necessary to change maladaptive self-knowledge in effective treatment. However, it presents a more detailed specification of the nature of self-knowledge and offers a means of understanding processes influencing belief change. We must look beyond the declarative content of thought and beliefs and begin to examine the feedback cycles within and between cognitive and meta-cognitive processing that sustain emotional disorder.

CONCLUSION

Explanation of the interplay between emotion and attention requires the adoption of an explicit cognitive science framework, distinguishing biological, architectural and knowledge levels of explanation. We have emphasized especially the distinction between cognitive descriptions of phenomena, in terms of information-processing models, and explanations for *why* emotion and attentional functions are interlinked. Empirical studies of negative emotions and attention generate descriptively rich information-processing accounts of the phenomena. However, it is often unclear whether emotion is associated with variation in the formal properties of the cognitive architecture, or with use of the same architecture to support differing strategies. There is considerable evidence suggesting that anxiety and depression effects on both intensive and selective aspects of attention are under strategic control. Strategic intervention may be described within information-processing models, but we also require knowledge level explanations for the person's strategy choice. The Wells & Matthews S-REF model specifies the cognitive–attentional syndrome underpinning dysfunctional negative emotion states in terms of both the processing routines which implement coping strategies, and the self-knowledge which drives processing. In clinical practice, it is important to address failures to adapt to real-world environments directly, by reconstructing self-knowledge to reduce unrealistic goals, false negative appraisals of goal attainment, and the use of plans for coping and meta-cognition which generate coping strategies which serve to perpetuate the problem. Both theory and clinical practice require understanding of the mutual interdependence between plans for adaptation and specific processing routines called to implement those plans, successfully or otherwise.

ACKNOWLEDGEMENT

We are grateful to Trevor Harley for comments on a previous draft of this chapter.

REFERENCES

Allport, A. (1989). Visual attention. In M. I. Posner (ed.), *Foundations of Cognitive Science*. Cambridge, MA: MIT Press.

Anderson, J. R. (1982). Acquisition of cognitive skill. *Psychological Review*, **89**, 369–406.

Bakan, P. (1959). Extroversion–introversion and improvement in an auditory vigilance task. *British Journal of Psychology*, **50**, 165–178.

Bargh, J. A. (1992). The ecology of automaticity: toward establishing the conditions needed to produce automatic processing effects. *American Journal of Psychology*, **105**, 181–200.

Beck, A. T. (1967). *Depression: Causes and Treatment*. Philadelphia, PA: University of Pennsylvania Press.

Bower, G. H. (1981). Mood and memory. *American Psychologist*, **36**, 129–148.

Brand, N. & Jolles, J. (1987). Information processing in depression and anxiety. *Psychological Medicine*, **17**, 145–153.

Broadbent, D. E. (1971). *Decision and Stress*. London: Academic Press.

Broadbent, D. E. & Broadbent, M. H. P. (1988). Anxiety and attentional bias: state and trait. *Cognition and Emotion*, **2**, 165–183.

Calvo, M. G. & Castillo, M. D. (1997). Mood-congruent bias in interpretation of ambiguity: strategic processes and temporary activation. *Quarterly Journal of Experimental Psychology*, **50A**, 163–182.

Calvo, M. G., Eysenck, M. W. & Castillo, M. D. (1997). Interpretation bias in test anxiety: the time course of predictive inferences. *Cognition and Emotion*, **11**, 43–63.

Carver, C. S., Peterson, L. M., Follansbee, D. J. & Scheier, M. F. (1983). Effects of self-directed attention and resistance among persons high and low in test-anxiety. *Cognitive Therapy and Research*, **7**, 333–354.

Carver, C. S. & Scheier, M. F. (1981). *Attention and Self-regulation: A Control-theory Approach to Human Behavior*. Berlin: Springer-Verlag.

Carver, C. S. & Scheier, M. F. (1990). Origins and functions of positive and negative affects: a control-process view. *Psychological Review*, **97**, 19–35.

Clark, D. M. (1986). A cognitive model of panic. *Behaviour Research and Therapy*, **24**, 461–470.

Clark, D. M. & Wells, A. (1995). A cognitive model of social phobia. In R. G Heimberg, M. R Liebowitz, D. A Hope & R. R. Schneier (eds), *Social Phobia: Diagnosis, Assessment and Treatment*. New York: Guilford.

Cohen, J. D., Dunbar, K. & McClelland, J. L. (1990). On the control of automatic processes: a parallel distributed processing account of the Stroop effect. *Psychological Review*, **97**, 332–361.

Coyne, J. C. (1976). Toward an interactional description of depression. *Psychiatry*, **39**, 28–40.

Deary, I. J., Blenkin, H., Agius, R. M., Endler, N. S., Zealley, H. & Wood, R. (1996). Models of job-related stress and personal achievement among consultant doctors. *British Journal of Psychology*, **87**, 3–30.

Eysenck, M. W. (1982). *Attention and Arousal: Cognition and Performance*. New York: Springer.

Eysenck, M. W. (1992). *Anxiety: The Cognitive Perspective*. Hillsdale, NJ: Erlbaum.

Fenigstein, A., Scheier, M. F. & Buss, A. H. (1975). Public and private self-consciousness: assessment and theory. *Journal of Consulting and Clinical Psychology*, **43**, 522–527.

Foulds, G. A. (1952). Temperamental differences in maze performance. II: The effect of distraction and of electroconvulsive therapy on psychomotor retardation. *British Journal of Psychiatry*, **43**, 33–41.

Fox, E. (1996). Selective processing of threatening words in anxiety: the role of awareness. *Cognition and Emotion*, **10**, 449–480.

Geen, R.G. (1985).   Test anxiety and visual vigilance. *Journal of Personality and Social Psychology*, **49**, 963–970.

Gray, J. A. (1982).   *The Neuropsychology of Anxiety: An Enquiry into the Functions of the Septo-hippocampal System*. Oxford: Oxford University Press.

Hartlage, S., Alloy, L. B., Vazquez, C. & Dykman, B. (1993).   Automatic and effortful processing in depression. *Psychological Bulletin*, **113**, 247–278.

Hewitt, P. L. & Flett, G. L. (1993).   Dimensions of perfectionism, daily stress, and depression: a test of the specific vulnerability hypothesis. *Journal of Abnormal Psychology*, **102**, 58–65.

Higgins, E. T. (1990).   Personality, social psychology, and person–situation relations: standards and knowledge activation as a common language. In L. A. Pervin (ed.), *Handbook of Personality Theory and Research*. New York: Guilford.

Hockey, G. R. J. (1984).   Varieties of attentional state: the effects of the environment. In R. Parasuraman & D. R. Davies (eds), *Varieties of Attention*. New York: Academic Press.

Humphreys, M. S. & Revelle, W. (1984).   Personality, motivation and performance: a theory of the relationship between individual differences and information processing. *Psychological Review*, **91**, 153–184.

Ingram, R. E. (1984).   Toward an information-processing analysis of depression. *Cognitive Therapy and Research*, **8**, 443–478.

Ingram, R. E. (1990).   Self-focused attention in clinical disorders: review and a conceptual model. *Psychological Bulletin*, **107**, 156–176.

Johnson, M. H. & Magaro, P. A. (1987).   Effects of mood and severity on memory processes in depression and mania. *Psychological Bulletin*, **101**, 28–40.

Kitayama, S. (1991).   Impairment of perception by positive and negative affect. *Cognition and Emotion*, **5**, 255–274.

Kluger, A. N. & DeNisi, A. (1996).   The effects of feedback interventions on performance: a historical review, a meta-analysis, and a preliminary feedback intervention theory. *Psychological Bulletin*, **119**, 254–284.

Lazarus, R. S. & Folkman, S. (1984).   *Stress, Appraisal and Coping*. New York: Springer.

LeDoux, J. E. (1995).   Emotion: clues from the brain. *Annual Review of Psychology*, **46**, 209–235.

Lesch, K.-P., Bengel, D., Heils, A., Sabol, S. Z., Greenberg, B. D., Petri, S., Benjamin, J., Müller, C. R., Hamer, H. D. & Murphy, D. L. (1996).   Association of anxiety-related traits with a polymorphism in the serotonin transporter gene regulatory region. *Science*, **274**, 1527–1531.

Loehlin, J. C. (1992).   *Genes and Environment in Personality Development*. Newbury Park, CA: Sage.

MacLeod, C. & Mathews, A. (1991).   Cognitive–experimental approaches to the emotional disorders. In P. R. Martin (ed.), *Handbook of Behaviour Therapy and Psychological Science: An Integrative Approach*. Oxford: Pergamon.

Martin, M., Williams, R. M. & Clark, D. M. (1991).   Does anxiety lead to selective processing of threat-related information? *Behaviour Research and Therapy*, **29**, 147–160.

Mathews, A. & MacLeod, C. (1985).   Selective processing of threat cues in anxiety states. *Behaviour Research and Therapy*, **23**, 563–569.

Mathews, A., May, J., Mogg, K. & Eysenck, M. W. (1990).   Attentional bias in anxiety: selective search or defective filtering? *Journal of Abnormal Psychology*, **98**, 131–138.

Matthews, G. (1992).   Mood. In A. P. Smith & D. M. Jones (eds), *Handbook of human performance. Vol. 3: State and Trait*. London: Academic Press.

Matthews, G., Davies, D. R. & Lees, J. L. (1990).   Arousal, extraversion, and individual differences in resource availability. *Journal of Personality and Social Psychology*, **59**, 150–168.

Matthews, G. & Dorn, L. (1995).   Cognitive and attentional processes in personality and intelligence. In D. H. Saklofske & M. Zeidner (eds), *International Handbook of Personality and Intelligence*. New York: Plenum.

Matthews, G. & Harley, T. A. (1996). Connectionist models of emotional distress and attentional bias. *Cognition and Emotion*, **10**, 561–600.

Matthews, G., Mohamed, A. & Lochrie, B. (1998). Dispositional self-focus of attention and individual differences in appraisal and coping. In J. Bermudez, A. M. Perez, A. Sanchez-Elvira & G. L. van Heck (eds), *Personality Psychology in Europe*, Vol. 6. Tilburg: Tilburg University Press.

Matthews, G., Pitcaithly, D. & Mann, R. L. E. (1995). Mood, neuroticism, and the encoding of affective words. *Cognitive Therapy and Research*, **19**, 563–587.

Matthews, G. & Southall, A. (1991). Depression and the processing of emotional stimuli: a study of semantic priming. *Cognitive Therapy and Research*, **15**, 283–302.

Matthews, G., Sparkes, T. J. & Bygrave, H. M. (1996). Stress, attentional overload and simulated driving performance. *Human Performance*, **9**, 77–101.

Matthews, G. & Wells, A. (1996). Attentional processes, coping strategies and clinical intervention. In M. Zeidner & N. S. Endler (eds), *Handbook of Coping: Theory, Research, applications*. New York: Wiley.

Matthews, G. & Wells, A. (in press). Attention, automaticity and affective disorder. *Behavior Modification*.

Matthews, G. & Westerman, S. J. (1994). Energy and tension as predictors of controlled visual and memory search. *Personality and Individual Differences*, **17**, 617–626.

Mayo, P. R. (1989). A further study of the personality-congruent recall effect. *Personality and Individual Differences*, **10**, 247–252.

McNally, R. J. (1995). Automaticity and the anxiety disorders. *Behaviour Research and Therapy*, **33**, 747–754.

McNally, R. J. & Ricciardi, J. N. (1996). Suppression of negative and neutral thoughts. *Behavioural and Cognitive Psychotherapy*, **24**, 17–25.

Morgan, I. A., Matthews, G. & Winton, M. (1995). Coping and personality as predictors of post-traumatic intrusions, numbing, avoidance and general distress: a study of victims of the Perth flood. *Behavioural and Cognitive Psychotherapy*, **23**, 251–264.

Neisser, U. (1976). *Cognition and Reality*. San Francisco, CA: Freeman.

Neely, J. H. (1991). Semantic priming effects in visual word recognition: a selective review of current findings and theories. In D. E. Besner & G. Humphreys (eds), *Basic Processes in Reading*. Hillsdale, NJ: Erlbaum.

Newell, A., Rosenbloom, P. S. & Laird, J. E. (1989). Symbolic architectures for cognition. In M. I. Posner (ed.), *Foundations of Cognitive Science*. Cambridge, MA: MIT Press.

Norman, D. A. & Shallice, T. (1985). Attention to action: willed and automatic control of behaviour. In R. J. Davidson, G. E. Schwartz & D. Shapiro (eds), *Consciousness and Self-regulation: Advances in Research*, Vol. 4. New York: Plenum.

Oatley, K. (1992). *Best Laid Schemes: the Psychology of Emotions*. Cambridge: Cambridge University Press.

Oatley, K. & Johnson-Laird, P. (1987). Towards a cognitive theory of emotions. *Cognition and Emotion*, **1**, 29–50.

Pashler, H. (1994). Dual-task interference in simple tasks: data and theory. *Psychological Bulletin*, **116**, 220–244.

Posner, M. (1975). Psychobiology of attention. In M. Gazzaniga & C. Blakemore (eds), *Handbook of Psychobiology*. New York: London.

Pylyshyn, Z. W. (1984). *Computation and Cognition: Toward a Foundation for Cognitive Science*. Cambridge, MA: MIT Press.

Revelle, W. (1993). Individual differences in personality and motivation: "non-cognitive" determinants of cognitive performance. In A. Baddeley & L. Weiskrantz (eds), *Attention: Selection, Awareness and Control*. Oxford: Oxford University Press.

Richards, A. & French, C. C. (1992). An anxiety-related bias in semantic activation when processing threat/neutral homographs. *Quarterly Journal of Experimental Psychology*, **40A**, 503–528.

Richards, A., French, C. C., Johnson, W., Naparstek, J. & Williams, J. (1992). Effects of mood manipulation and anxiety on performance of an emotional Stroop task. *British Journal of Psychology*, **83**, 479–491.

Richards, A., French, C. C. & Randall, F. (1995). Anxiety and the use of strategies in the performance of a sentence–picture verification task. *Journal of Abnormal Psychology*, **105**, 132–136.

Sarason, I. G. (1988). Anxiety, self-preoccupation and attention. *Anxiety Research*, **1**, 3–7.

Schneider, W. & Detweiler, M. (1987). A connectionist/control architecture for working memory. In G. H. Bower (ed.), *The Psychology of Learning and Motivation*, Vol. 21. San Diego, CA: Academic Press.

Schneider, W., Dumais, S. T. & Shiffrin, R. M. (1984). Automatic and control processing and attention. In R. Parasuraman & D. R. Davies (eds), *Varieties of Attention*. New York: Academic Press.

Segal, Z. V. & Vella, D. D. (1990). Self-schema in major depression: replication and extension of a priming methodology. *Cognitive Therapy and Research*, **14**, 161–176.

Shallice, T. (1988). *From Neuropsychology to Mental Structure*. Cambridge: Cambridge University Press.

Small, S. A. & Robins, C. J. (1988). The influence of induced depressed mood on visual recognition thresholds: predictive ambiguity of associative network models of mood and cognition. *Cognitive Research and Therapy*, **12**, 295–304.

Van der Heijden, A. H. C. (1992). *Selective Attention in Vision*. London: Routledge.

Watts, F. N., McKenna, F. P., Sharrock, R. & Tresize, L. (1986). Colour naming of phobia-related words. *British Journal of Psychology*, **25**, 253–261.

Wells, A. (1990). Panic disorder in association with relaxation induced anxiety: an attentional training approach to treatment. *Behavior Therapy*, **21**, 273–280.

Wells, A. (1995). Meta-cognition and worry: a cognitive model of generalised anxiety disorder. *Behavioural and Cognitive Psychotherapy*, **23**, 301–320.

Wells, A. (1997a). *Cognitive Therapy of Anxiety Disorders: A Practice Manual and Conceptual Guide*. Chichester: Wiley.

Wells, A. (1997b). A cognitive model of generalized anxiety disorder. *Behavior Modification*, in press.

Wells, A., Clark, D. M. & Ahmad, S. (1995). How do I look with my mind's eye? Perspective taking in social phobic imagery. Paper presented at the Annual Conference of the British Association of Behavioural and Cognitive Psychotherapy, Southampton University.

Wells, A., Clark, D. M., Salkovskis, P., Ludgate, J., Hackmann A. & Gelder, M. (1995). Social phobia: the role of in-situation safety behaviors in maintaining anxiety and negative beliefs. *Behavior Therapy*, **26**, 153–161.

Wells, A. & Matthews, G. (1994a). *Attention and Emotion: A Clinical Perspective*. Hove: Erlbaum.

Wells, A. & Matthews, G. (1994b). Self-consciousness and cognitive failures as predictors of coping in stressful episodes. *Cognition and Emotion*, **8**, 279–295.

Wells, A. & Matthews, G. (1996). Modelling cognition in emotional disorder: The S-REF model. *Behaviour Research and Therapy*, **34**, 881–888.

Wells, A. & Papageorgiou, C. (1998). Social phobia: effects of external attention focus on anxiety, negative beliefs and perspective taking. *Behavior Therapy*, **29**, 357–370.

Wells, A. & Papageorgiou, C. (1995). Worry and the incubation of intrusive images following stress. *Behaviour Research and Therapy*, **33**, 579–583.

Wells, A., White, J. & Carter, K. (1997). Attention training: effects on anxiety and beliefs in panic and social phobia. *Clinical Psychology and Psychotherapy*, **4**, 226–232.

Wickens, C. D. (1992). *Engineering psychology and human performance*, 2nd edn. New York: Harper Collins.

Williams, J, M. G., Watts, F. N., MacLeod, C. & Mathews, A. (1988). *Cognitive Psychology and Emotional Disorders*. Chichester: Wiley.
Wine, J. D. (1981). Test anxiety and direction of attention. *Psychological Bulletin*, **76**, 92–104.

Chapter 10

Mood and Memory

Henry C. Ellis* *and* **Brent A. Moore**
University of New Mexico, Albuquerque, NM, USA

Research on the relationship between mood and memory has rapidly developed over the past 20 years into a vigorous and active domain. Although prior to 1970 there were occasional studies of mood and memory, it was not an active area of research. This picture has changed dramatically since 1975 for a variety of reasons, one being the acceptance by many cognitive psychologists of the importance of affect in memory, which had been recognized earlier by clinical and social psychologists. Another factor was the development of experimental procedures which allow mood and memory to be studied in the laboratory as well as in clinical settings, and a third factor has been the development of theoretical frameworks that encompass both emotion and cognition, topics that had earlier seen a largely independent theoretical development.

The terms "affect", "emotion" and "mood" are sometimes used interchangeably, although they do differ. We shall follow the convention suggested by Bower & Forgas (in press), in which "affect" is the more general term, encompassing both emotions and moods (Forgas, 1995). In contrast, "emotion" is regarded as having the properties of a reaction, sometimes an intense response to a specific stimulus. In turn, "mood" is regarded as a more subtle, longer-lasting and less intense experience and tends to be more general or non-specific.

This chapter addresses four topics in the domain of mood-memory research: (a) mood-congruent memory; (b) mood-dependent memory; (c) theoretical issues and approaches to mood and memory; and (d) mood-related impairments in memory for neutral material. These topics represent four important as well as substantive areas of work. Our review of mood-congruent memory indicates that

---

* To whom correspondence should be addressed.

Handbook of Cognition and Emotion. Edited by T. Dalgleish and M. Power.
© 1999 John Wiley & Sons Ltd.

this is a robust phenomenon with only a few exceptions to this general picture. Mood-dependent memory has had a somewhat volatile history, with an early promising beginning (e.g. Bower, Monteiro & Gilligan, 1978) followed by a decade of negative or equivocal results (e.g. Bower & Mayer, 1989; Leight & Ellis, 1981). Recently, Eich (1995) has presented a more optimistic portrayal of mood-dependent memory, indicating the conditions in which it is likely to occur. Next, we examine six theoretical issues and approaches noting a trend towards identifying the processes underlying mood–memory effects. Finally, we very briefly summarize some of the principal generalizations regarding mood-related impairments in memory for neutral material. We do not, of course, provide a full review of the literature, neither have we discussed a number of other topics which are important such as memory for emotional events, including eyewitness testimony, recovery of repressed memories and flashbulb memories, because these topics are extensively discussed elsewhere in this volume and in Christianson (1992), Ellis & Hertel (1993) and Mathews (1996).

MOOD-CONGRUENT MEMORY

Mood-congruent processing occurs when material is selectively encoded or retrieved while individuals are in a mood state consistent with the affective tone of the material. Thus, an individual in a happy mood would encode or retrieve more information if that material was also affectively positive than if the material was depressing or affectively negative. Mood-congruent processing can be divided into mood-congruent encoding or mood-congruent learning and mood-congruent retrieval.

In mood-congruent encoding, material is learned better because the affective tone of that material is consistent with an individual's mood state. In the typical experiment (Bower, Gilligan & Monteiro, 1981; Mayer & Salovey, 1988), participants are first induced into a particular mood state through the use of a procedure such as hypnosis, retelling emotional autobiographical events, listening to affect-laden music, or reading self-referential statements. This is followed by a learning task such as memorizing a sad or happy word list, including words such as "death" or "joy", or reading an affect-laden story. At a later point, when individuals are in a neutral mood state, their memory for the material is measured. Increased recall is found in conditions congruent with the mood state at encoding as compared with incongruent mood states.

Mood-congruent encoding has been shown with both direct memory tests, such as word list recall (Bower, Gilligan & Monteiro, 1981; Rinck, Glowalia & Schneider, 1992), and indirect memory tests, such as word-stem completion (Ruiz-Caballero & Gonzalez, 1994; Tobias, Kihlstrom & Schacter, 1992). Researchers have generally explained these results by suggesting that individuals experiencing a particular mood state generate more elaborative associations to information in agreement with that mood state. Such theories are supported by findings that individuals in a particular mood state (generally happy or sad) spend more time studying material that is congruent with their mood state and less time with incongruent material (Forgas, 1995; Forgas & Bower, 1987).

While it is clear that emotional mood states affect encoding of affect-laden material, mood-congruent retrieval is less frequently evidenced. Mood-congruent retrieval is defined as increased recall for material that is of the same affective tone as the mood experienced (Blaney, 1986). In typical experiments, after a mood state is measured (or induced) the participant recalls autobiographical memories and the amount recalled or speed of recall are measured (Bullington, 1990; Teasdale & Fogarty, 1979). For example, Burke & Mathews (1992) found that anxious individuals retrieved more anxious memories than normal participants. In general, participants show a bias for retrieving autobiographical memories consistent or congruent with their current mood, although a few studies have found better memory for personal events that are incongruent with the current mood (Parrott & Sabini, 1990). Nevertheless, studies of autobiographical event memory are problematic as evidence for mood-congruent retrieval, since the affective valence of the material is almost always associated with the emotional state at the time of the event. Thus, the results of autobiographical memory studies may be instances of mood-dependent memory or mood-congruent encoding, rather than mood-congruent retrieval (see Blaney, 1986).

Studies examining mood-congruent retrieval, in which the participants learn affectively laden material in a neutral mood and retrieve in a mood either congruent or incongruent with the material, are less conclusive that those examining mood-congruent encoding. Some have found support for mood-congruent retrieval (Teasdale & Russell, 1983), while others have found little or no support (Bower, Gilligan & Monteiro, 1981; Fiedler & Stroehm, 1986; Gotlib & McCann, 1984). In contrast, Clark et al. (1983) found mood-incongruent recall with happy and sad participants.

In general, mood-congruent effects occur reliably under most mood states, as well as in clinical, subclinical and induced depression (for reviews, see Blaney, 1986; Matt, Vazquez & Campbell, 1992), although mood-congruent memory with clinical anxiety is less clear (Dalgleish & Watts, 1990; Mathews & MacLeod, 1994). However, there are several factors that regulate the conditions and the strength of the effect. First, mood-congruent memory is found when individuals are aware that the material they are learning is consistent with their current mood (Perrig & Perrig, 1988; Rothkopf & Blaney, 1991). Second, the to-be-remembered information may need to be self-referential as well as related to the current mood for mood-congruent memory to be demonstrated (Bradley & Mathews, 1983; Nasby, 1994). Kuiper & Derry (1982) and Pietromonaco & Markus (1985), among others, have found that both happy and sad participants learned more self-referential words consistent rather than inconsistent with their mood. These studies failed to find a mood-congruent effect for words that were not self-referential. Although other studies have found mood-congruent memory with non-self-referential materials (see Matt, Vazquez & Campbell, 1992), the effect appears to be stronger with self-referential material. Finally, both the mood experienced and the to-be-remembered material have to be of sufficient affective strength for mood-congruent learning to be shown. For example, Rinck, Glowalia & Schneider (1992) found the classic mood-congruent effect when the words to be learned were highly affectively toned, but when the words were mildly affective they found mood-incongruent learning. Thus, when the strength of an individual's mood state and the affective tone of the material are more intense, individuals may be more likely to notice the relationship between the mood and the material and to generate more elaborate associations to the information.

With the exception of anxiety, mood-congruent memory is a robust effect which occurs with most mood states. Although mood-congruent encoding is a stronger and more reliable effect than mood-congruent retrieval, and likely the dominant factor in demonstrations of mood-congruent memory, there is also evidence for mood-congruent retrieval. Conditions which favor individuals noticing the relationship between their current mood state and the memory material are more likely to show mood-congruent effects.

MOOD-DEPENDENT MEMORY

Mood-dependent memory (MDM) refers to the increased likelihood of remembering material that was learned in a particular mood state. Thus, if an individual heard a particular story while in a sad or depressed mood, such as at a funeral, the story would be more likely to be recalled when the individual was again in a depressed mood, rather than some other mood state. MDM differs from mood-congruent memory in that the important relationship is the consistency of the mood state at encoding and retrieval, rather than between the material and the current mood state. MDM is a specific case of the more general state-dependent memory which has primarily involved studies with drug-induced states of consciousness. However, while drug-induced state-dependent memory has been found to be a strong and reliable effect, evidence for the MDM effect is less strong (see Eich, 1995).

The classic study by Bower, Montiero & Gilligan (1978) provides a good example of a typical experiment examining MDM. Participants were required to learn two word lists, one while in a happy mood and one while in a sad mood. At a later time, the participants recalled as many words as possible while in one of the two mood states. Thus, the mood state at retrieval could be consistent or inconsistent with the mood state at encoding. Given this procedure, they found that individuals who were in the same mood state at encoding and retrieval (whether happy or sad) recalled more than individuals who were in different moods at encoding and retrieval. Although this and other early experiments found evidence for MDM (Weingartner, Miller & Murphy, 1977), many researchers have been unable to replicate these findings (e.g. Bower & Mayer, 1989). Using the same procedures as those described above, Bower & Mayer, in a series of six experiments, found no support for MDM effects, with the exception of one study. Although these findings indicate that the general MDM effect is weak, there may be circumstances in which MDM is more readily evoked. Thus, recent work has focused on the circumstances in which MDM is most likely to occur (Eich, 1995).

Two areas have been the focus for explaining mood-dependent effects. The first concerns specific aspects of mood states and the second relates to the type or nature of the memory material. Concerning mood states, MDM is not significantly affected by the type of mood induction procedure used (Haaga, 1989), although only a few mood states (e.g. happy, sad, angry) have been examined. MDM is also more likely to occur when contrasting mood states, such as sad vs. happy, are used rather than comparing some mood state with a neutral mood (Ucros, 1989). MDM is also more evident when mood states are stronger (see Eich, 1995). Researchers hypothesize that stronger mood states lead to stronger associations with the material, and thus, when mood states at testing match those at encoding, the mood provides a stronger cue to retrieve the target material (Bower, 1981, 1992).

Regarding the type of memory material, Ucros (1989), in a meta-analysis of the research on MDM from 1975 to 1985, found that MDM was less likely to occur with laboratory memory tasks than with real-life events which are more meaningful. Supporting this conclusion, Eich, Macaulay & Ryan (1994) asked participants first to generate autobiographical events in a particular mood state and then to recall the events several days later in the same or different mood state. MDM was indicated such that, when the mood state was consistent at generation and recall, participants were more likely to recall autobiographical items than when the moods were inconsistent. However, as noted above, most studies examining MDM with real-life events fail to separate the mood at encoding from the affective tone of the event; thus, these findings may be a result of mood-congruent memory rather than MDM (see Blaney, 1986).

An alternative explanation for why MDM effects are more likely to occur with real-life events is that such events are more likely to have internally generated retrieval cues than externally generated cues. In a direct test of this hypothesis, Eich & Metcalfe (1989) used the "generate" vs. "read" procedures in four experiments. For "read" items, participants read a category list of word pairs, such as precious metals: silver–GOLD where GOLD was the target item. For the "generate" condition, the same category word pairs were used but the participant had to generate the target word, as in precious metals: silver–G_____. Generated items were better recalled than read items when the mood at generation and recall matched, supporting the hypothesis that internal events, those created by the mental activities of the individual, are better associated with the current mood state and thus are more likely to show MDM (Eich, 1995).

Several other researchers have made suggestions similar to those of Eich and his colleagues. Bower (1981; Bower & Forgas, in press) suggested that, for mood-dependent effects to be witnessed, the individual must perceive that the mood state and the material "causally belong" together. In a similar vein, Kihlstrom and his colleagues (Kihlstrom, 1989; Tobias, Kihlstrom & Schacter; 1992) suggested that mood should be viewed as a feature of an individual's general environmental context, albeit an internal feature. The effects of environmental context, however, have frequently been found to be weak, suggesting that mood as a part of context may also be a weak retrieval cue. Such retrieval cues act more strongly, compared with other retrieval cues in situations in which the relationship of the context and the to-be-remembered material is made explicit or when there are few other cues available. Generally, mood states provide only implicit retrieval cues and thus mood-dependent effects are less robust. However, when an individual's mood state is explicitly associated with the material, then the mood state can function as a reliable retrieval cue and produce the pattern of findings indicative of MDM.

In a concise summary of MDM research, Eich (1995) concluded that the problem of unreliability with MDM lies not with the phenomenon itself but rather with the methods used to detect it. He believes that robust and reliable MDM effects can be revealed, but only within a restricted range of conditions. Eich (1995) further notes that, "under conditions in which subjects (a) experience strong, stable, sincere moods; (b) play an active part in generating the target events; and (c) take responsibility for producing the cues required to retrieve these events, evidence of MDM seems clear and consistent" (p. 74).

THEORETICAL ISSUES AND APPROACHES TO MOOD AND MEMORY

A variety of theoretical approaches exist concerning the effects of mood states on cognitive processes. These range from theories designed to address specific aspects of mood and memory, such as mood-congruent processing (Bower, 1981; Bower, Gilligan & Monteiro, 1981; Bower & Forgas, in press; Forgas, 1995; Mathews & MacLeod, 1994; Ruiz-Caballero & Gonzalez, 1994; Schwarz & Clore, 1988) and mood state-dependency (Bower, 1981; Clark & Isen, 1982; Eich, 1995; Eich, Macaulay & Ryan, 1994; Forgas, 1995). In addition, there are theories designed to account for memory deficits associated with mood states (Ellis, 1990; Ellis & Ashbrook, 1988; Ellis et al., 1997; Hertel, 1994; Hertel & Rude, 1991) and complex multi-level theories (see Teasdale, this volume; Teasdale & Barnard, 1993).

Some theories are general, in that they attempt to account for mood–memory effects from a comprehensive framework encompassing a variety of phenomena, such as the affect-infusion model (Bower & Forgas, in press), the associative network model (Bower, 1981; Bower & Forgas, in press), the resource allocation model and cognitive interference theory (Ellis & Ashbrook, 1988; Ellis et al. 1997; Gotlib, Roberts & Gilboa, 1996; Sarason, Pierce & Sarason, 1996; Seibert & Ellis, 1991), schema theory (Teasdale & Russell, 1983) and information processing (Gotlib & McCabe, 1992). Other theories are more restricted in scope and address specific phenomena such as cognitive initiative (Hertel, 1994) and arousal processes (Clark, Milberg & Erber, 1988; Revelle & Loftus, 1992). In general, all these theories have focused on depression or other mood states as they affect memory, on the role of anxiety as it affects cognitive processes, or on cognitive biases (Gilboa & Gotlib, in press; Gotlib, Gilboa & Kaplan, in press; Mineka, 1992).

In this section we examine six such theoretical approaches only as they directly address mood and memory: (a) associative network theory, (b) schema theory, (c) the resource allocation model and cognitive interference theory, (d) motivational theory, (e) cognitive initiative theory and (f) arousal theory. Although this treatment is not exhaustive, we have selected five theories that currently receive attention and one (schema theory) which has a long history. Additional general theories of cognition and emotion are addressed elsewhere (Part IV, this volume).

Associative Network Theory

A prominent view of the role of mood and memory is the associative network theory, proposed independently by Bower (1981) and by Clark & Isen (1982). This view assumes that emotional states are represented as nodes in semantic memory and that specific emotions, such as depression, joy or anxiety, are represented by a specific node or unit including related aspects of each emotion. Each emotion node is thought to be linked with propositions that describe events from a person's life, during which time that emotion was aroused. About six basic emotion nodes are thought to be biologically wired into the brain. Emotion nodes can be activated by many events and are subject to the spread of activation, in that when an emotion is aroused, that emotion node spreads excitation to a variety of indicators to which it is connected (see Bower & Forgas, in press). These emotion nodes can be activated by many stimuli, such as physiological states or verbal labels for one's state, and ". . . when activated above a threshold, the emotion unit transmits excitation to those nodes that produce the pattern of autonomic arousal and expressive behavior commonly assigned to that emotion" (Bower, 1981, p. 135).

The network model has been successfully used to account for a variety of mood–memory effects, including mood-congruent effects (Burke & Mathews, 1992; Watkins et al., 1992; Watts & Dalgleish, 1991), mood state-dependent effects (Beck & McBee, 1995; Bower, 1992; Eich, 1995; Eich, in press; Fiedler, 1990) and autobiographical memories (Snyder & White, 1982), as well as other phenomena. In addition, the network model can account for mood-congruence effects in implicit memory (Ruiz-Caballero & Gonzalez, 1994; Tobias, Kihlstrom & Schacter, 1992), mood-congruent priming (Bower, 1981; Mayer et al., 1992), the effect of a person's mood on interpreting ambiguous stimuli (Eysenck, MacLeod & Mathews, 1987; McNally, 1994; Watts et al., 1988) and mood management (Smith & Petty, 1995). Both the power and limitations of the network approach have been carefully documented by Bower & Forgas (in press). Some of the expected memory effects are not as strong as originally anticipated

(Blaney, 1986) and a major problem lies in the difficulty of identifying when mood-congruence will and will not occur. Despite an earlier critical review by Singer & Salovey (1988), the associative network theory continues to be one of the three principal theoretical accounts of mood and memory.

Schema Theory

A somewhat related idea to network theory is the long-standing idea of schema. With respect to mood, schema theory proposes that a person's prevailing mood state functions as a structure for processing and organizing information, as well as guiding retrieval. Sad or depressed individuals are thus thought to have a prevailing depressive schema which selectively organizes information and directs retrieval of specific mood-related memories. The idea of a negative schema has been prevalent in cognitive theories of depression, and Beck et al. (1979) proposed that depression is caused by specific stressors that activate a prevailing schema. Beck's approach to schema theory proposes that depression is associated with biased attention and memory for affectively negative information, and continues to be a useful framework. Recently, Hedlund & Rude (1995) reported evidence for latent depressive schemas in remitted depressives, who recalled a greater number of negative words and showed more negative interpretative biases than non-depressed controls.

Although the schema concept continues to be employed in general theories of cognition and emotion, particularly depression, it has received somewhat less experimental attention in recent years, principally because it has been used in a variety of ways, there is some lack of agreement regarding the definition of the concept, and its empirical implications do not easily distinguish it from more formal theories such as network theory.

Resource Allocation Model and Cognitive Interference Theory

A principal task in much mood–memory research is to account for mood-produced decrements in memory. A prominent explanation of such decrements is the resource allocation model of Ellis & Ashbrook (1988), which is based on the concepts of *attention* and *cognitive interference*. This model assumes that the induction of a sad mood, or any emotional state, will reduce the likelihood that a person will allocate or deploy attentional resources to some memory task. This occurs because the emotional state leads to an increase in irrelevant thoughts that compete with relevant cognitive activities important for memory. These intrusive, irrelevant thoughts pre-empt allocation of attention to the memory task, and thus impair performance. Ellis & Ashbrook (1988) proposed two mechanisms to account for mood-related decrements in memory: (a) depressed people allocate more attentional resources to processing irrelevant features of the memory task; and (b) depressed people think more about their moods (Salovey,

1992) and this reduces the cognitive resources available to allocate to the memory task. With either mechanism, any reduction in attentional capacity will impair performance on the memory task (see Kihlstrom, 1989). This view further contends that mood states produce their effects on memory, not by way of emotion *per se*, but by way of distracting, competing, irrelevant thoughts and by lack of attention given to relevant features of the memory task. Thus, it is the *cognitive consequences* of mood states that impact on memory, as distinct from the affective state itself, a position in general agreement with Riskind's cognitive priming position (1989).

One prediction of the Ellis–Ashbrook (1988) model is that the debilitating effects of a depressed mood will be greater when the encoding demands of the memory task are more difficult or demanding. Support for this prediction was obtained by Ellis, Thomas & Rodriguez (1984), who found that college students with depressed mood showed greater impairment in more difficult, effortful memory tasks. In a somewhat related study, Dalgleish (1995) found that a stimulus presentation that facilitated more elaborate processing appeared to produce a larger difference in performance between people with an emotional disorder and normal subjects, compared with a stimulus presentation that did not encourage elaborate processing. Another prediction is that happy (elated) as well as sad moods will lead to memory impairment, which was found by Seibert & Ellis (1991) in a perceptual grouping task and Ellis, Seibert & Varner (1995) in a surprise, delayed recall task. Similarly, Ingram, Bernet & McLaughlin (1994) demonstrated changes in attentional allocation processes in individuals at risk for depression, as reflected in enhanced attention to emotional stimuli following a negative mood indication. In addition, Ellis et al. (1995) found that depressed-mood college students were less effective in predicting their recall of passages than neutral mood students. The cognitive interference assumption of the model has been examined by demonstrating that the production of irrelevant thoughts is negatively correlated with recall performance. In two experiments, Seibert & Ellis (1991) found correlations of −0.72 and −0.67 between irrelevant thoughts and recall. Similarly, negative correlations between irrelevant thoughts and recall were obtained by Ellis et al. (1997). Although negative correlations are expected by the resource allocation model, thoughts may not always necessarily be the determinants of recall because both thoughts and recall may reflect an underlying difficulty in comprehending the memory material.

The resource allocation model does not assume that mood states will uniformly impair memory and Ellis (1990) has noted that there is no empirical basis for assuming across-the-board decrements in memory. Several studies have failed to find mood-related decrements in memory (e.g. Bower, Gilligan & Monteiro, 1981) and the evidence indicates interactions between mood states and task variables and argues for the task-sensitivity of mood effects (Ellis & Ashbrook, 1988, 1989; Hertel & Rude, 1991). Finally, the resource allocation model continues to be a principal approach in accounting for mood-related deficits in memory, primarily because it focuses on the processes of attention and cognitive interference that underlie mood–memory effects.

Motivational Theory

Another explanation of depressive deficits in memory is based on motivation. Persons in a depressed mood may simply be less energized to perform well in effortful tasks. A motivational account contends that depressed individuals could possess the cognitive resources to carry out the task but they are insufficiently motivated to do so. Talland (1965) made such a proposal regarding patients with amnesia and argued that motivational deficits might explain a variety of psychological deficits. Although there can be no doubt that motivational deficits may be present in depressed individuals, this explanation appears insufficient to account for all mood-related impairments in memory.

Kihlstrom (1989) proposed an interesting way to evaluate the motivational hypothesis. He suggested that it would be useful to examine the effects of elation and happiness on memory, and further suggested that positive and negative moods might have similar effects on memory, in that *both* mood states should induce extra-task processing, reduce attentional capacity and impair performance on effortful memory tasks, in accordance with the Ellis–Ashbrook (1988) model. He further noted that, "On the other hand, the motivational hypothesis seems to suggest that these effects should be specific to depression and sadness" (p. 25). This issue was quickly addressed in two studies. First, Seibert & Ellis (1991) found, in two experiments, that both positive and negative mood states produced a comparable reduction in recall compared with a neutral-mood control condition. Moreover, both positive and negative moods led to a comparable increase in irrelevant thoughts. Similarly, Ellis, Seibert & Varner (1995) found that positive and negative mood states produced a comparable reduction in recall in a surprise, delayed free-recall test. In short, symmetry of mood effects is not what would be expected from a motivational account of depressive deficits in memory, according to Kihlstrom.

We do not, or course, contend that symmetry of mood effects in memory is a general finding, and Isen (1987) has reported asymmetrical effects in some circumstances. Our conclusion is simply that a purely motivational account is incomplete and insufficient.

Cognitive Initiative Theory

Another view of mood-related decrements in memory concerns what Hertel (1994; Hertel & Rude, 1991) has called "cognitive initiative". She contends that depressed individuals may lack the necessary cognitive initiative to carry out memory tasks and that if properly constrained, deficits in memory performance can be eliminated. This position focuses on the use of cognitive strategies that might be employed to remediate memory deficits. What is significant about this view is that it also attempts to identify a specific mechanism that underlies depressive deficits, just as the resource allocation model identifies the processes of attention and cognitive interference. Although numerous studies have demon-

strated mood-related decrements in memory, a major theoretical task is to identify the mechanisms or processes that underlie such decrements.

In a test of this view, Hertel & Rude (1991) demonstrated that the typical
depressive-deficit in memory could be eliminated by requiring depressed subjects
to pay focused attention to the task. Their subjects were given a surprise recall
test after they had read incomplete sentence frames, in which they determined
whether a word properly completed a sentence. In one condition, subjects simply
read the sentence and decided if the word fitted; in the focused attention condition, subjects were required to read aloud the words at the beginning and end
of the presentation. Subjects who were required to pay attention showed none
of the usual depressive-deficit in recall. Hertel (1994) has summarized results of
several studies that show that depression does not always impair memory if
subjects are required to pay attention to the task.

It should be pointed out that, although the finding of remediation of impairments in memory through attentional control is supportive of cognitive initiative,
it is also what would be expected from the resource allocation model. This model
would also contend that the focused attention procedure produces improved
recall precisely because it encourages the increased allocation of attentional
resources to the task (Ellis, 1990).

Finally, it is the case that encouraging subjects to pay attention to a task does
not always reduce or eliminate depressive-deficits in performance. In a study of
mood effects on comprehension of stories, Ellis et al. (1997) found that subjects
who were encouraged to look for contradictions in stories were better at detecting contradictions than those not encouraged; however, depressed subjects were
still poorer at detecting contradictions than neutral mood subjects. In addition,
depressed subjects had a higher level of false detections, indicating that although
they were trying, that is, they were showing cognitive initiative with the task, their
comprehension was still poorer due to the depressed mood. This simply means
that, although the cognitive initiative idea is useful and important, it, like many
theories, has some constraints.

The significance of the cognitive initiative view is that it emphasizes the role
of cognitive strategies as a factor in mood–memory deficits, and that such deficits
can be remediated. In addition, it will likely be viewed as an important process
in understanding mood-related impairments in memory, principally because it
focuses on attentional control as an important process in remediating memory.

Arousal Theory

Several general theories of cognition and emotion have proposed a role for
arousal. For example, Clark, Milberg & Erber (1988) argued that arousal can cue
information stored in memory with a similar level of arousal. Similarly, Revelle &
Loftus (1992) proposed a general theory of anxiety in which arousal is a key
component. The role of arousal has been controversial and over the years researchers have proposed views ranging from Zajonc's (1984) primacy-of-affect
view to that of Lazarus (1991) and Riskind (1989), who argued that cognition is

primary in understanding emotion–cognition relationships. In the context of mood–memory research, the theoretical issue is: are mood–memory relationships dependent upon arousal, or upon cognitive (thought) processes, or upon both components?

Riskind (1989) has summarized a large amount of evidence which argues that the critical mediating mechanism is *cognitive priming*, as distinct from arousal. In experiments that pit cognitive priming against an arousal factor, the pattern of results was fairly consistent in support of cognitive priming. Similarly, Bower & Forgas (in press) reached a parallel conclusion in their analysis of this literature.

Further support of the cognitive priming view is seen in a recent study by Varner & Ellis (1998), who compared the relative effects of cognitive priming vs. arousal induced by stepping up and down a cinder block. They first demonstrated that free recall of a categorical word list was better for those words primed either by a sad-mood induction procedure or by reading an explanation of how to plan and write an essay. Subjects in a sad mood recalled more of the negative words in the list, whereas subjects in the essay-reading condition recalled more of the essay-related words in the list. In contrast, arousal produced no effect in recall, as the exercise subjects showed no difference in recall of either of the two types of words.

In contrast, an earlier study by Clark, Milberg & Ross (1983) provided evidence in support of the role of arousal. Their subjects learned two lists for free recall, one while relaxing and the other after exercising. Later, they attempted to recall both lists after watching a relaxing nature film or a sexually-arousing erotic film. They found that subjects better recalled the list learned while relaxed after viewing the relaxing nature film, whereas subjects better recalled the list learned earlier after exercising and while aroused from watching the erotic film. Importantly, their study indicated that arousal may prime the memory of arousing events. However, Bower & Forgas (in press) reported the results of an unpublished study by Van Aken (1995), which was a systematic replication of the Clark, Milberg & Ross (1993) study, in which no arousal-dependent memory was found.

In summary, we are left with a somewhat uncertain picture regarding the role of arousal, with some doubt placed on the robustness of arousal effects and on the general importance of arousal as a factor accounting for mood–memory findings.

SUMMARY OF MOOD-RELATED IMPAIRMENTS IN MEMORY FOR NEUTRAL MATERIALS

There is now a vast literature on mood-related effects on memory, including the conditions under which mood affects memory. This research has been described in various sources (e.g. Bower 1992; Bower & Forgas, in press; Christianson, 1992; Eich, in press; Ellis & Ashbrook, 1988, 1989; Ellis & Hertel, 1993; Fiedler & Forgas, 1988; Forgas, 1995; Gotlib, 1992; Kuiken, 1989, 1991; Mathews, 1996;

Mathews & MacLeod, 1994; Teasdale & Barnard, 1993; Williams et al., 1988; Winograd & Neisser, 1992) and continues to grow at a rapid pace. Space limitations preclude any systematic or detailed examination of this research on mood-related decrements in memory. Instead, we shall briefly summarize 15 of the major generalizations that emerge from this research on memory for neutral material.

The principal generalizations regarding mood-related decrements in memory are as follows:

1. As a general rule, depressive mood states will impair memory, and do so because of several processes operating, including attentional deficits, cognitive interference, negative schemata, lack of motivation and impaired cognitive initiative.
2. Similarly, happy or elated moods can impair memory and may do so by way of some of the same processes.
3. Memory performance is not always impaired by depressive mood states. When mood fails to affect memory, this may be the result of many possible factors, including weak mood manipulations, relatively easy memory tasks, and the operation of mood-repair processes.
4. Mood-related deficits in memory can be remediated by procedures designed to encourage or force a person to pay attention to the memory task.
5. Research shows that mood-state, memory-task and subject-condition interactions occur with some frequency. For example, mood effects appear greatest with more effortful, demanding tasks.
6. Implicit as well as explicit memory may be impaired by depressive mood states; however, the effects on implicit memory appear to be weaker and not as reliable.
7. Mood states are frequently accompanied by intrusive irrelevant and/or negative thoughts which, in turn, may produce decrements in memory.
8. Similarly, mood-related deficits in memory may be the result of a failure in cognitive initiative, that is, the spontaneous use of cognitive strategies.
9. Mood effects appear most likely to be the result of cognitive priming, that is, the activation of thoughts as a result of a person's prevailing mood state.
10. Mood effects in memory cannot be attributed simply to a motivation-deficit explanation.
11. Likewise, mood impairments in memory appear not to be the simple result of arousal.
12. Mood states can impair both encoding and retrieval processes in memory.
13. Mood effects appear in everyday memory situations with emotional as well as neutral materials, including false memories, autobiographical memory (including flashbulb memories) and eyewitness testimony.
14. Experimentally induced and naturally occurring depressive mood states frequently, but not always, produce similar decrements in memory performance. Similar decrements in performance do not, of course, necessarily imply similar processes underlying such effects.

15.   Finally, mood-related impairments in memory cannot be attributed simply
       to the demand characteristics of the task.

REFERENCES

Beck, A. T., Rush, A. J., Shaw, B. F. & Eméry, B. (1979).   *Cognitive Therapy of Depres-
    sion.* New York: Guilford.
Beck, R. C. & McBee, W. (1995).   Mood-dependent memory for generated and repeated
    words: replication and extension. *Cognition & Emotion*, **9**, 289–307.
Blaney, P. H. (1986).   Affect and memory: a review. *Psychological Bulletin*, **99**, 229–246.
Bower, G. H. (1981).   Mood and memory. *American Psychologist*, **36**, 129–148.
Bower, G. H. (1992).   How might emotions affect learning? In S. A. Christianson (ed.),
    The Handbook of Emotion and Memory: Research and Theory. Hillsdale, NJ: Erlbaum,
    pp. 3–31.
Bower, G. H., Gilligan, S. G. & Monteiro, K. P. (1981).   Selectivity of learning caused by
    affective states. *Journal of Experimental Psychology: General*, **110**, 451–473.
Bower, G. H. & Forgas, J. P. (in press).   Affect, memory, and social cognition. In E. Eich
    (ed.), *Counter-points: Cognition and Emotion*. New York: Oxford University Press.
Bower, G. H. & Mayer, J. D. (1989).   In search of mood-dependent retrieval. In D.
    Kuiken (ed.), *Mood and Memory: Theory, Research and Applications*. Special issue of
    Journal of Social Behavior and Personality, **4**, 121–156.
Bower, G. H., Monteiro, K. P. & Gilligan, S. G. (1978).   Emotional mood as a context
    for learning and recall. *Journal of Verbal Learning and Verbal Behavior*, **17**, 573–585.
Bradley, B. & Mathews, A. (1983).   Negative self-schemata in clinical depression. *British
    Journal of Clinical Psychology*, **22**, 173–181.
Bullington, J. C. (1990).   Mood congruent memory: a replication of symmetrical effects
    for both positive and negative moods. *Journal of Social Behavior and Personality*, **5**,
    123–134.
Burke, M. & Mathews, A. M. (1992).   Autobiographical memory and clinical anxiety.
    Cognition and Emotion, **6**, 23–35.
Christianson, S. A. (ed.) (1992).   *The Handbook of Emotion and Memory: Research and
    Theory*. Hillsdale, NJ: Erlbaum.
Clark, D. M, Teasdale, J. D., Broadbent, D. E. & Martin, M. (1983).   Effect of mood on
    lexical decisions. *Bulletin of the Psychonomic Society*, **21**, 175–178.
Clark, M. S. & Isen, A. M. (1982).   Towards understanding the relationship between
    feeling states and social behavior. In A. H. Hastorf & A. M. Isen (eds), *Cognitive Social
    Psychology*. New York: Elsevier-North Holland, pp. 73–108.
Clark, M. S., Milberg, S. & Erber, R. (1988).   Arousal-state-dependent memory: evi-
    dence and implications for understanding social judgments and social behavior. In K.
    Fiedler & J. P. Forgas (eds), *Affect, Cognition, and Social Behavior*. Toronto: Hogrefe,
    pp. 63–86.
Clark, M. S., Milberg, S. & Ross, J. (1983).   Arousal cues arousal-related material in
    memory: implication for understanding effects of mood on memory. *Journal of Verbal
    Learning and Verbal Behavior*, **22**, 633–649.
Dalgleish, T. (1995).   Performance of the emotional Stroop task in groups of anxious,
    expert, and control participants: a comparison of computer and card presentation
    formats. *Cognition & Emotion*, **9**, 326–340.
Dalgleish, T. & Watts, F. N. (1990).   Biases of attention and memory in disorders of
    anxiety and depression. *Clinical Psychology Review*, **10**, 589–604.
Eich, E. (1995).   Searching for mood dependent memory. *Psychological Science*, **6**, 67–75.
Eich, E. (ed.) (in press).   *Counter-points: Cognition and Emotion*. New York: Oxford
    University Press.

Eich, E., Macaulay, E. & Ryan, L. (1994). Mood dependent memory for events of the personal past. *Journal of Experimental Psychology: General*, **123**, 201–215.

Eich, E. & Metcalfe, J. (1989). Mood dependent memory for internal versus external events. *Journal of Experimental Psychology: Learning, Memory & Cognition*, **15**, 443–455.

Ellis, H. C. (1990). Depressive deficits in memory: processing initiative and resource allocation. *Journal of Experimental Psychology: General*, **119**, 60–62.

Ellis, H. C. & Ashbrook, P. W. (1988). Resource allocation model of the effects of depressed mood states on memory. In K. Fiedler & J. P. Forgas (eds), *Affect, Cognition, and Social Behavior*. Toronto: Hogrefe, pp. 25–43.

Ellis, H. C. & Ashbrook, P. W. (1989). The "state" of mood and memory research: a selective review. In D. Kuiken (ed.), *Mood and Memory: Theory, Research and Applications*. Special issue of *Journal of Social Behavior and Personality*, **4**, 1–21.

Ellis, H. C. & Hertel, P. T. (1993). Cognition, emotion and memory: some applications and issues. In C. Izawa (ed.), *Cognitive Psychology Applied*. Hillsdale, NJ: Erlbaum, pp. 199–215.

Ellis, H. C., Moore, B. A, Varner, L. J., Ottaway, S. A. & Becker, A. S. (1997). Depressed mood, task organization, cognitive interference, and memory: irrelevant thoughts predict recall performance. *Journal of Social Behavior and Personality*, **12**, 453–470.

Ellis, H. C., Ottaway, S. A., Varner, L. J., Becker, A. S. & Moore, B. A. (1997). Emotion, motivation and text comprehension: the detection of contradictions in passages. *Journal of Experimental Psychology: General*, **126**, 131–146.

Ellis, H. C., Seibert, P. S. & Varner, L. J. (1995). Emotion and memory: Effects of mood states on immediate and unexpected delayed recall. *Journal of Social Behavior and Personality*, **10**, 349–362.

Ellis, H. C., Thomas, R. I. L. & Rodriguez, I. A. (1984). Emotional mood states and memory: elaborative encoding, semantic processing, and cognitive effort. *Journal of Experimental Psychology: Learning, Memory & Cognition*, **10**, 470–482.

Ellis, H. C., Varner, L. J., Becker, A. S. & Ottaway, S. A. (1995). Emotion and prior knowledge in memory and judged comprehension of ambiguous stories. *Cognition & Emotion*, **9**, 363–382.

Eysenck, M. W., MacLeod, C. & Mathews, A. M. (1987). Cognitive functioning in anxiety. *Psychological Research*, **49**, 189–195.

Fiedler, K. (1990). Mood-dependent selectivity in social cognition. In W. Stroebe & M. Hewstone (eds), *European Review of Social Psychology*, Vol. 1. Chichester: Wiley, pp. 1–32.

Fiedler, K. & Forgas, J. P. (eds) (1988). *Affect, Cognition and Social Behavior*. Toronto: Hogrefe.

Fiedler, K. & Stroehm, W. (1986). What kind of mood influences what kind of memory: the role of arousal and information structure. *Memory & Cognition*, **14**, 181–188.

Forgas, J. P. (1995). Mood and judgment: the Affect Infusion Model (AIM). *Psychological Bulletin*, **117**, 1–28.

Forgas, J. P. & Bower, G. H. (1987). Mood effects on person perception judgments. *Journal of Personality and Social Psychology*, **53**, 53–60.

Gilboa, E. & Gotlib, I. H. (in press). Cognitive biases and affect persistence in previously dysphoric and never-dysphoric individuals. *Cognition & Emotion*.

Gotlib, I. H. (1992). *Psychological Aspects of Depression: Toward a Cognitive Interpersonal Integration*. Chichester: Wiley.

Gotlib, I. H. & McCabe, S. B. (1992). An information processing approach to the study of cognitive functioning in depression. In E. Walker, B. Cornblatt & R. Dworkin (eds), *Progress in Experimental Personality and Psychopathology Research*. New York: Springer, pp. 131–161.

Gotlib, I. H. & McCann, C. D. (1984). Construct accessibility and depression: an examination of cognitive and affective factors. *Journal of Personality and Social Psychology*, **47**, 427–439.

Gotlib, I. H., Gilboa, E. & Kaplan, B. L. (in press). Cognitive functioning in depression: nature and origins. In R. J. Davidson (ed.), *Wisconsin Symposium on Emotion*, Vol. 1. New York: Oxford University Press.

Gotlib, I. H., Roberts, J. E. & Gilboa, E. (1996). Cognitive interference in depression. In I. G. Sarason, G. R. Pierce & B. R. Sarason (eds), *Cognitive Interference: Theories, Methods, and Findings*. Mahwah, NJ: Erlbaum, pp. 347–378.

Haaga, D. A. F. (1989). Mood state-dependent retention using identical or non-identical mood inductions at learning and recall. *British Journal of Clinical Psychology*, **28**, 75–83.

Hedlund, S. & Rude, S. S. (1995). Evidence of latent depressive schemas in formerly depressed individuals. *Journal of Abnormal Psychology*, **104**, 517–525.

Hertel, P. T. (1994). Depressive deficits in word identification and recall. *Cognition & Emotion*, **8**, 313–327.

Hertel, P. T. & Rude, S. S. (1991). Depressive deficits in memory: focusing attention improves subsequent recall. *Journal of Experimental Psychology: General*, **120**, 301–309.

Ingram, R. E., Bernet, C. Z. & McLaughlin, S. C. (1994). Attentional allocation processes in individuals at risk for depression. *Cognitive Therapy and Research*, **18**, 317–332.

Isen, A. (1987). Positive affect, cognitive processes and social behavior. In L. Berkowitz (ed.), *Advances in Experimental Social Psychology*, Vol. 20. New York: Academic Press, pp. 203–253.

Kihlstrom, J. F. (1989). On what does mood-dependent memory depend? In D. Kuiken (ed.), *Mood and Memory: Theory, Research and Applications*. Special issue of *Journal of Social Behavior and Personality*, **4**, 23–32.

Kuiken, D. (ed.) (1989). *Mood and Memory: Theory, Research and Applications*. Special issue of *Journal of Social Behavior and Personality*, **4**.

Kuiken, D. (1991). *Mood and Memory*. Newbury Park, CA: Sage.

Kuiper, N. A. & Derry, P. A. (1982). Depressed and non-depressed content self-reference in mild depressives. *Journal of Personality*, **50**, 67–80.

Lazarus, L. S. (1991). *Emotion and Adaptation*. New York: Oxford University Press.

Leight, K. A. & Ellis, H. C. (1981). Emotional mood states, strategies, and state-dependency in memory. *Journal of Verbal Learning and Verbal Behavior*, **20**, 251–266.

Mathews, A. (1996). Selective encoding of emotional information. In D. Herrmann, C. McEvoy, C. Hertzog, P. Hertel & M. K. Johnson (eds), *Basic and Applied Memory Research: Practical Applications*, Vol. 2. Mahwah, NJ: Erlbaum, pp. 287–300.

Mathews, A. M. & MacLeod, C. (1994). Cognitive approaches to emotion and emotional disorders. *Annual Review of Psychology*, **45**, 25–50.

Matt, G. E., Vazquez, C. & Campbell, W. K. (1992). Mood-congruent recall of affectively toned stimuli: a meta-analytic review. *Clinical Psychology Review*, **12**, 227–255.

Mayer, J. D., Gaschke, Y. N., Braverman, D. L. & Evans, T. W. (1992). Mood congruent judgment is a general effect. *Journal of Personality and Social Psychology*, **63**, 119–132.

Mayer, J. D. & Salovey, P. (1988). Personality moderates the interaction of mood and cognition. In K. Fiedler & J. P. Forgas (eds), *Affect, Cognition, and Social Behavior*. Toronto: Hogrefe, pp. 87–99.

McNally, R. J. (1994). Cognitive bias in panic disorders. *Current Directions in Psychological Science*, **3**, 129–132.

Mineka, S. (1992). Evolutionary memories, emotional processing, and the emotional disorders. In D. L. Medin (ed.), *The Psychology of Learning and Motivation: Research and Theory*. Hillsdale, NJ: Erlbaum, pp. 245–268.

Nasby, W. (1994). Moderators of mood-congruent encoding: self-/other-reference and affirmative/non-affirmative judgment. *Cognition & Emotion*, **8**, 259–278.

Parrott, W. G. & Sabini, J. (1990). Mood and memory under natural conditions: Evidence for mood incongruent recall. *Journal of Personality and Social Psychology*, **59**, 321–336.

Perrig, W. J. & Perrig, P. (1988). Mood and memory: mood-congruity effects in absence of mood. *Memory & Cognition*, **16**, 102–109.

Pietromonaco, P. R. & Markus, H. (1985). The nature of negative thoughts in depression. *Journal of Personality and Social Psychology*, **48**, 799–807.

Revelle, W. & Loftus, D. A. (1992). The implications of arousal effects for the study of affect and memory. In S. A. Christianson (ed.), *The Handbook of Emotion and Memory: Research and Theory*. Hillsdale, NJ: Erlbaum, pp. 113–149.

Rinck, M., Glowalia, U. & Schneider, K. (1992). Mood-congruent and mood-incongruent learning. *Memory & Cognition*, **20**, 29–39.

Riskind, J. H. (1989). The mediating mechanisms in mood and memory: a cognitive-priming formulation. In D. Kuiken (ed.), *Mood and Memory: Theory, Research and Applications*. Special issue of *Journal of Social Behavior and Personality*, **4**, 39–43.

Rothkopf, J. S. & Blaney, P. H. (1991). Mood-congruent memory: the role of affective focus and gender. *Cognition & Emotion*, **5**, 53–64.

Ruiz-Caballero, J. A. & Gonzalez, P. (1994). Implicit and explicit memory bias in depressed and non-depressed subjects. *Cognition and Emotion*, **8**, 555–570.

Salovey, P. (1992). Mood-induced self-focused attention. *Journal of Personality and Social Psychology*, **62**, 699–707.

Sarason, I. G., Pierce, G. R. & Sarason, B. R. (eds) (1996). *Cognitive Interference: Theories, Methods and Findings*. Mahwah, NJ: Erlbaum.

Schwarz, N. & Clore, G. L. (1988). How do I feel about it? The informative function and directive functions of affective states. In K. Fiedler & J. P. Forgas (eds), *Affect, Cognition, and Social Behavior*. Toronto: Hogrefe, pp. 44–62.

Seibert, P. S. & Ellis, H. C. (1991). Irrelevant thoughts, emotional mood states, and cognitive task performance. *Memory and Cognition*, **19**, 507–513.

Singer, J. A. & Salovey, P. (1988). Mood and memory: evaluating the network theory of affect. *Clinical Psychology Review*, **8**, 211–251.

Smith, S. M. & Petty, R. E. (1995). Personality moderators of mood congruency effects on cognition: the role of self-esteem and negative mood regulation. *Journal of Personality and Social Psychology*, **68**, 1092–1107.

Snyder, M. & White, P. (1982). Moods and memories: elation, depression and the remembering of the events of one's life. *Journal of Personality*, **50**, 149–167.

Talland, G. A. (1965). *Deranged Memory: A Psychonomic Study of the Amnesic Syndrome*. New York: Academic Press.

Teasdale, J. D. & Barnard, P. G. (1993). *Affect, Cognition, and Change: Remodeling Depressive Thought*. Hillsdale, NJ: Erlbaum.

Teasdale, J. D. & Fogarty, S. J. (1979). Differential effects of induced mood on retrieval of pleasant and unpleasant events from episodic memory. *Journal of Abnormal Psychology*, **88**, 248–257.

Teasdale, J. D. & Russell, M. L. (1983). Differential effects of induced mood on the recall of positive, negative and neutral words. *British Journal of Clinical Psychology*, **22**, 163–171.

Tobias, B. A., Kihlstrom, J. F. & Schacter, D. L. (1992). Emotion and implicit memory. In S. A. Christianson (ed.), *The Handbook of Emotion and Memory: Research and Theory*. Hillsdale, NJ: Erlbaum, pp. 67–92.

Ucros, C. G. (1989). Mood state-dependent memory: a meta-analysis. *Cognition & Emotion*, **3**, 139–169.

Van Aken, C. (1995). Mood-Dependent Memory: Is Arousal State the Underlying

Mechanism? Unpublished Honors Thesis, Department of Psychology, Stanford University, Stanford, CA.

Varner, L. J. & Ellis, H. C. (1998). Cognitive activity and physiological arousal: processes that mediate mood-congruent memory. *Memory & Cognition*, **26**, 939–950.

Watkins, T., Mathews, A. M., Williamson, D. A. & Fuller, R. D. (1992). Mood congruent memory in depression: emotional priming or elaboration? *Journal of Abnormal Psychology*, **101**, 581–586.

Watts, F. N. & Dalgleish, T. (1991). Memory for phobia related words in spider phobics. *Cognition & Emotion*, **5**, 313–329.

Watts, F. N., McKenna, F. P., Sharrock, R. & Trezise, L. (1988). Color naming of phobia related words. *British Journal of Psychology*, **77**, 97–108.

Weingartner, H., Miller, H. & Murphy, D. L. (1977). Mood-state-dependent retrieval of verbal associations. *Journal of Abnormal Psychology*, **86**, 276–284.

Williams, J. M. G., Watts, F. N., MacLeod, C. & Mathews, A. (1988). *Cognitive Psychology and Emotional Disorders*. Chichester: Wiley.

Winograd, E. & Neisser, U. (1992). *Affect and Accuracy in Recall*. New York: Cambridge University Press.

Zajonc, R. B. (1984). On the primacy of affect. *American Psychologist*, **39**, 117–123.

Chapter 11

Organization of Emotional Memories

Sven-Åke Christianson *and* **Elisabeth Engelberg**
Stockholm University, Stockholm, Sweden

From an evolutionary perspective it is essential to recognize and remember emotional events and, in particular, unpleasant situations in order to ensure appropriate responses in maintaining protective, withdrawing or defensive behavior. Thus, survival has, to a great extent, hinged on some sort of emotional system that is fast enough to alert us to threatening or disturbing stimuli. The ability to quickly identify and recognize stimuli indicative of threatening situations seems to be based on partly an intentional recollection, mediated by phylogenetically and ontogenetically sophisticated memory systems (cf. episodic and semantic memory, see Tulving, 1972; explicit memory, see Graf & Schacter, 1985; reflective memory, see Johnson & Multhaup, 1992), and partly by mechanisms which do not involve consciously controlled processes (cf. implicit memory, see Schacter 1987; perceptual representation system, see Tulving & Schacter, 1990; evolutionary early perceptual subsystems, see Johnson & Multhaup, 1992).

With evolution, we also seem to have developed mechanisms which help us to inhibit or "forget" unpleasant experiences. To "forget" does not necessarily mean that the information is lost forever. Rather, we sometimes may have great difficulties accessing these events and bringing them up to a level of conscious awareness. There is extensive documentation showing that memories can be lost through trauma, for example victims of rape, torture, sexual abuse and war may show an initial psychogenic amnesia, but these memories may be successfully retrieved later on. Thus, memory of emotional events could be said to be organized along dimensions of consciousness. This chapter aims at elaborating on the thesis that emotionally valenced information is sometimes organized to favour conscious access routes and sometimes to favour non-conscious access routes.

Handbook of Cognition and Emotion. Edited by T. Dalgleish and M. Power.
© 1999 John Wiley & Sons Ltd.

We review some recent research that points to how a different organization of memory components may give rise to either dissociative kinds of remembering or a more complete retrieval of an emotional episode.

RECOLLECTION OF EMOTIONAL EVENTS AMONG CHILDREN AND ADULTS

A sizable body of research exists on memory for emotional events, in which the approach is taken to eocamine the subject's intentional effort to recall some previous episode. Even though explicit recall is undertaken for events that have occurred in early childhood, it is still possible to retrieve rather accurate details pertaining to these events (e.g. Brewin, Andrews & Gotlib, 1993; Goodman, Hepps & Reed, 1986; Goodman et al., 1996; Ornstein et al., 1993; Sheingold & Tenney, 1982). Usher & Neisser (1993) studied, for example, the earliest memories possible to retrieve among adults with regard to four different events having occurred during the first 5 years. The type of events consisted of the birth of a younger sibling, an overnight stay at a hospital, the death of a family member and the family moving to another location. A few hundred students reported that they had experienced at least one of these four events, and either the mother or a close relative could corroborate the time and place that the event had occurred. Results showed that a hospital stay and the birth of a sibling was remembered mainly if experienced after the age of 2–3 years, whereas the death of a family member and moving house tended to be remembered mostly if they had occurred after 3–4 years of age.

Less developed functions in the child, such as cognitive abilities, may account for the less complete encoding of events occurring in early childhood. More specifically, the self-concept, Howe & Courage (1993) argue, is a necessary reference point for organization of personal experiences in memory. The knowledge of one's own self is, according to Howe, Courage & Peterson (1996), under a gradual development between 18 and 24 months of age. Prior to 24 months, it is nevertheless possible to observe long-term memory retention in the form of habituation, preference for new objects, emotion-laden associations or idiosyncratic behavior. For example, an 18 month-old girl had a fish bone stuck in her throat and had to have it removed by a physician. The girl was described as "hysterical" during the removal of the fish bone. Seven months later she was unable to relate verbally any details about this event, but she was nevertheless able to recognize the physician. She further refused to eat fish and was very reluctant to have her throat examined (Howe, Courage & Peterson, 1996). At the time of the event, the girl had developed neither a sufficient verbal ability nor a full blown self-concept, and she therefore could not encode and store the event as a distinct episode. Her experience had instead become encoded as a schematic representation that could only be retrieved indirectly through the behavior that she exhibited.

Although expressed behaviorally, the critical detail information about the stressful event, that is, information that elicited the emotional reaction, was well retained at an implicit level in the memory of the 18 month-old girl. On the basis of 25 cases of young children's long-term retention of early traumatic events, involving emergency room treatment, Howe, Courage & Peterson (1996) concluded that central features of the incident, as well as the post-event treatment, were extremely well remembered, both immediately and at a 6-month recall, but the amount of peripheral information that was freely recalled declined over a 6-month retention interval. This pattern is consistent with laboratory-based studies of long-term retention (Christianson, 1992; Heuer & Reisberg, 1990; Rudy & Goodman, 1991; Terr, 1990). Such central or critical detail information tends to be specifically retained from traumatic experiences. Lenore Terr (1979, 1983), for instance, points to the accuracy with which the children in Chowchilla could verbally recall the gist in the sequence of events of their kidnapping, but they were often mistaken in their recall of peripheral details. A high degree of accuracy of central details, as compared to peripheral details, has also been seen among adult witnesses to violent crimes, who were interviewed by Yuille and his colleagues (Yuille & Cutshall, 1986, 1989; Yuille & Tollestrup, 1992) soon after the crime and again 4–5 months later.

In cases of very strong emotions, the individual most often thinks about and reacts to certain emotionally stressful aspects that are central to the traumatic experience. The individual is also often preoccupied with intrusive thoughts about the threatening event. This type of processing will result in narrowed attention and heightened psychological focusing on those critical details that are the source of the emotional stress. We might refer to this process as "tunnel memory". In this stage of processing, the subject engages in an emotional mode of processing, where "controlled" mechanisms, such as post-stimulus elaboration, are allocated to the emotion-provoking information. Compared to a neutral event, subjects exposed to an emotionally stressful event, such as an accident or a crime, are more concerned with what they have just experienced, which will lead to increased post-stimulus elaboration. Heuer (1987) argues that the recall pattern for emotional events and associated details is different from that of neutral events in that emotional memories center around the causes of the emotions—the thoughts, feelings, and reactions of the subject—and thus cause the subject to personalize a narrative account around the central elements of the emotional experience. Emotional events also have greater implications for the individual's sense of self, which promotes elaborative rehearsal. A failure to integrate a traumatic experience with the sense of self is sometimes observed in dissociative reactions, such as psychogenic amnesia, psychogenic fugue or multiple personality disorder. Thus, the process of elaboration, such as thinking about and reacting to the emotion-provoking information, will promote memory of central detailed information and the gist of the emotional event, but actively inhibit processing of details that are irrelevant, spatially peripheral to the emotion-eliciting event or the source of emotional stress, or both. A strong affective reaction after an event may also act as a cue and cause reactivation of the emotion-provoking event information. That is, a negative emotional reaction like fear, disgust or anger would cue a person to remember the negative or upsetting in what he/she had just experienced. In contrast to neutral situations, where the detailed information normally does not elicit feelings that are intrinsic to the event information, there is a natural correspondence between what a person feels and the emotion-eliciting information in emotionally arousing situations. Criminal psychopaths, who do not experience emotional reactions to emotionally valenced events, show no differential processing of emotional information, and thus may fail to show enhanced memory for central details of a traumatic event (Christianson et al., 1996).

The tunnel memory effects as described above, resulting from emotional/ traumatic experiences, appear to lessen over time, perhaps as the original emotional stress lessens. One implication of this change in memory representation is that the individual may regain access to peripheral information in a traumatic event. Research has also shown that the favorable central details effects found with immediate testing increased with delayed testing, compared to the neutral condition, whereas the peripheral details disadvantage in the emotional condition decreased (see e.g. Burke, Heuer & Reisberg, 1992). In conclusion, emotional stress may in some instances inhibit initial retrieval of certain detailed information, or the whole event in cases of traumatic amnesia, but helps long-term remembering of certain core information of emotional events. Equally important, emotional memories contain errors and will in many cases be lost, that is, emotion provides no guarantee of permanent or perfectly accurate recall, but, as stated by Heuer & Reisberg (1992), ". . . we believe it likely that we can largely trust our vivid memories" (p. 176).

NON-CONSCIOUS ACCESS ROUTES TO TRAUMATIC MEMORY

The rare case of a very persistent inability to recall certain events, and of course in the absence of any organic memory deficits, is usually an indicator of long-standing or repeated trauma that involves severe intimidation or a violation of integrity. A study by Williams (1994) showed that 38% of women who had been treated for rape or sexual abuse prior to 12 years of age, could not remember the abuse or the treatment 17 years later when interviewed about it. Such experiences may, however, sometimes be expressed through emotional reactions triggering avoidance behavior to trauma-related types of stimuli. That is, an emotional response to some stimulus may reveal the experience of a previous event that is not explicitly recalled. This was seen in a case study of a woman who had been brutally assaulted and raped, and as a result suffered from psychogenic amnesia (Christianson & Nilsson, 1989). Three weeks after the rape, the woman was escorted by the police through the area of woods where she had been found shortly after the assault. She reacted with great anxiety to specific places and spontaneously uttered: "And then there is the brick", but could not explain why these details crossed her mind. In guiding her onto a path, she got very distressed at the sight of crumbled bricks spread over the path and into the wooded environment. Upon reaching a nearby meadow, she began to cry, perspire profusely and feel very nauseous. As the rapist had confessed a few days earlier, the police knew that she had been running along the path in an attempt to escape the rapist before he had caught up with her and forced her out onto the meadow, where the rape took place.

Both classic and contemporary observations among mainly amnesics (e.g. Christianson & Nilsson, 1989; Claparede, 1911, 1951; Levinson, 1967), have shown that the memory of emotional aspects of an event may be available through non-intentional, non-conscious expressions. The phenomenon in which affective components of an emotional event are retrieved beyond the specific details of the event itself is further illustrated by the following case study. A 17 year-old man was jailed and tortured in Argentina for 6 years. Barely alive, he was saved through Amnesty International. After residing in Sweden for 20 years, he recounted the following about his memories of the years of torture:

> Memories come over me, not when I try to remember or want to . . . . We were going to play indoor hockey. I was there with a few friends from work and we were sitting in the locker room, changing clothes and waiting for a couple playing badminton to finish their game. It was a big hall where there was a powerful echo to every loud sound. The two people playing badminton seemed to be at it quite intensely.
>
> There I was in the locker room chatting with my colleagues. All of a sudden, I could feel how I started to perspire. I felt my heart beating faster and this nauseous feeling. I felt as if I was going to faint. I could definitely feel that something was happening to me. I could not control it. I thought to myself: "What is happening to me?"
>
> Then, all these sensations started to fade. My colleagues asked me: "What's the matter?" "I'm okay", I said. And a few minutes later, I understood. The sounds from the hall, where it echoed, were identical to the sound that I had heard a thousand times in jail, where they tortured people. The badminton players screamed very loudly when they missed the ball or something, and indeed screamed pretty ferociously. There was also the noise of an almost naked body falling to the floor, which was exactly the same sound that you could hear in the isolation unit in the jail in Argentina (Christianson, 1994, p. 360).

Another example that similarly illustrates partly independent memory functions, is provided in the case study of a 19 year-old woman. She had been raped by a group of men in an unusually brutal and sadistic fashion, resulting in various injuries, of which some had to be surgically amended. Although she was constantly preoccupied in her thoughts with the rape incident, she would go through emotions of intense anxiety, along with shaking and palpitations, only when seeing people that were of the same ethnic background as the rapists (Hartman & Burgess, 1993).

Several cases in the literature suggest an interesting double dissociation between memory for emotional information and memory for specific event information. That is, sometimes people seem to exhibit retention of the emotional component of an event without having access to specific event information, or remember specific event information without having access to the emotional component of the event. A few laboratory studies (Christianson, Säisä & Silfvenius, 1995; see Johnson & Multhaup, 1992) have investigated the implication that affective responses may reflect the acquisition of emotionally valenced information at a previous episode. In a study by Johnson, Kim & Risse (1985), Korsakoff patients were presented with two pictures, each portraying a different male face. The subjects were then asked to rate the two faces on several characteristics pertaining to personality (e.g. honesty, generosity). After having made the impression ratings, the Korsakoffs were asked to listen to a tape containing fictional biographical information, which depicted the person on each picture as either a "good guy" or a "bad guy". The impact of the biographical information on later affective memory of the pictures was measured by repeated impression ratings. When the Korsakoffs were tested after a 20-day interval, they recognized both target pictures, but were unable to recall the biographical information. Although the patients did not have voluntary access to the biographical information, 78% of these had more favorable impression ratings of the "good guy" than of the "bad guy".

In a neuropsychological study using a similar design to that of Johnson, Kim & Risse (1985), emotional reactions and memory were studied in patients with unilateral temporal and/or frontal lobe epilepsy, using a sodium amytal testing procedure (Christianson, Säisä & Silfvenius, 1995). The patients were presented with pictures of ordinary faces and accompanying biographical descriptions while either the right or the left cerebral hemisphere was deactivated. Results showed a superior recognition of faces that were associated with unpleasant biographies following left hemisphere injection (i.e. testing the non-speech-dominant right hemisphere). Although the content of the biographical information could not be recognized, the ratings of the faces associated with the unpleasant biographies were less favorable. The finding of this study is consistent with that of Johnson, Kim & Risse (1985), that is, emotional information may be retrieved by mechanisms at a different, non-verbal level of consciousness.

Marcia Johnson more specifically envisions such retrieval mechanisms to be mediated by non-verbal, so-called "perceptual subsystems" of the brain, that stem from the early evolution of man (Johnson, 1990; Johnson & Multhaup, 1992), as opposed to the later developed "reflective subsystems". In different classifications of memory, there is an implication that emotional information may be acquired, apart from semantically mediated processes, also as perceptually based changes in stored memory representations at a non-declarative or procedural level, and be expressed through behavior or performance (e.g. Squire, 1995). Other researchers emphasize the role of implicit retrieval mechanisms when emotional aspects of a traumatic event have become dissociated (see e.g. Tobias, Kihlstrom & Schacter, 1992). Another view is that a non-conscious, emotional processing takes place simultaneously with a conscious, conceptual processing (Leventhal, 1984). In consistency with the views mentioned above, yet other researchers have proposed dual representations of autobiographical events. Conway (1992), for instance, has proposed a kind of representation that consists, on the one hand, of a "phenomenological record" containing on-line phenomenal experience of specific events and, on the other hand, of "thematic knowledge" containing more semantic or abstract knowledge about events in the personal history of an individual. Brewin, Dalgleish & Joseph (1996; see also Brewin, 1989) have, however, more specifically focused upon trauma in formulating their dual representation consisting of "situationally accessible knowledge" and "verbally accessible knowledge". The former indeliberately triggers emotional responses, as originally conditioned, in situations where some aspects may be reminiscent of the traumatic event. Situationally accessible knowledge is not available to consciousness via so-called "verbally accessible knowledge", which is generic knowledge that enables an individual to appraise the implications of the traumatic event and to integrate it with existing schemata of self-image and the world in general. A dual representation theory neatly ties into observations that traumatic experiences are generally represented as memories of feelings and bodily sensations. Christianson & Engelberg (1996) have, therefore, argued that the kind of emotionally monitored memory response that is difficult to express verbally is a rudiment of earlier stages in evolution, i.e. a type of "hard-wired" mechanism that ensures automatic and non-conscious retention of distinct emotional information from stressful events, in order to react to threatening stimuli and maintain a defensive behavior. More sophisticated mechanisms have developed with evolution, either to integrate an experience with relevant schemata at a cognitive level, or to block experiences from consciousness that would otherwise impede normal functioning in contemporary life.

Research has given support to the different interpretations basically emanating from an idea that emotional processing would take place in two different systems and, further, that these are hierarchically organized as a result of evolution (see Gainotti, Caltagirone & Zoccolotti, 1993, for an overview). Emotion and memory are, as pointed out by Joseph LeDoux (1992), nonetheless often discussed as unitary phenomena. There is generally an assumption that feelings either facilitate or inhibit memory (e.g. mood state-dependent theories, Bower, 1981; Ellis & Ashbrook, 1989; theories of repression, Freud, 1915/1957; Rapaport, 1942). Emotions *per se* may, however, constitute a form of memory that the brain may encode and store, particularly memories of negative valence. When such memories are established merely by means of subcortical mechanisms, they may be encoded through non-conscious processing and become very resistant to extinction, as illustrated above with, for example, the man formerly tortured in an Argentine prison.

INTERCONNECTED REPRESENTATION OF AN AFFECTIVE EXPERIENCE

Apart from contextual cues associated with critical event information, such as auditory details (as in the case of the formerly tortured man), and visual details (the brutally raped woman), smell sensations may elicit memories of emotional salience. Such odor-evoked memory experiences are usually accompanied by a feeling reminiscent of the "tip of the tongue" (Lawless & Engen, 1977), which suggests that odors are not primarily represented at a verbal level of memory. Recent studies consistently suggest that the effectiveness by which odors trigger an enhancement in memory performance is not semantically mediated (Schab, 1990; Herz & Cupchik, 1992). There is an abundance of anecdotal information about odor-evoked recollection, but only recently has research provided some experimental evidence for the importance of odor-related sensations for emotions and emotional memories. In a study by Herz & Cupchik (1995), it was interestingly shown that the outstanding characteristic of odor-evoked memories is their emotional quality. Subjects looked at 16 different paintings of evocative emotional quality while either smelling or being told to imagine in total eight different odors. Two days later, memory for the paintings and the feelings that had been associated with them were tested by cued recall. Results not only revealed that when paintings were correctly recalled with an odor cue instead of an odor name, descriptions of the paintings were significantly more emotional, but also that more emotions were evoked and rated as more intense.

There is a certain limitation to retrieval by cognitive means alone, as seen by the significant memory enhancement obtained with the *in vivo* odor cue, instead of the semantic type of odor name cue. The re-experiencing to a sufficient extent of the original context, for instance being exposed anew to an associated odor as above (Herz & Cupchik, 1995), has been shown to decrease any contextual discrepancy and consequently improve recall (Bower, 1981; Eich, 1980; Ellis & Ashbrook, 1989). The implication that perceptual details of the original context may trigger and enhance verbal retrieval of detailed event information suggests the existence of a certain interactive connection between levels or systems of memory (see Johnson & Multhaup, 1992; Leventhal, 1984). This sort of interconnected representation of an affective experience at different memory levels could be said to be further revealed in the case of an amnesic patient who had once received an electric shock. On one occasion after this treatment, he was still amnesic but drew the conclusion that the presence of the case containing the shock apparatus was a likely indication that he would soon be electrified by the doctor (Korsakoff, 1889, cited in Tobias, Kihlstrom & Schachter, 1992). In other words, the perceptual detail consisting of the case triggered access to contextual information at a verbal level of the memory representation. Another case study similarly illustrates the effect of context-dependent cirumstances triggering access to a verbal level (cf. "verbally accessible knowledge") and consists of a woman in her 20s who was watching a TV program about incest. To her own amazement, she suddenly found herself exclaiming that it had really happened to her. This incident made it more difficult for her to suppress memories about her stepfather sexually abusing her between the ages of 8 and 14 years (Christianson & Engelberg, 1996).

In view of various indications that there seems to exist a certain interconnection between perceptual memory mediated by subcortical structures and cortical structures pertaining to recollection of temporal and spatial aspects, it should be possible among non-amnesics to activate a more complete recall of an event by conceptually probing emotional aspects associated with the episode. A study by Liwag & Stein (1995) showed precisely this. Their study aimed at investigating the memory of preschool children for a recent autobiographical event, when parents had reported seeing their child as either happy, sad, angry or afraid. Apart from a free recall condition, the study consisted of different cued recall conditions that contained various instructions encouraging children to recount the event by describing how they had felt, both verbally and by means of body language (e.g. by facial expressions corresponding to the feelings experienced at the event). The results showed that children in the cued recall conditions gave more detailed descriptions of the event that were also more causally structured, and also recounted about other similar autobiographical events that crossed their minds.

Preschool children have a limited ability for the organization and storage of episodic memories, mainly due to a limited ability to encode the aspects of "when" and "where" that are critical for event information (Friedman, 1991; Pillemer & White, 1989). Physical re-enactment, as compared to imagery, may therefore have a greater potential to access and activate non-verbal components of emotional experience in preschool children, as the storage of emotional events may not yet be supported to a sufficient degree by a conceptual memory level.

A consistent result was obtained among adults in a study by the authors (Engelberg & Christianson, 1997). This study aimed at exploring the ability to remember emotional reactions induced by a film sequence depicting a very unpleasant event. Emotional reactions were assessed by means of intensity ratings immediately upon presentation of the film, and recollected six weeks later either at free recall, or recall mediated by many of the memory-enhancing techniques underlying the Cognitive Interview (Fisher & Geiselman, 1992). At free recall, emotional reactions were significantly underestimated. However, by probing event information through instructions that encouraged imagery of the original physical and affective context, intensity of emotional reactions was rather accurately recalled. Results thus indicated that reinstatement of the original context in the mind of the subject facilitated recall of emotions evoked by the film (cf. the encoding specificity principle; Tulving & Thomson, 1973).

Memory for the occurrence of past events seems to be comprehensively explained by reconstructive theories, stating that temporal aspects of events are retrieved through a reconstructive application of a more generic type of knowledge about time patterns (Friedman, 1993). Interestingly, Friedman further stresses the importance of contextual information for temporal memory, which would plausibly play a greater role in children's ability to retrieve specific events, than in adults whose generic body of temporal knowledge is fully developed. The importance of contextual information is supported by a recent finding that correct recall of the day that an event occurred was enhanced with a vivid recollection of personal circumstances associated with the episode (Larsen & Thompson,

1995). The personal context surrounding an event may to some extent consist of sensorimotor-encoded aspects, such as experienced emotions, physical activity performed, or olfactory and other perceptual impressions.

REPRESENTATION OF EMOTIONAL EVENTS IN AN ASSOCIATIVE MEMORY MATRIX

Memory for emotional events could hence be conceptualized along the lines of the connectionist tradition (Bower, 1981) as ameliorated by a more thorough encoding due to the distinct and unique character of these sorts of episodes. During encoding, certain aspects of the event are specifically elaborated upon or associated with previous experiences or schematic knowledge in order to enable adequate behavioral responses, or to come to terms with emotional reactions. Emotion-inducing events generally also give rise to bodily reactions, such as changed cardiovascular activity. Taken together, cognitive and physiological aspects should increase the associative matrix by which the event eventually gains a representation in memory. The well-integrated representation permits an increased availability of different aspects of the event, which may automatically or with some effort trigger an activation of associated components for a more complete retrieval of the event. Reinstatement procedures consisting of either reenactment, imagery or other context-dependent cues should therefore activate the extraction of information from non-verbal and verbal components which, due to their associative links, trigger unabated retrieval.

A highly emotional or traumatic experience may nevertheless be difficult to access, and such a difficulty would then consist of a decreased availability of associated memory components. The affective salience or threatening character of an event results in the creation of fewer associative links to other stored representations in memory, and ultimately in its dissociation. Dissociative symptoms may take different forms, from occasional denial to pathological conditions such as psychogenic amnesia or dissociative identity disorder (see e.g. Putnam, 1989). Whereas semantically stored event information is not accessible, the availability of perceptual aspects often remains intact, as seen, for instance, in the case of a young man who sought therapy for depression, but also complained of peculiar sensations of "twisting" and "choking". These symptoms were later revealed to emanate from an episode in early childhood when he had witnessed his mother attempting suicide by hanging (Rosen, 1955, cited in Tayloe, 1995). This sort of dissociation could be described as a deficit in the association of remembered information with its context. That is, the separation of conceptual components from perceptual/behavioral memory could be seen as a failure to connect with a non-verbally organized network of associations.

This ability to separate temporal, spatial and semantic aspects of conceptual components may be due to the relative malleability of these (e.g. Bartlett, 1932; Hyman, Husband & Billings, 1995; Rumelhart, 1980; Thompson, Skowronski &

Lee, 1988). Conceptual memory components may change over time, for example, as a result of the inadvertent influence exerted by suggestive connotations in the way an interviewer phrases his questions (Loftus, 1979), or by different motivational and emotional states during the course of recounting the experience from time to time (Loftus & Kaufman, 1992). The recounting of traumatic memories may similarly alter their meaning and content, as pointed out by Krystal, Southwick & Charney (1995), particularly as a result of the focus on central details at the expense of peripheral information belonging to the original trauma-inducing event (Christianson, 1992).

It is well acknowledged that sharing emotional memories with others has a sound effect on mental health (Pennebaker & O'Heeron, 1984; Pillemer, 1992; Spiegel et al., 1989). In case a verbal account may trigger a re-experiencing of an emotionally painful event or may challenge schemata pertaining to self-image and life in general (Dyregrov, 1992; Horowitz & Reidbord, 1992), it may be just as healthy to share a memory that has been subject to some sort of alteration. For example, a boy who had witnessed his mother being raped later claimed that he had not been able to see anything, because his older sister had been standing in front of him (Pynoos & Nader, 1988). The emotional or affective content of certain memories hampers unmodified integration to decrease availability. Thus, in order to weaken associative ties of the memory representation, it is a reasonable conjecture that the event is less elaborated upon or rehearsed. For instance, a few studies have indicated that less effort is spent on recalling negative events among repressors (Holtgraves & Hall, 1995; Lorig et al., 1995). Other studies have shown that the lack of emotional support provided by the communication with relatives and friends about a trauma is a contributing factor for decreased availability of such memories, especially for children (e.g. Goodman et al., 1996). Children who have been involved in accidents, catastrophes or some other trauma usually process the experience by talking about it with their parents, who help them come to terms with the event. If a close relative, on the other hand, is responsible for inflicting the trauma, a child is not in the same position to deal with the experience. In the case of sexual abuse, the trauma may therefore be discarded from the reality as the child perceives it—the child may even deny that he/she is actually abused (see Fürniss, 1991). This has been observed among children exploited in pornography. Even when they have been shown the film sequence or photos depicting the sexual abuse, these children insist that they have never been part of it, maintain that they cannot remember or simply refuse to talk about it (Svedin & Back, 1996).

As emotional sensations are potent retrieval cues to the emotion-provoking event information, victims of trauma may exhibit emotional numbness or a sense of detachment. Thus, although the range of associations to emotional context is restricted at a conceptual level, suppression of the susceptibility to succumb to emotional stimuli may be a further necessary step to block out traumatic memories. In contrast to neutral situations, where the detailed information normally does not elicit feelings that are intrinsic to the event information, there is a natural correspondence between a person's feelings and the emotion-eliciting information in emotionally arousing situations. After an extended period of therapy sessions, clinicians therefore commonly observe that trauma-related memories are unblocked along with various expressions of emotional agony, or even sensations of pain.[1] Although neither emotions nor memories are blocked, it may initially be difficult to retrieve specific details, as trauma victims usually have access to only generalized types of memories. A plausible neuropsychological explanation is that very intense or prolonged stress may hamper the functioning of the hippocampus (Squire, 1987), which in turn may give rise to fearful feelings that are very difficult to pinpoint as originating from a specific episode. If the functioning of the hippocampus is not intact, however, perceptual aspects of an experience will not get associated with temporal and spatial aspects (van der Kolk & Saporta, 1993). Another explanation is that children who have experienced prolonged and repeated traumas have developed defenses in order to cope with the expectation of continued traumatization. Defenses may range from entering a different state of consciousness, in which they cannot take in and register what is happening to them, to intellectualization and projective identification (Terr, 1996).

CONCLUSION

Highly emotional events are retained differently to neutral events, as they usually carry greater implications for the individual's sense of self and integrity. Such event information therefore becomes encoded in more elaborate ways, which means that emotional events fall into oblivion to a lesser degree than neutral events. Both laboratory studies and studies of real-life events indicate that emotion promotes memory of central features or the gist of traumatic events, but may actively inhibit processing of details that are irrelevant, spatially peripheral to the emotion-eliciting event.

If an incident arouses extreme emotions, or when an individual sustains repeated trauma, we may tend to develop defensive reactions ranging from simple denial to psychogenic amnesia. The retrieval of emotion-laden memories is, however, a matter of a well-known and documented phenomena within memory research; there is an abundant storage of information that may not be accessible to consciousness without the proper contextual cues. Thus, the difficulty in recalling emotional events partly consists of insufficient access to event information stored at an explicit level of memory. Whereas temporal and spatial aspects require more intentional processing at the level of explicit recall, emotional aspects strongly associated to auditory, visual, olfactory or other perceptual details, or feelings and mood evoked at the time of the event, are less

---

[1] It should be noted that there are studies showing that we can erroneously remember whole sequences of events due to an inappropriate interviewing technique. As pointed out by Loftus (1993), research has shown that unrelated information may exert substantial influence on memory at recall, even to the extent that subjects claim to remember events that have never actually taken place.

amenable to explicit retrieval attempts. Such emotional aspects are, instead, more accessible under conditions of implicit recall. An apparently different organization of event information, although seemingly interconnected, may thus account for dissociative memory phenomena, whereby either the emotional component of an event is re-experienced in the absence of explicit event information, or specific event information is remembered without having access to emotional aspects.

ACKNOWLEDGMENTS

The preparation of this chapter was an equal collaborative effort and was supported by Grant F 793/95 from the Swedish Council for Research in the Humanities and Social Sciences to Sven-Åke Christianson.

REFERENCES

Bartlett, F. C. (1932). *Remembering: A Study in Experimental and Social Psychology*. London: Cambridge University Press.

Bower, G. H. (1981). Mood and memory. *American Psychologist*, **36**, 129–148.

Brewin, C. R. (1989). Cognitive change processes in psychotherapy. *Psychological Review*, **96**, 379–394.

Brewin, C. R., Andrews, B. & Gotlib, I. H. (1993). Psychopathology and early experience: a reappraisal of retrospective reports. *Psychological Bulletin*, **113**, 82–98.

Brewin, C. R., Dalgleish, T. & Joseph, S. (1996). A dual representation theory of posttraumatic stress disorder. *Psychological Review*, **103**(4), 670–686.

Burke, A., Heuer, F. & Reisberg, D. (1992). Remembering emotional events. *Memory and Cognition*, **20**, 277–290.

Christianson, S.-Å. (1984). The relationship between induced emotional arousal and amnesia. *Scandinavian Journal of Psychology*, **25**, 147–160.

Christianson, S.-Å. (1992)(ed.). *The Handbook of Emotion and Memory: Research and Theory*. Hillsdale, NJ: Erlbaum.

Christianson, S.-Å. (1994). *Traumatiska Minnen*. Borås: Natur och Kultur.

Christianson, S.-Å. & Engelberg, E. (1996). Remembering and forgetting traumatic experiences: a matter of survival. In M. A. Conway (ed.), *Recovered Memories and False Memories*. Oxford: Oxford University Press, pp. 230–250.

Christianson, S.-Å. & Nilsson, L.-G. (1989). Hysterical amnesia: a case of aversively motivated isolation of memory. In T. Archer & L.-G. Nilsson (eds), *Aversion, avoidance, and anxiety: perspectives on aversively motivated behavior*. Hillsdale, NJ: Erlbaum, pp. 289–310.

Christianson, S-Å., Forth, A. E., Hare, R. D., Strachan, C., Lidberg, L. & Thorell, L.-H. (1996). Remembering details of emotional events: a comparison between psychopathic and non-psychopatic offenders. *Personal and Individual Differences*, **20**, 437–443.

Christianson, S.-Å., Säisä, J. & Silfvenius, H. (1995). The right hemisphere recognises the bad guys. *Cognition and Emotion*, **9**(4), 309–324.

Claparede, E. (1911/1951). Recognition and "me"ness. In D. Rapaport (ed.), *Organization and Pathology of Thought*. New York: Columbia University Press, pp. 58–75. (Reprinted from *Archives de Psychologies*, 1911, **11**, 79–90.)

Conway, M. A. (1992). A structural model of autobiographical memory. In M. A. Conway, D. C. Rubin, H. Spinnler & W. A. Wagenaar (eds), *Theoretical Perspectives on Autobiographical Memory*. Dordrecht Kluwer, pp. 167–194.

Dyregrov, A. (1992). *Katastrofpsykologi*. Lund: Studentlitteratur.

Eich, J. E. (1980). The cue-dependent nature of state-dependent retrieval. *Memory and Cognition*, **8**, 157–173.

Ellis, H. C. & Ashbrook, P. W. (1989). The "state" of mood and memory research: a selective review. In D. Kuiken (ed.), *Mood and Memory: Theory, Research, and Applications*. Special issue of the *Journal of Social Behavior and Personality*, **4**, 1–21.

Engelberg, E. & Christianson, S.-Å. (1997). Recall of unpleasant emotion as experienced during an emotion-inducing event: Manuscript submitted for publication.

Fisher, R. P. & Geiselman, R. E. (1992). *Memory-enhancing Techniques for Investigative Interviewing*. Springfield, IL: Charles C. Thomas.

Freud, S. (1915/1957). Repression. In J Strachey (ed.), *The Standard Edition of the Complete Psychological Works of Sigmund Freud*, Vol. 14. London: Hogarth, pp. 146–158.

Friedman, W. J. (1991). The development of children's memory for the time of past events. *Child Development*, **62**, 139–155.

Friedman, W. J. (1993). Memory for the time of past events. *Psychological Bulletin*, **113**(1), 44–66.

Fürniss, T. (1991). *The Multiprofessional Handbook of Child Sexual Abuse: Integrated Management, Therapy and Legal Intervention*. London: Routledge.

Gainotti, G., Caltagirone, C. & Zoccolotti, P. (1993). Left/right and cortical/subcortical dichotomies in the neuropsychological study of human emotions. *Cognition and Emotion*, **7**, 71–93.

Goodman, G. S., Hepps, D. H. & Reed, R. S. (1986). The child victim's testimony. In A. Haralamic (ed.), *New Issues for Child Advocates*. Phoenix, AZ: Arizona Council of Attorneys for Children.

Goodman, G. S., Quas, J. A., Batterman-Faunce, J. M., Riddlesberger, M. M. & Kuhn, J. (1996). Predictors of accurate and inaccurate memories of traumatic events experienced in childhood. In K. Pezdek & W. P. Banks (eds), *The Recovered Memory/False Memory Debate*. San Diego, CA: Academic Press, pp. 3–28.

Graf, P. & Schacter, D. L. (1985). Implicit and explicit memory for new associations in normal and amnesic subjects. *Journal of Experimental Psychology: Learning, Memory, and Cognition*, **11**, 501–518.

Hartman, C. R. & Burgess, A. W. (1993). Treatment of victims of rape trauma. In J. P. Wilson & B. Raphael (eds), *International Handbook of Traumatic Stress Syndromes* New York: Plenum, pp. 507–516.

Herz, R. & Cupchik, G. C. (1995). The emotional distinctiveness of odor-evoked memories. *Chemical Senses*, **20**(5), 517–528.

Herz, R. S. & Cupchik, G. C. (1992). An experimental characterization of odor-evoked memories in humans. *Chemical Senses*, **17**(5), 519–528.

Heuer, F. (1987). *Remembering detail: the vole of emotion in long-term memory*. Unpublished dissertation. New School for Social Research, New York.

Heuer, F. & Reisberg, D. (1990). Vivid memories of emotional events: the accuracy of remembered minutiae. *Memory & Cognition*, **18**, 496–506.

Heuer, F. & Reisberg, D. (1992). Emotion, arousal, and memory for detail. In S.-Å. Christianson (ed.), *The Handbook of Emotion and Memory: Research and Theory*. Hillsdale, NJ: Erlbaum.

Holtgraves, T. & Hall, R. (1995). Repressors: what do they repress and how do they repress it ? *Journal of Research in Personality*, **29**, 306–317.

Horowitz, M. J. & Reidbord, S. P. (1992). Memory, emotion and response to trauma. In S.-Å. Christianson (ed.), *The Handbook of Emotion and Memory: Research and Theory*. Hillsdale, NJ: Erlbaum.

Howe, M. L. & Courage, M. (1993). On resolving the enigma of infantile amnesia. *Psychological Bulletin*, **113**(2), 305–326.

Howe, M. L., Courage, M., Peterson C. (1996). How can I remember when "I" wasn't there: long-term retention of traumatic experiences and emergence of the cognitive self. In K. Pezdek & W. P. Banks (eds), *The Recovered Memory/False Memory Debate*. San Diego, CA: Academic Press, pp. 121–149.

Hyman, I. E., Husband, T. H. & Billings, F. J. (1995). False memories of childhood experiences. *Applied Cognitive Psychology*, **9**, 181–197.

Janet, P. (1886). Les actes inconscients et le dédoublement de la personalité. *Revue Philosophiques*, **22**(2), 212–223.

Johnson, M. K. (1990). Functional forms of human memory. In J. L. McGaugh, N. M. Weinberger & G. Lynch (eds), *Brain Organization and Memory: Cells, Systems and Circuits*. New York: Oxford University Press, pp. 106–134.

Johnson, M. K., Kim, J. K. & Risse, G. (1985). Do alcoholic Korsakoff's syndrome patients acquire affective reactions? *Journal of Experimental Psychology: Learning, Memory, and Cognition*, **11**, 22–36.

Johnson, M. K. & Multhaup, K. S. (1992). Emotion and MEM. In S.-Å. Christianson (ed.), *The Handbook of Emotion and Memory: Research and Theory*. Hillsdale, NJ: Erlbaum.

Korsakoff, S. S. (1889). Etude medico-psychologique sur une forme des maladies de la memoire. *Revue Psychologique*, **28**, 501–530.

Krystal, J. H., Southwick, S. M. & Charney, D. S. (1995). Post-traumatic stress disorder: psychobiological mechanisms of traumatic remembrance. In D. L. Schacter (ed.), *Memory Distortions: How Minds, Brains, and Societies Reconstruct the Past*. Cambridge, MA: Harvard University Press, pp. 150–172.

Larsen, S. F. & Thompson, C. P. (1995). Reconstructive memory in the dating of personal and public news events. *Memory & Cognition*, **23**(6), 780–790.

Lawless, H. & Engen, T. (1977). Associations to odors: interference, mnemonics, and verbal labelling. *Journal of Experimental Psychology*, **3**, 52–59.

LeDoux, J. E. (1992). Emotion as memory: anatomical systems underlying indelible neural traces. In S.-Å. Christianson (ed.), *The Handbook of Emotion and Memory: Research and Theory*. Hillsdale, NJ: Erlbaum, pp. 269–288.

Leventhal, H. (1984). A perceptual-motor theory of emotion. In K. R. Scherer & P. Ekman (eds), *Approaches to Emotion*. Hillsdale, NJ: Erlbaum, pp. 271–291.

Levinson, B. W. (1967). States of awareness during general anesthesia. In J. Lassner (ed.), *Hypnosis and Psychosomatic Medicine*. New York: Springer-Verlag.

Liwag, M. & Stein, N. (1995). Children's memory for emotional events: the importance of emotion-related retrieval cues. *Journal of Experimental Child Psychology*, **60**, 2–31.

Loftus, E. F. (1979). *Eyewitness Testimony*. London: Harvard University Press.

Loftus, E. F. (1993). The reality of repressed memories. *American Psychologist*, **48**, 518–537.

Loftus, E. F. & Kaufman, L. (1992). Why do traumatic experiences sometimes produce good memory (flashbulbs) and sometimes no memory (repression)? In Winograd, E. & Neisser, U. (eds), *Affect and Accuracy in Recall: Studies of "Flashbulb" Memories* New York: Cambridge University Press, pp. 212–226.

Lorig, T. S., Singer, J. L., Bonnano, G. A., Davis, P. & Schwartz, G. E. (1995). Repressor personality style and EEG patterns associated with affective memory and thought suppression. *Imagination, Cognition, and Personality*, **14**(3), 203–210.

Ornstein, P. A., Gordon, B. N., Baker-Ward, L. E. & Merrit K. A. (1993). In D. P. Peters (ed.), *The Child Witness in Context: Cognitive, Social and Legal Perspectives*. Dordrecht: Kluwer.

Pennebaker, J. W. & O'Heeron, R. (1984). Confiding in others and illness rate among spouses of suicide and accidental-death victims. *Journal of Abnormal Psychology*, **93**, 473–476.

Pillemer, D. B. (1992).   Remembering personal circumstances: a functional analysis. In
    Winograd, E. & Neisser, U. (eds), *Affect and Accuracy in Recall: Studies of "Flashbulb"*
    Memories. New York: Cambridge University Press, pp. 236–264.
Pillemer, D. B. & White, S. H. (1989).   Childhood events recalled by children and adults.
    In H. W. Reese (ed.), *Advances in Child Development and Behavior, Vol. 21*. Orlando,
    FL: Academic Press, pp. 297–340.
Putnam, F. W. (1989).   *Diagnosis and Treatment of Multiple Personality Disorder*. New
    York: Guilford.
Pynoos, R. S. & Nader, K. (1988).   Children who witness the sexual assaults of their
    mothers. *Journal of the American Academy of Child Psychiatry*, **27**, 567–572.
Rosen, V. (1955).   The reconstruction of a traumatic childhood event in case of
    derealization. *Journal of the American Psychoanalytic Association*, **3**, 211–221.
Rapaport, D. (1942).   *Emotions and Memory*. New York: International Universities
    Press.
Rudy, L. & Goodman, G. S. (1991).   Effects of participation on children's reports: impli-
    cations for children's testimony. *Developmental Psychology*, **27**, 527–538.
Rumelhart, D. E. (1980).   Schemata: the building blocks of cognition. In R. Spiro, B.
    Bruce & W. Brewer (eds), *Theoretical Issues in Reading Comprehension*. Hillsdale, NJ:
    Erlbaum.
Schab, F. R. (1990).   Odors and the remembrance of things past. *Journal of Experimental*
    Psychology: Learning, Memory, and Cognition, **16**(4), 648–655.
Schacter, D. L. (1987).   Implicit memory: history and current status. *Journal of Experi-*
    mental Psychology: Learning, Memory, and Cognition, **13**, 501–518.
Sheingold, K. & Tenney, Y. J. (1982).   Memory for a salient childhood event. In U.
    Neisser (ed.), *Memory Observed: Remembering in Natural Contexts*. New York: Free-
    man, pp. 201–212.
Spiegel, D., Bloom, J. H. , Kraemer, H. C. & Gottheil, E. (1989).   Effects of psychosocial
    treatment of patients with metastatic breast cancer. *Lancet*, **2**, 888–891.
Squire, L. (1987).   *Memory and Brain*. New York: Oxford University Press.
Squire, L. (1995).   Biological foundations of accuracy and inaccuracy in memory. In D. L.
    Schacter (ed.), *Memory Distortions: How Minds, Brains, and Societies Reconstruct the*
    Past. Cambridge, MA: Harvard University Press, pp. 197–225.
Svedin, S. & Back, M. (1996).   *Barn som inte berättar: Om att utnyttjas i barnpornografi*.
    Scandbook, Falun: Rädda Barnen.
Tayloe, D. R. (1995).   The validity of repressed memories and the accuracy of their recall
    through hypnosis, A case study from the courtroom. *American Journal of Clinical*
    Hypnosis, **37**(3), 25–31.
Terr, L. (1979).   Children of Chowchilla: a study of psychic trauma. *Psychoanalytic Study*
    of the Child, **34**, 547–623.
Terr, L. (1983).   Chowchilla revisited: the effects of psychic trauma fours years after a
    schoolbus kidnapping. *American Journal of Psychiatry*, **140**, 1543–1550.
Terr, L. (1990).   *Too Scared to Cry: Psychic Trauma in Childhood*. New York: Harper &
    Row.
Terr, L (1996).   True memories of childhood trauma: flaws, absences, and returns. In K.
    Pezdek & W. P. Banks (eds), *The Recovered Memory/False Memory Debate*. San
    Diego, CA: Academic Press, pp. 69–80.
Thompson, C. P., Skowronski, J. J. & Lee, D. J. (1988).   Telescoping in dating naturally
    occurring events. *Memory & Cognition*, **16**, 461–468.
Tobias, B. A., Kihlstrom, J. F. & Schacter, D. L. (1992).   Emotion and implicit memory.
    In S.-Å Christianson (ed.), *The Handbook of Emotion and Memory*. Hillsdale, NJ:
    Erlbaum.
Tulving, E. (1972).   Episodic and semantic memory. In E. Tulving & W. Donaldson (ed.),
    Organization of Memory. New York: Academic Press.

Tulving, E. & Schacter, D. L. (1990). Priming and human memory systems. *Science*, **247**, 301–306.

Tulving, E. & Thomson, D. M. (1973). Encoding specificity and retrieval processes in episodic memory. *Psychological Review*, **80**, 352–373.

Usher, J. A. & Neisser, U. (1993). Childhood amnesia and the beginnings of memory for four early life events. *Journal of Experimental Psychology: General*, **122**, 155–165.

van der Kolk, B. A. & Saporta, J. (1993). Biological response to psychic trauma. In J. P. Wilson & B. Raphael B. (eds), *International Handbook of Traumatic Stress Syndromes*. New York: Plenum, pp. 19–27.

Williams, L. M. (1994). Recall of childhood trauma: A prospective study of Women's memories of child sexual abuse. *Journal of Consulting and Clinical Psychology*, **62**, 1167–1176.

Yuille, J. C. & Cutshall, J. L. (1986). A case study of eyewitness memory of a crime. *Journal of Applied Psychology*, **71**, 291–301.

Yuille, J. C. & Cutshall, J. L. (1989). Analysis of the statements of victims, witnesses and suspects. In J. C. Yuille (ed.), *Credibility Assessment*. Dordrecht: Kluwer.

Yuille, J. C. & Tollestrup, P. A. (1992). A model of the diverse effects of emotion on eyewitness memory. In S.-Å. Christianson (ed.), *The Handbook of Emotion and Memory Research and Theory*. Hillsdale, NJ: Erlbaum.

Chapter 12

Autobiographical Memory

Helen Healy *and* **J. Mark G. Williams**
University of Wales, Bangor, UK

Psychotherapy is the healing of memories. At first, this claim seems both extreme and outdated, referring to a type of analytic psychotherapy that faded once Freud had changed his mind about the power of reminiscence in therapy. It may be true that few psychologists still believe that conscious access to repressed traumatic memories is the sole key to therapeutic success, yet both prescriptive and exploratory therapies include a great deal of anamnesis: recalling and "revisiting" events, both recent and remote; for example, in cognitive therapy, such anamnesis occurs at a number of different points: giving a family history, reporting on week-by-week events, recalling homework assignments, revisiting past events to reality-test the validity of beliefs and interpretations, understanding the origins of dysfunctional attitudes, considering how previous life events have affected current functioning. Despite the importance of recollection of autobiographical memory, it is only relatively recently that experimental psychologists began to study it systematically. In this chapter, recent studies will be reviewed in the light of current models of autobiographical memory.

EARLY EXPERIMENTAL INVESTIGATIONS

Lloyd & Lishman (1975) were amongst the first to investigate personal memory experimentally. They used a list of neutral words as cues in clinically depressed patients who were instructed to think of either a pleasant or an unpleasant memory. They found that the more severe the depression, the quicker the patient retrieved an unpleasant memory. Further work in Oxford using non-depressed volunteers whose mood had been experimentally manipulated (Teasdale & Fogarty, 1979) found that latencies to remember positive or negative personal events were biased by mood, although most of this was due to slowed recall of

Handbook of Cognition and Emotion. Edited by T. Dalgleish and M. Power.

positive material in depressed mood, rather than speeded recall of negative material. Further research examined clinically depressed individuals selected for the presence of diurnal variation of mood (Clark & Teasdale, 1982). They found that happy memories were less probable (and depressing memories more probable) when patients were more depressed. When the same patients were at the less depressed point in their cycle, this picture was reversed.

Similar results have been found in parallel studies by Isen and her colleagues (Isen et al., 1978; Isen & Daubman, 1984; Isen, Daubman & Norwicki, 1987; Isen, 1990). A broad summary of these findings suggest that positive mood facilitates access to positive memories. Negative affect has, however, rarely been shown to have effects opposite and symmetrical to those obtained with positive affect inductions. Isen (1990) reported that negative affect either fails to facilitate the recall of negative material or acts as a less efficient retrieval cue than a positive mood state. A possible explanation for this finding is that the primary function of positive affect is to broaden the context in which stimuli are interpreted and act as a cue for a large variety of material (Isen & Daubman, 1984).

Early studies of autobiographical memory were carried out within the general framework of network models of memory. These suggested that emotions are represented in memory as part of a more general associative network (Bower, 1981). Bower proposed that emotions are represented by nodes in memory which send and receive spreading activation and are connected to other nodes with varying degrees of strength. Such an account is similar to that of semantic network theory (Collins & Quillian, 1969). Within such a system a particular affective state can be regarded as a node in a memory similar in character to the information originally encoded. Thus, a number of "emotional addresses" can exist in such networks, corresponding to different valences, and in turn can be activated by compatible sources.

Since the early research on personal memory was concerned with examining the speed of retrieval or preferential access to material congruent with encoding and retrieval mood, network models seemed to provide a useful heuristic framework. However, such models have increasingly appeared inadequate to explain results. If affective state is used primarily as a retrieval cue in a network, then it is surprising that negative affect would not trigger the retrieval of more associated material in the same manner as positive affect. Second, it has become apparent that different moods (e.g. anxiety and depression) affect information processing in different ways (Williams et al., 1997). It is difficult to understand how one emotion such as sadness/depression could be associated with a congruent bias in a particular encoding or retrieval operation, while another closely related emotion, such as fear/anxiety, is not. Third, network models proved to be poor in accounting for a number of specific sets of experimental results: self-reference mood–memory effects; the failure to show consistent mood-related lexical decision effects; mood-incongruent memory effects; and for evidence that mood affects schematic level rather than word-level processing (for a comprehensive review of these studies, see Teasdale & Barnard, 1993, and Williams et al., 1997).

The greatest challenge to network theory, however, has come from experi-mental and clinical findings that demand a framework that moves away from an emphasis on the quantitative aspects of memory: the probability or latency of recall of positive vs. negative events (a "horse-race model") towards the qualitative nature of what is recalled, whether positive or negative. Most recent research has focused on this aspect, particularly the generality or specificity with which events are recalled. We shall see that this phenomenon is to be found in a range of clinical conditions (e.g. patients showing suicidal behaviour, depression, PTSD and OCD) and that it has important consequences for other psychological functioning.

THE SPECIFICITY OF PERSONAL MEMORIES

Williams & Broadbent (1986) first identified the phenomenon of over-general retrieval as part of a study of mood and memory in parasuicide patients. They found that what appeared to be mood-congruent retrieval bias (delayed recall of positive memories) was in a large part due to the clinical group responding at first with inappropriately general memories. Whereas control subjects would respond to a cue word with an event that had occurred at a specific place and time (e.g. to the cue "happy" the response: "playing squash last Friday"), parasuicide patients tended to respond with a general category that summarized a number of specific memories (e.g. "Whenever I used to play squash").

A similar finding emerged from the study of autobiographical memory in depressed subjects (Moore, Watts & Williams, 1988). Moore and colleagues presented patients and matched controls with 16 situations involving social sup-port or lack of social support (e.g. "a neighbour helped me with some practical problem"; "my partner criticized me"). The percentage of first responses to these cues that were inappropriately general was 40% for depressives and 19% for controls. Further work has replicated this memory deficit in clinically diagnosed depressed patients (Williams & Scott, 1988; Puffet et al., 1991; Brittlebank et al., 1993; Kuyken & Dalgleish, 1995).

What aspect of the psychopathology is responsible for these effects? To date, the closest associations have been found with depression (although trait rather than state depression; Williams, 1996). Even when deficits have been found in other clinical groups, depression has been closely involved. For example, Wilhelm et al. (1997) found that patients with OCD had difficulty retrieving specific autobiographical memories (compared to healthy control participants), but it was the co-occurrence of depression and not the presence of OCD *per se* that was the critical variable associated with autobiographical memory deficits.

Deficits in autobiographical memory were also examined in a group of schizo-phrenic patients by Baddeley et al. (1996). The patients were divided into two groups (deluded and non-deluded) and their performances on the Autobio-graphical Memory Inventory (Kopelman, Wilson & Baddeley, 1989) compared.

In this task subjects were tested for both "personal semantic memory", (knowledge of facts about their early life, such as the names of teachers and schools) and also about personal episodes, with memory in each category probed for early life, mid-life and recent memories. The mean performance on the recall of autobiographical facts was reasonably good in both groups. However, the results of the autobiographical personal incident score suggested a difference, with the patients who were not deluded performing more poorly than the deluded group. Non-deluded schizophrenic patients tended to retrieve more general memories. While these results are preliminary due to small sample size, they warrant further investigation, particularly to examine associations with mood disorder.

Results from several studies suggest a connection between trauma history and memory dysfunction. They have raised the possibility that overgenerality may be present in emotional disorders where intrusive cognitions are present. For example, over-general memories have been found in Vietnam veterans who have PTSD (McNally et al., 1994, 1995).

Although the presence of discrete traumatic events may not be necessary for the occurrence of over-general memory, they may be sufficient if the events still have the capacity to intrude into consciousness. Kuyken & Brewin (1995) found that over-general memory is particularly severe in depressed women who have suffered physical and sexual abuse. The authors also found that over-general memory was related to more reported efforts to avoid these memories, as measured by the Impact of Event Scale (IES)[1] (Horowitz, Wilner & Alvarez, 1979). The association between over-generality and reports of attempting to avoid thinking about unpleasant events from the past were still significant after controlling for symptom severity. Similarly, Brewin et al. (in press), in a study of depressed cancer patients, found that reported attempts to avoid intrusive memories (often concerned with past losses through death) were significantly associated with greater over-general memory. Note that in both studies the over-general memories asked for, and those retrieved, were unrelated to the traumatic events.

These studies, even though correlational, suggest that patients' attempts to avoid intrusive autobiographical memories may be causally implicated in their overgeneral memory problems. Although the longer-term effects of intrusive memories have not been studied in depressed patients, evidence that the extent of the intrusion and avoidance of distressing memories may be associated with a worse outcome has come from studies of people involved in a variety of emotional situations (Joseph et al., 1996; McFarlane, 1992; Shalev et al., 1996). To explain the possible mechanisms underlying the construction of overgeneral memories and the relationship between intrusive thoughts and such overgeneral memories we need to examine current models of autobiographical memory.

---

[1] The Impact of Event Scale (IES) is a 15-item scale consisting of two sub-scales. It includes questions about the impact of a traumatic event, the degree of intrusions and extent to which the person attempts to avoid the unpleasant images.

STRUCTURAL OR HIERARCHICAL MODELS OF AUTOBIOGRAPHICAL MEMORY

Conway & Rubin (1993) suggests that autobiographical memory is highly structured and that an autobiographical knowledge base consists of three levels; lifetime periods, general events, and event-specific knowledge. Lifetime periods denote extended periods or thematic events in a person's autobiography. Similarly, Anderson & Conway (1993) propose that general events are organized in terms of contextually distinctive details that distinguish between different events. Knowledge of phenomenal experiences and associated thematic or general event knowledge combine in a highly dynamic and highly interconnected process to facilitate the retrieval and construction of specific autobiographical recollections. This entire process may be initiated around different levels of the hierarchy.

A number of independent studies support the notion that autobiographical memory is hierarchically organized (Linton, 1986; Conway & Bekerian, 1987; Conway, 1990; Schooler & Hermann, 1992). Thus, the construction of autobiographical memories depends upon access to an autobiographical knowledge base, and each layer of autobiographical knowledge, organized in an hierarchical fashion, provides indices to the other levels and thus facilitates access (Conway & Bekerian, 1987; Barsalou, 1988; Williams & Scott, 1988; Williams & Dritschel, 1992; Williams, 1996). Once access is gained to a particular level, a further process of retrieval is initiated. Retrieval of specific memories is thus mediated by a cyclical series of retrieval attempts until a suitable memory is accessed. So subjects typically generate a specific memory by first accessing an extended or general event theme, "e.g. that holiday in France", and the cycle proceeds by a progressive narrowing onto specific events and episodes (see Conway & Rubin, 1993).

The emphasis on the organization of retrieval processes has implications both for theory of mood and memory in general and for practical work with patients. Taking theory first, the early dependence on network models explained the prepotency of memories with a certain affective content in terms of the activation spreading from emotion nodes and other associated nodes. It focused on the single event as the unit of memory to be investigated. This concern with quantitative aspects of memory (how fast an individual could retrieve a memory, or how probable a negative or positive a memory was), ignored important aspects of both emotional disorders and memory theory. Such an over-narrow focus has not only been confined to studies in the field of cognition and emotion. For example, studies of the availability heuristic (Tversky & Kahneman, 1973) are premised on the accessibility of representations of specific events in memory. Yet if specific memories are not always the preferred output of the memory system, it becomes important to re-examine the effects these alternative outputs have on cognition (Williams et al. 1996). The pattern of data emerging from the clinical studies reviewed earlier suggests that reduced specificity in recollecting personal events is a frequent marker for a wider cognitive dysfunction in emotional disorders. The effects of such a retrieval style on successful therapeutic outcome demands that we understand the processes that underlie such over-general encoding and retrieval; its origins, its consequences and its underlying mechanism.

THE ORIGINS OF OVER-GENERAL MEMORY

An examination of developmental data (Williams, 1996) suggests that prior to the third and fourth years of life, normal children tend to retrieve events in a generic way. The ability to inhibit these relatively automatic categoric description processes develops at around three and a half years, allowing the child greater strategic control over the recollection process. Chronic stress in childhood, including failure to make satisfactory attachment relationships, may affect the ability to learn fully how to control these processes. First, a person growing up in such an environment may learn that specific event information is too negative, so passively avoids this punishing consequence of recollection. Whenever a mnemonic cue activates categoric intermediate descriptions which begin to construct fragments of an emotional episode, the search is aborted. Second, failure to access specific memories has further consequences for encoding and retrieving other (even positive) events. Failure to access specific information results in the retrieval process attempting to make further iterations with alternative intermediate descriptions.

The result of the tendency for negative early experiences to affect retrieval processes in this way is that the child will come to have a range of self-descriptions in a chronically activated state, so that new emotionally valent events will be encoded along with many general trait self-descriptors. These over-generic encoding retrieval cycles constitute the cognitive style which we later find in depressed, PTSD and suicidal patients. The exact extent of later difficulties will depend on the existence of facilitatory or inhibitory factors in the retrieval context. For example, if another negative life event has recently occurred, there may be very few positive mnemonic cues in the environment to help in the retrieval process. The more patients find themselves ruminating about past traumas, the greater difficulty they will have in retrieving specific positive events (Kuyken & Brewin, 1995; McNally et al., 1994).

THE CONSEQUENCES OF OVER-GENERAL MEMORY

A number of important consequences have been found to result from the difficulty in retrieving specific memories: these individuals are slower to recover from depression, they have deficits in solving interpersonal problems and experience vagueness and a sense of hopelessness in imagining the future. First, over-generality of memory in depression plays a mediating role in assisting or inhibiting recovery. Brittlebank et al. (1993) assessed depressed patients' autobiographical memory on their admission to a psychiatric unit and found that the extent of over-generality of their memory predicted whether they remained depressed 7 months later. Very recent evidence that this may not be true of depressed cancer patients (Brewin et al., in press) needs further work to determine whether the difference is due to differences in the patient sample, the measures used, or the time frame over which the study was conducted.

Second, deficits in problem solving skills are linked with such memory problems. Such deficits have been shown in both suicidal and depressed patients (Schotte, Cools & Payvar, 1990; Marx, Williams & Claridge, 1992; Goddard, Dritschel & Burton, 1996). Might this be due to the difficulties such patients have remembering their past sufficiently specifically? Problem solving skills may be inhibited because depressed patients attempt to use intermediate descriptions as a database in order to generate solutions. Such a database is limited and restricted because of a dearth of specific information. This account would be consistent with models proposed for analogical problem solving. In solving through analogy, individuals apply their knowledge of a base domain to a structurally similar target domain. Successful transfer requires that the base problem be disembedded from its specific context. This disembedding does not imply forgetting the original context, but rather recognizing the abstract relations that hold among elements of the problem (Brown, 1989). For many interpersonal problems, efficient access to a database and instances of structurally similar target domains or specific autobiographical event memories is necessary to generate adequate solutions.

Consistent with this hypothesis, Evans et al. (1992) found that parasuicide patients who had greatest difficulty in retrieving specific memories showed the most difficulty in producing effective solutions on the Means–Ends Problem Solving Task. Goddard, Dritschel & Burton (1996) replicated the findings of Evans et al. (1992) in depressed patients. They further suggested that it was the excessive rumination initiated and maintained by a generic retrieval style that creates an overwhelming preoccupation with the past, reducing the amount of cognitive resources available for problem solving.

Third, non-specificity in recalling the past limits the ability to imagine the future in a specific way, thereby exacerbating hopelessness. Williams et al. (1996) found that suicidal subjects had difficulty picturing the future in a specific way compared to matched controls. The degree of difficulty was significantly correlated with the specificity of their autobiographical memories. This study also used experimental induction of different retrieval styles to examine the causal link between memory style and future images. The results suggested that, as predicted, the induction of specific or generic retrieval styles influenced the specificity with which future events were imagined. This preliminary evidence of a link between specificity of retrieval and specificity of imagining the future has important clinical implications, since future perspectives play a central role in depression and suicide. A number of studies have found that hopelessness mediates the relationship between depression and suicidal intent within suicidal populations (see Salter & Platt, 1990; Wetzel et al., 1980). In addition, hopelessness has been found to predict repetition of parasuicide 6 months later (Petrie, Chamberlain & Clark, 1988) and completed suicides up to 10 years later (Beck, Brown & Steer, 1989). In summary, the evidence suggests that specific retrieval predicts good therapeutic outcome, enhances problem solving skills and allows the construction of more specific images of the future.

OVER-GENERAL MEMORY—POSSIBLE MECHANISMS

Hierarchical models of memory suggest that retrieval from autobiographical memory involves an intermediate stage in which a general context or description is framed to aid the search for a specific exemplar (e.g. Williams & Hollan, 1981; Norman & Bobrow, 1979; Reiser, Black & Abelson, 1985; Kolodner, 1983). The cue "happy" will first pose the question: "What sort of activities, people, places, objects make me happy?" These general descriptions are recursively refined until a specific example is retrieved, its appropriateness checked, and a suitable response made. It appears that the emotionally disturbed patients referred to earlier were accessing an "intermediate description" in memory retrieval, but were stopping short of a specific example. Successful retrieval of specific episodes requires initial access to categoric descriptions, but then rapid inhibition of these descriptions, so that contextual (time and place) information can be introduced into the mnemonic search. If the intermediate descriptions do not succeed in moving the search on to more specific information, the system tries further iterations with alternative intermediate descriptions.

After a number of such iterations, a more highly elaborated network of categoric intermediate descriptions will exist. For example, on the first iteration, a cue such as "unhappy" may have elicited the description, "I've always failed", which might normally have helped retrieve the event, "receiving the letter telling me that I had failed the exams". However, if the search is aborted at this stage, an alternative intermediate description will be derived, for example, "I was never good at school". Several such iterations may result in a host of negative categoric descriptions (e.g. "I never had many friends", "I always let my parents down"). The result is an over-elaboration of categories, encouraged by (and itself encouraging) ruminative self-focus.

These categoric descriptions are more likely to be encoded along with future event occurrences. In future attempts at retrieval, an initial cue is likely to activate an intermediate description which simply activates other self-descriptions. Williams (1996) coins the terms "mnemonic interlock" to describe the block in retrieval due to excessive access of "intermediate" mnemonic material at the expense of effective and directed search of specific event memory. Given the findings of a close association between past stress, current intrusions and categoric memory, we must also consider the possibility that the difficulty in recollecting specific autobiographical events experienced by depressed and suicidal patients is partly due to capacity limitations in working memory.

AUTOBIOGRAPHICAL MEMORY AND WORKING MEMORY

The excessive rumination initiated and maintained by generic retrieval styles may reduce the cognitive resources necessary for efficient access to specific memories. Is there any evidence for the supposition that working memory capacity is reduced by current preoccupations and the excessive ruminations which depressed and suicidal groups engage in? Previous work has shown that such stimulus-independent thoughts are heavily dependent upon central executive resources (Teasdale et al., 1995). Stimulus-independent thoughts are streams of thoughts and images unrelated to immediate sensory input, and are similar to the worrisome intrusive ruminations that preoccupy depressed and clinical groups. Evidence that the production of thoughts and images depend upon central executive resources suggests that clinical groups who suffer intrusive material and expend effort trying to avoid such material will indeed have reduced working memory capacity. The search for specific memories may simply be too effortful for these individuals.

This suggestion is consistent with the suggestion of Ellis & Ashbrook (1988) and Hertel & Hardin (1990) that depressed subjects show poor memory partly because of limited resources. However, these "cognitive effort" or "resource allocation" models of memory deficits in depression, despite their intuitive appeal, have not attempted to measure such deployment of resources independently. If future research is to examine directly the hypothesis that memory search is aborted because subjects find it too effortful relative to their working memory capacity (Williams & Dritschel, 1992; Williams, 1996), it will need to assess such capacity directly. Work in progress in our laboratory is using a random key pressing task (Baddeley et al., 1996) as an index of cognitive capacity. Participants are required to press buttons randomly and concurrently with a cued autobiographical memory task. Preliminary results suggest, as predicted, a trade-off between randomization performance and the level of generality in memory output. However, given the results showing that generic encoding and retrieval of memories can have its origins in childhood (Williams, 1996), reduced capacity during retrieval is unlikely to provide a complete explanation for the memory phenomena as it is observed in the laboratory. Of course, it remains possible that the original failures to encode and retrieve personal event memory in childhood may have been influenced by, and in turn come to influence, central executive capacity.

Under what conditions is autobiographical memory likely to proceed more smoothly (i.e. demand less effort)? There are some suggestions that the imageability of the cue available to a person is an important factor. We have found (Williams et al., 1996) that high-imageable cues mediate access to specific autobiographical memories more directly, while low-imageable cues tend to result in the recall of general memories. Why should this happen? Images represent summary information in autobiographical memory which can be used to direct memory searches. High-imageable cues contain information which is maximally informative about a represented event in the sense that information in the image has many connections with other related events and themes. The information contained in an image may be employed as a source of powerful cues by retrieval processes, with which to probe memory traces. Protocols provided by a number of subjects indicate that information in images can be elaborated upon in order to access further information related to an event (Whitten & Leonard, 1981).

Such evidence suggests that images may be employed to search complex memories and that images facilitate access to information within a complex memory trace. This argument was advanced by Conway (1988), who suggested that a major function of imagery is to facilitate memory retrieval in autobiographical memory. If images do contain information which can be exploited by retrieval processes to construct a specific memory, it must correspond to similar information stored in other parts of memory (Tulving & Thompson, 1973). To be effective retrieval cues, images should represent information which maps onto many parts of a memory trace. Thus, cues high in imageability which are also rich in semantic attributes and predicates readily access specific memories. How does this fit with models of retrieval in autobiographical memory?

We suggest that the retrieval strategies adopted by depressed and suicidal groups is comparable to that of normal participants when they are instructed to retrieve specific memories in response to low-imageable cues. Depressed and suicidal participants behave as if they are always having to work with impoverished and constrained cues, showing an inability to engage the mechanisms by which imageability mediates the construction of specific memories (image generation, context availability and the richness of semantic information). The tendency for clinical groups to find all cues impoverished and constrained (perhaps owing to current preoccupations) in turn activates indirect retrieval search strategies, resulting in an excess of intermediate descriptors that make the task of retrieval even more effortful.

CONCLUSION

The occurrence of past traumas and images of trauma have long been identified as important factors in the psychogenesis of anxiety and depression. However, many people suffer negative events yet seem able satisfactorily to "process" such events emotionally and cognitively. Where this does not occur, a high frequency of intrusive thoughts and images remain. Current research on memory is beginning to suggest that the specificity/generality of all autobiographical memories (not just those related to such negative events) is of critical importance. A long-term cognitive style of non-specificity in the encoding and retrieval of (even trivial) events affects, first, whether negative events are processed satisfactorily when they occur, and second, how much impact they subsequently have on current problem solving and hopelessness for the future. This research has direct implications for the design of interventions for the control of retrieval strategies in clinical groups, where the aim of such interventions is to maintain goal-directed behaviour in the specificity of personal recollections. Many psychotherapeutic strategies depend upon the ability of patients to retrieve specific events from the remote or recent past, or to keep diaries of day-to-day events. Current research is examining predictions from this memory research: that effectiveness of both prescriptive and exploratory psychotherapies is in large part determined by how well patients are able to bring about the specific recollection of current and past events. Perhaps successful therapeutic outcomes have relied implicitly on the identification and modification of maladaptive retrieval strategies in clinical groups. If so, future work should aim to make these processes explicit.

REFERENCES

Anderson, S. J. & Conway, M. A. (1993). Investigating the structure of autobiographical memories. *Journal of Experimental Psychology: Learning Memory and Cognition*, **19**, 1178–1196.

Baddeley, A. D. (1996). Exploring the central executive. *The Quarterly Journal of Experimental Psychology*, **49A**, 5–28.

Baddeley, A. D., Thornton, A., Eng Chua, S. & McKenna, P. (1996). Schizophrenic delusions and the construction of autobiographical memory. In D. Rubin (ed.), *Remembering Our Past: Studies in Autobiographical Memory*. Cambridge: Cambridge University Press, pp. 384–428.

Barsalou, L. W. (1988). The content and organization of autobiographical memories. In U. Neisser & E. Winograd (eds), *Remembering Reconsidered: Ecological and Traditional Approaches to the Study of Memory*. New York: Cambridge University Press, pp. 193–243.

Beck, A. T., Brown, G. & Steer, R. A. (1989). Prediction of eventual suicide in psychiatric inpatients by clinical ratings of hopelessness. *Journal of Consulting & Clinical Psychology*, **57**, 309–310.

Bower, G. H. (1981). Mood and memory. *American Psychologist*, **36**, 129–148.

Brewin, C. R., Watson, M., McCarthy, S., Hyman, P. & Dayson, D. (in press). Intrusive memories and depression in cancer patients. *Behaviour Research and Therapy*.

Brittlebank, A. D., Scott, J., Williams, J. M. G. & Ferrier, I. N. (1993) Autobiographical memory in depression: state or trait marker? *British Journal of Psychiatry*, **162**, 118–121.

Brown, A. L. (1989). Analogical learning and transfer: what develops? In S. Vosniadou & A. Ortony (eds), *Similarity and Analogical Reasoning*. Cambridge: Cambridge University Press, pp. 369–412.

Clark, D. M. & Teasdale, J. D. (1982). Diurnal variation in clinical depression and accessibility of memories to positive and negative experiences. *Journal of Abnormal Psychology*, **2**, 87–95.

Collins, A. M. & Quillian, M. R. (1969). Retrieval time from semantic memory. *Journal of Verbal Learning and Verbal Behaviour*, **8**, 240–247.

Conway, M. A. & Bekerian, D. B. (1987). Organization in autobiographical memory. *Memory and Cognition*, **15**, 119–132.

Conway, M. A. (1988). Images in autobiographical memory. In M. Denis, J. Engelkamp

& J. T. E. Richardson (eds), *Cognitive and Neuropsychological Approaches to Mental Imagery*. The Hague: Martinus Nijhoff, pp. 337–346.

Conway, M. A. (1990). *Autobiographical Memory: An Introduction*. Milton Keynes: Open University Press.

Conway, M. A. & Rubin, D. C. (1993). The structure of autobiographical memory. In A. E. Collins, S. E. Gathercole, M. A. Conway & E. M. Morris (eds), *Theories of Memory*. Hillsdale, NJ: Erlbaum, pp. 103–137.

Ellis, H. C. & Ashbrook, P. W. (1988). Resource allocation model of the effects of depressed mood states on memory. In K Fiedler & J. Forgas (eds), *Affect, Cognition and Social Behavior*. Toronto: Hogrefe, pp. 25–43.

Evans, J., Williams, J. M. G., O'Loughlin, S. & Howells, K. (1992). Autobiographical memory and problem-solving strategies of parasuicide patients. *Psychological Medicine*, **22**, 399–405.

Goddard, L., Dritschel, B. & Burton A. (1996). Role of autobiographical memory in social problem solving and depression. *Journal of Abnormal Psychology*, **105**, 609–616.

Hertel, P. T. & Hardin, T. S. (1990). Remembering with and without awareness in a depressed mood: evidence of deficits in initiative. *Journal of Experimental Psychology: General*, **119**, 45–59.

Horowitz, M. J., Wilner, N. & Alvarez, W. (1979). Impact of Event Scale: a measure of subjective stress. *Psychosomatic Medicine*, **41**, 209–218.

Isen, A. M., Shalker, T., Clark, M. & Karp, L. (1978). Affect, accessibility of material in memory and behaviour: a cognitive loop? *Journal of Personality and Social Psychology*, **36**, 1–12.

Isen, A. M., & Daubman, K. A. (1984). The influence of affect on categorisation. *Journal of Personality and Social Psychology*, **47**, 1206–1217.

Isen, A. M., Daubman, K. A., & Norwicki, G. P. (1987). Positive affect facilitates creative problem solving. *Journal of Personality and Social Psychology*, **52**, 1122–1131.

Isen, A. M. (1990). The influence of positive and negative affect on cognitive organization. Some implications for development. In N. L. Stein, B. Leventhal & T. Trabasso (eds), *Psychological and Biological Approaches to Emotion*. Hillsdale, NJ: Erlbaum, pp. 75–94.

Joseph, S. A., Dalgleish, T., Thrasher, S., Yule, W., Williams, R. & Hodgkinson, P. (1996). Chronic emotional processing in survivors of the Herald of Free Enterprise disaster: the relationship of intrusion and avoidance at 3 years to distress at 5 years. *Behaviour Research and Therapy*, **34**, 357–360.

Kolodner, J. L. (1983). Maintaining memory organization in dynamic long-term memory. *Cognitive Science*, **7**, 243–280.

Kopelman M. D., Wilson B. A. & Baddeley A. (1989). The autobiographical memory interview: a new assessment of autobiographical and personal semantic memory in amnesic patients. *Journal of Clinical and Experimental Neurology*, **11**, 724–744.

Kuyken, W. & Brewin, C. R. (1995). Autobiographical memory functioning in depression and reports of early abuse. *Journal of Abnormal Psychology*, **104**, 585–591.

Kuyken, W. & Dalgleish, T. (1995). Autobiographical memory and depression. *British Journal of Clinical Psychology*, **34**, 89–92.

Linton, M. (1986). Ways of searching and the contents of memory. In Rubin, D. C. (ed.). *Autobiographical Memory*. Cambridge: Cambridge University Press, pp 50–67.

Lloyd, G. G. & Lishman, W. A. (1975). Effects of depression on the speed of recall of pleasant and unpleasant experiences. *Psychological Medicine*, **5**, 173–180.

Marx, E. M., Williams, J. M. G. & Claridge, G. C. (1992). Social problem-solving in depression. *European Review of Applied Psychology*, **44**, 271–279: Special Issue: *Facets of Social Intelligence*.

McFarlane, A. C. (1992). Avoidance and intrusion in post-traumatic stress disorder. *Journal of Nervous and Mental Disease*, **180**, 439–445.

McNally, R., Lasko, N. B., Macklin, M. L. & Pitman, R. K. (1995). Autobiographical memory disturbance in combat-related post-traumatic stress disorder. *Behaviour Research and Therapy*, **33**, 619–630.

McNally, R., Litz, B. T., Prassas, A., Shin, L. M. & Weathers, F. W. (1994). Emotional priming of autobiographical memory in post-traumatic stress disorder. *Cognition and Emotion*, **8**, 351–367.

Moore, R. G., Watts, F. N. & Williams, J. M. G. (1988). The specificity of personal memories in depression. *British Journal of Clinical Psychology*, **27**, 275–276.

Norman, D. A. & Bobrow, D. G. (1979). Descriptions: an intermediate stage in memory retrieval. *Cognitive Psychology*, **11**, 107–123.

Petrie, K., Chamberlain, K. & Clarke, D. (1988). Psychological predictors of future suicidal behaviour in hospitalized suicide attempters. *British Journal of Clinical Psychology*, **27**, 247–258.

Puffet, A., Jehin-Marchot, D., Timsit-Berthier, M. & Timsit, M. (1991). Autobiographical memory and major depressive states. *European Psychiatry*, **6**, 89–137.

Reiser, B. J., Black, J. B. & Abelson, R. P. (1985) Knowledge structures in the organisation and retrieval of autobiographical memories. *Cognitive Psychology*, **17**, 89–137.

Salter, D. & Platt, S (1990). Suicidal intent, hopelessness and depression in a parasuicide population: the influence of social desirability and elapsed time. *British Journal of Clinical Psychology*, **29**, 361–371.

Schooler, J. W. & Hermann, D. J. (1992). There is more to episodic memory than just episodes. In M. A. Conway, D. C. Rubin, H. Spinnler & W. A. Wagenaar (eds), *Theoretical Perspectives on Autobiographical Memory*. London: Kluwer Academic, pp. 241–261.

Schotte, D. E., Cools, J. & Payvar, S. (1990). Problem-solving skills in suicidal patients: trait vulnerability or state-dependent phenomenon? *Journal of Consulting and Clinical Psychology*, **58**, 562–564.

Shalev, A., Peri, T., Canetti, L. & Schreiber, S. (1996). Predictors of PTSD in injured trauma survivors: a prospective study. *American Journal of Psychiatry*, **153**, 219–225.

Teasdale, J. D. & Fogarty, S. J. (1979). Differential effects of induced mood on retrieval of pleasant and unpleasant events from episodic memory. *Journal of Abnormal Psychology*, **3**, 248–257.

Teasdale, J. D. & Barnard, P. J. (1993). *Affect, Cognition and Change: Re-modeling Depressive Thought*. Hove: Erlbaum.

Teasdale, D., Dritschel, B. H., Taylor, M. J., Proctor, L., Lloyd, C. A., Nimmo-Smith, I. & Baddeley, A. D. (1995). Stimulus-independent thought depends on central executive resources. *Memory & Cognition*, **23**, 551–559.

Tulving, E. & Thompson, D. M. (1973). Encoding specificity and retrieval processes in episodic memory. *Psychological Review*, **80**, 353–373.

Tversky, A. & Kahneman, D. (1973). The belief in the law of small numbers. *Psychological Bulletin*, **33**, 233–242.

Wetzel, R. D., Marguiles, T., Davis, R. & Karam, E. (1980). Hopelessness, depression and suicidal intent. *Journal of Clinical Psychiatry*, **41**, 159–160.

Whitten, W. B. & Leonard, J. M. (1981). Directed search through autobiographical memory. *Memory and Cognition*, **9**, 566–579.

Wilhelm S., Mc Nally, R. J., Baer, L. & Florin I. (1997). Autobiographical memory in obsessive-compulsive disorder. *British Journal of Clinical Psychology*, **36**, 21–31.

Williams, D. M. & Hollan, J. D. (1981). The process of retrieval from very long-term memory. *Cognitive Science*, **5**, 87–119.

Williams, J. M. G. & Broadbent, K. (1986). Autobiographical memory in suicide attempters. *Journal of Abnormal Psychology*, **95**, 144–149.

Williams, J. M. G. & Dritschel, B. (1988). Emotional disturbance and the specificity of autobiographical memory. *Cognition and Emotion*, **2**, 221–234.

Williams, J. M. G. & Scott, J. (1988).   Autobiographical memories in depression. *Psychological Medicine*, **18**, 689–695.

Williams, J. M. G. & Dritschel, B. H. (1992).   Categoric and extended autobiographical memories. In M. A. Conway, D. C. Rubin, H. Spinnler & W. A. Wagenaar (eds), *Theoretical Perspectives on Autobiographical Memory*. London, Kluwer Academic, pp. 391–412.

Williams, J. M. G., Ellis, N. C., Tyers, C., Healy, H., Rose, G. & MacLeod, A. K. (1996).   The specificity of autobiographical memory and imageability of the future. *Memory & Cognition*, **24**, 116–125.

Williams, J. M. G. (1996).   The specificity of autobiographical memory in depression. In D. C. Rubin (ed.), *Remembering Our Past: Studies in Autobiographical Memory*. Cambridge: Cambridge University Press, pp. 244–267.

Williams, J. M. G., Watts, F. N., MacLeod, C. & Mathews, A. (1997).   *Cognitive Psychology and Emotional Disorders*, Chichester: Wiley.

Chapter 13

Inhibition Processes in Cognition and Emotion: A Special Case?

Tim Dalgleish*
Andrew Mathews
and
Jacqueline Wood
MRC Cognition and Brain Sciences Unit, Cambridge, UK

INTRODUCTION

The notion of inhibition as an explanatory heuristic for understanding aspects of mental life has considerable currency in paradigms ranging from the psychobiological to the socio-cultural. At a biological level it is commonly held that neurones exert both excitatory and inhibitory influences on one another. This dynamic is neatly reflected in both distributed and localist connectionist models of mental processes, with their emphasis on neural plausibility (Rumelhart & McClelland, 1986). Similarly, at a functional psychological level, processes of inhibition are cited in explanations of phenomena such as forgetting (Bjork, 1989), selective attention (Tipper et al., 1991) and selection for action (Tipper, Lortie & Baylis, 1992). Finally, at the socio-cultural level the notion of inhibition has been profitably employed in accounts of, for instance, the non-expression of anger in certain cultures (Briggs, 1970), or the phases of acceptance and denial of the reality of child sexual abuse in Western society over the last 100 years (Herman, 1992).

So far we have been careful to refer to inhibition as a useful tool or heuristic

* To whom correspondence should be addressed.

Handbook of Cognition and Emotion. Edited by T. Dalgleish and M. Power.
© 1999 John Wiley & Sons Ltd.

in generating explanations for mental phenomena, rather than as an actual process. This distinction between inhibition as a useful explanatory device and inhibition as an active process cuts to the heart of one of the key debates in the area. This is perhaps best illustrated by a consideration of the role of inhibition in explanations at the functional psychological level, which is conveniently the main focus of the present chapter. So, if we consider, as an example, the process of forgetting a piece of information, it would be possible to argue that there is some *direct* process of inhibition acting on the representation in memory of this information, such that it becomes more difficult to retrieve. Similarly, one could propose that, even if the representation itself is not directly inhibited, then retrieval pathways to the representation might be directly inhibited in some way. However, an alternative and clearly more parsimonious explanation is to say that retrievability from memory is a function of nothing more than differential activation. According to this account, the representation of the forgotten information is not inhibited at all, but merely receives relatively little activation. In contrast, other competing representations receive relatively greater activation and this means that they are more likely to be retrieved at any given time.

Elsewhere, we have called the first of these types of account, where there is a proposal of direct inhibition of a representation or pathway, a *strong* theory of inhibition. Where it is unclear whether any direct inhibition is taking place and it therefore may be only *as if* a representation is being inhibited (that is, where the term "inhibition" is only being used as a heuristic explanatory device), we have suggested the notion of a *weak* theory of inhibition (Dalgleish, 1991; Power, Dalgleish & Claudio, submitted). Although it is relatively straightforward to draw a theoretical distinction between these two uses of the term "inhibition", it is nevertheless very difficult to generate unequivocal evidence that decides between the two accounts (Anderson & Bjork, 1994). In practice, almost all of the empirical data can be accounted for in terms of processes akin to differential activation. In other words, there is very little to suggest that most accounts that utilize ideas of inhibition are anything other than theories of the weak type.

However, over the last 10–15 years a number of experimental methodologies have begun to emerge that do offer the potential to examine direct processes of inhibition, in that they generate data that cannot be adequately explained by, say, a differential activation account. Some of these methodologies, such as negative priming (Tipper, 1985), directed forgetting (Geiselman, Bjork & Fishman, 1983) and retrieval-induced inhibition (Anderson & Spellman, 1995) are discussed in more detail below.

So far we have been referring to inhibition as part of a set of dynamic processes that interact during perceiving, attending and remembering in everyday cognition. However, an additional question, and the one pertinent to the present chapter, concerns the issue of whether inhibition in the domain of cognition and emotion is in some way different to inhibition as it serves routine processing of emotionally neutral information, sensation or feeling. Is inhibition in cognition and emotion a special case?

In the clinical domain there are numerous phenomena that do suggest the existence of differential inhibition of emotional material or feelings. These phenomena include dissociative states, psychogenic amnesia, hysterical deafness and blindness, recovered memories, fugue states and the like. Although the exact nature of many of these presentations is embroiled in controversy, the fact that the clients we see in our clinical work so often manifest these constellations of symptoms provides a compelling motivation to examine more carefully, and therefore inevitably empirically, the processes that might underlie these clinical states. Furthermore, in the clinical literature, there are famous theories of inhibition, such as the Freudian notion of repression. However, despite these encouraging signs from the clinical domain, it is unclear whether these are examples of weak or strong inhibition. The reality seems to be that most proclamations of strong inhibition, for example the Freudian notion of repression, are so far no more than theoretical promise and that the majority of the data are unable to differentiate strong and weak accounts (Holmes, 1974; Holmes, 1990).

In the rest of the chapter we shall seek to draw out a number of threads identified in this Introduction as they pertain to cognition and emotion. We shall, as we have said, concentrate on the functional psychological level of explanation and, within that, largely concern ourselves with the effects of individual differences in emotional state or diagnostic status on putative inhibition processes acting on emotional feelings or emotion-related information. Lack of space precludes a detailed analysis of what is now a burgeoning literature. Rather, we shall seek to illustrate the important concepts and methodologies in each area with selected studies. As a way of organizing this varied literature, we shall attempt to provide a novel heuristic way of classifying inhibitory phenomena in cognition and emotion. Then, at the end of the chapter, we shall return to the two related questions raised here: (a) Is there anything quantitatively or qualitatively different about inhibition in the domain of cognition and emotion?; and, (b) is there any evidence for strong as opposed to weak inhibition in the domain of cognition and emotion?

A CLASSIFICATION OF INHIBITORY PHENOMENA IN COGNITION AND EMOTION

In this section we endeavour to provide an heuristic scheme within which to conceptualize putative processes of inhibition in cognition and emotion. The scheme is agnostic to whether we are referring to what we have called strong or weak theories of inhibition. That is, it is independent of the exact mechanics of the processes of inhibition. Instead, it focuses on the nature of what is inhibited and the extent to which the inhibitory process is automatic or controlled (Shiffrin & Schneider, 1977).

The first distinction we propose in this heuristic scheme is between inhibition of emotion-related information and inhibition of emotional feelings themselves.

So, for example, we may try not to think about an emotional event or even be unable to remember it. This would be seen as inhibition of emotional *information*. In contrast, we may be able to remember such an emotive event but still try to inhibit our feelings about that event. This can be seen as inhibition of *emotional feeling*.

This distinction mirrors ideas in the mainstream emotion literature that emotions can be deconstructed into a set of components (Dalgleish, 1997; Lang, 1988; Power & Dalgleish, 1997) such as behaviour, feelings and cognitive content. We are suggesting that, for the purposes of the present scheme, as far as inhibition from conscious awareness is concerned the most important of these factors are feelings and cognitive content. This is not to say that there is no evidence to suggest inhibition of emotion-related behaviour. On the contrary, there is a healthy literature on, for example, inhibition of emotional expression and its consequences to health (Pennebaker, 1995).

The proposal that there can be differential inhibition of both the feeling and cognitive content components of emotion is, in a sense, the other side of the coin from the literature that discusses differential activation of those same components. For example, work on desynchrony of fear reactions following exposure therapy (Rachman & Hodgson, 1974). Whether or not both sides of the coin have the same underlying processes, that is, whether the differential inhibition is only of the weak sort and therefore merely a variant of differential activation, is a question we shall return to in the sections that follow.

Orthogonal to this distinction between inhibition of emotion-related information and inhibition of emotional feelings, we propose a division between automatic and controlled processes of inhibition (Shiffrin & Schneider, 1977). This distinction has proved useful in cognitive psychology when referring respectively to rapid, parallel, non-conscious, resource-independent processing, on the one hand, and slower, serial, conscious, resource-dependent processing on the other. So, the example we used above of trying not to get upset about something, of "bottling up" feelings (Traue & Pennebaker, 1993), is an instance, we suggest, of the controlled inhibition of emotional feelings. In contrast, in cases where a person is unable to experience emotion about what is generally agreed to be an emotional event, we suggest that there is automatic inhibition of emotion.

Similarly, in the domain of inhibition of emotional information, an example of automatic inhibition would be psychogenic amnesia (American Psychiatric Association, 1994)—the inability to remember details, or indeed all, of emotional events. In contrast, deliberate attempts to not think about or to distract oneself from emotional information (Herman, 1992) would be an example of controlled inhibition. This two-by-two classification scheme of automatic vs. controlled inhibition and emotional information vs. emotional feelings is illustrated in Table 1.

The majority of theoretical speculation concerning automatic and controlled processing in the mainstream cognitive psychology literature proposes that controlled cognitive processes have the potential to become automatized with

Table 13.1 A two-by-two classification heuristic for examining inhibitory phenomena in the domain of cognition and emotion

	Emotional information	Emotional feelings
Automatic	e.g. Psychogenic amnesia; repression; derealization	e.g. Emotional numbing; peri-traumatic dissociation, repression, alexithymia
Controlled	e.g. Cognitive avoidance techniques, such as thought suppression and non-disclosure	e.g. "Bottling up of emotions"

constant repetition (Logan, 1988). So, continual practice at complex cognitive–behaviour interactions, such as driving, will lead to an ability to drive "automatically", in the sense that the processes will become relatively rapid, unconscious, parallel and resource-independent. The boundaries on what types of processes can become automatized in this way have been pushed back since the early 1980s by researchers such as John Bargh (1988; Bargh & Srull, 1984), who have provided compelling evidence of automatic social-cognitive processes, such as the activation of attitudes. Theoretical speculation that there is automatization of the inhibition of emotional information originates much earlier, in an altogether different theoretical paradigm—that of psychoanalysis. Psychoanalytic theorists have speculated that so-called "primary repression"—the unconscious inhibition of distressing memories—may develop following a period of "suppression" or "after expulsion", in which there are deliberate attempts to forget the information (Erdelyi, 1990). A research survey by Melchert (1996) speaks to this issue, in that a majority of 41 respondents who reported periods of amnesia for early abuse also stated that they had consciously attempted to avoid such memories in the past.

There has recently been something of a rapprochement of these two literatures on automaticity, such that old psychodynamic ideas have been reformulated in the language of cognitive science (Power & Dalgleish, 1997). Here the suggestion is that inhibition of information in memory can become automatized following a period of controlled inhibition. A similar argument has been put forward concerning the inhibition of emotions themselves (Power & Dalgleish, 1997; Traue & Pennebaker, 1993). It is suggested that continual attempts during development to inhibit the experience and expression of emotion lead to the automatization of this process, such that later an individual is unable to experience emotions to appropriate elicitors. Again, this is a familiar idea from the psychodynamic literature (Erdelyi, 1990).

It is important to point out that, although we are proposing that deliberate attempts to inhibit emotional feelings or emotional material from awareness can become automatized over time, we are not arguing for a clear-cut delineation between automatic and controlled processing. Rather, we endorse the popular view that they are useful ways of describing sets of processes that broadly conform to certain parameters and that are probably the end-points of a continuum rather than discrete categories.

We have already stated that the two-by-two classification we are proposing is agnostic with respect to the mechanics of inhibition; for example, whether inhibition is weak or strong. Having alluded to traditional theories in the psychodynamic literature, it is important to note that the proposed classification also holds no brief for any particular theory of inhibition such as a Freudian repression view (e.g. Freud, 1915/1949) or a dissociation model, derived from authors such as Janet (e.g. Janet, 1925).

In the following sections we shall consider in turn each cell of the two-by-two classification presented in Table 1 and selectively review the relevant literature. We shall begin by considering briefly the phenomena that need to be understood; in particular, those from the clinical domain. We shall then consider the empirical research, where it exists, that has sought to advance this understanding.

THE CONTROLLED INHIBITION OF EMOTIONAL FEELINGS

Most of us at some time attempt not to experience emotional feelings to certain events. We may try to distract ourselves—to think of other things. We may merely try to contain the feelings welling up inside us. Such controlled inhibition of emotional feelings usually occurs if a situation is perceived as an inappropriate forum in which to be emotional or where the feelings are just too aversive; for example, following trauma or bereavement. Similar techniques are also utilized in cognitive-behavioural treatments for emotional disorders, to enable individuals to deal with extreme emotional experiences (Beck et al., 1979). As well as these acute experiences of inhibition, it seems that the tendency towards such inhibition of emotional feelings can also be a trait-like structure, such that some people habitually inhibit such feelings where at all possible.

Much of the research that has looked at trait-like controlled inhibition of emotional feelings has used a variety of self-report measures of expressivity and has examined the consequences to health or future psychological status of failing to express what would be regarded as appropriate emotions in a given situation (Gross & Levenson, 1997; Paez et al., 1995; Schwartz & Kline, 1995). For example, we carried out a study with survivors of the *Herald of Free Enterprise* ferry disaster (Joseph et al., 1997), in which a sub-sample of survivors were given the Attitudes to Emotional Expression Questionnaire (AEQ) (Williams et al., 1995) at 30 months post-disaster and then followed up at 6 years. The AEQ assesses individuals' trait inclination to inhibit their own experience of emotions—to "bottle up" emotional feelings. The results indicated that the less inclined survivors were at 30 months to allow themselves to experience emotion, the greater their level of self-reported post-traumatic symptomatology at 6 years, even with earlier symptom levels partialled out. At the other end of the spectrum, research by Petrie, Booth & Davison (1995) has concentrated on the effects of suppression of emotion on the immune system, as revealed by variables such as proportions of blood lymphocyte sub-populations or natural killer cell activity, and has revealed that suppression of emotional feelings impairs immune system functioning.

THE AUTOMATIC INHIBITION OF EMOTIONAL FEELINGS

We shall use the label of automatic inhibition of emotional feelings to refer to instances in which an individual does not have any phenomenal experience of emotional affect in situations in which it would normally be seen (by an impartial observer) as appropriate for such affect to be present. In most cases in the literature, the individuals themselves also regard this lack of experience of affect as troublesome or unusual. However, this is not invariably the case, as evidenced by, for example, the presentation of psychopaths who do not seem to experience affect to emotive stimuli but who also feel that this is acceptable (Hare & Quinn, 1971).

A common example of automatic inhibition of emotion feelings is found in stages of bereavement, in which people report that they feel numb and are unable to cry or be upset about their loss (Shuchter & Zisook, 1993). Similarly, emotional numbing is often experienced following traumatic events (Litz, 1992). Automatic inhibition of emotional feelings can also occur at the time of an event's occurrence. The phenomena of peri-traumatic dissociation, in which an individual experiences depersonalization and derealization during a trauma, seems to involve inhibition of appropriate emotional experience (Marmar et al., 1994), and predicts poor long-term outcome (Shalev, Orr & Pitman, 1993). Similarly, individuals with dissociative disorder (American Psychiatric Association, 1994) seem to contain highly emotive information within the context of particular ego-states, such that it is inhibited from being accessed and experienced by alternative ego-states. Finally, damage to the medial–frontal region of the brain seems to lead to loss of affect in some patients when presented with highly emotive pictures, despite the patients realizing that the pictures *should* upset them (e.g. Damasio, Tranel & Damasio, 1991).

As well as these state-like instances of the automatic inhibition of emotional affect, it has been argued by a number of authors that there is a corresponding trait-like tendency. Perhaps the most systematically researched and carefully defined of these trait-like constructs has been the concept of so-called "repressive coping style" (Singer, 1990). Alexithymia is a label given to another trait-like construct, representing a tendency towards impoverished emotional experience. Alexithymia is characterized by inadequacy in describing one's own feelings or thoughts or in discriminating emotional states from bodily reactions (Taylor, 1984). However, despite numerous research articles, the question of whether alexithymia represents a truly independent construct, or whether it is merely a facet of repressive coping style, remains unanswered (Bonano & Singer, 1990) and we will not consider it further here.

"Repressors" have been operationally defined (Turvey & Salovey, 1994) as those individuals who score low on self-report measures of anxiety but high on self-report measures of defensiveness, such as the Marlowe–Crowne Social Desirability Scale (Crowne & Marlowe, 1964). As this operational definition implies, repressors are characterized by low levels of self-reported emotion; that is, as individuals who may be automatically inhibiting the experience of emotional affect. Much of the research on repressors in the cognition and emotion literature has also looked at putative inhibition of emotional *information* in repressors (Fox, 1993; Myers & Brewin, 1994), rather than of emotional feelings *per se*, and we consider these studies in the sections below.

A number of studies, however, have looked at inhibition of emotional feelings in repressors (Asendorpf & Scherer, 1983; Gudjonsson, 1981; Weinberger, Schwartz & Davidson, 1979). For example, Gudjonsson (1981) and Weinberger, Schwartz & Davidson (1979) measured electrodermal responses in repressors and found that, even though their self-reported anxiety was unusually low, they presented with a psychophysiological profile more consistent with high anxiety. Similar effects were found for heart rate and forehead muscle tension, as measured by frontalis EEG (Weinberger, Schwartz & Davidson, 1979). Despite these data, it does not appear to be the case that repressors are unaware of the physiological changes that are taking place. Results show that there is little difference between low-anxious subjects and repressors on somatic anxiety (Weinberger, Schwartz & Davidson, 1979) and repressors seem as good as other subjects at tracking changes in, for example, heart rate (Derakshan, personal communication). What repressors do differ on is the association of these bodily changes to emotion. This could be because the repressors choose not to label their experience as emotional; that is, they employ a deliberate strategy of denial in harmony with their augmented social desirability. In contrast, they may just not experience the bodily changes as emotion-related; that is, some automatic process of inhibition or desynchronization may be in operation.

CONTROLLED INHIBITION OF EMOTIONAL INFORMATION

Deliberate attempts not to represent emotional information, as opposed to emotional affect itself, in consciousness nevertheless utilize many of the same techniques (such as distraction). The term "suppression", originally derived from the psychodynamic literature, has become widely used (Horowitz, 1988) to refer to deliberate, conscious (controlled) attempts to inhibit emotional information from awareness. A number of clinical disorders are characterized by this process (see Tallis, this volume). In posttraumatic stress disorder (PTSD), survivors of trauma engage in continuous attempts to avoid unwanted intrusive thoughts or images of the trauma. Similarly, in obsessive–compulsive Disorder (OCD; Tallis, 1995) and generalized anxiety disorder (GAD), attempts are made to exclude obsessional or worrying thoughts from consciousness.

Much of the empirical research in this area has stemmed from the paradox that in order to deliberately exclude something from conscious awareness, you somehow have to represent the to-be-excluded information so as to carry out the task successfully (Wegner, 1994). Ironically, therefore, the very need to represent or "monitor" the information in this way means that it is susceptible to being activated, and therefore liable to intrude into consciousness when the system is placed under mental load. The majority of research into such "thought suppression" has been concerned with inhibiting emotionally neutral information, such as trying not to think of white polar bears in the prototypical experiments of Dan Wegner (1989). The basic design is that the subject is instructed to try and suppress all thoughts concerning a particular thing. The number of thoughts that the subject subsequently experiences are then monitored. The results indicate that subjects report being unusually sensitive to the unwanted thought throughout the period of suppression (Wegner et al., 1987). This has been verified by self-report and by psychophysiological measures (Wegner et al., 1990).

A number of these studies have concentrated on the suppression of emotionally negative thoughts and information (Wegner & Lane, 1995). For example Arndt et al. (1997) showed that, under conditions of high mental load, subjects experienced more death-related thoughts following a mortality salience intervention, compared with subjects under conditions of low mental load. The standard explanation for this type of effect (Wegner, 1994) is that conditions of mental load disrupt the process which monitors the to-be-suppressed information, thus causing that information to intrude into conscious awareness. Wegner (1994) has extended this argument to suggest that it is the very attempt to suppress emotive thoughts, under conditions of emotional stress, that leads to their intrusion in disorders such as depression, OCD and PTSD (see Tallis, this volume).

Another programme of research that has been concerned with the effects of suppressing emotional information is the work of James Pennebaker on disclosure (Pennebaker, 1995). This body of work indicates that disclosure of past traumatic experiences, either orally or in written form, promotes better health as measured by biological markers and prospective or retrospective self-report (Pennebaker, 1989, for a review). Arguing in reverse, the implication is that non-disclosure, and presumably therefore concomitant attempts at suppression, have adverse consequences for health.

AUTOMATIC INHIBITION OF EMOTIONAL INFORMATION

We shall apply the label of the automatic inhibition of emotional information to instances where an individual exhibits impoverished processing of emotional information and where the salience and/or the nature of the presentation of the information provides no indication as to why it should have been processed in an impoverished manner.

An example of the automatic inhibition of emotional information, then, is the experience of psychogenic amnesia following a trauma (Herman, 1992). In such cases, survivors of trauma experience periods of time when they report an inability to remember the details of what happened to them. This may occur after a period of intact memory and/or memory may return after a period of amnesia (Elliot & Briere, 1995; Feldman-Summers & Pope, 1994; Melchert, 1996). This latter possibility has recently become the subject of considerable controversy, particularly in North America, where the veracity of so-called "recovered" memories that emerge following periods of amnesia has been vociferously challenged (Loftus & Ketcham, 1994). The gist of the challenge is that for a proportion of recovered memories, the recalled experiences are "false" and may have been "implanted" in some way during psychotherapy, using what has been termed "long-term, multifaceted, suggestive memory work" (Lindsay & Read, 1995) (see Brewin & Andrews, 1998, for a review). These doubts have led to a spate of laboratory-based studies attempting to implant "false" memories (see Lindsay & Read, 1995, for a review). The consensus seems to be that some memories recovered in therapy are most likely veridical (e.g. Williams, 1994), but that it is eminently possible that some memories are false (for further discussion, see Bekerian & Goodrich, this volume).

There is a growing body of experimental research in mainstream cognitive psychology investigating automatic inhibition of affectively neutral information (see Anderson & Bjork, 1994, for a review of the memory literature). The question of whether such processes are either qualitatively or quantitatively different when the material is emotional is only beginning to be addressed. This area is potentially the most fruitful empirical interface between cognitive psychology and research on emotions and, consequently, we shall consider a number of studies in detail. For convenience we shall divide the studies into those that have purported to examine perceptual and attentional processes and those that have concerned themselves with memory, although we acknowledge that the distinction between these is somewhat arbitrary.

Automatic Inhibition of Emotional Information in Perception and Attention

The concept of perceptual defence has been invoked to explain experimental results in which stressful and non-stressful words are flashed on a screen at short presentation intervals. The standard finding has been that stressful words had to be presented for longer before subjects could read them (see Erdelyi, 1974, for a discussion). This was taken as evidence of primary repression; that is, the relegation of material to the unconscious before an individual has even become aware of its existence. A problem with the research demonstrating perceptual defence is that the frequency characteristics of the stressful words were not balanced with those of the control words. Furthermore, the social constraints on reading negatively emotional, often dirty, words, were not controlled for. Both of these artefacts of the design of the early experiments appear to have biased the data, because when stimuli are balanced and the social constraints of the situation removed, the perceptual defence effect disappears (Holmes, 1990). At present, then, there is little convincing evidence of differential inhibition of emotional information in perception.

Turning to the research on attention, the fact that stimuli having emotional significance often *attract* attention is hardly in doubt. For example, words chosen to match the emotional concerns of normal individuals produce more interference than do matched control words in a Stroop colour-naming task (e.g. Rieman & McNally, 1995). Similarly, pictures of stimuli associated with strongly polarized attitudes are more likely to be noticed when embedded in a larger set (Roskos-Ewoldsen & Fazio, 1992). This is particularly true for negative or threatening trait descriptors (Pratto & John, 1991) and in emotionally disordered individuals (for reviews, see Mathews & MacLeod, 1994; also Mogg & Bradley, and MacLeod, C., both this volume). Despite this general finding, attention to emotional stimuli is by no means universal, and can be abolished or even reversed under certain circumstances, and perhaps particularly in certain people. Such abolition may reflect either strong or weak inhibitory processes (see above), irrespective of whether it is controlled or automatic.

With attention being assessed with a visual probe, we found that high trait-anxious students about to take an important examination selectively attended to threatening words (MacLeod & Mathews, 1988; see also Mogg, Bradley & Hallowell, 1994). In contrast, low-trait anxious students did not show this effect and sometimes seemed to actively avoid attending to the same words. As we have suggested above, it is possible that the most avoidant individuals are not in fact truly low-anxious, but are those who tend to deny all negative emotion (so-called "repressors"). Studies in the attentional literature of repressors have been inconclusive. Some (but not all) studies using Stroop interference measures have suggested that repressors are similar to highly anxious individuals in attending to threatening stimuli (Dawkins & Furnham, 1989). In contrast, an experiment using visual probes (Fox, 1993; see also Fox, 1994) suggested that repressors were indeed avoidant, although only of socially threatening words. If so, the earlier finding of interference may partly reflect effortful avoidance (controlled inhibition), rather than automatic attentional selection.

We suggest here that it is not only a specific group of repressors who can inhibit emotionally disturbing material, but that everyone, even highly anxious individuals, can do so, at least transiently, when the cues involved are relatively weak. In support of this position, we first briefly review some studies suggesting that inhibition does indeed occur, albeit not always consistently.

In a study of colour-naming, MacLeod & Rutherford (1992) found more interference from threatening words in highly anxious students about to take an exam, although surprisingly only for words that were masked so that their content could not be reported. By implication, interference due to unmasked words could be controlled in some way (although see Mogg, Bradley & Hallowell, 1994, for evidence of attention to both masked and unmasked words). In three experiments, Fox (1996) also found interference from masked, but not unmasked, threat words in highly anxious subjects, and only when these conditions were mixed, or when masked exposures followed earlier unmasked exposures. These results seem to suggest the paradoxical conclusion that non-conscious interference effects depend on knowing that threatening words are sometimes present, and that interference can be suppressed only when the word is currently visible.

Other evidence of an apparent inhibition effect is the paradoxical abolition of colour-naming interference in phobic individuals under stress. Interference from words related to snakes in phobic students was eliminated when the test was in the presence of a real snake (Mathews & Sebastian, 1993; although see Chen, Lewin & Craske, 1996, for conflicting data). The same effect has been reported in social phobic patients who were expecting to give a speech in public (Amir et al., 1996). Although it is not yet certain why this phenomenon sometimes occurs, one view holds that it is due to competition for attention from task demands, and the mental representations of the real threat (see Williams, Mathews & MacLeod, 1996; Mathews, MacKintosh & Fulcher 1997). In this view, competition occurs between representations of the task target, the distracting word meaning, and the external threat. As each representation gains in activation, so it inhibits the others, until one becomes dominant. If activation of a threatening distracter exceeds that of the target stimulus, attention will be diverted from the task and interference occurs. With sufficient effort to attend to the task stimulus, however, the distracter can be inhibited. The presence of a severe external threat radically increases competition for attention, and forces drastic increases in task-related effort, sufficient to inhibit the lesser threat represented by word meanings.

There are thus two alternative explanations for the finding that high trait-anxious individuals (and anxious patients) show an attentional bias towards threat. One is that the activation of threat representations in such individuals is stronger, requiring more effort to inhibit them. The other is that their inhibitory capacity is defective, relative to less vulnerable people. Some evidence is available to support both of these possibilities.

In a study of attentional search, generalized anxiety disorder was found to be associated with slowing due to the presence of distracting words, even when these were neutral in meaning (Mathews et al., 1990). This did not happen when the location of the target was known in advance. The implication is that when searching for a target, anxious individuals have difficulty in preventing their attention being captured by any irrelevant stimuli that they encounter. In three related experiments with high trait-anxious subjects, Fox (1994) also found evidence supporting the idea that anxiety is associated with the defective inhibition of attention. Of particular relevance is the use of the negative priming paradigm, developed by Tipper (1985), in which a distracter that is ignored on one trial sometimes becomes the target on the next. Negative priming (inhibition) is revealed by the slowing on these critical trials relative to control trials when the same target had not been ignored previously. Even with neutral symbols as targets and distracters, high-trait anxious subjects showed less negative priming than other groups, suggesting a relative inability to inhibit irrelevant distracters. In another experiment, using threatening words as to-be-ignored distracters, there was no evidence of any negative priming in the same subjects, with low-anxious "repressors" showing the most. Fox (1994) concluded that anxiety-prone individuals may have a rather general defect in their ability to inhibit irrelevant information encountered during attentional search.

It may still be the case that this inhibitory defect is particularly problematic in the case of threatening distracters. Interference was greatest for these threatening stimuli during attentional search in anxious patients (Mathews et al., 1990), and having to ignore a threatening distracter also caused most slowing in the following trial, for anxious students (Fox, 1994). A tentative conclusion is that both the amplification of threat representations and an inhibitory defect may combine to cause attentional bias in anxiety. Although we have reviewed these studies in the section on automatic inhibition, the evidence does not permit a firm conclusion on the question of whether these processes are partly controlled or entirely involuntary. Perhaps interference effects can be inhibited by an increase in voluntary efforts to attend to the target, provided that the distracting stimulus is visible or in a known location. The hypothesis outlined above suggests that such inhibitory control must be limited, and will be overwhelmed by highly threatening events (Mathews, MacKintosh & Fulcher, 1997). Greater threat activation, and deficient inhibition, will thus result in such a failure of control occurring more readily in anxiety-prone individuals.

The Automatic Inhibition of Emotional Information in Memory

The last 65 years have witnessed a number of attempts to demonstrate in the laboratory the phenomena of automatic inhibition or repression of emotional information. A number of methodologies have been employed, such as autobiographical memory tasks and studies involving the introduction and elimination of stress. These are eloquently reviewed in a pair of essays by David Holmes (1974, 1990) and we will not repeat the details here. The bottom line is that, although many of the studies are ingenious, none provides convincing evidence of anything other than weak inhibition. In other words, all of the data can be explained in a way that does not call upon inhibition processes proper but instead relies upon differential activation.

To illustrate, let us consider the phenomenon of the "return of the repressed". In experiments concerned with this issue, subjects learned and were then tested on their memory for neutral materials. Half of the subjects were then exposed to a stress condition designed to make these, by now familiar, neutral materials aversive in some way. The subjects were then tested again and results typically showed that subjects in the stress manipulation now recalled fewer of the neutral materials compared to the non-stressed controls. The stress was then eliminated (for example, by exposure to success or by debriefing) and recall tested a third time. There were no longer any differences between the groups. These findings (Zeller, 1950, 1951) were widely cited as evidence for repression. However, an alternative explanation is that the stress manipulation merely interfered with the subjects' task performance and that there was no repression occurring. This alternative view was borne out in studies which have been able to demonstrate the so-called "return of the repressed" using non-stressful but equally interfering manipulations (Holmes, 1972). The take-home message of the numerous studies such as these on repression in memory appears to be that, although at first blush they seem to provide support for the concept of inhibition of emotional information in memory, closer examination reveals that they only substantiate a weak theory of inhibition.

Partly in reaction to similarly inconclusive studies in mainstream cognitive psychology, the last 15 years have seen an upsurge in interest in providing evidence of strong cognitive inhibition (see above) in memory. A number of methodologies, such as the directed forgetting paradigm (Bjork, 1989) and the retrieval-induced inhibition paradigm (Anderson & Spellman, 1995), have substantiated the empirical status of strong theories of cognitive inhibition at retrieval (see above). More recently, researchers have begun to employ these tasks with emotionally valent material to investigate whether there are any differences in the strong inhibition of this information. The most frequently employed methodology has been the directed forgetting paradigm. The standard procedure is to present a list of items in an intentional recall methodology. After presentation of half of this list, subjects are told that they should forget those items [the to-be-forgotten (TBF) material], as these were for practice; and only remember any subsequently presented stimuli [the to-be-remembered (TBR) items]. Subjects are then given a recall test of *all* of the items. The usual finding is that the TBR items are recalled well but that there is poor recall of the TBF items relative to a baseline condition where there is no instruction to forget half-way through the list (Geiselman, Bjork & Fishman, 1983). This type of result has been interpreted as evidence of strong inhibition at retrieval, first, as similar effects can be found for incidentally recalled items, thus mitigating against any explanation in terms of selective activation due to rehearsal, and second, as the effect disappears when memory is tested by recognition.

A series of experiments by Power et al. (submitted) used the directed forgetting task with emotional words. They found that normal subjects showed stronger directed forgetting for threat-related items relative to neutral material in a within-subject design. This suggests that negative (relative to neutral) material may be more easily inhibited at retrieval by normal subjects. However, when the neutral words were analysed separately, there was no evidence of a directed forgetting effect and this casts some doubt on the validity of the effect with the threat material. In another experiment, Power et al. also found that depressed subjects showed hypermnesia for TBF-negative items, relative to baseline. This effect was not seen in generally anxious and control subjects.

Cloitre et al. (1996) assessed performance on the directed forgetting task with positive and negative words in individuals with a diagnosis of borderline personality disorder, who either had or had not suffered early parental abuse, and compared them to matched, non-clinical controls. There was no evidence of differential directed forgetting across groups. Wilhelm et al. (1996) examined directed forgetting in individuals with obsessive–compulsive disorder (OCD). The results indicated that OCD sufferers showed *less* directed forgetting of words related to their concerns, mirroring the findings of Power et al. with depressed individuals.

Finally, the directed forgetting paradigm was used by Myers, Brewin & Power (1998) with repressors and controls. The results showed that repressors exhibited stronger directed forgetting of negative but not positive words that were self-rated, relative to controls. However, in this task there was no baseline condition in which repressors were instructed to remember all of the material (the only baseline condition involved non-repressors). The enhanced forgetting of negative information could therefore be due to poorer encoding on the part of the repressors, rather than inhibition at retrieval.

This research on repressors using the directed forgetting methodology follows on from work by Penny Davis (Davis, 1987; Davis, 1990; Davis & Schwartz, 1987) investigating autobiographical memory. During both free- and cued-recall tasks repressors had difficulty in recalling negative, relative to positive, autobiographical memories. On a similar note, Myers, Brewin & Power (1992) found that the age of repressors' earliest negative memories was significantly older than that of non-repressors, despite evidence that they had worse childhoods (Myers & Brewin, 1994). As with much of the work discussed above on repression, these autobiographical memory results are supportive of a weak theory of inhibition but do not really speak to the question of whether there is strong inhibition of emotional information in repressors.

DISCUSSION AND CONCLUSIONS

The notion that there are active processes in the mind concerned with the inhibition of emotional feelings or of emotional information was first introduced by Freud (1915/1949) around the turn of the century. More recently, the idea has gained currency in the cognition and emotion literature and a number of researchers in this domain have begun to take the idea of such inhibition seriously.

In this chapter we have endeavoured to provide a two-by-two taxonomy for classifying research on inhibition in cognition and emotion. We have suggested that a useful distinction can be made between inhibition of emotional feelings vs.

inhibition of emotional information or cognitive content, and between automatic vs. controlled processes of inhibition. The scheme was derived from componential theories of emotion, which suggest that emotions can usefully be deconstructed into discrete components such as behaviour, physiological change and cognitions (Lang, 1988). We have then discussed each of the cells of this two-by-two scheme with appropriate clinical and empirical examples.

There are three issues that we wish to address in this final section. The first concerns the possibility that processes of inhibition may be an indirect result of other forms of automatic or controlled processing on the part of the individual. The other two issues revolve around the questions that we raised in the Introduction: first, whether or not there is any evidence for differential strong inhibition of emotional feelings or information; and second, whether or not there is evidence to suggest that inhibition in the domain of cognition and emotion is in any way a special case.

The question of whether or not inhibition processes may be an indirect result of other automatic or controlled processing arises from the literature on mood repair. For example. Parrott & Sabini (1990) investigated the valency of autobiographical memories from high school during times of naturally occurring low- and high-mood (as they varied with weather, music and proximity to exams). They found that when subjects' prevailing mood was unhappy, the first memories that they retrieved were more likely to be happy. This phenomenon of mood repair can be conceptualized in terms of inhibition, in that retrieval of positive memories and/or the corresponding generation of positive mood may have an inhibitory effect on low mood.

Similarly, a number of studies using the emotional priming paradigm have shown that normal subjects, when presented with a negative prime, are slower at long latencies to endorse a negative trait adjective as self-referent (Power & Brewin, 1990; Power et al., 1991). The suggestion here is that efforts at mood repair make it harder to subsequently access negative aspects of the self. Similar instances of second-order inhibition are evident in the clinical presentations that we have reviewed above. For instance, many efforts at controlled inhibition, such as distraction, involve actively attending to non-emotional information in order to block the entry of emotional information into awareness.

In order to address the question of whether there is any convincing evidence of strong inhibition of emotional feelings or information, we must necessarily focus on the research on automatic inhibition of emotional information; what might be called repression. The reason for this is that in the cases of controlled inhibition and inhibition of emotional feelings, there have been no attempts to determine whether the underlying processes are of the strong or weak type. Only in the case of repression, and only relatively recently (see Holmes, 1990), has research focused its attention on this issue.

In the domain of automatic inhibition of emotional information, the relevant data are provided by the directed forgetting task. As we saw above, in all three of the studies with clinical groups using this paradigm (Cloitre et al., 1996; Power et al., submitted; Wilhelm et al., 1996), there was no suggestion of any enhanced

directed forgetting of emotional information. If anything, the data were supportive of impaired forgetting. The two studies that do show evidence of differential
forgetting of emotional information are Power et al. (submitted), experiment 2
and Myers, Brewin & Power (1998). As we have noted above, in the first of these,
the relatively enhanced directed forgetting effect for negative information was
due to a loss of directed forgetting for neutral material, rather than a particularly
strong effect for the valenced information. In the latter study by Myers et al., we
have perhaps the most convincing data of differential forgetting of emotional
information, this time in repressors. However, as we have discussed, the crucial
baseline condition, in which repressors were *not* asked to forget some of the
information, was not included in the design and thus it may be that the data
represent an effect of differential encoding. In summary, then, our view echoes
that of David Holmes in that there are, as yet, no data that clearly demonstrate
strong inhibition in the domain of cognition and emotion.

Irrespective of whether or not we can demonstrate differential strong inhibition in the domain of cognition and emotion, it is important to consider whether
the phenomena and research findings that we have reviewed suggest that inhibition (strong or weak) in cognition and emotion is in any way a special case. In the
case of the controlled inhibition of emotional information, the research by Dan
Wegner on thought suppression suggests that there is no difference between
suppression of emotional information and of any other information relevant to
the ongoing task demands. Similarly, there are no data to suggest differential
controlled inhibition of emotional feelings as compared to, for example, feelings
of pain or hunger. Indeed, a number of approaches to the inhibition or avoidance
of such phenomena treat them as equal (e.g. Hayes et al., 1996).

The case of the automatic inhibition of emotional feelings is somewhat different. Here, we have suggested that the concept of inhibition can be applied when
an impartial observer would deem it appropriate for emotional affect to be
experienced in a given situation but where there is an absence of such affect. As
we noted in the case of repressors, in a proportion of these situations there is
some phenomenal experience of physiological change, but it is not associated
with emotion by the observer. In these cases, it does not appear to be the case
that there is inhibition of emotional feelings *per se*. If there is any inhibition
operating, it is of the association between a particular set of feelings and the idea
that they might be emotional.

In other cases, where there does seem to be genuine lack of both affect and
physiological change associated with affect, there is a case for arguing that
inhibition here is merely a convenient label. There is no evidence that there is
anything that is being inhibited. Consequently, it may merely be the social construction of what is appropriate in a given situation that leads one to adopt terms
such as "inhibition" in such cases. This argument becomes somewhat harder to
maintain when the situation involves intense personal trauma, such as rape, and
the victim is describing dissociation from the experience at the time of its occurrence, with corresponding lack of affect. This type of account seems to suggest
strongly that some form of inhibition, via dissociation, must be involved. This

may well be the case and there are no data at present to decide either way. However, it is important to note that in similar circumstances, sufferers can also feel dissociated from pain and other bodily experiences and it is therefore not necessarily true that the inhibition process is unique to the domain of emotion.

Finally, we have reviewed a host of evidence that there is differential automatic inhibition of emotion-related information, even if the case for strong inhibition of such material is less convincing. However, although these data can be explained in terms of the emotional nature of the material causing it to be inhibited, an equally plausible, and more parsimonious, explanation is that there is inhibition of information that is incongruent with current dominant meaning structures, such as schemas (Power & Dalgleish, 1997). In this latter view, any information that does not fit in with current, active schematic representations, whether it is emotive or not, is likely to be inhibited.

To illustrate this point, consider a prototypical experiment by Anderson & Pichert (1978). Here subjects were presented with a story involving a detailed description of a house. They were encouraged to adopt the perspective of either a burglar or a potential house buyer and then asked to recall as much of the story as possible. Perhaps not surprisingly, the subjects recalled more information congruent to their adopted perspective; for example, the "burglars" were more likely to recall that the back window was slightly broken. Subjects were then asked to adopt the other perspective and to recall the story again. The results indicated that information relevant to the new perspective that had previously not been recalled was now remembered, whereas information that was no longer perspective-relevant was forgotten.

This sort of study illustrates that the schemas operating during a particular experimental task can influence the profile of information that is remembered and forgotten. If we apply this idea to, for instance, the data on repressors reviewed in the body of the paper, it could be argued that information associated with negativity is incongruent with the repressors' self-schemas and is therefore inhibited. In this analysis, it is not the negativity of the information *per se* that is crucial, but rather its incongruence with dominant schematic meaning.

There are few actual data that speak to this issue of self-schema incongruence vs. negative emotionality in repressors. One of the exceptions is the study by Myers, Brewin & Power (in press), who showed that whether material was rated as self-referent or not in repressors did not affect its likelihood of being forgotten in a directed forgetting paradigm. However, the ratings of self-relatedness in this study were collapsed to only an either/or categorization, and may not have been fine-tuned enough to detect the important differences. There is further support for this possibility in that the repressors in this study did not rate negative terms as self-referent any more than the controls on this dichotomous categorization, whereas there is a wealth of other evidence that indicates that this is exactly what repressors do most readily (Singer, 1990).

In summary, although there is plenty of evidence for inhibition (of the weak variety at least) in cognition–emotion interactions, it is not possible to put together a convincing argument that there is anything special about this particular domain. It is equally plausible that similar processes operate differentially on other forms of bodily experiences (e.g. pain and hunger) and on other forms of information discrepant from currently active meaning representations (cf. Anderson & Pichert, 1978).

REFERENCES

American Psychiatric Association (1994). *Diagnostic and Statistical Manual of Mental Disorders*, 4th edn. Washington DC: American Psychiatric Association.

Amir, N., McNally, F. J., Riemann, B. C., Burns, J., Loenz, M. & Mullen, J. T. (1996). Suppression of the emotional Stroop effect by increased anxiety in patients with social phobia. *Behaviour Research and Therapy*, **34**, 945–948.

Anderson, M. C. & Bjork, R. A. (1994). Mechanisms of inhibition in long-term memory: a new taxonomy. In D. Dagenbach & T. Carr (eds), *Inhibitory Processes in Attention, Memory and Language*. San Diego, CA: Academic Press, pp. 265–325.

Anderson, M. C. & Spellman, B. A. (1995). On the status of inhibitory mechanisms in cognition: memory retrieval as a model case. *Psychological Review*, **102**, 68–100.

Anderson, R. C. & Pichert, J. W. (1978). Recall of previously unrecallable information following a shift in perspective. *Journal of Verbal Learning and Verbal Behaviour*, **17**, 1–12.

Arndt, J., Greenberg, J., Soloman, S., Pyszczynski, T. & Simon, L. (1997). Suppression, accessibility of death-related thoughts, and cultural worldview defense: exploring the psychodynamics of terror management. *Journal of Personality and Social Psychology*, **73**, 5–18.

Asendorpf, J. A. & Scherer, K. R. (1983). The discrepant repressor: differentiation between low anxiety, high anxiety, and repression of anxiety by autonomic–facial–verbal patterns of behaviour. *Journal of Personality and Social Psychology*, **45**, 1334–1346.

Bargh, J. A. (1988). Automatic information processing: implications for communication and affect. In H. E. Sypher, L. Donohew & E. T. Higgins (eds), *Communication, Social Cognition, and Affect*. Hillsdale, NJ: Erlbaum. pp. 9–32.

Bargh, J. A. & Srull, T. R. (1984). Automatic and conscious processing of social information. In R. S. Wyer (ed.), *Handbook of Social Cognition*, Vol. 3. Hillsdale, NJ: Erlbaum, pp. 1–44.

Beck, A. T., Rush, A. J., Shaw, B. F. & Emery, G. (1979). *Cognitive Therapy of Depression: A Treatment Manual*. New York: Guilford.

Bjork, R. A. (1989). Retrieval inhibition as an adaptive mechanism in human memory. In H. L. Roediger III & F. L. M. Craik (eds), *Varieties of Memory and Consciousness: Essays in Memory of Endel Tulving*. Hillsdale, NJ: Erlbaum.

Bonano, G. A. & Singer, J. L. (1990). Repressive personality style: theoretical and methodological implications for health and pathology. In J. L. Singer (ed.), *Repression and Dissociation: Implications for Personality Theory, Psychopathology, and Health*. Chicago, IL: University of Chicago Press, pp. 435–470.

Brewin, C. R. & Andrews, B. (1998). Recovered memories of trauma: phenomenology and cognitive mechanisms. *Clinical Psychology Review*.

Briggs, J. L. (1970). *Never in Anger: Portrait of an Eskimo Family*. Cambridge, MA: Harvard University Press.

Chen, E., Lewin, M. R. & Craske, M. G. (1996). Effects of state anxiety on selective processing of threatening information. *Cognition & Emotion*, **10**, 225–240.

Cloitre, M., Cancienne, J., Brodsky, B., Dulit, R. & Perry, S. W. (1996). Memory performance among women with parental abuse histories: enhanced directed forgetting or directed remembering? *Journal of Abnormal Psychology*, **105**, 204–211.

Crowne, D. P. & Marlowe, D. (1964). *The Approval Motive: Studies in Evaluative Dependence*. New York: Wiley.

Dalgleish, T. (1991). The Processing of Emotional Information in Clinical and Subclinical Anxiety States. Unpublished Doctoral thesis, University of London.

Dalgleish, T. (1997). An anti-anti-essentialist theory of emotion: a reply to Kupperman. *Philosophical Psychology*, **10**, 85–90.

Damasio, A. R., Tranel, D. & Damasio, H. (1991). Somatic markers and the guidance of behaviour: theory and preliminary testing. In H. S. Levin, H. M. Eisenberg & A. L. Bemton (eds), *Frontal Lobe Function and Dysfunction*. New York: Oxford University Press, pp. 217–219.

Davis, P. J. (1987). Repression and the inaccessibility of affective memories. *Journal of Personality and Social Psychology*, **53**, 585–593.

Davis, P. J. (1990). Repression and the inaccessibility of emotional memories. In J. L. Singer (ed.), *Repression and Dissociation: Implications for Personality Theory, Psychopathology, and Health*. Chicago, IL: University of Chicago Press, pp. 387–403.

Davis, P. J. & Schwartz, G. E. (1987). Repression and the inaccessibility of affective memories. *Journal of Personality and Social Psychology*, **52**, 155–162.

Dawkins, K. & Furnham, A. (1989). The colour naming of emotional words. *British Journal of Psychology*, **80**, 383–389.

Elliot, D. M. & Briere, J. (1995). Posttraumatic stress associated with delayed recall of sexual abuse: a general population study. *Journal of Traumatic Stress*, **8**, 629–647.

Erdelyi, M. H. (1974). A new look at the new look: perceptual defense and vigilance. *Psychological Review*, **81**, 1–25.

Erdelyi, M. H. (1990). Repression, reconstruction and defense: history and integration of the psychoanalytic and experimental frameworks. In J. L. Singer (ed.), *Repression and Dissociation: Implications for Personality Theory, Psychopathology, and Health*. Chicago, IL: University of Chicago Press, pp. 1–32.

Feldman-Summers, S. & Pope, K. S. (1994). The experience of forgetting childhood abuse: a national survey of psychologists. *Journal of Consulting and Clinical Psychology*, **62**, 636–639.

Fox, E. (1993). Allocation of visual attention and anxiety. *Cognition and Emotion*, **7**, 207–215.

Fox, E. (1994). Attentional bias in anxiety: a defective inhibition hypothesis. *Cognition and Emotion*, **8**, 165–195.

Fox, E. (1996). Selective processing of threatening words in anxiety: the role of awareness. *Cognition and Emotion*, **10**, 449–480.

Freud, S. (1915/1949). *The Unconscious* (trans. J. Strachey). London: Hogarth Press.

Geiselman, R. E., Bjork, R. A. & Fishman, D. L. (1983). Disrupted retrieval in directed forgetting: a link with post-hypnotic amnesia. *Journal of Experimental Psychology: General*, **112**, 58–72.

Gross, J. J. & Levenson, R. W. (1997). Hiding feelings: the acute effects of inhibiting negative and positive emotion. *Journal of Abnormal Psychology*, **106**, 95–103.

Gudjonsson, G. H. (1981). Self-reported emotional disturbance and its relation to electrodermal reactivity, defensiveness and trait anxiety. *Personality and Individual Differences*, **2**, 47–52.

Hare, R. D. & Quinn, M. J. (1971). Psychopathy and autonomic conditioning. *Journal of Abnormal Psychology*, **77**, 223–235.

Hayes, S. C., Wilson, K. G., Strosahl, K., Gifford, E. V. & Follette, V. M. (1996). Experiential avoidance and behavioural disorders: a functional dimensional approach to diagnosis and treatment. *Journal of Consulting and Clinical Psychology*, **64**, 1152–1168.

Herman, J. L. (1992). *Trauma and Recovery: From Domestic Abuse to Political Terror*. London: Pandora.

Holmes, D. S. (1972). Repression or interference: a further investigation. *Journal of Personality and Social Psychology*, **22**, 163–170.

Holmes, D. S. (1974). Investigations of repression: differential recall of material experimentally or naturally associated with ego threat. *Psychological Bulletin*, **81**, 632–653.

Holmes, D. S. (1990). The evidence for repression: an examination of sixty years of research. In J. L. Singer (ed.), *Repression and Dissociation: Implications for Personality Theory, Psychopathology, and Health*. Chicago, IL: University of Chicago Press, pp. 85–102.

Horowitz, M. J. (1988). *Psychodynamics and Cognition*. Chicago, IL: University of Chicago Press.

Janet, P. (1925). *Psychological Healing: A Historical and Clinical Study* (trans, Eden and Cedar Paul). London: George Allen & Unwin.

Joseph, S. A., Dalgleish, T., Williams, R., Thrasher, S., Yule, W. & Hodgkinson, P. (1997). Attitudes towards emotional expression and post-traumatic stress at 5 years following the Herald of Free Enterprise disaster. *British Journal of Clinical Psychology*, **36**, 133–138.

Lang, P. J. (1988). What are the data of emotion? In G. H. Bower, V. Hamilton & N. H. Frijda (eds), *Cognitive Perspectives on Emotion and Motivation*. NATO ASI Series D: Behavioural and Social Sciences, Vol. 44. Dordrecht: Kluwer Academic, pp. 173–194.

Lindsay, D. S. & Read, J. D. (1995). "Memory work" and recovered memories of childhood sexual abuse: scientific evidence and public, professional and personal issues. *Psychology, Public Policy and the Law*, **1**, 846–908.

Litz, B. T. (1992). Emotional numbing in combat-related post-traumatic stress disorder: a critical review and reformulation. *Clinical Psychology Review*, **12**, 417–432.

Loftus, E. F. & Ketcham, K. (1994). *The Myth of Repressed Memory*. New York: St Martin's Press.

Logan, G. D. (1988). Toward an instance theory of automatisation. *Psychological Review*, **95**, 492–527.

MacLeod, C. & Mathews, A. (1988). Anxiety and the allocation of attention to threat. *Quarterly Journal of Experimental Psychology*, **40**, 653–670.

MacLeod, C. & Rutherford, E. M. (1992). Anxiety and the selective processing of emotional information: mediating roles of awareness, trait and state variables, and personal relevance of stimulus materials. *Behaviour Research and Therapy*, **30**, 479–491.

Marmar, C. R., Weiss, D. S., Schlenger, W. E., Fairbank, J. A., Jordan, K., Kulka, R. A. & Hough, R. L. (1994). Peritraumatic dissociation and posttraumatic stress in male Vietnam theater veterans. *American Journal of Psychiatry*, **151**, 902–907.

Mathews, A., MacKintosh, B. & Fulcher, E. (1997). Cognitive biases in anxiety and attention to threat. *Trends in Cognitive Science*, **1**, 340–345.

Mathews, A. & MacLeod, C. (1994). Cognitive approaches to emotion and emotional disorders. *Annual Review of Psychology*, **45**, 25–50.

Mathews, A., May, J., Mogg, K. & Eysenck, M. (1990). Attentional bias in anxiety: selective search or defective filtering? *Journal of Abnormal Psychology*, **99**, 166–173.

Mathews, A. & Sebastian S. (1993) Suppression of emotional Stroop effects by fear-arousal. *Cognition and Emotion*, **7**, 517–530.

Melchert, T. P. (1996). Childhood memory and a history of different forms of abuse. *Professional Psychology: Research and Practice*, **27**, 438–446.

Mogg, K., Bradley, B. P. & Hallowell, N. (1994). Attentional bias to threat: roles of trait anxiety, stressful events, and awareness. *Quarterly Journal of Experimental Psychology*, **47A**, 841–864.

Myers, L. B. & Brewin, C. R. (1994). Recall of early experience and the repressive coping style. *Journal of Abnormal Psychology*, **103**, 288–292.

Myers, L. B., Brewin, C. R. & Power, M. J. (1992). Repression and autobiographical memory. In M. A. Conway, D. C. Rubin, H. Spinnler & W. A. Wagenaar (eds), *Theoretical Perspectives on Autobiographical Memory*. Dordrecht: Kluwer.

Myers, L. B., Brewin, C. R. & Power, M. J. (1998). Repressive coping and the directed forgetting of emotional material. *Journal of Abnormal Psychology*, **107**, 141–148.

Paez, D., Basabe, N., Valdoseda, M., Velasco, C. & Iraurgi, I. (1995). Confrontation: inhibition, alexithymia, and health. In J. W. Pennebaker (ed.), *Emotion, Disclosure and Health*. Washington, DC: American Psychological Association, pp. 195–222.

Parrott, W. G. & Sabini, J. (1990). Mood and memory under natural conditions: evidence for mood incongruent recall. *Journal of Personality and Social Psychology*, **59**, 321–336.

Pennebaker, J. (ed.) (1995). *Emotion, Disclosure and Health*. Washington, DC: American Psychological Association.

Pennebaker, J. W. (1989). Confession, inhibition, and disease. *Advances in Experimental Social Psychology*, **22**, 211–244.

Petrie, K. J., Booth, R. J. & Davison, K. P. (1995). Repression, disclosure, and immune function: recent findings and methodological issues. In J. W. Pennebaker (ed.), *Emotion, Disclosure and Health*. Washington, DC: American Psychological Association, pp. 223–237.

Power, M. J. & Brewin, C. R. (1990). Self-esteem regulation in an emotional priming task. *Cognition and Emotion*, **4**, 39–51.

Power, M. J. & Dalgleish, T. (1997). *Cognition and Emotion: From Order to Disorder*. Hove: Psychology Press.

Power, M. J., Dalgleish, T. & Claudio, V. (submitted). The directed forgetting task: application to emotionally valent material.

Power, M. J., Stuessy, A., Mahony, T. & Brewin, C. R. (1991). The emotional priming task: results from a student population. *Cognitive Therapy and Research*, **14**, 21–31.

Pratto, F. & John, O. P. (1991). The attention-grabbing power of negative social information. *Journal of Personaality and Social Psychology*, **61**, 380–391.

Rachman, S. J. & Hodgson, R. I. (1974). Synchrony and desynchrony in fear and avoidance. *Behaviour Research and Therapy*, **12**, 311–318.

Riemann, B. C. & NcNally, R. J. (1995). Cognitive processing of personally relevant information. *Cognitive and Emotion*, **9**, 325–340.

Roskos-Ewoldsen, D. R. & Fazio, R. H. (1992). On the orienting value of attitudes: attitude accessibility as a determinant of an object's attraction of visual attention. *Journal of Personality and Social Psychology*, **63**, 198–211.

Rumelhart, D. E. & McClelland, J. L. (1986). *Parallel Distributed Processing: Explorations in the Microstructure of Cognition, Vol. 1: Foundations*. Cambridge, MA: MIT Press.

Schwartz, G. E. & Kline, J. P. (1995). Repression, emotional disclosure, and health: theoretical, empirical, and clinical considerations. In J. W. Pennebaker (ed.), *Emotion, Disclosure and Health*. Washington, DC: American Psychological Association, pp. 177–194.

Shalev, A. Y., Orr, S. P. & Pitman, R. K. (1993). Psychophysiologic assessment of traumatic imagery in Israeli civilian patients with posttraumatic stress disorder. *American Journal of Psychiatry*, **150**, 620–624.

Shiffrin, R. M. & Schneider, W. (1977). Controlled and automatic human information processing: II. Perceptual learning, automatic attending and a general theory. *Psychological Review*, **84**, 127–190.

Shuchter, S. R. & Zisook, S. (1993). The course of normal grief. In M. S. Stroebe, W. Stroebe & R. O. Hansson (eds), *Handbook of Bereavement: Theory, Research, and Intervention*. Cambridge: Cambridge University Press, pp. 23–43.

Singer, J. L. (ed.) (1990). *Repression and Dissociation: Implications for Personality Theory, Psychopathology, and Health*. Chicago, IL: University of Chicago Press.

Tallis, F. (1995). *Obsessive Compulsive Disorder: A Cognitive and Neuropsychological Perspective*. Chichester: Wiley.

Taylor, G. J. (1984). Alexythymia: concept, measurement, and implications for treatment. *American Journal of Psychiatry*, **141**, 727–732.

Tipper, S. P. (1985). The negative priming effect: inhibitory effects of ignored primes. *Quarterly Journal of Experimental Psychology*, **37A**, 571–590.

Tipper, S. P., Lortie, C. & Baylis, G. C. (1992). Selective reaching: evidence for action-centered attention. *Journal of Experimental Psychology: Human Perception and Performance*, **18**, 891–905.

Tipper, S. P., Weaver, B., Kirkpatrick, J. & Lewis, S. (1991). Inhibitory mechanisms of attention: locus, stability, and relationship with distractor interference effects. *British Journal of Psychology*, **82**, 507–520.

Traue, H. C. & Pennebaker, J. W. (eds) (1993). *Emotion, Inhibition and Health*. Seattle: Hogrefe & Huber.

Turvey, C. & Salovey, P. (1994). Measures of repression: converging on the same construct? *Imagination, Cognition and Personality*, **13**, 279–289.

Wegner, D. M. (1989). *White Bears and Other Unwanted Thoughts*. New York: Viking.

Wegner, D. M. (1994). Ironic processes of mental control. *Psychological Review*, **101**, 34–52.

Wegner, D. M. & Lane, J. D. (1995). From secrecy to psychopathology. In J. Pennebaker (ed.), *Emotion, Disclosure and Health*. Washington, DC: American Psychological Association, pp. 25–46.

Wegner, D. M., Schneider, D. J., Carter, S. I. & White, L. (1987). Paradoxical effects of thought suppression. *Journal of Personality and Social Psychology*, **53**, 5–13.

Wegner, D. M., Shortt, J. W., Blake, A. W. & Page, M. S. (1990). The suppression of exciting thoughts. *Journal of Personaility and Social Psychology*, **58**, 409–418.

Weinberger, D. A., Schwartz, G. E. & Davidson, R. J. (1979). Low-anxious, high-anxious and repressive coping styles: psychometric patterns and behavioural responses to stress. *Journal of Abnormal Psychology*, **88**, 369–380.

Wilhelm, S., McNally, R. J., Baer, L. & Florin, I. (1996). Directed forgetting in obsessive-compulsive disorder. *Behaviour Research and Therapy*, **34**, 633–641.

Williams, J. M. G., Mathews, A. & MacLeod, C. (1996). The emotional Stroop task and psychopathology. *Psychological Bulletin*, **120**, 3–24.

Williams, L. M. (1994). Recall of childhood trauma: a prospective study of women's memories of child sexual abuse. *Journal of Consulting and Clinical Psychology*, **62**, 1167–1176.

Williams, R., Hodgkinson, P., Joseph, S. & Yule, W. (1995). Attitudes to emotional expression, crisis support and distress 30 months after the capsize of a passenger ferry. *Crisis Intervention*, **1**, 209–214.

Zeller, A. (1950). An experimental analogue of repression. II. The effect of individual failure and success on memory measured by relearning. *Journal of Experimental Psychology*, **40**, 411–422.

Zeller, A. (1951). An experimental analogue of repression. III. The effect of induced failure and success on memory measured by recall. *Journal of Experimental Psychology*, **42**, 32–38.

Chapter 14

Prospective Cognitions

Andrew K. MacLeod
Royal Holloway College, University of London, Egham, UK

Plans, goals, expectancies, hopes, fears, dread and apprehension: these are just some of the many terms that exist for describing mental states that all have as their focus some future state of affairs. A quick glance at these terms reveals that many of them have a strong affective quality, and this chapter will be concerned with understanding these future-orientated, or prospective, cognitive–affective states and their relation to emotional disturbance. Prospective cognitions vary along many dimensions other than the affective dimension, such as the extent to which a goal is abstract rather than concrete, the degree to which a plan to achieve a goal is specific rather than general, and the extent to which expectancies about the future are represented at the level of conscious awareness, as opposed to unconscious assumptions (Austin & Vancouver, 1996; Emmons, 1992). Some of these dimensions, as will become apparent, are particularly important when considering the relationship between prospective cognitions and emotional disorders.

The study of prospective cognitions and their relation to emotion has been relatively neglected when compared with the study of other cognitive processes, such as memory or attention. Perhaps one reason for this relative neglect is psychology's preference for natural science-like, causal explanations of human behaviour and experience, rather than teleological accounts which explain behaviour by reference to mental representations about the future, such as goals, plans and expectations. However, there has been a lineage of teleologically minded theorists, such as McDougall and Tolman (Valentine, 1992) and some theorists have tried to integrate causal and teleological accounts in terms of self-regulating cybernetic systems (Miller, Galanter & Pribram, 1960; Carver & Scheier, 1990). The issue will not be addressed directly in this chapter, but it is an assumption of the chapter that prospective cognitions are important in influencing behaviour.

Handbook of Cognition and Emotion. Edited by T. Dalgleish and M. Power.
© 1999 John Wiley & Sons Ltd.

PROSPECTIVE COGNITION IN THEORIES OF EMOTIONAL DISORDER

Although the study of prospective cognitions has been relatively neglected, it would not be true to say that prospective cognitions have played no role in theories of emotional disorder. Beck et al. (1979) suggest that depression is characterized by the cognitive triad—a negative view of the self, the world and the future. Hopelessness about the future plays a key role in various accounts of depression (Beck et al., 1979; Brown & Harris, 1978; Melges & Bowlby, 1969). More recently, Abramson, Alloy & Metalsky (1989) have reformulated the revised learned helplessness theory in terms of hopelessness, a major part of which is an expectancy that positive outcomes will not occur and that negative outcomes will occur. Klinger's incentive-disengagement theory views depression as a period of disengagement from goals that are perceived to be unobtainable (Klinger, 1993). Theoretical views of anxiety have also emphasized the importance of prospective cognitions (Barlow, 1988; Mathews, 1990), but worry rather than hopelessness is the key construct here.

EMPIRICAL FINDINGS

Global Self-report

A number of attempts have been made to try to capture some of the global attitudes towards the future, represented by terms such as optimism, hope and worry. These constructs have been measured by self-report scales that are not always worded specifically about the future, but which certainly have as their major focus thoughts and attitudes towards the future. Scheier & Carver (1985) devised the Life Orientation Test (LOT), which assesses generalized expectancies for positive vs. negative outcomes. Snyder et al. (1991) have developed the Hope Scale to assess individual differences in the extent to which people perceive that goals can be met. Strathman et al. (1994) developed the Consideration of Future Consequences Scale, which is intended to measure individual differences in the extent to which someone considers distant vs. immediate consequences of behaviour. Research has been carried out correlating scores on these various constructs to mental and physical health outcomes.

In thinking specifically about emotional disturbance, the two scales of this type that are most relevant are the Beck Hopelessness Scale (BHS; Beck et al., 1974) and the Penn State Worry Questionnaire (PSWQ; Meyer et al., 1990). The BHS is a 20-item true/false questionnaire which measures global attitudes towards the future, such as, "My future seems dark to me" and "I can look forward to more good times than bad" (reversed scoring). The BHS has been found to be important in depression and, more particularly, in suicidal behaviour (MacLeod, Rose

& Williams, 1993). The PSWQ is most closely related to anxiety (Molina & Borkovec, 1994), which is consistent with the view of worry as representing the type of future-directed thinking found in anxiety.

Scales such as the ones described are useful in mapping out individuals' general attitudes or stances towards the future. However, other research has tried to look in more detail at the way individuals anticipate their future.

Subjective Probability Judgements

The most common way of examining prospective cognitions is by presenting individuals with a range of hypothetical future positive and negative events or outcomes and asking them to estimate how likely those events are to happen to them. Usually, likelihood is estimated by selecting a number on a scale of probability. The main aim has been to examine the degree to which people with emotional disturbance, such as anxiety and depression, differ from the norm (as represented by judgements of non emotionally-disturbed people) in their judgements. Some studies have also looked at judgements of the likelihood of those events happening to others, although differences between mood-disturbed and non-mood-disturbed individuals emerge most clearly when making self-relevant judgements.

The consistent finding is that mood-disturbed individuals differ from controls in such judgements. Mood-disturbed subjects have been found to judge negative future events as more likely to happen to them than do controls. This has been found when the subjects are chronically anxious worriers (MacLeod, Williams & Bekerian, 1991), high trait anxious students (Butler & Mathews, 1987) anxious patients (Butler & Mathews, 1983; MacLeod et al., 1997), mildly depressed (dysphoric) students (MacLeod & Cropley, 1995; Pietromonaco & Markus, 1985) and depressed patients (Butler & Mathews, 1983; MacLeod et al., 1997). Mood-disturbed subjects have also been found to show a reduction, relative to controls, in their perceived likelihood of positive future events, although this finding is less consistent than the finding of increased negative expectancies. Again, this effect has been found in a range of groups, including mildly depressed students (MacLeod & Cropley, 1995; Pysczcynski, Holt & Greenberg, 1987), depressed patients (MacLeod et al., 1997) and anxious patients (MacLeod et al., 1997). However, some studies have failed to find this effect in anxious or depressed patients (Butler & Mathews, 1983) or dysphoric students (Pietromonaco & Markus, 1985). In a variant of the procedure, where subjects are asked to say "yes" or "no" as to whether a number of future positive and negative events were likely to happen to them, similar results have been found (Andersen, Spielman & Bargh, 1992; Dunning & Story, 1991).

Although the question of accuracy of such judgements is of considerable interest, it has proved to be difficult to address. In almost all studies it is a typical finding that control subjects give higher likelihood estimates for positive events than they do for negative events, an effect that is attenuated or disappears in the mood-disturbed subjects. Does this represent a positive bias on the part of the controls that perhaps disappears at high levels of mood disturbance? It is not possible to say. Reference to a "bias" as a departure from an absolute norm can only be stated when there is an absolute norm to act as a reference point. Experimental studies using constrained situations where the prior probabilities can be controlled may be able to make statements about a bias, but studies asking for real-life judgements where all the relevant variables are neither specified nor controlled cannot. Therefore, the fact that controls make higher estimates for positive events than for negative events does not tell us that they have a positive bias, as positive events may actually be more likely than negative events. This questioning of "bias" as departure from a statistical norm is made forcefully by Tversky & Kahneman (1973) when they note that, "each occurrence of an economic recession, a successful medical operation or a divorce is essentially unique, and its probability cannot be evaluated by a simple tally of instances" (p. 228). The only warranted use of bias seems to be in describing a relative difference between mood-disturbed and non-mood-disturbed groups. A few studies, however, have measured the extent to which predicted events actually happened. Dunning & Story (1991) found that although controls predicted fewer negative events than mildly depressed subjects, they did actually experience fewer (as assessed by retrospective reports of what did happen to them during the follow-up period).

It is clear that there are differences between mood-disturbed and non-mood-disturbed individuals in their expectancies for future positive and negative events happening to them. It is a question of interest whether altered expectancies relate differentially to anxiety and depression. The findings across studies are rather inconsistent, which may in part be explained by studies using different sets of items. However, a more serious problem is that where investigators have measured both anxiety and depression levels in their subjects, the mood-disturbed subjects have always been found to have elevated levels of both anxiety and depression. The problem of the co-variation of anxiety and depression is not unique to this particular area and has been the topic of much discussion. Watson, Clark & Tellegen (1988) have suggested a way of understanding the overlap as well as the distinctiveness of anxiety and depression. This analysis relies on the distinction between two orthogonal dimensions of mood—positive affect (PA) and negative affect (NA). PA is a dimension ranging from pleasurable engagement (enthusiasm and alertness) to unpleasurable disengagement (bored, lethargic); NA covers affective states ranging from unpleasurable engagement (fearful, tense) to pleasurable disengagement (calm, peaceful). It has been argued that, whereas anxiety represents a state of high NA, depression represents a mixed state of high NA and low PA. It has also been suggested that PA and NA relate to reward-driven and punishment-driven motivational systems, such as Gray's (1982) behavioural approach and behavioural inhibition systems (Clark, Watson & Mineka, 1994; MacLeod, Byrne & Valentine, 1996). MacLeod et al. (1996) found in two studies that subjects' ratings of the likelihood of negative future events loaded onto a factor that included a measure of NA, anxiety, worry and depression, whereas their judgements of positive future events loaded onto a factor including PA (negative loading), hopelessness and depression. Similar results were found by MacLeod et al. (1997).

To summarize, mood-disturbed individuals differ from those who are not mood-disturbed in how likely they judge future positive and negative events are to happen to them, although the accuracy of such judgements is hard to assess. Negative affect (which is related to both anxiety and depression) seems to be more strongly correlated with the perceived likelihood of negative events, whereas positive affect (low levels of which relate to depression only) is related to expectancy of positive events.

Other Methods of Assessing Prospective Cognitions

As well as global self-report scales and subjective probability judgements for hypothetical positive and negative events, a number of other methods have been used to assess prospective cognitions. There has been a fairly long-standing interest in the prospective cognitions of suicidal individuals. As indicated earlier, prospective cognitions in suicidal individuals have tended to become synonymous with self-reported global levels of hopelessness, as measured by the BHS. However, early studies using methods less reliant on self-report found evidence that suicidal individuals were less orientated to the future generally, in that they provided less elaborate descriptions of future time periods (Yufit et al., 1970), had a reduced temporal extension into the future (Melges & Weisz, 1971) and used fewer future-tense verbs (Greaves, 1971).

More recently, I and my colleagues have examined prospective cognitions in suicidal individuals using an adapted verbal fluency paradigm (MacLeod, Rose & Williams, 1993; MacLeod et al., 1997). In this procedure, subjects are presented with time periods in the future, for example, the next week or the next year, and are asked to think of as many things that they are going to be doing or that are going to happen to them in each time period. They are given a set time, usually one minute, to generate as many events as possible and the total number of items generated is recorded. The time periods are presented twice—once to elicit positive items (things the person is looking forward to) and once to elicit negative items (things the person is worried about or not looking forward to). Parasuicide patients generate fewer positive items than matched controls do, but the groups do not differ on the number of negative items they are able to generate. The effect is found in parasuicides who are not depressed as well as those who are (MacLeod et al., 1997). This finding suggests that suicidality is specifically linked to a lack of positive cognitions about the future, rather than an increased presence of negative thoughts. As MacLeod, Rose & Williams (1993) point out, this lack of positive anticipation could have a cognitive explanation (inaccessibility of representations of positive future outcomes), an affective explanation (an inability to derive pleasure from what to other people would be pleasurable experiences) or a social explanation (living in circumstances where there is reduced accessibility to pleasurable experiences). It is likely that a complex interaction of factors is involved.

MacLeod & Byrne (1996) have applied the same fluency paradigm to a sample of students who were either only anxious, anxious and depressed, or neither anxious or depressed. In contrast to the parasuicide subjects of the previous studies, the anxious group showed an increased number of negative anticipated experiences and did not differ from controls on number of anticipated positive experiences. The subjects who were anxious and depressed showed both increased anticipation of negative experiences and decreased anticipation of positive experiences, relative to controls. MacLeod et al. (1997) found that anxious patients showed the same increase in negative anticipation in the absence of reduced positive anticipation, and their sample of depressed patients showed reduced positive anticipation in the absence of any increased negative anticipation. The results from this fluency paradigm suggest that anxiety is associated with an increase in negative anticipation, whereas the prospective cognitions of depression and suicidality represent primarily a lack of positive anticipation.

One method for looking at prospective cognitions derived from autobiographical memory research has been to present subjects with cues referring to a future outcome and to assess the speed with which they are able to generate a specific example in the future relating to that cue. For example, MacLeod & Cropley (1995) presented subjects with future positive and negative hypothetical outcomes. As well as being asked to say how likely those outcomes were, subjects were also asked to picture a specific situation in the future relating to each cue. Latency to bring to mind a specific example was recorded. Like the subjective probability ratings, mildly depressed students took longer to generate positive examples and were quicker to generate negative examples, relative to controls. Williams et al. (1996) also used a specific cueing procedure to assess prospective cognitions. Parasuicide subjects were found to have more difficulty in generating specific future outcomes relating to a cue, as indicated by a greater tendency to produce overly general responses, typically through giving examples covering a broad time period in the future, rather than referring to a specific occasion. This finding mirrors the findings on retrieval of specific past memories in parasuicides, which has been documented by Williams (1996), and the relationship between over-general memory and over-general prospective cognitions will be returned to.

Thus, on a range of different types of measures, including global self-report ratings, subjective probability judgements, self-generated fluency, reaction time and over-general responses to cues, mood-disturbed subjects have been found to differ from their non-mood-disturbed counterparts. In addition, the evidence points to positive and negative expectancies being independent and relating differentially to anxiety and depression. The next section will turn to addressing some of the processes which may underlie these differences.

PROCESSES AND MECHANISMS

Given the differences in the prospective cognitions of mood-disturbed individuals, the obvious question is what lies behind these differences. Probably the most influential account of how people anticipate future outcomes stems from the work of Tversky & Kahneman on judgement heuristics. In their early work, Tversky & Kahneman (1973) argued that, when asked to assess the likelihood of a particular future outcome, people often use the availability heuristic. The availability heuristic describes the process whereby people estimate the likelihood of a particular event happening in the future by how easily they are able to bring relevant instances to mind. Tversky & Kahneman (1973) suggested two classes of mental operations that bring things to mind—retrieval of past instances, where similar events are recalled from long-term memory, and construction of scenarios. The more easily past examples are recalled, or the easier it is to construct a scenario leading to the outcome happening, the more likely the event is judged to be. The second mechanism—scenario construction—will be used when the event in question is uncommon or even unique, in which case there will not be a data base of past experiences upon which to base the judgement.

This second aspect of the availability heuristic was renamed the "simulation heuristic", in recognition that as a mechanism it was sufficiently distinct from recall of past instances to warrant separate consideration (Kahneman & Tversky, 1982). The simulation heuristic describes the process of constructing a mental model of reality in which the hypothetical event takes place. An important component of the mental model being constructed is a set of causal explanations leading to the event's occurrence. The ease with which causal theories producing the outcome can be generated determines the judged likelihood of the outcome. The emphasis on causal explanations in predictive judgements is consistent with approaches to other areas of cognition, such as causal attribution, where it has been argued that information about causal mechanisms, rather than simply information about co-variation, is used to make attributional judgements (e.g. Ahn et al., 1995).

Memory Recall and Future Prediction

Is their any evidence that people use their memories of what has happened in the past in order to predict the future? Osberg & Shrauger (1986) asked college students to make subjective probability estimates on a range of future possible outcomes. Subjects were subsequently interviewed about the basis on which they had made their judgements. The most common basis for their judgement given by subjects made reference to the frequency with which the event had happened to them in the past. It should be noted that this does not necessarily imply that subjects were bringing to mind specific past instances, as opposed to utilizing some pre-computed index of frequency.

C. MacLeod & Campbell (1992) presented subjects with short descriptions of common pleasant (a welcome invitation) and unpleasant (a painful injury) events. Subjects were asked to retrieve a specific memory that fitted each event description and rate the probability of experiencing the event description within the next 6 months. There was a significant correlation between speed of retrieval of an example and how likely the event was judged to happen in the next 6 months. However, as in the Osberg & Shrauger (1986) study, C. MacLeod & Campbell did not check whether memories were actually being recalled, raising the possibility that what was being used as the basis for the judgement was a general impression memory (whether that particular event had happened often in the past), rather than recall of specific examples. This possibility seems even more likely, given the average recall latency of 2.5 seconds, which is extremely fast for recalling a specific autobiographical memory.

Several studies have shown parallel effects in remembering the past and anticipating the future. Williams et al. (1996) asked suicidal patients and controls to generate specific past events and possible future events in response to cues. Previous studies have found that suicidal subjects have greater difficulty in recalling specific autobiographical memories, instead tending to give overly general memories that do not refer to a specific event (Williams, 1996). Williams et al. (1996) found that the suicidal subjects' recall of past events and generation of future events were both more general than those of controls, and there was a significant correlation across subjects in how general past and future responses were. Follow-up experiments supported a direct link between retrieval and anticipation by showing that manipulations that increased over-general retrieval resulted in more over-general future anticipation. Williams et al. (1996) suggest that the intermediate descriptions used to search autobiographical memory are also used to generate images of possible future events.

MacLeod et al. (1997) also found parallels between memory recall and future anticipation. Anxious, depressed and control subjects were given the adapted verbal fluency paradigm described earlier, both in its original future anticipation version and also in a memory version. The memory version asked subjects to recall positive and negative experiences from the past week, the past year, and the past 5–10 years. The measure was again the total number of items subjects generated in the given time. The results for memory recall and future anticipation were almost identical. Anxious subjects anticipated and remembered more negative experiences than controls, whereas depressed subjects anticipated and remembered fewer positive experiences than controls.

In conclusion, there is some empirical evidence that supports the memory-based aspect of the availability heuristic. Subjects report using recall of past examples to make future predictions, there is some, albeit somewhat ambiguous, evidence of a correlation between speed of memory retrieval and future prediction, and over-general retrieval of the past is linked to over-general imagining of the future. Furthermore, the particular patterns of future anticipation shown by anxious and depressed patients is mirrored by how they remember the past. However, it is not clear that recall of specific examples are used directly as the basis for future prediction. It is possible, as Williams et al. (1996) suggest, that the same intermediate processes are used both to retrieve past instances and to generate possible future instances.

Simulation and Future Prediction

In contrast to studies suggesting a memory basis for future judgements, Buehler, Griffin & Ross (1994) found quite different results in trying to account for the "planning fallacy" (Kahneman & Tversky, 1979). The planning fallacy describes the phenomenon of believing that one's own project will proceed as planned and be finished on time, even whilst aware that the vast majority of similar plans have not been completed on time. In a series of studies, students were asked to predict completion times for various tasks, which were then compared with actual completion times. Consistent with the planning fallacy, subjects typically underestimated their completion times. Buehler, Griffin & Ross (1994) sampled subjects' thoughts when making predictions and found that their subjects focused on plan-based scenarios which described future actions and circumstances, rather than on past experiences. When past experiences of prediction failures were drawn to their attention, the subjects attributed those occasions to external, transient and specific factors, thus minimizing their relevance to the future. Thus, in these studies subjects were not only not using past experience to form future predictions but were, in fact, actively discounting the relevance of past experiences for predicting the future.

A number of other studies provide support for the idea that future expectancies are based on an active process of constructing causal explanations or plans which would lead to the event rather than simply retrieval of relevant past experiences. MacLeod (1994) reported the results of a study that found a significant correlation between perceived likelihood of negative events and the extent to which subjects could provide reasons why the events would happen, as opposed to reasons why the events would not happen. Thus, subjects who were able to think of many reasons why an event would happen, and few reasons why it would not, judged that event to be likely. Where anxious and depressed subjects differ in their subjective probability estimates for positive and negative events, they have also been found to show similar differences in the accessibility of reasons to explain the occurrence or non-occurrence of those events (MacLeod, Williams & Bekerian, 1991; MacLeod et al., 1997), providing further support for the link between causal explanations and perceived likelihood.

Strong support for the role of explanations in future judgements comes from studies which have observed effects on judgements through manipulating the accessibility of causal explanations. For example, Levi & Pryor (1987) asked subjects to provide explanations for why a particular candidate would win a forthcoming presidential debate. Estimates were more optimistic for the candidate who had been the focus of the explanation task. Interestingly, simply imagining a particular candidate winning did not affect the outcome, suggesting that constructing causal explanations rather than simply bringing to mind a mental picture of the outcome is important.

Hoch (1985) found that the over-optimistic judgements of final year business students about future job prospects (e.g. receiving three job offers on graduating, which could be compared with the lower base rates from previous years) were normalized by asking subjects to generate reasons why the positive outcomes would not happen. The ability to manipulate judgements by asking subjects to generate counter-explanations suggests the possibility of altering the relatively pessimistic judgements of mood-disturbed subjects. MacLeod and colleagues found that the relatively increased pessimism of anxious worriers (MacLeod, Williams & Bekerian, 1991) and parasuicide subjects (MacLeod & Tarbuck, 1994) for hypothetical future negative events could be reduced by asking those individuals to generate reasons why the negative events would not happen to them.

Other Mechanisms of Future Prediction

Although both memory recall and, in particular, simulation, may be used when thinking about what is going to happen in the future, other processes may also be important. One obvious source of information when someone is thinking about the likelihood of various outcomes in the future is the retrieval of a pre-formed judgement. Sherman et al. (1983) presented subjects with information about two football teams and asked them to explain a hypothetical victory by one of the teams in a forthcoming game. They were then asked to predict which team would win. In general, and consistent with other research findings (see Koehler, 1991), explaining the success of a particular team resulted in that team being judged to be more likely to win. However, this effect was not observed if subjects were encouraged to form their own opinion of which team would win prior to the explanation task. In this case, the explanation task had no effect on predictions. Sherman et al. (1983) conclude that in this case, subjects simply recalled their previous prediction when asked to make a prediction.

Andersen, Spielman & Bargh (1992) have put forward a similar view that also incorporates differences between depressed and non-depressed individuals. These authors have suggested that through negative rumination about the future, depressed individuals have developed a "future event schema". This means that judgements about the future are made relatively automatically, with little cognitive effort, rather than going through the process of memory recall or simulation. Evidence for this view comes from a study (Andersen, Spielman & Bargh, 1992) showing that reaction time of depressed subjects to make a future likelihood judgement was unaffected by performing a secondary distracting task, whereas the reaction time of non-depressed subjects was slowed.

A second alternative mechanism is that, instead of using specific cognitive information, people may use their mood state as a direct basis for the judgement. Schwarz & Clore (1983) suggest that under some circumstances people will make judgements directly on the basis of how they feel at the time. In this process, reasoning and judgement flow from affect rather than affect from reasoning. However, little research has actually looked at the direct effects of mood state on prospective cognitions. Such research would need to rule out the possibility that mood was affecting future judgements through altering the accessibility of other cognitions, for example, autobiographical memories. Perhaps mood is most likely to be used when the judgement to be made is very general, such as the sort of well-being judgements used by Schwarz & Clore (1983) and where there is little in the way of specific information that is relevant to the judgement.

CONCLUSIONS AND FUTURE RESEARCH

Prospective cognitions play an important role in theories of depression and anxiety, a role supported by the empirical evidence comparing the prospective cognitions of mood-disturbed and non-mood-disturbed subjects, using a variety of methods. Furthermore, there is evidence that the prospective cognitions of anxious and depressed individuals vary in an important way: anxiety is associated with increased negative anticipation, whereas depression appears to be predominantly a reduction in positive anticipation. Various mechanisms by which prospective cognitions are formed were suggested, mainly based on recall of relevant memories (the availability heuristic) or the simulation of future possibilities (the simulation heuristic). There is evidence to support the use of both the availability heuristic and the simulation heuristic.

It remains for future research to elucidate the conditions under which one or the other mechanism is used. An obvious possibility is that memories are used to think about the future when they are perceived as relevant, otherwise the simulation heuristic is employed. However, the work of Buehler, Griffin & Rose (1994) highlights the fact that even fairly similar past events can be discounted by the individual as being relevant to the future. Consequently, research could examine the attribution processes by which seemingly relevant past experiences are deemed not relevant to the future, and whether this "normal bias" is affected by mood disturbance. Future research also needs to devise more sophisticated ways of operationalizing and measuring mental simulation. Asking subjects to generate reasons for or against an event happening, or to volunteer their plans, almost certainly accesses the process of simulation but does so in a rather clumsy way. It should be possible to develop more elegant and sophisticated ways of measuring mental simulation.

A second major line of research could develop in relating prospective cognitions to actual experience. Oatley & Perring (1991) looked at the interaction of expectancies and actual experiences in recovery from depression. They interviewed a sample of depressed and/or anxious individuals about their plans for the next 6 months, and 6 months later assessed both the extent of their recovery and the degree to which initial plans had worked out. Having plans that did not work out predicted low recovery. Thus, the impact of life experiences and events needs to be understood in the context of the individual's prior expectancies. A study by Champion, Power & Rutter (in preparation) illustrated the potential beneficial effects of planning and anticipation. These authors were interested in factors affecting the relationship between having behavioural and emotional problems in childhood and experiencing adversity in adulthood. Although in their sample this relationship was generally found, the relationship was modified by the individual's capacity to form plans, particularly in the area of relationships. Individuals who, despite having troubled childhoods, were able to anticipate and plan their relationships developed better relationships in adulthood, which in turn protected them from adversity. Such planning, the content of which will also reflect the individual's developmental stage (Nurmi, 1991), may be a crucial link between the individual–cognitive and social–environmental factors that influence well-being. Life events and experiences, therefore, should be seen against a background of what was anticipated and planned, and the role of anticipation and planning needs to be understood in the context of what subsequently happens. In that way the the usefulness of teleological explanations of human behaviour will be most clearly seen.

REFERENCES

Abramson, L. Y., Alloy, L. B. & Metalsky, G. I. (1989). Hopelessness depression: a theory-based subtype of depression. *Psychological Review*, **96**, 358–372.

Ahn, W., Kalish, C. W., Medin, D. L. & Gelman, S. A. (1995). The role of covariation versus mechanism information in causal attribution. *Cognition*, **54**, 299–352.

Anderson, S. M., Spielman, L. A. & Bargh, J. A. (1992). Future-event schemas and certainty about the future: automaticity in depressives' future-event predictions. *Journal of Personality and Social Psychology*, **63**, 711–723.

Austin, J. T. & Vancouver, J. B. (1996). Goal constructs in psychology: structure, process, and content. *Psychological Bulletin*, **120**, 338–375.

Barlow, D. H. (1988). *Anxiety and Its Disorders*. New York: Guilford.

Beck, A. T., Rush, A. J., Shaw, B. F. & Emery, G. (1979). *Cognitive Therapy for Depression*. New York: Guilford.

Beck, A. T., Weissman, A., Lester, D. & Trexler, L. (1974). The measurement of pessimism: the hopelessness scale. *Journal of Consulting and Clinical Psychology*, **42**, 861–865.

Brown, G. & Harris, T. O. (1978). *Social Origins of Depression*. London: Tavistock.

Buehler, R., Griffin, D. & Ross, M. (1994). Exploring the planning fallacy: why people underestimate their task completion times. *Journal of Personality and Social Psychology*, **67**, 366–381.

Butler, G. & Mathews, A. (1983). Cognitive processes in anxiety. *Advances in Behaviour Research and Therapy*, **5**, 51–62.

Butler, G. & Mathews, A. (1987). Anticipatory anxiety and risk perception. *Cognitive Therapy and Research*, **11**, 551–565.

Carver, C. S. & Scheier, M. F. (1990). Origins and functions of positive and negative affect: a control process view. *Psychological Review*, **97**, 19–35.

Champion, L. A., Power, M. J. & Rutter, M. (in preparation).

Clark, L. A., Watson, D. & Mineka, S. (1994). Temperament, personality, and the mood and anxiety disorders. *Journal of Abnormal Psychology*, **103**, 103–116.

Dunning, D. & Story, A. L. (1991). Depression, realism, and the overconfidence effect:

are the sadder wiser when predicting future actions and events? *Journal of Personality and Social Psychology*, **61**, 521–532.

Emmons, R. A. (1992). Abstract versus concrete goals: personal striving level, physical illness, and psychological well-being. *Journal of Personality and Social Psychology*, **62**, 292–300.

Gray, J. A. (1982). *The Neuropsychology of Anxiety: An Enquiry into the Functions of the Septo-hippocampal System*. Oxford: Oxford University Press.

Greaves, G. (1971). Temporal orientation in suicidal patients. *Perceptual and Motor Skills*, **33**, 1020.

Hoch, S. J. (1985). Counterfactual reasoning and accuracy in predicting personal events. *Journal of Experimental Psychology, Learning, Memory, and Cognition*, **11**, 719–731.

Kahneman, D. & Tversky, A. (1982). The simulation heuristic. In D. Kahneman, P. Slovic & A. Tversky (eds), *Judgement under Uncertainty: Heuristics and Biases*. Cambridge: Cambridge University Press, pp. 201–208.

Kahneman, D. & Tversky, A. (1979). Intuitive prediction: biases and corrective procedures. *TIMS Studies in Management Science*, **12**, 313–327.

Klinger, E. (1993). Loss of interest. In C. Costello (ed.), *Symptoms of Depression*. New York: Wiley.

Koehler, D. J. (1991). Explanation, imagination, and confidence in judgement. *Psychological Bulletin*, **110**, 499–519.

Levi, A. S. & Pryor, J. B. (1987). Use of the availability heuristic in probability estimates of future events: the effects of imagining outcomes vs. imagining reasons. *Organizational Behaviour and Human Decision Processes*, **40**, 219–234.

MacLeod, A. K. (1994). Worry and explanation-based pessimism. In G. Davey & F. Tallis (eds), *Worrying: Perspectives on Theory, Assessment, and Treatment*. Chichester: Wiley, pp. 115–134.

MacLeod, A. K. & Byrne, A. (1996). Anxiety, depression and the anticipation of future positive and negative experiences. *Journal of Abnormal Psychology*, **105**, 286–289.

MacLeod, A. K., Byrne, A. & Valentine, J. D. (1996). Affect, emotional disorder and future-directed thinking. *Cognition and Emotion*, **10**, 69–86.

MacLeod, A. K. & Cropley, M. L. (1995). Depressive future-thinking: the role of valence and specificity. *Cognitive Therapy and Research*, **19**, 35–50.

MacLeod, A. K., Pankhania, B., Lee, M. & Mitchell, D. (1997). Depression, hopelessness and future-directed thinking in parasuicide. *Psychological Medicine*, **27**, 973–977.

MacLeod, A. K., Rose, G. S. & Williams, J. M. G. (1993). Components of hopelessness about the future in parasuicide. *Cognitive Therapy and Research*, **17**, 441–455.

MacLeod, A. K. & Tarbuck, A. (1994). Explaining why negative events will happen to oneself: parasuicides are pessimistic because they can't see any reason not to be. *British Journal of Clinical Psychology*, **33**, 317–326.

MacLeod, A. K., Tata, P., Kentish, J., Carroll, F. & Hunter, E. (1997). Anxiety, depression, and explanation-based pessimism for future positive and negative events. *Clinical Psychology and Psychotherapy*, **4**, 15–24.

MacLeod, A. K., Tata, P., Kentish, J. & Jacobsen, H. (1997). Retrospective and prospective cognitions in anxiety and depression. *Cognition and Emotion*, **11**, 467–479.

MacLeod, A. K., Williams, J. M. G. & Bekerian, D. A. (1991). Worry is reasonable: the role of explanations in pessimism about future personal events. *Journal of Abnormal Psychology*, **100**, 478–486.

MacLeod, C. & Campbell, L. (1992). Memory accessibility and probability judgements: an experimental evaluation of the availability heuristic. *Journal of Personality and Social Psychology*, **63**, 890–902.

Mathews, A. (1990). Why worry? The cognitive function of anxiety. *Behaviour Research and Therapy*, **28**, 455–468.

Melges, F. T. & Bowlby, J. (1969). Types of hopelessness in psychopathological process. *Archives of General Psychiatry*, **20**, 690–699.

Melges, F. T. & Weisz, A. E. (1971).   The personal future and suicidal ideation. *The Journal of Nervous and Mental Disease*, **153**, 244–250.

Meyer, T. J., Miller, M. L., Metzger, R. L. & Borkovec, T. D. (1990).   Development and validation of the Penn State Worry Questionnaire. *Behaviour Research and Therapy*, **28**, 487–495.

Miller, G. A., Galanter, E. H. & Pribram, K. (1960).   *Plans and the Structure of Behaviour*. New York: Holt, Rinehart, and Winston.

Molina, S. & Borkovec, T. D. (1994).   The Penn State Worry Questionnaire: psychometric properties and associated characteristics. In G. Davey & F. Tallis (eds), *Worrying: Perspectives on Theory, Assessment, and Treatment*. Chichester: Wiley, pp. 265–283.

Nurmi, J. (1992).   How do adolescents see their future? A review of the development of future orientation and planning. *Developmental Review*, **11**, 1–59.

Oatley, K. & Perring, C. (1991).   A longitudinal study of psychological and social factors affecting recovery from psychiatric breakdowns. *British Journal of Psychiatry*, **158**, 28–32.

Osberg, T. M. & Shrauger, J. S. (1986).   Self-prediction: exploring the parameters of accuracy. *Journal of Personality and Social Psychology*, **51**, 1044–1057.

Pietromonaco, P. & Markus, H. (1985).   The nature of negative thoughts in depression. *Journal of Personality and Social Psychology*, **48**, 799–807.

Pyszczynski, T., Holt, K. & Greenberg, J. (1987).   Depression, self-focused attention, and expectancies for positive and negative future life-events for self and others. *Journal of Personality and Social Psychology*, **46**, 14–25.

Scheier, M. F. & Carver, C. S. (1985).   Optimism, coping, and health: assessment and implications of generalized outcome expectancies. *Health Psychology*, **4**, 219–247.

Schwarz, N. & Clore, G. L. (1983).   Mood, misattribution, and judgements of well-being: informative and directive functions of affective states. *Journal of Personality and Social Psychology*, **45**, 513–523.

Sherman, S. J., Zehner, K. S., Johnson, J. & Hirt, E. R. (1983).   Social explanation: the role of timing, set and recall on subjective likelihood estimates. *Journal of Personality and Social Psychology*, **44**, 1127–1143.

Snyder, C. R., Harris, C., Anderson, J. R., Holleran, S. A., Irving, L. M., Sigmon, S. T., Yoshinobu, L., Gibb, J. Langelle, C. & Harney, P. (1991).   The will and the ways: development and validation of an individual-difference measure of hope. *Journal of Personality and Social Psychology*, **60**, 570–585.

Strathman, A., Gleicher, F., Boninger, D. S. & Edwards, C. S. (1994).   The consideration of future consequences: weighing immediate and distant outcomes of behaviour. *Journal of Personality and Social Psychology*, **66**, 742–752.

Tversky, A. & Kahneman, D. (1973).   Availability: a heuristic for judging frequency and probability. *Cognitive Psychology*, **5**, 207–232.

Valentine, E. R. (1992).   *Conceptual Issues in Psychology* 2nd edn. London: Routledge.

Watson, D., Clark, L. A. & Tellegen, A. (1988).   Development and validation of brief measures of positive and negative affect: the PANAS scales. *Journal of Personality and Social Psychology*, **54**, 1063–1070.

Williams, J. M. G. (1996).   Depression and the specificity of autobiographical memory. In D. Rubin (ed.), *Constructing Our Past: An Overview of Autobiographical Memory*. Cambridge: Cambridge University Press.

Williams, J. M. G., Ellis, N. C., Tyers, C., Healy, C., Rose, G. S. & MacLeod, A. K. (1996).   The specificity of autobiographical memory and imageability of the future. *Memory and Cognition*, **24**, 116–125.

Yufit, R. I., Benzies, B., Font, M. E. & Fawcett, J. A. (1970).   Suicide potential and time perspective. *Archives of General Psychiatry*, **23**, 158–163.

Chapter 15

Unintended Thoughts and Images

Frank Tallis
Charter Nightingale Hospital, London, UK

THE STREAM OF CONSCIOUSNESS

> ... the mysterious stream of consciousness. Immortal phrase of the immortal James!
> Oh stream of hell... (D. H. Lawrence, *Psychoanalysis and the Unconscious*,
> 1921).

Until the mid-1970s, information processing models of mental functioning shared a number of assumptions regarding the nature of thinking. Perhaps the most cherished of these was that the individual could exercise intentional control over the flow of thought and, subsequently, decision making (see review by Lachman, Lachman & Butterfield, 1979); however, as the decade progressed, a number of doubts were raised as to the accuracy of this view (Posner & Snyder, 1975; Langer, 1978). Although the intentional control of thought was a salient property of the processing system, it was becoming increasingly apparent that this same control was far from absolute. Although the 1970s marked something of a sea change in the understanding of the role of intentionality in mental life (Bargh & Uleman, 1989), the foundations of a more accurate framework were laid many years earlier.

In his *Principles of Psychology* (1890), James employed the term "stream of consciousness" to describe the fluid contents of awareness—the continuous flow of thoughts and images that constitutes mental life. Although it is possible to divert the course of thinking in the service of certain goals, for example as in

Handbook of Cognition and Emotion. Edited by T. Dalgleish and M. Power.
© 1999 John Wiley & Sons Ltd.

problem solving, most mental events are unintended and spontaneous. It might be argued that this undisciplined nature of mental life has been captured more successfully in works of art than in the laboratory. In Joyce's epic novel *Ulysses* (1922), the stream of consciousness is transferred to the page without compromise: "Bronze by gold heard the hoofirons, steelyrining Imperthnthn thnthnthn". Why should the contents of awareness be so chaotic? Why is it that even the most engaging lines of thought are often interrupted by trivial ideas or plain nonsense?

Given that most phenomena are best explained within an evolutionary framework, it must be assumed that the stream of consciousness, however turbulent or idiosyncratic, bestows some advantage on human beings (Humphrey, 1992). This advantage is most probably related to creative thinking and the generation of novel coping strategies.

It is interesting to note that there are numerous anecdotal accounts of revolutionary ideas occurring in the form of unintended thoughts or images. Individuals are "inspired" or experience a sudden moment of insight (the so-called "eureka" or "aha" phenomena). Perhaps the most compelling examples of creative thinking occur when intentional control of the cognitive system is abandoned completely. For example, the secrets of the molecular structure of organic material and the quantum model of atomic structure came to Friederich Kekule and Neils Bohr, respectively, in dreams (Carey, 1995: Stevens, 1996). Unintended mental events may be as important to human intellectual development as the random mutations of genes are to the process of evolution (Dawkins, 1976); however, the price paid for mental flexibility is the intrusion into awareness of unwanted thoughts and images—the writer D. H. Lawrence's "stream of hell".

UNINTENDED THOUGHT AND EMOTION

The relationship between unintended thought and emotion is clearly a close one. Indeed, all emotional states, to a greater or lesser extent, are attended by spontaneous "thinking" that arises irrespective of intention. Although such thinking occurs in both positive and negative mood states (Edwards & Dickerson, 1987), it is the relationship between negative mood and intrusive cognition that has received the greatest academic interest. Clearly, this bias is accounted for by the pressing need to understand those cognitive factors associated with clinical problems. Such understanding is a necessary first step if effective methods of remediation are to be developed.

Although the close relationship between thinking and feeling is now universally accepted, the controversy surrounding the issue of primacy has a long and distinguished history dating back to Aristotle. More recently, the primacy debate achieved prominence after the publication of key papers by Lazarus (1984) and Zajonc (1984), with the former favouring the primacy of cognition and the latter favouring the primacy of emotion. With the rise and expansion of "rational" schools of psychotherapy (Kelly, 1955; Ellis, 1956; Meichenbaum, 1977; Beck et al., 1979; Beck et al., 1990), in the clinic at least, the argument seems to have temporarily halted in favour of the primacy of cognition. Cognitive accounts of emotional disorders suggest that thoughts (Beck et al., 1979), appraisals (Lazarus, 1966), judgements (Tversky & Kahneman, 1973; Macleod, 1994), and beliefs (Beck et al., 1979; Guidano & Liotti, 1983), are the primary, if not necessarily the ultimate, cause of affective disturbance. This particular position is now very much linked with clinical practice and the influential work of Beck and his associates. However, it should also be noted that more complex accounts of the relationship between thinking and feeling promise renewed debate in the future, for example, the "somatic marker hypothesis" (Damasio, 1994) and Inter-acting Cognitive Subsystems theory (Teasdale & Barnard, 1993). As Lazarus (this volume) points out, emotion may now be considered a superordinate concept. Other constructs, such as cognition and motivation, can be subsumed under the "emotion" heading.

Given new developments in the field of cognition and emotion, it is no longer possible to posit a "direct" correspondence between thoughts and feelings. Never-theless, the presence of unintended thought in clinical problems is associated with considerable emotional distress. While accepting the apparent ubiquity of unintended thoughts, there are, however, a number of disorders in which invol-untary "thinking" is considered of particular relevance. These are post-traumatic stress disorder (PTSD), obsessive-compulsive disorder (OCD) and generalized anxiety disorder (GAD).

CLINICAL PROBLEMS ASSOCIATED WITH UNINTENDED THOUGHTS

Perhaps the most characteristic feature of PTSD is the persistent "re-experiencing" of a traumatic event (American Psychiatric Association, 1994). This re-experiencing may take the form of intrusive and distressing recollections of the traumatic event, "flashbacks" and recurrent dreams that are thematically related to the trauma.

The cardinal feature of GAD is worry. Although worry itself is not defined in current diagnostic systems, the fact that "The person finds it difficult to control the worry" is given considerable emphasis (American Psychiatric Association, 1994).

In the context of OCD, obsessions are defined as, "recurrent and persistent thoughts, impulses, or images that are experienced, at some time during the disturbance, as intrusive and inappropriate and that cause marked distress" (American Psychiatric Association, 1994). Although it is understood that obses-sions are not simply worries (Turner, Beidel & Stanley, 1992), it should be noted that there is considerable overlap between extreme forms of worrying in GAD and sub-classes of OCD, most notably, in those patients who suffer primarily from ruminations and morbid preoccupations (Rachman, 1973).

The three clinical conditions described above are each associated with unin-tended thoughts and/or images. Moreover, these cognitive events share a number of common features. They are unwanted, persistent, difficult to control and cause distress. Individuals suffering from PTSD, GAD and OCD recognize that unintended thoughts and images are generated internally, and insight is usually maintained. There is, however, some evidence to suggest that insight can be compromised in individuals suffering from OCD, albeit temporarily (Kozak & Foa, 1994; Tallis, 1995).

Broadly speaking, unintended thoughts and images occur in both static and flexible forms. Images can be experienced as both "snapshots" and "sequences", while thoughts can be experienced as either "sentences" or "narratives". More often than not, both static and flexible forms of these mental events occur together.

CAUSAL ANTECEDENTS

The presence of a clinical problem characterized by unintended thoughts and images seems to be very closely associated with prior stress. This is most obviously so in the case of PTSD; however, it is becoming increasingly clear that the same is also true with respect to GAD and OCD. Borkovec (1994) and colleagues found that individuals meeting criteria for GAD had experienced significantly more traumas (as defined by PTSD criteria), compared to normal controls. Moreover, Khanna et al. (1988) found that subjects with OCD experienced an excess of life events in the 6 months prior to the onset of the illness; particularly undesirable, uncontrolled events in the areas of health and bereavement. It might be alleged, of course, that all psychological problems, to a greater or lesser extent, are precipitated by stress. Future research will no doubt examine specific vulnerability factors in the individual, as well as salient features of the stressful event. Blanchard et al. (1996), for example, found that the belief that death was likely during road traffic accidents was the best predictor of subsequent development of PTSD. Other studies, for example Buttolph & Holland (1990), have found that pregnancy and childbirth are common precipitants of OCD in women.

Although it is relatively uncontentious to suggest that traumatic histories provide fertile ground for the development of disorders characterized by unintended thoughts and images, proximal triggers are less easy to specify. It is certainly the case that some situations will reliably precipitate episodes of uncontrollable thinking in PTSD, GAD and OCD. This is especially so when such situations evoke recollections of trauma or are in some way related to current preoccupations. For example, an individual traumatized by a work accident will be likely to suffer intrusive recollections on returning to the workplace, in the same way that an individual with contamination fears will become preoccupied with infection if forced to stand near a perceived contaminant.

Notwithstanding the above, episodes of uncontrollable thinking are also commonly reported under conditions where external cues are minimal or totally absent. Fifty-seven per cent of non-clinical subjects suggest that worry begins "in bed", with 59% of worrying occurring between the late hours of the evening and the early hours of the morning (Tallis, Davey & Capuzzo, 1994). The well-attested relationship between worrying and insomnia (Borkovec, 1979) suggests that when competing stimuli are removed, unwanted thoughts capture the processing system with relative ease. Borkovec and colleagues have postulated the existence of a permanently primed "worry area" in declarative memory to explain such phenomena (Borkovec, Metzger & Pruzinsky, 1986).

The concept of "primed areas" and chronic accessibility (cf. Higgins, 1989) may correspond with some underlying neuroanatomical substrate. A likely candidate is the self-sustaining fronto-striatal circuits favoured by biological theorists (cf. Baxter et al., 1992; Insel & Winslow, 1990). These are thought to be particularly relevant with respect to obsessional and ruminative phenomena. Indeed, the term "hyperfrontality" has been employed to describe a pattern of activation in neural pathways associated with increased worry, rumination and intense affect (Insel & Winslow, 1990).

UNINTENDED THOUGHTS AND ADAPTIVITY

It has already been suggested that one of the costs of a flexible cognitive system is the occasional admission into awareness of unintended thoughts; however, the fact that unintended thoughts are strongly associated with traumatic histories suggests that they may also have some functional significance. PTSD, GAD and OCD are all classified as anxiety disorders and it is therefore very likely that intrusive recollections, worries and obsessions are all cognitive features of a more general response to threat. As such, these mental events might be usefully construed as "alarms" (cf. Barlow, 1988). If unintended thoughts and images are construed as a cognitive feature of a primitive alarm system, this might go some way towards explaining why they are so difficult to control. An alarm that could be silenced without much effort would be of doubtful value if considered within a Darwinian framework.

Tallis & Eysenck (1994) and Eysenck (1992) have suggested that worry is a feature of the processing system, in which threat-related information is pre-sented—and then subsequently represented—into awareness. They suggest that non-pathological worry may be adaptive, serving three principle functions: alarm, prompt and preparation. If worry is triggered by a perceived threat and the individual does not respond, threat-related thoughts and images will be re-presented into awareness. These serve to remind the individual that a threat still exists and requires attention. Finally, repeated presentations may reduce the aversiveness of threat-related material due to a process of habituation. The notion that worrying can be adaptive was first suggested by Janis (1958), who introduced the concept of the "work of worrying". His initial studies suggested that moderate levels of worry were associated with more favourable post-operative recovery. More recently, support for the prompt and preparatory function of worry was gathered by Davey et al. (in press). A factor analysis of items reflecting the consequences of worry produced two factors which suggested that worry firstly motivates, and secondly encourages, problem solving.

A "cognitive alarm" account of unintended thoughts and images is particularly relevant with respect to OCD, in which thought content tends to reflect blasphemous, aggressive and sexual themes (Goodman et al., 1989a; Goodman et al., 1989b). Attempting to understand this specificity of content, Tallis (1995), has suggested that such thoughts might arise in certain high-risk situations in order to promote caution and deter inappropriate behaviour. The occurrence of intrusive thoughts in situations requiring high levels of control was noted by the seventeenth century preacher John Bunyan, who wrote: "When I have been preaching, I have been violently assaulted with thoughts of blasphemy, and strongly tempted to speak them with my mouth before the congregation" (cited by Toates, 1990, p. 76).

It should be noted that adaptivity has also been discussed with respect to the occurrence of unintended thoughts and images after traumatic stress. Although such thoughts and images are involuntary, several theorists have suggested that they play a crucial role in the "working through" of negative life events (Janis, 1972; Parkes, 1972; Silver, Boon & Stones, 1983; Horowitz, 1976, 1985). Summarizing this position, Wegner (1989) suggests that

> The reason we think about a trauma over and over may be that this thinking is good for us. The trauma may start in motion a natural process of self-healing or self-correction, in which the individual repeatedly reviews the trauma as a way of coming to terms with it (p. 164).

That certain types of unintended thought reflect the operation of largely adaptive "sub-routines" is appealing; however, in PTSD, GAD and OCD such "sub-routines" become dysregulated and are clearly non-adaptive. There are a number of cognitive and affective factors that may be relevant in accounting for this dysregulation and the subsequent compromise of mental control.

PERSISTENCE OF UNINTENDED THOUGHTS IN CLINICAL PROBLEMS

The process by which thoughts are generated and enter awareness is one that, even today, is poorly understood. However, contemporary models of the cognitive processing system acknowledge a hierarchical arrangement of "activation-driven" (cf. Collins & Loftus, 1975) processing units (Norman & Shallice, 1980; Fodor, 1983; Wells & Mathews, 1994). Processing may begin relatively low in the hierarchy; thus, information may remain outside awareness. However, after a threshold of activation is reached, the executive units become operational for the purpose of controlled processing.

Processing units low in the hierarchy are thought to operate "automatically"; however, it should be noted that the sharp distinction between automatic and controlled processing is probably misconceived (Bargh, 1989), especially when considering clinical phenomena. Indeed, ruminations may occupy a place on a continuum somewhere between purely automatic and intentional processes (Uleman, 1989). Although biases in the processing system might facilitate the entry into awareness of intrusive thoughts and images, the fact that they are held in awareness may be largely due to mental manoeuvres that are largely under conscious control (e.g. counter-productive coping strategies). In sum, the persistence of intrusive thoughts and images in clinical conditions should be understood in terms of both preconscious and volitional biases.

Failure of Inhibitory Mechanisms

The repeated entry into awareness of an unintended thought is not merely the result of increased activation in specialized processing units. Intrusive cognition is also due to the failure of inhibitory systems. Clearly, inhibitory systems are functioning all of the time. This is something of a necessity, because consciousness is of limited capacity and the contents of awareness must be limited to salient features of the environment and/or information drawn from memory (cf. Broadbent, 1958). A failure of the mechanisms that inhibit the products of preconscious processing has been implicated, most notably, in schizophrenia (Dixon, 1981; Frith, 1992).

With respect to OCD, the repeated presence of unintended thoughts, images, and particularly impulses, might be attributed, in part, to the failure of inhibitory mechanisms (cf. Tallis & Shafran, 1997). The principal biological loci of inhibitory mechanisms are thought to be situated in the frontal lobe. Both brain scanning studies (Baxter et al., 1992; Hoehn-Saric et al., 1991; McGuire et al., 1994) and neuropsychological tests (Harvey, 1987; Veale, 1994; Behar et al., 1984) suggest abnormal frontal lobe functioning in patients with OCD. In addition, some commentators have suggested that brain scan investigations of OCD patients show anomalies in the caudate nucleus of the basal ganglia, which might account for the repeated failure of sub-cortical "gating" mechanisms (Baxter et al., 1990). Thus, primitive urges on aggressive or sexual themes are frequently able to gain entry into awareness. This biological model thus accounts for the frequent report in OCD of morally unacceptable ideas, images and impulses.

Attentional Bias

It has already been suggested that threat-related information is of particular relevance with respect to unintended thought. There is now considerable evidence to suggest that anxiety states are characterized by an attentional bias toward threat-related information (see Dalgleish, 1994, for a comprehensive and critical review). Using Stroop-type stimuli (Stroop, 1935), attentional biases favouring the processing of threat-related information have been demonstrated in patients with PTSD (Thrasher, Dalgleish & Yule, 1994), GAD (Mathews & MacLeod, 1985) and OCD (Lavy, van Oppen & van den Hout, 1994). Moreover, the allocation of attentional resources probably begins with an analysis of stimulus features that occurs outside of awareness (Mathews & MacLeod, 1986). Presumably, this bias is in operation regardless of whether target stimuli occur in the form of internal or external events. Thus a key factor that determines whether unintended thought will enter awareness is the degree to which information is analysed and designated "threat-relevant" at an early stage of processing.

Another attentional feature of the processing system that may be relevant in explaining the tenacity of unintended thoughts is dispositional self-focus. The tendency to "introspect" may be a general risk factor related to affective disturbance; however, it may be of particular relevance with respect to obsessional and ruminative phenomena.

According to Ingram (1990), "self-absorption" is a dysfunctional state of self-focused attention in clinical conditions. It can be measured according to three parameters: (a) internal–external; (b) duration; and (c) flexibility. Thus, a worrier, for example, might be particularly self-absorbed; if attention is predominantly focused inward, the duration of the focus is extended and, further, the individual finds it difficult to disengage and redirect attention. In support of the importance of self-focused attention in ruminative problems, Wells (1985) reports a significant relationship between self-focused attention and worry.

In sum, unintended and repetitive thoughts may arise with greater frequency in the processing system of those suffering from a clinical condition. Moreover, threat-related information is more likely to receive an early analysis and further attentional resources will subsequently be recruited. Individuals with an internally biased attentional system are more likely to detect unwanted mental events. Finally, the ability to redirect attention may be impaired, so unwanted thoughts are preserved in awareness for longer durations.

The salience of information within the processing system is thought to be determined by representations and propositions that are encoded at the schematic level (Markus, 1977; Beck, Emery & Greenberg, 1985; Higgins, 1989). Thus, early analysis and attentional deployment may ultimately be guided by the individual's "assumptive world" (Cantril, 1950).

Learning Experiences and Schemata

Schemata are related sets of beliefs or representations that influence the organization of information in the processing system. The formation of schemata is closely associated with learning experiences. In the traditional cognitive model of emotional disorders (Beck, 1987), "dysfunctional" schemata represent knowledge in at least two ways; first, in terms of conditional propositions or assumptions, e.g. "If I am not loved then I can never be happy"; and second, in terms of unconditional statements such as, "I am unlovable". The latter are examples of core beliefs and are thought to be the most fundamental of schema components; however, recently, with the advent of "Schema-Focused Cognitive Therapy" (Young, 1990), the notion of pre-verbal schemas has gained considerable currency. Pre-verbal schemata are thought to form at a stage of development preceding the acquisition of language. They are therefore the oldest component of the cognitive architecture. Although knowledge encoded at the schematic level can be brought into awareness (particularly so during therapy), schemata more commonly exert their influence from below the awareness threshold. When schemata become "active" (usually because of a critical triggering event), their influence is detectable in the form of somatic change and biased appraisals. It should be noted that the elements of Beck's schemata are conceptualized largely as collections of propositional beliefs; however, as suggested earlier, different approaches, such as that of Teasdale & Barnard (1993), define schematic models in terms of supra-propositional meaning structures.

The relationship between beliefs and learning experiences can range from relatively straightforward to obscure. Perhaps the clearest relationship between belief formation and experience is observed in PTSD, where the elements of "danger schemata" (cf. Beck, Emery & Greenberg, 1985) are almost certainly elaborated during or immediately after the trauma itself. Stimuli associated with the trauma acquire great significance and may subsequently receive priority processing. This allocation of processing resources is as relevant to internal stimuli as external. Thus, unintended thoughts and images will also capture attention on account of their significance. The salience of unintended thoughts and images in the context of OCD and GAD is also determined by "danger schemata"; however, the links between schemata and experiences can be idiosyncratic.

Intrusive thoughts, particularly on aggressive, sexual or blasphemous themes, are a universal experience (Rachman & de Silva, 1978; Salkovskis & Harrison, 1984); however, in OCD such thoughts usually provoke an intense emotional reaction. In addition to anxiety, feelings of guilt are often described. Such reactions appear to be closely related to the presence of beliefs concerning an exaggerated sense of personal influence (Freud 1909; Tallis, 1995), inflated responsibility (Rachman, 1976; Salkovskis, 1985) and thought–action fusion (Salkovskis, 1985; Rachman, 1993). Exaggerated personal influence or the "omnipotence of thoughts", as it was termed in the early psychoanalytic literature, refers to the belief that mental events can actually influence events in the external world. Thought–action fusion refers primarily to the belief that the occurrence of an intrusive thought is the moral equivalent of undertaking a related act.

Tallis (1995), has suggested that schemata associated with the above concepts may be closely linked to idiosyncratic learning experiences; however, it should be noted that a very similar account was posited by Freud 1909; 1913; 1919 in several works. If an individual experiences an apparent causal relationship between mental events and events in the real world, this will potentiate the formation of beliefs concerning inflated personal influence. Case histories are cited by Tallis

(1994) and Freud (1919) in which unacceptable wishes preceded the actual occurrence of related events (e.g. wishing someone dead shortly before their sudden death). If an individual believes that thinking can influence events in the real world, such an individual will naturally feel a heightened sense of responsibility and perceive thoughts as the moral equivalent of related actions. Intrusive thoughts, therefore, become signals for reparative action, which usually takes the form of covert and overt anxiety-reducing rituals. Over time, the occurrence of intrusive thoughts, and the conjoint operation of appraisals, underlying beliefs and reparative actions, might result in the development of highly integrated and complex cognitive schemata (Tallis, 1995). The activation and operation of these complex schemata may become increasingly automated and thus more difficult to interrupt and control (cf. Norman & Shallice, 1980).

It is very likely that differences between normal and pathological worry are determined by the existence of particular beliefs. The psychoanalytic view of worry is that it represents a form of self-inflicted punishment; in effect, a method of "redemption through suffering" (cf. Challman, 1974). Although the psychodynamic view is not favoured by contemporary therapists, there are interesting parallels with recent work formulated within the cognitive–behavioural framework. GAD patients often describe initiating worry when life is untroubled. The underlying belief is that a certain amount of suffering is inevitable. Therefore, a trouble-free life is in some way "tempting fate". Engaging in worry is a method of experiencing modest levels of distress, so that a major cataclysmic event is avoided (cf. Wells, 1994; Butler, 1994). Once worry has been initiated, other factors may result in its continuation. Again, it is likely that these semi-superstitious beliefs are intimately linked with learning history and cultural orientation.

Mood and Arousal

The persistence and distress caused by intrusive thoughts is influenced by mood in a number of ways. First, it is likely that mood-congruent memory effects will increase the accessibility of unwanted thoughts (Bower, 1981). Eysenck (1984), for example, has shown that negative mood is capable of increasing worry frequency in laboratory conditions. Secondly, intrusive thoughts are more likely to cause discomfort in a depressed individual, due to the increased accessibility of negative automatic thoughts (Beck et al., 1979). Thus, intrusions are appraised as being of special significance to the individual (Salkovskis, 1985). This process is consistent with Kahneman's (1973) availability heuristic. Material that is more accessible will be given greater weight when judgements are being made. It is interesting to note that, in the context of OCD, judgments can be influenced profoundly by mood, and in some cases, severe depression can transform obsessions into delusions (Lewis, 1966; Ingram 1961). For example, doubts about having caused harm to others might be transformed into a rigid belief that harm was actually done (Gittleson, 1966). Thirdly, if intrusive thoughts and images are understood in terms of a traditional behavioural model, they can be construed as anxiety-evoking stimuli (Rachman & Hodgson, 1980; Marks & Tobena, 1990). Under normal circumstances, anxiety associated with repeated presentations of such mental events will decline due to habituation (cf. Marks & Tobena, 1990). Clinical work on treatment-resistant cases of OCD (Foa, 1979) strongly suggests that mood disturbance can result in a failure of anxiogenic stimuli to habituate. They thus continue to capture attentional resources. Finally, it is very likely that depressed mood has an effect on cognitive control mechanisms. For example, Edwards & Dickerson (1987) report that non-clinical subjects exhibited decreased control of both negative and positive intrusions when depressed.

Physiological arousal may also affect the processing system, leading to a loss of control (Rachman & Hodgson, 1980); however, with respect to unwanted thoughts, it is likely that arousal affects the process of attention, such that intrusions remain the principal focus of attention. Easterbrook (1959) suggested that the breadth of attention is inversely related to levels of arousal. Contemporary research has led to the modification of this position. Hypervigilence theory (Eysenck, 1992), for example, suggests that arousal may indeed reduce the breadth of attention, but only when peripheral stimuli are of little or no relevance. Thus, a generally aroused individual is likely to focus attention on the most significant event in the phenomenal field. If this is an intrusive thought, then attention may then narrow to the exclusion of other stimuli.

Arousal not only affects the breadth of the "attentional beam", but also its direction. This may be a direct effect, or indirect. With respect to the latter, perceived internal physiological changes may capture attentional resources and draw them generally inward. Wegner & Guiliano (1980) found that aroused subjects chose more self-relevant words on a sentence completion task than non-aroused subjects. Fenigstein & Carver (1978) report similar findings using a false feedback paradigm. It would appear that physiological sensations cause individuals to reflect more intensely about themselves in general, becoming more aware of affect, values, standards of behaviour and self-critical judgements (Duval & Wicklund, 1972). In Barlow's model of anxious apprehension (Barlow, 1988), increased arousal is given a central role to play in the modification of attentional parameters, most notably breadth and direction.

Counter-productive Coping Strategies

Perhaps the most influential concept to be introduced into the area of intrusive cognition in recent years is thought suppression. The notion that suppression may be associated with a range of psychological sequelae is an old psychoanalytic concept. Although Freud (1900) was the first to suggest that attempts to deny a thought might lead to subsequent obsession, other observers have consistently remarked on a similar class of effects (e.g. Lindermann, 1944; Janis, 1958; Polivy & Herman, 1985; Pennebaker, 1985). The revival of interest in thought suppression and its psychological sequelae is largely due to the work of Wegner and colleagues.

The original and influential paradigm devised by Wegner et al. (1987) to explore the effect of thought suppression involved subjects verbalizing their stream of consciousness under two conditions. In the initial suppression condition, subjects tried not to think of white bears (a stimulus chosen for its distinctiveness), whereas under the initial expression condition subjects were instructed to think about white bears. Subjects rang a bell whenever they experienced the target thought. After 5 minutes, conditions were reversed. Again, subjects verbalized their stream of consciousness and rang a bell when thinking of a white bear. The results showed that subjects who had suppressed thinking about white bears experienced a subsequent increase in the frequency of this thought during the expression period, compared with subjects who had not suppressed at first. This increased frequency of target thoughts after suppression has been termed the "rebound effect".

Shortly after conducting a preliminary series of investigations, Wegner proposed that suppression might play a key role in the development of clinical phenomena characterized by loss of mental control, most notably obsessions, worry and intrusive recollections of stressful events. He suggested that cycles of suppression and rebound combine in the manner of a positive feedback system, producing frequent intrusions and compromised control:

> The release of suppression leads to a rebound of expression, and this then requires a greater level of suppression to eliminate. The greater suppression, in turn, may yield a still greater rebound . . . to produce a thought that is alarmingly frequent and insistent (Wegner, 1989; p. 170).

This formulation has been particularly well-endorsed by clinicians favouring a cognitive–behavioural account of OCD (cf. Tallis, 1992; Wells & Mathews, 1994; Salkovskis et al., 1995).

Since Wegner's initial study, numerous replications and extensions of the initial paradigm have been undertaken (Lavy & van den Hout, 1990; Merkelbach et al., 1991; Muris et al., 1993; Clark, Ball & Pape, 1991; Clark, Winton & Thynn, 1993; Borkovec & Lyonfields, 1993; Salkovskis & Campbell, 1994; Trinder & Salkovskis, 1994; McNally & Ricciardi, 1996; van den Hout et al., 1996). These investigations have yielded a range of results both consistent and inconsistent with Wegner's original report. Interpretation is complicated by the fact that researchers have used differing target stimuli and methods of detecting their entry into awareness.

A trend in this research has been toward exploring the effect of suppressing personally relevant negative thoughts, as opposed to neutral thoughts. Results suggest that rebound effects are more likely to occur with respect to the former. For example, McNally & Ricciardi (1996) found that subjects asked to suppress a neutral thought experience a decline in thought occurrence as a function of time, irrespective of a subsequent expression period; however, subjects asked first to suppress a personally relevant negative thought experienced a nearly three-fold increase in occurrence when later given permission to express it. The authors conclude that negatively valent thoughts respond differently to neutral thoughts after attempts at suppression.

EMOTIONAL PROCESSING

In the preceding sections, particular factors thought to influence the occurrence and persistence of unwanted thoughts and images have been discussed. Although these various factors might be brought together within a unified model, such a model would lack parsimony. To date, the most successful, and arguably the most influential, attempt to provide a general framework within which the occurrence of intrusive thoughts and images can be understood is that of "emotional processing".

In his 1980 paper introducing the concept of emotional processing, Rachman suggested that "emotional processing" is a "process whereby emotional disturbances are absorbed, and decline to the extent that other experiences and behaviour can proceed without disruption" (p. 51). When emotional processing is unsatisfactory, the "central indispensable index" is "the persistence or return of intrusive signs of emotional activity" (p. 51). The principal intrusive signs include obsessions, nightmares, intrusive thoughts and a range of anxiety symptoms. Rachman suggests a range of state, personality and stimulus factors likely to impede or facilitate emotional processing. Stimulus factors likely to give rise to processing difficulties include: sudden stimuli, intense stimulation, signals of danger, uncontrollable stimuli, unpredictable stimuli, irregularity of presentation, and large "chunks" of stimulation. Concurrent stressors (thus giving rise to overload) might also impede processing further. Clearly, Rachman's formulation has relevance to the unwanted psychological sequelae of any traumatic event, but is of particular relevance with respect to PTSD.

In Rachman's original paper, the process whereby emotional experiences are "absorbed" is not detailed; however, Foa & Kozak (1986) have suggested that emotional processing involves the modification of memory structures that underlie emotions. Thus, corrective information is integrated at the schema level. Fear reduction is achieved when two conditions are met. First, fear-relevant information must be made available by activation of the fear structure; and second, information incompatible with those elements already activated must then be processed. In this way, a new memory can be formed. Foa & Kozak suggest that individuals make considerable use of their own physiological responding during emotional processing. For example, if a traumatized individual confronts a feared situation, arousal levels will eventually decrease because of habituation. This interoceptive information is encoded in the form of response propositions incompatible with the existing fear structure, thereby weakening the links that exist between stimulus and response elements. Foa & Kozak's formulation is not without precedent. A remarkably similar account of the mechanisms governing adjustment after trauma was given by Freud & Breuer in 1895. Moreover, the "working through" of traumatic experiences described above is understood by Horowitz (1975) as a process involving, "matching and integrating . . . new or massive information about the self or world", and including, "the assessment of meaning, interpretations and implications of incoming information" (p. 1462).

Dalgleish, Power & Bolton (1999) have attempted to flesh out further the factors that influence emotional processing and its success or failure. Their account is "discrepancy-driven" and linked with four fundamental assumptions shared by many cognitive models of emotion: that emotions are functional; that emotions are appraisal-driven; that emotions are a function of higher-order organizational meaning structures (cf. Teasdale & Barnard, 1993), and that the cognitive emotional system is self-organizing. With respect to the final assumption, this implies that the system will seek to resolve discrepancies between different representational elements so that all information is integrated. The "direction" of this process favours the assimilation of new representational information into higher-order organizational meaning structures.

Intrusive thoughts and images can occur as a function of discrepancies between representations in memory and models of how the world or self "should be". Information that cannot be easily assimilated (e.g. traumatic information) will subsequently intrude into awareness. This is a fundamentally adaptive process insofar as it facilitates the mobilization of strategies that might result in a resolution of current problems.

Unfortunately, traumatic or highly distressing information (which is profoundly discrepant with pre-existing meaning structures) cannot be easily assimilated. Under such conditions, information is represented in an unassimilated form in memory. Moreover, because the system is self-organizing, attempts to integrate discrepant information will continue. Unassimilated representations are frequently reactivated, and their "vivid" quality can be explained by the fact that they have not been "modified" by the process of assimilation. Employing this framework, Rachman's "processing" can be defined in terms of the assimilation of lower-level meaning representations into higher-order meaning structures.

Although emotional processing failure appears to be of particular relevance with respect to explaining intrusive thoughts after traumatic stress, the concept has also been implicated in the literature on pathological worrying. Borkovec and colleagues have suggested that the process of worrying impedes emotional processing, insofar as verbal linguistic mental activity does not evoke physiological arousal to the same extent as "imagery" (Lang, 1988). Therefore, fear structures are not activated and the critical changes in interoceptive information described by Foa & Kozak (1986) cannot be utilized in the modification of memories. This account has some experimental support, the most notable of which is reported by Butler, Wells & Dewick (1995), who found that subjects instructed to worry "verbally" about an aversive film experienced more intrusive thoughts in the subsequent 3 days than individuals who were instructed to visualize the film.

CONCLUSION

In sum, intrusive thoughts and images are the price humanity pays for a flexible cognitive system. Were it possible to exercise absolute control over mental events, creativity in both art and science might be the first casualty.

The entry into awareness of unwanted thoughts and images seems to be closely associated with a history of actual or perceived trauma. The repeated re-entry into awareness of unintended thoughts and images might reflect the operation of adaptive cognitive sub-routines. Such sub-routines would serve to alert the organism with respect to future danger and facilitate the "processing" of distressing emotional information. Clinical conditions arise when adaptive sub-routines become dysregulated. This dysregulation most probably arises due to both low-level (e.g. poor inhibitory functioning) and high-level (metacognitive functioning) features of an individual's processing system. "Emotional processing" is perhaps the most useful general framework within which to understand the loss of mental control in clinical conditions such as OCD, GAD and PTSD. This framework suggests that efforts to avoid "working through" emotional material (for example by suppression) will result in continued disturbance and distress.

REFERENCES

American Psychiatric Association (1994). *Diagnostic and Statistical Manual of Mental Disorders*, 4th edn (DSM IV). Washington, DC: American Psychiatric Association.

Bargh, J. A. (1989). Conditional automaticity: varieties of automatic influence in social perception and cognition. In J. S. Uleman & J. A. Bargh (eds), *Unintended Thought*. New York: Guilford.

Bargh, J. A. & Uleman, J. S. (1989). Introduction. In J. S. Uleman & J. A. Bargh (eds), *Unintended Thought*. New York: Guilford.

Barlow, D. (1988). *Anxiety and Its Disorders*. New York: Guilford.

Baxter, L. R., Schwartz, J. M., Bergam, K. S., Szuba, M. P., Guze, B. H., Mazziotta, J. C., Alazraki, A., Selin, C. E., Ferng, H., Munford, P. & Phelps, M. (1992). Caudate glucose metabolic rate changes with both drug and behavior therapy for obsessive-compulsive disorder. *Archives of General Psychiatry*, **49**, 681–689.

Baxter, L. R., Schwartz, J. M., Guze, B. H., Bergman, K. & Szuba, M. P. (1990). Neuroimaging in obsessive-compulsive disorder: seeking the mediating neuroanatomy. In M. A. Jenike, L. Baer & W. E. Minichiello (eds), *Obsessive-Compulsive Disorders: Theory and Management*, 2nd edn. London: Mosby Year Book.

Beck, A. T. (1987). Cognitive models of depression. *Journal of Cognitive Psychotherapy*, **1**, 5–37.

Beck, A. T., Emery, G. & Greenberg, R. L. (1985). *Anxiety Disorders and Phobias: A Cognitive Perspective*. New York: Basic Books.

Beck, A. T., Freeman, A. & Associates (1990). *Cognitive Therapy of Personality Disorders*. New York: Guilford.

Beck, A. T., Rush, A., Shaw, B. & Emery, G. (1979). *Cognitive Therapy of Depression*. New York: Guilford.

Behar, D., Rapoport, J. L., Berg, C. J. et al. (1984). Computerized tomography and neuropsychological test measures in adolescents with obsessive-compulsive disorder. *American Journal of Psychiatry*, **141**, 363–369.

Blanchard, E., Hickling, E., Taylor, A., Loos, W., Forneris, C. & Jaccard, J. (1996). Who develops PTSD from motor vehicle accidents? *Behaviour, Research & Therapy*, **34**, 1–10.

Borkovec, T. D. (1979). Pseudo (experimental)-insomnia and idiopathic (objective) insomnia: theoretical and therapeutic issues. In H. J. Eysenck & S. Rachman (eds), *Advances in Behaviour Research and Therapy*. London: Pergamon, pp. 27–55.

Borkovec, T. D. (1994). The nature, functions, and origins of worry. In G. C. L. Davey & F. Tallis (eds), *Worrying: Perspectives on Theory, Assessment and Treatment*. Chichester: Wiley.

Borkovec, T. D. & Lyonfields, J. D. (1993). Worry: thought suppression of emotional processing. In H. Krohne (ed.), *Vigilance and Avoidance*. Toronto: Hogrefe and Huber, pp. 101–118.

Borkovec, T. D., Metzger, R. L. & Pruzinsky, T. (1986). Anxiety, worry, and the self. In L. Hartman & K. R. Blankstein (eds), *Perception of Self in Emotional Disorder and Psychotherapy*. New York: Plenum.

Bower, G. H. (1981). Mood and memory. *American Psychologist*, **36**, 129–148.

Broadbent, D. E. (1958). *Perception and Communication*. London: Pergamon.

Butler, G. (1994). Treatment of worry in generalised anxiety disorder. In G. C. L. Davey & F. Tallis (eds), *Worrying: Perspectives on Theory, Assessment and Treatment*. Chichester: Wiley.

Butler, G., Wells, A. & Dewick, H. (1995). Differential effects of worry and imagery after exposure to a stressful stimulus: a pilot study. *Behavioural and Cognitive Psychotherapy*, **23**, 45–56.

Buttolph, L. & Holland, A. (1990). Obsessive-compulsive disorders in pregnancy and childbirth. In M. A. Jenike, L. Baer & W. Minichiello (eds), *Obsessive-Compulsive Disorders: Theory and Management*. Boston, MA: Year Book Medical Publishers.

Cantril, H. (1950). *The "Why" of Man's Experience*. New York: Macmillan.

Carey, J. (1995). Chains and rings: Kekule's dreams. In J. Carey (ed.), *The Faber Book of Science*. London: Faber & Faber.

Challman, A. (1974). The empirical nature of worry. *American Journal of Psychiatry*, **131**(10), 1140–1141.

Clark, D. M., Ball, S. & Pape, D. (1991). An experimental investigation of thought suppression. *Behaviour, Research, and Therapy*, **29**, 253–257.

Clark, D. M., Winton, E. & Thynn, L. (1993). A further experimental investigation of thought suppression. *Behaviour, Research, and Therapy*, **31**, 207–210.

Collins, A. M. & Loftus, E. F. (1975). A spreading activation theory of semantic processing. *Psychological Review*, **82**, 407–428.

Dalgleish, T. (1994). The appraisal of threat and the process of selective attention in clinical and sub-clinical anxiety states. I: Theoretical issues. *Clinical Psychology and Psychotherapy*, **1**, 153–164.

Dalgleish, T., Power, M. & Bolton, D. (1999). Discrepancy-based theories of emotions and their implications for the taxonomy of emotional disorders: a theoretical note. Manuscript submitted for publication.

Damasio, A. R. (1994). *Descartes' Error*. New York: Grosset/Putnam.

Davey, G. C. L., Tallis, F. & Capuzzo, N. (in press). Beliefs about the consequences of worrying. *Cognitive Therapy & Research*.

Dawkins, R. (1976). *The Selfish Gene*. Oxford: Oxford University Press.

Dixon, N. F. (1981). *Preconscious Processing*. London: Wiley.

Duval, S. & Wicklund, R. A. (1972). *Effects of Objective Self-awareness*. New York: Academic Press.

Easterbrook, J. A. (1959). The effect of emotion on cue utilisation and the organisation of behaviour. *Psychological Review*, **66**, 183–201.

Edwards, S. & Dickerson, M. (1987). On the similarity of positive and negative intrusions. *Behaviour, Research, & Therapy*, **25**, 207–211.

Ellis, A. (1956/1977). The basic clinical theory of rational emotive therapy. In A. Ellis & R. Grieger (eds), *Handbook of Rational Emotive Therapy* (1977). New York: Springer.

Eysenck, M. W. (1984). Anxiety and the worry process. *Bulletin of the Psychonomic Society*, **22**, 545–548.

Eysenck, M. W. (1992). *Anxiety: The Cognitive Perspective.* Hove: Erlbaum.

Fenigstein, A. & Carver, C. S. (1978). Self-focusing effects of heartbeat feedback. *Journal of Personality and Social Psychology*, **36**, 1241–1250.

Foa, E. (1979). Failure in treating obsessive-compulsives. *Behaviour, Research, & Therapy*, **17**, 169–176.

Foa, E. B. & Kozak, M. H. (1986). Emotional processing of fear: exposure to corrective information. *Psychological Bulletin*, **44**(99), 20–35.

Fodor, J. A. (1983). *The Modularity of Mind.* Cambridge, MA: MIT Press.

Frith, C. D. (1992). *The Cognitive Neuropsychology of Schizophrenia.* Hove: Erlbaum.

Freud, S. (1900). The interpretation of dreams. In A. Richards (ed.), *The Penguin Freud Library.* Harmondsworth: Penguin.

Freud, S. (1909). Notes upon a case of obsessional neurosis (the "rat man"). In A. Richards (ed.), *The Penguin Freud Library: Case Histories II.* Harmondsworth: Penguin.

Freud, S. (1913). The predisposition to obsessional neurosis. In *Collected Papers*, Vol. 2. London: Hogarth Press.

Freud, S. (1919). The "uncanny". In Angela Richards (ed.), *The Penguin Freud Library: Art and Literature.* Harmondsworth: Penguin.

Freud, S. & Breuer, J. (1895). On the physical mechanism of hysterical phenomena: preliminary communication. In *Studies on Hysteria: The Pelican Freud Library.* Harmondsworth: Pelican.

Gittleson, N. (1966). The fate of obsessions in depressive psychosis. *British Journal of Psychiatry*, **112**, 705–708.

Goodman, W. K., Price, L. H., Rassmussen, S. A. et al. (1989a). The Yale–Brown Obsessive-Compulsive Scale (Y-Bocs): Part I. Development, use, and reliability. *Archives of General Psychiatry*, **46**, 1006–1011.

Goodman, W. K., Price, L. H., Rassmussen, S. A. et al. (1989b). The Yale–Brown Obsessive Compulsive Scale (Y-Bocs): Part II. Validity. *Archives of General Psychiatry*, **46**, 1012–1016.

Guidano, V. L. & Liotti, G. (1983). *Cognitive Processes and Emotional Disorders.* New York: Guilford.

Harvey, N. S. (1987). Neurological factors in obsessive-compulsive disorder. *British Journal of Pychiatry*, **150**, 567–568.

Higgins, E. T. (1989). Knowledge, accessibility and activation: subjectivity and suffering from unconscious sources. In J. S. Uleman & J. A. Bargh (eds), *Unintended Thought.* New York: Guilford.

Hoehn-Saric, R. Pearlson, G. Harris, G. J. et al. (1991). Effects of fluoxetine on regional cerebral blood flow in obsessive-compulsive patients. *American Journal of Psychiatry*, **49**, 690–694.

Horowitz, M. J. (1975). Intrusive and repetitive thoughts after experimental stress: a summary. *Archives of General Psychiatry*, **32**, 1457–1463.

Horowitz, M. J. (1976). *Stress Response Syndromes.* New York: Jason Aronson.

Horowitz, M. J. (1985). Disasters and psychological response to stress. *Psychiatric Annals*, **15**, 161–167.

Humphrey, N. (1992). *A History of the Mind.* London: Chatto & Windus.

Ingram, I. M. (1961). Obsessional illness in mental hospital patients. *Journal of Mental Science*, **107**, 382–402.

Ingram, R. E. (1990). Self-focused attention in clinical disorders: review and a conceptual model. *Psychological Bulletin*, **107**, 156–176.

Insel, T. R. & Winslow, J. T. (1990). Neurobiology of obsessive-compulsive disorder. In M. A. Jenike, L. Baer & W. E. Minichiello (eds), *Obsessive-Compulsive Disorders: Theory and Management*, 2nd edn. London: Mosby Year Book.

James, W. (1890). *Principles of Psychology*. London: Macmillan.

Janis, I. L. (1958). *Psychological Stress*. New York: Wiley.

Janis, I. L. (1972). *Stress and Frustration*. New York: Harcourt Brace Jovanovich.

Joyce, J. (1922). Ulysses. Paris: Shakespeare.

Kahneman, D. (1973). *Attention and Effort*. Englewood Cliffs, NJ: Prentice-Hall.

Kelly, G. A. (1955). *The Psychology of Personal Constructs*. New York: Norton.

Khanna, S., Rajendra, P. N., Channabasavanna, S. M. et al. (1988). Life events and onset of obsessive-compulsive disorder. *International Journal of Social Psychiatry*, **34**, 305–309.

Kozak, M. J. & Foa, E. B. (1994). Obsessions, overvalued ideas and delusions in obsessive-compulsive disorder. *Behaviour, Research & Therapy*, **32**, 343–353.

Lachman, R. Lachman, J. L. & Butterfield, W. C. (1979). *Cognitive Psychology and Information Processing: An Introduction*. Hillsdale, NJ: Erlbaum.

Langer, E. J. (1978). Rethinking the role of thought in social interaction. In J. H. Harvey, W. J. Ickes & R. F. Kidd (eds), *New Directions in Attribution Research*, Vol. 2. Hillsdale, NJ: Erlbaum.

Lang, P. J. (1988). The image of fear: emotion and memory. Invited Address, World Congress of Behavior Therapy, Edinburgh, UK.

Lavy, E. & van den Hout, M. (1990). Thought suppression induces intrusions. *Behavioural Psychotherapy*, **18**, 251–258.

Lavy, E., van Oppen, P. & van den Hout, M. (1994). Selective processing of emotional information in obsessive-compulsive disorder. *Behaviour, Research, & Therapy*, **32**, 243–246.

Lazarus, R. S. (1966). *Psychological Stress and the Coping Process*. New York: McGraw-Hill.

Lazarus, R. S. (1984). On the primacy of cognition. *American Psychologist*, **39**, 124–129.

Lewis, A. (1966). Obsessional disorder. In R. Scott (ed.), *Price's Textbook of the Practice of Medicine*, 10th edn. London: Oxford University Press.

Linderman, E. (1944). Symptomatology and management of acute grief. *American Journal of Psychiatry*, **101**, 141–148.

MacLeod, A. K. (1994). Worry and explanation based pessimism. In G. C. L. Davey & F. Tallis (eds), *Worrying: Perspectives on Theory, Assessment and Treatment*. Chichester: Wiley.

Marks, I. & Tobena, A. (1990). Learning and unlearning fear: a clinical and evolutionary perspective. *Neuroscience & Behavioral Reviews*, **14**, 365–384.

Markus, H. (1977). Self-schemata and processing information about the self. *Journal of Personality and Social Psychology*, **35**, 63–78.

Mathews, A. & MacLeod, C. (1985). Selective processing of threat cues in anxiety states. *Behaviour, Research and Therapy*, **23**, 563–569.

Mathews, A. & MacLeod, C. (1986). Discrimination of threat cues without awareness in anxiety states. *Journal of Abnormal Psychology*, **95**, 131–138.

McGuire, P. K., Bench, C. J., Frith, C. D. et al. (1994). Functional anatomy of obsessive-compulsive phenomena. *British Journal of Psychiatry*, **164**, 459–468.

McNally, R. & Ricciardi, J. (1996). Suppression of negative and neutral thoughts. *Behavioural and Cognitive Psychotherapy*, **24**, 17–25.

Meichenbaum, D. (1977). *Cognitive-behavior Modification: An Integrative Approach*. New York: Plenum.

Merkelbach, H., Muris, P., van den Hout, M. & de Jong, P. (1991). Rebound effects of thought suppression: instruction dependent? *Behavioural Psychotherapy*, **19**, 225–238.

Muris, P. Merkelbach, H. and de Jong, P. (1993). Verbalisation and environmental cueing in thought suppression. *Behaviour, Research, & Therapy*, **31**, 609–612.

Norman, D. A. & Shallice, T. (1980). *Attention to Action: Willed and Automatic Control of Behaviour.* Center for Human Information Processing (Technical report No. 99). [Reprinted in revised form in R. J. Davidson, G. E. Schwartz & D. Shapiro (eds), *Consciousness and Self-regulation: Advances in Research and Theory*, Vol. 4 (1986). New York and London: Plenum, pp. 1–18.]

Parkes, C. M. (1972). Components of the reaction to loss of a limb, spouse or home. *Journal of Psychosomatic Research*, **16**, 343–349.

Pennebaker, J. W. (1985). Inhibition and cognition: toward an understanding of trauma and disease. *Canadian Psychology*, **26**, 82–95.

Polivy, J. & Herman, C. P. (1985). Dieting and binging: a causal analysis. *American Psychologist*, **40**, 193–201.

Posner, M. I. & Snyder, C. R. R. (1975). Attention and cognitive control. In R. L. Solso (ed.), *Information Processing and Cognition: The Loyola Symposium.* Hillsdale, NJ: Erlbaum.

Rachman, S. (1973). Some similarities and differences between obsessional ruminations and morbid preoccupations. *Canadian Psychiatric Association Journal*, **18**, 71–74.

Rachman, S. (1976). Obsessive-compulsive checking. *Behaviour, Research & Therapy*, **14**, 269–277.

Rachman, (1980). Emotional processing. *Behaviour, Research & Therapy*, **18**, 51–60.

Rachman, S. (1993). Obsessions, responsibility, and guilt. *Behaviour, Research & Therapy*, **31**, 149–154.

Rachman, S. J. & de Silva, P. (1978). Abnormal and normal obsessions. *Behaviour, Research and Therapy*, **16**, 233–248.

Rachman, S. & Hodgson, R. (1980). *Obsessions and Compulsions.* Hillsdale, NJ: Prentice-Hall.

Salkovskis, P. (1985). Obsessional-compulsive problems: a cognitive-behavioural analysis. *Behaviour, Research and Therapy*, **25**, 571–583.

Salkovskis, P. M. & Campbell, P. (1994). Thought suppression induces intrusion in naturally occurring negative intrusive thoughts. *Behaviour, Research and Therapy*, **32**, 1–8.

Salkovskis, P. M. & Harrison, J. (1984). Abnormal and normal obsessions: a replication. *Behaviour, Research and Therapy*, **22**, 549–552.

Salkovskis, P. M., Richards, H. C. & Forrester, E. (1995). The relationship between obsessional problems and intrusive thoughts. *Behavioural and Cognitive Psychotherapy*, **23**, 281–299.

Silver, R. L., Boon, C. & Stones, M. H. (1983). Searching for meaning in misfortune: making sense of incest. *Journal of Social Issues*, **39**(2), 81–102.

Stevens, A. (1996). *Private Myths.* Harmondsworth: Penguin.

Stroop, J. R. (1935). Studies of interference in serial verbal reactions. *Journal of Experimental Psychology*, **18**, 643–662.

Tallis, F. (1992). *Understanding Obsessions and Compulsions.* London: Sheldon Press.

Tallis, F. (1994). Obsessions, responsibility, and guilt: two case reports suggesting a common and specific aetiology. *Behaviour, Research & Therapy*, **32**, 143–145.

Tallis, F. (1995). *Obsessive Compulsive Disorder: A Cognitive and Neuropsychological Perspective.* Chichester: Wiley.

Tallis, F., Davey, G. C. L. & Capuzzo, N. (1994). The phenomenology of non-pathological worry: a preliminary investigation. In G. C. L. Davey & F. Tallis (eds), *Worrying: Perspectives on Theory, Assessment and Treatment.* Chichester: Wiley.

Tallis, F. & Eysenck, M. (1994). Worry: mechanisms and modulating influences. *Behavioural Psychotherapy*, **22**, 37–56.

Tallis, F. & Shafran, R. (1997). Schizotypal personality and obsessive compulsive disorder. *Clinical Psychology and Psychotherapy*, **4**, 172–178.

Teasdale, J. D. & Barnard, P. J. (1993). Affect cognition and change: re-modelling depressive thought. Hove: Erlbaum.

Thrasher, S. M., Dalgleish, T. & Yule, W. (1994). Information processing in posttraumatic stress disorder. *Behaviour, Research and Therapy*, **32**, 247–253.

Toates, F. (1990). *Obsessional Thoughts and Behaviour.* Wellingborough: Thorsons.

Trinder, H. & Salkovskis, P. M. (1994). Personally relevant intrusions outside the laboratory: long term suppression increases intrusion. *Behaviour, Research & Therapy*, **32**, 833–842.

Turner, S. M., Beidel, D. C. & Stanley, M. A. (1992). Are obsessional thoughts and worry different cognitive phenomena? *Clinical Psychology Review*, **12**, 257–270.

Tversky, A. & Kahneman, D. (1973). Availability: a heuristic for judging frequency and probability. *Cognitive Psychology*, **5**, 207–232.

Uleman, J. S. (1989). A framework for thinking intentionally about unintended thought. In J. S. Uleman & J. A. Bargh (eds), *Unintended Thought.* New York: Guilford.

van den Hout, M., Merckelbach, H. & Pool, K. (1996). Dissociation, reality monitoring, trauma, and thought suppression. *Behavioural and Cognitive Psychotherapy*, **24**, 97–108.

Veale, D. (1994). Cognitive deficits in obsessive-compulsive disorder in tests which are sensitive to frontal lobe dysfunction. Unpublished MD Thesis, University of London.

Wegner, D. (1989). *White Bears and Other Unwanted Thoughts: Suppression, Obsession, and the Psychology of Mental Control.* New York: Viking Penguin.

Wegner, D. M. & Giuliano, T. (1980). Arousal-induced attention to the self. *Journal of Personality and Social Psychology*, **38**, 719–726.

Wegner, D. M., Schneider, D. J., Carter, S. III & White, L. (1987). Paradoxical consequences of thought suppression. *Journal of Personality and Social Psychology*, **53**, 1–9.

Wells, A. (1985). Relationship between provate self-consciousness and anxiety scores in threatening situations. *Psychological Reports*, **57**, 1063–1066.

Wells. A. (1994). Attention and the control of worry. In G. C. L. Davey & F. Tallis (eds), *Worrying: Perspectives on Theory, Assessment and Treatment.* Chichester: Wiley.

Wells, A. & Matthews, G. (1994). *Attention and Emotion: A Clinical Perspective.* Hove: Earlbaum.

Young, J. E. (1990). *Cognitive Therapy for Personality Disorders: A Schema-focused Approach.* Sarasota, FL: Professional Resource Exchange.

Zajonc, R. B. (1984). On the primacy of affect. *American Psychologist*, **39**, 117–123.

Chapter 16

Facial Expressions

Paul Ekman
University of California, San Francisco, CA, USA

INTRODUCTION

The argument about whether facial expressions of emotion are universal or culture-specific goes back more than 100 years. For most of that time the evidence was sparse, but in the last 30 years there have been many research studies. That has not served to convince everyone, but it has sharpened the argument. I will review the different kinds of evidence that support universals in expression and cultural differences. I will present eight challenges to that evidence, and how those challenges have been met by proponents of universality. I conducted some of this research and have been active in answering the challenges, so I am not a disinterested commentator, but probably no-one is. I will try to present the evidence and counter-arguments as fairly as I can, so that readers can make up their own minds.

Most of the research on universals in facial expression of emotion has focused on one method—showing pictures of facial expressions to observers in different cultures, who are asked to judge what emotion is shown. If the observers in the different cultures label the expressions with the same term, it has been interpreted as evidence of universality. Most of the challenges have been against this type of evidence, arguing that the lack of total agreement is evidence of cultural difference.

There have been other types of studies relevant to universals, studies in which facial behavior itself is measured. This too has been challenged. Near the end of this chapter I will more briefly summarize still other research relevant to universals, evidence which heretofore has not been brought to bear: studies of other animals, studies of the relationship between expression and physiology, studies of the relationship between expression and self-report, and conditioning

Handbook of Cognition and Emotion. Edited by T. Dalgleish and M. Power.
© 1999 John Wiley & Sons Ltd.

studies. In the conclusion I will describe my reading of all the evidence, delineating where there are universals and the many aspects of facial expressions which differ within and between cultures.

THE EVIDENCE

1. Evidence from Darwin's Study

It begins with Charles Darwin's *The Expression of the Emotions in Man and Animals* (1872/1998). His evidence for universality was the answers to 16 questions he sent to Englishmen living or traveling in eight parts of the world: Africa, America, Australia, Borneo, China, India, Malaysia and New Zealand. Even by today's standard, that is a very good, diverse, sample. They wrote that they saw the same expressions of emotion in these foreign lands as they had known in England, leading Darwin to say: "It follows, from the information thus acquired, that the same state of mind is expressed throughout the world with remarkable uniformity . . .".

There are three problems that make Darwin's evidence on universality unacceptable by today's scientific standards. First, Darwin did not ask a sufficient number of people in each country to answer his questions. Second, Darwin relied upon the answers of these Englishmen, rather than asking the people who were native in each country (or asking his English correspondents to do so). Current research always studies the people who are native to each country, not a foreign observer's interpretation of their behavior. Third, the way in which Darwin worded his questions often suggested the answer he wanted. For example, Darwin asked, "Is astonishment expressed by the eyes and mouth being opened wide, and by the eyebrows being raised?". Instead Darwin should have asked, "What emotion is being shown when a person you observe has their eyes and mouth open wide and their eyebrows raised?" Even better would have been to show photographs of facial expressions to people in each country, asking them what emotion they saw. Although Darwin did use this method, he did so only in England.

Challenge 1: Examples of Cultural Differences

A very influential example of the challenge to Darwin's view that facial expressions are universal to the species was raised by the eminent social psychologist Otto Klineberg. While he acknowledged that a few patterns of behavior are universal, such as crying, laughing and trembling, Klineberg (1940) said that the expressions of anger, fear, disgust, sadness, etc. are not. Klineberg cited many observations of cultural differences in expressions noted by anthropologists, but the deciding evidence for Klineberg was a study which found that humans could not understand a chimpanzee's facial expressions. I describe this later in section 10.

The leading advocate of the view that expressions are specific to each culture in the 1960s and 1970s was the anthropologist/linguist Ray Birdwhistell. Birdwhistell (1970) attempted to prove that body movement and facial expression, what he called *kinesics*, can be best viewed as another language, with the same type of units and organization as spoken language. Birdwhistell wrote as follows:

> When I first became interested in studying body motion I was confident that it would be possible to isolate a series of expressions, postures and movements that were denotative of primary emotional states ... As research proceeded, and even before the development of kinesics, it became clear that this search for universals was culture-bound ... There are probably no universal symbols of emotional state. ... We can expect them [emotional expressions] to be learned and patterned according to the particular structures of particular societies (p. 126).

And again:

> Early in my research on human body motion, influenced by Darwin's *The Expression of the Emotions in Man and Animals*, and by my own preoccupation with human universals, I attempted to study the human smile. ... Not only did I find that a number of my subjects "smiled" when they were subjected to what seemed to be a positive environment but some "smiled" in an aversive one (pp. 29–30).

Birdwhistell failed to consider that there may be more than one form of smiling. He might not have made that mistake if he had read the work of Duchenne de Boulogne, a nineteenth century neurologist whom Darwin had quoted extensively. Duchenne (1862/1990) distinguished between the smile of actual enjoyment and other kinds of smiling. In the enjoyment smile, not only are the lip corners pulled up, but the muscles around the eyes are contracted, while non-enjoyment smiles involve just the smiling lips.

We should not fault Birdwhistell too much on this point, however, for up until 1982, no-one else who studied the smile had made this distinction. Many social scientists were confused by the fact that people smiled when they were not happy. In the last 10 years, my own research group and many other research groups have found very strong evidence to show that Duchenne was correct, there is not one smile, but different types of smiling, only one of which is associated with actual enjoyment (for a review, see Ekman, 1992).

2.   Evidence in Which Multiple Observers in Different Literate Cultures Judge Expressions

In is only in the last 30 years, nearly 100 years after Darwin wrote *The Expression of The Emotions in Man and Animals*, that psychologists finally focused their attention on the question of whether expressions are universal or specific to each culture. Darwin's method of showing photographs and asking people to judge the emotion shown in the photograph has been the principal method. Because there have been so many studies using this research approach, critics have often ignored the other evidence relevant to universals which used very different methods of research (see sections 7–10 below). But first, let us consider what have often been called "judgment studies", because people in each culture are asked to judge the emotion shown in each of a series of photographs.

Many countries were studied, and it was natives in each country who were examined. They were shown photographs of facial expression and asked, not told, what emotion was shown. Apart from technical problems—a particular photograph not being a very good depiction of a real emotional expression, the words for emotion not being well translated in a particular language, or the task of judging what emotion is being shown being very unfamiliar—people from different countries should ascribe the same emotion to the expressions if there is universality.

Figure 16.1 shows six of the photographs we (Ekman, Sorenson & Friesen, 1969) used in this type of research in 1966. These are all actors who were posed

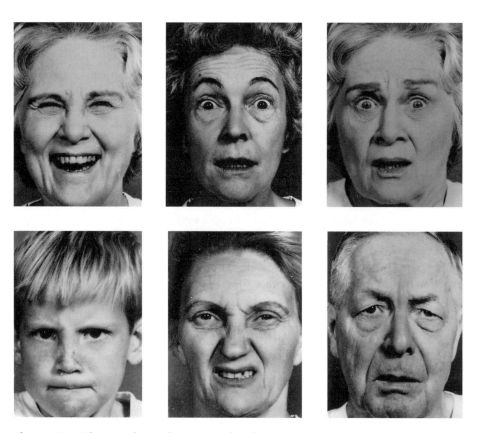

Figure 16.1 Photographs used in cross-cultural research

by Silvan Tomkins (1962), an emotion theorist who advised me, and also Carroll Izard (1971), on how to do cross-cultural research on emotional expression. Our research differed from previous work in how we selected the particular facial expressions we would show to people in various cultures.

Previous studies had uncritically accepted as satisfactory every one of the actor's attempts to pose an emotion, and had shown them to people in each culture. Inspecting the hundreds of poses Tomkin's actors had made, it was obvious that some were better than others. Rather than relying upon our intuitions, however, we scored the photographs with a new technique we had developed for measuring facial behavior (Ekman, Friesen & Tomkins, 1971), selecting the ones which met *a priori* criteria for what configurations should be present in each picture. Izard also selected the photographs to show in his experiments, but by a different procedure. He first showed many photographs to American students, and then chose only the ones which Americans agreed about to show to people in other cultures.

I have chosen as the data set to discuss the findings listed and discussed by Russell (1994) in his attack on universality (a detailed account of how Russell misunderstood those data can be found in my reply; Ekman, 1994). Usually there was only one group of people studied in each country, but in some instances there were two or three, so that the total number of groups is 31. I grouped together the different samples from the same countries, even though they had been gathered at different times, sometimes by different scientists. This results, then, in providing data on 21 literate countries: Africa (this included subjects from more than one country in Africa, and is the only group who were not tested in their own languages but in English), Argentina, Brazil, Chile, China, England, Estonia, Ethiopia, France, Germany, Greece, Italy, Japan, Kirghizistan, Malaysia, Scotland, Sweden, Indonesia (Sumatra), Switzerland, Turkey and the USA. This includes two studies which I led (Ekman, Sorenson & Friesen, 1969; Ekman et al., 1987), and separate independent studies by five other investigators or groups of investigators (Izard, 1971; Niit & Valsiner, 1977; Boucher & Carlson, 1980; Ducci, Arcuri, Georgis & Sineshaw, 1982; McAndrew, 1986).

In all of these studies the observers in each culture who saw the picture selected one emotion term from a short list of six to ten emotion terms, translated, of course, into their own language. I will focus on just the results for the photographs the scientists intended to show happiness, anger, fear, sadness, disgust and surprise, for these were included in all of the experiments.

There was an extraordinary amount of agreement about which emotion was shown in which photographs across the 21 countries. In *every* case, the majority in each of the 21 countries agreed about the pictures that showed happiness, those that showed sadness and those that showed disgust. For surprise expressions there was agreement by the majority in 20 out of the 21 countries, for fear on 19 out of 21, and for anger on 18 out of 21. In those 6 cases in which the *majority* did not choose the same emotion as was chosen in every other country, the *most frequent* response (although it was not the majority), was the same as was given by the majority in the other countries. In my own studies, the only studies in which the expressions were selected on the basis of measuring the muscle movements shown in the photographs, *all* the expressions were judged as showing the same emotion by the majority in *every* country we studied.

Contrary evidence, evidence against universality, would have been to find that the expressions that the majority of people in one country judged as showing one emotion (let us say anger) were judged as showing another emotion (fear) by the majority in another culture. This never happened.

Challenge 2: Not Every Culture was Studied

If the requirement is that every country must be studied, and every sub-culture in every country, then no-one could ever establish that anything is universal. The counter to this criticism is that it is not plausible for there to be such high agreement in so many different countries—for 21 is not a small number, and 10 of them were not Western—if expressions are not universal. The anthropologist Brown (1991) wrote on just this point:

> The first and most obvious point about the demonstration of universals is that it is never done by exhaustive enumeration, showing that a phenomenon exists and existed in each known individual, society, culture or language. There are too many known peoples to make this feasible . . . Thus all statements of universality are hypotheses or arguments based on various limited kinds of evidence . . . (p. 51).

Challenge 3: The Observers Couldn't Choose Their Own Words

A second challenge, which has been forcefully, but I believe fallaciously, made is that the appearance of universality was found only because the people in each culture were not allowed to say what emotion they really thought each expression showed. Recall that the people in every culture had to register their judgment about the emotion shown in an expression by choosing one emotion word from a list of emotion terms, such as anger, fear, sadness, disgust, etc. What if they had been given other words, Russell (1994) argued, might they have not disagreed? Perhaps those facial expressions really didn't show any of the emotions on the list, but instead showed quite unrelated emotions. If only the scientists had allowed them to choose their own words, rather than forcing them to choose from the scientists' list of emotion words, then evidence for cultural differences in emotional expression would have emerged.

There are two answers to this challenge, one logical and the other experimental. If words like fear, anger, disgust, and happiness are truly unrelated to the expressions, if they are as meaningless when it comes to registering the emotion shown in an expression as a set of nonsense syllables (oto, nim, faz, etc.), then widespread disagreement would have been found when people were asked to use this list to choose a word which fitted each expression. People within each culture would have disagreed with each other, and that is not what was found. And people across cultures would have disagreed with each other, and that also was not found. Just the opposite happened. In every culture the people agreed with each other in their choices of emotion words. And across cultures they agreed in their choice of emotion words. So it is unlikely that these emotion words are unrelated to the expressions they saw.

3. Evidence from Free Choice Judgments of Facial Expressions

Of course, the best rebuttal is to allow people to choose their own words in judging the emotion they see in each expression, and to determine whether the same results are obtained. Izard (1971) did just that in one of his studies. He allowed people in Britain, France, Greece and America to give their own word for each photograph. Boucher & Carlson (1980) did the same in America, Malaysia and among the Temuans, an aboriginal group in Malaysia. Rosenberg & Ekman (1994) did the same thing in the USA, comparing agreement when people choose their own words, with the agreement that is found when people were restricted to choosing one word from a list of six or seven emotions. Neither Izard nor Boucher & Carlson provided much information about how they classified the words their subjects gave them into categories, but the strength of their studies is they compared cultures. Rosenberg & Ekman provided the raw data in their report, but they only studied one culture.

In all of these studies in which people could choose their own word, the words they chose were quite similar, within and between cultures, and the words they chose were quite similar to the emotion words that had been used in the 21 countries in which people were given a list of words to choose from. Russell (1995) dismissed this evidence, because Rosenberg & Ekman had only studied one culture, ignoring the Boucher & Carlson and the Izard data on multiple cultures.

One of Russell's own studies (Russell, Suzuki & Ishida, 1993) in which observers were allowed to choose their own word to describe the emotion shown in a photograph, strongly supports universality. English-speaking Canadians, Greeks and Japanese were shown seven photographs from Ekman & Friesen's set (1976), and allowed to give their own response rather than choosing from a list (I will not report the findings on contempt, as I discuss that emotion later). There were 18 opportunities for disagreement (three cultures × six emotions); on 17 of those 18 opportunities the most frequent word the subjects gave was the emotion term that Ekman & Friesen had specified for the photographs. In further challenging the findings on universality, Russell (1995) only mentions the one disagreement out of 18 (the Japanese called the "fear" photograph "surprise"), and does not mention the high agreement that he had actually found in every other instance. Russell also cites a study using free response by Sorenson (1975), but Sorenson did not know well the languages of the cultures he studied, neither was he trained in how to conduct such a study. His experience at that time was solely as a cinematographer.

Challenge 4: Shared Visual Input Created the Appearance of Universality

A third and perhaps more serious challenge to the findings of universality was that all the people studied had the opportunity to learn these expressions from each other or from a common source. Perhaps everyone learned their "universal" expressions from watching *Sesame Street* on television! If people who were visually isolated were studied, this argument goes, if people who had seen no magazines, cinema or television were studied, they might show completely different facial expressions. Birdwhistell made this argument when I first showed him my cross-cultural findings.

4.   Evidence from Judgments by Observers in a Preliterate, Visually Isolated Culture

To answer this criticism I went to Papua New Guinea in 1967 to study the South Fore culture. These people were visually isolated; most had seen few or no outsiders. They were still using stone implements, and had never seen a photograph, magazine, film or television. I could not do what I and others had done in the 21 literate cultures. I could not give them a list of emotion words, since they had no written language. I could not ask one of the few translators to read these people the list of emotion words, since it is not easy for anyone to keep in mind the list of words, and it becomes tedious when it is read again and again. I needed a procedure in which the people who saw the photographs could make their judgment without having to speak.

The procedure I adopted had been used many years earlier (Dashiell, 1927) for studying young children who also can not read. My translator read the person a brief story, and asked the person to point to the picture which fitted that story. Before using this procedure I had to have a story which clearly described a situation in which an emotion was likely to occur for these people. To discover the stories I showed people one photograph at a time and asked them to make up a story which described what had happened to produce each expression. This was demanding on both the subject and the translator, and very time-consuming. Even if there is no language barrier, it is harder to make up a story than to hear a story and point to a picture. But I had to ask people to make up a story for each picture so that I could find out what themes are most common in this culture for each of the expressions, so I could use stories based on those themes in the main research study in which the stories were read and the people just had to point to the picture.

These stone-age people, who could not have learned expressions from the media, chose the same expressions for each emotion as had the people in the 21 literate cultures (Ekman & Friesen, 1971). The only exception was that they failed to distinguish the fear and surprise faces from each other, although both were distinguished from anger, happiness, sadness and disgust expressions.

I also did more informal studies, in which I arranged for something to happen and filmed how people acted. For example, I tape-recorded two men while they played their Jews' harp and talked to each other. Then when I had my motion picture film camera going, I played back the audio tape, filming how they acted when they heard their voices come out of this machine. They showed extreme happiness blended with surprise, just as it would be shown anywhere to an enjoyable novel occurrence. On another occasion I waited by the side of a road for people who had not seen each other for some time to meet. Again, I saw expressions of happiness. I could not safely provoke anger, but I inadvertently made a woman angry by looking directly at her in a public situation, and she showed exactly the configuration I had previously identified as anger. I also frightened some children, and their expressions showed the same facial configuration for fear found anywhere else in the world.

5. Evidence from Posing Facial Expressions by Members of a Visually Isolated Preliterate Culture

In another study I asked some of these people to show me what their face would look like if they were in one of the stories. I videotaped them as they enacted the emotions, and then showed these videotapes to Americans. Figure 16.2 shows some frames from the video. If expressions are universal, then the Americans who have never seen any people from this New Guinea culture should have no trouble judging what emotion they are showing. That is just what happened

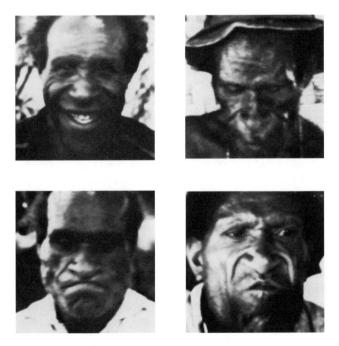

Figure 16.2   Emotion poses by New Guineans

except, once again, that fear and surprise were not distinguishable one from another (Ekman, 1972).

Challenge 5: Unwittingly Biasing the New Guinea Subjects

Although our New Guinea study was considered crucial evidence for universality by many social scientists who commented on our work, Russell criticized this work. He (Russell, 1995, p. 381) tried to dilute the extent of agreement we found by combining our study with a study conducted by Sorenson (1975) who, as I mentioned, did not use our procedures and was a cinematographer when he did that work, not a trained social scientist. But Russell's major attack on our New Guinea study was his claim that we had influenced our subjects to give the responses we wanted. Although we described in our published reports the many steps we took to ensure that neither our translators nor we acted in a way which could have suggested to the New Guineans which photograph was the "correct" choice for each photograph, Russell credited reports by Sorenson, who was present only in our first year study before we developed our procedures to guard against influencing our subjects. Sorenson was not present to see how we did the study reported above.

No matter how many precautions you take, it is impossible to prove that something might not have happened that you were unaware of and which could have biased your results. Fortunately, another study, conducted by a team which was trying to prove us wrong, provides the decisive answer to any such doubts about our work. For if an investigator's attitudes and expectations could influence the findings, then this team should have found results opposite to our own.

6. Evidence from a Second Preliterate, Visually Isolated Culture

Karl Heider, an anthropologist, and Eleanor Rosch, a psychologist, thought we were wrong about universals. The Dani people of West Irian, whom Heider had studied for many years, do not have words for all six emotions we had studied. When Heider heard about our findings in Papua New Guinea, he visited me to learn how to conduct our experiment so that he could go back to West Irian, use our methods and prove us wrong. Their results, with a people more isolated than those I had studied, were nearly identical to our findings (reported in Ekman, 1972).

Challenge 6: Only Posed Expressions Are Universal

Another challenge to the findings of universality came from the anthropologist Margaret Mead (1975). She pointed out that all of our evidence was on posed, not spontaneous, facial expression. Establishing that posed expressions are universal, she said, does not necessarily mean that spontaneous expressions are universal. I replied (Ekman, 1977) that it seemed illogical to presume that people can readily interpret posed facial expressions if they had not seen those facial expressions and experienced them in actual social life. Once again, the best answer to a challenge is not just logical argument, but to have findings that directly meet that challenge.

7. Evidence from Observers Judgments of Spontaneous Facial Behavior

We studied the spontaneous facial expressions shown by Japanese and American college students. We selected Japan as the comparison culture because of the popular notion of their inscrutability. We hoped to show that this was due to display rules about masking negative affect in the presence of an authority. Students in Tokyo and in California watched a neutral travelogue and stress-inducing films (of surgery, accidents, etc.) while a hidden camera recorded their facial expressions. Two studies were done of these materials. In the first, the videotapes were shown to people in the USA and Japan who were asked to guess whether the people they saw had been watching the stressful or the neutral film. In the second study, the actual facial expressions shown by the Japanese and American students when they had been watching the stressful and travelogue films were measured.

The first study of spontaneous facial expressions strongly supported universals. The judgments made by the Japanese and Americans who saw the videotapes of the spontaneous facial expressions were highly correlated. It didn't matter whether a Japanese or an American was judging someone from their own or another culture, they made virtually the same judgments. If the Japanese observers were correct in judging whether a Japanese student was watching a stressful or non-stressful film, so were the Americans. And so it was when Americans were judged by Americans and Japanese. We repeated this study a second time, with a new set of students in Japan and in California watching the stressful and non-stressful films, and a new group of observers in Japan and in California judging their spontaneous facial expressions. The results were the same. Neither the culture of the observer nor the culture of the person showing the facial expressions mattered in the accurate judgment of whether facial expressions had occurred during the stressful or neutral film. Facial expressions shown by Americans must have had the same meaning to Japanese observers as they had to American observers, and the same was true for the interpretation of the facial expressions of the Japanese subjects. This is very strong evidence, and it is evidence not on the judgment of still photographs of posed behavior, but on the judgment of videotapes showing spontaneous facial expressions.

Challenge 7: Agreement about Judgments Does Not Prove Identical Expressions

This criticism was not made by someone else, but is a problem we recognized when we did the study. Our results do not rule out the possibility that all the

Japanese showed disgust when they saw a surgical film, and the Americans all showed sadness. Remember that the observers were not asked what emotion they saw, but only when that expression was shown, during the stress or neutral film. Our results could have been found as long as both Japanese and Americans observers decided that the Americans' sadness occurred during the stressful, not the neutral, film, and the Japanese disgust similarly occurred during the stressful, not the neutral, film. To rule this out—to show that the same facial expressions were shown—a very different type of study had to be done in which the actual facial expressions themselves were measured, not what observers judged them to be.

8. Evidence from Measuring the Spontaneous Facial Behavior of Subjects in Two Cultures

This is the first study which does not rely upon observers' judgments of emotions, but instead measured the actual facial movements to see if they are the same or different in two cultures. The videotapes were measured by persons who did not know which film was being seen when the facial expressions occurred. A very high correlation was found in the particular facial movements shown by the American and Japanese students. Virtually the same repertoire of facial movements occurred at the same points in time. Later in the same experiment, a scientist dressed in a white coat entered the room and sat with the subject while he watched a stress film. We expected that now what we (Ekman & Friesen, 1969) had termed *display rules* for managing facial expressions in the presence of an authority figure would be operative, more so in Japan than in the USA. The Japanese did indeed show more positive emotions (masking the negative emotions) than the Americans, and less negative emotions.

Thus, this study showed that when spontaneous, not posed, facial expressions were studied, once again evidence of universals was obtained. Japanese and Americans interpreted the spontaneous behavior in the same way, regardless of whether they were judging the expressions of a Japanese or an American. When the students were alone, the facial expressions in response to the stress film were the same for the Japanese and the Americans. In the presence of another person, the Japanese subjects masked negative emotions with positive expressions more than did the Americans.

Challenge 8: Flaws in the Design and Contradictions in the Evidence

Fridlund (1994) has critized just the study (Section 8) in which we measured the facial expressions the students had shown when alone and when with another person. He complained that it was not easy to compare the facial behavior in the alone condition and in the condition in which they watched stress films in the presence of an authority figure, because we used different measurements in each. He is incorrect; we used the same measurement technique in both. Fridlund also objected that we reported only partial face findings in the alone condition, but he must have missed our report, which did also provide findings on the whole face.

Fridlund noted correctly that 20% of our subjects showed no facial activity and wondered why that would be so. Not everybody is expressive, but the key issue is that the same percentage of Japanese and Americans showed no expressions. Fridlund also correctly noted that there was a third condition in which Japanese and Americans showed similar facial behavior. After watching the films alone they were then interviewed by a graduate student (dressed in a white coat to enhance his authority), and then watched the stress films in the presence of that authority figure. The Japanese and Americans showed the same expressions when alone, and when being interviewed, but differed when watching the films in the presence of the authority, with the Japanese showing more positive and less negative expressions. Rather than regarding the similarity when being interviewed as further evidence of universality, Fridlund viewed it as a challenge to our findings of differences in the third condition, when watching the film with the authority figure present. Why did they not show differences in the second condition when being interviewed?, Fridlund asked. The answer is straightforward. The differences occur when negative emotions were being aroused—by a film— and managed, masked by smiling. The interview did not elicit sufficiently strong negative emotion, and was not intended to. It is only when they were viewing the very unpleasant films with the authority figure present, that the differences emerged.

Finally, and considered most important by Fridlund, we can not prove that the Japanese and Americans felt the same emotions when they were alone. He asked why we did not report the data we collected on what the students said after the experiment about how they felt. But these reports should also be influenced by cultural differences. The same display rules which cause the Japanese to mask negative expressions in the presence of an authority figure, would lead them not to report as much negative emotion in questionnaires given to them by that very same authority figure. For that reason we never analyzed those reports. Instead we used a very different strategy. The films we showed to these subjects we already knew had the same emotional impact, from prior research by Richard Lazarus and his colleagues, which found the same physiological response to these films in Japanese and American subjects. We selected these films precisely because of that fact, because we could be certain that they would arouse the same emotions.

9. Evidence from Measuring Spontaneous Facial Behavior in Infants

Camras et al. (1992) measured Japanese and American infants' facial responses to arm restraints with an adaptation of the Facial Action Coding System (Oster

& Rosenstein, 1991). Japanese and American infants displayed the same emotional expressions. There was a cultural difference in the latency of negative emotional expressions, with Americans responding more quickly than Japanese to the arm restraint procedure. This study has not yet been challenged by any of the critics of universality. It is an especially powerful study because it examined young infants, and directly measured facial behavior rather than being a judgment study.

A Concession by a Challenger

Russell, one of the most prominent critics of universals in facial expressions of emotion, recently conceded that the evidence from the judgment studies (Evidence in Sections 1–6; he does not deal with Evidence in Sections 7–9) allows us to rule out the possibility that facial expressions have no relationship to emotion, and are totally different in one culture as compared to another. Russell said: "So, we agree that the amount of universality is greater than 0% and less than 100%" (1995, page 382).

I believe this is the wrong way to think about the matter. I will suggest that the evidence strongly suggests universality on some aspects, and cultural differences on other aspects of facial expressions of emotion. But first, more briefly, let me summarize other relevant evidence.

10.   Other Evidence

Continuity of the Species

If the particular configuration of facial muscle movements that we make for each emotion are the product of our evolution, as Darwin suggested, it is likely that we might find evidence of these expressions in other primates. Evidence that some of our expressions are shared with other primates would therefore be consistent with the proposal that these expressions are shared by all human beings—universal.

Klineberg (1940, Challenge 1) also thought that commonality in expressions between humans and another primate, such as a chimpanzee, was crucial in deciding whether human expressions are universal: "If expression is largely biological and innately determined, we should expect considerable similarity between . . . two closely related species. If on the other hand culture is largely responsible for expression we should expect marked differences . . ." (p. 179). Citing a doctoral dissertation by Foley (1938), which found that humans' judgments of a chimpanzee's expressions were not accurate, Klineberg concluded: "[This research] . . . strengthens the hypothesis of cultural or social determination of the expressions of emotions in man. Emotional expression is analogous to language in that it functions as a means of communication, and that it must be learned, at least in part".

Foley had said the students were inaccurate because they disagreed with what the photographer who took the pictures said the chimp had been feeling. I showed Foley's pictures to a modern primatologist, Chevalier-Skolnikoff, and asked her to interpret the expressions based on the decades of research on chimpanzee expression since Foley's time. When I compared what Foley's college students had said the chimp was feeling with Chevalier-Skolnikoff's interpretations, I found that the students had been right all along (this is reported more fully in Ekman, 1973).

Chevalier-Skolnikoff (1973) and another primatologist, Redican (1982), each reviewed the literature on facial expressions in New and Old World monkeys. Each came to the conclusion that the same facial configurations can be observed in humans and a number of other primates.

Expression and Physiology

If the association between facial expressions and emotions is in some part given, then it is logical to expect that facial expressions should be related to changes in the physiology of emotion. Ekman and Davidson found such evidence examining EEG measures of cerebral brain activity while subjects watched emotionally provocative films. Different patterns of brain activity occurred when disgust or a Duchenne smile (i.e. smiling lips plus the contraction of the muscle orbiting the eye) was spontaneously shown (Davidson, Ekman, Saron, Senulis & Friesen, 1990; Ekman, Davidson & Friesen, 1990). These differences were consistent with previous findings on asymmetries in cerebral activity for negative and positive emotions. In another study they had subjects voluntarily make both a Duchenne smile and a non-Duchenne smile. Only the Duchenne smile generated the pattern of EEG activity previously found in many other studies for positive emotion (Ekman & Davidson, 1993). While Ekman & Davidson's findings are only for one culture, there is no reason to expect that these findings would be any different in any other culture.

In another set of studies, Ekman & Levenson found different patterns of autonomic nervous system (ANS) activity occurring with different facial expressions (Ekman, Levenson & Friesen, 1983; Levenson, Ekman & Friesen, 1990). They replicated their findings in a Moslem, matrilineal society in Western Sumatra (Levenson et al., 1992).

Subjective Experience

If facial expressions are universal signs of emotion, they should be related to the subjective experience of emotion. Until very recently it has been uncertain whether such a relationship was weak or strong. Two new studies have found evidence of a very strong relationship. Ruch (1995), studying German subjects, has shown that within subject designs, with aggregated data, yield quite high correlations between expression and self-report. Rosenberg & Ekman (1994) found that when subjects were provided with a means of retrieving memories for specific emotional experiences at specific points in time, there was a strong relationships between expression and self-report.

Conditioning

Further support for an evolutionary view of facial expressions of emotion comes from a series of studies by Dimberg & Öhman (1996). They did *not* find that different facial expressions are interchangeable, as one might expect if expressions are only arbitrarily linked to emotion. Instead, they found that an angry face is a more effective conditioned stimulus for an aversive unconditioned stimulus than a happy face. Conditioned responses could be established to masked angry but not to masked happy faces.

CONCLUSIONS

Taking account of the evidence, not just the judgment studies (Sections 1–6) but the other evidence (Sections 7–10) as well, I believe it is reasonable to propose that the universal in facial expressions of emotion is the connection between particular facial configurations and specific emotions. That does not mean that expressions will always occur when emotions are experienced, for we are capable of inhibiting our expressions. Nor does it mean that emotions will always occur when a facial expression is shown, for we are capable of fabricating an expression (but note that there is evidence to suggest that the fabrication differs from the spontaneous expression when emotion is occurring; Ekman, 1992). How did this universal connection between expression and emotion become established? In all likelihood it is by natural selection; however, we can not rule out the possibility that some of these expressions are acquired through species-constant learning (Ekman, 1979).

It is not certain how many different expressions are universal for any one emotion. There is some evidence to suggest there is more than one universal expression; both closed and open mouth versions of anger and disgust, and variations in the intensity of muscular contractions for each emotion. It is also not certain exactly how many emotions have a universal facial expression, but it is more than simply the distinction between positive and negative emotional states. The evidence is strongest for happiness, anger, disgust, sadness and fear/surprise. I believe that fear and surprise do have separate distinct expressions, but the evidence for that comes only from literate cultures. In preliterate cultures fear and surprise were distinguished from other emotions but not from each other. There is (Ekman & Friesen, 1986; Ekman & Heider, 1988; Matsumoto, 1992) also evidence that contempt, the emotion in which one feels morally superior to another person, has a universal expression. But this evidence is also only from literate cultures, as this research was done in the 1980s and it was not possible to find any visually isolated preliterate cultures. Keltner (1995), has evidence that there is a universal expression for embarrassment. In my chapter on basic emotions (Chapter 3, this volume) I listed 15 emotions which I believe have either a unique facial expression or a unique vocal expression.

To say that there is a universal connection between expression and emotion does not specify to what aspect of emotion the expression is connected. It may be the message that another person perceives when looking at the face (what has been studied in all the judgment studies), or it may be the feelings the person is experiencing, or the physiological changes which are occurring, or the memories and plans the person is formulating, or the particular social context in which the expression is shown.

Even if we limit ourselves just to the message that another person derives when looking at an expression, that itself is not a simple matter. Most of the judgment studies represented that message in a single word or two (e.g. angry, enraged), but such words are a shorthand, an abstraction that represents all of the other changes which occur during emotional experience. It is just as likely that the information typically derived from facial expressions is about the situational context; so that instead of thinking, "he is angry", the perceiver thinks, "he is about to fight", or "something provoked him". Elsewhere (Ekman, 1993, 1997) I have delineated seven classes of information which may be signaled by an expression.

Culture, social groupings within cultures, and individual differences all produce large differences in facial expressions of emotions. There are differences in the expression itself, and in what the expression signifies to the person showing the expression and to others. I expect the largest difference to be with regards to the words which represent emotions. I expect that languages differ not only in terms of how many words they have for each emotion, but the extent to which they have a word which gives subtle nuances, or combines emotions, or tells us about what caused the emotion or what behavior is most likely to be shown. The Germans have the word *Schadenfreude* for that distinctive enjoyment which comes when one learns about a misfortune which has befallen one's enemy. English speakers have no single word for that feeling, although they feel the emotion. Not having a word for an emotional state, or as many words, may well influence emotional experience. Without being able to name feelings, it is harder to distinguish them, think about them, plan regarding them, etc. Given the likelihood that the words used to refer to emotions are so permeated by culture-specific differences, it is amazing that agreement has been so high in the judgment studies (Evidence 2–6).

There are differences also in display rules, regarding the management of emotional expressions in specific social situations. Izard (1971) reported differences in attitudes about emotions, how positively or negatively the experience of one or another emotion was experienced. Gottman, Katz & Hooven (1996) have defined "meta-emotion philosophy" as one's organized set of feelings and thoughts about one's own and others' emotions. They have shown how individual differences in a parent's meta-emotion philosophy about their child's emotions related to how they parent, the child's regulatory abilities, and various child outcomes in middle childhood. Although the research has yet to be done, I believe it is very likely that, in addition to the individual differences they have observed, there are also social class differences and cultural differences in meta-emotion philosophies.

Cultures differ also in some of the specific events which are likely to call forth an emotion. For example, some of the foods which are prized in one culture may be repulsive in another cultural setting. Of course, such differences in food preferences and aversions are also found within a culture. Notice that, although the specific event varies—the type of food—the general theme—ingesting something repulsive as a cause for disgust, or ingesting something attractive as a cause of enjoyment—is universal. I think this is a good model for all the emotions. The specific event which gets an American angry may be different from what gets a Samoan angry, but the theme will be the same. Anger can be brought forth by something which is provocative, insulting or frustrating, to name just a few of the anger themes, although what each person finds provocative, insulting or frustrating may not be the same across or within cultures.

There are, then, major differences in facial expressions of emotion between cultures, and differences within any culture: in the words for emotions, in what is learned about the events which call forth an emotion, in display rules, in attitudes about emotions and, I expect, in meta-emotion philosophies. All these differences shape our emotional experience. Our evolution gives us universal expressions, which tell others some important information about us, but exactly what an expression tells us is not the same in every culture.

REFERENCES

Birdwhistell, R. (1970). *Kinesics and Context*, Philadelphia, PA: University of Pennsylvania Press.

Boucher, J. D. & Carlson G. E. (1980). Recognition of facial expression in three cultures. *Journal of Cross-cultural Psychology*, **11**, 263–280.

Brown, D. E. (1991). *Human Universals*. Philadelphia, PA: Temple University Press.

Camras, L. A., Oster, H., Campos, J. J., Miyake, K. & Bradshaw, D. (1992). Japanese and American infants' response to arm restraint. *Developmental Psychology*, **28**, 578–583.

Chevalier-Skolnikoff, S. (1973). Facial expression of emotion in non-human primates. In P. Ekman (ed.), *Darwin and Facial Expression*. New York: Academic Press, pp. 11–98.

Dashiell, J. F. (1927). A new method of measuring reactions to facial expression of emotion. *Psychological Bulletin*, **24**, 174–175.

Davidson, R. J., Ekman, P., Saron, C., Senulis, J. & Friesen, W. V. (1990). Emotional expression and brain physiology. I: Approach/withdrawal and cerebral asymmetry. *Journal of Personality and Social Psychology*, **58**, 330–341.

Darwin, C. (1872). *The Expression of the Emotions in Man and Animals*. New York: Philosophical Library. Darwin, C. (1998) 3rd edn with Introduction, Afterword and Commentary by Paul Ekman: London: Harper Collins; New York: Oxford University Press.

Dimberg, U. & Ohman, A. (1996). Behold the wrath: psychophysiological responses to facial stimuli. *Motivation and Emotion*, **20**, 149–182.

Ducci, L., Arcuri, L., Georgis, T. & Sineshaw, T. (1982). Emotion recognition in Ethiopia. *Journal of Cross-cultural Psychology*, **13**, 340–351.

Duchenne, B. (1862). *Mechanisme de la physionomie humaine ou analyse electrophysiologique de l'expression des passions*. Paris: Baillière; Duchenne, B. (1990) *The Mechanism of Human Facial Expression or an Electro-physiological Analysis of the Expression of the Emotions* (trans. A. Cuthbertson). New York: Cambridge University Press.

Ekman, P. (1972). Universals and cultural differences in facial expressions of emotion. In J. Cole (ed.), *Nebraska Symposium on Motivation, 1971*. Lincoln, NE: University of Nebraska Press, pp. 207–283.

Ekman, P. (1973). Cross-cultural studies of facial expression. In P. Ekman (ed.), *Darwin and Facial Expression: A Century of Research in Review*. New York: Academic Press, pp. 169–222.

Ekman, P. (1977). Biological and cultural contributions to body and facial movement. In J. Blacking (ed.), *Anthropology of the Body*. London: Academic Press, pp. 34–84.

Ekman, P. (1979). About brows: emotional and conversational signals. In M. von Cranach, K. Foppa, W. Lepenies & D. Ploog (eds), *Human Ethology*. Cambridge: Cambridge University Press, pp. 169–248.

Ekman, P. (1992). Facial expression of emotion: new findings, new questions. *Psychological Science*, **3**, 34–38.

Ekman, P. (1993). Facial expression of emotion. *American Psychologist*, **48**, 384–392.

Ekman, P. (1994). Strong evidence for universals in facial expressions: a reply to Russell's mistaken critique. *Psychological Bulletin*, **115**, 268–287.

Ekman, P. (1997). Expression or communication about emotion. In N. Segal, G. E. Weisfeld and C. C. Weisfeld (eds), *Genetic, Ethological and Evolutionary Perspectives on Human Development: Essays in Honor of Dr Daniel G. Freedman*. Washington, DC: American Psychiatric Association.

Ekman, P. & Davidson, R. J. (1993). Voluntary smiling changes regional brain activity. *Psychological Science*, **4**, 342–345.

Ekman, P., Davidson, R. J. & Friesen, W. V. (1990). The Duchenne smile: emotional expression and brain physiology II. *Journal of Personality and Social Psychology*, **58**, 342–353.

Ekman, P. & Friesen, W. V. (1969). The repertoire of nonverbal behavior: categories, origins, usage, and coding. *Semiotica*, **1**, 49–98.

Ekman, P. & Friesen, W. V. (1986). A new pan-cultural expression of emotion. *Motivation and Emotion*, **10**, 159–168.

Ekman, P. & Friesen, W. V. (1971). Constants across cultures in the face and emotion. *Journal of Personality and Social Psychology*, **17**, 124–129.

Ekman, P. & Friesen, W. V. (1976). *Pictures of Facial Affect*. Palo Alto, CA: Consulting Psychologists Press.

Ekman, P., Friesen, W. V. & Tomkins, S. S. (1971). Facial affect scoring technique: a first validity study. *Semiotica*, **3**, 37–58.

Ekman, P., Friesen, W. V., O'Sullivan, M., Chan, A., Diacoyanni-Tarlatzis, I., Heider, K., Krause, R., LeCompte, W. A., Pitcairn, T., Ricci-Bitti, P. E., Scherer, K. R., Tomita, M. & Tzavaras, A. (1987). Universals and cultural differences in the judgments of facial expressions of emotion. *Journal of Personality and Social Psychology*, **53**, 712–717.

Ekman, P. & Heider, K. G. (1988). The universality of contempt expression: a replication. *Motivation and Emotion*, **12**, 303–308.

Ekman, P., Levenson, R. W. & Friesen, W. V. (1983). Autonomic nervous system activity distinguishes between emotions. *Science*, **221**, 1208–1210.

Ekman, P., Sorenson, E. R. & Friesen, W. V. (1969). Pan-cultural elements in facial displays of emotions. *Science*, **164**(3875), 86–88.

Foley, J. P. Jr (1938). Judgments of facial expression of emotion in the champanzee. *Journal of Social Psychology*, **6**, 31–54.

Fridlund, A. (1994). *Human Facial Expression: An Evolutionary View*. San Diego, CA: Academic Press.

Gottman, J. M., Katz, L. F. & Hooven, C. (1996).   Parental meta-emotion philosophy and the emotional life of families: theoretical models and preliminary data. *Journal of Family Psychology*, **10**, 243–268.

Izard, C. (1971).   *The Face of Emotion*. New York: Appleton-Century-Crofts.

Keltner, D. (1995).   Signs of appeasement: evidence for the distinct displays of embarrassment, amusement, and shame. *Journal of Personality and Social Psychology*, **68**, 441–454.

Klineberg, O. (1940).   *Social Psychology*. New York: Holt.

Levenson, R. W., Ekman, P. & Friesen, W. V. (1990).   Voluntary facial action generates emotion-specific autonomic nervous system activity. *Psychophysiology*, **27**, 363–384.

Levenson, R. W., Ekman, P., Heider, K. & Friesen, W. V. (1992).   Emotion and autonomic nervous system activity in the Minangkabau of West Sumatra. *Journal of Personality and Social Psychology*, **62**, 972–988.

Matsumoto, D. R. (1992).   More evidence for the universality of a contempt expression. *Motivation and Emotion*, **16**, 363–368.

McAndrew, F. T. A Cross-cultural study of recognition thresholds for facial expression of emotion. *Journal of Cross-cultural Psychology*, **17**, 211–224.

Mead, M. (1975).   Review of *Darwin and Facial Expression*. *Journal of Communication*, **25**, 209–213.

Niit, T. & Valsiner, J. (1991).   Recognition of facial expressions: an experimental investigation of Ekman's model. *Acta et Commentationes Universitatis Tarvensis*, **429**, 85–107.

Oster, H. & Rosenstein, D. (1991).   Baby FACS: analyzing facial movement in infants. Unpublished manuscript.

Rosenberg, E. L. & Ekman, P. (1994).   Coherence between expressive and experiential systems in emotion. *Cognition and Emotion*, **8**, 201–229.

Redican, W. K. (1982).   An evolutionary perspective on human facial displays. In P. Ekman (ed.), *Emotion in the Human Face*, 2nd edn. Elmsford, New York: Pergamon, pp. 212–280.

Ruch, W. (1995).   Will the real relationship between facial expression and affective experience please stand up: the case of exhilaration. *Cognition and Emotion*, **9**, 33–58.

Russell, J. A. (1994).   Is there universal recognition of emotion from facial expression? A review of cross-cultural studies. *Psychological Bulletin*, **115**, 102–141.

Russell, J. A. (1995).   Facial expressions of emotion: what lies beyond minimal universality? *Psychological Bulletin*, **118**, 379–391.

Russell, J. A., Suzuki, N. & Ishida, N. (1993).   Canadian, Greek, and Japanese freely produced emotion labels for facial expression. *Motivation and Emotion*, **17**, 337–351.

Sorenson, E. R. (1975).   Culture and the expression of emotion. In T. R. Williams (ed.), *Psychological Anthropology*. Chicago, IL: Aldine, pp. 361–372.

Tomkins, S. S. (1962).   *Affect, Imagery, Consciousness, Vol 1. The Positive Affects*. New York: Springer.

Chapter 17

Distinguishing Unconscious from Conscious Emotional Processes: Methodological Considerations and Theoretical Implications

Arne Öhman
Karolinska Institute, Stockholm, Sweden

The distinction between the unconscious and the conscious being of the mental state. . . . is the sovereign means for believing what one likes in psychology, and of turning what might become a science into a tumbling-ground for whimsies (James, 1890/1950, p. 163).

UNCONSCIOUS PROCESSES: DEVELOPMENT OF THE CONCEPT

The Point of Departure: James and the Psychological Common Sense

For William James and his contemporaries, conscious thought was not simply the outflow of hidden psychological mechanisms, but the primary object of study for a science of psychology. Admitting the existence of unconscious mental states, therefore, threatened to strip psychology of its basic claim for legitimacy as a science, the data base. No wonder, therefore, that there was widespread skepticism to the notion of unconscious mental processes.

James's emphasis on conscious psychological activity is consistent with psy-

Handbook of Cognition and Emotion. Edited by T. Dalgleish and M. Power.

chological common sense, which has proven remarkably resistant to the influence of 100 years of psychoanalytic thought. In our daily life, we take for granted that people are transparent, at least to themselves, that they know what they are doing and the reason for doing so. If you need to know why someone does something, you need only ask and, most often, the answer can be trusted.

This chapter, however, focuses on the other side, what is missing in straight answers to the simple question "Why?", on unconscious psychological mechanisms and their role in emotion. "Unconscious psychological processes" has been an uncomfortable notion for laymen and professionals alike, and it has had a controversial history in psychology (as well as in a much broader cultural context). My treatment of the topic is restricted to academic psychology, and particularly to experimental psychology, because I shall review some of the hard evidence that has been generated during 100 years of scientific study of the unconscious. Therefore, the chapter starts with a brief historical outline of research into the nature of unconscious psychological processes.

A primary difficulty of my task is conceptual in nature. To discuss unconscious psychological processes, it is necessary to provide at least a tentative delineation of "unconscious", which hardly can be done without some notion of the opposite mental state, consciousness. Furthermore, because I am concerned with the subset of unconscious processes related to emotion, I have to interact with another conceptually difficult term, "emotion", which typically is taken to denote processes occurring in the focus of consciousness. These conceptual problems are addressed in two sections of the chapter. Then fear is discussed with emphasis on unconscious processes in its activation, and recent data are reviewed. The chapter ends with a discussion of the contribution of research on unconscious emotional processes to the theoretical understanding of emotion.

The Freudian Revolution

Against the background provided by the turn-of-the-century introspectionist psychology, Breuer & Freud's (1893/1955) conclusion that hysteria resulted from unconscious affective memories bordered on the heretic. Freud (1894/1962) pursued the analysis further by making it explicit that mental phenomena associated with strong affect could be pushed out of consciousness by an active process of defense:

> (The) ego was faced with an experience, an idea or a feeling which aroused such a distressing affect that the subject decided to forget about it because he had no confidence in his power to resolve the contradiction between the incompatible idea and his ego by means of thought-activity (p. 47).

In the present context, it is interesting to note that from the very beginning, Freud viewed unconscious mental mechanisms as intimately connected to emotion. In fact, emotion ruled the unconscious through instinctual impulses which could influence both mental and somatic conditions (as revealed for example by hysteric symptoms). In subsequent developments of his position, Freud elaborated the contrast between the conscious and the unconscious. Instead of the rational, temporally organized, reality-orientated secondary process thinking that characterized consciousness, the primary process of the unconscious was irrational, timeless and governed by the pleasure principle (see Power & Brewin, 1991, for a readable account of Freud's theory of the unconscious).

The threat to academic introspectionist psychology provided by the Freudian unconscious was primarily warded off by ignoring it. This was easily done because it originated in a completely different tradition of thought focused on clinical phenomena and hypnosis (see Perry & Laurence, 1984). However, only a decade or two later, the basic tenet of the introspectionist psychology of content was challenged from within by the results of the Würzburg school, demonstrating "image-less thoughts", i.e. "obscure, intangible, unanalyzable, indescribable (mental) contents that are neither sensation nor ideas" (Boring, 1950, p. 403). Soon the center-stage of psychology was to be moved to the USA and the functional spirit of psychology at this new continent was about to turn into behaviorism.

The Behaviorist Take-over

The main deliverer of data for the behaviorist revolution, Ivan Pavlov (1927), called the relation between the conscious and the unconscious, "one of the darkest sides of our subjective self" (p. 410), but still felt that it could be elucidated by some of his results from studies of conditioned reflexes. His Soviet followers accepted the usefulness of the conditioning methodology for studies of unconscious and conscious mechanisms and pursued experimental analyses of the "observable unconscious" and the "inferable conscious" through studies of interoceptive and semantic conditioning, respectively (Razran, 1961).

In the victorious movement of American behaviorism, the distinction between conscious and unconscious psychological processes lost its appeal, at least to a large part of the community of academic psychologists. With Skinner (1954/1972), Freud's discovery was given an interpretation that provided a radical break with the psychological common sense:

> "the Freudian distinction between the conscious and unconscious mind . . . has been widely misunderstood . . . Freud's argument that we need not be aware of important causes of conduct leads naturally to the broader conclusion that awareness of cause has nothing to do with causal effectiveness" (p. 247).

In Skinner's version, therefore, the invention of the unconscious reflected Freud's inability to free himself from traditional mentalist psychology, and this failure prevented him from realizing the real revolutionary potential of his observations. Thus, by postulating the unconscious, Freud could retain the more central idea firmly embedded within the world-view of his time, the mentalist theory of consciousness (Lang, 1978).

The New Look and the Dismissal of the Psychodynamics of Perception

By the middle of the century, Skinner's view had reached broad acceptance in mainstream American psychology. With the emergence of the "New Look" in perception (Bruner & Goodman, 1947), however, doors were opened for a constructivist view of perception which included motivational factors among its determinants. This stimulated studies of unconscious influences on perception, such as perceptual defense, i.e. the active blockage of threatening information from reaching consciousness (e.g. McGinnies, 1949). However, increased latency to indentify conflict-laden stimuli could more parsimoniously be intepreted as the effect of response bias, an unwillingness to utter the taboo words that often were critical components of the stimulus display (Howes & Solomon, 1950). To overcome some of the methodological problems plaguing earlier studies, Lazarus & McCleary (1951) developed a conditioning paradigm to demonstrate emotional responses to consciously non-recognized words, a phenomenon they called "subception". They conditioned skin conductance responses (SCRs) to a subset of nonsense syllables by pairing them with an annoying electric shock. In a subsequent test session, shocked and non-shocked syllables were tachisto-scopically exposed at durations varying from clearly below to clearly above the threshold for recognition. Assessing SCRs only from trials where the subjects failed to verbally recognize the stimulus, they nevertheless reported larger responses to shock-associated than to non-shock-associated syllables. This was taken as evidence of unconscious discrimination of emotionally relevant stimuli that the subjects were unable to discriminate consciously.

With a fervor that would have pleased William James, Eriksen (e.g. 1960) took on the task of dismissing the alleged evidence of unconscious perceptual mechanisms generated in the "New Look" tradition. For example, in an incisive analysis he argued that subception should be attributed more properly to psychometric necessities than to unconscious perception. Given the reasonable assumption that SCRs and verbal reports are imperfectly intercorrelated and only partly valid indicators of a common perceptual process, randomly determined dissociations between the two measures are inevitable. As a consequence, partial correlations will occur to the effect that, for instance, SCRs may distinguish between shock- and non-shock-associated words with verbal reports held constant (i.e. trials on which the subjects failed to recognize the stimuli) even without differential sensitivity of the two measures to the stimuli used. In several experiments from his own laboratory, Eriksen (1960) confirmed the subception effect reported by Lazarus & McCleary (1951), but in no case did he report that presumably emotionally relevant measures, such as the SCR, were more sensitive than verbal reports in responding to "marginally perceptible stimuli" (to use the term suggested by Greenwald, Klinger & Schuh, 1994). Eriksen's (1960) experimental work and intriguing analyses of the literature laid the idea of unconscious perceptual mechanisms to rest for more than a decade. He also inspired related work in the context of human classical conditioning that did away with the claims of unconscious emotional conditioning (e.g. Lacey & Smith, 1954) to reach the unanimous conclusion that awareness of the stimulus contingency is a necessary condition for classical conditioning to occur (e.g. Dawson, 1973; Dawson & Biferno, 1973; see Öhman, 1983, for a review).

The Cognitive Unconscious: Respectable and Probably Necessary

In the mid-1970s, Erdelyi (1974) realized that the information-processing models that were invading experimental psychology invariably involved assumptions of unconscious processing stages. This conclusion was reaffirmed both by observers centrally located in the psychodynamic tradition (Dixon, 1981; Shevrin & Dickman, 1980) and in textbooks in mainstream cognitive psychology:

> Most of what we do goes on unconsciously. It is the exception, not the rule, when thinking is conscious; but by its very nature, conscious thought seems the only sort. It is not the only sort; it is the minority (Lachman, Lachman & Butterfield, 1979, p. 207).

The theoretically argued points were supplemented by several bodies of data. One of them was firmly embedded in the psychodynamic tradition. Silverman & Weinberger (1985) reviewed a series of studies indicating that the activation of symbiotic fantasies by unconscious stimulation ("Mommy and I are one") had beneficial effects on many measures for different groups of normal and clinical subjects (see also Weinberger, 1992).

However, data supporting an important role for unconscious processes were presented also within the mainstream of experimental psychology. Since James (1890/1950), the concept of consciousness has been intertwined with the concept of attention. In the mid-1970s, research on attention introduced a distinction between automatic and conscious (Posner, 1978) or automatic and controlled (Shiffrin & Schneider, 1977) information processing. This distinction made use of a concept of "limited cognitive resources". This concept was developed to account for the fact that the selectivity of attention is better described in terms of a flexible and strategic distribution of limited processing resources across stimuli and tasks, than in terms of structural bottlenecks letting through only one of the potential inputs (Kahneman, 1973). Automatic processing was defined as resource independent, whereas controlled processing was defined as heavily dependent on resources (Schneider, Dumais & Shiffrin, 1984). This implies that tasks handled by automatic processes can be carried out concurrently without mutual interference; the performance in consciously controlled tasks, on the other hand, is severely degraded by forced time-sharing with other similarly

Table 17.1 Characteristics of automatic and controlled information processing

Characteristic	Automatic processing	Controlled processing
Cognitive resources	Independent	Heavily dependent
Intentional control	Incomplete	Complete
Attention	Not required, may be called	Required
Effort	Little if any	Much
Serial–parallel dependence	Parallel	Serial
Awareness	Little, if any	High
Indivisibility	Wholistic	Fragmentized
Storage in long-term memory	Little, if any	Large amounts
Performance level	High	Low, except for simple tasks
Practice	Gradual improvement	Little effect
Modification	Difficult	Easy

(adapted from Schneider, Dumais & Schiffrin, 1984)

controlled tasks. Table 17.1 summarizes some of the characteristics that differentiate automatic from controlled processes. It is evident that awareness of automatic processes is low and that it is high for controlled processes. Thus, these processes provide a coherent distinction between attentional control systems which appears related to unconscious and conscious mental processes. However, it has later been questioned whether these different characteristics provide a consistent differentiation between two separate systems (see the discussion by Bargh, 1989).

Memory processes are obviously related to conscious mental activity. For example, James's (1890/1950) version of short-term memory, primary memory, was defined as the phenomenological present in the sense that its content had never left consciousness. Similarly, the modern concept of working memory (Baddeley, 1992) is obviously related to conscious processes (e.g. Kihlstrom, 1987; LeDoux, 1996). In the early 1980s, the concept of "implicit memory" was introduced to describe instances of unconscious memory, that is, performance evidence of memory that subjects could not attribute to a consciously recalled learning episode (Graf & Schacter, 1985). For example, subjects shown a list of words were primed by this exposure in a subsequent word stem completion task even if they failed to remember the words in a recognition test. Furthermore, brain damage subjects with severe amnesia performed quite normally in this type of implicit memory task, whereas their explicit recognition performance was very poor (Warrington & Weiscrantz, 1974; see Schacter, 1987, for an early review of research on implicit memory).

Interest in mechanisms related to unconscious psychological processes also became evident in another main area of psychology, social psychology. Zajonc (1980) argued that we automatically assess stimuli in terms of whether we like them or not, whereas to determine what we think about them is a slower, erratic and deliberate process. To use his own phrase, "preference precedes inference".

Part of the empirical backing for this assertion came from new studies of the mere exposure effect (Zajonc, 1968). Kunst-Wilson & Zajonc (1980) first exposed subjects to very briefly presented (1 ms) visual stimuli (irregular geometric shapes), and then presented these stimuli in pairs with similar distractor stimuli, requiring the subjects to indicate which one they liked and recognized best. Even though recognition was at chance level, the subjects systematically preferred previously exposed stimuli to non-exposed distractors, thus demonstrating that mere exposure effects did not require conscious mediation. Other investigators reported that unconsciously presented trait information affected person impression (Bargh & Pietromonaco, 1982; Lewicki, 1986), and, indeed, that such effects could be mediated by complex but unconscious rule learning (Lewicki, 1986).

Unconsciously mediated psychological phenomena could also be demonstrated in a neuropsychological context. Prosopagnosia, an inability to recognize people from their visual appearance, may result from damage to visual association cortices (Damasio, Tranel & Damasio, 1990). In two independent case studies, it was demonstrated that prosopagnosics appeared to recognize familiar faces in terms of enhanced SCRs (compared to those shown to unfamiliar faces), even though they failed completely verbally to identify the persons (Bauer, 1984; Tranel & Damasio, 1985). Thus, the patients showed evidence of unconscious recognition that could not be accessed consciously. Conceptually similar findings were reported by Öhman (1986) from conditioning experiments with human subjects, conditioned to facial stimuli paired with electric shock. When previously conditioned angry faces were presented masked by neutral faces, which blocked their conscious recognition (see Esteves & Öhman, 1993), they nevertheless elicited conditioned SCRs.

By the mid-1980s, therefore, there was converging evidence of psychological systems that operate outside of awareness, even though the terms "conscious" and "unconscious" were seldom used explicitly. Marcel (1983), however, used these terms to characterize data on unconscious priming in lexical decision and the Stroop color-word interference tasks, and in presenting an ambitious theory giving unconscious processing a central role in perception. Some of these different bodies of evidence of unconscious mental mechanisms were communicated to the broader scientific community by the influential paper on "The cognitive unconscious" in *Science* by Kihlstrom (1987). Although this research primarily concerned "cold cognition" in the context of cognitive science, it nevertheless has profound implications for the psychology of emotion by demonstrating that conscious cognition results from the interaction of many unconscious processing systems (LeDoux, 1996).

However, even though the existence of unconscious effects was widely accepted, the question was still open concerning their importance. To use Loftus & Klinger's (1992) catchy phrase, how smart or dumb is the unconscious? How complicated a system is it, and can it handle complex information? How flexibly can it deal with novel situations? And does it do what is best for us? Greenwald (1992) reviewed the available evidence to address these questions. He concluded that there is substantial evidence for unconscious cognition but that its performance appears unimpressive: it can handle the semantics of single words but not of sentences.

THE BORDERLINE BETWEEN CONSCIOUS AND UNCONSCIOUS PSYCHOLOGICAL PROCESSES

An Objective Criterion of Consciousness

The data notwithstanding, there were still skeptics around following up on Eriksen's (1960) critical lead with regard to how the results should be interpreted. Holender (1986) published an extensive critical review of studies purporting to demonstrate semantic processing of consciously non-recognized stimuli. Examining evidence from several lines of study, he concluded that "none of these studies has included the requisite controls to ensure that semantic activation was not accompanied by conscious identification of the stimulus at the time of presentation" (p. 1). By default, then, if no unconscious effects had been demonstrated, he appeared to suggest that *all* reported effects must be consciously mediated. Such a conclusion appears consistent with the psychological common sense alluded to in the opening of this chapter, but for the skeptical scientist it is harder to digest. Taken at face value, claiming that all perceptual processes are consciously accessible appears at least as problematic as admitting that some of them are unconscious.

Several authors, including Eriksen (1960), have felt that there is a problem here, but it was most clearly articulated by Bowers (1984). Not surprisingly, it has to do with the definition of conscious awareness in the context of threshold intensity stimulation. A majority of authors, and in particular the most influential critics, Eriksen (1960) and Holender (1986), have subscribed to an *objectively* defined line of demarcation between the conscious and unconscious domains, operationalized in terms of discriminative behavior. Typically, subjects have been exposed to forced-choice identification tasks in which they are required to determine whether a stimulus is present or absent, or which stimulus out of a small set of known stimuli is presented. Subjects who correctly identify stimuli at an above-chance level on such a task are then, by definition, regarded as consciously aware of the stimuli. Because the statistical power of the procedure to discover above-chance performance increases substantially with the number of trials on which mean performance is based, this factor influences conscious accessibility according to this criterion.

Unconscious processing is demonstrated if stimuli that yield chance level identification performance in this task (given a sufficient number of trials) can be shown to affect reliably another psychological measure, which then reveals the unconscious effect. In other words, with our targeting on emotional processes, a demonstration of unconscious effects requires a *dissociation* between the perceptual and the emotional impact of a stimulus. For example, Öhman & Soares

(1994) showed that subjects were unable to distinguish between different visual stimuli followed by a masking stimulus in a forced choice discrimination task. However, enhanced SCRs were specifically observed to masked pictures of feared objects, suggesting that emotional activation did not require full perceptual analysis of the stimulus.

As pointed out by Bowers (1984), there is a serious risk with the objective definition of consciousness: it may come to include any evidence of discriminative behavior in relation to a stimulus as consciously mediated, and then, by definition, unconscious effects become logically excluded. This problem is compounded by the fact that perceptual measures typically are neither *exhaustive* nor *exclusive* measures of consciously mediated effects (Merikle & Reingold, 1992; Reingold & Merikle, 1988).

The exhaustiveness requirement involves that a particular measure of consciousness is sensitive to *all* types of conscious effects. This is often questionable. For example, in the experiment by Öhman & Soares (1994), the effectively masked stimuli had effects not only on the SCR but also on emotional ratings of the stimuli. Thus, even though they did not explicitly recognize the stimuli, the subjects somehow had conscious access to some aspect of them as revealed by their ratings. Because it is hard to be sure that the exhaustiveness criterion is met, one can not exclude that a presumed unconscious effect actually was consciously mediated by a process that was not captured in the measure of perceptual sensitivity.

The exclusiveness requirement states that the perceptual measure should be sensitive *only* to consciously mediated effects. As pointed out by Merikle & Reingold (1992) and by Jacoby, Yonellinas & Jennings (1997), it is more likely that a particular measure is affected by both conscious and unconscious processes than by conscious processes alone. If this is true, and investigators adjust their stimulus to yield no evidence of discrimination, then *both* consciously *and* unconsciously mediated effects are excluded, and therefore no unconscious effects can be observed (Merikle, 1992). Thus, by requiring that consciousness be defined in terms of objective evidence of discriminatory behavior, the odds become seriously biased in the direction of logically excluding observations of unconscious effects. "The solution to the dilemma may be to revise our criteria for the use of epistemic words such as *know, see,* or *understand*" (Kahneman & Treisman, 1984, p. 56).

The Phenomenology of Consciousness

Bowers (1984) proposed a distinction between perceiving and noticing, where noticing refers to the introspective awareness of perceiving. Thus, stimuli may be perceived without being registered in consciousness. Selective attention is a critical component in the transformation of a perception into something noticed. Perceiving is sufficient to influence behavior, for example, verbal reports in a forced-choice recognition paradigm, but in the absence of attention this influence remains inaccessible to consciousness. In Lundh's (1979) words, "introspective reports do not tell us about what the subject perceives, but only about what the subject is introspectively aware of having perceived. The criterion of what is perceived is not introspective, but behavior in a wider sense" (pp. 228–29). Note that instrospective awareness here is seen as retrospective, that it reflects integration over a time span ("aware of having perceived"). Examining the effect of thalamic stimulation in humans, Libet et al., (1991) concluded that, "Conscious sensory awareness can lag behind the real world by as much as 0.5 s" (p. 1754). This is consistent (except for the specific time window suggested) with Gray's (1995) hypothesis that consciousness has a monitoring rather than a guiding function in relation to mental activity and behavior. According to this hypothesis, consciousness lags behind events as they actually occur to compare the unfolding state of the perceptual world with that predicted on the basis of memorial information.

The distinction between perceiving and noticing is dramatized in "blindsight": patients with damage to visual cortices may respond quite accurately to visual events in the blind field even though they claim that they see nothing at all (Weiskrantz, 1986). Thus, it appears difficult to talk meaningfully about consciousness without implying some type of phenomenological experience on part of the observer.

Attention is necessary but perhaps not sufficient in this context, as implied in James's (1890/1950) statement that, "my experience is what I agree to attend to" (p. 402). In addition to "attend to", this statement involves an "I" and an "agree", implying a deliberately experiencing and intentional (Jacoby, Yonellinas & Jennings, 1997) self. Consistent with this analysis, Kihlstrom, Barnhardt & Tataryn (1992) argued that conscious experience of events necessarily involves the person, which they interpret to mean that representations of events, "fact nodes", contact the representation of oneself, "the self-node", in working memory (cf. Kihlstrom & Cantor, 1984).

To illustrate the necessity of the phenomenological level for talking meaningfully about consciousness, Bowers (1984) invoked the contrasting approaches of a hard-nosed experimental psychologist and an optometrist in deciding the eyesight of a person in need of glasses. Certainly, above-chance forced-choice discrimination between Os and Ws or Qs and Ds would provide evidence that the potential lens-bearer would be able to discriminate much smaller letters on the eye chart than revealed when the optometrist merely asks what the subject *sees*. Nevertheless, the phenomenologically based criterion is much more appropriate for the patient's need: lenses that make the world seeable rather than discriminable.

From the perspective of the distinction between perceiving and noticing, therefore, the critiques leveled by Eriksen (1960) and Holender (1986) miss the point. By identifying consciousness with differential behavior they make unconscious processing a logical impossibility or force the adoption of a threshold that necessarily excludes all unconscious effects. Furthermore, it misses the critical (albeit problematic) aspect of consciousness, its phenomenological quality.

A Subjective Criterion of Consciousness

To avoid these dilemmas, one has to accept a subjective definition of consciousness.

> The rough and ready criterion for . . . consciousness is that a person be able to *identify* specific features from an indeterminately large set of them (Bowers, 1984, p. 235).

Thus, above chance forced-choice performance is not a sufficient criterion of awareness but must be supplemented by, for instance, some measure of the subjects' confidence in their decisions. It has long been known that subjects may perform well above chance in discrimination-type tasks, yet subjectively feel that their performance is random (Pierce & Jastrow, 1884, as reviewed by Kihlstrom, Barnhardt & Tataryn, 1992). Eriksen (1960) dismissed confidence as a viable operationalization of awareness on the ground that measures of this type "place upon the individual subject the responsibility for establishing the criterion of awareness" (p. 293). Leaving the decision of what is conscious to the subject rather than retaining it for the experimenter to decide, is, of course, an inevitable consequence of accepting that what is conscious has to a include a phenomenological quality.

> Adopting such a criterion may complicate the researcher's life somewhat, but so be it; the alternative of garroting conceptual subtlety with method-ease, has, in the case of subliminal perception, obscured more than it has revealed (Bowers, 1984, p. 235).

Cheesman & Merikle (1984) assessed subjective thresholds by exposing subjects to a forced-choice identification procedure and requiring them to rate their level of performance after each block of trials. They found this subjective threshold to be above the objective threshold in terms of discriminatory behavior. Furthermore, they demonstrated that the effect of unconscious priming on subsequent decisions, reported by Marcel (1983), could be replicated when the threshold was subjectively defined, but not when an objective threshold was used. Cheesman & Merikle (1984, 1986) have argued that the subjectively defined threshold captures the intuitive phenomenological quality of consciousness advocated by Bowers (1984) and that, therefore, this is a satisfactory way of delineating conscious from unconscious perceptual processing. Furthermore, under the assumption that the studies reporting unconscious priming effects (Balota, 1983; Fowler et al., 1981; Marcel, 1983; McCauley et al., 1980) inadvertently measured subjective rather than objective thresholds, this is a proposition that brings some order to the otherwise inconsistent literature. Thus, Holender's (1986) conclusion that convincing demonstrations of unconscious processing remain to be performed is correct if consciousness is defined as objectively established discriminative behavior. However, if the subjective definition of consciousness is used, then the data quite consistently indicate that, for example, unconscious priming is an empirically valid phenomenon (Cheesman & Merikle, 1986).

As a consequence of adopting a subjective threshold, the distinction between unconscious and conscious processing comes more in line with the contrast proposed between automatic and strategic processing (Neely, 1977; Posner & Schneider, 1975). This distinction typically operates with a temporal line of demarcation between the two processes (300–500 ms) that is of sufficient duration to generate clearly above-chance performance in forced-choice identification tasks.

Convergent Operations: The Strong View of the Unconscious

The advantages of the subjective definition of consciousness notwithstanding, some of the problems with this approach that Eriksen (1960) pointed out remain unsolved in our discussion so far. Because the definition of the threshold is left to the subject, it can not be independently validated. For example, it can not be distinguished from response bias (Cheesman & Merikle, 1986). To address this problem, Cheesman & Merikle (1986) advocated a construct validity approach aimed at establishing qualitative differences between conscious and unconscious processing of a stimulus in terms of the effects of other independent variables (see Shevrin & Dickman, 1980, for a related point). If such qualitative differences could be demonstrated, then Eriksen's (1960) psychometrically based critique of dissociations between measures as a means of inferring unconscious effects could also be dealt with. For if the dissociation merely resulted from imperfect correlations between less than valid measures, then one would not expect an independent variable to have differential effects dependent on whether or not subjects passed the criterion of being conscious.

To test their idea, Cheesman & Merikle (1986) used the Stroop color-word interference paradigm, in which priming color-words (e.g. GREEN, YELLOW) were either congruent or incongruent with subsequently presented target color patches to which the subjects produced choice reaction times. The critical variables in the experiment were supra- or sub-(subjective)-threshold presentation of the color words, and the proportion of congruent word-color patch trials. The hypothesis was that subjects would be able consciously to use the probability of congruent trials to inform their performance, which would result in faster responses on congruent trials and slower on incongruent trials, the higher the probability. This consciously controlled strategy, however, would not operate on masked trials, which only could engage unconscious processes. These predictions were confirmed in two independent experiments.

In subsequent experiments, Merikle & Reingold (1992) used a two-step procedure in which the subjects first had to decide whether a word was presented or not in a particular interval. In the second step, in two different experiments, they then had to guess which of two words, or whether a word or a non-word, had been presented. With correct detections that a word (or a sequence of letters) had been presented, subjects performed at an above-chance level in correctly identifying both words and non-words. However, when they had missed that a word was presented in the first step (i.e. were unconscious about the word), they nevertheless were able to identify the stimulus at an above-chance level in the second step, but only if it was a real word. If it was a non-word, performance was at chance, which was attributed to prior memorial representations for words but not for non-words. Again, then, different principles appeared to organize conscious and unconscious perception when the threshold was subjectively defined, thus providing construct validity for this operational demarcation between conscious and non-conscious processes.

This discussion underlines that there is no rough-and-ready method available to delineate unconscious from conscious processes. Alternative approaches include relaxing the exclusiveness assumption by using comparable direct and indirect indices of perceptual processes (Reingold & Merikle, 1988), regression analytic techniques (Greenwald et al., 1994) or directly pitting conscious against unconscious processes (Jacoby et al., 1992). For example, Jacoby and coworkers (Jacoby et al., 1992; Jacoby, Yonellinas & Jennings, 1997) have presented a process- rather than a measure-based approach to the definition of unconscious and conscious processing in the context of memory. Thus, assuming that all measures are influenced by both conscious and unconscious processes, they have developed methods to assess directly the contribution of each process on, for example, recognition performance. Furthermore, they have provided consistent support for the hypothesis that conscious and non-conscious processes are independent from each other (Jacoby, Yonellinas & Jennings, 1997).

Varieties of Unconscious Effects: Failures of Attention and Failures of Memory

There are two principally different routes to unconscious psychological effects: attention and memory. One avenue examines stimuli that are, one way or the other, presented outside the subject's current focus of attention. Attention may be impeded or rendered impossible by the use of "subliminal" or "marginally perceptible" (Greenwald, Klinger & Schuh, 1994) stimuli, that is, stimuli that the subject will be unable to notice (cf. Bowers, 1984). Alternatively, stimuli may be presented at a clearly supraliminal intensity, but outside of a focus of attention that is tied up by some other task. Subjects may have to divide their attention across several stimulus channels (e.g. Jacoby, Yonellinas & Jennings, 1997), and critical word stimuli may be presented to one ear (the unattended ear) while subjects are busy shadowing (repeating aloud) other words presented to the other (attended) ear. For example, Corteen & Wood (1972) and Dawson & Schell (1982) reported that previously conditioned SCRs to city names could be elicited when the critical words were embedded among words presented in the non-attended ear during shadowing. Thus, regardless of the specific method used, the investigator hopes that the critical stimuli will fail to be noticed in consciousness, yet affect other psychological processes, e.g. of an emotional nature.

Another way that a person can be unconscious about an event is through failure of recall. Thus, the event may have been carefully attended to when first encountered, yet fail to be accessible for explicit memory at a later time. For example, the event may be related to an emotional episode, thus evoking an emotional response even though failing to be noticed when encountered at a later occasion. A potentially important distinction here concerns the nature of the forgetting process. As was clear in the quotation in the beginning of this chapter, the Freudian notion of repressed memories implies an active process in which an emotionally disturbing memory is actively warded off from consciousness. This requires that, at some level of unconscious mental activity, the event is re-cognized as threatening, and that active processes then are recruited for its repression. The implicit assumption, that the unconscious can deal with very complex events and actively control conscious access, has often been doubted. A simpler possibility that still may cover many instances of what looks like repression is to merely assume a passive process of forgetting: recall or recogni-tion fails, yet the event still has power to elicit, say, autonomic responses (e.g. Parra et al., 1997).

The discussion of the definition of unconscious effects in this section was mainly directed at the first type of unconscious effects, events that are unat-tended. Nevertheless, similar arguments are valid also with regard to the second type of unconscious effects, for example, when it comes to distinguishing between implicit and explicit memories (e.g. Jacoby, Yonellinas & Jennings, 1997).

CONCEPTUALIZING EMOTION

Emotion as Feeling and Unconscious Emotional Processes

For the layman, emotion is identified with *feeling*. Thus, it is inextricably linked to a subjectively defined consciousness, as previously described. As a subjective entity, feeling is in the focus of attention, and it involves the self. Many investiga-tors regard feeling as a necessary condition for emotion, particularly when it is linked to appraisal of something as good or bad (Clore, Schwartz & Conway, 1994). Explaining emotion as feeling has been viewed as the central task for the psychology of emotion since the pioneering theoretical propositions by James (1884). If the emphasis on feeling is accepted, then "unconscious emotion" be-comes logically impossible because it provides a contradiction in terms (Clore, 1994). However, by distinguishing between emotions and emotional processes, one can argue that emotion, as feeling, may result from processes (e.g. percep-tions or appraisals) that remain inaccessible to consciousness, i.e. are unconscious (Clore, 1994). For example, a particular feeling could result from the unconscious appraisal of a stimulus as emotionally significant, or from the implicit memory of an emotional event. From this perspective, unconscious emotional processes would be viable objects of scientific inquiry, even though the final product that would legitimate the modifier "emotional" in front of "processes" would be a conscious feeling.

However, denoting the elucidation of feelings as the central task for the psychology of emotion is not a preferred option by all investigators in the field. For example, Lang (1978) has argued that emotion is better viewed as a complex response with many observationally accessible components than as an exclusively felt inner state. LeDoux (1996) suggested that the focus on conscious content that goes with the emphasis of emotions as feelings has actually impeded progress in the scientific understanding of emotion. The lesson to be transferred from cognitive to affective science, according to him, is that the change of focus from conscious content to unconscious information processing mechanisms (e.g. Neisser, 1967) paved the way for new and more successful approaches to consciousness in cognitive science (e.g. Cohen & Schooler, 1997; Marcel & Bisiach, 1988). Similarly, LeDoux (1996) argued, emotion psychologists should free themselves from the constraints imposed by conscious feelings and try to delineate the emotional processes that we share with other members of the animal kingdom. In his view, emotional feelings result when such processes are activated in a brain capable of consciousness.

Components of Emotion

Even the most ardent phenomenologist would have to admit that the feeling denoting emotional experience has objective correlates, such as psychophysiological responses, expressive gestures and overt motor actions. For example, when in fear, a person is likely to exhibit increased heart rate, to show specific facial grimaces, and to try hard to get away from the situation. However, this set of facts can be interpreted in different ways.

In the more popular version, it is interpreted as providing means of operationalizing the emotion in order to allow its scientific study. Thus, the feeling, in this view, is isomorphic with a hypothetical inner state constituting the "real emotion" (e.g. Izard, 1991). Emotional ratings, psychophysiological responses, expressive gestures and overt behaviors then provide alternative operational routes to studying this state. In an alternative version, however, the different components would simply be seen as parallel, and easily dissociable, outflows from a centrally organized emotional response (Lang, 1978). For example, fear seems to be organized by a neural network centered on the amygdala, and providing efferent outflows to midbrain and brain stem regions controlling different aspects of the manifest fear response (e.g. Davis, 1992; 1996).

This system is assumed to be similar for most mammals, even though in humans, its activation would be represented in a brain system controlling consciousness (LeDoux, 1996). Because in this latter view, the observable fear responses (verbal reports of fear, psychophysiological activation, fear grimaces and avoidance behavior) would not be understood as alternative indicators of the felt state, dissociation between measures may be expected depending on circumstances. For example, if the fear is elicited by an escapable stimulus, such as a small animal, autonomic recruitment including cardiovascular activation and facilitation of defensive reflexes, such as startle, is observed (Hamm et al., 1997; Globisch et al., in press). However, if the fear object is a mutilated human body, it will not support flight but rather promote immobility and low cardiovascular activity, perhaps to minimize bleeding. Then heart rate decelerates but the fear network will still maintain elevated startle reactivity (Hamm et al., 1997).

From the perspective of a component view of emotion, which denies a special status to emotional feelings, unconscious emotion simply denotes a particular type of dissociation of emotional response system. For example, it could involve a situation with physiological and behavioral response activation in the absence of explicit emotional feelings. This could occur, for example, when an emotional stimulus is presented outside of the person's focus of attention or below the threshold for recognition (e.g. Öhman & Soares, 1994). Inferring unconscious emotion in this context is logically similar to inferring unconscious semantic activation from evidence of priming in the absence of recognition of the prime (Marcel, 1983). In both cases, a psychological state influencing, for example, response readinesses, is activated by a consciously inaccessible stimulus. However, theorists giving feeling a priviliged status in defining emotion would argue that the dissociation between emotional feeling and physiological responses would not reflect true emotion but rather, for example, unconscious emotional processing.

Contrasting Approaches to the Psychology of Emotion

If emotion is identified with conscious experience, then a primary task for research on emotion is to delineate the domain of emotional experience. We have an impressively rich vocabulary to talk about this domain, and typically attempts toward its formal delineation have used this "emotional lexicon" as their point of departure. The emotional terms that constitute this lexicon "refer to internal mental states that are focused on affect (where affect simply refers to the perceived goodness or badness of something)" (Clore, Schwartz & Conway, 1994, p. 325). To account for such states, Ortony, Clore & Collins (1988) developed a cognitive theory of emotion in which events, actions or objects can be appraised in terms of three concerns: goals, standards and attitudes. Thus, the consequences of events can be pleasing or displeasing and, depending on further evaluations, will result in emotions such as hope, fear, relief, happiness or sadness. Actions are evaluated in relation to standards, and will be approved or disapproved, eventually giving emotions such as pride, admiration, anger or gratitude. Objects, finally, are liked or disliked, with the evaluations leading to emotions such as love or hate. The model of Ortony, Clore & Collins (1988) provides a good example of an approach to emotion which explicitly and successfully aims to account for the whole variety of experienced emotions in humans.

However, contrasting approaches are available. If the requirement of feeling as a necessary condition of emotion is loosened, it is clear that emotions are commonplace among mammals. A pet owner surely distinguishes between emotional states in his/her darling creature. Indeed, an emotion such as fear is remarkably similar in its expression across mammalian species, and thus must have been resilient to evolutionary change. From the perspective provided by biological evolution, emotions can be understood in relation to a functional agenda set by the ecological demands imposed by the environment in which species evolved. Thus, emotions are embedded in tasks our forefathers had to solve in order to deliver genes to the next generation (Tooby & Cosmides, 1990). Recurrent adaptive demands, such as finding food and shelter, asserting oneself and finding protection among conspecifics, escaping dangers such as predation, finding sexual partners and producing children, caring for children, and so on, are all activities that are structured by emotion. An important function of emotion is to provide for flexibility in problem solving by defining emotional endstates that are worth striving for or avoiding by whatever means are at hand. Emotions make us want to do what our forefathers had to do in order to survive and deliver genes to the next generation. Thus, ecological pressures during evolution have shaped emotion systems in animals, including humans, to prepare them to deal with problems encountered in their life. From this perspective, different emotion systems have different evolutionary histories and are better viewed as independent than as parts of a general domain of emotion. In other words, rather than expecting a generalized mechanism of emotion the output of which accounts, for example, for happiness, anger, sadness, fear and disgust, one should expect to find different mechanisms behind different emotions.

An Evolutionary Perspective on the Fear Response

Because many emotional systems have their roots far back in mammalian evolution, their origin is with primitive organisms with much less neocortex than humans, and without any linguistic capability. Thus, they had functioned unconsciously for millions of years before they eventually came to exist in brains into which evolution gradually inserted capacities for language and conscious experience. In the evolutionary perspective, emotions may be viewed as independent modules that most often operate unconsciously, but which, in the human brain can be accessed by the brain systems responsible for consciousness (LeDoux, 1996).

To take fear as a prototypical example (Öhman, 1986; Öhman, Dimberg & Öst, 1985), its evolution can be understood in relation to three different behavior systems (Mayr, 1974): non-communicative fears (fears of non-living things), and two forms of communicative fears, interspecific fear (fear of other animals) and intraspecific fear (fear of other humans). Fear is modified depending on these behavioral system contexts, but it has a common core in an aversive behavior system which prompts physiological activation to support avoidance and escape

(LeDoux, 1996). This is an evolutionarily ancient system, whose roots when it comes to interspecific fear may originate in the need of early mammals to avoid reptile predators (Öhman, 1986). Hence, reptiles and reptile-like creatures still serve as the prototype of fear-inducing beasts.

It is likely that cues suggesting predators, hostile conspecifics and natural disasters have been evolutionarily preprogrammed to become easily associated with fear and defense (Öhman, Dimberg & Öst, 1985; Seligman, 1971). Thus, predator characteristics can be easily conditioned to activate the fear system (see Öhman, 1993b), as can characteristics such as eye-brows, which determine a hostile facial expression (Dimberg & Öhman, 1996).

Predators strike hard and fast, and therefore time has always been a primary consideration for the fear system. The faster it can be activated the better the odds of escaping the predator. Therefore, the system must be connected to perceptual mechanisms that automatically scan the environment for potential threat, particularly when suspicions that a predator may be present are warranted (Fanselow, 1994; Russell, 1979). When cues signal that predators are close, the fear system is instantaneously activated. Indeed, the eliciting stimulus does not have to be fully analyzed. Rather, it can be activated on the basis of only a rough, subcortical analysis which, via a monosynaptic link from the thalamus to the amygdala, provides information that is sufficient to start activating the fear response (LeDoux, 1987; 1990; 1996). Thus, when information about the fully analyzed stimulus reaches the amygdala via the temporal cortex, it serves to confirm (or disconfirm) the activation that is already set in motion by the subcortical route. Because "false negatives", i.e. failure of responding to an, in effect, dangerous stimulus, is evolutionarily more costly than "false positives", i.e. responding to an, in effect, non-harmful stimulus, this system is biased to make mistakes in the directions of responding rather than refraining from re-sponding (LeDoux, 1990; Mineka, 1992).

Because of the time constraints involved in predator–prey encounters, the rapid, automatic activation of the fear system has been resistant to evolu-tionary change and has been kept in the gene pool for virtually all mammals, including humans. Thus, the fact that humans have evolved brain systems for conscious access to perceptual and emotional information has not changed the operating characteristics of the fear system (LeDoux, 1996). This is because conscious mental activity is slow, and therefore conscious deliberation before defensive action is likely to leave the genes of the potential prey unrepresented in the next generation. Thus, even though the fear system can be accessed by consciousness, it operates independently of consciousness, and in this sense it is a prototypical unconscious emotional system. Indeed, if one follows Gray's (1995; Gray, this volume) line of thought, a general task of consciousness is to check retrospectively on the operation of a host of unconscious information-processing systems that manage the on-line interaction between persons and their environments.

The independence of the fear system from consciousness explains why rational thought has little influence on strong fears. A hallmark of "pathological fears", such as phobias, is that they are irrational and uncontrollable by volition (e.g. Marks, 1969). Thus, the fear system may be fully activated even though the person consciously realizes that the eliciting stimulus is an innocuous spider, hardly worth bothering about as a real threat. When spider phobics report that they think spiders are more dangerous than do normal controls (Thorpe & Salkovskis, 1995), this should be understood as an afterthought, that to make sense of their fear they have to think of the phobic stimulus as in effect dangerous.

EMPIRICAL FINDINGS

Unconscious Activation of the Fear System

The neurophysiology of the fear system has been well characterized at both the animal level (Davis, 1992, 1996; Fanselow, 1994; LeDoux, 1996) and the human level (Damasio, 1994; Lang, Bradley & Cuthbert, 1997; Öhman, Flykt & Lundqvist, in press). When a strong fear stimulus is presented to fearful subjects, they show a distinct psychophysiological response of sympathetic origin with large SCRs, heart rate accelerations, and blood pressure increases concomitantly with a facilitated startle reflex (e.g. Hamm et al., 1997; Globisch et al, in press), and increased activity in the corrugator muscle that controls the eye-brows (e.g. Dimberg & Öhman, 1996). This response pattern contrasts clearly with the response pattern shown to pleasant stimuli, which typically includes heart rate deceleration, inhibition of the startle and increased activity in the zygomaticus major muscle (which pulls the corners of the mouth upwards) rather than in the corrugator (e.g. Dimberg & Öhman, 1996; Hamm et al., 1997; Globisch et al., in press; Lang, Bradley & Cuthberg, 1997). These responses are controlled by efferent outflow from the amygdala, which activates sympathetic responses through nuclei in the lateral hypothalamus, achieves startle modulation via the reticular nucleus of the pons, and controls facial muscles through the facial motor nerve (Davis, 1992).

On the afferent side, activating the fear response does not require that the stimulus is consciously accessed. Öhman & Soares (1994) recruited subjects highly fearful of snakes but not of spiders, or vice versa, and also a control group of non-fearful subjects, from a large group of students. A forced-choice discrimination task was used to ascertain that the subjects were not able to recognize pictures of snakes, spiders, flowers and mushrooms when they were shown for 30 ms and immediately followed by a 100 ms masking stimulus. Nevertheless, with masked stimulus presentations, the snake-fearful subjects showed elevated SCRs specifically to snakes, and spider-fearful subjects to spiders, whereas the non-fearful subjects did not differentiate between the stimuli. Thus, even though the subjects were unable consciously to discriminate the stimuli, they showed enhanced sympathetic responding specifically to their feared stimulus.

Similar results were reported from conditioning experiments by Öhman &

Soares (1993). They conditioned subjects to pictures by pairing them with a mild electric shock to the fingers. After conditioning, masked presentation of the pictures revealed that subjects conditioned to snakes or spiders, but not those conditioned to flowers or mushrooms, showed reliable conditioned SCRs to stimuli that were below the recognition threshold. Similar data were reported by Soares & Öhman (1993a; b). Esteves, Dimberg & Öhman (1994) conditioned subjects to pictures of angry or happy faces and reported that conditioned SCRs survived backward masking, provided that the conditioned stimulus was an angry face. Similar data were reported by Parra et al. (1997). Thus, it appears that human SCRs conditioned to evolutionary fear-relevant stimuli are resistant to backward masking, whereas SCRs conditioned to neutral or pleasant stimuli (mushrooms, flowers, happy faces) are not.

LeDoux and co-workers (1984) found that conditioned emotional responses to auditory stimuli in the rat did not require an intact auditory cortex, but were disrupted by lesions in lower relay stations of the auditory pathway, such as the medial thalamus or the inferior colliculus. Similarly, Öhman & Soares (1998) reported that conditioned SCRs in humans could be acquired to masked presentations of snakes and spiders but not to masked presentations of flowers and mushrooms. Esteves et al. (1994) examined conditioning to masked faces and found reliable evidence of response acquisition to angry but not to happy faces. Thus, again, the masking procedure did not preclude acquisition of a conditioned fear response provided that the conditioned stimuli had some degree of evolutionarily determined fear relevance (snakes, spiders, angry faces). In other words, fear could be conditioned to such stimuli independently of their conscious recognition. Interestingly, however, Öhman & Soares (1998) found that subjects were able to develop differentiation between masked spiders and snakes in shock expectancy ratings during conditioning training, even though there was no evidence that they could consciously recognize the stimuli. This was taken to indicate that feedback from the conditioned fear response became available to the conscious system and could be used to govern expectancy ratings in the absence of conscious recognition of the stimuli. In accordance with LeDoux's theorizing, therefore, aspects of the unconscious fear response could be accessed by consciousness.

The unconscious processing of evolutionarily fear-relevant stimuli that has been documented in this series of studies (for further reviews, see, e.g. Öhman, 1996) supports the functional–evolutionary perspective on the fear response. Because of the need instantaneously to activate the response once a significant fear stimulus is located, consciousness is short-circuited, and the response is set in motion before the person knows which stimulus he/she is responding to. However, the evolutionary analysis suggests that fear-relevant stimuli should not only result in automatic elicitation of fear once the stimulus is located, but also that there should be perceptual systems for automatic and immediate location of fear stimuli. This question was addressed by Öhman, Flykt & Esteves (submitted). They had subjects search for stimuli of a deviant category among many instances of stimuli from the same category. For example, some stimulus displays contained a target snake stimulus among background stimuli of flowers, whereas others showed mushrooms against background spiders. In agreement with the evolutionary hypothesis, they reported that normal subjects were consistently faster to find deviant snakes and spiders among flowers and mushrooms, than vice versa. This bias for finding threatening stimuli was further enhanced in fearful subjects. Thus, snake-fearful subjects were faster to find snakes than spiders, and spider-fearful subjects were especially fast in finding spiders, irrespectively of the number of background stimuli. This finding suggests that there are perceptual systems that unconsciously direct attention toward biologically significant objects and events in the surrounding. What we attend to, therefore, is at least partly determined by the evolutionary history of the species we belong to.

Generalized Bias to Attend to Threat in Anxiety

The unconscious bias to attend to threat seen in animal fearful subjects has its counterpart in a generalized attentional bias for threatening stimuli in anxious subjects (for reviews, see, Dalgleish & Watts, 1990; MacLeod, this volume; Mathews, 1990; Mogg & Bradley, this volume; Williams, Mathews & MacLeod, 1996). For example, MacLeod, Mathews & Tata (1986) showed anxious and non-anxious subjects pairs of words on a computer screen, one of which was threatening (e.g. "disaster", "cancer") whereas the other was neutral (e.g. "monastery", "common"). One of these words was replaced by a dot to which the subject was instructed to produce a fast key-press. Anxiety patients pressed the key consistently faster when the dot replaced the threatening word than when it replaced the neutral word, indicating that they selectively attended to threat. Normals, however, tended to show a bias away from threat, that is, they were faster when the dot replaced the neutral word.

This bias for attending to threat appears to have an unconscious origin. MacLeod & Rutherford (1992) used the Stroop paradigm to study interference by word content in the color-naming of words in subjects high or low in trait anxiety. On half of the trials, the words were masked by letter fragments of the same color as the word. Nevertheless, anxious subjects showed slower reaction times in color-naming masked threatening words than did normal subjects, particularly when state anxiety was elevated because of examination stress. However, when the words were non-masked, and the subjects were in the high stress condition, both high and low state anxiety subjects tended selectively to avoid threat words related to examination (e.g. "failure"), that is, they were faster in color-naming examination-relevant words than neutral ones.

These results have been replicated by Bradley, Mogg and co-workers in studies on generalized anxiety disorder patients. Similar to MacLeod & Rutherford (1992) they used a modified Stroop interference task with half the trials masked and the other half non-masked, with stringent criteria for non-awareness on masked trials. Again high-anxiety participants showed a preconscious bias for negative words (Bradley et al., 1995; Mogg et al., 1993). However, in contrast to the avoidance of threat words on non-masked trials reported by MacLeod & Rutherford (1992), with anxiety patients as subjects there was a bias for attending to threat, not only on masked but also on non-masked trials. Essentially similar results were reported with a masked version of the MacLeod, Mathews & Tata (1986) dot probe paradigm by Mogg, Bradley & Williams (1995).

These studies all concur in demonstrating enhanced unconscious or automatic sensitivity for threat in high-anxiety subjects. Thus, the unconscious activation of the fear system appears not restricted to pictorial fear stimuli but may also result from the more indirect threat conveyed by word stimuli. When the stimulus presentation condition allowed conscious perception of the stimuli, however, anxiety patients continued to show a bias for threat (Bradley et al., 1995; Mogg et al., 1993; Mogg, Bradley & Williams, 1995), whereas students with high trait anxiety under examination stress showed specific avoidance of examination-related threat words (MacLeod & Rutherford, 1992). Even though highly anxious, these students managed a highly demanding medical training, and thus they appeared able adaptively to cope with the threat by strategic avoidance once it was allowed to enter awareness. This strategy may not be available to the less well-adjusted anxiety patients. The opposite biases toward and away from threat at the unconscious and conscious level is similar to psychodynamic defenses in combining unconscious activation of anxiety with defensive denial of the stimulus to become consciously represented. Indeed, subjects reporting low anxiety coupled with high social desirability have been regarded as "repressors" precisely because they systematically avoid and prefer non-threatening interpretation of information implying some degree of threat (see review by Derakshan & Eysenck, 1997).

THEORETICAL RELEVANCE OF UNCONSCIOUS ACTIVATION OF EMOTION

Unconscious Elicitation of Emotion in the Natural Environment

In the natural environment, it is probably on rare occasions that the fear system is triggered by stimuli of which the person remains unaware. An important point with the arrangement is that the stimulus which automatically activates fear also ends up in the center of voluntary attention, that is, for humans, in consciousness. In most instances, therefore, the automatic and conscious components of emotion are inextricably intertwined, and it is only by special methods such as backward masking that they can be teased apart. Even though the phobic may not stay around long enough to discover that the "snake" actually was a rope left in the grass by her kids, she will nevertheless have a conscious, albeit misinterpreted, perception of the object that she is escaping. However, in some situations, such as social interactions, rapidly passing stimuli in the form of individual facial gestures may not be consciously appraised, yet elicit emotional responses related to fear such as submissiveness and uncertainty. Socially anxious persons may consciously construe situations as involving social threat, but they may not be able to specify exactly what it is they are responding to. In such instances, therefore, unconscious stimulation may be important for the emotional outcome.

From Emotional Activation to Cognition

However, even though the fear stimulus typically ends up in the center of consciousness, the actual sequence of events is different from that presumed in everyday psychology. Fear is fast, and the response may be well on its way when the fear-evoking stimulus is eventually registered in consciousness. Thus, rather than the common sense sequence with fear activation following conscious processing of the stimulus, conscious processing will take place against a background of rising activation in the fear system triggered by the stimulus. In LeDoux's (1996) words: "the feeling of being afraid results when we become consciously aware that an emotion system in the brain, like the defense system, is active" (p. 268). This echoes James's (1884) famous assertion that we know that we are terrified by the bear because we are running away from him. It also underscores an important point made by Bargh (1992): the crucial question is not so much being aware of the stimulus as being aware of its effects. We must recognize that the fear is due to the bear rather than just recognizing that the bear, as a stimulus, is there. This implies that we sometimes may be unaware of the emotional effects of a clearly perceptible stimulus. For example, anxiety may be misattributed to worries raised by the topic of conversation, rather than to gestures of dominance conveyed by the fearsome authority figure who is part of the company.

In general, it appears that theorists giving bodily feedback an important role as input to emotional activation (e.g. Damasio, 1994; James, 1884; Mandler, 1975; Schachter & Singer, 1962) must assume that the bodily response is elicited before and more or less independently of the subsequent cognitive meaning analysis that it influences. Some, like Schachter & Singer (1962), merely specify that the psychophysiological arousal must be "unexplained", in order to prompt a search for explanation in the surroundings. Others, like Mandler (1975), are somewhat more specific in suggesting that the autonomic activation that triggers the cognitive meaning analysis resulting in emotion is due to the disruption of plans for action (see also Oatley & Johnson-Laird, 1987, reviewed below), violated expectancies or incongruities in the stimulus input. Damasio (1994) views emotion as resulting from "somatic markers" residing in a subcortical system centered on the amygdala, which assist the frontal lobe in evaluating the situation and taking decisions about various courses of action. Through learned association, the subcortical circuit may be activated by any stimulus, and when activated it may control the person's behavior toward this stimulus without having explicitly to reveal its influence to consciousness.

The Independence of Emotional Activation and Cognition

LeDoux (1996) distinguishes between natural triggers and learned triggers of emotional systems in the brain, such as the fear system. Natural triggers can be thought of as sign stimuli which have been selected by evolution to activate fear because they represent a recurrent threat to survival in the ecology of a particular species. Learned triggers, on the other hand, have acquired their power to activate the fear system through Pavlovian conditioning; that is, by being present when the system is activated by a natural trigger, they acquire potency to trigger the system by themselves. A central point in LeDoux's (1996) argument is that the fear system can be activated independently of consciousness, and new stimuli can become learned triggers of the system without any conscious representation of the learning episode. This is because the fear system is independent of the conscious memory system centered on the hippocampus that records episodes for later conscious retrieval. Because of this dissociation between implicit emotional memories capable of activating the fear system, and explicit memory of the emotional situation, persons may become emotionally aroused by situational cues without any conscious recollection of the reason for the arousal, similar to the results seen in the masking studies (e.g. Öhman, 1996). This is likely to happen with some frequency because forgetting is more common in the explicit memory system than in the fear-conditioning system controlling the fear response. When this happens, persons find themselves in a state of unexplained arousal, prompting need for explanation according to the theory suggested by Schachter & Singer (1962). In the perspective of LeDoux's (1996) theory, therefore, activation of emotional brain circuits may often occur unconsciously, leaving the person to consciously sort out what is going on.

Role of Attribution in Fear

Unconscious activation of emotion gives attribution an important role in the cognitive appraisal of the situation. Once the fear response is on its way, fear activation becomes consciously represented, and an explanation for the arousal has to be found. If a phobic stimulus is present, this is uncomplicated: the fear is due to the snake or to stimuli reminding one of snakes. Similarly, in the flashbacks of post-traumatic stress disorder, the fear and anxiety can be attributed to memories of the traumatic situation. However, in panic disorder the situation is different, because the triggering stimulus for a panic attack may be inconspicuous, or consist of, for example, an only unconsciously perceived sudden increase in heart rate. In other words, rather than an identifiable source of danger in the external world, the person has to deal with an enemy from within (Öhman,

1993a). Then the field is free for cognitive interpretation in order to understand what is going on. One possibility is that the fear response is attributed to the lack of a route to safety, thus laying the foundation for agoraphobia (Mathews, Gelder & Johnston, 1981). Another possibility is that a vicious circle is entered with panic provoking more panic (Clark, 1997). Because of the need for an explanation of the fear response, the person is open to cognitive influences. For example, the risk for panic may be curtailed by information about the likely course of events (Rapee, Mattick & Murrell, 1986) or by providing (illusory) assertions that the fear response can be controlled (Sanderson, Rapee & Barlow, 1989).

Thus, if emotions are assumed to result from the (unconscious) activation of ancient but functional neural networks in the brain, then an important task for the conscious cognitive system is to work out plausible explanations for the emotional activation. Thus, rather than being an important factor in the shaping of emotion, as assumed by most cognitively-orientated theorists of emotion (e.g. Ortony, Clore & Collins, 1988; Scherer, 1988; Smith & Ellsworth, 1985), from the present perspective, conscious cognitive mechanisms enter late in the sequence of events, with the primary aim of finding some order in and evaluating what is going on. Therefore, self-reports may be a misleading route to the understanding of emotion (cf. Nisbett & Wilson, 1977; LeDoux, 1987).

The Broader Emotional Context: The Theory of Oatley & Johnson-Laird

This discussion has been concentrated on one particular emotion, that of fear. The advantage with this limitation is that we have a good grasp of what we are talking about. Fear is well defined at the phenomenological, behavioral and neural level. This means, for example, that the often elusive discussion of the relationship between cognition and emotion can be anchored in neural systems subserving fear and conscious cognition (LeDoux, 1996), rather than being framed in terms of theoretical constructs with less precise meaning. At the same time, however, it means that the discussion is restricted to the quite limited context of one specific emotion, even though, to some extent, what we have learned about fear may generalize to other emotions. To broaden the relevance of the analysis, theoretical notions have to be developed that allow other emotional systems to be considered. In particular, a function has to be given to emotions that transcend the particulars of specifically evolved adaptations, such as the fear system.

Oatley & Johnson-Laird (1987) have developed a theoretical approach which views basic emotions as a means to disrupt cognitive processing in order to promote basic biosocial goals. Thus, for them, emotions are internal signals that set cognitive processing modules into specific modes, invoking "a limited suite of goals, action possibilities, and skills" (Oatley & Johnson-Laird, 1987, p. 37).

An important function of emotion, according to this theory, is to assist in the coordination of multiple plans and goals under the constraints of limited time and other resources. Thus, emotions are "part of the biological solution to the problem of how to plan and to carry out action aimed at satisfying multiple goals in environments which are not perfectly predictable" (Oatley & Johnson-Laird, 1987, p. 35). Basic emotions (happiness, sadness, anxiety, anger and disgust) are elicited at junctures between plans, prompting continuation or reorientation of sequences of plans. They are related to basic biological needs and they do not depend on conscious appraisal for their elicitation. In other words, they are sometimes elicited after merely an automatic, unconscious analysis of the situation.

To start with fear (or anxiety, as Oatley & Johnson-Laird prefer to call it), this is an emotion which is elicited when self-preservation goals are threatened during the pursuit of actions directed at other goals. For example, the slammed door announcing the appearance of an angry and potentially violent rival on the romantic scene exchanges the lovers' happiness ("continue with plan, modifying as necessary") with fear ("stop, attend vigilantly to environment and/or escape"). Alternatively, had the interference occurred at an earlier and less vulnerable stage of courting, and by a less fearsome rival, it would have frustrated the plan of seduction, and resulted in anger ("try harder and/or aggress"). Finally, had the whole enterprise failed because of an early rejection of the romantic approach, the emotional outcome would have been sadness ("do nothing, search for new plan") (all quotes from Oatley & Johnson-Laird, 1987, Table 1, p. 36).

The theory of Oatley & Johnson-Laird (1987) puts basic emotions into a coherent cognitive science frame of reference, while still retaining a biological perspective which is close to the one advocated in this chapter. In this sense, it provides a vehicle for dealing with a broader assortment of emotional phenomena than that restricted to fear. However, by invoking a generalized role for diverse emotion ("disrupt/change plans") it becomes removed from the evolutionary and neurological bedrock on which analyses of fear can be rested (LeDoux, 1996; Öhman, Dimberg & Öst, 1985). The more general appeal at the psychological level, therefore, has to be paid for by less specificity at the biological level.

ACKNOWLEDGMENTS

Preparation of this chapter was facilitated by grants from the Swedish Council for Research in the Humanities and Social Sciences and the Bank of Sweden Tercentennial Foundation.

REFERENCES

Baddeley, A. (1992). Working memory. *Science*, **255**, 556–559.
Balota, D. A. (1983). Automatic semantic activation and episodic memory encoding. *Journal of Verbal Learning and Verbal Behavior*, **22**, 88–104.

Bargh, J. A. (1989).   Conditional automaticity: varieties of automatic influence in social perception and cognition. In J. S. Uleman & J. A. Bargh (eds), *Unintended Thought*. New York: Guilford, pp. 3–51.

Bargh, J. A. (1992).   Does subliminality matter to social psychology? Awareness of the stimulus versus awareness of its influence. In R. F. Bornstein & T. S. Pittman (eds), *Perception Without Awareness: Cognitive, Clinical, and Social Perspectives*. New York: Guilford, pp. 236–258.

Bargh, J. A. & Pietromonaco, P. (1982).   Automatic information processing and social perception: the influence of trait information presented outside of conscious awareness on impression formation. *Journal of Personality and Social Psychology*, **43**, 437–449.

Bauer, R. M. (1984).   Automatic recognition of names and faces in prosopagnosia: a neuropsychological application of the Guilty Knowledge Test. *Neuropsychologia*, **22**, 457–469.

Boring, E. G. (1950).   *A History of Experimental Psychology*, 2nd edn. New York: Appleton-Century-Crofts.

Bowers, K. S. (1984).   On being unconsciously influenced and informed. In K. S. Bowers & D. Meichelbaum (eds), *The Unconscious Reconsidered*. New York: Wiley, pp. 227–272.

Bradley, B. P., Mogg, K., Millar, N. & White, J. (1995).   Selective processing of negative information: effects of clinical anxiety, concurrent depression, and awareness. *Journal of Abnormal Psychology*, **104**, 532–536.

Breuer, J. & Freud, S. (1893/1955).   On the psychical mechanism of hysterical phenomena. In J. Strachey (ed.), *The Standard Edition of the Complete Psychological works of Sigmund Freud*, Vol. 2. London: Hogarth.

Bruner, J. S. & Goodman, C. C. (1947).   Value and need as organizing factors in perception. *Journal of Personality*, **16**, 69–77.

Cheesman, J. & Merikle, P. M. (1984).   Priming with and without awareness. *Perception and Psychophysics*, **36**, 387–395.

Cheesman, J. & Merikle, P. M. (1986).   Distinguishing conscious from unconscious perceptual processes. *Canadian Journal of Psychology*, **40**, 343–367.

Clark, D. M. (1997).   Panic disorder and social phobia. In D. M. Clark & C. G. Fairburn (eds), *Science and Practice of Cognitive Behaviour Therapy*. Oxford: Oxford University Press, pp. 121–153.

Clore, G. L. (1994).   Why emotions are never unconscious. In P. Ekman & R. J. Davidson (eds), *The Nature of Emotion. Fundamental Questions*. New York: Oxford University Press, pp. 285–290.

Clore, G. L., Schwartz, N. & Conway, M. (1994).   Affective causes and consequences of social information processing. In R. S. Wyer & T. Scull (eds), *Handbook of Social Cognition*, 2nd edn. Hillsdale, NJ: Erlbaum, pp. 323–417.

Cohen, J. D. & Schooler, J. W. (eds) (1997).   *Scientific Approaches to Consciousness*. Hillsdale, NJ: Erlbaum.

Corteen, R. S. & Wood, B. (1972).   Autonomic response to shock-associated words in a non-attended message. *Journal of Experimental Psychology*, **94**, 308–313.

Dalgleish, T. & Watts, F. N. (1990).   Biases of attention and memory in disorders of anxiety and depression. *Clinical Psychology Review*, **10**, 589–604.

Damasio, A. R. (1994).   *Descartes' Error: Emotion, Reason, and the Human Brain*. New York: G. Putnam's Sons.

Damasio, A. R., Tranel, D. & Damasio, H. (1990).   Face agnosia and the neural substrates of memory. *Annual Review of Neuroscience*, **13**, 89–109.

Davis, M. (1992).   The role of amygdala in conditioned fear. In J. P. Aggleton (ed.), *The Amygdala: Neurobiological Aspects of Emotion, Memory, and Mental Dysfunction*. New York: Wiley-Liss, pp. 255–306.

Davis, M. (1996).   Fear-potentiated startle in the study of animal and human emotion. In

R. D. Kavanaugh, B. Zimmerberg & S. Fein, (ed.), *Emotion: Interdisciplinary Perspectives*. Hillsdale, NJ: Erlbaum, pp. 61–90.

Dawson, M. E. (1973). Can classical conditioning occur without contingency learning? A review and evaluation of the evidence. *Psychophysiology*, **10**, 82–86.

Dawson, M. E. & Biferno, M. A. (1973). Concurrent measurement of awareness and electrodermal classical conditioning. *Journal of Experimental Psychology*, **101**, 55–62.

Dawson, M. E. & Schell, A. M. (1982). Electrodermal responses to attended and nonattended significant stimuli during dichotic listening. *Journal of Experimental Psychology: Human Perception and Performance*, **8**, 315–324.

Derakshan, N. & Eysenck, M. W. (1997). Return of the repressed. *European Psychologist*, **2**, 235–246.

Dimberg, U. & Öhman, A. (1996). Behold the wrath: psychophysiological responses to facial stimuli. *Motivation and Emotion*, **20**, 149–182.

Dixon, N. F. (1981). *Preconscious Processing*. Chichester: Wiley.

Erdelyi, M. H. (1974). A new look at The New Look: perceptual defense and vigilance. *Psychological Review*, **81**, 1–25.

Eriksen, C. W. (1960). Discrimination and learning without awareness: a methodological survey and evaluation. *Psychological Review*, **67**, 279–300.

Esteves, F., Dimberg, U. & Öhman, A. (1994). Automatically elicited fear: conditioned skin conductance responses to masked facial expressions. *Cognition and Emotion*, **8**, 393–413.

Esteves, F., Parra, C., Dimberg, U. & Öhman, A. (1994). Non-conscious associative learning: Pavlovian conditioning of skin conductance responses to masked fear-relevant facial stimuli. *Psychophysiology*, **31**, 375–385.

Esteves, F. & Öhman, A. (1993). Masking the face: recognition of emotional facial expresssions as a functions of the parameters of backward masking. *Scandinavian Journal of Psychology*, **34**, 1–18.

Fanselow, M. S. (1994). Neural organization of the defensive behavior system responsible for fear. *Psychonomic Bulletin & Review*, **1**, 429–438.

Fowler, C. A., Wolford, G., Slade, R. & Tassinary, L. (1981). Lexical access with and without awareness. *Journal of Experimental Psychology: General*, **110**, 341–362.

Freud, S. (1894/1962). The neuro-psychoses of defense. In J. Strachey (ed.), *The Standard Edition of the Complete Psychological Works of Sigmund Freud*, Vol. 3. London: Hogarth.

Globisch, J., Hamm, A. O., Esteves, F. & Öhman, A. (in press). Fear appears fast: temporal course of startle reflex potentiation in animala fearful subjects. *Psychophysiology*.

Graf, P. & Schacter, D. L. (1985). Implicit and explicit memory for new associations in normal and amnesic subjects. *Journal of Experimental Psychology: Learning, Memory, and Cognition*, **11**, 501–518.

Gray, J. A. (1995). Contents of consciousness: a neuropsychological conjecture. *Behavioral and Brain Sciences*, **18**, 659–676.

Greenwald, A. G. (1992). New Look 3. Unconscious cognition reclaimed. *American Psychologist*, **47**, 766–769.

Greenwald, A. G., Klinger, M. R. & Schuh, E. S. (1994). Activation by marginally perceptibel ("subliminal") stimuli: dissociation of unconscious from conscious cognition. *Journal of Experimental Psychology: General*, **124**, 22–42.

Hamm, A. O., Cuthbert, B. N., Globisch, J. & Vaitl, D. (1997). Fear and the startle reflex: blink modulation and autonomic response patterns in animal and mutilation fearful subjects. *Psychophysiology*, **34**, 97–107.

Holender, D. (1986). Semantic activation without conscious identification in dichotic listening, parafoveal vision, and visual masking: a survey and appraisal. *Behavioral and Brain Sciences*, **9**, 1–66.

Howes, D. H. & Solomon, R. L. (1950). A note on McGinnies' "Emotionality and perceptual defense". *Psychological Review*, **57**, 229–234.

Izard, C. E. (1991). *The Psychology of Emotion*. New York: Plenum.

Jacoby, L. L., Toth, J. P., Lindsay, D. S. & Debner, J. A. (1992). Lectures for the layperson: methods for revealing unconscious processes. In R. F. Bornstein & T. S. Pittman (eds), *Perception without Awareness: Cognitive, Clinical, and Social Perspectives*. New York: Guilford, pp. 81–122.

Jacoby, L. L., Yonellinas, A. P. & Jennings. J. M. (1997). The relation between conscious and unconscious (automatic) influences: a declaration of independence. In J. D. Cohen & J. W. Schooler (eds), *Scientific Approaches to Consciousness*. Hillsdale, NJ: Erlbaum, pp. 13–48.

James, W. (1890/1950). *The Principles of Psychology*, Vol. 1. New York: Dover.

James, W. (1884). What is an emotion? *Mind*, **9**, 188–205.

Kahneman, D. (1973). *Attention and Effort*. Englewood Cliffs, NJ: Prentice-Hall.

Kahneman, D. & Treisman, A. (1984). Changing views of attention and automaticity. In R. Parasuraman & D. R. Davies (eds), *Varieties of Attention*. New York: Academic Press, pp. 29–62.

Kihlstrom, J. F. (1987). The cognitive unconscious. *Science*, **237**, 1445–1452.

Kihlstrom, J. F., Barnhardt, T. M. & Tataryn, D. J. (1992). Implicit perception. In R. F. Bornstein & T. S. Pittman (eds), *Perception without Awareness: Cognitive, Clinical, and Social Perspectives*. New York: Guilford, pp. 17–54.

Kihlstrom, J. F. & Cantor, N. (1984). Mental representations of the self. In L. Berkowitz (ed.), *Advances in Experimental Social Psychology*, Vol. 17. Orlando, FL: Academic Press, pp. 1–47.

Kunst-Wilson, W. R. & Zajonc, R. B. (1980). Affective discrimination of stimuli that cannot be recognized. *Science*, **207**, 557–558.

Lacey, J. L. & Smith, R. L. (1954). Conditioning and generalization of unconscious anxiety. *Science*, **120**, 1045–1052.

Lachman, R., Lachman, J. L. & Butterfield, E. C. (1979). *Cognitive Psychology and Information Processing: An Introduction*. Hillsdale, NJ: Erlbaum.

Lang, P. J. (1978). Anxiety: toward a psychophysiological definition. In H. S. Akiskal & W. L. Webb (eds), *Psychiatric Diagnosis: Explorations of Biological Predictors*. New York: Spectrum.

Lang, P. J., Bradley, M. M. & Cuthbert, B. N. (1997). Motivated attention: affect, activation, and action. In P. J. Lang, R. F. Simons & M. T. Balaban (eds), *Attention and Orienting: Sensory and Motivational processes*. Hillsdale, NJ: Erlbaum.

Lazarus, R. S. & McCleary, R. A. (1951). Autonomic discrimination without awareness: a study of subception. *Psychological Review*, **58**, 113–122.

LeDoux, J. E. (1987). Emotion. In F. Plum (ed.), *Handbook of Physiology. 1: The Nervous System*, Vol. V, Higher functions of the brain. Bethesda, MD: American Physiological Society, pp. 419–460.

LeDoux, J. E. (1990). Fear pathways in the brain: implications for a theory of the emotional brain. In P. F. Brain, S. Parmigiani, R. J. Blanchard & D. Mainardi (eds), *Fear and Defense*. London: Harwood, pp. 163–178.

LeDoux, J. (1996). *The Emotional Brain. The Mysterious Underpinnings of Emotional Life*. New York: Simon and Schuster.

LeDoux, J. E., Sakaguchi, A. & Reiss, D. J. (1984). Subcortical efferent projections of the medial geniculate nucleus mediate emotional responses conditioned by acoustic stimuli. *Journal of Neuroscience*, **4**, 683–698.

Lewicki, P. (1986). *Nonconscious Social Information Processing*. Orlando, FL: Academic Press.

Libet, B., Pearl, D. K., Morledge, D. E., Gleason, C. A., Hosobuchi, Y. & Barbaro, N. M. (1991). Control of the transition from sensory detection to sensory awareness in man by the duration of a thalamic stimulus. *Brain*, **114**, 1731–1757.

Loftus, E. F. & Klinger, M. R. (1992). Is the unconscious smart or dumb? *American Psychologist*, **47**, 761–765.

Lundh, L.-G. (1979). Introspection, consciousness, and human information processing. *Scandinavian Journal of Psychology*, **20**, 223–238.

MacLeod, C., Mathews, A. & Tata, P. (1986) Attentional bias in anxiety disorders. *Journal of Abnormal Psychology*, **95**, 15–20.

MacLeod, C. & Rutherford, E. (1992). Anxiety and the selective processing of emotional information: mediating roles of awareness, trait and state variables, and personal relevance of stimulus material. *Behaviour Research and Therapy*, **30**, 479–491.

Mandler, G. (1975). *Mind and Emotion*. New York: Wiley.

Marcel, A. (1983). Conscious and unconscious perception: an approach to the relations between phenomenal experience and perceptual processes. *Cognitive Psychology*, **15**, 238–300.

Marcel, A. J. & Bisiach, E. (1988). *Consciousness in Contemporary Science*. Oxford: Oxford University Press.

Marks, I. M. (1969). *Fears and Phobias*. London: Heinemann.

Mathews, A. (1990). Why worry? The cognitive function of anxiety. *Behaviour Research and Therapy*, **28**, 455–468.

Mathews, A., Gelder, M. G. & Johnston, D. W. (1981). *Agoraphobia: Nature and Treatment*. London: Tavistock.

Mayr, E. (1974). Behavior programs and evolutionary strategies. *American Scientist*, **62**, 665–659.

McCauley, C., Parmelee, M., Sperber, C. D. & Carr, T. H. (1980). Early extraction of meaning from pictures and its relation to conscious identification. *Journal of Experimental Psychology: Human Perception and Performance*, **6**, 265–276.

McGinnies, E. (1949). Emotionality and perceptual defense. *Psychological Review*, **56**, 244–251.

Merikle, P. M. (1992). Perception without awareness: critical issues. *American Psychologist*, **47**, 792–795.

Merikle, P. M. & Reingold, E. M. (1992). Measuring unconscious perceptual processes. In R. F. Bornstein & T. S. Pittman (eds), *Perception without Awareness: Cognitive, Clinical, and Social Perspectives*. New York: Guilford, pp. 55–80.

Mineka, S. (1992). Evolutionary memories, emotional processing, and the emotional disorders. In D. Medin (ed.), *The Psychology of Learning and Motivation*, Vol. 28. New York: Academic Press, pp. 161–206.

Mogg, K., Bradley, B. P. & Williams, R. (1995). Attentional bias in anxiety and depression: the role of awareness. *British Journal of Clinical Psychology*, **34**, 17–36.

Mogg, K., Bradley, B. P., Williams, R. & Mathews, A. (1993). Subliminal processing of emotional information in anxiety and depression. *Journal of Abnormal Psychology*, **102**, 304–311.

Neely, J. H. (1997). Semantic priming and retrieval from lexical memory: roles of inhibitionless spreading activation and limited-capacity attention. *Journal of Experimental Psychology: General*, **106**, 226–254.

Neisser, U. (1967). *Cognitive Psychology*. New York: Appleton-Century-Crofts.

Nisbett, R. E. & Wilson, T. D. (1977). Telling more than we can know: verbal reports on mental processes. *Psychological Review*, **84**, 231–259.

Oatley, K. & Johnson-Laird, P. N. (1987). Towards a cognitive theory of emotions. *Cognition and Emotion*, **1**, 29–50.

Öhman, A. (1983). The orienting response during Pavlovian conditioning. In D. A. T. Siddle (ed.), *Orienting and Habituation: Perspectives in Human Research*. Chichester: Wiley, pp. 315–369.

Öhman, A. (1986). Face the beast and fear the face: animal and social fears as prototypes for evolutionary analyses of emotion. *Psychophysiology*, **23**, 123–145.

Öhman, A. (1993a). Fear and anxiety as emotional phenomena: clinical phenomenology, evolutionary perspectives, and information-processing mechanisms. In M. Lewis & J. M. Haviland (eds), *Handbook of Emotions*. New York: Guilford, pp. 511–536.

Öhman, A. (1993b). Stimulus prepotency and fear: data and theory. In N. Birbaumer & A. Öhman (eds), *The Organization of Emotion: Cognitive, Clinical and Psychophysiological Perspectives*. Toronto: Hogrefe, pp. 218–239.

Öhman, A. (1996). Preferential preattentive processing of threat in anxiety: preparedness and attentional biases. In R. M. Rapee (ed.), *Current Controversies in the Anxiety Disorders*. New York: Guilford, pp. 253–290.

Öhman, A., Dimberg, U. & Öst, L.-G. (1985). Animal and social phobia: biological constraints on learned fear responses. In S. Reiss & R. R. Bootzin (eds), *Theoretical Issues in Behavior Therapy*. New York: Academic Press, pp. 123–178.

Öhman, A., Flykt, A. & Esteves, F. (submitted). Snakes in the grass: evolutionary threats, attention, and emotion in a visual search task.

Öhman, A., Flykt, A. & Lundqvist, D. (in press). Unconscious emotion: evolutionary perspectives, psychophysiological data, and neuropsychological mechanisms. In R. Lane and L. Nadel (eds), *The Interface between Emotion and Cognitive Neuroscience*. New York: Oxford University Press.

Öhman, A. & Soares, J. (1993). On the automaticity of phobic fear: conditioned skin conductance responses to masked phobic stimuli. *Journal of Abnormal Psychology*, **102**, 121–132.

Öhman, A. & Soares, J. J. F. (1994). Unconscious anxiety: phobic responses to masked stimuli. *Journal of Abnormal Psychology*, **103**, 231–240.

Öhman, A. & Soares, J. J. F. (1998). Emotional conditioning to masked stimuli: expectancies for aversive outcomes following non-recognized fear-relevant stimuli. *Journal of Experimental Psychology: General*.

Ortony, A., Clore, G. & Collins, A. (1988). *The Cognitive Structure of Emotion*. New York: Cambridge University Press.

Parra, C., Esteves, F., Flykt, A. & Öhman, A. (1997). Pavlovian conditioning to social stimuli: backward masking and the dissociation of implicit and explicit cognitive processes. *European Psychologist*, **2**, 106–117.

Pavlov, I. P. (1927). *Conditioned Reflexes* (trans. Anrep, G. V.). Oxford: Oxford University Press.

Perry, C. & Laurence, J.-R. (1984). Mental processing outside of awareness: the contribution of Freud and Janet. In K. S. Bowers & D. Meichelbaum (eds), *The Unconscious Reconsidered*. New York: Wiley, pp. 9–48.

Pierce, C. S. & Jastrow, J. (1884). On small differences in sensation. *Memoirs of the National Academy of Science*, **3**, 75–83.

Posner. M. I. (1978). *Chronometric Explorations of mind*. Hillsdale, NJ: Erlbaum.

Posner, M. I. & Snyder, C. R. (1975). Attention and cognitive control. In R. L. Solso (ed.), *Information Processing and Cognition: The Loyola Symposium*. Hillsdale, NJ: Erlbaum, pp. 55–85.

Power, M. & Brewin, C. R. (1991). From Freud to cognitive science: a contemporary account of the unconscious. *British Journal of Clinical Psychology*, **30**, 289–310.

Rapee, R. M., Mattick, R. & Murrell, E. (1986). Cognitive mediation in the affective component of spontaneous panic attacks. *Journal of Behavioral Therapy and Experimental Psychiatry*, **17**, 245–253.

Razran, G. (1961). The observable unconscious and the inferrable conscious in current Soviet psychophysiology: interoceptive conditioning, semantic conditioning, and the orienting reflex. *Psychological Review*, **68**, 81–147.

Reingold, E. M. & Merikle, P. M. (1988). Using direct and indirect measures to study perception without awareness. *Perception and Psychophysics*, **44**, 563–575.

Russell, P. A. (1979). Fear-evoking stimuli. In W. Sluckin (ed.), *Fear in Animals and Man*. New York: Van Nostrand einhol.

Sanderson, W. C., Rapee, R. M. & Barlow, D. H. (1989). The influence of an illusion of control on panic attacks induced via inhalation of 5.5% carabon dioxide-enriched air. *Archives of General Psychiatry*, **46**, 157–162.

Schachter, S. & Singer, J. E. (1962). Cognitive, social and physiological determinants of emotional state. *Psychological Review*, **69**, 379–399.

Schacter, D. L. (1987). Implicit memory: history and current status. *Journal of Experimental Psychology: Learning, Memory, and Cognition*, **13**, 501–518.

Scherer, K. R. (1988). Criteria for emotion-antecedent appraisal: a review. In V. Hamilton & G. H. Bower (eds), *Cognitive Perspective on Emotion and Motivation*. Dordrecht: Kluwer Academic, pp. 89–126.

Schneider, W., Dumais, S. T. & Shiffrin, R. M. (1984). Automatic and control processing and attention. In R. Parasuraman & D. R. Davies (eds), *Varieties of Attention*. New York: Academic Press, pp. 1–28.

Seligman, M. E. P. (1971). Phobias and preparedness. *Behavior Therapy*, **2**, 307–320.

Shevrin, H. & Dickman, S. (1980). The psychological unconscious: a necessary assumption for all psychological theory. *American Psychologist*, **35**, 421–434.

Shiffrin, R. M. & Schneider, W. (1977). Controlled and automatic human information processing. II. Perceptual learning, automatic attending, and a general theory. *Psychological Review*, **84**, 127–190.

Silverman, L. H. & Weinberger, J. (1985). "Mommy and I are one". Implications for psychotherapy. *American Psychologist*, **40**, 1296–1308.

Skinner, B. F. (1954/1972). A critique of psychoanalytic concepts and theories. In B. F. Skinner, *Cumulative Record. A Selection of Papers*, 3rd edn. New York: Appleton-Century-Crofts, pp. 239–248.

Smith, C. A. & Ellsworth, P. C. (1985). Patterns of cognitive appraisal in emotion. *Journal of Personality and Social Psychology*, **48**, 813–838.

Soares, J. J. F. & Öhman, A. (1993a). Backward masking and skin conductance responses after conditioning to non-feared but fear-relevant stimuli in fearful subjects. *Psychophysiology*, **30**, 460–466.

Soares, J. J. F. & Öhman, A. (1993b). Preattentive processing, preparedness, and phobias: effects of instruction on conditioned electrodermal responses to masked and non-masked fear-relevant stimuli. *Behaviour Research and Therapy*, **31**, 87–95.

Thorpe, S. J. & Salkovskis, P. M. (1995). Phobic beliefs: do cognitive factors play a role in specific phobias? *Behaviour Research and Therapy*, **33**, 805–816.

Tooby, J. & Cosmides, L. (1990). The past explains the present: emotional adaptations and the structure of ancestral environment. *Ethology and Sociobiology*, **11**, 375–424.

Tranel, D. & Damasio, A. R. (1985). Knowledge without awareness: an autonomic index of facial recognition. *Science*, **228**, 1453–1454.

Warrington, E. K. & Weiscrantz, L. (1974). The effect of prior learning on subsequent retention in amnesic patients. *Neuropsychologia*, **12**, 419–428.

Weinberger, J. (1992). Validating and demystifying subliminal psychodynamic activation. In R. F. Bornstein & T. S. Pittman (eds), *Perception Without Awareness: Cognitive, Clinical, and Social Perspectives*. New York: Guilford, pp. 170–190.

Weiskrantz, L. (1986). *Blindsight. A Case Study and Implications*. Oxford: Oxford University Press.

Williams, J. M. G., Mathews, A. & MacLeod, C. (1996). The emotional Stroop task and psychopathology. *Psychological Bulletin*, **120**, 3–24.

Zajonc, R. B. (1968). Attitudinal effects of mere exposure. *Journal of Personality and Social Psychology*, **9** suppl.

Zajonc, R. B. (1980). Feeling and thinking: preferences need no inferences. *American Psychologist*, **35**, 151–175.

Chapter 18

Self-regulation, Affect and Psychosis: The Role of Social Cognition in Paranoia and Mania

Richard P. Bentall
Department of Clinical Psychology, University of Liverpool, UK
and
Peter Kinderman
School of Psychiatry and Behavioural Sciences, University of Manchester, UK

INTRODUCTION

In this chapter we will describe a programme of research that has highlighted the role of social cognition in persecutory (paranoid) delusions and mania. We will argue that both of these symptoms can be understood in terms of disorders of those mechanisms that normal individuals use to maintain a positive sense of self, and hence a positive mood, and that they are close relatives in a family of psychiatric disorders that also includes depression. If this argument is correct, the findings from paranoid and manic patients have important implications for the understanding of self-regulatory processes in normal individuals. Before reviewing the relevant research findings, however, it will first be useful to say something about the general characteristics of our approach, and about research on the role of affect in psychotic disorders in general.

Handbook of Cognition and Emotion. Edited by T. Dalgleish and M. Power.
© 1999 John Wiley & Sons Ltd.

Psychosis and Affect: Limitations of the Kraepelinian Approach

The term "psychosis" refers to the most severe of psychiatric disorders, in which the individual is often thought to lose touch with reality. The most common "positive" symptoms of psychosis (so called because they take the form of behaviours and experiences that would preferably be absent) include delusions (bizarre beliefs that appear to be resistant to counter-argument, often with persecutory or grandiose themes), auditory hallucinations (hearing voices when no-one is in fact present), disorders of speech and communication (which may render the individual incoherent to the listener) and mania (at first sight, characterized by an extreme positive mood coupled with excitement and hyperactivity; but see below). Some patients also experience "negative" symptoms (so called because they are manifested as the absence of desirable behaviours), such as apathy, social withdrawal and flat affect. Patients who experience some combination of these symptoms are usually assigned to one of two diagnostic classes: "schizophrenia", if hallucinations and delusions are prominent, and "bipolar affective disorder" (also called "manic depression"), if abnormal mood is prominent. However, the term "schizo-affective disorder" is often used to describe patients who appear to suffer from some combination of these two groups of symptoms, and the term "delusional disorder" is also sometimes used to describe patients who suffer from delusions in the absence of other psychotic symptoms.

Operational definitions of these disorders have appeared in diagnostic handbooks such as the recent 4th edition of the American Psychiatric Association's Diagnostic and Statistical Manual (DSM-IV; American Psychiatric Association, 1994) and the 10th edition of the World Health Organization's International Classification of Disease (ICD-10; World Health Organization 1992). These definitions are conceptually descendant from principles of psychiatric taxonomy first elucidated by Emil Kraepelin who, in 1896, argued that psychotic illnesses fell into the two major classes of schizophrenia (termed by him "dementia praecox") and manic depression. Research on the role of affect in the psychoses has for the most part adhered to the Kraepelinian model, and affect has therefore been seen as a central feature of bipolar disorder but not schizophrenia. Leonhard's (1957) observation that mania nearly always occurs in the context of a history of depression, so that unipolar mania is rare, indeed seems consistent with the hypothesis that the underlying psychopathology in mania is affective in nature. However, there is also substantial evidence of affective disturbance in patients who meet the criteria for schizophrenia. For example, Norman & Malla (1991) measured both depression and anxiety in a population of currently ill schizophrenia patients and found that these emotions were highly correlated in their sample and especially evident in those suffering mainly from positive symptoms. Longitudinal studies have also shown that both depression and anxiety are often prominent during the weeks preceding a psychotic relapse (Birchwood, Macmillan & Smith, 1992). As Norman & Malla (1991) note, the presence of anxiety and depression together in both acutely ill and relapsing schizophrenia patients mirrors the findings from research into non-psychotic disorders, in which depression and anxiety are commonly observed together (Clark, Watson & Reynolds, 1995; Goldberg & Huxley, 1992; Tyrer, 1990).

The fact that affect seems to play a prominent role in both bipolar disorder and schizophrenia alerts us to the possibility that these may not be separate syndromes after all. Indeed, it has become increasingly evident that the division of the psychoses into these two main types is problematic. The evidence that has accumulated against the Kraepelinian model has been reviewed in detail elsewhere (Bentall, 1990; Blashfield, 1984) but can be summarized as follows. First, studies in which multivariate statistical techniques have been used to assess the co-variance of psychotic symptoms have revealed that they do not segregate into two main clusters (Blashfield, 1984; Kendell, 1989). Second, Kraepelinian diagnoses are poorly associated with specific pathological and aetiological factors (Bentall, Jackson & Pilgrim, 1988). Third, these diagnoses are poor predictors of outcome (Ciompi, 1984; Kendell & Brockington, 1980) and response to treatment (Johnstone et al., 1988; Kendell, 1989).

Faced with these kinds of findings, researchers have adopted a number of strategies. Some have continued to employ Kraepelinian diagnoses in order to classify subjects for the purpose of research. However, this is clearly a hazardous strategy, as even the authors of DSM-IV acknowledge that these diagnostic categories may be arbitrary and may eventually be superseded by dimensional classification systems (American Psychiatric Association, 1994). Others have suggested that there may be a continuum of psychosis running from "pure" manic depression to "pure" schizophrenia (Crow, 1986; Kendell & Brockington, 1980). A third approach, which has been increasingly advocated by psychological researchers in Europe and North America, has been to focus on specific psychological phenomena or symptoms, rather than on broad diagnostic categories (Bentall, 1990; Costello, 1992; Frith, 1992; Persons, 1986). The work described in the main part of this chapter, which focuses on paranoid (persecutory) delusions and mania, falls within this latter approach.

Common Characteristics of Paranoia and Mania

Although paranoid delusions and manic states are usually attributed to the two different diagnostic categories of schizophrenia and manic depression, respectively, Zigler & Glick (1988) have listed a number of reasons for supposing that they have much in common, and have suggested that both are therefore types of camouflaged depression.

The first and most obvious similarity concerns clinical presentation. Patients who are paranoid, whether they receive a primary diagnosis of schizophrenia or delusional disorder, by definition are characterized by persecutory delusions which are often accompanied by grandiose delusions (for example, when a patient makes claim to supernatural powers and at the same time believes that he is being persecuted by envious others as a consequence). In a systematic review of data from 26 studies of the phenomenology of mania, Goodwin & Jamison (1990) found that grandiose delusions were present in 48% of patients and persecutory delusions were present in 28%. In a similar analysis of data from four studies of bipolar depression, Goodwin & Jamison found that delusions were reported to be present in 33–56% of depressive episodes. In the majority of cases of bipolar depression, the delusions are persecutory (Freedman & Schwab, 1978), grandiose delusions being almost never evident during depressive episodes.

Zigler and Glick argue that salience of the self is a further characteristic that both paranoia and mania have in common with depression. In paranoia the patient is typically preoccupied with slights against the self, in mania the preoccupation usually concerns positive characteristics of the self, and in depression the patient is usually preoccupied by low self-esteem, self-devaluation and a view of the self as insufficient to meet the patient's aspirations.

Further similarities between these conditions highlighted by Zigler & Glick concern the premorbid characteristics of patients and the typical age at which symptoms first appear. In a series of studies, Zigler and his colleagues showed that both paranoid and affective disorder patients, in contrast to patients who are diagnosed as suffering from non-paranoid schizophrenia, are older at initial hospitalization and score higher on measures of premorbid social competence (Glick, Zigler & Zigler, 1985; Zigler & Glick, 1986; Zigler & Levine, 1981), observations that have been replicated by other investigators (Lewine et al., 1980).

Paranoia and Mania as Defences

As Zigler & Glick (1988) have noted, some psychological theories of paranoia and mania have emphasized common processes. The idea that persecutory delusions have a defensive function can be traced at least as far back as Freud's (1911/1950) celebrated analysis of the autobiography of the eminent German Judge Daniel Schreber (1842–1911). Schreber first suffered a nervous breakdown in 1884 at the age of 42, after failing to be elected to the Reichstag. Following hospitalization for 6 months, he returned to live normally with his wife for a period of 8 years before experiencing his second breakdown several weeks after he took up the position of President of the Supreme Court in Saxony. This time he was hospitalized for 9 years, during which period he wrote the book *Memoirs of My Nervous Illness* (Schreber, 1903/1955), which was to make him "the most frequently quoted patient in psychiatry" (Macalpine & Hunter, 1955). Schreber's paranoid beliefs, described at length in his autobiography, were so bizarre that they defy brief summary, but began with the belief that his former psychiatrist, Flechsig, was transforming him into woman for the purposes of sexual abuse, and evolved into highly complex theological ideas concerning the effects of "rays" from God on his body. Freud's ingenious explanation of these symptoms, like Schreber's autobiography, has to be read in full to be properly appreciated.

In brief, Freud maintained that Schreber's homosexual desire towards his father had been defensively transferred from their true object to Flechsig and that, in a further series of defensive manoeuvres, Schreber's love for Flechsig was transformed into Flechsig's supposed hatred of the judge.

Later, psychodynamically-inspired theorists have tended to agree that paranoid delusions serve a defensive function, while stressing the wider utility of projection for ego-protection. Kretschmer (1927), Henderson & Gillespie (1936), Mayer-Gross, Slater & Roth (1954) and even Bleuler (1911/1950) all saw delusions as the results of attempts to attribute internal ideas to external agencies, but believed that these ideas were not necessarily homosexual in nature (see Winters & Neale, 1983, for a detailed review of these theories). In an attempt to operationalize this general model, and to bring it into line with modern cognitive psychology, Colby and his colleagues proposed a computer simulation of paranoid ideation (Colby, Faught & Parkinson, 1979). Colby's programme assumes that paranoid individuals have a tendency to perceive or generate threats to their self-esteem and that they then protect themselves against these threats by projection and externalization of the threat to others.

The idea that mania serves a similar defensive function also originated with the early psychoanalysts (Neale, 1988). Abraham (1911/1927) held that both phases of manic depression reflected the same psychological complexes but that, during depression, the patient is weighed down by the complexes, whereas in mania they are treated with indifference, an account which was later elaborated by Freud (1917/1950). Rado (1928) subsequently argued that intense narcissism rendered the manic-depressive patient vulnerable to events that threaten self-esteem and that the function of mania is to destroy the introjected "bad object" that would otherwise cause melancholia. In a modern, cognitive reformulation of this account, Neale (1988) has proposed that unstable self-esteem, coupled to unrealistic standards for success, are predisposing factors for manic depression. On this account, intensification of low self-regard in the vulnerable patient (which may be precipitated by either biological, environmental or cognitive processes) leads to grandiose ideas which have the function of keeping distressing cognitions out of consciousness. These ideas in turn may lead to mood elevation and hence to manic episodes.

Although psychoanalytic hypotheses have often been ignored by cognitive psychologists (largely because they are held to be difficult to test), they might be seen as having much in common with cognitive models, in that emotional and behavioural disturbances are seen as arising from underlying distortions of thinking, reasoning and information processing. Indeed, Power & Brewin (1991) have recently suggested that it is time for a rapprochement between the two approaches. Certainly, the work of Colby, Faught Parkinson (1979) and Neale (1988) shows how psychoanalytic accounts can be reformulated in cognitive terms. As we will see later in this chapter, subsequent empirical studies which have focused on the attributional and self-representational processes in these disorders have produced evidence that is broadly consistent with these accounts.

PSYCHOLOGICAL PROCESSES AND PARANOID IDEATION

A delusion is defined in DSM-IV as, "A false personal belief based on incorrect inference about external reality that is firmly sustained in spite of what almost everyone else believes and in spite of what usually constitutes incontrovertible and obvious proof or evidence to the contrary" (American Psychiatric Association, 1994, p. 765). Within that broad classification, a persecutory or paranoid delusion is one in which the central theme is that the patient (or someone to whom the patient is close) is being attacked, harassed, cheated, persecuted or conspired against.

Despite the substantial distress caused by delusions in general and paranoia in particular, psychological research has only focused on these phenomena during the last 10 years or so. There appear to be two main reasons for this relative lack of attention. First, delusions and paranoia are typically viewed as symptoms of illnesses such as schizophrenia or delusional disorder, and patients have therefore usually been classified according to these broader diagnostic concepts for the purposes of research. Second, researchers in the psychiatric tradition have tended to see delusional beliefs as qualitatively different from normal beliefs and attitudes. This assumption has followed from the highly influential account of Karl Jaspers (1912/1963), who suggested that the abnormal beliefs of psychiatric patients are not only held with extraordinary conviction, have bizarre or impossible content, and are impervious to counter-argument, but are also "ununderstandable" in the sense that they cannot be understood by reference to the patient's background and experience (see Walker, 1991, for a detailed explanation of Jaspers' argument). Jaspers' approach (which implies that the models of normal cognition have few implications for the study of delusions) is clearly exemplified by the recent work of Berrios (1991), who has asserted that delusions are, "Empty speech acts, whose informational content refers to neither world or self. They are not the symbolic expression of anything".

In contrast to Jaspers' account, phenomenological studies have shown that there is a continuum that runs from normal beliefs and attitudes to fully-fledged delusions (Kendler, Glazer & Morgenstern, 1983; Strauss, 1969) and that quasi-psychotic delusion-like beliefs are often reported by people who do not meet standard criteria for psychiatric disorder (Chapman & Chapman, 1988). Moreover, far from being meaningless speech acts, the most common delusions observed in psychiatric patients seem to reflect the same existential issues (Musalek, Berner & Katschnig, 1989) or concerns about the individual's position in the social universe (Bentall, 1994) that preoccupy normal people.

Recent research into the role of cognitive processes in delusions have highlighted a number of factors. Some, but by no means all, delusional beliefs appear to be the consequence of relatively rational attempts to explain anomalous experiences (Maher, 1988). For example, studies have shown that delusional misidentifications (such as the Capgras delusion, in which the individual believes that a loved one has been replaced by an imposter, doppelganger or robot) at least partially reflect deficits in face perception that lead the individual to experience the loved one as unfamiliar (Ellis & Young, 1990). Deluded patients in general also experience difficulty when reasoning about probabilities (Dudley et al., 1997; Fear & Healy, 1997; Garety, Hemsley & Wessely, 1991; Huq, Garety & Hemsley, 1988; John & Dodgson, 1994; Young & Bentall, 1995, 1997). However, in the present context we will focus particularly on evidence about selective information processing, attributional and self-representational processes in paranoid patients.

Selective Information Processing in Paranoia

The hypothesis that paranoid delusions reflect abnormal information processing was first advanced by Ullmann & Krasner (1969), who argued that selective attention to threatening information could lead an individual to form conclusions about the environment which appear delusional to others. The first empirical study of selective attention in paranoid subjects was carried out by Bentall and Kaney (1989) using the emotional Stroop paradigm. In a Stroop task subjects are shown words written in various ink colours and are asked to name the colours without reading the word. It has generally been found that colour-naming is slower for emotionally salient material, reflecting the extent to which subjects experience conflict between naming the colour and reading the word (Williams, Mathews & MacLeod, 1996). Bentall & Kaney (1989) found that paranoid patients showed slowed colour-naming for threat-related words (e.g. spy, persecute) but not depression-related words, a result that was later replicated by Fear, Sharp & Healy (1996).

Kinderman (1994) used a similar methodology to investigate paranoid patients' colour-naming of positive and negative trait words (e.g. wise, capable; lazy, foolish). In this study, in addition to being given the Stroop task, the subjects were also asked to indicate in a questionnaire whether or not the words were self-descriptive. In general, both the paranoid subjects and the normal controls endorsed as true of themselves many more positive trait words than negative trait words, indicating high self-esteem. However, during the Stroop task, the paranoid patients, in comparison with the normal controls, showed slowed slow-colour naming for both positive and especially negative trait words.

In a single case-study that investigated the relationship between selective attention and active delusional symptomatology, Leafhead, Young & Szulecka (1996) repeatedly administered an emotional Stroop task to a 29 year-old woman who had a 4-year history of psychotic episodes. When ill, the woman reported the belief that she was dead (known as the Cotard delusion). She also claimed that her body was about to explode, and that her mother and brother had changed and were no longer the people they had been before (the Capgras delusion). On the first test, when she was most severely ill and preoccupied with the idea that she might be dead, she showed slowed colour-naming for both death-related (e.g. coffin, died, funeral) and duplicate-related words (e.g. copy, double, impostors), in comparison with a small control group. By the second testing, at which point her condition had improved, she showed slowed colour-naming for the duplicate-related words only. On the final testing, when she was well, she showed no selective Stroop effect at all.

Given that deluded patients selectively attend to stimuli that are relevant to their delusions, it might also be expected that they would preferentially recall such information. This prediction was tested by Kaney et al. (1992) using a story recall task. When compared to control subjects, the paranoid patients recalled less of the stories overall. However, they recalled more information that was specifically threat-related. In a subsequent study of free recall of a mixed list of threat-related, depression-related and neutral words, Bentall, Kaney & Bowen-Jones (1995) found that paranoid patients, in comparison with controls, selectively recalled both the threat-related and depression-related words in preference to the neutral words.

Overall, therefore, the available data consistently supports the hypothesis that delusions are associated with selective attention for delusion-related stimuli. Although it seems likely that this bias in information processing will lead to the maintenance of delusional beliefs once established, it is important to acknowledge that such biases are not an exclusive characteristic of deluded patients. Williams, Mathews & MacLeod (1996) have noted that most psychiatric disorders seem to be associated with selective attention towards stimuli congruent with patients' psychopathological concerns.

Causal Attributions in Paranoia

Causal attributions (explanations for everyday events) are common elements of cognition (Zullow et al., 1988). Psychologists such as Heider (1958) and Weiner (1986) have regarded a person's conception of why significant events have occurred as important in determining their emotional and behavioural reactions to those events. Most of the research which has so far been conducted on the role of attributions in psychopathology has focused on depression.

In their "learned helplessness" model of depression, Abramson, Seligman & Teasdale (1978) argued that depressed patients tend to make abnormally internal (self-blaming), stable (unchangeable) and global explanations for negative events. (For example, exam failure might be attributed to "stupidity", a cause which is internal to the individual, unchangeable and likely to affect other areas of life.) Subsequent research has consistently supported the general hypothesis that attributions are abnormal during depression (Brewin, 1985; Sweeny, Anderson & Bailey, 1986), although the exact nature of these abnormalities remains a matter of some debate. In a later revision of the learned helplessness model, Abramson, Metalsky & Alloy (1989) argued that hopelessness is a proximal cause of depressed mood, but that abnormally stable and global attributions for negative events play a causal role in hopelessness; on this account, internality judgements play little or no role in depression. Other researchers have suggested that the attributional style seen in depressed patients may be related to low self-esteem rather than to depression (Tennen & Herzenberger, 1987; Tennen, Herzenberger & Nelson, 1987). Moreover, the *causal* status of attributions in depressive symptomatology has yet to be firmly established, as it is not clear whether attributional abnormalities are present before the onset of depression, as both the helplessness and hopelessness models suggest (Robins & Hayes, 1995).

Kaney & Bentall (1989) used the Attributional Style Questionnaire (ASQ: Peterson et al., 1982) to investigate the causal attributions of paranoid patients. The ASQ requires respondents to generate likely explanations for hypothetical positive and negative events affecting themselves, and then to rate their own causal statements on three bipolar scales of internality (the degree to which the cause implicates the self as opposed to other people or circumstances), stability (the degree to which the cause is likely to be present in the future) and globalness (the degree to which the cause influences a wide range of events in the individual's life, or only particular events). Kaney & Bentall found that paranoid patients, in comparison with non-patient and depressed controls, tended to make abnormally internal attributions for positive events and abnormally external attributions for negative events. This finding has been substantially replicated by Candido & Romney (1990), Fear et al. (1996) and Sharp, Fear & Healy (1997). In a subsequent experimental investigation using computer games which were "rigged" so that participants either won or lost, Kaney & Bentall (1992) reported a result that was consistent with the findings from studies employing the ASQ. While depressed patients reported little control in either condition, normal subjects demonstrated a robust "self-serving bias", reporting more control in the (contrived) win condition than the lose condition. As might be expected on the basis of the previous findings, paranoid patients reported a significantly greater self-serving bias than the normal subjects.

Interestingly, this excessive self-serving attributional bias appears to be present in paranoid patients only on explicit measures. Winters & Neale (1985) developed a non-obvious measure of attributional style, the Pragmatic Inference Task (PIT). This is presented as a test of memory, so that on each item subjects are asked to recall which of two explanations (one internal and one external) was responsible for the good or bad outcome described in a self-referent story they have just heard (the stories are carefully constructed so that neither answer is more correct than the other). Lyon, Kaney & Bentall (1994) found that both deluded and depressed patients responded similarly on the PIT, making internal attributions for negative events. On an explicit measure of attributional style, the same deluded patients made external attributions for negative events, as observed in previous research (see Figure 18.1). This pattern of

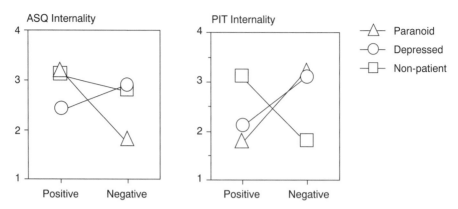

Figure 18.1 Ratings of internal (self-blaming) attributions for positive and negative events made by deluded, depressed and non-patient participants on the ASQ (Attributional Style Inventory) and the PIT (Pragmatic Inference Task). Reproduced from Lyon, Kaney & Bentall (1994), with permission

results can be interpreted as reflecting paranoid patients' explicit attempts to maintain a positive view of the self under the threat of implicit negative self-representations.

Self-representations in Paranoid Patients

Clearly, the attributional data is consistent with the hypothesis that paranoia functions as a defence against low self-esteem. Research on self-esteem in paranoid patients is similarly consistent with this general model. Although psychotic patients, in general, score low on measures of self-esteem (Ibelle, 1961; Kaplan, 1975; Rogers, 1958; Silverstone, 1991; Wylie, 1979) and have poorly elaborated (Robey, Cohen & Gara, 1989) or contradictory (Gruba & Johnson, 1974) self-concepts, paranoid patients appear to be an exception and tend to report high levels of self-esteem (Havner & Izard, 1962).

Bentall, Kinderman & Kaney (1994) recently proposed a detailed model of persecutory delusions that builds on the earlier insights of Colby, Faught & Parkinson (1979) and Zigler & Glick (1988) and which incorporates certain features of "self-discrepancy theory" (Higgins, 1987), a theory which has developed to explain the role of abnormal self-representations in depression and anxiety, and which is a codification of the long-held view that individuals' self-representations have multiple aspects (Markus & Wurf, 1987). According to this theory, discrepancies may exist between different domains of the self (the actual-self, ideal-self and ought-self) and different perspectives on these domains (e.g. beliefs about how others view the self, how they would like the individual to be, how they think the individual ought to be) and these discrepancies have important psychological consequences. Clinically depressed and dysthymic

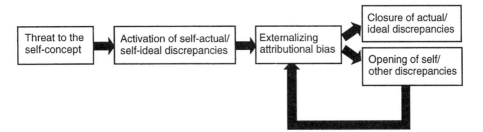

Figure 18.2 Diagram indicating initial hypothesized relationships between self-discrepancies and attributional styles. Reproduced from Bentall, Kinderman & Kaney (1994), with permission

non-clinical subjects report discrepancies between the actual-self and the ideal-self, whereas socially phobic or clinically anxious patients report discrepancies between the actual-self and the ought-self (Scott & O'Hara, 1993; Strauman, 1989; Strauman & Higgins, 1988). Manipulations of these self-discrepancies in normal subjects have been shown to lead to predictable changes in mood (Strauman & Higgins, 1987), autobiographical memory (Strauman, 1992) and even physiological functioning (Strauman & Higgins, 1987; Strauman, Lemieux & Coe, 1993).

In the Bentall, Kinderman & Kaney (1994) model, shown diagrammatically in Figure 18.2, persecutory delusions are seen as the consequence of an attributional process which minimizes potential self-actual:self-ideal discrepancies. It is assumed that the person prone to paranoid delusions has an implicit negative self-schema which, when activated by some kind of threatening event (e.g. a negative social interaction), would ordinarily lead to discrepancies between self-actual and self-ideal representations. However, in the paranoid individual the event is rendered personally benign by explaining it in terms of external factors. Although these external attributions apparently minimize self-actual:self-ideal discrepancies ("I am not to blame—therefore I am as I would like to be"), they also open discrepancies between self-representations and the views other people are believed to hold about the self ("Other people are to blame—they must hate me").

Specific predictions stemming from this model have been empirically tested. Kinderman & Bentall (1996a) elicited paranoid, depressed and normal subjects' actual-self, ideal-self and ought-self representations, and also their beliefs about how their parents viewed them. The data from this study are shown in Figure 18.3, which shows the degree of consistency between the different types of representations (low consistency scores indicate high discrepancy). In keeping with previous clinical research, the normal subjects showed high consistencies between all domains of the self-concept, while depressed patients showed marked self-discrepancies, particularly between the self-actual and self-ideal representations. Paranoid patients alone displayed small self-actual: self-ideal and self-actual:self-ought discrepancies, together with large discrepancies

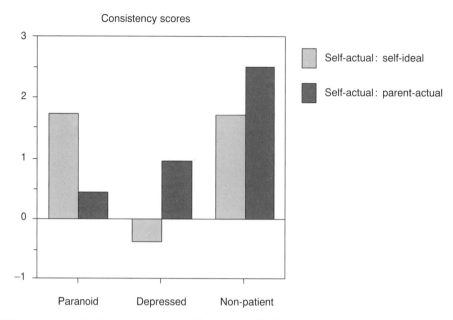

Figure 18.3 Consistency between self-actual and self-ideal and self-actual and parent-actual domains for paranoid, depressed and non-patient participants. Data from Kinderman & Bentall (1996a).

between self-perceptions and the believed perceptions of parents about the self. Examination of the content of the paranoid patients' responses indicated that they believed that their parents held exceptionally negative views about them. These findings are clearly consistent with the Bentall, Kinderman & Kaney (1994) model.

The model also proposes that paranoid patients have implicit negative self-representations perhaps similar to the explicit negative self-representations reported by depressed patients. Lyon et al.'s (1994) observation that paranoid patients make *internal* attributions for negative events on an implicit test is clearly consistent with this hypothesis, as is Kinderman's (1994) observation that paranoid patients show slowed Stroop colour-naming for both positive and especially negative trait words.

In a recent attempt to test further this hypothesis, Bentall & Kaney (1996) administered paranoid and control subjects the Dysfunctional Attitude Scale, a questionnaire measure of perfectionist standards for evaluating self-worth. Both non-depressed paranoid patients and depressed paranoid patients scored higher than normal controls on this test, as did depressed psychiatric controls, suggesting that paranoid patients, like depressed patients, are vulnerable to self-ideal discrepancies by virtue of having very high ideals.

More equivocal evidence of abnormal self-representations was obtained from a second test administered in this study. Subjects were given a self-referent encoding task in which they were first required to state whether positive and negative trait words described themselves before trying to recall the words in a surprise test. On this kind of test, subjects usually preferentially recall words they have endorsed. As predicted, the paranoid and normal patients in contrast to the depressed controls endorsed more positive than negative words as true of themselves. It was predicted that both the paranoid and depressed patients would recall more negative than positive words overall, but this proved not to be the case. However, when words which had been endorsed as true of self were examined, it was found that only the normal subjects recalled more positive than negative words, the paranoid and depressed patients recalling an equal number of words of either type.

Types of External Attribution and Theory of Mind

Overall, the evidence described so far is consistent with the hypothesis that paranoia reflects an abnormal attributional strategy that serves the function of maintaining self-esteem. However, all of these studies of causal attribution, following the tradition of the learned helplessness theory of depression, have treated internality–externality as a bipolar dimension. Some authors have noted that responses on bipolar scales of this sort tend to be inconsistent and have proposed alternative ways of categorizing attributions for internality (Stratton et al., 1986; White, 1991). Moreover, the ASQ internality dimension has been criticized because of its poor psychometric reliability (Reivich, 1995) and it is possible that this is because the bipolar format does not reflect psychological reality.

In fact, three distinct attributional loci can be identified in the attributional classification developed by Seligman, Peterson and their colleagues: an internal locus (attributing the causes of events to self), an external-personal locus (attributing the causes of events to the actions or omissions of identifiable others) and an external-situational locus (attributing the causes of events in terms of circumstances or chance). For this reason Kinderman & Bentall (1996b) developed the Internal, Personal and Situational Attributions Questionnaire (the IPSAQ), which independently measures attributions for positive and negative events made to internal, external-personal and external-situational loci. Kinderman & Bentall found that, in normal subjects, the subscales of the questionnaire had significantly better internal consistency than those of the ASQ.

It is likely that the two types of external attribution assessed by the IPSAQ have differential effects on psychological functioning. After all, external-situational attributions are the hallmark of normal excuse making ("I was late because of the traffic") and only external-personal attributions ("It was his fault") are likely to lead to the kinds of persecutory beliefs and self–other discrepancies observed in paranoid patients. To test this hypothesis, Kinderman & Bentall (1997) administered the IPSAQ to paranoid, depressed and normal subjects. Both the paranoid and the normal subjects in this study showed a robust self-serving bias, attributing more positive events than negative events to internal loci, whereas the depressed patients attributed as many negative as positive events to internal causes. Uniquely, the paranoid patients also showed a highly abnormal personalizing bias, allocating the majority of their external attributions to personal as opposed to situational loci. In fact, they made few external-situational attributions for either positive or negative events. It was as if they were unable to generate appropriate excuses for negative events and so, faced with the dilemma of choosing between blaming themselves or blaming other people, they almost invariably blamed other people. These findings confirm that it is useful to separate out the two distinct external attributional loci, but raise questions about why paranoid patients are unable to make use of external-situational attributions.

Despite the considerable research that has been carried out into the role of attributions in psychopathology—especially depression—there has been very little research into the aetiology of particular attributional styles. However, there is at least some evidence that attributional abnormalities may begin in childhood and that, in the case of psychosis at least, they may predict future psychopathology. In a study of normal families using the bipolar format for assessing internality, Seligman et al. (1984) reported that childrens' attributional styles correlated with those of their mothers (but not their fathers). Frenkel et al. (1995), in a longitudinal study of adolescents vulnerable to psychosis because they had psychotic parents, found that external locus of control (not dissimilar from an externalizing attributional bias) predicted later mental ill-health. However, although these findings suggest a family origin for the excessive need to make external attributions for negative events, they do not explain why paranoid patients make exclusively external-*personal* attributions for such events.

It is possible that the tendency to make external-personal attributions is a consequence of failure of those cognitive systems required to make external-situational attributions. On experiencing some kind of negative social interaction (e.g. when being ignored by a friend), a common response is to make an external-situational attribution for the other person's behaviour ("He must be having a bad day"). However, a response of this sort requires that some effort is taken to appreciate the other person's perspective and to see his/her point of view. Without taking this perspective, the offending person's behaviour can only be attributed to some kind of general disposition ("He's a *******!").

The ability to take someone else's perspective (somewhat misleadingly termed "theory of mind" (ToM), as it implies having theories about other peoples' minds) is believed to play an important role in ordinary social interactions (for a review, see Baron-Cohen, 1995) and has been extensively studied in the fields of autism and Asperger's syndrome (Baron-Cohen, Leslie & Frith, 1985; Frith, 1989; Happé & Frith, 1994; Leslie, 1991), as people with these conditions seem to have severe and enduring deficiencies in this domain. Although the hypothesis that ToM deficits contribute to the abnormal attributional style of the paranoid patient must remain tentative at present, there are at least two lines of evidence in its favour. First, Frith and his colleagues (Corcoran, Frith & Mercer, 1995; Frith & Corcoran, 1996) have found that symptomatically paranoid but not remitted patients perform badly on ToM tasks. Second, in a study of normal subjects, Kinderman, Dunbar & Bentall (1998) found the predicted relationship between performance on ToM tasks and scores on the IPSAQ—those who performed worst on the ToM task made the least number of external-situational attributions and the most number of external-personal attributions.

Frith's observation that remitted psychotic patients perform normally on ToM tasks suggests that difficulties in perspective-taking are episodic and correlate with paranoid symptomatology. Psychotic episodes are associated with fairly severe dysfunctions of working memory and attentional capacity (Green, 1992). As ToM tasks appear to make considerable demands on cognitive resources it is possible that the ToM deficits experienced by paranoid patients reflect these more general psychological impairments.

Generalizing from the Attributional Account of Paranoia

The evidence outlined above indicates that paranoid ideation reflects the interaction of several of domains of cognition. In particular, it would seem that paranoid individuals attend excessively to threatening stimuli, implicitly hold a negative view of the self rather similar to the negative view of the self held by depressed patients, but unlike depressed patients make excessively external-personal attributions for negative events, in order to prevent the experience of a discrepancy between how they are and they would like to be. Although we can only speculate at present, it seems likely that this style of making attributions reflects both family processes and specific deficits in the ability to appreciate the point of view of others. A tentative model linking these observations, and which expands on the model presented in Figure 18.2, is shown in Figure 18.4.

Before moving on to consider mania, one further question needs to be addressed. Throughout the preceding sections we have been careful to stress that the data we have described has been almost exclusively obtained from patients suffering from paranoid delusions. However, we have also pointed out that most types of delusional system reflect concerns about the individual's position in the social universe (Bentall, 1994), and therefore the possibility that attributional processes may play a role in other types of delusional systems must be considered. Young (1994), for example, has suggested that, although visual information-processing abnormalities seem to play an important role in the Capgras and Cotard delusions, attributional abnormalities may also be implicated. However, the only studies so far undertaken that have tested the generality of the attributional account have been reported by Fear and his colleagues (Fear, Sharp & Healy, 1996; Sharp, Fear & Healy, 1997), who assessed attributional style in two groups of psychiatric patients suffering from a variety of delusional ideas (although the Capgras and Cotard delusions were not represented in either sample). The data from these two studies indicated that attributional

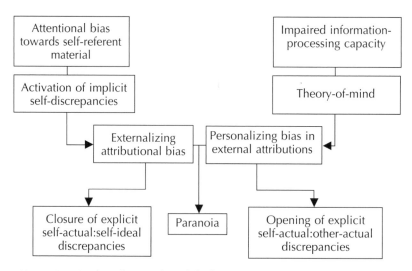

Figure 18.4 A revised attributional model of paranoia

abnormalities were most evident in those patients who suffered from persecutory or grandiose delusions. As grandiose delusions are often prominent in patients who are experiencing a manic episode, this observation has obvious implications for the understanding of psychological processes involved in mania.

PSYCHOLOGICAL PROCESSES IN MANIA

Mania, which has been even more neglected by psychological researchers than paranoia, is usually regarded as a state that exists at the opposite end to depression on a spectrum of affect. This assumption is implied by the term "bipolar affective disorder", which is now more commonly used than "manic depression".

However, the assumption that mania and depression are opposites is probably misleading. Some observers have argued that increased activity rather than abnormal mood is the most important feature of mania (Bauer et al., 1991). Others have suggested that mania is an extreme end-state of depression, an idea that can be traced at least as far back as the second century AD (Goodwin & Jamison, 1990). This idea is reflected in the theoretical accounts offered by those psychoanalytic writers who have argued that mania is an extreme defence against depression and is implicit in Neale's (1988) more recent reformulation of the manic-defence hypothesis.

Contrary to the common view that mood is usually euphoric during the manic state, phenomenological studies indicate that, overall, depression is as evident as euphoria (Goodwin & Jamison, 1990). On the basis of careful observation, Carlson & Goodwin (1973) have argued that manic episodes typically progress through three stages, with euphoria characteristic only of the first. The emotions most characteristic of the second are anger and irritability and, in the third, depression, panic and delirium are most evident. When patients have been followed over several episodes, it has been observed that their depression scores are sometimes higher when they are manic than when they are depressed (Kotin & Goodwin, 1972).

These observations suggest that the cognitive processes involved in mania, like those involved in paranoia, may have much in common with those implicated in depression. Some psychological studies have indicated that manic patients are highly distractible and suffer from problems of memory and attention, whereas others have focused on linguistic and other processes that appear to play a specific role in the manic patient's communication difficulties (Goodwin & Jamison, 1990; Grossman & Harrow, 1991). However, for the present purposes we will focus on those aspects of cognition that we have considered earlier when reviewing the psychological literature on paranoia.

Selective Information Processing in Mania

In an attempt to test the manic-defence hypothesis, Bentall & Thompson (1990) conducted an analogue study using the emotional Stroop paradigm with student subjects selected according to their scores on Eckblad & Chapman's (1986) Hypomanic Personality Scale. High scores on this scale reflects the positive endorsement of grandiose ideas, such as the belief that one can be successful in several careers. One set of Stroop stimuli consisted of depression-related words, another set consisted of euphoria-related words, and a third set consisted of emotionally neutral words. As predicted by the manic-defence hypothesis, the hypomanic students showed abnormally slowed colour-naming for the depression-related words but not for the euphoria-related words. French, Richards & Scholfield (1996) argued that this finding might reflect high anxiety in the hypomanic group, a possibility that was not considered by Bentall & Thompson. However, when French et al. replicated the study controlling for anxiety, they similarly observed slowed colour-naming for depression-related words in their hypomanic group.

Lyon, Startup & Bentall (in press) recently administered a similar Stroop task to clinically manic, bipolar-depressed and normal subjects. In this study, care was taken to match the depression-related and euphoria-related words for emotionality. The results, shown in Figure 18.5, were comparable to those obtained from the two earlier analogue studies. As others had previously found in studies of depression (Gotlib & Hammen, 1992), the depressed patients showed slowed colour-naming for the depression-related words. The same finding was observed for the manic patients in contrast with the normal controls. No difficulty in colour-naming the euphoria-related words was observed in any of the three groups.

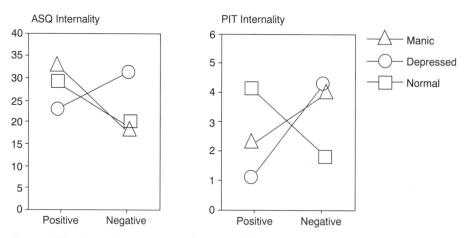

Figure 18.5 Internality scores on the ASQpf (left panel) and the PIT (right panel) for manic, bipolar-depressed and normal subjects. Reproduced from Lyon, Startup & Bentall (in press), with permission

Causal Attributions in Mania

The first attempt to systematically assess the role of causal attributions in mania was carried out by Winters & Neale (1985), who used the Pragmatic Inference Task (PIT) to compare remitted manic patients, depressed patients and normal controls. It will be recalled that the PIT (which was subsequently used with paranoid patients by Lyon, Kaney & Bentall, 1994) is an implicit test which is presented in the form of an assessment of memory. Winters & Neale found that the remitted manic patients, like their depressed controls (and also like the paranoid patients subsequently tested by Lyon et al.) made predominantly internal attributions for negative events and external attributions for positive events.

Winters & Neale's study was groundbreaking because of its focus on mania and its use of an implicit measure. However, it suffered from two obvious limitations. First, because of the difficulty of assessing currently manic patients, only remitted manic patients, were tested. Second, an explicit measure of attributional style was not administered. Lyon, Startup & Bentall (in press) recently administered the PIT and a version of the ASQ to currently manic, depressed and normal subjects. The currently manic patients scored similarly to Winters & Neale's remitted patients on the PIT, but showed a normal self-serving bias on the ASQ, on which they attributed negative events more to external causes than positive events. This pattern of results was similar to that previously observed for paranoid patients, with one exception: although the manic patients showed a robust self-serving bias on the ASQ, the bias was not significantly greater than that shown by the normal controls. Nonetheless, the difference between the manic patients' performance on the implicit and the explicit measures is clearly consistent with the manic-defence hypothesis.

Self-representations in Mania

The manic-defense hypothesis implies that manic patients, like paranoid patients, should show high consistency between their self-representations and their ideals. Research on self-esteem in bipolar patients has revealed evidence consistent with this prediction. Owen & Nurcombe (1970) used semantic differentials to assess constructs for self and others in a 13 year-old bipolar girl. Although her self-construct was much more negative in the depressed state than in the manic state, her constructs for others did not change between the two types of episode. In a similar study with manic depressive adults, Ashworth, Blackburn & McPherson (1982) measured self-esteem using repertory grids, finding abnormally high self-esteem during mania and abnormally low self-esteem during depression. Follow-up observations of some of the patients revealed that self-esteem returned to normal levels after either kind of episode.

In a recent study conducted using the theoretical framework provided by self-discrepancy theory, Bentall, Kinderman & Manson (submitted) investigated discrepancies between different domains and perspectives of self-representation in manic, depressed, remitted-bipolar and normal subjects. Whereas depression was characterized by abnormally high discrepancies between self-actual representations and self-ideals, mania was associated by an abnormal lack of self-discrepancies. The remitted patients, like the normal subjects, showed a low level of self-actual:self-ideal discrepancies that nonetheless exceeded those of the currently manic patients. In contrast to the data obtained from paranoid patients by Kinderman & Bentall (1996a), the manic patients, like the normal controls, showed little evidence of discrepancies between how they viewed themselves and how they thought they were viewed by other people—they believed that other people shared their positive view of themselves.

Consistent with this last observation, there is evidence that individuals prone to mania score highly on "social desirability", a construct that refers to an abnormal need to present the self in a positive light to others. Donnelly & Murphy (1973) compared bipolar patients and unipolar depressed patients (i.e. patients who were depressed but who had never suffered from mania) and observed higher social desirability scores in their bipolar group. Winters & Neale (1985) similarly found that social desirability scores were abnormally high in remitted manic patients.

Evidence of an implicit negative self-representation in manic patients is available from Lyon, Startup & Bentall's (in press) study, in which subjects were presented with a self-referent encoding measure in addition to the Stroop and attributional measures already described. It will be recalled that, on this type of test, subjects are first required to state whether positive and negative trait words describe themselves before trying to recall the words in a surprise test. The test used by Lyon et al. was identical to that used by Bentall & Kaney (1996) in their study of paranoia, but the results were much less equivocal. Whereas the manic patients endorsed positive words as true of themselves almost exclusively, like depressed patients they recalled more of the negative than the positive words.

COMMON MECHANISMS IN DEPRESSION, PARANOIA AND MANIA?

Biases in selective attention (Gotlib & Hammen, 1992), attributional abnormalities (Abramson, Metalsky & Alloy, 1989; Abramson, Seligman & Teasdale, 1978; Robins & Hayes, 1995) and abnormal self-representations (Higgins, 1987; Strauman & Higgins, 1988) have long been known to play an important role in depression. The evidence reviewed in this chapter indicates that abnormalities in these same cognitive systems are also implicated in both mania and paranoia. This evidence therefore supports Zigler & Glick's (1988) argument that depression, paranoia and mania are related phenomena. If correct, this hypothesis would further justify a radical rethinking of current methods of psychiatric classification but would also have several other important implications.

Why are Depression, Paranoia and Mania Different?

The observation that depression, paranoia and mania reflect abnormalities in the same cognitive domains implies that they are related conditions but not that they are identical. The most obvious way of accounting for the phenomenological differences between these conditions is in terms of the precise nature of the cognitive abnormalities involved in each.

The differences obtained from psychological studies of depression, paranoia and mania are most striking on tests requiring explicit judgements and are least striking on implicit tests. On measures of self-discrepancy, depressed patients show discrepancies between self-actual representations and self-ideals (Higgins, 1987; Strauman & Higgins, 1988), normal and paranoid individuals show substantial consistency between their perceived selves and their ideals (Kinderman & Bentall, 1996a), whereas manic patients show an abnormal degree of consistency between these representations (Bentall, Kinderman & Manson, submitted).

On questionnaire measures of attributional style, depressed patients abnormally attribute negative events to internal causes (Robins & Hayes, 1995), normal and manic patients show a self-serving bias and attribute negative events more than positive events to external causes (Lyon, Startup & Bentall, in press), and in paranoid patients the self-serving bias appears to be amplified. These findings must be qualified in the light of Kinderman & Bentall's (1996b) proposal that external attributions fall into two separate classes: those that implicate the actions of others and those that implicate circumstances or chance. The study by Kinderman & Bentall (1997) has indicated that paranoid patients are poor at making situational attributions and make excessive use of external-personal attributions. Unfortunately, this typology of internality judgements has not yet been studied in manic patients. It seems likely that such patients will not make excessive external-personal attributions for negative events (in which case they would be expected to develop persecutory delusions) but will make excessive external-situational attributions in comparison with normal subjects.

In contrast to the differences observed between depression, paranoia and mania on explicit tests, implicit tests reveal evidence of common mechanisms in the three conditions. For example, evidence of latent negative self-representations similar to those observed on explicit tests in depression has been reported for both paranoia (Bentall & Kaney, 1996; Kinderman, 1994; Lyon, Kaney & Bentall, 1994) and mania (Lyon, Startup & Bentall, in press). Moreover, on Winters & Neale's (1985) implicit measure of attributional style, depressed, paranoid, currently manic and remitted manic patients have all been found to exhibit a self-deprecating bias, attributing negative outcomes to self more than positive outcomes. These similarities must not be overstated (after all, the findings from Stroop and self-referent encoding measures are similar but not identical for paranoid and manic patients) but, nonetheless, the evidence as a whole points to problems of self-esteem in all three conditions.

The Dynamics of Attribution and Self-representation

It is possible that the phenomenological differences between depressed, paranoid and manic patients reflect not only the precise nature of their abnormal attributions and self-representations, but also differences in the way that these cognitive domains are coupled to each other. After all, the hypotheses we have so far discussed in relation to these conditions (in particular the Bentall, Kinderman & Kaney model of paranoia) all assume that self-representations and causal attributions are dynamically interrelated. Specifically, internal attributions for negative events (as made by depressed patients) should be associated with increases in self-actual:self-ideal and self-actual:self-ought discrepancies, whereas external attributions for negative events (as made by paranoid and manic patients) should be associated with a closure or a minimization of such discrepancies. In the case of paranoid patients (who make external-personal attributions for negative events) this minimization of self-actual:self-ideal and self-actual:self-ought discrepancies should be accompanied by an increased conviction that others hold negative views about the self, whereas in mania (which, we have assumed but not yet shown, is predominately associated with external-situational attributions for negative events) no such increase in self:other discrepancies should be observed.

A preliminary attempt to explore the validity of these assumptions has been made in two experimental studies involving non-patient participants by

Kinderman & Bentall (submitted). In both studies, participants completed a self-discrepancies questionnaire before and after completing a measure of causal attribution and, in both, internal attributions for negative events were, as predicted, associated with increases in self-actual:self-ideal discrepancies. However, in the first study the Peterson–Seligman bipolar internality scale was employed and the predicted consequences of excessively external attributions were not found. External attributions for negative events, instead of being associated with increases in self-actual:other-actual discrepancies, were actually associated with a decrease in those discrepancies. Subjects who made predominantly external attributions for negative events were therefore broken down into two groups according to whether the majority of these attributions were external-situational or external-personal. As predicted, external-personal attributions were then found to be associated with an increase in self-actual:other-actual discrepancies, whereas a reduction of those discrepancies was observed in those making mainly external-situational attributions.

The second study was conducted following the development of the IPSAQ and therefore subjects' attributions could more readily be allocated to the three attributional loci, with results that were entirely as predicted. Attributions made to internal (self-blaming) loci were associated with increased self-actual:self ideal and increased self-actual:other-actual discrepancies. Attributions made to external personal (other-blaming) loci were associated with reduced self-actual: self-ideal discrepancies, together with increased self-actual:other-actual discrepancies. In contrast, attributions made to external-situational loci were relatively benign and were associated with reduced self-actual:self-ideal and reduced self-actual:other-actual discrepancies.

These findings suggest that the cognitive processes involved in generating attributions and self-representations are closely coupled in normal individuals. Whether the way that they are coupled is identical in clinical subjects has yet to be established. Clearly, there is a need for more detailed studies of these interactions, especially with psychiatric patients. Such studies will not be easy to carry out as they will involve the repeated testing of people who, by virtue of their conditions, are difficult to recruit to research projects. However, the evidence that is already available indicates that it would be quite wrong to focus on a single cognitive domain—whether attributions or self-representations—in order to explain psychiatric disorders. Rather, there is a need for sophisticated models of how different types of cognitive abnormalities are interrelated.

Cognitive Abnormalities and the Course of Psychiatric Disorders

The above discussion about the ways in which attributions and self-representations may interact raises important questions about the causal status of abnormalities in these cognitive domains. This is a complex issue, and only a few brief words can be addressed to it here.

Debates about the causal role of attributions in depression have usually fo-cused on whether attributional style is best considered a trait or a state. It is assumed that, if attributional style is a trait, it can be considered to be a diathesis that precedes psychiatric breakdown, whereas if it is a state that co-varies with depression, it must be an epiphenomenon of depressive episodes. Attempts to resolve this debate empirically have usually involved complex longitudinal de-signs and have yielded ambiguous results (Robins & Hayes, 1995). Nonetheless, we have pointed to some evidence that suggests that, in psychotic patients at least, abnormal attributional processes may be present some years before a psychiatric breakdown occurs (Frenkel et al., 1995).

It is worth considering whether, for the purpose of determining causation, the distinction between traits and states is over-simplistic. After all, we have argued that self-representations may change as a consequence of certain kinds of attribu-tions and it is also possible that attributions are affected by the current state of self-representations. Consistent with this latter possibility, Forgas, Bower & Moylan (1990) found that normal subjects given contrived failure experiences afterwards showed evidence of a more pessimistic attributional style than beforehand.

It would appear, therefore, that attributions and self-representations are in a constant state of flux, influenced by each other, and also by various positive and negative events that the individual is exposed to. Of course, this does not mean that different clinical groups, all other things being equal, will settle into the same pattern of attributions and self-representations. That group designs reveal overall differences on these measures between different clinical groups is clear evidence that this is not the case. However, the particular "attributional style" recorded in a particular patient at a particular point in time is likely to be influenced by a range of factors (the current status of the individual's self-representations, recent life experiences, etc.) and this may explain the considerable within-group vari-ance typically observed in group comparison studies.

Developmental psychologists who have attempted mathematical models of multiple interacting cognitive systems have shown that, even in the case of quite simple systems, relatively small cognitive differences at an early point of time may herald quite dramatic and non-linear cognitive changes later (van Geert, 1994). This argument implies that quite subtle abnormalities in cognitive status may be all that is required to render someone vulnerable to a later breakdown characterized by very abnormal performance on cognitive tests. In these circum-stances cognitive abnormalities may be neither trait-like or state-like, but some-where in between. It may, therefore, be extremely difficult to detect cognitive abnormalities that precede a breakdown, even if the presence of those abnor-malities is essential for a breakdown to occur.

The studies which we have carried out to date, like most investigations in psychopathology, have provided "snapshots" of individuals' cognitive and affec-tive processes as they experience various types of psychiatric symptoms. How-ever, the above observations suggest that, in future research, it will be important to pay much more attention to the ways in which cognitive processes, affective states and symptoms of psychopathology vary across time. Studies of this sort will require sophisticated longitudinal designs which will not be easy to implement. However, it is only by adding these kinds of designs to our repertoire of methodologies that further progress will be achieved in understanding severe mental illness.

REFERENCES

Abraham, K. (1911/1927).   Notes on the psychoanalytic investigation and treatment of manic-depressive insanity and allied conditions. In E. Jones (ed.), *Selected Papers of Karl Abraham*. London: Hogarth.

Abramson, L. Y., Metalsky, G. I. & Alloy, L. B. (1989).   Hopelessness depression: a theory-based subtype of depression. *Psychological Review*, **96**, 358–372.

Abramson, L. Y., Seligman, M. E. P. & Teasdale, J. D. (1978).   Learned helplessness in humans: critique and reformulation. *Journal of Abnormal Psychology*, **78**, 40–74.

American Psychiatric Association (1994).   *Diagnostic and Statistical Manual for Mental Disorders*, 4th edn. Washington, DC: American Psychiatric Association.

Ashworth, C. M., Blackburn, I. M. & McPherson, F. M. (1982).   The performance of depressed and manic patients on some repertory grid measures. *British Journal of Medical Psychology*, **55**, 247–255.

Baron-Cohen, S. (1995).   *Mindblindness: An Essay on Autism and Theory of Mind*. Cambridge, MA: MIT Press.

Baron-Cohen, S., Leslie, A. M. & Frith, U. (1985).   Does the autistic child have a "theory of mind"? *Cognition*, **21**, 37–46.

Bauer, M. S., Crits-Christoph, P., Ball, W. A., Dewees, E., McAllister, T., Alahi, P., Cacciola, J. & Whybrow, P. C. (1991).   Independent assessment of manic and depressive symptoms by self-rating: scale characteristics and implications for the study of mania. *Archives of General Psychiatry*, **48**, 807–812.

Bentall, R. P. (1990).   The syndromes and symptoms of psychosis: or why you can't play 20 questions with the concept of schizophrenia and hope to win. In R. P. Bentall (ed.), *Reconstructing Schizophrenia*. London: Routledge.

Bentall, R. P. (1994).   Cognitive biases and abnormal beliefs: towards a model of persecutory delusions. In A. S. David & J. Cutting (eds), *The Neuropsychology of Schizophrenia*. London: Erlbaum.

Bentall, R. P., Jackson, H. F. & Pilgrim, D. (1988).   Abandoning the concept of schizophrenia: some implications of validity arguments for psychological research into psychotic phenomena. *British Journal of Clinical Psychology*, **27**, 303–324.

Bentall, R. P. & Kaney, S. (1989).   Content-specific information processing and persecutory delusions: an investigation using the emotional Stroop test. *British Journal of Medical Psychology*, **62**, 355–364.

Bentall, R. P. & Kaney, S. (1996).   Abnormalities of self-representation and persecutory delusions. *Psychological Medicine*, **26**, 1231–1237.

Bentall, R. P., Kaney, S. & Bowen-Jones, K. (1995).   Persecutory delusions and recall of threat-related, depression-related and neutral words. *Cognitive Therapy and Research*, **19**, 331–343.

Bentall, R. P., Kinderman, P. & Kaney, S. (1994).   The self, attributional processes and abnormal beliefs: towards a model of persecutory delusions. *Behaviour Research and Therapy*, **32**, 331–341.

Bentall, R. P., Kinderman, P. & Manson, K. (submitted). Self-discrepancies in bipolar-affective disorder.

Bentall, R. P. & Thompson, M. (1990).   Emotional stroop performance and the manic defence. *British Journal of Clinical Psychology*, **29**, 235–237.

Berrios, G. (1991). Delusions as "wrong beliefs": a conceptual history. *British Journal of Psychiatry*, **159**, 6–13.

Birchwood, M., Macmillan, F. & Smith, J. (1992). Early intervention. In M. Birchwood & N. Tarrier (eds), *Innovations in the Psychological Management of Schizophrenia*. Chichester: Wiley.

Blashfield, K. (1984). *The Classification of Psychopathology: NeoKraepelinian and Quantitative Approaches*. New York: Plenum.

Bleuler, E. (1911/1950). *Dementia Praecox or the Group of Schizophrenias* (trans. Zinkin, E.). New York: International Universities Press.

Brewin, C. R. (1985). Depression and causal attributions: what is their relation? *Psychological Bulletin*, **98**, 297–309.

Candido, C. L. & Romney, D. M. (1990). Attributional style in paranoid vs. depressed patients. *British Journal of Medical Psychology*, **63**, 355–363.

Carlson, G. A. & Goodwin, F. K. (1973). The stages of mania. *Archives of General Psychiatry*, **28**, 221–228.

Chapman, L. J. & Chapman, J. P. (1988). The genesis of delusions. In T. F. Oltmanns & B. A. Maher (eds), *Delusional Beliefs*. New York: Wiley.

Ciompi, L. (1984). Is there really a schizophrenia? The long-term course of psychotic phenomena. *British Journal of Psychiatry*, **145**, 636–640.

Clark, L. A., Watson, D. & Reynolds, S. (1995). Diagnosis and classification on psychopathology: challenges to the current system and future directions. *Annual Review of Psychology*, **46**, 121–153.

Colby, K. M., Faught, W. S. & Parkinson, R. C. (1979). Cognitive therapy of paranoid conditions: heuristic suggestions based on a computer simulation. *Cognitive Therapy and Research*, **3**, 55–60.

Corcoran, R., Frith, C. D. & Mercer, G. (1995). Schizophrenia, symptomatology and social inference: Investigating "theory of mind" in people with schizophrenia. *Schizophrenia Research*, **17**, 5–13.

Costello, C. G. (1992). Research on symptoms versus research on syndromes: arguments in favour of allocating more research time to the study of symptoms. *British Journal of Psychiatry*, **160**, 304–308.

Crow, T. J. (1986). The continuum of psychosis and its implication for the structure of the gene. *British Journal of Psychiatry*, **149**, 419–429.

Donnelly, E. F. & Murphy, D. L. (1973). Social desirability and bipolar affective disorder. *Journal of Consulting and Clinical Psychology*, **41**, 469.

Dudley, R. E. J., John, C. H., Young, A. W. & Over, D. E. (1997). Normal and abnormal reasoning in people with delusions. *British Journal of Clinical Psychology*, **36**, 243–258.

Eckblad, M. & Chapman, L. J. (1986). Development and validation of a scale for hypomanic personality. *Journal of Abnormal Psychology*, **95**, 214–222.

Ellis, H. D. & Young, A. W. (1990). Accounting for delusional misidentifications. *British Journal of Psychiatry*, **157**, 239–248.

Fear, C. F. & Healy, D. (1997). Probabilistic reasoning in obsessive-compulsive and delusional disorders. *Psychological Medicine*, **27**, 199–208.

Fear, C. F., Sharp, H. & Healy, D. (1996). Cognitive processes in delusional disorder. *British Journal of Psychiatry*, **168**, 61–67.

Forgas, J. P., Bower, G. H. & Moylan, S. J. (1990). Praise or blame? Affective influences on attributions for achievement. *Journal of Personality and Social Psychology*, **59**, 809–819.

Freedman, R. & Schwab, P. J. (1978). Paranoid symptoms in patients on a general hospital psychiatric unit. *Archives of General Psychiatry*, **35**, 387–390.

French, C. C., Richards, A. & Scholfield, E. J. C. (1996). Hypomania, anxiety and the emotional Stroop. *British Journal of Clinical Psychology*, **35**, 617–626.

Frenkel, E., Kugelmass, S., Nathan, M. & Ingraham, L. J. (1995). Locus of control and mental health in adolescence and adulthood. *Schizophrenia Bulletin*, **21**, 219–226.

Freud, S. (1911/1950). Psychoanalytic notes upon an autobiographical account of a case of paranoia (Dementia Paranoides). In: *Collected Papers*. London: Hogarth.

Freud, S. (1917/1950). *Mourning and Melancholia*. London: Hogarth.

Frith, C. & Corcoran, R. (1996). Exploring "theory of mind" in people with schizophrenia. *Psychological Medicine*, **26**, 521–530.

Frith, C. D. (1992). *The Cognitive Neuropsychology of Schizophrenia*. Hillsdale, NJ: Erlbaum.

Frith, U. (1989). *Autism: Explaining the Enigma*. Oxford: Blackwell.

Garety, P. A., Hemsley, D. R. & Wessely, S. (1991). Reasoning in deluded schizophrenic and paranoid patients. *Journal of Nervous and Mental Disease*, **179**, 194–201.

Glick, M., Zigler, E. & Zigler, B. (1985). Developmental correlates of age on first hospitalization in non-schizophrenic psychiatric patients. *Journal of Nervous and Mental Disease*, **173**, 677–684.

Goldberg, D. & Huxley, P. (1992). *Common Mental Disorders: A bio-social Model*. London: Routledge.

Goodwin, F. K. & Jamison, K. R. (1990). *Manic-depressive Illness*. Oxford: Oxford University Press.

Gotlib, I. H. & Hammen, C. L. (1992). *Psychological Aspects of Depression: Towards a Cognitive–Interpersonal Integration*. Chichester: Wiley.

Green, M. F. (1992). Information processing in schizophrenia. In D. J. Kavanagh (ed.), *Schizophrenia: An Overview and Practical Handbook*. London: Chapman and Hall.

Grossman, L. S. & Harrow, M. (1991). Thought disorder and cognitive processes in mania. In P. A. Magaro (ed.), *Annual Review of Psychopathology*. Newbury Park, CA: Sage.

Gruba, F. P. & Johnson, J. E. (1974). Contradictions within the self-concepts of schizophrenics. *Journal of Clinical Psychology*, **30**, 253–254.

Happé, F. & Frith, U. (1994). Theory of mind in autism. In E. Schopler & G. B. Mesibov (eds), *Learning and Cognition in Autism*. New York: Plenum.

Havner, P. H. & Izard, C. E. (1962). Unrealistic self-enhancement in paranoid schizophrenics. *Journal of Consulting Psychology*, **26**, 65–68.

Heider, F. (1958). *The Psychology of Interpersonal Relations*. New York: Wiley.

Henderson, D. K. & Gillespie, R. D. (1936). *A Textbook of Psychiatry*, 4th edn. London: Oxford University Press.

Higgins, E. T. (1987). Self-discrepancy: a theory relating self and affect. *Psychological Review*, **94**, 319–340.

Huq, S. F., Garety, P. A. & Hemsley, D. R. (1988). Probabilistic judgements in deluded and non-deluded subjects. *Quarterly Journal of Experimental Psychology*, **40A**, 801–812.

Ibelle, B. P. (1961). Discrepancies between self-concepts and ideal self-concepts in paranoid schizophrenics and normals. *Dissertation Abstracts*, **21**, 2004–2005.

Jaspers, K. (1912/1963). *General Psychopathology* (trans. Hoenig, J. & Hamilton, M. W.). Manchester: Manchester University Press.

John, C. H. & Dodgson, G. (1994). Inductive reasoning in delusional thought. *Journal of Mental Health*, **3**, 31–49.

Johnstone, E. C., Crow, T. J., Frith, C. D. & Owens, D. G. C. (1988). The Northwick Park "functional" psychosis study: diagnosis and treatment response. *Lancet*, **ii**, 119–125.

Kaney, S. & Bentall, R. P. (1989). Persecutory delusions and attributional style. *British Journal of Medical Psychology*, **62**, 191–198.

Kaney, S. & Bentall, R. P. (1992). Persecutory delusions and the self-serving bias. *Journal of Nervous and Mental Disease*, **180**, 773–780.

Kaney, S., Wolfenden, M., Dewey, M. E. & Bentall, R. P. (1992). Persecutory delusions and the recall of threatening and non-threatening propositions. *British Journal of Clinical Psychology*, **31**, 85–87.

Kaplan, H. B. (1975). *Self-attitudes and Deviant Behaviour*. Pacific Pallisades: Goodyear.

Kendell, R. E. (1989). Clinical validity. In L. N. Robins & J. E. Barrett (eds), *The Validity of Psychiatric Diagnosis*. New York: Raven.

Kendell, R. E. & Brockington, I. F. (1980). The identification of disease entities and the relationship between schizophrenic and affective psychoses. *British Journal of Psychiatry*, **137**, 324–331.

Kendler, K. S., Glazer, W. & Morgenstern, H. (1983). Dimensions of delusional experience. *American Journal of Psychiatry*, **140**, 466–469.

Kinderman, P. (1994). Attentional bias, persecutory delusions and the self concept. *British Journal of Medical Psychology*, **67**, 53–66.

Kinderman, P. & Bentall, R. P. (1996a). Self-discrepancies and persecutory delusions: evidence for a defensive model of paranoid ideation. *Journal of Abnormal Psychology*, **105**, 106–114.

Kinderman, P. & Bentall, R. P. (1996b). The development of a novel measure of causal attributions: the Internal Personal and Situational Attributions Questionnaire. *Personality and Individual Differences*, **20**, 261–264.

Kinderman, P. & Bentall, R. P. (1997). Causal attributions in paranoia: internal, personal and situational attributions for negative events. *Journal of Abnormal Psychology*.

Kinderman, P. & Bentall, R. P. (submitted). The self and explanatory style: the impact of internality judgements on the accessibility of self-discrepancies. *Journal of Personality and Social Psychology*.

Kinderman, P., Dunbar, R. I. M. & Bentall, R. P. (1998). Theory of mind deficits and causal attributions. *British Journal of Psychology*, **89**, 191–204.

Kotin, J. & Goodwin, F. K. (1972). Depression during mania. *American Journal of Psychiatry*, **129**, 679–686.

Kretschmer, E. (1927). *Der Sensitive Bezeihungswahn*, 2nd edn. Berlin: Springer.

Leafhead, K. M., Young, A. W. & Szulecka, T. K. (1996). Delusions demand attention. *Cognitive Neuropsychiatry*, **1**, 5–16.

Leonhard, K. (1957). *The Classification of Endogenous Psychoses*, 5th edn. New York: Irvington.

Leslie, A. M. (1991). The theory of mind impairment in autism: evidence for a modular mechanism of development? In A. Whiten (ed.), *Natural Theories of Mind*. Oxford: Blackwell.

Lewine, R. R. J., Watt, N. F., Pretky, R. A. & Fryer, J. H. (1980). Childhood social competence in functionally disordered psychiatric patients and in normals. *Journal of Abnormal Psychology*, **89**, 132–138.

Lyon, H., Startup, M. & Bentall, R. P. (in press). Social cognition and the manic defense. *Journal of Abnormal Psychology*.

Lyon, H. M., Kaney, S. & Bentall, R. P. (1994). The defensive function of persecutory delusions: evidence from attribution tasks. *British Journal of Psychiatry*, **164**, 637–646.

Macalpine, I. & Hunter, R. (1955). Preface. In I. Macalpine & R. Hunter (eds), *Daniel Paul Schreber's "Memoirs of My Nervous Illness"*. London: Dawson.

Maher, B. A. (1988). Anomalous experience and delusional thinking: the logic of explanations. In T. F. Oltmanns & B. A. Maher (eds), *Delusional Beliefs*. New York: Wiley.

Markus, H. & Wurf, E. (1987). The dynamic self-concept: a social psychological perspective. *Annual Review of Psychology*, **38**, 299–337.

Mayer-Gross, W., Slater, E. & Roth, M. (1954). *Clinical Psychiatry*. London: Cassell.

Musalek, M., Berner, P. & Katschnig, H. (1989). Delusional theme, sex and age. *Psychopathology*, **22**, 260–267.

Neale, J. M. (1988). Defensive function of manic episodes. In T. F. Oltmanns & B. A. Maher (eds), *Delusional Beliefs*. New York: Wiley.

Norman, R. M. G. & Malla, A. K. (1991). Dysphoric mood and symptomatology in schizophrenia. *Psychological Medicine*, **21**, 897–203.

Owen, S. E. & Nurcombe, B. (1970). The application of the Semantic Differential Test in a case of manic-depressive psychosis. *Australian and New Zealand Journal of Psychiatry*, **4**, 148–154.

Persons, J. B. (1986). The advantages of studying psychological phenomena rather than psychiatric diagnoses. *American Psychologist*, **41**, 1252–1260.

Peterson, C., Semmel, A., Von Baeyer, C., Abramson, L., Metalsky, G. I. & Seligman, M.E.P. (1982). The Attributional Style Questionnaire. *Cognitive Therapy and Research*, **3**, 287–300.

Power, M. J. & Brewin, C. R. (1991). From Freud to cognitive science: a contemporary account of the unconscious. *British Journal of Clinical Psychology*, **30**, 289–310.

Rado, S. (1928). The problem of melancholia. *International Journal of Psychoanalysis*, **9**, 420–438.

Reivich, K. (1995). The measurement of explanatory style. In G. M. Buchanan & M. E. P. Seligman (eds), *Explanatory Style*. Hillsdale, NJ: Erlbaum.

Robey, K. L., Cohen, B. D. & Gara, M. A. (1989). Self-structure in schizophrenia. *Journal of Abnormal Psychology*, **98**, 436–442.

Robins, C. J. & Hayes, A. H. (1995). The role of causal attributions in the prediction of depression. In G. M. Buchanan & M. E. P. Seligman (eds), *Explanatory Style*. Hillsdale, NJ: Erlbaum.

Rogers, A. H. (1958). The self-concept in paranoid schizophrenia. *Journal of Clinical Psychology*, **14**, 365–366.

Schreber, D. (1903/1955). *Memoirs of My nervous Illness* (trans. I. Macalpine & R. A. Hunter). London: Dawson.

Scott, L. & O'Hara, M. W. (1993). Self-discrepancies in clinically anxious and depressed university students. *Journal of Abnormal Psychology*, **102**, 282–287.

Seligman, M. E., Peterson, C., Kaslow, N. J., Tanenbaum, R. L., Alloy, L. B. & Abramson, L. B. (1984). Attributional style and depressive symptoms among children. *Journal of Abnormal Psychology*, **93**, 235–238.

Sharp, H. M., Fear, C. F. & Healy, D. (1997). Attributional style and delusions: an investigation based on delusional content. *European Psychiatry*, **12**, 1–7.

Silverstone, P. H. (1991). Low self-esteem in different psychiatric conditions. *British Journal of Clinical Psychology*, **30**, 185–188.

Stratton, P., Heard, D., Hanks, H. G., Munton, A. G., Brewin, C. & Davidson, I. (1986). Coding causal beliefs in natural discourse. *British Journal of Social Psychology*, **25**.

Strauman, T. J. (1989). Self-discrepancies in clinical depression and social phobia: cognitive structures that underlie emotional disorders? *Journal of Abnormal Psychology*, **98**, 14–22.

Strauman, T. J. (1992). Self-guides, autobiographical memory, and anxiety and dysphoria: toward a cognitive model of vulnerability to emotional distress. *Journal of Abnormal Psychology*, **101**(1), 87–95.

Strauman, T. J. & Higgins, E. T. (1987). Automatic activation of self-discrepancies and emotional syndromes: when cognitive structures influence affect. *Journal of Abnormal Psychology*, **98**, 14–22.

Strauman, T. J. & Higgins, E. T. (1988). Self-discrepancies as predictors of vulnerability to distinct syndromes of chronic emotional distress. *Journal of Personality*, **56**, 685–707.

Strauman, T. J., Lemieux, A. M. & Coe, C. L. (1993). Self-discrepancy and natural killer cell activity: immunological consequences of negative self-evaluation. *Journal of Personality and Social Psychology*, **64**, 1042–1052.

Strauss, J. S. (1969). Hallucinations and delusions as points on continua function: rating scale evidence. *Archives of General Psychiatry*, **21**, 581–586.

Sweeny, P., Anderson, K. & Bailey, S. (1986). Attributional style and depression: a meta-analytic review. *Journal of Personality and Social Psychology*, **50**, 774–791.

Tennen, H. & Herzenberger, S. (1987). Depression, self-esteem and the absence of self-protective attributional biases. *Journal of Personality and Social Psychology*, **52**, 72–80.

Tennen, H., Herzenberger, S. & Nelson, H. F. (1987). Depressive attributional style: the role of self-esteem. *Journal of Personality*, **55**, 631–660.

Tyrer, P. (1990). The division of neurosis: a failed classification. *Journal of the Royal Society of Medicine*, **83**, 614–616.

Ullmann, L. P. & Krasner, L. (1969). *A Psychological Approach to Abnormal Behaviour*. Englewood Cliffs, NJ: Prentice-Hall.

van Geert, P. (1994). *Dynamic Systems of Development: Change Between Complexity and Chaos*. New York: Harvester Wheatsheaf.

Walker, C. (1991). Delusions: what did Jaspers really say? *British Journal of Psychiatry*, **159**, 94–103.

Weiner, B. (1986). Cognition, emotion and action. In R. M. Sorrentino & E. T. Higgins (eds), *Handbook of Motivation and Cognition: Foundations of Social Behaviour*. New York: Guilford.

White, P. A. (1991). Ambiguity in the internal/external distinction in causal attribution. *Journal of Experimental Social Psychology*, **27**, 259–270.

Williams, J. M. G., Mathews, A. & MacLeod, C. (1996). The emotional Stroop task and psychopathology. *Psychological Bulletin*, **120**, 3–24.

Winters, K. C. & Neale, J. M. (1983). Delusions and delusional thinking: a review of the literature. *Clinical Psychology Review*, **3**, 227–253.

Winters, K. C. & Neale, J. M. (1985). Mania and low self-esteem. *Journal of Abnormal Psychology*, **94**, 282–290.

World Health Organization (1992). *ICD-10: International Statistical Classification of Diseases and Related Health Problems*, 10th edn, revised. Geneva: World Health Organization.

Wylie, R. C. (1979). *The Self-concept*, revised edn. Lincoln, NE: University of Nebraska Press.

Young, A. W. (1994). Recognition and reality. In E. M. R. Critchley (ed.), *The Neurological Boundaries of Reality*. London: Farrand.

Young, H. F. & Bentall, R. P. (1995). Hypothesis testing in patients with persecutory delusions: comparison with depressed and normal subjects. *British Journal of Clinical Psychology*, **34**, 353–369.

Young, H. F. & Bentall, R. P. (1997). Probabilistic reasoning in deluded, depressed and normal subjects: effects of task difficulty and meaningful versus non-meaningful materials. *Psychological Medicine*, **27**, 455–465.

Zigler, E. & Glick, M. (1986). *A Developmental Approach to Psychopathology*. New York: Wiley.

Zigler, E. & Glick, M. (1988). Is paranoid schizophrenia really camouflaged depression? *American Psychologist*, **43**, 284–290.

Zigler, E. & Levine, J. (1981). Age of first hospitalization of male and female paranoid and non-paranoid schizophrenics: a developmental approach. *Journal of Abnormal Psychology*, **90**, 458–467.

Zullow, H. M., Oettingen, G., Peterson, C. & Seligman, M. E. P. (1988). Pessimistic explanatory style in the historical record: CAVing LBJ, Presidential candidates, and East versus West Berlin. *American Psychologist*, **43**, 673–682.

Chapter 19

The Early Emergence of Emotional Understanding and Appraisal: Implications for Theories of Development

Nancy L. Stein
University of Chicago, Chicago, IL, USA
and
Linda J. Levine
University of California, Irvine, CA, USA

INTRODUCTION

This chapter presents an essay on the nature and emergence of emotional understanding. By focusing on understanding, we describe how children and adults make sense of those events that evoke emotion, the types of appraisals that lead to the experience of emotion, the role that preferences and goals play in evoking emotion, and the ways in which emotion influences subsequent thinking and behavior. In essence, we describe the unfolding of emotion in terms of the causal sequence of mental processes that occur when emotion is experienced. Because we focus on development, we address the issue of how children may or may not differ from adults in their experience of emotion. We speak to the complex relationship between cognition and emotion, the need to describe the contents of the inferences made during emotional experience, and understanding of the "basic" emotions (e.g. happiness, anger, sadness and fear).

Children and adults use both conscious and unconscious processes to understand, evaluate and respond to events that evoke emotion. From the very beginning, emotional understanding is goal- and preference-based. Even the youngest

Handbook of Cognition and Emotion. Edited by T. Dalgleish and M. Power.
© 1999 John Wiley & Sons Ltd.

children who experience and express what we consider to be the "basic" emotions make inferences about the harms and benefits of emotion-laden situations. Very young children also engage in planful action to attain or eliminate states that are pleasurable or aversive. Thus, the mental structures that govern and regulate emotional understanding are in place well before children begin to talk. We will argue that the types of appraisals that children carry out in emotion situations are similar to those that adults carry out.

To document the early emergence of emotional understanding, we present a model that operates from at least 2 years of age, when children begin to talk consistently and communicate about their understanding of emotional events. We describe how these young children evaluate events, goals, plans and actions during the retrospective recall of emotional events. We also discuss studies in which young children narrate on-line during the experience of emotion.

The early emergence of emotional understanding does not negate the existence of developmental differences in the depth of understanding of emotion-eliciting events. Typically, adults have been exposed to more situations, and as a result have broader knowledge of the causes and consequences of emotion-eliciting events than do younger children. The question we pose, however, is whether these developmental changes influence the basic organization of emotional thinking, or whether they influence the specific types of appraisals made, the specific coping strategies used and the speed with which retrieval of information occurs.

A MODEL OF EMOTIONAL EXPERIENCE AND UNDERSTANDING

Four dimensions characterize the process of understanding that accompanies emotional experience. First, the evocation of emotion always signals that some type of change has been perceived in a personally significant goal. That is, children and adults who experience an emotion have perceived some type of change in one of their goals, such that the goal has been attained, blocked or threatened (Folkman & Stein, 1997; Stein & Levine, 1987, 1989, 1990; Stein, Trabasso & Liwag, 1992).

Second, a one-to-one correspondence between a given event and a specific emotion does not exist. The experience of emotion depends upon the prior knowledge, beliefs and appraisals used to assess the status of personally significant goals. The appraisals made about the causes and consequences of an event, rather than the event itself, determine whether and which emotion will be experienced. The lack of a direct correspondence between an event and an emotion holds even for young children (Stein & Levine, 1989; Stein, Liwag & Wade, 1995). For example, Sroufe (1979) notes that very young infants can have a variety of reactions to the game of peek-a-boo. At one time, an infant may respond to the game with a startle response, followed by a fearful expression and crying. At another time, the same infant may display gleeful laughter when engaged in the game of peek-a-boo. The critical factors believed to regulate the experience of an emotion are the initial psychological state of the infant, in terms of the goals and beliefs operating at the onset of a specific event, and the inferences made about the consequences the event will have for a valued goal state.

The involuntary nature of emotional experience is the third dimension that characterizes the process of understanding. We do not plan to experience an emotion. We can anticipate how we might react when an emotion-laden event occurs, and we can even carry out an enactment of how we might respond to a specific event (as therapists are wont to have their patients do in practicing emotion regulation). However, emotions occur involuntarily and unexpectedly, in response to novel aspects of an event or situation. The presence of information that violates prior expectations is a critical component of emotional experience (e.g. Mandler, 1984; Stein & Levine, 1987). For example, when children and adults are presented with the same event repeatedly, they experience an emotion the second time the event is presented because they perceive a new element in the event that was not encoded during the first presentation. If children and adults fail to notice a novel aspect of an event, they do not experience the same intensity of emotion, and sometimes they report not experiencing any emotion (Stein & Trabasso, 1989).

The fourth dimension that characterizes emotional understanding is the causal thinking, goal-appraisal and planning processes that operate continually throughout the experience of an emotion. Current theories of cognition and emotion have accepted the importance of goal appraisal processes (Frijda, 1995; Johnson-Laird & Oatley, 1989; Lazarus, 1991; Oatley & Johnson-Laird, 1987; Roseman, Antoniou & Jose, 1996; Smith & Lazarus, 1993). Frijda (1995) uses the word "concerns" to illustrate the focus on goals; Oatley & Johnson-Laird examine goals that differentiate among the emotions; Smith & Lazarus (1993) speak to the importance of linking appraisals to the goals of well-being. We focus on the goal appraisal processes that are carried out throughout the experience of emotion, and we describe the ways in which thinking and appraisal unfold during emotional experience (Folkman & Stein, 1997; Levine, 1996; Stein et al., in press; Stein & Levine, 1987, 1990; Stein, Trabasso & Liwag, 1992, 1994).

The model that we present in this chapter is distinct from other models in the following ways. We address issues related to the *development* of emotional understanding. Thus, we examine understanding in very young children (Levine, 1995; Levine & Stein, 1997; Liwag & Stein, 1995; Stein & Levine, 1989; Stein & Liwag, 1997; Stein, Trabasso & Liwag, 1994: Trabasso, Stein & Johnson, 1981) and in adults (Levine, 1996; Stein & Levine, 1989; Stein, Trabasso & Liwag, 1994; Stein et al., in press). Rather than proceed with the assumption that children are fundamentally different thinkers than adults, we use our theory of the understanding process to examine the similarities and differences between children's and adults' thinking. In this way, we are able to speak to the universals associated with emotional understanding as well as to the differences that may occur.

We also describe appraisal, thinking and planning, as these processes occur *on-line* during the experience of an emotion (Stein, Bernas & Calicchia, 1997; Stein & Boyce, 1995; Trabasso & Ozyureck, 1997) or *retrospectively*, as people engage in recalling events that are emotionally meaningful (Levine, 1996, Levine & Bluck, in press; Levine & Stein, 1997; Liwag & Stein, 1995; Stein & Liwag, 1997; Stein, Liwag & Wade, 1995; Stein, Wade & Liwag, 1997). The emphasis on content, causal sequencing and function allows us to describe the "unfolding" of an emotion episode.

In our analysis of the non-verbal dimensions of emotion, we focus on the expressive systems of the face, voice and hands, as well as the sequence of non-verbal actions that children and adults carry out during the "narration" of emotional experience (Boyce et al., 1991; Stein & Boyce, 1995).

Finally, we have examined the accuracy of memory for emotional events, the ways in which memory affects subsequent states of psychological well-being, and the ways in which emotions affect thinking and strategic interaction during conflicts (Albro & Stein, 1997; Folkman & Stein, 1997; Levine, in press; Levine & Burgess, 1995; Stein, Bernas & Calicchia, 1997; Stein et al., in press; Stein & Trabasso, 1992). We have also begun to characterize individual differences in emotional experience and to describe the impact these differences have on memory for emotional events (Stein & Boyce, 1995).

THE EMERGENCE OF EMOTIONAL UNDERSTANDING

Given that thinking and appraisal are integral to emotional experience, what can we say about their development? The experience and expression of emotion change significantly during the first 6 months of life. At birth, the infant's affective repertoire includes a set of behaviors for responding to different types and intensities of stimulation. Some of these behaviors are reflexive in nature (e.g. the startle, orientating, blinking and sucking reflexes) and are followed by general affective responses like distress (e.g. volatile activity and crying), quieting (e.g. the absence of volatile activity) and pleasure.

Some researchers take a reflexive response, coupled with a general affective response such as distress or quieting, to be indicative of emotion (LeDoux, 1996). In our theory (Stein & Levine, 1987, 1989; Stein, Trabasso & Liwag, 1992), these general affective responses are not defined as emotions. The experience of emotion requires that infants be able to represent a goal state and the changes that occur in these goal states. The ability to represent a state that is not yet present (e.g. a goal state) gradually emerges between the ages of 2–6 months (Stenberg & Campos, 1990; Stem, 1985, 1992; Sroufe, 1979). The ability to exhibit a preference for one state vs. another also emerges at approximately the same time. It is when infants acquire the capability to represent an absent goal state, prefer one state over another, and invoke action in the service of getting from one state to another, that they begin to experience and express emotion. An important source of evidence for this development is that generalized negative reactions, such as the distress expression, gradually give way to discrete facial expressions of anger, sadness and fear which are accompanied by actions appropriate to these emotional states (e.g. Stenberg & Campos, 1990; Izard, Hemsbree & Heubner, 1987).

LeDoux's (1996) finding of a direct connection between the sensory thalamus and the amygdala is not evidence that emotional responses are "hard-wired" or that emotional responses bypass the cortex. The level of behavior LeDoux describes is considered "reflexive" by many, and much of his data are drawn from research on the behavior of rats. What LeDoux defines as "emotional" we define as "affective". The critical data that LeDoux needs in humans are those from decerebrate infants, and the few inquiries that exist indicate that expressions of discrete emotions never emerge in these infants (Kolb & Taylor, 1990).

The fact that newborn infants express pleasure and distress does not mean that they prefer or desire to shift from one state to another. Having preferences requires the ability to represent, remember, compare and choose between two different states, and to express a desire to orientate more toward one state than toward another. Although newborns display pleasure or distress in direct response to different events, they have yet to achieve the capacity to represent a state different from the one currently directing their behavior. The time between birth and 6 months of age is believed to be essential for acquiring the prerequisite knowledge necessary to experience and express emotion as we define it. Several milestones can be observed. The infant's ability to habituate to and remember different classes of events increases in breadth. Habituation signals that infants can form predictable representations of an event and that they can detect discrepant information in the event (or dishabituate) when novelty is introduced (Alessandri, Sullivan & Lewis, 1990; Lewis, Alessandri & Sullivan, 1990).

Infants also become capable of sustained attention to objects, people and events, and they begin to exhibit "anticipatory" behaviors in viewing and responding to a sequence of actions and events (Haith, 1994; Reznick, 1994; von Hofsten, 1994). These anticipations indicate that a set of expectations and causal inferences have developed concerning the upcoming event. Infants also learn that certain actions result in aversive outcomes and that others result in pleasurable outcomes (Alessandri, Sullivan & Lewis, 1990; Lewis, Alessandri & Sullivan, 1990). As a consequence of drawing causal inferences between outcomes and the resulting affective states, they learn to change their plans of action so that they can escape aversive states and reinstate pleasurable states.

According to the literature on infant development (e.g. Alessandri, Sullivan & Lewis, 1990; Fernald, 1984; Haith, 1994; Lewis, Alessandri & Sullivan, 1990), these skills cohere and become integrated somewhere between the second and seventh month of life. By 8–12 months of age (Stenberg & Campos, 1990; Duncan

& Farley, 1990; Willats, 1990), the non-verbal precursors of children's understanding of emotional experience are solidly in place. Young children rapidly
shift the focus of their attention when a novel stimulus is introduced; they attend
to the novelty before expressing their emotion (Sroufe, 1979; Stenberg &
Campos, 1990); they focus on the object or person who has directly blocked or
facilitated their goals (Alessandri, Sullivan & Lewis, 1990; Stenberg & Campos,
1990); they repeat or generate different plans of actions until they are able to
attain a desired state; and they express discrete emotions as a direct function of
the outcome of their actions.

When asked to construct a temporal sequence of events they have observed, 1-
year-old children are able to reconstruct specific types of temporal sequences,
and 16–20-month-old children are able to reproduce causal sequences of events,
even after delays of 2 and 6 weeks (Bauer & Mandler, 1989, 1990; Bauer & Shore,
1987). Myers, Clifton & Clarkson (1987) also report that one 33 month-old child
who returned to their laboratory after participating in a study was able to recall
verbally a picture of a whale that he had seen in the lab at 9 months of age. The
memory of the whale was preserved despite the fact that the child had no word
for "whale" at the time he saw the picture (see Mandler & McDonough, 1997, for
an extensive discussion of non-verbal memory in young children).

In summary, infant studies show that the experience of discrete emotions
emerges gradually within in the first 6 months of life. Young infants rapidly
develop the skills needed to monitor the status of personally meaningful goals, to
recognize when goals succeed, fail or are threatened, to assess the consequences
of their actions, and to create alternative plans of action to achieve a goal. The
fact that infants are in a pre-verbal state does not preclude their ability to engage
in complex thinking and planning (Baldwin & Moses, in press). Using sophisticated methodology to examine the planning and action capabilities of pre-verbal
infants, researchers have shown that infants exhibit excellent skill at tracking and
responding to other people's actions and behavior, especially when they are
intent upon achieving a very specific goal (Duncan & Farley, 1990; Haith, 1994;
Willats, 1990). Although we do not have verbal evidence of infant's understanding of emotion situations until approximately 2 years of age, we do have good
evidence from non-verbal observations of emotional understanding that infants
engage in complex thinking and planning behavior.

THE EMERGENCE OF VERBAL EMOTIONAL UNDERSTANDING

When children begin to talk about their own and other people's emotional
states, how do they talk about emotional experience? How do they understand,
remember and recount emotional events that affect themselves and other
people? If toddlers have acquired the requisite non-verbal knowledge to appraise and evaluate changes in their goal states, we should observe a very

fast mapping of non-verbal emotion concepts onto language. In particular, children should use their knowledge of emotion to talk about six different components of experience:

1. What happened?
2. How did the event affect my goals?
3. How do I feel about it?
4. What do I want to do about it?
5. What did I do?
6. What were the results of my actions?

These questions reflect the temporal and causal constraints in the mental schemas used to interpret and respond to emotion-laden events. The questions also reflect the typical sequence and content of talk that children and adults generate when recounting emotional experiences.

Figure 19.1 illustrates our general model of the sequence of processes carried out during the experience of emotion. Although we do not describe each component of the general model in this chapter, the emotional understanding process captured by our model can be summarized succinctly by focusing on the answers to the questions listed above. The following tenets are critical to our model of the understanding process. First, we define appraisal as the process of evaluating the significance and worth of any event, either external or internal to the person.

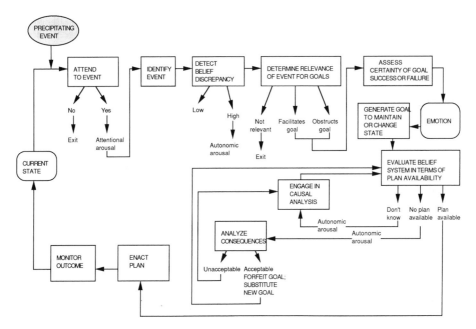

Figure 19.1 A general model of evaluation, planning, and decision making during emotional experience

Thus, everything that a narrator includes in a description of an emotional experience is considered "technically" to be an appraisal. We use the verb "appraise" as synonymous with the verb "evaluate". Some appraisals focus on the identification and status of an event without reference to the impact the event had on a person's goals. Other appraisals include explicit statements concerning the impact of an event on a person's values, preferences and goals. We distinguish between these two types of appraisals throughout our analysis of emotional experience.

Second, the process of appraisal and evaluation has a large non-verbal component, even for adults. Appraisals of value are based upon states of liking and states of preference. Both liking and preference are intimately linked to the sensory and physiological experiences of pleasure and pain. Thus, physiological information from the body serves as a primary source in regulating the value assigned to a particular event or state. Indeed, when uncontrollable "bad" events happen to adults, they will often state how much pain they are in over a loss or unavoidable tragedy, even though physical pain and damage are technically absent from the experience (Stein, Trabasso, and Albro, 1997).

Much of the procedural knowledge activated during planning and goal-related action is also non-verbal in nature. Infants are continually engaged in constructing plans of action and solving problems, even though these plans are restricted to specific domains. Several infant researchers (see Alessandri, Sullivan & Lewis, 1990; Gergely et al., in press; Emde, 1980; Haith, 1994; Reznick, 1994; Stenberg & Campos, 1990; von Hofsten, 1994; Willats, 1990), have established that infants form expectations and carry out goal-directed action quite early in life. Although researchers debate about the exact onset and meaning of goal-directed action, most argue that it is causally linked to emotional expression between the ages of 4 and 8 months. Evidence for earlier problem-solving skills in emotional situations has been reported by Lewis and his colleagues (Lewis, Alessandri & Sullivan 1990; Alessandri, Sullivan & Lewis, 1990).

In describing the development of emotional understanding, we focus on a set of studies carried out in our laboratories. In these studies, children aged 2.5–6 years were asked to recall events that evoked four different emotions: happiness, sadness, anger and fear. The unique aspect of these studies is that children and their parents engaged in several different recall tasks that focused on these four emotions. Thus, we obtained several observations of the same child, but in different contexts. In this chapter, we report data from the following contexts: (a) children recalled situations in which they had felt each emotion; (b) children recalled situations in which they had observed their best friend or sibling experience each emotion; (c) children recalled events reported by their parents concerning times that the children had experienced each emotion; and (d) children described events that could evoke each of the four emotions in themselves and in others. Because of space limitations, we report the results from three questions that summarize most of the appraisals in children's narratives: What happened; How were my goals affected; and What do I want to do about it?

WHAT HAPPENED?

Memories of what happened focus on a specific event or set of conditions that evoked an emotion. Attending to and identifying the precipitating event is critical to emotional experience. Precipitating events are used as markers to signal the initial or pivotal cause of the changes that occurred with respect to valued goals. The precipitating event is often cited as the reason for an emotional response, without including reference to the intermediate, more proximal, appraisals that have been made about the changes in personally significant goals. For example, when asked why he was so angry at a little girl he had just met, one of our 3 year-old boys said, "She broke my gun!" as he yelled at the experimenter and at the video camera. This statement, standing alone (without the non-verbal cues), tells us only that one of this little boy's possessions was destroyed. It does not tell us how the boy appraised the destruction with respect to his goals or preferences.

Without the occurrence of a pivotal initiating event, however, the little boy's goals would not have changed. Thus, the event that begins the change is highly salient, and children in each of our studies (Levine & Stein, 1997; Stein & Liwag, 1997) could describe initiating events that resulted in the experience of emotion. Children were able to describe events that had evoked emotions in themselves over 82% of the time. Children corroborating the occurrence of events nominated by parents agreed 87% of the time that the events had indeed occurred. Further, all children could then produce a narrative that described how they felt, why they felt that way, and what they did about the situation (Liwag & Stein, 1995; Stein & Liwag, 1997).

Table 19.1 contains the 22 different event categories that were generated when children were asked to recall events that had made them or another person feel happy, sad, angry and afraid. The data show that events that elicited happiness did not overlap with events that elicited the three negative emotions. Among the three negative emotions, fear events were discriminable from those that elicited anger and sadness. Being threatened, encountering a supernatural creature and having nightmares were specific only to fear. Experiencing undesirable sensory stimuli was also highly specific to fear. The cluster analysis in Figure 19.2 supported this assertion by showing that the statistical distance among the four categories was the greatest when happiness was compared to the three negative emotions. Within the negative emotions, fear was more distant from anger and sadness than these two emotions were from one another. Clearly, anger and sadness had much greater overlap in precipitating events than the other two emotions.

We have replicated these results over four different studies with both children and adults (Levine & Stein, 1997; Liwag & Stein, 1995; Stein, Trabasso & Liwag,

Table 19.1 Percentage of children nominating events in each category

Event categories	Emotion			
	Happy (%)	Angry (%)	Sad (%)	Afraid (%)
CHILD . . .				
Is reunited with significant others	3			
Plays	23			
Celebrates birthdays/holidays	3			
Gives or receives affection	10			
Gets desirable objects	25			
Engages in desirable activities	15			
Avoids a bad situation	8			
Is denied desirable objects		6	5	
Is prohibited from desirable activities		11	9	
Is denied affection/companionship			2	
Has goals in conflict with others'		2		
Is unable to get desirable objects		2	8	
Is unable to engage in desirable activities		2	3	
Is separated from significant others			3	
Has possessions taken away/destroyed		2	3	
Has expectations not met		3	2	
Is forced to do something		3		
Is punished		5	8	
Is intruded upon		31	19	10
Is physically harmed		20	23	9
Has experience related to death		2	2	2
Sees others harmed or in pain			2	2
Is left alone			2	3
Has nightmares/bad dreams				3
Experiences undesirable sensory stimuli		2		15
Perceives a threat				12
Encounters supernatural creatures				30

1994; Trabasso, Stein & Johnson, 1981). The data speak clearly to our assertion that appraisals of an event, rather than the event itself, are the critical components regulating emotion. The fact that an event can result in either anger or sadness speaks to the necessity of examining appraisals to determine which emotion will be experienced.

HOW WERE MY GOALS AFFECTED?

Goal–Outcome Appraisals

From our previous studies (Liwag & Stein, 1995; Stein & Levine, 1989; Trabasso, Stein & Johnson, 1981), we knew that 3 year-old children are able to label

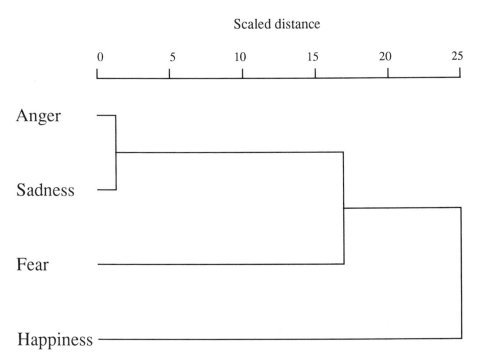

Figure 19.2 A cluster analysis of the events nominated that evoked the emotions of happiness, fear, anger and sadness

emotion faces correctly, and that they are able to generate the causes and consequences of the basic emotions of happiness, sadness, fear and anger (Stein & Levine, 1989; Trabasso, Stein & Johnson, 1981). The next set of findings speak to whether children, as they recount real life events, talk about goals and changes in the status of their goals as reasons for experiencing an emotion. According to our theory of emotional understanding, talk about liking, disliking and the attainment of goals emerges roughly at the same time. Statements of liking are the simplest appraisal of value that can be made. Preferences are also value-laden, but require a contrast between two different states of liking, such that one state is preferred over the other. Liking and preference appraisals do not carry goal information. They set the stage for the selection and setting of a goal.

Children are most likely to talk about liking, preferences and goals when their current goal has been disrupted or when they unexpectedly attain a goal that is highly valued (Stein & Levine, 1989; Stein & Liwag, 1997). Both children and adults, however, must often be probed to elicit the inferences they have made about values and goals. The easiest way that we have found to get children to talk about internal states is to ask them for explanations for their emotional reactions (Levine & Stein, 1997; Stein & Levine, 1989; Stein & Liwag, 1997). Children and adults often delete explicit mention of goals and preferences during spontaneous conversation because these internal states can be inferred easily from non-verbal expressions and from discourse about the precipitating events and actions accompanying an emotional experience (Stein & Glenn, 1979; Stein & Liwag, 1997).

If probed, however, even very young children's explanations for their emotions refer to preferences and goal states. Typically, their explanations focus on changes induced by the precipitating event and the goal state they desired at the time the precipitating event occurred. The following example occurred in the interview with the 3 year-old boy whose toy was broken: "She broke my toy [spontaneous speech] and I was real mad [response to: How did you feel?]. I didn't want her to do that [response to: Why did her breaking your toy make you mad?]. I like fixed guns, not broken ones [response to: Why didn't you want her to do that?]". Thus, this child understood the relationship between the outcome and his preferences, but this knowledge was demonstrated only in response to probe questions rather than in spontaneous unprobed speech.

Table 19.2A shows the specific combinations of goals and outcomes generated by children in their descriptions of each of four emotions. Goal–outcome states reported for happiness are distinct from those reported for the three negative emotions. Children most often associate getting something that they want (e.g. a desired toy or favorite food, a special treat) with the experience of happiness. Although the prevention of undesirable states (e.g. "I didn't want him to hit me,

Table 19.2   (A) Percentage of children mentioning goal/outcome appraisals and reasons for emotions. (B) Percentage of children mentioning reasons for emotions

(A)	Goal–outcome appraisals	Emotion			
		Happy (%)	Angry (%)	Sad (%)	Afraid (%)
	Want–have	74		2	
	Not want–not have	15			
	Want–not have	7	43	62	
	Not want–have	2	57	29	29
	Not want–have (uncertain)			2	71

(B)	Reasons	Emotion			
		Angry (%)	Sad (%)	Afraid (%)	Happy (%)
	Precipitating event	22	8	14	9
	Preferences	44	39	7	40
	Consequences	0	31	61	30
	Violations	11	8	4	8
	Agent	56	33	43	29

and my brother stopped him") was also associated with happiness, these goal–outcome states were talked about less frequently than the attainment of desired states.

Goal–outcome states associated with anger and sadness were: (a) desired states that were not attained ("My mom wouldn't let me watch my favorite video") and (b) aversive states that had to be tolerated ("I had to eat the spaghetti all mixed up with the peas, and I don't like it when they're mushed together"). Although these goal–outcome combinations were generated for both anger and sadness, aversive states were associated with anger more frequently than with sadness. Conversely, children associated the lack or loss of a desired state with sadness more often than with anger. These results replicate those reported by Stein & Levine (1989), who examined children's and adults' causal understanding of anger, sadness and happiness. Both children and adults were more likely to respond to aversive states with anger and to loss states with sadness, irrespective of the type of agent and the intent of the agent who caused the negative outcome (see also Levine, 1995).

According to several models of emotion, people get angry when they trace the cause of a negative outcome to the external agent who acted intentionally (e.g. Smith & Lazarus, 1993; Roseman, 1991). Our studies have shown that with increasing age, children become more sensitive to an agent who caused them to experience a negative outcome, and they are more likely to respond with anger when harm is intentionally caused by another person. For 3 year-old children, however, the presence of a human agent did not increase the likelihood that anger would be expressed when compared with older children and adults. Rather, 3 year-old children expressed anger more often when they believed that they could reinstate the goal that had been obstructed. They expressed sadness most often when they believed that nothing could be done to reinstate an obstructed goal (Levine, 1995; Stein & Liwag, 1997; Stein & Levine, 1989; Stein & Liwag, 1997).

These data suggest that theories that define anger in terms of its relationship to human agency do not apply to the emotional understanding of preschool children. Making agency a prerequisite for the experience of anger may unnecessarily complicate the conceptual representation of anger in theories of both children's and adults' emotional understanding. Like children, adults express anger in response to aversive events that involve no animate agent (Berkowitz, 1990) and when they can generate a plan to reinstate obstructed goals (Levine, 1996; Stein & Levine, 1989).

For fear, the most frequent goal–outcome states reported were the desire to avoid an aversive state, where the outcome was uncertain. When talking about fear, even 3 year-old children talked about future outcomes that could occur but that were not desirable. The use of the future tense, such as, "He's going to hit me", or the use of the perfect conditional, "He was going to hit me", signaled outcome states that had not yet occurred. Interestingly, narratives about fear were the longest, most elaborated narratives for young children.

Causal Orientation Appraisals

Table 19.2B shows the types of appraisals that were included in children's explanations for their emotional reactions, in addition to the focus on goal-outcome states. These appraisals are important because they show that children focus on different parts of an emotional experience as reasons for each emotion. For example, anger and sadness, even though their goal–outcome states are similar, differ not only in beliefs about being able to reinstate a goal, but also in the focus of attention during the reporting of each experience. Children who experience anger refer to the agent who caused their anger more frequently than children who experience sadness. Sadness, on the other hand, occurs because of the orientation to the consequences of goal failure. Thus, when feeling sad, children not only refer to the irrevocable nature of goal failure, but they also refer to more general consequences that will occur because of goal failure. After expressing her sadness at being left home alone, one 4 year-old girl then focused on the fact that she would not get to see her mother, and that she could not have any of her friends spend time with her.

Children describing fear also focused on the consequences that would occur if they did not successfully remove a threat or prevent goal failure from occurring. A focus on consequences was even more frequent for fear than for sadness. Children expressing fear, however, also focused on the human agent who had caused their fear. Thus, fear accounts involved an orientation to both the causes and consequences of the emotion. The fact that both past and future orientations were included may be the reason that children generate their longest narratives when describing fear experiences.

Appraisals made about happy experiences focused on three different dimensions: the human agent responsible for goal attainment, the fact that the resulting outcome was preferred over the existing lack state that had been present previously, and the positive outcomes that would occur given that a specific goal had been attained.

It should be noted that the types of goal–outcome combinations and the causal orientation inferences that children made about the four basic emotions remained constant over the different types of emotion situations that children recounted. Thus, children talked about each emotion in the same way, independent of whether they or their parents nominated the emotion-eliciting events. The important dimension that discriminated among the appraisals made were the specific emotions recounted in each narrative.

Evaluative Beliefs

Evaluative beliefs refer to children's appraisals of events, people, places and objects when they recalled how their goals had been affected by an emotion-eliciting event. Although a focus on changes in the status of goals was the predominant mode of appraisal, children also generated evaluative beliefs throughout their narratives. The types of beliefs generated in emotion narratives are shown in Table 19.3. The table includes specific examples of each of nine classes of "State of the World" beliefs. Children generated these beliefs at the rate of one for every six clauses in their narration. Neither the total number nor the total proportion of beliefs generated during narration were significantly correlated with the children's ages in months. The relative rate of belief generation was stable across the contexts in which emotion narratives were generated, and again, the focus of beliefs was highly related to the specific emotion described.

Table 19.3 and Table 19.4 illustrate the varied nature of these beliefs (Stein & Liwag, 1997). Children appraised almost everything pertinent to an emotion-eliciting event, including the internal states of other people and themselves. Although they focused primarily on their own feeling states (especially when they unexpectedly attained or failed to attain a goal), they readily appraised the mental states of others, especially if they had been misunderstood.

Reports of happy experiences focused primarily on positive beliefs, but they also included *negative beliefs* that occurred primarily *at the beginning* of the narratives. As children began their reports of happy feelings, they sometimes focused first on the lack states that motivated them to take action. They reported their dislike of these lack states and their reasons for wanting to change these states. When children related their plans of action with respect to existing lack states, they switched their focus from a negative to a positive evaluation stance. They often related how valuable the goal under consideration was and the number of other goals that could be attained if the primary goal was accomplished. When children reported success in accomplishing their goals, they often focused on the unexpected benefits of goal success, and they generated evaluations of the people who had helped them attain their goals.

Table 19.3 Percentage of "state of the world" beliefs in each of children's emotion narratives

Content categories	Child's emotion			
	Angry (%)	Sad (%)	Afraid (%)	Happy (%)
Beliefs about harm	7	14	52	2
Beliefs about gains or benefits	34	27	3	47
Beliefs about losses or denials	0	37	11	9
Beliefs about child's obligations or appropriate behavior of others	13	5	0	2
Beliefs about child's abilities	0	3	0	11
Beliefs about the status of a relationship	27	3	0	5
Beliefs about ownership	7	3	0	2
Beliefs about the state of the world or the nature of things	0	5	29	2

Narratives about negative emotional experiences also included both positive and negative beliefs. In anger, sadness and fear narratives, *positive appraisals* were often generated *at the beginning* of the narrative and indicated how valuable a goal was or how satisfied the narrator was before the state of the world changed in response to loss or an impending loss. The value of the lost or blocked goal was explicitly stated and beliefs about goals were also stated, especially in terms of the positive moral evaluations children associated with the attainment of desired goals. Once a goal was blocked, however, negative beliefs about other people and the state of the world were then expressed. Thus, in narratives about negative emotional experiences, negative beliefs were generated primarily *after* an undesired change of state occurred.

Table 19.3 also illustrates that the types of beliefs expressed differed significantly for the four emotions. In anger narratives, children expressed their beliefs about the moral obligations of others who broke their promises, and they also talked about not being sure whether they could ever trust these people again. In fact, beliefs about the possibility of terminating relationships were expressed primarily in anger narratives. In sad narratives, the focus was primarily on beliefs about losses that were incurred or that would be incurred given that a pivotal goal was blocked. In fear narratives, the focus was on the uncertain nature of the world, given that harm either had occurred or would occur in the very near future. Finally, in happy narratives, children often expressed their beliefs about their emerging positive abilities.

Although the beliefs that children expressed focused primarily on what the children themselves believed to be true about their world, some children focused on what they thought other people believed to be true about the state of the world. For example, one child who was yelled at by her mother explained how her mother had mistakenly thought that she had dropped a cup: "*She thought that I was making the noise. And that's what she thought. I was dropping the cup. That's why she yelled at me . . .*" (girl, 5.2 years old). This young girl also recalled how she corrected her mother's false belief by telling her mother that it was her little brother who had made the noise. Other children expressed awareness of what others might think and do in response to their own actions: "My mama says

Table 19.4 Percentage of personal evaluations in children's emotion recall

Personal evaluation categories	Emotion			
	Angry (%)	Sad (%)	Afraid (%)	Happy (%)
Preferences	50	37	26	37
Personality traits/enduring attributes	4	4	6	6
Specific or habitual behaviors	29	29	30	26
Mental states	13	13	6	11
Qualities/characteristics of objects/events	4	17	32	20

she gonna get me a costume, and when I go under the water, boy, *everybody, they think, it's the killer whale, a real one. 'Cause I'm gonna have sharp teeth*" (boy, 3.8 years old); and, "Well, *I was just very quiet* when my mom was driving home, in the back, *and she thought I was asleep*" (boy, 6.0 years old).

The most interesting set of appraisals, with respect to children's understanding of other people's beliefs, were generated during children's reports about obligations they had to uphold. Children most often talked about these obligations when relating conversations with one of their parents. For example, in relating why she had to go school, one little girl reported: "One day, my mom was just saying, '*But, darling, you* **have to** *go to school*'"(girl, 4.0). Another little boy reported: "I haven't saw him, and mamma said, **I gotta stay here and go to school**" (boy, 3.4). A 3 year-old boy reported: "My mom said I don't hafta play with him". All of these children stated their evaluations about their parents' beliefs in the form of obligatory conversational statements made by their parents. Upon probing these children further and asking, "Did your mom think you should go to school", the answer was yes.

These data are critical in understanding how children express their knowledge about other people's beliefs. Although children will sometimes use the words: "He thought", "He believed", "He knew", children (and adults) will frequently quote snippets of conversation they have had with the person whose mental states they are attempting to represent. Reporting other people's beliefs in the form of conversation is a more powerful way of presenting evidence to persuade a listener about the truth value of what another person thinks or believes. The uncertainty associated with mental state verbs ("think", "believe", etc.) disappears, and the beliefs being attributed to another person increases in certainty and validity.

Narrative Functions of Beliefs and Evaluations

When children talk about beliefs in the context of an emotion episode, what functions do these evaluative statements serve? We found that *explanation* was the most common function of these appraisals. About 50% of the time, children expressed a belief or a judgment in order to explain or justify their own emotions (e.g. "I was sad *because I thought I was staying at my cousin's forever*"); desires (e.g. "I want to go to the circus *because circuses are fun*"); and behaviors (e.g. "My mother . . . um, I woke up her *because I thought she'd probably go on back up to sleep*"). Children also used other people's beliefs to provide explanations for a person's goals and actions (e.g. "And actually, see 'cause, um, *my mom got in my way cause she thought I was going to go under* [the water]. And I said stop, cause I wasn't going to go under"). Another 25% of beliefs and evaluations focused on the negative or positive outcomes that had occurred and served to provide evidence for the goals and plans that were activated as a result of the precipitating event. Thus, the belief data, by the inclusion of causal markers and relationships to outcomes and goals, clearly supports the hypothesis that preschoolers understand the links among beliefs, emotions, and behaviors and that they make continual use of the explanatory power of appraisals.

WHAT DO I WANT TO DO ABOUT IT?

Table 19.5 contains the types of wishes that children generated when describing happiness, sadness, anger, and fear. The wishes that accompanied happiness did not overlap with the wishes for any other emotion. All wishes generated in response to feeling happy were either to maintain the present goal state or to attain new goals as a function of attaining the focal goal. Fear was quite distinct from anger and sadness in that over 90% of all subjects wanted to prevent an undesirable state from occurring. Thus, on every dimension, happiness and fear are clearly separable from one another, and they were distinct from the emotions of anger and sadness.

The greatest amount of overlap in wishes occurred between anger and sadness. Each emotion, however, resulted in the generation of a unique wish. Anger resulted in two primary wishes: the desire to reinstate the original goal and the desire to seek revenge. Sadness, on the other hand, resulted in the desire to reinstate the original goal or to substitute new goals. The fact that approximately half the children who experienced sadness already planned to substitute another goal implies that they were aware that they could never reinstate their original goal.

Functional Significance of Expressed Emotions

As we have illustrated throughout our description of children's understanding of emotion situations, each of the four specific emotions carries with it specific patterns of antecedent appraisals and plans (see Ekman, 1977, for a similar

Table 19.5 Percentage of children mentioning wishes

Wishes	Emotion			
	Angry (%)	Sad (%)	Afraid (%)	Happy (%)
Maintain original goal				37
Attain new goal				47
Reinstate original goal	40	36	8	
Substitute new goal	20	46		
Abandon original goal		2		
Revenge	40	8		
Prevent undesirable state		8	92	

argument). The specific emotions children express in their interactions with one another and their parents thus become critical for predicting future behavior during social interactions. In one study (Stein & Albro, 1997), we examined the emotions children and their parents expressed when each was asked to recall a recent conflict that they had had with each other. Thirty mothers described an ongoing conflict with their preschool children. Mothers reported what and who initiated the conflict, what happened as a result of the disagreement, and how the conflict was resolved. They also reported what their beliefs, emotions, goals and plans were at the time that the conflict erupted. We then presented children with the conflict topics that their mothers had nominated. If children agreed that they did have the specific disagreement with their mother, they narrated about the conflict in the same manner as their mothers had. They were then brought together with their mothers to discuss how the conflict could be resolved. Both children and mothers participated in an individual post-test interview, where each appraised and assessed their face-to-face interaction.

When children and mothers both reported feeling angry in reaction to their original conflict, the probability of the two resolving the ongoing conflict was 42%. The remainder ended in stand-offs, with the conflict still unresolved. A conversational analysis of negotiations that ended in stand-offs revealed that both children and mothers focused on blaming each other for the onset of the original conflict. Rarely did children or mothers focus on their own role in starting the conflict or on the reasons that the other might have had for getting mad at them.

When mothers and children both expressed sadness in their original conflict memories, they were able to come to a mutually agreed-upon resolution in face-to-face interaction 68% of the time. Of these acceptable resolutions, 60% were compromises and 40% were resolutions that involved a win–loss outcome. The sadness reported by both children and mothers was significantly associated with a focus on consequences in memories for the original conflict. The sadness reflected a future-orientated concern for the consequences that the conflict would have for their relationship.

The fact that acceptable resolutions included win–loss outcomes as well as compromise solutions suggests that sadness may predispose children and mothers to being more open to persuasion by the other to substitute a new goal. We also found that some win–loss solutions evolved without confrontation or hostility being expressed. When mothers and children expressed combinations of anger and sadness in their pre-negotiation memory reports, the probability of resolving the conflict in a mutually satisfactory way was 55%. The mutually satisfactory solutions were evenly distributed between compromises and win–loss outcomes.

These data illustrate the important role that expressed emotions play in determining future interaction strategies and negotiation behaviors. Expressed emotions were also significantly correlated with the beliefs, goals and plans reported during the original conflict. The expression of anger by either child or mother was highly correlated with beliefs of moral righteousness and with an insistence that the other person change their behavior to conform to "expected goals and behavior". When sadness was expressed, beliefs about the self being wrong were expressed more frequently, as were strategies for changing one's own behavior.

CONCLUSIONS

From the very beginning, newborn infants are active processors of events in their environment (see also Spelke & Newport, 1997). Although the newborn does not express discrete emotions in reaction to specific events (see Camras, 1992, for a discussion of discrete emotion faces displayed to varying types of stimulation), the beginning organization of emotional experience is present in terms of the affective responses of distress, quieting, and pleasure. The missing components are knowledge about events that lead to positive vs. negative outcomes and strategies for evaluating plans and actions that can be used to attain valued goal states. During the first 6 months of life, infants acquire a rich array of knowledge that allows them to engage in active appraisal processes focused on maintaining personally significant goals and positive states of psychological well-being. The important consequence of acquiring this knowledge is the expression and experience of basic emotions.

Specific inferences about goal success or failure are *always* made when happiness, sadness, anger or fear are evoked. Further, almost as soon as they begin to speak, children make the same types of inferences regarding success and failure of goals as adults do. They focus on reinstating their goals, activating plans to achieve these goals, and learning how to cope with obstacles that block goal success. When personally significant goals cannot be achieved, children abandon their goals and determine whether or not a new goal can be substituted for a failed goal (Trabasso & Stein, 1994, 1997).

One reason that appraisals of emotion situations emerge early and retain their similarity over the life span is that goal-directed thinking is highly constrained. Only three outcomes are possible when goal attainment is desired: success, failure and uncertain goal attainment. Given that infants monitor personally significant goals very early in development, the number of times they observe success and failure during everyday interaction is exceedingly high. If we actually counted the number of times goals were monitored over the course of a week, the frequency would be astonishing. Thus, the schemes that are used to monitor and understand emotion situations become highly rehearsed and easily accessible. Although children are exposed to different contexts across development and cultures, they still evaluate outcomes in terms of pleasure and pain, and they actively construct plans to attain states that lead to personal satisfaction. Thus, the tightly constrained causal structure of intentional action is one reason emotional understanding emerges rapidly and provides common ground for understanding both the self and other people.

In the types of appraisals that elicit emotion, we have found only one consistent developmental difference. Although young children are able to make causal inferences about the role of an agent intentionally blocking their goals, they often choose to disregard intentionality in their expression of anger. This disregard of intentionality, however, does not mean that young children are incapable of imputing blame or expressing anger. In their narratives about real-life personal experiences, they frequently describe situations where a sibling or friend made them "really" angry because of physical aggression or violation of a promise (Liwag & Stein, 1995; Stein & Liwag, 1997). They just express anger less frequently than older children and adults do when intentional harm is present. Rather, they choose to focus on the consequences of goal failure instead of the causes.

Using personal narratives to evaluate children's understanding of emotions has also proved to be important in documenting the growth of person knowledge (Stein, 1996). When children talk about specific situations where personally meaningful goals were at stake, they demonstrate an understanding of their own internal states, and they show a rich understanding of other people's internal states. The inclusion of probe questions that focus directly on their knowledge of other people beliefs, goals, and emotions is essential for determining precisely what children know about themselves and others (Stein & Liwag, 1997). Children often delete explicit references to people's internal states because these dimensions can be inferred from the prosody of speech, from non-verbal gestures, and from conversational quotes that children use to represent the beliefs of other people. Thus, emotional understanding is often far more complex than data from analyses of spontaneous conversation suggests.

Finally, the existing data on children's emotional understanding suggests that emotion concepts like happiness, anger, sadness and fear are not fuzzy in nature and do not correspond to the notion of a family resemblance conceptual scheme, as some researchers have claimed (see Shaver et al., 1987; Tangney & Fischer, 1995). When children talk about the causes and consequences of basic emotions, each emotion carries with it specific conditions that do not occur in the representation of other emotions. The appraisals and wishes associated with happiness do not overlap with those associated with the three negative emotions. Fear is also distinct from the emotions of anger and sadness because it carries the element of uncertainty and threat. Sadness and anger are the only emotions that carry some features in common, and even they can be distinguished by beliefs about goal reinstatement and permanent goal failure (Levine, 1995; Stein & Levine, 1989).

The belief in a theory of family resemblance may stem more from the ambiguity concerning how the "self-conscious" emotions are understood. Although these emotions are exceedingly important, especially in predicting the functional significance of an emotional event (Barrett, 1995; Lewis, 1995; Tangney & Fischer, 1995), the definition of each self-conscious emotion may not be as widely shared as the definition of each basic emotion. Further research will be necessary to examine how children's emerging appraisals of themselves are related to the expression of self-conscious emotions. Although self-conscious emotions may emerge later than basic emotions, they may be fully understood quite early in development. The task for us will be to separate children's use of emotion language (e.g. "guilt", "shame", "pride") from their non-verbal conceptual understanding of emotional states.

Finally, the study of children's understanding of emotion situations strongly suggests that children are aware of the causes and antecedents of emotion, and that they have little difficulty verbalizing the causes of their feelings. Although Frijda (1995) has argued that people are often unaware of the causes of their emotional reactions, our data does not support this hypothesis. By using on-line talk-aloud procedures (Stein & Boyce, 1995) and a narrative analysis of emotional memories (Levine & Stein, 1997; Stein et al., in press; Stein & Liwag, 1997), we have found that the first appraisal process that people typically carry out is focused on what happened and what specifically caused their emotion. In future studies, it will become imperative to examine more closely the on-line inferences made during the experience of emotion. Then, we can specify more accurately the types and rapidity of causal thinking that occurs throughout development and the experience of emotion.

ACKNOWLEDGEMENTS

This research was funded in part by grants from the Smart Foundation on Early Learning, the National Institute of Child Health and Human Development (Grant No. HD 25742) and the Spencer Foundation. Our thanks are due Liz Albro and Lisa Moskalski for their comments on an earlier version of this draft. We wish to thank all of the preschools, parents and children in Hyde Park who have so generously given their time, memories and support throughout our projects on everyday memory for emotional and harmful events.

REFERENCES

Albro, E. R. & Stein, N. L. (1997).   Children's memory for conflict as a function of liking. Unpublished manuscript, University of Chicago.
Alessandri, S. M., Sullivan, M. W. & Lewis, M. (1990).   Violation of expectancy and frustration in early infancy. *Developmental Psychology*, **26**(5), 738–744.
Baldwin, D. A. & Moses, L. J. (in press).   The ontogeny of social information-gathering. *Child Development*.
Barrett, K. C. (1995).   A functionalist approach to shame and guilt. In J. P. Tangney & K. W. Fischer (eds), *Self-conscious Emotions: The Psychology of Shame, Guilt, Embarrassment, and Pride*. New York: Guilford, pp. 25–63.
Bauer, P. & Mandler, J. M. (1989).   One thing follows another. Effects of temporal structure on 1 to 2 year-olds' recall of events. *Developmental Psychology*, **25**, 197–206.
Bauer, P. & Mandler, J. M. (1990).   Remembering what happened next: very young children's recall of event sequences. In R. Fivush & J. A. Hudson (eds), *Knowing and Remembering in Young Children*. New York: Cambridge University Press, pp. 9–29.
Bauer, P. & Shore, C. M. (1987).   Making a memorable event: the effects of familiarity and organization of young children's recall of action sequences. *Cognitive Development*, **2**, 327–338.

Berkowitz, L. (1990). On the formation and regulation of anger and aggression: a cognitive-neoassociationistic analysis. *American Psychologist*, **45**, 494–503.

Boyce, W. T., Chesterman, E. A., Martin, N., Folkman, S., Cohen, F. & Wara, D. (1991). Immunological changes occurring in kindergarten entry predict respiratory illness following the Loma Prieta Earthquake. Paper presented at the Annual Meeting of the Society of Pediatric Research. New Orleans, April 30.

Camras, L. (1992). Expressive development and basic emotions. *Cognition & Emotion*, **6**(3/4), 269–283.

Duncan, S. & Farley, A. (1990). Achieving parent–child co-ordination through convention: fixed- and variable-sequence conventions. *Child Development*, **61**, 742–753.

Ekman, P. (1977). Biological and cultural contributions to body and facial movement. In J. Blacking (ed.), *Anthropology of the Body*. London: Academic Press, pp. 34–84.

Emde, R. (1980). Levels of meaning in infant development. In W. A. Collins (ed.), *Minnesota Symposium on Child Psychology*, Vol. 13. Hillsdale, NJ: Erlbaum, pp. 1–38.

Fernald, A. (1984). The perceptual and affective salience of mothers' speech to infants. In L. Feagans, C. Garvey & R. Golinkoff (eds) with M. T. Greenberg, C. Harding & J. Bohannon, *The Origins and Growth of Communication*. Norwood, NJ: Ablex, pp. 5–29.

Folkman, S. & Stein, N. L. (1997). A goal-process approach to analyzing narrative memories for AIDS-related stressful events. In N. L. Stein, P. A. Ornstein, B. Tversky & C. Brainerd (eds), *Memory for Everyday and Emotional Events*. Hillsdale, NJ: Erlbaum.

Frijda, N. H. (1995). Passions and socially consequential behavior. In R. Kavanaugh, B. Zimmerberg-Glick & S. Fein (eds), *Emotion: A Multidisciplinary Perspective*. The G. Stanley Hall Symposium. Hillsdale, NJ: Erlbaum, pp. 1–28.

Gergely, G., Nadasdy, Z., Csibra, G. & Biro, S. (in press). Taking the intentional stance at 12 months of age. *Cognition*.

Haith, M. M. (1994). Visual expectations as the first step toward the development of future-oriented processes. In M. M. Haith, J. B. Benson, R. J. Roberts & B. F. Pennington (eds), *The Development of Future-oriented Processes*. Chicago, IL: University of Chicago Press.

Izard, C. E., Hemsbree, E. A. & Huebner, R. R. (1987). Infant's emotional expressions to acute pain: developmental change and stability of individual differences. *Developmental Psychology*, **23**, 105–113.

Johnson-Laird, P. N. & Oatley, K. (1989). The language of emotion: an analysis of a semantic field. *Cognition and Emotion*, **3**, 81–123.

Kolb, B. & Taylor, L. (1990). Neocortical substrates of emotional behavior. In N. L. Stein, B. Leventhal & T. Trabasso (eds), *Psychological and Biological Approaches to Emotion*. Hillsdale, NJ: Erlbaum, pp. 97–114.

Lazarus, R. S. (1991). *Emotion & Adaptation*. New York: Oxford University Press.

LeDoux, J. (1996). *The Emotional Brain*. New York: Simon & Schuster.

Levine, L. J. (1995). Young children's understanding of the causes of anger and sadness. *Child Development*, **66**, 697–709.

Levine, L. J. (1996). The anatomy of disappointment: a naturalistic test of appraisal models of sadness, anger, and hope. *Cognition and Emotion*, **10**, 337–359.

Levine, L. J. (in press). Reconstructing memory for emotions. *Journal of Experimental Psychology: General*.

Levine, L. J. & Bluck, S. (in press). Experienced and remembered emotion intensity in older adults. *Psychology and Aging*.

Levine, L. J. & Burgess, S. L. (1995). Beyond arousal: effects of specific emotions on memory. Paper presented at the Society for Applied Research on Memory and Cognition, Vancouver, Canada, July.

Levine, L. & Stein, N. L. (1997). "I'm not his brain": the emergence of young children's understanding of emotions in themselves and their friends. Unpublished manuscript, University of Chicago.

Lewis, M. (1995). Self-conscious emotions. *American Scientist*, **83**(Jan–Feb), 68–78.

Lewis, M., Alessandri, S. M. & Sullivan, M. W. (1990). Violation of expectancy, loss of control, and anger expressions in young infants. *Developmental Psychology*, **26**(5), 745–751.

Liwag, M. D. & Stein, N. L. (1995). Children's memory for emotional events: the importance of emotion enactment cues. *Journal of Experimental Child Psychology*, **60**, 2–31.

Mandler, G. (1984). *Mind and Body: Psychology of Emotion and Stress*. New York: Norton.

Mandler, J. M. & McDonough (1997). Non-verbal recall. In N. L. Stein, P. A. Ornstein, B. Tversky & C. Brainerd (eds), *Memory for Everyday and Emotional Events*. Hillsdale, NJ: Erlbaum.

Myers, N. A., Clifton, R. K. & Clarkson, M. G. (1987). When they were young: almost threes remember two years ago. *Infant Behavior and Development*, **10**, 123–132.

Oatley, K. & Johnson-Laird, P. N. (1987). Towards a cognitive theory of emotion. *Cognition and Emotion*, **1**, 29–50.

Reznick, J. S. (1994). In search of infant expectation. In M. M. Haith, J. B. Benson, R. J. Roberts & B. F. Pennington (eds), *The Development of Future-oriented Processes*. Chicago, IL: University of Chicago Press.

Roseman, I. J. (1991). Appraisal determinants of discrete emotions. *Cognition & Emotion*, **5**, 161–200.

Roseman, I. J., Antoniou, A. A. & Jose, P. E. (1996). Appraisal determinants of emotions: constructing a more accurate and comprehensive theory. *Cognition and Emotion*, **10**(3), 241–277.

Shaver, P., Schwartz, J., Kirson, D. & O'Connor, C. (1987). Emotion knowledge: further explorations of a prototype approach. *Journal of Personality & Social Psychology*, **52**(6), 1061–1086.

Smith, C. A. & Lazarus, R. S. (1993). Appraisal components, core relational themes, and the emotions. *Cognition and Emotion*, **7**(3/4), 233–269.

Spelke, E. S. & Newport, E. L. (1997). Nativism, empiricism, and the development of knowledge. In W. Damon (ed.-in-chief), *Handbook of Child Psychology*, 5th edn, Vol. 1. New York: Wiley.

Sroufe, A. (1979). Socioemotional development. In J. Osofsky (ed.), *The Handbook of Infant Development*, New York: Wiley, pp. 462–516.

Stenberg, C. R. & Campos, J. J. (1990). The development of anger expressions in infancy. In N. L. Stein, B. Leventhal & T. Trabasso (eds), *Psychological and Biological Approaches to Emotion*. Hillsdale, NJ: Erlbaum, pp. 247–282.

Stein, N. L. (1996). Children's memory for emotional events. In K. Pezdek & W. P. Banks (eds), *The Recovered Memory/False Memory Debate*. San Diego, CA: Academic Press, pp. 169–194.

Stein, N. L. & Albro, E. R. (1997). Children's understanding of conflict: evidence from past memories and on-line negotiated resolutions. Paper presented at the Society for Research on Child Development. Washington, DC, April.

Stein, N. L., Bernas, R. & Calicchia, D. (1997). Conflict talk: understanding and resolving arguments. In Tom Givon (ed.), *Typological Studies in Language: Conversational Analysis*. Amsterdam: John Benjamins.

Stein, N. L. & Boyce, W. T. (1995). The role of physiological reactivity in attending to, remembering, and responding to an emotional event. Paper presented at the Society for Research in Child Development. Indianapolis, IN, April.

Stein, N. L., Folkman, S., Trabasso, T. & Richards, T. A. (in press). Appraisal and goal Processes as predictors of psychological well-being in bereaved caregivers. *Journal of Personality and Social Psychology*.

Stein, N. L. & Glenn, C. G. (1979). An analysis of story comprehension in elementary school children. In R. O. Freedle (ed.), *New Directions in Discourse Processing*,

Vol. 2. Series on Advances in Discourse Processes. Norwood, NJ: Ablex, pp. 53–120.

Stein, N. L. & Levine, L. J. (1987). Thinking about feelings: the development and organization of emotional knowledge. In R. E. Snow & M. J. Farr (eds), *Aptitude, Learning, and Instruction. Vol. 3: Conative and Affective Process Analyses*. Hillsdale, NJ: Erlbaum.

Stein, N. L. & Levine, L. (1989). The causal organization of emotion knowledge: a developmental study. *Cognition and Emotion*, **3**(4), 343–378.

Stein, N. L. & Levine, L. (1990). Making sense out of emotional experience: the representation and use of goal-directed knowledge. In N. L. Stein, B. Leventhal & T. Trabasso (eds), *Psychological and Biological Approaches to Emotion*. Hillsdale, NJ: Erlbaum, pp. 45–74.

Stein, N. L. & Liwag, M. D. (1997). A goal-appraisal process approach to understanding and remembering emotional events. In P. van den Broek, P. Bauer & T. Bourg (eds), *Developmental Spans in Event Comprehension and Representation*. Hillsdale, NJ: Erlbaum.

Stein, N. L., Liwag, M. D. & Wade, E. (1995). A goal-based approach to memory for emotional events: implications for theories of understanding and socialization. In R. Kavanaugh, B. Zimmerberg-Glick & S. Fein (eds), *Emotion: A Multidisciplinary Perspective*. The G. Stanley Hall Symposium, Hillsdale, NJ: Erlbaum, pp. 91–118.

Stein, N. L. & Trabasso, T. (1989). Children's understanding of changing emotion states. In C. Saarni & P. Harris (eds), *The Development of Emotional Understanding*. New York: Cambridge University Press.

Stein, N. L. & Trabasso, T. (1992). The organization of emotional experience: creating links among emotion, thinking, language and intentional action. *Cognition and Emotion* (Special Issue on Basic Emotions), **6**(3/4), 225–244.

Stein, N. L., Trabasso & Albro, E. R. (1997). The course of caregiving in an ever-worsening illness. Unpublished manuscript, University of Chicago.

Stein, N. L., Trabasso, T. & Liwag, M. (1992). The representation and organization of emotional experience: unfolding the emotion episode. In M. Lewis & J. Haviland (eds), *Handbook of Emotions*. New York: Guilford, pp. 279–300.

Stein, N. L., Trabasso, T. & Liwag, M. D. (1994). The Rashomon phenomenon: personal frames and future-oriented appraisals in memory for emotional events. In M. Haith, J. Benson, R. Roberts & B. Pennington (eds), *The Development of Future-oriented Processes*. Chicago, IL: University of Chicago Press, pp. 323–349.

Stein, N. L., Wade, E. & Liwag, M. D. (1997). A theoretical approach to understanding and remembering emotional events. In N. L. Stein, P. A. Ornstein, B. Tversky & C. Brainerd (eds), *Memory for Everyday and Emotional Events*. Hillsdale, N.J: Erlbaum, pp. 15–48.

Stern, D. (1985). *The Interpersonal World of the Infant*. New York: Basic Books.

Stern, D. (1992). *Diary of a Baby*. New York: Basic Books.

Tangney, J. P. & Fischer, K. W. (1995). *Self-conscious Emotions: The Psychology of Shame, Guilt, Embarrassment, and Pride*. New York: Guilford.

Trabasso, T. & Stein, N. L. (1994). Using goal-plan knowledge to merge the past with the present and the future in narrating events on-line. In M. Haith, J. Benson, R. Roberts & B. Pennington (eds), *The Development of Future-oriented Processes*. Chicago, IL: University of Chicago Press, pp. 323–349.

Trabasso, T. & Stein, N. L. (1997). Narrating, representing, and remembering event sequences. In P. van den Broek, P. Bauer & T. Bourg (eds), *Developmental Spans in Event Comprehension and Representation*. Hillsdale, NJ: Erlbaum.

Trabasso, T., Stein, N. L. & Johnson, N. (1981). Children's knowledge of events: a causal analysis of story structure. *The Psychology of Learning and Motivation*, **15**, 237–282.

Trabasso, T. & Ozyurek, A. (1997). Communicating evaluation in narrative understanding. In T. Givon (ed.), *Spontaneous Conversation*. Philadelphia, PA: John Benjamins, pp. 269–302.

von Hofsten, C. (1994). Planning and perceiving what is going to happen next. In M. M. Haith, J. B. Benson, R. J. Roberts & B. F. Pennington (eds), *The Development of Future-oriented Processes*. Chicago, IL: University of Chicago Press, pp. 63–86.

Willatts, P. (1990). The development of problem-solving strategies in infancy. In D. Bjorklund (ed.), *Children's Strategies: Contemporary Views of Cognitive Development*. Hillsdale, NJ: Erlbaum, pp. 23–66.

Part III

Emotions

Chapter 20

Anger

Leonard Berkowitz
University of Wisconsin-Madison, Madison, WI, USA

The term "anger" has a multiplicity of meanings in psychology, as in everyday language, and can refer to an experience or feeling, internal bodily reactions, an attitude toward others, an instigation to aggression, an overt assault on some target, and to various combinations of these different reactions. Since these responses are only imperfectly correlated, it is usually unclear just what people have in mind when they speak of "anger". This chapter will review how investigators concerned with the psychology of emotions define the concept. Nothing will be said about the measurement of anger and, because of space limitations, we will also not look at the research into the consequences of expressing or not expressing anger feelings.

But although this chapter will concentrate on this one particular affective state, it will take up matters that are relevant to many other emotions as well. The study of anger raises issues that should be considered by theories of emotion generally. Some of these have to do with the phenomenology of the emotional state and the influences shaping the nature of this experience, others with the conditions that give rise to the emotion, and still others with the relation between the affective experience and overt behavior. The present chapter will survey the research and theories bearing on each of these topics and, in doing this, will highlight questions that are pertinent to many other emotions as well.

SOCIAL REPRESENTATIONS OF ANGER

Mental Representations of Physiological Reactions

A good deal of research has focused on the mental representations of the bodily reactions in anger. The results have been quite similar in many of these investi-

---

Handbook of Cognition and Emotion. Edited by T. Dalgleish and M. Power.

gations: experienced increases in cardiovascular and muscular activity. For example, according to Davitz (1969), his male and female students reported feeling greater blood pressure and heightened bodily tension when angry, while for Shield's (1984) undergraduates the most common symptoms of anger included muscle tension, general restlessness, an increase in heart rate and the face feeling hot. Much the same pattern of experienced muscular and cardiovascular symptoms was reported by the students in the Shaver et al. (1987) analysis, as well as by the randomly selected telephone subscribers in the survey conducted by Scherer & Tannenbaum (1986). It is especially worth noting here that felt heat seems to be an important aspect of many people's mental representation of anger. Lakoff & Kovecses (1987; cited in Shaver, Wu & Schwartz, 1992, p. 204) have pointed out that the prevailing metaphor in the public's conception of anger is that of a hot liquid in a closed container, as when we say an angry person is "hot under the collar", or "all steamed up". At any rate, taken together, the findings are consistent with the marked dilation of the blood vessels and heightened stimulation of the voluntary muscles that Lange (1885; cited in Rimé & Giovannini, 1986, pp. 85–86) believed was characteristic of anger.

Anger seems to be associated with emotion-specific autonomic changes as well as with relatively distinct peripheral sensations, challenging the once popular cognitive analysis of emotion offered by Schachter & Singer (1962) and Mandler (1975). Where this latter formulation held that all emotions have much the same pattern of peripheral bodily reactions, there is now evidence that at least the negative emotions of anger—disgust, fear and sadness—can be differentiated physiologically (Ekman, Levenson & Friesen, 1983; Levenson, Ekman & Friesen, 1990). According to Ekman, Levenson & Friesen (1983), as an example, both anger and fear lead to a rise in heart rate, but there is a fairly sharp jump in finger temperature under anger, but not fear. This last-mentioned observation is of course consistent with the widespread characterization of anger as a "hot" feeling.

Yet another issue here has to do with the comparative roles of biology and culture in the experience of emotions. For social constructivists, mostly in anthropology and sociology but also in psychology (Averill, 1982, 1983; Gergen, 1985, Rimé, Philippot & Cisamolo, 1990), people's cultural learning shapes just what they feel when they are emotionally aroused. The emotion-specific autonomic differences just mentioned presumably derive from this cultural learning. However, proponents of such a view are hard-pressed to account for the remarkable similarity in the nature of many emotional experiences across different societies.

Scherer, Wallbott, Rimé and their colleagues have highlighted these similarities. In one of their first investigations (Scherer, Wallbott & Summerfield, 1986; Rimé & Giovannini, 1986), based on university students in Belgium, France, the UK, Israel, Italy, Spain, Switzerland and West Germany, the participants had to describe their sensations when experiencing various emotions. They typically reported themselves as unpleasantly aroused, feeling hot, having muscular symptoms and an increased blood pressure when they were angry.

There were some cultural differences in addition to these commonalities; when the investigators compared the descriptions given by the students residing in the northern countries with those made by their southern counterparts, more of the northerners indicated having muscular symptoms, whereas the southerners were more apt to report a rise in blood pressure (see Rimé & Giovannini, 1986, pp. 89–90).

Rimé, Philippot & Cisamolo (1990) added to this line of research by asking US and Belgian university students to rate the intensity of various peripheral symptoms when they were in a given emotional state, and also noted the national similarities. In both groups, both anger and fear were accompanied by heart rate and breathing changes as well as by muscular tension, although feeling hot was more characteristic of anger and there was more perspiration when afraid. Despite these findings, however, Rimé, Philippot & Cisamolo (1990) argued that the national similarities do not necessarily prove that biology is paramount in determining the emotional experience. Maintaining that peripheral changes are usually only poorly detected (p. 47), these writers held that people actually refer to their "social schemata" of emotions, rather than to their memories of specific emotional episodes, when they report how they had felt during earlier emotional events (p. 39). The cross-cultural similarities found in the various studies just cited could then be due to common ideas about the nature of emotional experiences, ideas that have spread across the modern world, and not to a common physiology. Rimé and his colleagues (1990) then adopted the social constructivist position, and suggested that culturally developed emotional schemata could shape just how one felt when emotionally aroused, as well as affecting one's memory of past feelings.

Scherer & Wallbott (1994) have questioned this constructivist view of emotional reactions. In their analysis of questionnaire data from some 2900 university students in 37 countries on five continents, the cross-national similarities were again pronounced; independently of the country sampled, there were significant differences among the seven emotions studied with regard to what peripheral reactions were reported. As Scherer & Wallbott (1994) concluded:

> The results for the three response domains investigated—feeling, physiological symptoms, and expression—show consistently strong effects for universal, emotion-specific effects and small to medium effects for country and the Emotion × Country interaction. The data reported here do not support an extreme position of cultural relativism with respect to emotional experience (p. 324).

The reported physiological symptoms of anger were very much in accord with the symptoms described by other investigations: in particular, marked indications of sympathetic arousal, such as a substantial increase in heart rate (although less than that in fear), and a relatively great increase in muscle tension (again, less than that in fear). Also, as other studies had found (and in line with previously mentioned observations), anger was typically felt as relatively "hot" (along with joy), whereas fear was experienced as "colder". The time duration of the anger feelings is also of some interest. Ekman (1984) had argued that since facial muscle action rarely lasted for longer than 4 seconds, it was advisable to think of emotions as only very short-lived. Long-lasting feelings should be regarded as "moods", he said, rather than as "emotions". Nonetheless, Scherer & Wallbott (1994) observed, as did the Scherer, Wallbott & Summerfield (1986) team earlier, that many of their participants experienced angry feelings for minutes and even hours.

Scherer & Wallbott were impressed by the extent to which the reported peripheral symptoms were consistent with what has been found in studies of emotion-specific autonomic reactions (p. 326). For them, it was therefore "premature" to claim, much as Rimé, Philippot & Cisamolo (1990) had done, "that self-reported reactions only exist as socially constituted representations in our heads" (p. 326). There are "important cultural differences in emotion elicitation, regulation [and] symbolic representation", they recognized, but they believed that it was "the common experience of powerful basic emotions" that produces the social representations that permit people to "abstractly report on emotional patterning" (p. 326). Lakoff & Kovecses (1987; cited in Shaver, Wu & Schwartz, 1992, pp. 204–205) reached much the same conclusion with regard to the "hot liquid" metaphor of anger. "If we look at metaphors and metonymies for anger in the languages of the world", they proposed, "we [probably] will not find any that contradict the physiological results that [researchers] have found" (cited in Shaver, Wu & Schwartz, 1992, p. 205). Biology evidently plays a considerable, but certainly not exclusive, role in emotional experience.

Representations Emphasizing External, Largely Causal, Influences

Emotion characterizations vary in the extent to which they focus on the internal aspects of the affective states or also refer to more externally-based considerations (Johnson-Laird & Oatley, 1989). The early formulations published by Lange (1885; cited in Rimé & Giovannini, 1986) and James (1890) are prime examples of internally focused accounts, but several contemporary writers have also emphasized internal reactions, although not necessarily only those related to the autonomic nervous system. Izard (1991), to cite one example, noted how, in anger, "the blood 'boils', the face becomes hot, the muscles tense. There is a feeling of power and an impulse to strike out . . ." (p. 241).

However, many other students of the emotions place considerable emphasis on external considerations or even give external factors overriding importance. Whatever the details in their theoretical positions, it seems fair to say, with Mandler (1975), that most of the theorists in this camp seek "to be consistent with 'common knowledge'" about emotions (p. 1), much as if ordinary language usage contains some special wisdom about emotions, their antecedents, and their consequences (see Mandler, 1975, pp. 6–7). Oversimplifying somewhat, they have sought this consistency in two different ways. The classical approach, according to Russell & Fehr (1994), is to define anger "by a set of common features, each necessary and together sufficient to determine membership" (p. 186), with these features usually identified by public knowledge. Proponents of this view contend that it is not the physiology or the subjective feelings that define an emotional state but the interpretation of the cause that is vital. The other perspective maintains that the everyday conceptions of anger are best regarded as prototypes, typical examples known to most persons.

Appraisal Conceptions of Anger

Most appraisal-based views of anger are externally focused conceptions within the classical tradition. Regarding emotion as arising from the meaning given to perceived occurrences, they basically contend that anger exists only when outside events are understood in a particular manner. More specifically, appraisal conceptions typically maintain that the precipitating incident has to be seen as an offense or mistreatment. Solomon (1993), a philosopher, took this position when he insisted that, "if there is nothing objectionable, frustrating or offensive (to the person), then those feelings do not count as . . . anger (or even as 'feeling angry') . . ." (p. 10) and that "all emotions presuppose or have as their preconditions certain sorts of cognitions . . . recognition of an offense in anger . . ." (p. 11). Averill's (1983) argument that anger "for the person in the street, is an accusation" that "accepted social norms" have been violated (p. 1149) is essentially much the same kind of statement, as is the Ortony, Clore & Collins (1988) contention that anger requires the disapproval of someone's blameworthy action as well as displeasure at the undesirable event.

Many appraisal formulations go well beyond this basic claim. Although there are a good many appraisal analyses worthy of consideration here (e.g. Frijda, 1986; Roseman, Spindel & Jose, 1990; Scherer, 1993), space limitations permit a summary of only three of these theoretical schemes. From his social constructivist perspective, Averill (1982, 1983) viewed anger as a "syndrome" (or "transitory social role") having biological, psychological and social components, including appraisals. The organization of these components is not "hard-wired" into the person, he believed, and is "not explicable in strictly mechanistic (e.g. physiological) terms" (1982, p. 9), but is culturally determined. In agreement with a number of other appraisal theorists, he also held that anger must have an object. "A person cannot be angry without being angry *at* [italics in original] something" (1982, p. 10). Averill's survey of students and community residents also led him to maintain that "the person in the street" typically regards anger as being different from annoyance. Anger was not only more intense, more serious than annoyance, he claimed, but also "involves one's self and one's principles in a way that annoyance does not" (1983, p. 1152).

The appraisal analysis offered by Ortony, Clore & Collins (1988) emphasizes that emotional states are organized hierarchically. With the other writers sharing their perspective, they believed that any given emotion cannot be defined in terms of physiology, feelings, or behavior alone, but only through those reactions that are triggered by "appropriate cognitive analyses". In their view, these analyses occur in sequence. The appraisal first gives rise to either a positive or a negative affective reaction, and the more differentiated states then come into being as additional factors are considered. In the case of anger, the afflicted person presumably has to think that the agent (cause) of the undesirable event behaved in a blameworthy manner. Anger is elicited, then, according to Ortony, Clore & Collins (1988), if *both* the blameworthiness of the agent's action *and* [emphases in original] the incident's undesirableness are considered together. Focusing on one or the other of these constituents rather than on both presumably would activate affective states other than anger. Ortony, Clore & Collins, and the other appraisal theorists as well, thus dispute Berkowitz's (1993a,b) supposition that any strong negative affect can give rise to anger. For the Ortony–Clore team, intense displeasure alone would produce other states, such as distress or even indignation or resentment, but not anger (see Clore et al., 1993, p. 65). In saying this, though, these writers did not distinguish between anger and annoyance, as Averill did. Their anger concept embraces terms such as "rage" and "fury" as well as "annoyance", "irritation", and even "exasperation" (Ortony, Clore & Collins, 1988, p. 148).

Lazarus's (1991) well-known analysis is very similar to the Ortony, Clore, & Collins formulation in its essential details. He too maintained that anger has defining characteristics, but he spoke of these features in terms of primary and secondary appraisals. If there is to be anger, he said, there must be, first, the primary appraisal that a given incident threatens or assaults the person's "ego identity" (p. 222). Secondary appraisals can then combine with this initial evaluation to help form the anger and influence what action is taken. One of these is blame; some external agent is viewed as having been able to control the threatening occurrence and is thus held accountable for it. If the afflicted person also believes that "the demeaning offense is best ameliorated by attack" (another secondary appraisal), the anger is theoretically "potentiated" and open aggression becomes more likely (p. 225).

There have now been a good many attempts to test the various appraisal conceptions of emotion (see Roseman, Spindel & Jose, 1990; Scherer, 1993; Smith & Ellsworth, 1985, for lists of these studies and interpretations of the findings). It is clear from this research that appraisal formulations can indeed account for the preponderance of emotional occurrences. Nonetheless, there do seem to be exceptions, and I will discuss some of these anomalies later in the chapter.

Emphasizing Goal-structured Knowledge

Several appraisal formulations do not regard anger as basically an "accusation" of a perceived mistreatment and/or norm violation (e.g. Johnson-Laird & Oatley, 1989; Stein & Levine, 1990). However, I will here talk about only one of these schemes because, like the other theories just reviewed, it, too, postulates some necessary antecedent conditions. For Stein & Levine (1990; Stein, Trabasso & Liwag, 1993) these have to do with the desire to maintain or attain a desired state (or goal). Anger occurs, they proposed, when people: (a) think they can accomplish a particular goal/attain a desired state; (b) find that the desired goal is lost or an aversive condition cannot be avoided; and (c) firmly believe that the desired state can be reinstated. Should these persons focus on the loss and not believe that they can regain what they were striving for, theoretically they will become sad rather than angry. Differentiating themselves even further from the other appraisal formulations, Stein & Levine (1990) questioned whether anger requires the perception of an intentional misdeed. They suggested that angry people tend to say (and believe) that they had been deliberately wronged, because they had learned in growing up that such a claim makes anger permissible (p. 65).

The writers pointed to a study with children and college students (Stein & Levine, 1989) to support their reasoning. When the participants reported their reactions to a number of hypothetical emotional episodes, all having to do with goal–outcome relations, they were most likely to indicate they would be angry in response to an aversive state of affairs, a condition they would have preferred to avoid. Many of the participants said they would be angry even when the aversive event had arisen naturally or had been accidental but, of course, anger was reported most often if the harm had been described as intentional, especially in the case of the older respondents. Also, in accord with the authors' theorizing, most of those saying they would be angry (76%) evidently focused on the goal rather than on their loss by indicating they would want to reinstate the desired state of affairs. Levine (1995) corroborated the latter findings in a later study with kindergarten children. When the youngsters were queried about a series of hypothetical situations, they did not employ the criterion of intentional harm in distinguishing between anger- and sadness-arousing events. Instead, they typically believed that anger would be most likely to arise when people: (a) could change undesirable situations and reinstate their goals; and (b) focused their attention on the agent producing the undesirable occurrence.

Prototypic Conceptions of Anger

Much as has been emphasized by Scherer (1992) and Rimé, Philippot & Cisamolo (1990), people's reports of their emotional experiences—and appraisal theorists' analyses as well—are generally based on widely shared mental representations of the emotions, whether these representations arise from cultural learning, from one's past history, or both. Following the lead provided by cognitive psychologists, several emotion researchers have argued that these representations should be understood in prototypic terms. They note that when people think of an emotion or when they encounter an emotion-producing episode, they typically have an implicit model, or prototype, of the relevant emotional state in mind, and organize their interpretations and reports in terms of this guiding conception. Affect-related experiences are then categorized in terms of their "family resemblance" to this best-case model, the prototype.

When Shaver et al. (1987) analyzed their students' accounts of emotional experiences from the prototype perspective, they found that the anger prototype included features in accord with appraisal theorizing, especially in regard to eliciting conditions. However, this prototype apparently also had characteristics generally neglected in most appraisal formulations (but recognized by Izard, 1991, as mentioned above): as the authors put it, "the angry person reports becoming stronger (higher in potency) and more energized in order to fight or rail against the cause of anger" (p. 1078). Also going beyond most appraisal conceptions, Shaver et al. (1987) noted that the students' implicit model of anger frequently included aggression-related physical actions, such as fist clenching, pounding on things, and even attacks against inanimate objects. For the Shaver group (Shaver, Wu & Schwartz, 1992), these last-mentioned features of the public's prototypic conception of anger are very much in line with Frijda's (1986; Frijda, Kuipers & ter Schure, 1989) contention that emotions have more to do with a change in action readiness than with feelings *per se*.

Russell & Fehr (1994) have published the most important, and most provocative, applications of the prototype approach to the study of emotions. Their objection to the classical view is especially significant. Rather than saying that each of the emotional states possesses certain necessary defining features, they maintained that an affective state's membership in a given emotion category is a matter of degree, how closely it resembles the emotion exemplar on a pattern of features. The intensity of the feelings associated with the concept is one of these features, but only one (see p. 193). Moreover, not only can there be varieties of anger graded in terms of how good an example they are of the anger prototype, but the "borders separating anger from 'not-anger' are fuzzy" (p. 186).

We can illustrate this notion of "degrees of prototypicality" by considering the relation between "anger" on one hand and "annoyance" and "irritation" on the other. Averill (1983) had maintained that for "the person in the street, the difference between anger and annoyance is intuitively clear" (p. 1151). The Russell & Fehr (1994) data question such a statement; in one of their studies (see p. 197), 81% of the participants indicated that annoyance was a member of the category "anger" (and 91% agreed that irritation was a category member). Then too, Clore et al. (1993) regarded contempt as "anger-like" but not really anger because, they suggested, it does not necessarily have to do with negative outcomes (p. 71). It might be better to say that contempt has a moderately good resemblance to people's implicit model of anger, since 80% of the Russell & Fehr (1994) sample placed contempt within the anger category (see p. 197).

Johnson-Laird & Oatley (1989) have argued that some emotion-related phenomena cannot be understood in prototype terms. They maintained that people cannot have a prototype for subjective feelings, since these are "unanalysable primitive experiences", but can have a prototype involving the antecedents and consequences of emotions (p. 93). Russell & Fehr might agree; for them, the anger prototype is essentially script-like in nature. To know "a concept of anger", they said, "is to know a script . . . in which prototypical antecedents, feelings, expressions, behaviors, physiological changes and consequences are laid out in causal and temporal sequence" (p. 202).

SOME QUESTIONS ABOUT APPRAISAL ANALYSES OF ANGER

There Are Exceptions

Appraisal theories probably can account for most emotional experiences. However, they do not always work, as if some emotional episodes are governed by processes not dreamt of in the appraisal philosophy. Thus, in one study, the Johnson-Laird & Oatley theory "correctly predicted [only] about 69% of the basic emotions arising from goal-relevant events" (Oatley & Johnson-Laird, 1996, p. 369), while in the appraisal-orientated investigation by Smith & Ellsworth (1985), [only] "44% of their subjects' appraisals were assigned by discriminant analysis to the correct emotion category" (Frijda, Kuipers & ter Schure, 1989, p. 212).

A number of writers, including—but not only—Izard (e.g. 1991, 1993), Panksepp (1994) and Zajonc (1984), would not be surprised at these exceptions, since they do not believe that appraisals, or any other cognitive processes, are necessary for all emotions. In regard to anger more specifically, Berkowitz (1993a,b; 1994) has pointed to a number of instances in which anger arousal was not clearly anticipated by standard appraisal theorizing. Some of these question the contention that an unpleasant event will arouse anger only when the perceived cause is interpreted as blameworthy. And so, to cite only one example, close to 40% of the respondents in Averill's (1982, 1983) survey said they had been angered by another person's action, even though they had not regarded that behavior as socially improper, and 12% even viewed the eliciting action as having been justified.

Can Anger Arise Independently of Goal-orientated Evaluations?

Although appraisal theories are virtually unanimous in holding that emotions result from an evaluation of a given event's goal relevance, one can ask whether goal-orientated evaluations are necessarily involved in every instance of anger. The prototype approach suggests that this need not be so. The public apparently recognizes that aversive states of affairs sometimes generate anger, even though these events have little directly to do with the blocking of goal attainment and/or are not illegitimate. We saw this in the Stein & Levine (1989) study mentioned earlier, and can also find further indications in the Russell & Fehr (1994) Study 3. When the participants were asked to think of an occasion in which they experienced anger and rate how good an example of anger this was, the following instance was judged to be a "slightly good example" (a rating of 4 on the 6-step scale):

> I went swimming at a pool. I was swinging on a rope, then my arm slipped, and I
> bashed my knee-cap on the edge (p. 194).

Many people seem to know that unexpected painful happenings can produce anger at times—that is, these events have a low to moderate prototypicality—even though these occurrences do not closely resemble the anger-eliciting examplars they have in mind.

Aversive Events as Anger Sources

This last-mentioned observation raises a matter that in my view is not adequately addressed by most appraisal formulations: A rapidly growing number of investigations show that people exposed to unpleasant conditions are apt to become angry and aggressively inclined. The Stein & Levine (1989) study mentioned above indicates that many people are aware of the anger-enhancing effect of aversive conditions. Laboratory experiments testify to the reality of this shared mental representation (see Berkowitz, 1989; 1993a,b,c; 1994). Physical pain is perhaps the best example of a decidedly unpleasant state of affairs, and we now know that people in pain often display anger and hostility (Berkowitz, 1993c; Fernandez & Turk, 1995). Izard has recognized this, remarking that:

> ... pain is a direct and immediate cause of anger. Even in very young infants, we see anger expression to inoculation long before they can appraise or understand what has happened to them (1991, p. 237).

Other aversive conditions that do not produce sharp physical pain can also give rise to anger and an instigation to aggression. Citing only some of the findings showing this, laboratory studies have demonstrated that exposure to irritable cigarette smoke, foul odors, high room temperatures, and unpleasantly cold water can generate anger and aggression. And so, in Anderson's research into the effects of uncomfortable heat on affective aggression, high temperatures led to anger and hostility even when this manipulation was regarded as socially justified (e.g. Anderson, Deuser & DeNeve, 1995; also see Anderson & Anderson, 1996), and similarly, in the experiments by Berkowitz, Cochran & Embree (1981), in which the participants kept a hand in cold water in the course of a legitimate scientific study, the uncomfortable cold made the participants highly irritable and annoyed.

The Cognitive–Neoassociationistic Approach

Berkowitz (1989, 1993a,b,c) has offered what he terms a cognitive–neoassociationistic (CNA) model to account for these and similar findings. In his early versions of this formulation (e.g. Berkowitz, 1989, 1993b) he suggested that any decidedly unpleasant state of affairs—whether physical pain, high temperatures, unpleasant cold, a frustration, social stress, depressive feelings, or even the death of a loved one—could give rise to anger and aggressive inclinations through a multi-stage process. Figure 20.1 summarizes this theoretical model. The initial reaction to the negative condition is negative affect. According to CNA, as the figure indicates, this decidedly unpleasant feeling then automatically generates at least two emotional syndromes consisting of expressive-motor and physiological reactions, feelings, thoughts and memories. One of these syndromes is associated with fight inclinations and the other with flight tendencies. The anger experience presumably grows out of the awareness of the aggression-related reactions, whereas fear derives from the awareness of the flight-linked responses.

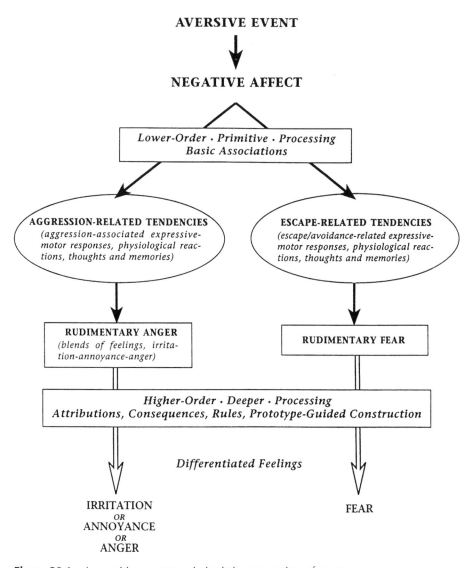

Figure 20.1   A cognitive–neoassociationistic conception of anger

Situational influences, prior learning and inherited dispositions determine the relative strengths of these two opposing syndromes. However, even when the flight syndrome is dominant, theoretically there is also some inclination to aggression which could become manifest if escape from the aversive situation is not possible.

In this formulation, associative mechanisms dominate at first, right after the initial experience, but cognitive processes dominate in the later stages as the person thinks about what is happening. It is at this later time, CNA proposes, that appraisals and attributions come into play, guiding the further construction of the emotional experience based on the person's schemata/scripts regarding the situational origins and experiential nature of particular emotions.

Some Questions

Where the first versions of the cognitive–neoassociationistic analysis tentatively proposed that virtually any kind of negative affect could activate the "fight"- and "flight"-orientated syndromes, Berkowitz now suggests that the unpleasant feeling is most likely to have this effect if it is of an agitated nature. It might be appropriate to term this feeling "distress". Whatever the exact label Berkowitz would give to the initial affective reaction to the aversive condition, Clore et al. (1993) questioned whether anger arises in the conjectured multi-stage sequence; for them, it will be recalled, anger exists only when an actor's behavior has negative consequences and is appraised as being blameworthy. Russell & Fehr (1994) attempted to resolve the difference between Berkowitz and Clore et al. by saying that each of them employed the concept "anger" in a legitimate, although different, manner; both specified a class of events having some relationship to occurrences in the public's anger script. But even though Berkowitz and the appraisal theorists may be talking about different classes of events, is it not important, as Berkowitz (1994) has noted, that these different occurrences may have similar consequences, at least in some respects?

Emotional Syndromes as Associative Networks

This formulation is similar in many respects to Bower's (1981) semantic network model of emotions, and indeed, is greatly indebted to Bower's writings. Extending Bower's original associative network conception, I have argued elsewhere (Berkowitz, 1993b) that emotion theorists would do well to recognize the important role played by associative processes in emotional phenomena. CNA, as its name implies, gives very great—but not complete—weight to these processes in its interpretations of conditions that generate anger and affective aggression. Thus, in conceiving of emotional syndromes as associative networks that can be activated by internal or external stimulation associated with these syndromes, CNA can accommodate the research showing that the facial expressions and bodily postures characteristic of anger can generate angry feelings (DuClos et al., 1989).

CNA also holds that external stimuli having strong associative links to previous anger-arousing experiences are capable of eliciting anger fairly automatically, and assumes that people are not always fully aware of why or how these situational stimuli are affecting them. Oatley & Johnson-Laird (1996) have noted this occasional lack of complete awareness. For them, the "basic" emotions (which they believe are happiness, anger, disgust, sadness and fear) can sometimes be triggered by stimuli that are outside awareness, and that may even have little or nothing to do with an evaluation, so that the emotional experience is essentially "free-floating". Hostility displacement, a phenomenon not adequately explained by most appraisal theorizing, could arise in such a manner. In reacting to some negative stimulus outside their full awareness, people might develop angry feelings and hostile thoughts before they have anyone to blame. Now primed to anger and hostility, they conceivably could then accuse some appropriate target of wrongdoing—after their anger had arisen. At least two studies have obtained findings consistent with such a possibility. In one, when Quigley & Tedeschi (1996) analyzed their respondents' self-reported angry incidents, they concluded that anger can lead to blame rather than being a consequence of blame. Earlier, Keltner, Ellsworth & Edwards (1993) induced angry or sad feelings in their participants and showed that the people in the former condition were more apt to blame others for mishaps that occurred.

Responding to Possible Responses by Appraisal Theorists

Whether or not they believe that blame appraisals are necessary for anger to arise (and I noted before that some appraisal theorists do not have such a view), proponents of the appraisal perspective typically respond to observations such as those just reported by raising two possibilities: For one, they maintain that cognition is necessarily involved in emotional experience and that an appraisal might actually have been made in these situations, since such a mental operation need not be conscious. For other emotions researchers, such as Izard (1993), Panksepp (1994) and Zajonc (1984) such a contention requires overly-broad definitions of "cognition" and "appraisal", definitions that are so diffuse that theories employing these extremely broad concepts are ultimately non-testable. Thus, Panksepp (1994) argues for restricting the notion of a cognitive process to those operations that are based on neocortical and hippocampal functioning. If their narrower conception of what is a cognitive process were to be followed, one would not say, for example, that unpleasantly high temperatures give rise to irritability, annoyance or even anger because of appraisals. Furthermore, not only is there no independent evidence of appraisals leading to the anger-related affect in many of these cases, but, as Anderson, Deuser & DeNeve (1995) have suggested, the unpleasant feelings can produce whatever hostile appraisals are made so that these interpretations then accompany (rather than cause) the anger that is experienced. The Keltner, Ellsworth & Edwards (1993) findings mentioned above support such a possibility.

But then, appraisal advocates sometimes deal with this latter argument by taking another definitional tack. Some of them say that the negative affect generated by non-appraised stimuli is only a mood and not a true emotion. Emotions, they maintain, require a perceived, and thus an appraised, source. Here I would only wonder if this distinction between "mood" and "emotion" is not too arbitrary. People afflicted by decidedly unpleasant conditions often say they are "irritated" or "annoyed" (mood-like terms for some writers) but they are also apt to describe themselves as feeling "angry". Is this reported "anger" only a mood? And moreover, as the studies by Berkowitz and by Anderson have shown, the supposedly mood-like feelings generated by supposedly mood-arousing conditions typically lead to many of the same behavioral and cognitive reactions one would ordinarily expect of the anger-emotion state.

ANGER EXPERIENCE AND BEHAVIOR

Emotion theorists are by no means agreed as to what is the relation between the emotional experience and overt behavior. Many of them, especially those who are cognitively-orientated, contend that emotions function generally to promote particular plans and goals, but their analyses of how this comes about do not always emphasize the same psychological processes. For some, such as Clore et al. (1993), emotions influence actions by affecting cognitive mechanisms—including attention, judgment, decision-making and memory—rather than by directly priming a class of behaviors. By contrast, other writers, most notably Frijda (1986; Frijda, Kuipers & ter Schure 1989), hold that this priming does occur in many emotional states. In these cases, according to Frijda, an emotionally relevant appraisal elicits not only specific physiological and experiential reactions but also a particular action readiness, a "readiness to engage in or disengage from interaction with some goal object in some particular fashion" (Frijda, Kuipers & ter Schure 1989, p. 213). The term "readiness" here might be taken as referring only to a latent disposition, but for Frijda the notion also involves active motor responses. Thus, where in his research (e.g. Frijda, Kuipers & ter Schure 1989) he typically assessed action readiness by asking the participants what they wanted to do when they were in particular emotional states, he at times indicated that these wants can also involve "impulses" and involuntary skeletal—muscular reactions. As an example, he has cited findings pointing to the activated motor reactions that frequently accompany angry feelings (see Frijda, Kuipers & ter Schure 1989, p. 226), findings that I noted earlier in this chapter. In the case of anger, according to Frijda, this desire has to do largely with "moving against" someone.

We can ask, however, whether the phrases "moving against" and "action readiness" adequately characterize the impulses activated in the anger state. More than a mere "readiness", there may be an active urge to attack, even to hurt, someone. Izard (1991) thought so when he spoke of anger being accompanied by "an impulse to strike out, to attack the [perceived] source of the anger" (p. 241). Spielberger's (1996, personal communication) factor analysis of responses to his latest questionnaire assessing individual differences in experienced anger testifies to such an aggressive urge. He found three intercorrelated clusters, one dealing with angry feelings (composed of items such as, "I am furious"), one with a felt pressure to verbal expression (items such as, "I feel like screaming") and the third reflecting an urge to physical aggression (items such as, "I feel like kicking somebody"). These results, along with the indications of heightened motor activity mentioned earlier in this chapter, show that angry feelings are paralleled by aggression-related motor impulses. Furthermore, these impulses could have the aim of doing injury. Berkowitz (1993a,b) has suggested that the anger experience accompanies an activated motor program orientated toward the injury (or even destruction) of an available target. Roseman, Wiest & Swartz (1994) obtained evidence of this desire to hurt someone when they asked their respondents to indicate what they felt like doing when they were angry. Many of these people answered that in such a state they characteristically thought "how unfair something was". But more importantly, quite a few of them also said that they felt "like hitting someone", and that they wanted "to hurt someone". The experimental results published by Berkowitz, Cochran & Embree (1981) also point to such an aggressive goal. In their two studies the participants (women) were most apt to punish a peer when: (a) they were exposed to presumably legitimate but physically painful stimulation; and (b) had been told that their punishment would hurt, rather than help, the target. It is as if these suffering, and angry, persons were most likely to act on their aggressive urge when they believed they had an opportunity to reach their goal of inflicting hurt.

CONCLUSION

The available research into the nature and origin of anger clearly calls for an eclectic approach to the understanding of this emotional state. None of the now-dominant theoretical approaches are correct in every respect. Or, to put this more kindly, they are all right—in some ways but not necessarily in others. The anger experience apparently grows to a considerable extent out of biological processes, but it is also shaped to some degree by cultural learning. Appraisals and attributions clearly play a major role in many (if not most) instances of anger arousal, but there also seem to be times when anger is a relatively thoughtless reaction to aversive environmental conditions. Furthermore, as the frequently-made distinction between moods and emotions indicates, it probably is often worth identifying how clear it is to the experiencing persons just what is the cause of their affective state, but this causal–clarity dimension may not be important in some emotional reactions. Surely, a very important task for future research on anger, and for emotion research generally, is to determine the conditions under which the affective state is governed largely by cognitive processes (narrowly defined) and just when other processes not under neocortical control play a dominant part.

REFERENCES

Anderson, C. A. & Anderson, K. B. (1996). Violent crime rate studies in philosophical context: a destructive testing approach to heat and southern culture of violence effects. *Journal of Personality and Social Psychology*, **70**, 740–756.

Anderson, C. A., Deuser, W. E. & DeNeve, K. M. (1995). Hot temperatures, hostile affect, hostile cognition, and arousal: tests of a general model of affective aggression. *Personality and Social Psychology Bulletin*, **21**, 434–448.

Averill, J. R. (1982). *Anger and Aggression: An Essay on Emotion*. New York: Springer-Verlag.

Averill, J. R. (1983). Studies on anger and aggression: implications for theories of emotion. *American Psychologist*, **38**, 1145–1160.

Berkowitz, L. (1989). Frustration–aggression hypothesis: examination and reformulation. *Psychological Bulletin*, **106**, 59–73.

Berkowitz, L. (1993a). *Aggression: Its Causes, Consequences, and Control*. New York: McGraw-Hill.

Berkowitz, L. (1993b). Towards a general theory of anger and emotional aggression: implications of the cognitive-neoassociationistic perspective for the analysis of anger and other emotions. In R. S. Wyer Jr & T. K. Srull (eds), *Perspectives on Anger and Emotion: Advances in Social Cognition*, Vol. VI. Hillsdale, NJ: Erlbaum, pp. 1–46.

Berkowitz, L. (1993c). Pain and aggression: some findings and implications. *Motivation and Emotion*, **17**, 277–293.

Berkowitz, L. (1994). Is something missing: some observations prompted by the cognitive-neoassociationist view of anger and emotional aggression. In L. R. Huesmann (ed.), *Aggressive Behavior: Current Perspectives*. New York: Plenum, pp. 35–57.

Berkowitz, L., Cochran, S. & Embree, M. (1981). Physical pain and the goal of aversively stimulated aggression. *Journal of Personality and Social Psychology*, **40**, 687–700.

Bower, G. H. (1981). Mood and memory. *American Psychologist*, **36**, 129–148.

Bower, G. H. (1992). How might emotions affect learning? In S.-A. Christianson (ed.), *Handbook of Emotion and Memory: Research and Theory*. Hillsdale, NJ: Erlbaum, pp. 3–31.

Clore, G. L., Ortony, A., Dienes, B. & Fujita, F. (1993). Where does anger dwell? In R. S. Wyer Jr & T. K. Srull (eds), *Perspectives on Anger and Emotion: Advances in Social Cognition*, Vol. VI. Hillsdale, NJ: Erlbaum, pp. 57–88.

Davitz, J. R. (1969). *The Language of Emotion*. New York: Academic Press.

DuClos, S. E., Laird, J. D., Schneider, E., Sexter, M., Stern, L. & Van Lighten, O. (1989). Emotion-specific effects of facial expressions and postures on emotional experience. *Journal of Personality and Social Psychology*, **57**, 100–108.

Ekman, P. (1984). Expression and the nature of emotion. In K. R. Scherer & P. Ekman (eds), *Approaches to Emotion*. Hillsdale, NJ: Erlbaum, pp. 319–344.

Ekman, P., Levenson, R. W. & Friesen, W. V. (1983). Autonomic nervous system activity distinguisher between (sic) emotions. *Science*, **221**, 1208–1210.

Fernandez, E. & Turk, D. C. (1995). The scope and significance of anger in the experience of chronic pain. *Pain*, **61**, 165–175.

Frijda, N. H. (1986). *The Emotions*. Cambridge/New York: Cambridge University Press.

Frijda, N. H., Kuipers, P. & ter Schure, E. (1989). Relations among emotion, appraisal, and emotional action readiness. *Journal of Personality and Social Psychology*, **57**, 212–228.

Gergen, K. J. (1985). The social constructionist movement in modern psychology. *American Psychologist*, **40**, 266–275.

Izard, C. E. (1991). *The Psychology of Emotions*. New York: Plenum.

Izard, C. E. (1993). Four systems for emotion activation: cognitive and noncognitive processes. *Psychological Review*, **100**, 68–90.

James, W. (1890). *Principles of Psychology*. New York: Holt.

Johnson-Laird, P. N. & Oatley, K. (1989). The language of emotions: an analysis of a semantic field. *Cognition and Emotion*, **3**, 81–123.

Keltner, D., Ellsworth, P. C. & Edwards, K. (1993). Beyond simple pessimism: effects of sadness and anger on social perception. *Journal of Personality and Social Psychology*, **64**, 740–752.

Lazarus, R. S. (1991). *Emotion and Adaptation*. New York: Oxford University Press.

Levenson, R. W., Ekman, P. & Friesen, W. V. (1990). Voluntary facial action generates emotion-specific autonomic nervous system activity. *Psychophysiology*, **27**, 363–384.

Levine, L. J. (1995). Young children's understanding of the causes of anger and sadness. *Child Development*, **66**, 697–709.

Mandler, G. (1975). *Mind and Emotions*. New York: Wiley.

Oatley, K. & Johnson-Laird, P. N. (1996). The communicative theory of emotions: empirical tests, mental models, and implications for social interaction. In L. L. Martin & A. Tesser (eds), *Striving and Feeling*. Mahwah, NJ: Erlbaum, pp. 363–393.

Ortony, A., Clore, G. L. & Collins, A. (1988). *The Cognitive Structure of Emotions*. Cambridge/New York: Cambridge University Press.

Panskepp, J. (1994). A proper distinction between affective and cognitive process is essential for scientific progress. In P. Ekman & R. J. Davidson (eds), *The Nature of Emotion: Fundamental Questions*. New York/Oxford: Oxford University Press, pp. 224–226.

Quigley, B. M. & Tedeschi, J. T. (1996). Mediating effects of blame attributions on feelings of anger. *Personality and Social Psychology Bulletin*, **22**, 1280–1288.

Rimé, B. & Giovannini, D. (1986). The physiological patterns of reported emotional states. In K. R. Scherer, H. G. Wallbott & A. B. Summerfield (eds), *Experiencing Emotion: A Cross-cultural Study*. Cambridge: Cambridge University Press, pp. 84–97.

Rimé, B., Philippot, P. & Cisamolo, D. (1990). Social schemata of peripheral changes in emotion. *Journal of Personality and Social Psychology*, **59**, 38–49.

Roseman, I. J. (1991). Appraisal determinants of discrete emotions. *Cognition and Emotion*, **5**, 161–200.

Roseman, I. J., Spindel, M. S. & Jose, P. E. (1990). Appraisals of emotion-eliciting events: testing a theory of discrete emotions. *Journal of Personality and Social Psychology*, **59**, 899–915.

Roseman, I. J., Wiest, C. & Swartz, T. S. (1994). Phenomenology, behaviors and goals differentiate discrete emotions. *Journal of Personality and Social Psychology*, **67**, 206–221.

Russell, J. A. & Fehr, B. (1994). Fuzzy concepts in a fuzzy hierarchy: varieties of anger. *Journal of Personality and Social Psychology*, **67**, 186–205.

Schachter, S. & Singer, J. (1962). Cognitive, social, and physiological determinants of emotional state. *Psychological Review*, **69**, 379–399.

Scherer, K. R. (1992). On social representations of emotional experience: stereotypes, prototypes, or archetypes? In M. Von Cranach, W. Doise & G. Mugny (eds), *Social Representations and the Social Bases of Knowledge*. Gottingen: Hogrefe & Huber, pp. 30–36.

Scherer, K. R. (1993). Studying the emotion-antecedent appraisal process: an expert system approach. *Cognition and Emotion*, **7**, 325–355.

Scherer, K. R. & Tannenbaum, P. H. (1986). Emotional experiences in everyday life: a survey approach. *Motivation and Emotion*, **10**, 295–314.

Scherer, K. R. & Wallbott, H. G. (1994). Evidence for universality and cultural variation of differential emotion response patterning. *Journal of Personality and Social Psychology*, **66**, 310–328.

Scherer, K. R., Wallbott, H. G. & Summerfield, A. B. (1986). *Experiencing Emotion: A Cross-cultural Study*. Cambridge: Cambridge University Press.

Shaver, P., Schwartz, J., Kirson, D. & O'Connor, C. (1987).   Emotion knowledge: further
    exploration of a prototype approach. *Journal of Personality and Social Psychology*, **52**,
    1061–1086.
Shaver, P., Wu, S. & Schwartz, J. C. (1992).   Cross-cultural similarities and differences in
    emotion and its representation: a prototype approach. In M. Clark (ed.), *Review of
    Personality and Social Psychology,* Vol. 13 Emotion. Newbury Park, CA: Sage, pp.
    175–212.
Shields, S. A. (1984).   Reports of bodily changes in anxiety, sadness, and anger. *Motiva-
    tion and Emotion*, **8**, 1–21.
Smith, C. A. & Ellsworth, P. C. (1985).   Patterns of cognitive appraisal in emotion.
    Journal of Personality and Social Psychology, **48**, 813–838.
Solomon, R. C. (1993).   The philosophy of emotions. In M. Lewis & J. M. Haviland (eds),
    Handbook of Emotions. New York/London: Guilford, pp. 3–15.
Stein, N. L. & Levine, L. J. (1989).   The causal organization of emotional knowledge: a
    developmental study. *Cognition and Emotion*, **3**, 343–378.
Stein, N. L. & Levine, L. J. (1990).   Making sense out of emotion: the representation and
    use of goal-structured knowledge. In N. L. Stein, B. Leventhal & T. Trabasso (eds),
    Psychological Approaches to Emotion. Hillsdale, NJ: Erlbaum, pp. 45–73.
Stein, N. L., Trabasso, T. & Liwag, M. (1993).   The representation and organization of
    emotional experience: unfolding the emotion episode. In M. Lewis & J. Haviland (eds),
    Handbook of Emotions. New York: Guilford, pp. 279–300.
Zajonc, R. B. (1984).   On the primacy of affect. *American Psychologist*, **39**, 117–123.

Chapter 21

Disgust: The Body and Soul Emotion

Paul Rozin
University of Pennsylvania, Philadelphia, PA, USA
Jonathan Haidt
University of Virginia, Charlottesville, VA, USA
and
Clark R. McCauley
Bryn Mawr College, Bryn Mawr, PA, USA

Disgust is on virtually every list of "basic emotions", from the second century *Natyashastra* from India (Masson & Patwardhan, 1970; Hejmadi, 1998; Shweder, 1993), through Darwin's (1872) *Expression of the Emotions in Man and Animals* and on to contemporary textbooks. Like other basic emotions, disgust links together cognitive and bodily responses; it can be well analyzed within the Tomkins/Ekman (Ekman, 1984) framework as an affect "program", in which outputs (behaviors, expressions, physiological responses) are triggered by inputs (cognitive appraisals of environmental events). It is the thesis of this chapter that disgust, as experienced by humans around the world, shows a high degree of constancy or conservatism on the output side (i.e. expression, nausea and behavioral tendency), but has undergone an extraordinary transformation and expansion on the appraisal side (Rozin, Haidt & McCauley, 1993; 1997a; Haidt et al., 1997). This expansion varies with history and culture in a way that takes disgust far beyond its animal precursors on the appraisal side.

THE DISGUST PROGRAM

The constellation of responses associated with the emotion of disgust is relatively stable across situations, cultures and even species, and consists of expressive

Handbook of Cognition and Emotion. Edited by T. Dalgleish and M. Power.
© 1999 John Wiley & Sons Ltd.

movements (particularly in the face), certain physiological events, and behaviors or behavioral tendencies.

The Expression of Disgust

The disgust face is familiar and recognized in many and perhaps all cultures (Ekman, 1984; Ekman et al., 1987; Izard, 1971; Haidt & Keltner, 1998). The three major muscle groups involved (Darwin, 1872; Ekman & Friesen, 1975; Izard, 1971) are the gape (lowering of the lower jaw), with or without tongue extrusion, the nose wrinkle, and the upper lip raise. The gape and nose wrinkle are most associated with disgust situations related to food. The upper lip raise, the movement least related functionally to eating or rejection of food, is most associated with what we call elaborated disgust (elicitors like dead bodies, physical contact with strangers, and certain moral violations) (Rozin, Lowery & Ebert, 1994).

Physiology

Unlike other emotions, disgust has a unique physiological signature, associated with the experience of nausea. Also, whereas anger and fear involve sympathetic arousal, disgust may be parasympathetically organized and sympathetically neutral or de-arousing (Ekman, Levenson & Friesen, 1983; Levenson, Ekman & Friesen, 1990).

Behavior

The behavior associated with disgust is typically a distancing from the disgusting situation or object. Distancing may be accomplished by an expulsion or removal of an offending stimulus (as in spitting out or washing) or by a removal of the self from the situation (turning around, walking away) or by withdrawal of attention (closing or covering the eyes, engaging in some distraction or changing the topic of a conversation).

THE EXPERIENCE OF DISGUST: QUALIA

There is a sense of "offense" associated with disgust, related to a sense of deviance or imperfection: something is not as it should be. Scherer & Walbott (1994) report, based on questionnaires from college students from 37 countries on five continents, that in comparison to most other basic emotions, disgust is reported to be relatively short in duration and relatively low in experienced intensity.

PREADAPTATION AND THE EXPANSION OF DISGUST ELICITORS

We describe the expansion of disgust elicitors in cultural evolution as an instance of the evolutionary concept of preadaptation (Mayr, 1960): the use and modification of an already existing structure/system that had evolved for a different purpose (Rozin, Haidt & McCauley, 1993; 1997a). For example, the mouth evolved as an aperture involved in eating and breathing. The tongue and teeth are adaptations for handling food. However, as language evolved in humans, the expressive aspect co-opted the mouth, conveniently located as the output of the breathing system, and employed the tongue, teeth and muscular control over the oropharynx in the service of speech. Hence, the mouth can be said to have been preadapted to take on a speech function.

We propose that disgust originated in the widespread distaste/oral rejection response seen in many mammals in response to certain categories of tastes, e.g. bitter tastes, and that the output side of this distaste program was appropriated by a wide range of elicitors, appraisals and meanings. We trace a trajectory from animal disgust origins centered on food selection and protecting the body from harmful ingestants to ideational disgust serving to protect the soul from harmful influences. Disgust expands from "out of mouth" to "out of mind". This general pattern of extension has also been suggested by Oatley & Johnson-Laird (1987) as characteristic of evolution of the emotions. The same pattern may also be manifested in development, a process which may parallel preadaptation, and may be described as increased accessibility (Rozin, 1976).

CORE DISGUST

Early landmarks in consideration of disgust are the contributions of Charles Darwin (1872), from the evolutionary standpoint, and of Andras Angyal (1941), from a psychoanalytic perspective. Both of these penetrating analyses recognize the broad range of meanings and elicitors of disgust, yet conceptualize the food system as the phylogenetic and ontogenetic origin of disgust. We concur and describe *core disgust* as the prototype and origin of disgust (Rozin & Fallon, 1987). Our definition of core disgust derives from Angyal (1941): "Revulsion at the prospect of (oral) incorporation of an offensive substance. That substance has contamination properties: if it contacts an otherwise edible substance, it renders it inedible" (Rozin & Fallon, 1987, p. 23: the first sentence is from Anygal, 1941). Our argument for this definition, and the feeding system as the origin of disgust, is as follows (Rozin & Fallon, 1987):

1. The physical signature of disgust is nausea, a gastro-intestinal, usually food-related sensation, which discourages ingestion and may lead to ejecting (vomiting) something already ingested.

2. The facial expression of disgust focuses on the mouth and nose, and has strong components of rejection of tastes and smells.
3. The parallel manifestation of gaping and vomiting in non-human mammals is clearly and virtually exclusively associated with the food system.
4. Etymologically, the word "disgust" (or its relative, *degout* in French) literally means bad taste.

In our view, the disgust emotion program evolved from a pre-adapted part of the feeding system: the mammalian distaste response (Rozin & Fallon, 1987). This response involves the gape and related facial expressions, is linked to behavioral withdrawal, and is probably associated with nausea. It is widespread in mammals (see Grill & Norgren, 1977, for detailed description for *Rattus norvegicus*), and clearly manifested in newborn human infants (Steiner, 1979; Rosenstein & Oster, 1988). It is present as well in adult humans in their reactions to bad-tasting food, such as foods that are very bitter.

But distaste is quite different from disgust. For distaste, the rejection is made on the basis of sensory properties; there is no sense of offense if the bad-tasting substance is introduced into the stomach in a way that bypasses the oral senses (e.g. a pill). Neither does distaste involve contamination; people rarely reject a desired food if a distasteful food merely touched it. In our taxonomy of food rejections (Rozin & Fallon, 1980; Fallon & Rozin, 1983), *distaste* is motivated by undesirable sensory properties, *danger* by undesirable consequences of ingestion, and *disgust* by offensive properties having to do with the nature or origin of the potential food.

We consider disgust, including core disgust, to be uniquely human. The complex conceptual apparatus required for reactions based on the nature and origin of disgust elicitors, and for ideas of contamination that do not depend on sensory qualities, are unavailable to non-human animals. We now consider three critical aspects of core disgust, all deriving from the definition provided above (see Rozin & Fallon, 1987, for a fuller discussion).

Oral Incorporation

Core disgust can be thought of as a gatekeeper for the mouth, guarding against oral incorporation of improper substances. Eating is the principal process through which materials outside of the self are taken into the self. This extremely intimate act, accomplished almost always through the mouth, activates a deep, strongly felt cognition: "you are what you eat". Based on everyday experiences with mixing of substances, it is entirely reasonable to believe that mixing a body with a food will impart some properties of the food to the body. The "you are what you eat" principle is overt and salient in traditional cultures (see review in Nemeroff & Rozin, 1989). We have shown using indirect methods that this belief is also present in college undergraduates (Nemeroff & Rozin, 1989): people eating wild boar are seen as more aggressive and hairier than people eating sea turtles. "You are what you eat" explains why people feel so strongly about consuming offensive substances: they will make the consumer offensive!

Animals as the Source of Offensive Substances

We have argued that elicitors of core disgust are generally of animal origin (Rozin & Fallon, 1987). Virtually all food-related items of disgust, cross-culturally, are of animal origin. Plant foods that are disliked are generally regarded as distasteful, but not disgusting (i.e. they don't contaminate everything they touch). Our more recent description of core disgust (Rozin, Haidt & McCauley, 1993) describes the elicitors of core disgust as animals (roaches, maggots, rats), food (monkey meat, ketchup on ice-cream), and body products (feces, vomit, saliva).

Contagion

Anthropologists at the turn of the century (Tylor, 1871/1974; Frazer, 1890/1959; Mauss, 1902/1972) described contagion as one of the laws of sympathetic magic. The basic idea is "once in contact, always in contact". When two entities make contact, there is a permanent passage of properties. Hence, when an earthworm briefly contacts a food, the earthworm "properties" enter the food. The critical properties of contagion (Rozin & Nemeroff, 1990) seem to be that: (a) physical contact is required; (b) the effect of contact is dose-insensitive—very brief contact suffices to accomplish most of the potential effect; (c) the effect is permanent; and (d) that negative contagious effects are more common and more powerful than positive contagious effects. We have shown, contrary to the original claim that sympathetic magical thinking is characteristic only of people in traditional cultures, that it is widespread in Western-developed cultures (Rozin, Millman & Nemeroff, 1986).

Contagion is a defining feature of disgust, and extends throughout the varied domains of disgust. The negative contagion produced by disgust elicitors seems to be universal among adults but absent in young children (Fallon, Rozin & Pliner, 1984) and, so far as we know, any non-human species (see Rozin & Nemeroff, 1990, for a review). Initial research on the cognitions involved in contagion suggests that "mental models" of contagion include principles of association, the idea of a "material essence" transferred by contact, and the idea of a non-material, "spiritual essence", also transferred by contact (Nemeroff & Rozin, 1994).

Core disgust is only the beginning of the story of disgust. When we asked Americans and Japanese (Imada, Yamada & Haidt, 1993) to give three examples of what is disgusting (*ken'o* in Japanese), core disgust items (foods, animals, body products) accounted for only 24% of American responses and 27% of Japanese responses. The majority of responses illustrated the expansion of disgust into other domains of life, to which we now turn.

ANIMAL-NATURE DISGUST

In our various open-ended studies we have found frequent references to four additional kinds of elicitors: poor hygiene (body odor, not washing frequently); inappropriate sex (as with animals or siblings); body envelope violations (as with gaping wounds, or amputated limbs); and contact with death (as with touching a corpse). These four domains, together with the core domains (animals, food, body products), have in common that they deal with essentials of animal life: eating, excreting, grooming, reproduction, injury, death and decay. Given the ethnographic prominence of the assertions that humans are not animals, and that humans are above animals, we can summarize a possible meaning for the seven domains of elicitors as reminders of our animal nature (Rozin & Fallon, 1987; Rozin, Haidt & McCauley, 1993). If humans are to convince themselves that they are different from animals, these are seven areas in which work must be done to hide (as with defecation and menstruation for Americans) or humanize (as with table manners and funeral rites) biological necessities.

The rejection/withdrawal/offense response previously used for offensive foods is now harnessed to the offensive idea that we are animals. The contagion properties of core disgust elicitors are also extended to the animal nature elicitors, such that a sweater worn by a person who has an amputated leg is less desirable than a sweater worn by a normally equipped person (Rozin, Markwith & McCauley, 1994).

Disgust is thus the emotion of civilization, and of socialization. It is part of affirming our unique humanity. This conception of disgust as a rejection of our animal nature is congruent with Norbert Elias' (1939/1978) ideas on the civilizing process, and the development of sensitivities in Europe from medieval to modern times. Elias (1939/1978) argues that: ". . . people in the course of the civilizing process seek to suppress in themselves every characteristic that they feel to be 'animal'" (p. 120). We call this expanded form of disgust "animal-nature disgust" (Rozin, Haidt & McCauley, 1993; 1997; Haidt et al. 1997). This framing of disgust is very much in keeping with the concept of disgust as it is elaborated in Miller's book, *The Anatomy of Disgust* (1997) and with Kass' (1994) treatment of the extension of food as a body related entity to food as a soul-related entity.

There is one property that humans share with animals that is particularly upsetting to the self conscious *Homo sapiens*. It is mortality—death and decay of the flesh. Humans are presumably the only species that understands this extremely threatening state of affairs, and it seems reasonable to assume that distancing the self from animals and animal properties might be a way of dealing with fear of death. The psychoanalyst Ernest Becker, in *The*

Denial of Death (1973), argues that mortality is *the* great human problem. He suggests that the elaborate psychological defense machinery proposed by Freud, including mechanisms of repression and denial, serve principally to deal with the prospect of death, rather than with sexual desires and aggressive impulses. If Becker is right, then disgust at animality, and at corpses in particular, should play an important role in the mental economy of humankind.

The analysis of item intercorrelations in a disgust sensitivity scale that we created reveals that items dealing with contact with death are among the most predictive of total disgust sensitivity (Haidt, McCauley & Rozin, 1994). This argues for an important role for attitudes to death, as does the fact that the quintessential odor of disgust is the odor of decay, a result of microbial action and, in particular, of death.

We propose animal nature disgust as the first major elaboration of disgust in its cultural evolution; in this scheme, the function of disgust moves further toward protecting the soul, as well as the body (Rozin, Haidt & McCauley, 1993; 1997a; Haidt et al., 1997).

INTERPERSONAL DISGUST

There are many disgust experiences that are not easily understood in terms of core or animal-nature disgust. Many of these experiences involve interactions or contact with other persons. Contact or intimacy with persons outside of one's social circle is often aversive and disgusting, at least to the Americans, Japanese and Indians we have studied. For this reason, many people in these countries are reluctant to wear clothing bought in used clothing stores. In a study on aversion to people with AIDS, Rozin, Markwith & McCauley (1994) found that unknown people were contaminating; subjects were less willing to wear a washed sweater worn briefly by a healthy stranger than the same sweater new. Unknown people who had experienced a misfortune (e.g. a limb amputation as a result of a car accident) were more contaminating, and people with infectious diseases (like tuberculosis) or moral taints (e.g. a convicted murderer) were still more contaminating.

We call what we have been discussing "interpersonal disgust". We think interpersonal disgust makes sense as a re-use of the original disgust "program" applied to the social domain. Just as core disgust rejects most animals and animal products for consumption, and sexual disgust rejects most potential sexual objects, so interpersonal disgust rejects most people as partners for intimate social contact (e.g. sharing food, clothing, linens and casual touch). In all three cases, disgust makes us extremely selective, critical and judgmental. Interpersonal disgust is particularly salient in Hindu India, since the caste system is in large measure defined and maintained by transaction rules, primarily for food. One's purity and status are lowered by eating food prepared by someone of lower caste (Appadurai, 1981).

SOCIO-MORAL DISGUST

There is one final category of situations cited by subjects as elicitors of disgust. This is a large and puzzling category: socio-moral violations. Most socio-moral violations are not disgusting (e.g. robbing a bank) and many of the most disgusting socio-moral violations appear to be disgusting because they involve aspects of core or animal-nature disgust (e.g. the sexual molestation of children, or brutal murders that involve mutilation or other body envelope violations). However, whenever we ask people to describe disgusting situations, we get frequent descriptions of situations that do not seem to make contact with the concerns of core or animal-nature or interpersonal disgust: situations such as hypocrisy, racism, betrayal and disloyalty, or "sleazy" behavior, such as lawyers who chase ambulances.

When we began our research on socio-moral disgust we thought that this category might just reflect an exaggerated or metaphoric use of the English language, in which certain kinds of violations are called "disgusting" even though the reaction will never involve a disgust expression or nausea. However, most of the other languages we have looked at have a word expressing a similar compound of bodily concerns (about food, feces, sex) with social and moral concerns, for example French *degout*, German *Ekel*, Spanish *asco*, Russian *otvrastchenie*, Hebrew *go-al*, Japanese *ken-o*, Oriya (India) *ghrna*, and Chinese *aw-shin*. We therefore believe that socio-moral disgust is not a quirk of the English language. We believe it reflects a common path in the cultural evolution of many societies in which disgust is extended into the social domain, and used to reject certain classes of violators who are beyond redemption (Kekes, 1992). A bank-robber has a normal (human) desire for money; he uses unacceptable means to get money, and for his crime he must "pay back" society in some way. However, people who reveal themselves to have deep characterological flaws that make them unfit for participation in society are rejected and ostracized by the socio-moral disgust of their peers. Thus, racism (for liberals) or lack of loyalty (for conservatives) makes a person revolting and perhaps contaminating in a way that a bank-robber is not.

With interpersonal and moral disgust we complete our description of elaborated disgust. We suggest that interpersonal and moral disgust are the latest additions to the disgust elicitors, in cultural evolution and perhaps even in individual development, but we acknowledge that evidence for this suggestion is meagre.

AN ALTERNATIVE FRAMING OF DISGUST

Miller (1997) proposes a different way of categorizing kinds of disgust. He proposes that there are two basic kinds of disgust: a "Freudian" kind, which acts as a barrier to satisfying unconscious desire, and the "disgust of surfeit", which is activated by overindulgence in food, drink, sex, or other areas of desire that are consciously acted upon. We think that the disgust of surfeit is an important kind of disgust not previously attended to by disgust researchers. However, we do not see the need to bring in a Freudian apparatus of conscious vs. unconscious desires. We think it more parsimonious to view surfeit-disgust as another example of pre-adaptation. If disgust already functioned to discourage the eating of potentially contaminated foods, then it was well-suited as an "off switch" to discourage eating excessive amounts of uncontaminated foods, especially for an omnivorous species that seeks wide variety in diet. Surfeit disgust may have also taken on additional meanings during the civilizing process as people developed disgust for the over-indulgence of basic animal appetites. A popular stereotype conceives many animals as voracious and gluttonous in feeding and promiscuous in mating. Gluttons may therefore disgust by appearing animal-like.

DISGUST IN CULTURAL PERSPECTIVE

We have described disgust as closely linked to the protection and internalization of culture-based sensitivities, in accord with Elias (1939/1978) and Miller (1997). However, cultural sensitivities vary greatly across cultures and historical eras, and we have some indications that disgust and its role in society does, too. Our comparison of American disgust with Japanese *ken-o* (Haidt et al., 1997) found that the kinds of experiences subjects described were very similar in the core and animal reminder domains, but they diverged greatly for socio-moral events. Americans described reactions to people who grossly violate the autonomy or dignity of other individuals (e.g. senseless murders and acts of cruelty and racism), particularly helpless individuals such as children, while Japanese were more likely to describe situations from everyday life in which their own fit into the social order was blocked or threatened (e.g. being criticized, or failing to live up to important standards). This pattern of similarity in core disgust and divergence in socio-moral disgust fits with Oatley & Johnson-Laird's (1987) cognitive theory of emotions, in which universal basic emotions are elaborated into culturally variable complex emotions.

One way to make sense of cultural variations in moral life is through Shweder's theory of the Three Ethics of Morality (Shweder et al., 1997). This theory proposes that moral thought and discourse can be conducted in three different languages, or ethics. The ethic of autonomy focuses on the autonomous individual as the central entity and tries to maximize the rights, freedom and welfare of that individual. This is the dominant moral ethic in the modern Western world. A second system, the ethic of community, focuses on collective entities (e.g. family, community, nation) and strives to maximize the integrity and honor of those entities against such affronts as disorder and disrespect. A third system, the ethics of divinity, focuses on the spark of divinity that exists in all people, and strives to protect that divinity from pollution and degradation while guiding people to live in an elevated and god-like way. All three ethics may be available to individuals in all cultures, but cultures appear to show preferences and differential patterns of use of the three ethics.

We have suggested that Shweder's three moral systems map on to the three other-directed moral emotions, with anger linked to autonomy, contempt to community, and disgust to divinity (Rozin et al., 1999a). Since the ethics of divinity focuses on purity, and is concerned that people behave like gods rather than like animals, it makes sense that disgust and its rejection of animality becomes a central moral emotion in this ethic. We have gathered supporting evidence for this moral–emotional mapping: among Japanese and American subjects, short scenarios describing one or the other type of Shweder violation are generally assigned to the appropriate emotion word (from a choice of the three) or to the corresponding facial expression of that emotion.

It seems that the contemporary Western devotion to a rights–justice ethics of autonomy severely restricts the moral domain of disgust. Haidt, Koller & Dias (1993) asked Brazilians and Americans of upper and lower social class about a variety of disgusting yet harmless actions, such as eating one's pet dog (after it was killed by a car) and having sexual intercourse with a dead chicken. All groups agreed that the actions were disgusting, but the upper-class groups, particularly the American college students, said that the actions were not wrong, since they did not hurt anyone. That is, these subjects separated their personal emotional reactions (disgust) from their moral judgments. Miller (1997) suggests that this separation may be driven by a kind of liberal discomfort with the breadth of a disgust-based morality, under which people who elicit disgust would be declared morally deficient through no fault of their own (e.g. the handicapped, the retarded, the ugly and, for many people, homosexuals).

If upper-class Americans have a narrow moral domain limited to the ethics of autonomy, then the opposite end of the spectrum is represented by traditional Hindu India, where the ethics of community and divinity are extremely well elaborated. In such a society, interpersonal and sociomoral disgust appear to work somewhat differently. The moral domain seems particularly large for Hindus, for whom almost every aspect of daily life can be imbued with moral significance and socially regulated (Shweder, Mahapatra & Miller, 1987). The issues of core disgust (food, animals and body products) become central to the mechanics of purity and pollution. Appadurai (1981) describes food, for Hindus, as a "bio-moral" substance. Thus, although there are things that are disgusting to Hindus and not to Americans, and vice versa, the big differences between the cultures may be the much wider range of entities, disgusting in both cultures, which enter the moral domain in Hindu India.

THE DEVELOPMENT OF DISGUST

It seems that up to about two years of age, children show no aversion to feces and other "primary" disgust elicitors (Rozin, Hammer, Oster, Horowitz & Marmara,

1986). Toilet training may be the primal socialization into core disgust (Angyal, 1941; Rozin & Fallon, 1987).

Although the development of disgust has been little studied, the development of contagion, a proposed criterial feature of disgust, has been explored. Contagion is not present in young preschool children, even though they may reject the contaminating substance itself. Original studies on American children indicated an onset of contagion thinking in the context of disgust or toxins in the 6–7 year-old range (Fallon, Rozin & Pliner, 1984; Rozin, Fallon & Augustoni-Ziskind, 1985), but later studies on Australian children, using more sensitive measures, provide evidence for some contagion sensitivity by the age of four years (Siegal & Share, 1990).

In early as well as in later development, it often happens that an event or object that was previously morally neutral becomes morally loaded. We have called this process "moralization" (Rozin, 1997). In the course of this process, as for example in the case of cigarette smoking in the USA, or meat-eating among vegetarians, the emotion of disgust is recruited. Thus moral vegetarians find meat more disgusting than do "health" vegetarians (Rozin, Markwith & Stoess, 1997b).

At this time, there is little evidence for or against our suggestion that child development recapitulates the cultural expansion of disgust elicitors, beginning with core disgust. What is clear, primarily from common sense and common observation, is that disgust becomes a major, if not *the* major force for negative socialization in children; a very effective way to internalize culturally prescribed rejections (perhaps starting with feces) is to make them disgusting.

THE NEUROBIOLOGY OF DISGUST

A recent series of studies adds an important new dimension to the understanding of disgust from a neurobiological perspective. Sprengelmeyer et al. (1996) have described a striking deficit in the recognition of facial and vocal expressions of disgust in patients with Huntington's disease. This deficit, presumably resulting from damage to the basal ganglia, is noticeably more severe for disgust expressions than for those of any other basic emotion. Disgust sensitivity, measured by a paper and pencil test, was intact. The specificity of this syndrome offers intriguing and unexpected possibilities concerning both the neural and psychological organization of emotion. There is also evidence for a link between disgust (perhaps via contagion sensitivity) and the cleaning compulsions that are common symptoms of obsessive-compulsive disorder (OCD) (Ware et al., 1994). This has neurological significance, since the basal ganglia are implicated in obsessive-compulsive disorder (Rapoport, 1988). The disgust–OCD link has been confirmed and expanded by a recent study reporting that people with OCD show a severe deficit in the recognition of disgust faces (like the Huntington's disease patients) (Sprengelmeyer et al., 1998). The suggestion of a disgust recognition deficit in OCD patients is surprising, since one might expect that the presumed higher disgust sensitivity of OCD patients would be linked to higher sensitivity in recognizing disgust expressions.

THE ALLURE OF DISGUST

Although we have emphasized withdrawal as the behavioral manifestation of disgust, disgust elicitors can be attractive or entertaining in some circumstances. Novelty stores sell realistic imitations of vomit, mucus and slime (apparently mostly to young boys). *Beavis and Butthead*, a television show popular with adolescents, often dwells on disgusting situations (e.g. inappropriate excretion of body fluids; Oppliger & Zillmann, 1995). There is a whole genre of jokes that center on disgust, and disgust humor is particularly salient, perhaps dominant, in young children (Dunn, 1988). In our laboratory experiments on disgust, in which subjects are asked to engage in disgusting experiences up to the point where they don't want to continue, we observe a mixture of disgust expressions and laughter, and subjects rate their laboratory experience overall as interesting and enjoyable (Rozin, Haidt, McCauley, Dunlop & Ashmore, 1999b).

The allure, or perhaps ambivalence, of disgust has been well-articulated by Miller (1997), who takes a Freudian approach to understanding the complexity of human reactions to disgust. From our point of view, the allure of disgust is an instance of a large set of human activities that involve playing with and testing the limits of propriety or safety established by culture (see Apter, 1992). We have described this type of enjoyment with regard to liking for chilli pepper (Rozin, 1990), for roller coasters and for horror movies (McCauley, 1998). In all cases, the body responds with withdrawal and/or negative autonomic events but the mind knows the threat is not real. This disparity between body and mind, or mind over body, seems to produce pleasure. Only constrained or apparent risks are attractive, however; real, out-of-control experiences of disgust or fright are rarely sought or enjoyed (see Miller, 1997, for a similar perspective).

INDIVIDUAL DIFFERENCES IN SENSITIVITY TO DISGUST

We constructed a paper-and-pencil scale to measure individual differences in disgust in the USA and in Japan (Haidt, McCauley & Rozin, 1994). The 32-item Disgust Scale included four items for each of the seven core and animal-nature disgust domains, and four similar items tapping sympathetic magical thinking. In addition to revealing wide variation in disgust sensitivity, the Disgust Scale demonstrated positive intercorrelations of disgust sensitivities across the different domains of elicitors—that is, evidence that the domains converged on a common dimension of sensitivity to disgust. Some behavioral validation emerged from a series of "hands on" laboratory experiences in which the Disgust Scale predicted the degree to which subjects would actually engage in a wide range of disgust activities ($r = -0.41$; Rozin, Haidt, McCauley, Dunlop & Ashmore, 1999b).

Correlations with other scales have begun to locate disgust sensitivity in relation to other individual difference measures (Haidt, McCauley & Rozin, 1994). The Disgust Scale showed a moderate positive correlation (0.39) with fear of death and a moderate negative correlation (−0.46) with sensation seeking.

Davey and his colleagues argue that phobias involving predatory animals (sharks or lions) invoke fear, whereas phobias involving animals that do not threaten significant physical harm (rat, spider, snake, slug, maggot) are motivated primarily by disgust (Matchett & Davey, 1991; Webb & Davey, 1993; Ware et al., 1994). This distinction is buttressed by a number of experimental and psychometric findings, including relations between disgust sensitivity and non-predatory animal phobias.

In our initial Disgust Scale research (Haidt, McCauley & Rozin, 1994), women were substantially more sensitive to disgust than men; the mean difference amounted to more than half a standard deviation in the distribution of Disgust Scale scores. Other work has corroborated this gender difference (Druschel & Sherman, 1994; Oppliger & Zillmann, 1995; Quigley, Sherman & Sherman, 1996).

Besides gender, the demographic variable most correlated with Disgust Scale scores is social class. We were surprised to find that blue-collar workers in our initial studies were more disgust-sensitive than students and middle-class managers (Haidt McCauley & Rozin, 1994). This result was confirmed by Doctoroff & McCauley (1996), who found education negatively correlated with Disgust Scale scores ($r = -0.32$).

Individual differences in disgust are probably related to psychopathology. We have already mentioned links between animal phobias or obsessive compulsive disorder and disgust. These and related psychopathological aspects of disgust are richly discussed by Power and Dalgleish (1997).

CONCLUSION

Disgust is basic, pervasive, and extraordinarily broad in its domain. The interaction of biology and culture is clear, because the output side of disgust remains largely ruled by the biological forces that originally shaped it, while the input/appraisal/meaning part has been greatly elaborated, and perhaps transformed in some cases—so much so that in Miller's (1997) extended analysis, a case is made that its deep meaning is perhaps qualitatively transformed from its animal or infantile origins. Although the range of disgust, as applied to matters as diverse as social miss-steps in Japan, or excess indulgence in Western countries, is indeed daunting, we feel that a preadaption/cultural-evolution framework can account for most of the substantial history of the meanings of disgust. The rich and varied meanings, and the contrasting conservativeness of the response side of disgust, make the study of disgust a particularly promising road toward integrating the biological and cultural roots of emotion.

ACKNOWLEDGEMENTS

We are grateful for grants from the Whitehall Foundation and from the National Institute of Drug Abuse (R21-DA10858-0) for supporting some of the research cited, and the preparation of this chapter.

REFERENCES

Angyal, A. (1941). Disgust and related aversions. *Journal of Abnormal and Social Psychology*, **36**, 393–412.

Appadurai, A. (1981). Gastro-politics in Hindu South Asia. *American Ethnologist*, **8**, 494–511.

Apter, M. J. (1992). *The Dangerous Edge: The Psychology of Excitement*. New York: Free Press.

Becker, E. (1973). *The Denial of Death*. New York: Free Press.

Darwin, C. R. (1872/1965). *The Expression of the Emotions in Man and Animals*. London: John Murray, 1872 (reprinted Chicago: University of Chicago Press, 1965).

Doctoroff, G. & McCauley, C. (1996). Demographic Differences in Sensitivity to Disgust. Poster presented at the annual meeting of the Eastern Psychological Association, Philadelphia, PA, March.

Douglas, M. (1966). *Purity and Danger*. London: Routledge & Kegan Paul.

Druschel, B. & Sherman, M. F. (1994). Disgust Sensitivity as a Function of Personality Characteristics and Gender. Poster presented at the annual meeting of the Eastern Psychological Association, Providence, RI, March.

Dunn, J. (1988). *The Beginnings of Social Understanding*. Cambridge, MA: Harvard University Press.

Ekman, P. (1984). Expression and the nature of emotion. In K. Scherer & P. Ekman (eds), *Approaches to Emotion*. Hillsdale, NJ: Erlbaum.

Ekman, P. (1992). An argument for basic emotions. *Cognition and Emotion*, **6**, 169–200.

Ekman, P. & Friesen, W. V. (1975). *Unmasking the Face*. Englewood Cliffs, NJ: Prentice-Hall.

Ekman, P., Friesen, W. V., O'Sullivan, M. et al. (1987). Universals and cultural differences in the judgments of facial expressions of emotion. *Journal of Personality & Social Psychology*, **53**, 712–717.

Ekman, P., Levenson, R. W. & Friesen, W. V. (1983). Autonomic nervous system activity distinguishes among emotions. *Science*, **221**, 1208–1210.

Elias, N. (1939/1978). *The History of Manners. The Civilizing Process*, Vol. I (trans. E. Jephcott). New York: Pantheon Books, 1978 (original work published 1939).

Fallon, A. E. & Rozin, P. (1983). The psychological bases of food rejections by humans. *Ecology of Food and Nutrition*, **13**, 15–26.

Fallon, A. E., Rozin, P. & Pliner, P. (1984). The child's conception of food: the development of food rejections with special reference to disgust and contamination sensitivity. *Child Development*, **55**, 566–575.

Frazer, J. G. (1890/1959). *The Golden Bough: A Study in Magic and Religion*. New York: Macmillan (1959 reprint of 1922 abridged edition, edited by T. H. Gaster; original work published 1890).

Grill, H. J. & Norgren, R. (1977). The taste reactivity test. I. Oro-facial responses to gustatory stimuli in neurologically normal rats. *Brain Research*, **143**, 263–279.

Haidt, J., Imada, S., McCauley, C. & Rozin, P. (1999). Disgust and individual differences in disgust in Japan (manuscript in preparation).

Haidt, J. & Keltner, D. (1998). Culture and emotion: multiple methods find new faces and a gradient of universality (manuscript under review).

Haidt, J., Koller, S. H. & Dias, M. G. (1993). Affect, culture, and morality, or is it wrong to eat your dog? *Journal of Personality and Social Psychology*, **65**, 613–628.

Haidt, J., McCauley, C. R. & Rozin, P. (1994). A scale to measure disgust sensitivity. *Personality and Individual Differences*, **16**, 701–713.

Haidt, J., Rozin, P., McCauley, C. R. & Imada, S. (1997). Body, psyche and culture: The relationship between disgust and morality. *Psychology and Developing Societies*, **9**, 107–131.

Hejmadi, A. (1998). Rasa or aesthetic emotion as mentioned in the Natyasastra of Bharata (manuscript).

Imada, S., Yamada, Y. & Haidt, J. (1993). The differences of Ken'o (disgust) experiences for Japanese and American students. *Studies in the Humanities and Sciences, Hiroshima-Shudo University*, **34**, 155–173.

Izard, C. E. (1971). *The Face of Emotion*. New York: Appleton-Century-Crofts.

Kass, L. (1994). *The Hungry Soul*. New York: Free Press.

Kekes, J. (1992). Disgust and moral taboos. *Philosophy*, **67**, 431–446.

Levenson, R. W., Ekman, P. & Friesen, W. V. (1990). Voluntary facial action generates emotion-specific autonomic nervous system activity. *Psychophysiology*, **27**, 363–384.

Masson, J. L. & Patwardhan, M. V. (1970). *Aesthetic Rapture: the Rasadhyaya of the Natyasastra*. Poona, India: Deccan College.

Matchett, G. & Davey, G. C. L. (1991). A test of a disease-avoidance model of animal phobias. *Behaviour Research & Therapy*, **29**, 91–94.

Mauss, M. (1902/1972). *A General Theory of Magic* (trans. R. Brain). New York: W.W. Norton, 1972 (original work published 190: *Esquisse d'une theorie generale de la magie. L'Annee Sociologique*, 1902–1903).

Mayr, E. (1960). The emergence of evolutionary novelties. In S. Tax (eds), *Evolution after Darwin, Vol. 1. The Evolution of Life*. Chicago, IL: University of Chicago Press.

McCauley, C. (1998). When screen violence is not attractive. In J. H. Goldstein (ed.), *The Attractions of Symbolic Violence*. Oxford: Oxford University Press, pp. 144–162.

Miller, W. I. (1997). *The Anatomy of Disgust*. Cambridge, MA: Harvard University Press.

Nemeroff, C. & Rozin, P. (1989). "You are what you eat". Applying the demand-free "impressions" technique to an unacknowledged belief. *Ethos: The Journal of Psychological Anthropology*, **17**, 50–69.

Nemeroff, C. & Rozin, P. (1994). The contagion concept in adult thinking in the United States: transmission of germs and interpersonal influence. *Ethos: The Journal of Psychological Anthropology*, **22**, 158–186.

Oatley, K. & Johnson-Laird, P. N. (1987). Towards a cognitive theory of emotions. *Cognition & Emotion*, **1**, 29–50.

Oppliger, P. A. & Zillmann, D. (1995). Disgust in humor: its appeal to adolescents (manuscript).

Power, M. & Dalgleish, T. (1997). *Cognition and Emotion: From Order to Disorder*. Hove: Psychology Press.

Quigley, J. F., Sherman, M. & Sherman, N. (1996). Personality Disorder Symptoms, Gender, and Age as Predictors of Adolescent Disgust Sensitivity. Poster presented at the annual meeting of the Eastern Psychological Association, Philadelphia, PA, March.

Rapoport, J. (1988). The neurobiology of obsessive compulsive disorder. *Journal of the American Medical Association*, **260**, 2888–2890.

Rosenstein, D. & Oster, H. (1988).   Differential facial responses to four basic tastes in
    newborns. *Child Development*, **59**, 1555–1568.
Rozin, P. (1976).   The evolution of intelligence and access to the cognitive unconscious.
    In J. A. Sprague & A. N. Epstein (eds), *Progress in Psychobiology and Physiological
    Psychology*, Volume 6. New York: Academic Press, pp. 245–280.
Rozin, P. (1990).   Getting to like the burn of chili pepper: biological, psychological and
    cultural perspectives. In B. G. Green, J. R. Mason & M. R. Kare (eds), *Chemical
    Senses, Vol. 2: Irritation*. New York: Marcel Dekker, pp. 231–269.
Rozin, P. (1996).   Towards a psychology of food and eating: from motivation to model
    to meaning, morality and metaphor. *Current Directions in Psychological Science*, **5**,
    1–7.
Rozin, P. (1997).   Moralization. In A. Brandt & P. Rozin (eds), *Morality and Health*. New
    York: Routledge, pp. 379–401.
Rozin, P. & Fallon, A. E. (1980).   The psychological categorization of foods and non-
    foods: a preliminary taxonomy of food rejections. *Appetite*, **1**, 193–201.
Rozin, P. & Fallon, A. E. (1987).   A perspective on disgust. *Psychological Review*, **94**,
    23–41.
Rozin, P. Fallon, A. E. & Augustoni-Ziskind, M. (1985).   The child's conception of food:
    the development of contamination sensitivity to "disgusting" substances. *Developmen-
    tal Psychology*, **21**, 1075–1079.
Rozin, P., Haidt, J. & McCauley, C. R. (1993).   Disgust. In M. Lewis & J. Haviland (eds),
    Handbook of Emotions. New York: Guilford, pp. 575–594.
Rozin, P., Haidt, J., McCauley, C. R. & Imada, S. (1997a).   The cultural evolution of
    disgust. In H. M. Macbeth (ed.), *Food Preferences and Taste: Continuity and Change*.
    Oxford: Berghahn, pp. 65–82.
Rozin, P., Haidt, J., McCauley, C. R., Dunlop, L. & Ashmore, M. (1999b).   An ecologi-
    cally valid set of measures of disgust sensitivity and a validation of the Disgust Scale
    (completed manuscript).
Rozin, P., Hammer, L., Oster, H., Horowitz, T. & Marmara, V. (1986).   The child's
    conception of food: differentiation of categories of rejected substances in the 1.4 to 5
    year age range. *Appetite*, **7**, 141–151.
Rozin, P., Lowery, L. & Ebert, R. (1994).   Varieties of disgust faces and the structure of
    disgust. *Journal of Personality & Social Psychology*, **66**, 870–881.
Rozin, P., Lowery, L., Imada, S. & Haidt, J. (1999a).   The CAD triad hypothesis: a
    mapping between the other-directed moral emotions, disgust, contempt, and anger,
    and Shweder's three universal moral codes. *Journal of Personality and Social
    Psychology*, (in press).
Rozin, P., Markwith, M. & McCauley, C. R. (1994).   The nature of aversion to
    indirect contact with another person: AIDS aversion as a composite of aversion to
    strangers, infection, moral taint and misfortune. *Journal of Abnormal Psychology*, **103**,
    495–504.
Rozin, P., Markwith, M. & Stoess, C. (1997b).   Moralization: becoming a vegetarian, the
    conversion of preferences into values and the recruitment of disgust. *Psychological
    Science*, **8**, 67–73.
Rozin, P., Millman, L. & Nemeroff, C. (1986).   Operation of the laws of sympathetic
    magic in disgust and other domains. *Journal of Personality and Social Psychology*, **50**,
    703–712.
Rozin, P. & Nemeroff, C. J. (1990).   The laws of sympathetic magic: a psychological
    analysis of similarity and contagion. In J. Stigler, G. Herdt & R. A. Shweder (eds),
    Cultural Psychology: Essays on Comparative Human Development. Cambridge:
    Cambridge University Press, pp. 205–232.
Scherer, K. R. & Wallbott, H. G. (1994).   Evidence for universality and cultural variation
    of differential emotion response patterning. *Journal of Personality & Social Psychol-
    ogy*, **66**, 310–328.

Sherman, N. (1996). Disgust Sensitivity Among College Women by Major. Poster presented at the annual meeting of the Eastern Psychological Association, Philadelphia, PA, March.

Shweder, R. A. (1993). Cultural psychology of the emotions. In M. Lewis & J. A. Haviland (eds), *Handbook of the Emotions*. New York: Guilford, pp. 417–431.

Shweder, R. A., Mahapatra, M. & Miller, J. G. (1987). Culture and moral development. In J. Kagan & S. Lamb (eds), *The Emergence of Moral Concepts in Young Children*. Chicago: University of Chicago Press, pp. 1–82.

Shweder, R. A., Much, N. C., Mahapatra, M. & Park, L. (1997). The "big three" of morality (autonomy, community and divinity), and the "big three" explanations of suffering, as well. In A. Brandt & P. Rozin (eds), *Morality and Health*. New York: Routledge (in press).

Siegal, M. S. & Share, D. L. (1990). Contamination sensitivity in young children. *Developmental Psychology*, **26**, 455–458.

Sprengelmeyer, R., Young, A. W., Calder, A. W. et al. (1996). Loss of disgust. Perception of faces and emotions in Huntington's disease. *Brain*, **119**, 1647–1665.

Sprengelmeyer, R., Young, A. W., Pundt, I. et al. (1998). Disgust: implicated in obsessive-compulsive disorder. *Proceedings of the Royal Society, Series B* (in press).

Steiner, J. E. (1979). Human facial expressions in response to taste and smell stimulation. In H. W. Reese & L. P. Lipsitt (eds), *Advances in Child Development and Behavior*, Vol. 13. New York: Academic Press, pp. 257–295.

Tomkins, S. (1963). *Affect, Imagery, Consciousness, Vol. II. The Negative Affects*. New York: Springer.

Tylor, E. B. (1871/1974). *Primitive Culture: Researches into the Development of Mythology, Philosophy, Religion, Art and Custom*. New York: Gordon, 1974. (original work published 1871).

Ware, J., Jain, K., Burgess, L. & Davey, G. C. L. (1994). Disease-avoidance model: Factor analysis of common animal fears. *Behaviour Research & Therapy*, **32**, 57–63.

Webb, K. & Davey, G. C. L. (1993). Disgust sensitivity and fear of animals: effect of exposure to violent or repulsive material. *Anxiety, Coping, & Stress*, **5**, 329–335.

Wronska, J. (1990). Disgust in relation to emotionality, extraversion, psychoticism and imagery abilities. In P. J. Dret, J. A. Sergent & R. J. Takens (eds), *European Perspectives in Psychology,* Vol. 1. Chichester Wiley, pp. 125–138.

Chapter 22

Anxiety and Anxiety Disorders

Colin MacLeod
The University of Western Australia, Perth, WA, Australia

The study of cognitive functioning in anxious individuals has a long history within experimental psychology. However, until 15 or so years ago, most of this research focused principally upon delineating and explaining the patterns of cognitive deficits commonly displayed by clinically anxious patients, and by normal individuals reporting high levels of state or trait anxiety. This early research revealed performance decrements in anxious subjects on a broad range of cognitive tasks. It now has been established, for example, that anxious individuals exhibit deficient inductive reasoning (Reed, 1977), slowed decision latencies (Volans, 1976), shallow depth of processing (Fransson, 1977) and reduced memory span (Idzihowski & Baddeley, 1987). They also demonstrate impaired attentional control (Broadbent, Broadbent & Jones, 1986), displaying particular problems in the execution of attentional inhibition (Fox, 1994).

Perhaps the most influential account of these performance deficits is that introduced by M. W. Eysenck (e.g. Eysenck, 1982, 1992; Eysenck & Calvo, 1992), which implicates a functional restriction in working memory capacity. Specifically, Eysenck draws attention to the characteristic cognitive preoccupations with emotionally negative concerns commonly displayed by highly anxious individuals. Collectively, such preoccupations represent the "worry" symptoms of anxiety, as distinct from the "somatic" symptoms, which principally reflect elevated sympathetic arousal (cf. Deffenbacher, 1980). According to Eysenck, worrying represents a resource-consuming task-irrelevant cognitive process, maintained by the allocation of working memory capacity, and it is this depletion of working memory that underpins anxiety-related cognitive deficits.

Consistent with Eysenck's hypothesis, there is indeed evidence that anxiety-related performance deficits may be restricted to those cognitive tasks which

Handbook of Cognition and Emotion. Edited by T. Dalgleish and M. Power.

make demands upon working memory (e.g. Darke, 1988). Furthermore, MacLeod & Donnellan (1993) have observed that, as predicted by Eysenck's account, the performance of highly anxious subjects on a simple verbal reasoning task is more greatly impaired than that of less anxious subjects when working memory capacity is reduced further by the simultaneous addition of a digit-load task. This finding, that the effect of an experimental restriction in working memory capacity interacts with the effect of anxiety, lends weight to the proposal that anxiety-linked performance deficits reflect reductions in working memory capacity.

Despite such supportive evidence, Eysenck's task-irrelevant processing account of anxiety-related cognitive deficits has not gone unchallenged (cf. Leon & Revelle, 1985). Nevertheless, this model highlights the interesting possibility that anxious individuals may be poor at performing certain cognitive tasks because they selectively process something else instead. That is, anxiety may be associated not with the general impairment of information processing, but with unusual patterns of processing selectivity. Those who are highly anxious may preferentially allocate resources to sustain the processing of information that is relevant to their anxiety, even though this information may be irrelevant to experimental tasks they have been asked to perform.

Over the past 15 years or so, cognitive research into anxiety has been marked by a new focus upon the patterns of selective information processing that are associated with high levels of anxiety (cf. Mathews & MacLeod, 1994). Indeed, there now exists a wealth of clinical accounts which not only promote the view that vulnerability to anxiety may be associated with cognitive biases that selectively favour the processing of emotionally threatening information, but which also propose that these selective processing biases may causally underpin such anxiety vulnerability (e.g. Beck, Emery & Greenberg, 1985; Teasdale & Barnard, 1993; Williams et al., 1988, 1997). This chapter will review experimental evidence, concerning different domains of cognitive functioning, that pertains to this theoretical position, provided by studies that have examined clinically anxious patients or normal individuals differing in their trait vulnerability to anxiety. Following this review, consideration will be given both to the theoretical and to the clinical implications of observed associations between anxiety vulnerability and selective information processing.

ATTENTIONAL BIAS IN ANXIETY

Researchers often have employed interference paradigms to investigate the patterns of attentional bias displayed by clinically anxious individuals. This approach involves presenting subjects with some central task to perform in the presence of distracting information. By assessing the extent to which different types of distracting information interferes with performance on the central task, researchers have been able to draw inferences concerning the degree to which these types of distracters recruit selective attention. Interference tasks employing emotionally valenced distracter stimuli frequently have demonstrated that individuals with high levels of anxiety vulnerability show disproportionately large interference effects from threat-related distracters, suggesting that they display an attentional bias towards threatening stimuli (cf. MacLeod, 1990, 1995).

By far the most popular interference methodology within this field of research has been the adaptation of the classic Stroop colour-naming paradigm (Stroop, 1938), which has become known as the emotional Stroop task (cf. Matthews & Harley, 1996; Williams, Mathews & MacLeod, 1996). In this variant, subjects are shown emotionally threatening words (e.g. "death" or "failure") and emotionally non-threatening words (e.g. "chair" or "picture") in different coloured print, and are required to name the colour of each stimulus item as quickly as possible. Consistent with the hypothesis that they should have difficulty ignoring threat word content, clinically anxious patients, when compared with non-anxious control subjects, repeatedly have been found to display disproportionately long colour-naming latencies on the threat words. First demonstrated with generalized anxiety disorder (GAD) patients (e.g. Mathews & MacLeod, 1985), this phenomenon has now also been observed with many other clinically anxious populations, including specific phobics (e.g. Lavy, van den Hout & Arntz, 1993), social phobics (e.g. Mattia, Heimberg & Hope, 1993), panic disorder patients (e.g. McNally et al., 1994); post-traumatic stress disorder (PTSD) sufferers (e.g. Thrasher, Dalgleish & Yule, 1994), and obsessive-compulsive patients (e.g. Lavy, van Oppen & van den Hout, 1994).

Many investigators report that the interference effects shown by clinically anxious individuals differ maximally from those displayed by control subjects on those specific threat words that are of greatest relevance to the concerns of that particular patient group. Thus, for example, Mogg, Mathews & Weinman (1989) found that those GAD patients who reported worrying most about physical concerns showed the greatest colour-naming interference on threat words related to physical dangers (such as "injury"), while those who reported worrying most about social concerns showed the greatest interference on words related to social threat (such as "humiliated"). Similarly, the greatest level of interference has been found on social threat words for social phobics (e.g. Hope et al., 1990), on physical threat words for panic disorder patients (e.g. Ehlers et al., 1988), on words related to their feared stimuli for specific phobics (e.g. Watts et al., 1986), on words related to their obsessive concerns for obsessive compulsive patients (e.g. Foa et al., 1993), and on words related to their original traumatic event for PTSD patients (e.g. Kaspi, McNally & Amir, 1995).

The conclusion that such interference studies support the existence of an anxiety-linked attentional bias towards threatening information is premised on the assumption that increased colour-naming interference on threat words reflects increased attention towards word content. Some researchers, however, question the validity of this assumption, pointing out that a tendency to divert attention *away from* words with particular content also could retard the colour-naming of such stimuli (e.g. MacLeod, 1990; de Ruiter & Brosschot, 1994). Consistent with this possibility, there is evidence that individuals classed as "repressers" on the basis of questionnaire scores, a group commonly assumed to selectively avoid processing aversive information, also show high levels of colour-naming interference on threat words (e.g. Dawkins & Furnham, 1989). Furthermore, when subjects have been explicitly instructed to make a particular effort to avoid processing certain classes of word content, then this does indeed serve to increase colour-naming interference on such words (Lavy & van den Hout, 1994).

In order to assess attentional distribution more directly than is permitted by interference paradigms, a number of investigators have adopted variants of a dot probe methodology introduced by MacLeod, Mathews & Tata (1986), who briefly presented GAD patients and non-anxious control subjects with pairs of words, separated vertically on a VDU screen. Subjects were required to press a response button whenever they detected small dot probes, which could occur in either the upper or lower screen location following the disappearance of any word pair. Critical word pairs consisted of one threat-related word, and one length and frequency matched neutral word, and the probes presented immediately after these critical word pairs could appear in the spatial vicinity of either the threat or the non-threat word. It was reasoned that probes appearing in attended screen areas would be detected more rapidly than probes appearing in unattended screen areas, making it possible to infer subjects' attentional responses to the emotional word pairs by examining their patterns of probe detection latencies. MacLeod et al. found that their anxiety patients detected probes fastest when these appeared in the vicinity of the threat words, supporting the hypothesis that these anxious individuals systematically directed attention towards the threat-related stimuli. In contrast, control subjects demonstrated a strong trend in the reverse direction, suggesting a tendency for these individuals to divert attention away from threat-related stimuli. Such effects have been replicated by other researchers using this paradigm, not only with GAD patients (e.g. Mogg, Mathews & Eysenck, 1992), but also with other forms of anxiety pathology, such as obsessive-compulsive disorder (Tata et al., 1996).

There is considerable evidence that the initiation of this anxiety-linked attentional bias towards threat-related stimuli occurs at a very early point in the processing continuum. Indeed, a number of researchers have presented data suggesting that the bias may operate quite automatically, prior to subjects becoming consciously aware of stimulus identity (cf. McNally, 1995). For example, in an early interference study using a dichotic listening procedure, Mathews & MacLeod (1986) demonstrated that GAD patients showed disproportionate interference from threat-related distracter words, yet displayed no ability to either identify these words or to correctly classify their emotional valence. More recently, a number of researchers have used backward pattern masking to more rigorously preclude awareness of stimulus content (cf. Turvey, 1973). This approach involves briefly exposing stimulus words (for 20 ms or less) before replacing them with random patterns, usually consisting of inverted and rotated letter fragments. Although such a procedure typically prevents conscious awareness of stimulus identity, a considerable body of data suggests that semantic processing of such masked stimuli still takes place (cf. MacLeod, 1998). Using this backward masking procedure to successfully eliminate awareness of word content in the colour-naming interference paradigm, several studies have found that GAD patients continue to display disproportionately long colour-naming latencies on those trials when threat words have been exposed (e.g. Mogg et al., 1993).

A fuller account of those studies that have examined anxiety-linked attentional bias under masked exposure conditions can be found in Chapter 11 (this volume). For the moment, however, it is interesting to note that the specificity effects mentioned earlier, involving the restriction of such biases to stimuli associated with domains of personal concern, are far less evident under masked than under unmasked exposure conditions. Under unmasked exposure conditions, for example, Thorpe & Salkovskis (1997) observed in spider phobics the usual elevated colour-naming interference specifically shown on spider-related threat words, but found no evidence of such an effect under masked exposure conditions. MacLeod & Rutherford (1992) also employed masked and unmasked trials within a colour-naming interference task, to examine the patterns of interference shown by high and low anxious individuals on threatening and non-threatening words that were related or unrelated to their domain of current concern. They found that the pattern of interference effects shown under the unmasked exposure condition was most pronounced on those stimuli relevant to subjects' current concerns. However, under the masked exposure condition this was not the case, with the high anxiety subjects showing the same elevated colour-naming interference on all threat-related stimuli, regardless of whether or not these were concern-relevant. MacLeod & Rutherford concluded that specificity effects are likely to be strategically mediated, while at an automatic level of processing anxiety appears to be associated with an attentional bias towards *all* classes of threat-related stimuli.

Virtually all of the studies reported above have examined clinically anxious populations, making it difficult to determine whether the observed patterns of attentional bias represent markers of anxiety vulnerability, or are better construed as the cognitive correlates of anxious mood state. Treatment research reveals that attentional biases are not invariant within clinically anxious individuals, but become less pronounced as their anxiety symptoms decline. Thus, in Mogg et al.'s (1992) dot probe study, a group of recovered GAD patients failed to show speeding to probes in the vicinity of threat words. Effective therapeutic interventions also serve to reduce or eliminate the elevated colour-naming interference shown on threat words by spider phobics (Lavy, van den Hout & Arntz, 1993), obsessive-compulsive patients (Foa & McNally, 1986), social phobics (Mattia, Heimberg & Hope, 1993) and GAD patients (Mathews et al., 1995). In the only published study yet to have compared the effects of treatment on the patterns of colour-naming interference displayed under masked and unmasked exposure conditions, Mogg et al. (1995) observed that cognitive therapy served to reduce threat interference under both exposure conditions. Interestingly, however, these researchers found that only those reductions in threat interference observed under the masked exposure condition were correlated with reductions in patients' anxious thoughts and worries. On the basis of this finding, Mogg et al. suggest that automatically-mediated patterns of attentional bias may most directly contribute to the production of such cognitive symptomatology.

This observation, that attentional bias to threat declines as clinically anxious patients recover, can sustain three interpretations. First, it is possible that attentional bias to threat could be a first-order correlate of anxious mood state, having no direct association with anxiety vulnerability. Second, it could be suggested that attentional bias to threat may be a direct correlate of anxiety vulnerability, and declines in these studies only because effective treatments successfully reduce such vulnerability. Third, it may be the case that attentional bias to threat is an enduring feature of trait vulnerability to anxiety, but one that is manifested only when state anxiety is elevated. According to this last possibility, treatment may not reduce the vulnerable individual's abnormal disposition to display an attentional orientation towards threat stimuli when state anxious, but instead may only attenuate the manifestation of this trait-linked attentional bias by removing the state anxiety elevation required to trigger its expression. Research on attentional bias in non-clinical subjects, who differ in levels of state and trait anxiety, lends considerable empirical support to this third account.

MacLeod & Mathews (1988) employed the dot probe paradigm to examine the patterns of attentional allocation displayed by high and low trait anxious students, when their levels of state anxiety were either low or high as a consequence of differing temporal proximity to examinations. On the low state anxiety test occasion, the high and low trait anxious subjects displayed equivalent patterns of probe detection latencies, neither group showing evidence of a biased attentional response to these emotional stimuli. On the high state anxiety test occasion, however, the high trait anxious subjects now displayed a pronounced speeding to detect probes in the vicinity of threat words, suggesting an attentional bias towards threat stimuli. In contrast, on this high state anxiety test occasion, the low trait anxious subjects now showed a slowing to detect probes in the vicinity of threat words, suggesting an attentional bias away from threat stimuli. Thus, the differential patterns of attentional allocation which served to discriminate the high and low trait anxious subjects were manifested only when state anxiety was elevated.

Similar results were obtained by MacLeod & Rutherford (1992), who adopted a parallel experimental design, but employed a colour-naming interference task with masked and unmasked exposure conditions to dissociate automatic from strategic patterns of attentional selectivity. Under the masked exposure condition, the findings provided a conceptual replication of MacLeod & Mathews' earlier results. On the low state anxiety test occasion, the high and low trait subjects showed equivalent patterns of colour-naming latencies, with neither group displaying the differential latencies for threat and non-threat stimulus words that would suggest the presence of attentional bias. In contrast, on the high state anxiety test occasion, high trait anxious subjects now showed longer colour-naming latencies on the masked threat words than on the masked non-threat words, suggesting an automatic attentional bias towards threat word content; while low trait anxious subjects showed faster colour-naming latencies on the masked threat words than on the masked non-threat words, suggesting the reverse automatic attentional bias. Thus, MacLeod & Rutherford concluded that high and low trait anxious individuals differed in terms of the automatic attentional biases elicited by elevated state anxiety. Only in high trait anxious individuals does state anxiety elevation trigger the automatic allocation of attention towards threat-related information.

Somewhat surprisingly, MacLeod & Rutherford found that in the unmasked version of their colour-naming task, which permitted a degree of strategic attentional control, high and low trait anxious subjects now showed an equivalent cognitive response to the state anxiety elevation, which involved a speeding of colour-naming latencies on those particular threat words relevant to examination stress. This finding led these researchers to suggest that, regardless of trait anxiety level, individuals exposed to an anxiety-inducing stressor may be able to strategically avoid processing threat stimuli associated with the source of this anxiety. Consistent with this possibility, Mathews & Sebastian (1993) observed that when snake-fearful students were rendered highly state anxious through exposure to a live snake, this served to suppress colour-naming interference on unmasked snake-related words. Similarly, Amir et al. (1996) have reported that their clinical population of social phobics also responded to a social stressor that elevated state anxiety (i.e. threat of public speaking) by showing suppression of their normally elevated colour-naming interference effect on unmasked socially threatening words. It seems likely that a more complete understanding of the conditions which permit strategic suppression of threat interference effects, and of the mechanisms through which this suppression operates, may prove valuable to those clinicians who endeavour to treat anxiety disorders through the strategic manipulation of cognition.

Before leaving this consideration of anxiety-linked patterns of attention, it is appropriate to recognize that some researchers have questioned whether the observed effects do represent an abnormal attentional bias towards threat stimuli in anxious subjects. Two alternative points of view have been put forward. The first is that the experimental findings simply reflect the general tendency for all individuals to attend to information that they consider to be personally relevant, regardless of stimulus valence. Certainly, there is evidence that "personal relevance" interference effects do exist, that are unrelated to stimulus valence effects. For example, Riemann & McNally (1995) found normal subjects to show increased colour-naming interference on words that they judged to be personally relevant, regardless of whether these were positive or negative in emotional tone. Indeed, stimulus words pertaining to domains of personal expertise can elicit colour-naming interference even when they are emotionally neutral, as evidenced by Dalgleish's (1995) finding that ornithologists display disproportionately long colour-naming latencies on bird names. Thus, it is possible to suggest that anxious individuals may be "experts" with respect to threat domains and, instead of showing abnormalities in attentional control, they display only the normal tendency to allocate attention towards stimuli which fall within their personal domain of expertise. However, Dalgleish (1995) points out several lines of evidence that appear inconsistent with such an account. For example, he argues that this expertise proposal does not accord with the observation that the degree of threat-interference shown by anxiety patients typically reduces with treatment, which is unlikely to affect personal expertise (e.g. Lavy, van den Hout & Arntz, 1993; Mogg et al., 1995). Dalgleish also notes that those trauma victims who develop PTSD typically show greater colour-naming interference on trauma-related threat words than do those victims of the same trauma who do not develop PTSD (e.g. Foa et al., 1991), although it is likely that both groups will have similar levels of expertise concerning the trauma-related information. Therefore, while expertise might underpin certain attentional biases towards stimuli associated with the expert domain, it is unlikely that this phenomenon can fully explain the attentional bias to threat displayed by anxious individuals.

Another proposal, challenging the view that anxiety is associated with an abnormal attentional bias towards threat stimuli, comes from Martin, Williams & Clark (1991), who argue that anxious individuals may attend selectively to *any* emotional stimuli, regardless of whether these are negative or positive in emotional valence. When they employed positive stimulus words, as well as threat-related words and neutral words, Martin et al. found their GAD patients to display greater colour-naming interference than control subjects on both categories of emotional stimuli. However, this has not proved to be an easy finding to replicate. Although Mathews & Klug (1993) have reported that their GAD patients showed increased colour-naming interference on both threat words and their direct antonyms, most studies either have failed to observe an anxiety-linked elevation in the level of colour-naming interference shown on positive stimuli (e.g. McNally, English & Lipke, 1993; Richards et al., 1992), or have shown that the magnitude of this interference effect is greater on threat words than on positive words (e.g. Cassiday, McNally & Zeitlin, 1992). A potential explanation for inconsistencies across studies is provided by Rutherford & MacLeod's (submitted) recent finding that different dimensions of anxiety serve to mediate alternative patterns of colour-naming interference. Specifically, these researchers observed that across both high and low trait anxious subjects, elevations in state anxiety served to increase colour-naming interference on both negative and positive words. However, in high trait anxious individuals this state anxiety elevation increased interference on negative words more than on positive words, while in low trait anxious subjects it increased interference on positive words more than on negative words. Thus, while elevated state anxiety may increase the degree to which everyone attends to emotional information in general, it appears to elicit preferential attention towards negative information rather than positive information only in high trait anxious individuals.

BIASED JUDGEMENT AND INTERPRETATION IN ANXIETY

Anxious subjects also have been found to show biases in a variety of judgement tasks, usually suggesting the disproportionately threatening appraisal of their environments. For example, when asked to estimate the future probability of specified event categories, clinically anxious patients, unlike non-anxious control subjects, provide elevated risk estimates for more threatening classes of events (Butler & Mathews, 1983; McNally & Foa, 1987). The breadth of this bias is directly associated with anxiety vulnerability. Thus, although an impending stressor appears to elevate the subjective risk of experiencing negative events closely related to this stressor for both low and high trait individuals, only in high trait anxious individuals does this inflated subjective risk extend to classes of negative events unrelated to the source of this current stress (Butler & Mathews, 1987).

In certain situations, anxious individuals' elevated expectations of experiencing a negative event may reflect biased perception of environmental contingencies. When Tomarken, Cook & Mineka (1989) presented fearful individuals with slides containing fear-related stimuli or neutral stimuli, and followed 30% of all presentations with a mild electrical shock, these subjects later judged the contingent probability of shock to have been higher following fear-related slides than following neutral slides. Furthermore, they erroneously appraised the shock as having been more severe when it followed the fear-related images. Subsequent research has supported Tomarken et al.'s observation that the magnitude of this co-variation bias is closely related to subjects' fear levels (e.g. Sutton & Mineka, submitted; Amin & Lovibond, submitted). As yet, it remains unclear whether the co-variation bias represents an ever-present feature of anxiety vulnerability, or is displayed only when state anxiety is elevated, as studies differ in their conclusions concerning whether or not the effect is still evident following treatment (de-Jong & Merckelbach, 1991; de-Jong et al., 1992).

A good deal of research has now investigated the patterns of interpretations imposed by anxious subjects on ambiguous stimuli that permit alternative interpretations that differ in their aversiveness. It has consistently been observed that, when overtly asked to report the meanings they impose on such stimuli, clinical anxiety patients show an increased tendency to report the more aversive interpretations. Thus, when Butler & Mathews (1983) presented short ambiguous scenarios, together with sets of possible interpretations differing in emotional valence, their GAD patients showed an elevated tendency to endorse the more negative options as being their own most likely interpretations. Related effects have been obtained more recently by Winton, Clark & Edelmann (1995) in a rather different study that required the forced-choice classification of briefly displayed facial expressions. These researchers found that socially anxious subjects displayed an increased tendency explicitly to classify these expressions as negative, rather than neutral, in emotional tone.

It might reasonably be argued that tasks which involve directly instructing subjects to report their interpretations of ambiguity could be overly vulnerable to experimental demand effects. However, experimental approaches that have less obtrusively required subjects to interpret ambiguous stimuli also have revealed anxiety-related biases. One such approach has employed a simple spelling task, in which subjects are required to write down auditorally presented words. Embedded among a large number of filler words are homophones that have differentially-valenced possible meanings, distinguished by alternative spellings (e.g. die/dye, groan/grown, pain/pane). Responses on this spelling task, therefore, provide a plausible index of interpretation, without subjects being alerted to the fact that interpretation is being assessed. Using this methodology, it has been established that GAD patients display an elevated tendency to respond with the threat spellings of these ambiguous verbal stimuli (Mathews, Richards & Eysenck, 1989; Mogg et al., 1994).

It seems likely that this tendency to spell such homophones in their more threatening form is a function of trait anxiety level, rather than a direct correlate of anxious mood state. Correlational analysis carried out by Eysenck, MacLeod & Mathews (1987) revealed that the proportion of threat spellings produced was highly correlated with trait anxiety, but was uncorrelated with state anxiety. Nevertheless, there is some evidence that mood state may play a role in governing the expression of this trait-linked bias. For example, Mathews et al. (1989) found that a group of recovered GAD patients did not produce significantly more threat spellings on this homophone task than did never-anxious control subjects. However, this finding is rendered difficult to interpret by the fact that neither did this recovered group produce significantly less threat spellings than currently anxious patients (who did display significantly more threat spellings than the control subjects). It seems possible that, as with the anxiety-linked attentional bias discussed earlier, the tendency to impose threat word spellings on homophones may be a feature of trait anxiety, which is manifested only during periods of stress. Consistent with this account, MacLeod (1990) reports a homophone study in which a stress manipulation served to increase the proportion of threat spelling produced by high trait anxious subjects while decreasing the proportion of threat spellings produced by low trait anxious subjects.

While the homophone spelling task may assess interpretation in a less obtrusive manner than the self-report methodologies described earlier, all of these experimental techniques share a common methodological limitation, which compromises confidence in their capacity to illuminate interpretative processing. Specifically, in each of the reported studies, subjects' interpretations have been inferred on the basis of the frequency with which these individuals emit, or endorse, differentially valenced response options. Consequently, it is possible that these tasks may tap an anxiety-linked response bias rather than an interpretative bias (MacLeod & Mathews, 1991; Mogg et al., 1994). That is, the observed pattern of findings can be explained, without implicating interpretation, by postulating that when subjects recognize the need to select between alternative response options, anxious individuals consistently opt for the more negatively-toned response categories.

In order to avoid this methodological problem, a variety of techniques have been developed for assessing anxious individuals' interpretation while requiring all subjects to emit precisely the same responses. Collectively, these techniques represent variants on priming methodologies, with interpretation being inferred from the observed impact of previously presented ambiguous information on the speed with which responses to target stimuli can be executed. For example, MacLeod & Cohen (1993) employed a text comprehension paradigm that required high and low trait anxious subjects to read short passages by presenting them, at a self-paced rate, sentence by sentence on a VDU screen. Within critical passages, an initial ambiguous sentence permitted two differentially valenced alternative interpretations (e.g. "the two men discussed the best way to blow up the dingy"). By manipulating a single word in the immediately subsequent sentence, this could be made to provide a plausible continuation for either one of each possible interpretation (e.g. "they decided to use a pump" vs. "they decided to use a bomb"). Given that the continuation sentence should be harder to understand when inconsistent with the meaning imposed on the preceding ambiguous sentence, MacLeod & Cohen were able to infer the interpretations imposed on ambiguous sentences by examining how long their subjects paused to comprehend each type of continuation sentence. The observed patterns of comprehension latencies across threat-consistent and threat-inconsistent continuation sentences suggested that high trait anxious subjects, but not low trait anxious subjects, did indeed impose the more negative meanings on the ambiguous sentences. Recently, Calvo, Eysenck & Castillo (1997) have conceptually replicated this finding, using a slightly different method of measuring comprehension latency on the continuation sentences.

More conventional priming methodologies also have been employed to assess anxiety-linked interpretation, in studies that have examined the degree to which ambiguous textual "primes" serve to facilitate lexical decisions on target words related to each of their possible meanings. For example, Calvo, Eysenck & Estevaz (1994) found that, immediately following exposure to ambiguous prime paragraphs, test anxious subjects showed disproportionate facilitation of lexical decisions on target words related to the more negative meanings, but not on those relating to the more neutral meanings, of the ambiguous primes. Similar results have been obtained by Hirsch (1995), who also used ambiguous passages as primes, and by Richards & French (1992), who employed single ambiguous words as their prime stimuli. Once again, there is evidence from priming studies of this type that a negative interpretative bias might represent a trait-linked effect that is triggered by state anxiety. MacLeod (1990) reports finding that it is only when subjects report elevated levels of state anxiety that high trait anxious individuals, relative to low trait anxious individuals, show a disproportionately large priming effect on target words related to the more negative meanings of ambiguous primes.

In addition to excluding trivial response bias accounts of the data, priming methodologies of this type also have permitted researchers to begin investigating the automaticity of anxiety-linked interpretative biases, by manipulating the temporal intervals between the priming context and the target words. There is good evidence that priming effects obtained at prime-target stimulus onset asynchronies (SOA) of 250 ms or less represent automatic cognitive effects, while those which occur only at SOAs of 500 ms or more can be influenced by intentional cognitive strategies (e.g. Neely, 1977). Patterns of priming suggesting that anxiety is associated with a negative interpretative bias have not been obtained when the priming context and the target words have been separated by 500 ms or less, but occur only when this interval is extended to 750 ms (Richards & French, 1992) or 1250 ms (Calvo & Castillo, in press). Therefore, it can be suggested that anxious individuals' tendency to impose threatening interpretations upon ambiguity may represent a strategic aspect of their cognitive style. However, the alternative possibility should be noted that, while interpretation itself may not occur with the rapidity required to class this as an entirely automatic process, nevertheless anxiety-related *influences* on interpretation still might function in an entirely automatic manner.

MEMORY BIAS IN ANXIETY

In contrast to the fairly consistent patterns of findings that have been obtained across studies of attention and interpretation, collectively supporting the presence of an anxiety-linked processing advantage for threatening information within these domains of cognitive functioning, there has been less consistent evidence of an anxiety-linked memory advantage for such information. Certainly, it does appear to be the case that both high trait anxious normals and GAD patients can very readily retrieve threat-related events from autobiographical memory. Mayo (1989), for example, observed in an autobiographical memory task that increased levels of trait anxiety were associated with better cued recall of negative past events and poorer cued recall of positive past events. Similarly, Burke & Mathews (1992) found that, in response to cue words, GAD patients, relative to non-anxious control subjects, recalled significantly more negative autobiographical memories. However, it is by no means clear that such differences in autobiographical memory represent biased mnemonic functioning. It is equally plausible that individuals with heightened vulnerability to anxiety may simply tend to have experienced an inordinate number of negative events in their pasts.

The possibility that anxiety vulnerability may be associated with enhanced recall and recognition memory for threatening information is addressed more appropriately by examining people's abilities to remember emotionally-toned stimuli encountered within the experimental session. Studies adopting this methodological approach have revealed little evidence to support the existence of such anxiety-linked memory biases. For example, immediately after performing emotional Stroop tasks, on which GAD and phobic patients have shown increased colour-naming interference on threatening stimulus words, these patients typically show no enhanced ability to recall such threat-related stimuli (e.g. Mathews & MacLeod, 1985; Mogg, Mathews & Weinman, 1989; Watts et al., 1986). Furthermore, in a program of research designed specifically to investigate anxious subjects' memory for emotionally toned trait adjectives presented within experimental sessions, Mogg (1988) failed in four separate studies to reveal any tendency for GAD patients to display enhanced selective recall or recognition memory for anxiety-related stimuli. Even when asked to report only whether stimulus words feel familiar, GAD patients show no heightened tendency for prior exposure to enhance the familiarity of anxiety-related words more than neutral words (Mogg et al., 1992).

Although some data have been put forward as evidence of a recall advantage for threat-related information in agoraphobics (Nunn, Stevenson & Whalan, 1984) and social phobics (Lundh & Ost, 1996), these studies suffer from rather serious methodological limitations. One problem is that the "threat-related" stimuli employed were selected because of their specific relevance to the patients' domains of concern, and may not have been at all threatening for the non-anxious control subjects. In Lundh & Ost's social phobia study, for example, subjects were presented with photographs of people posing normally, and a photo was classed as a "threat" stimulus if subjects judged it to be of "a person who is generally critical towards others". In Nunn, Stevenson & Whalan's (1984) agoraphobia study, the "threat" stimuli were words such as "cinema" and "street". If, as seems likely, control subjects did not find such stimuli threatening, then no conclusions can be drawn concerning differences between the patterns of recall for threatening information shown by the anxiety patients and the controls. An additional problem with Lundh & Ost's study, acknowledged by the authors, is that the memory measure they used could not exclude the possible influence of response bias. Thus, what looked like better recognition memory for "critical" individuals, could have resulted from a tendency for social phobics simply to endorse, in the recognition memory task, all those photos they considered to be of "critical" individuals, regardless of their actual presentation status. Experiments with less methodological limitations typically have failed to find that either agoraphobics or social phobics display relatively better recall of threatening information than is shown by control subjects. In a conceptual replication of Nunn et al.'s original experiment, Pickles and van den Broeck (1988) failed to find any recall bias in agoraphobic patients. Likewise, rigorous programs of experimentation carried out independently by Rapee et al. (1994) and Cloitre et al. (1995) have revealed no sign of any recall advantage for threat stimuli in social phobics.

Perhaps the strongest evidence for the existence of such a recall advantage for threatening stimuli in anxiety patients has come from studies that have examined individuals suffering from panic disorder. There now exist several well-designed experiments which have found that panic disorder patients, when compared with non-anxious controls, display enhanced recall of threat-related stimulus words (McNally, Foa & Donnell, 1989; Cloitre & Liebowitz, 1991; Cloitre et al., 1994;

Becker, Margraf & Rinck, 1994). While some studies have failed to replicate even this effect (e.g. Beck et al., 1992), it does seem possible that the facilitated recall of threatening information may be a peculiar feature of panic disorder. Nevertheless, there is very little convincing evidence to suggest that a recall advantage for threatening information is a general characteristic of anxiety pathology.

Indeed, a fair number of studies have observed quite the reverse pattern of biased memory in anxious subjects. Thus, when Mogg, Mathews & Weinman (1987) used recognition and recall tasks to assess memory for negative and neutral trait adjectives in GAD patients and non-anxious controls, they found the patients to display a relative *impairment* in the retrieval of the negative words, particularly those most closely associated with anxiety-relevant traits. Parallel effects have been obtained with other categories of anxiety disorder. For example, impaired recall of feared stimuli has been observed in spider phobics (Watts, 1986; Watts & Dalgleish, 1991), while Sanz (1996) has recently reported that social phobics display a positive recall bias which favours the retrieval of more positively-toned trait adjectives. Within a population of speech-fearful subjects exposed to an anxiety manipulation, Foa, McNally & Murdock (1989) found that those individuals who showed the greatest evidence of elevated anxiety displayed the poorest relative ability to recall anxiety-related trait words. Although this selective impairment in the recall of threatening information may not be a highly reliable characteristic of anxious individuals, the fact that it has often been obtained suggests that the common failure to observe an anxiety-linked recall or recognition memory advantage for threatening information has not resulted simply from underpowered experiments. Rather, the weight of evidence now appears to require the conclusion that anxiety generally is not associated with the facilitated retrieval of threat-related information on tasks assessing either recall or recognition memory.

Despite this apparent lack of a negative retrieval bias on such measures of explicit memory, Williams et al. (1988) proposed that anxious individuals may display a mnemonic advantage for threat-related information on tests that assess implicit memory performance (cf. Schacter, 1987). Although this area of research has been marked by inconsistent findings, considerable evidence has accrued in recent years which offers a fair degree of support for this hypothesis (cf. MacLeod & Rutherford, 1998). The first study to contrast anxious individuals' explicit and implicit memory for emotional stimulus words was conducted by Mathews et al. (1989). These researchers presented GAD patients and control subjects with emotional words in an initial encoding task. Subsequently, subjects were given three-letter word stems that could be completed to yield either previously seen or unseen words, and these were accompanied by either explicit or implicit memory instructions. The former instructions required subjects to intentionally search memory, by telling them to complete the stems to yield words seen during the earlier encoding phase, and explicit memory was revealed by the numbers of such words they were able to produce correctly. The latter instructions required no intentional memory search, as subjects were told to complete stems simply with the first words that came to mind, and implicit memory was revealed by the degree to which previously seen words were produced more frequently than unseen words. Mathews et al. found that, relative to the control subjects, the GAD patients showed no evidence of elevated explicit memory for threat words, but displayed disproportionately great implicit memory for such stimuli. This finding was conceptually replicated by MacLeod & McGlaughlin (1995), using rather different types of explicit and implicit memory tasks. These researchers observed that GAD patients showed no enhanced memory for threat words on a recognition task used to assess explicit memory. However, they found such patients to display disproportionately good implicit memory for previously presented threat words on a perceptual identification task, which revealed implicit memory through increased tachistoscopic identification accuracies for previously seen, relative to unseen, stimulus words.

An anxiety-linked implicit memory advantage for threat-related stimuli has been reported in studies assessing other anxious populations also. For example, using the word stem completion task previously employed by Mathews at al. (1989), Cloitre et al. (1994) obtained evidence that panic disorder patients show enhanced implicit memory for emotionally threatening stimulus words. Amir et al. (1996) reached the same conclusion using a very different method of assessing implicit memory. In this procedure, subjects were required to assess, on each trial, the volume of an auditory white noise signal, which was superimposed on a recorded word. Implicit memory was revealed by a reduction in the subjective volume of the white noise accompanying previously presented, rather than previously unseen, stimulus words. Amir et al. found that the magnitude of this reduction was disproportionately great for threat words in panic disorder patients, indicating superior implicit memory for negative stimuli within this population of anxious subjects.

Studies conducted on normal individuals with high levels of anxiety vulnerability also have provided evidence that they display an implicit memory bias favouring threatening information. For example, although Richards & French (1991) found no evidence of any explicit memory bias in their high trait anxious subjects, a word stem completion task revealed that these individuals did show greater implicit memory for previously exposed threat-related words than was observed in a low trait anxious group. More recently, Lang & Craske (1997) obtained similar results with normal subjects reporting high levels of anxiety sensitivity (cf. Reiss et al., 1986). On the free recall task used to assess explicit memory, these subjects showed the same pattern of memory for exposed emotional words as was displayed by subjects reporting low levels of anxiety sensitivity. However, on a word stem completion task designed to assess implicit memory, they displayed an implicit memory advantage for the more negative stimulus words. This finding, that vulnerability to anxiety in normal subjects is associated with enhanced implicit memory for threat-related stimuli, has not been restricted to studies that have employed the word fragment completion procedure to assess retention. MacLeod (1995) has reported finding an implicit memory advantage for threat stimuli in high trait anxious subjects using the same perceptual identification task as MacLeod & McGlaughlin (1995) employed to assess implicit memory in GAD patients. No such bias was shown by these high trait anxious subjects on a recognition task employed to assess explicit memory.

Despite this burgeoning evidence to support the existence of an anxiety-linked implicit memory bias, a troubling number of well-designed experiments have failed to obtain such an effect. A study carried out on GAD patients by Mathews et al. (1995), using the same word stem memory tests originally employed by Mathews et al. (1989), failed to replicate this earlier experiment's finding that such patients show enhanced implicit memory for threat stimuli. Becker, Margraf & Rinck (1994) found no evidence of any such implicit memory bias in panic disorder patients, again using the word stem completion approach. In a more recent study using the perceptual identification index of implicit memory, McNally & Amir (1996) were unable to detect an implicit memory advantage for trauma-related information in PTSD patients. Two separate word stem completion experiments carried out by Nugent & Mineka (1994) each revealed no difference in implicit memory for threatening and non-threatening information between high and low trait anxious students.

Such inconsistencies within the literature suggest that it may be premature to draw firm conclusions concerning the existence of an implicit memory advantage for threat-related information in anxious individuals. For the moment, explaining the basis of these inconsistencies should represent a major goal for researchers working within this field. It seems unlikely that discrepancies between findings concerning the presence of this implicit memory bias can be attributed to cognitive differences between subtypes of anxious individuals. Both positive findings and null results have been reported within equivalent anxious populations, including GAD patients, panic disorder patients and high trait anxious normals. Likewise, it is not obvious that differences in methods of assessing implicit memory can account for the divergent results obtained. The same word stem completion measure has been employed in studies that have revealed an anxiety-linked implicit memory advantage for threat (e.g. Mathews et al., 1989) and in studies which have obtained no such effect (e.g. Becker, Margraf & Rinck, 1994). The same is true of the perceptual identification measure, which sometimes has revealed an implicit memory bias in anxious subjects (e.g. MacLeod & McGlaughlin, 1995) and sometimes has failed to do so (e.g. McNally & Amir, 1996). Even the more far-fetched hypothesis, that alternative implicit memory tasks might be differentially sensitive to the implicit memory biases shown by alternative categories of anxious subjects, does not accord with the data. For example, using the same implicit memory measure to study the same population of high trait anxious students, Richards & French (1991) found evidence of an implicit memory bias, while Nugent & Mineka (1994) did not. Similarly, this same measure revealed an implicit memory bias in GAD patients within Mathews et al.'s (1989) original study, yet failed to detect this effect when Mathews et al. (1995) attempted a replication using the same clinical population.

Perhaps the most promising candidate explanation to account for discrepancies across anxiety-related implicit memory findings is that they may stem from differences in the nature of the encoding tasks that have been employed (Eysenck & Byrne, 1994). Cognitive-experimental researchers recently have recognized that traditional implicit memory tests typically assess perceptual processing, while traditional explicit memory tests commonly assess conceptual processing (cf. Roediger & Blaxton, 1987). There is now evidence that memory tests which assess perceptual processing are rendered more sensitive when structural, rather than conceptual, processing has been encouraged during stimulus encoding, while memory tests assessing conceptual processing are most sensitive when conceptual stimulus processing has been favoured during encoding (Blaxton, 1989). Eysenck & Byrne (1994) reasoned, therefore, that anxiety-linked effects on traditional implicit memory measures, such as the word fragment completion task, may be most evident following an encoding procedure that favours structural over conceptual processing. These researchers obtained experimental support for this position in a study, carried out using normal individuals differing in levels of trait anxiety, within which a manipulation was introduced to vary the degree to which conceptual processing was encouraged during initial encoding. A subsequent word fragment completion task revealed an anxiety-linked implicit memory advantage for threat stimuli only after the encoding condition which favoured structural stimulus processing. No anxiety-linked bias in explicit memory performance was observed under either encoding condition.

Eysenck & Byrne's data highlight the likely importance of considering encoding procedures when investigating implicit and explicit memory biases in anxious subjects. However, their proposal that structural encoding will routinely elicit an anxiety-linked implicit memory bias is not fully consistent with the overall pattern of implicit memory findings observed across all other studies. For example, using the word stem completion task, Mathews et al. (1989) observed an implicit memory bias in GAD patients following an encoding task which, by requiring subjects to imagine themselves in situations involving the referents of each word, clearly encouraged conceptual processing. However, when this encoding task was later amended to a procedure which directly encouraged structural processing, by requiring subjects to count the number of times the letter "e" appeared in each presented word, Mathews et al. (1995) found no evidence of any implicit memory bias in this patient population. Such results clearly sit at odds with the view that anxiety-linked implicit memory biases will be most pronounced following structural encoding tasks.

Progress towards a clearer picture of mnemonic functioning in anxious individuals will rely partly upon the introduction of more powerful experimental designs. Among these, almost certainly, will figure approaches that systematically cross the conceptual vs. structural processing requirements of encoding tasks, the conceptual vs. structural processing requirements of memory tasks, and the degree to which such memory tasks assess intentional or unintentional retrieval. As data accumulates from such future studies, it seems probable that some results already reported within the literature may prove to be unreliable. Ultimately, this will lead to a fuller understanding of the association between anxiety vulnerability and selective memory. For the moment, however, it must be concluded that there is little convincing evidence to suggest that anxiety vulnerability generally is associated with enhanced explicit memory for threat-related stimuli. In contrast, the majority of published studies support the existence of enhanced implicit memory for threat-related stimuli in individuals with elevated vulnerability to anxiety.

ACCOUNTING FOR OBSERVED ASSOCIATIONS BETWEEN SELECTIVE INFORMATION PROCESSING AND ANXIETY VULNERABILITY

The reviewed evidence demonstrates clearly that vulnerability to anxiety is indeed associated with the biased processing of emotional information, but indicates that the occurrence of this bias is not equivalent across all cognitive operations. Within encoding operations, clinically anxious patients display an attentional bias towards threat stimuli, which functions automatically at a very early stage of processing. High trait anxious normals also show this automatic attentional bias, particularly when under stress. Interpretative processing, too, is characterized by an anxiety-linked processing bias. In both clinical anxiety patients and high trait anxious normals, this interpretative bias operates to selectively impose threatening meanings on ambiguous information. However, there is a striking dearth of evidence to indicate that vulnerability to anxiety is associated with any bias favouring the retrieval of threat-related information on explicit memory tasks. Indeed, a number a studies suggest that quite the reverse explicit memory bias may operate, serving to selectively suppress the recall and recognition of threatening stimuli. Only on implicit memory tests, which assess the automatic impact of initial stimulus exposure on later task performance, does the balance of evidence indicate that clinically anxious patients and high trait anxious normals may display a memorial advantage for threat-related information. Consider how this observed pattern of associations between anxiety vulnerability and selective information processing might best be explained.

The findings present considerable difficulties for theoretical accounts of cognition and emotion, such as those of Bower (1981, 1987) or Beck (Beck, Emery & Greenberg, 1985; Beck & Clark, 1988), which predict that anxiety-linked advantages in the processing of threatening information should be evident across all classes of cognitive operations. According to Bower's network model, for example, representations of threatening information are primed within anxious individuals' semantic memories, thus rendering such information disproportionately available to every cognitive process that requires access to this data base, which should include explicit memory. Beck's schema model holds that, in individuals with elevated vulnerability to anxiety, high level "danger schemata" operate to selectively facilitate the processing of threatening information throughout the cognitive continuum. The apparent absence of an anxiety-linked explicit memory advantage for threatening information is inconsistent with such theoretical conceptions. To accommodate this pattern of findings, it becomes necessary to model the cognitive characteristics of emotional vulnerability within a framework that draws clearer distinctions between processing subsystems. Perhaps it is not surprising, therefore, that such theoretical approaches to modelling the association between cognition and emotion have become increasingly common in recent years (e.g. Oatley & Johnson-Laird, 1987; Teasdale & Barnard, 1993). One such model, put forward by Williams et al. (1988, 1997), offers a specific explanation for the profile of cognitive biases associated with anxiety vulnerability.

Williams et al.'s account draws upon the distinction, introduced by Graf & Mandler (1984), between the processes of "integration" and "elaboration", each of which operate on mental representations in quite different ways. The former is an automatic process that serves to strengthen the internal organization of a mental representation. Because of its increased internal cohesion, a highly integrated representation will more readily come to mind when only some of its features have been extracted from the stimulus environment. In contrast, elaboration is a strategic process through which new associations are formed between one mental representation and others within the cognitive system, resulting in the establishment of richer relationships linking such representations together. Highly elaborated representations are more retrievable, therefore, in tasks which require subjects to intentionally search memory, given the greater richness of associative pathways that lead to such representations. A central proposal within Williams et al.'s model of emotion and cognition is that anxiety vulnerability is associated specifically with the enhanced integrative processing of threat representations, but with no increased elaborative processing of such representations. Such a position goes a considerable way towards explaining the observed pattern of findings.

Given that highly integrated representations will be accessed with disproportionate ease when minimal evidence of their features has been extracted from the environment, it would be expected that stimuli presenting such evidence will selectively capture attention. In interference tasks, for example, the stimulus information extracted from unattended distractors will be more likely to result in representational access when the relevant representations are characterized by a high level of integration. Thus, if threat representations are more highly integrated in individuals with elevated vulnerability to anxiety, then unattended threat stimuli should produce increased interference for such individuals, as has been observed. Likewise, interpretation should be influenced by level of representational integration because, as extraction of information from an ambiguous stimulus proceeds, this should result in representational access at an earlier point for those candidate representations which are characterized by the highest levels of integration. Thus, if those who are most vulnerable to anxiety tend to have threat representations in the most highly integrated states, then threatening interpretations of ambiguity should be disproportionately likely for such individuals, once again as has been observed. Performance on implicit memory tests also should be affected by representational integration. Such procedures typically assess which representations are accessed when presented stimulus information is impoverished, either by exposing stimulus items very briefly or by providing only incomplete stimulus fragments. Therefore, if threat representations are more highly integrated in individuals with elevated anxiety vulnerability, then those individuals should show an implicit memory advantage for threatening information, once more as has been observed. However, level of representational integration will have no impact upon the probability that an intentional memory search will identify a retrieval pathway that leads to a representation. Therefore, even if individuals vulnerable to anxiety do possess highly integrated threat representations, this would not lead to them displaying an explicit memory advantage for threat-related information, and indeed such individuals show little evidence of any such effect.

While Williams et al.'s proposal, that high levels of anxiety vulnerability are associated with enhanced integration of threat representations, may explain why high trait anxious normals and most clinically anxious patients show no explicit memory advantage for threatening information, it does not account for the observation that such subjects occasionally display disproportionately poor explicit memory for such stimuli. In their original model, Williams et al. (1988) suggested that this may reflect a tendency for such anxious individuals to demonstrate, under certain circumstances, reduced elaborative processing of representations associated with their fears and concerns. For example, spider-phobic patients, when they encounter spider-related stimuli, may deliberately avoid the strategically-mediated reflection required to elaboratively develop and strengthen associations between the aversive representations of these stimuli and other representations within the cognitive system. Such impoverished elaboration would result in impaired explicit memory for the threat-related stimuli. In a more recent version of their model, Williams et al. (1997) note that such an account may seem inconsistent with the anecdotal observation that anxious individuals often appear to ruminate upon, and worry about, negatively-toned information in a way that may seem to resemble elaborative processing. Consequently, they revise their model in a manner that builds upon the distinction between memorial and non-memorial elaboration, invited by Johnson & Hirst's (1993) multiple-entry memory (MEM) framework of mnemonic functioning. MEM delineates 16 basic memory processes that operate within four separate memory subsystems. Only some of the processes which involve elaboration, such as "rehearsal" and "reactivation", concern elaborative processing of representations corresponding to presented stimuli, and so have consequences for the memorability of such stimuli. Other forms of elaborative processing, such as "discovering" and "shifting", although evoked by presented stimuli, do not directly implicate their representations, and so do not affect their memorability. These latter forms of elaborative processing, which involve creative mental activities that Johnson & Hirst liken to "problem solving or brain storming", are not bound by the stimulus materials themselves. In their revised model, Williams et al. propose that, for individuals with high levels of anxiety vulnerability, there is an increased likelihood that threat-related stimuli will evoke such non-memorial elaborative processing (manifesting itself subjectively as worry), rather than memorial elaborative processes such as rehearsal and reactivation. This attenuation of memorial elaboration accounts for the finding that threat-related stimuli often are not well retrieved by such anxious individuals on explicit memory tasks.

Williams et al.'s account construes the enhanced integrative processing of threatening representations to be a stable characteristic of trait vulnerability to anxiety. However, their model functions in a manner that means the ease with which this trait-linked bias can be detected is increased when state anxiety is elevated. In the 1988 version of the model, this resulted from state anxiety operating to increase the gain of the affective decision mechanism, through which stimuli are judged to be threatening or not. Thus, according to this position, heightened state anxiety magnifies the subjective threat value of negative stimuli, and so elevates the likelihood of eliciting subjects' characteristic emotional processing biases. In the 1997 version of the model, which represents a parallel distributed processing implementation (cf. McLelland, 1995), state anxiety exerts transient neuromodulatory control in a manner that increases the tagging of threat stimuli, again inflating the probability that individuals will display their characteristic selective processing responses to threatening information.

Williams et al. therefore provide a theoretical framework that can accommodate the observed pattern of associations between processing selectivity and anxiety vulnerability. However, they go further, to propose that elevated trait vulnerability to anxiety may represent the direct causal result of this tendency to selectively process threat-related information. Evidence pertaining to this possibility, together with its clinical implications, now will be considered in the final section of the chapter.

CLINICAL IMPLICATIONS

The proposal that individual differences in the tendency to automatically favour the selective processing of threatening information may represent the causal substrate of individual differences in trait anxiety is of more than theoretical interest. Should this position be valid, then it would seem likely that clinical practice could be enriched by taking fuller account of the processing selectivity shown by anxious patients. The most immediate applied benefits of such an approach might involve the development of more objective, and perhaps more precise, assessment measures.

Recent research already has established that selective processing indices may represent sensitive measures of clinical change in response to therapeutic interventions for the anxiety disorders. Interference measures of selective attention have received the greatest empirical scrutiny in this regard. The finding that recovered GAD patients fail to display the exaggerated threat interference effect shown by currently anxious patients (e.g. Mogg, Mathews & Eysenck, 1992) is consistent with the possibility that clinical recovery might be indexed by change in this attentional variable. Firmer support for this proposal comes from the many studies to have found that threat interference declines with treatment, in cohorts of GAD patients (Mathews et al., 1995), obsessive-compulsive patients (Foa & McNally, 1986) and specific phobics (Lavy, van den Hout & Arntz, 1993). The strongest evidence, however, comes from those experiments which not only have reported reduced threat interference with treatment, but also have demonstrated that the magnitude of this reduction is directly related to the efficacy of the intervention. Thus, for example, Mattia, Heimberg & Hope (1993) found that, following clinical intervention, it was only those social phobics who showed a good response to treatment who evidenced a decline in the magnitude of their threat interference effect. Similarly, Mogg et al. (1995) observed that post-treatment changes in the level of threat interference shown on masked stimulus words were directly correlated with post-treatment changes in the clinical symptomatology reported by their GAD patients.

As yet, little research has examined the possibility that indices of selective interpretation indices also might be employed as measures of clinical change, but early findings provide a basis for optimism. It has already been mentioned that Mathews et al. (1989) found a group of recovered GAD patients not to display current patients' elevated tendencies to spell ambiguous homophones in their more threatening form. More recently, Westling & Ost (1995) used a different measure to assess changes in interpretative bias within a cohort of panic disorder patients undergoing psychological treatment. These researchers not only found that the patients' initial tendencies to impose threat interpretations on ambiguous stimuli were reduced following treatment, but also observed that this reduction was greatest in those individuals who showed the best treatment outcomes. As yet, it remains to be seen whether measures of implicit memory bias, too, may serve as indicators of therapeutic efficacy within clinical intervention studies. Collectively, however, the above findings already lend substantial weight to the proposal that measures of selective information processing might enable the relatively precise assessment of clinical change within anxiety-disordered patients, in a manner likely to bypass the usual demand effects and reactivity problems associated with self-report indices.

Should it be correct that selective processing biases causally underpin anxiety vulnerability, then it is reasonable to expect that measures of such biases may do more than index potentially important clinical change. Additionally, they should be capable of powerfully predicting which individuals are most at risk of developing anxiety problems, serving to identify those who are likely to respond to future stressful events with disproportionately intense dysphoric reactions. Evidence now exists to suggest that this is indeed the case. MacLeod & Hagan (1992) employed a masked version of the colour-naming interference task to assess individual differences in the automatic selective processing of threatening information within a population of women, stressed by the proximity of an imminent colposcopy investigation conducted to screen for cervical pathology. At this same time, these women were also given traditional questionnaire measures of emotional vulnerability, such as the Spielberger Trait Anxiety Inventory (Spielberger et al., 1983). Approximately 8 weeks later, those women who later received a diagnosis of cervical pathology completed a questionnaire assessing the emotional impact of this subsequent negative life event. MacLeod & Hagan found that the only measure, taken on the initial test session, to significantly predict individual differences in the intensity of the women's dysphoric reactions to this later life event, was the magnitude of the threat interference effect shown on the masked colour-naming trials. Those women who displayed the greatest level of threat interference on this initial assessment task reported experiencing greater levels of emotional distress when they subsequently received the diagnosis of cervical pathology.

In a replication study, van den Hout et al. (1995) have confirmed this finding that threat interference on masked colour-naming trials serves as a powerful predictor of trait vulnerability to anxiety. Recently, MacLeod & Ng (submitted) have provided additional evidence that early measures of threat interference on the colour-naming task can powerfully predict later emotional responses to stressful life events. These researchers employed this interference task, together with questionnaire measures of emotional vulnerability, to screen a population of recent Singaporean high school graduates, who were assessed in their home country several weeks prior to their departure to commence tertiary studies in Australia. Measures of state anxiety, taken both on this initial test session and on the day of subjects' subsequent arrival in Australia, permitted assessment of the degree to which this later transition experience served to elevate anxious mood state. The single best predictor of individual differences in state anxiety responses to this subsequent life stress was the magnitude of the threat interference effect elicited in the original test session by a minor stressor. Those individuals who showed the largest threat interference effects on this initial session responded to their subsequent migration with the greatest elevations in state anxiety. Thus, it does indeed appear to be the case that measures of selective processing may enable clinicians to better predict which individuals, approaching a stressful event, are most likely to respond with problematic levels of anxiety. Such predictive capacity could enable early prophylactic procedures, including preparatory counselling, to be directed effectively towards those who may benefit most from such psychological input.

The finding that initial individual differences in the tendency to selectively process threat-related information can precede, and predict, later individual differences in emotional reactions to subsequent life events is fully consistent with the notion that selective processing biases may make a causal contribution to anxiety vulnerability. However, such observations do not necessitate this conclusion. It remains possible that some third individual difference factor could independently mediate both selective processing and anxiety vulnerability, resulting in a strong statistical association between these latter two dimensions of individual difference despite the existence of no causal relationship between them. A more direct test of the hypothesis that selective processing of threat-related information can cause anxiety vulnerability, and one which could yield results with immediate and important therapeutic implications, would be provided by studies designed to directly manipulate selective information processing, in order to test the prediction that this should serve to modify anxiety vulnerability. MacLeod, Rutherford & Campbell (1997) have recently reported results from a research program designed with such an aim, which offer considerable support for this prediction.

For example, they describe a study, carried out in conjunction with Greg Ebsworthy, that employed an adaptation of the dot probe procedure to train different patterns of attentional bias within two groups of normal subjects. Each trial briefly presented a word pair, containing both a threat and non-threat member, on a VDU screen. Following this word pair presentation, a linear probe stimulus always appeared in one of the two screen locations, and this line could slant either left or right. Subjects were required to rapidly discriminate the slope of each probe. Although the threat member of each word pair appeared with equal frequency in either the upper or lower screen location, the positions of the probes were contingent upon the positions of the threat words, with this contingency differing for each of two subject groups. For one group, across the set of 684 training trials, virtually all the probes appeared in the same screen location as the preceding threat word, and it was intended that this would induce an attentional bias towards the more threatening stimuli. For the other group, in contrast, virtually all these probes appeared in the opposing screen location to that previously occupied by the threat word, and it was intended that this would induce attentional avoidance of the threat stimuli. Discrimination latencies observed on those few trials to violate these training contingencies served to confirm that, across the 45-minute training procedure, the two subject groups did come to acquire these tendencies to orient attention towards or away from the threat words, even on word pairs not previously presented during attentional training.

Following this attentional training procedure, all subjects were exposed to a stress manipulation, which involved their being videotaped while completing a difficult anagram task, under timed conditions and while receiving failure feedback. This manipulation served to elevate dysphoric mood state across both subject groups. Of most importance, however, was the critical finding that the magnitude of this dysphoric response was attenuated for those subjects who had experienced the training procedure that induced attentional avoidance of threat. A replication study, just completed in collaboration with Lin Hokker, now has confirmed this central findings. This replication once again employed the dot probe attentional training procedure, and found that an induced attentional bias away from threat stimuli served to reduce subjects' vulnerability to experience state anxiety elevations in response to a subsequent stress task. These demonstrations, that the direct manipulation of subjects' selective information processing can serve to modify their levels of anxiety vulnerability, lend strong support to the hypothesis that processing selectivity can make a causal contribution to such emotional vulnerability.

MacLeod, Rutherford & Campbell (1997) have reported recent extensions to this research program, the results of which suggest that prolonged exposure to attentional training procedures of this sort might even reduce problematically high levels of anxiety outside the laboratory. In one such study, 30 high trait anxious students were exposed to over 6000 trials of the dot probe training task across a 3-week period, during which time they also reported their trait anxiety levels using a modified version of the Spielberger Trait Anxiety Inventory. For half of these subjects, virtually all of the dot probe training trials presented probes in the opposing screen location to that occupied by the threat-related word stimuli, a contingency designed to induce attentional avoidance of threat. The remaining subjects experienced no such contingency, and probes occurred with equivalent frequencies in the vicinities of the threat-related and the neutral word stimuli. Probe discrimination latencies indicated that the former group did, as intended, develop an attentional bias away from the threat stimuli across the weeks of attentional training. Interestingly, evidence of this induced attentional bias was obtained even on test trials in which the word pairs were backwardly masked to prevent their conscious identification, suggesting that the extended training procedure may have established an attentional bias at an automatic level of processing. Most importantly, across the 3 weeks of the study, those subjects exposed to the training procedure designed to induce attentional avoidance of threat stimuli showed evidence of a decline in their trait anxiety scores, relative to those who experienced the non-contingent version of the dot probe task. In addition to lending further strong support to the hypothesis that selective processing biases can contribute causally to anxiety vulnerability, this finding also suggests that attentional training procedures may represent effective therapeutic tools, which might serve a useful function within intervention programs designed to reduce such vulnerability to anxiety.

This evidence that emotional vulnerability might be modified by directly manipulating patterns of selective information processing, using variants of those same cognitive-experimental tasks which previously have been employed only to assess processing selectivity, brings research on the association between cognition and emotion to a new threshold. It remains to be seen whether the direct manipulation of selective processing can make a potent contribution to the treatment of clinical anxiety disorders. Candidate processes for manipulation include not only attention, but also interpretation and implicit memory, and the types of training tasks most likely to efficiently modify such operations have yet to be developed. Doubtless, this will require a concerted research effort that will span many laboratories and will extend across future years. However, the conceptual and methodological foundations needed to support this program of investigation are now set firmly in place. These foundations have been established by a fruitful collaboration between cognitive–experimental researchers and clinical investigators which, across these past 15 years, has greatly illuminated our understanding of the cognitive factors that underlie anxiety vulnerability. It seems likely that this same collaboration will continue to play a central role within future research on this exciting topic, which now may usefully focus upon identifying creative ways to transform this enriched understanding into more effective clinical procedures.

ACKNOWLEDGEMENT

This chapter was prepared with support from an Australian Research Council Grant held by the author.

REFERENCES

Amin, J. & Lovibond, P. F. (submitted). Covariation bias and expectancy bias for biological and technological fear-relevant stimuli.

Amir, N., McNally, R. J., Riemann, B. C. & Clements, C. (1996). Implicit memory bias for threat in panic disorder: application of the "white noise" paradigm. *Behaviour Research & Therapy*, **34**, 157–162.

Amir, N., McNally, R. J., Riemann, B. C., Burns, J., Lorenz, M. & Mullen, J. T. (1996). Suppression of the emotional Stroop effect by increased anxiety in patients with social phobia. *Behaviour Research & Therapy*, **34**, 945–948.

Beck, A. T. & Clark, D. M. (1988). Anxiety and depression: an information processing perspective. *Anxiety Research*, **1**, 23–36.

Beck, A. T., Emery, G. & Greenberg, R. C. (1985). *Anxiety Disorders and Phobias: A Cognitive Perspective*. New York: Basic Books.

Beck, J. G., Stanley, M. A., Averill, P. M., Baldwin, L. E. & Deagle, E. A. (1992). Attention and memory for threat in panic disorder. *Behaviour Research & Therapy*, **30**, 619–629.

Becker, E., Margraf, J. & Rinck, M. (1994). Memory bias in panic disorder. *Journal of Abnormal Psychology*, **103**, 396–399.

Blaxton, T. A. (1989). Investigating dissociations among memory measures: support for a transfer-appropriate processing framework. *Journal of Experimental Psychology: Learning, Memory, and Cognition*, **15**, 657–668.

Bower, G. H. (1987). Commentary on mood and memory. *Behaviour Research and Therapy*, **25**, 443–456.

Bower, G. H. (1981). Mood and memory. *American Psychologist*, **36**, 129–148.

Broadbent, D. E., Broadbent, M. H. P. & Jones, J. L. (1986). Performance correlates of self-reported cognitive failure and obsessionality. *British Journal of Clinical Psychology*, **25**, 285–299.

Burke, M. & Mathews, A. (1992). Autobiographical memory and clinical anxiety. *Cognition & Emotion*, **6**, 23–35.

Butler, G. & Mathews, A. (1983). Cognitive processes in anxiety. *Advances in Behaviour Research and Therapy*, **5**, 51–62.

Butler, G. & Mathews, A. (1987). Anticipatory anxiety and risk perception. *Cognitive Therapy & Research*, **91**, 551–565.

Calvo, M. G. & Castillo, D. (in press). Mood-conguent bias in interpretation of ambiguity: strategic processes and temporary activation. *The Quarterly Journal of Experimental Psychology*.

Calvo, M. G., Eysenck, M. W. & Estevaz, A. (1994). Ego-threat interpretative bias in test anxiety: on-line inferences. *Cognition & Emotion*, **2**, 127–146.

Calvo, M. G., Eysenck, M. W. & Castillo, M. D. (1997). Interpretative bias in test anxiety: the time course of predictive inference. *Cognition & Emotion*, **11**, 43–63.

Cassiday, K. L., McNally, R. J. & Zeitlin, S. B. (1992). Cognitive processing of trauma cues in rape victims with post-traumatic stress disorder. *Cognitive Therapy & Research*, **16**, 283–295.

Cloitre, M. & Liebowitz, M. R. (1991). Memory bias in panic disorder: an investigation of the cognitive avoidance hypothesis. *Cognitive Therapy & Research*, **15**, 371–386.

Cloitre, M., Cancienne, J., Heimberg, R. G., Holt, C. S. & Liebowitz, M. (1995). Memory bias does not generalise across anxiety disorders. *Behaviour Research & Therapy*, **33**, 305–307.

Cloitre, M., Shear, K., Cancienne, J. & Zeitlin, S. (1994). Implicit and explicit memory for catastrophic associations to bodily sensation words in panic disorder. *Cognitive Therapy & Research*, **18**, 225–240.

Dalgeish, T. (1995). Performance on the emotional Stroop task in groups of anxious, expert and control subjects: a comparison of computer and card presentation formats. *Cognition & Emotion*, **9**, 341–362.

Darke, S. (1988). Anxiety and working memory capacity. *Cognition and Emotion*, **2**, 145–154.

Dawkins, K. & Furnham, A. (1989). The colour naming of emotional words. *British Journal of Psychology*, **80**, 383–389.

de Ruiter, C. & Brosschot, J. F. (1994). The emotional Stroop interference effect in anxiety: attentional bias or cognitive avoidance? *Behaviour Research and Therapy*, **32**, 315–319.

Deffenbacher, J. L. (1980). Worry and emotionality in test anxiety. In I. G. Sarason (ed.), *Test Anxiety: Theory, Research and Applications*. Hillsdale, NJ: Erlbaum.

de-Jong, P. J., Merckelbach, H., Arntz, A. & Nijman, J. (1992). Covariation detection in treated and untreated spider phobics. *Journal of Abnormal Psychology*, **101**, 724–727.

de-Jong, P. & Merckelbach, H. (1991). Covariation bias and electrodermal responding in spider phobics before and after behavioural treatment. *Behaviour Research & Therapy*, **29**, 307–314.

Ehlers, A., Margraf, J., Davies, S. & Roth, W. T. (1988). Selective processing of threat cues in subjects with panic attacks. *Cognition and Emotion*, **2**, 201–220.

Eysenck, M. W. (1982). *Attention and Arousal: Cognition and Performance*. Berlin: Springer.

Eysenck, M. W. (1992). *Anxiety: The Cognitive Perspective*. Hove: Erlbaum.

Eysenck, M. W. & Byrne, A. (1994). Implicit memory bias, explicit memory bias and anxiety. *Cognition & Emotion*, **8**, 415–432.

Eysenck, M. W. & Calvo, M. G. (1992). Anxiety and performance: the processing efficiency theory. *Cognition & Emotion*, **6**, 409–434.

Eysenck, M. W., MacLeod, C. & Mathews, A. (1987). Cognitive functioning in anxiety. *Psychological Research*, **49**, 189–195.

Foa, E. B., Feske, U., Murdock, T. B., Kozak, M. J. & McCarthy, P. R. (1991). Processing of threat-related information in rape victims. *Journal of Abnormal Psychology*, **100**, 156–162.

Foa, E. B., Ilai, D., McCarthy, P. R., Shoyer, B. & Murdock, T. (1993). Information processing in obsessive compulsive disorder. *Cognitive Therapy & Research*, **17**, 173–189.

Foa, E. B., McNally, R. J. & Murdock, T. B. (1989). Anxious mood and memory. *Behaviour Research and Therapy*, **27**, 141–147.

Foa, E. G. & McNally, R. J. (1986). Sensitivity to feared stimuli in obsessive-compulsives: a dichotic listening analysis. *Cognitive Therapy and Research*, **10**, 477–486.

Fox, E. (1994). Attentional bias in anxiety: a defective inhibition hypothesis. *Cognition & Emotion*, **8**, 165–195.

Fransson, A. (1977). On qualitative differences in learning IV: effects of intrinsic motivation and extrinsic anxiety on process and outcome. *British Journal of Educational Psychology*, **47**, 244–257.

Graf, P. & Mandler, G. (1984). Activation makes words more accessible, but not necessarily nore retrievable. *Journal of Verbal Learning and Verbal Behaviour*, **23**, 553–568.

Hirsch, C. (1995). Anxiety and Cognitive Schemata. Unpublished PhD Thesis, University of Cambridge.

Hope, D. A., Rapee, R. M., Heimberg, R. G. & Dombeck, M. J. (1990). Representations of the self in social phobia: vulnerability to social threat. *Cognitive Therapy & Research*, **14**, 177–189.

Idzihowski, C. & Baddeley, A. (1987). Fear and performance in novice parachutists. *Ergonomics*, **30**, 1463–1474.

Johnson, M. K. & Hirst, W. (1993). MEM: Memory subsystems as processes. In A. F. Collins, S. E. Gathercole, M. A. Conway, & P. E. Morris (eds), *Theories of Memory*. Hove: Erlbaum.

Kaspi, S. P., McNally, R. J. & Amir, N. (1995). Cognitive processing of emotional information in posttraumatic stress disorder. *Cognitive Therapy & Research*, **19**, 433–444.

Lang, A. J. & Craske, M. (1997). Information processing in anxiety and depression. *Behaviour Research & Therapy*, **35**, 451–455.

Lavy, E. H. & van den Hout, M. A. (1994). Cognitive avoidance and attentional bias: causal relationships. *Cognitive Therapy & Research*, **18**, 179–191.

Lavy, E. H., van Oppen, P. & van den Hout, M. (1994). Selective processing of emotional information in obsessive compulsive disorder. *Behaviour Research and Therapy*, **32**, 243–246.

Lavy, E., van den Hout, M. & Arntz, A. (1993). Attentional bias and spider phobia: conceptual and clinical issues. *Behaviour Research and Therapy*, **31**, 17–24.

Leon, M. R. & Revelle, W. (1985). Effects of anxiety on analogical reasoning: a test of three theoretical models. *Journal of Personality and Social Psychology*, **49**, 1302–1315.

Lundh, L. G. & Ost, L. G. (1996). Recognition bias for critical faces in social anxiety. *Behaviour Research & Therapy*, **34**, 787–794.

MacLeod, C. & Cohen, I. (1993). Anxiety and the interpretation of ambiguity: a text comprehension study. *Journal of Abnormal Psychology*, **102**, 238–247.

MacLeod, C. & Donnellan, A. M. (1993). Individual differences in anxiety, and the restriction of working memory capacity. *Personality and Individual Differences*, **15**, 163–173.

MacLeod, C. & Hagan, R. (1992). Individual differences in selective processing of threatening information, and emotional responses to a stressful life event. *Behaviour Research & Therapy*, **30**, 151–161.

MacLeod, C. & Mathews, A. (1991). Cognitive-experimental approaches to emotional disorders. In P. Martin (ed.), *Handbook of Behaviour Therapy and Psychological Science*. New York: Pergamon.

MacLeod, C. & McGlaughlin, K. (1995). Implicit and explicit memory bias in anxiety: a conceptual replication. *Behaviour Research & Therapy*, **33**, 1–14.

MacLeod, C. & Rutherford, E. M. (1998). Automatic and strategic cognitive biases in anxiety and depression. In K. Kirsner, C. Speelman, M. Maybery, A. O'Brien-Malone, M. Anderson & C. MacLeod. (eds), *Implicit and Explicit Mental Processes*. Mahwah, NJ: Erlbaum.

MacLeod, C. (1990). Mood disorders and cognition. In M. W. Eysenck (ed.), *Cognitive Psychology: An International Review*. Chichester: Wiley.

MacLeod, C. (1995). Anxiety and cognitive processes. In I. G. Sarason, B. P. Sarason & G. R. Pierce (eds), *Cognitive Interference: Theories, Methods & Findings*. Hillsdale, NJ: Erlbaum.

MacLeod, C. (1998). Implicit perception: perceptual processing without awareness. In K. Kirsner, C. Speelman, M. Maybery, A. O'Brien-Malone, M. Anderson & C. MacLeod. (eds), *Implicit and Explicit Mental Processes*. Mahwah, NJ: Erlbaum.

MacLeod, C. & Ng., V. (submitted). Initial attentional bias to threat predicts later emotional response to acculturation stress.

MacLeod, C. & Mathews, A. (1988). Anxiety and the allocation of attention to threat. *Quarterly Journal of Experimental Psychology: Human Experimental Psychology*, **38**, 659–670.

MacLeod, C. & Rutherford, E. M. (1992). Anxiety and the selective processing of emotional information: mediating roles of awareness, trait and state variables, and personal relevance of stimulus materials. *Behaviour Research and Therapy*, **30**, 479–491.

MacLeod, C., Mathews, A. & Tata, P. (1986). Attentional bias in emotional disorders. *Journal of Abnormal Psychology*, **95**, 15–20.

MacLeod, C., Rutherford, E. M. & Campbell, L. (1997). Modification of anxiety vulnerability through direct manipulation of selective processing bias. Paper presented to 2nd Australian Anxiety Disorders Conference, Port Douglas, Queensland, July.

Martin, M., Williams, R. M. & Clark, D. M. (1991). Does anxiety lead to selective processing of threat-related information? *Behaviour Research & Therapy*, **29**, 147–160.

Mathews, A., Mogg, K., May, J. & Eysenck, M. W. (1989). Implicit and explicit memory bias in anxiety. *Journal of Abnormal Psychology*, **98**, 236–240.

Mathews, A. M. & Sebastian, S. (1993). Suppression of emotional Stroop effects by fear arousal. *Cognition & Emotion*, **7**, 517–530.

Mathews, A. & Klug, F. (1993). Emotionality and interference with color naming in anxiety. *Behaviour Research & Therapy*, **31**, 57–62.

Mathews, A. & MacLeod, C. (1985). Selective processing of threat cues in anxiety states. *Behaviour Research and Therapy*, **23**, 563–569.

Mathews, A. & MacLeod, C. (1986). Discrimination of threat cues without awareness in anxiety states. *Journal of Abnormal Psychology*, **95**, 131–138.

Mathews, A. & MacLeod, C. (1994). Cognitive approaches to emotion. *Annual Review of Psychology*, **45**, 25–50.

Mathews, A., Mogg, K., Kentish, J. & Eysenck, M. (1995). Effect of psychological treatment on cognitive bias in generalised anxiety disorder. *Behaviour Research & Therapy*, **33**, 293–303.

Mathews, A., Richards, A. & Eysenck, M. (1989). Interpretation of homophones related to threat in anxiety states. *Journal of Abnormal Psychology*, **98**, 31–34.

Matthews, G. & Harley, T. A. (1996). Connectionist models of emotional distress and attentional bias. *Cognition & Emotion*, **10**, 561–600.

Mattia, J. I., Heimberg, R. G. & Hope, D. A. (1993). The revised Stroop color-naming task in social phobics. *Behaviour Research and Therapy*, **31**, 305–313.

Mayo, P. R. (1989). A further study of the personality-congruent recall effect. *Personality and Individual Differences*, **10**, 247–252.

McLelland, J. (1995). A connectionist perspective on knowledge and development. In T. J. Simon & G. S. Halford (eds), *Developing Cognitive Competence: New Approaches to Process Modelling*. Hillsdale, NJ: Erlbaum.

McNally, R. J. (1995). Automaticity and the anxiety disorders. *Behaviour Research & Therapy*, **33**, 747–754.

McNally, R. J. & Amir, N. (1996). Perceptual implicit memory for trauma-related information in post-traumatic stress disorder. *Cognition & Emotion*, **10**, 551–556.

McNally, R. J. & Foa, E. B. (1987). Cognition and agoraphobia: bias in the interpretation of threat. *Cognitive Therapy & Research*, **11**, 567–581.

McNally, R. J., Amir, N., Louro, C. E., Lukach, B. M., Riemann, B. C. & Calamari, J. E. (1994). Cognitive processing of idiographic emotional information in panic disorder. *Behaviour Research & Therapy*, **32**, 119–122.

McNally, R. J., English, G. E. & Lipke, H. J. (1993). Assessment of intrusive cognition in PTSD: use of the modified Stroop paradigm. *Journal of Traumatic Stress*, **6**, 33–241.

McNally, R. J., Foa, E. B. & Donnell, C. D. (1989). Memory bias for anxiety information in patients with panic disorder. *Cognition and Emotion*, **3**, 27–44.

Mogg, K. (1988). *Processing of Emotional Information in Clinical Anxiety States*. Unpublished PhD thesis, University of London.

Mogg, K., Bradley, B. P., A., Miller, T., Potts, H., Glenwright, J. & Kentish, J. (1994).

Interpretation of homophones related to threat: anxiety or response bias effects. *Cognitive Therapy & Research*, **18**, 461–477.

Mogg, K., Bradley, B. P., Millar, N. & White, J. (1995). A follow-up study of cognitive bias in generalised anxiety disorder. *Behaviour Research & Therapy*, **33**, 927–935.

Mogg, K., Bradley, B. P., Williams, R. & Mathews, A. (1993). Subliminal processing of emotional information in anxiety and depression. *Journal of Abnormal Psychology*, **102**, 304–311.

Mogg, K., Gardiner, J. M., Starron, A. & Golombok, S. (1992). Recollection experience and recognition memory for threat in clinical anxiety states. *Bulletin of the Psychonomic Society*, **30**, 109–112.

Mogg, K., Mathews, A. & Eysenck, M. W. (1992). Attentional bias to threat in clinical anxiety states. *Cognition & Emotion*, **6**, 149–159.

Mogg, K., Mathews, A. & Weinman, J. (1987). Memory bias in clinical anxiety. *Journal of Abnormal Psychology*, **96**, 94–98.

Mogg, K., Mathews, A. & Weinman, J. (1989). Selective processing of threat cues in anxiety states: a replication. *Behaviour Research and Therapy*, **27**, 317–323.

Neely, J. H. (1977). Semantic priming and retrieval from lexical memory: roles on inhibitionless spreading activation and limited capacity attention. *Journal of Experimental Psychology: General*, **106**, 226–254.

Nugent, K. & Mineka, S. (1994). The effect of high and low trait anxiety on implicit and explicit memory tasks. *Cognition & Emotion*, **8**, 147–164.

Nunn, J. D., Stevenson, R. & Whalan, G. (1984). Selective memory effects in agoraphobic patients. *British Journal of Clinical Psychology*, **23**, 195–201.

Oatley, K. & Johnson-Laird, P. (1987). Towards a cognitive theory of emotions. *Cognition & Emotion*, **1**, 29–50.

Pickles, A. J. & van den Broeck, M. D. (1988). Failure to replicate evidence for phobic schemata in agoraphobic patients. *British Journal of Clinical Psychology*, **27**, 271–272.

Rapee, R. M., McCallum, S. L., Melville, L. F., Ravenscroft H. & Rodney, J. M. (1994). Memory bias in social phobia. *Behaviour Research & Therapy*, **32**, 89–99.

Reed, G. F. (1977). Obsessional cognition: performance on two numerical tasks. *British Journal of Psychiatry*, **130**, 184–185.

Reiss, S., Peterson, R. A., Gursky, D. M. & McNally, R. J. (1986). Anxiety sensitivity, anxiety frequency and the prediction of fearfulness. *Behaviour Research & Therapy*, **24**, 1–8.

Richards, A. & French, C. C. (1991). Effects of encoding and anxiety on implicit and explicit memory performance. *Personality and Individual Differences*, **12**, 131–139.

Richards, A., French, C. C., Johnson, W., Naparstek, J. & Williams, J. (1992). Effects of emotion manipulation and anxiety on performance of an emotional Stroop task. *British Journal of Psychology*, **83**, 479–491.

Richards, A. & French, C. C. (1992). An anxiety related bias in semantic activation when processing threat/neutral homographs. *Quarterly Journal of Experimental Psychology*, **45A**, 503–525.

Riemann, B. C. & McNally, R. J. (1995). Cognitive processing of personally relevant information. *Cognition & Emotion*, **9**, 325–340.

Roediger, H. L. & Blaxton, T. A. (1987). Retrieval modes produce dissociations in memory for surface information. In D. Gorfein & R. R. Hoffman (eds), *Memory and Cognitive Processes: The Ebbinghaus Centennial Conference*. Hillsdale, NJ: Erlbaum.

Rutherford, E. M. & MacLeod, C. (submitted). Discriminating anxiety-linked emotionality effects from anxiety-linked valence effects on the colour naming interference task.

Sanz, J. (1996). Memory biases in social anxiety and depression. *Cognition & Emotions*, **10**, 87–105.

Schacter, D. L. (1987). Implicit memory: history and current status. *Journal of Experimental Psychology: Learning, Memory & Cognition*, **13**, 501–518.

Spielberger, C. D., Gorsuch, R. C., Lushene, R., Vagg, P. R. & Jacobs, G. A.

(1983). *Manual for the State-Trait Anxiety Inventory*. Palo Alto, CA: Consulting Psychologists Press.

Stroop, J. R. (1938). Factors affecting speed in serial verbal reactions. *Psychological Monographs*, **50**, 38–48.

Sutton, S. K. & Mineka, S. (submitted). Naturalistic priming of covariation bias for fear-relevant stimuli and aversive outcomes.

Tata, P., Leibowitz, J. A., Prunty, M. J., Cameron, M. & Pickering, A. D. (1996). Attentional bias in obsessional compulsive disorder. *Behaviour Research & Therapy*, **34**, 53–60.

Teasdale, J. D. & Barnard, P. J. (1993). *Affect, Cognition and Change: Re-modelling Depressive Thought*. Hillsdale, NJ: Erlbaum.

Thorpe, S. & Salkovskis, P. M. (1997). Information processing in spider phobics. *Behaviour Research & Therapy*, **35**, 131–144.

Thrasher, S. M., Dalgleish, T. & Yule, W. (1994). Information processing in post-traumatic stress disorder. *Behaviour Research & Therapy*, **32**, 247–254.

Tomarken, A. J., Cook, M. & Mineka, S. (1989). Fear-relevant selective associations and covariation bias. *Journal of Abnormal Psychology*, **98**, 381–394.

Turvey, M. (1973). On peripheral and central processes in vision: inferences from an information-processing analysis of masking with patterned stimuli. *Psychological Review*, **80**, 1–52.

van den Hout, M., Tenney, N., Huygens, K., Merckelbach, H. & Kindt, M. (1995). Responding to subliminal threat cues is related to trait anxiety and emotional vulnerability: a successful replication of MacLeod and Hagan (1992). *Behaviour Research and Therapy*, **33**, 451–454.

Volans, P. J. (1976). Styles of decision-making and probability appraisal in selected obsessional and phobic patients. *British Journal of Social & Clinical Psychology*, **15**, 305–317.

Watts, F. N. (1986). Cognitive processing in phobias. *Behavioural Psychotherapy*, **14**, 295–301.

Watts, F. N. & Dalgleish, T. (1991). Memory for phobia related words in spider phobics. *Cognition & Emotion*, **5**, 313–329.

Watts, F. N., McKenna, F. P., Sharrock, R. & Trezise, L. (1986). Colour naming of phobia related words. *British Journal of Psychology*, **77**, 97–108.

Westling, B. E. & Ost, L. G. (1995). Cognitive bias in panic disorder patients and changes after cognitive-behavioural treatments. *Behaviour Research & Therapy*, **33**, 585–588.

Williams, J. M. G., Mathews, A. & MacLeod, C. (1996). The emotional Stroop task and psychopathology. *Psychological Bulletin*, **120**, 3–24.

Williams, J. M. G., Watts, F. N., MacLeod, C. & Mathews, A. (1988). *Cognitive Psychology and the Emotional Disorders*. New York: Wiley.

Williams, J. M. G., Watts, F. N., MacLeod, C., Mathews, A. (1997). *Cognitive Psychology and the Emotional Disorders*, 2nd edn. New York: Wiley.

Winton, E. C., Clark, D. M. & Edelmann, R. (1995). Social anxiety, fear of negative evaluation and the detection of negative emotion in others. *Behaviour Research & Therapy*, **33**, 193–196.

Chapter 23

Panic and Phobias

Richard J. McNally
*Department of Psychology, Harvard University,
Cambridge, MA, USA*

Psychopathologists have used two primary approaches to study aberrant cognition in people with anxiety disorders. One approach requires patients to disclose their beliefs about fear-evoking objects on structured self-report instruments (e.g. McNally & Steketee, 1985; Thorpe & Salkovskis, 1995) and on questionnaires, such as the Anxiety Sensitivity Index (ASI; Reiss et al., 1986). Studies in this tradition rest on the assumption that people are capable of describing what they dread and why they dread it. Patients' beliefs, in turn, presumably figure in the maintenance and perhaps the etiology of their disorder.

The second approach to studying aberrant cognition entails the application of experimental psychology methods (e.g. Williams et al., 1997; McNally, 1996). These laboratory-based studies emphasize behavioral measures (e.g. reaction time) as a means of making inferences about information-processing derangements that presumably generate the signs and symptoms of anxiety disorders. Unlike self-report methods that tap propositional abnormalities (e.g. "If my heart beats too fast, I may have a heart attack"), they instead capture on-line processing abnormalities in attention, memory and so forth.

These approaches have deep roots in our field's two great traditions of psychometric and experimental psychology (Cronbach, 1957). But some psychopathologists doubt whether the first tradition is capable of providing a credible basis for a cognitive science of anxiety disorders. In a characteristically brilliant essay, MacLeod (1993) argued that self-report approaches to cognition signify a return to the discredited introspectionism that derailed psychology in the early twentieth century. Accordingly, he holds, contemporary attempts to elucidate cognitive abnormalities via self-report are doomed to repeat the mistakes of the past. MacLeod urged psychopathologists to remain rigorously experimental and to use behavioral data as the chief basis for inferring cognitive dysfunction.

Handbook of Cognition and Emotion. Edited by T. Dalgleish and M. Power.
© 1999 John Wiley & Sons Ltd.

MacLeod's (1993) arguments notwithstanding, there are at least two ways that researchers might use self-reports to study cognition, and only one is fully susceptible to the force of his critique. As MacLeod emphasizes, because information-processing mechanisms are usually inaccessible to awareness, introspection is rarely helpful as an investigative strategy. On the other hand, self-report methods are acceptable, indeed unavoidable, if one desires to characterize abnormal beliefs held by patients about their feared objects.

Moreover, even the most rigorously experimental scholars rely on self-report instruments to select their research subjects. For example, psychologists often identify individuals with high trait anxiety on the basis of self-report. Thus, although self-report is clearly inadequate for some purposes, it is essential for others.

A vast literature has emerged on the cognitive aspects of anxiety. For example, according to the computer database *PsycLit*, over 150 publications have appeared on the Anxiety Sensitivity Index *alone* as of June 1997, and research on the historically older topic of trait anxiety is far more extensive. Because comprehensive reviews are available elsewhere (e.g. Eysenck, 1992; McNally, 1994; Power & Dalgleish, 1997; Wells & Matthews, 1994), I have confined this chapter to work on panic disorder and phobias, and have primarily addressed studies in the information-processing, not self-report, tradition. My purpose is to review research on interpretive, attentional, memory and interoceptive biases favoring threat in people with these syndromes. But before doing so, I will briefly describe their clinical characteristics as summarized in the *Diagnostic and Statistical Manual of Mental Disorders* 4th edn (American Psychiatric Association, 1994).

PANIC DISORDER, SOCIAL PHOBIA, AND SPECIFIC PHOBIA

Panic attacks are unexpected surges of terror involving such symptoms as breathlessness, racing heart, dizziness, trembling and fears of dying, fainting or "going crazy". People who experience recurrent panic attacks, and who have a persistent fear of experiencing further attacks, qualify for a diagnosis of panic disorder. Individuals who experience panic attacks may begin to avoid situations in which panic would prove embarrassing or otherwise incapacitating. If behavioral avoidance becomes widespread, a diagnosis of panic disorder with agoraphobia would be warranted. Although agoraphobia was once conceptualized as an irrational fear of open or public places, most contemporary theorists consider it a fear of experiencing panic attacks in these places.

People with social phobia fear, and often avoid, situations in which they will be exposed to the scrutiny of other people (Mathews & MacLeod, 1994). More specifically, they are concerned that they will embarrass or humiliate themselves by blushing, trembling, or otherwise behaving in a socially ungraceful way. When exposed to unavoidable critical scrutiny, people with social phobia may experience symptoms akin to panic attacks.

People with specific phobia exhibit intense fear of circumscribed situations or objects. Phobias of animals, heights, enclosed places, blood-related cues and flying in airplanes are among the most common specific phobias.

Occasional panic attacks and moderately intense fears are not uncommon in the general population. Only when these symptoms become so intense as to handicap a person's ability to function in everyday life are formal diagnoses justified.

INTERPRETIVE BIAS

People routinely encounter situations whose meaning is not obvious. A tendency to interpret these ambiguous stimuli as threatening ought to increase the likelihood of a person repeatedly experiencing episodes of elevated anxiety. Researchers have tested whether patients with panic disorder and with social phobia are characterized by a bias for interpreting ambiguous stimuli as threatening. Unique among studies on information-processing abnormalities, studies addressing interpretive bias have relied on the self-reports of subjects.

Inspired by work by Butler & Mathews (1983), McNally & Foa (1987) developed a booklet comprising a series of ambiguous scenarios, involving external stimuli (e.g. "You smell smoke. What do you think is burning?") and internal stimuli (e.g. "You are having difficulty breathing. Why?"). Agoraphobic (with panic), recovered agoraphobic and healthy control subjects completed this task. The results revealed that patients with agoraphobia interpreted external as well as internal scenarios as threatening more than did either recovered agoraphobics or control subjects.

Harvey and her colleagues replicated these findings in panic patients, and observed similar, but less pronounced, biases in social phobics whose ASI scores were as high as those of their panic patients (Harvey et al., 1993). Likewise, Portuguese panic patients with varying degrees of agoraphobia exhibited biases favoring threat on a translation of Butler & Mathews's (1983) instrument (Baptista et al., 1990).

Modifying McNally & Foa's instrument, Clark et al. (1997) found that panic patients (mostly non-agoraphobic) interpreted only ambiguous scenarios concerning bodily sensations having an abrupt onset (e.g. skipped heartbeat) as threatening, but did not do so for ambiguous scenarios involving general events, social events, or bodily signs not having an abrupt onset (e.g. spot on one's hand). Panic patients were also distinguished by their strength of belief in their favored interpretations. Clark et al., moreover, demonstrated that this interpretive bias associated with internal scenarios was more pronounced in panic patients than in patients with either generalized anxiety disorder (GAD) or social phobia, a finding consistent with Clark's (1988) cognitive theory of panic.

Westling & Öst (1995) administered the Swedish version of Clark et al.'s

(1997) questionnaire to panic patients with little or no agoraphobia and to healthy control subjects. They replicated Clark et al.'s finding of a specific interpretive bias for internal but not external ambiguous stimuli, and discovered that both successful cognitive-behavioral therapy and applied relaxation treatment abolished this bias. Moreover, elimination of panic attacks was linked to the abolition of interpretive bias.

Studying interpretive bias with different methods, Stoler & McNally (1991) asked agoraphobics, recovered agoraphobics and healthy control subjects to complete a series of sentence stems with the first thought that came to mind, and then to jot down a few additional sentences elaborating on their first response. The sentence stems were either ambiguous or unambiguous, and either related or unrelated to threat. So, for example, interpretation of the stem "Knowing that entering the store would produce a sure fit, I . . ." might entail disambiguation of "fit" as referring either to clothes or to a panic attack.

The results indicated that agoraphobics exhibited biases for interpreting stems as threatening, relative to healthy control subjects, and that the interpretations of recovered agoraphobics were similar to those of symptomatic agoraphobics more than those of control subjects, suggesting that interpretive bias may persist after recovery. Although first responses to ambiguous information did not differ between recovered and symptomatic agoraphobics, the additional sentences written by recovered agoraphobics indicated a tendency to cope adaptively with threat, whereas those of the symptomatic agoraphobics did not. Perhaps cognitive-behavioral treatment furnishes patients with strategic coping skills which they apply after first automatically misinterpreting ambiguous stimuli as threatening.

In the most recent study on interpretive bias, panic/agoraphobia patients and healthy control subjects completed one questionnaire requiring them to provide interpretations of anxiety-like sensations in non-anxious contexts, and another questionnaire requiring them to interpret ambiguous internal and external scenarios (Kamieniecki, Wade & Tsourtos, 1997). The first questionnaire contained items such as:

> You water the plants and then do some physical exercises for 15 minutes. You then have a glass of cold water, rearrange some magazines on the coffee table and turn on the television. You suddenly realize that you are short of breath and your heart is beating fast (p. 144).

Subjects were given 10 seconds to provide the first interpretation that came to mind, and these were classified as either anxiety-related (e.g. impending panic), harm-related (e.g. impending heart attack) or benign (e.g. exercise-induced).

The second questionnaire contained internal scenarios such as, "You have just got out of bed in the morning and notice you are trembling and shaking" (p. 145) external scenarios were similar to McNally & Foa's (1987). Subjects were given 20 seconds to provide their first interpretation, and then to provide any other interpretations that came to mind. They also rated the subjective cost (negative valence) of their first interpretation.

Relative to control subjects, panic patients provided fewer innocuous (e.g. exercise) explanations and more anxiety-related explanations for physical sensations (but not more harm-related ones) on the first questionnaire. On the second questionnaire, 87% of the panic patients provided at least one costly anxiety-related interpretation for which they were unable to provide an alternative benign interpretation, whereas only 7% of control subjects did so. The groups did not differ in their interpretation of ambiguous external stimuli.

Taken together, these data indicate that panic disorder (and perhaps social phobia) is associated with a bias for interpreting ambiguous autonomic cues as threatening, and that successful treatment may eliminate this bias. But as MacLeod (1991) observed, such results are also consistent with a response bias explanation. Patients may entertain a range of interpretive options, some non-threatening, but affirm a catastrophic interpretation in response to implicit experimental demand. To be sure, feeling compelled to nominate catastrophic alternatives is itself a clinically significant phenomenon, but it need not signify an automatic (rapid, involuntary) interpretive processing bias. Panic researchers have yet to use MacLeod & Cohen's (1993) ingenious text comprehension procedure—a paradigm capable of discriminating interpretive biases from response biases.

ATTENTIONAL BIAS

Capacity limitations of the human information-processing system require people to attend to some stimuli and ignore others. Any bias for selectively attending to potentially threatening cues should increase the frequency of anxiety episodes. Threat detection surely has adaptive significance, but a low threshold for shifting into a defensive mode would produce unnecessary anxiety. If the cognitive system associated with pathological anxiety is excessively primed for threat detection, individuals with panic and phobic disorders ought selectively to process threat cues relative to non-threat cues and relative to people without these disorders.

Detection Paradigms

Burgess and his associates used dichotic listening procedures to study attentional biases for threat in social phobics, agoraphobics and control subjects (Burgess et al., 1981). Subjects were asked to listen to two different prose passages, one presented to each ear, to repeat aloud (shadow) one passage while ignoring the other, and to push a button whenever they heard threat (e.g. "shopping alone") and neutral (e.g. "pick") targets occurring out of context in either passage. The results indicated that both social phobic and agoraphobic patients, but not control subjects, detected more threat targets than neutral targets in the unattended passage, consistent with an attentional bias for threat.

Interference Paradigms

Detection paradigms provide data consistent with both attentional and response bias accounts (MacLeod, 1991). Hence, researchers have used interference paradigms to triangulate putative attentional biases for threat. Interference paradigms require subjects to perform a primary task while ignoring distractor stimuli that vary in valence. Attentional capture by distractor stimuli is inferred from performance decrements on the primary task.

The emotional Stroop color-naming task has been the most popular interference paradigm (Williams, Mathews & MacLeod, 1996). It requires subjects to name the colors of words varying in emotional significance while ignoring the meanings of the words. Delays in color-naming (i.e. Stroop interference) occur when the meaning of a word captures the subject's attention despite the subject's effort to attend to its color. If patients with panic or phobic disorders are characterized by an attentional bias for processing threatening information, they ought to take longer to color-name threat words than other words, and ought to take longer to do so than should people without these disorders. This hypothesis has been repeatedly confirmed for every anxiety disorder diagnostic category (Williams, Mathews & MacLeod, 1996) including spider phobia (Watts et al., 1986), social phobia (Hope et al., 1990), and panic disorder (e.g. Ehlers et al., 1988a; McNally, Riemann & Kim, 1990). Moreover, the closer a word relates to the patient's primary fears, the more often it provokes interference. Thus, panic patients exhibit more interference for physical threat words (e.g. "fatal") than for social threat words (e.g. "stupid"), whereas social phobics exhibit the opposite pattern (Hope et al., 1990). "Emotionality" *per se*, independent of valence, does not seem to account for the effect. For example, McNally et al. (1992) found that panic patients rated positive words (e.g. "cheerful") as more emotional than catastrophe words (e.g. "collapse"), but took longer to color-name the latter than the former. Moreover, McNally et al. (1994) found that even positive words 180 degrees conceptually removed from threat (e.g. "relaxed") failed to produce interference in panic patients.

New findings continue to emerge that further illuminate the boundaries of the emotional Stroop effect. Maidenberg and his colleagues had panic patients, social phobics and healthy controls color-name words related to a range of negative, positive and neutral themes (Maidenberg et al., 1996). The results revealed that panic patients exhibited significant interference for general threat words (e.g. "destructive"), social threat words (e.g. "inept"), and panic threat words (e.g. "suffocate") more than to neutral words (e.g. "ceiling"). Panic patients did not exhibit interference for general positive words (e.g. "creative"), social positive words (e.g. "praise") or panic positive words (e.g. "relaxed"). In contrast to panic patients, who exhibited interference to all threat words, social phobics exhibited interference only to social threat words. Control subjects exhibited no differential interference as a function of word type. Maidenberg et al. concluded that the fear network associated with panic disorder extends beyond concern about physical symptoms and their presumed associated catastrophes. These data only partly replicate Hope et al. (1990), who reported content-specificity effects for panic disorder as well as for social phobia.

McNeil et al. (1995) studied content specificity effects in social phobia. They found that subjects with generalized social phobia (regardless of the presence of co-morbid avoidant personality disorder) exhibited interference for general social words (e.g. "date"), negative social evaluative words (e.g. "boring"), and public speaking words (e.g. "audience"). In contrast, subjects with specific (speech) social phobia exhibited interference for only negative social evaluative words and public speaking words. McNeil et al. interpreted these experimental data as support for the nosologic distinction between generalized and specific social phobia.

Anxiety patients appear to exhibit more disorder-relevant Stroop interference when threat words appear blocked together rather than when intermixed with non-threat words. Indeed, in one study, social phobics exhibited *no* interference for social threat words when the computer presented these stimuli intermixed with other words, whereas interference did occur for social phobics who viewed the social threat words in a blocked format (Holle, Heimberg & Neely, 1997). Interestingly, apart from Maidenberg et al.'s (1996) study, experiments documenting emotional Stroop effects in social phobia have only involved blocked presentations of social threat words (Hope et al., 1990; Mattia, Heimberg & Hope, 1993; McNeil et al., 1995). Inter-item semantic priming, maximized in a blocked format, may exacerbate interference effects for threatening material.

Although Stroop interference sometimes occurs in response to words relevant to a subject's positive as well as negative current concerns (Riemann & McNally, 1995), threat-related cues usually provoke the most interference in people with anxiety disorders (Williams, Mathews & MacLeod, 1996). Based on this assumption, researchers have explored how induction of arousal or anxiety affects processing of threat cues in Stroop tasks. McNally et al. (1992) found that exercise-induced arousal did not selectively enhance interference for threat words in patients with panic disorder, and Hayward, Ahmad & Wardle (1994) found that agoraphobic patients exhibited similar degrees of threat-related interference regardless of whether patients were tested at home or in a (presumably threatening) public setting. Strikingly, though, Mathews & Sebastian (1993) reported that the presence of a snake (or a tarantula) *abolished* interference for snake-related words in snake-fearful college students. Likewise, we found that patients with social phobia exhibited reductions in Stroop interference for social threat words when informed they would soon be asked to give a speech (Amir et al., 1996a). As Mathews & Sebastian suggested, the presence of a veridical threat may shift processing priorities so that phobic individuals no longer selectively attend to verbal representations of threat on the emotional Stroop task. Chen and her associates, however, found that the presence of a spider enhanced interference for threat words in students afraid of spiders (Chen, Lewin & Craske, 1996). Taken together, it remains unclear what variables determine whether anxiety enhances (or diminishes) selective processing of threat.

Facilitation Paradigms

Attention to threat disrupts performance on interference tasks, but enhances performance on facilitation tasks. For example, on MacLeod, Mathews & Tata's (1986) dot-probe attention deployment task, selective processing of threat words speeds detection of a dot probe that replaces threat words on a computer screen. Using such a task, Asmundson & Stein (1994) found that patients with generalized social phobia responded faster to dot probes that followed social threat words than to probes that followed neutral and physical threat words. Likewise, they found that panic patients responded faster to dot probes that replaced physical threat words, but not to those that replaced social threat words (Asmundson et al., 1992). In neither of these studies, however, was there evidence of patients *shifting* attention to threat cues. Moreover, Asmundson & Stein (1994/1995) failed to replicate these effects in a new group of panic patients despite having used bodily sensation threat words (e.g. "suffocating") that should have provoked more bias than the general physical threat words they had used in their previous research (e.g. "cancer"). This finding runs counter to most studies, which have uncovered strong content-specificity effects whereby the closer the word matches the chief concerns of the diagnostic group, the stronger the selective processing effect.

Employing a similar task, Beck and her associates found that panic patients selectively attend to positive as well as physically threatening words, whereas healthy control subjects do not (Beck et al., 1992). Like Asmundson et al., Beck et al. were unable to document attention shifts to threat cues in panic patients.

MEMORY BIAS

People with panic disorder are plagued by unwanted thoughts about harm, especially during periods of physiological arousal. Thus, the phenomenology of panic implies that information about threat is notable for its ease of accessibility. To test this hypothesis, McNally, Foa & Donnell (1989) asked panic patients and healthy control subjects to rate the self-descriptiveness of adjectives related to anxiety (e.g. "nervous") and adjectives unrelated to anxiety (e.g. "polite") prior to performing either a high-arousal (i.e. exercise step-test) or a low-arousal (i.e. relaxation) task. After the arousal manipulation, subjects received a surprise free recall test which revealed that panic patients recalled more anxiety than non-anxiety words, whereas control subjects recalled more non-anxiety words than anxiety words. This bias was non-significantly ($p < 0.11$) enhanced in the high arousal condition, but only for panic patients. Further analyses confirmed that these results could not be attributed merely to a self-descriptive recall bias or to a response bias for guessing anxiety-relevant words.

Others have reported memory biases for threat in panic disorder. Relative to healthy control subjects, panic patients exhibited a free recall bias for panic-related words (e.g. "madness") but not for positive words (e.g. "sweet") or for generally negative words unrelated to panic (e.g. "murder"; Becker, Rinck & Margraf, 1994). Cloitre & Liebowitz (1991) found that panic patients disproportionately recalled panic-related threat words (e.g. "collapse") relative to positive (e.g. "pleasure") and neutral (e.g. "magazine") words. Additional analyses ruled out a possible response bias interpretation of these results. Healthy control subjects did not exhibit differential recall as a function of word type.

Using a word-pair association task, Cloitre et al. (1994) exposed panic patients, therapists who treat panic disorder, and healthy control subjects to pairs of words that were either related or unrelated, and had either negative, positive or neutral valence. For example, one related threat word-pair was breathless–suffocate, and one unrelated positive word-pair was cheerful–bureau. Subjects rated the relatedness of each word pair, and later performed a cued recall test. Panic patients recalled more threat than neutral or positive word pairs, and more neutral than positive word pairs, whereas neither control group exhibited this memory bias for threat.

Although conventional recognition memory tests do not reveal memory biases for threat in panic disorder (Beck et al., 1992; Ehlers et al., 1988a), Cloitre & Liebowitz (1991) found that panic patients exhibited superior recognition memory for threat words relative to positive and neutral words when test items appeared for very short durations (35 ms). Anxiety-congruent recognition memory biases, therefore, emerged only under degraded stimulus conditions.

Memory biases for threat in panic disorder have not always replicated (Otto et al., 1994; Rapee, 1994a). Procedural differences may explain some differences across studies. The effect appeared in one study that involved self-descriptive anxiety/threat words (e.g. "fearful"), induced physiological arousal, and free recall (McNally, Foa & Donnell, 1989), whereas it failed to emerge in another study that involved abstract threat words (e.g. "coronary"), no induced arousal, and cued recall (Otto et al. 1994). Alternatively, neuropsychological individual difference variables may modulate memory biases. Thus, Otto et al. reported that auditory perceptual asymmetries associated with relative left hemisphere activation strongly predicted cued recall for threat words in panic patients, but not in healthy control subjects. Left hemisphere biases may reflect verbal processing superiority for emotionally relevant material (i.e. threat words for panic patients) that becomes apparent during recall. Our group recently found once again that hemispheric laterality was differentially associated with memory for threat words in panic disorder and normal control groups (McNally et al., in press). Recall of threat words subjects had been told to forget was negatively and significantly associated with greater left hemisphere bias in the control group, and positively (albeit non-significantly) associated with greater left hemisphere bias in the panic group.

There is no evidence that people with either social phobia (Cloitre et al., 1995; Rapee et al., 1994) or spider phobia (Watts & Coyle, 1993) exhibit biases favoring recall of threat words. Lundh & Öst (1996), however, recently reported that social phobics exhibit a recognition memory bias favoring photographs of threatening faces.

Most studies in this area concern explicit rather than implicit memory biases. Memory is expressed explicitly by tasks such as free recall, cued recall and recognition that require subjects consciously to recollect their previous experiences. Memory is expressed implicitly when previous experiences influence performance on a task that does not require subjects to recollect these previous experiences.

Few studies have addressed whether panic and phobic patients are characterized by implicit memory biases for threatening material. Using a word-stem completion paradigm, Otto et al. (1994) did not find an implicit memory bias for threat words in panic patients. On the other hand, Cloitre et al. (1994) reported an implicit as well as explicit memory bias for threat in panic disorder when they used the word-pair association method. The exceptionally strong effect on the implicit version of this test implies that contamination by recollective strategies may have occurred.

It has now become apparent that certain implicit tasks, such as word-stem completion, often reflect perceptual rather than semantic memory (e.g. Schacter, 1992). That is, the magnitude of "priming" (i.e. implicit memory effects) can be reduced by alterations in the physical aspects of the input. For example, priming on visual word-stem completion tests often declines if subjects have heard, not seen, words on the study list. Because psychopathologists are interested in the emotional meaning of threat words, tests that mainly tap perceptual implicit memory are less relevant than those that mainly tap conceptual implicit memory.

To test for implicit memory of conceptually complex input, Amir (1996b) adapted Jacoby's "white noise" paradigm (Jacoby et al., 1988). In this study, panic patients and healthy control subjects first heard a series of threat (e.g. "The anxious woman panicked in the supermarket") and neutral (e.g. "The shiny apple sat on the table") sentences presented by a computer. Subjects later heard these old sentences intermixed with new threat and neutral sentences, each embedded in white noise that varied in volume. Subjects were asked to judge the volume of white noise accompanying each sentence. In this paradigm, implicit memory for old sentences is evinced by subjects judging the noise accompanying these sentences as less loud than the noise accompanying new sentences. An implicit memory bias for threat appears if the difference between volume judgments for new minus old sentences is greater for threat sentences than for neutral sentences. The results revealed trends for panic patients to exhibit greater priming for threat sentences than for neutral sentences, whereas control subjects tended to exhibit the opposite pattern. Whether this task taps conceptual implicit memory or whether it merely constitutes a perceptual task involving conceptually complex input remains to be determined.

INTEROCEPTIVE ACUITY BIAS

Because panic patients fear certain bodily sensations, any enhanced interoceptive acuity for detecting such sensations means that patients would have abundant opportunities for experiencing fear. Just as some people have better vision than others, so might panic patients be better than other people at detecting internal perturbations.

One early report suggested that anxiety neurotics (panic patients?) and hypo-chondriacs were better than phobic patients at estimating their heart rate (Tyrer, Lee & Alexander, 1980), whereas another study uncovered no differences be-tween agoraphobics and normal control subjects in the ability to estimate heart rate (Ehlers et al., 1988b). Unfortunately, in both studies subjects could have based their estimates on knowledge of their average heart rates. Hence, neither study tested optimally for interoceptive acuity *per se*.

In a 24-hour ambulatory monitoring study, Pauli et al. (1991) asked panic patients and normal control subjects to rate their anxiety in response to cardiac events (e.g. acceleration in heart rate). Although patients detected no more events than did control subjects, they became more anxious when they did detect them. Only patients routinely experienced further heart rate increases following detection of cardiac events; control subjects typically experienced a decrease in heart rate upon detection of a cardiac event. Pauli et al. concluded that panic patients are more afraid of these events, but are no better at detecting them, than are healthy control subjects.

Ehlers & Breuer (1992), however, did find that panic patients exhibited en-hanced interoceptive acuity in a "mental tracking" paradigm. They recorded subjects' heart rates while having them count their heartbeats during periods of 35, 25 and 45 seconds. Panic patient were more accurate than control subjects but not more accurate than patients with GAD. These data imply that both clinical groups are quite good at detecting bodily sensations, but that only the group with elevated fear of these sensations are prone to panic in response to them.

Rapee (1994b), however, found that panic patients were no better than normal control subjects at detecting increasing concentrations of carbon dioxide in in-haled air. Because carbon dioxide produces dose-related increases in a wide range of bodily sensations, Rapee questioned whether panic patients are, indeed, characterized by enhanced interoceptive acuity.

In summary, there is inconsistent evidence that panic patients are notable for a bias in the detection of internal perturbations. But since this acuity persists after recovery (Antony et al., 1994), the catastrophic meaning that patients assign to these sensations, rather than their ability to detect them, is what is probably most important in the maintenance of panic disorder.

THEORETICAL IMPLICATIONS

The core idea underlying all theories on cognitive bias in panic and phobias is that people with these disorders process information differently than do people without these disorders (e.g. Beck, Emery & Greenberg, 1985; Clark, 1988; Foa & Kozak, 1986; Williams et al., 1988). That is, the defining phenomenologic features of these syndromes themselves arise because of aberrant processes in the brain, but characterized at the informational, not neural, level of analysis. During the past 15 years, a fruitful dialectic between theory and data has unfolded. Global theories of cognitive abnormality (e.g. Beck, Emery & Greenberg, 1985; Foa & Kozak, 1986) inspired experiments designed to test for biases throughout the information-processing system, biases that presumably affected attention (e.g. Watts et al., 1986), interpretation (e.g. McNally & Foa, 1987) and memory (e.g. McNally, Foa & Donnell, 1989). Subsequent theoretical endeavors, enriched by the first generation of experiments, sharpened predictions. Thus, Williams et al. (1988) suggested that pathological anxiety states ought to be linked to attentional and interpretive biases, but not to explicit memory biases for threat.

Researchers have approached the issue of cognitive abnormality from diverse perspectives, yet data from many, perhaps most, experiments cannot readily adjudicate among competing theories; many make the same predictions. For example, memory biases for threat are equally consistent with Foa & Kozak's (1986) fear network approach and with Beck, Emery & Greenberg (1985) schema theory.

Another issue concerns whether biases map on to psychiatric diagnostic categories. Some theorists have stressed emotion-related biases while de-emphasizing nosology (Williams et al., 1988), whereas others have endeavored to elucidate biases that are strongly linked to certain syndromes. For example, Clark (1988) has argued that a specific bias involving catastrophic misinterpretation of certain bodily sensations is perhaps uniquely linked to panic disorder.

In summary, experimental cognitive research on panic and phobias has been characterized by an iterative process whereby global cognitive theories making broad predictions have begun to undergo successive theoretical sharpening as data emerge from experiments inspired by these theories. Theories that characterize where in the cognitive system dysfunctions lie are likely to become common as further experiments are conducted.

FUTURE DIRECTIONS

Research on cognitive biases associated with panic and phobic disorders has proliferated during the past 10–15 years. Many salient issues remain unresolved, however.

Automatic vs. Strategic Processing Biases

In their attempts to elucidate cognitive biases associated with pathological anxiety, psychopathologists have distinguished between automatic and strategic (also called "effortful" or "controlled") processing (Wells & Matthews, 1994; Williams et al., 1997). Convention holds that an automatic process does not require cognitive capacity (i.e. resources, effort), does not require awareness (i.e. can occur unconsciously) and does not involve volition (i.e. is involuntary or obligatory). Hence, a modal instance of automaticity is capacity-free, unconscious and involuntary (e.g. Shiffrin & Schneider, 1977). In contrast, convention holds that a strategic process requires cognitive capacity, requires conscious attention, and is amenable to voluntary control.

Interest in automaticity stems from the "ego-dystonic" phenomenology of pathological anxiety. Panic attacks and phobic fear, for example, seem involuntary, implying that their underlying mechanisms are automatic, not strategic. However, given that putative attributes of automaticity do not necessarily co-vary (Bargh, 1989), researchers must specify in what sense anxiety-linked cognitive biases are "automatic".

Certainly emotional Stroop tasks indicate that processing threat cues captures cognitive capacity in that their presence disrupts performance on the primary task of color-naming. Therefore, this attribute of automaticity does not seem to apply.

Some studies involving patients with anxiety disorders other than panic or phobias (e.g. GAD) imply that processing threat cues outside of awareness occurs (e.g. "subliminal" Stroop task; Mogg et al., 1993), whereas others do not (e.g. McNally, Amir & Lipke, 1996). Thus, at least some studies indicate that biases are automatic in the sense of operating in the absence of awareness (but see Wells & Matthews, 1994, pp. 103–106, for a critique of the "subliminal" Stroop studies).

But perhaps the attribute of automaticity most relevant to understanding anxiety disorders is that of being obligatory or involuntary (McNally, 1995). Patients seemingly cannot help but process threat cues selectively. Automaticity in the anxiety disorders, then, is chiefly a form of involuntary processing.

Do Cognitive Biases Remit Following Recovery?

Studies suggest that at least some cognitive biases may disappear following successful treatment of pathological anxiety (McNally, 1996). Data are scarce, though, and not all studies have concerned panic and phobic disorders. Successful treatment of spider phobia is associated with diminished Stroop interference for spider-related threat words (Lavy, van den Hout & Arntz, 1993; Watts et al., 1986). Social phobics who respond to either cognitive-behavioral therapy or phenelzine exhibit loss of disorder-specific Stroop interference, whereas patients who remain symptomatic do not (Mattia, Heimberg & Hope, 1993).

Most studies on patients whose panic disorder has remitted suggest that interpretive bias diminishes (Clark et al., 1997; McNally & Foa, 1987; Westling & Öst, 1995), whereas another did not (Stoler & McNally, 1991). There are no data on memory bias in recovered panic patients.

It is likely that treatment studies will increasingly include measures of cognitive bias among their outcome measures. It remains to be seen whether residual cognitive bias predicts relapse after successful treatment.

Are Cognitive Biases Risk Factors?

Research on college students with high trait anxiety strongly suggests that attentional biases precede the development of formal anxiety disorders (Eysenck, 1992; Wells & Matthews, 1994). Some theorists believe high trait anxiety may increase risk for GAD. There are no data, however, on whether people at risk for panic exhibit the information-processing biases present in people who already have panic disorder. An obvious group to study would be people who have high ASI scores but no history of panic. Indeed, confirming early predictions that elevated anxiety sensitivity in non-clinical subjects is a risk factor for panic (McNally & Lorenz, 1987), Schmidt, Lerew & Jackson (1997) found that elevated ASI scores independently predicted the subsequent occurrence of spontaneous panic attacks during basic training ("boot camp") in a cohort of over 1110 United States Air Force Academy cadets, even after they partialled out the effects of previous panic and trait anxiety. It remains to be seen whether people identified as at-risk for panic on the basis of their ASI scores also exhibit cognitive abnormalities on attention, interpretation and memory tasks.

Finally, research on children may illuminate whether cognitive biases on laboratory tasks predict the onset of subsequent anxiety disorders. Children characterized as "behaviorally inhibited" as infants tend to show Stroop interference for threat words at early adolescence (Schwartz, Snidman & Kagan, 1996). Young, spider-fearful children exhibit interference for spider related words (Martin, Horder, & Jones, 1992). Using variants of MacLeod, Mathews & Tata's (1986) dot probe paradigm, Vasey and his colleagues have reported attentional bias for threat words in test-anxious children (Vasey, Elhag & Daleiden, 1996) and in children diagnosed with a range of anxiety disorders (Vasey et al., 1995). Taken together, these studies indicate that cognitive biases appearing in adult phobics appear as well in children with similar phobias. Researchers need to determine, though, whether children merely at risk for anxiety disorders (e.g. Schwartz, Snidman & Kagan, 1996) exhibit these biases as consistently as do children who have already developed them.

ACKNOWLEDGEMENT

Preparation of this chapter was supported in part by NIMH Grant MH51927 awarded to the author.

REFERENCES

American Psychiatric Association (1994). *Diagnostic and Statistical Manual of Mental Disorders*, 4th edn. Washington, DC: American Psychiatric Association.
Amir, N., McNally, R. J., Riemann, B. C., Burns, J., Lorenz, M. & Mullen, J. T.

(1996a). Suppression of the emotional Stroop effect by increased anxiety in patients with social phobia. *Behaviour Research and Therapy*, **34**, 945–948.

Amir, N., McNally, R. J., Riemann, B. C. & Clements, C. (1996b). Implicit memory bias for threat in panic disorder: application of the "white noise" paradigm. *Behaviour Research and Therapy*, **34**, 157–162.

Antony, M. M., Meadows, E. A., Brown, T. A. & Barlow, D. H. (1994). Cardiac awareness before and after cognitive-behavioral treatment for panic disorder. *Journal of Anxiety Disorders*, **8**, 341–350.

Asmundson, G. J. G., Sandler, L. S., Wilson, K. G. & Walker, J. R. (1992). Selective attention toward physical threat in patients with panic disorder. *Journal of Anxiety Disorders*, **6**, 295–303.

Asmundson, G. J. G. & Stein, M. B. (1994). Selective processing of social threat in patients with generalized social phobia: evaluation using a dot-probe paradigm. *Journal of Anxiety Disorders*, **8**, 107–117.

Asmundson, G. J. G. & Stein, M. B. (1994/1995). Dot-probe evaluation of cognitive processing biases in patients with panic disorder: A failure to replicate and extend. *Anxiety*, **1**, 123–128.

Baptista, A., Figueira, M. L., Lima, M. L. & Matos, F. (1990). Bias in judgment in panic disorder patients. *Acta Psiquiátrica Portuguesa*, **36**, 25–35.

Bargh, J. A. (1989). Conditional automaticity: varieties of automatic influence in social perception and cognition. In J. S. Uleman & J. A. Bargh (eds), *Unintended Thought*. New York: Guilford, pp. 3–51.

Beck, A. T., Emery, G. & Greenberg, R. L. (1985). *Anxiety Disorders and Phobias*. New York: Basic Books.

Beck, J. G., Stanley, M. A., Averill, P. M., Baldwin, L. E. & Deagle, E. A. III (1992). Attention and memory for threat in panic disorder. *Behaviour Research and Therapy*, **30**, 619–629.

Becker, E., Rinck, M. & Margraf, J. (1994). Memory bias in panic disorder. *Journal of Abnormal Psychology*, **103**, 396–399.

Burgess, I. S., Jones, L. M., Robertson, S. A., Radcliffe, W. N. & Emerson, E. (1981). The degree of control exerted by phobic and non-phobic verbal stimuli over the recognition behaviour of phobic and non-phobic subjects. *Behaviour Research and Therapy*, **19**, 233–243.

Butler, G. & Mathews, A. (1983). Cognitive processes in anxiety. *Advances in Behaviour Research and Therapy*, **5**, 51–62.

Chen, E., Lewin, M. R. & Craske, M. G. (1996). Effects of state anxiety on selective processing of threatening information. *Cognition and Emotion*, **10**, 225–240.

Clark, D. M. (1988). A cognitive model of panic attacks. In S. Rachman & J. D. Maser (eds), *Panic: Psychological Perspectives*. Hillsdale, NJ: Erlbaum, pp. 71–89.

Clark, D. M., Salkovskis, P. M., Öst, L.-G., Breitholz, E., Koehler, K. A., Westling, B. E., Jeavons, A. & Gelder, M. (1997). Misinterpretation of body sensations in panic disorder. *Journal of Consulting and Clinical Psychology*, **65**, 203–213.

Cloitre, M., Cancienne, J., Heimberg, R. G., Holt, C. S. & Liebowitz, M. (1995). Memory bias does not generalize across anxiety disorders. *Behaviour Research and Therapy*, **33**, 305–307.

Cloitre, M. & Liebowitz, M. R. (1991). Memory bias in panic disorder: an investigation of the cognitive avoidance hypothesis. *Cognitive Therapy and Research*, **15**, 371–386.

Cloitre, M., Shear, M. K., Cancienne, J. & Zeitlin, S. B. (1994). Implicit and explicit memory for catastrophic associations to bodily sensation words in panic disorder. *Cognitive Therapy and Research*, **18**, 225–240.

Cronbach, L. J. (1957). The two disciplines of scientific psychology. *American Psychologist*, **12**, 671–684.

de Ruiter, C. & Brosschot, J. F. (1994). The emotional Stroop interference effect in anxiety: attentional bias or cognitive avoidance? *Behaviour Research and Therapy*, **32**, 315–319.

Ehlers, A. & Breuer, P. (1992).   Increased cardiac awareness in panic disorder. *Journal of Abnormal Psychology*, **101**, 371–382.

Ehlers, A., Margraf, J., Davies, S. & Roth, W. T. (1988a).   Selective processing of threat cues in subjects with panic attacks. *Cognition and Emotion*, **2**, 201–219.

Ehlers, A., Margraf, J., Roth, W. T., Taylor, C. B. & Birbaumer, N. (1988b).   Anxiety induced by false heart rate feedback in patients with panic disorder. *Behaviour Research and Therapy*, **26**, 1–11.

Eysenck, M. W. (1992).   *Anxiety: The Cognitive Perspective*. Hillsdale, NJ: Erlbaum.

Foa, E. B. & Kozak, M. J. (1986).   Emotional processing of fear: exposure to corrective information. *Psychological Bulletin*, **99**, 20–35.

Harvey, J. M., Richards, J. C., Dziadosz, T. & Swindell, A. (1993).   Misinterpretation of ambiguous stimuli in panic disorder. *Cognitive Therapy and Research*, **17**, 235–248.

Hayward, P., Ahmad, T. & Wardle, J. (1994).   Into the dangerous world: an *in vivo* study of information processing in agoraphobics. *British Journal of Clinical Psychology*, **33**, 307–315.

Holle, C., Heimberg, R. G. & Neely, J. H. (1997).   The effects of blocked versus random presentation and semantic relatedness of stimulus words on response to a modified Stroop task among social phobics. *Cognitive Therapy and Research*, **21**, 681–697.

Hope, D. A., Rapee, R. M., Heimberg, R. G. & Dombeck, M. J. (1990).   Representations of the self in social phobia: Vulnerability to social threat. *Cognitive Therapy and Research*, **14**, 177–189.

Jacoby, L. L., Allan, L. G., Collins, J. C. & Larwill, L. K. (1988).   Memory influences subjective experience: noise judgments. *Journal of Experimental Psychology: Learning, Memory, and Cognition*, **14**, 240–247.

Kamieniecki, G. W., Wade, T. & Tsourtos, G. (1997).   Interpretive bias for benign sensations in panic disorder and agoraphobia. *Journal of Anxiety Disorders*, **11**, 141–156.

Lavy, E., van den Hout, M. & Arntz, A. (1993).   Attentional bias and spider phobia: conceptual and clinical issues. *Behaviour Research and Therapy*, **31**, 17–24.

Lundh, L.-G. & Öst, L.-G. (1996).   Recognition bias for critical faces in social phobics. *Behaviour Research and Therapy*, **34**, 787–794.

MacLeod, C. (1991).   Clinical anxiety and the selective encoding of threatening information. *International Review of Psychiatry*, **3**, 279–292.

MacLeod, C. (1993).   Cognition in clinical psychology: measures, methods or models? *Behaviour Change*, **10**, 169–195.

MacLeod, C. & Cohen, I. L. (1993).   Anxiety and the interpretation of ambiguity: a text comprehension study. *Journal of Abnormal Psychology*, **102**, 238–247.

MacLeod, C., Mathews, A. & Tata, P. (1986).   Attentional bias in emotional disorders. *Journal of Abnormal Psychology*, **95**, 15–20.

Maidenberg, E., Chen, E., Craske, M., Bohn, P. & Bystritsky, A. (1996).   Specificity of attentional bias in panic disorder and social phobia. *Journal of Anxiety Disorders*, **10**, 529–541.

Martin, M., Horder, P. & Jones, G. V. (1992).   Integral bias in the naming of phobia-related words. *Cognition and Emotion*, **6**, 479–486.

Mathews, A. & MacLeod, C. (1994).   Cognitive approaches to emotion and emotional disorders. *Annual Review of Psychology*, **45**, 25–50.

Mathews, A. & Sebastian, S. (1993).   Suppression of emotional Stroop effects by fear-arousal. *Cognition and Emotion*, **7**, 517–530.

Mattia, J. I., Heimberg, R. G. & Hope, D. A. (1993).   The revised Stroop color-naming task in social phobics. *Behaviour Research and Therapy*, **31**, 305–313.

McNally, R. J. (1994).   *Panic Disorder: A Critical Analysis*. New York: Guilford.

McNally, R. J. (1995). Automaticity and the anxiety disorders. *Behaviour Research and Therapy*, **33**, 747–754.

McNally, R. J. (1996). Cognitive bias in the anxiety disorders. *Nebraska Symposium on Motivation*, **43**, 211–250.

McNally, R. J., Amir, N. & Lipke, H. J. (1996). Subliminal processing of threat cues in posttraumatic stress disorder? *Journal of Anxiety Disorders*, **10**, 115–128.

McNally, R. J., Amir, N., Louro, C. E., Lukach, B. M., Riemann, B. C. & Calamari, J. E. (1994). Cognitive processing of idiographic emotional information in panic disorder. *Behaviour Research and Therapy*, **32**, 119–122.

McNally, R. J. & Foa, E. B. (1987). Cognition and agoraphobia: Bias in the interpretation of threat. *Cognitive Therapy and Research*, **11**, 567–581.

McNally, R. J., Foa, E. B. & Donnell, C. D. (1989). Memory bias for anxiety information in patients with panic disorder. *Cognition and Emotion*, **3**, 27–44.

McNally, R. J. & Lorenz, M. (1987). Anxiety sensitivity in agoraphobics. *Journal of Behavior Therapy and Experimental Psychiatry*, **18**, 3–11.

McNally, R. J., Otto, M. W., Yap, L., Pollack, M. H. & Hornig, C. D. (in press). Is panic disorder linked to cognitive avoidance of threatening information? *Journal of Anxiety Disorders*.

McNally, R. J., Riemann, B. C. & Kim, E. (1990). Selective processing of threat cues in panic disorder. *Behaviour Research and Therapy*, **28**, 407–412.

McNally, R. J., Riemann, B. C., Louro, C. E., Lukach, B. M. & Kim, E. (1992). Cognitive processing of emotional information in panic disorder. *Behaviour Research and Therapy*, **30**, 143–149.

McNally, R. J. & Steketee, G. S. (1985). The etiology and maintenance of severe animal phobias. *Behaviour Research and Therapy*, **23**, 431–435.

McNeil, D. W., Ries, B. J., Taylor, L. J., Boone, M. L., Carter, L. E., Turk, C. L. & Lewin, M. R. (1995). Comparison of social phobia subtypes using Stroop tests. *Journal of Anxiety Disorders*, **9**, 47–57.

Mogg, K., Bradley, B. P., Williams, R. & Mathews, A. (1993). Subliminal processing of emotional information in anxiety and depression. *Journal of Abnormal Psychology*, **102**, 304–311.

Otto, M. W., McNally, R. J., Pollack, M. H., Chen, E. & Rosenbaum, J. F. (1994). Hemispheric laterality and memory bias for threat in anxiety disorders. *Journal of Abnormal Psychology*, **103**, 828–831.

Pauli, P., Marquardt, C., Hartl, L., Nutzinger, D. O., Holzl, R. & Strian, F. (1991). Anxiety induced by cardiac perceptions in patients with panic attacks: a field study. *Behaviour Research and Therapy*, **29**, 137–145.

Power, M. & Dalgleish, T. (1997). *Cognition and Emotion: From Order to Disorder*. Hove: Psychology Press.

Rapee, R. M. (1994a). Failure to replicate a memory bias in panic disorder. *Journal of Anxiety Disorders*, **8**, 291–300.

Rapee, R. M. (1994b). Detection of somatic sensations in panic disorder. *Behaviour Research and Therapy*, **32**, 825–831.

Rapee, R. M., McCallum, S. L., Melville, L. F., Ravenscroft, H. & Rodney, J. M. (1994). Memory bias in social phobia. *Behaviour Research and Therapy*, **32**, 89–99.

Reiss, S., Peterson, R. A., Gursky, D. M. & McNally, R. J. (1986). Anxiety sensitivity, anxiety frequency and the prediction of fearfulness. *Behaviour Research and Therapy*, **14**, 1–8.

Riemann, B. C. & McNally, R. J. (1995). Cognitive processing of personally relevant information. *Cognition and Emotion*, **9**, 325–340.

Schacter, D. L. (1992). Understanding implicit memory: a cognitive neuroscience approach. *American Psychologist*, **47**, 559–569.

Schmidt, N. B., Lerew, D. R. & Jackson, R. L. (1997). The role of anxiety sensitivity in the pathogenesis of panic: prospective evaluation of spontaneous panic attacks during acute stress. *Journal of Abnormal Psychology*, **106**, 355–364.

Schwartz, C. E., Snidman, N. & Kagan, J. (1996). Early temperamental predictors of Stroop interference to threatening information at adolescence. *Journal of Anxiety Disorders*, **10**, 89–96.

Shiffrin, R. M. & Schneider, W. (1977). Controlled and automatic human information processing: II. Perceptual learning, automatic attending, and a general theory. *Psychological Review*, **84**, 127–190.

Stoler, L. S. & McNally, R. J. (1991). Cognitive bias in symptomatic and recovered agoraphobics. *Behaviour Research and Therapy*, **29**, 539–545.

Thorpe, S. J. & Salkovskis, P. M. (1995). Phobic beliefs: Do cognitive factors play a role in specific phobias? *Behaviour Research and Therapy*, **33**, 805–816.

Tyrer, P. J., Lee, I. & Alexander, J. (1980). Awareness of cardiac function in anxious, phobic and hypochondriacal patients. *Psychological Medicine*, **10**, 171–174.

Vasey, M. W., Daleiden, E. L., Williams, L. L. & Brown, L. M. (1995). Biased attention in childhood anxiety disorders: a preliminary study. *Journal of Abnormal Child Psychology*, **23**, 267–279.

Vasey, M. W., Elhag, N. & Daleiden, E. L. (1996). Anxiety and the processing of emotionally-threatening stimuli: distinctive patterns of selective attention among high- and low-test-anxious children. *Child Development*, **67**, 1173–1185.

Watts, F. N. & Coyle, K. (1993). Phobics show poor recall of anxiety words. *British Journal of Medical Psychology*, **66**, 373–382.

Watts, F. N., McKenna, F. P., Sharrock, R. & Trezise, L. (1986). Colour naming of phobia-related words. *British Journal of Psychology*, **77**, 97–108.

Wells, A. & Matthews, G. (1994). *Attention and Emotion: A Clinical Perspective*. Hove: Erlbaum.

Westling, B. E. & Öst, L.-G. (1995). Cognitive bias in panic disorder patients and changes after cognitive-behavioral treatments. *Behaviour Research and Therapy*, **33**, 585–588.

Williams, J. M. G., Mathews, A. & MacLeod, C. (1996). The emotional Stroop task and psychopathology. *Psychological Bulletin*, **120**, 3–24.

Williams, J. M. G., Watts, F. N., MacLeod, C. & Mathews, A. (1988). *Cognitive Psychology and the Emotional Disorders*. Chichester: Wiley.

Williams, J. M. G., Watts, F. N., MacLeod, C. & Mathews, A. (1997). *Cognitive Psychology and the Emotional Disorders*, 2nd edn. Chichester: Wiley.

Chapter 24

Sadness and Its Disorders

Mick J. Power
*University of Edinburgh, Royal Edinburgh Hospital,
Edinburgh, UK*

INTRODUCTION

> Crying, fear and anger are so common as to be virtually ubiquitous and most
> cultures provide social sanction for the expression of these emotions in the funeral
> rites and customs of mourning which follow bereavement. In this respect, Western
> cultures, which tend to discourage the overt expression of emotion at funerals, are
> highly deviant. They differ from most other societies and from our own society as it
> was a hundred years ago (Parkes, Laungani & Young, 1997, p. 5).

The more extreme variants of sadness, such as grief, bereavement and mourning,
or disorders derived from sadness, such as depression, have been widely studied
in psychology, although the milder everyday variants have received little attention (cf. Stearns, 1993). Power & Dalgleish (1997) have suggested that the focus
on the extreme and the abnormal may perhaps represent something of our
cultural problems with sadness and its expression. It must be noted, though, that
much of what we think about as sadness should more correctly be viewed as
sadness combined with other basic emotions, such as fear, anger or disgust,
because of the fact that sadness seems to be the basic emotion that most readily
combines with the other basic emotions (Oatley & Duncan, 1992). For example,
a common procedure used to study "sadness" in the laboratory is to use a mood
induction procedure such as the Velten card technique (Velten, 1968), in which
the subject reads through a list of statements along the lines of "I'm worthless",
"I'm a failure" and so on. Such lists encourage a state of self-criticism which is not
a defining feature of sadness, although it is a defining feature of the more complex
state of depression. The experience of "pure" sadness without such self-criticism
is phenomenologically very distinct from depression; for example, when the

Handbook of Cognition and Emotion. Edited by T. Dalgleish and M. Power.
© 1999 John Wiley & Sons Ltd.

lovers part at the end of David Lean's film *Brief Encounter*, never again to meet, we are left with tears streaming down our faces, but only for a minute or so until we move on to our next activity. Much mood induction work, therefore, may have studied sadness in complex states in conjunction with other cognitive and emotional factors rather than sadness itself.

A second point that we must note is that sadness, like many other so-called "negative" emotions, is not necessarily negative; thus, even though we associate sadness with predominantly negative phenomenological states, we watch films such as *Brief Encounter* because they are effective at making us feel sad. It will also be argued later, when combinations of basic emotions are considered, that sadness and the "opposite" emotion of happiness can combine together in complex emotional states such as nostalgia, in which the person may feel sad at the memory of a previous time of happiness.

In order to define sadness a number of important features must be considered, which we have previously identified as the key external or internal event, an interpretation, an appraisal, a physiological state, an action potential, conscious awareness and overt behaviour (Power & Dalgleish, 1997). These points are elaborated below.

1. There is an appraisal of loss or failure, in which the lost object or goal varies in degree of importance and type; it could be a person, a place, an ambition that has not been attained, an object of personal value (e.g. a special pen, an important gift), or a loss of an ideal or moral value. The focus of sadness is therefore on the appraisal of loss of one or more goals across one or more domains.

2. The loss need not be permanent, but could be a temporary separation from a loved one or a loved place or even a sadness experienced at the return to a loved one or a loved place following a period of separation. We would disagree, therefore, with analyses of loss that suggest that the loss needs to be permanent or irrevocable (e.g. Lazarus, 1991; Oatley & Johnson-Laird, 1987).

3. The focus of the loss may be on a significant other rather than oneself, for example, one's child failing an examination or being ill or injured. Indeed, the loss may be communal rather than personal, as in the loss of a Head of State, a favourite film star, or failure by one's National team in the World Cup.

4. The temporal frame of the loss may vary from past to present to future. One may reminisce and feel sad about the loss of childhood or of schooldays, just as one may feel sad about a current loss. However, the loss could be an imagined one that has not yet happened, as in the imagined future loss of one's parents or, indeed, it might never happen except in a dream or a daydream. Some of the most poignant experiences of basic emotions may be in dream states during which complex cognitive appraisals may be absent, although this possibility remains to be tested.

5. The phenomenological experience of sadness thereby differs considerably both in intensity and in duration according to these and other factors. Sad-

ness can be mild and last a few seconds, as in the mention of an emotion-laden name during conversation; it can last minutes when the hero dies at the end of a novel; it can last hours because of breaking a favourite ornament; and, in some senses, it can last a lifetime because of the loss of a significant other such as a partner or child.

In relation to the key question that has to be addressed to all of the emotions, we must ask what might be the functions of sadness and what are its adaptive features? In many cultures sadness is not considered to be inherently negative, because sadness, or states akin to sadness, are highly valued (e.g. Kleinman & Good, 1985; Lutz, 1985); for example, a state of sad reflectiveness may be considered a step along the road to salvation in many Asian societies. As Stearns (1993) emphasizes, the variation across cultures in the approach to sadness reflects a culture's view of the perceived lack of self-mastery, and the perceived "demands" that may thereby be placed on others in the social network as a consequence of sadness. Both lack of self-mastery and demandingness on others are viewed negatively in those cultures which emphasize individuality rather than collectivity and activity rather than passivity. In Western cultures, when a soccer player such as Paul Gascoigne sheds tears in public, he becomes headline news. One important social function of sadness, therefore, is that it may lead the individual to make emotional and practical demands on others; it can thereby strengthen social bonds and lead to altruism in which others feel sympathy or pity (Izard, 1993).

In addition to its social functions, sadness also serves a more personal function, although this may be over-emphasized in our culture because of the emphasis on the active individual. This personal function is the increase in self-focus that may occur in sadness; in such a state of self-focused sadness the individual may review priorities given to important goals and roles in the light of an experienced loss or the possibility of such loss. Such reviews may enable individuals to alter the balance of their lives, for example, to reassess the overvaluing of one goal, such as work, at the expense of others, such as personal relationships (Champion & Power, 1995). Following an irrevocable loss such as that of a partner, the implications for shared goals and plans may be so all-encompassing that the individual may take a considerable length of time to realize the extent of the loss and its implications for future events, such as holidays or the first Christmas without that person, and so on.

SADNESS: SOME THEORETICAL CONSIDERATIONS

Following the outline general model presented in Power & Dalgleish (1997) of the so-called SPAARS (Schematic Propositional Associative Analogical Representation Systems) approach to emotion (see also Teasdale, Chapter 31, for additional discussion of the SPAARS model), the application of the model to sadness will now be briefly considered. The focus will initially be on all forms of sadness, but in subsequent sections we will briefly examine how the model applies to the extreme forms of sadness seen in grief, and to the sadness-based disorder of depression.

Three of the key points that were proposed in Power & Dalgleish (1997) were: (a) that basic emotions have the potential to develop in a modular fashion; (b) that multiple levels of meaning must be considered, especially in relation to important roles and goals across the domains of self, world and other; and (c) that we must take account of the considerable range of inhibitory and facilitatory processes that occur both within and between different levels of processing. The application of some of these points is presented in Figure 24.1, which takes as its starting point an appraisal of loss or the potential for loss. As the Figure shows, the generation of sadness can occur either as a function of the appraisal (schematic model) route or the automatic (associative) route. For example, sadness might be generated by the automatic route because of an innate aspect of sadness linked to the loss of any key attachment figure (see later), or because of an automated sequence in which, for example, a particular place becomes associated with the emotion of sadness. It is likely that low-level automatic activation of emotion modules occurs continually throughout both our waking and our sleeping lives, the large part of which goes unnoticed except perhaps in research on videotaping and psychophysiological recording of emotional responses.

A second level of possible initial activation of the emotion module is through the propositional level of input, although, as we have noted elsewhere (Power & Dalgleish, 1997), propositional input could lead to the generation of emotion through either the appraisal or the automatic route. Many of the so-called "aesthetic" emotions are likely to be experienced through this level because they are encoded in propositional form; the novel, play or film causes some transient experience of sadness in us because of its propositional content, which may then be coded into a schematic model.

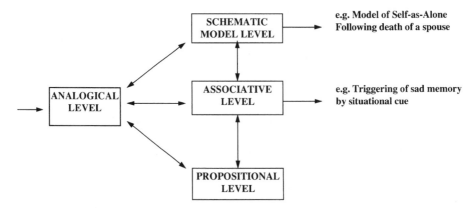

Figure 24.1 The generation of sadness via two different routes within the SPAARS approach

A third level of activation occurs at the schematic model level. At this level a whole variety of sources of information, both external and internal to the individual, may be combined into a holistic representation; thus, a schematic model associated with sadness could incorporate propositional material, body-state input and mnemonic material, none of which in themselves might be sufficient to activate a schematic model associated with sadness. For example, as the widow sits back in her armchair to watch her favourite television programme, she might suddenly be reminded of how her husband too used to sit in that particular armchair; even though the memory in itself might be a happy one, she might nevertheless feel sad *because* it was something that was in the past.

Following the initial activation of the sadness module, a range of possible facilitatory or inhibitory processes may then come into effect. The activated module includes physiological change, the biasing of processing at different levels within the system, and a potential for action associated with sadness. Figure 24.2 presents examples of possible facilitatory effects within a module.

A series of positive feedback loops may maintain and even enhance the activation of the sadness module; thus, stored representations at the associative level may trigger off sadness-related propositions which, in turn, can serve to

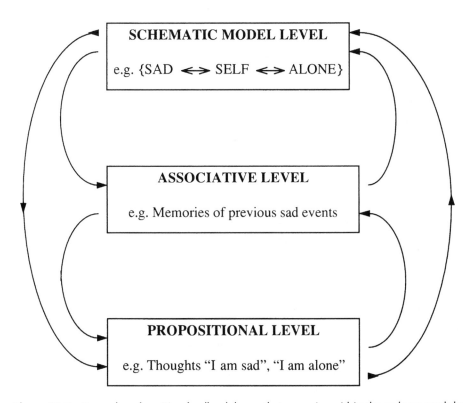

Figure 24.2 Examples of positive feedback loops that can arise within the sadness module

maintain the activation of the schematic model of being in a state of sadness. In fact, as will be presented subsequently, one of the problems with extreme grief reactions and severe forms of depression is that the individual feels unable to shift to a different state or to a different emotion; these positive feedback loops can maintain the activation of the module for months or even years under certain conditions.

In normal individuals, mild activation of the sadness module is typically very transient; thus, in mood induction studies subjects may begin to recall mood-incongruent happy memories and generate positive self-related propositions in order to inhibit the unwanted mood and replace it with a more positive one (e.g. Isen, 1984; Parrott & Sabini, 1990). Under normal circumstances individuals may use a variety of strategies that operate at one or more levels. These strategies can operate at an associative level, such as recalling something pleasant; at the propositional level by having positive thoughts about oneself; or at the schematic level by generating a different emotional self-model (see Figure 24.2). Of course, in practice an effective strategy will operate at all levels, for example, a pleasant memory may generate a series of positive propositions, and include the recollection of the self with a different schematic model.

In some individuals the inhibitory processes may be so strong that there is considerable difficulty in experiencing an emotion such as sadness, even when it is appropriate to do so and even though an appropriate physiological state for the emotion may be present. One such group are so-called repressors, who may recall little if anything negative from their past, endorse few negative trait adjectives, and show poor retention of self-related negative material (e.g. Myers, Brewin & Power, 1992).

Although we have focused on facilitatory and inhibitory processes occurring primarily *within* the sadness module, it is also important to consider facilitatory and inhibitory processes that can occur *between* emotion modules: herein may lie the royal road to emotional disorder, therefore, it will provide a key focus for the remainder of this chapter. We turn next, therefore, to a consideration of how sadness may interact with other basic emotions.

COMBINATIONS OF SADNESS AND OTHER BASIC EMOTIONS

One of the possibilities suggested previously (Power & Dalgleish, 1997) was that two or more basic emotions could, under certain circumstances, continuously activate each other. This "coupling" between emotion modules can be considered to work in a similar way to the within-module activation that was outlined earlier. The proposal does, of course, run counter to a number of emotion theories such as that of Oatley & Johnson-Laird (1987), in which it is argued that even complex emotions are derived from only one basic underlying emotion. We hope, however, to demonstrate that there is much to be gained from taking a different line; namely, that the coupling of two or more basic emotions may lock the individual into a complex emotional state from which it may be difficult to escape.

The fact that even under normal circumstances sadness can readily be experienced together with other basic emotions is illustrated by the examples presented in Figure 24.3. By "experienced together" we literally mean simultaneously, rather than in succession. All emotion theorists acknowledge that one emotion can be replaced by a succession of others as circumstances or appraisals change; for example, the student who feels disappointed at getting a lower mark than hoped for on a test may subsequently feel overjoyed on finding out that she actually came top of the class. The first example in Figure 24.3 shows a combination of Sadness and Disgust and an example under which such a combination might occur; namely, someone feeling self-disgust following the break-up of a relationship. Such a combination may be central to the experience of depression, so we will return to the pairing of Sadness and Disgust in the subsequent section on depression. The second example is that of the combination of Sadness and Anger, a pairing that used to be thought pathological in the experience of bereavement, but which, from the work of Bowlby (e.g. 1980) and others, is now known to be a common experience in both children and adults following temporary or permanent breaks in attachment relationships. The third example is that of Sadness and Anxiety which, again, may be a common combination following a loss in which the individual feels depleted of resources and therefore fears for his/her capacity to deal with future demands. The final combination, that of Sadness and Happiness, is probably best known to us in forms such as nostalgia, homesickness and love-sickness, and at the end of Hollywood movies. In addition to our own anecdotal experience of combined basic emotions, there is empirical evidence of the types of combinations that may occur. Keith Oatley has carried

	EXAMPLE
SADNESS - DISGUST	He left me because I am such an awful person.
SADNESS - ANGER	Why did he leave me, the ******?!
SADNESS - ANXIETY	How will I cope now that he's gone?
SADNESS - HAPPINESS	Oh, how I miss the good times we had.

Figure 24.3 Examples of phrases in which sadness is combined with other basic emotions

out a number of diary studies in which individuals were asked to make detailed recordings of emotions that they experienced over a number of days (Oatley & Duncan, 1992). Despite having claimed in earlier theoretical work cited above that basic emotions cannot be combined, Oatley & Duncan reported that more than a third of everyday experiences of the basic emotions of fear, anger, sadness and love were found to be simultaneously accompanied by the experience of one of the other basic emotions. In fact, sadness was found to be the emotion that was most likely to occur in combination, providing 77% of all such examples. Furthermore, where emotions were found to change over the course of an incident, the commonest change was found to occur between sadness and anger (with 33% of such changes being accounted for by this pairing). The predilection for sadness to combine with other basic emotions may provide some clue as to why conditions such as grief and depression can be so long-standing.

It seems, therefore, that the combination or coupling of basic emotions is a common everyday experience and that sadness is more likely than any of the other basic emotions to be involved in such coupling. We will proceed to examine, therefore, two particularly insidious combinations, those of Sadness–Anger and Sadness–Disgust which, we suggest, may underlie atypical grief reactions and some forms of depression, respectively. Before doing so, however, we must emphasize that because combinations of basic emotions occur so readily within the bounds of normal experience, we reiterate that our approach emphasizes that the emotional disorders are extreme variants of normal experience rather than being qualitatively different.

Grief

In this section we will examine an extreme variant of sadness that most people will experience at some time, that is, grief. The importance of sadness and grief, both in childhood and adulthood, can probably best be understood in terms of attachment theory (e.g. Bowlby, 1988), although it must be noted that recent work has broadened this focus to emphasize more general aspects of stress and coping (e.g. Stroebe, Stroebe & Hansson, 1993). One of the key innate systems is that of attachment to the primary caretaker, threats to which are experienced with considerable distress by the child. There is good evidence that problems can develop early on in attachment style and that these problems may be associated with later psychopathology; thus, so-called anxious attachment and avoidant attachment styles may be associated with a range of later adult attachment problems. We can certainly predict that longitudinal studies from early childhood onwards of attachment style and adult studies with the so-called adult attachment interview (e.g. Main, 1991) should increase our understanding of a range of problems, including both normal and abnormal reactions to grief.

In an attempt to understand both the lengthy nature of the normal grief reaction and the even lengthier nature of abnormal reactions, studies of children's separations from their primary caretakers provide considerable information. Bowlby's (1980) excellent summary of this work showed that the child initially goes through stages of protest and despair because of the separation, but, eventually, if the mother (or other primary caretaker) returns, the child may treat her as if she were a stranger. In contrast, a non-primary caretaker (perhaps the father) may be greeted with warmth and relief over the same length of separation. Bowlby's interpretation of these different reactions is that the child reacts to the separation or loss of the mother eventually by "defensively excluding" or inhibiting the negative emotions. Even with very short separations of a few minutes studied in the laboratory, for example with the Strange Situation Test (Ainsworth et al., 1978), a proportion of children as young as 12 months show ambivalent positive and negative reactions to the mother's return.

A second related area from work with children focuses not so much on whether children *express* ambivalent feelings, but on whether they can *conceptualize* such ambivalence. Harter (1977) observed that many children she saw clinically were unable to admit to ambivalent feelings towards primary caretakers. In her subsequent work with normal children, she found that only at about 10 years of age can children acknowledge and describe ambivalent feelings (Harter & Buddin, 1987).

The conclusion that we draw from these findings and our previous proposals (Power & Dalgleish, 1997) is that the loss of the main attachment figure, whether in childhood or adulthood, leads to not only the emotion of sadness, but frequently also to anger at that person for abandoning the individual to an uncertain fate. The expression and conceptualization of such ambivalence requires a developmentally sophisticated level of maturity that many individuals fail to achieve; thus, the individual may feel sadness following such a loss, but feel extreme guilt about feelings of anger, or, psychologically, go one step further and idealize the lost person so that no feelings of anger could even be imaginable towards such a perfect individual. In addition, the combination of pressures on an individual in Western and other cultures to inhibit the expression of both sadness and anger following loss may all lead to the result that grief runs an atypical course.

The experience of extreme grief consequent on the loss of an attachment figure can be seen as the major loss of mutual goals, roles and plans that the loss of attachment figures entails. Because of the evolutionary base to attachment, the universal experience of grief across cultures must in part have an innate basis and must, therefore, involve operation of an automatic or direct access route to emotion. However, the impact of the loss of a significant other is so wide-ranging on the individual's life that multiple and continued appraisals will accompany any automatic reactions. For example, studies of the impact of bereavement in our culture show that the nature of the impact and its consequences may differ for widows and widowers; Wortman, Silver & Kessler (1993) reported that widowers were particularly vulnerable to limited social relationships and problems with taking on tasks that their wives had handled, whereas widows were more vulnerable to financial strain following the death of their husbands. The net effect of these and other problems is that bereaved individuals may make appraisals that they will be unable to cope with the practical and emotional burden that they have been left with. In addition, if the bereaved appraise the grief reaction itself as weak or not allowed, because of a more general rejection of negative emotions, then a more atypical course may be likely for grief.

This atypical course may be more likely to occur, we would speculate, if the coupling of the basic emotions of sadness and anger occurs, as shown in Figure 24.4, given that many grief reactions have, in addition to the primary emotion of sadness, other appraisals that lead to anger (see Power & Dalgleish, 1997). The anger may be directed at the lost individuals themselves, be directed at others who caused the loss or did not offer enough to prevent the loss; anger is more likely to occur where deaths are sudden and unexpected (e.g. Vargas, Loye & Hodde-Vargas, 1989) and may thereby explain in part why sudden, untimely or unexpected deaths may lead to more chronic or difficult grief reactions. Once such couplings of activated basic emotions occur, they may reciprocally activate each other and thereby prolong the emotional state. In the case of grief, however, we must also emphasize the internal and external pressures to inhibit not only the expression of sadness, but especially the expression of anger towards the lost

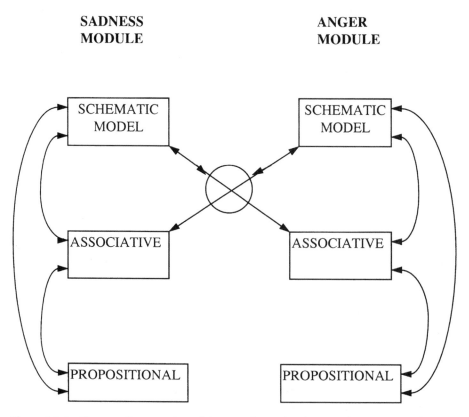

Figure 24.4   The coupling together of the emotions of sadness and anger in grief

individual. The greater the attempts to inhibit one or both of the emotions of sadness and anger involved in grief, therefore, the longer the course that the grief reaction will run. The loss of the main attachment figure, whether in childhood or in adulthood, involves nothing less than a redefinition of the self; an individual who prevents, whether consciously or unconsciously, such a process from occurring, who attempts to deny the loss of the key other, will be left with a model of the self that is maladaptive, inaccurate and out-of-date.

In conclusion, grief is a powerful and universal reaction to the loss of attachment figures in particular. The experience of loss leads to overwhelming sadness and, in addition, a myriad of accompanying appraisals that revolve around the loss of mutual goals, roles and plans, together with bereaved individuals' appraisals of whether or not they will be able to cope without the lost person. Theorists such as Bowlby (e.g. 1980) who have proposed that the grief reaction follows a series of stages have also emphasized the angry protests that the bereaved individual typically goes through. Although recent theorists present more flexible models with, for example, the possibility that stages overlap (e.g. Shuchter & Zisook, 1993), nevertheless anger is a very frequent accompaniment of grief. We have speculated, therefore, that, in terms of the SPAARS model (Power & Dalgleish, 1997), the duration and outcome of grief will depend on whether basic emotions such as sadness and anger become coupled together and thereby sustain each other. In order to explore speculations such as these, it will be necessary to consider pre-existing characteristics of individuals and their typical styles of coping with emotion. It will also be necessary for bereavement researchers to distinguish more carefully between bereavement and depression, rather than treat one as if it might be the same as the other. As Clayton (1990) reported, bereavement depressions show lower levels of hopelessness, worthlessness and loss of interest in friendships, which would be expected if the basic emotion of disgust (in the form of self-disgust) is an essential part of depression, but not of bereavement. Moreover, Clayton's comparison of a group of recently bereaved individuals and a group of matched community controls showed near-identical levels of worthlessness, with 14% in the bereaved and 15% in the controls, even though the overall rates of "depression" were 47% for the bereaved vs. 8% for controls. We will examine these differences in more detail in the next section.

Depression

One of the most widespread emotional disorders that is based in part on the basic emotion of sadness is that of depression. Although other chapters in this *Handbook* deal in more detail with depression and accompanying cognitive biases (see e.g. Chapters 10, 12 and 14), it will be briefly discussed here because of the significant role of sadness and the appraisal of loss in its onset and maintenance.

The epidemiology of depression provides such a puzzling picture that almost any simple model can be eliminated by one or other of the statistics. One of the most cited and replicated findings is that there is a 2 : 1 ratio of women to men who experience the disorder (e.g. Weissman & Klerman, 1977), a ratio that holds for both clinical samples and untreated community cases (Cochrane, 1983). However, any simplistic biological explanation can be discounted by the fact that the ratio differs significantly according to marital status; thus the rates for *single* men and women are about the same, whereas the rates for married women are highest and those for married men lowest (Champion, 1992). Additional problems are that, first, prior to mid-adolescence there is more depression in boys than in girls with upwards of twice as many boys as girls being treated for depression (Harrington, 1993); that the rates of depression appear to be increasing in younger as compared to older age groups, especially for men, and that the rates for depression appear to even out for older adults (Nolen-Hoeksema, 1990). In addition, cross-cultural studies further demonstrate that the 2 : 1 ratio is not obtained consistently either between or within cultures; for example, Jenkins, Kleinman & Good (1991) reported a number of studies that have found higher rates of depression for women in cultures where the female role is devalued, but significantly lower rates amongst women in the same culture who reject the traditional roles.

There are now a considerable number of cognitive and social models of depression, so to make matters easy a brief overview will be provided of the Champion & Power (1995) model which attempts to integrate many of the other models. The key points from the Champion & Power (1995) model of depression are presented in Figure 24.5. Along with a number of social and social–cognitive accounts of depression, one of the key components of the model relates to the roles and goals that are available to the individual. Unlike purely social accounts, however (e.g. Becker, 1964; Thoits, 1986), the theory focuses on the perceived value of roles and goals and not simply their availability or mere existence. It is proposed that vulnerable individuals typically over-invest in one role or goal, but under-invest in, and do not value, other areas of their lives. Lam & Power (1991) reported supporting evidence for this proposal using the Roles and Goals questionnaire, which was in part designed to test the model. They found, as predicted, that the proposed pattern of over- and under-investment was more typical of depressed than non-depressed adult and elderly community samples. The studies were, however, cross-sectional, so it was unclear whether the pattern was a cause or a consequence of depression. Lam et al. (1994; 1996) have more recently reported evidence in a longitudinal study of depressed outpatients that the further occurrence of negative events in the most invested domain delays recovery from depression or increases the likelihood of relapse in someone who has already recovered.

A second component of the model presented in Figure 24.5 is highlighted in the contrast between vulnerable and non-vulnerable individuals and concerns the self-protective function that the over-valued role or goal provides. The proposal is that, while the over-valued role or goal is being successfully pursued, the vulnerable individual may stave off self-negativity (cf. Bentall & Kinderman's discussion of paranoia and mania in Chapter 18). However, if the role or goal is

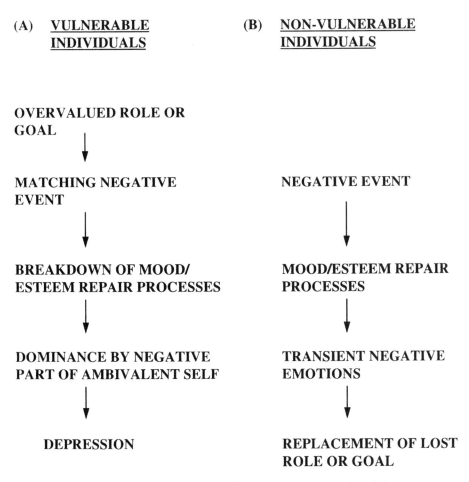

(A) VULNERABLE   (B) NON-VULNERABLE
    INDIVIDUALS   **INDIVIDUALS**

**OVERVALUED ROLE OR
GOAL**

**MATCHING NEGATIVE   NEGATIVE EVENT
EVENT**

**BREAKDOWN OF MOOD/   MOOD/ESTEEM REPAIR
ESTEEM REPAIR PROCESSES   PROCESSES**

**DOMINANCE BY NEGATIVE   TRANSIENT NEGATIVE
PART OF AMBIVALENT SELF   EMOTIONS**

**DEPRESSION   REPLACEMENT OF LOST
                            ROLE OR GOAL**

Figure 24.5 The Champion & Power (1995) social–cognitive model of depression

threatened or subsequently lost, the consequent combination of sadness and self-negativity (primarily, that is, the predominance of self-disgust) will lead to depression. Although, as highlighted in Figure 24.5, non-vulnerable individuals also experience a range of emotions at the loss of important roles and goals (see the earlier section on grief), such individuals are less likely to experience self-disgust or self-negativity and are more likely to replace the lost role or goal from a range of other valued roles and goals.

There are two further points that we should make about the loss of a valued role or goal. First, the loss may of course occur late in life: the individual may have pursued a highly successful career or have been involved in a long and satisfying relationship, before tragedy in one form or another strikes. Indeed, the very fortunate though vulnerable individual may skate on thin ice for a lifetime and be lucky enough to escape depression. Nevertheless, there is a substantial amount of first onset depression in later life (Murphy, 1982), which can come as a particular shock to an individual who may have taken pride in a belief in his/her emotional strength.

The second point that we would like to make is that the apparent "loss" of a role or goal can also occur because of its successful completion (e.g. Champion, 1992) in addition to the more commonplace meaning of loss that we have used until now. The philosopher John Stuart Mill reported in his autobiography (1853) on an episode of depression that occurred when he was already in a low mood, but he then imagined the following:

> In the frame of mind it occurred to me to put the question directly to myself, "Suppose that all your objects in life were realized; that all the changes in institutions and opinions which you are looking forward to, could be completely effected at this very instant: would this be a great joy and happiness to you?" And an irrepressible self-consciousness distinctly answered, "No"! At this my heart sank within me: the whole foundation on which my life was constructed fell down.

In Mill's case, therefore, merely imagining the successful completion of his goals and plans was sufficient to lead to a severe episode of depression. Although the evidence for so-called "success depression" is primarily anecdotal and clinical and its existence has been disputed on theoretical grounds by behavioural theorists (Eastman, 1976), one area deserving of further research is that of the "Golden Boy" and "Golden Girl" syndrome identified by Seligman (1975) in his classic book on learned helplessness. Seligman's proposal was that so-called "Golden Boys" and "Golden Girls" had experienced non-contingent *positive* reinforcement throughout their lives, because their parents had indulged them completely, but without ever requiring anything of them. When they then entered the "real world", however, they were unable to cope with the fact that rewards were no longer non-contingent but, instead, were very much contingent on their own actions, and as a consequence became depressed. An alternative interpretation is suggested by Lorna Champion's proposals about the importance of life-stage transitions in relation to roles and goals (Champion, Goodall & Rutter, 1995; Champion & Power, 1995; Maughan & Champion, 1990); namely, that the transition from adored-child-cum-adolescent may require the individual to relinquish the role in which they starred and, hence, require them to abandon the role that gave them most satisfaction. Many such individuals may, therefore, attempt to delay the transition rather than face up to it, rather like Hilde Bruch's *Golden Cage* (1978) interpretation of anorexia as an attempt to prevent or delay the onset of maturity and adulthood. To return, though, to the possibility of "success depression", this proposal, therefore, runs counter to any straightforward cognitive account of emotion which equates happiness with the achievement of goals and sadness with their loss (e.g. Oatley & Johnson-Laird, 1987); occasionally, the reverse may be true or there may be both joy and sadness at goal completion.

The attempt to "eliminate" emotions and needs that are labelled as "weak" and as "negative" is a common feature of depression and other emotional disorders, as revealed, for example, by the endorsement of such attitudes on the "Self-Control" subscale of the 24-item Dysfunctional Attitude Scale (Power et al., 1994). The expression of disgust by significant others, therefore, towards aspects of the child's self, needs and expression of emotion seems a crucial area for research in relation to disorder. Indeed, in extremely vulnerable adults such expression by significant others has been shown to lead to relapse in both depression and in schizophrenia; thus, in the work on expressed emotion (EE), Vaughn & Leff (1976) originally reported that the occurrence of "critical comments" by significant others greatly increased the chance of relapse in both depression and in schizophrenia. Although most of the subsequent work has focused on schizophrenia (e.g. Lam, 1991), the important point is that many of the critical comments are expressions of disgust by a significant other directed at the vulnerable person.

On a more general level it should also be noted that a positive self that is unfettered by negativity is as pathological as a negative self unfettered by positivity. Such extreme positive selves may, for example, be seen in some manic conditions in which the self can become grandiose, powerful and invulnerable. Although there is a psychoanalytic clinical tradition (e.g. Lewin, 1951) and some empirical data (Winters & Neale, 1985) that such states are a "manic defence" against depression, the argument here is that, sure, the positive state inhibits the negative state, but the obverse is also true in that the negative state can inhibit the positive state. Both the positive and the negative states have "validity", therefore, but they inhibit the expression of the other state because they are unintegrated and work antagonistically, rather than the positive state being simply a defence against the "true" state of depression. Power (1987) proposed that the overall self-concept in depression might best be described as "self-ambivalent", with a split between positive and negative aspects of the self. Under appropriate circumstances or in certain moods or emotional states, therefore, either the positive or the negative side of the self may dominate. More recently, Showers (e.g. Showers & Kling, 1996) has developed an empirical method for testing what she has labelled "compartmentalized" vs. "integrative" self-organization and has found interesting supportive evidence for a compartmentalized or self-ambivalent structure in individuals prone to more intense negative emotions.

In contrast to grief, therefore, which we derived from the basic emotions of sadness and anger, Power & Dalgleish (1997) argue that depression may be derivable primarily from the basic emotions of sadness and disgust. This proposal offers an alternative to that for example suggested by Freud in *Mourning and Melancholia* (1917/1984), in which mourning was derived from sadness whereas depression was derived from sadness in conjunction with anger that was turned against the self. The key rejection of Freud's proposal for retroflective anger occurred in Bibring's (1953) classic ego psychoanalytic reanalysis of depression, a paper that anticipated all of the major cognitive approaches to the disorder. Nevertheless, our proposal does hold some similarities to Freud's in that we emphasize self-condemnation, guilt and shame as defining characteristics of depression, the crucial difference being that we derive them from the basic emotion of disgust rather than from anger. We would also point out that since Bibring's paper, most cognitive models have focused on the role of low self-esteem in depression; thus, in both Beck's (1976) cognitive therapy and in Abramson, Seligman & Teasdale's (1978) learned helplessness reformulation, the self is seen as culpable for negative events, and is considered to be shameful, worthless, failed or bad. All of these aspects of the self can be derived from the turning of the basic emotion of disgust against the self, such that aspects of the self are seen as bad and have to be eliminated or rejected from the self.

The key coupling of the basic emotions of sadness and disgust that we argue is the basis of some presentations of depression is shown in Figure 24.6. So why have we given disgust such a central role? For this choice we offer a number of reasons, some of which are more speculative than others, although we accept that the overall proposal requires direct empirical testing. Nevertheless, we are persuaded by ideas from a number of different areas that the role of disgust has largely been unrecognized in the development of emotional and other disorders (Power & Dalgleish, 1997).

In support of the proposal we should note, first, that the basic emotions of

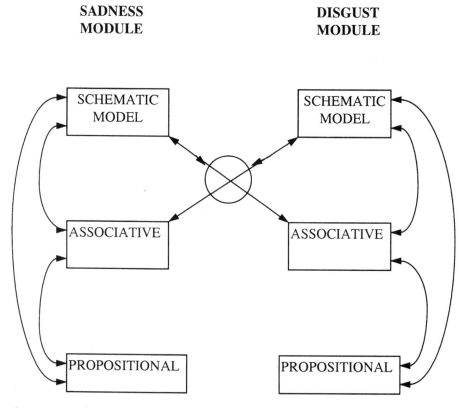

Figure 24.6 The coupling together of the emotions of sadness and disgust in depression

sadness, disgust and happiness appear within the first 3 months of infancy, with sadness appearing, for example, at the withdrawal of positive stimuli, disgust in relation to unpleasant foodstuffs, and happiness, for example, in reaction to familiar faces (e.g. Fischer, Shaver & Carnochan, 1990; Lewis, 1993). As Fischer, Shaver & Carnochan (1990) argue, the early appearance of the basic emotions in the first year of life indicate that they provide important guiding principles around which development is organized, in particular, the development of the self and interpersonal relationships. However, it is a mistake to focus on disgust primarily as a reaction to food or excrement in the way that some analyses of the term suggest (e.g. Rozin & Fallon, 1987). Disgust is used by significant others to socialize the developing child in a range of permissible expressions and activities, not simply those related to food and the contents of nappies.

Our final line of argument is a definitional one, although it also draws on the phenomenology of depression. It is clear that the phenomenological "taste" of dysphoric mood or of depression is not one of sadness, although sadness is there as a component. Nor, as we have argued above, is it anxiety that adds the missing ingredient. The additional ingredient is in fact a loathing of the self. We suggest, therefore, that the core phenomenological state in depression is a combination of sadness and self-disgust.

COGNITIVE BIASES AND DEPRESSION

The question of cognitive biases and distortions has long held interest in the study of depression with, for example, the emphasis on logical distortions and irrational beliefs in the early work of Beck (e.g. 1976) and of Ellis (e.g. 1962). However, as Haaga, Dyck & Ernst (1991) have pointed out, the terms "bias" and "distortion" were not distinguished in this early work, and it has only been recently that care has been taken with this distinction. A bias is a proclivity to take one direction over another which, under some conditions, will lead to accuracy or realism, but under other conditions will lead to inaccuracy or distortion (see Power, 1991). In contrast, distortion is invariably wrong. For example, if a group of depressed and a group of normal individuals are given a set of positive and negative adjectives to recall, then the depressed are typically found to recall more negative adjectives and the normal controls more positive adjectives (e.g. Derry & Kuiper, 1981). Neither group is *distorting* reality, but, rather, the depressed group are showing a negative bias and the normal group a positive bias: they are presenting different views of the *same* reality in what has been called a "Rashomon effect", in reference to Akira Kurosawa's film masterpiece in which four witnesses recount contrasting views of the same event, a murder in a forest. The debate between proponents of the so-called "depressive realism" position vs. cognitive therapy's proposed "depressive distortion" view has been an artificial one in which oranges have been compared with apples: both positions are "true", but under appropriate conditions. Nevertheless, even if it is now accepted that emotional disorders such as depression and anxiety are associated with cognitive biases rather than distortions, the question remains of the extent of such biases. For example, the network theories of Bower and the schema theories of Beck lead to predictions for pervasive biases in a range of cognitive processes in emotional disorders which, unfortunately for the theories, have not been supported; thus, in their summary of the evidence, Williams et al. (1988; 1997) argued that the biases most apparent in anxiety were those concerned with automatic preattentive processes, whereas those most apparent in depression were controlled mnemonic processes. Again, we argue that these discrepant theories may have approached the problem of bias from the wrong angle: that whether or not bias is evident in a pre-attentive, mnemonic or other cognitive process depends in part on the content, and the appraised relevance of that content, as we have outlined elsewhere (Power & Dalgleish, 1997).

A further key problem that has arisen with the cognitive bias approach is whether observed cognitive biases are merely state-dependent consequences of depression or whether they are vulnerability factors that are causal antecedents in the development of depression. As with many national economies, this area has been through a number of boom-and-bust cycles. Much of the initial work focused on global self-report measures such as of dysfunctional attitudes, automatic thoughts and hopelessness. Typical findings showed that depressed individuals scored significantly higher than normal controls on these measures. Unfortunately, subsequent studies which followed up depressed individuals until they were fully recovered showed that levels of global self-reported attitudes and automatic thoughts return to those shown by normal controls. Such findings have led some (e.g. Coyne & Gotlib, 1983) to question the whole basis of the cognitive approach, but they have led others (e.g. Power, 1987; Williams et al., 1988) to call for the use of more sophisticated measures of cognitive vulnerability that can assess automatic as well as controlled processes. The results that have been obtained so far from this enterprise suggest a more complex view of vulnerability than the results from the self-report measures would suggest. Because there a number of relevant chapters elsewhere in this *Handbook* (see Chapters 9, 10, 12 and 14), this evidence will not be reviewed again in this chapter. Instead, some further issues will be raised.

GENERAL COMMENTS ON BIAS RESEARCH

The findings from studies of cognitive biases in depressed and normal moods show that there are a number of effects. Perhaps the strongest evidence for bias in depression comes from work on explicit memory including word-list and autobiographical memory tasks (see Chapter 10). These studies, however, emphasize that the clearest biases are obtained in the processing of self-related negative material rather than *any* negative material. The fact that findings for biases in implicit memory tasks have been less consistent probably indicates that the mechanisms involved in such biases are more poorly understood, in particular, in the way in which mood and other factors combine. This problem also seems to be have been evident in studies of attentional biases in depression, where there is evidence both for and against bias. Again, it must be emphasized that factors such as the personal relevance of the materials have not been properly considered in many of the studies. The problem also arises of whether evidence of a positive bias in normals and of apparent "even-handedness" in depressed individuals should be interpreted as evidence for depressive realism or for depressive negative bias. As we argued above, under certain circumstances biases lead to accurate or realistic responses; thus, conclusions of even-handedness in depression and positive bias in normal individuals should, in our view, be seen as evidence for a negative bias in depression. This recommendation applies not only to the contingency judgement studies of Alloy, Abramson and colleagues (e.g. Alloy & Abramson, 1979; Vazquez, 1987), but also to studies of attentional bias (e.g. Gotlib, McLachlan & Katz, 1988).

FURTHER COMMENTS AND CONCLUSIONS

In relation to the more general SPAARS theory presented by Power & Dalgleish (1997), we suggest that in depression-prone individuals there is a preoccupation with an over-invested role or goal. A major threat to or loss of this dominant role or goal leads the individual to focus on the aspects of the self-concept that are normally rejected and the lost role or goal that was central to self-worth (Champion & Power, 1995). This preoccupation with the lost role or goal leads to working memory resources being allocated primarily to working through the loss and, therefore, an apparent emphasis on the past. The individual may, therefore, allocate fewer resources to non-goal-relevant tasks, in part because of reduced capacity (Hasher & Zacks, 1988; Ellis & Ashbrook, 1988), but also because of the depressed individual's proclivity to under-value non-goal relevant tasks or information; this combination leads to an appearance of reduced initiative for allocating resources to other tasks (Hertel & Hardin, 1990) as well as reduced working memory capacity.

One of the more interesting predictions from our proposal about the modularization of basic emotions in depression-prone individuals concerns the processing of self-related positive material in recovered depressives. Following, for example, our demonstration of priming effects for positive material in depression (Power et al., 1996), our prediction would be that recovered depressives should under some conditions be "too positive" and, might, for example, find it more difficult to moderate a positive mood, under conditions in which such a mood would interfere with a cognitively demanding task; thus, normal individuals may use mood-incongruent recall under such conditions in order to modify positive distractions (Erber & Erber, 1994). If, however, there is a failure of integration of positive and negative aspects of the self in depression, then during recovery, when the positive aspects of the self predominate, there should be less regulation of the positive state because negative aspects of the self may be unavailable or excluded at such time. At their most extreme, such uncontrollable positive mood states are, as we have noted, present in mania and hypomania.

Finally, we reiterate that the emotional disorders related to sadness often run a long and complicated course. These disorders, in particular grief and depression, reflect the fact that sadness is a response to the failure of our most important goals and our most cherished relationships. In addition, these losses leave the vulnerable individual prone to feelings of anger or self-disgust which, we suggest, may prolong grief and depression when they become coupled with sadness.

REFERENCES

Abramson, L. Y., Seligman, M. E. P. & Teasdale, J. D. (1978).   Learned helplessness in humans: critique and reformulation. *Journal of Abnormal Psychology*, **87**, 49–74.
Ainsworth, M. D. S., Blehar, M. C., Waters, E. & Wall, S. (1978).   *Patterns of Attachment: A Psychological Study of the Strange Situation*. Hillsdale, NJ: Erlbaum.
Alloy, L. B. & Abramson, L. Y. (1979).   Judgment of contingency in depressed and nondepressed students: sadder but wiser? *Journal of Experimental Psychology: General*, **108**, 441–485.
Beck, A. T. (1976).   *Cognitive Therapy and the Emotional Disorders*. New York: Meridian.
Becker, E. (1964).   *The Revolution in Psychiatry*. New York: Free Press.
Bibring, E. (1953).   The mechanism of depression. In P. Greenacre (ed.), *Affective Disorders*. New York: International Universities Press.
Bowlby, J. (1980).   *Attachment and Loss: Vol. 3, Sadness and Depression*. London: Hogarth.
Bowlby, J. (1988).   *A Secure Base: Clinical Applications of Attachment Theory*. London: Routledge.
Bruch, H. (1978).   *The Golden Cage: The Enigma of Anorexia Nervosa*. Shepton Mallet: Open Books.
Champion, L. A. (1992).   Depression. In L. A. Champion & M. J. Power (eds), *Adult Psychological Problems: An Introduction*. London: Falmer.
Champion, L. A., Goodall, G. & Rutter, M. (1995).   Behavioural problems in childhood and stressors in early adult life: I. A 20 year follow-up of London school children. *Psychological Medicine*, **25**, 231–246.
Champion, L. A. & Power, M. J. (1995).   Social and cognitive approaches to depression: towards a new synthesis. *British Journal of Clinical Psychology*, **34**, 485–503.
Clayton, P. J. (1990).   Bereavement and depression. *Journal of Clinical Psychiatry*, **51**(suppl.), 34–40.
Cochrane, R. (1983).   *Social Creation of Mental Illness*. London: Longman.
Coyne, J. C. & Gotlib, I. H. (1983).   The role of cognition in depression: a critical appraisal. *Psychological Bulletin*, **94**, 472–505.
Derry, P. A. & Kuiper, N. A. (1981).   Schematic processing and self-reference in clinical depression. *Journal of Abnormal Psychology*, **90**, 286–297.
Eastman, C. (1976).   Behavioural formulations of depression. *Psychological Review*, **83**, 277–291.
Ellis, A. (1962).   *Reason and Emotion in Psychotherapy*. New York: Lyle Stuart.
Ellis, H. C. & Ashbrook, P. W. (1988).   Resource allocation model of the effects of depressed mood states on memory. In K. Fiedler & J. Forgas (eds), *Affect, Cognition, and Social Behavior*. Toronto: Hogrefe.

Erber, R. & Erber, M. W. (1994). Beyond mood and social judgment: Mood incongruent recall and mood regulation. *European Journal of Social Psychology*, **24**, 79–88.

Fischer, K. W., Shaver, P. R. & Carnochan, P. (1990). How emotions develop and how they organise development. *Cognition and Emotion*, **4**, 81–127.

Freud, S. (1917/1984). *Mourning and Melancholia*. Pelican Freud Library, Vol. 11. Harmondsworth: Penguin.

Gotlib, I. H., MacLachlan, A. L. & Katz, A. N. (1988). Biases in visual attention in depressed and nondepressed individuals. *Cognition and Emotion*, **2**, 185–200.

Haaga, D. A. F., Dyck, M. J. & Ernst, D. (1991). Empirical status of cognitive therapy of depression. *Psychological Bulletin*, **110**, 215–236.

Harrington, R. (1993). *Depressive Disorder in Childhood and Adolescence*. Chichester: Wiley.

Harter, S. (1977). A cognitive-developmental approach to children's expression of conflicting feelings and a technique to facilitate such expression in play therapy. *Journal of Consulting and Clinical Psychology*, **45**, 417–432.

Harter, S. & Buddin, B. (1987). Children's understanding of the simultaneity of two emotions: a five-stage developmental acquisition sequence. *Developmental Psychology*, **23**, 388–399.

Hasher, L. & Zacks, R. T. (1988). Working memory, comprehension, and aging: a review and a new view. In G. H. Bower (ed.), *The Psychology of Learning and Motivation: Advances in Research and Theory*, Vol. 22. New York: Academic Press.

Hertel, P. T. & Hardin, T. S. (1990). Remembering with and without awareness in a depressed mood; evidence of deficits in initiative. *Journal of Experimental Psychology: General*, **119**, 45–59.

Isen, A. M. (1984). Toward understanding the role of affect in cognition. In R. Wyer & T. Srull (eds), *Handbook of Social Cognition*, Vol. 3. Hillsdale, NJ: Erlbaum.

Izard, C. E. (1993). Four systems for emotion activation: cognitive and noncognitive processes. *Psychological Review*, **99**, 561–565.

Jenkins, J. H., Kleinman, A. & Good, B. J. (1991). Cross-cultural studies of depression. In J. Becker & A. Kleinman (eds.), *Psychosocial Aspects of Depression*. Hillsdale, NJ: Erlbaum.

Kleinman, A. & Good, B. (eds) (1985). *Culture and Depression: Studies in the Anthropology and Cross-cultural Psychiatry of Affect and Disorder*. Berkeley: University of California Press.

Lam, D. H. (1991). Psychosocial family interventions in schizophrenia: review of empirical studies. *Psychological Medicine*, **21**, 423–441.

Lam, D. H. & Power, M. J. (1991). A questionnaire designed to assess role and goals: a preliminary study. *British Journal of Medical Psychology*, **64**, 359–373.

Lam, D. H., Green, B., Power, M. J. & Checkley, S. (1994). The impact of social cognitive variables on the initial level of depression and recovery. *Journal of Affective Disorders*, **32**, 75–83.

Lam, D. H., Green, B., Power, M. J. & Checkley, S. (1996). Dependency, matching adversities, length of survival and relapse in major depression. *Journal of Affective Disorders*, **37**, 81–90.

Lazarus, R. S. (1991). *Emotion and Adaptation*. New York: Oxford University Press.

Lewin, B. D. (1951). *The Psychoanalysis of Elation*. London: Hogarth.

Lewis, M. (1993). The emergence of human emotions. In M. Lewis & J. M. Haviland (eds), *Handbook of Emotions*. New York: Guilford.

Lutz, C. A. (1985). Ethnopsychology compared to what? Explaining behavior and consciousness among the Ifaluk. In G. White & J. T. Kirkpatrick (eds), *Person, Self, and Experience: Exploring Pacific Ethnopsychologies*. Berkeley, CA: University of California Press.

Main, M. (1991). Metacognitive knowledge, metacognitive monitoring, and singular (coherent) vs. multiple (incoherent) model of attachment: findings and directions for future research. In C. M. Parkes, J. Stevenson-Hinde & P. Marris (eds), *Attachment Across the Life Cycle*. London: Routledge.

Maughan, B. & Champion, L. A. (1990). Risk and protective factors in the transition to young adulthood. In P. B. Baltes & M. M. Baltes (eds), *Successful Aging: Perspectives from the Behavioral Sciences*. Cambridge: Cambridge University Press.

Mill, J. S. (1853/1991). Autobiography. In R. Porter (ed.) (1991), *The Faber Book of Madness*. London: Faber and Faber (1991).

Murphy, E. (1982). Social origins of depression in old age. *British Journal of Psychiatry*, **141**, 135–142.

Myers, L. B., Brewin, C. R. & Power, M. J. (1992). Repression and autobiographical memory. In M. A. Conway, D. C. Rubin, H. Spinnler & W. A. Wagenaar (eds), *Theoretical Perspectives on Autobiographical Memory*. Dordrecht: Kluwer.

Nolen-Hoeksema, S. (1990). *Sex Differences in Depression*. Stanford: Stanford University Press.

Oatley, K. & Duncan, E. (1992). Incidents of emotion in daily life. In K. T. Strongman (ed.), *International Review of Studies on Emotion*, Vol. 2. Chichester: Wiley.

Oatley, K. & Johnson-Laird, P. N. (1987). Towards a cognitive theory of emotions. *Cognition and Emotion*, **1**, 29–50.

Parkes, C. M., Laungani, P. & Young, B. (1997). *Death and Bereavement Across Cultures*. London: Routledge.

Parrott, W. G. & Sabini, J. (1990). Mood and memory under natural conditions: evidence for mood incongruent recall. *Journal of Personality and Social Psychology*, **59**, 321–336.

Power, M. J. (1987). Cognitive theories of depression. In H. J. Eysenck & I. Martin (eds), *Theoretical Foundations of Behaviour Therapy*. New York: Plenum.

Power, M. J. (1991). Cognitive science and behavioural psychotherapy: where behaviour was, there shall cognition be? *Behavioural Psychotherapy*, **19**, 20–41.

Power, M. J., Cameron, C. M. & Dalgleish, T. (1996). Emotional priming in clinically depressed subjects. *Journal of Affective Disorders*, **38**, 1–11.

Power, M. J. & Dalgleish, T. (1997). *Cognition and Emotion: From Order to Disorder*. Hove: Psychology Press (Erlbaum, UK).

Power, M. J., Katz, R., McGuffin, P., Duggan, C. F., Lam, D. & Beck, A. T. (1994). The Dysfunctional Attitude Scale (DAS): a comparison of forms A and B and proposals for a new subscaled version. *Journal of Research in Personality*, **28**, 263–276.

Rozin, P. & Fallon, A. E. (1987). A perspective on disgust. *Psychological Review*, **94**, 23–41.

Seligman, M. E. P. (1975). *Helplessness: On Depression, Development and Death*. San Francisco, CA: Freeman.

Showers, C. J. & Kling, K. C. (1996). Organization of self-knowledge: implications for recovery from sad mood. *Journal of Personality and Social Psychology*, **70**, 578–590.

Shuchter, S. R. & Zisook, S. (1993). The course of normal grief. In M. S. Stroebe, W. Stroebe & R. O. Hansson (eds), *Handbook of Bereavement: Theory, Research, and Intervention*. Cambridge: Cambridge University Press.

Stearns, C. S. (1993). Sadness. In M. Lewis & J. M. Haviland (eds), *Handbook of Emotions*. New York: Guilford.

Stroebe, M. S., Stroebe, W. & Hansson, R. O. (1993). Bereavement research and theory: an introduction to the handbook. In M. S. Stroebe, W. Stroebe & R. O. Hansson (eds), *Handbook of Bereavement: Theory, Research, and Intervention*. Cambridge: Cambridge University Press.

Thoits, P. A. (1986). Multiple identities: examining gender and marital status differences in distress. *American Sociological Review*, **51**, 259–272.

Vargas, L. A., Loye, F. & Hodde-Vargas, J. (1989). Exploring the multidimensional aspects of grief reactions. *American Journal of Psychiatry*, **146**, 1484–1488.

Vaughn, C. E. & Leff, J. P. (1976). The influence of family and social factors on the course of psychiatric illness: a comparison of schizophrenic and depressed neurotic patients. *British Journal of Psychiatry*, **129**, 125–137.

Vazquez, C. (1987). Judgement of contingency: cognitive biases in depressed and nondepressed subjects. *Journal of Personality and Social Psychology*, **52**, 419–431.

Velten, E. (1968). A laboratory task for induction of mood states. *Behaviour Research and Therapy*, **6**, 473–482.

Weissman, M. M. & Klerman, G. L. (1977). Sex difference and the epidemiology of depression. *Archives of General Psychiatry*, **34**, 98–111.

Williams, J. M. G., Watts, F. N., MacLeod, C. & Mathews, A. (1988). *Cognitive Psychology and Emotional Disorders*. Chichester: Wiley.

Williams, J. M. G., Watts, F. N., MacLeod, C. & Mathews, A. (1997). *Cognitive Psychology and Emotional Disorders*, 2nd edn. Chichester: Wiley.

Winters, K. C. & Neale, J. M. (1985). Mania and low self-esteem. *Journal of Abnormal Psychology*, **94**, 282–290.

Wortman, C. B., Silver, R. C. & Kessler, R. C. (1993). The meaning of loss and adjustment to bereavement. In M. S. Stroebe, W. Stroebe & R. O. Hansson (eds), *Handbook of Bereavement: Theory, Research, and Intervention*. Cambridge: Cambridge University Press.

Chapter 25

Positive Affect

Alice M. Isen
Cornell University, Ithaca, NY, USA

INTRODUCTION

A growing body of research indicates that mild positive affect (happy feelings), induced in subtle, common ways that can occur frequently in everyday life, has a marked influence on a broad range of social behavior and thought processes. This work has shown that an event such as unexpectedly finding a coin in the return-slot of a public telephone, seeing a few minutes of a comedy film, receiving a small gift (valued at only a few cents), or learning that one has performed well on a seemingly inconsequential task, is sufficient to bring about significant changes in behavior and thinking.

Not only are social phenomena such as interpersonal interaction and social categorization influenced, but several aspects of cognitive processing itself, including memory, learning, problem solving and creativity and flexibility in thinking, just to name a few, are also affected significantly by simple happy feelings. In addition, more complex processes, based on these fundamental cognitive processes, such as categorization, decision making, risk assessment, creative problem solving and preference for variety, have also been shown to be influenced by positive affect. Further, this down-to-earth state has also been found to influence people's motivations for certain kinds of activities, and the way they go about even more complex tasks such as negotiation, work-task performance and appraisals, and a host of other activities, from medical diagnosis by physicians to product choice by consumers.

It should be noted that the results of these studies indicate that in the vast majority of situations, positive affect typically facilitates efficient, but at the same

Handbook of Cognition and Emotion. Edited by T. Dalgleish and M. Power.
© 1999 John Wiley & Sons Ltd.

time careful and thorough, thinking and problem solving. It is not usually found to be disruptive or impairing of thought processes, as many people may assume would be true of any emotion's effect on organized cognitive functioning or complex cognitive processing.

These effects, and especially how all of this occurs, are of keen interest to people in the research community, as well as to the general public. In addition, there is a growing interest in these phenomena among clinicians and brain researchers, who are trying to understand processes that enable people to cope effectively, and ways in which constructive happy states may differ from superficially similar, but destructive, states such as mania, substance abuse and addiction. In our consideration of positive affect, we will try to pay some attention to these issues, although the major focus will be on the effect of normal, happy feeling states. In addition, our consideration of each topic must be brief here; but hopefully it will stimulate further work on these and related issues, and aid in integrating these perspectives.

BACKGROUND

Before moving to a discussion of the effects that have been found, a few words of background information will be helpful.

Mild Positive Affect

This chapter considers work on mild positive affect, of the kind that is induced by the small interventions or events described above. We do not know what the effects of intense or extreme positive affect, such as might be described as "euphoria" or strong elation, would be. Some people may assume that the effects of very exciting events and extremely positive feelings would be the same, or even greater than those observed with mild affect. However, there is some reason to believe that the effects of intense affect may be quite different—different in kind, rather than just in magnitude—from the effects of mild, pleasant affect.

This is because a key to positive affect's facilitating influence on thinking and social interaction may be that it occurs without interrupting the ongoing activity. Intense affect, or focused emotion, in contrast, may be distracting or demanding of attention; and this aspect of intense affect may cause it to have quite a different impact on cognition from that which follows from mild positive affect. Thus, from the standpoint of facilitating one's decision making or creative problem solving at the particular moment in time, it may be better to find $5.00 than to win $5,000,000 in the lottery. This, however, remains to be explored.

Nonetheless, what we know is that a happy state sufficient to influence behavior and facilitate thinking can be induced by small, frequently encountered events in everyday life. Thus, additionally, such states are quite likely actually to be encountered and to play a role in people's lives.

Conceptual Validation of Affect Induction

One question that may arise is how we know that these inductions bring about the intended affective states and that the behavioral and cognitive effects observed are caused by the affect induced (rather than, say, by some other influence of the intended affect inducer). One way in which researchers sometimes address these kinds of issues is to use so-called "manipulation checks" to confirm that the desired feeling state was induced. Usually these take the form of self-report questionnaires asking people to indicate the degree of the feeling state, or of several states, that they are experiencing.

In some instances in the studies described in this chapter, such checks on the manipulation of affect were employed. But most often, a different method—the conceptual one, of triangulation on the construct of affect—was used, rather than asking people to report their feeling states. This was done for several reasons. First, asking people to focus on their feeling states, as such self-report measures do, may interfere with performance on the task being studied, or may make people more conscious of their affect than they would normally be. Thus, it may be too reactive a method for use in studies designed to investigate the effects of naturally occurring, everyday feelings. Second, it has not been established that such self-reported affect is a valid indicator of a person's feeling states. People may be unwilling, or unable, to report their true feelings, and in some cases may comply with "experimenter demand" and respond in ways that they surmise the experimenter would like them to respond. For these reasons, in much of the research described, a different plan for validating the affect inductions was employed, one based on the conceptual tool of converging operations, using different forms of affect induction to triangulate on the constructs involved.

For example, over the body of research, several divergent methods of inducing positive affect were employed while investigating the impact of each on the same dependent variable/measure, such as helping. Even though any one induction method, such as success or receiving an unexpected small gift, or seeing 5 minutes of a comedy film, could be open to the alternative interpretation that something other than affect was also induced and caused the observed effect, taken together, these various treatments are not easily interpreted in that way. That is, because the several treatments are very different and do not share the same alternative interpretation, when they are observed to have the same impact on the dependent variable of interest (for example, helping or creative problem solving), the most parsimonious interpretation for their impact on the dependent measure is in terms of the one quality or factor they share, induction of happy feelings.

Another aspect of this validation process is the compatibility of the outcomes or effects with theoretical expectations. In addition, theoretical compatibility is sometimes addressed by discriminant validation. This technique involves the inclusion of dependent measures, or conditions, that are *not* expected to be influenced by the affective state, along with some that *are* expected to be influenced (and a statistical interaction is predicted). Thus, over programs of research, or several studies cumulatively, the fact that positive affect is the cause of the observed effects is established conceptually and empirically.

Also, over several studies different methods of verification of affect's influence have been used, thus providing further converging evidence of the role of affect. For example, in some studies (i.e. those involving use of films to induce affect), requests that participants fill out self-report affect questionnaires can more unobtrusively be used, because they fit in with the task the participants are focused on (e.g. evaluation of how the film made them feel). If such opportunities are utilized, then it is often possible to have self-reports of affect as well as the other behavioral evidence mentioned. Where all of these indicators of affect converge, the evidence that it is affect that is producing the observed impact is most clear. In addition, this process can provide some validation of the use of the self-report questionnaire, at least in situations where it fits with the participant's understanding of the task he/she is carrying out.

Positive and Negative Affect

The next background point that needs to be made is that one cannot assume that negative affect will have the inverse effect of positive feelings (see Isen, 1984, 1987, 1990, for discussions of this point). Sometimes people assume that the opposite of what is true of positive affect will hold true for negative feeling states. The research literature on the influence of affect, however, indicates that positive and negative feelings are not usually symmetrical or parallel in their effects. This is true for their impacts on both social behavior and cognition.

For example, while positive affect has been found to promote sociability and helpfulness over a wide range of situations, negative affect has not always been found to reduce performance of those behaviors. Sometimes studies report that people in whom negative affect has been induced help less than controls, but some studies find they help more than controls (e.g. Cialdini, Darby & Vincent, 1973), and sometimes negative-affect and control groups do not differ (e.g. Isen, 1970).

Likewise, the lack of symmetry between the two kinds of states has been noted in the literature on affect and *cognition*. For example, a substantial body of research indicates that positive affect facilitates retrieval of positive material in memory (e.g. Isen et al., 1978; Teasdale & Fogarty, 1979). However, most of the studies that report such effects, and that attempt simultaneously to investigate the influence of negative affect on recall of negative material, do not find parallel effects. Sadness (rather than fear or anger, which might also be considered "negative affective states") is usually assumed to be the opposite affective state from happiness, and therefore sadness or depression has often been investigated in this context, in search of effects parallel to those found with happiness. However, most of these studies that attempt to examine the effects of sadness on memory report that sadness either fails to facilitate the recall of negative material, or that the effect is slight in comparison with that of positive feelings (e.g. Isen, 1987; Isen et al., 1978; Snyder & White, 1982; Teasdale & Fogarty, 1979; Teasdale, Taylor & Fogarty, 1980; see also Isen, 1990, for discussion). So, the effects of positive and negative affect on cognition do not appear to be parallel, either.

There are many possible reasons one can see for this. First, the structure of negative and positive affect is not similar. For example, one can immediately think of three distinct basic affects that are usually considered negative (anger, fear and sadness), but only one that is positive (joy). Even beyond that, however, the research indicates that the cognitive structures associated with negative and positive material, as well as with negative and positive feelings, are quite different. At least for normal people, positive affect appears to be extensive, integrated, well-interconnected and broadly organized (e.g. Cramer, 1968; Isen et al., 1985), whereas negative material and affect are more limited and discretely organized (see also Isen, 1985, 1990, for discussion). Anecdotal information suggests that this may not be true for clinical depressives. That is, for clinically depressed people, in contrast to non-depressives, it may be that it is negative material, rather than positive, that is more extensive, well-interconnected and integrated, and negative affect that is a better retrieval cue for a wide range of material. But this hypothesis is yet to be established.

It is interesting to think about why this situation may exist, but for the moment, the point that needs to be made is only that one should not assume that negative affect will necessarily have the inverse, or a parallel, effect to positive. Sometimes it does, but sometimes it does not; and illuminating this phenomenon is one topic for additional future research.

Is Positive Affect Facilitating or Disrupting of Systematic Cognitive Processing?

One question that often arises in consideration of the influence of positive affect is whether it is generally facilitating or impairing of thought processes (and, especially, of systematic thinking). As with most questions phrased in that way, the answer is, "it depends." It depends on many things, including the specific task that the person is asked to undertake, the circumstances and context, the goals of the person that are engendered by that context, the range of other tasks that need to be performed simultaneously, and what the questioner means by "facilitating" or "disrupting," to name just a few. Recent work has begun to focus on these interactions, and show that specifics of the situation make a real difference (see e.g. Bodenhausen, Kramer & Susser, 1994; Forgas, 1995; Isen, 1987, 1993; Martin et al., 1993). But some more specific answers are also emerging.

In general, the research suggests that positive affect has a salutory effect on thinking, problem solving, creative problem solving and innovation, as well as on social interaction, and on motivation for many kinds of tasks (see Isen, 1987, 1993, for reviews). While this improved motivation and approach to tasks may not extend to all activities, it does include a wide range, not just "fun" or easy tasks. Tasks that are interesting, those that are important, as well as some that are humanistic have been found to be fostered by positive affect. Happy feelings seem to help us as we interact and engage things we are interested in. There is even evidence that it can help us cope with situations that are otherwise problematic (see Aspinwall & Taylor, 1997; Taylor & Aspinwall, 1996, for reviews).

Nonetheless, a case has also been made by some authors that positive affect impairs "systematic" processing, either because of depleting cognitive resources or because of undermining the motivation to think carefully by, for example, signaling safety (e.g. Mackie & Worth, 1991; Schwarz & Bless, 1991). In addition, as noted previously, some people wonder about whether positive affect causes, or is similar to, some abnormal and self-destructive states such as mania, addiction and other psychopathological states.

This chapter will give some consideration to these divergent points of view and will review recent data suggesting that normal positive affect does not impair functioning under most conditions, but instead usually is facilitating. It will delineate what some of the exceptions to this generalization may be, and why; and, last, it will consider some possible theoretical conceptualizations that may aid in our understanding of these issues and distinctions.

Given the space limitations of the current volume, it will not be possible in this chapter to review in detail the basic findings of the influence of affect on memory and social behavior. For this, the reader is referred to earlier works such as that by Blaney (1986) and Isen (1984, 1987). The chapter continues, then, with only a brief review of some of the major findings with regard to the basic influence of positive affect on social behavior and cognitive processes, before moving on to the more central focus described above.

POSITIVE AFFECT FACILITATES PRO-SOCIAL BEHAVIOR

A large body of work in both laboratory and organizational settings indicates that positive affect promotes helpful and sociable behavior towards others, reduces interpersonal conflict, and leads to better outcomes for both parties in interactions such as bargaining and negotiation (e.g. Carnevale & Isen, 1986; Isen & Baron, 1991; Isen, 1987). For example, in one series of studies, people who had received information that they had succeeded on an inconsequential task donated more to a charity collection can, and showed more willingness to help a stranger who was loaded down with books and papers, in comparison with a control group or with people who had received a report of failure. In another series of studies, shoppers in a mall who used a public telephone and unexpectedly found a dime in the coin-return, relative to those whose coin return was empty, were more likely to help a person who dropped a sheaf of papers as she passed by (Isen, 1970; Isen & Levin, 1972).

It is well established by now that, under most circumstances, people who are feeling happy are more friendly, sociable and helpful. However, there are some circumstances—for example, when the plight of the person in need is not serious and the helping task will clearly undermine the positive-affect state—under which people in positive affect will help less than controls (e.g. Isen & Simmonds, 1978). It has also been found that there are times when people who are feeling sad will also help more than controls; but this is a different phenomenon, since, as discussed above, positive and negative affect are not simply "opposites" and should not be expected to have inverse effects (e.g. Cialdini, Darby & Viacent, 1973; see Isen, 1987, for review and discussion). But the general rule, for which there is a considerable amount of research support, is that positive affect promotes helpful, friendly and socially responsible behavior.

POSITIVE AFFECT INFLUENCES COGNITION

One way of understanding this effect on social interaction has been in terms of the impact of positive affect on cognitive processing. That is, it has been proposed that the decision to help is the result of a cognitive process of decision making (e.g. Latané & Darley, 1970), and that positive affect influences helping by influencing that decision-making process (Isen & Levin, 1972; Isen et al., 1978). This, then, would explain why different details of a situation could result in changes in whether or not helping actually does occur. People decide, on the basis of their assessment of a large variety of factors, whether helping is the best course of action in the situation. The particular factors considered, and perhaps the relative weightings of the various factors, may be influenced by positive affect to produce the effects observed.

Memory and Complex Cognitive Context

Further, it was proposed that one important component of the process by which positive affect influences decision making is through the subset of material that is recruited from memory by a positive feeling state (Isen et al., 1978). The finding that positive affect facilitates recall of positive material in memory, together with recognition of the extensive, integrated nature of that material (e.g. Cramer, 1968; Isen et al., 1985), suggests two important aspects of the process by which positive affect influences decision making: memory and the complexity of the subset of material cued by positive affect.

That is, it is widely acknowledged that not everything that is stored in memory comes to mind at the same time. Material relevant to the task and situation comes to mind, and not even all of that may reach awareness in any given situation. The presence of a mild positive affect state at the time one is working on a problem, or considering a course of action, insures that, in addition to material relevant to the task, situation, possible outcomes, goals and so forth, positive material also comes to mind. The fact that positive material is extensive, diverse and well-integrated means that a rich, complex cognitive context is present during a positive state. Such a complex cognitive context has been found to promote creative responding (e.g. Cramer, 1968). Consequently, decision making and problem solving under conditions of positive affect are likely to be more rich, flexible and innovative.

Not Simply "Bias" or "Response Bias"

Thus, the decision process under conditions of positive affect can be influenced or clarified, as people see more positive aspects, but also more diverse aspects, of the situation and of their considered behavior, more positive possible outcomes, but also more different possible outcomes, and so forth. Consequently, one should expect, and the research has generally supported this point, that this retrieval of positive material should *not* result in a blinding bias, something akin to seeing all situations through "rose-colored glasses," as might have been assumed initially. Rather, positive affect's influence on retrieval of material from memory leads to elaboration, more thinking about more different aspects of situations and, possibly as a result of this, more creative, effective problem solving.

As the research has accumulated, it has become clear that the process by which positive affect influences decision making and thought processes is a subtle, complex and responsive one, not just a simple, grossly biasing effect. While it is true that positive affect causes more pleasant thoughts to come to mind and the contents of thought to be more positive than at other times, it does not appear that the effect of this is simply to bias indiscriminately people's perceptions and decisions in a positive direction.

For example, it has repeatedly been shown that positive affect does not influence all material equally, but has its greatest influence on specific kinds of material, depending in part on the situation. One type that is more affected by positive feelings is ambiguous material, where there are different aspects or types of thoughts that can be cued by the affective state. In one study, for instance, the evaluation of ambiguous or neutral slides was influenced most by positive affect (Isen & Shalker, 1982). In contrast, negative, and to some extent positive, material is not as readily influenced. Positive material may not be seen as ever more positive, and truly negative material will not be judged as acceptable, under conditions of mild positive affect. For example, for most people, positive affect would not improve their evaluation of the Nazi reign of terror, or lead them to feel that it wasn't so bad. For a more mild example, a study investigating categorization of people into person-type categories, found that positive affect influenced perception (classification) of marginal category representatives into positive person categories, such as "bartender" into the category "nurturant people," but not of marginal category representatives into negative person categories, such as "genius" into the category "unstable people" (Isen, Niedenthal & Cantor, 1992). Similarly, a study on the influence of positive affect on word associations showed that positive affect resulted in more extensive and diverse word associations to neutral words, but not to negative or even positive words (Isen et al., 1985). The important point here is that positive affect cues positive material about items for which positive thoughts exist in the person's mind, and does not simply result in a global perceptual or response bias (the "rose-colored glasses" effect). The findings, which have been obtained in many studies, of significant interactions between induced affect and valence of the material under consideration support this point.

It might be added, here, that the failure of positive affect to influence unusual responses to negative words in the study mentioned above (Isen et al., 1985) argues against an interpretation in terms of simple cognitive priming (that is, without an intervening affect component). This is because, through priming alone, one would expect all word-valence types to be influenced similarly. Only when affective processes are called into play would differential responses to negatively valenced material be expected.

Further, the significant interactions between positive affect and other aspects of the situation also suggest that affect's influence is not simply to influence decisions in a positive direction regardless of the dangers or other factors that may be present in a situation. For example, one study set in an organizational context showed that positive affect influenced task perceptions and satisfaction for an enriched task, but not for an unenriched task (Kraiger, Billings & Isen, 1989). In the organizational behavior literature, an "enriched task" is one that allows employees an opportunity for some autonomy, diversity of activity and sense of control and meaningfulness, whereas an unenriched task is one that requires only relatively routine, scripted activity and/or allows little sense of control or meaningfulness.

Two more illustrations that the impact of positive affect on decision making and behavior is complex, responsive to the situation and task demands, and the product of thought rather than of simple bias, come from the variety-seeking and the risk-taking literatures. There, a significant interaction has been found between affective state and the amount of potential unpleasantness of the outcome under consideration. In the variety-seeking work, in three studies looking at consumers' choices in the snack-food product class, Kahn & Isen (1993) found that, as long as the products promised to be enjoyable, positive affect led to increased preference for variety, as measured by number of alterations between products (higher), diversity of the set of items considered (larger) and "market share" of the most preferred item (smaller). ("Market share" refers to the percentage of the total number selected that is captured by one alternative; market share of the most preferred item would be the percentage of choices that goes to the most preferred item; and variety seeking, or preference for variety, would be reflected by the most preferred brand/item receiving a smaller market share or percentage of the total number of choices.) This was not true, however, where the items were unfamiliar and the description of them (e.g. low salt) suggested that they might taste bad. In that circumstance, the positive affect and control groups did not differ in their degrees of variety seeking. This suggests that the increase in variety preference that results from positive affect arises because of greater anticipated enjoyment, but that this assessment is quite responsive to the details of the situation.

Studies on positive affect's influence on risk preference also indicate an interaction between affect and level of risk or chance of a genuine, meaningful loss. That is, studies show that while positive affect may appear to increase risk taking in a low-risk or hypothetical situation, it actually leads to risk avoidance or decreased risk preference in situations of high, real risk or possible genuine, meaningful loss (e.g. Isen & Geva, 1987; Isen & Patrick, 1983). Again, this significant interaction indicates that positive affect influences thinking in a complex way involving elaboration and evaluation of expected feeling states, rather than just by biasing responding blindly in a positive direction. In fact, in one study, where a high risk of a genuine loss was involved, people in the positive affect condition, relative to controls, had significantly more thoughts about the potential loss, as reflected in a thought-listing task following the risk measure (Isen & Geva, 1987). This indicates that positive affect fosters thinking about whatever needs to be thought about in the situation, and does not lead people to downplay, ignore or distort potential negative information.

Positive Affect Fosters Cognitive Flexibility and Creativity

Much research, using varied affect inductions and varied measures of creativity and flexibility, now supports the conclusion that positive affect fosters cognitive flexibility, creativity and innovation (see Isen (1998) for further discussion). As already noted, people in whom positive affect has been induced show more unusual (but still reasonable and sensible) word associations to neutral words, more liking for unusual, non-typical products, and more flexible categorization of both neutral words into topic categories and products into product classes (Isen et al., 1985; Isen & Daubman, 1984; Kahn & Isen, 1993; Murray et al., 1990; see also Showers & Cantor, 1985). As described above, this effect also applies to people's classification of person-types into positive categories (but not into negative categories; Isen et al., 1992). Relative to control groups, people in positive affect have better negotiation outcomes and enjoy the task more, where the bargaining situation requires a problem-solving approach and they can take the other person's perspective (Carnevale & Isen, 1986); and they show greater variety seeking among safe, enjoyable alternatives (Kahn & Isen, 1993). It will be recalled that this preference vanishes if the taste quality of the products is questionable. All of these findings are indicative of increased flexibility in thinking; and, again, the process seems to be one of purposive decision making, based on flexible consideration of available evidence, not just bias.

Further, however, several studies, from two separate research groups studying diverse populations that include not only college students (Isen, Daubman & Nowicki, 1987) but also young adolescents (Greene & Noice, 1988) and practicing medical doctors (Estrada, Young & Isen, 1994), have found that people in positive affect perform better on tasks commonly acknowledged to require creative problem-solving ability. The tasks used in this research were Duncker's (1945) Candle Problem and the Mednicks' (Mednick, Mednick & Mednick, 1964) Remote Associates Test. In the Candle Task, the participant is asked to affix a candle to the wall (a corkboard) and light it safely, using only the materials available, which include a candle, a box of tacks, and a book of matches. In the Remote Associates test, respondents are shown a stem consisting of three remotely-associated words and are asked to provide a fourth word that fits with each of the other three. This test has been validated and used as an individual-difference measure of creativity (Mednick et al., 1964). The positive-affect research uses seven items of moderate difficulty from this test. These studies have repeatedly shown that positive affect induced as described above, by receipt of a gift of a small bag of candy (which is not eaten during the session), by watching 5 minutes of a comedy film, or the like, results in significantly improved performance on these tasks.

The work on positive affect's influence on word association, which was used earlier to illustrate the fact that positive affect does not simply bias all thinking in a positive direction, also points the way to understanding how positive affect influences cognitive flexibility, creativity and innovation, as well. Recall that the word associations of people in the positive affect condition were not only more unusual than those of neutral-affect subjects, they were also more diverse. Consequently, we know that not only is it true that positive affect cues positive material in memory, but also that positive material is more diverse, extensive and well-interconnected than other material. Thus, more positive material comes to mind when one is happy, and since positive material is diverse and extensive, that means that a rich, complex, extensive set of ideas is more likely to come readily to mind when one is feeling happy. This, a complex cognitive context, is thought to promote creativity and innovation.

Another way of understanding this effect of positive feelings has been suggested recently by Ashby, Isen & Turken (in press). These authors have proposed that the influence of positive affect on creativity may be mediated by release of the neurotransmitter, dopamine, which accompanies positive affect. They point out that the presence of dopamine in the brain, which is known from animal studies to be released in response to reward, is correlated with cognitive flexibility in humans. In addition, reductions in dopamine, as occur, for example, in Parkinson's disease, are associated with impaired ability to switch "set" as measured by tasks such as the Wisconsin Card Sort Task. While direct evidence is yet to be obtained for the hypothesis that dopamine release mediates the creativity resulting from positive affect, it is plausible; and one interesting by-product of it may be a change in the way we understand the types of tasks that will, or will not, be influenced by positive affect.

Enhanced Cognitive Flexibility May Mediate Affect's Influence on Social Tasks

This recognition of the complex influence of positive affect on cognitive processes suggests that the social effects that have been reported to result from positive affect may be attributable, at least in part, to these affect-induced changes in cognitive flexibility. As has been described, many studies confirm that when we feel happy, we can be more creative and innovative, more thorough yet at the same time more efficient in considering alternatives and making decisions; and we are more flexible and open to different ideas and to the perspectives of others (e.g. Estrada, Young & Isen, 1994; Estrada, Isen & Young, 1997; Green & Noice, 1988; Isen, Ashby & Waldron, 1997; Isen, Daubman & Nowicki, 1987; Isen & Means, 1983; Isen, Rosenzweig & Young, 1991). Perhaps because of these tendencies, people who are feeling happy are also less likely to distort or ignore evidence that doesn't fit with their preconceptions, and they show superior coping skills and styles (Aspinwall & Taylor, 1997; Carnevale & Isen, 1986; Estrada, Isen & Young, 1997; Showers & Cantor, 1985; Taylor & Aspinwall, 1996). Thus, this cognitive flexibility may play a crucial role not only in cognitive processing and in producing the effects of positive affect on thinking, but also in producing the social effects of positive affect described earlier, as well as others.

When one is more flexible, more open to information and the perspective of others, less "defensive" or rigid, it follows that social interaction may be facilitated. Certainly, negotiation processes may be expected to improve. For example, in the bargaining study reported by Carnevale & Isen (1986), not only were the outcomes better for both of the face-to-face negotiating parties in the positive-affect condition (indeed, they were optimal), but analyses of the negotiation process revealed that those in the positive-affect condition showed a greater tendency than controls to adopt a problem-solving approach to the negotiation task. That is, they looked for innovative, "win–win" possibilities. This is in contrast to the other strategies they might have adopted, such as going for some obvious but mutually unsatisfactory compromise, withdrawing, or contending for their own position, as was typical in the control condition. Each of these latter strategies leads to less than optimal negotiation outcomes (Pruitt, 1983); and in fact in the control condition bargaining was characterized by hostility and contention, and the modal response was to break off negotiation without reaching agreement. In contrast, in the positive affect condition, not only was the negotiation characterized by more pleasantness and enjoyment for the bargainers, but also there seemed to be more insight. While one's preconception might be that the good outcome could be attributable to the improved social feeling alone, the evidence seems more to point to the importance of the cognitive factor—the adoption of a problem-solving approach. For example, there was evidence that those in the positive-affect state were better able to see their opponent's perspective, because when asked at the end of the session, they correctly reported the other person's payoff matrix, a fact not itself given in the negotiation process.

Other cognitive processes that are promoted by positive affect, and that arise from increased flexibility, may also play a role in improved social interaction. For example, in one study, Dovidio et al. (1995) found that people in a positive affect state were more likely than were controls to categorize members of another group as similar to themselves, through membership in an overarching superordinate group of which they, too, were members. This enabled them to see the commonalties between the groups and, as confirmed by path analyses, led to increased acceptance and liking of the members of that other group, relative to the control condition.

Positive Affect and Decision Making

Positive feelings have also been found to lead to efficient decision making, and three protocol-analysis studies indicate that it promotes decision making and problem solving that is more thorough and careful at the same time that it is more efficient, if the task is one that is interesting or important (e.g. Estrada, Isen & Young, 1997; Isen & Means, 1983; Isen, Rosenzweig & Young, 1991). In one study, people choosing a fictitious car for purchase made their choices earlier (although their choices did not differ, on average, from those of the control group), and went about making the choice more efficiently, showing, for example, less redundancy in the search process (Isen & Means, 1983). When this same choice problem was re-cast as a disease/patient-selection task and given to medical-student subjects, it was again found that people in the positive-affect condition, in contrast to controls, solved the assigned problem earlier, in this case identifying the correct patient earlier in their protocols. However, in this instance, they did not stop working on the materials once the assigned task was completed, but instead, significantly more than controls, went beyond the assigned task (doing things like diagnosing the other patients or suggesting treatments), integrated the material more, and showed less confusion in their decision-making protocols (Isen, Rosenzweig & Young, 1991).

Most recently, a protocol-analysis study examining the influence of positive affect on physicians' diagnostic processes showed that doctors in the positive-affect condition recognized the correct domain of the disease earlier in their protocols and showed significantly less "anchoring" to an initial hypothesis than controls. That is, they were significantly less likely than doctors in the control condition to distort or ignore information that would not fit with their existing hypothesis (Estrada, Isen & Young, 1997). It was also observed, as would fit with such a finding, that they were not likely to jump to conclusions, show premature closure, or display any evidence of superficial or faulty processing.

Positive Affect's Influence on Risk Taking

Another type of decision making that has been studied in the context of an influence of positive affect has been risk preference, or decision making under risk. This work has already been mentioned in other contexts in this chapter. However, some attempts to understand the possible causes of this effect can now be described, as this will lead into the next section of the chapter, on Motivation.

As noted, several studies indicate that positive affect leads people to avoid risks, where there is danger of a real, meaningful loss. This may seem surprising, because of people's assumptions about happy feelings, and especially in view of the data on positive affect and creative problem solving. (People often assume that creativity involves or requires taking risks; however, it is not clear that desire to take a risk, or risk preference, is essential for creativity.) In contrast, the data indicate that even though positive affect may improve subjective probability of a good outcome (e.g. Johnson & Tversky, 1983; Nygren et al., 1996), it also influences, in the opposite direction, perceived *utility* of the outcomes, particularly negative outcomes. That is, positive affect increases the negative utility of a loss, meaning that a potential loss seems worse under conditions of positive affect than it might at another time (Isen, Nygren & Ashby, 1988). There is also some evidence that positive affect may cause utility to be weighted more than probability in the consideration of risky situations (Nygren et al., 1996). These changes that follow from positive affect suggest that motivations (in the sense of what one cares about) may be influenced by positive affect.

POSITIVE AFFECT AND MOTIVATION

A few studies suggest that positive affect influences motivation, as well as cognition and social behavior. While this can be mentioned only briefly here, it is worth noting the kinds of effects that have been observed, as well as the kinds that have *not* been found. First, there is no evidence that positive affect has any influence on general motivation, in the sense of "trying harder" or "not trying as hard." However, there is evidence of particular kinds of motivational influences. Three different kinds of effects have been found so far.

First, there is evidence that people who are feeling happy are motivated to maintain that state, and they behave in ways that will enable them to do so (e.g. Isen & Simmonds, 1978). The risk data may be understood in this way. For example, as noted earlier, without some good reason to do so, people who are feeling happy are less likely to take risks, if faced with the probability of genuine, meaningful loss. Possibly for the same reason, they seek variety among safe, enjoyable products, but not where the products are questionable. Similarly, they seek to have fun, but not if there is danger or if serious or interesting work needs to be done.

Further, people in positive affect show more intrinsic motivation, and are more humanistic in orientation. For example, related to intrinsic motivation, as mentioned earlier, one study found that positive affect promotes, in an organizational context, improved task perceptions and satisfaction from enriched tasks, but not for dull tasks (e.g. Kraiger, Billings & Isen, 1989). In another study, physicians in a positive-affect condition, compared to controls, endorsed more humanistic, relative to extrinsic, sources of satisfaction (motivations) from the practice of medicine (Estrada, Young & Isen, 1994).

CONCLUSION

As this brief consideration of the literature has indicated, positive affect is not similar to mania or other disordered states such as drug abuse or addiction. Many studies on cognition, as well as decision-making and problem-solving, have shown that positive affect fosters problem solving and thinking, and is generally facilitating. For example, it enables creative problem solving on tasks that are otherwise very difficult, and promotes thinking that is not only efficient but also careful, open-minded and thorough (e.g. Estrada, Young & Isen, 1994; Estrada, Isen & Young, 1997; Isen & Means 1983; Isen, Rosenzweig & Young, 1991).

Although some earlier papers suggested that positive affect impaired systematic processing either because of draining limited cognitive capacity or interfering with motivation to process carefully (e.g. Mackie & Worth, 1989; Bless et al., 1990), many authors did not find compatible results (e.g. Smith & Shaffer, 1991; Staw & Barsade, 1993), and others reported findings pertaining to deployment of attention that would lead to an opposite conclusion (e.g. Derryberry, 1993). More recently, many authors have found that the impairing effects that were reported tend to be observed primarily when the task is dull, unpleasant or unimportant, or for some other reason subjects don't realize that they need to engage the task seriously (e.g. Bodenhausen, Kramer & Susser, 1994[1]; also see Isen, 1993, for discussion).

Thus, one exception to the generalization that positive affect facilitates systematic, careful processing may be where the task is not pleasant or interesting *and* where, at the same time, people are not told it is important to perform the task. Under this kind of circumstance, positive affect may lead to impaired performance, compared with that of controls. But there is ample evidence that if the task is presented as important, or if it is one that is of interest (not necessarily "fun"), people in positive affect will engage it seriously; and when they do, they are more efficient, more thorough, and more creative and integrative in solving it. The evidence supports the view that people's thinking is purposive, and thus many details of situations and people's goals contribute to the ultimate outcome in any given task-situation.

---

[1] Although Bodenhausen, Kramer & Susser (1994) offer a different interpretation of their findings, their data actually fit with the formulation being put forth here.

As noted earlier, a hypothesis has been proposed that at least some of the effects of positive affect may depend on the neurotransmitter, dopamine (Ashby, Isen & Turken, 1997). This hypothesis suggests that positive affect may especially influence tasks that are controlled by brain regions that contain dopamine receptors, and it may lead us to more specific ways of defining the kinds of tasks that may, or may not, be facilitated, or impaired, by positive affect. Most likely, the full picture will be even more complex than this, and the effects of combinations of different neurotransmitters will have to be considered. Certainly, too, it will take some time to develop these insights. When that is done, moreover, the purposive nature of people's thinking and behavior will need to be integrated into our understanding of the effects of various neurotransmitters, singly or in concert. That is, the fact that people's goals influence their interpretation of situations, and their behavior in those situations, is supported by so much evidence that such processes will not be able to be ignored by neurological analyses; rather, insights from these different levels of analysis will have to be integrated.

Finally, it should be emphasized again that all of these effects that have been described have resulted from mild, everyday affect inductions. Further, they have been observed when people were randomly assigned to treatment groups. This indicates that these effects, many of which are beneficial and highly sought-after (such as creative problem solving, helpfulness, improved conflict resolution), can be induced readily in almost everyone. While there may be individual differences among people in abilities and skills underlying these processes, those are not sufficient to negate the power of simply-induced, mild, happy feelings to enhance performance measurably. Thus, the currently popular focus on genetic endowment, or emphasis on early-childhood experience, should not obscure the fact that people respond to their surroundings and that a small positive event can have powerful, facilitating effects on many important processes.

REFERENCES

Ashby, F. G., Isen, A. M. & Turken, A. (1997). A neuropsychological theory of positive affect and its influence on cognition, *Psychological Review*.

Aspinwall, L. G. & Taylor, S. E. (1997). A stitch in time: self-regulation and proactive coping. *Psychological Bulletin*, **121**, 417–436.

Blaney, P. H. (1986). Affect and memory: a review. *Psychological Bulletin*, **99**, 229–246.

Bless, H., Bohner, G., Schwarz, N. & Strack, F. (1990). Mood and persuasion: a cognitive response analysis. *Personality and Social Psychology Bulletin*, **16**, 331–345.

Bodenhausen, G. V., Kramer, G. P. & Susser, K. (1994). Happiness and stereotypic thinking in social judgment. *Journal of Personality and Social Psychology*, **66**(4), 621–632.

Carnevale, P. J. D. & Isen, A. M. (1986). The influence of positive affect and visual access on the discovery of integrative solutions in bilateral negotiation. *Organizational Behavior and Human Decision Processes*, **37**, 1–13.

Cialdini, R. B., Darby, B. & Vincent, J. (1973). Transgression and altruism: a case for hedonism. *Journal of Experimental Social Psychology*, **9**, 502–516.

Cramer, P. (1968). *Word Association*. New York: Academic Press.

Derryberry, D. (1993). Attentional consequences of outcome-related motivational states: congruent, incongruent, and focusing effects. *Motivation and Emotion*, **17**(2), 65–90.

Dovidio, J. F., Gaertner, S. L., Isen, A. M. & Lowrance, R. (1995). Group representations and intergroup bias: positive affect, similarity, and group size. *Personality & Social Psychology Bulletin*, **21**, 856–865.

Duncker, K. (1945). On problem-solving. *Psychological Monographs*, **58** (whole No. 5).

Estrada, C. A., Isen, A. M. & Young, M. J. (1997). Positive affect facilitates integration of information and decreases anchoring in reasoning among physicians. *Organizational Behavior and Human Decision Processes*, **72**, 117–135.

Estrada, C. A., Young, M. J. & Isen, A. M. (1994). Positive affect influences creative problem solving and reported source of practice satisfaction in physicians. *Motivation and Emotion*, **18**, 285–299.

Forgas, J. P. (1995). Mood and judgment: the affect infusion model (AIM). *Psychological Bulletin*, **117**(1)(January), 39–66.

Greene, T. R. & Noice, H. (1988). Influence of positive affect upon creative thinking and problem solving in children. *Psychological Reports*, **63**, 895–898.

Isen, A. M. (1970). Success, failure attention and reactions to others: the warm glow of success. *Journal of Personality and Social Psychology*, **17**, 107–112

Isen, A. M. (1984). Toward understanding the role of affect in cognition. In R. Wyer & T. Srull (eds), *Handbook of Social Cognition*. Hillsdale, NJ: Erlbaum, pp. 179–236.

Isen, A. M. (1985). The asymmetry of happiness and sadness in effects on memory in normal college students. *Journal of Experimental Psychology: General*, **114**, 388–391.

Isen, A. M. (1987). Positive affect, cognitive processes and social behavior. In L. Berkowitz (ed.), *Advances in Experimental Social Psychology*. New York: Academic Press, pp. 203–253.

Isen, A. M. (1990). The influence of positive and negative affect on cognitive organization: implications for development. In N. Stein, B. Leventhal & T. Trabasso (eds), *Psychological and Biological Processes in the Development of Emotion*. Hillsdale, NJ: Erlbaum, pp. 75–94.

Isen, A. M. (1993). Positive affect and decision making. In M. Lewis & J. Haviland (eds), *Handbook of Emotion*. New York: Guilford, pp. 261–277.

Isen, A. M. (1998). On the relationship between affect and creative problem solving. In S. W. Russ (ed.), *Affect, Creative Experience, and Psychological Adjustment*. Philadelphia, PA: Brunner/Mazel, pp. 3–17.

Isen, A. M., Ashby, F. G. & Waldron, E. (1997). The sweet smell of success. *Aromacology Review*, **VI**(3), 1, 4–5.

Isen, A. M. & Baron, R. A. (1991). Positive affect in organizations. L. Cummings & B. Staw (eds), *Research in Organizational Behavior*. Greenwich, CT: JAI, pp. 1–52.

Isen, A. M. & Daubman, K. A. (1984). The influence of affect on categorization. *Journal of Personality and Social Psychology*, **47**, 1206–1217.

Isen, A. M., Daubman, K. A. & Nowicki, G. P. (1987). Positive affect facilitates creative problem solving. *Journal of Personality and Social Psychology*, **52**, 1122–1131.

Isen, A. M. & Geva, N. (1987). The influence of positive affect on acceptable level of risk: the person with a large canoe has a large worry. *Organizational Behavior and Human Decision Processes*, **39**, 145–154.

Isen, A. M., Johnson, M. M. S., Mertz, E. & Robinson, F. G. (1985). The influence of positive affect on the unusualness of word association. *Journal of Personality and Social Psychology*, **48**, 1413–1426.

Isen, A. M. & Levin, P. F. (1972). The effect of feeling good on helping: cookies and kindness. *Journal of Personality and Social Psychology*, **21**, 384–388.

Isen, A. M. & Means, B. (1983). The influence of positive affect on decision-making strategy. *Social Cognition*, **2**, 18–31.

Isen, A. M., Niedenthal, P. & Cantor, N. (1992). The influence of positive affect on social categorization. *Motivation and Emotion*, **16**, 65–78.

Isen, A. M., Nygren, T. E. & Ashby, F. G. (1988). The influence of positive affect on the perceived utility of gains and losses. *Journal of Personality and Social Psychology*, **55**, 710–717.

Isen, A. M. & Patrick, R. E. (1983). The effect of positive feelings on risk-taking: When the Chips are down. *Organizational Behavior and Human Performance*, **31**, 194–202.

Isen, A. M., Shalker, T. E., Clark, M. & Karp, L. (1978). Affect, accessibility of material in memory and behavior: A cognitive loop? *Journal of Personality and Social Psychology*, **36**, 1–12.

Isen, A. M. & Shalker, T. E. (1982). Do you "accentuate the positive, eliminate the negative" when you are in a good mood? *Social Psychology Quarterly*, **45**, 58–63.

Isen, A. M. & Simmonds, S. F. (1978). The effect of feeling good on a helping task that is incompatible with good mood. *Social Psychology Quarterly*, **41**, 345–349.

Isen, A. M., Rosenzweig, A. S. & Young, M. J. (1991). The influence of positive affect on clinical problem solving. *Medical Decision Making*, **11**, 221–227.

Johnson, E. & Tversky, A. (1983). Affect generalization, and the perception of risk. *Journal of Personality and Social Psychology*, **45**, 20–31.

Kahn, B. & Isen, A. M. (1993). The influence of positive affect on variety-seeking among safe, enjoyable products. *Journal of Consumer Research*, **20**, 257–270.

Kraiger, K., Billings, R. S. & Isen, A. M. (1989). The influence of positive affective states on task perceptions and satisfaction. *Organizational Behavior and Human Decision Processes*, **44**, 12–25.

Latané, B. & Darley, J. (1970). *The Unresponsive Bystander: Why Doesn't He Help?* New York: Appleton-Century-Crofts.

Mackie, D. M. & Worth, L. T. (1989). Cognitive deficits and the mediation of positive affect in persuasion. *Journal of Personality and Social Psychology*, **57**, 27–40.

Mackie, D. M. & Worth, L. (1991). Feeling good but not thinking straight: the impact of positive mood on persuasion. In J. P. Forgas (ed.), *Emotion and Social Judgment*. Oxford: Pergamon, pp. 201–220.

Martin, L. L., Ward, D. W., Achee, J. W. & Wyer, R. S. Jr (1993). Mood as input: people have to interpret the motivational implications of their moods. *Journal of Personality and Social Psychology*, **64**, 317–326.

Mednick, M. T., Mednick, S. A. & Mednick, E. V. (1964). Incubation of creative performance and specific associative priming. *Journal of Abnormal and Social Psychology*, **69**, 84–88.

Murray, N., Sujan, H., Hirt, E. R. & Sujan, M. (1990). The influence of mood on categorization: a cognitive flexibility interpretation. *Journal of Personality and Social Psychology*, **59**, 411–425.

Nygren, T. E., Isen, A. M., Taylor, P. J. & Dulin, J. (1996). The influence of positive affect on the decision rule in risk situations: focus on outcome (and especially avoidance of loss) rather than probability. *Organizational Behavior and Human Decision Processes*, **66**(1), 59–72.

Pruitt, D. G. (1983). Strategic choice in negotiation. *American Behavioral Scientist*, **27**, 167–194.

Schwarz, N. & Bless, H. (1991). Happy and mindless, but sad and smart? The impact of affective states on analytic reasoning. In J. P. Forgas (ed.), *Emotion and Social Judgment.* Oxford: Pergamon, pp. 55–71.

Showers, C. & Cantor, N. (1985). Social cognition: a look at motivated strategies. *Annual Review of Psychology*, **36**, 275–305.

Smith, S. M. & Shaffer, D. R. (1991). The effects of good moods on systematic processing: "Willing but not able, or able but not willing?" *Motivation and Emotion*, **15**, 243–279.

Staw, B. M. & Barsade, S. G. (1993). Affect and managerial performance: a test of the sadder-but-wiser vs. happier-and-smarter hypotheses. *Administrative Science Quarterly*, **38**, 304–331.

Snyder, M. & White, E. (1982). Moods and memories: elation, depression, and remembering the events of one's life. *Journal of Personality*, **50**, 149–167.

Taylor, S. E. & Aspinwall, L. G. (1996). Mediating and moderating processes in psychosocial stress: appraisal, coping, resistance and vulnerability. In H. B. Kaplan (ed.), *Psychosocial Stress: Perspectives on Structure, Theory, Life-course, and Methods*. San Diego, CA: Academic Press, pp. 71–110.

Teasdale, J. D. & Fogarty, S. J. (1979). Differential effects of induced mood on retrieval of pleasant and unpleasant events from episodic memory. *Journal of Abnormal Psychology*, **88**, 248–257.

Teasdale, J. D., Taylor, R. & Fogarty, S. J. (1980). Effects of induced elation-depression on the accessibility of memories of happy and unhappy experiences. *Behavior Research and Therapy*, **18**, 339–346.

Chapter 26

The Self-conscious Emotions: Shame, Guilt, Embarrassment and Pride

June Price Tangney
George Mason University, Fairfax, VA, USA

Publication of this *Handbook* is especially timely for the self-conscious emotions. The past decade has seen a tremendous increase in attention to these long-neglected siblings of the basic emotions. In the span of little more than 10 years, researchers from a diversity of disciplines have developed new measurement methods to assess shame, guilt, embarrassment and pride. At the same time, theoretical perspectives on these emotions have become increasingly sophisticated (paralleling the study of emotions, in general). And these developments, together, have led to a remarkable body of rich empirical work where before there was so little. In this chapter, I attempt to summarize current perspectives and findings on the self-conscious emotions, highlighting key controversies facing researchers in this field.

WHAT ARE SELF-CONSCIOUS EMOTIONS?

Shame, guilt, embarrassment and pride are members of a family of "self-conscious emotions". Each involves, as a central feature, some form of self-reflection and self-evaluation. This self-evaluation may be implicit or explicit, consciously experienced or silently transpiring below conscious awareness. But these emotions are fundamentally about the self. For example, when good things happen, we may feel a range of positive emotions—joy, happiness, satisfaction or contentment. But we feel pride in our *own* positive

Handbook of Cognition and Emotion. Edited by T. Dalgleish and M. Power.
© 1999 John Wiley & Sons Ltd.

attributes or actions.[1] By the same token, we feel ashamed of ourselves, guilty over our behavior, and embarrassed by our pratfalls. In one way or another, the self is the object of these self-conscious emotions.

SOME GENERAL DEVELOPMENTAL CONSIDERATIONS

In contrast to the "basic" emotions (e.g. anger, fear, joy) which emerge very early in life, the self-conscious emotions have been described as "secondary", "derived" or "complex" emotions because they emerge later and hinge on several key cognitive abilities (Lewis, 1992; Lewis et al., 1989; Fischer & Tangney, 1995). Most notably, these emotions require a developed self—a clear recognition of the self as separate from others (Lewis et al., 1989), as well as a set of standards against which the self is evaluated. In fact, most emotions theorists believe that a recognized self is a *prerequisite* for emotions such as embarrassment, shame, guilt and pride (Lewis, 1992, 1994, 1995; Stipek, 1995; Stipek, Gralinski & Kopp, 1990; Stipek, Recchia & McClintic, 1992; Wallbott & Scherer, 1995; see Barrett, 1995, however, for an opposing view). According to this view, very young children simply haven't developed the cognitive capacity to experience self-conscious emotions. That is, before a certain point in development, there isn't a self to be conscious of.

In support of this view, Lewis et al. (1989) reported an inventive series of developmental studies showing that the capacity to experience embarrassment directly parallels the emergence of self-recognition. Very young children first showed behavioral signs of embarrassment (smiling coupled with gaze aversion, touching the face, etc.) at precisely the same phase of development in which a rudimentary sense of self emerges—between 15 and 24 months. Moreover, within this span of development, those children who displayed self-recognition (in a "rouge" test; Amsterdam, 1972; Bertenthal & Fischer, 1978) were the very same children who displayed signs of embarrassment in an unrelated task. In other words, kids who didn't recognize the self in one context, didn't show embarrassment in another context.

There continues to be some debate regarding the precise timing of the onset of self-conscious emotions (Barrett, 1995; Kagan, 1984; Lewis 1992, 1994; Lewis et al., 1989; Tangney, in press). Do toddlers begin to experience shame, guilt and pride at about the same point in development as embarrassment? Or is the development of additional, later, cognitive abilities (e.g. distinction between self and behavior, consideration of intentions, etc.) necessary? From the perspective of some developmentalists, the basic premise of these "onset" questions is

---

[1] On some occasions we may feel pride over another person's behavior; that person, however, is typically someone with whom we are closely affiliated or identified (e.g. a family member, friend or colleague closely associated with the self). We experience pride because that person is part of our self-definition.

misguided (e.g. Barrett, 1995; Mascolo & Fischer, 1995). A larger, more pertinent issue concerns developmental changes in the nature and functions of these emotions across the lifespan. Certainly, the nature and structure of the self evolves considerably beyond age 15 months (Damon & Hart, 1982), as do critical aspects of our social and moral standards, our points of reference, etc. So it's not difficult to argue that there are parallel shifts in the experience of self-conscious emotions and their role in daily life. The question then isn't so much, "*When* do children begin experiencing guilt (or shame or pride)?" but "*How* do children experience guilt (or shame or pride) at a given age, and what functions does it serve at this particular developmental period?" (Barrett, 1995; Mascolo & Fischer, 1995). Mascolo & Fischer (1995) have laid out an especially detailed developmental sequence for shame, guilt and pride (see also Barrett, 1995; Ferguson & Stegge, 1995; Griffin, 1995; Heckhausen, 1984; Lewis, 1992; Tangney, in press).

SELF-CONSCIOUS EMOTIONS ARE INTERPERSONAL, TOO

The self-conscious emotions are not only intimately connected to the self. They are also intimately connected to our relationships with others. In fact, Barrett (1995; Barrett & Campos, 1987) underscores the many interpersonal features of these emotions by referring to this family not as "self-conscious" emotions, but as "social" emotions.

First, our earliest and most important interpersonal relationships form the foundation for experiencing emotions such as shame, guilt, pride and embarrassment. These emotions typically arise when we meet, surpass or violate our standards and goals. And in turn, our moral and social standards, our hopes and ideals for the self, are shaped by key socialization experiences with parents, teachers, peers and others (Barrett, 1995; Lewis, 1992; Tangney, 1995).

Second, the "self-conscious" emotions are "social" in the sense that they typically arise in interpersonal contexts (Barrett, 1995; Baumeister, Reis & Delespaul, 1994; Jones, Kugler & Adams, 1995; Lewis, 1992; Miller, 1995a; Tangney, 1992; Tangney et al., 1994, 1996b). Embarrassment, in particular, seems to be the quintessential social emotion, occurring almost without exception in the company of others (Miller, 1995a; Tangney Miller et al., 1996b).

Third, these "self-conscious", "social" emotions motivate important and very different behaviors in the interpersonal realm (Barrett, 1995; Miller, 1995a; Tangney, 1995). The "action tendencies" of shame, guilt, embarrassment and (to a lesser extent) pride are very much interpersonally focused. For example, shame seems to motivate interpersonal avoidance or interpersonal hostility aggression, whereas guilt appears to motivate confession, apology and reparation (H. B. Lewis, 1971; Lindsay-Hartz, 1984; Tangney, 1995; Tangney et al., 1992, 1996b; Wicker, Payne & Morgan; 1983). In fact, in their extensive review, Baumeister,

Stillwell & Heatherton (1994) presented a compelling argument that guilt's primary function is to protect and enhance our close relationships.

In sum, when considering the self-conscious emotions, both theory and empirical research have focused a great deal on interpersonal aspects of these emotions. In what interpersonal contexts do these emotions arise? What roles do they play in our relationships with others? What are their implications for long-term social adjustment?

These are some of the common themes shared by psychologists interested in the self-conscious emotions. But, in addition, rather separate literatures have emerged for shame/guilt, pride and embarrassment, respectively, as theorists and researchers have grappled with issues and controversies somewhat unique to each emotion.

SHAME AND GUILT

What's the Difference?

A fundamental question facing theorists and researchers in this area over the past several decades concerns the distinction between shame and guilt. Is there any appreciable difference between these two emotions? And, if so, what is it?

Many people—scientists and laypersons alike—tend to use these emotion terms interchangeably. In the clinical literature, especially, it's not uncommon to see psychologists refer to "feelings of shame and guilt" or to discuss the "effects of shame and guilt" without making any distinction between the two emotions. In everyday discourse, people typically avoid the term "shame", referring instead to "guilt" when they mean shame, guilt or some combination of the two.

Nonetheless, there have been a number of attempts to differentiate between shame and guilt over the years. Two bases for distinguishing between shame and guilt stand out as especially influential—the anthropologists' focus on public vs. private transgressions (e.g. Benedict, 1946), and Helen Block Lewis's (1971) focus on self vs. behavior.[2]

The anthropological approach to distinguishing between shame and guilt focuses on differences in the content or structure of events eliciting these emotions. The notion is that *certain kinds of situations* lead to shame, whereas *other kinds of situations* lead to guilt. In a nutshell, shame is construed as a more "public" emotion than guilt (Benedict, 1946). Shame presumably arises from public exposure and disapproval of some shortcoming or transgression, whereas guilt is a more "private" experience arising from self-generated

---

[2] Although many psychoanalytically-orientated theories have considered shame and guilt, their conceptualization of these emotions has been erratic, and the bases for distinguishing between the two affective states have proved empirically elusive (see H. B. Lewis, 1971; Morrison, 1987; and Tangney, 1994, in press, for a more detailed analysis of psychoanalytic approaches to shame and guilt).

pangs of conscience. Gehm & Scherer (1988), for example, recently speculated that:

> Shame is usually dependent on the public exposure of one's frailty or failing, whereas guilt may be something that remains a secret with us, no-one else knowing of our breach of social norms or of our responsibility for an immoral act (p. 74).

As it turns out, empirical research has consistently failed to support this public/ private distinction (Tangney et al., 1994, 1996b). For example, we recently conducted a systematic analysis of "audiences" to shame- and guilt-eliciting events (Tangney et al., 1994). We asked several hundred children and adults to describe recent events in which they had experienced shame, guilt and pride, and then examined just how public or private these events really were. Although shame and guilt were *each* most often experienced in the presence of others (among both children and adults), a substantial number of respondents (17.2% of children and 16.5% of adults) reported shame experiences occurring alone—when *not* in the presence of others. More important, "solitary" shame was about as common as "solitary" guilt. And the frequency with which others were *aware* of the respondents' behavior did not vary as a function of shame and guilt.

We've also assessed whether shame and guilt might differ in terms of the *types* of the transgressions or failures that elicit them. Analyses of personal shame and guilt experiences provided by both children and adults indicated that there are very few, if any, "classic" shame-inducing or guilt-inducing situations (Tangney, 1992; Tangney et al., 1994). Most types of events (e.g. lying, cheating, stealing, failing to help another, disobeying parents, etc.) were cited by some people in connection with feelings of shame and by other people in connection with guilt. Similarly, Keltner & Buswell (1996) reported a high degree of overlap in the types of events that cause shame and guilt.

How do shame and guilt differ, if not in terms of the types of situations that elicit them? Empirical research has been much more supportive of Helen Block Lewis's (1971) emphasis on self vs. behavior; according to her, shame involves a negative evaluation of the global self; guilt involves a negative evaluation of a specific behavior. Although this distinction may, at first glance, appear rather subtle, this differential emphasis on self ("I did that horrible thing") vs. behavior ("I did that horrible thing") leads to very different phenomenological experiences.

Shame is an acutely painful emotion that is typically accompanied by a sense of shrinking or of "being small", and by a sense of worthlessness and powerlessness. Shamed people also feel exposed. Although shame doesn't necessarily involve an actual observing audience, present to witness one's shortcomings, there is often the imagery of how one's defective self would appear to others. H. B. Lewis (1971) described a split in self-functioning in which the self is both agent and object of observation and disapproval. An observing self witnesses and denigrates the focal self as unworthy and reprehensible. Not surprisingly, shame often leads to a desire to escape or to hide—to sink into the floor and disappear.

In contrast, guilt is typically a less painful and devastating experience because the primary concern is with a specific, rather than the entire self. So guilt doesn't affect one's core identity. Instead, there's a sense of tension, remorse and regret over the "bad thing done". People in the midst of a guilt experience often report a nagging focus or pre-occupation with the transgression—thinking of it over and over, wishing they had behaved differently or could somehow undo the harm that was done. Rather than motivating an avoidance response, guilt motivates reparative behavior.

There is now considerable empirical support for this distinction between shame and guilt from studies employing a range of methodologies—including qualitative case study analyses (H. B. Lewis, 1971; Lindsay-Hartz, 1984; Lindsay-Hartz, Mascolo & DeRivera, 1995), content analyses of shame and guilt narratives (Ferguson, Stegge & Damhuis, 1990a,b; Tangney, 1992; Tangney et al., 1994), participants' quantitative ratings of personal shame and guilt experiences (e.g. Ferguson, Stegge & Damhuis, 1991; Tangney, 1993; Tangney et al., 1996b; Wallbott & Scherer, 1988, 1995; Wicker, Payne & Morgan, 1983) and analyses of participants' counterfactual thinking (Niedenthal, Tangney & Gavanski, 1994).

Implications of Shame and Guilt for Interpersonal Behavior and Adjustment

One of the consistent themes emerging from empirical research on shame and guilt is that these emotions have important and very different implications for interpersonal behavior and adjustment. On balance, guilt appears to be the more adaptive emotion, benefiting relationships in a variety of ways (Baumeister, Stillwell & Heatherton, 1994, 1995a,b; Tangney, 1991, 1995). Three sets of findings help to illustrate the adaptive, "relationship-enhancing functions" of guilt (Baumeister, Stillwell & Heatherton, 1994, 1995a; Tangney, 1991, 1995), in contrast to the hidden costs of shame (Tangney, 1995; Tangney, Wagner & Gramzow, 1992; Tangney et al., 1992).

First, phenomenological studies of shame and guilt consistently find that these emotions lead to contrasting motivations or "action tendencies" relevant to the interpersonal context (H. B. Lewis, 1971; Lindsay-Hartz, 1984; Ferguson, Stegge & Damhuis, 1991; Tangney, 1993; Tangney et al., 1996b; Wallbott & Scherer, 1995; Wicker, Payne & Morgan, 1983). Shame typically leads to attempts to deny, hide or escape the interpersonal situation; guilt typically leads to reparative action—confessing, apologizing, undoing. Thus, guilt appears to orientate people in a more constructive, proactive, future-orientated direction, whereas shame orientates people toward separation, distancing and defense.

Second, there appears to be a special link between guilt and empathy, observed both in studies of affective styles or dispositions and in studies of emotion states. Regarding dispositions, numerous independent studies have examined the relationship of shame-proneness and guilt-proneness to a dispositional capacity for interpersonal empathy, drawing on substantial samples of children, college students and adults (Leith & Baumeister, in press; Tangney, 1991, 1994, 1995; Tangney et al., 1991; Tangney, Wagner & Barlow, in preparation). The results are quite consistent. Guilt-prone individuals are generally empathetic individuals. In contrast, shame-proneness has been repeatedly associated with an impaired capacity for other-orientated empathy and a propensity for "self-orientated" personal distress responses. Similar findings are evident when considering feelings of shame and guilt "in the moment". Individual differences aside, when people describe personal guilt experiences, they convey greater empathy for others involved, than when they describe shame experiences (Leith & Baumeister, in press; Tangney et al., 1994). In contrast, people induced to feel shame exhibit less empathy (Marschall, 1996). A number of factors, no doubt, contribute to this link between guilt and empathy. As noted by several prominent developmentalists, guilt and empathy appear to emerge along a common developmental pathway (Eisenberg, 1986; Hoffman, 1982; Zahn-Waxler & Robinson, 1995). In addition, by focusing on a bad behavior (as opposed to a bad self), people experiencing guilt are relatively free of the egocentric, self-involved process of shame. Instead, their focus on a specific behavior is likely to highlight the consequences of that behavior for distressed others, further facilitating an empathetic response (Tangney, 1991, 1995).

Finally, there appears to be a special link between shame and anger, again observed at both the dispositional and state levels. Helen Block Lewis (1971) first noted the link between shame and anger (or humiliated fury) in her clinical case studies. In years since, numerous empirical studies of both children and adults indicate that shame-prone individuals are also prone to feelings of anger and hostility (Tangney, 1994, 1995; Tangney et al., 1991, 1992). Not only are shame-prone individuals more prone to anger, in general, than their non-shame-prone peers. Once angered, they are also more likely to manage their anger in an unconstructive fashion. In a recent cross-sectional developmental study of substantial samples of children, adolescents, college students and adults (Tangney et al., 1996c), proneness to shame was clearly related to maladaptive and non-constructive responses to anger, across individuals of all ages, consistent with Scheff's (1987, 1995) and Retzinger's (1987) descriptions of a "shame–rage spiral". In contrast, guilt was generally associated with constructive means of handling anger. Similar findings have been observed at the situational level, too. For example, Wicker, Payne & Morgan (1983) found that college students re-ported a greater desire to punish others involved in personal shame vs. guilt experiences. And in a study of specific real-life episodes of anger among romantically involved couples, shamed partners were significantly more angry, more likely to engage in aggressive behavior, and less likely to elicit conciliatory behavior from their significant other (Tangney, 1995). What accounts for this rather counter-intuitive link between shame and anger? When feeling shame, people initially direct hostility inward ("I'm such a bad person"). But this hostility can easily be redirected outward in a defensive attempt to protect the self, "turn the tables" and shift the blame elsewhere—something along the lines of, "Oh, what a horrible person I am, and damn it, how could you make me feel that way!" (Tangney, 1995; Tangney et al., 1992).

In sum, a range of research studies—employing diverse samples, measures and methods—converge at the same practical bottom line: all things being equal, it's better if your friend, partner, child or boss feels guilt than shame. Shame often motivates behaviors that, in one way or another, are likely to sever or interfere with interpersonal relationships. In contrast, guilt helps keep people constructively engaged in the relationship at hand.

Implications of Shame and Guilt for Psychological Adjustment

The research reviewed thus far suggests that guilt is, on balance, the more "moral" or adaptive emotion—at least when considering social behavior and interpersonal adjustment. But is there a trade-off *vis-à-vis* individual psychological adjustment? Does the tendency to experience guilt over one's transgressions, to feel empathy for one's victims, and to set aside one's own needs and desires in favor of the needs of others, ultimately lead to increases in anxiety and depression, or decreases in self-esteem? And what about shame? Does the tendency to experience shame about the entire self leave one vulnerable to psychological problems?

There is a clear consensus on the latter question. Researchers consistently report a relationship between proneness to shame and a whole host of psychological symptoms, including depression, anxiety, eating disorder symptoms, subclinical sociopathy and low self-esteem (Allan, Gilbert & Goss, 1994; Brodie, 1995; Cook, 1988, 1991; Gramzow & Tangney, 1992; Harder, 1995; Harder, Cutler & Rockart, 1992; Harder & Lewis, 1987; Hoblitzelle, 1987; Sanftner et al., 1995; Tangney, 1993; Tangney, Burggraf & Wagner, 1995; Tangney et al., 1992; Tangney, Wagner & Gramzow, 1992). This relationship appears to be robust across a range of measurement methods and across diverse age groups and populations. Moreover, the link between shame-proneness and depression is robust, even after controlling for attributional style (Tangney, Wagner & Gramzow, 1992). People who frequently experience feelings of shame about the entire self seem vulnerable to a range of psychological symptoms.

There is much more controversy regarding the relationship of guilt to psychopathology. In fact, two very different views of guilt are represented in the current literature. The traditional view, rooted in a long clinical tradition (e.g. Freud), is that guilt contributes significantly to psychological distress and symptoms of psychopathology (Harder, 1995; Harder & Lewis, 1987). Clinical theory and clinical case studies make frequent reference to a maladaptive guilt characterized by chronic self-blame and obsessive rumination over one's transgressions (Blatt, D'Afflitti & Quinlin, 1976; Bush, 1989; Ellis, 1962; Freud, 1909/1955, 1917/1957, 1924/1961; Hartmann & Loewenstein, 1961; Rodin,

Silbertstein & Striegel-Moore, 1985; Weiss, 1993; Zahn-Waxler et al., 1990). On the other hand, recent theory and research has emphasized the adaptive functions of guilt, particularly for interpersonal behavior (Baumeister, Stillwell & Heatherton, 1994, 1995a; Hoffman, 1982; Tangney, 1991, 1994, 1995). Tangney and colleagues (Tangney, Wagner & Gramzow, 1992; Tangney, Burggraf & Wagner, 1995) have argued that once one makes the critical distinction between shame and guilt, there's no compelling theoretical reason to expect tendencies to experience guilt over specific behaviors to be associated with poor psychological adjustment.

The empirical research on guilt and psychopathology is similarly mixed. Studies employing adjective checklist-type (and other globally-worded) measures of shame and guilt have found that both shame-prone and guilt-prone styles are associated with psychological symptoms (Harder, 1995; Harder, Cutler & Rockart, 1992; Harder & Lewis, 1987; Jones & Kugler, 1993; Meehan et al., 1996). On the other hand, a very different pattern of results emerges when measures are used that are sensitive to H. B. Lewis's (1971) self vs. behavior distinction (e.g. Tangney's scenario-based methods assessing shame-proneness and guilt-proneness with respect to specific situations). Across studies of both children and adults, the tendency to experience "shame-free" guilt is essentially unrelated to psychological symptoms, whereas people prone to experience shame appear vulnerable to a range of psychological problems (Burggraf & Tangney, 1990; Gramzow & Tangney, 1992; Tangney, 1994; Tangney, Burggraf & Wagner, 1995; Tangney et al., 1991; Tangney, Wagner & Gramzow, 1992).

Is there Maladaptive Guilt?

What is the chronic, ruminative, problematic guilt described by so many clinicians? One possibility is that these problematic guilt reactions are actually feelings of guilt fused with feelings of shame (Tangney, 1995, 1996b). It seems likely that when a person begins with a guilt experience ("Oh, look at what a horrible *thing* I have *done*") but then magnifies and generalizes the event to the self ("... and aren't I a horrible *person*"), many of the advantages of guilt are lost. Not only is a person faced with tension and remorse over a specific behavior that needs to be fixed; he/she is also saddled with feelings of contempt and disgust for a bad, defective self. In effect, shame-fused guilt may be just as problematic as shame itself.

There may, however, be problematic guilt reactions that are not simply due to an overlay of shame. Recently, researchers interested in guilt—Roy Baumeister, Jane Bybee, Tamara Ferguson, David Harder and June Tangney—came together in a symposium to grapple with the question of maladaptive guilt (Bybee & Tangney, 1996). It was clear that researchers in the field are moving away from a "black-or-white" conceptualization of guilt. The question is no longer "Is guilt good or bad—adaptive or maladaptive?" Rather, the next challenge is to clarify for whom, and under what conditions, guilt serves adaptive as opposed to maladaptive functions. Here, no doubt, both situational factors (e.g. events with immutable causes, events with immutable or irreversible consequences) and person variables (e.g. individual differences in the tendency to take on "misplaced responsibility" [Zahn-Waxler & Robinson, 1995], rigid inflexible notions of what constitutes adequate "atonement", limited ability to envision future-orientated solutions, or a tendency to fuse shame and guilt) come in to play. This is an area that will attract much theoretical and empirical attention in the coming decade.

Is there Adaptive Shame?

A related issue concerns the potential positive functions of shame. Much recent theory and research has emphasized the dark side of shame (e.g. Harder & Lewis, 1987; Harder, 1995; H. B. Lewis, 1971; Tangney, 1995; Tangney, Burggraf & Wagner, 1995; Tangney et al., 1996c), underscoring negative consequences of this emotion for both psychological adjustment and interpersonal behavior. An obvious question, then, is—Why do we have the capacity to experience this emotion anyway? What adaptive purpose might it serve now? Or what purpose might it have served at earlier stages of development?

Several decades ago, Tomkins (1963) suggested that shame serves an adaptive function by regulating experiences of excessive interest and excitement. This perspective has since been embraced and elaborated by Nathanson (1987) and Schore (1991). A common theme is that, particularly at very early stages of development, some mechanism is needed to "put the brakes on" interest and excitement in social interactions (especially *vis-à-vis* the mother). Feelings of shame ensue when a child's bid for attention is rebuffed or when a significant social exchange is interrupted (e.g. when a mother is distracted from focusing on the infant). According to this view, feelings of shame then help the very young child disengage when it is appropriate to do so.

Taking a sociobiological approach, Gilbert (1997) has discussed the appeasement functions of shame and humiliation displays, noting continuities across human and non-human primates. Gilbert's approach in many ways echoes Leary's (1989; Leary, Landel & Patton, 1996) analysis of the appeasement functions of blushing and embarrassment (see also Keltner, 1995). Both perspectives emphasize the communicative aspects of shame/embarrassment displays and their role in diffusing expressions of anger and aggression among conspecifics.

And finally, there is the widely held assumption that, because shame is such a painful emotion, feelings of shame help people to avoid "doing wrong" (Barrett, 1995; Ferguson & Stegge, 1995; Zahn-Waxler & Robinson, 1995), decreasing the likelihood of transgression and impropriety. As it turns out, there is surprisingly little direct evidence supporting this adaptive function of shame. But indirect evidence suggests that shame is not as effective as guilt in serving this moral, self-regulatory function. In one study (Tangney, 1994), we examined the relationship of individual differences in proneness to shame and guilt to self-reported moral behavior (assessed by the Conventional Morality Scale; Tooke & Ickes, 1988). We found that self-reported moral behaviors were substantially positively correlated with proneness to guilt, but unrelated to proneness to shame. Together with other results showing that guilt *but not shame* is associated with enhanced empathy, a tendency to take responsibility and constructive responses to anger, these findings really raise questions about the "moral", self-regulatory functions of shame.

Implications for Treatment

Given the obvious clinical relevance of shame and guilt, surprisingly little research has been directed toward treatment-related issues. Two areas merit attention. First, more work is needed to identify and evaluate effective treatment strategies for individuals who are burdened with excessive feelings of shame or who struggle with chronic, maladaptive experiences of guilt. In recent years, clinicians have begun to propose specific therapeutic approaches for shame- and guilt-related problems, drawing on both psychodynamic and cognitive-behavioral principles (e.g. Gilbert, 1997, in press; Kaufman, 1996; Klass, 1990; Weiss, 1993), but outcome studies have yet to be conducted to evaluate the effectiveness of these treatments. A second area concerns the effects of guilt and (especially) shame on the *process* of psychotherapy. Several decades ago, Helen Block Lewis (1971) presented a compelling analysis of the numerous ways in which shame can interfere with, interrupt or, in some cases, terminate treatment. Her clinical case studies provided rich illustrations of shame wreaking havoc in the client–therapist relationship, but larger, more systematic "process" studies have yet to follow up on this ground-breaking and intriguing work.

Developmental Issues

In addition to the general developmental issues concerning the nature and functions of shame and guilt at different points in the lifespan (see above), there is the question of how shame-prone and guilt-prone styles develop. Empirical research has shown that there are reliable individual differences in the degree to which people are prone to shame or guilt (Harder & Lewis, 1987; Tangney, 1990, 1992; Tangney, Wagner & Gramzow, 1992). These moral affective styles appear to be well established by at least middle childhood (Burggraf & Tangney, 1989; Tangney et al., 1991) and are moderately stable from childhood into adolescence, and highly stable over a two to three year period in adulthood (Tangney, unpublished data).

What accounts for these individual differences in proneness to shame and proneness to guilt? Psychologists have speculated about both socialization (especially parenting) factors (e.g. Barrett, 1995; Ferguson & Stegge, 1995; Hoffman, 1982; Lewis, 1992; Miyake & Yamazaki, 1995; Potter-Efron, 1989; Rosenberg, 1997; Tangney et al., 1991; Zahn-Waxler & Robinson, 1995) and temperament factors (e.g. Dienstbier, 1984; Kochanska, 1991, 1993). But systematic empirical research—especially research that makes an explicit distinction between shame and guilt—has only recently begun.

In a recent study of twins, Zahn-Waxler & Robinson (1995) found a strong genetic component for shame, with correspondingly weak shared environment effects. For guilt, the opposite pattern was observed. Individual differences in guilt-proneness appear strongly tied to socialization factors and little affected by genetic factors.

Unfortunately, we know little about what socialization factors specifically contribute to these moral affective styles. Initial reports have been mixed. In a multigenerational study of about 364 families, Tangney et al. (1991) found little evidence of direct intergenerational transmission of shame and guilt. For example, shame-prone mothers were no more likely to have shame-prone daughters than their non-shame-prone peers. There was some evidence for a link between fathers' and sons' guilt-proneness, but this relationship was not replicated in a follow-up two years later (Tangney, unpublished data). In addition, the Tangney et al. (1991) study found few consistent relationships between parenting attitudes and behaviors (as assessed by the Block Child-rearing Practices Report) and children's shame- and guilt-proneness. Recently, Rosenberg et al. (1994) developed a series of inventories to assess more specific parental disciplinary behavior theoretically linked to shame and guilt (e.g. negative evaluations of specific behaviors vs. the child's self, ridicule and humiliation, other-orientated induction). In a study of elementary school-aged children and their parents, children's shame- and guilt-prone styles were moderately associated with children's *perceptions* of their parents' behavior, but not with parents' own self-reported behaviors (Rosenberg, 1997). Ferguson & Stegge (1995), however, found that children's guilt was associated with parents' reports of induction and parental anger in negative situations, whereas children's shame was associated with parental hostility, little recognition of positive outcomes and a lack of discipline. Drawing on observations of parental behavior, Alessandri & Lewis (1996) found that negative maternal behavior was correlated with children's shame reactions during laboratory tasks. However, Alessandri & Lewis (1993) reported that, contrary to their hypotheses, parents' specific but not global negative comments were associated with children's displays of shame. In an analysis of retrospective reports of parents' behavior, Gilbert, Allan & Goss (1996) found that recalled put-downs and shaming were associated with shame-proneness in adulthood. Finally, Zahn-Waxler, Cole & Barrett (1991; Zahn-Waxler & Robinson, 1995) have presented evidence suggesting that children of depressed mothers may be at special risk for developing "maladaptive" patterns of guilt. In sum, although some studies have been conducted in this area, more research is needed to clarify how individual differences in proneness to shame and proneness to guilt develop.

Directions for Future Research

Several important directions have already been mentioned. What specific factors shape shame-prone and guilt-prone styles? For whom and under what conditions does guilt become maladaptive? Under what conditions is shame adaptive? What are the most effective strategies for treating people with shame and guilt-related difficulties? What roles do shame and guilt play in the dynamics of the therapeutic process itself?

Three other areas ripe for research spring to mind. The first concerns the dynamics involved in people's attempts to use guilt as a form of interpersonal control. To date, only a handful of studies have explicitly examined the phenomena of guilt induction (Baumeister, Stillwell & Heatherton, 1995a; Vangelisti, Daly & Rudnick, 1991). These initial studies indicate that conscious attempts to induce guilt occur relatively frequently, particularly in the context of close relationships, and especially in response to real or perceived periods of neglect. But other questions remain. For example, do attempts to induce guilt in others vary with the stage of a relationship? What are the costs and benefits of guilt induction, and how do these vary as a function of transgression, relationship and individual factors involved? Are some people more vulnerable than others to guilt inductions?

Second, more cross-cultural research is needed. Researchers have just begun to examine how the nature, functions and psychosocial implications of self-conscious emotions might vary across cultural groups (Bierbrauer, 1992; Chiang & Barrett, 1989; Johnson et al., 1987; Kitayama, Markus & Matsumoto, 1995; Lebra, 1973; Shaver et al., 1987; Wallbott & Scherer, 1988, 1995). Kitayama, Markus & Matsumoto (1995) make the compelling argument that because there are cultural variations in the construction of the *self*, itself (e.g. independent vs. interdependent selves, cf. Markus & Kitayama, 1991), *self*-conscious emotions may show especially marked variations across cultural contexts.

Finally, there continue to be significant challenges in the assessment of shame and guilt. Although quite a number of promising new measures have been developed during the past decade (see Ferguson & Crowley, in press; Kugler & Jones, 1992; and Tangney, 1990, 1995, 1996a, for reviews and analyses of measurement issues in this area), shame and guilt are difficult constructs to assess and the coming decade will no doubt see improvements in our ability to capture these self-conscious emotions. In particular, more work is needed: (a) to tease out adaptive from maladaptive forms of guilt (Tangney et al., 1996a, recently constructed a pilot version of the TOSCA-2 to take a first stab at this); and (b) to reliably assess *state* shame and guilt (feelings of shame and guilt "in the moment").

EMBARRASSMENT

The study of embarrassment has a long and illustrious history dating back to Darwin (1872/1965), and continuing with the pioneering work of Goffman (1956), Sattler (1963), Modigliani (1968), Edelmann (1981, 1982; Edelmann & Hampson, 1981a,b) and Miller (1987, 1996). Miller (1995a) defines embarrassment as "an aversive state of mortification, abashment and chagrin that follows public social predicaments" (p. 322). Indeed, embarrassment appears to be the most "social" of the self-conscious emotions. Unlike shame and guilt, it occurs almost without exception in the company of other people (Parrott & Smith, 1991; Tangney et al., 1996b). Beyond this public feature of embarrassment, however, there are few situational factors that consistently define an embarrassing situation. Analyzing personal accounts of embarrassment from hundreds of high school students and adults, Miller (1992; see also Cupach & Metts, 1992) attempted to catalogue the types of situations that cause people to feel embarrassment. At the top of the list were "normative public deficiencies"—situations in which the individual behaved in a clumsy, absent-minded or hapless way. These are the types of situations that one typically thinks of as embarrassing—tripping in front of a large class, forgetting someone's name, unintended bodily-induced noises. But, in addition, Miller's "catalogue" covers a very broad range of circumstances, from awkward social interactions, to conspicuousness in the absence of any deficiency, to "team transgressions" (embarrassed by a member of one's group), to "empathic" embarrassment.

The diversity of situations that lead to embarrassment has posed a challenge to theorists attempting to construct a comprehensive "account" of embarrassment. What core psychological process or dilemma leads to embarrassment? Some theorists believe that the crux of embarrassment is negative evaluation by others (Edelmann, 1981; Miller & Leary, 1992; Miller, 1996; Semin & Manstead, 1981) or transient drops in self-esteem secondary to negative evaluation by others (Modigliani, 1968). This social evaluation account highlights the fact that embarrassment occurs almost without exception in the company of others, but it runs into difficulty with embarrassment events that do not involve any apparent deficiency (e.g. being the center of attention during a chorus of "Happy Birthday"). Other theorists subscribe to the "dramaturgic" account of embarrassment (Goffman, 1956; Gross & Stone, 1964; Silver, Sabini & Parrott, 1987). According to this view, embarrassment occurs when implicit social roles and scripts are disrupted and social interactions go awry. A flubbed performance, an unanticipated belch, *and* being the focus of "Happy Birthday" each present a dilemma in the sense that these situations deviate from accustomed social scripts. A related but distinct view is Babcock's (1988) "personal account" of embarrassment, which holds that embarrassment occurs when one acts in a way that is inconsistent with one's *persona*, or personal standards that help form a person's identity. From this perspective, too, one's behavior may not necessarily be negative in any objective or social sense. Rather, it is incongruent with a person's own standards of conduct.

Finally, Lewis (1992) has distinguished between two types of embarrass-ment—embarrassment due to exposure and embarrassment due to negative self-evaluation. According to Lewis (1992), embarrassment due to exposure emerges early in life, once children develop a rudimentary sense of self. Toddlers begin to show signs of embarrassment in a range of situations that involve public "exposure" and scrutiny, but which do not involve any apparent negative self-evaluation. As children develop standards, rules and goals (SRGs), a second type of embarrassment emerges—"embarrassment as mild shame" associated with some failure in relation to SRGs. Lewis notes that as adults, we continue to experience both types of embarrassment—embarrassment over obvious partfalls and blunders, and a more purely "self-conscious" type of embarrassment (e.g. upon receiving high compliments, as the center of attention at a birthday celebration.)

These contrasting "accounts" of embarrassment have led to a lively debate in the theoretical and empirical literature. Researchers have devised some very inventive experiments in an attempt to tease out the "essence" of this very common affective reaction (e.g. Leary, Landel & Patton, 1996; Parrott, Sabini & Silver, 1988; Parrott & Smith, 1991). The jury is still out, however, and as the debate continues a multifactor account of embarrassment seems most likely.

Functions of Embarrassment

Although there is some debate about the fundamental *causes* of embarrassment, there is much more agreement about the adaptive significance, or functions, of embarrassment. Leary (1989; Leary & Meadows, 1991; Leary, Landel & Patton, 1996) and others (Gilbert, 1997; Keltner, 1995; Keltner & Buswell, in press; Miller, 1996) have suggested that embarrassment serves an important social function by signaling *appeasement* to others. When a person's untoward behavior threatens his/her standing in an important social group, visible signs of embarrassment function as a non-verbal acknowledgment of shared social standards. Leary argues that embarrassment displays thus diffuse negative social evaluations and the likelihood of retaliation. There's a good deal of empirical evidence to support this "appeasement" or remedial function of embarrassment from studies of both humans and non-human primates (for reviews, see Gilbert, 1997; Keltner & Buswell, in press; Leary & Meadows, 1991). For example, Semin & Manstead (1982) found that people reacted more positively to others following a social transgression if the transgressors were visibly embarrassed, and in an inventive series of studies, Leary, Landel & Patton (1996) presented evidence that people are actually *motivated* to convey embarrassment to others as a way of repairing their social image.

A second function, suggested by Lewis (1995), is that embarrassment serves to prevent undue self-reflection. The notion is that feelings of embarrassment interrupt cycles of "meta" reflection (thinking about the self thinking about the self thinking about the self).

Embarrassment and Shame

Is there a difference between shame and embarrassment, or are these two terms for the same affective experience? Some theorists have essentially equated the two emotions. Izard (1977), for example, conceptualized embarrassment as an element of shame. Kaufman (1989) asserted that "however mild or intense, embarrassment is not a different affect" (p. 24) from shame. And H. B. Lewis (1971), in her extensive treatment of shame and guilt, only briefly mentioned embarrassment as a "shame variant".

A more dominant view is that shame and embarrassment can be distinguished in terms of intensity of affect (e.g. Borg et al., 1988) and/or severity of transgression (Buss, 1980; Lewis, 1992; Ortony, Clore & Collins, 1988). Shame is generally assumed to be a more intense emotion than embarrassment, and it has been suggested that shame results from more serious failures and moral transgressions, whereas embarrassment follows relatively trivial social transgressions or untoward interactions.

Still others have suggested that different patterns of *attributions* for negative events are associated with shame and embarrassment. Modigliani (1968), Shott (1979) and Klass (1990) all proposed that shame is tied to perceived deficiencies of one's *core* self, whereas embarrassment results from deficiencies in one's *presented* self. Thus, shame is presumably associated with more global and enduring negative attributions about oneself, whereas embarrassment is tied to more transient, situation-specific failures and pratfalls.

Although many opinions have been offered about the potential differences between shame and embarrassment, empirical research has only recently been conducted to address the issue systematically (Babcock & Sabini, 1990; Manstead & Tetlock, 1989; Miller & Tangney, 1994; Mosher & White, 1981; Tangney et al., 1996b). Together, these studies suggest that shame and embarrassment are indeed quite different emotions—more distinct, even, than shame and guilt! For example, in a study comparing young adults' personal shame, guilt and embarrassment experiences, Tangney et al. (1996b) found that, compared to embarrassment, shame was a more intense, painful emotion that involved a greater sense of moral transgression. But even with intensity and morality controlled, shame and embarrassment differed markedly along a range of affective, cognitive and motivational dimensions. For example, shamed participants felt greater responsibility and regret. They felt more angry and disgusted with themselves and believed that others, too, felt anger towards them. In contrast, embarrassment events involved more humor and occurred more suddenly and with a greater sense of surprise. Embarrassment was also accompanied by more obvious physiological changes (e.g. blushing) and by a greater sense of exposure and conspicuousness. On the other hand, there was little support for the assumption (Modigliani, 1968; Shott, 1979; Klass, 1990) that embarrassment (as compared to shame) results from larger losses of perceived approval from others than from changes in self-appraisal.

Individual Differences in Embarrassability

As with shame and guilt, there are individual differences in the degree to which people are prone to experience embarrassment. These individual differences are evident within the first few years of life and appear to be quite stable by at least three years of age (Lewis et al., 1991). Research has shown that people who are prone to frequent and excessive embarrassment reactions tend to be more *self-conscious* than the average person, and they are more concerned about receiving negative evaluations from *others* (Leary & Meadows, 1991; Miller, 1995b). Miller (1995b) has shown that this heightened self-consciousness and fear of negative evaluation is not simply due to the fact that embarrassable people have poor social skills. In a study of several hundred young adults, proneness to embarrassment was not related to a measure of global social skills. Rather, a key factor was sensitivity to social norms. People who are prone to embarrassment tend to be highly aware of and concerned with social rules and standards. Research also suggests that frequent and excessive episodes of embarrassment may put people at risk for other social and emotional difficulties. For example, embarrassability has been linked to neuroticism and high levels of negative affect (Edelmann & McCusker, 1986; Miller, 1995b). On the other hand, an impaired capacity to experience or express embarrassment appears to be detrimental, as well. Keltner, Moffitt & Stouthamer-Loeber (1995) found that aggressive and delinquent boys showed less embarrassment on a cognitive task than well-adjusted boys.

Directions for Future Research

Initial research on embarrassment focused on the phenomenology of embarrassment and its causes. More recently, researchers have begun to examine the range of behaviors that people engage in, once embarrassed (Cupach & Metts, 1990, 1992; Miller, 1996; Sharkey & Stafford, 1990). What are the costs and benefits of these strategies for managing embarrassment—for the individual and for the interpersonal relationships involved? A second, related issue concerns intervention. How can people troubled by excessive embarrassment learn to develop more effective responses to the inevitable pratfalls of everyday life? Third, researchers have only recently begun to examine embarrassment across cultures (e.g. Cupach & Imahori, 1993; Edelmann & Iwawaki, 1987; Haidt & Keltner, 1996; Hashimoto & Shimizu, 1988; Sueda & Wiseman, 1992). How does the experience, meaning and functions of embarrassment vary across different cultural contexts?

PRIDE

Of the self-conscious emotions, pride is the neglected sibling, having received the least attention by far. Most research comes from developmental psychology, particularly in the achievement domain (Heckhausen, 1984; Lewis, Alessandri & Sullivan, 1992; Stipek, 1983; Stipek, Recchia & McClintic, 1992).

Mascolo and Fischer (1995) define pride as an emotion "generated by appraisals that one is responsible for a socially valued outcome or for being a socially valued person" (p. 66). From their perspective, pride serves to enhance people's self-worth and, perhaps more importantly, to encourage future behavior that conforms to social standards of worth or merit (see also Barrett, 1995).

Developmental Issues

Developmental psychologists have discussed substantial developmental shifts, from early childhood into adolescence, in the types of situations that induce pride, the nature of the pride experience itself, and the ways in which pride is expressed (Heckhausen, 1984; Lewis, 1994; Mascolo & Fischer, 1995; Stipek, 1995; Stipek, Recchia & McClintic, 1992). For example, Stipek, Recchia & McClintic's (1992) research suggests that there are developmental changes in the criteria children use for evaluating success and failure—and, by extension, changes in the types of situation that lead to pride experiences. Children under 33 months of age clearly respond positively to task-intrinsic criteria (e.g. completing a tower of blocks), but they do not seem to grasp the concept of competition (e.g. winning or losing a race to complete a tower of blocks). It is only after 33 months that children show enhanced pride responses in the event of a competitive win.

There also appear to be developmental shifts in the importance of praise from others. In a study of children aged 13–39 months, Stipek et al. (1992) reported that across all ages, children smiled and exhibited pleasure with their successes. But there were significant developmental changes in social referencing behavior. As children neared age 2, they began to seek eye contact with parents upon completing a task, and in many cases actively solicited parental recognition. In turn, parental praise seemed to enhance children's pleasure with their achievements. Similarly, Alessandri & Lewis (1993) found that parental praise was inversely related to 3 year-olds' expressions of shame, although in this study praise was unrelated to children's expressions of pride. Taking a broader developmental perspective, Stipek (1995) has suggested that the importance of external praise may follow a curvilinear pattern across the lifespan. Very young children take pleasure in simply having some immediate effect on their environment but, as they develop self-consciousness and a broader concern with social evaluation (about age 2), others' reactions play an important role in shaping their affective reactions to success and failure. Still later, as they move into middle to late childhood, their standards become increasingly internalized and experiences of pride become again more autonomous, less contingent on others' praise and approval.

Stipek et al. (1992) have examined the implications of parental goal-setting, in addition to parental praise. In their study of mothers and 13–39 month-old children they found that, whereas maternal expressions of praise for children's accomplishments enhanced children's pride responses, maternal goal-setting seemed to actually interfere with children's pleasure in their achievements. Across all ages, children expressed more joy and more frequently called attention to achieved goals they had set for themselves, compared to goals their mothers had proposed.

Two Types of Pride?

Researchers have identified different types of negative self-conscious emotions— shame, guilt and embarrassment. Are there different forms of positive self-conscious emotions, as well? Both Tangney (1990) and Lewis (1992) have suggested that there may be two types of pride. Paralleling the self vs. behavior distinction of guilt and shame, Tangney (1990) distinguished between pride in self ("alpha" pride) and pride in behavior ("beta" pride). The Self-conscious Affect and Attribution Inventories (SCAAI: Tangney et al., 1988; SCAAI-C: Burggraf & Tangney, 1989) and the Tests of Self-conscious Affect (TOSCAs: Tangney et al., 1989) each contain measures of individual differences in the tendency to experience alpha pride and beta pride, respectively. However, neither Tangney nor any other investigators have made much use of these ancillary scales, perhaps in part owning to their rather modest reliability (the pride scales draw on a rather small subset of SCAAI and TOSCA scenarios).

In a similar vein, Lewis (1992) distinguished between pride and hubris. According to Lewis, pride is experienced when one's success is attributed to a specific action or behavior. Hubris (pridefulness) arises when success is attributed to the global self. Lewis (1993) views hubris as a largely maladaptive reaction. Most of his discussions appear to focus on hubris as a trait (tendencies to experience hubris frequently across multiple situations) rather than as a state (e.g. momentary feelings of pride in self). From Lewis's perspective, hubris is "something dislikeable and to be avoided" (1993, p. 570), in part because of the "addictive" quality of hubris. Such global feelings of pride are highly reinforcing, yet difficult to sustain. As a consequence, Lewis suggests, hubristic individuals are inclined to distort and invent situations to recreate this transient emotion. Further, Lewis notes, people do not like hubristic individuals. Hubris brings with it a range of interpersonal problems.

Little empirical research has been conducted to examine individual differences in proneness to pride in self (or pride in behavior, for that matter). My impressions from unpublished data utilizing our SCAAI and TOSCA measures of alpha pride across many samples of adults is that individual differences in proneness to alpha pride (hubris) are not markedly adaptive or maladaptive. Whether this is the case in clinical samples (e.g. those including individuals with narcissistic traits) remains to be seen.

Directions for Future Research

Pride remains an area wide open for empirical research. The pioneering work of Stipek (1995; Stipek, Recchia & McClintic, 1992) has begun to map out developmental changes in the situations and social contexts that shape children's experiences of pride, but clearly more work remains to be done, particularly regarding interpersonal aspects of positive self-evaluation. Second, very little work has addressed individual differences in the tendency to take pride in one's self or one's accomplishments. What are the implications of such individual differences for children's achievement motivation and behavior as they negotiate the challenges of elementary school and beyond? What socialization factors contribute to the emergence of these individual differences? And is the proposed distinction between global vs. specific pride empirically useful? No doubt, the next decade will see exciting advances in our understanding of this long-neglected but very important self-conscious emotion.

REFERENCES

Alessandri, S. & Lewis, M. (1993). Parental evaluation and its relation to shame and pride in young children. *Sex Roles*, **29**, 335–343.

Alessandri, S. & Lewis, M. (1996). Differences in pride and shame in maltreated and nonmaltreated preschoolers. *Child Development*, **67**, 1857–1869.

Allan, S., Gilbert, P. & Goss, K. (1994). An exploration of shame measures: II. Psychopathology. *Personality and Individual Differences*, **17**, 719–722.

Amsterdam, B. (1972). Mirror self-image reactions before age two. *Developmental Psychobiology*, **5**, 297–305.

Babcock, M. K. (1988). Embarrassment: a window on the self. *Journal for the Theory of Social Behavior*, **18**, 459–481.

Babcock, M. K. & Sabini, J. (1990). On differentiating embarrassment from shame. *European Journal of Social Psychology*, **20**, 151–169.

Barrett, K. C. (1995). A functionalist approach to shame and guilt. In J. P. Tangney & K. W. Fischer (eds), *Self-conscious Emotions: Shame, Guilt, Embarrassment, and Pride*. New York: Guilford, pp. 25–63.

Barrett, K. C. & Campos, J. J. (1987). Perspectives on emotional development: II. A functionalist approach to emotions. In J. Osofsky (ed.), *Handbook of Infant Development*, 2nd edn. New York: Wiley, pp. 555–578.

Baumeister, R. G., Reis, H. T. & Delespaul, P. A. E. G. (1995). Subjective and experiential correlates of guilt in everyday life. *Personality and Social Psychology Bulletin*, **117**, 1256–1268.

Baumeister, R. F., Stillwell, A. M. & Heatherton, T. F. (1994). Guilt: an interpersonal approach. *Psychological Bulletin*, **115**, 243–267.

Baumeister, R. F., Stillwell, A. M. & Heatherton, T. F. (1995a). Interpersonal aspects of guilt: evidence from narrative studies. In J. P. Tangney & K. W. Fischer (eds), *Self-conscious Emotions: Shame, Guilt, Embarrassment, and Pride*. New York: Guilford, pp. 255–273.

Baumeister, R. F., Stillwell, A. M. & Heatherton, T. F. (1995b). Personal narratives about guilt: role in action control and interpersonal relationships. *Basic and Applied Social Psychology*, **17**, 173–198.

Benedict, R. (1946). *The Chrysanthemum and the Sword*. Boston, MA: Houghton Mifflin.

Bertenthal, B. L. & Fischer, K. W. (1978). Development of self-recognition in the infant. *Developmental Psychology*, **14**, 44–50.

Bierbrauer, G. (1992). Reactions to violation of normative standards: a cross-cultural analysis of shame and guilt. *International Journal of Psychology*, **27**, 181–193.

Blatt, S. J., D'Afflitti, J. P. & Quinlin, D. M. (1976). Experiences of depression in normal young adults. *Journal of Abnormal Psychology*, **86**, 203–223.

Borg, I., Staufenbiel, T. & Scherer, K. R. (1988). On the symbolic basis of shame. In K. R. Scherer (ed.), *Facets of Emotion: Recent Research*. Hillsdale, NJ: Erlbaum, pp. 79–98.

Brodie, P. (1995). How Sociopaths Love: Sociopathy and Interpersonal Relationships. Unpublished doctoral dissertation, George Mason University, Fairfax, VA.

Burggraf, S. A. & Tangney, J. P. (1989). Proneness to Shame, Proneness to Guilt, and Self-concept. Poster presented at the meetings of the American Psychological Society, Alexandria, VA, June.

Burggraf, S. A. & Tangney, J. P. (1990). Shame-proneness, Guilt-proneness, and Attributional Style Related to Children's Depression. Poster presented at the meetings of the American Psychological Society, Dallas, June.

Bush, M. (1989). The role of unconscious guilt in psychopathology and psychotherapy. *Bulletin of the Menninger Clinic*, **53**, 97–107.

Buss, A. H. (1980). *Self-consciousness and social anxiety*. San Francisco, CA: W. H. Freeman.

Bybee, J. & Tangney, J. P. (chairs) (1996). Is Guilt Adaptive? Functions in Interpersonal Relationships and Mental Health. Symposium presented at the meetings of the American Psychological Association, Toronto, August.

Chiang, T. & Barrett, K. C. (1989). A cross-cultural comparison of toddlers' reactions to the infraction of a standard: a guilt culture vs. a shame culture. Paper presented at the meeting of the Society for Research in Child Development, Kansas City, MO, April.

Cook, D. R. (1988). The measurement of shame: the Internalized Shame Scale. Paper presented at the annual meetings of the American Psychological Association, Atlanta, GA, August.

Cook, D. R. (1991). Shame, attachment, and addictions: implications for family therapists. *Contemporary Family Therapy*, **13**, 405–419.

Cupach, W. R. & Imahori, T. T. (1993). Managing social predicaments created by others: a comparison of Japanese and American facework. *Western Journal of Communication*, **57**, 431–444.

Cupach, W. R. & Metts, S. (1990). Remedial processes in embarrassing predicaments. In J. Anderson (ed.), *Communication Yearbook 13*. Newbury Park, CA: Sage, pp. 323–352.

Cupach, W. R. & Metts, S. (1992). The effects of type of predicament and embarrassability on remedial responses to embarrassing situations. *Communications Quarterly*, **40**, 149–161.

Damon, W. & Hart, D. (1982). Development of self-understanding from infancy through adolescence. *Child Development*, **53**, 841–864.

Darwin, C. R. (1965). *The Expression of Emotions in Man and Animals*. Chicago: University of Chicago Press. (Original work published 1872.)

Dienstbier, R. A. (1984). The role of emotion in moral socialization. In C. Izard, J. Kagan & R. B. Zajonc (eds), *Emotions, Cognitions, and Behaviors* (pp. 484–513).

Edelmann, R. J. (1981). Embarrassment: the state of research. *Current Psychological Reviews*, **1**, 125–138.

Edelmann, R. J. (1982). The effect of embarrassed reactions upon others. *Australian Journal of Psychology*, **34**, 359–367.

Edelmann, R. J. & Hampson, R. J. (1981a). Embarrassment in dyadic interaction. *Social Behavior and Personality*, **9**, 171–177.

Edelmann, R. J. & Hampson, R. J. (1981b). The recognition of embarrassment. *Personality and Social Psychology Bulletin*, **7**, 109–116.

Edelmann, R. J. & Iwawaki, S. (1987). Self-reported expression and consequences of embarrassment in the United Kingdom and Japan. *Psychologia*, **30**, 205–216.

Edelmann, R. J. & McCusker, G. (1986). Introversion, neuroticism, empathy, and embarrassability. *Personality and Individual Differences*, **7**, 133–140.

Eisenberg, N. (1986). *Altruistic Cognition, Emotion, and Behavior*. Hillsdale, NJ: Erlbaum.

Ellis, A. (1962). *Reason and Emotion in Psychotherapy*. New York: Lyle Stuart.

Ferguson, T. J. & Crowley, S. L. (in press). Measure for measure: guilt is not a unitary construct. *Journal of Personality Assessment*.

Ferguson, T. J. & Stegge, H. (1995). Emotional states and traits in children: the case of guilt and shame. In J. P. Tangney & K. W. Fischer (eds), *Self-conscious Emotions: Shame, Guilt, Embarrassment, and Pride*. New York: Guilford, pp. 174–197.

Ferguson, T. J., Stegge, H. & Damhuis, I. (1990a). Guilt and shame experiences in elementary school-age children. In R. J. Takens (ed.), *European Perspectives in Psychology*, Vol. 1. New York: Wiley, pp. 195–218.

Ferguson, T. J., Stegge, H. & Damhuis, I. (1990b). Spontaneous and Elicited Guilt and Shame Experiences in Elementary School-age Children. Poster presented at the Southwestern Society for Research in Human Development, Dallas, TX, March.

Ferguson, T. J., Stegge, H. & Damhuis, I. (1991). Children's understanding of guilt and shame. *Child Development*, **62**, 827–839.

Fischer, K. W. & Tangney, J. P. (1995). Self-conscious emotions and the affect revolution: framework and overview. In J. P. Tangney & K. W. Fischer (eds), *Self-conscious Emotions: Shame, Guilt, Embarrassment, and Pride*. New York: Guilford, pp. 3–22.

Freud, S. (1909/1955). Notes upon a case of obsessional neurosis. In J. Strachey (ed. and trans.), *The Standard Edition of the Complete Psychological Works of Sigmund Freud*, Vol. 10. London: Hogarth, pp. 155–318. (original work published 1909).

Freud, S. (1917/1957). Mourning and melancholia. In J. Strachey (ed. and trans.), *The Standard Edition of the Complete Psychological Works of Sigmund Freud*, Vol. 14. London: Hogarth, pp. 243–258 (original work published 1917).

Freud, S. (1924/1961). The dissolution of the Oedipus Complex. In J. Strachey (ed. and trans.), *The Standard Edition of the Complete Psychological Works of Sigmund Freud*, Vol. 19. London: Hogarth, pp. 173–182 (original work published 1924).

Gehm, T. L. & Scherer, K. R. (1988). Relating situation evaluation to emotion differentiation: nonmetric analysis of cross-cultural questionnaire data. In K. R. Scherer (ed.), *Facets of Emotion: Recent Research*. Hillsdale, NJ: Erlbaum, pp. 61–77.

Gilbert, P. (1997). The evolution of social attractiveness and its role in shame, humiliation, guilt, and therapy. *British Journal of Medical Psychology*, **70**, 113–147.

Gilbert, P. (in press). Shame and humiliation in the treatment of complex cases. In N. Tarrier, G.T. Haddock & A. Wells (eds), *Complex Cases: Clinical Challenges for Cognitive Behavior Therapy*. Chichester: Wiley.

Gilbert, P., Allan, S. & Goss, K. (1996). Parental representations, shame, interpersonal problems, and vulnerability to psychopathology. *Clinical Psychology and Psychotherapy*, **3**, 23–34.

Goffman, E. (1956). Embarrassment and social organization. *American Journal of Sociology*, **62**, 264–271.

Gramzow, R. & Tangney, J. P. (1992). Proneness to shame and the narcissistic personality. *Personality and Social Psychology Bulletin*, **18**, 369–376.

Griffin, S. (1995). A cognitive-developmental analysis of pride, shame, and embarrassment in middle childhood. In J. P. Tangney & K. W. Fischer (eds), *Self-conscious Emotions: Shame, Guilt, Embarrassment, and Pride.* New York: Guilford, pp. 219–236.

Gross, E. & Stone, G. P. (1964). Embarrassment and the analysis of role requirements. *American Journal of Sociology*, **70**, 1–15.

Haidt, J. & Keltner, D. (1996). Culture and emotion: new methods and new emotions (manuscript in preparation).

Harder, D. W. (1995). Shame and guilt assessment and relationships of shame and guilt proneness to psychopathology. In J. P. Tangney & K. W. Fischer (eds), *Self-conscious Emotions: Shame, Guilt, Embarrassment, and Pride.* New York: Guilford, pp. 368–392.

Harder, D. W., Cutler, L. & Rockart, L. (1992). Assessment of shame and guilt and their relationship to psychopathology. *Journal of Personality Assessment*, **59**, 584–604.

Harder, D. W. & Lewis, S. J. (1987). The assessment of shame and guilt. In J. N. Butcher & C. D. Spielberger (eds), *Advances in Personality Assessment*, Vol. 6. Hillsdale NJ: Erlbaum, pp. 89–114.

Hartmann, E. & Loewenstein, R. (1961). Notes on the superego. *The Psychoanalytic Study of the Child*, **17**, 42–81.

Hashimoto, E. & Shimizu, T. (1988). A cross-cultural study of the emotion of shame/ embarrassment: Iranian and Japanese children. *Psychologia*, **31**, 1–6.

Heckhausen, H. (1984). Emergent achievement behavior: some early developments. In J. Nicholls (ed.), *Advances in Motivation and Achievement, Vol. 3. The development of achievement motivation.* Greenwich, CT: JAI, pp. 1–32.

Hoblitzelle, W. (1987). Attempts to measure and differentiate shame and guilt: the relation between shame and depression. In H. B. Lewis (ed.), *The Role of Shame in Symptom Formation.* Hillsdale, NJ: Erlbaum, pp. 207–235.

Hoffman, M. L. (1982). Development of prosocial motivation: empathy and guilt. In N. Eisenberg-Berg (ed.), *Development of Prosocial Behavior.* New York: Academic Press, pp. 281–313.

Izard, C. E. (1977). *Human Emotions.* New York: Plenum.

Johnson, R. C., Danko, G. P., Huang, Y. H., Park, J. Y., Johnson, S. B. & Nagoshi, C. T. (1987). Guilt, shame and adjustment in three cultures. *Personality and Individual Differences*, **8**, 357–364.

Jones, W. H. & Kugler, K. (1993). Interpersonal correlates of the Guilt Inventory. *Journal of Personality Assessment*, **61**, 246–258.

Jones, W. H., Kugler, K. & Adams, P. (1995). You always hurt the one you love: guilt and transgressions against relationship partners. In J. P. Tangney & K. W. Fischer (eds), *Self-conscious Emotions: Shame, Guilt, Embarrassment, and Pride.* New York: Guilford, pp. 301–321.

Kagan, J. (1984). *The Nature of the Child.* New York: Basic Books.

Kaufman, G. (1989). *The Psychology of Shame: Theory and Treatment of Shame-based Syndromes.* New York: Springer.

Kaufman, G. (1996). *The Psychology of Shame*, 2nd edn. New York: Springer.

Keltner, D. (1995). Signs of appeasement: evidence for the distinct displays of embarrassment, amusement, and shame. *Journal of Personality and Social Psychology*, **68**, 441–454.

Keltner, D. & Buswell, B. N. (1996). Evidence for the distinctness of embarrassment, shame, and guilt: a study of recalled antecedents and facial expressions of emotion. *Cognition and Emotion*, **10**, 155–171.

Keltner, D. & Buswell, B. N. (in press). Embarrassment: its distinct form and appeasement functions. *Psychological Bulletin.*

Keltner, D., Moffitt, T. & Stouthamer-Loeber, M. (1995). Facial expressions of emotion and psychopathology in adolescent boys. *Journal of Abnormal Psychology*, **104**, 644–652.

Kitayama, S., Markus, H. R. & Matsumoto, H. (1995). Culture, self, and emotion: a cultural perspective on "self-conscious" emotion. In J. P. Tangney & K. W. Fischer (eds), *Self-conscious Emotions: Shame, Guilt, Embarrassment, and Pride.* New York: Guilford, pp. 439–464.

Klass, E. T. (1990). Guilt, shame, and embarrassment: cognitive-behavioral approaches. In H. Leitenberg (ed.), *Handbook of Social and Evaluation Anxiety.* New York: Plenum, pp. 385–414.

Kochanska, G (1991). Socialization and temperament in the development of guilt and conscience. *Child Development*, **62**, 1379–1392.

Kochanska, G. (1993). Toward a synthesis of parental socialization and child temperament in early development of conscience. *Child Development*, **64**, 325–347.

Kugler, K. & Jones, W. H. (1992). On conceptualizing and assessing guilt. *Journal of Personality and Social Psychology*, **62**, 318–327.

Leary, M. R. (1989). Fear of exclusion and appeasement behaviors: the case of blushing. In R. F. Baumeister (Chair), The Need to Belong. Symposium presented at the annual meeting of the American Psychological Association, New Orleans, LA, August.

Leary, M. R., Landel, J. L. & Patton, K. M. (1996). The motivated expression of embarrassment following a self-presentational predicament. *Journal of Personality*, **64**, 619–637.

Leary, M. R. & Meadows, S. (1991). Predictors, eliciters, and concomitants of social blushing. *Journal of Personality and Social Psychology*, **60**, 254–262.

Lebra, T. S. (1973). The social mechanism of guilt and shame: the Japanese case. *Anthropological Quarterly*, **44**, 241–255.

Leith, K. P. & Baumeister, R. F. (in press). Empathy, shame, guilt, and narratives of interpersonal conflicts: guilt-prone people are better at perspective taking. *Journal of Personality*.

Lewis, H. B. (1971). *Shame and Guilt in Neurosis.* New York: International Universities Press.

Lewis, M. (1992). *Shame: The Exposed Self.* New York: Free Press.

Lewis, M. (1993). Self-conscious emotions: embarrassment, pride, shame, and guilt. In M. Lewis & J. Haviland (eds), *Handbook of Emotions.* New York: Guilford.

Lewis, M. (1994). Emotional development in the preschool child. In H. Nuba, M. Searson & D. L. Sheiman (eds), *Resources for Early Childhood: A Handbook.* New York: Garland.

Lewis, M. (1995). Embarrassment: the emotion of self-exposure and evaluation. In J. P. Tangney & K. W. Fischer (eds), *Self-conscious Emotions: Shame, Guilt, Embarrassment, and Pride.* New York: Guilford, pp. 198–218.

Lewis, M., Alessandri, S. M. & Sullivan, M. W. (1992). Differences in shame and pride as a function of children's gender and task difficulty. *Child Development*, **63**, 630–638.

Lewis, M., Stanger, C., Sullivan, M. W. & Barone, P. (1991). Changes in embarrassment as a function of age, sex and situation. *British Journal of Developmental Psychology*, **9**, 485–492.

Lewis, M., Sullivan, M. W., Stanger, C. & Weiss, M. (1989). Self-development and self-conscious emotions. *Child Development*, **60**, 146–156.

Lindsay-Hartz, J. (1984). Contrasting experiences of shame and guilt. *American Behavioral Scientist*, **27**, 689–704.

Lindsay-Hartz, J., de Rivera, J. & Mascolo, M. (1995). Differentiating shame and guilt and their effects on motivation. In J. P. Tangney & K. W. Fischer (eds), *Self-conscious Emotions: Shame, Guilt, Embarrassment, and Pride.* New York: Guilford, pp. 274–300.

Manstead, A. S. R. & Tetlock, P. E. (1989). Cognitive appraisals and emotional experience: further evidence. *Cognition and Emotion*, **3**, 225–240.

Markus, H. R. & Kitayama, S. (1991). Culture and the self: implications for cognition, emotion, and motivation. *Psychological Review*, **98**, 224–253.

Marschall, D. E. (1996).   Effects of Induced Shame on Subsequent Empathy and Altru-
    istic Behavior. Unpublished Masters' thesis, George Mason University, Fairfax VA.
Mascolo, M. F. & Fischer, K. W. (1995).   Developmental transformation in appraisals
    for pride, shame, and guilt. In J. P. Tangney & K. W. Fischer (eds), *Self-conscious
    Emotions: Shame, Guilt, Embarrassment, and Pride*. New York: Guilford, pp.
    64–113.
Meehan, M. A., O'Connor, L. E., Berry, J. W., Weiss, J., Morrison, A. & Acampora, A.
    (1996).   Guilt, shame, and depression in clients in recovery from addiction. *Journal of
    Psychoactive Drugs*, **28**, 125–134.
Miller, R. S. (1987).   Empathic embarrassment: situational and personal determinants of
    reactions to the embarrassment of another. *Journal of Personality and Social Psychol-
    ogy*, **53**, 1061–1069.
Miller, R. S. (1992).   The nature and severity of self-reported embarrassing circum-
    stances. *Personality and Social Psychology Bulletin*, **18**, 190–198.
Miller, R. S. (1995a).   Embarrassment and social behavior. In J. P. Tangney & K. W.
    Fischer (eds), *Self-conscious Emotions: Shame, Guilt, Embarrassment, and Pride*.
    New York: Guilford, pp. 322–339.
Miller, R. S. (1995b).   On the nature of embarrassability: shyness, social-evaluation, and
    social skill. *Journal of Personality*, **63**, 315–339.
Miller, R. S. (1996).   *Embarrassment: Poise and Peril in Everyday Life*. New York:
    Guilford.
Miller, R. S. & Leary, M. R. (1992).   Social sources and interactive functions of embar-
    rassment. In M. Clark (ed.), *Emotion and Social Behavior*. New York: Sage.
Miller, R. S. & Tangney, J. P. (1994).   Differentiating embarrassment and shame. *Journal
    of Social and Clinical Psychology*, **13**, 273–287.
Miyake, K. & Yamazaki, K. (1995).   In J. P. Tangney & K. W. Fischer (eds), *Self-
    conscious Emotions: Shame, Guilt, Embarrassment, and Pride*. New York: Guilford,
    pp. 488–504.
Modigliani, A. (1968).   Embarrassment and embarrassability. *Sociometry*, **31**, 313–326.
Morrison, N. K. (1987).   The role of shame in schizophrenia. In H. B. Lewis (ed.), *The
    role of Shame in Symptom Formation*. Hillsdale, NJ: Erlbaum, pp. 51–87.
Mosher, D. L. & White, B. B. (1981).   On differentiating shame and shyness. *Motivation
    and Emotion*, **1**, 61–74.
Nathanson, D. L. (1987).   A timetable for shame. In D. L. Nathanson (ed.), *The Many
    Faces of Shame*. New York: Guilford, pp. 1–63.
Niedenthal, P. M., Tangney, J. P. & Gavanski, I. (1994).   "If only I weren't" versus "If
    only I hadn't": distinguishing shame and guilt in counterfactual thinking. *Journal of
    Personality and Social Psychology*, **67**, 585–595.
Ortony, A., Clore, G. L. & Collins, A. (1988).   *The Cognitive Structure of Emotions*.
    Cambridge: Cambridge University Press.
Parrott, W. G., Sabini, J. & Silver, M. (1988).   The roles of self-esteem and social inter-
    action in embarrassment. *Personality and Social Psychology Bulletin*, **14**, 191–202.
Parrott, W. G. & Smith, S. F. (1991).   Embarrassment: actual vs. typical cases, classical vs.
    prototypical representations. *Cognition and Emotion*, **5**, 467–488.
Potter-Efron, R. T. (1989).   *Shame, Guilt and Alcoholism: Treatment Issues in Clinical
    Practice*. New York: Haworth.
Retzinger, S. R. (1987).   Resentment and laughter: video studies of the shame–
    rage spiral. In H. B. Lewis (ed.), *The Role of Shame in Symptom Formation*. Hillsdale,
    NJ: Erlbaum, pp. 151–181.
Rodin, J., Silberstein, L. & Striegel-Moore, R. (1985).   Women and weight: a normative
    discontent. In T. B. Sondregger (ed.), *Psychology and Gender: Nebraska Symposium
    on Motivation, 1984*. Lincoln, NE: University of Nebraska Press.
Rosenberg, K. L. (1997).   The Socialization of Shame and Guilt. Unpublished doctoral
    dissertation, George Mason University, Fairfax, VA.

Rosenberg, K. L., Tangney, J. P., Denham, S., Leonard, A. M. & Widmaier, N. (1994). *Socialization of Moral Affect—Parent of Children Form* (SOMA-PC). George Mason University, Fairfax, VA.

Sanftner, J. L., Barlow, D. H., Marschall, D. E. & Tangney, J. P. (1995). The relation of shame and guilt to eating disorders symptomotology. *Journal of Social and Clinical Psychology*, **14**, 315–324.

Sattler, J. M. (1963). The relative meaning of embarrassment. *Psychological Reports*, **12**, 263–269.

Scheff, T. J. (1987). The shame–rage spiral: a case study of an interminable quarrel. In H. B. Lewis (ed.), *The Role of Shame in Symptom Formation*. Hillsdale, NJ: Erlbaum, pp. 109–149.

Scheff, T. J. (1995). Conflict in family systems: the role of shame. In J. P. Tangney & K. W. Fischer (eds), *Self-conscious Emotions: Shame, Guilt, Embarrassment, and Pride*. New York: Guilford, pp. 393–412.

Schore, A. N. (1991). Early superego development: the emergence of shame and narcissistic affect regulation in the practicing period. *Psychoanalysis and Contemporary Thought*, **14**, 187–250.

Semin, G. R. & Manstead, A. S. R. (1982). The social implications of embarrassment displays and restitution behavior. *European Journal of Social Psychology*, **12**, 367–377.

Shaver, P., Schwartz, J., Kirson, D. & O'Connor, C. (1987). Emotional knowledge: further exploration of a prototype approach. *Journal of Personality and Social Psychology*, **52**, 1061–1086.

Sharkey, W. F. & Stafford, L. (1990). Responses to embarrassment. *Human Communication Research*, **17**, 315–342.

Shott, S. (1979). Emotion and social life: a symbolic interactionist analysis. *American Journal of Sociology*, **84**, 1317–1334.

Silver, M., Sabini, J. & Parrott, W. G. (1987). Embarrassment: a dramaturgic account. *Journal for the Theory of Social Behaviour*, **17**, 47–61.

Stipek, D. J. (1983). A developmental analysis of pride and shame. *Human Development*, **26**, 42–54.

Stipek, D. (1995). The development of pride and shame in toddlers. In J. P. Tangney & K. W. Fischer (eds), *Self-conscious Emotions: Shame, Guilt, Embarrassment, and Pride*. New York: Guilford, pp. 237–252.

Stipek, D. J., Gralinski, J. H. & Kopp, C. B. (1990). Self-concept development in the toddler years. *Developmental Psychology*, **26**, 972–977.

Stipek, D., Recchia, S. & McClintic, S. (1992). *Self-evaluation in Young Children*. Monographs of the Society for Research in Child Development, **57** (1, Serial No. 226).

Sueda, K. & Wiseman, R. L. (1992). Embarrassment remediation in Japan and the United States. *International Journal of Intercultural Relations*, **16**, 159–173.

Tangney, J. P. (1990). Assessing individual differences in proneness to shame and guilt: development of the self-conscious affect and attribution inventory. *Journal of Personality and Social Psychology*, **59**, 102–111.

Tangney, J. P. (1991). Moral affect: the good, the bad, and the ugly. *Journal of Personality and Social Psychology*, **61**, 598–607.

Tangney, J. P. (1992). Situational determinants of shame and guilt in young adulthood. *Personality and Social Psychology Bulletin*, **18**, 199–206.

Tangney, J. P. (1993). Shame and guilt. In C. G. Costello (ed.), *Symptoms of Depression*. New York: Wiley, pp. 161–180.

Tangney, J. P. (1994). The mixed legacy of the super-ego: adaptive and maladaptive aspects of shame and guilt. In J. M. Masling & R. F. Bornstein (eds), *Empirical Perspectives on Object Relations Theory*. Washington, DC: American Psychological Association, pp. 1–28.

Tangney, J. P. (1995). Shame and guilt in interpersonal relationships. In J. P. Tangney &

K. W. Fischer (eds), *Self-conscious Emotions: Shame, Guilt, Embarrassment, and Pride*.
New York: Guilford, pp. 114–139.

Tangney, J. P. (1996a). Conceptual and methodological issues in the assessment of shame and guilt. *Behaviour Research and Therapy*, **34**, 741–754.

Tangney, J. P. (1996b). *Functional and Dysfunctional Guilt*. In J. Bybee & J. P. Tangney (Chairs), Is Guilt Adaptive? Functions in Interpersonal Relationships and Mental Health. Symposium presented at the meetings of the American Psychological Association, Toronto, August.

Tangney, J. P. (in press). How does guilt differ from shame? In J. A. Bybee (ed.), *Guilt and Children*. New York: Academic Press.

Tangney, J. P., Burggraf, S. A., Hamme, H. & Domingos, B. (1988). Assessing individual differences in proneness to shame and guilt: the Self-Conscious Affect and Attribution Inventory. Poster presented at the meetings of the Eastern Psychological Association, Buffalo, NY.

Tangney, J. P., Burggraf, S. A. & Wagner, P. E. (1995). Shame-proneness, guilt-proneness, and psychological symptoms. In J. P. Tangney & K. W. Fischer (eds), *Self-conscious Emotions: Shame, Guilt, Embarrassment, and Pride*. New York: Guilford, pp. 343–367.

Tangney, J. P., Ferguson, T. J., Wagner, P. E., Crowley, S. & Gramzow, R. (1996a). The Test of Self-Conscious Affect—2. George Mason University, Fairfax, VA.

Tangney, J. P., Marschall, D. E., Rosenberg, K., Barlow, D. H. & Wagner, P. E. (1994). Children's and Adults' Autobiographical Accounts of Shame, Guilt and Pride Experiences: An Analysis of Situational Determinants and Interpersonal Concerns (unpublished manuscript).

Tangney, J. P., Miller, R. S., Flicker, L. & Barlow, D. H. (1996b). Are shame, guilt and embarrassment distinct emotions? *Journal of Personality and Social Psychology*, **70**, 1256–1269.

Tangney, J. P., Wagner, P. E. & Barlow, D. H. (in preparation). The relation of shame and guilt to empathy: an intergenerational study.

Tangney, J. P., Wagner, P. E., Barlow, D. H., Marschall, D. E. & Gramzow, R. (1996c). The relation of shame and guilt to constructive vs. destructive responses to anger across the lifespan. *Journal of Personality and Social Psychology*, **70**, 797–809.

Tangney, J. P., Wagner, P. E., Burggraf, S. A., Gramzow, R. & Fletcher, C. (1991). Children's Shame-proneness, but not Guilt-proneness, Is Related to Emotional and Behavioral Maladjustment. Poster presented at the meetings of the American Psychological Society, Washington, DC, June.

Tangney, J. P., Wagner, P. E., Fletcher, C. & Gramzow, R. (1992). Shamed into anger? The relation of shame and guilt to anger and self-reported aggression. *Journal of Personality and Social Psychology*, **62**, 669–675.

Tangney, J. P., Wagner, P. & Gramzow, R. (1989). *The Test of Self-Conscious Affect (TOSCA)*. George Mason University, Fairfax, VA.

Tangney, J. P., Wagner, P. E. & Gramzow, R. (1992). Proneness to shame, proneness to guilt, and psychopathology. *Journal of Abnormal Psychology*, **103**, 469–478.

Tooke, W. S. & Ickes, W. (1988). A measure of adherence to conventional morality. *Journal of Social and Clinical Psychology*, **6**, 310–334.

Tomkins, S. (1963). *Affect, Imagery, Consciousness: Vol. 2. The Negative Affects*. New York: Springer.

Vangelisti, A. L., Daly, J. A. & Rudnick, J. R. (1991). Making people feel guilty in conversations: techniques and correlates. *Human Communication Research*, **18**, 3–39.

Wallbott, H. G. & Scherer, K. R. (1988). How universal and specific is emotional experience? Evidence from 27 countries and five continents. In K. R. Scherer (ed.), *Facets of Emotion: Recent Research*. Hillsdale, NJ: Erlbaum, pp. 31–56.

Wallbott, H. G. & Scherer, K. R. (1995). Cultural determinants in experiencing shame and guilt. In J. P. Tangney & K. W. Fischer (eds), *Self-conscious Emotions: Shame, Guilt, Embarrassment, and Pride.* New York: Guilford, pp. 465–487.

Weiss, J. (1993).   *How Psychotherapy Works.* New York: Guilford.

Wicker, F. W., Payne, G. C. & Morgan, R. D. (1983).   Participant descriptions of guilt and shame. *Motivation and Emotion*, **7**, 25–39.

Zahn-Waxler, C., Cole, P. & Barrett, K. C. (1991).   Guilt and empathy: sex differences and implications for the development of depression. In K. Dodge & J. Garber (eds), *Emotion Regulation and Dysregulation.* New York: Cambridge University Press, pp. 243–272.

Zahn-Waxler, C., Kochanska, G., Krupnick, J. & McKnew, D. (1990).   Patterns of guilt in children of depressed and well mothers. *Developmental Psychology*, **26**, 51–59.

Zahn-Waxler, C. & Robinson, J. (1995).   Empathy and guilt: early origins of feelings of responsibility. In J. P. Tangney & K. W. Fischer (eds), *Self-conscious Emotions: Shame, Guilt, Embarrassment, and Pride.* New York: Guilford, pp. 143–173.

Chapter 27

Jealousy and Envy

Martin P. East
and
Fraser N. Watts
University of Cambridge, Cambridge, UK

INTRODUCTION

In this chapter, we provide an overview of two of the most intriguing of the so-called "complex" emotions. Both jealousy and envy are concerned with possessing some valued thing. Jealousy typically concerns what one possesses and fears to lose, whereas envy concerns what one does not have but would like to have. In practice, however, the "what" in question is different: while there are many things we can envy a person for possessing, jealousy, especially as discussed in the psychological literature, usually takes place in the context of a threat to a valued romantic/sexual relationship. Research on jealousy and envy has been carried out largely separately, apart from a small quantity of work looking at how people distinguish between them; consequently, they will be dealt with mainly separately here. Although emotional reactions labelled as "jealous" may occur in other situations, such as between siblings or friends, due to a paucity of work in these areas we confine ourselves to a discussion of the jealousy which occurs within romantic/sexual relationships. Romantic jealousy is probably also the most powerful and salient form of the emotion (Bringle, 1991).

In contrast with the copious attention which both jealousy and envy have received in prose and poetry, they have been neglected in the research literature in comparison with emotions such as depression, anxiety and anger. Part of the explanation for this lies in the difficulty of establishing any consensus about what jealousy and envy actually are. Van Sommers (1988) has argued that the range of jealous experience is such that we will never attain a single all-encompassing theory to account for it. Moreover, both jealousy and envy are complex and inextricable from the social structures and rules in which they are embedded.

Handbook of Cognition and Emotion. Edited by T. Dalgleish and M. Power.
© 1999 John Wiley & Sons Ltd.

There need to be other people to arouse our jealousy or envy. Also, the social antecedents of jealousy in one group or culture may be very different from another.

A further problem is that jealousy and envy may be difficult to study "on-line" using either naturally-occurring or induced mood states. The vast majority of research is based on retrospective self-report of past situations, or judgements of likely responses to hypothetical situations.

In this review we first look at the nature and aetiology of jealousy. Psychological theories of jealousy are discussed and evaluated by considering research findings. The nature and aetiology of envy is dealt with separately. Finally, relationships between the two emotions are discussed.

JEALOUSY

Definitions of Jealousy

Definitions of jealousy tend to be couched in terms of aetiology rather than emotional topography. Most propose that jealousy may result when the jealous person perceives a threat of loss of a valued (romantic) relationship to a real or imagined rival. A number of theorists have extended this definition in various ways. Clanton & Kosins (1991) note that the threat may be to the existence of the relationship or to its quality. For example, while there may be no danger of losing the beloved to the rival, trust may diminish, emotional support may be disrupted, or there may be a loss of a sense of specialness or uniqueness about the relationship.

White & Mullen's (1989) definition includes a further aetiological component:

> Romantic jealousy is a complex of thoughts, emotions, and actions that follows loss of or threat to self-esteem and/or the existence or quality of the romantic relationship. The perceived loss or threat is generated by the perception of a real or potential romantic attraction between one's partner and a (perhaps imaginary) rival (p. 9).

In this definition, there are two conceptually distinct psychological mechanisms which may result in a jealousy complex, neither of which is held to be primary. A close romantic relationship, as well as providing resources and rewards, may help to create and maintain certain aspects of self-concept and self-esteem; a threat of or actual loss of the relationship is thus likely to disrupt both of these.

Other definitions of jealousy encompass a greater range of potential jealousy-inducing situations. Gurnee (1936) describes jealousy as arising whenever another person receives attention or recognition that one feels rightly belongs to oneself. Buunk (1991) sees jealousy as ". . . aversive emotional reactions evoked by the real, imagined, or expected attraction between one's current or former partner and a third person". By emphasizing attention and attraction, these definitions acknowledge that emotional reactions commonly labelled as jealousy may occur as a result of relatively innocuous events, such as the beloved looking at pictures of someone of the opposite sex in a magazine or flirting light-heartedly with another, events which perhaps may not signal real threat to relationship or to self-esteem.

Classification of Normal Jealousy

A number of researchers have argued that jealousy should be divided into two or more subtypes. Indeed, it has become apparent that jealousy is a heterogeneous construct, and that subdivision may be necessary.

Within the range of normal jealousy (pathological jealousy will be discussed later), Parrott (1991) draws the distinction between suspicious and *fait accompli* jealousy. When a threat to the relationship is unclear or only suspected, suspicious jealousy is the result, with the predominant emotional reactions being anxiety and insecurity. It occurs ". . . when a person believes that a partner may be transferring to a rival the type of attention that is formative in a relationship". Cognitive symptoms may include suspiciousness, inability to concentrate on other matters, ruminations and preoccupations, fantasies of the partner and rival enjoying a wonderful relationship, etc. Parrott sees suspicious jealousy as the prototypical form of jealousy. With *fait accompli* jealousy, a real threat to the relationship has occurred; the damage has been done, so to speak. This jealousy is relatively free of anxiety, and includes emotional reactions such as sadness, anger and hurt, depending on the focus of attention.

Buunk (1991), outlines two further varieties which are again conceptually distinct from the above. "Preventive" jealousy is different from other types of jealousy mentioned here in that it is not an emotional reaction to perceived threatening events, but behaviour aimed at preventing such events. The jealous person may go to considerable efforts to control and influence the behaviour of the partner, for instance to prevent contact of the partner with a particular third person. "Self-generated" jealousy occurs when the individual tends to generate images and thoughts of the beloved's infidelity, which leads to obsessive anxiety and worrying. As in reactive forms of jealousy, negative affect is evoked by some event, but here the events are generated in imagination by the individual.

Finally, Van Sommers (1988) notes that there may be cases of what he calls "spiteful" jealousy, in which the jealous person is not interested in the rewards and resources the partner has to offer, yet resents intrusions upon it. This may occur in relationships in which there is little sexuality or affection left. There may also be "retrospective jealousy" in which the person is hurt by the past sexual involvements of the partner. As Van Sommers notes, "One agonizes not over present or future deprivations arising from another's gains, but over events that no longer affect the quantity and duration of access to one's partner". These two forms of jealousy pose a particular challenge to theories of jealousy because it is at least not obvious how they involve a threat to rewards and resources, and to self-esteem.

Emotional Responding and Jealousy

Jealousy is often associated with intense affect. Anxiety, anger and depression are the three most often mentioned emotions in relation to jealousy. Parrott (1991) sees these as separate emotions that occur when the jealous person shifts the focus of attention to different aspects of the jealousy situation. Similarly, White & Mullen (1989) note that there may be different phases of emotional responding to an appraisal of threat to the relationship. First, there may be an initial autonomic response characteristic of sudden perceived threat or harm. This so-called "jealous flash" is a common initial experience of the jealous (Pines & Aronson, 1983). The initial response is most often fear or anger, although a minority of jealous individuals also report sexual arousal.

The second phase of emotional responding is a result of secondary appraisal of the situation. Feelings of intense emotion and relative quiescence may alternate. There may be sadness and a sense of loss and a depleted future. There may be feelings of shame, brought about through exposure of private vulnerabilities and feelings that an outsider has been introduced into the intimacy of the relationship. A study by Hupka (1984) supports the idea of shifting emotions in jealousy. He asked subjects to focus on different aspects of several jealousy scenarios. He found that different appraisals called for in the scenarios produced different attributions of emotion to the story's jealous character. For example, focusing on the partner's sharing of secrets with a romantic rival produced attributions of anger to the jealous person; focusing on the prospect of having to make do on one's own after depending on the partner produced attributions of fear.

A number of studies have factor- or cluster-analysed emotion ratings of jealous subjects or of subjects who were predicting what emotions they would feel. The commonly emerging factors are Anger/Revenge, Sadness/Depression, Fear/Anxiety, Envy, Sexual Arousal and Guilt (Amstutz, 1982; Buunk, Bringle & Arends, 1984; Salovey & Rodin, 1986). Mathes (1992) suggests that anger is one of the most important components of (reactive) jealousy. Mathes, Adams & Davies (1985) had subjects rate their levels of depression, anxiety and anger to four hypothetical loss situations: "fate" (the beloved is killed in an accident); "destiny" (the beloved takes a job elsewhere); "rejection" (the beloved does not love the person any more); and "rival" (the beloved is lost to a rival). While depression was high and anxiety moderately high across the four conditions, anger was low for the fate condition, moderate for the destiny and rejection conditions, and high in the rival (jealousy) condition.

Theoretical Perspectives on Normal Jealousy

White & Mullen's Model

White & Mullen's (1989) model of romantic jealousy is perhaps the most well-developed psychological theory of jealousy. They view jealousy as a "complex of thoughts, emotions and actions", rather than an emotion as such, which may be precipitated by threat to the relationship, threat to self-esteem, or both. Romantic relationships confer a range of resources and rewards, such as emotional support, sex, companionship, use of material goods, etc. A threat to the relationship may signal possible loss of these resources.

In addition, a romantic relationship is a powerful source of meaning about the self. A relationship may foster self-esteem regarding one's lovableness, sexual potency, competence, sense of humour, etc. It may also strengthen self-concept in that a partner may confirm one's beliefs about oneself. Conversely, if one's partner is attracted to another person, this may signal the partner's devaluation of central aspects of oneself.

The model has two main theoretical aspects. First, it is a *cognitive* model in that generation of negative affect depends upon certain appraisals of threat, and appraisals of the ability to cope with the threat. Second, it is a *systemic* theory in that the jealousy complex occurs within an "interpersonal jealousy system" comprising the jealous, the beloved and the rival, each of which have their own support system. Also relevant is the larger system of meanings, values and norms which may be called "culture".

The cognitive model borrows heavily from Lazarus's cognitive-transactional theory of stress and coping (Lazarus & Folkman, 1984). Cognitive process are differentiated into "primary appraisal", which determines initial emotional responses, and "secondary appraisal", which concerns the development of strategies to cope with jealousy. The primary appraisals assumed to generate jealousy are about the potential for a rival relationship to exist, whether such a relationship actually exists, and the degree of harm posed by an actual or potential rival relationship. However, there is no mention of how threats to self-esteem or self-concept enter into the primary appraisal process. Secondary appraisal processes involve a detailed assessment of the threatening situation and how to cope with it. These processes are thought to be: "motives assessment" ("Why is my partner interested in the rival?"); "social comparison to rival" ("What does my rival have that I don't, and vice versa?"); "alternatives assessment" ("What is going to happen to me if I get left?"); and "loss assessment" ("What might I lose or have lost?"). Secondary appraisal also comprises planning coping efforts and assessing the results of such efforts.

From these appraisals, the individual may develop and initiate coping strategies. For example, as a result of motives assessment and social comparison to rival, the person may decide that he/she should make the relationship more attractive to the partner by increasing the partner's rewards and lowering the costs (e.g. making oneself more physically attractive, doing more household chores, etc.), thus engaging in the strategy of "improving the relationship". The other strategies mentioned by White & Mullen are "interfering with the rival relationship" (increasing costs and lowering rewards of rival relationship), "demanding commitment" (forcing the partner into a choice that would erect social and emotional barriers to leaving the relationship, e.g. marriage), "derogating the partner and/or rival" (discrediting the relationship, thereby reducing threat to self-esteem), "developing alternatives" (as sources of self-esteem), "denial/avoidance" (primarily to manage negative affect), "self-assessment" (trying to change oneself in order to manage the threat better), and "support/catharsis" (strategies directed toward the management of emotions through their safe expression).

This model is clearly a comprehensive account of the psychological processes involved in jealousy, although it is probably best viewed as a framework, rather than a theory that will turn out to be either true or false. One weakness is that it is not explicit about the factors which determine whether the existence of a potential rival will initially be appraised as threatening. Furthermore, given the supposed importance of threat to self esteem and concept, little is said about how this threat is evaluated, and how jealousy which is primarily a threat to the self differs from jealousy which is primarily a threat to relationship outcomes. Finally, the theory cannot account for situations in which, although the jealous person believes at the "intellectual" level that there is no threat, he/she is still disturbed by attention that the beloved is receiving or giving. In other words, in some cases conscious appraisal and emotional responding may be dissociated, a phenomenon which is starting to gain more attention in the cognition and emotion literature (Teasdale & Barnard, 1993).

Mathes' Cognitive Theory

This theoretical framework is similar to White & Mullen's, and is also based on the work of Richard Lazarus. Mathes (1991, 1992) views jealousy as a process of appraisal, coping and reappraisal, although he emphasizes different kinds of appraisal and coping (especially primary appraisal), and his account is generally less exhaustive. Reappraisal is also included, i.e. an assessment of how successful coping strategies have been, and decisions about what further action to take. Interestingly, whereas White & Mullen emphasize attraction between beloved and rival, Mathes sees the intention of the rival to acquire the beloved as the typical threat event.

A strength of the theory is that it describes in more detail the factors which mediate the primary appraisal of a potential jealousy situation as threatening. Five factors are thought to be important: P's (the person's) assessment of the probability that R (the rival) will take away the beloved; the level of P's love for B (the beloved); P's values regarding relationships; P's psychological health and self-esteem; and P's trait jealousy. In some situations, these mediating factors will be such that the presence of R is not viewed as threatening. If P decides that the rival is unlikely to succeed in taking away B, for example if B is a primary school teacher and R is a pupil with a crush, R's presence may be evaluated as irrelevant. If P no longer loves and is trying to get rid of B, R's presence may be viewed as positive/benign. Finally, if P values individual sexual freedom and sharing, P may evaluate R's presence as positive/benign because it offers a chance for B to be sexually free.

The mediating factors of psychological health, self-esteem and trait jealousy are relatively stable intrapsychic/personality factors that may influence the perception of threat. If P is psychologically healthy and has high self-esteem, P will be more optimistic about keeping B, or finding a replacement for B, and will thus appraise R's presence as being less stressful. If P is high in trait jealousy, P will be more likely to judge the situation as stressful. Note that Mathes' emphasis is on self-esteem as a mediator of perception of threat to the relationship, rather than something which is itself threatened in jealousy-inducing situations.

The secondary appraisal processes emphasized by Mathes are "reward", assessment of who has most to offer the beloved, (which is similar to White & Mullen's "social comparison to rival"), "punishment", which is an assessment of whether punishment would be effective in causing the beloved to remain in the relationship, something not really considered as a coping strategy by White & Mullen, and "moral and legal power", which is an assessment of whether P has legal or social rights to B, and is in the same domain as the coping strategy "demanding commitment".

While not providing as exhaustive an account of secondary appraisal and coping as White & Mullen, Mathes' theory supplements the former by providing a fuller exploration of the components involved in primary processes, thus enhancing a cognitive perspective on jealousy. However, it shares some of the problems of the previous theory in that, although particular elements of the theory may be refuted, the cognitive processes which result in jealous affect are are not addressed at a level which makes the theory as a whole disprovable.

Bringle's Transactional Model

As in the above formulations, Bringle sees jealousy as an outcome of an interpretation of or a transaction with the environment (Bringle, 1991). Bringle outlines how three "constructs" affect the probability of a jealous response occurring in the presence of a jealousy-evoking event: commitment, insecurity and arousability. Each of these constructs is a function of variables from three different loci: the person (stable traits and belief as well as less stable aspects), the relationship (stable aspects of the relationship such as history, as well as transient states), and the situation (the social circumstances which may imply changes in relationship outcomes).

"Commitment" refers to the person's degree of involvement and dependence in a relationship and expectation of future outcomes, which may be in jeopardy if the relationship is threatened.

"Insecurity" is a function of the jealous person's appraisal of the partner's commitment to the relationship. Arousability is more or less synonymous with emotionality, and refers to the intensity of the emotions a person tends to experience.

The strengths of Bringle's approach are its simplicity, intuitive plausibility, and the fact that it generates clear and readily testable predictions. For example, one could attempt to measure "commitment" using subjective questions (i.e. perceived commitment) or objective indicators (e.g. joint purchasing of goods, sacrifices made to maintain relationship, etc.), and then relate this to jealous responses. However, virtually nothing is said about how the perception of a rival and the vulnerability factors interact as a process to produce jealousy. Also, little reason is given for why this combination of constructs are held to be primary in determining jealousy responses.

An Exchange Perspective on Jealousy

Buunk (1991) has discussed how exchange theories can throw light on some of the processes involved in jealousy. Exchange theories assume that people form and continue close relationships on the basis of the rewards these relationships offer. To obtain rewards, individuals have to provide rewards themselves and make sure that the costs of providing rewards by the other are not too high. A central assumption is that a relationship is more satisfying and stable if outcomes (rewards, punishments and costs) are more or less equal. However, the exchange of rewards may be rather complex; for example, temporary inequalities may be tolerated for the sake of later rewards, and positive experiences of one partner may vicariously become rewards for the other.

When a partner becomes involved with somebody else, it is likely that the rewards provided by the partner will decrease, giving rise to jealousy. However, such a "zero-sum" situation—in which one person's gain is another's loss—is not inevitable. For example, there may be situations in which a partner ". . . for reasons either of guilt or of personal consideration, lavishes extra loving attention on a partner while developing an outside attachment" (Van Sommers, 1988, p. 16). Nevertheless, this attachment may still evoke intense jealousy. According to Thibaut & Kelley (1986), satisfaction or dissatisfaction within a relationship reflects not only the outcomes generated by the behaviours of the other, but also the meaning attached to these behaviours. Where exclusivity is lost, these outcomes may lose much of their meaning, and therefore their reward value.

Exchange theory provides a parsimonious explanation of why partners may prefer to equate their degree of extradyadic involvement (such as having friends of the opposite sex, having an "open" relationship, etc.). What one feels that the partner "deserves" will be determined by what one obtains oneself. Buunk (1980, 1983) tested the hypothesis that an individual will be jealous by partner involvement with another to the extent that the person has not been involved in extramarital relationships of his/her own. Both men and women were more jealous if they themselves had been involved in fewer affairs. However, while the exchange view on jealousy is attractive in some respects, there is little evidence that perception of unequal outcomes is a major factor in determining jealousy responses. Furthermore, the theory would have to be significantly elaborated to account for certain jealousy phenomena, such as "spiteful" jealousy, in which levels of exchange in the relationship are presumably so minimal that further decreases in outcomes would not be significant.

In summary, while White & Mullen, and Mathes, offer analyses of jealous appraisal and coping which together constitute a rich and thorough account of the emotion, Bringle & Buunk offer more focused and perhaps more readily testable accounts which emphasize particular aspects of jealousy-evoking situations. Before reviewing research findings, it should be noted that at present the theories are probably both too underspecified or too multifaceted to be strongly supported or refuted by empirical evidence. Certainly, none of the evidence reviewed below gives cause to prefer one theory over another, although it will be clear that support is found for various aspects of the different theories.

Causal Antecedents of Jealousy—Research Findings

Situational Factors

Situational factors in jealousy are those aspects of the jealousy-evoking event which influence the appraisal of threat and therefore the intensity of the jealous reaction. Research has focused on the beloved's behaviour in relation to the rival, characteristics of the rival, characteristics of the relationship, and cross-cultural variation in situational antecedents. It should be noted that this research is mostly based on subjects *predicting how they would react to hypothetical situations.* It is a moot point whether these predictions accurately reflect real reactions. As negative attitudes exist towards jealousy in our culture, they are likely to be subject to a degree of social desirability response bias. Furthermore, people are often asked to comment on experiences they may not have actually had. In a minority of studies, subjects have been required to report on actual jealousy experiences that occurred within a relationship.

The study by Mathes, Adams & Davies (1985) already mentioned suggests that loss of one's partner to a rival is different from other kinds of loss, such as loss due to fate, destiny or rejection: loss to a rival evokes more anger. As the loss in rewards and resources is the same in all four conditions, this study provides support for the idea that some other factor, for example self-esteem, must be involved in determining jealousy responses. However, the threat posed by a rival can take several forms, and a number of studies have examined this. Studies are in agreement that a rival's interaction with the beloved is most upsetting when it involves some erotic or sexual component; sexual intercourse, especially within an ongoing relationship, is most upsetting (Hansen, 1982, 1983; Buunk, 1980, 1982).

Sharpsteen (1995) attempted to study more directly the effects of both self-esteem and relationship threat on jealousy by creating scenarios in a 2 × 2 design. For example, "For financial reasons, your partner has to move back to his/her home where his/her former lover lives" formed a *low self-esteem, high relation-ship threat* scenario. He found that increases in either type of threat were associ-ated with increased likelihood of becoming fearful, angry and sad, emotions commonly associated with jealousy.

Research has also looked at attractiveness of the rival and how well the rival is known by the jealous person. Apparently, jealousy is more intense when the potential rival is physically or socially unattractive (Shettel-Neuber, Bryson & Young, 1978; Buunk, 1982). This finding supports the role of threat to the self in jealousy. It may be a greater blow to one's self-concept or self-esteem for a partner to be attracted to somebody who does not seem attractive, because it implies that this person may be comparable or preferable to oneself. On the other hand, Pines & Aronson (1983) found that known rivals, rivals who are friends and admired rivals elicit more jealousy. Mathes (1992) suggests that in some situa-tions preservation of self-esteem is most important, and there is preference for an attractive rival; in others there may be a focus on preserving the relationship, and an unattractive rival will be preferred. Anyhow, the studies reviewed above do suggest that factors which are likely to increase threat to self-esteem are also likely to intensify jealous responding, which clearly supports White & Mullen's view of the importance of threat to self-esteem in jealousy.

The interaction of relationship characteristics and jealousy has also been investigated. Intensity of romantic love is positively related to questionnaire measures of jealousy in both men and women (Mathes & Severa, 1981; White, 1984). However, satisfaction with the relationship is associated with less jealousy (Bringle, 1986; Bringle, Evenbeck & Schmedel, 1977). The former correlation may derive from intensity of love being associated with rewards and the extent to which self-concept and self-esteem are defined or enhanced by the relationship. The latter correlation is perhaps more difficult to interpret, but may partly reflect lower levels of jealousy leading to a more harmonious and therefore satisfying relationship.

"Dependence" refers to the extent to which the person believes that outcomes in the current relationship are superior to those in alternative relationships, and correlates with jealousy (White, 1981a, 1981b; Bringle & Gray, 1986). The possibility of loss of relationship rewards may be more threatening when the rewards are not readily available elsewhere. Since those that are dependent on a relationship are also likely to be committed, this provides partial support for Bringle's view that commitment is a determinant of jealousy. "Relative dependence" refers to the degree to which one partner is dependent on the relationship compared to the other, and was also found to be related to jealousy, providing support for Bringle's idea that insecurity is important in determining jealous responses.

Cross-cultural Factors

There is substantial cross-cultural variation in the kinds of extra-dyadic behav-iour which evoke jealousy (Hupka, 1981). For instance, among the Pawnee

Indians a request by another male for a cup of water from one's wife is viewed as a signal of sexual interest in the wife, and may evoke intense jealousy. In other cultures, a spouse may have sexual intercourse with another person under certain circumstances which do not lead to jealousy. While an Ammassalik Eskimo may invite a guest to have sexual intercourse with his wife by means of "putting out the lamp", it would not be unusual for the husband to kill the visitor if intercourse occurred without the prior ritual (Mirsky, 1937). Among the Lesu men of New Ireland in Melanesia, jealousy is allayed by an exchange of gifts from the wife's lover to the wife and then to the husband. This may be a way ensuring that outcomes between spouses are equitably maintained, the importance of which is suggested by Buunk's theory.

Presumably, there is cultural variation in the situations which lead to an appraisal of threat to relationship or self-esteem. To an extent, these variations may reflect different values regarding relationships, with values of sexual sharing (perhaps in particular circumscribed situations) resulting in less threat, as suggested by Mathes (1991).

In their study of 92 cultures, Hupka & Ryan (1981) found three cultural variables which were related to severity of male responses to adultery. These were importance of marriage for social status, importance of private ownership of property, and restriction of sex to marriage. These findings are at least consistent with the idea of jealousy being the result of threats to relationship or self-esteem. For instance, valuing private ownership is likely to increase perceived seriousness of a loss of relationship; furthermore, to the extent that infidelity undermines marriage, it will also threaten social status and therefore self-esteem associated with it.

Appraisal and Coping Processes

Surprisingly, there has been virtually no research on the primary appraisal processes which determine the initial jealousy response. As a result, little is known about such matters as how the person assesses whether a rival relationship exists, how the degree of threat is assessed, how the person comes to focus on either threat to self-esteem or threat to the relationship, etc.

Research of secondary appraisal and coping has thrown some light on how people respond to and cope with jealousy. For example, White (1981c) had subjects indicate which dimensions of comparison they used when worried about losing their partners to rivals. Responses were concerned with physical/sexual attractiveness, personality, similarity to partner, job/professional position, willingness to form a long-term relationship, or sensitivity to partner's ideas or emotions. Sharpsteen & Schmalz (1988) coded reports of actual jealousy episodes, and reported that over half the subjects tried to conceal their jealousy. Possibly concealment is related to shame about jealousy, or fear about the consequences of its expression.

More is known about the domains of secondary appraisal and coping than how these processes actually arise and evolve. However, Schmitt (1988) found that subjects derogated actual romantic rivals only on those traits they thought were important to their romantic partners. This suggests that derogation may partly function to maintain self-esteem because it promotes a more flattering comparison with the rival in important domains. White (1981c) found that the method of coping chosen was often related to secondary appraisal of the situation, for example "developing alternatives" was a coping strategy associated with an appraisal that attraction was the motive for the partner's involvement with the rival. In general, there is support for a number of the coping processes proposed in the two cognitive theories of jealousy, and evidence that the style of coping used follows as a consequence of secondary appraisal.

Personality Factors

A number of personality trait measures have been found to be related to measures of jealous responding. In general, this research has been carried out in an *ad hoc* fashion and not been guided by theories of personality. The highest correlations (around 0.40) have been found with trait neuroticism, which is thought to be a measure of emotionality (e.g. Rosmarin, Chambless & LaPointe, 1980). This provides some support for Bringle's contention that "arousability" is an important determinant of jealousy. External locus of control is also related to jealousy (Bringle et al., 1977; White, 1984), which suggests that people who feel they have little control over their lives are more likely to feel jealous. Possibly they feel that they have no control over their partner's behaviour and therefore feel more insecure. They may feel that they are less able to stop a rival from taking the beloved away, an aspect of the primary appraisal process mentioned in Mathes' theory.

The relationship of self-esteem to jealousy is a particularly interesting and problematic issue. Although people who are experiencing jealousy may appear to have low self-esteem, the causal direction is ambiguous. Sullivan (1953) has hypothesized that jealous reactions derive from people's feelings of inadequacy, because the individual feels unworthy and believes others are more deserving of the beloved. However, there is evidence that people high in self-esteem may be more sensitive to esteem threats in many circumstances (Bringle, 1981; Tesser & Paulus, 1983).

A further complication is that self-esteem is related to other variables that affect jealousy. For example, people high in self-esteem score as more in love with their current partners; since love is correlated with jealousy measures, those high in self-esteem are more likely to score as jealous. On the other hand, people with high self-esteem may compare themselves favourably with rivals and thus the appraised degree of threat may be low. In fact, evidence for a relationship between these two constructs is mixed, with some studies showing an effect and others showing none (White & Mullen, 1989). It may be fruitful to investigate the factors which affect when attention is directed to esteem-enhancing vs. esteem-threatening aspects of the jealousy situation.

Pathological Jealousy

Pathological jealousy may be distinguished from normal jealousy by the intensity and readiness of emotional responding (White & Mullen, 1989) or by an apparent unreasonableness or lack of objectivity in the response (Tarrier et al., 1990). Many cases of pathological jealousy may simply present as more extreme forms of normal jealousy. The pathologically jealous person may appraise minor occurrences as evidence of betrayal; affects related to these events may be abnormally painful and intense; the imagination may be plagued with fantasies of the beloved's unfaithfulness or the jealous lover's plans of retribution. Attendant behaviours may include incessant checking of mail, clothing and bed linen for signs of unfaithfulness. The lover may be pestered to account for behaviour, give a confession of infidelity, or give reassurance. Jealous partners may feel disgust at their own activities, but nevertheless find it difficult to resist the urge to check and question. Delusions of infidelity may accompany these symptoms.

A number of authors have distinguished between jealousy in which delusions of infidelity form part of a generalized psychiatric state, and more circumscribed forms of jealousy involving intense reaction and in some cases specific jealous delusions (Mairet, 1908; White & Mullen, 1989). White & Mullen call the former type of jealousy "symptomatic jealousy", and its occurrence and course is thought to be tightly linked to the presence and progress of mental disorder. For example, delusions of infidelity in schizophrenia would occur alongside other symptoms, perhaps other types of delusion, and these would be expected to remit with successful treatment of the psychosis. They refer to the latter as "reactive jealousy", in which there is an exaggerated response to a provoking event with "an excessive ensuing disturbance in state of mind and behavioural turmoil" (p. 200). Rather than being associated with mental illness, the jealous reaction depends on the situation or aspects of the relationship. The person may have a predisposition to such reaction through previous experience with desertion or infidelity, personality disorder or some other mental disorder.

ENVY

Envy has received even less attention than jealousy in the psychological literature, and there are very few studies dedicated to its examination. Here, we discuss how envy may be defined, different varieties of envy, how envy is experienced, and finally its relationship with jealousy.

Definition of Envy

According to Parrott & Smith (1993), "... envy occurs when a person lacks another's superior quality, achievement, or possession and either desires it or wishes that the other lacked it". Envy thus involves social comparison, which may be a powerful influence on self-concept (Festinger, 1954; Heider, 1958). When one's abilities, achievements or possessions compare unfavourably with someone else's, there may be a decrease in self-esteem, and this may be one route to envy (Parrott, 1991).

However, it seems important that the shortcoming exists in a domain which is important to self-concept. For instance, a professional athlete is more likely to be envious of the performance of his gold medal-winning team-mate than the musical performance of a concert pianist (Salovey & Rothman, 1991). Similarly, Salovey & Rodin (1984) found that envy was only experienced when students received negative feedback in a self-relevant domain, and also anticipated meeting a student who excelled in that domain. Furthermore, it is only when comparison in a "self-definitional" domain serves to call attention to one's shortcomings that envy results (Parrott, 1991). For example, a young piano student may not be envious of a concert pianist because he could not be expected to perform at that level.

Varieties of Envy

A number of authors have made the distinction between "malicious envy" and more benign forms of envy, called "admiring envy" (Neu, 1980) or "emulating envy" (Taylor, 1988). In malicious envy, there is the sense of "I wish you did not have what you do" (Neu, 1980). The person may desire the removal or destruction of the envied object or quality, even though the envious person may not actually desire the object or quality for him/herself. However, in non-malicious forms of envy, the sense is of "I wish I had what you have", which may lead to feelings of resignation and inferiority, or determination to improve oneself, or admiration of the envied person. A further distinction is that the latter form of envy may be viewed as morally acceptable, although the former variety may not be (Parrott, 1991).

A further distinction is that made by Rawls (1971) between malicious envy and resentment. Anger and hostility may be a component in both of these experiences, but in resentment the superiority is construed as resulting from unfair or unjustified actions, and the anger elicited is considered to be justified. Parrott (1991) considers that ". . . the distinction between resentment and malicious envy is one that is made using the objective facts of the social world". It may happen that while the person views his/her feelings as justified, and therefore experiences "righteous indignation", others may not see that there has been any transgression or injustice, and judge that the person is experiencing malicious envy. In other cases of malicious envy, the person may to some extent realize that the anger felt is unjustified. This perception may dampen the anger, or evoke feelings of guilt (Parrott, 1991).

Cognition–Emotion Relationships in Envy

Parrott (1991) has discussed how focusing on different aspects of the envy situation may elicit different emotional experiences. When the focus is on the desired object or quality, there may be feelings of longing or frustrated desire. When the person focuses on his/her own shortcomings, there may be feelings of inferiority, sadness and anxiety, and perhaps awareness of diminished public stature. The person may perceive another's superiority as the result of unfairness, which will evoke anger and resentment. If the transgression was caused by the envied individual, anger and possibly hatred will be felt towards the individual. However, there may be a focus on the unfairness of "life itself", leading to what Parrott calls "global resentment", which is accompanied by a sense that no-one in particular is responsible for the unfairness. A search for the cause of the inequality may lead to the conclusion that the cause is oneself, leading to further feelings of sadness.

Attention may be directed towards the idea that the ill-will borne against the envied person is not warranted. There may be feelings of guilt or shame when the person realizes that his/her malicious thoughts are wrong or sinful, which may help to inhibit the thoughts. Finally, focusing on particular qualities of the envied person may produce admiration, the experience of which may be part of the blend or progression of emotions. It would be interesting to determine the differences between the kind of processing and attention to the desired quality which produces longing and that which produces admiration. Parrott does not suggest how these differences may occur.

Recent work by Smith (1991; Smith et al., 1994) has examined the origins of hostile feelings in envy. He acknowledges a number of possible origins of these feelings. The envied person may draw attention to or somehow represent an obstacle to a desired or important goal; the blocking of this goal may produce anger or frustration (Berkowitz, 1972, 1989). Rawls (1971) suggests that it is the sense of hurt and loss arising from the unflattering comparison that arouses rancour and hostility, perhaps because the other person is seen as the cause of this hurt. Aided by references to pieces of literature, Smith argues persuasively that it is the (private) sense of injustice, the sense that the superiority is undeserved, that arouses hostility.

Smith et al. had students remember in detail an episode of envy they had experienced. Following this they were given a questionnaire about the experience with items designed to tap a sense of "subjective injustice" (e.g. "it seemed unfair that the good fortune of the person I envied came naturally to him/her"), "inferiority beliefs" (e.g. "the person I envied made me feel inferior"), hostile and depressive feelings, and "objective injustice", which tap the perception that others would also view the situation as unfair. Hostile feelings were strongly associated with beliefs of subjective injustice, and were even more strongly associated with "objective injustice", which provides support for Smith's position. Depressed feelings were highly associated with "inferiority beliefs", supporting

Parrott's contention that depressed feelings in envy may result from focusing on one's inferiority.

Differences and Similarities between Envy and Jealousy

Although jealousy and envy are generally distinguished as qualitatively different emotions in the psychological literature, they would certainly seem to be associated in a number of respects. Their association would seem to be implied by the fact that whereas the word "envious" has a relatively specific meaning, the word "jealous" has come to mean either jealous or envious (Smith, Kim & Parrott, 1988).

There are certainly a number of similarities between the two emotions. Both may involve interpersonal hostility and threats to self-esteem brought about by social comparison. Furthermore, envy and jealousy may co-occur. A partner's preference for a rival may provoke jealous feelings, but also envy of the success or qualities of the rival. Conversely, envy of a person's qualities may lead to thinking of that person as a possible rival for one's partner, leading to a suspicious sort of jealousy. In fact, some authors have argued against the usefulness of the distinction. For example, Bers & Rodin (1984) feel that it is more useful to differentiate between social-comparison jealousy/envy, which refers to situations that "challenge one's superiority or equality", and social-relations jealousy/envy, which refers to situations that "challenge one's exclusivity in a relationship".

Salovey & Rodin (1986) cite three studies in which subjects reported probable emotional reactions and thoughts in hypothetical situations and vignettes. The results seemed to suggest that envy and jealousy are experienced in basically the same way, except that jealousy was more intense than envy. Parrott (1991) suggested that the results may reflect the greater intensity of jealousy obscuring differences in the quality of the two. To test this hypothesis, Parrott & Smith (1993) had subjects recall an instance of jealousy and envy and found qualitative differences between them. In jealousy, feelings that others would disapprove and feelings of longing and wanting to improve were more salient, whereas in envy, feelings of distrust, fear and uncertainty were more salient. They also found that 59% of accounts of jealousy included envy, while only 11% of the accounts of envy included jealousy. The overlap between jealousy and envy was accounted for by feelings of envy towards the rival.

FINAL CONCLUSIONS

In recent years, theoretical and empirical work on jealousy has grown considerably, and there are now a number of psychological theories of jealousy which have a degree of support from empirical findings. For example, there is indirect evidence of the involvement of both threat to self-esteem and to the relationship in the production of jealousy. We know something about the personality and situational factors which modulate jealousy, and these tend to be consistent with theoretical assumptions. We know a little about how people re-appraise and cope with their jealousy. Work on envy has been more fragmentary, and no unified psychological theory of envy yet exists, although there have been a number of proposals about its psychological nature. However, recent studies suggest that envy may be as amenable to psychological investigation as jealousy.

It is clear that the terms "jealousy" and "envy" encompass a range of psychological states, behaviours, social situations, etc. This is particularly true for jealousy, which may range from normal reactive forms such as Parrott's (1991) suspicious and *fait accompli* jealousy, through to forms which reflect a degree of neuroticism, such as Buunk's "preventive" and "self-generated" types, through to pathological jealousy and delusions of infidelity. Finally, there may be spiteful and retrospective forms of jealousy (Van Sommers, 1988). On the whole, psychological theories have failed to address these distinctions. They have not, for example, described the distinguishing antecedents and processes of different varieties of jealousy. Some varieties pose a particular problem. In retrospective jealousy, for instance, the models offer little help in explaining the nature of the perceived threat and the processes underlying its perception.

A further concern is the relatively little attention given to primary appraisal in theoretical and empirical work. Description of the process has probably been underspecified. For example, how does a person assess the probability of a relationship developing with the rival, what factors affect whether self-esteem or relationship threat determines jealousy response, and are there qualitative or quantitative differences in affect according to whether the perceived threat is to self-esteem or to the relationship? It seems essential that these processes should be studied to determine the importance of perceived threat to relationship and to self-esteem, given that current ideas of jealousy hinge on these processes. It may turn out to be the case that jealousy is elicited in situations in which there is no (conscious) appraisal of threat to relationship or self-esteem. There is no direct evidence either way on this issue.

One way forward in jealousy research may be to develop paradigms which get a better handle on the initial processes involved in jealous appraisal. Guessing one's reactions to hypothetical situations, which perhaps depends on acute faculties of introspection, memory and prediction and is susceptible to a number of biases, may not be the best tool for this. It may be possible to develop a jealousy mood induction paradigm, which would enable analysis of jealous processes as they occur using methods other than self-report. Alternatively, the processes of chronically or pathologically jealous individuals could be studied if their emotional states were sufficiently continuous. They may be able to provide powerful analogues of normal jealousy.

REFERENCES

Amstutz, D. (1982). Androgyny and Jealousy. Unpublished doctoral dissertation, Northern Illinois University, IL.

Berkowitz, L. (1972). Frustrations, comparisons, and other sources of emotional arousal as contributors to social unrest. *Journal of Social Issues*, **28**, 77–91.

Berkowitz, L. (1989). Frustration–aggression hypothesis: examination and reformulation. *Psychological Bulletin*, **106**, 59–73.

Bers, S. A. & Rodin, J. (1984). Social-comparison jealousy: a developmental and motivational study. *Journal of Personality and Social Psychology*, **47**, 766–779.

Bringle, R. G. (1981). Conceptualizing jealousy as a disposition. *Alternative Lifestyles*, **4**, 274–290.

Bringle, R. G. (1986). Effects of dispositional jealousy on marital quality. Unpublished manuscript, Indiana University at Indianapolis, IN.

Bringle, R. G. (1991). Psychosocial aspects of jealousy: a transactional model. In P. Salovey (ed.), *The Psychology of Jealousy and Envy*. New York: Guilford.

Bringle, R. G., Evenbeck, S. E. & Schmedel, K. (1977). The role of jealousy in marriage. Paper presented at the annual meeting of the American Psychological Association, San Francisco, CA.

Bringle, R. G., Roach, S., Andler, C. & Evenbeck, S. (1977). Correlates of jealousy. Paper presented at the 49th Annual Convention of the Midwestern Psychological Association, Chicago, IL.

Bringle, R. G. & Gray, K. (1986). Jealousy and the third person in the love triangle. Unpublished manuscript, Indiana University at Indianapolis, IN.

Buunk, B. (1980). *Intieme relaties met derden: Een sociaal psychologische studie* [*Multiple Intimate Relationships: A Social Psychological Study*]. Alphen aan de Rijn, The Netherlands: Samsom.

Buunk, B. (1982). Strategies of jealousy: styles of coping with extramarital involvement of the spouse. *Family Relations*, **31**, 13–18.

Buunk, B. (1983). De rol van attributies en afhankelijkheid bij jaloezie [The role of dependency and attributions in jealousy]. *Nederlands Tijdschrift voor de Psychologie*, **38**, 301–311.

Buunk, B. P. (1991). Jealousy in close relationships: an exchange-theoretical perspective. In P. Salovey (ed.), *The Psychology of Jealousy and Envy*. New York: Guilford.

Buunk, B., Bringle, R. G. & Arends, H. (1984). Jealousy—a response to threatened self-concept? Paper presented at the International Conference on Self and Identity, Cardiff, Wales.

Clanton, G. & Kosins, D. J. (1991). Developmental correlates of jealousy. In P. Salovey (ed.), *The Psychology of Jealousy and Envy*. New York: Guilford.

Festinger, L. (1954). A theory of social comparison processes. *Human Relations*, **7**, 117–140.

Gurnee, H. (1936). *Elements of Social Psychology*. New York: Farrar & Rinehart.

Hansen, G. L. (1982). Reactions to hypothetical jealousy producing events. *Family Relations*, **31**, 513–518.

Hansen, G. L. (1983). Marital satisfaction and jealousy among men. *Psychological Reports*, **52**, 363–366.

Heider, F. (1958). *The Psychology of Interpersonal Relations*. New York: Wiley.

Hupka, R. B. (1981). Cultural determinants of jealousy. *Alternative Lifestyles*, **4**, 310–356.

Hupka, R. B. (1984). Jealousy: compound emotion or label for a particular situation? *Motivation and Emotion*, **8**, 141–155.

Hupka, R. B. & Ryan, J. M. (1981). The cultural contribution to emotions: cross-cultural aggression in sexual jealousy situations. Paper presented at the annual meeting of the Western Psychological Association, Los Angeles, CA.

Lazarus, R. S. & Folkman, S. (1984). *Stress, Appraisal and Coping.* New York: Springer.

Mairet, A. (1908). *La jalousie: Étude psycho-physiologique, clinique et médico-légale.* Paris: Montpellier.

Mathes, E. W. (1991). A cognitive theory of jealousy. In P. Salovey (ed.), *The Psychology of Jealousy and Envy.* New York: Guilford.

Mathes, E. W. (1992). *Jealousy: The Psychological Data.* Maryland: University Press of America.

Mathes, E. W., Adams, H. E. & Davies, R. M. (1985). Jealousy: loss of relationship rewards, loss of self-esteem, depression, anxiety, and anger. *Journal of Personality and Social Psychology,* **42**, 1227–1231.

Mathes, E. W. & Severa, N. (1981). Jealousy, romantic love, and liking: theoretical considerations and preliminary scale development. *Psychological Reports,* **49**, 23–31.

Mirsky, J. (1937). The Eskimo of Greenland. In M. Mead (ed.), *Cooperation and Competition Among Primitive Peoples.* New York: McGraw-Hill.

Neu, J. (1980). Jealous thoughts. In A. O. Rorty (ed.), *Explaining Emotions.* Berkeley, CA: University of California Press, pp. 425–463.

Parrott, W. G. (1991). The emotional experiences of jealousy and envy. In P. Salovey (ed.), *The Psychology of Jealousy and Envy.* New York: Guilford.

Parrott, W. G. & Smith, R. H. (1993). Distinguishing the experiences of envy and jealousy. *Journal of Personality and Social Psychology,* **64**, 906–920.

Pines, A. & Aronson, E. (1983). Antecedents, correlates, and consequences of sexual jealousy. *Journal of Personality,* **51**, 108–136.

Rawls, J. (1971). *A Theory of Justice.* Cambridge, MA: Harvard University Press.

Rosmarin, D. M., Chambless, D. L. & LaPointe, K. (1980). The survey of interpersonal reactions: an inventory for the measurement of jealousy. Paper presented at the Annual Convention of the Western Psychological Association.

Salovey, P. & Rodin, J. (1984). Some antecedents and consequences of social-comparison jealousy. *Journal of Personality and Social Psychology,* **47**, 780–792.

Salovey, P. & Rodin, J. (1986). The differentiation of social-comparison jealousy and romantic jealousy. *Journal of Personality and Social Psychology,* **50**, 1100–1112.

Salovey, P. & Rothman, A. (1991). Envy and jealousy: self and society. In P. Salovey (ed.), *The Psychology of Jealousy and Envy.* New York: Guilford.

Schmitt, B. H. (1988). Social comparison in romantic jealousy. *Personality and Social Psychology Bulletin,* **14**, 374–387.

Sharpsteen, D. J. (1995). The effects of relationship and self-esteem threats on the likelihood of romantic jealousy. *Journal of Social and Personal Relationships,* **12**, 89–101.

Sharpsteen, D. J. & Schmalz, C. M. (1988). Romantic jealousy as a blended emotion. Unpublished manuscript, University of Denver, CO.

Shettel-Neuber, J., Bryson, J. B. & Young, C. E. (1978). Physical attractiveness of the "other person" and jealousy. *Personality and Social Psychology Bulletin,* **4**, 612–615.

Smith, R. H. (1991). Envy and the sense of injustice. In P. Salovey (ed.), *The Psychology of Jealousy and Envy.* New York: Guilford.

Smith, R. H., Kim, S. H. & Parrott, W. G. (1988). Envy and jealousy: semantic problems and experiential distinctions. *Personality and Social Psychology Bulletin,* **14**, 401–409.

Smith, R. H., Parrott, W. G., Ozer, D. & Moniz, A. (1994). Subjective injustice and inferiority as predictors of hostile and depressive feelings in envy. *Personality and Social Psychology Bulletin,* **20**, 705–711.

Sullivan, H. S. (1953). *The Interpersonal Theory of Psychiatry.* New York: Norton.

Tarrier, N., Beckett, R., Harwood, S. & Bishay, N. (1990). Morbid jealousy—A review and cognitive behavioural formulation. *British Journal of Psychiatry,* **157**, 319–326.

Taylor, G. (1988). Envy and jealousy: emotions and vices. *Midwest Studies in Philosophy*, **13**, 233–249.

Teasdale, J. D. & Barnard, P. J. (1993). *Affect, Cognition and Change*. Hove: Erlbaum.

Tesser, A. & Paulus, D. (1983). The definition of self: private and public self-evaluation management strategies. *Journal of Personality and Social Psychology*, **44**, 672–682.

Thibaut, J. W. & Kelley, H. H. (1986). *The Social Psychology of Groups*, 2nd edn. New Brunswick, NJ: Transaction Books.

Van Sommers, P. (1988). *Jealousy: What Is It and Who Feels it?* London: Penguin.

White, G. L. (1981a). Jealousy and partner's perceived motives of attraction to a rival. *Social Psychology Quarterly*, **44**, 24–30.

White, G. L. (1981b). A model of romantic jealousy. *Motivation and Emotion*, **5**, 295–310.

White, G. L. (1981c). Social comparison, motive attribution, alternatives assessment and coping with jealousy. Paper presented at the annual meeting of the American Psychological Association.

White, G. L. (1984). Comparison of four jealousy scales. *Journal of Research in Personality*, **18**, 115–130.

White, G. L. & Mullen, P. E. (1989). *Jealousy: Theory, Research, and Clinical Strategies*. New York: Guilford.

Part IV

Theories in Cognition and Emotion

Chapter 28

Network Theories and Beyond

Joseph P. Forgas
University of New South Wales, Sydney, Australia

INTRODUCTION

The relationship between feeling and thinking, cognition and affect has been the source of enduring fascination to philosophers, writers and artists since time immemorial. Indeed, cognition and affect have long been assumed to represent basic yet interrelated faculties of the human mind (Hilgard, 1980). During the last two decades or so, interest in the role of affect in cognition and behavior has increased dramatically. Contemporary theories guiding this work are predominantly based on cognitive principles and often rely on models of information storage and retrieval—that is, memory mechanisms—for their explanatory frameworks (Bower, 1981, 1991; Clore, Schwarz & Conway, 1994; Fiedler, 1990, 1991; Forgas, 1992a, 1995a; Singer & Salovey, 1988). Perhaps the most parsimonious and influential theory for explaining affective influences on cognition and judgments has been the network theory of affect. According to this view, the arousal of an affective state spreads activation throughout a network of cognitive associations linked to that emotion (Bower, 1981; Bower & Cohen, 1982; Clark & Isen, 1982; Isen, 1984). As a result, material that is associatively linked to the current mood is more likely to be activated, recalled and used in various constructive cognitive tasks, leading to a marked mood congruency in constructive associations, evaluations and judgments.

The main objective of this chapter is to provide a timely review and update of the associative network theory of affect and cognition. The first half of the chapter will review the basic conceptual foundations of this model, and some of the empirical evidence supporting the theory will be considered. The

Handbook of Cognition and Emotion. Edited by T. Dalgleish and M. Power.

second half of the chapter will update the network theory in view of the empirical evidence now available, and will place it within the broader theoretical context of contemporary theorizing about the links between affect to cognition. Some of the criticisms of the network theory will be considered, together with some competing explanations for mood-congruity effects. The chapter concludes with the outline of a revised theory, the Affect Infusion Model (AIM), that attempts to locate network explanations within an integrated theory linking affect and cognition.

Most of this discussion is concerned with the consequences of affect on cognition, rather than the cognitive antecedents of affect. However, network theories suggest a bidirectional rather than a unidirectional link between affect and cognition. Thus, there is much evidence for affect influencing attention, memory, thinking, associations and judgments in ways that are consistent with associative network models. Equally, however, associative processes are also integral to the elicitation of affective states, as people's cognitive analysis of situational information activates appropriate emotional responses. Recent work by Ortony, Clore & Collins (1988) sought to systematize some of these elicitation rules, and Bower & Cohen (1982) in their "blackboard model" also focus on how production rules can trigger particular affective responses. Such associative "emotion production rules" were further elaborated in recent appraisal theories of emotion (Lazarus, 1991; Ortony, Clore & Collins, 1988; Roseman, 1984; Smith & Ellsworth, 1985). Thus, associative network models seek to link affect and cognition within a single, integrated and bi-directional representational system. However, as most of the research evidence to date deals with the cognitive consequences of affect, this chapter cannot but reflect this orientation.

Terms such as affect, emotion and mood continue to suffer from the absence of clear definitions. For our purposes, "affect" may be used as the more general term, to include both emotions and moods (Forgas, 1995a). In contrast, "emotion" refers to more intense, brief and target-specific affective reactions. Emotions involve highly elaborate and consciously available cognitive information about antecedents, consequences and reactions. Moods, on the other hand, tend to be weaker, more enduring and less consciously accessible affective states that are more general and usually lack specific and readily available cognitive content (Forgas, 1995a). Despite these differences, it is difficult to draw a sharp distinction between these states. Strong emotions often leave a lingering mood state in their wake, and moods can impact on how emotional stimuli are responded to. Network theories can apply to both emotions and moods, as well as to other affective states. Accordingly, no clear distinction between these terms will be attempted here. Interestingly, much research stimulated by network theories looked at the cognitive consequences of moods, rather than emotions. As moods tend to be more enduring, less specific and less conscious than are specific emotions, they appear to have more widespread and insidious consequences for cognition than is the case with specific emotions.

THE ASSOCIATIVE NETWORK MODEL

The idea that affect and cognition may become linked within an integrated cognitive representational system was first suggested by Isen and her colleagues (e.g. Isen et al., 1978) and by Bower and his collaborators (e.g. Bower, 1981). However, the roots of network theories can be traced to earlier associationist principles embodied in conditioning paradigms (Berkowitz, 1993). It was Gordon Bower at Stanford University who most clearly specified and elaborated this model, proposing a series of testable hypotheses derivable from it. The associative network principle suggests that the links between affect and cognition are neither motivationally based, as psychodynamic theories suggest, nor are they the result of merely incidental environmental associations, as conditioning theories imply. Rather, affect and cognition are integrally linked within an associative network of cognitive representations.

In other words, affect is not an incidental, but an inseparable part of how we see and represent the world around us, the way we select, store and retrieve information, and the way we use stored knowledge structures in the performance of cognitive tasks. The model assumes that some affective nodes are biologically wired into the brain, activated by a range of situational triggers which become greatly elaborated as a result of cultural learning. Affective states can spread activation to related physiological and autonomic reactions, facial and postural expressions, verbal labels, action tendencies, and memories associated with that affect in the past. When trying to retrieve a memory, affect-related information is more likely to be accessed as it receives more total activation, from the retrieval cue plus the current affective state. As a result of such summation of activation, affect can infuse cognitive processes through facilitating access to related cognitive categories (Bower, 1981; Isen, 1987). As Bower (1981) suggests, affective states have a "specific node or unit in memory that . . . is also linked with propositions describing events from one's life during which that emotion was aroused . . . Activation of an emotion node also spreads activation throughout the memory structures to which it is connected" (p. 135). Several important consequences follow from this basic principle.

BASIC PREDICTIONS AND THE EMPIRICAL EVIDENCE

Most evidence for network theories comes from experiments involving two separate stages. Subjects are first induced to experience an affective state, usually happy or sad mood, using hypnotic suggestions or exposure to happy or sad movies, music, autobiographic memories, or positive or negative feedback about a recently performed task or test. Following mood induction, aspects of cognitive performance (memories, associations, judgments, attention) are assessed in what subjects believe is a separate, unrelated experiment (Bower, 1981, 1991; Forgas, 1992a, 1995a). Naturally occurring moods following attendance at movies, sports events and the like can also be used to study mood effects on various aspects of cognitive performance (Forgas & Moylan, 1987; Mayer et al., 1992). The following are some of the main predictions and research areas stimulated by network theories.

Mood-state dependent retrieval is a core prediction of network theories, suggesting that memory should be enhanced when retrieval mood matches the original encoding mood, consistent with the Encoding Specificity Principle proposed by Tulving (1983). Laboratory studies found that memory for word lists is better when recall mood matches encoding mood (Bower, Monteiro & Gilligan, 1978). People also seem selectively to recall autobiographical memories that match their prevailing mood, whether from the previous week or from their early childhood (Bower, 1981; Snyder & White, 1982). Depressed people show a similar pattern, preferentially remembering aversive childhood experiences, a memory bias that disappears once depression is brought under control (Lewinsohn & Rosenbaum, 1987).

There have been some problems in reliably replicating mood-state dependent memory effects in studies using simple stimuli such as word lists (Bower & Mayer, 1985). However, research with more complex social stimuli and using more realistic encoding and recall contexts than word lists tended to reliably produce mood-state dependent retrieval (Fiedler, 1990; 1991; Forgas, 1991c; 1992d; 1993a; Forgas & Bower, 1987). These studies provided subjects with a much richer set of encoding and retrieval cues than is commonly available in standard memory experiments, allowing affective cues to more effectively function as a differentiating context in learning and recall, as originally suggested by Bower (1981). In these more elaborate contexts, subjects may also be more likely to assume that there is a causal belonging between their temporary mood and surrounding information (Eich, 1995; Munakata & Bower, 1992).

Mood-congruent retrieval occurs when affective state facilitates the recall of affectively congruent material from memory. Thus, depressed subjects take less time to retrieve unpleasant rather than pleasant memories, while non-depressed subjects show the opposite pattern (Lloyd & Lishman, 1975; Teasdale & Fogarty, 1979). Others reported that anxious patients show a similar bias for recalling negative autobiographic memories (Burke & Mathews, 1992). However, these studies may confound mood-state-dependent retrieval with mood-congruent retrieval. A more convincing demonstration of mood-congruent retrieval requires that subjects experience no specific affect during encoding, yet still show better retrieval for information that is consistent with the retrieval mood later on. Such results were obtained by Teasdale & Russell (1983).

Support for network theories also comes from some implicit memory tasks, where people are not consciously trying to recall information. For example, depressed people tend to complete word stems to produce negative rather than positive words they have seen before (Ruiz Caballero & Gonzalez, 1994). This implicit memory bias occurs following both explicit or surreptitious exposure to words, suggesting that this is a mood-congruent recall effect, as implied by network theories. Stem-completion and sentence-completion tasks were also found to indicate an implicit memory bias by Tobias, Kihlstrom & Schacter (1992). However, mood-priming effects seem often difficult to demonstrate in word recognition tasks, although Niedenthal & Setterlund (1994) found evidence for category-specific mood-congruity effects in lexical decisions.

Selective attention and learning effects. In complex cognitive tasks people often experience information overload and need to select a small subsample of the rich variety of information available to them for further processing. It appears that affect can have a significant influence on what people will pay attention to (Niedenthal & Setterlund, 1994). As a result of the selective activation of a mood-related associative base, affect-congruent information tends to receive greater attention and is more likely to be processed than are affectively neutral or incongruent details (Bower, 1981; Forgas & Bower, 1987). Several experiments show that people spend longer reading affect-congruent information, linking it into a richer network of primed associations and as a result, and are better able to remember such information (Bower, 1981; Forgas & Bower, 1987; Forgas, 1992b). These effects occur because "concepts, words, themes, and rules of inference that are associated with that emotion will become primed and highly available for use ... [in] ... top-down or expectation-driven processing ... [acting] ... as interpretive filters of reality" (Bower, 1983, p. 395). Thus, people process mood-congruent material more deeply, with greater associative elaboration, and thus learn it better (Forgas & Bower, 1987; Gilligan, 1982). In terms of the network model these findings suggest that people more readily access elaborative associations to information that is congruent rather then incongruent with their affective state (Anderson, 1976; Forgas, 1992d). Depressed psychiatric patients also show better learning and memory for depressive words (Watkins et al., 1992), a bias that disappears once the depressive episode is over (Bradley & Mathews, 1983). However, mood-congruent learning seems a less robust phenomenon in patients suffering from anxiety (Burke & Mathews, 1992; Watts & Dalgleish, 1991), perhaps because anxious patients use particularly vigilant processing strategies to defend themselves against anxiety-arousing information (Mathews & MacLeod, 1994). This account suggests that processing strategies could play a crucial role in mediating affect priming processes.

Associations and interpretations. Many cognitive tasks require people to "go beyond the information given", and use associations, inferences and interpretations to construct a judgment or a decision, particularly when dealing with complex and ambiguous social information (Heider, 1958). Affect can prime the kind of associations used in the interpretation and evaluation of a stimulus (Clark & Waddell, 1983). The greater availability of mood-consistent associations can influence the top-down, constructive processing of complex or ambiguous details (Bower, 1981; 1991). For example, in word associations to an ambiguous word like "life", happy subjects generate more positive associations (love, freedom), while sad subjects produce words like "struggle", "death" (Bower, 1981). Mood-congruent associations also emerge when emotional subjects daydream or make up stories about fictional characters on the Thematic Apperception Test (Bower, 1981). These associative effects also influence affect-congruent distortions in many real-life situations due to naturally occurring moods (Mayer & Volanth, 1985; Mayer et al., 1992).

Associative mood effects can have a marked impact on many social judgments, such as perceptions of human faces (Schiffenbauer, 1974), impressions about people (Forgas, Bower & Krantz, 1984, Forgas & Bower, 1987) and self-perceptions (Sedikides, 1995). However, recent experiments suggest that this effect is diminished as the targets to be judged become more clear-cut and thus require less constructive processing (Forgas, 1994b, 1995b, 1997b,c). Such a diminution in the associative consequences of mood with increasing stimulus clarity again suggests that constructive processing is an important prerequisite for affect infusion to occur (Fiedler, 1991). The critical role of different processing styles in mediating affect priming effects will be further developed in the Affect Infusion Model (AIM). Mood-primed associations can also play a role in clinical states. Anxious people tend to interpret spoken homophones such as pane/pain or die/dye in the more anxious, negative direction (Eysenck, MacLeod & Mathews, 1987), consistent with the greater activation these affect-consistent concepts receive.

CRITICAL EVALUATION

Despite strong cumulative evidence supporting the associative network model from a wide variety of studies, there are also several problems that research has highlighted.

The replicability of mood-priming effects. Some of the predicted memory effects, such as lexical priming and mood-state dependent recall, initially appeared less robust than expected (Blaney, 1986; Bower & Mayer, 1985; Morris, 1989). Mood effects on lexical priming seem to occur as long as not only the valence, but also the affective category of the words matches the affective state (Niedenthal & Setterlund, 1994). The difficulty of obtaining reliable mood-state dependent memory effects was variously explained as due to the lack of sufficiently *intense* mood manipulations (Bower & Mayer, 1985), the lack of *causal belonging* between mood induction and the experimental task (Bower, 1991) and the fact that mood-priming may be difficult to obtain in conditions that are "antithetical to self-referencing" (Blaney, 1986, p. 232). Interestingly, these problems seem to be confined to standard memory tasks, where people try to learn and recall relatively meaningless word lists. In studies using more complex and realistic stimuli, such as person perception, impression formation or similar tasks, mood-state dependent retrieval has been a reliable phenomenon (cf. Bower, 1991; Forgas, 1990, 1991a, 1992b; Forgas & Bower, 1987; 1988; Mayer et al., 1992; Salovey et al., 1991). These tasks provide people with a richer and more elaborate set of encoding and retrieval cues, and thus allow affect to more readily function as a differentiating context (Bower, 1981) (see Neisser, 1982, for a related argument). Somewhat similar conclusions were reached by Eich (1995; Eich, Macaulay & Ryan, 1994), suggesting that mood-dependent retrieval is a robust effect that best appears when the moods induced are strong, when free recall rather than recognition is called for, and when the memories are self-generated rather than externally imposed.

The fan effect. Another frequent criticism of network theories is that they imply that all "positively valenced material is more accessible . . . in positive . . . moods, and negatively valenced material is more accessible [in] negative moods" (Schwarz, 1990, p. 528). If this were so, spreading activation to all similarly valenced contents should rapidly dissipate the priming effects of moods (a so-called fan effect). In fact, this criticism is based on a misunderstanding of network models. Network models do not imply that affect should prime all similarly valenced cognitions indiscriminately. Rather, affect is supposed to function as an additional source of selective activation among constructs already primed by specific situational and contextual associations (Bower, 1981). The accumulated evidence for mood-congruency in numerous memory as well as other processing tasks is clearly inconsistent with the presumed operation of such a diffusive "fan effect" (Forgas, Bower & Krantz, 1984; Forgas, Bower & Moylan, 1990; Mayer et al., 1992; Sedikides, 1992).

Clinical issues. Difficulties in obtaining attention effects in clinical disorders such as depression have also been interpreted as presenting problems for network theories. Williams et al. (1988) proposed a distinction between integrative priming and elaboration to account for the fact that attention effects appear to be more easily obtained in anxiety disorders, while depressive states seem to influence memory rather than attention. This may occur because anxiety mainly affects "the passive, automatic aspect of encoding and retrieval", whereas depression impacts on the "more active, effortful aspects of encoding and retrieval" (pp. 173–174). The proposed distinction between these two mechanisms is a useful one, and to some extent will be reflected in the different kinds of processing mechanisms proposed in the Affect Infusion Model to be described below.

Falsifiability. A major advantage of the associative network account is that it is based on a rich tradition of research on memory and information processing (Anderson, 1976), and can provide a relatively simple and parsimonious framework for understanding a wide variety of affective influences on cognition. However, this is also a model that is notoriously difficult to falsify, as most outcomes of mood congruency can be potentially explained in terms of network principles. This problem has been clearly acknowledged in various reformulations of the theory (e.g. Bower & Cohen, 1982), and is certainly not limited to associative network theories. The problem of falsifiability mainly arises because in practice it is difficult to provide a complete *a priori* specification of the kind of cognitive contents likely to be activated in any particular cognitive task.

Variations in affect congruence. Two additional kinds of empirical findings have presented particular difficulties for the associative network model. Firstly, several experiments in the literature show that mood congruence is not always obtained when, according to network principles, it should occur (e.g. Parrott & Sabini, 1990). Second, numerous studies suggest that the degree and quality of affect priming is not universal, as implied by network models, and can vary widely depending on contextual factors such as the nature of the task, the complexity of the information, the motivation of the subjects and the features of the situation (Blaney, 1986; Fiedler, 1991; Forgas, Bower & Krantz, 1984). Consequently, there has been a premature tendency to criticize the network model as too simplistic to provide an adequate explanation for the range of mood congruity effects reported in the literature.

This appears to be an unwarranted conclusion. In fact the associative network model continues to be the most robust, parsimonious and well-supported explanation for a wide variety of mood congruity effects reported. However, it now seems that the kind of affect priming processes predicted by the network model—not surprisingly—only occur in circumstances that are conducive to open, constructive information processing that allows the generative use of previously stored and affectively primed information in computing an outcome (Fiedler, 1991). The network model thus needs to be supplemented by a more careful specification of the processing conditions under which it is most likely to apply.

BEYOND NETWORK THEORIES: THE AFFECT INFUSION MODEL (AIM)

The idea that good or bad moods should "color" cognitions through associative processes has been so powerful that most research was focused on demonstrating mood-congruity effects in memory, associations and evaluations (Forgas & Bower, 1988). The need for a reformulation became clear as empirical evidence over the past decade or so indicated that affect priming is not an invariable or universal phenomenon—instead, it seems rather context-sensitive (Blaney, 1986; Erber & Erber, 1994; Forgas, 1991b,c; Sedikides, 1994, 1995; Parrott & Sabini, 1990). This part of the chapter seeks to locate the associate network model within the broader landscape of contemporary affect-cognition theorizing. It is proposed here that, although affect-priming is a robust and powerful phenomenon, it most reliably occurs in circumstances when people employ substantive, constructive processing strategies that allow the infusion of affect-linked information into cognitive processing (Fiedler, 1991). An integrative multi-process theory, the Affect Infusion Model (AIM), has been developed to specify the conditions under which affect-priming is more or less likely to occur.

Affect infusion may be defined here as the process whereby affective information influences and becomes incorporated into people's constructive processing, selectively influencing their learning, memory, attention and associative processes, and eventually coloring the outcome of their deliberations in an affect-congruent direction (Forgas, 1995a, p. 39). The evidence suggests that affect-priming is the major mechanism producing mood-congruity effects in cognition. However, similar effects can also occur when people directly use affect as information in circumstances that call for simple, heuristic processing (Clore, Schwarz & Conway, 1994). Within the AIM, these two explanations can be integrated as complementary rather than competing accounts, both capable of explaining mood congruity effects, albeit under different processing conditions. The AIM also seeks to account for instances in which affect infusion does not occur, or indeed, when mood-incongruent outcomes are generated, because subjects either directly access a pre-existing opinion, or engage in targeted, motivated processing that is incompatible with affect infusion.

The Multi-process Approach: Features and Assumptions.

In order to achieve these objectives, the Affect Infusion Model is based on a strong assumption of *process mediation*. That is, the nature and extent of mood effects on cognition should depend on the particular kind of processing strategy used to deal with a given task. A corollary assumption is that, other things being equal, people will try to minimize cognitive effort, adopting the simplest and least effortful processing strategy that satisfies minimal contextual requirements. Most information processing models in cognitive psychology—such as the network model—start out as implicit "single process" theories: they assume robust, universal and context-insensitive cognitive mechanisms. As evidence accumulates, the "boundary conditions" for the theory become more and more salient. This is, indeed, what happened as the network theory has been extended to deal with an increasingly broad and heterogeneous set of phenomena (Forgas & Bower, 1988). The Affect Infusion Model seeks to define and systematize what is now known about the boundary conditions of mood congruity effects as predicted by network theories. What started as a robust, single-process explanation—the network model—now has to be seen as operating only under certain conditions, as part of a more complex, multi-process theory. Such multi-process explanations have become common in social cognition research dealing with cognitive processes in such areas as persuasive communication, attitude formation and change, self-perception, stereotyping and related fields (Brewer, 1988; Chaiken, 1980; Fiedler, 1991; Kruglanski, 1989; Petty, Gleicher & Baker, 1991). We shall next describe the four processing strategies as identified by the AIM, before turning to a brief discussion of the eliciting conditions that recruit each of these processing styles.

The Four Processing Strategies

A schematic outline of the four basic information processing strategies identified by the AIM, and the contextual variables that trigger their use, is presented in Figure 28.1. Two of these strategies (direct access and motivated processing) involve relatively closed, directed information search processes that limit the opportunity for affect-infusion. The other two strategies (heuristic and substan-

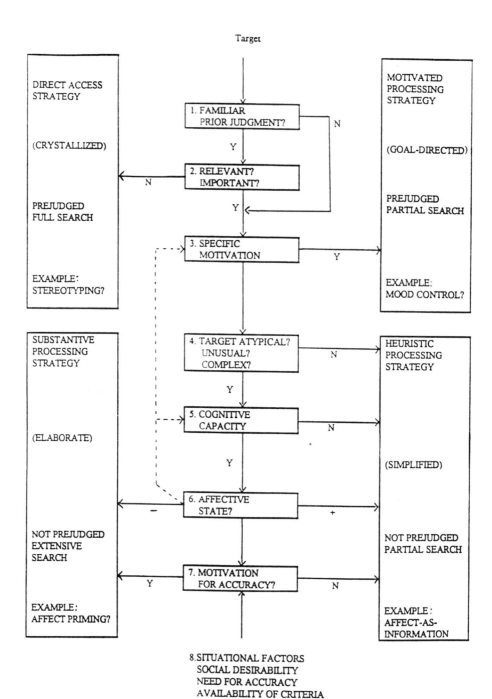

Figure 28.1 Schematic outline of the multiprocess affect infusion model (AIM): affect infusion in social judgements depends on which of four alternative processing strategies is adopted in response to target, judge and situational features. The flowchart illustrates the hierarchical relationships among factors determining processing choices, and the multiple informational and processing effects influence of affect on judgements. After Forgas (1995a)

tive processing) require more constructive and open-ended thinking allowing multiple avenues for affect infusion. The kind of affect-priming processes predicted by network theories are most likely to occur in circumstances that are conducive to substantive processing according to the AIM.

The *direct access strategy* is the simplest method of performing a cognitive task, based on the strongly cued retrieval of stored cognitive contents. Most people have a rich repertoire of such crystallized, predetermined reactions and evaluations to draw on when conditions do not warrant more extensive processing. For example, producing evaluations about familiar objects, responding to well-rehearsed survey questions, or dealing with routine information can be performed by simply retrieving pre-existing reactions. Direct access is most likely to be used when the task is familiar, there is little or no personal involvement, and there are no other motivational, cognitive, affective or situational forces mandating more elaborate processing. The direct access strategy is, by definition, a robust process that resists affect infusion, as little constructive thinking is required.

The *motivated processing strategy* occurs when information processing is guided by a strong, pre-existing objective, and thus little constructive ("unguided") processing occurs, reducing the likelihood of affect infusion. Motivated processing is most likely when a specific outcome is desired, and information processors employ highly selective, motivated information search and integration strategies designed to produce a preferred outcome (Kunda, 1990). Moods themselves often have motivational consequences, directed at achieving mood maintenance as well as mood repair (Clark & Isen, 1982; Erber & Erber, 1994; Berkowitz & Troccoli, 1990). Motivated processing involves more than just a motivation to be accurate (cf. Kunda, 1990): it occurs when a specific directional goal dominates and guides information search and evaluations. The variables that lead to motivated processing may include enduring personality and individual differences in how people approach a cognitive task (Rhodewalt, Strube & Wysocki, 1988; Smith & Petty, 1995; Forgas, 1997a), as well as such specific and situationally induced motives as self-enhancement, ego-defense, self-evaluation maintenance and the like.

Heuristic processing occurs when subjects have neither a crystallized response nor a strong motivational goal to influence their processing strategies and they lack either personal involvement or sufficient processing resources. Therefore, they follow a heuristic strategy to compute a response with the least amount of effort, relying on limited information and using whatever shortcuts are available to them (Brewer, 1988; Chaiken, 1980; Petty, Gleicher & Baker, 1991). Heuristic processing is likely to be adopted when the task is relatively simple or typical, personal relevance is low, specific motivational objectives are absent, cognitive capacity is limited and the situation does not demand accuracy or substantive processing (Figure 28.1). During heuristic processing, reactions may be based on irrelevant associations with environmental variables (Griffitt, 1970) and may also be informed by one's prevailing mood, according to the affect-as-information model (cf. Clore, Schwarz & Conway, 1994).

Substantive processing is the last, and most constructive information-processing strategy allowing the greatest likelihood of affect infusion. In terms of the AIM, network theories are most likely to apply to circumstances when substantive processing is adopted. During substantive processing, people need to select, learn, interpret and process information about a task, and relate this information to pre-existing knowledge structures using memory processes. Most single-process models imply that such vigilant, careful information processing is the norm. In contrast, within the AIM substantive processing is essentially a default option, adopted only when simpler and less effortful processing strategies cannot be employed. The likelihood of substantive processing is greater when the task is complex or atypical, is personally relevant, when subjects have adequate processing capacity, and have no specific motivational goal guiding them. It is during substantive processing that memory mechanisms such as affect-priming are most likely to influence the selection, learning, interpretation and assimilation of information into pre-existing knowledge (Bower, 1991; Forgas, 1995a). In terms of the AIM, the more extensive processing is required to compute a judgment, the more likely it is that affect infusion will influence the outcome. This counter-intuitive prediction has been supported in several recent experiments showing greater mood congruity due to extended substantive processing (Fiedler, 1991; Forgas, 1992a,b; 1993a,b; 1995a).

Factors Influencing Processing Choices

This section will summarize the role of various antecedent variables associated with the task, the person, and the situation that determine subjects' selection of different processing choices, thus mediating mood effects. The schematic relationship between these variables is summarized in Figure 28.1.

Task Familiarity

Familiar tasks are most likely to be processed using the direct access strategy, as long as personal relevance is low and further processing is not demanded. Since people possess extensive and accessible information for responding to familiar issues, mood-congruence will not occur. Research found no mood effects when people think about highly familiar products, their living quarters, or familiar health issues; however, mood-congruent distortions occur when people evaluate little-known products, global life satisfaction, and judgments about unfamiliar health states (Salovey & Birnbaum, 1989; Schwarz et al., 1987; Srull, 1983, 1984).

Complexity and Typicality of Task

Complex, atypical or otherwise problematic tasks do require more substantive processing, enhancing affect infusion effects. Experiments show that atypical tasks, such as thinking about unusual people, forming impressions about mismatched couples, or making attributions for complex conflicts, take longer to complete and produce significantly greater mood-priming effects than do simple or typical tasks (thinking about typical people, well-matched couples or simple conflicts) (Forgas, 1992c,d; 1993b; 1994b; 1995b).

Personal Relevance

Tasks of low personal relevance tend to be processed using effort-minimizing strategies such as direct access or heuristic processing. High personal relevance combined with specific motivation should lead to motivated processing, while high personal relevance in the absence of specific motivation should lead to substantive processing (Figure 28.1). Even slight changes in personal relevance can have quite dramatic consequences for how people deal with information (Brewer, 1988; Neisser, 1982). We have found that as soon as a judgmental task became more personally relevant, motivated processing was adopted, thereby reducing mood-priming effects (Forgas, 1989; 1991b; Forgas & Fiedler, 1996).

Personal Motivation

When a strong personal goal guides information search and processing, affect infusion is unlikely. Positive or negative affect itself can be a source of motivated processing (mood maintenance or mood repair), often leading to mood-incongruent outcomes in memory and judgments (Erber & Erber, 1994). Individual differences can also be linked to habitual motivated processing strategies. Several studies suggest that mood congruency is reduced for subjects who score high on such individual difference measures as Type-A personality, self-esteem, macchiavellism and need for approval (Forgas, 1997a; Rhodewalt et al., 1988; Smith & Petty, 1995) and thus have a habitual tendency to approach certain cognitive tasks from a motivated perspective. Such trait/state interactions probably play a critical role in triggering motivated processing and mediating mood effects on cognition (Mayer & Salovey, 1988).

Processing Capacity

Impaired information processing capacity due to overload or distractions should trigger simpler, heuristic processing, even if more substantive processing would be used otherwise. Under such conditions priming effects are less likely, as people rely on simple, ready-made information such as stereotypes (Bodenhausen, 1993) or the affect-as-information heuristic (Clore, Schwarz & Conway, 1994).

Mood Effects on Processing

Mood itself can play a dual role in influencing cognition: affect can impact both on *what* people think (informational effects) and *how* people think (processing effects). Good moods often lead to faster, simpler and more flexible and super-ficial processing strategies (Isen, 1987; Mackie & Worth, 1991; Fiedler, 1991; Hertel & Fiedler, 1994). In turn, negative moods cause slower, more systematic and vigilant processing strategies (Ellis & Ashbrook, 1988; Forgas & Bower, 1987; Forgas, 1994a; Schwarz & Bless, 1991). This processing asymmetry has been attributed to at least three possible causes—evolutionary/functional reasons, capacity effects and motivational effects. (a) *Functional-evolutionary explana-tions* suggest that affective states "exist for the sake of signaling states of the world that have to be responded to" (Frijda, 1988, p. 354). Relaxed, superficial information processing in a good mood, and systematic, vigilant processing in a bad mood seem consistent with such a functional account, although conclusive evidence for such evolutionary explanations is notoriously difficult to obtain. (b) *Capacity explanations* suggest that thoughts associated with good or bad moods intrude on people's attentional and cognitive resources, taking up scarce process-ing capacity (Ellis & Ashbrook, 1988; Isen, 1987; Mackie & Worth, 1991). How-ever, since both positive and negative moods may impair processing capacity, it isn't clear how capacity effects could explain the asymmetric processing conse-quences of good and bad moods. (c) *Motivational explanations* suggest that bad moods motivate people to engage in controlled processing in the service of mood repair, while good moods motivate subjects to engage in simplified, heuristic processing in order to avoid cognitive effort and maintain a pleasant affective state (Clark & Isen, 1982). Overall, the evidence suggests that happy people are more likely to process information heuristically, whereas sad people will process it more substantively.

Multiple Influences on Processing Strategies

According to the AIM, there is a hierarchical relationship between variables in determining processing outcomes (Figure 28.1). For example, the processing effects of mood tend to be weaker and secondary to other processing influences. Several studies found that complex or atypical tasks will be processed slowly and substantively by both happy and by sad subjects, showing strong affect-priming effects; in other words, task characteristics rather than mood was the primary determinant of processing strategies (Forgas, 1995b).

In terms of the AIM, both heuristic and substantive processing can produce mood congruent outcomes, through either the affect-as-information or the affect-priming mechanism. Whether heuristic or substantive processing was used can be empirically distinguished in terms of processing variables, such as memory and latency data, making the processing predictions of the AIM empirically falsifiable (Forgas & Bower, 1987). The evidence suggests that affect-priming typically occurs in the course of substantive, elaborate processing, and disappears when other (heuristic, direct access or motivated) processing strategies are used (Forgas, 1990, 1994b, 1995a,b). In fact, the AIM has the important and counter-intuitive implication that the more extensively people need to think about an atypical or complex task, the more likely that affect infusion due to network principles will occur. In several studies, happy or sad subjects encoded, and later recalled and evaluated more or less typical others (Forgas, 1992b,d), formed impressions about more or less well-matched couples (Forgas, 1993a, 1995b; Forgas & Moylan, 1991; Forgas, Levinger & Moylan, 1994) and explained more or less serious relationship conflicts (Forgas, 1994b). In all cases, affect priming was observed, but only in circumstances conducive to substantive processing consistent with the AIM. Further, greater mood-congruity effects were consistently related to more elaborate and substantive processing, as indicated by processing latency data. Thus, the AIM provides a more general framework within which network theories can be located, suggesting that affect priming effects are most likely to occur in conditions conducive to substantive, elaborate processing strategies (Fiedler, 1991; Forgas, 1995a).

SUMMARY AND CONCLUSIONS

Philosophers, artists and laypersons have long assumed a close interdependence between feeling and thinking, affect and cognition (Hilgard, 1980). Associative network theories provide a robust and universal conceptual framework for understanding the mechanisms that link affect and cognition, and have stimulated an impressive amount of research during the last few decades. The associative network model (Bower, 1981, 1991) explains how affect can facilitate access to related cognitions, and thus offers a simple and parsimonious explanation for a broad range of mood congruity effects. The first part of this chapter reviewed the major implications of this theory, and considered some of the empirical evidence supporting it. As accumulating empirical evidence showed the absence, or even reversal, of mood congruity effects in some circumstances, a critical review and re-assessment of the model has become necessary. In the second half of the chapter a broader, multi-process theory linking affect and cognition was outlined, the Affect Infusion Model (Forgas, 1995a). This model defines some important boundary conditions for the network theories, suggesting that network predictions should apply when open, constructive and substantive processing is adopted by people (Fiedler, 1991). Affect priming is unlikely to occur when heuristic, direct access or motivated processing strategies are adopted by a person, strategies that constrain the kind of open, constructive information processing that appears to be a prerequisite for affect infusion (Forgas, 1995a). The Affect Infusion Model also links network theories, and alternative models capable of predicting mood-congruent outcomes, such as the affect-as-information model (Clore, Schwarz & Conway, 1994), within a comprehensive conceptual framework.

Based on the available evidence, associative network theories continue to provide the most general and parsimonious explanation for the influence of affective states on cognitive processes. Specifically, some counter-intuitive results show that more extensive, substantive processing enhances mood congruity, providing strong support for network models (Forgas, 1992d; 1994b; 1995b). The implications of network theories apply not only in the laboratory, but also in many real-life cognitive tasks. Numerous studies found affect infusion effects in organizational decisions, personnel selection choices, consumer preferences, in clinical practice, and in health-related judgments that support network theories (Baron, 1987; Forgas & Moylan, 1987; Mayer et al., 1992; Salovey et al., 1991; Sedikides, 1992). Paradoxically, the more people need to engage in open, constructive processing in order to deal with a problem, the more likely that their affective state may influence the information they consider and the responses they make. These effects can even influence such involved and complex tasks as seeking an explanation for difficult relationship conflicts (Forgas, 1994b).

Most of the evidence considered here deals with valence effects, showing how good or bad moods influence the accessibility of positively or negatively valenced cognitions. Other features of affective state may also become associated with people's thoughts and judgments. For example, affect may directly prime motivational states that impact on thoughts and behaviours without the need for higher level substantive processing (Berkowitz, 1993). Affective states may also have direct appraisal properties that activate relevant information about situational contingencies and likely consequences (Smith & Ellsworth, 1985). Although these effects are certainly interesting, it appears that general valence effects linked to good or bad moods are likely to be the most important influence on cognitive processes. In any case, the four processing strategies identified by the AIM are also likely to be highly relevant to our understanding of the motivational and appraisal effects of affective states.

To conclude, associative network explanations currently provide perhaps the most universal mechanism for understanding affect infusion effects. However, these effects are not context independent: in circumstances when substantive, elaborate processing requiring memory mechanisms is inhibited, affect priming is also unlikely to occur. The Affect Infusion Model proposes a more inclusive, updated theory that recognizes the complex, constructive character of many cognitive processes, and identifies the circumstances most likely to permit affect priming. Empirical evidence suggesting the absence, or even reversal, of mood congruity effects in the past has been mistakenly interpreted as inconsistent with associative network explanations. The AIM offers an integrative framework for understanding the boundary conditions under which associative network models are applicable. By clarifying the characteristics and conditions conducive to the operation of associative network mechanisms, it is hoped that this chapter will encourage further research in this important domain.

ACKNOWLEDGEMENTS

Support from the Australian Research Council and the Alexander von Humboldt Foundation, Germany, are gratefully acknowledged.

REFERENCES

Anderson, J. R. (1976). *Language, Memory and Thought*. Hillsdale, NJ: Erlbaum.

Baron, R. (1987). Interviewers' moods and reactions to job applicants: the influence of affective states on applied social judgments. *Journal of Applied Social Psychology*, **16**, 16–28.

Berkowitz, L. (1993). Towards a general theory of anger and emotional aggression. In T. K. Srull & R. S. Wyer (eds), *Advances in Social Cognition*, Vol. 6. Hillsdale, NJ: Erlbaum, pp. 1–46.

Berkowitz, L. & Troccoli, B. T. (1990). Feelings, direction of attention, and expressed evaluations of others. *Cognition and Emotion*, **4**, 305–325.

Blaney, P. H. (1986). Affect and memory: a review. *Psychological Bulletin*, **99**, 229–246.

Bodenhausen, G. V. (1993). Emotion, arousal and stereotypic judgment: a heuristic model of affect and stereotyping. In D. Mackie & D. Hamilton (eds), *Affect, Cognition and Stereotyping: Interactive Processes in Intergroup Perception*. San Diego: Academic Press, pp. 13–37.

Bower, G. H. (1981). Mood and memory. *American Psychologist*, **36**, 129–148.

Bower, G. H. (1983). Affect and cognition. *Philosophical Transactions of the Royal Society of London B*, **302**, 387–402.

Bower, G. H. (1991). Mood congruity of social judgments. In J. P. Forgas (ed.), *Emotion and Social Judgments*. Oxford: Pergamon, pp. 31–53.

Bower, G. H. & Cohen, P. R. (1982). Emotional influences in memory and thinking: data and theory. In M. S. Clark & S. T. Fiske (eds), *Affect and Cognition*. Hillsdale, NJ: Erlbaum, pp. 291–332.

Bower, G. H. & Mayer, J. D. (1985). Failure to replicate mood-dependent retrieval. *Bulletin of the Psychonomic Society*, **23**, 39–42.

Bower, G. H., Monteiro, K. P. & Gilligan, S. G. (1978). Emotional mood as a context for learning and recall. *Journal of Verbal Learning and Verbal Behavior*, **17**, 573–585.

Bradley, P. P. & Mathews, A. M. (1983). Negative self-schemata in clinical depression. *British Journal of Clinical Psychology*, **22**, 173–181.

Brewer, M. (1988). A dual-process model of impression formation. In T. K. Srull & R. S. Wyer (eds), *Advances in Social Cognition*, Vol. 1. Hillsdale, NJ: Erlbaum, pp. 1–36.

Burke, M. & Mathews, A. M. (1992). Autobiographical memory and clinical anxiety. *Cognition and Emotion*, **6**, 23–35.

Chaiken, S. (1980). Heuristic versus systematic information processing and the use of source versus message cues in persuasion. *Journal of Personality and Social Psychology*, **39**, 752–766.

Clark, M. S. & Isen, A. M. (1982). Towards understanding the relationship between feeling states and social behavior. In A. H. Hastorf & A. M. Isen (eds), *Cognitive Social Psychology*. New York: Elsevier-North Holland, pp. 73–108.

Clark, A. M. & Waddell, B. A. (1983). Effects of moods on thoughts about helping, attraction and information acquisition. *Social Psychology Quarterly*, **46**, 31–35.

Clore, G. L., Schwarz, N. & Conway, M. (1994). Affective causes and consequences of social information processing. In R. S. Wyer & T. K. Srull (eds), *Handbook of Social Cognition*, 2nd edn. Hillsdale, NJ: Erlbaum.

Eich, E. (1995). Searching for mood dependent memory. *Psychological Science*, **6**, 67–75.

Eich, E., Macaulay, E. & Ryan, L. (1994). Mood-dependent memory for events of a personal past. *Journal of Experimental Psychology: General*, **123**, 201–215.

Ellis, H. C. & Ashbrook, P. W. (1988). Resource allocation model of the effects of depressed mood state on memory. In K. Fiedler & J. P. Forgas (eds), *Affect, Cognition and Social Behaviour*. Toronto: Hogrefe, pp. 25–43.

Erber, R. & Erber, M. W. (1994). Beyond mood and social judgment: mood incongruent recall and mood regulation. *European Journal of Social Psychology*, **24**, 79–88.

Eysenck, M. W., MacLeod, C. & Mathews, A. M. (1987). Cognitive functioning in anxiety. *Psychological Research*, **49**, 189–195.

Fiedler, K. (1990). Mood-dependent selectivity in social cognition. In W. Stroebe & M. Hewstone (eds), *European Review of Social Psychology*, Vol. 1. Chichester: Wiley, pp. 1–32.

Fiedler, K. (1991). On the task, the measures and the mood in research on affect and social cognition. In J. P. Forgas (ed.), *Emotion and Social Judgments*. Oxford: Pergamon, pp. 83–104.

Forgas, J. P. (1989). Mood effects on decision-making strategies. *Australian Journal of Psychology*, **41**, 197–214.

Forgas, J. P. (1990). Affective influences on individual and group judgments. *European Journal of Social Psychology*, **20**, 441–453.

Forgas, J. P. (ed.) (1991a). *Emotion and Social Judgments*. Oxford: Pergamon.

Forgas, J. P. (1991b). Mood effects on partner choice: role of affect in social decisions. *Journal of Personality and Social Psychology*, **61**, 708–720.

Forgas, J. P. (1991c). Affect and cognition in close relationships. In G. Fletcher & F. Fincham (eds), *Cognition in Close Relationships*. Hillsdale, NJ: Erlbaum, pp. 151–174.

Forgas, J. P. (1992a). Affect in social judgments and decisions: a multi-process model. In M. Zanna (ed.), *Advances in Experimental Social Psychology*, Vol. 25. New York: Academic Press, pp. 227–275.

Forgas, J. P. (1992b). On bad mood and peculiar people: affect and person typicality in impression formation. *Journal of Personality and Social Psychology*, **62**, 863–875.

Forgas, J. P. (1992c). Affect and social perceptions: research evidence and an integrative model. In W. Stroebe & M. Hewstone (eds), *European Review of Social Psychology*, Vol. 3. Chichester: Wiley, pp. 183–224.

Forgas, J. P. (1992d). Mood and the perception of unusual people: affective asymmetry in memory and social judgments. *European Journal of Social Psychology*, **22**, 531–547.

Forgas, J. P. (1993a). On making sense of odd couples: mood effects on the perception of mismatched relationships. *Personality and Social Psychology Bulletin*, **19**, 59–71.

Forgas, J. P. (1993b). Affect, appraisal and action: towards a multi-process framework. In R. S. Wyer & T. K. Srull (eds), *Advances in Social Cognition*, Vol. 6. Hillsdale, NJ: Erlbaum, pp. 89–108.

Forgas, J. P. (1994a). The role of emotion in social judgments: an introductory review and an Affect Infusion Model (AIM). *European Journal of Social Psychology*, **24**, 1–24.

Forgas, J. P. (1994b). Sad and guilty? Affective influences on the explanation of conflict episodes. *Journal of Personality and Social Psychology*, **66**, 56–68.

Forgas, J. P. (1995a). Mood and judgment: the Affect Infusion Model (AIM). *Psychological Bulletin*, **117**, 1–28.

Forgas, J. P. (1995b). Strange couples: mood effects on judgments and memory about prototypical and atypical targets. *Personality and Social Psychology Bulletin*, **21**, 747–765.

Forgas, J. P. (1997a). Feeling good and getting your way: mood effects on negotiating strategies and outcomes (manuscript under review).

Forgas, J. P. (1997b). On being sad and polite: the effects of mood on request strategies (manuscript under review).

Forgas, J. P. (1997c). Affective influences on the perception of more or less ambiguous facial expressions (manuscript, University of New South Wales).

Forgas, J. P. & Bower, G. H. (1987). Mood effects on person perception judgements. *Journal of Personality and Social Psychology*, **53**, 53–60.

Forgas, J. P. & Bower, G. H. (1988). Affect in social judgements. *Australian Journal of Psychology*, **40**, 125–145.

Forgas, J. P. & Fiedler, K. (1996). Us and Them: mood effects on intergroup discrimination. *Journal of Personality and Social Psychology*, **70**, 36–52.

Forgas, J. P. & Moylan, S. J. (1987). After the movies: the effects of transient mood states on social judgments. *Personality and Social Psychology Bulletin*, **13**, 478–489.

Forgas, J. P. & Moylan, S. J. (1991). Affective influences on stereotype judgments. *Cognition and Emotion*, **5**, 379–397.

Forgas, J. P., Bower, G. H. & Krantz, S. (1984). The influence of mood on perceptions of social interactions. *Journal of Experimental Social Psychology*, **20**, 497–513.

Forgas, J. P., Bower, G. H. & Moylan, S. J. (1990). Praise or Blame? Affective influences on attributions for achievement. *Journal of Personality and Social Psychology*, **59**, 809–818.

Forgas, J. P. Levinger, G. & Moylan, S. (1994). Feeling good and feeling close: mood effects on the perception of intimate relationships. *Personal Relationships*, **2**, 165–184.

Frijda, N. (1988). The laws of emotion. *American Psychologist*, **43**, 49–358.

Gilligan, S. G. (1982). Mood Intensity and Learning of Congruous Material. PhD thesis, Psychology Department, Stanford University, CA.

Griffitt, W. (1970). Environmental effects on interpersonal behavior: ambient effective temperature and attraction. *Journal of Personality and Social Psychology*, **15**, 240–244.

Heider, F. (1958). *The Psychology of Interpersonal Relations*. New York: Wiley.

Hertel, G. & Fiedler, K. (1994). Affective and cognitive influences in a social dilemma game. *European Journal of Social Psychology*, **24**, 131–146.

Hilgard, E. R. (1980). The trilogy of mind: cognition, affection, and conation. *Journal of the History of the Behavioral Sciences*, **16**, 107–117.

Isen, A. (1987). Positive affect, cognitive processes and social behaviour. In L. Berkowitz (ed.), *Advances in Experimental Social Psychology*, Vol. 20. New York: Academic Press, pp. 203–253.

Isen, A. M. (1984). Toward understanding the role of affect in cognition. In R. S. Wyer & T. K. Srull (eds), *The Handbook of Social Cognition*, Vol. 3. Hillsdale, NJ: Erlbaum, pp. 179–236.

Isen, A. M., Shalker, T. E., Clark, M. & Karp, L. (1978). Affect, accessibility of material and memory, and behavior: a cognitive loop? *Journal of Personality and Social Psychology*, **36**, 1–12.

Kruglanski, A. W. (1989). *Lay Epistemics and Human Knowledge: Cognitive and Motivational Bases*. New York: Plenum.

Kunda, Z. (1990). The case for motivated reasoning. *Psychological Bulletin*, **108**, 331–350.

Lazarus, R. S. (1991). *Emotion and Adaptation*. New York: Oxford University Press.

Lewinsohn, P. M. & Rosenbaum, M. (1987). Recall of parental behavior by acute depressives, remitted depressives, and nondepressives. *Journal of Personality and Social Psychology*, **52**, 611–619.

Lloyd, G. G. & Lishman, W. A. (1975). Effect of depression on the speed of recall of pleasant and unpleasant experiences. *Psychological Medicine*, **5**, 173–180.

Mackie, D. & Worth, L. (1991). Feeling good, but not thinking straight: the impact of positive mood on persuasion. In J. P. Forgas (ed.), *Emotion and Social Judgments*. Oxford: Pergamon, pp. 201–220.

Mathews, A. M. & McLeod, C. (1994). Cognitive approaches to emotion and emotional disorders. *Annual Review of Psychology*, **45**, 25–50.

Mayer, J. D. & Salovey, P. (1988). Personality moderates the interaction of mood and cognition. In K. Fiedler & J. P. Forgas (eds), *Affect, Cognition and Social Behaviour*. Toronto: Hogrefe, pp. 87–99.

Mayer, J. D. & Volanth, A. J. (1985). Cognitive involvement in mood response system. *Motivation and Emotion*, **9**(3), 261–275.

Mayer, J. D., Gaschke, Y. N., Braverman, D. L. & Evans, T. W. (1992). Mood congruent judgment is a general effect. *Journal of Personality and Social Psychology*, **63**, 119–132.

Morris, W. N. (1989). *Mood: The Frame of Mind*. New York: Springer.

Munakata, Y. & Bower, G. H. (1992). Mood effects on recall of successes and failures. Unpublished manuscript, Stanford University, CA.

Neisser, U. (1982). Memory: what are the important questions? In U. Neisser (ed.), *Memory Observed*. San Francisco: Freeman.

Niedenthal, P. M. & Setterlund, M. B. (1994). Emotion congruence in perception. *Personality and Social Psychology Bulletin*, **20**(4), 401–411.

Ortony, A., Clore, G. L. & Collins, A. (1988). *The Cognitive Structure of Emotion*. Cambridge: University Press.

Parrott, W. G. & Sabini, J. (1990). Mood and memory under natural conditions: evidence for mood incongruent recall. *Journal of Personality and Social Psychology*, **59**, 321–336.

Petty, R. E., Gleicher, F. & Baker, S. (1991). Multiple roles for affect in persuasion. In J. P. Forgas (ed.), *Emotion and Social Judgments*. Oxford: Pergamon, pp. 181–200.

Rhodewalt, F., Strube, M. J. & Wysocki, J. (1988). The Type A behaviour pattern, induced mood, and the illusion of control. *European Journal of Personality*, **2**, 231–237.

Roseman, I. J. (1984). Cognitive determinants of emotion: a structural theory. *Review of Personality and Social Psychology*, **5**, 11–36.

Ruiz Caballero, J. A. & Gonzalez, P. (1994). Implicit and explicit memory bias in depressed and non-depressed subjects. *Cognition and Emotion*, **8**, 555–570.

Salovey, P. & Birnbaum, D. (1989). Influence of mood on health-related cognitions. *Journal of Personality and Social Psychology*, **57**, 539–551.

Salovey, P., O'Leary, A., Stretton, M., Fishkin, S. & Drake, C. A. (1991). Influence of mood on judgments about health and illness. In J. P. Forgas (ed.), *Emotion and Social Judgments*. Oxford: Pergamon, pp. 241–262.

Schiffenbauer, A. I. (1974). Effect of observer's emotional state on judgments of the emotional state of others, *Journal of Personality and Social Psychology*, **30**(1), 31–35.

Schwarz, N. (1990). Feelings as information: informational and motivational functions of affective states. In E. T. Higgins & R. Sorrentino (eds), *Handbook of Motivation and Cognition: Foundations of Social Behaviour*, Vol. 2. New York: Guilford, pp. 527–561.

Schwarz, N. & Bless, H. (1991). Happy and mindless, but sad and smart? The impact of affective states on analytic reasoning. In J. P. Forgas (ed.), *Emotion and Social Judgments*. Oxford: Pergamon, pp. 55–71.

Schwarz, N., Strack, F., Kommer, D. & Wagner, D. (1987). Soccer, rooms and the quality of your life: mood effects on judgments of satisfaction with life in general and with specific life domains. *European Journal of Social Psychology*, **17**, 69–79.

Sedikides, C. (1992). Changes in the valence of self as a function of mood. *Review of Personality and Social Psychology*, **14**, 271–311.

Sedikides, C. (1994). Incongruent effects of sad mood on self-conception valence: it's a matter of time. *European Journal of Social Psychology*, **24**, 161–172.

Sedikides, C. (1995). Central and peripheral self-conceptions are differentially influenced by mood: tests of the differential sensitivity hypothesis. *Journal of Personality and Social Psychology*, **69**(4), 759–777.

Singer, J. A. & Salovey, P. (1988). Mood and memory: evaluating the network theory of affect. *Clinical Psychology Review*, **8**, 211–251.

Smith, C. A. & Ellsworth, P. C. (1985). Patterns of cognitive appraisal in emotion. *Journal of Personality and Social Psychology*, **48**, 813–838.

Smith, S. M. & Petty, R. E. (1995). Personality moderators of mood congruency effects on cognition: the role of self-esteem and negative mood regulation. *Journal of Personality & Social Psychology*, **68**, 1092–1107.

Snyder, M. & White, P. (1982). Moods and memories: elation, depression and the remembering of the events of one's life. *Journal of Personality*, **50**, 149–167.

Srull, T. K. (1983). Affect and memory: the impact of affective reactions in advertising on the representation of product information in memory. In R. Bagozzi & A. Tybout (eds), *Advances in Consumer Research*, Vol. 10. Ann Arbor, MI: Association for Consumer Research, pp. 244–263.

Srull, T. K. (1984). The effects of subjective affective states on memory and judgment. In T. Kinnear (ed.), *Advances in Consumer Research*, Vol. 11. Provo, UT: Association for Consumer Research, pp. 530–533.

Teasdale, J. D. & Forgarty, S. J. (1979). Differential effects on induced mood on retrieval of pleasant and unpleasant events from episodic memory. *Journal of Abnormal Psychology*, **88**, 248–257.

Teasdale, J. D. & Russell, M. L. (1983). Differential effect on induced mood on the recall of positive, negative, and neutral words. *British Journal of Clinical Psychology*, **22**, 163–171.

Tobias, B. A., Kihlstrom, J. F. & Schacter, D. L. (1992). Emotion and implicit memory. In S. A. Christianson (ed.), *The Handbook of Emotion and Memory: Research and Theory*. Hillsdale, NJ: Erlbaum, pp. 67–92.

Tulving, E. (1983). *Elements of Episodic Memory*. Oxford: Oxford University Press.

Watkins, T., Mathews, A. M., Williamson, D. A. & Fuller, R. (1992). Mood congruent memory in depression: emotional priming or elaboration. *Journal of Abnormal Psychology*, **101**, 581–586.

Watts, F. N. & Dalgleish, T. (1991). Memory for phobia related words in spider phobics. *Cognition and Emotion*, **5**, 313–329.

Williams, J. M. G., Watts, F. N., MacLeod, C. & Mathews, A. (1988). *Cognitive Psychology and Emotional Disorders*. Chichester, Wiley.

Chapter 29

Attributional Theories of Emotion

Ian H. Gotlib
Stanford University, Stanford, CA, USA
and
Lynn Y. Abramson
University of Wisconsin-Madison, Madison, WI, USA

Over the past two decades, theorists and researchers alike have become increasingly interested in trying to understand the nature of the links between cognitive and emotional functioning. Indeed, the publication of this *Handbook* is clear evidence of this endeavor. As part of this general trend, investigators interested in clinical phenomena have begun to examine more specifically the association between biased cognitive functioning and emotional disturbance. In this context, a number of researchers have formulated cognitive theories of emotional disorders. These theories, in turn, have provided the impetus for a large body of empirical work examining the nature of the association between cognitive dysfunction and emotional difficulties.

As is described in detail in several other chapters in this volume, a number of these theories focus on the content, structure and function of schemata of individuals who are experiencing such emotional disorders as depression and anxiety (e.g. Beck, 1976; Segal, 1988) or on the nature of the cognitive associative networks of depressed or anxious persons (e.g. Bower, 1981). Other cognitive theories of emotional disorders, however, focus more specifically on the ways in which individuals explain their world, the events that happen to them, or even the emotional disturbance itself that they are experiencing. These theories, broadly described as attributional theories, contend that the explanations an individual makes for events, and particularly for negative events, affect both the likelihood that the person will experience emotional distress and the severity and duration of this distress. Indeed, there is a growing consensus among clinical researchers

Handbook of Cognition and Emotion. Edited by T. Dalgleish and M. Power.
© 1999 John Wiley & Sons Ltd.

that some forms of emotional disorder, particularly depression and anxiety, are caused or sustained by biases in attributions. Moreover, consistent with this perspective, a number of psychological therapies attempt to reduce or ameliorate emotional distress by helping clients to become more "rational" or "realistic" in their perceptions and interpretations of their social worlds.

There is now a large body of empirical research examining hypotheses derived from attributional theories of emotional functioning. The results of these investigations, in turn, have led to subsequent refinements and extensions of the theories. The purpose of this chapter is to present and discuss the most prominent of these theories, highlighting and evaluating the nature of the associations they posit between cognition and emotion. Because the vast majority of the theoretical and empirical work in this area has focused on the relation between attributions and depression, in this chapter we focus primarily on depression and depressive affect as we discuss attributional theories of emotion. In addition, however, because of the high co-morbidity of depression and anxiety, where appropriate we also discuss the relevance of these theories to anxiety.

Given this focus on depression and anxiety, we begin this chapter with a brief discussion of the symptomatology and epidemiology of these two emotional disorders. Then, in order to provide an historical context and foundation for the chapter, we present a brief overview of the development of cognitive theories of emotional dysfunction. We continue more specifically with a discussion of the major theoretical attributional formulation of depression, the learned helplessness model, and the more recent expansion of this model, the hopelessness model of depression. We review the tenets of these models and highlight the results of research testing these theories. We conclude the chapter with a discussion of three broader issues in the area of attributional models of emotions: modifications that might be made to cognitive therapies on the basis of the hopelessness theory; the possible origins of an explanatory style that leads to difficulties in emotional functioning; and directions for future research that we believe would be fruitful for the field. We begin with a brief discussion of depression and anxiety.

DEPRESSION AND ANXIETY

Symptoms, Prevalence and Co-morbidity

Of all the psychiatric disorders, depressive and anxiety disorders are by far the most common. Depressive disorders are characterized by depressed mood or a loss of interest or pleasure in almost all daily activities, as well as a number of associated symptoms, such as weight loss or gain, loss of appetite, sleep disturbance, psychomotor agitation or retardation, fatigue, feelings of guilt or worthlessness, and concentration difficulties. To receive a clinical diagnosis of major depression, an individual must experience a constellation of these symptoms persistently over at least a two-week period. Based on this symptom pattern, it is estimated that 8–18% of the general population will experience at least one clinically significant episode of depression during their lifetime (Kessler et al., 1993; Weissman et al., 1991) and that approximately twice as many women than men will be affected by this disorder (Blehar & Oren, 1995; Weissman et al., 1991). Depression is also a recurrent disorder: over 80% of depressed patients have more than one depressive episode (Belsher & Costello, 1988). In fact, over 50% of depressed patients have been found to relapse within 2 years of recovery (e.g. Keller & Shapiro, 1981); individuals with three or more previous episodes of depression may have a relapse rate as high as 40% within only 12–15 weeks after recovery (Keller et al., 1992; Mueller et al., 1996). This high rate of recurrence of depression suggests that there are individuals who are prone to experience depression repeatedly because of the presence of a stable vulnerability factor, or diathesis, for this disorder. We will address this formulation in greater detail later in this chapter.

Importantly, some of the symptoms of major depression are also characteristic of anxiety disorders. For example, DSM-IV criteria for generalized anxiety disorder (GAD) include excessive anxiety and worry about a number of events or activities more days than not for at least 6 months, as well as a number of associated symptoms, such as restlessness, fatigue, concentration difficulties, irritability, muscle tension, and sleep disturbance. The prevalence of the anxiety disorders, when considered as an entire category, is at least as great as that of the mood disorders. The Epidemiologic Catchment Area (ECA) study, conducted in the 1980s, reported 6-month prevalence rates of any anxiety disorder at 8.9% and lifetime prevalence rates at 14.6% (cf. Robins & Regier, 1991). More recent estimates using more stringent criteria were 3.1% for 12-month prevalence and 5.1% for lifetime prevalence (Wittchen et al., 1994). Like depression, GAD is approximately twice as common in females as in males (Robins & Regier, 1991).

In recent years, considerable attention has been paid to findings that depression and anxiety commonly co-occur, at both the symptom and syndrome levels (cf. Gotlib & Cane, 1989). For example, estimates from the ECA study for 6-month prevalence rates showed that 33% of those with an affective disorder also had an anxiety disorder, and that 21% of those with an anxiety disorder also had an affective disorder. Not surpisingly, these numbers are even higher when one examines lifetime prevalence rates for depression and anxiety co-morbidity (Regier, Narrow & Rae, 1990). Indeed, these high levels of co-morbidity have been part of the impetus for the inclusion in DSM-IV of an Appendix describing a mixed anxiety–depressive disorder (Zinbarg et al., 1994).

The high incidence and prevalence rates of depression and anxiety in the general population, combined with the high rates of relapse in the depressive disorders, have spurred theorists and researchers to formulate explanations for these emotional disorders, and to examine factors that might play a causal role in the onset or recurrence of depression and anxiety. In this context, investigators have formulated a number of biological and genetic theories of these two disorders (see Barlow, 1991, Brawman-Mintzer & Lydiard, 1997; Goodman &

Gotlib, in press, for reviews of these theories). The largest body of empirical literature, however, has grown out of theoretical formulations of depression and anxiety that implicate cognitive functioning as being causally related to these two disorders. In the remainder of this chapter we examine briefly the development of cognitive theories of depression and anxiety, and then turn more specifically to a discussion of attributional theories of emotional disorder.

COGNITIVE THEORIES OF DEPRESSION AND ANXIETY

Schema and Network Theories

As a major part of the "cognitive revolution" (Dember, 1974) in psychology, Aaron Beck formulated the first systematic cognitive theory of the emotional disorders of depression and anxiety (e.g. Beck, 1967, 1976; Beck et al., 1979). Beck first formulated a cognitive theory of depression, in which he implicated three cognitive constructs in the onset and maintenance of this disorder: schemas, the negative cognitive triad, and cognitive distortions or errors. These constructs are described and discussed in detail in other chapters in this volume; consequently, we will be brief in our presentation here. Essentially, schemas are cognitive structures that serve to filter incoming information; they guide attention, expectancies, interpretation and memory functioning. According to Beck, individuals who are vulnerable to experiencing depression have developed negative schemas, "chronically atypical" cognitive structures that represent "a stable characteristic of (the depressive's) personality" (Kovacs & Beck, 1978, p. 530). Moreover, these negative schemas are postulated to serve as causal factors for depression by leading the individual to perceive and interpret environmental stimuli in a negative and pessimistic direction.

Beck also postulated that depressed persons are characterized by a negative cognitive triad and by negative cognitive distortions. The negative cognitive triad consists of negative views of the self, the world and the future, leading to depressive symptoms of low self-esteem, self-criticism and hopelessness. Similarly, the negative cognitive distortions, or errors, made by depressed persons are hypothesized to maintain or exacerbate symptoms of depression.

Beck (1976) extended these constructs and postulation, particularly those involving the concept of negative schemas, to the anxiety disorders. Essentially, Beck hypothesized that whereas the schemas of individuals who are vulnerable to depression involve concepts of loss and failure, the schemas of individuals at risk for experiencing anxiety involve themes of danger and threat. Thus, although the *content* of the relevant schemas differs for depression and anxiety, the *functional role* of the schemas is postulated to be the same for both these disorders. In both cases, Beck suggests that the presence of these negative schemas increases the likelihood that, in the face of a "schema-congruent" stressful life event (e.g. an event involving loss or failure for depression, and threat or danger for anxiety), individuals will become depressed or anxious (cf. Gotlib & MacLeod, 1997).

A formulation that is similar in a number of respects to Beck's schema theories of depression and anxiety has been presented by Bower (1981, 1992). Bower extended an earlier general theory of human associative memory (Anderson & Bower, 1973) to include processing of emotional information. Bower conceptualized memory as a collection of nodes, each containing discrete representations. Accessing any representation involves activating that node to some threshold level, and associative connections develop and strengthen between those nodes that are frequently activated simultaneously. Through this network, activation of any node will lead, through "spreading", to the partial activation (or "priming") of other nodes that share associative connections with the original node. The representations contained within these primed nodes will then be disproportionately easy to access, because less additional activation will be required to bring these nodes to the threshold level for such access to occur.

In this network formulation, emotion nodes each correspond to discrete emotional states and become active whenever that state is experienced. Over time, each emotion node will come to develop associative connections with those nodes that are most often activated simultaneously with it. Thus, because individuals will often experience depression when processing information related to loss or failure, associative connections will develop between the depression node and nodes containing this class of negative information. Similarly, because individuals will often experience anxiety when processing information related to threat and danger, associative connections will develop between the anxiety node and nodes containing information about threat and danger. Bower postulates that once such associative networks have developed, the experience of a mood state will introduce a systematic bias into the memory system. Different classes of emotionally negative representations will be made more available to the cognitive system when anxiety and when depression are elevated—threat and danger representations for anxiety, and loss and failure representations for depression. Thus, like Beck's formulation, Bower's mood–memory model of cognitive functioning suggests that depression and anxiety are both associated with biases in memory functioning and, although the content differs in depressed and anxious individuals, the process underlying these biases is the same.

These and other related schema and network theories of depression and anxiety (e.g. Teasdale, 1988) assume that individuals who are experiencing depression and/or anxiety are characterized by a negative automaticity in their processing of environmental stimuli. Indeed, studies conducted to examine postulates of these theories typically assess reaction times of depressed or anxious subjects in processing valenced stimuli that are either congruent or incongruent with their disorder. In general, the results of these investigations indicate that anxious persons selectively attend to anxiety-relevant stimuli, and that depressed individuals demonstrate better memory for negative than for positive stimuli (for reviews, see Gotlib, Roberts & Gilboa, 1996; Gotlib & MacLeod, 1997). There is little direct evidence from this literature, however, that these biases in cognitive information processing play a causal role in depression or anxiety (for a notable exception, see MacLeod & Hagan, 1992). In contrast, theories of emotional disorders that implicate more strategic or controlled, as opposed to automatic, cognitive processes have provided the foundation for studies that have yielded more promising results with respect to the role of cognitive functioning in the onset of emotional disturbance. In particular, attributional theories have been formulated that posit that the explanations individuals make for the occurrence of negative events in their lives affects not only the likelihood that they will experience depression, but the severity and duration of depression as well. Importantly, there is a growing literature demonstrating that such attributions might indeed play a role in the onset and maintenance of depressive affect. We now turn to a discussion of these attributional theories.

ATTRIBUTIONAL THEORIES OF DEPRESSION

The most systematically formulated and broadly tested attributional theory of depression currently is the hopelessness theory of depression (Abramson, Metalsky & Alloy, 1989). The hopelessness theory represents a theory-based approach to the classification of a subset of the depressive disorders that is process-rather than symptom-orientated. In essence, the hopelessness theory postulates the existence of a specific subtype of depression, *hopelessness depression*, that has not yet been identified empirically. Indeed, Abramson et al. suggest that hopelessness depression might not map directly onto any currently diagnosed category of depression, but instead, that it likely cuts across current categories of depression. To provide a context for understanding hopelessness theory, as well as to document the evolution of the development of this attributional approach to understanding depression, we now trace its historical development, beginning with the original helplessness theory.

Helplessness Theory of Depression (1975)

The earliest direct precursor of hopelessness theory was Seligman's (1975) helplessness theory of depression, which was rooted in laboratory studies of animal learning. In the initial studies, dogs were immobilized and exposed to a series of painful, uncontrollable, electric shocks. A striking phenomenon occurred 24 hours later when these dogs were exposed to subsequent electric shocks that now could be terminated by a simple response. Dogs who had been previously exposed to controllable shocks or to no shocks at all exhibited vigorous responding and quickly learned the response necessary to turn off the shocks. In contrast, dogs who had the "pretreatment" experience with uncontrollable shocks passively accepted the shock and made little effort to learn how to terminate it (Overmier & Seligman, 1967; Seligman & Maier, 1967).

To explain the maladaptive passivity of these dogs, Seligman (1975) proposed the learned helplessness hypothesis. According to this hypothesis, when organisms are exposed to uncontrollable aversive events, they learn accurately that they have no control. Seligman suggested that such learning can be maladaptive if the organism forms an expectation of no control that generalizes to new situations, including those in which the organism actually *does* have control. Thus, Seligman hypothesized that the dogs who were exposed to uncontrollable shocks in the original situation learned to expect to have no control in future situations, and that this expectation led to their maladaptive passivity and to other symptoms of learned helplessness.

Noting the parallels between helplessness induced in the laboratory by exposure to uncontrollable, aversive events and symptoms exhibited by individuals experiencing depressive episodes, Seligman (1975) proposed that this laboratory phenomenon represented a model of the development of human depression. In part because of its intuitive appeal and scientific testability, this learned helplessness theory of depression generated a large body of research. Consistent with the theory, numerous studies demonstrated that beliefs that events are uncontrollable lead individuals to experience increased emotional distress (e.g. Glass, Reim & Singer, 1971; for review, see Seligman, 1975).

Despite this growing body of research, theorists and researchers became increasingly disenchanted with the applicability of the learned helplessness model to human depression. Although the model was able to account for the behavioral and affective symptoms of depression in humans, it was less able to explain several other important characteristics of depression. For example, the learned helplessness model did not explain the loss of self-esteem commonly observed in depressed individuals, the generalization of depression across situations, or the experience of depressive affect as a primary symptom of depression. Moreover, the foundation of the learned helplessness model appeared to be inconsistent with the frequently reported finding that, rather than experiencing feelings of "no control" in their environment, depressives often blame themselves for their failures. Finally, the learned helplessness model could not explain individual differences in the *persistence* of depression; whereas some depressive episodes last for 2 weeks, others may last for 2 years (e.g. Mueller et al., 1996). These limitations of the original learned helplessness model led Abramson, Seligman & Teasdale (1978) to reformulate this model.

Reformulated Theory of Helplessness and Depression (1978)

To address these shortcomings, Abramson, Seligman & Teasdale (1978) substantially changed the original learned helplessness theory of depression by introducing an attributional component to the model. The reformulation drew heavily on attribution theory in social psychology (e.g. Jones et al., 1971; Kelley, 1967; Weiner, 1974). The central assumption in the reformulation was that when people are confronted with an uncontrollable event, they often ask themselves why the event occurred. This assumption is consistent with research in social psychology demonstrating that the occurrence of uncontrollable events frequently induces peoples to engage in causal analysis (e.g. Pittman & Pittman, 1980). For Abramson et al., the results of this causal analysis are critical in understanding the onset and maintenance of depressive symptoms. In brief, the reformulated learned helplessness theory of depression postulated that attributing lack of control to *internal* factors leads to lowered self-esteem, whereas attributing lack of control to external factors does not. The theory also postulated that attributing lack of control to *stable* factors leads to an expectation of uncontrollability in future situations and, consequently, to helplessness and depressive deficits that are extended across time. Similarly, attributing lack of control to *global* factors was posited to lead to an expectation of uncontrollability in other situations and, consequently, to helplessness and depressive deficits extended across situations. In contrast, attributing lack of control to unstable, specific factors was hypothesized to lead to helplessness and depressive deficits that are short-lived and situation-specific. Finally, Abramson et al. postulated that only those cases in which the expectation of uncontrollability concerns the loss of a highly desired outcome or the occurrence of a highly aversive outcome are sufficient to cause depressive affect. In short, according to the reformulation, the sweeping, maladaptive generalization of helplessness to new situations that so captured Seligman in his early experiments is not a necessary outcome of an experience with an uncontrollable event. Rather, such generalization only should occur when people believe that an important initial uncontrollable, aversive event is caused by a stable and global factor.

Addressing the vulnerability issue we raised earlier in this chapter, Abramson, Seligman & Teasdale (1978) also suggested that there are important individual differences in the causal attributions that people typically use to explain the occurrence of uncontrollable, aversive events. They hypothesized that some people tend to exhibit a "depressive attributional style"—the tendency to attribute uncontrollable, negative events to internal, stable, and global factors (see also Ickes & Layden, 1978, for a parallel development of the concept of attributional style within social psychology). Interestingly, Dykman & Abramson (1990) suggested that the concept of attributional style provided a contemporary specification of one facet of the concept of "depressive personality", discussed in detail in psychoanalytic and neopsychoanalytic writings (e.g. Freud, 1917/1957). Dykman & Abramson speculated further that describing a facet of the depressive personality in terms of attributional style may have been particularly appealing because it integrated an important psychoanalytic concept with basic research in contemporary social psychology.

In testing the reformulated learned helplessness theory, numerous studies used cross-sectional designs to compare the attributional styles of depressed and non-depressed individuals. Based on the theory, investigators predicted that, compared to non-depressed individuals, depressed individuals would make more internal, stable, global causal attributions for negative events and, perhaps, more external, unstable, specific attributions for positive events. In large part, this prediction was supported across a variety of participant samples, including hospital inpatients, college students, and children (for detailed reviews and meta-analyses of these studies, see Gotlib & Hammen, 1992; Joiner & Wagner, 1995; Peterson & Seligman, 1984; Sweeney, Anderson & Bailey, 1986).

It is important to note that these predictions, as well as the tests of these hypotheses, involve *between-groups comparisons* of attributions, i.e. comparing the attributions of depressed and non-depressed participants. One of the most clinically interesting aspects of the reformulated learned helplessness theory, however, also concerns *within-group comparisons*, that is, the hypothesized difference in the nature of the attributions made by depressed individuals for negative vs. positive events, and the manner in which they differ from their non-depressed counterparts with respect to this pattern of attributions. As we noted above, the reformulated learned helplessness theory postulated that depressed individuals would show a "self-derogating" attributional style, attributing negative events to internal, stable and global causes and positive events to external, unstable and specific causes. Although the tenets of other clinically-based theories of depressive cognition (e.g. Beck, 1967) are consistent with these hypothesized attributions, these theories differ from the reformulation with respect to expectations of the nature of the attributions of *non-depressed* individuals for positive and negative events. The reformulation hypothesizes that non-depressed individuals should make attributions that are the mirror image of those made by depressed persons, that is, external, unstable, and specific attributions for negative events and internal, stable, and global attributions for positive events. Indeed, it is this "positive attributional style" that is hypothesized to keep non-distressed persons from becoming emotionally distressed (cf. Taylor & Brown, 1988). In this context, therefore, it is instructive to note that Beck, Ellis, and many other cognitive theorists depicted depressed individuals as biased in their cognitive functioning and non-depressed individuals as rational and unbiased. This view would lead to the prediction that whereas depressed persons should demonstrate a negative attributional style, non-depressed individuals should show a more even-handed attributional style, making relatively similar causal attributions for positive and negative events.

Contrary to the clinically intuitive position of the rationality of non-depressed persons, the results of relevant studies in this area suggest that non-depressed individuals do, in fact, demonstrate a bias in their attributions, tending to attribute negative events to external, unstable, specific factors and positive events to internal, stable, global factors. In fact, some theorists contend that this "positivity" bias, a pattern referred to by some social psychologists as a self-serving attributional style (e.g. Miller & Porter, 1988), is a commonly observed characteristic of nondepressed individuals. In fact, the results of these studies of the different patterns of attributions of depressed and nondepressed persons complement, and are generally consistent with, research in social psychology that demonstrates pervasive optimistic biases in normal (i.e. non-depressed) individuals (e.g. Taylor & Brown, 1988; Weinstein, 1980). For example, nondepressed people often exhibit an "illusion of control", in which they believe they control outcomes over which they objectively have no control; depressed individuals, in contrast, seem to be less susceptible to this illusion (e.g. Alloy et al., 1990; Golin, Terrell & Johnson, 1977). Such social psychological research on optimistic biases among normal people suggests that in formulating theories of depressive cognition, clinical researchers may have been wrong in assuming accuracy as the baseline of "normal" cognitive functioning.

Indeed, the results of studies in this area have given rise to a lively debate concerning whether, in a complete reversal of Beck's (1967, 1987) original characterization of "depressive cognitive distortion", depressives actually may be *more accurate* than non-depressed persons in their perceptions and interpretations of their environment. Of course, from a non-justificationist philosophical perspective (e.g. Lakatos, 1978; Popper, 1962), it is impossible to know with absolute certainty which of the two groups is ultimately more accurate in their perceptions (cf. Kruglanski & Jaffe, 1988). However, consistent with Coyne & Gotlib's (1983) conceptual analysis, recent laboratory work has demonstrated that both depressed and non-depressed people show cognitive biases and illusions that are consistent with their preconceived notions, or schemas (Dykman et al., 1989; Gotlib, McLachlan & Katz, 1988; McCabe & Gotlib, 1995). In response to this work, modifications of Beck's theory have been proposed that emphasize differences in the *content*, rather than in the *process*, of depressed and non-depressed persons' cognitions (e.g. Dykman et al., 1989; Haack et al. 1996; Hollon & Garber, 1988). Thus, although research examining depressive realism and optimistic biases in normal cognition has not established that depressed individuals are always more accurate than are non-depressed persons, the results of these studies have nevertheless posed an important challenge to Beck's original portrayal of depressives as either impervious to environmental information or hopelessly biased by pervasive negative schemas, and of non-depressives as completely data-driven and free of the influence of biasing schemas. These contemporary reformulations of Beck's theory provide a necessary integration of work on depressive cognition with studies of normal cognition and emotion by social and experimental psychologists.

Hopelessness Theory of Depression (1989)

Although the 1978 reformulation of the learned helplessness theory of depression represented an important advancement over the original model, and provided the impetus for a great number of empirical studies, it suffered from three major shortcomings: (a) it did not present an explicitly articulated theory of depression; (b) it did not incorporate insights from descriptive psychiatry concerning the heterogeneity of depression; and (c) although the reformulation relied heavily on attribution theory, it did not incorporate other relevant work in social, personality and cognitive psychology. Consequently, Abramson, Metalsky & Alloy (1989) revised the reformulated helplessness theory and developed the hopelessness theory of depression. This theory was developed to describe and explain one hypothesized subtype of depression—hopelessness depression—and to specify a chain of distal and proximal causes of its symptoms.

Drawing on and integrating basic research in psychopathology, animal learning, cognition, personality, psychiatry and social psychology, Abramson, Metalsky & Alloy (1989) hypothesized that hopelessness depression is characterized by 12 symptoms: retarded initiation of voluntary responses; lack of energy; apathy; psychomotor retardation; sad affect; suicide; brooding; sleep disturbance; difficulty in concentration; mood-exacerbated negative cognitions; and, less consistently, lowered self-esteem or dependency.

Cause

In contrast to symptom-based classifications of depression, *cause* figures prominently in the definition of hopelessness depression. According to the theory, hopelessness results from the expectation that highly desired outcomes will not occur, or that highly aversive outcomes will occur, and that one cannot change this situation. This hopelessness is a proximal and sufficient cause of the broader symptoms of hopelessness depression. The evolution from a helplessness to a hopelessness theory of depression is consistent with analyses in both social (Weiner & Litman-Adizes, 1980) and experimental (Mandler, 1972) psychology that suggest that hopelessness, but not helplessness, is a sufficient cause of a wide range of depressive symptoms, if not a full-scale clinical depressive disorder.

How does a person become hopeless and develop the symptoms of hopelessness depression? The causal chain begins with the occurrence of negative life events. Three kinds of inferences that people may make when confronted with these events contribute to the development of hopelessness and, in turn, the symptoms of hopelessness depression: causal attributions, inferred consequences, and inferred characteristics about the self. In brief, relatively generalized hopelessness and, consequently, symptoms of hopelessness depression, are likely to occur when negative life events are attributed to causes that are stable (enduring) and global (likely to affect many outcomes), and that are viewed as important, as likely to lead to other negative consequences or outcomes, and as implying that the person is deficient or unworthy. Moreover, when negative life events are attributed to internal, stable, and global causes, hopelessness will be accompanied by lowered self-esteem. In the reformulation, internal attributions for negative events alone were postulated to lead to lower self-esteem. In contrast, in the more recent hopelessness theory, internal, stable, and global attributions are posited to be necessary for lowering self-esteem. This revision was prompted by the results of studies demonstrating that internal attributions *per se* do not necessarily lower self-esteem and, in some cases, may even be adaptive (e.g. Dweck & Licht, 1980; Janoff-Bulman & Lang-Gunn, 1988).

What influences the kinds of inferences people make about causes, about consequences, and about themselves when they experience negative life events?

Perhaps because the attributional reformulation was the immediate theoretical precursor of the hopelessness theory, Abramson, Metalsky & Alloy (1989) focused primarily on the determinants of causal attributions, rather than on the inferences about consequences and the self. An important shortcoming of the 1978 reformulation was that it ignored both research demonstrating that the environment constrains the content of people's attributions, and the results of investigations indicating that depressed individuals are often faced with environmental adversities that may shape their current cognitions in important ways (e.g. Barnett & Gotlib, 1988; Gotlib & Hammen, 1992; Krantz & Gallagher-Thompson, 1990).

Abramson, Metalsky & Alloy (1989) addressed this limitation by incorporating situational determinants of causal attributions into the hopelessness theory. According to Kelley's (1967) model of the attribution process, people's causal attributions are affected by three types of situational information: (a) consensus (Is this event happening only to me, or is it happening to other people as well?); (b) consistency (Have similar events happened to me in the past?); and (c) distinctiveness (Is this event distinctive in my life?). Consensus, consistency, and distinctiveness information is relevant to the attributional dimensions of internality, stability, and globality, respectively. In the hopelessness theory, Abramson et al. hypothesize that individuals are likely to make depressogenic (i.e. internal, stable, global) attributions for a negative event (e.g. break-up of an important relationship) when they are confronted with situational information that suggests that the event is low in consensus (e.g. others in their social networks are in satisfying relationships), high in consistency (they have a pattern of failed relationships), and low in distinctiveness (e.g. many of their interpersonal relationships are unsatisfying). Clearly, more theoretical and empirical work is required to explicate both environmental factors that influence people's inferences about the nature and consequences of negative events, and the implications of the occurrence of such events for individuals' self-concepts. Nevertheless, the incorporation in the hopelessness theory of findings from research in social psychology concerning situational influences on attributions is a critical advance, because it began to broaden the cognitive focus in depression research to include the possibility of a "hopelessness-inducing" environment.

The hopelessness theory also clarified and elaborated the vulnerability–stress component that was implied, but not explicitly articulated, in the 1978 reformulation. According to this aspect of the theory, the content of people's causal attributions is a function not only of environmental information, but also of dispositional individual differences in attributional style. Individuals who exhibit a general style to attribute negative life events to internal, stable, global causes and to view these events as important are hypothesized to be characterized by a "cognitive vulnerability", and should be more likely than are "non-vulnerable" individuals to make this depressogenic causal attribution about a given negative life event. Integrating research on situational determinants of causal attributions with the concept of individual differences in attributional style suggests that people's attributions for a particular event should be a joint function of situational information and person characteristics. Consistent with this hypothesis, Haack et al. (1996) found that among a college sample of both dysphoric and non-dysphoric students, causal attributions for laboratory events were a joint function of manipulated environmental information concerning consensus, consistency and distinctiveness, and the students' prior beliefs.

Addressing the general notion of cognitive vulnerability, Abramson, Metalsky & Alloy (1989) further postulated the existence of individual differences in the tendency to infer negative consequences and/or negative characteristics about the self when faced with the occurrence of a negative life event. Thus, cognitively vulnerable individuals should be more likely than their non-vulnerable counterparts to make depressogenic inferences about the cause and consequence of a negative life event, and to infer negative characteristics of the self. Importantly, in the absence of negative life events cognitively vulnerable individuals should be no more likely than non-vulnerable persons to develop hopelessness and symptoms of hopelessness depression. This aspect of the theory is clearly a diathesis–stress component (Metalsky, Halberstadt & Abramson, 1987). Moreover, consistent with a "matching" hypothesis, cognitive vulnerability in a particular content domain (e.g. interpersonal) should provide "specific vulnerability" when a person is confronted with negative events in that same domain (e.g. social rejection). This specific vulnerability hypothesis requires that, for the cognitive vulnerability–stress interaction to occur and lead to hopelessness and depressive symptoms, there must be a match between the content areas of an individual's cognitive vulnerability and the negative life events he/she encounters (see also Beck, 1983).

Finally, Abramson, Metalsky & Alloy (1989) proposed a "titration" aspect of their cognitive vulnerability–stress model. Specifically, the less negative a person's cognitive style, the more negative an event must be to interact with that style and contribute to symptom formation (cf. Zubin & Spring, 1977). Thus, although many cases of hopelessness depression will occur among cognitively vulnerable people when they face negative life events, people who do not exhibit cognitive vulnerability also may develop hopelessness depression when they are confronted with events that are sufficiently powerful to engender hopelessness in many or most people (e.g. death camp imprisonment).

Empirical Tests of the Hopelessness Theory's Cognitive Vulnerability Hypothesis of Depression Onset

While a number of studies have been conducted to test various aspects of the hopelessness theory (see Abramson, Alloy & Metalsky, 1995, for a review), we focus here on research that we believe provides the most compelling test of the cognitive vulnerability hypothesis of depression onset. A powerful method for testing the cognitive vulnerability hypothesis of hopelessness theory is the "behavioral high-risk design" (e.g. Depue et al. 1981). Similar to the genetic high-risk paradigm, the behavioral high-risk design involves studying participants who do not currently have the disorder of interest but who are hypothesized to be at high or low risk for developing the disorder. In contrast to the genetic high-risk paradigm, in the behavioral high-risk study individuals are selected on the basis of hypothesized psychological, rather than genetic, vulnerability or invulnerability to the disorder. Thus, to test the vulnerability predictions of the hopelessness theory, non-depressed individuals who either do or do not exhibit the hypothesized cognitive vulnerability for depression, specifically hope-lessness depression, would be selected and then compared on their likelihood of exhibiting depression, both in the past in a retrospective version of the design, and in the future, in a prospective version of the design. It is important to note here that one important drawback of the retrospective design is that the cognitive "vulnerability" that is assessed might actually be a *scar* of a previous depressive episode rather than a *causal* factor in depression (cf. Rohde, Lewinsohn & Seeley, 1991).

The results of studies that have utilized less optimal methods to test the vulnerability predictions of the hopelessness theory have been equivocal (see, for example, Barnett & Gotlib, 1988). In contrast, recent studies that have used variants of the prospective behavioral high-risk design have consistently found that people who exhibit the hypothesized cognitive vulnerability are more likely to develop depressive moods and/or depressive symptoms when they experience negative life events, such as a failing grade on a mid-term examination, than are individuals who do not demonstrate this vulnerability, even after statistically controlling for severity of initial depressive symptoms (e.g. Alloy et al., 1996; Metalsky, Halberstadt & Abramson, 1987; Metalsky et al., 1993).

Using a retrospective behavioral high-risk design, Alloy, Lipman & Abramson (1992) tested the attributional vulnerability hypothesis of the hopelessness theory for clinically significant depression. In this study, currently non-depressed college students who either did or did not exhibit attributional vulnerability for depres-sion with low self-esteem (tendency to attribute negative life events to internal, stable, global causes) were compared with respect to the probability that they had experienced major depressive disorder, as well as the hypothesized subtype of hopelessness depression, over the past 2 years. Alloy et al.'s results supported the applicability of the hopelessness theory to clinical depression: compared with attributionally invulnerable students, attributionally vulnerable students were more likely to have exhibited major depressive disorder and hopelessness depres-sion over the previous 2 years and to have experienced a greater number of episodes of these disorders.

The ongoing Temple–Wisconsin Cognitive Vulnerability to Depression (CVD) Project (Alloy & Abramson, 1998) is a two-site study that utilizes the prospective behavioral high-risk strategy and provides a test of the vulnerability and causal mediation hypotheses of both hopelessness theory and Beck's (1967, 1976) cognitive theory of depression. Moreover, it assesses both depressive symp-toms and clinically significant depressive episodes. As we noted above, Beck's theory is similar to the hopelessness theory in that it, too, is a cognitive vulner-ability–stress theory: individuals who exhibit dysfunctional attitudes are hypothesized to be vulnerable to depressive episodes when they encounter stressors that impinge on, or match, their specific dysfunctional attitudes. In the CVD Project, university freshmen who were currently non-depressed and had no other current Axis I psychopathology were followed every 6 weeks for 2.5 years with self-report and structured interview assessments of stressful life events, cognitions, and symptoms and diagnosable episodes of psychopathology. The subjects were then followed for an additional 3 years, with assessments occurring every 4 months.

Because the cognitively high-risk (HR) participants were required to score in the highest quartile on measures of the cognitive vulnerabilities described in both the hopelessness theory (Cognitive Style Questionnaire) and Beck's theory (Dysfunctional Attitude Scale), and the cognitively low risk (LR) participants were required to score in the lowest quartile on both these measures, the CVD Project provides a broad test of "generic" cognitive vulnerability hypotheses. A strength of this study is that the two sites permit a built-in assessment of replicability of results. Whereas the University of Wisconsin sample has a high representation of Caucasian individuals from rural, farming, small town and suburban backgrounds, the Temple University sample is more urban, with a high representation of minority (largely African-American) and lower socio-economic participants. Importantly, all of the results reported below replicated across the two sites.

Consistent with the vulnerability hypotheses of the cognitive theories, preliminary analyses based on the first 2.5 years of prospective follow-up data indicated that, compared with the LR participants, the HR participants showed a greater prospective incidence of DSM-III-R major depression (23% vs. 3%), RDC minor depression (45% vs. 14%), and the syndrome of hopelessness depression (49% vs. 11%). Moreover, in a prospective test of the cognitive vulnerability hypothesis, Alloy & Abramson examined the prospective incidence rates of depression among the subsample with no prior lifetime history of depression (i.e. examination of *first onsets* of clinically significant depression). Even among these participants with no lifetime history of depression, HR participants were far more likely than were their LR counterparts to have a first onset of DSM-III-R or RDC major depression (17% vs. 1%), RDC minor depression (39% vs. 6%), and the syndrome of hopelessness depression (41% vs. 5%).

The finding that cognitively vulnerable individuals exhibited greater prospective incidence of both first onsets and recurrences of depressive disorders than did cognitively low-risk individuals, even when controlling for initial differences in depressive symptoms, provides the first demonstration that negative cognitive style may confer risk for full-blown, clinically significant depressive disorders and, in particular, for the hypothesized subtype of hopelessness depression. This is particularly important because a criticism leveled at the cognitive theories of depression is that they may apply to mild, but not to clinically significant, depression. These results suggest that this criticism is not warranted, and that these theories are relevant to explaining more severe, clinically significant forms of depression. The initial findings from this project also provide preliminary support for the hypothesis that the specific subtype of hopelessness depression exists in nature and conforms to theoretical description. Further analyses of this data set will provide tests of the hypothesized cognitive–vulnerability–stress interaction in predicting onset of clinical depression.

We believe it is clear from this discussion that attributional theories and, in particular, the hopelessness theory of depression, have considerable promise to contribute to our understanding of both the development of symptoms of depressive disorders and the onset of more severe depressive disorders. Moreover, with respect to therapy, the tenets of hopelessness theory and findings from empirical studies in this area suggest a number of ways in which traditional cognitive therapies can be modified and enhanced. In the next section of this chapter, we discuss several of these modifications.

MODIFICATIONS TO COGNITIVE THERAPY BASED ON THE HOPELESSNESS THEORY

The therapeutic predictions of the hopelessness theory generally are consistent with the theory and practice of cognitive therapy. However, the hopelessness theory suggests a number of interventions that depart from the emphases of cognitive therapy as it is currently conceptualized and practiced. For example, because of its acknowledgment of "hopelessness-inducing" environments, the hopelessness theory suggests a greater focus on environmental modifications than is currently practiced in cognitive therapy (see also Gotlib & Colby, 1987). Clearly, the hopelessness theory contends that individuals' environments must be changed if the environments are found to contribute to the individuals' vulnerability to depression.

In addition, because the hopelessness theory does not postulate that depressogenic inferences necessarily are unrealistic or distorted (and allows for non-depressive cognitive distortions), the focus of therapy for hopelessness depressives would be on the content, rather than the realism, veridicality or rationality, of their inferences and beliefs (see also Hollon & Garber, 1988; Kruglanski & Jaffe, 1988). This position stands in contrast to more traditional approaches to cognitive therapy, which focus on correcting the cognitive distortions and biases of depressed patients. Finally, hopelessness theory calls for a more explicit focus on changing the attributions of depressed patients in order to both improve their current emotional functioning and reduce the risk of recurrence or relapse of disorder. For example, research indicating that early experience of neglect and/or abuse may contribute to the formation of a cognitive vulnerability to depression suggests that adopting a stronger focus on the past than is currently the case in cognitive therapy for depression may be beneficial to these patients. Thus, it may be therapeutic for such individuals, who might believe that they were maltreated or neglected because they were inherently bad or defective, or because their parents did not care for them, to reinterpret their traumatic developmental histories in terms of being raised by parents or others who, for whatever reason, did not have the psychological competence to raise a child in a more adaptive way.

This potential therapeutic benefit of focusing on changing perceptions of, and attributions for, early adverse experiences suggests that it is important to try to understand how early experience might contribute to cognitive vulnerability. Indeed, an outstanding issue in the area of cognitive vulnerability and emotional dysfunction concerns the origins of cognitive vulnerability. This question is of critical importance, because it both informs theoretical formulations of the nature of the relation between cognition and emotion, and has implications for prevention of emotional dysfunction. We now turn to a consideration of this issue.

THE ORIGINS OF COGNITIVE VULNERABILITY TO DEPRESSION

The question of the origin of the patterns of biased attributions described in this chapter has received relatively little empirical attention. Gotlib, Gilboa & Sommerfeld (in press) recently highlighted the importance of examining the origin of cognitive vulnerability to emotional disorders, but did not focus specifically on attributional models of emotion. The original learned helplessness theory posited that helplessness has its origins in learning that outcomes are independent of responses, but did not specify the kinds of early conditions that might give rise to this learning. Both the 1978 and the 1989 reformulations clearly emphasize the importance of a "depressogenic attributional style" in the onset of depression, but neither theory explicitly discussed the developmental origin of this type of explanatory style.

Recently, Rose & Abramson (1997) addressed this question, hypothesizing that the formation of cognitive risk for depression might have its origins in a developmental history of maltreatment and neglect. In presenting this hypothesis, Rose & Abramson integrate studies examining the attributional styles, or cognitive functioning more broadly, of depressed persons, with investigations demonstrating that individuals who experience episodes of depression often report having been exposed to adverse family environments (cf. Brewin, Andrews & Gotlib, 1993). Rose & Abramson reasoned that the paradigm utilized in the original learned helplessness experiments, in which animals were exposed to uncontrollable electric shocks (Seligman, 1975), is analogous to a laboratory model of abuse or maltreatment. They also noted that research examining "depressive realism" suggests that depressives may not be as irrational as originally portrayed in Beck's cognitive distortion theory of depression (e.g. Alloy et al., 1990). Rose & Abramson suggest that the negative cognitive and attributional styles exhibited by depressives might be the internal representations of maltreatment or adverse environments they actually experienced, rather than cognitive distortions. This position is clearly consistent with models formulated by a number of theorists (e.g. Gotlib & Whiffen, 1991; Gotlib & Beach, 1995; Joiner, Alfano & Metalsky, 1992) that emphasize the importance of the quality and nature of the individual's interpersonal environment in contributing to vulnerability to depression.

Consistent with their formulation, Rose & Abramson (1997) found that adults who exhibited cognitive vulnerability for depression reported growing up in environments characterized by emotional, sexual, and physical abuse, and neglect. Four findings from Rose & Abramson's study are particularly relevant to the issue of the origins of a depressogenic attributional style. First, depressed participants reported significantly higher rates of neglect and emotional, physical and sexual abuse during their childhoods than did non-depressed controls. Second, reported severity of abuse in childhood predicted lifetime history of clinical depression. Third, participants with childhood onset of clinical depression reported more severe overall abuse than did participants with later-onset depression, who in turn reported more severe abuse than did never-depressed participants. In fact, in the vast majority of cases (92%), the age of first maltreatment preceded the onset of the first depression, a pattern of results consistent with the hypothesis that developmental maltreatment contributes to risk for depression. Finally, greater severity of childhood maltreatment was associated with a more negative cognitive style (cognitive vulnerability) in adulthood.

These findings demonstrate important associations among childhood maltreatment, cognitive vulnerability to depression, and lifetime history of depression. The correlational data obtained in Rose & Abramson's (1997) study cannot establish that the association between early maltreatment and risk for depression is causal, nor can they demonstrate that this association is mediated by increased cognitive vulnerability. Nevertheless, the results of this investigation are clearly consistent with the hypothesis that developmental maltreatment predisposes cognitive vulnerability to depression. They are also consistent with other data suggesting that the early environments of individuals who subsequently experience depression are more negative than are those of individuals who do not become depressed (e.g. Gotlib et al., 1988). Rose & Abramson suggest that emotional abuse may contribute to cognitive vulnerability to depression through the explicit transmission of negative cognitions to the victim. For example, the individual may be told why negative events happen (e.g. "Of course you didn't get invited to the prom. You're ugly.") and internalize or "introject" these attributions. Anecdotally, Rose & Abramson noted that participants spontaneously reinforced this position while they were being interviewed about their early maltreatment. Participants who had experienced multiple forms of abuse made comments such as, "Bruises heal. Unless you end up needing reconstructive surgery, getting beaten isn't the worst thing. But I could not forget those terrible things my mother said to me. I can't get the names she called me out of my head". Such anecdotal reports are valuable sources of data in generating hypotheses concerning the development of dysfunctional attributional styles; clearly, however, much more empirical research is required to examine more systematically the origins of cognitive vulnerability for emotional disorders.

COGNITIVE AND BIOLOGICAL VULNERABILITY TO DEPRESSION: TOWARD AN INTEGRATION

In closing, we would like to offer what we believe is an important direction for further research in this area. Much important work has been conducted on both attributional and biological vulnerability to depression. Nevertheless, these two lines of research have proceeded in relative isolation from each other. Recently, however, Davidson et al. (1997) have begun to provide an empirical integration of the hopelessness theory with biological approaches to vulnerability to depression. Davidson and his colleagues have demonstrated that depressed individuals exhibit greater relative right-sided anterior activation of their cerebral hemispheres than do non-depressed individuals—a pattern consistent with behavioral withdrawal from the environment. Interestingly, these cerebral activation differences appear to be largely state-independent. For example, Gotlib, Ranganath & Rosenfeld (1998) found that asymptomatic remitted depressives exhibit greater relative right-sided anterior activation than do never-depressed controls—the same pattern of hemispheric asymmetry exhibited by currently depressed individuals. Based on these and other findings Davidson and colleagues (e.g. Davidson, 1992) and Gotlib et al. have suggested that relative right anterior hemispheric activation may represent a vulnerability to depression.

In their integrative study, Davidson et al. (1997) examined the association between this hemispheric lateral asymmetry and the presence of hopelessness cognitions. These investigators found that, as expected, non-depressed individuals with relative right anterior hemispheric activation also exhibited a depressogenic attributional style, attributing negative life events to internal, stable and global causes. Thus, individuals who were identified as being at risk for depression because they exhibited the depressogenic attributional vulnerability hypothesized by the hopelessness theory also exhibited the cerebral hemispheric activation pattern postulated to represent biological risk for depression. This is a particularly important finding given that Gotlib et al. (1998) failed to find a significant association between hemispheric asymmetry and cognitive vulnerability to depression measured by scores on the Dysfunctional Attitudes Scale. This discrepancy between the results of these two studies suggests that attributional vulnerability and vulnerability defined by elevated levels of dysfunctional attitudes may be independent risk factors for depression, and differentially related to other, more biologically based, risk factors for emotional disorder. This hypothesis is clearly speculative and awaits further research designed to examine this formulation more explicitly.

Moreover, it will also be important to conduct studies designed explicitly to compare different measures of "cognitive vulnerability", such as dysfunctional attitudes, attributional style, and negative information-processing biases and, further, to examine the differential associations of these cognitive vulnerabilities to depression and anxiety. In this regard, Alloy et al. (1997) recently presented promising results indicating that the cognitively vulnerable subjects in the Temple–Wisconsin CVD Project were characterized by negative biases on self-referent information-processing tasks. Clearly, further research examining the comparability among different types of cognitive vulnerability is warranted. At the least, it does appear that attributional vulnerability and right anterior hemispheric asymmetry may share a common bio-cognitive process that increases individuals' risk for depression. In our opinion, the integration of cognitive and biological perspectives on risk for emotional disorders represents an important direction for future research.

REFERENCES

Abramson, L. Y., Alloy, L. B. & Metalsky, J. I. (1995). Hopelessness depression. In G. M. Buchanan & M. E. P. Seligman (eds), *Explanatory Style*. Hillsdale, NJ: Erlbaum, pp. 113–134.

Abramson, L. Y., Metalsky, G. I. & Alloy, L. B. (1989). Hopelessness depression: a theory-based subtype of depression. *Psychological Review*, **96**, 358–372.

Abramson, L. Y., Seligman, M. E. P. & Teasdale, J. D. (1978). Learned helplessness in humans: critique and reformulation. *Journal of Abnormal Psychology*, **87**, 49–74.

Alloy, L. B. & Abramson, L. Y. (1998). The Temple–Wisconsin Cognitive Vulnerability to Depression (CVD) Project: conceptual background, design, and methods (manuscript in preparation, Temple University).

Alloy, L. B., Abramson, L. Y., Hogan, M. E., Murray, L. A. & Whitehouse, W. G. (1997). Self-referent information-processing in individuals at high and low cognitive risk for depression. *Cognition and Emotion*, **11**, 539–568.

Alloy, L. B., Albright, J. S., Abramson, L. Y. & Dykman, B. M. (1990). Depressive realism and non-depressive optimistic illusions. The role of the self. In R. E. Ingram (ed.), *Contemporary Psychological Approaches to Depression*. New York: Plenum, pp. 71–86.

Alloy, L. B., Kayne, N. T., Romer, D. & Crocker, J. (1996). Predicting depressive reactions in the classroom: a test of a cognitive diathesis-stress theory of depression with causal modeling techniques (unpublished manuscript, Temple University).

Alloy, L. B., Lipman, A. J. & Abramson, L. Y. (1992). Attributional style as a vulnerability factor for depression: validation by past history of mood disorders. *Cognitive Therapy and Research*, **16**, 391–407.

Anderson, J. & Bower, G. H. (1973). *Human Associative Memory*. Washington, DC: Winston.

Barlow, D. H. (1991). Towards a new integration of psychology and pharmacology. *Journal of Psychopharmacology*, **5**, 286–287.

Barnett, P. A. & Gotlib, I. H. (1988). Psychosocial functioning and depression: distinguishing among antecedents, concomitants, and consequences. *Psychological Bulletin*, **104**, 97–126.

Beck, A. T. (1967). *Depression*. New York: Hoeber Medical.

Beck, A. T. (1976). *Cognitive Therapy and the Emotional Disorders*. New York: International Universities Press.

Beck, A. T. (1983). Cognitive therapy of depression: new perspectives. In P. J. Clayton

& J. E. Barrett (eds), *Treatment of Depression: Old Controverises and New Approaches*. New York: Raven Press, pp. 265–284.

Beck, A. T. (1987). Cognitive models of depression. *Journal of Cognitive Psychotherapy: An International Quarterly*, **1**, 5–37.

Beck, A. T., Rush, A. J., Shaw, B. F. & Emery, G. (1979). *Cognitive Therapy of Depression*. New York: Guilford.

Belsher, G. & Costello, C. G. (1988). Relapse after recovery from unipolar depression: a critical review. *Psychological Bulletin*, **104**, 84–96.

Blehar, M. C. & Oren, D. A. (1995). Women's increased vulnerability to mood disorders: integrating psychobiology and epidemiology. *Depression*, **3**, 3–12.

Bower, G. H. (1981). Mood and memory. *American Psychologist*, **36**, 129–148.

Bower, G. H. (1992). How might emotions affect learning? In S. A. Christianson (ed.), *Handbook of Emotion and Memory*. Hillsdale, NJ: Erlbaum, pp. 3–31.

Brawman-Mintzer, O. & Lydiard, R. B. (1997). Biological basis of generalized anxiety disorder. *Journal of Clinical Psychiatry*, **58**, 16–25.

Brewin, C. R., Andrews, B. & Gotlib, I. H. (1993). Psychopathology and early experience: a reappraisal of retrospective reports. *Psychological Bulletin*, **113**, 82–98.

Coyne, J. C. & Gotlib, I. H. (1983). The role of cognition in depression: a critical appraisal. *Psychological Bulletin*, **94**, 472–505.

Davidson, R. J. (1992). Anterior cerebral asymmetry and the nature of emotion. *Brain and Cognition*, **20**, 125–151.

Davidson, R. J., Abramson, L. Y., Tomarken, A. J. & Wheeler, R. E. (1997). Asymmetrical anterior temporal brain activity predicts beliefs about the causes of negative life events (manuscript in preparation, University of Wisconsin-Madison).

Dember, W. (1974). Motivation and the cognitive revolution. *American Psychologist*, **29**, 161–168.

Depue, R. A., Slater, J., Wolfstetter-Kausch, H., Klein, D., Goplerud, E. & Farr, D. (1981). A behavioral paradigm for identifying persons at risk for bipolar disorder: a conceptual framework and five validation studies (Monograph). *Journal of Abnormal Psychology*, **90**, 381–437.

Dweck, C. S. & Licht, B. (1980). Learned helplessness and intellectual achievement. In J. Garber & M. E. P. Seligman (eds), *Human Helplessness*. New York: Academic Press, pp. 197–221.

Dykman, B. M. & Abramson, L. Y. (1990). Contributions of basic research to the cognitive theories of depression. *Personality and Social Psychology Bulletin*, **16**, 42–57.

Dykman, B. M., Abramson, L. Y., Alloy, L. B. & Hartlage, S. (1989). Processing of ambiguous feedback among depressed and non-depressed college students: schematic biases and their implications for depressive realism. *Journal of Personality and Social Psychology*, **56**, 431–455.

Freud, S. (1917/1957). Mourning and melancholia. In J. Strachey (ed. and trans.), *The Standard Edition of the Complete Psychological Works of Sigmund Freud*, Vol. 14. London: Hogarth (original work published in 1917).

Glass, D. C., Reim, B. & Singer, J. E. (1971). Behavioral consequences of adaptation to controllable and uncontrollable noise. *Journal of Experimental Social Psychology*, **7**, 244–257.

Golin, S., Terrell, F. & Johnson, B. (1977). Depression and the illusion of control. *Journal of Abnormal Psychology*, **86**, 440–442.

Goodman, S. H. & Gotlib, I. H. (in press). Risk for psychopathology in the children of depressed mothers: A developmental model for understanding mechanisms of transmission. *Psychological Review*.

Gotlib, I. H. & Beach, S. R. H. (1995). A marital/family discord model of depression: implications for therapeutic intervention. In N. S. Jacobson & A. S. Gurman (eds), *Clinical Handbook of Couple Therapy*. New York: Guilford, pp. 411–436.

Gotlib, I. H. & Cane, D. B. (1989). Self-report assessment of depression and anxiety. In

P. C. Kendall & D. Watson (eds), *Anxiety and Depression: Distinctive and Overlapping Features*. Orlando, FL: Academic Press, pp. 131–169.

Gotlib, I. H. & Colby, C. A. (1987). *Treatment of Depression: An Interpersonal Systems Approach*. New York: Pergamon.

Gotlib, I. H., Gilboa, E. & Sommerfeld, B. K. (in press). Cognitive functioning in depression: nature and origins. In R. J. Davidson (ed.), *Wisconsin Symposium on Emotion*, Vol. 1. New York: Oxford University Press.

Gotlib, I. H. & Hammen, C. L. (1992). *Psychological Aspects of Depression: Toward a Cognitive–Interpersonal Integration*. Chichester: Wiley.

Gotlib, I. H. & MacLeod, C. (1997). Information processing in anxiety and depression: a cognitive developmental perspective. In J. Burack & J. Enns (eds), *Attention, Development, and Psychopathology*. New York: Guilford, pp. 350–378.

Gotlib, I. H., McLachlan, A. L. & Katz, A. N. (1988). Biases in visual attention in depressed and non-depressed individuals. *Cognition and Emotion*, **2**, 185–200.

Gotlib, I. H., Mount, J. H., Cordy, N. I. & Whiffen, V. E. (1988). Depressed mood and perceptions of early parenting: a longitudinal investigation. *British Journal of Psychiatry*, **152**, 24–27.

Gotlib, I. H., Ranganath, C. & Rosenfeld, J. P. (1998). Frontal EEG alpha asymmetry, depression, and cognitive functioning. *Cognition and Emotion*, **12**, 449–478.

Gotlib, I. H., Roberts, J. E. & Gilboa, E. (1996). Cognitive interference in depression. In I. G. Sarason, G. R. Pierce & B. R. Sarason (eds), *Cognitive Interference: Theories, Methods, and Findings*. (pp. 347–377). Mahwah, NJ: Erlbaum.

Gotlib, I. H. & Whiffen, V. E. (1991). The interpersonal context of depression: Implications for theory and research. In W. H. Jones & D. Perlman (eds), *Advances in Personal Relationships*, Vol. 3. London: Jessica Kingsley, pp. 177–206.

Haack, L. J., Metalsky, G. I., Dykman, B. M. & Abramson, L. Y. (1996). Use of current situational information and causal inference: do dysphoric individuals make "unwarranted" causal inferences? *Cognitive Therapy and Research*, **20**, 309–331.

Hollon, S. D. & Garber, J. (1988). Cognitive therapy: a social-cognitive perspective. In L. Y. Abramson (ed.), *Social Cognition and Clinical Psychology: A Synthesis*. New York: Guilford, pp. 204–253.

Ickes, W. & Layden, M. A. (1978). Attributional styles. In J. Harvey, W. Ickes & R. Kidd (eds), *New Directions in Attribution Research*, Vol 2. Hillsdale, NJ: Erlbaum, pp. 119–152.

Janoff-Bulman, R. & Lang-Gunn, L. (1988). Coping with disease, crime, and accidents: the role of self-blame attributions. In L. Y. Abramson (ed.), *Social Cognition and Clinical Psychology: A Synthesis*. New York: Guilford, pp. 116–147.

Joiner, T. E., Alfano, M. S. & Metalsky, G. I. (1992). When depression breeds contempt: reassurance seeking, self-esteem, and rejection of depressed college students by their roommates. *Journal of Abnormal Psychology*, **101**, 165–173.

Joiner, T. E. & Wagner, K. D. (1995). Attributional style and depression in children and adolescents: a meta-analytic review. *Clinical Psychology Review*, **15**, 777–798.

Jones, E. E., Worchel, S., Goethals, G. R. & Grumet, J. F. (1971). Prior expectancy and behavioral extremity as determinants of attitude attribution. *Journal of Experimental Social Psychology*, **7**, 59–80.

Keller, M. B. & Shapiro, R. W. (1981). Major depressive disorder: initial results from a one-year prospective naturalistic follow-up study. *Journal of Nervous and Mental Disorders*, **169**, 761–768.

Keller, M. B., Lavori, P. W., Mueller, T. I., Endicott, J., Coryell, W., Hirschfeld, R. M. A. & Shea, T. (1992). Time to recovery, chronicity, and levels of psychopathology in major depression: a 5-year prospective follow-up of 431 subjects. *Archives of General Psychiatry*, **49**, 809–816.

Kelley, H. H. (1967). Attribution theory in social psychology. In D. Levine (ed.), *Nebraska Symposium on Motivation*, Vol. 15. Lincoln: University of Nebraska Press, pp. 192–240.

Kessler, R. C., McGonagle, K. A., Swartz, M., Blazer, D. G. & Nelson, C. B. (1993). Sex and depression in the National Comorbidity Survey I: lifetime prevalence, chronicity and recurrence. *Journal of Affective Disorders*, **29**, 85–96.

Kovacs, M. & Beck, A. T. (1978). Maladaptive cognitive structures in depression. *American Journal of Psychiatry*, **135**, 525–533.

Krantz, S. E. & Gallagher-Thompson, D. (1990). Depression and information valence influence depressive cognition. *Cognitive Therapy and Research*, **14**, 95–108.

Kruglanski, A. W. & Jaffe, Y. (1988). Curing by knowing: the epistemic approach to cognitive therapy. In L. Y. Abramson (ed.), *Social Cognition and Clinical Psychology: A Synthesis*. New York: Guilford, pp. 254–291.

Lakatos, I. (1978). Falsification and the Methodology of Scientific Research Programs. In J. Worral & G. Currie (eds), *The Methodology of Scientific Research Programs: Imre Lakatos Philosophical Papers*, Vol 1. Cambridge: Cambridge University Press, pp. 8–101.

MacLeod, C. & Hagan, R. (1992). Individual differences in selective processing of threatening information, and emotional responses to a stressful life event. *Behaviour Research & Therapy*, **30**, 151–161.

Mandler, G. (1972). Helplessness: theory and research in anxiety. In C. D. Spielberger (ed.), *Anxiety: Current Trends in Theory and Research*. New York: Academic Press, pp. 359–374.

McCabe, S. B. & Gotlib, I. H. (1995). Selective attention and clinical depression: Performance on a deployment-of-attention task. *Journal of Abnormal Psychology*, **104**, 241–245.

Metalsky, G. I., Halberstadt, L. J. & Abramson, L. Y. (1987). Vulnerability to depressive mood reactions: toward a more powerful test of the diathesis-stress and causal mediation components of the reformulated theory of depression. *Journal of Personality and Social Psychology*, **52**, 386–393.

Metalsky, G. I., Joiner, T. E., Hardin, T. S. & Abramson, L. Y. (1993). Depressive reactions to failure in a naturalistic setting: a test of the hopelessness and self-esteem theories of depression. *Journal of Abnormal Psychology*, **102**, 101–109.

Miller, D. T. & Porter, C. A. (1988). Errors and biases in the attribution process. In L. Y. Abramson (ed.), *Social Cognition and Clinical Psychology: A Synthesis*. New York: Guilford, pp. 3–30.

Mueller, T. I., Keller, M. B., Leon, A. C., Solomon, D. A., Shea, M. T., Coryell, W. & Endicott, J. (1996). Recovery after five years of unremitting major depressive disorder. *Archives of General Psychiatry*, **53**, 794–799.

Overmier J. B. & Seligman, M. E. P. (1967). Effects of inescapable shock upon subsequent escape and avoidance learning. *Journal of Comparative and Physiological Psychology*, **63**, 23–33.

Peterson, C. & Seligman, M. E. P. (1984). Casual explanations as a risk factor for depression: theory and evidence. *Psychological Review*, **91**, 347–374.

Pittman, T. S. & Pittman, N. L. (1980). Deprivation of control and the attribution process. *Journal of Personality and Social Psychology*, **39**, 377–389.

Popper, K. R. (1962). *Conjectures and Refutations*. New York: Basic Books.

Regier D. A., Narrow W. E. & Rae, D. S. (1990). The epidemiology of anxiety disorders: the Epidemiologic Catchment Area (ECA) experience. *Journal of Psychiatric Research*, **24**, 3–14.

Robins, L. N. & Regier, D. A. (eds) (1991). *Psychiatric Disorders in America*. New York: Free Press.

Rohde, P., Lewinsohn, P. M. & Seeley, J. R. (1991). Are people changed by the experience of having an episode of depression? A further test of the scar hypothesis. *Journal of Abnormal Psychology*, **99**, 264–271.

Rose, D. T. & Abramson, L. Y. (1997). Developmental maltreatment and cognitive vulnerability to depression (manuscript in preparation, University of Wisconsin-Madison).

Segal, Z. V. (1988).   Appraisal of the self-schema construct in cognitive models of depression. *Psychological Bulletin*, **103**, 147–162.

Seligman, M. E. P. (1975).   *Helplessness: On Depression, Development, and Death*. San Francisco, CA: W. H. Freeman.

Seligman, M. E. P. & Maier, S. F. (1967).   The alleviation of learned helplessness in the dog. *Journal of Experimental Psychology*, **74**, 1–9.

Sweeney, P., Anderson, K. & Bailey, S. (1986).   Attributional style in depression: a meta-analytic review. *Journal of Personality and Social Psychology*, **50**, 974–991.

Taylor, S. E. & Brown, J. D. (1988).   Illusion and well-being: a social psychological perspective on mental health. *Psychological Bulletin*, **103**, 193–210.

Teasdale, J. D. (1988).   Cognitive vulnerability to persistent depression. *Cognition and Emotion*, **2**, 247–274.

Weiner, B. (1974).   *Achievement Motivation and Attribution Theory*. Morristown, NJ: General Learning Press.

Weiner, B. & Litman-Adizes, T. (1980).   An attributional, expectancy-value analysis of learned helplessness and depression. In J. Garber & M. E. P. Seligman (eds), *Human Helplessness: Theory and Application*. Orlando, FL: Academic Press, pp. 35–57.

Weinstein, N. D. (1980).   Unrealistic optimism about future life events. *Journal of Personality and Social Psychology*, **39**, 806–820.

Weissman, M. M., Bruce, M. L., Leaf, P. J., Florio, L. P. & Holzer, C. III (1991).   Affective disorders. In L. N. Robins & D. A. Regier (eds), *Psychiatric Disorders in America*. New York: Free Press, pp. 53–80.

Wittchen, H., Zhao, S., Kessler, R. C. & Eaton, W. W. (1994).   DSM-III-R generalized anxiety disorder in the National Comorbidity Survey. *Archives of General Psychiatry*, **51**, 355–364.

Zinbarg, R. E., Barlow, D. H., Liebowitz, M., Street L., Broadhead E., Katon W., Roy-Byrne P., Lepine, J. P., Teherani, M. & Richards, J. (1994).   The DSM-IV field trial for mixed anxiety–depression. *American Journal of Psychiatry*, **151**, 1153–1162.

Zubin, J. & Spring, B. J. (1977).   Vulnerability: a new view of schizophrenia. *Journal of Abnormal Psychology*, **86**, 103–126.

Chapter 30

Appraisal Theory

Klaus R. Scherer
University of Geneva, Geneva, Switzerland

HISTORY AND BASIC ASSUMPTIONS

A central tenet of appraisal theory is the claim that emotions are elicited and differentiated on the basis of a person's subjective evaluation or appraisal of the personal significance of a situation, object, or event on a number of dimensions or criteria. Implicitly, this assumption is found in many of the classic philosophical treatments of emotion antecedents (e.g. in Aristotle, Spinoza, Descartes, Hume: see Lyons, this volume). Even William James, whose revolutionary emotion theory suggested that emotion differentiation is based on feedback from peripheral systems, had to acknowledge the importance of appraisal (James, 1894; see also Ellsworth, 1994a; Scherer, 1996b). Although the German psychologist Stumpf suggested a rudimentary version of appraisal theory at the beginning of the century (Reisenzein & Schönpflug, 1992), the history of this tradition begins with Magda Arnold (1960), who first used the term "appraisal" to explain the elicitation of differentiated emotions. She suggested that events are appraised with respect to three dimensions: beneficial vs. harmful, presence vs. absence of some object, and relative difficulty to approach or avoid the latter. Richard Lazarus (1966) had the most direct influence on the theoretical approach labeled "appraisal theory". He argued that both stress and emotion are elicited by a two-stage process of appraisal: primary appraisal (i.e. the positive or negative significance of an event for one's well-being), and secondary appraisal (the ability to cope with the consequences of an event). In addition, he acknowledged the dynamic nature of appraisal by specifically allowing for re-appraisals of objects or events based on new information or re-evaluation.

Following these pioneering leads, during the last 20 years a number of authors have suggested, quite independently of each other, that the nature of an emo-

Handbook of Cognition and Emotion. Edited by T. Dalgleish and M. Power.
© 1999 John Wiley & Sons Ltd.

tional reaction can be best predicted on the basis of the individual's subjective appraisal or evaluation of an antecedent situation or event (De Rivera, 1977; Ellsworth, 1991; Frijda, 1986; Oatley & Johnson-Laird, 1987; Roseman, 1984, 1991; Scherer, 1982, 1984a,b, 1986; Smith & Ellsworth, 1985; Solomon, 1976; Stein & Levine, 1987; Weiner, 1982, 1986).

REVIEW OF THEORIES

It is possible to distinguish four major strands of theoretical approaches to appraisal. These approaches can be characterized by the nature of the appraisal dimensions postulated by the respective theorists: criteria, attributions, themes or meanings.

Criteria

The classic approach to appraisal, as based on the early work of Arnold and Lazarus, suggests that individuals use a fixed set of dimensions or criteria in evaluating the significance of the events that happen to them. These criteria can be categorized into four major classes:

1. Intrinsic characteristics of objects or events, such as novelty or agreeableness.
2. The significance of the event for the individual's needs or goals.
3. The individual's ability to influence or cope with the consequences of the event, including the evaluation of "agency".
4. The compatibility of the event with social or personal standards, norms, or values.

Table 30.1 shows a comparative listing of the major criteria as postulated by the theorists in this tradition (Frijda, 1986; Roseman, 1984, 1991; Roseman, Antoniou & Jose, 1996; Scherer, 1984a,b, 1986, 1988; Smith & Ellsworth, 1985). Typically, theorists in this tradition postulate that specific *profiles* of appraisal outcomes on these criteria determine the nature of the ensuing emotion. Table 30.2 shows examples of such theoretically postulated profiles for several emotions.

Attributions

Another group of theorists focuses exclusively on the nature of the causal attributions that are involved in emotion-antecedent appraisal. Weiner (1982, 1986), who emphasizes the motivational nature of attribution, has shown the extent to which a number of major emotions, such as anger, pride or shame, can be distinguished solely on the basis of internal vs. external attribution of responsibility (for example, external attribution leading to anger, internal attribution to

Table 30.1 Comparison of the appraisal criteria postulated by different theorists

Scherer	Frijda	Roseman	Smith/Ellsworth
Novelty	Change		Attentional activity
• Suddenness			
• Familiarity	Familiarity		
• Predictability			
Intrinsic pleasantness	Valence		Pleasantness
Goal significance		Appetitive/aversive	
• Concern relevance	Focality	motives	Importance
• Outcome probability	Certainty	Certainty	Certainty
• Expectation	Presence		
• Conduciveness	Open/closed	Motive consistency	Perceived obstacle/
• Urgency	Urgency		Anticipated effort
Coping potential			
• Cause: agent	Intent/self–other	Agency	Human agency
• Cause: motive			
• Control	Modifiability	Control potential	Situational control
• Power	Controllability		
• Adjustment			
Compatibility standards			
• External	Value relevance		Legitimacy
• Internal			

Table 30.2 Examples of theoretically postulated appraisal profiles for different emotions

Stimulus evaluation checks	Anger/rage	Fear/panic	Sadness
Novelty			
• Suddenness	High	High	Low
• Familiarity	Low	Open	Low
• Predictability	Low	Low	Open
Intrinsic pleasantness	Open	Open	Open
Goal significance			
• Concern relevance	Order	Body	Open
• Outcome probability	Very high	High	Very high
• Expectation	Dissonant	Dissonant	Open
• Conduciveness	Obstruct	Obstruct	Obstruct
• Urgency	High	Very high	Low
Coping potential			
• Cause: agent	Other	Other/nature	Open
• Cause: motive	Intent	Open	Chance/neg
• Control	High	Open	Very low
• Power	High	Very low	Very low
• Adjustment	High	Low	Medium
Compatibility with standards			
• External	Low	Open	Open
• Internal	Low	Open	Open

Note: Open-different appraisal results are compatible with the respective emotion.

shame) and the degree of perceived control. Abelson (1983), in a pioneering paper that strongly influenced later work, also focuses mostly on agency and intentionality.

Themes

Theorists in this tradition attempt to link the elicitation of a specific emotion to the identification of a specific pattern of goal-relatedness of an event. Lazarus (1991) proposed to add "core-relational themes" (e.g. "loss of a valued person or object") to the more abstract criteria of goal significance and coping potential that he had proposed in his pioneering work in this area. Smith & Lazarus (1993) have suggested a two-step model, combining both molecular (appraisal criteria) and molar (relational themes) elements. In this scheme, the molar themes are considered to summarize the combined patterns of outcomes in terms of the more molecular appraisal criteria that are proposed to be associated with specific emotions. Although stemming from rather different traditions, the suggestions made by Oatley & Johnson-Laird (1987) and Stein & Levine (1987) offer rather comparable accounts of emotion–antecedent evaluations of significant events, focusing primarily on the implications for the individual's goals.

Meanings

The protagonists of the approaches summarized in this category seem mostly interested by an analysis of the propositional nature of the semantic fields that underlie the use of specific emotion terms, almost in the sense of definitions. In other words, they attempt to show the logical operations that determine the labeling of a feeling state with a specific emotion word. As one might imagine, this direction has been particularly interesting to philosophers and cognitive scientists (De Rivera, 1977; Ortony, Clore & Collins, 1988; Solomon, 1976).

In spite of the differences in underlying philosophy, there is a high degree of convergence with respect to the nature of the appraisal dimensions postulated by these different theories, in spite of widely divergent disciplinary and historical traditions (for reviews see Karasawa, 1995; Lazarus & Smith, 1988; Manstead & Tetlock, 1989; Reisenzein & Hofmann, 1990, 1993; Roseman, Spindel & Jose, 1990; Roseman, Antoniou & Jose, 1996; Scherer, 1988).

EMPIRICAL EVIDENCE

Traditionally, a variety of different paradigms have been used to empirically buttress the relationship between particular configurations of appraisal results and the nature of the ensuing emotional reaction. The most frequently used strategy consists of asking subjects to recall specific emotional experiences and questioning them about the outcome of antecedent evaluation processes (Ellsworth & Smith, 1988a,b; Fitness & Fletcher, 1993; Folkman & Lazarus, 1988; Frijda, Kuipers & ter Schure, 1989; Gehm & Scherer, 1988; Mauro, Sato & Tucker, 1992; Reisenzein & Hofmann, 1993; Reisenzein & Spielhofer, 1994; Roseman, Antoniou & Jose, 1996; Roseman, Spindel & Jose, 1990; Scherer, 1997a; Smith & Ellsworth, 1985; Smith et al., 1993; Tesser, 1990). Another possibility is to use naturally occurring events such as examinations, or to induce emotions experimentally, and to obtain verbal reports on the appraisal processes (Folkman & Lazarus, 1985; Scherer & Ceschi, 1997; Smith, 1989; Smith & Ellsworth, 1987). A technique that is more closely related to the "meanings approach" as described above consists of having emotion words judged with respect to the appraisal implications that underlie the respective concept (Conway & Bekerian, 1987; Frijda, 1987; Ortony, Clore & Collins, 1988; Parkinson & Lea, 1991; Smolenaars & Schutzelaars, 1986/87). Finally, one can use vignettes or scenarios that have been systematically manipulated with respect to appraisal-relevant dimensions, asking subjects to indicate the emotional reactions that they—or a fictitious other—might experience in this situation (McGraw, 1987; Roseman, 1984; Russel & McAuley, 1986; Borg, Staufenbiel & Scherer, 1988; Smith et al., 1993; Smith & Lazarus, 1993; Stipek, Weiner & Li, 1989; Weiner et al., 1987; Weiner, Graham & Chandler, 1982; Weiner, Russell & Lerman, 1979). On the whole, these studies provided substantial support for many of the theoretical predictions made by appraisal theorists. For example, the limited set of predictor dimensions generally allows correct classification of about 40–50% of the emotional states studied in this research (see below).

The use of self-report of emotion–antecedent appraisal has given rise to repeated criticism. In most of the studies reported above, subjects are required to engage in conscious, complex inference or imagination processes, followed by verbalization. Subjects are generally asked to recall or infer the nature of their event or situation appraisal, mostly with the help of rating scales or questionnaire items constructed on the basis of the theoretically assumed appraisal dimensions. Obviously, all of these processes require a fairly high level of conceptual processing. It can be argued that participants are unlikely to be able to report upon antecedent appraisal processes which mostly occur outside awareness (Frijda, 1993; Parkinson, 1996, 1997; Nisbett & Wilson, 1977; Parkinson & Manstead, 1992, 1993).

In addition, these critics argue that the process of imagining an emotional event may depend to a large extent upon cognitive interpretation and memory and participants may construct a rationale for their emotional response or take recourse to social representations of emotional meaning. Furthermore, approaches using content analysis of narratives or interviews are subject to the criticism that, in addition to using verbal report of conscious experience, researchers impose the interpretative schemes of their respective theoretical systems. Lazarus (1995) has recently questioned some of the classic appraisal notions and methodological approaches by arguing that much of appraisal is unconscious and thus particularly susceptible to ego-defense mechanisms.

While many appraisal theorists admit that verbal report procedures need to be complemented by other approaches, they muster support for the dominant methodology from other areas of cognitive science. Smith (personal communication) argues that what is generally tapped is recognition memory rather than recall memory, since there are specific probes for the postulated appraisal dimensions. Therefore, many inferential processes that are potentially available to consciousness can be expected to be reported fairly accurately. Furthermore, in spite of the generally accepted fact that many appraisal processes may occur below the level of consciousness or may be difficult to verbalize, critics should realize that so far there is precious little alternative to study these processes at all.

Apart from the difficulties of assessing a process which, at least in part, is likely to happen at unconscious levels, appraisal theorists are faced with a number of issues that remain to be settled in the future—defining the precise object of the respective theories, the number and type of the criteria required for emotion differentiation, different levels of appraisal, the detailed nature of the appraisal process, and links to other components of the emotion process. These issues will be discussed below.

NUMBER AND TYPE OF APPRAISAL CRITERIA NEEDED FOR DISCRIMINATION

While converging with respect to the general principles, appraisal theories vary widely with respect to the number and definition of appraisal dimensions that are proposed. Scherer (1997a) has suggested distinguishing three different approaches:

1. A "reductionist" or, rather, a minimalist approach, postulating a minimal number of dimensions, often based on the assumption of fundamental motive constellations or prototypic themes (Oatley & Johnson-Laird, 1987; Lazarus, 1991; Stein & Trabasso, 1992).
2. An "eclectic" approach, attempting to include as many appraisal dimensions as needed to maximize the differentiation between types of emotional states (Frijda, 1986, 1987).
3. A "principled" approach (e.g. Roseman, 1991; Scherer, 1984a, 1986, 1993b; Smith & Ellsworth, 1985) postulating, on the basis of *psycho-logical* considerations, a restricted number of abstract dimensions considered necessary and sufficient to predict the occurrence of the major emotion categories.

A few recent studies have attempted to compare different appraisal theories and to empirically determine how many dimensions are needed and which dimensions seem to account for most of the variance (Manstead & Tetlock, 1989; Mauro, Sato & Tucker, 1992; Reisenzein & Hofman, 1990; Roseman, Spindel & Jose, 1990). While a larger set of non-redundant appraisal dimensions is likely to explain a larger proportion of the variance in a given set of emotion categories, an argument can be made for an attempt to predict the general nature of the emotional reaction on the basis of a relatively small set of appraisal dimensions (sacrificing some discrimination power).

In any case, it is likely that differentiation success will rise asymptotically with the increase of predictor criteria. Reisenzein & Hofmann (1993) have shown that the maximum level of discrimination that human judges can achieve on the basis of a full description of an emotional event by the individual who experienced the situation does not exceed 65–70%, averaged over different emotions. Consequently, this might be the upper limit of what appraisal theories could ideally achieve. If only a small set of abstract appraisal dimensions are used, the hit rate of the predictions should be even lower.

A number of authors have used discriminant analysis algorithms to examine this issue. Smith & Ellsworth (1985) correctly classified 42% of 15 emotions, using six predictors (factor scores); Frijda, Kuipers & ter Schure (1989) reported 32% (Study 1, 32 emotions, 19 appraisal variables) and 43% (Study 2, 32 emotions, 23 appraisal variables); Reisenzein & Spielhofer (1994) found 43% (chance corrected) for 30 emotions, 58% for 22 emotions (using 22 appraisal variables in both cases). Scherer (1997a), using the criterion of classification success in a cross-validation sample, reports around 40% accuracy in differentiating seven emotions with seven dimensions and 32% with only four dimensions.

It is an important issue for further work in this area to determine how many appraisal dimensions (and which particular set of them) are required to attain a realistic criterion value. Since this question depends on the number of different emotions to be classified, an agreement between appraisal researchers on a standard set of emotions to compare the predictive power of different appraisal theories would greatly improve the comparability of theories and studies.

Apart from the number of necessary criteria, a major issue for further research is the relative importance of particular criteria, i.e. their contribution to classification success. Smith & Ellsworth (1985, 1987), Folkman & Lazarus (1988), Mauro, Sato & Tucker (1992), and Roseman, Spindel & Jose (1990) all indicate that the criterion of agency or causation is one of the strongest prediction criteria (as one might have predicted from Weiner's, 1982, 1986, work). Scherer (1997a) also finds causation, followed by unfairness and immorality, to be the most important predictors.

It is possible that appraisal theorists have failed to specify some important dimensions. In particular, it has been suggested that appraisal theory has largely neglected the social context in which emotions are elicited, possibly requiring appraisal criteria relevant to relationships and interaction strategies (Kappas, 1996; Karasawa, 1995; Parkinson, 1996, see below).

THE ROLE OF THEORETICAL PREDICTIONS

Most of the studies reported above are limited to *post hoc* evaluation of how well the dimensions studied explain differentiation between the emotions reported by the subjects. In other words, the same group of subjects provides both the emotion and the appraisal information. In consequence, statistical analysis is limited to identifying the shared variance. Needless to say, the results cannot be generalized beyond the respective set of emotions and dimensions studied. While such information is eminently useful for the further development of appraisal theories, it seems desirable to develop a model that emphasizes the *prediction* of emotional states on the basis of a minimal set of necessary and sufficient dimensions or criteria of appraisal. Among the principles underlying the selection and definition of the appraisal criteria are stimulus features, personal relevance and coping potential, as well as normative context.

Only relatively few appraisal theorists have proposed detailed and concrete theoretical predictions as to which emotional state is expected to occur as a consequence of a particular configuration of appraisal results (see also Roseman, 1991, p. 167). Theory testing in a strict sense, generating cumulative research, requires concrete hypotheses, based on a theoretically derived set of appraisal dimensions that can be empirically tested. Not surprisingly, the proponents of a principled approach have been most prone to venture detailed prediction tables (see Roseman, 1984; Scherer, 1984b, 1988).

Understandably, it has been the same authors who have been concerned with the falsifiability of these theoretical prediction patterns by submitting them to empirical testing. Roseman and his collaborators have tested his predictions using (a) vignette studies (Roseman, 1991), and (b) recall of past events (Roseman, Antoniou & Jose, 1996). Scherer tested his predictions in a study using a computer expert system to obtain reports of past experiences and submit the systems' emotion postdictions to the participant's evaluation for correctness (Scherer, 1993b). In a large-scale study of emotion–antecedent appraisal Scherer (1997b) was able to show that the *modal* emotions studied (see Scherer, 1994) are universally associated with specific appraisal profiles, generally confirming the theoretical predictions. Similarly, Smith & Lazarus (1990) ventured specific hypotheses about appraisal–emotion linkages and expressly designed a study (Smith & Lazarus, 1993) to test these.

While conducted in the spirit of hypothesis testing, the studies reported above provide only indirect evidence, since the appraisal–emotion links are studied via *post-hoc* verbal reports on the evaluation of past events. A more direct test of the hypotheses presented by certain appraisal theorists obviously requires experimental manipulation of the appraisal mechanism. Recently, a number of studies have been reported in which the experimenters have attempted to systematically manipulate a variety of appraisal dimensions. Roseman & Evdokas (1995) conducted experimental studies in the laboratory in which participants' expectations relative to specific foods to be test-eaten were systematically varied in relation to real outcomes. Smith and his collaborators have used cognitive tasks to manipulate appraisals in a quasi-experimental fashion which also allows an examination of the dispositional and situational antecedents that contribute to the generation of the appraisal itself (Kirby & Smith, 1996; Pecchinenda & Smith, 1996; Pecchinenda, Kappas & Smith, 1997; Smith & Pope, 1992). Another possibility is to use computer games to induce emotions (MacDowell & Mandler, 1989). In appraisal research, typically various aspects of computer games (of the Pacman or the space exploration type) are manipulated in such a way as to affect intrinsic pleasantness, goal conduciveness, control and/or power (Banse et al., 1996; Johnstone, 1996; Kaiser & Wehrle, 1996; Kaiser, Wehrle & Edwards, 1994; Kappas & Pecchinenda, submitted; Schmidt, Wehrle & Kaiser, 1997; van Reekum, Johnstone & Scherer, 1997)

Another possibility to experimentally manipulate appraisal dimensions has been chosen by Ellsworth (1997). This author varied elements of moving cartoon images in a systematic fashion, requiring subjects (including children of various ages in several cultures) to report on their appraisals of the underlying intentions of the respective protagonists.

LEVELS OF APPRAISAL

The reliance in appraisal research upon questionnaire data, which by its very nature reflects high-level, conscious processes, combined with the large number of relatively sophisticated appraisal dimensions typically posited, has led many critics erroneously to deduce that appraisal processes are necessarily deliberate, conscious and thus "cognitivistic". In addition, many of the appraisal theories are worded in such a way as to reinforce this preconception. In consequence, appraisal theorists often find themselves accused of "excessive cognitivism". Critics question the likelihood that elaborate cognitive evaluations are performed during the few milliseconds that seem sufficient to bring about an emotion episode. It is claimed that, while appraisal theory may explain some types of emotional reactions, in many cases emotions are produced by unconscious, non-deliberate, non-voluntary—perhaps non-cognitive—factors. It has been claimed that affective arousal can be triggered without any cognitive–evaluative processing at all on the basis of processing by a primary "affect system" (Zajonc, 1984) or simple association processes (Berkowitz, 1994; see Berkowitz, this volume). Recently, Izard (1993) has suggested that there are several different activation systems for emotion, of which cognitive appraisal is only one.

The debate about the minimal cognitive prerequisites for emotion, often inaccurately labeled "cognition–emotion controversy" (Ekman & Davidson, 1994, Question 5; LeDoux, 1987, 1989; Leventhal & Scherer, 1987; Lazarus, 1984; Scherer, 1993a; Zajonc, 1980, 1984; Zajonc & Markus, 1984), has generated much attention (see Lazarus, this volume). This is in spite of the fact that the debate, fundamentally, seems to be mostly concerned with semantic issues. In trying to disambiguate the positions, two issues need to be clearly distinguished: (a) the target of the appraisal theory predictions; and (b) the meaning of cognition, evaluation or appraisal.

As to (a) it should be noted that appraisal theory does not attempt to explain all types of affective phenomena. For example, free-floating moods, preferences, reflexive pain reactions or emotional memories are not generally among the targets of appraisal theorists' predictive ambitions. Rather, the attention is focused on the reaction to significant stimulus events that impinge on organismic equilibrium or that change the organism–environment relationship (where the stimulus could range from a sudden thought, over proprioceptive perceptions, to a large class of external events). The target of the prediction is a full-blown emotion, such as the states that are labeled "anger", "fear", "sadness" and so on (see Scherer, 1984b, 1993a, for an attempt to define such full-blown emotions in more general terms as episodes of synchronization or coupling of all organismic subsystems). In consequence, ephemeral preferences for generally neutral stimuli, as produced by repeated exposure or subliminal priming (Kunst-Wilson & Zajonc, 1980; Murphy, Monahan & Zajonc, 1995), may not be considered to belong to the domain of appraisal theory (although it may well be argued that there are emotional states for which only some appraisals, e.g. valence, are made; see Ellsworth, 1991). Neither may be immediate, reflexive reactions to pain (as discussed by Berkowitz, 1994, see also Berkowitz, this volume). Thus, it seems advisable to first stake the claims of respective theoretical approaches before debating which account is more appropriate or economical.

With respect to (b), much of the debate hinges on definition of "cognition" (on which there seems to be just as little consensus as there is for the definition of emotion) or on the connotations of the concepts "appraisal" or "evaluation". The categorizing of appraisal theory as a "cognitive theory of emotion" and the unfortunate tendency to equate "cognitive" with "conscious, cortical" has led to serious misunderstandings. The debate becomes quite meaningless once one assumes that a substantial part of the appraisal processes occurs in an unconscious fashion, perhaps solely mediated via subcortical, e.g. limbic system, structures (Scherer, 1984a,b). Leventhal & Scherer (1987) have suggested the adoption of a "levels of processing" approach to more precisely specify the mechanisms underlying appraisal. Concretely, these authors have suggested that all of the standard appraisal criteria, exemplified by Scherer's (1982, 1984a) stimulus evaluation checks (SECs), can be processed on a sensorimotor, schematic or conceptual level, albeit in more or less rudimentary form and with different effects on the ensuing emotion. This proposal to view appraisal as a multi-level process corresponds to a number of similar approaches in other traditions, including the area of clinical psychology and the study of memory. The rapid development in this area has resulted in increasing interest in such *multi-level theories* (see overview by Teasdale, this volume). van Reekum and Scherer (1997) discuss the pertinence of such models for appraisal processes in greater detail. Recently, Smith and his collaborators have presented the outline of a multi-level process theory of appraisal (Smith et al., 1996).

Given the combined effect of the renewed interest in the issues of consciousness and unconsciousness in psychology and cognitive science as a whole, and the increasing sophistication of multi-level models of emotion-antecedent processing, it may not be too optimistic to hope that the oversimplified "cognition–emotion controversy" will finally fade into oblivion. There seems to be increasing agreement that emotion–antecedent information processing can occur at many different levels and that the question of how much of that can be called "cognitive" is a pseudo-issue.

However, this problem dealt with, another pseudo-issue arrives on the scene. Again, semantics and connotations are involved, revolving around the meaning of the term "appraisal". Should it not be reserved to the highest level of clearly cortical, conscious, propositional processing? Would not, otherwise, almost every type of information processing become "appraisal"? This renewed concern with the semantics of the central concepts in the area divides even the small group of appraisal theorists. Some (e.g. Frijda, personal communication) believe that this issue goes beyond semantics in that the use of words like "appraisal" or "evaluation" prejudges the nature of the underlying processes (e.g. excluding Gibsonian "pick-up" theories or universal effects of specific stimuli, such as sudden sounds or movement restraint).

However, one can argue that we need a general, overarching term to cover the fundamental fact that it is not the objective nature of a stimulus but the organism's "evaluation" of it that determines the nature of the ensuing emotion. A completely automatic, reflexive defense reaction of the organism also constitutes an intrinsic assessment, a valuation, of the noxiousness of the stimulus (although it may not necessarily produce a full-fledged emotion; see above). Even if simple feature detection is involved, the outcome of the process constitutes an assessment of the significance of the detected stimulus to the organisms, given that feature detectors that have any behavioral consequences are automatically "significance detectors". Obviously, this is a different process from the one that allows us to infer that a particular bit of news, given its ramifications, may have negative impact on our plans. And, obviously, the resulting emotional state and the action tendencies produced are different. Yet, both types of emotion–antecedent processing share a number of central functional-adaptational aspects. Does one want to emphasize this communality by talking about significance detection as "appraisal" or "evaluation" in the widest sense (without prejudging the nature of the underlying processes)? Or does one want clearly to demarcate the different processes by applying different concepts? The answer depends on the desired level of analysis, on the clarity of the respective definitions, and on the consensus on the conceptual distinctions made. In any case, researchers in this field need to undertake the in-depth study of the precise mechanisms that are involved. It would seem that this is where future efforts should be undertaken.

A better understanding of such processes may help to disambiguate some of the current controversies within the appraisal theory domain. For example, Lazarus (this volume) justifies the assumption of the centrality of *core-relational themes* by arguing that the personal meaning of a transaction between person and environment for well-being "can often be sensed in an instant without serial processing of the individual components which have contributed to that meaning". There seem to be two issues at stake: speed and synthetic apperception. With respect to speed, it is surprising how many psychologists, including appraisal theorists, seem to think of the appraisal process, particularly the sequential checking hypothesis, as a slow, laborious cranking-cogwheel process. Obviously, even sequential checking occurs in the context of the massively parallel architecture of cognitive processing and may take only milliseconds, thus also allowing effects to occur "in an instant". With respect to analytical vs. holistic or synthetic apperception, the processes of automatization or schematization, referred to above, may go a long way towards explaining the routinization of the appraisal processing of recurring situations and events (see Scherer's, 1994, suggestion of the *modality* of emotion–antecedent situations). While the existence of such processes do not rule out the existence of *themes* in the sense of Lazarus, they do not require them either (unless one wants to define a theme as a schema or a frequently occurring standard configuration of appraisal results). It is difficult to see how a very small number of pan-cultural themes can explain the large variety of differentiated emotional states.

THE PROCESS OF APPRAISAL

Many emotion theories give the impression that emotions are static states that can be conveniently labeled with a single term. However, it can be easily demonstrated that we need to talk about *emotion episodes* that are characterized by continuously occurring changes in the underlying appraisal and reaction processes (see Folkman & Lazarus, 1985; Frijda, 1986; Scherer, 1984a,b, 1993b; Scherer & Tannenbaum, 1986). Thus, to specify a pattern of appraisal results that is supposed to explain a static emotion as indexed by a label, is at best a first entry point into the complexity of the underlying mechanism. The nature of the appraisal *process* and the immediate effects of the evaluation results on the other components of emotion (such as subjective feeling, physiological responses, motor expression, and action tendencies) need to be explored. Even though most theorists pay lip service to the idea that emotions and, consequently, emotion–antecedent appraisal are processes, there has been little interest in, and even less work on, the specification of the *microgenetic process* of appraisal and the reaction patterning produced by it.

A first attempt in this direction has been made by the component process theory suggested by Scherer (1984a,b, 1986, 1988), which postulates that the appraisal criteria (stimulus evaluation checks, SECs) are evaluated in an invariant *sequence*. This sequence model, based on phylogenetic, ontogenetic and microgenetic considerations, assumes that the appraisal process is *constantly operative*, with evaluations being continuously performed to update the organism's information on an event or situation (including the current needs or goals of the organism and the possibility to act on these). In analogy to a rotating radar antenna updating the reflection patterns on the screen, the sequential stimulus evaluation checks are expected to occur in very rapid succession (see Scherer, 1984a,b, 1993a, for further details on the hypothesized sequential processing). Recently, the complex, dynamic nature of emotion, with appraisal and reaction processes intertwined, has received increasing attention (see Lewis, 1996; Lewis, this volume; Frijda, 1993; Scherer, 1996a; Smith et al., 1996).

LINKS BETWEEN APPRAISAL AND OTHER COMPONENTS OF EMOTION

One of the most serious criticisms leveled against appraisal theories is that much of this work remains exclusively in the domain of conceptual analysis, including most of the empirical work, and is thus subject to the problem of circular or tautological reasoning (Matsumoto, 1995; Parkinson, 1997). One way to escape from the dangers of circular reasoning within an exclusively conceptual analysis and to anchor appraisal processes in more directly measurable components of the emotion process, is to link the results of the appraisal process to consequences in other emotion modalities, such as motor expression or physiological responses. Such an integration of appraisal into a more comprehensive theory of emotion is an essential prerequisite if appraisal theory is to go beyond an explanation of the application of particular linguistic labels to instances of emotional experiences.

Several appraisal theories have linked the appraisal mechanism directly to other components of the emotion process. Generally, these theorists argue that, from a functional point of view, appraisal outcomes should bring about an appropriate adaptive reaction in the other emotion modalities. Scherer, postulating in his component process theory that each individual outcome of a stimulus evaluation check (SEC) directly affects the other subsystems (e.g. the somatic and autonomic nervous systems), has presented detailed prediction tables for the presumed effects of appraisal outcomes on facial and vocal expression, physiological responses and behavior tendencies (Scherer, 1984b, 1986, 1987, 1992). Similar attempts to link appraisal outcomes to response patterns have been suggested by Smith & Ellsworth (1985) and Frijda (1986). The former theorists have mainly focused on facial expression and Smith (1989), using EMG measurement, was able to demonstrate the presumed link between effort appraisal and corrugator activity. Frijda (1986, 1987) has mainly focused on the relationship between appraisal outcomes and action tendencies and has demonstrated the existence of appraisal-action tendency links with the help of verbal report research (Frijda, Kuipers & ter Schure, 1989). More recently, Ortony & Turner (1990) and Roseman (1996) have also suggested direct links between appraisal categories and response patterns.

The overall patterning predicted in this fashion for a number of modal emotions (see Scherer, 1994) has received support in empirical studies on vocal expression (using acoustic analyses of actor portrayals; Banse & Scherer, 1996) and facial expression (using dynamic synthesis of facial expression; Wehrle et al., submitted). A series of detailed studies on the isolated effects of experimentally manipulated appraisal outcomes on physiological responses as well as vocal and facial expression are currently being conducted by Smith and collaborators, using problem-solving tasks and cognitive attention-regulation tasks (Pecchinenda & Smith, 1996; Kirby & Smith, 1996). Both Kappas and Scherer, with their collaborators, use the computer games paradigm mentioned above (see references above) to study the effects of experimentally manipulated appraisal variables on a large variety of reaction modalities, including physiological responses, facial and vocal expression, and subjective report of feeling state.

UNIVERSALITY VS. CULTURAL SPECIFICITY OF APPRAISAL

Emotion psychology is currently dominated by a debate opposing *universalists*, claiming a phylogenetically based psychobiological emotion mechanism, and *cultural relativists*, assuming that emotions are part of cultural meaning structures (Mesquita & Frijda, 1992; Russell, 1994; Ekman, 1994). This issue is of central importance to appraisal theory since, even if emotion were to be considered a relatively universal psychobiological mechanism, one can assume that the nature of the eliciting events and the type and intensity of emotional reactions to similar events would be highly different across different cultures (see Mesquita, Frijda & Scherer, 1997).

There is some evidence that differences across cultures, (a) in the actuarial frequency of particular events (e.g. crime, see Scherer et al., 1988); (b) in the relative importance of particular aspects of social life, such as the family (see Mesquita, in press); (c) in the definition of self-identity (Markus & Kitayama, 1991); or (d) in the nature of cultural value systems (see Shweder, 1993), all play an important role in the elicitation and differentiation of emotional reactions.

However, such differences might be limited to the surface structure of the emotion-eliciting events, such as type of situation or type of cultural value involved, whereas the nature of the appraisal process and the set of evaluative criteria used (defined in a relatively abstract fashion) might well be part of the universal psychobiological mechanism. Thus, while specific goals are likely to be strongly determined by cultural values (e.g. raising fat pigs, honouring one's ancestors, or achieving maximal self-realization), the abstract appraisal of the goal conduciveness of an event might not be.

While there have been only few attempts to empirically study this issue, a number of preliminary patterns emerge. Among the most extensive data sets available today is a series of cross-cultural studies conducted by Scherer and several groups of collaborators. In a first series of studies, eight European countries, the USA and Japan were compared (Scherer, Wallbott & Summerfield, 1986; Scherer et al., 1988), followed by a large-scale study of 37 countries on all five continents (Scherer & Wallbott, 1994). Matsumoto et al. (1988) reported cultural differences with respect to the number of respondents readily attributing responsibility for antecedent situations to either themselves or other people (the Japanese students checking the "not pertinent" response category much more frequently than other nationalities for the causal attribution question). A preliminary analysis of the differences between rich vs. poor countries (based on Gross National Product) found that in rich countries fear- and sadness-evoking events are usually described as occurring more unexpectedly than in poor countries. This was speculatively interpreted as a greater need for controllability in rich countries (Gehm & Scherer, 1988; Wallbott & Scherer, 1988).

Recently, an exhaustive analysis of the appraisal data from this long-term research program has become available (Scherer, 1997a,b). The overall conclusion is that the appraisal mechanism itself seems to be universal—the appraisal profiles for the major emotions are very similar across the large number of rather diverse countries studied. However, the data also show rather important cultural differences in the appraisal patterns. While there are isolated effects on expectedness, coping potential and self consistency, the most consistent and powerful differences are represented by the appraisal of high immorality, unfairness and external causation by African respondents, and the appraisal of low immorality by Latin-American respondents (across all emotions studied). One possible explanation for this result is urbanism—African countries are generally low, Latin American countries high on this factor. The data reflect a tendency for respondents in highly urbanized countries to attribute less immorality to emotion-eliciting events than respondents in less urbanized regions of the world. In addition, the hyper-appraisal of external causation, unfairness and immorality in the African countries is attributed to the importance of witchcraft beliefs in those countries. The use of witchcraft explanations as a means of attributing causation for misfortunes is consistently mentioned by anthropologists studying this phenomenon (see review of the anthropological literature in Scherer, 1997b).

Both cultural similarities and differences have also been found by a growing number of cross-cultural studies by other investigators. Mauro, Sato & Tucker (1992) studied the differentiation of 14 emotions by a set of 10 appraisal dimensions in a comparative study using students in the USA, Japan, the People's Republic of China and Hongkong. They concluded that few differences between cultures are observed for the more "primitive" dimensions, such as pleasantness, attentional activity, certainty, coping ability and goal/need conduciveness, but that there are differences for more complex dimensions. For example, students from the USA made more use of the responsibility dimension than students from Japan (a finding that confirms the pattern found by Matsumoto et al., 1988). Haidt, Koller & Dias (1993) found that social transgressions and unconventional food and sex practices were more readily appraised as immoral by Brazilians than by Americans, and less appraised in terms of morality by highly educated than by less educated respondents in both cultures. Mesquita (in press) asked Dutch, Surinamese and Turkish people living in The Netherlands to rate a list of appraisal questions for six standard situations, such as "receiving compliments or admiration", "success", "offense by a non-intimate other" and "offense by an intimate other". While the appraisals in the three cultures were quite similar, differences were found with respect to the nature and social context of the eliciting situation and in the focality of the concerns upon which appraisal is based.

Studies of the emotion vocabulary in different languages have shown that lexically equivalent emotion words imply comparable appraisal patterns (Ellsworth & Smith, 1988a,b; Frijda et al., 1995; Mees, 1985; Roseman, 1991; Roseman, et al., 1995).

Most of these approaches rely on verbal report of appraisal processes in personal emotional experiences. Recently, Ellsworth and her collaborators (Ellsworth, 1997) have used subtly manipulated cartoon films to investigate potential cross-cultural differences in the appraisal of simple events, particularly in children.

While the cultural differences in the use of appraisal dimensions found in the intercultural studies reported above are generally smaller than the emotion differences, they are nevertheless, at least for some emotions and for some appraisal dimensions, rather sizable. Even though these cross-cultural differences do not call into question the existence of universal emotion-specific appraisal profiles, they do show that members of different cultures seem to appraise emotion–antecedent events somewhat differently on at least some of the major dimensions.

As expected, "complex" appraisal dimensions, requiring the use of cultural schemata, are more affected by intercultural differences than relatively basic dimensions related to stimulus characteristics or individual well-being (Ellsworth, 1994b; Frijda & Mesquita, 1994; Haidt et al., 1993; Mauro, Sato & Tucker, 1992; Mesquita, in press; Scherer, 1997b). Clearly, both the nature, i.e. the content, of culturally shared norms or standards and the focalization on legitimacy or morality as a major factor in event evaluation can vary widely between cultures. It is thus not surprising that several studies show immorality to be the dimension that shows the strongest culture effects and that the emotions most affected by such differences are shame and guilt, often considered as "social emotions".

Which determinants are responsible for the cross-cultural differences found? Because of the correlational nature of most studies, no causal inferences can be drawn. Furthermore, so far, no agreed-upon set of "culture factors or determinants" has been established that would allow researchers to move from a comparison of countries or geo-political regions (e.g. Africa vs. Latin America, see Scherer, 1997b) to truly "cultural" comparisons. The studies in this area show that among the dimensions to be considered are climate, socio-economic factors, value systems, social structure and language. An issue that also deserves research interest is the potential existence of *subcultural* differences in appraisal patterns, e.g. between rural and urban populations, between generations, or between specific subgroups.

INDIVIDUAL DIFFERENCES AND PATHOLOGY IN APPRAISAL

Appraisal theory stresses that the evaluation of emotion-eliciting objects or events is highly subjective and depends on the individual's perceived goals, values and coping potential, rather than objective characteristics (Smith & Pope, 1992). This is one of the major strengths of appraisal theory, explaining why seemingly similar events can trigger highly disparate emotions in different persons. Surprisingly, so far there has been little attempt to identify individual difference factors that might underlie systematic appraisal tendencies or biases. However, a review of the literature on individual differences (see van Reekum & Scherer, 1997) in cognitive processing suggests that quite a number of established trait dimensions are likely to consistently affect appraisal processes. The thoroughness or completeness of the appraisal may also be subject to individual differences. Whereas one individual may rapidly accept the result of an initial appraisal, another may engage in repeated re-appraisals before settling on one interpretation. One of the underlying variables might be the amount of cognitive effort that is characteristically expended. Furthermore, the relative complexity of the appraisal may depend on the cognitive style of the individual, i.e. gross vs. more fine-grained appraisal, particularly with respect to the width of the categories used in inference and classification. Appraisal tendencies or biases may also differ with respect to content, i.e. a systematic sensitization or distortion with respect to particular criteria in the appraisal process. A well-known example of such an individual difference variable is external vs. internal control or attribution bias, i.e. to attribute responsibility to oneself rather than others, or vice versa. It can be shown that such potential appraisal biases are likely to affect all the major appraisal criteria (see van Reekum & Scherer, 1997). So far, there has been little systematic research on such individual differences in appraisal. First efforts are being made by Smith and his collaborators, who are studying the effects of differences in performance goals and motivational styles on appraisal (Kirby & Smith, 1996; Smith & Haynes, 1996).

It is readily possible to conceptualize different types of emotional disorders on the basis of such appraisal biases or malfunctioning (see Kaiser & Scherer, 1997; Scherer, 1987). While appraisal is subjective and may exhibit major individual variations due to appraisal biases, it must be considered, at least by an individual's social environment, if not by him/herself, as more or less appropriate to the objective situation and the individual's realistic coping potential. If the appraisal deviates too strongly from such reality constraints, the resulting emotion will be seen as abnormal or disordered. Using this approach one can attempt to more theoretically link appraisal malfunctions to clinically relevant affect disorders.

Clinicians may object that these suggestions are little more than reformulations of syndrome definitions. However, the effort to link theories of normal emotion to an understanding of the etiology of affect disturbance may help, beyond a symptom description, to encourage more general studies on cognitive functioning and appraisal styles in patients suffering from affective illness in order to better understand the underlying mechanisms. In a similar vein, Watts (1992) provides an overview of potential applications of current cognitive theories of emotion to the conceptualization of emotional disorders. Clearly, once the role of appraisal biases in the etiology and maintenance of affective illness are better understood, it may become possible to develop appropriate remedial or therapeutic approaches to eliminate pathogenic appraisal biases (something that is consistently practiced, under somewhat different theoretical auspices, in cognitive-behavioral therapy; e.g. Beck, 1967).

CONCLUSIONS

Appraisal theories neither claim to be able to explain all types of affective phenomena (e.g. reflexive reactions, preferences, or moods) nor pretend that the occurrence of these altered states cannot be explained by mechanisms other than appraisal (e.g. induction by drugs, memories, proprioceptive feedback). Neither do appraisal theories claim to provide comprehensive models of emotion. However, as far as the explanation of the *elicitation and differentiation* of event-generated episodes commonly called *emotions* (what, in the honor of William James, one might call the *bear-out-of-the-woods* variety) are concerned, appraisal theory currently does not seem to have any serious rivals. This is not surprising, given that present-day appraisal theories can be considered the culminating formalization of two centuries of philosophical notions that have always insisted on significance evaluation as the core process of emotional reactions (see Lyons, this volume, and the beautiful quote from Robertson found in Lazarus, this volume).

Apart from lacking rivals, the domain of appraisal theories boasts an impressive convergence of independently developed theoretical models and a sizable number of empirical studies supporting the basic tenets of the theories. Furthermore, the generality of the appraisal model is confirmed by recent evidence on a large degree of cultural universality of appraisal–emotion links, as described above.

One of the persistent criticisms of this tradition—that of "excessive cognitivism"—is slow to subside in spite of the early insistence of many appraisal theorists that appraisal can occur at very low levels of the central nervous system (e.g. Scherer, 1984b; Leventhal & Scherer, 1987). Unfortunately, these arguments have often remained unacknowledged by the critics. Hopefully, the current buoyancy and rapid development of *multi-level theories* (see above; Teasdale, this volume) will change this unsatisfactory state of affairs and clear the way for more differentiated discussions. However, in addition to focusing on different levels of processing, more attention—both in theory and research—needs to be directed at the dynamic nature of these processes, particularly with respect to interlevel interaction (i.e. top-down priming, bottom-up elaboration) and the automatization of appraisals, such as schematization (see van Reekum & Scherer, 1997, for a more detailed discussion).

A more serious problem for appraisal theory is the criticism that the reliance on *post-hoc* verbal inference of appraisal processes is potentially tautological, since it might do little more than explicate the implicational semantic structures of our emotion vocabulary (see above). To rule out this possibility, appraisal theories need to invest strongly in four major lines of theoretical and empirical development: (a) further refinement of concrete, falsifiable predictions; (b) systematic experimental induction of specific appraisal outcomes; (c) use of more sophisticated verbal elicitation routines; and, most importantly, (d) the elaboration of non-verbal indicators for specific appraisal outcomes, such as physiological reactions, expression patterns or action tendencies. As shown above, recently there have been some promising research activities in this direction, combined with renewed efforts at the development of more complex theoretical models (Roseman, 1996; Scherer, 1984b, 1986; Smith et al., 1996). Theory development in this area may benefit from efforts to use computer modeling of appraisal theory, helping to test consistency of predictions, simulate alternative outcomes, and evaluate alternative versions of theories (Chwelos & Oatley, 1994; Scherer, 1993b; Wehrle, 1996; Wehrle & Scherer, 1995).

An important shortcoming of all current appraisal theories that has been recently highlighted by critics, is their predominantly intrapsychic orientation, tending largely to neglect the social context in which emotion–antecedent appraisal and the ensuing responses are often embedded (Kappas, 1996; Parkinson, 1997). While the criticism is well taken, suggesting the need for a major extension of the current theories, some of the suggested remedies need to be developed further to demonstrate their usefulness. For example, Parkinson's (1996) suggestion to include the strategic dimension of emotion in social interaction might be more pertinent for the study of emotional response regulation than for the study of appraisal processes antecedent to the initial emotional response. Obviously, regulation attempts will also partly depend on the outcome of appraisal processes. However, it seems doubtful whether it is useful to subsume all cognitive activity linked to emotional processes under the appraisal concept.

Another dimension that will require increasing attention from appraisal theorists concerns individual differences with respect to cognitive processing giving rise to dispositional appraisal tendencies or biases. Since it is one of the central tenets of appraisal theory to explain why, in the face of the very same event, different individuals are likely to respond with rather different emotions, one would have thought that the issue of individual differences might have played a larger part in this field than it actually did (Smith & Pope, 1992). As shown above, the study of idiosyncratic appraisal tendencies or biases is of major importance for the application of appraisal theory to clinical questions, particularly with respect to affective disorders.

The clinical domain is only one of the areas in which appraisal theory can be usefully applied. Other areas include health psychology (Fernandez & Turk, 1995; Jerusalem, 1993; Omdahl, 1995) and sports (e.g. Biddle & Hill, 1992; McAuley & Duncan, 1990)—to name but a few in which efforts are currently under way. Concern with applied issues may also foster the development of research paradigms that will search for ecological validity of the situation studied, such as earlier studies on emotions generated by university examinations (Folkman & Lazarus, 1985; Smith & Ellsworth, 1987) or the study of emotions following the discovery upon arriving at an airport that one's luggage has been lost (Scherer & Ceschi, 1997).

In sum, while over 2000 years old, appraisal theory is only now being systematically developed and given appropriate attention in the field. In spite of the awesome methodological difficulties of assessing the complex evaluation processes, occurring in a very rapid fashion on several levels of processing, recent appraisal research promises to progress beyond the retrospective verbal report data that have been the mainstay of this research tradition. In particular, experimental manipulation of appraisal in realistic settings and the measurement of non-verbal correlates or consequences of specific appraisal results start to yield interesting results. Further investments along these lines and the application of appraisal theory to emotional experiences in real-life settings promise rich yields for the next generation of appraisal researchers.

ACKNOWLEDGEMENTS

The author gratefully acknowledges comments and suggestions by Tania Bänziger, Phoebe Ellsworth, Nico Frijda, Susanne Kaiser, Leslie Kirby, Carien van Reekum, Susanne Schmidt and Craig Smith.

REFERENCES

Abelson, R. P. (1983). Whatever became of consistency theory? *Personality and Social Psychology Bulletin*, **9**, 37–54.
Arnold, M. B. (1960). *Emotion and Personality. Vol. 1, Psychological Aspects*. New York: Columbia University Press.
Banse, R., Etter, A., van Reekum, C. & Scherer, K. R. (1996). Psychophysiological responses to emotion-antecedent appraisal of critical events in a computer game. Poster presented at the 36th Annual Meeting of the Society for Psychophysiological Research, Vancouver, Canada, 16–20 October.
Banse, R. & Scherer, K. R. (1996). Acoustic profiles in vocal emotion expression. *Journal of Personality and Social Psychology*, **70**, 614–636.
Beck, A. T. (1967). *Depression: Clinical, Experimental and Theoretical Aspects*. New York: Harper & Row.
Berkowitz, L. (1994). Is something missing? Some observations prompted by the cognitive-neoassociationist view of anger and emotional aggression. In L. R. Huesmann (ed.), *Aggressive Behavior: Current Perspectives*. New York: Plenum. pp. 35–57.
Biddle, S. J. & Hill, A. B. (1992). Attributions for objective outcome and subjective

appraisal of performance: their relationship with emotional reactions in sport. *British Journal of Social Psychology*, **31**(3), 215–226.

Borg, I., Staufenbiel, Th. & Scherer, K. R. (1988).   On the symbolic basis of shame. In K. R. Scherer (ed.), *Facets of Emotion: Recent Research*. Hillsdale, NJ: Erlbaum, pp. 79–98.

Chwelos, G. & Oatley, K. (1994).   Appraisal, computational models, and Scherer's expert system. *Cognition and Emotion*, **8**, 245–257.

Conway, M. A. & Bekerian, D. A. (1987).   Situational knowledge and emotions. *Cognition and Emotion*, **1**, 145–191.

De Rivera, J. (1977).   A structural theory of the emotions. *Psychological Issues*, **10**(4), Monograph 40.

Ekman, P. (1994).   Strong evidence for universals in facial expression: a reply to Russell's mistaken critique. *Psychological Bulletin*, **115**, 268–287.

Ekman, P. & Davidson, R. J. (eds) (1994).   *The Nature of Emotion: Fundamental questions*. New York: Oxford University Press.

Ellsworth, P. C. (1991).   Some implications of cognitive appraisal theories of emotion. In K. Strongman (ed.), *International Review of Studies on Emotion*. New York: Wiley, pp. 143–161.

Ellsworth, P. C. (1994a).   William James and emotion: is a century of fame worth a century of misunderstanding? Special Issue: The Centennial Issue of the *Psychological Review*. *Psychological Review*, **101**, 222–229.

Ellsworth, P. C. (1994b).   Sense, culture and sensibility. In S. Kitayama & M. R. Markus (eds), *Emotion and Culture. Empirical Studies of Mutual Influence*. Washington, DC: American Psychological Association, pp. 23–50.

Ellsworth, P. C. (1997).   Chinese and American emotional responses to basic social situations. Paper presented at the Fifth Geneva Emotion Week, Geneva, Switzerland, April 19–23.

Ellsworth, P. C. & Smith, C. A. (1988a).   Shades of joy: patterns of appraisal differentiating pleasant emotions. *Cognition and Emotion*, **2**, 301–331.

Ellsworth, P. C. & Smith, C. A. (1988b).   From appraisal to emotion: differences among unpleasant feelings. *Motivation and Emotion*, **12**, 271–302.

Fernandez, E. & Turk, D. C. (1995).   The scope and significance of anger in the experience of chronic pain. *Pain*, **61**(2), 165–175.

Fitness, J. & Fletcher, G. J. O. (1993).   Love, hate, anger, and jealousy in close relationships: a prototype and cognitive appraisal analysis. *Journal of Personality and Social Psychology*, **65**, 942–958.

Folkman, S. & Lazarus, R. S. (1985).   If it changes it must be a process: study of emotion and coping during three stages of a college examination. *Journal of Personality and Social Psychology*, **48**, 150–170.

Folkman, S. & Lazarus, R. S. (1988).   Coping as a mediator of emotion. *Journal of Personality and Social Psychology*, **54**, 466–475.

Frijda, N. H. (1986).   *The Emotions*. Cambridge and New York: Cambridge University Press.

Frijda, N. H. (1987).   Emotion, cognitive structure, and action tendency. *Cognition and Emotion*, **1**, 115–143.

Frijda, N. H. (1993).   The place of appraisal in emotion. *Cognition and Emotion*, **7**, 357–387.

Frijda, N. H., Kuipers, P. & ter Schure, E. (1989).   Relations among emotion, appraisal, and emotional action readiness. *Journal of Personality and Social Psychology*, **57**, 212–228.

Frijda, N. H., Markam, S., Sato, K. & Wiers, R. (1995).   Emotions and emotion words. In J. A. Russell, J. M. Fernandez-Dols, A. S. R. Manstead & J. C. Wellenkamp (eds), *Everyday Conceptions of Emotion: An Introduction to the Psychology, Anthropology and Linguistics of Emotion*, Vol. 81. Dordrecht: Kluwer Academic, pp. 121–143.

Frijda, N. H. & Mesquita, B. (1994). The social roles and functions of emotions. In S. Kitayama & H. Markus (eds), *Emotion and Culture. Empirical Studies of Mutual Influence*. Washington, DC: American Psychological Association, pp. 51–88.

Gehm, T. L. & Scherer, K. R. (1988). Relating situation evaluation to emotion differentiation: non-metric analysis of cross-cultural questionnaire data. In K. R. Scherer (ed.), *Facets of Emotion: Recent Research*. Hillsdale, NJ: Erlbaum, pp. 61–78.

Haidt, J., Koller, S. H. & Dias, M. G. (1993). Affect, culture and morality, or is it wrong to eat your dog? *Journal of Personality and Social Psychology*, **65**, 613–628.

Izard, C. E. (1993). Four systems for emotion activation: cognitive and non-cognitive processes. *Psychological Review*, **100**, 68–90.

James, W. (1894). The physical basis of emotion. *Psychological Review*, **1**, 516–529.

Jerusalem, M. (1993). Personal resources, environmental constraints, and adaptational processes: the predictive power of a theoretical stress model. *Personality and Individual Differences*, **14**(1), 15–24.

Johnstone, T. (1996). Emotional speech elicited using computer games. In H. T. Bunnell & W. Idsardi (eds), *Proceedings of the Fourth International Conference on Spoken Language Processing, Philadelphia, PA*. New Castle: Citation Delaware, pp. 1985–1988.

Kaiser, S. & Scherer, K. R. (1997). Models of "normal" emotions applied to facial and vocal expressions in clinical disorders. In W. F. Flack Jr & J. D. Laird (eds), *Emotions in Psychopathology*. New York: Oxford University Press, pp. 81–98.

Kaiser, S. & Wehrle, T. (1996). Situated emotional problem solving in interactive computer games. In N. H. Frijda (ed.), *Proceedings of the VIIIth Conference of the International Society for Research on Emotions, ISRE '96*. Toronto: ISRE, pp. 276–280.

Kaiser, S., Wehrle, T. & Edwards, P. (1994). Multi-modal emotion measurement in an interactive computer-game: a pilot-study. In N. H. Frijda (ed.), *Proceedings of the VIIIth Conference of the International Society for Research on Emotions*. Storrs, CT: ISRE.

Kappas, A. (1996). The sociality of appraisals: impact of social situations on the evaluation of emotion antecedent events and physiological and expressive reactions. In N. H. Frijda (ed.), *Proceedings of the IXth Conference of the International Society for Research on Emotions, ISRE '96*. Toronto: ISRE, pp. 116–120.

Kappas, A. & Pecchinenda, A. Don't wait for the monsters to get you: manipulating appraisals in an ongoing interactive video-game task (manuscript submitted for publication).

Karasawa, K. (1995). Cognitive antecedents of emotions: findings and future directions. *Japanese Psychological Research*, **37**, 40–55.

Kirby, L. D. & Smith, C. A. (1996). Freaking, quitting, and staying engaged: patterns of psychophysiological response to stress. *Proceedings of the Ninth Conference of the International Society for Research on Emotions*. Toronto: International Society for Research on Emotions, pp. 359–363.

Kunst-Wilson, W. R. & Zajonc, R. B. (1980). Affective discrimination of stimuli that cannot be recognized. *Science*, **207**, 557–558.

Lazarus, R. S. (1966). *Psychological Stress and the Coping Process*. New York: McGraw Hill.

Lazarus, R. S. (1984). Thoughts on the relation between emotion and cognition. In K. R. Scherer & P. Ekman (eds), *Approaches to Emotion*. Hillsdale, NJ: Erlbaum, pp. 247–258.

Lazarus, R. S. (1991). *Emotion and Adaptation*. New York: Oxford University Press.

Lazarus, R. S. (1995). Vexing research problems inherent in cognitive-mediational theories of emotion and some solutions. *Psychological Inquiry*, **6**, 183–196.

Lazarus, R. S. & Smith, C. A. (1988). Knowledge and appraisal in the cognition–emotion relationship. *Cognition and Emotion*, **2**, 281–300.

LeDoux, J. E. (1987). Emotion. In V. Mountcastle & F. Plum (eds), *Handbook of*

Physiology, Nervous System. Vol. 5, Higher Function. Washington, DC: American Physiological Society, pp. 419–459.

LeDoux, J. E. (1989). Cognitive–emotional interactions in the brain. *Cognition and Emotion*, **3**, 267–289.

Leventhal, H. & Scherer, K. R. (1987). The relationship of emotion to cognition: a functional approach to a semantic controversy. *Cognition and Emotion*, **1**, 3–28.

Lewis, M. D. (1996). Self-organising cognitive appraisals. *Cognition and Emotion*, **10**, 1–25.

MacDowell, K. A. & Mandler, G. (1989). Constructions of emotion: discrepancy, arousal, and mood. *Motivation and Emotion*, **13**, 105–124.

Manstead, A. S. R. & Tetlock, P. E. (1989). Cognitive appraisals and emotional experience: further evidence. *Cognition and Emotion*, **3**, 225–240.

Markus, H. R. & Kitayama, S. (1991). Culture and the self: implications for cognition, emotion, and motivation. *Psychological Review*, **98**, 224–253.

Matsumoto, D. (1995). Lazarus's vexing research problems are even more vexing than he thinks. *Psychological Inquiry*, **6**, 228–230.

Matsumoto, D., Kudoh, T., Scherer, K. & Wallbott, H. (1988). Antecedents of and reactions to emotions in the United States and Japan. *Journal of Cross-Cultural Psychology*, **19**, 267–286.

Mauro, R., Sato, K. & Tucker, J. (1992). The role of appraisal in human emotions: a cross-cultural study. *Journal of Personality and Social Psychology*, **62**, 301–317.

McAuley, E. & Duncan, T. E. (1990). Cognitive appraisal and affective reactions following physical achievement outcomes. *Journal of Sport and Exercise Psychology*, **12**, 415–426.

McGraw, K. M. (1987). Guilt following transgression: an attribution of responsibility approach. *Journal of Personality and Social Psychology*, **53**, 247–256.

Mees, U. (1985). Was meinen wir, wenn wir von Gefühlen reden? Zur psychologischen Textur von Emotionswörtern. [What Do We Mean when We Talk about Emotion? On the Psychological Implications of Emotion Words]. *Sprache und Kognition*, **1**, 2–20.

Mesquita, B. (in press) *Cultural Variations in Emotions: A Comparative Study of Dutch, Surinamese, and Turkish People in The Netherlands*. New York: Oxford University Press.

Mesquita, B. & Frijda, N. H. (1992). Cultural variations in emotions: a review. *Psychological Bulletin*, **112**, 179–204.

Mesquita, B., Frijda, N. H. & Scherer, K. R. (1997). Culture and emotion. In J. E. Berry, P. B. Dasen & T. S. Saraswathi (eds), *Handbook of Cross-cultural Psychology. Vol. 2, Basic Processes and Developmental Psychology*. Boston: Allyn & Bacon, pp. 255–297.

Murphy, S. T., Monahan, J. L. & Zajonc, R. B. (1995). Additivity of nonconscious affect: combined effects of priming and exposure. *Journal of Personality and Social Psychology*, **69**, 589–602.

Nisbett, R. E. & Wilson, T. D. (1977). Telling more than we can know: verbal reports on mental processes. *Psychological Review*, **84**, 231–259.

Oatley, K. & Johnson-Laird, P. N. (1987). Towards a cognitive theory of emotions. *Cognition and Emotion*, **1**, 29–50.

Omdahl, B. L. (1995). *Cognitive Appraisal, Emotion, and Empathy*. Mahwah, NJ: Erlbaum.

Ortony, A. & Turner, T. (1990). What's basic about basic emotions? *Psychological Review*, **97**, 315–331.

Ortony, A., Clore, G. L. & Collins, A. (1988). *The Cognitive Structure of Emotions*. New York: Cambridge University Press.

Parkinson, B. (1996). Emotions are social. *British Journal of Psychology*, **87**, 663–683.

Parkinson, B. (1997). Untangling the appraisal–emotion connection. *Personality and Social Psychology Review*, **1**, 62–79.

Parkinson, B. & Lea, M. F. (1991).   Investigating personal constructs of emotion. *British Journal of Psychology*, **82**, 73–86.

Parkinson, B. & Manstead, A. S. R. (1992).   Appraisal as a cause of emotion. *Review of Personality and Social Psychology*, **13**, 122–149.

Parkinson, B. & Manstead, A. S. R. (1993).   Making sense of emotions in stories and social life. *Cognition and Emotion*, **7**, 295–323.

Pecchinenda, A., Kappas, A. & Smith, C. A. (1997).   Effects of difficulty and ability in a dual-task video game paradigm on attention, physiological responses, performance, and emotion-related appraisal. *Psychophysiology*, **34**, 534.

Pecchinenda, A. & Smith, C. A. (1996).   The affective significance of skin conductance activity during a difficult problem-solving task. *Cognition and Emotion*, **10**, 481–503.

Reisenzein, R. & Hofmann, T. (1990).   An investigation of dimensions of cognitive appraisal in emotion using the repertory grid technique. *Motivation and Emotion*, **14**, 1–26.

Reisenzein, R. & Hofmann, T. (1993).   Discriminating emotions from appraisal-relevant situational information: baseline data for structural models of cognitive appraisals. *Cognition and Emotion*, **7**, 271–294.

Reisenzein, R. & Schönpflug, W. (1992).   Stumpf's cognitive-evaluative theory of emotion. *American Psychologist*, **47**, 34–45.

Reisenzein, R. & Spielhofer, C. (1994).   Subjectively salient dimensions of emotional appraisal. *Motivation and Emotion*, **18**, 31–77.

Roseman, I. J. (1984).   Cognitive determinants of emotion: a structural theory. In P. Shaver (ed.), *Review of Personality and Social Psychology*, Vol. 5. Beverly Hills, CA: Sage, pp. 11–36.

Roseman, I. J. (1991).   Appraisal determinants of discrete emotions. *Cognition and Emotion*, **5**, 161–200.

Roseman, I. J. (1996).   Why these appraisals? Anchoring appraisal models to research on emotional behaviour and related response systems. In N. H. Frijda (ed.), *Proceedings of the IXth Conference of the International Society for Research on Emotions, ISRE '96*. Toronto: ISRE, pp. 106–110.

Roseman, I. J., Antoniou, A. A. & Jose, P. E. (1996).   Appraisal determinants of emotions: constructing a more accurate and comprehensive theory. *Cognition and Emotion*, **10**, 241–277.

Roseman, I. J., Dhawan, N., Rettek, S. I., Naidu, R. K. & Thapa, K. (1995).   Cultural differences and cross-cultural similarities in appraisals and emotional responses. *Journal of Cross-Cultural Psychology*, **26**, 23–48.

Roseman, I. J. & Evdokas, A. (1995).   Appraisals do cause real emotions: experimental evidence. Paper presented at the Seventh Annual Convention of the American Psychological Society, New York.

Roseman, I. J., Spindel, M. S. & Jose, P. E. (1990).   Appraisal of emotion-eliciting events: testing a theory of discrete emotions. *Journal of Personality and Social Psychology*, **59**, 899–915.

Russel, D. & McAuley, E. (1986).   Causal attributions, causal dimensions, and affective reactions to success and failure. *Journal of Personality and Social Psychology*, **50**, 1174–1185.

Russell, J. (1994).   Is there universal recognition of emotion from facial expression? A review of cross-cultural studies. *Psychological Bulletin*, **115**, 102–141.

Scherer, K. R. (1982).   Emotion as a process: function, origin, and regulation. *Social Science Information*, **21**, 555–570.

Scherer, K. R. (1984a).   Emotion as a multicomponent process: a model and some cross-cultural data. In P. Shaver (ed.), *Review of Personality and Social Psychology*, Vol. 5. Beverly Hills, CA: Sage, pp. 37–63.

Scherer, K. R. (1984b).   On the nature and function of emotion: a component process approach. In K. R. Scherer & P. Ekman (eds), *Approaches to Emotion*. Hillsdale, NJ: Erlbaum, pp. 293–318.

Scherer, K. R. (1986). Vocal affect expression: a review and a model for future research. *Psychological Bulletin*, **99**, 143–165.

Scherer, K. R. (1987). Vocal assessment of affective disorders. In J. D. Maser (ed.), *Depression and Expressive Behavior*. Hillsdale, NJ: Erlbaum, pp. 57–82.

Scherer, K. R. (1988). Criteria for emotion-antecedent appraisal: a review. In V. Hamilton, G. H. Bower & N. H. Frijda (eds), *Cognitive Perspectives on Emotion and Motivation*. Dordrecht: Nijhoff, pp. 89–126.

Scherer, K. R. (1992). What does facial expression express? In K. Strongman (ed.), *International Review of Studies on Emotion*, Vol. 2. Chichester: Wiley, pp. 139–165.

Scherer, K. R. (1993a). Neuroscience projections to current debates in emotion psychology. *Cognition and Emotion*, **7**, 1–41.

Scherer, K. R. (1993b). Studying the emotion-antecedent appraisal process: an expert system approach. *Cognition and Emotion*, **7**, 325–355.

Scherer, K. R. (1994). Toward a concept of "modal emotions". In P. Ekman & R. J. Davidson (eds), *The Nature of Emotion: Fundamental Questions*. New York/Oxford: Oxford University Press, pp. 25–31.

Scherer, K. R. (1996a). Emotions couple mind–body oscillators. In N. H. Frijda (ed.), *Proceedings of the IXth Conference of the International Society for Research on Emotions, ISRE '96*. Toronto: ISRE, pp. 69–73.

Scherer, K. R. (1996b). Emotion. In M. Hewstone, W. Stroebe & G. M. Stephenson (eds), *Introduction to Social Psychology*. Oxford: Blackwell, pp. 279–315.

Scherer, K. R. (1997a). Profiles of emotion–antecedent appraisal: testing theoretical predictions across cultures. *Cognition and Emotion*, **11**, 113–150.

Scherer, K. R. (1997b). The role of culture in emotion–antecedent appraisal. *Journal of Personality and Social Psychology*, **73**, 902–922.

Scherer, K. R., Banse, R., Wallbott, H. G. & Goldbeck, T. (1991). Vocal cues in emotion encoding and decoding. *Motivation and Emotion*, **15**, 123–148.

Scherer, K. R. & Ceschi, G. (1997). Lost luggage emotion: a field study of emotion–antecedent appraisal. *Motivation and Emotion*, **21**, 211–235.

Scherer, K. R. & Tannenbaum, P. H. (1986). Emotional experiences in everyday life: a survey approach. *Motivation and Emotion*, **10**, 295–314.

Scherer, K. R. & Wallbott, H. G. (1994). Evidence for universality and cultural variation of differential emotional response patterning. *Journal of Personality and Social Psychology*, **66**, 310–328.

Scherer, K. R., Wallbott, H. G., Matsumoto, D. & Kudoh, T. (1988). Emotional experience in cultural context: a comparison between Europe, Japan, and the USA. In K. R. Scherer (ed.), *Facets of Emotion: Recent Research*. Hillsdale, NJ: Erlbaum, pp. 5–30.

Scherer, K. R., Wallbott, H. G. & Summerfield, A. B. (eds), (1986). *Experiencing Emotion: A Cross-cultural Study*. Cambridge: Cambridge University Press.

Schmidt, S., Wehrle, T. & Kaiser, S. (1997). Appraisal profiles of positive and negative emotions elicited by a video-game. Poster presented at the 7th European Conference on Facial Expression—Measurement and Meaning, 16–20 July 1997, Salzburg.

Shweder, R. A. (1993). The cultural psychology of the emotions. In M. Lewis & J. M. Haviland (eds), *Handbook of Emotions*. New York: Guilford, pp. 417–434.

Smith, C. A. (1989). Dimensions of appraisal and physiological response in emotion. *Journal of Personality and Social Psychology*, **56**, 339–353.

Smith, C. A. & Ellsworth, P. C. (1985). Patterns of cognitive appraisal in emotion. *Journal of Personality and Social Psychology*, **48**, 813–838.

Smith, C. A. & Ellsworth, P. C. (1987). Patterns of appraisal and emotion related to taking an exam. *Journal of Personality and Social Psychology*, **52**, 475–488.

Smith, C. A., Griner, L. A., Kirby, L. D. & Scott, H. S. (1996). Toward a process model of appraisal in emotion. In N. H. Frijda (ed.), *Proceedings of the IXth Conference of the International Society for Research on Emotions, ISRE '96*. Toronto: ISRE, pp. 101–105.

Smith, C., A. & Haynes, K. N. (1996). Attributional antecedents of appraisal in anger and guilt. Paper presented at the 104th Convention of the American Psychological Association, Toronto.

Smith, C. A., Haynes, K. N., Lazarus, R. S. & Pope, L. K. (1993). In search of the "hot" cognitions: attributions, appraisals, and their relation to emotion. *Journal of Personality and Social Psychology*, **65**, 916–929.

Smith, C. A. & Lazarus, R. S. (1990). Emotion and adaptation. In L. A. Pervin (ed.), *Handbook of Personality: Theory and Research*. New York: Guilford, pp. 609–637.

Smith, C. A. & Lazarus, R. S. (1993). Appraisal components, core relational themes, and the emotions. *Cognition and Emotion*, **7**, 233–269.

Smith, C. A. & Pope, L. K. (1992). Appraisal and emotion: the interactional contributions of dispositional and situational factors. In M. S. Clark (ed.), *Review of Personality and Social Psychology, Vol. 14: Emotion and Social Behavior*. Newbury Park, CA: Sage, pp. 32–62.

Smolenaars, A. J. & Schutzelaars, A. J. H. (1986/87). On "cognitive" semantics of emotion words: Solomon quasi-ecologically tested. *Journal of Semantics*, **5**, 207–231.

Solomon, R. C. (1976). *The Passions: The Myth and Nature of Human Emotion*. Garden City, NY: Doubleday.

Stein, N. L. & Trabasso, T. (1992). The organisation of emotional experience: creating links among emotion, thinking, language, and intentional action. *Cognition and Emotion*, **6**, 225–244.

Stein, N. L. & Levine, L. J. (1987). Thinking about feelings: the development and organization of emotional knowledge. In R. E. Snow & M. Farr (eds), *Aptitude, Learning, and Instruction: Cognition, Conation and Affect*, Vol. 3. Hillsdale, NJ: Erlbaum, pp. 165–198.

Stipek, D., Weiner, B. & Li, K. (1989). Testing some attribution-emotion relations in the People's Republic of China. *Journal of Personality and Social Psychology*, **56**(1), 109–116.

Tesser, A. (1990). Smith and Ellsworth's appraisal model of emotion: a replication, extension, and test. *Personality and Social Psychology Bulletin*, **16**, 210–223.

van Reekum, C. M., Johnstone, T. & Scherer, K. R. (1997). Multimodal measurement of emotion induced by the manipulation of appraisals in a computer game. Paper presented at the 3rd European Congress of Psychophysiology, Konstanz, Germany, 28–31 May.

van Reekum, C. M. & Scherer, K. R. (1997). Levels of processing for emotion-antecedent appraisal. In G. Matthews (ed.), *Cognitive Science Perspectives on Personality and Emotion*. Amsterdam: Elsevier Science, pp. 259–300.

Wallbott, H. G. & Scherer, K. R. (1988). Emotion and economic development: data and speculations concerning the relationship between economic factors and emotional experience. *European Journal of Social Psychology*, **18**, 267–273.

Watts, F. N. (1992). Applications of current cognitive theories of the emotions to the conceptualization of emotional disorders. *British Journal of Clinical Psychology*, **31**, 153–167.

Wehrle, T. (1996). Computer simulation of appraisal theories. Abstracts of the XXVI International Congress of Psychology. *International Journal of Psychology*, **31**, 484.157.

Wehrle, T., Kaiser, S., Schmidt, S. & Scherer, K. R. Studying dynamic models of facial expression of emotion using synthetic animated faces (Submitted for publication).

Wehrle, T. & Scherer, K. R. (1995). Potential pitfalls in computational modelling of appraisal processes: a reply to Chwelos and Oatley. *Cognition and Emotion*, **9**, 599–616.

Weiner, B. (1982). The emotional consequences of causal attributions. In M. S. Clark & S. T. Fiske (eds), *Affect and Cognition*. Hillsdale, NJ: Erlbaum, pp. 185–209.

Weiner, B. (1986). *An Attributional Theory of Motivation and Emotion*. New York: Springer.

Weiner, B., Amirkhan, J., Folkes, V. S. & Verette, J. A. (1987). An attributional analysis of excuse giving: studies of a naive theory of emotion. *Journal of Personality and Social Psychology*, **52**, 316–324.

Weiner, B., Graham, S. & Chandler, C. (1982). Pity, anger, and guilt: an attributional analysis. *Personality and Social Psychology Bulletin*, **8**, 226–232.

Weiner, B., Russel, D. & Lerman, D. (1979). The cognition–emotion process in achievement-related contexts. *Journal of Personality and Social Psychology*, **37**, 1211–1220.

Zajonc, R. B. (1980). Feeling and thinking: preferences need no inferences. *American Psychologist*, **2**, 151–176.

Zajonc, R. B. (1984). On the primacy of affect. In K. R. Scherer & P. Ekman (eds), *Approaches to Emotion*. Hillsdale, NJ: Erlbaum, pp. 259–270.

Zajonc, R. B. & Markus, H. (1984). Affect and cognition: the hard interface. In C. E. Izard, J. Kagan & R. B. Zajonc (eds), *Emotions, Cognition, and Behavior*. Cambridge: Cambridge University Press, pp. 73–102.

Chapter 31

Multi-level Theories of Cognition–Emotion Relations

John D. Teasdale
MRC Cognition and Brain Sciences Unit, Cambridge, UK

WHAT ARE MULTI-LEVEL THEORIES AND WHY DO WE NEED THEM?

Multi-level theories of cognition and emotion recognize qualitatively distinct kinds, or "levels", of information and representation. Within such theories, representations of a given event or topic at different levels of information can have quite different functional relationships to emotion.

Multi-level theories suggest that, in attempting to understand the emotional effects of events, it is helpful to consider separately the contributions from different kinds of information, and their interactions, rather than to lump them all together in some general concept of "cognition".

There are many potential advantages to such multi-level approaches. They immediately allow us to side-step some of the unhelpful aspects of the Zajonc–Lazarus debate on the primacy of affect vs. the primacy of cognition in the generation of emotion. As Leventhal & Scherer (1987) have pointed out, much of this argument actually boiled down to a semantic controversy about whether the word "cognition" could be applied to more "sensory–perceptual" aspects of experience, or whether it should be restricted to more consciously accessible "appraisals". Multi-level theories treat both appraisals and perceptual features simply as information at different levels of abstraction. In this way, these theories allows us to focus clearly on the central tasks of characterizing those levels, and their relationship to emotion, rather than on arguing about the boundary conditions for the use of the term "cognition".

Dissociations in cognition–emotion relationships are not uncommon. For

Handbook of Cognition and Emotion. Edited by T. Dalgleish and M. Power.

example, we can think relatively "coolly" *about* emotive topics or past events such as "failures" or "catastrophes" without the affect that would normally occur if we actually *experienced* events that might be interpreted using those same concepts.

Such a simple observation poses profound difficulties for uni-level theories of emotion that suggest that "hot" affect is produced simply by activation of the same concepts or representations of events in memory that are involved in the "cool", "rational" consideration or discussion of related topics. For example, Bower's (1981) highly influential associative network theory of mood and memory used effectively only one level of representation, and relied on this same level to account for both "hot" and "cold" processing. The difficulty with such an approach was that the activation of, for example, a fear-related concept in the course of dispassionately thinking about fear, involved exactly the same process as the mechanism through which, it was proposed, fear was normally generated by a fear-related interpretation or appraisal of experience. As Bower himself subsequently noted, this leads to "the absurd implication that people always feel afraid when they refer to the concept" (Bower & Cohen, 1982, p. 308).

Multi-level theories avoid this difficulty by suggesting that the same topic can be represented in *qualitatively* different ways at different levels of information, and that some of those levels may be directly linked to emotion, whereas others may not. From this perspective, different types of information are involved in "cool" consideration of emotive material than in affect generation. For example, several theories suggest that the purely "conceptual" or "propositional" representations of affect-related material processed in "cool" thought are not directly linked to affect generation. These theories suggest that only representations of the same topics at a more schematic level have the power to elicit emotion. In this way, the dissociation between "hot" and "cold" processing of a topic is explained in terms of the level of representation of that topic that is being processed.

Related dissociations, between "intellectual" and "emotional" belief, and between the effects of "rational" vs. "experiential" interventions, frequently arise in therapy. For example, in attempting to change a depressed patient's belief that he/she is a total failure as a person, a cognitive therapist might help the patient review evidence of recent successes or achievements quite inconsistent with his/her extreme negative view of him/herself. After such an intervention patients often respond with something along the lines of: "I agree, intellectually, that it is not true that I am a total failure as a person, but that still doesn't alter my 'gut' belief that I am, nor does it affect my depression". This contrast is accommodated comfortably within multi-level theories that suggest that "intellectual" and "emotional" or "gut" beliefs reflect differences between *qualitatively* distinct levels of representation, only the level corresponding to "gut" or "emotional" belief having direct links to affect (Teasdale, 1993).

The "cognitive impenetrability" of certain emotional reactions poses similar problems. For many years, I knew Mrs Thatcher as the Prime Minister of the UK. On the basis of media reports a few years ago, I updated the database in my long-term memory so that when asked for the name of the Prime Minister, I said,

"John Major". More recently, this information has been further updated so that I now say "Tony Blair". This provides an example of the "cognitive penetrability" of learned action tendencies to new factual information; it was not necessary for me to visit these notables at 10 Downing Street to check out this evidence "experientially"—the written information was sufficient. And yet, if I had a phobia of spiders, I could read repeated accounts that reassured me that any spider that I might normally encounter in England was totally harmless, but my underlying fear might remain unchanged. In order to reduce my fear, I would have to have repeated experiences of being actually exposed (in imagination, or in reality) to spiders without any dire consequences obtaining. Within cognition–emotion theories that recognize qualitatively different and functionally "insulated" levels of information, such cognitive impenetrability is not unexpected. By contrast, uni-level explanations are challenged to account for the "cognitive penetrability" of some categories of information, but not others.

Finally, it is important to remember that the development of theories of cognition–emotion relationships is likely to proceed most effectively if it proceeds in parallel with developments in theory in cognitive psychology, more generally. Within cognitive psychology, there is a widely accepted consensus that the cognitive system as a whole should be conceptualized in terms of interactions between a number of distinct subsystems, each of which is relatively autonomous and specialized for dealing with only certain aspects of certain types of information (e.g. Baddeley, 1986; Shallice, 1988). Within mainstream cognitive psychology, a multi-level approach is normative. Accordingly, it is prudent to assume a multi-level approach if we wish to integrate cognition–emotion relations into any more comprehensive view.

WHAT MULTI-LEVEL THEORIES?

I shall review four approaches that have attempted to provide relatively comprehensive multi-level accounts of cognition–emotion relations. Other multi-level approaches that have focused on more specific aspects of cognition and emotion will not be considered, e.g. Brewin's (1989) valuable discussion of verbally accessible vs. situationally accessible knowledge in psychotherapy change processes.

Leventhal's Perceptual Motor Processing Model of Emotion

> The central postulate of the perceptual motor model of emotion is that adult emotions are complex behavioral reactions that reflect the constructive activity of a multi-component, hierarchical processing system, all of whose levels and components are involved in virtually all emotional experiences and reactions (Leventhal, 1979, 1980, 1984) (Leventhal & Scherer, 1987, p. 8).

The model proposes that the components which process emotion are organized at three levels: (a) sensori-motor; (b) schematic; and (c) conceptual.

The sensori-motor level includes a set of innate expressive-motor pro-grammes. In the neonate, these automatically generate distinctive sets of expres-sive reactions and feelings in response to specific external and internal releasing stimuli (e.g. smiling facial expressions in carers, "looming" objects, and temporal sequences of reward followed by non-reward). Sensori-motor modules are the "seeds" on which experience builds more complex, emotional responses.

The schematic level of processing:

> . . . integrates sensori-motor processes with image-like prototypes of emotional situ-ations. Schemata are created in emotional encounters with the environment and are conceptualized as memories of emotional experiences: they are concrete analogue representations in memory of specific perceptual, motor (expressive, approach–avoidance tendencies and autonomic reactions) and subjective feelings, each of which were components of the reactions during specific emotional episodes . . . Generalized schemata, i.e. prototypes, will emerge as similar, motor and subjec-tive states are evoked and combined in memory with the perceptual features derived from multiple situations (Leventhal & Scherer, 1987, p. 10).

Schematic emotional memory is seen as providing a rapid, automatic, perceptual–emotional appraisal of current situations, shaping our subjective ex-perience of events without effort or awareness of their activity, just as perceptual memory schemata shape the organization of objects in our perceptual field. The generation of virtually all post-neonatal emotional reactions involves activation of affective schematic structures.

The conceptual level of processing arises as the growing infant comes to reflect upon, abstract, and draw conclusions about the environment and his/her emo-tional reactions to it. Processing at this level involves:

> propositionally organized memory structures which have been formed by compari-son over two or more emotional episodes. Conceptual processing is also volitional and can evoke emotions by accessing schemata. Thus, conceptual processing in-volves memories *about* emotion and mechanisms or procedures for the volitional use of these memory structures (Leventhal & Scherer, 1987, p. 11).

Leventhal's model provides an heuristic account of the way more complex, schematically driven, emotional states might develop from the prepared sensorimotor emotional reactions with which an infant enters the world. These developments include both an extension of the range of sensory–perceptual features that will elicit emotion, and changes in the form of response. For example, it is suggested that, in a child who is regularly tickled or swung in the air when it smiles at its parents, its memory schema for happiness might be described as "euphoric" or excited. By contrast, in a child whose parents respond to smiles with soft coos and gentle endearments, a schema of calm happiness is more likely to develop.

Although recognizing that most adult emotional reactions will involve contri-butions from all three levels, Leventhal's model makes a clear distinction between the schematic level, which includes memories *of* emotional experience, and is, itself, capable of directly eliciting emotion, and the conceptual level, which includes memories *about* emotion, and can only elicit emotion indirectly, by "calling up" the schematic level. It follows that this model has no difficulty in handling the dissociation between "hot" and "cool" processing of emotional material; indeed, Leventhal's observation of related dissociations in the area of health psychology was one of the main sources leading to the development of the model in the first place.

Interacting Cognitive Subsystems (ICS)

Interacting cognitive subsystems (ICS), first described by Barnard (1985), is a comprehensive conceptual framework within which, in principle, accounts of all aspects of information processing can be developed. The framework was applied to emotion by Barnard & Teasdale (1991). Teasdale & Barnard (1993) provide an extended description of the framework and its application to understanding cognition–emotion relationships: moods and their effects on memory; depressive thinking and its role in the maintenance of depression; and the mechanisms of action of psychological treatments (see also Teasdale, 1996, 1997).

ICS is based on a few, basically simple, ideas. The first is that qualitatively different kinds of information, or mental codes, each represent a distinct aspect of experience. Sensory (visual, acoustic and body-state) codes represent the information of relatively "raw" "undigested" sensory experience. Speech-level and visual object codes represent regularities extracted from recurring patterns of sensory codes over an individual's life experience. Recurring patterns in speech-level and visual object codes are, themselves, represented by codes encoding meanings. ICS distinguishes two levels of meaning. Propositional code patterns represent specific explicit meanings of the kind that are conveyed by a single sentence in language. Implicational code represents a more generic, holistic, implicit level of meaning that encodes, in schematic models, recurring regularities and interdependencies across constellations of specific meanings and patterns of sensory codes. Subjectively, synthesis of implicational meanings is marked by experience of "senses" or "feelings" with implicit meaning content: "something wrong", "confidence", "on the right track", "hopelessness". Finally, effector codes control muscular and autonomic responses.

The second basic idea of ICS is that there are specific processes that transform information from one kind of code to another. In the ICS framework, such transformations represent the basic operation through which information processing occurs.

The third basic idea of the ICS approach is that there are separate memory systems for each of the different mental codes.

Transformation processes and code-specific memory stores are arranged in nine cognitive subsystems. Each subsystem is specialized for processing input in one information code. Such processing is constrained by a set of explicit operating principles. Extended information processing involves a continuing flow and exchange of data between subsystems.

In ICS, emotion is generated when appropriate patterns of implicational code are processed. Generally, these patterns will represent schematic models encoding recurring themes and regularities extracted from the patterns of propositional and sensory codes synthesized in previous situations that have elicited a given emotion. For example, schematic models encoding themes such as "globally negative view of self" or "hopeless, highly aversive, uncontrollable situation that will persist indefinitely" will be extracted as prototypical of depressing situations. When, subsequently, high-level meanings related to these themes are synthesized, a depressive emotional response will arise.

ICS proposes that emotional responses to basic sensory input (e.g. a blood-curdling shriek), and emotions reflecting complex, subtle patterns of meaning (e.g. embarrassment) are ultimately mediated through the same point in the system: "The implicational code provides a 'common currency' in which 'sensory' and 'cognitive' contributions can be expressed, integrated, and can modulate the production of emotion" (Teasdale & Barnard, 1993, p. 91).

Like Leventhal's earlier approach, ICS identifies a schematic level as the most direct influence on adult emotion, and suggests that the propositional level, concerned with concepts and specific meanings, has no direct influence, mediating, instead, "cool" thinking about emotion-related topics. In both accounts, the schematic level receives contributions directly from sensory–perceptual level features, sensory feedback from emotion-related body changes making particularly important contributions to emotion-related schemata. Unlike Leventhal's schematic level (at least the original presentations of it; but see Leventhal & Scherer, 1987) ICS's implicational schematic models include, in addition to sensory-perceptual elements, elements reflecting recurring constellations of specific meanings. Consequently, in ICS, the schematic level driving emotion generation is particularly sensitive to the thematic semantic content of situations (e.g. whether they are perceived as controllable or uncontrollable, whether they involve success or failure to achieve specified goal states, whether they imply an improving or worsening situation).

In contrast to the specific, explicit, propositional level of meaning, implicational level representations are holistic and implicit (cf. Gendlin's, 1981, "felt sense"). This distinction between explicit and implicit levels of meaning allows ICS to explain the frequently observed refractoriness of emotional responses to simple verbal–propositional interventions; change in emotional response depends on change at the implicit implicational level, requiring change in a wider and more sensorily influenced context than a few "helpful words of advice" may effect (see Teasdale & Barnard, 1993, Chapter 16).

By proposing separate memory stores for implicational and propositional representations, affect being linked directly only to the former, ICS provides a way to explain the variability of the effects of mood on memory biases. The ICS analysis proposes that a mood state will only enhance the encoding or retrieval of affectively congruent material if implicational representations of the material have been created at encoding, a proposal that can account for much of the variability apparent in the experimental literature (Teasdale & Barnard, 1993, Part III).

The ICS approach to emotion is nested within a dynamic, systemic approach to information processing in general. This facilitates accounts of the effects of mood on cognitive processes, such as memory. This aspect of ICS also enables us to formulate accounts of the dynamic processes through which "cognitive" and "affective" factors can interact to establish self-organizing, self-perpetuating, processing configurations that act to maintain persistent affective states, such as moods or emotional disorders. For example, it is suggested that the "depressive interlock" configuration, illustrated in Figure 31.1, plays an important role in the maintenance of clinical depression (Teasdale & Barnard, 1993; Teasdale 1996).

The Multiple-Entry, Modular Memory System Approach (MEM)

The multiple-entry, modular memory system approach (MEM) was initially proposed as a framework for understanding memory and related phenomena (Johnson, 1983). It was subsequently applied to emotion and cognition–emotion relationships (Johnson & Multhaup, 1992; Johnson, 1994).

According to MEM, "memory is organized into distinct but interacting subsystems, each made up of component cognitive processes" (Johnson, 1994, p. 88). Two perceptual subsystems (P-1 and P-2) process external stimuli, and store the results of such processing. P-1 handles relatively basic aspects of perceptual processing, of which we are often unaware. P-2 processes give rise to our phenomenal perceptual experiences of meaningful objects interacting in meaningful ways, e.g. identifying a scene as a table on which objects are placed in a particular spatial arrangement.

Two reflective subsystems (R-1 and R-2) process and store internally, or self-generated material, such as that involved in imagination, fantasy and problem-solving. These subsystems allow us to sustain, transform and organize information. R-1 processes are essentially "supervisory" (e.g. reactivating information), whereas R-2 processes operate at a more "executive" strategic level (e.g. discovering relations among aspects of experience).

Within MEM, all four subsystems can contribute to emotion, and similar emotions can be associated with different subsystems. Certain emotions, such as anger or fear, are likely to be "computed" in all subsystems. However, the exact character of an emotion will depend on the specific processes from which it was derived; the fear experienced from seeing a fist come towards you (arising from P-1 activity) and the fear experienced from imagining yourself speechless at a party (arising from R-1 activity) differ in important ways.

It is suggested that the variety of possible emotions increases progressively from the P-1 subsystem to the R-2 subsystem. For example, an emotion such as remorse depends on R-1 and R-2 activity re-activating and retrieving a prior

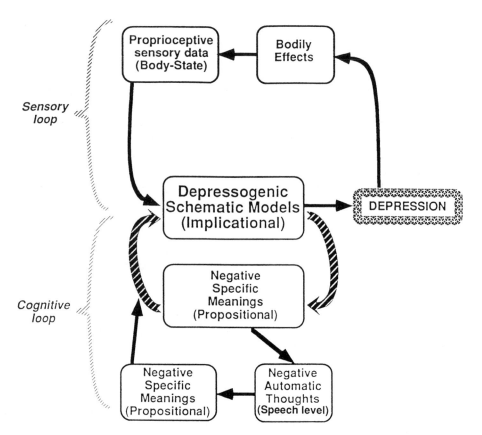

Figure 31.1 A sketch of the ICS "Depressive Interlock" configuration, which, it is suggested, plays a major role in the maintenance of clinical depression. The figure illustrates the following key features of the ICS analysis: (1) two levels of meaning—a specific (Propositional) level, and a more schematic (Implicational) level; (2) Implicational meanings (schematic mental models) may reflect contributions from both patterns of specific (Propositional) meanings, and patterns of sensory information (e.g. from bodily sensations); (3) emotion (depression) is generated directly only from the Implicational level of meaning—specific (Propositional) meanings and (speech level) negative automatic thoughts only contribute indirectly to emotion generation, to the extent that they affect the schematic meanings synthesized; (4) processing involves the dynamic exchange of information between subsystems—in the depressive interlock configuration, sensory and cognitive feedback loops can become established that "lock" subsystems into a self-perpetuating configuration that maintains depression. Reproduced from Teasdale (1996), by permission of Guilford Press.

commitment, along with the knowledge that one has failed to keep it, and could not be the result of activity in perceptual subsystems alone. Relatedly, Johnson (1994) has suggested that emotions arising from P-1 and P-2 activity correspond to basic or biologically primitive emotions, whereas emotions requiring R-1 and R-2 processing correspond to "secondary" or "derived" emotions.

In MEM, as in other multi-level theories: "different, and perhaps conflicting, emotional responses to the same nominal stimulus may co-exist, mediated by different subsystems; which of these would be active would depend on contextual factors, such as the type of cue, that might favor one or the other" (Johnson, 1994, p. 89).

Johnson's application of the MEM framework to her own studies of memory illustrates important implications of multi-level approaches to understanding cognition–emotion relationships. In one study (see Johnson & Multhaup, 1992, for a more detailed discussion), amnesic Korsakoff patients and control subjects heard brief sections of unfamiliar melodies, and, subsequently, rated how much they liked both these (now, potentially, familiar) melodies, and a set of new, unfamiliar, melodies. Both groups showed a greater liking for the previously experienced melodies than for the totally novel melodies. The extent of this preference was similar in both groups, suggesting that the (largely perceptual-level) processes responsible for the initial affective evaluation of the music, and for the retention of that evaluation, were unimpaired in the amnesic patients. By contrast, when asked to indicate whether they had heard the melodies before, the patients showed marked deficits compared to the controls. Such a dissociation is, of course, exactly what would be predicted from an approach which recognized the existence of separate memory systems specialized for encoding and retaining different aspects of experience.

The second study used a situation in which, it was assumed, reflective-level rather than perceptual-level processes largely accounted for the evaluations made. Subjects were shown pictures of two men, Bill and John, and asked to rate their honesty, intelligence, etc. both before and after hearing factual information about the behaviour of the two (e.g. "broke his wife's arm in a fight") that depicted John as a "good guy" and Bill as a "bad guy". Twenty days later, the evaluations were repeated. Although the Korsakoff patients could remember virtually nothing of the specific factual information about the two characters (compared to 35% recall in controls), they still gave the good guy higher ratings than the bad guy, again suggesting a dissociation between the retention of factual and affective information.

The SPAARS (Schematic, Propositional, Analogical and Associative Representation Systems) Approach

SPAARS (Power & Dalgleish, 1997) is the most recent of the multi-level approaches under review. As the name of the framework suggests, the different levels recognized within this framework are similar to those of earlier accounts: "Analogical" refers to sensory–perceptual levels; "propositional" to a propositional-conceptual level, and "schematic" to a type of representation identical to the implicational schematic models of the ICS account (we shall return to the Associative level shortly). The strength of Power & Dalgleish's (1997) presentation of this approach is to position it clearly in a philosophical and psychological historical context, and to accept the challenge of actually applying the SPAARS framework to the phenomena of ordered and disordered emotion.

Power & Dalgleish (1997) describe the varied appraisals that, within SPAARS, elicit different types of emotion. Current goals are central to those appraisals, and, it is suggested, these goals themselves are a function of the schematic model "in place" at a given time. In SPAARS, as in ICS, affect-related schematic models play a central role in emotion generation, propositional representations, alone, having no direct role:

> Events and interpretations can only be appraised with respect to the individual's goals, such that emotions are generated at the schematic model level of meaning ... although goals can be represented propositionally they can only be the subjects of an *emotion-related appraisal* process at the schematic model level ... propositional processing will be merely semantic—it will be cold and non-emotional (Power & Dalgleish, 1997, p. 170, original italics).

In SPAARS, the associative level provides a further route through which emotion may be generated "automatically" without concurrent access to the schematic model level of meaning. "Automatic" is used here as a contrast to "controlled" (Shiffrin & Schneider, 1977), in the sense proposed by Logan (1988):

> Automaticity is memory retrieval: performance is automatic when it is based on single-step direct-access retrieval of past solutions from memory.... Automatization reflects a transition from algorithm-based performance to memory-based performance (cited by Power & Dalgleish, 1997, p. 175).

Noting that almost all cognitive and social cognitive processes (e.g. attitude activation, Bargh & Gollwitzer, 1995) can become automatized, Power & Dalgleish suggest that the same is true of the processes involved in the generation of emotion. That is, with sufficient repetition of a provoking situation, elements of that situation that have been repeatedly paired with the emotional response eventually become able to elicit emotion themselves, "automatically", without the mediation of any extended appraisal process. Within SPAARS, such automatized emotional responses are mediated by an associative level, distinct from the schematic level, so allowing, within this framework, two distinct routes to emotion production. It is proposed that associatively mediated emotional responses are particularly easily established to certain pairings of biologically prepared event and response classes, such as taste aversions to tastes paired with nausea, or phobic responses to animals such as spiders and snakes. The "impenetrability" of such prepared conditioned emotional responses to corrective "rational" information arises, it is suggested, because these responses are mediated through prepared links at the associative level rather than through appraisals involving the synthesis of schematic models.

Figure 31.2 indicates the relationships between the basic components of the SPAARS framework.

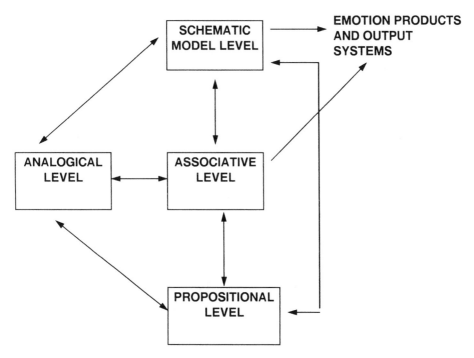

Figure 31.2 The SPAARS model of emotion showing the four representational systems. The figure shows the relationships between the different levels of this multi-level framework, and indicates that only the Schematic and Associative levels are directly linked to generation of emotion. Reproduced from Power & Dalgleish (1997), by permission of Psychology Press, Hove, UK.

STRENGTHS AND WEAKNESSES OF MULTI-LEVEL THEORIES

The richness of multi-level theories, with their separate levels, information codes, types of representation and processes, each level having different functional relationships to emotion, allows us to do justice to the observed variations in the ways that emotion can be elicited, and to the dissociations and functional independence often observed between different aspects of processing of the same topic. However, there is a danger that the advantages that such complexity in theorizing can buy us may be offset by the difficulty of distinguishing, empirically, between a multiplicity of explanatory accounts for any given phenomenon that different models, or indeed the same model, can provide. Put bluntly, if we can "explain" all aspects of cognition–emotion relations, simply by an unconstrained re-description of those relations in the language of a complex framework which does not yield verifiable predictions, then we may have really explained very little. The reality of this danger is a function of the level of precision of our theorizing, and of the number of constraints that our accounts of any phenomena have to satisfy.

The continuing development of our understanding of cognition–emotion relationships is a "boot-straps" operation, in which we need frameworks to guide the thinking that will lead to the experimental investigations that will, in turn, lead to findings that will force us to modify, or even abandon, our existing frameworks for something better. Viewed in this spirit, each of the approaches I have reviewed has something to offer to this unfolding endeavour, the contributions of the different approaches often being complementary.

As an illustration of the way that a multi-level framework can operate as a "tool for thought" the final section of this chapter illustrates the application of the ICS framework to a topic to which it has not previously been applied. I choose to focus on ICS as, of the frameworks that have been presented, it is both the most tightly constrained by explicit operating principles and the one with which I am most familiar.

MULTI-LEVEL THEORIES AND THE NEUROBIOLOGY OF EMOTION

Multi-level theories of cognition and emotion offer explanatory accounts at a functional, psychological level of analysis. Accounts can also be offered at a level that is more concerned with the actual neural mechanisms and brain machinery that mediate the production of emotion. Ideally, accounts at these two levels would complement each other, so that by mapping from one level to another and back, both types of explanation could be constrained and refined.

Multi-level theories can act as useful tools for thought in mediating the communication between psychological and more biological levels of analysis. I shall illustrate this possibility in relation to ICS and LeDoux's (1989, 1995) analysis of cognitive–affective interactions in the brain.

LeDoux distinguishes two classes of computation: cognitive and affective. Cognitive computations yield information about a stimulus itself and its relationship to other stimuli. Affective computations, on the other hand, yield information about the biological significance of the stimulus for the individual in that moment (e.g. of a snake, that it is a threat to personal safety) and lead to some form of behavioural, autonomic or humoral response (e.g. increased heart rate, and running away).

LeDoux proposes that, for fear and probably also other emotions, emotional responses and conscious emotional experiences are consequences of the affective computations performed on stimuli by a network in the amygdala. The amygdala receives inputs from the visual, auditory, somatosensory, gustatory and olfactory areas of the cerebral cortex, as well as inputs reflecting interoceptive sensory information. Interruption of the inputs to the amygdala from the modality-specific cortical areas leads to an inability to compute the emotional significance of stimuli in the corresponding modality.

The amygdala also receives sensory information (reflecting simple stimulus features) directly from thalamic sensory relay structures. Thus, there is both a "quick-and-dirty" and a slower and more accurate route to the computation of the affective significance of stimuli in the amygdala. Both routes can support simple conditioning of emotional responses, but the longer, cortical, route is required for more complex conditioning (e.g. learning that one stimulus is associated with the unconditioned stimulus, but another is not).

In addition to the affective computations performed on sensory and perceptual stimuli, it is suggested that the amygdala also evaluates the affective significance of "cognitive" inputs, received from the hippocampus. Such inputs have largely transcended their initial sensory modality, and reflect an integration across sensory modalities in complex association cortex before reaching the hippocampus.

LeDoux (1989) further proposed that the hippocampus allows cognitive modulation of the processing of affect in the amygdala. For example, although hippocampal lesions do not interfere with emotional conditioning, such lesions do interfere with the modulation of conditioned emotional responses by cognitive (contextual) information, "allowing the amygdala to respond to a stimulus as threatening in one situation and not in another" (LeDoux, 1995, p. 224). In the absence of cortical modulation (whether mediated through the hippocampus or elsewhere), learned emotional responses established through the thalamo-amygdala route are "relatively indelible" and do not extinguish (LeDoux, Romanski & Xagoraris, 1989).

In summary, the following key points emerge from LeDoux's analysis:

1. Sensory, perceptual, and cognitive inputs converge on the amygdala, where their affective significance is evaluated and emotional responses are generated.
2. There is a "quick-and-dirty" direct route through which crude aspects of sensory stimuli can elicit emotion production.
3. There is a longer, less direct route through which more detailed, complex perceptual features of stimuli can elicit emotion.
4. Cognitive inputs, reflecting inputs over multiple sensory–perceptual modalities, are fed to the amygdala from the hippocampus (where they may have been derived from/related to episodic memories of events, or mental maps of situations).
5. Cognitively derived inputs from the hippocampus can modulate the effects of inputs derived from sensory–perceptual aspects of stimuli (e.g. by influences of the wider context in which isolated sensory–perceptual features occurred).
6. Emotional responses learned to simple sensory–perceptual stimuli are relatively indelible; their extinction or modification depends on cortically derived "cognitive" modulation.

The essential features of the ICS framework for present purposes can be summarized as follows:

1. Emotion is generated when, in response to appropriate input, transformation processes specialized for processing implicational code produce patterns of effector code that control aspects of emotional response.

2. These transformation processes are biologically prepared to respond to certain sensorily derived patterns of implicational code, and "learn" to respond to patterns of implicational code that have been associatively linked with the production of emotion in the past.

3. Affect-related patterns of implicational code may contain contributions derived directly from low-level sensory information (e.g. the distinctive sound qualities of a shriek) by transformation processes that take one of the ICS sensory codes (acoustic, visual, and body-state) as input and produce, as output, elements of implicational code. Affect-related patterns of implicational code may also contain contributions derived from transformation processes that take as input recurring complexes of specific propositional meanings (themselves derived, initially, from external sensory input, or from internal cognitive processing) and produce, as output, elements of implicational code: "The implicational code provides a 'common currency' in which 'sensory' and 'cognitive' contributions can be expressed, integrated, and can modulate the production of emotion" (Teasdale & Barnard, 1993, p. 91).

4. The affective significance of sensorily derived implicational elements (e.g. from a shriek) can be modulated by meaning-derived elements (e.g. indicating the basic safety of a rough-and-tumble play situation in which the shriek was emitted) but only where implicational schematic models integrating the two classes of elements have been extracted from repeated experiences.

5. The processes that derive elements of implicational code from complexes of specific meanings depend on access to propositional memory records of autobiographical events.

We can now make the following speculative cross-mappings between ICS and LeDoux's neurobiological analysis:

1. Computation of the affective significance of stimuli in the amygdala is carried out by emotion-specific transformation processes that, on receiving appropriate patterns of implicational code as input, produce patterns of effector code controlling specific emotional responses as output.

2. In the amygdala's "quick-and-dirty" assessment of the affective significance of stimuli, transformation processes rely for input primarily on implicational elements derived directly from acoustic, sensory, or body-state sensory codes.

3. In the amygdala's "slow and careful" assessment of the affective significance of stimuli, the relevant implicational elements are derived only after the sensory codes have been further transformed into the "perceptual" visual object code (in non-primates) or, further, in humans, through speech-level (morphonolexical) or visual object code, and thence to specific meaning (propositional) code.

4. The "cognitive" inputs to the amygdala will be derived from the transformation process that converts patterns of (in humans) propositional code to elements of implicational code; as the development of these processes depends on extracting regularities from stored patterns of propositional code (and the process can also take stored patterns as input), the association of the hippocampus with explicit, episodic memory is particularly interesting.

5. The cognitive modulation of sensory–perceptual affective computations depends on transforming cognitive inputs into the same (implicational) code in which the sensory-derived elements are expressed. The affective computation can then be based on the total pattern of implicational code, reflecting both sensory- and meaning-derived elements.

6. Meaning-derived implicational elements can only modulate sensory-derived elements if they have repeatedly occurred together in situations where emotional responses have not been elicited.

I only have space to illustrate a few of the potential benefits that this type of exercise might afford. First, and very obviously, it brings very forcefully to our awareness the fact that the sequence of transformations through which, in the ICS analysis, a complex emotive situation is "appraised" in humans involves, crucially, patterns of propositional code (and, often, patterns of speech-level code from which the propositional patterns were derived). By contrast, these codes cannot play this role in animals such as rats, where these codes simply do not exist (Barnard & Teasdale, 1991, p. 39). It is striking that there is little mention of speech-level or propositional–conceptual processing in LeDoux's accounts.

Second, this analysis provides a clear explanation of the "cognitive impenetrability" of affect-related processing to "rational" information that is often observed. In order to modulate the affective computations of the amygdala, "cognitive" information has to be transformed into the (implicational) code in which the amygdala works; this will depend on repeated experiences that provide the basis for the relevant propositional–implicational transformations to be learned, and for their resulting products to be integrated into coherent implicational schematic models. Without such transformations, verbal-conceptual (propositional) information will not impact on emotion production.

Third, and relatedly, this analysis casts light on the persistence of affective responses in the face of attempts to modify them. LeDoux's work suggests that learned (or biologically prepared) emotional responses based on the "quick-and-dirty" route are essentially "indelible", and that their modification will depend on "cognitive" modulation, rather than simple "unlearning". The ICS analysis suggests that the "indelible" learning occurs at the level of the transformation process that takes patterns of implicational code as input and creates, as output, patterns of effector code controlling emotional responses. The modification and modulation of these responses will depend on the creation of new, coherent implicational schematic models, that integrate meaning- and sensory-derived elements. The creation of such modified models is likely to depend on arranging new experiences, rather than simply providing "corrective" information at a verbal-propositional level (see Teasdale & Barnard 1993, Chapter 16, for a related discussion).

The advantages of multi-level approaches to understanding cognition–emotion relations have, in fact, been well described by LeDoux himself. His views provide a fitting summary with which to conclude this chapter:

> In the past, cognitive–emotional interactions have often been discussed without much consideration of what the terms "cognition" and "emotion" mean. I have limited this discussion to the emotion of fear and have examined how specific cognitive processes (such as sensory processing in the thalamus, perceptual processing in the neocortex, spatial and contextual processing in the hippocampus, or mnemonic processing in the hippocampus) can influence the amygdala and thereby elicit fear responses. This perspective forces us to abandon discussion of cognitive–emotional interactions in terms of vague monolithic cognitive processes and instead consider exactly which cognitive processes are involved in fear reactions. This is a more practical and tractable problem than the problem of how cognition and emotion, in the broader sense of the terms, interact. (LeDoux, 1995, p. 224).

REFERENCES

Baddeley, A. D. (1986). *Working Memory*. Oxford: Oxford University Press.

Bargh, J. A. & Gollwitzer, P. M. (1995). Environmental control of goal-directed action: automatic and strategic contingencies between situations and behaviour. In W. D. Spaulding (ed.), *Integrative Views of Motivation, Cognition and Emotion*. Lincoln, NE: University of Nebraska Press.

Barnard, P. (1985). Interacting cognitive subsystems: a psycholinguistic approach to short-term memory. In A. Ellis (ed.), *Progress in the Psychology of Language*, Vol. 2. London: Erlbaum, pp. 197–258.

Barnard, P. J. & Teasdale, J. D. (1991). Interacting cognitive subsystems: a systemic approach to cognitive–affective interaction and change. *Cognition and Emotion*, **5**, 1–39.

Bower, G. H. (1981). Mood and memory. *American Psychologist*, **36**, 129–148.

Bower, G. H. & Cohen, P. R. (1982). Emotional influences in memory and thinking: Data and theory. In M. S. Clark & S. T. Fiske (eds), *Affect and Cognition*. Hillsdale, NJ: Erlbaum.

Brewin, C. R. (1989). Cognitive change processes in psychotherapy. *Psychological Review*, **96**, 379–394.

Gendlin, E. (1981). *Focusing*. New York: Bantam Books.

Johnson, M. K. (1983). A multiple-entry, modular memory system. In G. H. Bower (ed.), *The Psychology of Learning and Motivation: Advances in Research and Theory*, Vol. 17. New York: Academic Press, pp. 81–123.

Johnson, M .K. (1994). Some thoughts on emotion, consciousness, and MEM. In N. H. Frijda (ed.), *Proceedings of the VIIIth Conference of the International Society for Research on Emotions, ISRE '94*. Storrs, CT: ISRE, pp. 88–93.

Johnson, M. K. & Multhaup, K. S. (1992). Emotion and MEM. In S.-A. Christiansen (ed.), *The Handbook of Emotion and Memory: Current Research and Theory*. Hillsdale, NJ: Erlbaum, pp. 33–66.

LeDoux, J. E. (1989). Cognitive–emotional interactions in the brain. *Cognition and Emotion*, **3**, 267–289.

LeDoux, J. E. (1995). Emotion: clues from the brain. *Annual Review of Psychology*, **46**, 209–235.

LeDoux, J. E., Romanski, L. M. & Xagoraris, A. (1989).   Indelibility of subcortical emotional memories. *Journal of Cognitive Neuroscience*, **1**, 238–243.

Leventhal, H. (1979).   A perceptnal-motor processing model of emotion. In P. Pilner, K. Blankstein & I. M. Spigel (eds), *Perception of Emotion in Self and Others*, Vol. 5. New York: Plenum, pp. 1–46.

Leventhal, H. (1980).   Toward a comprehensive theory of emotion. In L. Berkowitz (ed.), *Advances in Experimental Social Psychology*, Vol. 13. New York: Academic Press, pp. 139–207.

Leventhal, H. (1984).   A perceptnal-motor theory of emotion. In L. Berkowitz (ed.), *Advance in Experimental Social Psychology*, Vol. 17. New York: Academic Press, pp. 117–182.

Leventhal, H. & Scherer, K. (1987).   The relationship of emotion to cognition: a functional approach to a semantic controversy. *Cognition and Emotion*, **1**, 3–28.

Logan, G. D. (1988).   Toward an instance theory of automatisation. *Psychological Review*, **95**, 492–527.

Power, M. & Dalgleish, T. (1997).   *Cognition and Emotion: From Order to Disorder*. Hove: Psychology Press.

Shallice, T. (1988).   *From Neuropsychology to Mental Structure*. Cambridge: Cambridge University Press.

Shiffrin, R. M. & Schneider, W. (1977).   Controlled and automatic human information processing: II. Perceptual learning, automatic attending and a general theory. *Psychological Review*, **84**, 127–190.

Teasdale, J. D. (1993).   Emotion and two kinds of meaning: cognitive therapy and applied cognitive science. *Behaviour Research and Therapy*, **31**, 339–354.

Teasdale, J. D. (1996).   Clinically relevant theory: integrating clinical insight with cognitive science. In P. M. Salkovskis (ed.), *Frontiers of Cognitive Therapy*, New York: Guilford.

Teasdale, J. D. (1997).   The relationship between cognition and emotion: the mind-in-place in mood disorders. In D. M. Clark & C. G. Fairburn (eds), *Science and Practice of Cognitive Behaviour Therapy*. Oxford: Oxford University Press, pp. 67–93.

Teasdale, J. D. & Barnard, P. J. (1993).   *Affect, Cognition and Change: Remodelling Depressive Thought*. Hove: Erlbaum.

Chapter 32

Self-organization of Cognition–Emotion Interactions

Marc D. Lewis
and
Isabela Granic
University of Toronto, Toronto, Canada

The computer metaphor for human cognition has been in decline—albeit a slow decline—since the early 1980s. Cognitive scientists are no longer content to characterize thought as a step-by-step computational sequence. In place of computation, current approaches highlight the dynamic, distributed, and non-linear aspects of a thought process that is rooted in context and embodied in a biological system (Port & van Gelder, 1995; Varela, Thompson & Rosch, 1991). Traditional AI has been all but replaced by neural network models, and the structure and function of the nervous system have become rigorous criteria for plausibility. From this perspective, cognition builds on itself, biasing its own outcomes, and changes unpredictably and unevenly from moment to moment. In short, cognition is becoming recognized as a process of self-organization in a complex dynamical system.

Self-organization means the spontaneous emergence of orderly patterns out of recurring interactions among lower-order elements. The emergence of new forms in embryogenesis, evolution, ecology and social organization exemplifies biological self-organization. Similarly, the emergence of complex, orderly patterns of cognition exemplifies psychological self-organization. At the cognitive level, coherent images, ideas and plans spontaneously assemble out of multiple associations. At the underlying neural level, the phasing or synchronization of brain

Handbook of Cognition and Emotion. Edited by T. Dalgleish and M. Power.
© 1999 John Wiley & Sons Ltd.

activity self-organizes from the coordination of local sites of activation. The appeal of viewing cognition as a self-organizing process goes back to the cognitive revolution, when Ashby (1952), McCulloch (McCulloch & Pitts, 1943) and von Neumann (1958) explored the surprising properties of processing networks and feedback loops. However, it is not until recent years, with growing acceptance of neural networks, embodied cognition and non-linear dynamics for modeling complex processes, that the idea of cognitive self-organization has come into its own.

This trend should be good news for emotion theorists, and particularly those interested in the relations between cognition and emotion. Rule-based cognition was never easily amenable to emotional influences. To make ends meet, traditional models of cognition–emotion interaction might insert emotion boxes in cognitive flow charts, as though emotion must be computational in order to participate in a computational cognitive process. However, this solution encounters a logical impasse: computational approaches to cognition are premised on the idea that the mind is functionally independent of its operational medium, and silicon is as good as flesh when it comes to manipulating symbols. Yet silicon has no emotions. Emotions have to do with the significance of actions for beings who have bodies and whose bodies have survival requirements. In fact, emotion has no role to play in computational systems, where prespecified goals and truth tables govern processing.[1] But in embodied cognitive systems, emotions are well suited to guide or bias the flow of cognitive self-organization over time. We assume that, if cognition is self-organizing rather than computational, the relations between cognition and emotion must be self-organizing as well.

In recent years, many emotion theorists have circumvented traditional computationalism in their approach to cognition–emotion relations. Some make explicit use of constructs such as graded influences, non-linearity, feedback, emergence and context-sensitivity which are antithetical to computationalism and suggestive, instead, of cognition–emotion self-organization. Our first goal in this chapter is to provide a brief compendium of self-organization principles for psychological systems and then to show how recent accounts of cognition–emotion relations have adopted some of these principles—implicitly or explicitly—in their move toward more powerful explanations. Our second goal is to introduce a theoretical model of cognition–emotion interactions which makes use of these principles in a comprehensive scheme. Third, we shift the focus to emotional development, where complex systems ideas concerning cognition–emotion have been elaborated more thoroughly and applied to such issues as

---

[1] The simulation of emotions on computers can take many forms, but none is critical to the way computers themselves process information. For example, the function of emotions has been described as selecting among multiple, competing goals (Oatley & Johnson-Laird, 1987). Computers may be programmed to have multiple goals, yet a computational sequence does not actually encounter ambiguous choices where emotions must make a difference. At any point in a processing sequence there is only one correct next step, at least for traditional systems, just as there is only one permissible outcome for the sequence as a whole (given a particular set of inputs). Computation is either correct or not.

personality and social development. Finally, we extend our own theoretical model to fashion a comprehensive picture of cognition–emotion relations in personality self-organization.

PRINCIPLES OF SELF-ORGANIZATION FOR PSYCHOLOGICAL SYSTEMS

A number of general principles and definitions are extremely useful for understanding the mind as a self-organizing system. Some of these are enumerated in greater detail in dynamical systems approaches to cognitive and social psychology (e.g. Killeen, 1989; Port & van Gelder, 1995; Vallacher & Nowak, 1997) and developmental psychology (Fogel & Thelen, 1987; Thelen & Smith, 1994; van Geert, 1994). Here we include four core principles that will help make sense of cognition and emotion as a self-organizing interaction in a complex psychological system:

1. *Recursion.*   Self-organizing systems are recursive. They continually rework or revise their own products. Recursion in physical systems is usually described as feedback. In biological systems, recursion takes many forms, such as autocatalysis in biochemical reactions and genetic inheritance in evolution (Kauffman, 1993). In psychological systems, recursion can be observed in the flow of cognition revising itself over time. The "outcome" of any cognitive activity is always the condition for subsequent cognitive activity. For example, the monitoring of a plan leads to its adjustment, and that adjusted plan is then further monitored. Similarly, motor behaviours produce changes in the world which cause sensory alterations as the basis for subsequent behaviours. As emphasized by Piaget, such recursive processes are the fundamental source of developing epistemic structures.

2. *Emergence.*   The importance of recursion is that it augments or amplifies change in dynamic systems. On each iteration, some part of a recent change feeds back to its source and undergoes further change; thus, change is multiplied by itself. In complex systems, where many components interact with each other, this multiplicative process becomes strongly non-linear. Some changes cancel themselves out but others grow abruptly and exponentially. Such non-linear relations in the interactions of multiple components produce novel or emergent forms (Prigogine & Stengers, 1984), such as the patterning of an insect swarm engendered by the interactions of many individuals. The mind is clearly a system of multiple interacting constituents. Perceptions, memories, associations, expectancies, propositions, script elements and schemas, not to mention emotions, all influence one another at every moment. The interplay of these psychological constituents is the condition for the emergence of novel interpretations and behaviours in *real time* (i.e. in the moment).

3. *Consolidation.*   The next principle concerns the profile of self-organization.

Unpredictability and sensitivity characterize self-organizing processes early on, providing their essential creativity and adaptiveness (Prigogine & Stengers, 1984). But as the elements of the system interact recursively, they begin to cooperate and become synchronized, leading finally to coherence or self-consistency as the system stabilizes. In dynamic systems terminology, such stable states are described as *attractors* in the *state space* of the system. All the potential states of a given system comprise its state space, yet highly coherent states are more probable than others, and self-organizing systems repeatedly fall into—or are mathematically "attracted" to—those states. Psychological systems epitomize the flow from turbulent to coherent states. The flights and perchings of birds, William James' grand metaphor for the dispersion and concentration of attention from moment to moment, captures this progression exquisitely. Psychologists pay much more attention to the perchings than the flights—so much so that the temporary coherences of self-organization are usually regarded as steps in computed solutions. Yet even the most stationary states can be seen to be temporary perchings whose endurance and recurrence depend on dynamic processes.

4. *Time scales.*   The final principle is concerned with different time scales of self-organization. These embedded and interacting time scales are typical of natural, self-organizing systems, and they are related to the beautiful shapes of fractal geometry. In psychological systems, time scales of self-organization are typically seen in the emergence of behaviour in real time situations and the emergence of behavioural traits or habits in developmental time (Thelen & Smith, 1994). Most importantly, self-organization at each scale influences self-organization at the other (Port & van Gelder, 1995). That is, the structural changes in system constituents over developmental time both result from and contribute to the emergence of coherent forms (attractors) in real time. The interplay of these resonating time scales sculpts detailed orderliness in the psychological state space of developing humans.

RECURSION, EMERGENCE, AND CONSOLIDATION OF COGNITION–EMOTION RELATIONS

A number of accounts of cognition–emotion interactions have adopted one or more of the above principles. Most prominent has been the idea that some sort of recursion or looping is involved in cognitive appraisals as they give rise to emotions. From this perspective, a single cognitive appraisal step is insufficient to generate a full-blown emotion. Thus, the outcome of an appraisal–emotion process feeds back to a subsequent, secondary appraisal. For Lazarus (1966), primary appraisals assess whether an event is relevant to a person's well-being and goals, and secondary appraisals assess the implications of that event, given a person's expectations and coping potential. Kagan (1978) also postulates an initial registration of an emotional event followed by an evaluative appraisal, both of which are needed to produce a full-blown emotion. A related idea is posited by Fischer, Shaver & Carnochan (1990), who propose a secondary appraisal loop in which emotion itself is the object of appraisal.

For several authors, cognition–emotion interactions evolve over more than one loop. Scherer's (1984) cognitive appraisals involve a progression of increasingly comprehensive evaluative checks operating recursively throughout the duration of an emotion-producing event. Thus, the appraisal process is recursive for Scherer, and this view is endorsed by Ellsworth (1991) as well. For other authors, it is the cognition–emotion cycle that is recursive. Teasdale (1983) describes a "vicious cycle" or "positive feedback" loop between negative thoughts (appraisal) and depression (an emotional state), and this cycle amplifies and maintains depression. Mathews (1990) proposes a circular relationship between the selective processing of threat-related information and a persistent anxious mood. Malatesta & Wilson (1988) note a recursive and sustaining relation between cognitive interpretations and emotions, and Tomkins (1984) claims that positive feedback between affects and their amplifiers promotes the endurance of affective states. Lazarus (1991) and Smith & Lazarus (1990) also touch on the idea of feedback when they describe cognition–emotion interaction as a system that processes its own products.

Recursion in cognition–emotion interactions goes some way toward a complex systems formulation, but the principle of emergence is a second necessary ingredient. The idea that cognition–emotion interactions are emergent rather than sequential is still relatively new. However, its antecedents can be found in models in which emotional elicitation builds on itself, moving from small beginnings to more elaborate and comprehensive outcomes. Buck (1991) emphasizes that emotional states are continuously reactivated until they achieve consciousness at particular thresholds of intensity. For Parkinson & Manstead (1993), emotion episodes evolve through complex social interactions on their way to acquiring their characteristic depth and richness. Scherer's (1984) appraisal checks also assume a cumulative profile, although they are characterized as incremental rather than emergent.

In order to release the genie of self-organization from its lamp, the principles of recursion and emergence must be combined. This was partly accomplished in a theoretical article by Frijda (1993b). Frijda's central contention is that a preliminary cognitive appraisal precedes emotion, while a secondary, more comprehensive appraisal follows from emotion. Thus a conventional "linear model", in which appraisal causes emotion, is replaced by the idea of a two-way causal relation between appraisal and emotion. Moreover, in Frijda's view, appraisals resulting from emotion elaborate the emotional experience and provide it with its integral character or content. The outcome of this process is a cognitive Gestalt, integrating all previous appraisal events, in which cognitive and emotional constituents "coalesce" into a "sense of reality" (p. 383). By linking the notion of emergent structure with the theme of reciprocal causation, Frijda uncovers an important theoretical conjunction which puts him on the doorstep of self-organization (Lewis, 1996).

Frijda seems well-attuned to concepts of non-linearity, sensitivity and emergence, but without explicit use of dynamic systems terminology. In contrast, this terminology has recently been adopted by Scherer (1996), who now refers explicitly to emotions as self-organizing systems. Scherer claims that appraisal consists of a series of stimulus evaluation checks, each of which modifies a number of organismic subsystems (e.g. neurophysiological, motor, etc.) in an incremental fashion. Over time, feedback and feedforward among these subsystems bring them into synchrony with each other. Appraisal thus results in the entrainment (or coupling) among several subsystems, providing a state of temporary stability. This entrainment is the condition for emotion. Emotion then increases the coupling of subsystems already in synchrony, and perhaps maintains this synchrony, although Scherer is not specific in this regard. Modal emotions are described as frequent occurrences of particular patterns of synchronization, triggered by frequently recurring appraisals. In keeping with complex systems terminology, these patterns are regarded as attractors, and they reflect regularities in environmental contingencies rather than basic emotions. Thus, Scherer's account integrates notions of recursion, coupling and coherent states or attractors. The pattern of synchronization which induces emotion is cumulative, it rests on a temporary coupling among organismic subsystems, and it is driven or triggered by recursive appraisal events. In short, Scherer's cognition–emotion interactions are explicitly self-organizing.

What remains problematic in Scherer's model is the incremental nature of a preordained sequence of "executed" appraisal steps. This step-wise progression follows the computational assumptions underlying traditional cognitivism, rather than the assumptions of complexity, sensitivity and non-linearity underlying the rest of his model. Scherer also says little about the influence of emotion on cognitive processes. Emotion clearly increases the coupling of organic subsystems, but its influence on cognitive appraisal is less explicit; thus appraisal remains essentially antecedent to emotion. However, Scherer's idea of the growing synchrony of coupled components, inducing an emotion which then enhances that coupling and recurs over occasions, elegantly captures many of the principles of self-organization. Similarly, as argued elsewhere (Lewis, 1996), Frijda's assumption of two appraisal steps, one preceding and one following emotion, falls back on the incremental assumptions that characterize traditional accounts. As a result, appraisal–emotion processes seem to require definitive beginning and ending points, and these are not clearly defined in Frijda's model. Yet Frijda's final "Gestalt" may indeed be regarded as an emergent coherence, collapsing variability and enduring over time, very much in keeping with the spirit of complex systems theory.

The model developed by the first author over the last 3 years works at resolving such discrepancies by wiping the slate clean and beginning with the premises of complex systems theory. Specifically, the computational metaphor is replaced by the assumption of cognitive self-organization, and reciprocal causation is specified between cognition and emotion—viewed as mutual participants in a recursive, emergent process.

Before going on, it should be noted that the premise of reciprocal causation requires a view of cognition and emotion as separate subsystems. We thus regard emotions as primitives, along the lines of basic or discrete emotions. We define an emotion as a global, non-reducible affective state that is non-specific as to semantic content (Izard, 1984), similar physiologically and phenomenologically across individuals and cultures (Ekman, 1984), elicited by a specific class of situations related to the organism's goals (Oatley & Johnson-Laird, 1987) and that motivates behavioral responses to these situations (Frijda, 1986). All of these features imply an adaptive biological function, and emotions are therefore considered to be phylogenetically specified and unlearned (Izard & Malatesta, 1987).

A MODEL OF SELF-ORGANIZING COGNITION-EMOTION INTERACTIONS

The model begins with the idea of reciprocal causation between cognitive appraisal and emotion. As in conventional emotion theory, cognitive appraisal gives rise to emotion when it denotes a class of situations relevant to the self and its goals (e.g. Lazarus, 1966; Stein & Trabasso, 1992). Emotion, in turn, directs perceptual and cognitive activity to possibilities for influencing those situations through adaptive behavior (Frijda, 1986; Izard & Malatesta, 1987). As argued by Frijda (1993b), these cognitive activities *following* emotion can be regarded as an additional appraisal step, incorporating further aspects of the present situation. However, in our view, cognitive appraisal does not take place in steps but constitutes a continuous process, as does emotion itself. Emotion is continuously enhanced or modified by changes in appraisal, while appraisal is progressively updated by cognitive adjustments resulting from emotional highlighting (Lewis, 1995). As shown in Figure 32.1, this constitutes a recursive loop. Moreover, rather than viewing appraisal as a computation, we view appraisal as an emergent form—an emerging interpretation of a particular situation. Over several iterations, appraisal grows through the coordination of cognitive and perceptual elements which are themselves activated by a consolidating emotional state. Because appraisal dovetails with emotion and both cohere at the same time, we characterize the emergent macrocosm as an appraisal–emotion amalgam or an *emotional interpretation* (Lewis & Junyk, 1997).

Given that emotional interpretations (EIs) are emergent forms, how do they consolidate and what are their constituents? In our view, the cognitive system, like any self-organizing system, tends toward coherence spontaneously as its elements become coupled or synchronized through recursive adjustments. Coherence depends on the reduction of discrepancies among reciprocally coactivating elements—that is, on self-consistency. This principle underlies constraint satisfaction solutions in neural networks. These networks "settle" into configurations in which the activation strengths of the units fit (as well as possible) the constraints imposed by the excitatory and inhibitory connections among them. Discrepancies are minimized over several iterations, and the network

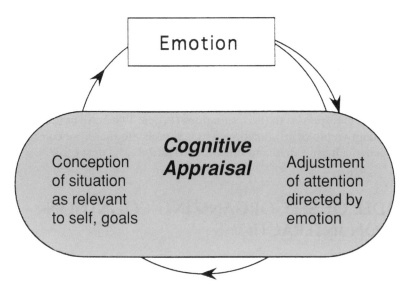

Figure 32.1 Recursive interaction between cognitive appraisal and emotion. A coherent interpretation of an emotion-eliciting situation emerges from reciprocal adjustments among cognitive constituents activated through this recursive process.

"discovers" a state of self-consistency which is difficult to perturb and therefore stable over time (Bechtel & Abrahamsen, 1991). Similarly, in psychological systems, the coupling of microscopic cognitive elements—including images, associations, propositional forms, script elements and concepts—minimizes discrepancy by arriving at a self-consistent, "sensible" interpretation of the emotion-eliciting situation. Such interpretations may include past memories along with immediate perceptual and attentional processes, adjusted and concatenated on the fly. As noted by Scherer (1996), synchrony among constituent elements emerges over time, and this synchrony determines the stability of emotional states.

Emotional interpretations satisfy not only the requirements of self-consistency but also the requirements for attending and responding to the most relevant features of situations. We follow Ekman & Izard in postulating a biological function for basic emotions. In serving that function, emotions steer cognitive activity in particular directions, toward interpretations, plans and often behaviours which can favourably influence those situations. Basic emotions favour the emergence of cognitive combinations that are consonant with the class of situations and responses they have evolved to serve. In anger, for example, attention to impediments and to available means of overcoming those impediments are templates for cognitive coupling. Concepts of goal, barrier, self-efficacy and potential action mutually select and activate each other, arriving at self-consistency in a plan or script.

Thus, cognitive self-consistency and emotion-related selectivity provide dual sets of constraints on self-organizing EIs. Consequently, EIs consolidate and endure when appraisal elements align, not only with themselves but also with a particular emotional state. This global cognition–emotion coupling continues as long as the emotion and the cognitive interpetation continue to perpetuate each other.

The consolidation of an EI within a situation traces the typical profile of self-organization. Many possibilities are briefly available until components couple and stabilize. The sudden smile of an approaching stranger sends a parade of possibilities rapidly through the mind. Fragments of cognitive interpreta-tions—is he friendly, devious, hostile?—correspond with fluctuating emotions—pleasure, anger, and fear—with attention to the eyes and bodily posture, and with overlapping memories of past encounters. Before long, however, a coherent interpretion congeals along with its corresponding emotion, and other possible construals vanish. It is not until some new event or behaviour injects discrepancy into the system that this interpretation becomes disrupted and another can take its place.

Emotional interpretations that stabilize repeatedly for a particular individual can be described as attractors on a state space (Lewis & Douglas, 1998). Within situations, the trajectory taken by cognition–emotion self-organization often progresses to one of several attractors, representing a range of conceivable interpretations of that situation. Particular attractors may be more or less access-ible at given times, depending on recent events and associations, present circum-stances, physiological and mood states, and so forth. However, an individual's overall repertoire of attractors defines his/her personality as a set of recurring cognition–emotion coherences. This notion is consistent with Izard's (1984) pic-ture of enduring affective–cognitive structures and with Magai's view of emotion traits accompanied by recurrent interpretations (Malatesta & Wilson, 1988). Yet it is also consistent with personality research that indicates high behavioural variability corresponding with situational and contextual factors (Wright & Mischel, 1987).

Self-organizing EIs help explain the coherence and duration of cognition–emotion assemblies. According to Ekman (1984), emotions are brief responses to events, generally lasting only a matter of seconds. Yet, as noted by Frijda (1993a), individuals often report "instances" of an emotion lasting over an hour, with a median of 3–6 hours in one study. Ekman (1984) has proposed that long-lasting emotions result from enduring elicitors or from summation over several brief emotion episodes. Yet this explanation implies a passive individual responding to objectively-defined events of varying frequencies and durations. Instead, we regard EIs as enduring elicitors in their own right, actively created by the indi-vidual, and keeping the world in focus in a particular way. Like Frijda et al. (1991), we see typical emotion episodes as processes rather than states (although they include states)—specifically, self-organizing processes that supply their own coherence and relevance.

An interesting problem arises from these considerations. In essence, we claim that emotions catalyze links among cognitive elements in a self-organizing processs. How, then, does cognitive self-organization proceed without this influence? We believe that it does not. Rather, the recursive cycle of human cognition may require at least low levels of emotion to proceed at all. Recent developments in neuroscience suggest that some emotion is necessary to hold images in mind and to combine them or select among them in a plan (Damasio, 1994). According to Edelman (1989), the matching of the limbic/brain stem (motivational) system with the thalamocortical system is the evolutionary foundation for conceptual learning. This matching permits perceptual and conceptual categorization to arise from a recursive loop of cortical, motivational and sensorimotor activities. Tucker (1992) provides a detailed model of the cycling of information through a similar loop, from perceptual processing to integration across perceptual modalities to gist-like appraisal, and then to increasing motor articulation, behaviour, and further perceptual processing. Rich emotional innervation of the paralimbic cortex is the condition for the gist-like appraisal at the centre of this loop. As we stated in the introduction, emotion is well suited to guide or bias the flow of self-organization in an embodied cognitive system. Here we are suggesting that it may also be mandatory.

SELF-ORGANIZING PROCESSES IN SOCIO-EMOTIONAL DEVELOPMENT

As previously mentioned, an important principle of complex systems is the notion of embedded and interacting time scales of self-organization. The idea that developmental change results from, as well as contributes to, the emergence and coherence of real time patterns has powerful implications for developmentalists. Thus far, our discussion has focused on the self-organizing process through which emotion and cognition interact from moment to moment, producing emergent forms which crystallize within situations. Now we extend our focus to the scale of developmental self-organization, wherein cognition–emotion processes evolve and stabilize over the course of months and years.

Recently, a number of theorists have begun to view socio-emotional development as a self-organizing process (e.g. Camras, 1992; Fogel, 1993; Lewis, 1995; Magai & Nusbaum, 1996). This work parallels a more elaborate line of dynamic systems models of motor and cognitive development that began in the mid-1980s (Kelso, 1984; Thelen & Ulrich, 1991; Thelen & Smith, 1994; van Geert, 1991). Perhaps the most prolific of these writers has been Alan Fogel, a social developmentalist who is concerned with the development of self and emotion within the context of interpersonal relationships.

Fogel (1993) approaches his work from a number of related theoretical perspectives including Piaget's theory, ecological psychology, sociocultural theory, as well as dynamic systems theory. He views human development as a dynamic flow of processes including, but not limited to, emotion, cognition and action, and claims that these processes cannot be understood as independent entities. Consistent with systems thinking, Fogel maintains that no one component of the psychological system takes primacy over others or, for that matter, is definable except through its relations to others. Cognition includes feeling, as well as perception and action, and emotions emerge "from the coming together of a brain, a body that moves and senses, and an environment" (Fogel et al., 1992, p. 149). Fogel posits no core set of emotions; instead, from infancy, emotions emerge creatively through interactions with other persons. In a related claim, Camras (1992) argues that basic emotions do not express a pre-given program but, rather, assemble dynamically out of hedonic, motor, appraisal and expressive constituents. According to Fogel, cognition–emotion interaction is the wrong idea; rather, cognition and emotion are two aspects of an emergent system sensitive to environmental influences. Moreover, not only are cognition and emotion inseparable, but so are the developing child and the social surround. All emotional and cognitive processes are considered inherently relational.

Where, then, do the principles of self-organization come into play in Fogel's work? Fogel (1993) suggests that developmental change occurs through communication, and this communication involves the co-regulation of individuals engaged in the mutual adjustment of joint actions. Thus, there is a distinct recursive process but it is interpersonal, not intrapersonal. Moreover, this recursive process is the vehicle of reciprocal adjustments and the source of emergent order. Consensual frames—Fogel's candidate for attractors—are created through this dance of reciprocal adjustments. These interpersonal attractors are the states towards which participants' emotional–cognitive systems jointly gravitate. They are stable constellations of cognition and emotion which give shape to social transactions within situations and which evolve and change over development. Fogel's empirical work (e.g. Fogel, 1993; Fogel et al., in press) has demonstrated how consensual frames manifest themselves through the mother–infant relationship and, in turn, influence the course of development. Information is created through self-organized interaction, not transmitted from partner to partner, and its meaning is the catalyst for the development of the self.

Fogel's work has contributed a great deal to the understanding of emotional development as a complex, dynamic process. His conceptualization of emotional development as a whole system comprising actions, cognitions and emotions, and his notion of consensual frames as interpersonal wholes "attracting" that system, provide refreshing and even radical alternatives to the atomistic models dominating mainstream developmental psychology. However, the mechanisms through which developmental forms self-organize and stabilize are not clearly spelled out. Part of the problem may be Fogel's reluctance to acknowledge the distinctness of subsystems or components, such as cognition and emotion or self and other. A complex systems account should be able to accommodate parts and wholes without ignoring process. Self-organizing forms at one level (e.g. consensual frames) imply interacting constituents at a lower level: systems imply subsystems.

It may be possible to identify the constituents from which Fogel's wholes emerge and to describe how, precisely, they interact.

A dynamic systems approach to cognition–emotion interactions in personality development has been suggested by Magai. Following Izard (1977), Magai takes a discrete emotions, functionalist perspective on emotional development. Individual differences in emotional development are the basis of personality, and these differences are understood as emotion traits which select and are selected by recurrent cognitive interpretations (Magai & McFadden, 1995). In earlier work, Malatesta & Wilson (1988) described a recursive and sustaining relationship between cognitive interpretations and emotions. This idea is obviously compatible with a complex systems account, as defined here, but we would emphasize that such recursion is also the foundation of novel forms in development. It is not until recently that Magai has begun to utilize dynamic systems notions explicitly, particularly in her examination of personality change (Magai & Nusbaum, 1996). She suggests that personality change can be modeled as a *phase transition* (abrupt reorganization of the state space), when sudden intense emotional experiences catalyze cognitive reorganization. Consistent with dynamic systems principles, Magai maintains that a seemingly minor event (or "small change") may elicit a strong emotional response that potentially galvanizes the emergence of system-wide changes through the amplifying process of feedback (Lewis, 1995). In order for this change to crystallize, "cognitive–emotional work" must take place in conjunction with interpersonal support. Haviland likewise incorporates the concept of emergence in her study of identity formation (Haviland & Kalbaugh, 1993). She views identity as a dynamic rather than a static structure, and suggests that "small" emotional experiences can produce large cognitive effects resulting in the reconstruction of identity.

To comprehend the process of change, Magai is most concerned with the principle of sensitivity—the system's non-linear response to small effects. Through examples that range from religious conversion to the moment of insight in psychotherapy, Magai provides vivid illustrations of phase shifts that are triggered by emotional experiences. Similar to Fogel, however, Magai paints a dynamic picture of personality development without a close look at underlying mechanisms. Precisely how do minor events result in new and enduring personality forms? Magai provides some promising suggestions for answering this question: in particular, a social support process in which novel emotion–cognition structures are elaborated through interpersonal interaction. The coupling or coordination of constituents is a key explanatory principle for self-organization, and for both Fogel and Magai interpersonal support may be its vehicle.

The search for developmental models of cognition–emotion self-organization is still in its early stages. We suggest that: (a) specification of system constituents and their means of interaction; (b) close examination of mechanisms of recursion, reciprocal modification, coupling and consolidation; and (c) analysis of embedded, interacting time scales will help bring greater precision and power to this evolving branch of theory. In the following section, we outline our own efforts to move in this direction.

A MODEL OF SELF-ORGANIZING COGNITION–EMOTION INTERACTIONS IN PERSONALITY DEVELOPMENT

In an earlier section of this chapter, we introduced a model showing how cognition–emotion interactions self-organize in real time (i.e. in the moment). The essence of this self-organizing process was the emergence of an emotional interpretation (EI) over continuous iterations of appraisal–emotion recursion. EIs were shown to consolidate and stabilize under the influence of two sets of constraints: those of cognitive self-consistency and those of emotion-related selectivity. Consistent with basic emotions accounts (Izard, 1977), our assumption is that the second set of constraints—emotion-related selectivity—is relatively fixed by our biological heritage. However, the first set of constraints—cognitive self-consistency—is the tip of a large and complex iceberg.

In this section, we suggest that the factors which guide cognitive consistency and coherence can be analyzed, not only in terms of situational features, but also in terms of a unique developmental history. We learn over development to make sense of situations in particular ways. These familiar cognitive construals, described as attractors on a state space, self-organize on each occasion in interaction with emotion. Yet the recurrence, amplification and consolidation of these attractors over months and years constitute self-organization at a developmental scale (Thelen & Ulrich, 1991). We view the consolidation of cognition–emotion attractors as the essence of personality development. Thus, as stated earlier, self-organizing processes can be conceived at embedded, interacting time scales. Emotional interpretations, self-organizing in real time, are embedded in personality formation, self-organizing in developmental time, and each contributes to the other in ways we shall now examine.

We suggest that habitual EIs evolve and coalesce over development through changes in the constraints on cognitive self-consistency. How, precisely, does this occur? Coupling or cooperation of cognitive elements on each occasion influences the way those elements fit together on subsequent occasions (Thelen & Smith, 1994). Particular concepts, micropropositions, images and associations become more congruent with each other and fit more quickly and easily together (e.g. in scripts, plans or propositions) as they co-occur repeatedly (e.g. Nelson, 1986). Others become incompatible with each other (e.g. mothers and army boots) because of their inclusion in competing or discrepant assemblies. Underlying these emergent tendencies is the strengthening of excitatory and inhibitory neural connections brought about by their repeated activation. Such changes form the basis of learning and concept formation (Hebb, 1949; Edelman, 1987). Thus, constraints on cognitive self-consistency evolve through the enhancement of complementarities and incongruities among underlying conceptual constituents.

Of particular importance to social and personality development is the complementarity that evolves between evaluations of the self and evaluations of the other (Sullivan, 1965). For example, a view of the self as needy emerges alongside a view of the other as unavailable, or of the self as "bad" and the other as rejecting. These concepts of self and other seem to be key semantic sub-systems which become adjusted to each other over occasions in the presence of strong emotions. They result in predictable and rapidly emerging EIs which probably take the form of relational schemas (Baldwin, 1992) or scripts (Shank & Abelson, 1977). Moreover, a number of such scripts may be available to each individual, giving the impression of a multiplicity of selves (Hermans, 1996).

Returning to the central importance of cognition–emotion interactions, we postulate emerging conceptual complementarities which select, and are selected by, particular emotions over repeated occasions. Thus, a likely interpretation of an emotional event grows out of the increasing compatibility of an ensemble of cognitive constituents with each other *and* with an emotion. At the same time, this emotion arises more rapidly and more predictably whenever this cognitive ensemble reconverges. Eventually, emotions may arise "automatically" from well-practiced associations (Power & Dalgleish, 1997). This view of recurrent co-selection is consistent with evidence for enduring emotional biases and attributions resulting from repeated negative emotional experiences (Cicchetti et al., 1991; Dodge, 1991). But normative forms may arise through the same process. Most children begin to claim, "It's not fair!" at about the age of 5 or 6 (Case, 1988). This interpretation arises from constituents which are all compatible with anger (e.g. loss to self, thwarted agency, violation of standards, inaccessibility of resources) and with each other. Thus, in both normative and individual development, the honing of cognitive connections, and the real-time coupling between cognitive ensembles and emotions, allow for a crystallizing repertoire of interpretations.

We believe that these self-organizing processes are at the core of personality development. Specifically, recurrent interpretations of emotional experiences converge to pervasive themes, characterized by emotion theorists as affective–cognitive structures (Izard, 1984) or emotion traits (Malatesta & Wilson, 1988). These themes represent a set of construals that all satisfy the requirements of cognitive self-consistency, given the underlying complementarities (and incongruities) among conceptual elements and the constraints of recurrent emotions. Moreover, these themes can be represented as families of attractors on the psychological state space. As these attractors become more refined in development and show up more quickly in real time, they also become enacted in increasingly diverse situations—and hence more "trait-like". This is because they converge given fewer contextual cues; or, in dynamic systems language, their basins extend further across the state space. However, in our view, context always plays a role, and the notion of traits needs to allow for indeterminacy and stochasticity in real-time processes.

In sum, emotional interpretations of the social world self-organize on two time scales. They self-organize in real time with the convergence of an EI to an attractor. They self-organize in development as particular attractors become increasingly influential. To the extent that these attractors are idiosyncratic, they give rise to descriptions of personality development. To the extent that they are shared among members of a culture or among all humans, they give rise to descriptions of normative conceptual and emotional development.

Finally, the consolidation of cognition–emotion attractors probably does not proceed in a smooth, linear fashion with development. Development is marked by periods of rapid change and reorganization (Emde, Gaensbauer & Harmon, 1976; Kagan, 1984; Spitz, 1965) and these reorganizations have been described as phase transitions by dynamic systems theorists (van der Maas & Molenaar, 1992; van Geert, 1991). It is this idea that Magai has utilized in her recent conceptualization of personality changes as abrupt reconfigurations of a dynamic system (Magai & Nusbaum, 1996). We have also described junctures in personality development as phase transitions at which novel cognition–emotion attractors emerge (Lewis, 1995, 1997). By this account, there are critical fluctuations in development, including cognitive/maturational and environmental changes (e.g. the onset of operational thought, puberty, parental divorce). At these nodal points, familiar configurations of cognitive constituents fail to cohere due to new incongruities among previously coupled elements or new complementarities among previously competing elements. At puberty, for example, concepts of friendship and intimacy become compatible with images of sexuality for the first time. The emotional concomitants of habitual configurations are now freed up (e.g. it is no longer always the case that "girls stink!"), and the psychological system acquires additional degrees of freedom. New appraisals, co-assembling with emotions, can build on themselves over a small number of occasions. Coupling on each of these occasions engenders the consolidation of one or more new EIs and reduces the degrees of freedom once again. We thus agree with Magai & Nusbaum (1996) that abrupt personality reorganizations are based on the shake-up of conceptualizations in the presence of strong emotions.

CONCLUSION

Computational cognitive systems require no emotions. There is only one way to proceed in a computation, and that is to arrive at a solution that satisfies some prespecified criterion for correctness. However, a self-organizing cognitive system has tremendous capacity for flexibility and variability. Constrained only by the requirements of self-consistency, such a system could end up almost anywhere. A self-organizing cognitive system is exactly the sort of system that can effectively make use of, and perhaps even require, the guiding constraints of emotions. Self-organizing cognitions must be linked with emotional agendas in order to keep our minds on the business of living. Also, as we have demonstrated, the critical role of emotion in shaping cognitive orderliness can be understood at time scales ranging from situations to lifetimes. Thus, the decline of the computational metaphor permits a new appreciation of the importance of cognition–emotion interactions in all psychological activity.

Emotion theorists studying cognition–emotion interactions are moving toward this vision from different directions, using different terminologies and highlighting different key constructs. For Frijda, it is the assumption of linear appraisal processes which must be overturned. For Scherer, the move to non-linear dynamics is a paradigm shift required by contradictions within conventional emotion theory. For Fogel, the components of emotional development cannot be viewed in isolation because of their constant connection and interaction. For Magai & Haviland, unpredictable changes in personality are incomprehensible without a dynamic systems perspective. We have emphasized principles of recursion, emergence, coupling and consolidation as well as interacting time scales in order to provide a unifying conceptual repertoire for this family of models. As emotion theorists come to apply these principles more rigorously, the scope and power of such models will become increasingly clear.

REFERENCES

Ashby, W. R. (1952). *Design for a Brain*. New York: Wiley.

Baldwin, M. W. (1992). Relational schemas and the processing of social information. *Psychological Bulletin*, **112**, 461–484.

Bechtel, W. & Abrahamsen, A. (1991). *Connectionism and the Mind: An Introduction to Parallel Processing in Networks*. Cambridge, MA: Basil Blackwell.

Buck, R. (1991). Motivation, emotion and cognition: a developmental–interactionist view. In K. T. Strongman (ed.), *International Review of Studies on Emotion*. Chichester: Wiley.

Camras, L. A. (1992). Expressive development and basic emotions. *Cognition and Emotion*, **6**, 269–283.

Case, R. (1988). The whole child: toward an integrated view of young children's cognitive, social, and emotional development. In A. D. Pellegrini (ed.), *Psychological Bases for Early Education*. New York: Wiley.

Cicchetti, D., Beeghly, M., Carlson, V., Coster, W., Gersten, M., Rieder, C. & Toth, S. (1991). Development and psychopathology: lessons from the study of maltreated children. In D. P. Keating & H. Rosen (eds), *Constructivist Perspectives on Developmental Psychopathology and Atypical Development*. Hillsdale, NJ: Erlbaum, pp. 69–102.

Damasio, A. R. (1994). *Descartes' Error*. New York: Avon.

Dodge, K. A. (1991). Emotion and social information processing. In J. Garber & K. A. Dodge (eds), *The Development of Emotion Regulation and Dysregulation*. Cambridge: Cambridge University Press, pp. 159–181.

Edelman, G. M. (1987). *Neural Darwinism*. New York: Basic Books.

Edelman, G. M. (1989). *The Remembered Present: A Biological Theory of Consciousness*. New York: Basic Books.

Ekman, P. (1984). Expression and the nature of emotion. In K. Scherer & P. Ekman (eds), *Approaches to Emotion*. Hillsdale, NJ: Erlbaum.

Ellsworth, P. C. (1991). Some implications of cognitive appraisal theories of emotion. In K. T. Strongman (ed.), *International Review of Studies on Emotion*. Chichester: Wiley.

Emde, R., Gaensbauer, T. & Harmon, R. (1976). *Psychological Issues: Vol. 10. Emotional Expression in Infancy: A Biobehavioral Study*. New York: International Universities Press.

Fischer, K. W., Shaver, P. R. & Carnochan, P. (1990). How emotions develop and how they organise development. *Cognition and Emotion*, **4**, 81–127.

Fogel, A. (1993). *Developing through Relationships: Origins of Communication, Self, and Culture*. Chicago: University of Chicago Press.

Fogel, A., Dickson, K. L., Hsu, H., Messinger, D., Nelson, G. C. & Nwokah, E. (in press). Communication of smiling and laughter in mother–infant play: research on emotion from a dynamic systems perspective. In K. Barrett (ed.), *New Directions in Child Development: Emotion and Communication*.

Fogel, A., Nwokah, E., Dedo, J. Y., Messinger, D., Dickson, K. L., Matusov, E. & Holt, S. A. (1992). Social process theory of emotion: a dynamic systems approach. *Social Development*, **1**, 122–142.

Fogel, A. & Thelen, E. (1987). Development of early expressive and communicative action: reinterpreting the evidence from a dynamic systems perspective. *Developmental Psychology*, **23**, 747–761.

Frijda, N. H. (1986). *The Emotions*. Cambridge: Cambridge University Press.

Frijda, N. H. (1993a). Moods, emotion episodes, and emotions. In M. Lewis & J. M. Haviland (eds), *Handbook of Emotions*. New York: Guilford.

Frijda, N. H. (1993b). The place of appraisal in emotion. *Cognition and Emotion*, **7**, 357–387.

Frijda, N. H., Mesquita, B., Sonnemans, J. & van Goozen, S. (1991). The duration of affective phenomena, or emotions, sentiments and passions. In K. T. Strongman (ed.), *International Review of Studies on Emotion*. New York: Wiley, pp. 187–225.

Haviland, J. M. & Kalbaugh, P. (1993). Emotion and identity processes. In M. Lewis & J. Haviland (eds), *The Handbook of Emotion*. New York: Guilford, pp. 327–338.

Hebb, D. O. (1949). *The Organization of Behavior*. New York: Wiley.

Hermans, H. J. M. (1996). Voicing the self: from information processing to dialogical interchange. Psychological Bulletin, **119**, 31–50.

Izard, C. E. (1977). *Human Emotions*. New York: Plenum.

Izard, C. E. (1984). Emotion–cognition relationships and human development. In C. E. Izard, J. Kagan & R. B. Zajonc (eds), *Emotion, Cognition, and Behavior*. Cambridge: Cambridge University Press, pp. 17–37.

Izard, C. E. & Malatesta, C. (1987). Perspectives on emotional development, I: differential emotions theory of early emotional development. In J. D. Osofsky (ed.), *Handbook of Infant Development*. New York: Wiley, pp. 494–554.

Kagan, J. (1978). On emotion and its development: a working paper. In M. Lewis & L. Rosenblum (eds), *The Development of Effect*. New York: Plenum.

Kagan, J. (1984). *The Nature of the Child*. New York: Basic Books.

Kauffman, S. A. (1993). *The Origins of Order*. New York: Oxford University Press.

Kelso, J. A. S. (1984). Phase transitions and critical behavior in human bimanual coordination. *American Journal of Physiology*, **15**, A1000–A1004.

Killeen, P. R. (1989). Behavior as a trajectory through a field of attractors. In J. R. Brink & C. R. Haden (eds), *The Computer and The Brain: Perspectives on Human and Artificial Intelligence*. Amsterdam: Elsevier.

Lazarus, R. S. (1966). *Psychological Stress and the Coping Process*. New York: McGraw-Hill.

Lazarus, R. S. (1991). *Emotion and Adaptation*. New York: Oxford University Press.

Lewis, M. D. (1995). Cognition–emotion feedback and the self-organization of developmental paths. *Human Development*, **38**, 71–102.

Lewis, M. D. (1996). Self-organising cognitive appraisals. *Cognition and Emotion*, **10**, 1–25.

Lewis, M. D. (1997). Personality self-organization: cascading constraints on cognition–emotion interaction. In A. Fogel, M. C. Lyra & J. Valsiner (eds), *Dynamics and Indeterminism in Developmental and Social Processes*. Mahwah, NJ: Erlbaum.

Lewis, M. D. & Douglas, L. (1998). A dynamic systems approach to cognition–emotion interactions in development. In M. F. Mascolo & S. Griffin (eds), *What Develops in Emotional Development?* New York: Plenum, pp. 159–188.

Lewis, M. D. & Junyk, N. (1997). The self-organization of psychological defenses. In F. Masterpasqua & P. Perna (eds), *The Psychological Meaning of Chaos: Self-organization in Human Development and Psychotherapy*. Washington, DC: American Psychological Association, pp. 41–73.

Magai, C. & McFadden, S. H. (1995). *The Role of Emotions in Social and Personality Development: History, Theory, and Research*. New York: Plenum.

Magai C. & Nusbaum, B. (1996). Personality change in adulthood: dynamic systems, emotions, and the transformed self. In C. Magai & S. H. McFadden (eds), *Handbook of Emotion, Adult Development, and Aging*. San Diego: Academic Press, pp. 403–420.

Malatesta, C. Z. & Wilson, A. (1988). Emotion/cognition interaction in personality development: a discrete emotions, functionalist analysis. *British Journal of Social Psychology*, **27**, 91–112.

Mathews, A. M. (1990). Why worry? The cognitive function of anxiety. *Behaviour Research and Therapy*, **28**, 455–468.

McCulloch, W. & Pitts, W. (1943). A logical calculus of the ideas immanent in nervous activity. *Bulletin of Mathematical Biophysics*, **5**, 115–133.

Nelson, K. (1986). Event knowledge and cognitive development. In K. Nelson (ed.), *Event Knowledge: Structure and Function in Development*. Hillsdale, NJ: Erlbaum, pp. 231–247.

Oatley, K. & Johnson-Laird, P. N. (1987). Towards a cognitive theory of emotions. *Cognition and Emotion*, **1**, 29–50.

Parkinson, B. & Manstead, A. S. R. (1993). Making sense of emotion in stories and social life. *Cognition and Emotion*, **7**, 295–323.

Port, R. F. & van Gelder, T. (1995). *Mind as Motion: Explorations in the Dynamics of Cognition*. Cambridge, MA: MIT Press.

Power, M. J. & Dalgleish, T. (1997). *Cognition and Emotion: From Order to Disorder*. Hove: Psychology Press.

Prigogine, I. & Stengers, I. (1984). *Order Out of Chaos*. New York: Bantam.

Scherer, K. R. (1984). On the nature and function of emotions: a component process approach. In K. R. Scherer & P. Ekman (eds), *Approaches to Emotion*. Hillsdale, NJ: Erlbaum.

Scherer, K. R. (1996). Emotions couple mind–body oscillators. Paper presented at the Biennial Meeting of the International Society for Research on Emotions, Toronto, August.

Shank, R. C. & Abelson, R. P. (1977). *Scripts, Plans, Goals and Understanding*. Hillsdale, NJ: Erlbaum.

Smith, C. A. & Lazarus, R. S. (1990). Emotion and adaptation. In L. A. Pervin (ed.), *Handbook of Personality: Theory and Research*. New York: Guilford, pp. 609–637.

Spitz, R. (1965). *The First Year of Life*. New York: International Universities Press.

Stein, N. L. & Trabasso, T. (1992). The organisation of emotional experience: creating links among emotion, thinking, language, and intentional action. *Cognition and Emotion*, **6**, 225–244.

Sullivan, H. S. (1965). *Personal Psychopathology: Early Formulations*. New York: Norton.

Teasdale, J. D. (1983). Negative thinking in depression: cause, effect, or reciprocal relationship? *Advances in Behaviour Research and Therapy*, **5**, 3–25.

Thelen, E. & Smith, L. B. (1994). *A Dynamic Systems Approach to the Development of Cognition and Action*. Cambridge, MA: Bradford/MIT Press.

Thelen, E. & Ulrich, B. D. (1991). Hidden skills: a dynamic systems analysis of treadmill stepping during the first year. *Monographs of the Society for Research in Child Development*, **56**(1) (Serial No. 223).

Tomkins, S. S. (1984). Affect theory. In K. R. Scherer & P. Ekman (eds), *Approaches to Emotion*. Hillsdale, NJ: Erlbaum.

Tucker, D. M. (1992). Developing emotions and cortical networks. In M. R. Gunnar & C. Nelson (eds), *Minnesota Symposia on Child Psychology. Vol 24, Developmental Behavioral Neuroscience*. Hillsdale, NJ: Erlbaum, pp. 75–128.

Vallacher, R. R. & Nowak, A. (1997). The emergence of dynamical social psychology. *Psychological Inquiry*, **8**, 73–99.

van der Maas, H. L. J. & Molenaar, P. C. M. (1992). Stagewise cognitive development: an application of catastrophe theory. *Psychological Review*, **99**, 395–417.

van Geert, P. (1991). A dynamic systems model of cognitive and language growth. *Psychological Review*, **98**, 3–53.

van Geert, P. (1994). *Dynamic Systems of Development: Change Between Complexity and Chaos*. New York: Prentice Hall/Harvester Wheatsheaf.

Varela, F. J., Thompson, E. & Rosch, E. (1991). *The Embodied Mind: Cognitive Science and Human Experience*. Cambridge, MA: MIT Press.

Von Neumann, J. (1958). *The Computer and the Brain*. New Haven, CT: Yale University Press.

Wright, J. C. & Mischel, W. (1987). A conditional approach to dispositional constructs: the local predictability of social behavior. *Journal of Personality and Social Psychology*, **53**, 1159–1177.

Part V

Applied Issues

Chapter 33

Cognition and Emotion Research and the Practice of Cognitive-behavioural Therapy

Zindel V. Segal
Mark A. Lau
Clarke Institute of Psychiatry, University of Toronto, Ontario,
Canada
and
Paul D. Rokke
Department of Psychology, North Dakota State University, Fargo,
ND, USA

INTRODUCTION

The role of thinking and reasoning in psychotherapy has gained increased legitimacy over the past 30 years. Current therapies' explorations of the particular meanings that patients assign to the events in their lives include information on both cognitive and affective aspects of experience. One of the historical reasons for this change was an expanding interface in the late 1960s and early 70s between basic learning models and complex clinical problems. This led learning based theories of behaviour change to evolve away from simplistic stimulus–response models to frameworks emphasizing cognitive mediation. Bandura's influential work (1969), for example, legitimized the study of cognitive variables such as expectancies, self-verbalizations, predictions and other covert processes

Handbook of Cognition and Emotion. Edited by T. Dalgleish and M. Power.

that had previously been excluded from accounts of human behaviour and learning.

In tandem with this, there was an influx of information from the neurosciences and computer sciences that focused the study of behaviour change on questions of representation, the role of memory in learning and the constructive-processes in perception (Pribram, 1986). Loosely termed the information-processing perspective, this viewpoint emphasized that humans are active and selective seekers, creators and users of information (Mahoney, 1990). Accounts of how people learn which had previously only accepted stimuli, responses and contingencies, started to consider deliberate cognitive activity as consequential. The application of these principles to the treatment of emotional disorders led to the development of different interventions emphasizing patients' thinking and reasoning as legitimate treatment targets, to complement performance-based strategies.

Cognitive therapy is a product of this mediationally based view of behaviour change. It is an intensive, short-term psychotherapy which focuses on how patients make use of the information at hand in arriving at idiosyncratic interpretations and the effects of these views on their emotional experience. Patients are asked to assess and evaluate their thoughts, attitudes and beliefs, especially those accessed in the midst of problematic situations. Many of the interventions in cognitive therapy have as their goal helping patients to "take a step back from" or to "distance themselves from" their thinking so that new information can be considered. A patient with panic disorder, for example, might be asked to monitor what he/she says to him/herself when experiencing sensations such as tingling skin or a racing heart. The patient is encouraged to treat these beliefs as hypotheses and to devise strategies for subjecting these views to empirical confirmation or disconfirmation. In doing so, patients may come to recognize the powerful, but often selective, ways in which they choose to understand these sensations. Once this bias is brought to light, the possibility of addressing these habitual patterns of thinking through explicit cognitive and behavioural interventions is enhanced.

The effectiveness of cognitive therapy has been evaluated in an impressive number of clinical trials (for comprehensive reviews of this literature see Hollon & Najavits, 1988; Hollon, Shelton & Loosen, 1991). Most of these studies have employed clinically diagnosed patient groups and many included a pharmacotherapy comparison group. In general, there is significant empirical support for the application of cognitive therapy to a variety of emotional disorders, particularly the affective disorders, eating disorders, hypochondriasis and somatization difficulties.

While the data on efficacy are encouraging for continued implementation of this approach in the clinic, the mechanisms by which these outcomes are achieved is still unclear. One possibility is that patients receiving CBT might be learning techniques that allow them to directly address cognition–emotion linkages which are relevant to symptom maintenance. In this case it should be possible to demonstrate that the processes which underlie change in cognitive therapy are closely related to those studied in more basic research into the relationship between thinking and feeling. There now exists good support for the notion that dysfunctional thinking in clinical disorders occurs at a number of levels and that different processes may be relevant to each problem. For example, Hollon & Kriss (1984) and others (Ingram, 1990) have suggested looking at cognitive products, processes and operations or structures. In what follows, we adopt this conceptual heuristic division among cognitive variables to illustrate how research in cognition and emotion can be applied to the practice of cognitive-behavioural therapy (CBT).

COGNITIVE PRODUCTS

Cognitive models of psychopathology tend to emphasize the role of dysfunctional thinking patterns in the development and maintenance of emotional disorders. Most typically, these models posit an incrementally cycling interaction among cognition, affect and behaviour. These cycles have been termed "downward spirals" of depression and guilt, or "upward spirals" of anxiety and anger. To illustrate, having the thought "I am hopelessly unattractive" in response to a disappointing social encounter may generate feelings of dysphoria or apathy. In turn, these emotions could stimulate withdrawal, or efforts to avoid situations involving risk-taking and challenge. Ultimately, such behaviour reinforces the plausibility of the original self-disparaging belief.

Cognitively-orientated psychopathologists have identified a number of levels at which dysfunctional thinking may occur (Hollon & Kriss, 1984; Segal, 1988). At the most manifest, symptomatic level are automatic thoughts. These are thoughts or visual images that occur in a seemingly involuntary fashion as part of an individual's ongoing stream of consciousness. They are characterized by: (a) their instantaneous arousal in response to an external stimulus; (b) their unquestioned plausibility to the patient; and (c) the fact that while not always in the patient's focal awareness, they can be detected by shifting attention to how one is interpreting a given situation.

Automatic thoughts contrast with deliberate information processing, which represents a more effortful, normative examination of input information. It is likely that most people rely primarily on automatic information processing much of the time and there is no current reason to presume that those suffering from emotional disorders differ in their propensity to engage in one mode or the other (Hollon & Garber, 1990). Rather, it is the content of automatic thinking that is hypothesized to differ in psychopathology. This section will examine a review of selected, relevant findings related to cognitive content in psychopathology, along with a discussion of how this literature may help elucidate possible change mechanisms that may account for the effectiveness of cognitive therapy.

Content Specificity in Automatic Thinking

The cognitive content-specificity hypothesis, one of the central tenets of the cognitive model, states that every psychological disorder has a distinctive cognitive profile (Beck, 1967; Beck, 1987). Considerable research demonstrates differences of cognitive content between depression and the anxiety disorders. In depression, the content of automatic thoughts is predominantly negative, stressing past losses and failures (Beck, 1967). For example, a depressed individual tends to interpret personally negative experiences as evidence to support the view of oneself as a failure. The cognitive profile in the anxiety disorders, on the other hand, is characterized by future-orientated automatic thoughts about potential physical or psychological threats or danger (Beck & Clark, 1988). For example, the cognitive theory of panic states that recurrent panic attacks result from a tendency to misinterpret benign changes in sensation as indicative of imminent and catastrophic health consequences (Clark, 1988). Studies on the relationship between cognitions and symptoms have verified a specific relationship of thoughts of loss and failure with depressive disorders, symptoms and mood state, while thoughts of harm and danger tend to be more highly associated with anxious symptoms and syndromes (for reviews see Clark & Beck, 1989; Haaga, Dyck & Ernst, 1991).

Research has provided good support for the content specificity hypothesis. In effect, this validates the emphasis that cognitive therapy places on identification and modification of dysfunctional cognitions. Several therapeutic strategies correspond with this unfolding literature. The first occurs during the assessment process, where the therapist identifies and organizes the cognitive patterns that may be contributing to the maintenance of the individual's disorder in order to formulate a treatment plan. The cognitive patterns are derived, in part, by identifying situation-specific cognitions associated with problematic emotional reactions. An "A–B–C" model is used in which affective reactions, at point C, to events, at point A, are seen as being, at least in part, determined by the interpretations made at point B of those events. For example, a patient suffering from panic attacks might reveal upon inquiry that an increase in heart rate was interpreted as, "I must be having a heart attack", and was followed by overwhelming fear.

During therapy, this emphasis is continued as the patient learns to identify and monitor dysfunctional thoughts in problematic situations so as to identify the targets for subsequent evaluation and modification. For example, the patient with recurrent panic attacks learns that a rapid heart rate can be understood as being excited or energized instead of a sign of an impending heart attack. Once the target thoughts have been identified, therapists encourage patients to regard their automatic thoughts as scientific hypotheses that then can be subjected to empirical (rather than strictly logical) examination. For example, the automatic thought "An increase in heart rate means I am having a heart attack" can be empirically tested by designing the appropriate experiment. In this case, the therapist might have the patient test the thought out by having him/her increase his/her heart rate with exercise in the session in order to determine whether his/her automatic thought is true.

Over-general Autobiographical Memory

A second way in which thought content may differ in psychopathology is in the specificity of autobiographical memory. This phenomenon has been studied most thoroughly in depressed individuals (Williams, 1996a). Autobiographical memory in depression is biased in that there are delays in the recall of positive vs. negative events. In addition, depressed individuals are more likely to provide over-general responses which summarize events (e.g. going for walks) rather than by giving specific events (e.g. going for a walk last Tuesday with Bill). This is a robust phenomenon that is found also in suicidal and post-traumatic clients, as well as in parents who have had difficulties controlling their children (Williams, 1996b).

Deficits in personal memories have two important consequences. They impair the reinterpretation of past events. For example, a patient might encode being ignored by someone on the street as "people not bothering with me" or "disliking me". However, an exploration of more specific details might lead to an alternative interpretation of that event. Second, over-general retrieval might impair the generation of alternative means of coping with current problems. Problem solving depends in part on articulating the problem as precisely as possible and generating as many alternative solutions as possible. The use of over-general memory as a database to generate effective solutions would severely restrict this database. In fact, increased difficulty in being specific in memory is correlated with decreased efficacy in problem solving (Evans et al., 1992).

Cognitive therapy addresses this phenomenon in two ways. Thought monitoring is designed in part to ensure an accurate and specific description of events, rather than relying on the patient's recall of what happened in a problematic situation. This record is then followed up in the therapy session, where the patient is further encouraged to provide specific details in response to the therapist's guided questions. Retrieval of specific details may then suggest alternative interpretations of that event.

Rumination

Negative automatic thoughts can also elicit characteristic response styles which serve to maintain psychopathology. This has been shown for the ruminative response style of depression and worry in the anxiety disorders.

Depressed individuals tend to be more self-focused or self-conscious than those who are not depressed (e.g. Ingram & Smith, 1984). Several theorists have argued that the tendency to self-focus, rather than engage in active coping, may influence the course of depression (e.g. Ingram, 1990; Lewinsohn et al., 1985). Specifically, ruminative responses have been shown to lead to longer periods of depressive affect (Morrow & Nolen-Hoeksema, 1990; Nolen-Hoeksema, 1991). While the content of these responses come to resemble negative automatic thoughts as described by Beck et al. (1979), it is the ruminative response style, a pattern of behaviours and thoughts that focus the individual's attention on his/her emotional state, that is thought to maintain dysphoric mood. For example, Morrow & Nolen-Hoeksema (1990) showed that depressed individuals were more depressed when they engaged in a ruminative task than those who engaged in a distracting task. No changes in mood were noted for non-depressed individuals in either condition. These results suggest that rumination can prolong an existing depressed mood but is not inherently depressing.

The tendency to engage in a ruminative response to depression appears to be a stable coping style (Nolen-Hoeksema, Parker & Larson, 1994). Furthermore, a ruminative coping style may lead typical periods of dysphoria to grow into more serious or prolonged depression. For example, recently bereaved adults who became mildly dysphoric after the death of their loved one suffered longer periods of depressed mood if they had a ruminative coping style (Nolen-Hoeksema et al., 1994).

One explanation for how rumination can maintain or exacerbate dysphoria is that it enhances the effects of depressed mood on thinking and interferes with good problem solving. Support for the notion that rumination leads to more negative, biased interpretations of situations, increased pessimism and decreased effectiveness of solutions to interpersonal problems was obtained by Lyubomirsky & Nolen-Hoeksema (1995). These authors investigated the effects of self-focused rumination on interpretations of events and interpersonal problem solving in a series of three studies. Dysphoric and non-dysphoric participants were induced to either ruminatively self-focus on their feelings and personal characteristics or to distract themselves by focusing their attention on thoughts that were focused external to the self. The results of these studies demonstrated that dysphoric participants induced to ruminate: (a) endorsed more negative, biased interpretations of hypothetical situations than dysphoric participants induced to distract themselves from their mood or non-dysphoric participants; (b) were more pessimistic about positive events in their future; (c) generated less effective solutions to interpersonal problems; and (d) offered the most pessimistic explanations for interpersonal problems and hypothetical negative events. In all these studies, dysphoric participants who were distracted were as optimistic and effective in problem solving as non-dysphoric participants.

Nolen-Hoeksema (1991), therefore, proposed that those with ruminative response styles must either be distracted from their ruminative thoughts long enough for their depressed mood to be relieved substantially or to cultivate the belief that they can change the situations thought to contribute to their depressed mood. Teaching one to use pleasant distractions to lift mood before thinking about problems might lead to fewer biased interpretations of problems.

This might also allow the individual to be more effective in overcoming problems and be less pessimistic about the future.

This suggestion is consistent with the use of behavioral intervention strategies like activity scheduling and graded task assignment. These strategies involve working with patients to establish a schedule where patients designate specific time slots for engaging in activities selected to include both pleasure- and mastery-related events. In selecting these tasks, it is important for therapists to attempt to maximize the likelihood of successful completion. This can be done by grading tasks such that patients start with the easiest and then move on to greater challenges. In this way, patients may ultimately succeed at tasks that were previously unattainable. One possibility is that behavioral change may act as an active distraction that can interrupt the vicious cycle of thoughts, which may effect synchronous change at the affective and cognitive levels. In addition, successful completion of these tasks, resulting in mobilization and improvement in mood, may demonstrate to the patient that he/she can change his/her mood with methods other than attempting to develop insight into his/her difficulties.

Worry

The study of self-referent negative rumination in anxiety states, or worry, also suggests that the manner in which individuals deal with worry may serve to maintain symptoms. While both normal and clinical populations experience un-wanted and intrusive thoughts about possible negative outcomes (Rachman, 1982), it is the continuing repetitious nature that distinguishes worry from the short-lived thoughts and images of normal populations. A common response to worry is to attempt to suppress it (Wegner, 1989). However, suppression may in fact lead to continuation of the undesired thought. Empirical research has revealed that suppression generally leads to increases in target thoughts for emotionally neutral material (e.g. Wegner et al., 1987, 1991) as well as emotional material (Roemer & Borkovec, 1994). Furthermore, suppression may also have subsequent negative effects. For example, suppression of thoughts about past traumatic events has been associated with increased illness and subjective distress (Pennebaker, 1989). More generally, suppressing thoughts about a situation leads to increased subjective anxiety about that situation (Roemer & Borkovec, 1994). These authors propose that deliberate suppression may begin a cycle in which the suppressed thought leads to that thought becoming associated with negative emotion (or arousal), which is more likely to be intrusive (Rachman, 1982), which is likely to lead to further attempts to suppress that thought.

Moreover, Roemer & Borkovec (1994) suggest the cycle begun by deliberate suppression can be reversed when repeated exposure to unwanted thoughts leads to habituation and a reduced emotional response to those thoughts. This leads to the thought becoming less intrusive, thereby eliminating any need for suppression. Keeping in mind the discussion in the previous section, it may appear as contradictory to suggest that distraction is better than rumination, but that suppression is worse than repeated exposure. One reason for this is that rumination does not offer exposure to unwanted thoughts in a way that is arousal-reducing. In fact, depressed patients do not see rumination as unwanted. They often view it as a form of focused problem solving which could be potentially helpful, if only they could derive the solution to their problems (Nolen-Hoeksema, 1991). This works against habituation of arousal to the content of worry and maintains the material's emotional significance.

Cognitive therapy utilizes a number of techniques, including thought monitoring, imaginal exposure and thought challenging that facilitate exposure to unwanted thoughts. The first two facilitate exposure to the thoughts by having the patient write them down or talking about them. Thought challenging offers the patient an alternative way to deal with his/her thoughts other than suppressing them. More recent approaches, currently in development, emphasize exposure to fearful images in the worry sequence (Brown, O'Leary & Barlow, 1993).

COGNITIVE PROCESSES

The types of cognitions discussed above are thought to represent the end product of a number of elemental psychological faculties, such as attention, memory and judgment. In the next section we will examine how cognitive therapy interventions impact on these more basic cognitive processes.

Attentional Bias

In the stream of thought processes which ultimately lead to a decision or judgment about oneself or one's behaviour, the first step involves attention, to notice and select those pieces of the available information which are important. In tasks which present words in a tachistoscopic or degraded fashion, depressed and anxious individuals appear to detect negatively valenced words more readily than neutral words and more readily than individuals in a euthymic mood state (Powell & Hemsley, 1984; Foa & McNally, 1986). Use of the emotional Stroop task has shown that anxious individuals have longer color-naming latencies for threat-related words (Mathews & MacLeod, 1985; Hope et al., 1990; Foa et al., 1991). Likewise, depressed individuals also have slower responses to depression-related words in comparison to neutral stimuli (Gotlib & McCann, 1984; Williams & Nulty, 1986).

Although many of these studies suggest biases in attention, the exact nature of the attentional problems have not been determined. Preferential attention to some information may result from biased searching strategies. Alternatively, bias could result from the inability to inhibit attention to the target stimuli. In a unique study of visual attention, Mathews & Antes (1992) tracked eye movements while mildly depressed subjects viewed a series of pictures with both happy and sad content. They found that, like non-depressed persons, depressed participants fixated happy regions significantly sooner, more often, and longer than they fixated sad regions. However, depressed participants fixated sad regions significantly more often than the non-depressed. Gotlib, McLachlan & Katz (1988) also did not find a bias favouring attention to negative information in depression, but rather that normal mood was associated with a bias toward attending to positive stimuli. In both of these cases, it could be argued that depression is associated with an inability to maintain a focus on positive information. While it appears that anxiety is associated with selective attention to negative information, and thus subject to an encoding bias, the research on depression is more mixed (Mathews & MacLeod, 1994).

Memory Bias

The processing of attended information, either for making a current decision or for committing it to memory for later retrieval, depends on the effortful and efficient use of limited attentional resources. Models of working memory have been proposed which allow for the separation of various components of the complex process of keeping some information in mind, while retrieving other information from memory, or manipulating parts of the information (e.g. summing, comparing, organizing), in order to perform the task at hand (Baddeley, 1992; Salthouse, 1990). These models have also been applied to the study of anxiety and depression.

In the case of anxiety, it has been observed that task performance often suffers to the extent that the task is complex and has high attentional demands. Some have suggested that performance decrements are due to increased worrying, which reduces task-related storage and processing capacity (Humphreys & Revelle, 1984; Sarason, 1988). Eysenck & Calvo (1992) have proposed some refinements to this perspective. They suggest that worry also serves a motivational function. In order to avoid the aversive consequences of poor performance, anxious individuals will increase their effort and may initiate other cognitive strategies. Thus, depending on the task and the individual, performance outcomes may not be impaired, but processing efficiency (considering the amount of effort relative to the outcome) will be lowered. This perspective may also help distinguish between anxious and depressive states. Depression also involves worry and, thus, may reduce processing capacity. However, depression may not be associated with the same motivation to avoid negative consequences, since affects of failure and hopelessness are expected to occur (Andersen, Spielman & Bargh, 1992; Beck, 1967). Depression may impair processing effort and efficiency as well as impede the use of alternative cognitive strategies (Hertel & Rude, 1991).

Different approaches have been taken to investigate the potential limitations in processing resources associated with depression. Following Kahneman (1973) and Hasher & Zacks (1979), some investigators have reasoned that it should be possible to demonstrate limitations in attentional capacity by varying the amount of effort required to process the information to be retained and remembered. Automatic processing tasks that do not require attention should not yield memory deficits in depression, whereas effortful tasks should reveal deficits as they demand increasing amounts of attention. In a review of this literature, Hartlage et al. (1993) concluded that depression does not interfere with automatic processing, but that performance on effortful tasks decreases with increases in effort required and with severity of depression.

Ellis & Ashbrook (1988) proposed a resource allocation model of depression in which they suggested that attentional capacity should be reduced in depression primarily because depressed individuals ruminate about their sad state, often do not put forth the required cognitive effort to actively process or encode task-related information, and are often engaged in processing irrelevant features of the task as well as information unrelated to the task at hand. In a limited capacity system, each of these activities will reduce the attentional resources available to devote to the criterion task.

In a series of studies, Ellis and his colleagues have found that, following a depressing mood induction, participants have poorer recall, especially on tasks requiring high effort, than those in a neutral mood condition (Ellis, Thomas & Rodriguez, 1984). They have also found that those undergoing a mood induction procedure (happy or sad) reported a higher proportion of task-irrelevant thoughts than those undergoing a neutral mood induction procedure (Seibert & Ellis, 1991). In this study, amount of irrelevant thinking was negatively correlated with recall performance.

Hertel and her colleagues have taken a slightly different approach to this problem (Hertel & Hardin, 1990; Hertel & Rude, 1991). They have shown that either providing retrieval strategies during recognition, or directing attention during learning, eliminated memory differences between depressed and non-depressed participants. They have argued that, since recall performance is the same under some conditions, depression may not fundamentally reduce attentional resources but rather may impair the manner in which those resources are used. They suggest that depression is associated with a deficit in initiating useful encoding and retrieval strategies.

There is a considerable literature on memory deficits associated with depression (Burt, Zembar & Niederehe, 1995; Johnson & Magaro, 1987; Mathews & MacLeod, 1994). Although the results have been less than consistent, there are enough studies which report recall differences that investigators have begun to look for potential explanations of these differences, i.e. when and why do they occur? Again, several different processes and different theories have been proposed. In addition to impairments in memory that may be produced by deficient or biased encoding strategies (Ellis & Ashbrook, 1988; Hertel & Rude, 1991), recall is likely to be affected by the mood state associated with learning and the mood state present at recall, especially if the information is autobiographical in nature (Bower, 1991; Ellis & Moore, 1997). Teasdale, for example, has shown that the ease and likelihood of recalling either pleasant or unpleasant memories depends on the current mood state, e.g. depression makes the recall of extremely unhappy memories more probable (Teasdale & Fogarty, 1979; Teasdale & Taylor, 1981; Teasdale, Taylor & Fogarty, 1980).

In summary, basic cognitive research has suggested that negative mood states are likely to lead to biases in attention, less efficient processing of information, and poorer memory for mood-incongruent information, or perhaps selective memory for mood-congruent information. These findings map onto clinical phenomena very well. Impairments in attention, concentration and memory are frequent complaints of those suffering from anxiety disorders and depression.

Clinical observations are full of examples of the ways in which reported events and their interpretations appear to be negatively biased. As in the laboratory (e.g. Bargh & Tota, 1988; Gotlib, McLachlan & Katz, 1988; Mogg et al., 1991), patients often report negative perspectives to their therapists in a fashion that is automatic and apparently without an awareness that there might be alternative points of view. Much of the work in CBT is designed to break the automaticity of negative thoughts and assumptions.

For example, treatments for anxiety and depression often begin with assignments for self-monitoring of critical events (Beck et al., 1979; Beck & Emery, 1985). The act of writing down thoughts associated with changes in mood can serve several purposes. When done in a systematic fashion, this can help counteract the assumed biases in information gathering. Monitoring can direct attention to the positive events that do occur, helps to avoid recall biases often present in retrospective reports, and can provide a more accurate and complete picture for therapist and client. The act of writing down one's thoughts when experiencing negative emotions may help to slow down the process of thinking about and evaluating circumstances. The automatic, habitual pattern of assumptions and interpretations that lead to and maintain negative mood states may be interrupted. Self-monitoring can provide useful assessment data for the therapist and client. Monitoring records help to identify the particular thoughts (specific content and erroneous decision heuristics) which lead to negative emotional consequences. The monitoring of variations in mood and cognition can also serve to reinforce the rationale and credibility of CBT by providing a first-hand demonstration of the correspondence between one's mood and interpretation of events.

Another technique which can be interpreted in light of cognitive research is activity scheduling. A patient is encouraged to schedule and engage in simple time-limited activities which are enjoyable and diverting. To the extent that these activities are pleasant and lead to positive variations in mood, positive memories and adaptive associations are likely to be more available. This would facilitate efforts to consider alternative perspectives and encourage active coping.

In addition, successfully engaging in a pleasant activity may serve to enhance one's expectancies for change. For example, anxiety and depression are often associated with poor social skill performance or performance on cognitive tasks. However, the deficits are often due to avoidance or lack of initiation rather than lack of competence. Encouragement to engage in a well-specified, time-limited activity which is under the control of the patient and has a high probability for successful outcomes can also provide strong experiential evidence to bolster a sense of self-competence and weaken expectations of failure or harm.

Many of the effective therapies for depression (Beck et al., 1979; Lewinsohn et al., 1984; Rehm & Rokke, 1988) are highly structured and directive in nature. This structure may play an important role in their effectiveness. To the extent that negative moods are made more probable and maintained by inefficient and unsuccessful coping, structure and direction may help to organize cognitive effort. Written homework assignments, to be completed on a schedule with built-in prompts and reminders, help redirect attention and initiate systematic problem-solving attempts. Activities which lead to mastery and pleasure (Beck et al., 1979) or self-reinforcement (Rehm, 1977) serve to supply motivation for counteracting tendencies for withdrawal, avoidance or low effort.

Cognitive therapeutic techniques, such as consequential analysis (examining the possible consequences of thinking or feeling certain thoughts), reattribution (generating alternative causal explanations to negative events), cost–benefit analysis (enumerating and comparing pros and cons of maintaining certain beliefs and behaviour patterns) and instruction in problem-solving strategies may all serve to make information processing more efficient and emotionally beneficial. These techniques help to redirect attention away from self-focused worries and rumination, organize information into balanced and meaningful units, and provide strategies, which depressed patients are unlikely to initiate on their own, for approaching problem solving in a more productive fashion.

COGNITIVE STRUCTURES OR ORGANIZATIONS

Changes at the level of automatic thoughts and cognitive distortions can effect rapid and marked symptomatic improvement. However, remission is likely to be short-lived where therapy has failed to address the enduring beliefs, rules and attitudes that underlie the patient's emotional disturbance (Williams et al., 1990). One approach to describing these cognitive organizations is the schema model proposed by Beck (1967), in which self-schemas comprise a highly organized network of stored personal information. Self-schemas are responsible for the selective encoding and retrieval of information which is congruent with the current mood state, by providing contextual cues that result in the activation of mood-congruent memories. Schemas make it more likely that information, especially if it is ambiguous, is interpreted in manner which is consistent with current beliefs and expectations (Derry & Kuiper, 1981; Segal, 1988). In the case of depression, the activation of negative self-schemas, judgments about oneself and one's relations to others are likely to be made in a decidedly biased fashion. Furthermore, because negative information is more readily available and accessible, recalled negative instances will be judged to be more representative of all instances, and opinions are not adjusted to fit new information, but rather are given over completely to expected negative initial impressions (cf. Kahneman, Slovic & Tversky, 1982).

Schema-congruent Processing Biases

Among the earliest attempts to measure the operation of knowledge structures in a clinical context was a self-report measure, the Dysfunctional Attitude Scale (DAS; Weissman & Beck, 1978), designed to assess the rigid, absolutistic standards for self-worth thought to represent an important component of depressive self-schemas. DAS items are stated such that self-worth and happiness are contingent upon meeting unrealistic standards of interpersonal approval (e.g. "I am nothing if a person I love doesn't love me") and perfectionistic standards of achievement (e.g. "If I fail partly, it is as bad as being a complete failure"). The question of whether dysfunctional attitudes represent a stable self-schema component or, alternately, another cognitive manifestation (i.e. product) of depression, has generated a good deal of controversy in the cognitive literature. The latter position is supported by studies showing that dysfunctional attitudes correlate with depression (e.g. Dobson & Shaw, 1986), but do not distinguish between individuals who will go on to become depressed and those who will not (Lewinsohn et al., 1981) or between recovered depressives and normals (Hamilton & Abramson, 1983). More recent work, however (Miranda & Persons, 1988; Segal, Gemar & Williams, 1997), indicates that individuals prone to developing depressive symptoms do obtain higher DAS scores, but only in the presence of a negative mood. These findings suggest that transient negative mood states may serve to prime negative self-schemas, thereby increasing the accessibility of dysfunctional attitudes.

Self-scenarios

Another self-report-based approach to assessing self-schemas, or more particularly schematic change over the course of treatment, involves the use of self-scenarios (Muran & Segal, 1994). Self-scenarios are vignettes which are ideographically constructed for each subject by expert observers on the basis of assessment interviews. Each vignette presents a stimulus situation which the subject typically finds distressing (e.g. being in a social setting). In addition, the scenarios include several other components thought to reflect the content of the self-schema: a cognitive response (e.g. "I wonder if others like me"), an affective response (e.g. "I feel anxious") and a motoric response (e.g. "I withdraw"). Subjects, their therapists and independent observers all rate the clinical relevance, or "goodness of fit" of each scenario (and its components).

Subjects then rate the two most relevant scenarios on eight dimensions: frequency, preoccupation, accessibility, alternatives, self-efficacy, self-view, interpersonal view and chronicity. These ratings can be interpreted as a baseline schematic measure against which to compare subsequent weekly ratings and can serve as an indirect measure of the extent to which treatment is altering the patient's view of self as defined by the scenarios being rated. Utilizing a repeated single-subject design, Muran & Segal (1994) analysed data from eight cases and found that patient ratings of relevant scenarios across treatment were significantly associated with outcome in short-term CBT.

Experimental evidence for schema-driven processing comes from a variety of sources, most of which have adopted measures from cognitive psychology or social cognition to the study of emotional disorders.

The Self-referent Encoding Task (SRET) (Derry & Kuiper, 1981)

This is an adaptation of a laboratory paradigm, originally developed by cognitive psychologists to test a "levels-of-processing" model of memory (Craik & Tulving, 1975). In the SRET, subjects are serially presented with a number of personal adjectives (positive and negative) and asked to decide, in a categorical fashion (i.e. yes or no), whether the adjective is self-descriptive. After all the adjectives have been rated, an incidental recall test is administered.

The SRET yields several schema-related measures. First, the number of positive and negative words rated as self-descriptive may provide an index of the relative proportion of negative and positive information stored in the self-schema. Consistent with schema-based models of depression, empirical work suggests that depressed subjects endorse more negative adjectives than do non-depressed controls, who tend to rate more positive adjectives as self-descriptive (MacDonald & Kuiper, 1984).

A second, and certainly less transparent, index of schematic processing relates to the time required for subjects to make their "yes–no" judgments. Theoretically, schemas are thought to facilitate the processing of schema-congruent information. As such, individuals with self-schemas comprising predominantly negative information should exhibit enhanced processing of negative adjectives. This notion is supported in SRET studies, demonstrating quicker rating times by non-depressed subjects for positive adjectives (Kuiper & MacDonald, 1982) and by depressed subjects for negative adjectives (MacDonald & Kuiper, 1984).

The third self-schema measure yielded by the SRET relates to incidental recall. Specifically, schema-congruent information ought to be processed at a relatively deep level, and, according to the levels of processing model, should be better recalled. Consistent with this notion, depressed subjects have been shown to recall more negative adjectives following the SRET, whereas non-depressives recall more positive ones (Derry & Kuiper, 1981).

Taken together, results from studies employing the SRET provide evidence for the operation of a negative self-schema in depression. Moreover, they suggest that the SRET may represent a useful strategy for mapping out the parameters of this cognitive structure. More recently, however, the SRET's validity as a measure of self-schema content and function has been questioned (see Segal, 1988). One of the more serious concerns, for example, relates to the possibility that the depression-related differences outlined above may reflect mood congruency effects rather than structural differences.

The Stroop Color-naming Paradigm

Another approach to the measurement of negative self-schemas, also borrowed from cognitive psychology, is the Stroop color-word test (Stroop, 1935). In this task, subjects are asked to name the color of the ink in which a stimulus word is presented, while attempting to ignore the meaning of the word itself. Longer latencies are thought to reflect the greater effort required to suppress the meaning of highly accessible or salient stimulus words—such as those congruent with the content of the self-schema. Conversely then, the content of the self-schema can be inferred by noting the stimulus words associated with longer latencies.

There have been numerous studies measuring Stroop-based interference in anxiety disorders, since it is hypothesized that anxious individuals have "danger" or "threat" schemas (Beck & Emery, 1985). This should produce an attentional bias for threat stimuli, leading to longer color-naming latencies for threat words relative to neutral words. That is, the meaning of the threat word should interfere with the primary task of color naming.

In the original demonstration of the effect, Mathews & MacLeod (1985) applied the modified Stroop color-naming paradigm to investigate selective processing of words related to social and physical threat with generalized anxiety disorder (GAD) patients. They found that GAD patients, relative to normal control subjects, evidenced greater interference for threat-related words than for neutral words. Moreover, although anxious subjects showed interference effects with social threat words, only those with physical concerns were equally disrupted by physical threat words. Accordingly, the bias for selective processing of threat information seems specific to a particular threat and not to threatening information in general.

Evidence of Stroop interference for threat has been found in all the anxiety disorders. In each case, patients have evidenced delayed color-naming for disorder-specific, threat-related words (e.g. in patients with simple phobia, Lavy, van den Hout & Arntz, 1993; social phobia, Hope et al., 1990; OCD, Foa et al., 1993; panic disorder, Ehlers et al., 1988; and PTSD, Thrasher, Dalgleish & Yule, 1994).

Turning to depression, evidence for the schematic organization of negative self-referent constructs obtains from the use of a modified version of the Stroop task in which the target words to be color named were primed by preceding presentations of either unrelated words or by other self-descriptive words. Segal et al. (1995) reasoned that, if self-representations are organized schematically, then self-descriptive primes should activate related self-referent information, thereby increasing the meaning of the target word and leading to even longer color-naming latencies for that information. Segal et al. (1995) reported longer latencies when the prime and the stimulus word were both self-descriptive. These results support the notion that self-referent information may be clustered or interrelated (i.e. schematically) to a greater degree than information that is not self-descriptive.

Cognitive Treatment Strategies Targeting Schematic Change

The best description of interventions used in facilitating change at the level of schematic organization comes from the work on cognitive therapy for personality disorders (Beck et al., 1990). It should be noted, however, that data on the efficacy of these procedures comes largely from anecdotal sources and, as explanations of how these effects are achieved, lack the specificity associated with descriptions of change in CBT for Axis 1 disorders. A common goal for all these strategies is to weaken the patient's belief that negative schemas are absolutely true and to work towards the construction of alternative schemas, so that the patient can become aware of and draw upon other available information which may disconfirm his/her pre-existing expectations (Padesky, 1994).

Rule-breaking Experiments

Dysfunctional schemas are commonly articulated in the form of general rules (e.g. "To be average is to be a nobody"; "People will reject you if you make a mistake"). Unfortunately, patients rarely, if ever, expose themselves to the possibility of disconfirming evidence. One way of addressing these beliefs is to design experiments in which patients deliberately seek out opportunities to break these fundamental rules, and note the outcomes. For example, an experiment might be designed to test a perfectionistic belief that being average leads to mediocrity and rejection. The patient could be asked to make an effort to be as average as possible for a given period of time (e.g. 1 week). Patients typically discover, contrary to expectation, that this experience has no untoward effects; and, once unburdened of the pressure to be perfect, may even find it enjoyable. The ultimate goal, of course, is to weaken core beliefs by providing evidence that does not support the perfectionism schema. Once enough instances of disconfirming evidence have been stored in memory, it is possible for patients to draw on these experiences as a way of facilitating more adaptive interpretations of events. According to construct accessibility theory (Higgins & Bargh, 1987), the more frequently this new information is utilized, the more accessible and interconnected with other networks it will become. Rule-breaking experiments, therefore, allow the patient to gather enough examples of counter-schematic behaviour to facilitate a novel cognitive organization of self-referent information.

Cost–Benefit Analysis

As core dysfunctional beliefs are identified and challenged, therapists may be surprised to discover that patients can be reluctant to give them up. Often, this persistence is due to the fact that the beliefs or rules have served a self-protective function, or provided patients with some important benefits. To illustrate, perfectionistic core beliefs (e.g. "If you can't do something perfectly, then don't bother doing it at all") can motivate impressive achievements. Patients are often loath to tamper with such beliefs, fearing that doing so may result in mediocrity or failure. In such cases, the costs and the benefits of maintaining such a belief system can be enumerated and compared.

Techniques such as this serve an elaborative function for information within the newly formed schema. Elaboration plays an important role in the establishment of new knowledge structures, as it enables the activation of related representations or units within a network which can lead to new relationships being formed between previously unconnected elements (Williams et al., 1988). Once this is achieved, there will be more competition within the system and the activation of earlier schematic elements may becomes less automatic over time.

Continuum Work

The use of continua is an additional way for patients to actively construct new elements of meaning, which can then be rehearsed and integrated into a new self-representation or schema. Because negative schemas tend to be dichotomous in nature, asking patients to rate how much they believe a certain view of themselves can be helpful as a way of introducing the notion of relativity into their thinking (Padesky & Greenberger, 1995). This provides patients with an additional standpoint from which to evaluate more automatic, and schema-driven, meanings and can prevent them from endorsing these views if an alternative graded interpretation can be constructed. For example, in accepting the view "I am a total failure" vs. stopping and asking oneself how much one believes this to be true, even a rating of 80–90% true still leaves open the possibility of an alternative construal. Once again, construct accessibility theory would predict that the more frequently an alternative construal is considered, the more this could weaken the automatic activation of the earlier schema.

Adopting a graduated approach to the evaluation of experiences also helps patients to synchronize the rate at which change is occurring in their lives and the time needed for the consolidation of a new self-view, estimated by Padesky & Greenberger (1995) as taking 6 months or longer.

CONCLUSIONS

Cognitive therapy is premised on a theoretical model which posits a reciprocally escalating relationship between affect and cognition. The application of this framework to the amelioration of emotional disorders entails examining the type of cognitive mediation underlying the production and maintenance of dysfunctional affects. Some of the more evident points of contact between basic research in cognition and emotion and cognitive therapy can be found in: (a) the reliance on cognitive models of emotion to account for dysphoric mood states; (b) the prominent role of schema theory in explaining the self-perpetuating nature of maladaptive self-representations, especially in the face of disconfirmatory evidence; (c) the distinction between effortful and automatic cognitive processing; and (d) the use of a semantic network model to describe how changes in activation levels for earlier and newly constructed views of self can be achieved. While many of the standard interventions used in cognitive therapy draw heavily upon these principles, it is less clear whether the outcomes from the use of these methods impact on the basic research domains from which they are derived. Perhaps with time, and with the continued demonstration of cognitive therapy's empirical efficacy, researchers working in the area of cognition and emotion will come to consider the clinical context as offering a naturalistic laboratory for the experimental study of change in these two basic human faculties.

REFERENCES

Andersen, S. M., Spielman, L. A. & Bargh, J. A. (1992). Future-event schemas and certainty about the future: automaticity in depressives' future-event predictions. *Journal of Personality and Social Psychology*, **63**, 711–723.

Baddely, A. (1992). Working memory. *Science*, **255**, 556–559.

Bandura, A (1969). *Principles of Behavior Modification*. New York: Holt, Rinehart and Winston.

Bargh, J. A. & Tota, M. E. (1988). Context-dependent automatic processing in depression: accessibility of negative constructs with regard to self but not to others. *Journal of Personality and Social Psychology*, **54**, 925–939.

Beck, A. T. (1967). *Depression: Clinical, Experimental and Theoretical Aspects*. New York: Harper & Row.

Beck, A. T. (1987). Cognitive models of depression. *Journal of Cognitive Psychotherapy*, **1**, 2–27.

Beck, A. T. & Clark, D. A. (1988). Anxiety and depression: an information processing perspective. *Anxiety Research*, **1**, 23–36.

Beck, A. T. & Emery, G. (1985). *Anxiety Disorders and Phobias*. New York: Basic Books.

Beck, A. T., Freeman, A. et al. (1990). *Cognitive Therapy of Personality Disorders*. New York: Guilford.

Beck, A. T., Rush, A. J., Shaw, B. F. & Emery, G. (1979). *Cognitive Therapy of Depression*. New York: Guilford.

Bower, G. H. (1981). Mood and memory. *American Psychologist*, **36**, 129–148.

Brown, T., O'Leary, T. & Barlow, D. (1993). Generalized anxiety disorder. In D. Barlow (ed.), *Clinical Handbook of Psychological Disorders*, 2nd edn. New York: Guilford, pp. 137–188.

Burt, D. B., Zembar, M. J. & Niederehe, G. (1995). Depression and memory impairment: a meta-analysis of the association, its pattern, and specificity. *Psychological Bulletin*, **117**, 285–305.

Clark, D. A. & Beck, A. T. (1989). Cognitive theory and therapy of anxiety and depression. In P. C. Kendall & D. Watson (eds), *Anxiety and Depression: Distinctive and Overlapping Features*. San Diego, CA: Academic Press, pp. 379–411.

Clark, D. M. (1988). A cognitive model of panic. In S. J. Rachman & J. Maser (eds), *Panic: Psychological Perspectives*. Hillsdale, NJ: Erlbaum.

Craik, F. I. M. & Tulving, E. (1975). Depths of processing and the retention of words in episodic memory. *Journal of Experimental Psychology General*, **104**, 268–294.

Derry, P. A. & Kuiper, N. A. (1981). Schematic processing and self-reference in clinical depression. *Journal of Abnormal Psychology*, **90**, 286–297.

Dobson, K. S. & Shaw, B. F. (1986). Cognitive assessment with major depressive disorders. *Cognitive Therapy and Research*, **10**, 13–29.

Ehlers, A., Margraf, J., Davies, S. & Roth, W. T. (1988). Selective processing of threat cues in subjects with panic attacks. *Cognition and Emotion*, **2**, 201–219.

Ellis, H. C. & Ashbrook, P. W. (1988). Resource allocation model of the effects of depressed mood states on memory. In K. Fiedler & J. Forgas (eds), *Affect, Cognition and Social Behavior*. Toronto: Hogrefe.

Ellis, H. C., Thomas, R. L. & Rodriguez, I. A. (1984). Emotional mood states and memory: elaborative encoding, semantic processing, and cognitive effort. *Journal of Experimental Psychology: Learning, Memory, and Cognition*, **10**, 470–482.

Ellis, H. C. & Moore, B. A. (1997). Mood and memory. In T. Dalgleish & M. Power (eds), *The Handbook of Cognition and Emotion*. Chichester: Wiley.

Evans, J., Williams, J. M. G., O'Loughlin, S. & Howells, K. (1992). Autobiographical memory and problem solving strategies of parasuicide patients. *Psychological Medicine*, **22**, 399–405.

Eysenck, M. W. & Calvo, M. G. (1992). Anxiety and performance: the processing efficiency theory. *Cognition and Emotion*, **6**, 409–434.

Foa, E. B., Feske, U., Murdock, T. B., Kozak, M. J. & McCarthy, P. R. (1991). Processing of threat-related information in rape victims. *Journal of Abnormal Psychology*, **100**, 156–162.

Foa, E. B., Ilai, D., McCarthy, P. R., Shoyer, B. & Murdock, T. (1993). Information processing in obsessive-compulsive disorder. *Cognitive Therapy and Research*, **17**, 173–189.

Foa, E. B. & McNally, R. J. (1986). Sensitivity to feared stimuli in obsessive-compulsives: a dichotic listening analysis. *Cognitive Therapy and Research*, **10**, 477–486.

Gotlib, I. H. & McCann, C. D. (1984). Construct accessibility and depression: an examination of cognitive and affective factors. *Journal of Personality and Social Psychology*, **47**, 427–439.

Gotlib, I. H., McLachlan, A. L. & Katz, A. N. (1988). Biases in visual attention in depressed and non-depressed individuals. *Cognition and Emotion*, **2**, 185–200.

Haaga, D. A., Dyck, M. J. & Ernst, D. (1991). Empirical status of cognitive theory of depression. *Psychological Bulletin*, **110**, 215–236.

Hamilton, E. W. & Abramson, L. Y. (1983). Cognitive patterns and major depressive disorder: a longitudinal study in a hospital setting. *Journal of Abnormal Psychology*, **92**, 173–184.

Hartlage, S., Alloy, L. B., Vasquez, C. & Dykman, B. (1993). Automatic and effortful processing in depression. *Psychological Bulletin*, **113**, 247–278.

Hasher, L. & Zacks, R. (1979). Automatic and effortful processes in memory. *Journal of Experimental Psychology: General*, **108**, 356–388.

Hertel, P. T. & Hardin, T. S. (1990). Remembering with and without awareness in a depressed mood: evidence of deficits in initiative. *Journal of Experimental Psychology: General*, **119**, 45–59.

Hertel, P. T. & Rude, S. S. (1991). Depressive deficits in memory: focusing attention improves subsequent recall. *Journal of Experimental Psychology: General*, **120**, 301–309.

Higgins, E. T. & Bargh, J. A. (1987). Social cognition and social perception. *Annual Review of Psychology*, **38**, 369–425.

Hollon, S. D. & Garber, J. (1990). Cognitive therapy for depression: a social cognitive perspective. *Personality and Social Psychology Bulletin*, **16**, 58–73.

Hollon, S. D. & Kriss, M. R. (1984). Cognitive factors in clinical research and practice. *Clinical Psychology Review*, **4**, 35–76.

Hollon, S. D. & Najavits, L. (1988). Review of empirical studies on cognitive therapy. In A. Francs & R. Hales (eds), *Annual Review of Psychiatry*, Vol. 7. Washington, DC: American Psychiatric Press, pp. 643–666.

Hollon, S. D., Shelton, R. C. & Loosen, P. T. (1991). Cognitive and pharmacotherapy for depression. *Journal of Consulting and Clinical Psychology*, **59**, 88–99.

Hope, D. A., Rapee, R. M., Heimberg, R. G. & Dombeck, M. J. (1990). Representations of the self in social phobia: vulnerability to social threat. *Cognitive Therapy and Research*, **14**, 177–189.

Humphreys, M. S. & Revelle, W. (1984). Personality, motivation, and performance: a theory of the relationship between individual differences and information processing. *Psychological Review*, **91**, 153–184.

Ingram, R. E. (1990). Self-focused attention in clinical disorders: review and a conceptual model. *Psychological Bulletin*, **109**, 156–176.

Ingram, R. E. & Smith, T. W. (1984). Depression and internal versus external locus of attention. *Cognitive Therapy and Research*, **8**, 139–152.

Johnson, M. H. & Magaro, P. A. (1987). Effects of mood and severity on memory processes in depression and mania. *Psychological Bulletin*, **101**, 28–40.

Kahneman, D. (1973). *Attention and Effort*. Englewood Cliffs, NJ: Prentice-Hall.

Kahneman, D., Slovic, P. & Tversky, A. (eds) (1982). *Judgment under Uncertainty: Heuristics and Biases*. Cambridge: Cambridge University Press.

Lavy, E., van den Hout, M. & Arntz, A. (1993). Attentional bias and spider phobia: conceptual and clinical issues. *Behaviour Research and Therapy*, **31**, 17–24.

Lewinsohn, P. M., Antonuccio, D. O., Steinmetz, J. L. & Teri, L. (1984). *The Coping with Depression Course*. Eugene, OR: Castalia.

Lewinsohn, P. M., Hoberman, H., Teri, L. & Hautzinger, M. (1985). An integrative theory of depression. In S. Reiss & R. Bootzin (eds), *Theoretical Issues in Behavior Therapy*. New York: Academic Press, pp. 331–359.

Lewinsohn, P. M., Steinmetz, J. L., Larson, D. W. & Franklin, J. (1981). Depression-related cognitions: antecedent or consequence? *Journal of Abnormal Psychology*, **90**, 213–219.

Lyubomirsky, S. & Nolen-Hoeksema, S. (1995). Effects of self-focused rumination on negative thinking and interpersonal problem solving. *Journal of Personality and Social Psychology*, **69**, 176–190.

Kuiper, N. A. & MacDonald, M. R. (1982). Self and other perception in mild depressives. *Social Cognition*, **1**, 223–239.

MacDonald, M. R. & Kuiper, N. A. (1984). Self-schema decision consistency in clinical depressives. *Journal of Social and Clinical Psychology*, **2**, 264–272.

Mahoney, M. J. (1990). *Human Change Processes*. New York: Basic Books.

Mathews, A. M. & MacLeod, C. (1985). Selective processing of threat cues in anxiety states. *Behaviour Research and Therapy*, **23**, 563–569.

Mathews, A. & MacLeod, C. (1994). Cognitive approaches to emotion and emotional disorders. *Annual Review of Psychology*, **45**, 25–50.

Mathews, G. R. & Antes, J. R. (1992). Visual attention and depression: cognitive biases in the eye fixations of the dysphoric and the non-depressed. *Cognitive Therapy and Research*, **16**, 359–371.

Miranda, J. & Persons, J. B. (1988).   Dysfunctional attitudes are mood-state dependent. *Journal of Abnormal Psychology*, **97**, 76–79.

Mogg, K., Mathews, A. M., Eysenck, M. & May, J. (1991).   Biased cognitive operations in anxiety: artefact, processing priorities or attentional search? *Behaviour Research and Therapy*, **29**, 459–467.

Morrow, J. & Nolen-Hoeksema, S. (1990).   Effects of responses to depression on the remediation of depressive affect. *Journal of Personality and Social Psychology*, **58**, 519–527.

Muran, J. C. & Segal, Z. V. (1994).   Self-scenarios as a repeated measures outcome measurement of self-schemas in short-term cognitive therapy. *Behavior Therapy*, **25**, 255–274.

Nolen-Hoeksema, S. (1991).   Responses to depression and their effects on the duration of depressive episodes. *Journal of Abnormal Psychology*, **100**, 569–582.

Nolen-Hoeksema, S., Parker, L. & Larson, J. (1994).   Ruminative coping with depressed mood following loss. *Journal of Personality and Social Psychology*, **67**, 92–104.

Padesky, C. (1994).   Schema change processes in cognitive therapy. *Clinical Psychology and Psychotherapy*, **1**, 267–278.

Padesky, C. & Greenberger, D. (1995).   *Clinician's Guide to Mind over Mood*. New York: Guilford.

Pennebaker, J. W. (1989).   Confession, inhibition and disease. *Advances in Experimental Social Psychology*, **22**, 211–244.

Powell, M. & Hemsley, D. R. (1984).   Depression: a breakdown of perceptual defence? *British Journal of Psychiatry*, **145**, 358–362.

Pribram, K. H. (1986).   The cognitive revolution and mind/brain issues. *American Psychologist*, **41**, 507–520.

Rachman, S. (1982).   Part I. Unwanted intrusive cognitions. *Advances in Behaviour Research & Therapy*, **3**, 89–99.

Rehm, L. P. (1977).   A self-control model of depression. *Behavior Therapy*, **8**, 787–804.

Rehm, L. P. & Rokke, P. (1988).   Self-management therapies. In K. S. Dobson (ed.), *Handbook of Cognitive-behavioral Therapies*. New York: Guilford, pp. 136–166.

Roemer, L. & Borkovec, T. D. (1994).   Effects of suppressing thoughts about emotional material. *Journal of Abnormal Psychology*, **103**, 467–474.

Salthouse, T. A. (1990).   Working memory as a processing resource in cognitive aging. *Developmental Review*, **10**, 101–124.

Sarason, I. G. (1988).   Anxiety, self-preoccupation and attention. *Anxiety Research*, **1**, 3–7.

Segal, Z. V. (1988).   Appraisal of the self-schemata construct in cognitive models of depression. *Psychological Bulletin*, **103**, 147–162.

Segal, Z. V., Gemar, M., Truchon, C., Guirguis, M. & Horowitz, L. (1995).   A priming methodology for studying self-representation in major depressive disorder. *Journal of Abnormal Psychology*, **104**, 205–213.

Segal, Z. V., Gemar, M. & Williams, S. (in press).   Differential cognitive effects to a mood challenge following response to either cognitive therapy or pharmacotherapy for unipolar depression, *Journal of Abnormal Psychology*.

Seibert, P. S. & Ellis, H. C. (1991).   Irrelevant thoughts, emotional mood states, and cognitive task performance. *Memory and Cognition*, **19**, 507–513.

Stroop, J. R. (1935).   Studies of interference in serial verbal reactions. *Journal of Experimental Psychology*, **18**, 643–662.

Teasdale, J. D. & Fogarty, S. J. (1979).   Differential effects of induced mood on retrieval of pleasant and unpleasant events from episodic memory. *Journal of Abnormal Psychology*, **88**, 248–257.

Teasdale, J. D. & Taylor, R. (1981).   Induced mood and accessibility of memories: an effect of mood state or of induction procedure. *British Journal of Clinical Psychology*, **20**, 39–48.

Teasdale, J. D., Taylor, R. & Fogarty, S. J. (1980). Effects of induced elation-depression on the accessibility of memories of happy and unhappy experiences. *Behaviour Research and Therapy*, **18**, 339–346.

Thrasher, S. M., Dalgleish, T. & Yule, W. (1994). Information processing in post-traumatic stress disorder. *Behaviour Research and Therapy*, **32**, 247–254.

Weissman, A. & Beck, A. T. (1978). The development and validation of the Dysfunctional Attitudes Scale. Paper presented at the annual meeting of the American Educational Research Association, Toronto.

Wegner, D. M. (1989). *White Bears and Other Unwanted Thoughts*. New York: Viking.

Wegner, D. M., Schneider, D. J., Carter, S. R. & White, T. L. (1987). Paradoxical effects of thought suppression. *Journal of Personality and Social Psychology*, **53**, 5–13.

Wegner, D. M., Schneider, D. J., Knutson, B. & McMahon, S. R. (1991). On polluting the stream of consciousness: the effect of thought suppression on the mind's environment. *Cognitive Therapy and Research*, **15**, 141–152.

Williams, J. M. G. (1996a). The specificity of autobiographical memory in depression. In D. C. Rubin (ed.), *Remembering Our Past: Studies in Autobiographical Memory*. Cambridge: Cambridge University Press, pp. 271–296.

Williams, J. M. G. (1996b). Memory processes in psychotherapy. In P. M. Salkovskis (ed.), *Frontiers of Cognitive Therapy*. New York: Guilford, pp. 97–113.

Williams, J. M. G., Healy, D., Teasdale, J., White, W. & Paykel, G. (1990). Dysfunctional attitudes and vulnerability to persistent depression. *Psychological Medicine*, **20**, 375–381.

Williams, J. M. G. & Nulty, D. D. (1986). Construct accessibility, depression and the emotional Stroop task: transient mood or stable structure? *Personality and Individual Differences*, **7**, 485–491.

Williams, J. M. G., Watts, F. N., MacLeod, C. & Mathews, A. (1988). *Cognitive Psychology and Emotional Disorders*. Chichester: Wiley.

Chapter 34

Psychodynamic Theory and Technique in Relation to Research on Cognition and Emotion: Mutual Implications

Drew Westen*

Department of Psychiatry, Harvard Medical School and The Cambridge Hospital, Cambridge, MA, USA

The interaction of cognition and affect has always been at the center of psychodynamic theory and practice. Although psychoanalysis has never developed a systematic, empirically informed portrait of cognition and affect, psychodynamic clinicians and theorists have been studying complex cognitive–affective interactions for over a century. Their observations provide a useful counterpoint to experimental models that frequently address less emotionally significant, less complex phenomena that may not operate on the same principles as the kinds of highly charged psychological events that occur in everyday life, particularly in intimate relationships. The main contention of this chapter is that an integration of contemporary research with psychoanalytic clinical observation and theory provides a more sophisticated and comprehensive approach to cognition and emotion than either tradition can produce alone.

The chapter begins by briefly tracing psychodynamic concepts of cognitive–affective interaction and the data that inform them. It then describes a series of propositions about cognitive–affective interaction that integrate psychodynamic clinical observation with experimental research in cognitive psychology and cog-

* Correspondence should be addressed to: Drew Westen PhD, Department of Psychiatry, The Cambridge Hospital, 1493 Cambridge St., Cambridge, MA 02139, USA

Handbook of Cognition and Emotion. Edited by T. Dalgleish and M. Power.
© 1999 John Wiley & Sons Ltd.

nitive neuroscience. Next it briefly describes some of the empirical evidence supporting these propositions. It concludes with a clinical case example that illustrates ways in which psychoanalytic theory and clinical observation may help to refine contemporary experimentally derived concepts of cognition, affect and their interaction.

COGNITION AND AFFECT IN PSYCHOANALYTIC THEORY

From its earliest days, psychoanalysis focused on the way patients' symptoms and behavior reflected associations among thoughts, feelings and motives stored in memory. Freud emphasized in *The Interpretation of Dreams* (1900/1953) that these associations are often unconscious, so that a patient might avoid a common stimulus, obsessively wash his hands, dream about something seemingly "meaningless", or make a slip of the tongue that provides data about the affective "charge" attached to a particular thought or memory. For a century, psychoanalytic supervisors have urged their trainees to "go where the affect is"— or where it consciously *is not* but seems like it *should be* (as when a patient who has been publicly chastised by a spouse claims not to have felt angry or humiliated).

Despite the centrality of affect to psychoanalytic practice, Freud's theory of emotion, and particularly its relation to cognition, was never particularly coherent (for reviews, see Rapaport, 1953; Spezzano, 1993). Freud initially tried to derive a theory of affect from his theory of drives, viewing anxiety, for example, as a residue of unfulfilled drive energy. His early theories never meshed well with either the data of clinical observation or the evolving technique of psychoanalysis as a treatment mode, and gradually he and later analytic theorists developed more useful formulations. Freud's most important reformulation occurred in 1926 with his concept of signal anxiety—the notion that anxiety is a signal that indicates to the person that something is wrong. This signal, in turn, can motivate behavior or defensive alterations of conscious cognition. Thus, a patient whose successes trigger fears that he will outdo his father may develop a work inhibition or convince himself that his accomplishments are meager (an alteration of a conscious self-representation).

Following Freud, three major theoretical currents have allowed a much more sophisticated understanding of the interaction of cognition and affect. The first was the rise of ego psychology in the late 1930s. Heinz Hartmann (1939), among others, shifted psychoanalytic theory away from its primary emphasis on drives and motivation and toward a more balanced portrait of an organism that not only wishes but thinks. Hartmann and other ego psychologists studied the work of Piaget, Werner, and other cognitive-developmentalists, and they attempted to develop a theory of cognition 30 years before the cognitive revolution in psychology. What was perhaps most important about this effort was that the interaction of affect and cognition was built into their models from the start, not appended to a model in which affect was not easy to accommodate. Thus, the issues the ego psychologists addressed centered on questions such as how attention is regulated by affective and motivational concerns, how thought is organized in patients with severe psychopathology, how cognitive development influences the development of motives, and how thinking is shaped or distorted by wishes, fears and other emotional states.

The second major development was within what is known as "classical" psychoanalytic theory, the branch of psychoanalysis that remains closest to Freud's initial models and emphasizes motivation and conflict. Since Freud, classical theorists have emphasized what they call "unconscious fantasies". The use of the term "fantasy" is misleading to readers outside psychoanalysis, since unconscious fantasies can be wishes, fears or cognitive constructions, and typically involve all three. Thus, the child of a depressed mother may have the "unconscious fantasy" (translation: schema or belief that influences the way she hears relevant information or feels in certain circumstances) that the reason her mother is so depressed is that she is a bad girl. This could lead to persistent guilt and efforts at reparation that may themselves include unconscious components (on relevant empirical data, see O'Connor et al., 1997).

Another central feature of classical psychoanalytic theory is its emphasis on conflict and compromise—that is, on the notion that multiple motives may be operative outside of awareness, which may be mutually incompatible. The result is known as a compromise formation (Brenner, 1982)—a thought, feeling, or behavior that reflects the combination of motivational pulls operating simultaneously in parallel. For example, a patient who felt guilty about leaving his wife but wanted to be free to date moved out into an apartment, but chose one far below his means in an undesirable area of town. Exploration of his conflicting motives led to the hypothesis that he had chosen a compromise between two motives, his wish to move out and have his "bachelor pad", and his attempt to regulate his guilt by choosing a place that would likely decrease his success at dating and more generally make him uncomfortable, allowing him to atone for his "sin".

The third development was the rise of object relations theories. "Object relations" refers to the cognitive, affective, motivational and behavioral patterns involved in close relationships (see Greenberg & Mitchell, 1983; Westen, 1991). From the present perspective, the most important aspect of object relations theory was the development in the 1960s of some complex notions about the cognitive–affective organization of representations of the self, others and relationships. Sandler and his colleagues (see Sandler, 1987; Sandler & Rosenblatt, 1962) developed the concept of the "representational world"—the inner world of affectively charged representations that guide interactions with others and influence many forms of psychopathology, such as depression and personality disorders. Around the same time, Bowlby (1969), also an analyst, was developing his concept of "internal working models" of attachment figures. Both of these concepts stressed the fact that representations of self, others and relationships are always highly charged emotionally, ambivalent (since interactions with significant others are never all roses) and influenced not only by efforts to see the person accurately but by affective and motivational pulls toward seeing the person as one would like to see him/her. Thus, it is not surprising that surveys of university students find that a hefty percentage report that the person they most admire is their same-sex parent. Surely not *everyone's* same-sex parent is among the most admirable people in the world.

Other object relations theorists, such as Kernberg (1984), have described the structure of representations in patients with personality disorders, such as the tendency of patients with borderline personality disorder to have difficulty maintaining representations of significant others that are balanced (as opposed to emotionally one-sided, that is, good or bad) in the face of pressing affects. Empirical investigations have tended to support many of these hypotheses, such as the tendency of borderline patients to produce cognitive-developmentally immature and malevolent representations (Baker et al., 1992; Nigg et al., 1992; Westen, 1991). Kernberg—like Sandler, Bowlby, and all other psychodynamic theorists and clinicians since Freud—also takes it as axiomatic that affective processes can influence conscious thought and behavior outside of awareness, and that affects themselves can be generated by events that occur outside of awareness.

PROPOSITIONS TOWARD AN INTEGRATED COGNITIVE-PSYCHODYNAMIC MODEL OF COGNITION AND AFFECT

Just 10 years ago, the concepts described above would have seemed nonsensical to most cognitive scientists, even those interested in affect. Until the mid-1980s, for example, the notion that most mental processes are implicit or unconscious was a peculiarly psychoanalytic notion. Today, experimental researchers are studying not only implicit thought and memory but implicit affect and motivation (see Bargh & Barndollar, 1996; McClelland, Koestner & Weinberger, 1989). The concept of conflict, however, is still not thoroughly ensconced in cognitive or social-cognitive models; neither is the notion that cognitions can be defensively distorted to avoid unpleasant feelings (e.g. Kihlstrom, 1987).

Elsewhere (Westen, 1992a) I have detailed some of the complementary strengths and weaknesses of psychodynamic and cognitive approaches to the interaction of cognition and affect, and I will not repeat those remarks here. I also will not attempt to defend all or most of what Freud or more recent psychoanalytic theorists have written about affect or cognition, since I think a much more fruitful path is to integrate the best of psychoanalytic thinking in this regard with the best of what cognitive science and, more broadly, cognitive neuroscience, has to offer. Others have attempted integrations of this sort as well (Bucci, 1997; Erdelyi, 1985; Epstein, 1990, 1994; Horowitz, 1987, 1988; Singer & Salovey, 1991). Below I present a list of five propositions that represent steps toward a psychodynamically informed cognitive neuroscience that might be useful for both psychoanalytic theorists and researchers studying cognition and affect.

1. Conscious, explicit processes typically reflect the interaction of neural circuits that operate in parallel outside of awareness. This is as true of affective and motivational as of cognitive processes. The mind does not have a parallel architecture for cognition but a serial architecture for affect and motivation. The mental contents that enter into conscious awareness reflect not only level of activation of implicit component processes but also the affective consequences of allowing a representation to become conscious. On the one hand, attention tends to turn toward stimuli that are relevant to adaptation and hence affectively salient. On the other hand, regulation of aversive affect states often involves regulation of attention to these states and to the cognitions that generate them. An integrated cognitive–dynamic connectionist perspective would suggest that among the constraints that must be satisfied to produce a particular cognition are *affective constraints*, namely, how the cognition would make the person feel.

2. Representations include implicit and explicit cognitive and affective processes, and neither the representation nor its affective components or associations need be conscious to influence behavior. Affects typically become associatively linked with representations (or, perhaps more precisely, affective dispositions become *part of* representations) just as other information becomes associatively connected, namely through experience. Representations that are of any significance to a person are affect-laden, often associated with multiple affects. In fact, the same representation can be associated with diametrically opposed affects at different levels of consciousness, as in the case of discrepancies between explicit and implicit attitudes toward ethnic minority groups assessed by self-report and priming procedures, respectively (Devine, 1989; Fazio et al., 1995).

3. Feelings (including both emotions and other sensory feeling states, such as pleasure and pain caused by tactile stimulation) are mechanisms for the selective retention of behavioral and mental responses, including behaviors, coping strategies and defensive processes. Just as selection pressures in the environment naturally select organisms, emotional states "naturally select" behavioral and mental processes associated with enhancing pleasurable feelings and diminishing painful ones (Westen, 1985, 1994; Westen et al., 1997). Thus, emotions tend to channel behavior in adaptive directions (see Plutchik, 1980; Tomkins, 1962). Naturally selected affective proclivities—such as the tendency to enjoy power or status, to become sexually jealous under certain circumstances (Buss et al., 1992), to feel empathic distress for others in pain (Hoffman, 1978), to find the cry of an infant aversive, and to develop strong

feelings toward attachment figures (Bowlby, 1969)—reflect thousands of genetically encoded adaptations to the environment that interact with learning experiences to lead people away from dangerous situations, reinforce sexual behavior, lead them to protect their offspring, motivate them to stay in close proximity to attachment figures when they are vulnerable and dependent, etc. The association between feelings and outcomes is the mechanism responsible for selecting affect-regulatory responses and behaviors.

4. Affect regulation mechanisms constitute a form of procedural knowledge. That is, they are procedures elicited by specific triggers, such as the matching of a current state with components of an emotion or with a situation-prototype associated with a pleasant or unpleasant emotion. These mechanisms are selectively maintained—that is, reinforced—by their association with reduction of aversive affect states or generation or maintenance of pleasurable states. Mental processes, like behaviors, can also be conditioned or selectively retained by their association with emotion, particularly by its diminution or enhancement. An internal "behavior" (such as repression, denial, or other distortions of conscious beliefs) will be negatively reinforced if it leads to avoidance of aversive affect (see Dollard & Miller, 1950; Wachtel, 1977; Westen, 1985, 1994).

5. Because many of the processes that generate conscious thought, feeling and behavior occur outside awareness, and because associative networks that guide information processing and behavior are not accessible to introspection, psychotherapy for many problems will require: (a) techniques for accessing implicit networks of association, notably implicit connections among affects and cognitive representations; and (b) a sophisticated set of interpretive principles akin to a "transformational grammar" for moving from the manifest level of explicit thought, feeling and behavior to the implicit level of affect-laden associational networks. Some forms of psychopathology can be addressed by relatively simple and direct alteration of associations (such as in vivo exposure techniques that lead to desensitization or habituation—that is, to an attenuated connection between a representation and an associated set of affective processes, including those at subcortical levels). Others can be addressed by altering conscious components of schemas or conscious affect-regulatory processes (coping strategies).

For more complex forms of psychopathology, however, effective therapy may require the therapist and patient to collaborate to map some of the patient's salient cognitive–affective networks of association in order to understand why the patient appears to be repeatedly pursuing or avoiding thoughts, feelings or experiences in ways that are dysfunctional. For example, one patient would begin to get involved with a potential mate but would then find that her feelings had completely changed, often quite suddenly ("I just, thought, yuck, I don't think I'm attracted to him anymore"). Exploration of her associations led to recognition of a clear pattern that made sense of a diverse set of symptoms and allowed her to begin to stop a pattern of avoidance that prevented her from developing new, more benign and less dysfunctional associations. Often, as in this case, "insight-orientated" work is essential for allowing the person to alter behavior or thought patterns in ways that create new associations, so that insight and conditioning processes (involving connections of representations with affects) may both be key components to therapeutic change (see Wachtel, 1977, 1987).

From the standpoint of therapeutic technique, not only is exploration of associations extremely important for accessing the structure of implicit representations and motives, but so is attention to patients' *narratives*. Clinical observation suggests that strong affects are generally attached to representations at more concrete than abstract levels—specific experiences and memories rather than abstractions and generalizations. Patients who are uncomfortable with affect often prefer to give the "headlines" than to tell the stories that give meaning to the headlines, because in the story lies the feeling. Implicit affective processes are much more accessible through examination of the stories patients tell about their interactions with others than through their conscious generalizations (e.g. "my mother and I have a very good relationship"). The themes and feeling-states that repetitively emerge in these narratives tend to provide a useful guide to the structure of patients' enduring ways of processing affectively meaningful information about themselves and relationships. For example, research suggests that the malevolent expectations of relationships expressed in the early memories and Thematic Apperception Test stories of patients with borderline personality disorder differentiate them from other patients, including patients currently in a major depressive episode, whose representations are negatively toned but not malevolent (Nigg et al., 1992; Westen et al., 1990).

EMPIRICAL SUPPORT

Elsewhere (Westen, 1985, 1991, 1992a, 1992b, 1994, 1997a, 1997b, 1998) I have presented in detail the empirical data supporting these propositions. Here I will briefly describe some of the most relevant lines of research. Dual- and multi-level processing theories of emotion (Epstein, 1994; Leventhal & Everhart, 1979; Teasdale, this volume; Westen, 1985, Chapter 2) tend to rest on the assumption that many affective processes are implicit or unconscious, and that these processes can influence thought and behavior without ever attaining consciousness. This supposition has now received ample support.

Implicit Affective Processes

Data from individuals with neurological damage provide some of the most compelling evidence. Patients with bilateral hippocampal damage can produce conditioned emotional responses to stimuli even though they have no recollection of the stimuli, if their amygdala is intact (Bechara et al., 1995). Korsakoff's patients, who also experience deficits in explicit memory, similarly express affective preferences toward stimuli they have encountered previously but cannot explicitly remember (Johnson, Kim & Risse, 1985). Prosopagnosics (who may lose the capacity to recognize familiar faces, at least consciously) nevertheless demonstrate distinct electrophysiological responses to familiar and unfamiliar faces (Bruyer, 1991).

A considerable body of research documents similar processes in normal subjects. Participants develop preferences for stimuli presented in the unattended channel in dichotic listening tasks and subliminally in visual priming tasks through mere exposure, even though their explicit recognition of these stimuli is at chance (Murphy & Zajonc, 1993; Wilson, 1975). Subliminal priming with happy faces prior to exposure to other stimuli similarly leads to affective preferences for those associated with happy faces (Eagle, 1959; Murphy, Monahan & Zajonc, 1995). Normal subjects show conditioned emotional responses (measured electrophysiologically, with measures ranging from brain evoked-related potentials to electrodermal activity) to subliminally presented stimuli previously associated with electric shock, even though they are unaware of either the stimulus or the contingency between the conditioned stimulus (CS) and the unconditioned stimulus (US); conditioned responses can even be acquired outside of awareness (see Öhman, this volume; Bunce et al., 1995).

Implicit Affect Regulation

A uniquely psychodynamic hypothesis is that people can regulate affects outside of awareness through unconscious defensive processes. Several lines of evidence now support this hypothesis as well. Wegner (1994) has shown that conscious efforts to suppress a thought lead to both a conscious process aimed at stopping the thought once it begins to intrude on consciousness and an automatic, unconscious search process aimed at detecting it. Paradoxically, this automatic process keeps the thought activated, and when the thought is associated with feeling—such as an exciting, sexual thought—subjects instructed to suppress the thought remain psychophysiologically aroused even while the thought is outside awareness (Wegner et al., 1990).

More direct evidence for unconscious affect regulation comes from studies of affect-regulatory styles aimed at keeping unpleasant thoughts and feelings out of awareness. Research on repressive coping styles (Dalgleish, Mathews & Wood, this volume; Weinberger, 1990), avoidant/dismissing attachment styles (Dozier & Kobak, 1992), and illusory mental health (the tendency to self-report low levels of negative affect while demonstrating high levels of implicit negative affect in narratives; Shedler, Mayman & Manis, 1993) all demonstrate not only that such processes occur outside awareness but that they influence a range of outcomes, from inhibition of memory for unpleasant childhood experiences to negative health outcomes.

A CASE EXAMPLE

The empirical evidence is clear that affective processes can occur unconsciously and that people can regulate their affects outside of awareness. I will conclude with a detailed clinical example to illustrate how the propositions outlined here might be useful for researchers whose primary interest is in affect and cognition, and how an integrated cognitive–psychodynamic model might differ from models that are not informed by psychoanalytic theory and clinical observation. The dual aim of examining a case in detail is to illustrate for researchers the kinds of complex, naturalistic data that any theoretical approach to cognition and emotion must be able to address, and for clinicians to suggest some of the ways in which more integrated, empirically informed theory can influence clinical practice.

An extended clinical example of this sort may appear jarring or irrelevant to some readers, who may perceive this as an attempt to argue by anecdote. Except where the data are neurological (and hence have the imprimatur of "hard science"), case studies are rarely presented in any of the major scientific journals in psychology, even in personality, which has a strong narrative tradition and the twin goals of understanding personality nomothetically and idiographically. We teach our students *explicitly* from the introductory level on up that case studies, like naturalistic observation, are among the methods psychologists use to understand psychological phenomena, recognizing that case studies cannot yield as definitive data as can controlled experiments. The *implicit* attitude of many researchers toward case material, however, is often quite different.

Just as research on implicit racial stereotypes points to the need for those of us with the best of explicit intentions to monitor our implicit affective biases, I would suggest that the same is true in our emotional reactions to data bearing on affect and cognition "from the other side of the tracks". Many important psychological processes are not likely to be revealed in controlled settings with strangers in the laboratory, just as the clinical setting does not provide optimal opportunities for rigorously testing hypotheses. Theories of cognition and emotion that can account for both experimental findings and clinical observations are likely to be more powerful than those that draw upon, and can account for, data from only the laboratory or the clinic.

The Case of Mr D

The patient, Mr D, was a man in his late 30s, a talented journalist who maintained a low-paying job at a small-town newspaper despite numerous possibilities of deploying his considerable skills elsewhere. He was intensely distraught at his fate, alternatively voicing feelings that he was better than his station in life and that he was worthless and untalented, as evidenced by his dismal salary and "local fishwrap" employment, as he called it. He had, on several occasions, had opportunities at more prestigious newspapers, including the *Boston Globe*, where a friend from college who admired his work was on the staff, but "something" always intervened to stop him. He would fail to meet application deadlines, retract his application after sending it, or fail to ask journalist friends who admired his work to recommend him for open positions at their papers. Thus, he felt like a failure, but he created the conditions for those feelings by maintaining external circumstances that would seemingly confirm his view of himself.

Mr D apparently came by his low self-confidence and self-criticism honestly. He reported an intensely critical, unempathic relationship with his parents, who were demanding of success but rarely seemed to reward it. As a middle-school child, when he brought home report cards with all As and A – s, his father would shake his head and ask, "What's this A– in English about? Can't you read?". By high school, his grades had dropped and he had become a chronic underachiever, despite his obvious talents as a writer. He developed his writing skills on the side by writing science fiction, which he never showed to anyone.

Although therapists rarely have access to anything more than patients' reports of their experience of childhood events, an adult experience that occurred during the first year of his treatment offered some sense of his parents' actual behavior. The patient won a journalism award for which he was honored at a ceremony. His parents, who lived one town over, were planning to attend, but "something else" came up that night. Some time later, they invited him to dinner and asked him to bring the story for which he had been honored so they could read it. On his way to their house, he realized he had forgotten it, so he returned home to pick it up. He did so, but they forgot to ask him for it. When he volunteered it toward the end of the evening, they began to read it. His father remarked, "There's a typo— see, there?" His mother read a paragraph and then began clearing the table. Within days of this interchange, the patient became very depressed, and the parents became alarmed and contacted his therapist. During the brief conversation, his father complained that "We didn't raise him to wallow in self-pity like this".

The patient kept a notebook that he would sometimes bring into therapy to remind himself of things he wanted to talk about, and the therapist noticed that tucked inside the notebook was a copy of the article for which he had received the award. When the therapist inquired about it, and wondered if the patient had thought of showing it to him, the patient became anxious, and ultimately divulged a mix of conflicting feelings. He had wanted to show his therapist the article, but "somehow felt really uncomfortable about it" in ways he could not specify, so he had decided against it. Curiously, however, he had not removed the article from the notebook, despite his clear conscious intention to do so lest the therapist "happen" to notice it. When they explored together his associations to his unease at showing the article to his therapist, Mr D's first thoughts were worries that he would be "bragging", as well as a fear that the therapist would find fault with it. His first association to the latter was the memory of his father and the report card.

The therapist formulated the case psychodynamically but worked in an integrative mode therapeutically. Part of the treatment was insight-orientated, helping Mr D to see how he was contributing to his own unhappiness, understand his conflicting feelings toward success and recognize the way he had taken on his parents' role as critic. A crucial piece of insight-orientated work involved helping him to understand how he was continuing to rely on solutions he had developed as a child to deal with his painful relationship with his parents (such as not trying to achieve), which may have been the best options available to him at the time but were now perpetuating the problem.

Another therapeutic strategy combined the psychodynamic construct of "corrective emotional experience"—providing a different kind of experience for the patient (in this case, a kinder, more empathic and respectful one) than he had come to expect—with the behavioral concept of exposure (confronting the person with a feared stimulus for purposes of desensitization or habituation). For this patient, as for many depressed patients, positive self-representations are tantamount to phobic stimuli, and they avoid them at all cost (Westen, 1985). Mr D was distinctly uncomfortable with any expressions of praise by the therapist (or by anyone else), as when the therapist happened to see occasional articles the patient wrote that were reprinted in the *Boston Globe* and commented on them. For patients who are afraid of hearing positive things about themselves (for reasons to be discussed shortly), a crucial part of the treatment, as in the treatment of any phobia, is to expose them to the feared "stimulus" in ways they can hear and not escape (cognitively or behaviorally)(Westen, in press). The therapist also relied at times on more strictly cognitive techniques, helping the patient problem-solve some of his work difficulties and ways of handling his parents, but exploring simultaneously the dynamic interplay of thought, feeling and motivation as Mr D invariably found ways to sabotage their best-laid plans.

Several features of this case highlight central issues at the intersection of psychoanalysis and the study of cognition and emotion and demonstrate the importance for both of their integration. I present them as hypotheses because in clinical work, as in research, we never have certainty, and in clinical practice we have no formal tests of significance or effect size. Formulating a case is like writing a review article: one looks at the preponderance of the evidence to see what trends one can find, and a good clinician never makes too much of any single data-point, any more than a good researcher makes too much of a single study. But across and within patients patterns do emerge, and with luck clinicians, like researchers, sometimes see what is in front of them and overcome their biases to see what they expect.

Ambivalence, Associationism, and the Nature of Representations

The first point to note is the conflicting feelings associated with Mr D's self-schemas or self-representations. On the one hand, he perceived himself as lowly, worthless and deserving of his fate. On the other, he perceived himself as too good for the "fishwrap", and in fact, his self-criticism was predicated on a view that he should—and could—do better. From time to time, exploration of some encounter led to his sheepish admission of an exalted view of his own talents, which may have been betrayed as well by his fear of "bragging" if he were to show his award-winning article to his therapist. Despite his generally low self-esteem, the patient appeared afraid of his own secret hubris.

From a psychodynamic point of view, this state of affairs represents a typical example of ambivalence, in which conflicting feelings and beliefs are associated with the same object (in this case, himself). Mr D did not always have conscious access to both sides of his ambivalence, however, so that he was likely to alternate between the two rather than to maintain a more cognitively complex conscious representation.

From a cognitive perspective, the fact that he would have conflicting views of himself, including conflicting feelings, is basic associationism: at various points in his lifetime, beginning in his childhood, he had occasion to associate himself with two very different sets of feelings and ideas, and through repeated experiences, he formed a complex implicit representation of himself with many sides. Unfortunately, he appeared to lack dense interconnections between the positive and negative sides of his representation of himself and was unable to use conscious control strategies to bring to mind the positive to offset or counterbalance the negative when the latter were evoked. Developing such control strategies became an explicit therapeutic goal. As an adult, different aspects of his self-representation would thus become active, depending on the match between the circumstance and the encoded, affectively polarized (and usually negative, since that was the more accessible representation) prototype. From a connectionist standpoint, Mr D's representation of self-as-failure was readily activated by any situation that even vaguely resembled a potential failure situation. This is because his representation of failure situations was well elaborated and salient and hence required only a small part of the network to activate the rest of the network and guide interpretation—and affective judgment. In connectionist terms, this is what one might mean by a chronically accessible schema (to use Higgins's term, 1990).

From an integrated cognitive–psychodynamic perspective, we would do well not to speak of representations or schemas without specifying several of their qualities, such as their affective valence or valences, the strength of these affective associations, the denseness of connections among aspects of the representation with differing affective valence, and the degree to which components of these representations are conscious. Further, we need to consider the extent to which affective qualities encoded in both cortical and subcortical neural circuits should be included as part of what we often think of as "cold" cognitive categories or representations. To the extent that an object in our lives is significant and is one with which we have repeated experience, it will be associated with affect. And to the extent that it is repeatedly associated with particular affective states, the neural units that provide affective coloring to these states—from the evaluative tone added by activation of circuits involving the amygdala to the autonomic responses set in motion by the hypothalamus and pituitary—will become chronically activated in tandem with the more cold cognitive aspects of the representation. Thus, when a Black student walks into an achievement situation and has his schemas or stereotypes about Blacks and achievement (and hence himself) activated (Steele, 1997), the activated representation is not simply a cognitive structure but a complex amalgam of thought, feeling and (as we shall shortly see) ways of responding to the feelings engendered that are routinely activated in tandem. Further, to the extent that the individual is not conscious of these processes—and may even consciously deny having any such thoughts or feelings—describing their level of consciousness is essential.

Affect Regulation, Associative Networks, and Motivation

A second point to note about the case of Mr D pertains to the relations among cognition, motivation and affect regulation strategies. In Mr D's narratives about significant occupational events (and events in his personal life as well), "something" would always intervene to block his attaining a goal of success. The goal of achieving was consciously represented (experienced as a conscious intention) but, at the beginning of treatment, he did not have any awareness of the shared structure of his failure narratives, and particularly of his contribution to the "something" that would impede his success and reconfirm his view of himself as a failure. (Freud called this experience of some unacknowledged aspect of self that feels like non-self the "it", translated into English as "id", although he emphasized the wishful side of the "it" rather than other ways in which aspects of self can be disavowed). Part of the role of the therapist in a case like this is to bring cognitive order to chaos, to make what felt like ground into figure, and to note recurring story schemas of this sort, which have been variously described as core conflictual relationship themes (Luborsky & Crits-Cristoph, 1990), relationship schemas (Baldwin, 1992; Horowitz, 1987), nuclear scenes (Tomkins, 1962) or dominant interpersonal concerns (Conklin & Westen, in press).

Given that Mr D did not hold a conscious goal of self-sabotage, the only possible explanation for the myriad things he did that ran counter to his conscious goal of success—failing to follow through with job applications or recommendations from friends, retracting applications and then offering elaborate rationalizations about why this was not a good time to apply, etc.—is that an unconscious counter-force was leading him in an opposing direction (see Erdelyi, 1985). How can we understand implicit motivational counter-forces, which are strong enough to disable and override seemingly sensible conscious intentions?

One way, as suggested above, is to view feelings (including both emotions and sensory feeling-states of pleasure and pain) and anticipated feelings as responsible for approach and avoidance, a position similar to that offered by Lewin (1935) many years ago, as well as by Gray (1990) in the behavioral literature and

Sandler (1987) in the psychoanalytic literature. If a schema or representation can have opposing affects associated with it (built up through positive and negative experiences) and can be expressed even when it is not conscious (as shown in the research on implicit racism, for example), then the affects associated with it can impel contradictory actions outside of awareness. Thus, if Mr D consciously wanted a better job but repeatedly thwarted himself from accomplishing this goal, one might hypothesize that his representation of either the process of trying to attain the goal or of the goal-state itself has multiple, contradictory affective meanings to him.

To imagine how Mr D could have developed such conflicting affective evaluations, and hence conflicting motives, is not difficult, especially in light of the interaction with his parents around his award. He wanted to please them and have them acknowledge his success, so he told them about the award. They rebuffed him, however, by skipping the ceremony, leading him to associate success—and his wish to have them *acknowledge* his success—with emotional pain (sadness, anger, or some other unpleasant admixture of feelings). His parents then essentially reactivated his wish for their respect by asking him to bring the article to dinner. His conflict around doing so, however, may have been expressed in his "forgetting" to bring the article and having to go back home to pick it up. One can certainly see why he might have wanted to "forget" the story: he had a history of experiences with his parents in which displaying his achievements led to more pain than pleasure, as when he would proudly bring home a report card and be criticized for its minor imperfections—or when his parents ultimately acted with such utter indifference when he brought home his "A+" story.

Note here the association that would naturally develop in his mind between a feeling—pride—and a punishing external response. Repeated experiences of this sort would produce an aversion toward feeling proud of his accomplishments—and hence a discomfort with compliments, which elicit pride. To succeed, then, and to feel proud of success, were associated with emotional pain. So, too, were the wish to be complimented by an authority figure and the effort required to achieve. The dangers of wishing, trying, succeeding and feeling proud were all reconfirmed when his parents failed to come to the ceremony honoring his achievement. His parents' ultimate reaction—their failing to ask to see the story, his father criticizing it for typographical errors, and his mother paying it little attention—only reinforced these negative associations (in connectionist terms, increased their weights). These associations, in turn, could be expected to reinforce certain behavioral and cognitive responses—reduced effort, avoidance of feeling proud, avoidance of receiving compliments, and efforts to shut off wishes for praise—and lead more generally to a fear of, and hence avoidance of, success.

Mr D's attitude toward compliments, which is common in chronically dysphoric patients, reflects similar cognitive–affective interactions and efforts to regulate aversive affective states. Because compliments (and pride in himself) have been associated with psychological pain, over time he has developed affect-regulatory processes to deflect them, such as automatic activation of negative self-representations to counterbalance them, inhibition of recognition of complimentary communications, and distortion of their content. Thus, as a communication begins to match a prototype of a compliment (i.e. activates some part of the neural network that represents the concept of "compliment", with its attendant feelings), he might begin to think of negative examples or alternative interpretations that place him in a more negative light. Bringing negative self-representations to consciousness is an implicit procedure—a form of procedural knowledge—that is automatically triggered, much as other cognitive processes are automatically activated when current situations match a prototype of a situation in which these procedures have provided a successful solution to a problem (see Anderson, 1995). In this case, the problem is an affective one. The process is little different from what Bargh (1997; Bargh & Barndollar, 1996) has documented experimentally for implicitly activated motives and behaviors, namely that surreptitiously priming a motive can lead to alterations in behavior, even when the person is entirely unaware of what is happening.

With this groundwork laid, we can now see the psycho-logic behind some self-defeating compromise formations, in which Mr D allowed himself only limited success. As an adolescent, he developed his writing skills—reflecting his wishes to achieve and to develop his talents—while simultaneously not showing his stories to anyone and hence avoiding possible criticism. As an adult, he kept his wishes and positive self-representations alive by staying at a newspaper at which he was the best writer and not subjecting himself to potential rejection at a better paper. He probably feared success as much as failure, because with success comes expectations of further success as well as wishes for recognition, both of which he had learned to associate with unpleasant feelings. Thus, his compromise with respect to his wishes to succeed and his fears of succeeding or being rejected was to keep his eyes open for potential jobs and even to apply for them, but not to follow through. His conflicting motives left him in an unsatisfying emotional stalemate.

A similar dynamic was apparently operative in Mr D's conflict about showing his story to his therapist. On the one hand, he wanted to share the story with the therapist, and hence to receive approval and validation, since the therapist was an important person in his life who could potentially provide the kind of validation he had so seldom received from his parents. On the other, he feared that he would not be validated, and instead would be seen as "bragging" about a story that the therapist would find unimpressive. The affective power and strength of activation of his unconscious fears are demonstrated in two ways. First, he had a strong conscious wish, yet this was apparently not strong *enough* to override a countervailing affective response (feeling "somehow uncomfortable") whose basis was outside his awareness. Thus, despite one motive being consciously accessible, another motive (avoidance) prevailed.

Second, his therapist had previously, on more than one occasion, spontaneously commented positively on stories he had written. Thus, on the basis of his experience with his therapist, he had no reason to expect a negative response to his story. Yet that was precisely what he feared—enough to inhibit himself from obtaining potential gratification from the therapist's response to the story. From a psychodynamic perspective, this is a classic example of transference: the patient brought wishes, fears and expectations from significant relationships from the past into the therapy relationship and played out a way of handling the situation, however dysfunctional in the present context, that had minimized his pain in the past. Transferential processes of this sort have now been documented empirically, both experimentally (Andersen, Reznik & Manzella, 1996) and in the relationship narratives patients tell (Luborsky & Crits-Cristoph, 1990). Transferential processes also make sense, from a cognitive–psychodynamic perspective, in terms of schematic processes and networks of association (see Singer, 1985; Wachtel, 1981; Westen, 1988): Just as a schema or network of associations can be activated in a priming study, leading to a pattern of inference, interpretation or expectation in line with activated cognitive contents, so, too, can situations that resemble prior situations in some way (such as interactions with authority figures), prime particular interpretations, expectations, affects, fears, wishes, defenses, behaviors and so forth.

For Mr D, the conflict between strong but opposing wishes and fears led to a compromise formation: do not deliberately show the story to the therapist but bring the story into the therapist's sight anyway. In the process, his conflicted *wish* for his therapist to see the story was transformed into a conscious *fear* that his therapist would notice it. Had the therapist not asked about it, the therapist would have inadvertently recapitulated Mr D's painful experience with his parents, who rarely noticed his accomplishments and in fact failed to ask to see the story when it was in their presence. Wachtel (1993, 1997) has described "cyclical psychodynamic" processes of this sort, in which a person begins with an expectation (in this case, that significant others will not notice or comment on successes), behaves in ways that follow from that expectation (not showing the story to the therapist), consequently experiences confirming events (the therapist does not ask to see the story, which is in fact in view), and then has the schema or association reinforced. Swann and Colleagues (1992) have documented similar self-verification processes empirically in numerous studies.

CONCLUSION

The experimental study of cognition and emotion has come a long way in a very short span of time. Yet some of the most important interactions of affect and cognition are not readily reproducible in the laboratory. Ex-spouses often hate each other with the same degree of passion that once united them, and their representations of the other may shift 180 degrees; children in the midst of divorce often feel intense loyalty conflicts and not only feel intense hostility toward one parent but manifest polarized representations of their parents; and people often find themselves repeating painful interpersonal patterns without any awareness of why their choices keep pulling them in uncomfortable, if familiar, places. Phenomena such as these suggest that progress in the understanding of cognition, affect and their interaction might be spurred by greater cross-fertilization between the laboratory and the clinic.

REFERENCES

Andersen, S., Reznik, I. & Manzella, L. (1996). Eliciting facial affect, motivation, and expectancies in transference: significant-other representations in social relations. *Journal of Personality and Social Psychology*, **71**, 1108–1129.

Anderson, J. R. (1995). *Learning and Memory: An Integrated Approach*. New York: Wiley.

Baker, L., Silk, K. R., Westen, D., Nigg, J. T. & Lohr, N. E. (1992). Malevolence, splitting, and parental ratings by borderlines. *Journal of Nervous and Mental Disease*, **180**, 258–264.

Baldwin, M. (1992). Relational schemas and the processing of social information. *Psychological Bulletin*, **112**, 461–484.

Bargh, J. & Barndollar, K. (1996). Automaticity in action: the unconscious as repository of chronic goals and motives. In P. M. Gollwitzer & J. Bargh (eds), *The Psychology of Action*. New York: Guilford, pp. 457–481.

Bargh, J. (1997). The automaticity of everyday life. In J. S. Wyer Jr (ed.), *Advances in Social Cognition*, Vol. 10. Hillsdale, NJ: Erlbaum, pp. 1–61.

Bechara, A., Tranel, D., Damasio, H., Adolphs, R., Rockland, C. & Damasio, A. (1995). Double dissociation of conditioning and declarative knowledge relative to the amygdala and hippocampus in humans. *Science*, **29**, 1115–1118.

Bowlby, J. (1969). *Attachment and Loss, Vol. 1, Attachment*. New York: Basic Books.

Brenner, C. (1982). *The Mind in Conflict*. New York: International Universities Press.

Bruyer, R. (1991). Covert face recognition in prosopagnosia: a review. *Brain and Cognition*, **15**, 223–235.

Bucci, W. (1997). *Psychoanalysis and Cognitive Science: A Multiple Code Theory*. New York: Guilford Press.

Bunce, S., Bernat, E., Wong, P. & Shevrin, H. (1995). Event-related potential and facial EMG indicators of emotion-relevant unconscious learning. Paper presented at the 103rd Annual Convention of the American Psychological Association, New York.

Buss, D. M., Larsen, R. J., Westen, D. & Semmelroth, J. (1992). Sex differences in jealousy: evolution, physiology, and psychology. *Psychological Science*, **3**, 251–255.

Conklin, A. & Westen, D. (in press). Thematic apperception test. In W. Dorfman & M. Hersen (eds), *Understanding Psychological Assessment*. New York: Plenum.

Devine, P. (1989). Stereotypes and prejudice: their automatic and controlled components. *Journal of Personality and Social Psychology*, **56**, 5–18.

Dollard, J. & Miller, N. (1950). *Personality and Psychotherapy: An Analysis in Terms of Learning, Thinking, and Culture*. New York: McGraw-Hill.

Dozier, M. & Kobak, R. (1992). Psychophysiology in attachment interviews: converging evidence for deactivating strategies. *Child Development*, **63**, 1473–1480.

Eagle, M. (1959). The effects of subliminal stimuli of aggressive content upon conscious cognition. *Journal of Personality*, **27**, 678–688.

Epstein, S. (1990). Cognitive-experiential self-theory. In L. Pervin (ed.), *Handbook of Personality: Theory and Research*. New York: Guilford, pp. 165–192.

Epstein, S. (1994). Integration of the cognitive and the psychodynamic unconscious. *American Psychologist*, **49**, 709–724.

Erdelyi, M. (1985). *Psychoanalysis: Freud's Cognitive Psychology*. San Francisco, CA: W. H. Freeman.

Fazio, R., Jackson, J. R., Dunton, B. & Williams, C. J. (1995). Variability in automatic activation as an unobtrusive measure of racial attitudes: a bona fide pipeline? *Journal of Personality and Social Psychology*, **69**, 1013–1027.

Freud, S. (1926/1953). Inhibitions, symptoms, and anxiety. In J. Strachey (ed. & trans.), *The Standard Edition of the Complete Psychological Works of Sigmund Freud*, Vol. 14. London: Hogarth, pp. 113–205 (original work published 1923).

Freud, S. (1900/1953). The interpretation of dreams. In J. Strachey (ed. & trans.), *The Standard Edition of the Complete Psychological Works of Sigmund Freud*, Vol. 4. London: Hogarth, pp. 1–338. (original work published 1900).

Gray, J. A. (1990). Brain systems that mediate both emotion and cognition. *Cognition and Emotion*, **4**, 269–288.

Greenberg, J. R. & Mitchell, S. (1983). *Object Relations in Psychoanalytic Theory*. Cambridge: Harvard University Press.

Hartmann, H. (1939). *The Ego and the Problem of Adaptation*. New York: International Universities Press.

Higgins, E. T. (1990). Personality, social psychology, and person-situation relations: standards and knowledge activation as a common language. In L. Pervin (ed.), *Handbook of Personality: Theory and Research*. New York: Guilford, pp. 301–338.

Hoffman, M. (1978). Toward a theory of empathic arousal and development. In M. Lewis and L. Rosenbaum (eds), *The Development of Affect*. New York: Plenum.

Horowitz, M. J. (1987). *States of Mind: Configurational Analysis of Individual Psychology*, 2nd edn. New York: Plenum.

Horowitz, M. J. (1988). *Introduction to Psychodynamics: A Synthesis*. New York: Basic Books.

Johnson, M. K., Kim, J. K. & Risse, G. (1985). Do alcoholic Korsakoff's syndrome patients acquire affective reactions? *Journal of Experimental Psychology: Learning, Memory, and Cognition*, **11**, 22–36.

Kernberg, O. (1984). *Severe Personality Disorders*. New Haven, CT: Yale University Press.

Kihlstrom, J. (1987). The cognitive unconscious. *Science*, **237**, 1445–1452.

Leventhal, H., Everhart, D. (1979). Emotion, pain, and physical illness. In C. E. Izard (ed.), *Emotion in Personality and Psychopathology*. New York: Plenum.

Lewin, K. (1935). *A Dynamic Theory of Personality*. New York: McGraw-Hill.

Luborsky, L. & Crits-Christoph, P. (1990). *Understanding Transference: The Core Conflictual Relationship Theme Method*. New York: Basic Books.

McClelland, D. C., Koestner, R. & Weinberger, J. (1989). How do self-attributed and implicit motives differ? *Psychological Review*, **96**, 690–702.

Murphy, S. T. & Zajonc, R. (1993). Affect, cognition, and awareness: affective priming with optimal and suboptimal stimulus exposures. *Journal of Personality and Social Psychology*, **64**, 723–739.

Murphy, S. T., Monahan, J. L. & Zajonc, R. (1995). Additivity of nonconscious affect: combined effects of priming and exposure. *Journal of Personality and Social Psychology*, **69**, 589–602.

Nigg, J., Lohr, N. E., Westen, D., Gold, L. & Silk, K. R. (1992). Malevolent object representations in borderline personality disorder and major depression. *Journal of Abnormal Psychology*, **101**, 61–67.

O'Connor, L., Berry, J. W., Weiss, J., Bush, M. & Sampson, H. (1997). Interpersonal guilt: the development of a new measure. *Journal of Clinical Psychology*, **53**, 73–89.

Plutchik, R. (1980). A general psychoevolutionary theory of emotion. In R. Plutchik & H. Kellerman (eds), *Emotion, Vol. 1. Theories of Emotion*. New York: Academic Press.

Rapaport, D. (1953). On the psychoanalytic theory of affects. *International Journal of Psychoanalysis*, **34**, 177–198.

Sandler, J. (1987). Toward a reconsideration of the psychoanalytic theory of motivation. In J. Sandler, *From Safety to the Superego: Selected papers of Joseph Sandler*. New York: Guilford.

Sandler, J. & Rosenblatt, B. (1962). The concept of the representational world. *Psychoanalytic Study of the Child*, **17**, 128–145.

Shedler, J., Mayman, M. & Manis, M. (1993). The illusion of mental health. *American Psychologist*, **48**, 1117–1131.

Singer, J. (1985). Transference and the human condition: a cognitive–affective perspective. *Psychoanalytic Psychology*, **2**, 189–219.

Singer, J. & Salovey, D. (1991). Organized knowledge structures and personality: person schemas, self-schemas, prototypes, and scripts. In M. Horowitz (ed.), *Person Schemas and Recurrent Maladaptive Interpersonal Patterns*. Chicago: University of Chicago Press.

Spezzano, C. (1993). *Affect in Psychoanalysis: A Clinical Synthesis*. Hillsdale, NJ: Analytic Press.

Steele, C. (1997). A threat in the air: how stereotypes shape intellectual identity and performance. *American Psychologist*, **52**, 613–629.

Swann, W., Stein-Seroussi, A. & Geisler, R. (1992). Why people self-verify. *Journal of Personality and Social Psychology*, **62**, 392–401.

Tomkins, S. S. (1962). *Affect, Imagery, Consciousness*, Vol. 1. New York: Springer.

Wachtel, P. (1977). *Psychoanalysis and Behavior Therapy*. New York: Basic Books.

Wachtel, P. (1981). Transference, schema, and assimilation: the relationship of Piaget to the psychoanalytic theory of transference. *Annual of Psychoanalysis*, **8**, 59–76.

Wachtel, P. (1993). *Therapeutic Communication*. New York: Guilford.

Wachtel, P. (1997). *Psychoanalysis, Behavior Therapy, and the Relational World*. Washington, DC: American Psychological Association Press.

Wegner, D. (1994). Ironic processes of mental control. *Psychological Review*, **101**, 34–52.

Wegner, D., Shortt, J., Blake, A. W. & Page, M. S. (1990). The suppression of exciting thoughts. *Journal of Personality and Social Psychology*, **58**, 409–418.

Weinberger, D. (1990). The construct validity of the repressive coping style. In J. Singer (ed.), *Repression and Dissociation*. Chicago: University of Chicago Press.

Westen, D. (1985). *Self and Society: Narcissism, Collectivism, and the Development of Morals*. New York: Cambridge University Press.

Westen, D. (1988). Transference and information processing. *Clinical Psychology Review*, **8**, 161–179.

Westen, D. (1991). Social cognition and object relations. *Psychological Bulletin*, **109**, 429–455.

Westen, D. (1992a). Social cognition and social affect in psychoanalysis and cognitive science: from analysis of regression to regression analysis. In J. W. Barron, M. N. Eagle & D. L. Wolitzky (eds), *The Interface of Psychoanalysis and Psychology*. Washington, DC: American Psychological Association.

Westen, D. (1992b). The cognitive self and the psychoanalytic self: can we put our selves together? *Psychological Inquiry*, **3**, 1–13.

Westen, D. (1994). Toward an integrative model of affect regulation: applications to social-psychological research. *Journal of Personality*, **62**, 641–647.

Westen, D. (1995). A clinical-empirical model of personality: life after the Mischelian ice age and the NEO-lithic era. *Journal of Personality*, **63**, 495–524.

Westen, D. (1997a). Toward an empirically and clinically sound theory of motivation. *International Journal of Psychoanalysis*, **78**, 521–548.

Westen, D. (1997b). Implicit cognition, affect, and motivation: the end of a century-long debate. In R. Bornstein & J. Masling (eds), *Empirical Studies of Unconscious Processes*. Washington, DC: American Psychological Association Press.

Westen, D. (1998). The scientific legacy of Sigmund Freud. Toward a psychodynamically informed psychological science. *Psychological Bulletin*, **124**, 333–361.

Westen, D. (in press). Integrative psychotherapy: integrating psychodynamic and cognitive-behavioral theory and technique. In C. R. Snyder & R. Ingram (eds), *Handbook of Psychological Change: Psychotherapy Processes and Practices for the 21st century.* New York: Wiley.

Westen, D., Lohr, N., Silk, K., Gold, L. & Kerber, K. (1990). Object relations and social cognition in borderlines, major depressives, and normals: a TAT analysis. *Psychological Assessment: A Journal of Consulting and Clinical Psychology, 2,* 355–364.

Westen, D., Muderrisoglu, S., Fowler, C., Shedler, J. & Koren, D. (1997). Affect regulation and affective experience: individual differences, group differences, and measurement using a Q-sort procedure. *Journal of Consulting and Clinical Psychology,* **65**, 429–439.

Wilson, W. R. (1975). Unobtrusive induction of positive attitudes. Unpublished doctoral dissertation, University of Michigan.

Chapter 35

Mechanisms of Change in Exposure Therapy for Anxiety Disorders

Susan Mineka
Northwestern University, Evanston, IL, USA
and
Cannon Thomas
University of Virginia, Charlottesville, VA, USA

The logic behind exposure treatments for the anxiety disorders is simple: anxious people avoid what they fear. By exposing them over a sustained period of time to the things they fear, their sense that avoidance is necessary to protect them from harm will be disconfirmed. Despite its simplicity, this basic method has proved to be perhaps the most powerful, specific intervention produced by psychologists to date. For all of the DSM-IV anxiety disorders, therapies which rely on exposure have produced large effects in the reduction of symptoms. They have performed at least as well as cognitive and generally better than non-directive interventions. Exposure plus response-prevention treatment has proved quite successful for obsessive-compulsive disorder, a disorder previously considered to be virtually intractable to psychological treatment (Abramowitz, 1996; Riggs & Foa, 1993). The relatively recently introduced, exposure-based treatment for panic disorder, which combines interoceptive and exteroceptive exposure, results in virtually complete remission of panic attacks in 75–90% of the patients treated, a rate high enough to support the position of this therapy as one of the treatments of choice for this disorder (Barlow, 1988; Margraf & Schneider, 1991; Margraf & Schneider, 1995; Telch, 1995). Simple phobias can be virtually cured by these means (e.g. Emmelkamp, 1994). And even for disorders such as social phobias, generalized anxiety disorder (GAD) and post-traumatic stress disorder (PSTD), in which avoidance involves more subtle patterns of thought and behavior,

Handbook of Cognition and Emotion. Edited by T. Dalgleish and M. Power.
© 1999 John Wiley & Sons Ltd.

exposure-based methods have been incorporated and play a central role in effective therapeutic packages (Calhoun & Resick, 1993; Feske & Chambless, 1995;
Keane et al., 1992). It is true that effect sizes for change are generally smaller for
the latter disorders, which tend to involve more diffuse emotional difficulties.
Additionally, for many of these disorders the reduction of specific symptoms does
not always translate into high end-state functioning because some level of avoidance, as well as elevated levels of general anxiety and depression, often remain.
Nevertheless, the success of these relatively simple exposure-based methods has
been remarkable. The question of current interest is *why* it works, a question
which has proved far more complex than one might have expected, given the
relatively simple procedures involved.

Traditionally, two explanations for the change process were seriously considered. One accounts for change during exposure as occurring through a habituation process (e.g. Lader & Wing, 1966; Watts, 1979). Habituation is a decrement
in fear, especially its psychophysiological aspects, when exposure to fear provoking situations occurs repeatedly. The process appears to have a physiological
basis and to be controlled by relatively primitive neurological structures such
as the brain stem (Davis et al., 1982; Groves & Thompson, 1970). Nevertheless,
simple habituation as studied in laboratory experiments of animals or humans
has difficulty accounting for therapeutic changes in phobic fears and other
anxiety disorders (Barlow, 1988; Rachman, 1990) because the type of changes
which occur during habituation are generally short-term (Watts, 1979) and are
thought to occur only in response to unconditioned or innately feared stimuli
(Davis et al., 1982). In addition, habituation, which has more typically been
proposed as the mechanism underlying systematic desensitization, would have
great difficulty explaining how more intense exposure-based treatments would
work, because the more intense stimuli should lead to sensitization—an incremental process—rather than habituation.

A second traditional explanation for change is extinction, a process which
involves a decrement in *learned* responses due to repeated, non-reinforced exposures to a conditioned stimulus. The process was traditionally thought to result
in a gradual weakening of the association between the stimulus and the anxiety
response. In more current learning theory terminology, extinction involves a
learned change in the expectancy that aversive consequences follow the
conditioned stimulus (Mackintosh, 1983). This theory has the advantage of
explaining long-term gains, because extinction is believed to be more long-lasting
than habituation. However, more complex factors appear to be involved in the
process of exposure than a simple Pavlovian fear extinction account can easily
accommodate (e.g. Barlow, 1988; Rachman, 1990). For example, this theory
does not do justice to the complex dissociations that occur following exposure-
based treatments between the different components of fear or anxiety
(behavioral, subjective and psychophysiological) (Lang, 1971; Rachman, 1990).
In addition, several studies have shown that exposure can be effective even when
avoidance responses are not prevented (e.g. Rachman et al., 1986). It is difficult
to explain how expected aversive consequences could be disconfirmed if patients

are still allowed to avoid the situation in which the expected consequence would occur.

Recent accounts of exposure have continued to focus on learning during the therapeutic process. However, the learning appears to be more complex than the weakening of simple associations that traditional models of extinction posited. Most current theories have assimilated habituation into their models, claiming that habituation provides information which alters higher-level cognitive representations of feared stimuli (Bandura, 1977; 1986; Barlow, 1988; Foa & Kozak, 1986; Lang, 1985; Rachman, 1990). However, these perspectives vary considerably in terms of the particular nature of this integration. The issues of contention between theories appear to revolve primarily around how fear representations are organized mentally and how they can be modified. For example, Foa & Kozak (1986), in an elaboration of the model of fear originally developed by Lang (1977, 1985), view fear as a structure of associated memory propositions, including both cognitive and affective information. By contrast, the self-efficacy theory, originally developed by Bandura, emphasizes an individual's beliefs about his/her ability to interact effectively with the environment in the fear-producing situation (Bandura, 1977, 1986; Williams, 1996). Although Bandura's theory recognizes habituation-type processes as one means by which information might be provided that would result in changing beliefs, the importance of subjective and psychophysiological measures of emotion are de-emphasized. The primary focus in self-efficacy theory is on behavior and beliefs about behavior. In our opinion, both theories have brought into focus important issues in understanding exposure. These two basic lines of inquiry seem to represent, at least in part, distinct levels of analysis rather than competing theories, and an improved understanding of the exposure process might result from exploring their integration.

In this chapter, we present a perspective that is generally consistent with both of these approaches and that provides a partial integration of them. Following Foa & Kozak (1986), we recognize the central role that elicitation of anxiety itself plays in the exposure process. The dysfunctional perceptions and beliefs associated with anxiety are interdependent with the emotion. Foa & Kozak, following Lang (1985), refer to the representations of emotional information as well as the thoughts and beliefs associated with an anxiety-provoking situation as "cognitive–affective structures". To access these beliefs in order to disconfirm them in a given context, it is important also to access the emotion. Foa & Kozak (1986) also go further, suggesting specific situations under which the emotions are accessed but the "meaning" of a situation may not be altered through exposure. Their discussion of the "meaning" of anxiety-provoking situations focuses primarily on changing the evaluative errors regarding the actual danger posed by feared stimuli (internal or external), as well as on changing the valence of the stimuli (Foa & McNally, 1996). This position seems unduly limited to us. We argue that an additional, fundamental aspect of the meaning of situations that are anxiety-provoking is that individuals perceive these situations to be out of their control. In other words, they feel they are unable to establish a contingent relationship between their intentions and their environment. (We are here referring to environment inclusively. Thoughts and emotions, as well as situations in the external environment, can operate independently of, or counter to, an individual's intentions and desires.) It is our belief that disconfirming this low sense of perceived control is one of the critical cognitive changes that occurs in exposure treatments (see also Barlow, 1988; Mineka & Kelly, 1989).

CURRENT THEORIES ON THE PSYCHOLOGICAL ORGANIZATION OF FEAR AND ANXIETY

Lang's theory of fear and anxiety was originally developed in part to accommodate evidence indicating that emotion is a complex rather than a unitary phenomenon. Correlations between behavioral, subjective and psychophysiological responses to emotion-provoking stimuli are often very low (Lang, 1971, 1985). Bioinformational theory (Lang, 1977; 1985) attempted to explain such results in terms of multiple response systems, which collectively define the emotional experience. Emotion is viewed as a highly integrative process. Responses to a given stimulus include information about valence (Bargh et al., 1989), autonomic responses (Levenson, 1992), facial responses (Ekman, 1992), escape or avoidance tendencies and so forth. A critical aspect of the model is that these responses actually serve a representational function in the emotional state; the responses act as *input* information in the definition of the final emotion (see Zajonc & Markus, 1984). For example, Ekman, Levenson & Friesen (1983) showed that manipulating the position of specific facial muscles into positions exhibited during certain emotional expressions resulted in changes in emotional states in the direction of the manipulated expression. Moreover, the effect of autonomic activity on emotional experience is well-established (e.g. Reisenzein, 1983). Lang's perspective was that the aggregate of these different response components are relevant to the full experience of an emotional state. The implication for understanding treatment of fear and anxiety was that treatment would require the full accessing of the "fear structure", which would ideally involve accessing all of the response systems simultaneously. For example, in the case of phobic anxiety, Lang showed that the simple phobic patients who improved the most across the course of treatment were the ones for whom these various "response systems" to fearful stimuli were activated simultaneously during exposure therapy. Specifically, subjects who showed elevations only in subjective fear or in heart rate improved less from treatment than subjects who showed both subjective fear and elevated heart rate together (e.g. Lang, Melamed & Hart, 1970; see Foa & McNally, 1996, for further examples). The coordination of response systems in this fashion is expected to be easier in some disorders than others because some disorders are hypothesized to have more or less "diffuse" cognitive–affective structures. It may be difficult to provide good matching input for a particularly diffuse structure (Drobes & Lang, 1995). For instance, in disorders such as generalized anxiety, which is relatively difficult to treat, correlations between subjective and psychophysiological indices of fear or anxiety are much lower than in other anxiety disorders.

To us, one of the most critical contributions of Lang's (1985) theory to understanding fear and anxiety has been his clear articulation of the kinds of information represented in memory that underlie these emotional states. However, it remained to later theorists to try to explain how, once accessed, this information was changed. Foa & Kozak (1986; see also Foa & McNally, 1996) reviewed extensive evidence indicating that psychophysiological arousal during exposure is an important predictor of therapy outcome in a number of anxiety disorders. In their view, there are specific expectations and beliefs associated with the arousal of this anxious emotional state during exposure. Once evoked, the emotion involves misconceptions such as the possibility that the anxiety will have catastrophic consequences, that it will spiral upward indefinitely, or that harmful or threatening consequences are more likely to occur (Foa & McNally, 1996). There is ample evidence in the literature that anxious emotion is associated with such biased perceptions (Beck & Emery, 1985; Clark, 1988). However, Foa & Kozak (1986) also noted that habituation occurs with prolonged exposure to a feared stimulus, resulting in a lowered anxiety level. They argue that this change in anxiety can in turn result in an attenuation of biased, negative thoughts and perceptions. The more neutral perceptions following habituation can provide more objective information about actual risk associated with the stimulus, thus disconfirming the high perceived risk which was associated with the anxious perception of the stimulus. This newly available information can then be assimilated into the cognitive–affective representation of the situation, thus leading to long-term change. In this way, the within-session habituation can result in between-sessions habituation due to an altered cognitive representation of the event.

Consistent with this position, there is substantial evidence that between-session habituation, but not within-session habituation, is reduced when circumstances interfere with the assimilation of new information into the fear structure during the process of exposure. For example, being distracted during exposure does not affect the reduction in fear occurring during the session but results in no improvement from one session to the next (Borkovec & Sides, 1979). Presumably, distraction interferes with the process by which new information would be assimilated into the cognitive–affective memory structure. The extent to which attention can be focused on relevant information has been shown to have a substantial impact on the extent to which information can be encoded in long-term memory (Tulving & Thomson, 1973). Depression also interferes with both within- and between-session habituation (Foa & Kozak, 1986). This is quite possibly due both to altered autonomic states in depressed individuals, which interfere with the possibility of processing interoceptive information, and to the high degree of self-focused attention seen in depression (e.g. Ingram, 1990; Pyszczynski & Greenberg, 1992), which also diverts attention from the information relevant to the feared stimulus. Other interesting conditions interfering with treatment include "overvalued ideation". Individuals with obsessive-compulsive disorder who believe their fears are realistic do not tend to show a diminution of fear with treatment (Foa, 1979). In PTSD, guilt appears to lead to poor within-session habituation as well as poor overall outcome (Pitman et al., 1991). It is easy to see how these conditions could lead to impaired assimilation of altered expectations of the situation. On the basis of this and other evidence, Foa & Kozak (1986) effectively demonstrated both the importance of eliciting the fear, including psychophysiological as well as subjective responses, and the importance of providing a context in which the implicit expectations associated with that fear can be disconfirmed.

The Role of Perceived Lack of Control in Fear and Anxiety

The above findings and perspectives persuasively demonstrate that theories of change in exposure therapy which focus on changes in internal representations of fear have distinct advantages over earlier models. Simpler extinction models cannot explain the relatively consistent finding across different forms of exposure that activation of both psychophysiological and subjective fear responses are important preconditions of change. Similarly, simple habituation models cannot easily explain findings showing that certain conditions such as distraction result in dissociations between within-session habituation and long-term change. A model which includes interrelationships between emotional responses and cognitive representations of information appears to be more useful (Foa & Kozak, 1986; Lang, 1985; Drobes & Lang, 1995). Nevertheless, there does still appear to be room for further refinement in these models. Foa & Kozak (1985, 1986; Foa & McNally, 1996) refer to the process of change as a modification of "cognitive–affective structures"; yet we think that their model misses a key component of the specific representations typical of a dysfunctional fear structure that must be modified for exposure therapy to be effective. Moreover, it may be changes in this key component that mediate changes in the other components such as evaluative errors.

We propose that some of the most crucial information represented in cognitive–affective fear structures is the individual's belief regarding his/her ability to regulate potentially threatening or aversive situations. We further argue that motivation to reduce anxiety, if successful, results in individuals establishing a sense of control over potentially aversive situations. The idea that anxiety is a motivational state is by no means a new one. This possibility has been presented from a variety of theoretical perspectives (Barlow, 1988, 1991; Gray, 1976; Gray & McNaughton, 1996; Mowrer, 1947). To our minds, framing this motivation as directed, at least in part, towards the establishment of control is justified by the substantial literature demonstrating that: (a) the lack or loss of perceived control is associated with increased anxiety; and (b) therapies which are directed at raising individuals' perceptions of control over a situation are associated with the remission of anxiety.

We have reviewed evidence of the causal relationship between low perceived control and anxiety more thoroughly elsewhere (Mineka, 1985; Mineka & Hendersen, 1985; Mineka & Kelly, 1989, Mineka & Zinbarg, 1996; see also Barlow, 1988; Barlow, Chorpita & Turovsky, 1996). In the current context, only a few points need be emphasized in order to establish some of the characteristics of the relationship between control and anxiety. First, it is important to understand what is meant by "control". Control is operationally defined as a contingent relationship between a response and the consequent outcome (Seligman, 1975). Research indicates that when an organism is given a means to terminate an aversive event, this control will attenuate both conditioned and unconditioned anxiety associated with that event. Such effects are established relative to appropriate comparison groups: participants who receive the same aversive stimulation but do not control the onset and/or the termination of that stimulation (Mineka & Hendersen, 1985). Although the majority of research of this sort has been performed on non-human animals, correlational research has also demonstrated the importance of perceived lack of control over highly aversive events in the establishment of long-term anxiety symptoms in humans (Barlow, 1988, 1991; Basoglu & Mineka, 1992; Foa, Zinbarg & Olasov-Rothbaum, 1992; Mineka & Kelly, 1989; Mineka & Zinbarg, 1996). Additionally, the mere perception of control, i.e. the belief that the individual can perform a response which will affect a feared or aversive event, even when such control does not actually exist, has been shown to have a powerful anxiety-reducing effect in humans. For example, Sanderson, Rapee & Barlow (1989) showed that the illusion of control reduced behavioral, subjective and physiological symptoms of panic resulting from a panic provocation procedure. In that study, the panic provocation involved breathing carbon dioxide-enriched air. Participants who believed they could control the level of carbon dioxide in the air if they so desired suffered substantially fewer panic symptoms than those without perceived control, even though the controlling response was not actually used. Moreover, a smaller percentage of those with perceived control had a full-blown panic attack. Such findings emphasize the important role that perceptions or beliefs play in exacerbating or reducing anxiety. A similar conclusion might be drawn from the fact that *general* experience with control, such as control over various positive aspects of one's environment, can decrease an organism's susceptibility to fear or anxiety (e.g. Mineka, Gunnar & Champoux, 1986). Such findings indicate that a more broad expectation that the organism's actions will have the intended effect on the environment can have the same impact on anxiety as knowledge that a specific course of action will alter or reduce the aversive situation.

Research on the attenuation of existing fears or anxiety indicates that control may also be a critical aspect of what is learned in causing this fear attenuation. In animal studies, the reduction of fear which occurs over the course of learning of an effective avoidance response has been shown to be a consequence of the contingent relationship between the response and the absence of aversive stimulation (e.g. Cook, Mineka & Trumble, 1987; Starr & Mineka, 1977). In essence, the response appears to become a safety signal for a non-threatening situation. The animal learns this relationship and thus does not anticipate threat to the same degree when the response can be performed. This finding stands in contrast to the possibility that fear attenuation occurs over the course of avoidance learning as a result of a simple Pavlovian fear extinction process, occuring because the CS is no longer followed by the UCS when successful avoidance occurs. The point is important, because it is precisely this more simple Pavlovian extinction- or habituation-type process which Foa & Kozak (1986) suggest underlies much of the process of change in exposure therapy.

Actually, a recent revision of the Foa & Kozak theory has modified this position somewhat to indicate that it *is* the learning of new associations, rather than the weakening of old associations, that occurs during exposure (Foa & McNally, 1996), although the focus of the new learning they discuss is not about perceived control. Their change in position was prompted by evidence from the animal literature which showed that, when a conditioned fear is extinguished, the extinction does not generalize well across contexts (Bouton, 1988, 1993). These findings indicate that, during extinction, information about the context in which the conditioned stimulus appears is learned by the animal and is very important in determining the conditions under which the once-feared stimulus will or will not elicit fear. One way of viewing this research is to think of contextual information as providing a discriminative cue which indicates to the individual that the feared stimulus is safe in this context. We mention this research because the process appears to parallel what was observed in the avoidance learning studies mentioned above: in both cases, new information is learned which provides the individual with signals of safety against threat. In general, however, the positive effects of gaining a sense of control do generalize well across situations (e.g. Mineka, Gunnar & Champoux, 1986; Mineka & Zinbarg, 1996; Williams & Maier, 1977). Thus, it seems likely that learning an effective coping response will provide more generalizable safety information than is provided simply by context alone following simple Pavlovian fear extinction.

Perceived Control and the Treatment of Anxiety Disorders

Relevant treatment research also tends to support this idea that learning an effective coping response enhances the effectiveness of exposure treatments. For example, providing a phobic with experience of coping effectively with threat provides stronger and/or more generalizable behavioral improvement than merely exposing the individual to the previously feared object or situation for the same period of time (e.g. Bandura, Jeffrey & Wright, 1974; Bourque & Ladouceur, 1980; Öst, Salkovskis, & Hellstrom, 1991; Williams & Zane, 1989). Research on treatment of phobia via participant modeling is also consistent with the position that the learning of appropriate responses to threat can be more useful than merely being exposed to information indicating that a feared situation is nonthreatening. For example, phobics improve more from watching models who overcome a threatening situation by determined effort than from watching adept models perform effective coping strategies in a nonchalant manner (Kazdin, 1973). This is in spite of the fact that, from the Foa & Kozak perspective, one would tend to expect that more information relevant to the non-threatening nature of the stimulus would be provided by the adept models than by the less adept models, because the adept models experienced less fear in facing the feared situation. However, as predicted from a perceived control or self-efficacy perspective, if it is primarily learning effective coping strategies which is important, these findings make sense. That is, the less adept models would provide relevant examples of effective coping in situations where fear is aroused and this would lead to greater improvements in the phobic participants.

Nevertheless, the Foa & Kozak (1986) model might be able to account for these findings if more fear is aroused when watching the frightened model (cf. Mineka & Cook, 1993). Thus, the fear structure might be more fully activated and relevant learning might occur more easily. However, the Foa & Kozak model is less effective in accounting for other findings arising from the same body of literature. For example, watching a group of models perform effective coping strategies is more effective than watching a single model perform identical behaviors (Kazdin, 1975, 1976), although it seems unlikely that watching a variety of models would arouse substantially more fear in the subject. Rather, it seems the individual watching a group of models would be more likely to attribute "safety" to the response patterns than to the models performing them, since the level of safety was constant across a number of individuals (Kelley, 1967). Thus, the individual could more easily learn that the response is an effective signal of "non-threat".

Unfortunately, the ideal modeling study for our purposes has not to our knowledge been performed. In that study, observed anxiety levels in a model (or group of models) would be constant across conditions, and the phobics' levels of arousal and subjective fear while watching the models would be measured, to ensure there were no differences across groups. Given these conditions, we would predict that watching one or more models actively perform coping strategies would lead to greater improvement in the phobics than watching one or more models who become less afraid at an equal rate but who do not perform active coping strategies.

So, to summarize our perspective briefly, anxiety is a motivational state; and when some response results in a reduction in this negative emotion, the individual begins to establish a sense of control over the aversive situations which caused the anxiety. The responses which follow from this motivation can be functional or dysfunctional attempts to regulate threatening or aversive circumstances. In the case of anxiety disorders, prior to treatment there is generally some form of response to the anxiety-provoking situation (Barlow, 1988) that, virtually by definition, is dysfunctional. The most common form of response in the anxiety disorders is passive or active avoidance of the aversive situation. It is the purpose of exposure therapy to prevent these dysfunctional patterns of response so that new, more functional response patterns can be learned. As discussed above, information is learned during the treatment of fear or anxiety which establishes conditions under which the individual can expect the feared aversive outcome not to occur. This information may merely be contextual information which provides the person with specific conditions under which the feared outcome will not occur. Or it may be a sense that the individual can perform an effective response which acts as a "safety signal."

How does this perspective relate to the Foa & Kozak (1986) model? According to their model, the process of change can be blocked in two ways: (a) activation of the relevant fear structure may not occur during exposure; and/or (b) the alteration of an activated fear structure may not occur because disconfirming information is not integrated into the structure. However, we suggest that another possibility is that an escape or avoidance response (overt or covert) intended to reduce the experience of negative emotion blocks or prevents its activation. In this case, the process of change may be impeded for two reasons: first, the relevant information about fear is not adequately accessed; and, second, the inhibition of anxiety by a dysfunctional response blocks the learning of new responses. Any success in regulating anxiety is attributed to the dysfunctional response, and alternate response patterns cannot be learned.

The possibility that overt or covert responses of this sort can have a substantial impact on the maintenance and treatment of anxiety has recently been receiving increasing attention. For example, Borkovec (1994; Borkovec & Hu, 1990; Borkovec et al., 1993) has recently suggested that worry, a process so common in anxiety that it is even the central defining symptom of generalized anxiety disorder, reduces psychophysiological responses to frightening stimuli. His studies have shown that, when anxious subjects undergo a worry induction, they show decreased autonomic responses to visually presented, threatening stimuli (Borkovec & Hu, 1990; Borkovec et al., 1993). The suggestion is that the primarily verbal nature of worry (Borkovec & Inz, 1990) decreases emotional processing of frightening stimuli, since verbal representations of a feared stimulus are only weakly associated with psychophysiological responses (Vrana, Cuthbert & Lang, 1986). Thus, the individual experiences less fear in the short term but does not fully emotionally process the stimulus, so the negative/threatening nature of the stimulus is maintained. Recent research has also indicated that worry about a stressful event can lead to "tagging" of the representation of the stressor in memory, leading to an actual incubation effect (Wells & Papageorgiou, 1995; Wells & Butler, 1997). Nevertheless, because the individual may feel that some degree of control over the anxiety is exerted by worrying, he/she may be unwilling to give up that control in order to see if a new means of control is more effective. One focus of treatment must therefore be to teach new forms of control that do not have these paradoxical effects of maintaining or even exacerbating anxiety.

Related findings have also been reported regarding treatment of social phobia. Wells et al., (1995) identified idiosyncratic safety behaviors that each of eight social phobics employed in anxiety-provoking situations. They then compared the effects of simple exposure to these situations with the effects of exposure plus an assigned decrease in safety behaviors. Results indicated that exposure plus decreased safety behaviors produced greater decreases in anxiety and beliefs in feared catastrophes than did exposure alone. One implication of these results is that the most effective forms of exposure may involve preventing subtle, dysfunctional means of controlling anxiety, so that the fear structure can be more fully accessed and new, more effective means of control can be learned.

Self-efficacy and What It Measures

Bandura's self-efficacy theory asserts that the process of improvement during therapy for anxiety disorders, most specifically phobic disorders, is mediated by an individual's beliefs about the ability to cope effectively with the anxiety-provoking situation. The core postulate of self-efficacy theory is that expectations of self-efficacy are a primary determinant of coping behavior in stressful situations. Self-efficacy is defined in relation to expectancies for outcomes as follows:

> An outcome expectancy is defined as a person's estimate that a given behavior will lead to certain outcomes. An efficacy expectation is the conviction that one can successfully execute the behavior required to produce the outcomes (Bandura, 1977, p. 193).

Thus, the emphasis in this theory is clearly on a sense of perceived control over *behavior* as the determinant and behavioral performance as the outcome measure (Bandura, 1986).

With regard to anxiety disorders, the self-efficacy construct has proved somewhat useful. In terms of simple correlations between a given index and final outcome in therapy, self-efficacy has done quite well. Measures of self-efficacy are more highly correlated with the ability of an individual to perform approach behaviors post-treatment than are measures of anticipated anxiety or perceived danger. Additionally, these beliefs are a better predictor of performance at post-test than are prior behavior or prior level of fear (e.g. Williams, 1996).

However, the primary purpose of all the theories discussed here is to define specific processes which mediate change during treatment. Mediation in this context means that general change is caused by an alteration in a more specific process (e.g. Hollon, DeRubeis & Evans, 1987). Of course, correlational evidence is not sufficient to establish a causal relationship of this sort. Unfortunately, at this point most of the available evidence for *all* theories in this area is merely correlational. However, the primary support for the importance of efficacy beliefs is their relationship to actual behavior in anxiety-producing contexts. Similarly, Foa & Kozak (1986) also support their theory through correlations between patterns of psychophysiological responding and final outcome. Obviously these simple correlations are not adequate to indicate what mediates the changes seen during treatment.

Moreover, neither efficacy expectations nor psychophysiological responding are perfect predictors of therapeutic outcome. It is interesting to look for a moment at the exceptions to these general trends. As noted by Barlow (1988), it seems problematic for the Foa & Kozak (1986) model that there are a substantial proportion of individuals who experience large reductions in subjective levels of fear but who do not show any change in the level of psychophysiological responsiveness in a feared situation (e.g. Vermilyea, Boice & Barlow, 1984). This pattern of desynchrony between response systems also appears to be relatively stable over time (Vermilyea et al., 1984). One descriptive explanation for this pattern of desynchrony is the phenomenon of courage, which has been examined in some detail by Rachman (1990), who has looked specifically at data on soldiers in combat situations. Soldiers who showed courage in a combat situation sometimes continued to have elevated levels of autonomic responsiveness. Nevertheless, over time, they quickly developed reductions in their levels of self-reported fear and, perhaps more importantly, they were able to function without impairment. Such an explanation is consistent with the position that it is fundamentally perceptions of control (or self-efficacy) which develop as at least subjective fears are reduced. These individuals continued to be aroused by a situation which was demanding of resources. However, they had also developed a sense that they could nevertheless effectively cope with the contingencies that arise.

On the other hand, efficacy expectations also do not seem to be able to account adequately for the levels of fear in a threatening situation in all cases. One example that makes this point salient was presented by Rachman (1990) in his re-examination of data on World War II soldiers. He noted, on the one hand, that the degree to which basic training instilled self-confidence through preparing the soldier to handle himself during battle was closely related to anxiety in combat. This "self-confidence", noted by officers during the war (Stouffer et al., 1949), appears to anticipate the self-efficacy theory of fear management. On the other hand, however, 38% of the soldiers with high self-confidence subsequently exhibited a high degree of fear. Six per cent with little or no self-confidence exhibited little or no fear during battle. Also, nearly 20% of soldiers reported dropping self-confidence during battle without any change in fear level; and conversely, roughly the same number of soldiers reported increasing confidence with battle experience but no change in fear level (Rachman, 1981).

It is possible that the self-confidence indicated in this sample does not adequately tap the construct intended by Bandura and his colleagues. However, the measure as described by Rachman does appear to be quite similar to the operationalization Bandura gives for self-efficacy. In our opinion, it may be the narrowness of the efficacy construct itself which is at fault. Below, we discuss two distinct but interrelated ways in which we differ from the self-efficacy position in our understanding of perceived control. For us, the fundamental issue is that self-efficacy theory has not adequately accounted for the central role that emotion plays in anxiety disorders and in the perceptions of control which are most directly relevant to anxiety.

First, the extent to which an individual outside of an extremely stressful situation is able to gain insight into what his/her perceptions within the situation will be seems to us to be potentially limited. In some ways, soldiers preparing for combat are the extreme case in which this limitation would be apparent. These soldiers simply do not have sufficient information to determine how they will feel during combat. As noted by the Foa & Kozak (1986; Foa & McNally, 1996) perspective, it is beliefs which occur in the context of anxious emotions which are most relevant to these disorders. Outside of the situation in which anxiety is provoked, it may be unlikely that an individual will be able to adequately access the feelings and perceptions he/she is likely to have when faced with that situation.

The second issue is actually intimately tied to the point that perceptions of control cannot be adequately understood outside of the context of precipitating emotions. In our opinion, the emphasis on *behavior* in self-efficacy theory is unnecessarily restrictive (see also Barlow, 1988, for related views). There are many times an organism can adequately perform behavioral responses but still not experience a "sense" of being in control of its *emotional response*. Thus, the emotions aroused by a situation may not be consistent with objective judgments about behavioral effectiveness (a point Bandura, 1986, himself acknowledged when he noted that self-efficacy scales were not designed to predict the ability to perform non-anxiously). For example, Mineka, Keir & Price (1980; Mineka & Keir, 1983) showed that monkeys could readily learn to perform approach behaviors to a feared stimulus (live snake) in order to obtain a food reward. These monkeys, however, still exhibited substantial evidence of fear behaviors during the performance of the task and showed no reduction in these fear behaviors across sessions, even though they became more and more adept at performing the appropriate behaviors (i.e. behavioral avoidance decreased). Moreover, substantial, long-lasting changes even in the behavioral avoidance component were only evidenced in a minority of the subjects, presumably because fear levels continued to be high in these animals. This is very consistent with human research also showing that subjective fear and behavioral avoidance are often dissociated following exposure therapy. Thus, an organism may not be able to control the experience of subjective fear, even if a behavior can be performed effectively in the presence of a feared stimulus. In our opinion, it is this feeling of being unable to control one's emotional state that in many cases may be the more dysfunctional aspect of most anxiety disorders than is the inability to control behavioral approach vs. avoidance. Accordingly, we believe that Bandura's theory is too restrictive in focusing on perceived efficacy in approaching a feared situation and would benefit from an expanded focus of perceived ability to control emotions (see Rapee, Craske, Brown & Barlow, 1996, for such a measure).

CONCLUSIONS

In conclusion, it is worth noting that none of the perspectives proposed here has been adequately tested. The next stage of research in this area will necessarily involve more careful studies in order to establish whether or not changes in a particular measure do indeed mediate a more broad range of changes. For example, one could easily wonder currently whether or not efficacy expectations are highly correlated with therapeutic outcome only because people have a high level of insight into the change that has occurred. The correlation certainly does not necessarily mean that it is the beliefs about change themselves which cause the improvement to occur. Likewise, the between-sessions habituation proposed by Foa & Kozak (1986) as mediating therapeutic outcome does not immediately appear to be distinct from outcome measures themselves. However, their position could be supported on empirical grounds if between-sessions habituation is shown through path analyses to unidirectionally predict change in a broader range of fear responses. The application of structural equation modeling to mediational research in this area of therapy will be particularly important, in part because of the loosely connected nature of the different manifestations of fear. It may be at the level of underlying, latent variables, rather than in terms of specifically operationalized measures, that the structure of fear and the course of change becomes most readily apparent. In our opinion, our understanding the mechanisms underlying change can only improve by exploring these mediational processes.

REFERENCES

Abramowitz, J. S. (1996).   Variants of exposure and response prevention in the treatment of obsessive–compulsive disorder. *Behavior Therapy*, **27**, 583–600.

Bandura, A. (1977).   Self-efficacy: towards a unifying theory of behavioral change. *Psychological Review*, **84**, 191–215.

Bandura, A. (1986).   *Social Foundations of Thought and Action: A Social Cognitive Theory*. Englewood Cliffs, NJ: Prentice-Hall.

Bandura, A., Jeffrey, R. W. & Wright, C. L. (1974).   Efficacy of participant modeling as a function of response induction aids. *Journal of Abnormal Psychology*, **83**, 56–64.

Barlow, D. H. (1988).   *Anxiety and Its Disorders: The Nature and Treatment of Anxiety and Panic*. New York: Guilford.

Barlow, D. H. (1991).   Disorders of emotion. *Psychological Inquiry*, **2**, 58–71.

Barlow, D. H., Chorpita, B. F. & Turovsky, J. (1996).   Fear, panic, anxiety, and disorders of emotion. In D. A. Hope (ed.), *Nebraska Symposium on Motivation: Perspectives on Anxiety, Panic, and Fear*, Vol. 43. Lincoln, NE: University of Nebraska Press, pp. 251–328.

Bargh, J. A., Litt, J., Pratto, F. & Spielman, L. A. (1989).   On the preconscious evaluation of social stimuli. In A. F. Bennett & K. M. McConkey (eds), *Cognition in Individual and Social Contexts*. Amsterdam: Elsevier/North-Holland, pp. 357–370.

Basoglu, M. & Mineka, S. (1992).   The role of uncontrollable and unpredictable stress in post-traumatic stress responses in torture survivors. In M. Basoglu (ed.), *Torture and Its Consequences: Current Treatment Approaches*. Cambridge: Cambridge University Press, pp. 182–225.

Beck, A. T. & Emery, G. (1985).   *Anxiety Disorders and Phobias: A Cognitive Perspective*. New York: Basic Books.

Borkovec, T. M. (1994).   The nature, functions, and origins of worry. In G. C. I. Davey & F. Tallis (eds), *Worrying: Perspectives On Theory, Assessment, and Treatment*. New York: Wiley, pp. 3–33.

Borkovec, T. M. & Hu, S. (1990).   The effect of worry on cardiovascular response to phobic imagery. *Behaviour Research and Therapy*, **28**, 69–73.

Borkovec, T. M. & Inz, J. (1990).   The nature of worry in generalized anxiety disorder: a predominance of thought activity. *Behaviour Research and Therapy*, **28**, 153–158.

Borkovec, T. M., Lyonfields, J. D., Wiser, S. L. & Deihl, L. (1993).   The role of worrisome thinking in the suppression of cardiovascular response to phobic imagery. *Behaviour Research and Therapy*, **31**, 321–324.

Borkovec, T. D. & Sides, J. K. (1979).   The contribution of relaxation and expectance to fear reduction via graded imaginal exposure to feared stimuli. *Behaviour Research and Therapy*, **17**, 529–540.

Bourque, P. & Ladouceur, R. (1980).   An investigation of various performance-based treatments with agoraphobics. *Behaviour Research and Therapy*, **18**, 161–170.

Bouton, M. E. (1988).   Context and ambiguity in the extinction of emotional learning: implications for exposure therapy. *Behaviour Research and Therapy*, **26**, 137–149.

Bouton, M. E. (1993).   Context, time, and memory retrieval in the interference paradigms of Pavlovian learning. *Psychological Bulletin*, **114**, 80–99.

Calhoun, K. & Resick, P. (1993).   Post-traumatic stress disorder. In D. Barlow (ed.), *Clinical Handbook of Psychological Disorders*. New York: Guilford, pp. 48–98.

Clark, D. M. (1988).   A cognitive model of panic attacks. In S. Rachman & J. Maser (eds), *Panic: Psychological Perspectives*. Hillsdale, NJ: Erlbaum, pp. 71–89.

Cook, M., Mineka, S. & Trumble, D. (1987).   The role of response produced and exteroceptive feedback in the attenuation of fear over the course of avoidance learning. *Journal of Experimental Psychology: Animal Behavior Processes*, **13**, 239–249.

Davis, M., Parisi, T., Gendelman, D., Tischler, M. & Kehne, J. (1982).   Habituation and sensitization of startle reflexes elicited electrically from the brainstem. *Science*, **218**, 688–690.

Drobes, D. J., Lang, P. J. (1995).   Bioinformational theory and behavior therapy. In W. O'Donohue & L. Krasner (eds), *Theories of Behavior Therapy: Exploring Behavior Change*. Washington, DC: American Psychological Association, pp. 229–257.

Ekman, P. (1992).   Facial expressions of emotion: new findings, new questions. *Psychological Science*, **3**, 34–38.

Ekman, P., Levenson, R. W. & Friesen, W. V. (1983).   Autonomic nervous system activity distinguishes between emotions. *Science*, **221**, 1208–1210.

Emmelkamp, P. (1994).   Behavior therapy with adults. In A. Bergin & S. Garfield (eds), *Handbook of Psychotherapy and Behavior Change*, 4th edn. New York: Wiley, pp. 379–427.

Feske, U. & Chambless, D. (1995).   Cognitive behavioral versus exposure only treatment for social phobia: a meta-analysis. *Behavior Therapy*, **26**, 695–720.

Foa, E. B. (1979).   Failure in treating obsessive-compulsives. *Behaviour Research and Therapy*, **16**, 391–399.

Foa, E. B. & Kozak, M. J. (1985).   Treatment of anxiety disorders: implications for psychopathology. In A. H. Tuma & J. D. Maser (eds), *Anxiety and the Anxiety Disorders*. Hillsdale, NJ: Erlbaum, pp. 451–462.

Foa, E. B. & Kozak, M. J. (1986).   Emotional processing of fear: exposure to corrective information. *Psychological Bulletin*, **99**, 20–35.

Foa, E. B. & McNally, R. J. (1996).   Mechanisms of change in exposure therapy. In R. Rapee (ed.), *Current Controversies in the Anxiety Disorders*. New York: Guilford, pp. 329–343.

Foa, E., Zinbarg, R. & Olasov-Rothbaum, B. (1992).   Uncontrollability and unpredictability in post-traumatic stress disorder: an animal model. *Psychological Bulletin*, **112**, 218–238.

Gray, J. A. (1976).   The behavioural inhibition system: a possible substrate for anxiety. In M. P. Feldman & A. M. Broadhurst (eds), *Theoretical and Experimental Bases of Behaviour Modification*. London: Wiley, pp. 3–41.

Gray, J. A. & McNaughton, N. (1996). The neuropsychology of anxiety: reprise. In D. A. Hope (ed.), *Nebraska Symposium on Motivation: Perspectives on Anxiety, Panic, and Fear*, Vol. 43. Lincoln, NE: University of Nebraska Press, pp. 61–134.

Groves, P. M. & Thompson, R. F. (1970). Habituation: a dual-process theory. *Psychological Review*, **77**, 429–450.

Hollon, S. D., DeRubeis, R. J. & Evans, M. D. (1987). Causal mediation of change in treatment for depression: discriminating between non-specificity and non-causality. *Psychological Bulletin*, **102**, 139–149.

Ingram, R. E. (1990). Self-focused attention and clinical disorders: review and a conceptual model. *Psychological Bulletin*, **107**, 156–176.

Kazdin, A. E. (1973). Covert modeling and the reduction of avoidance behavior. *Journal of Abnormal Psychology*, **81**, 87–95.

Kazdin, A. E. (1975). Covert modeling, imagery assessment, and assertive behavior. *Journal of Consulting and Clinical Psychology*, **43**, 716–724.

Kazdin, A. E. (1976). Effects of covert modeling, multiple models, and model reinforcement on assertive behavior. *Behavior Therapy*, **7**, 211–222.

Keane, T., Gerardi, R., Quinn, S. & Litz, B. (1992). Behavioral treatment of post-traumatic stress disorder. In S. Turner, K. Calhoun & H. Adams (eds), *Handbook of Clinical Behavior Therapy*, 2nd edn. New York: Wiley, pp. 87–97.

Kelley, H. H. (1967). Attribution theory in social psychology. In D. Levine (ed.), *Nebraska Symposium on Motivation*, Vol. 15. Lincoln, NE: University of Nebraska Press, pp. 192–241.

Lader, M. H. & Wing, L. (1966). *Physiological Measures, Sedative Drugs, and Morbid Anxiety*. London: Oxford University Press.

Lang, P. J. (1971). The application of psychophysiological methods to the study of psychotherapy and behavior modification. In A. E. Bergin & S. L. Garfield (eds), *Handbook of Psychotherapy and Behavior Change*. New York: Wiley, pp. 75–125.

Lang, P. J. (1977). Imagery in therapy: an information processing analysis. *Behavior Therapy*, **8**, 862–886.

Lang, P. J. (1985). The cognitive psychophysiology of emotion: fear and anxiety. In A. H. Tuma & J. D. Maser (eds), *Anxiety and the Anxiety Disorders*. Hillsdale, NJ: Erlbaum, pp. 131–170.

Lang, P. J., Melamed, B. J. & Hart, J. D. (1970). A psychophysiological analysis of fear modification using an automated desensitization procedure. *Journal of Abnormal Psychology*, **31**, 221–234.

Levenson, R. W. (1992). Autonomic nervous system differences among emotions. *Psychological Science*, **3**, 23–27.

Mackintosh, N. (1983). *Conditioning and Associative Learning*. New York: Oxford University Press.

Margraf, J. & Schneider, S. (1995). Psychological treatment of panic: What works in the long run? Paper presented at the World Congress of Behavioural and Cognitive Therapies. Copenhagen, Denmark.

Margraf, J. & Schneider, S. (1991). Outcome and active ingredients of cognitive-behavioral treatments for panic disorder. Paper presented at the Association for the Advancement of Behavior Therapy, New York.

Mineka, S., Keir, R. & Price, V. (1980). Fear of snakes in wild- and lab-reared rhesus monkeys. *Animal Learning and Behavior*, **8**, 653–663.

Mineka, S. (1985). Animal models of anxiety-based disorders: their usefulness and limitations. In J. Maser & A. Tuma (eds), *Anxiety and the Anxiety Disorders*. Hillsdale, NJ: Erlbaum, pp. 199–244.

Mineka, S. & Cook, M. (1993). Mechanisms involved in the observational conditioning of fear. *Journal of Experimental Psychology: General*, **122**, 23–38.

Mineka, S., Gunnar, M. & Champoux, M. (1986). Control and early socio-emotional development: infant rhesus monkeys reared in controllable versus uncontrollable environments. *Child Development*, **57**, 1241–1256.

Mineka, S. & Hendersen, R. (1985). Controllability and predictability in acquired motivation. *Annual Review of Psychology*, **36**, 495–530.

Mineka, S. & Keir, R. (1983). The effects of flooding on reducing snake fear in rhesus monkeys: 6-month follow-up and further flooding. *Behaviour Research and Therapy*, **21**, 527–535.

Mineka, S. & Kelly, K. A. (1989). The relationship between anxiety, lack of control, and loss of control. In A. Steptoe & A. Appels (eds), *Stress, Personal Control, and Health.* Brussels: Wiley, pp. 163–191.

Mineka, S. & Zinbarg, R. (1996). Models of anxiety disorders: Stress-in-dynamic-context anxiety models. In D. A. Hope (ed.), *Nebraska Symposium on Motivation: Perspectives on Anxiety, Panic, and Fear*, Vol. 43. Lincoln, NE: University of Nebraska Press, pp. 135–210.

Mowrer, O. H. (1947). On the dual nature of learning: a reinterpretation of "conditioning" and "problem-solving". *Harvard Educational Review*, **17**, 102–148.

Öst, L.-G., Salkovskis, P. & Hellstrom, K. (1991). One-session therapist-directed exposure vs. self-exposure in the treatment of spider phobia. *Behavior Therapy*, **22**, 407–422.

Pitman, R. K., Altman, B., Greenwald, E., Longpre, R. E., Macklin, M. L., Poire, R. E. & Steketee, G. S. (1991). Psychiatric complications during flooding therapy for posttraumatic stress disorder. *Journal of Clinical Psychiatry*, **52**, 17–20.

Pyszczynski, T. A. & Greenberg, J. (1992). *Hanging On and Letting Go: Understanding the Onset, Progression, and Remission of Depression.* New York: Springer-Verlag.

Rachman, S. J. (1981). The primacy of affect: some theoretical implications. *Behaviour Research and Therapy*, **19**, 279–290.

Rachman, S. J. (1990). *Fear and Courage.* New York: Freeman.

Rachman, S. J., Craske, M., Tallman, K., Solyom, C. (1986). Does escape behavior strengthen agoraphobic avoidance? A replication. *Behaviour Therapy*, **17**, 366–384.

Rapee, R. M., Craske, M. E., Brown, T. A. & Barlow, D. H. (1996). Measurement of perceived control over anxiety related events. *Behavior Therapy*, **27**, 279–293.

Reisenzein, R. (1983). The Schachter theory of emotion: two decades later. *Psychological Bulletin*, **94**, 239–264.

Riggs, D. S. & Foa, E. B. (1993). Obsessive compulsive disorder. In D. H. Barlow (ed.), *Clinical Handbook of Psychological Disorders.* New York: Guilford, pp. 189–239.

Sanderson, W. C., Rapee, R. M. & Barlow, D. H. (1989). The influence of an illusion of control on panic attacks induced via inhalation of 5.5% carbon dioxide-enriched air. *Archives of General Psychiatry*, **46**, 157–162.

Seligman, M. E. P. (1975). *Helplessness: On Depression, Development, and Death.* San Francisco: W. H. Freeman.

Starr, M. D. & Mineka, S. (1977). Determinants of fear over the course of avoidance learning. *Learning and Motivation*, **8**, 332–350.

Stouffer, S., Lumsdaine, A., Williams, R., Smith, M., Janix, I., Star, S. & Cottrell, L. (1949). *The American Soldier: Combat and Its Aftermath.* Princeton, NJ: Princeton University Press.

Telch, M. (1995). Singular and combined efficacy of in vivo exposure and CBT in the treatment of panic disorder with agoraphobia. Paper presented at the World Congress of Behavioural and Cognitive Therapies. Copenhagen, Denmark.

Tulving, E. & Thomson, D. M. (1973). Encoding specificity and retrieval processes in episodic memory. *Psychological Review*, **80**, 352–373.

Vermilyea, J. A., Boice, R. & Barlow, D. H. (1984). Rachman and Hodgson (1974) a decade later: how do desynchronous response systems relate to the treatment of agoraphobia? *Behaviour Research and Therapy*, **22**, 615–621.

Vrana, S. R., Cuthbert, B. N. & Lang, P. J. (1986). Processing fearful and neutral sentences: memory and heart rate change. *Cognition and Emotion*, **3**, 179–195.

Watts, F. N. (1979). Habituation model of systematic desensitization. *Psychological Bulletin*, **86**, 627–637.

Wells, A., Clark, D. M., Salvoskis, P., Ludgate, J., Hackmann, A. & Gelder, M. (1995). Social phobia: the role of in-situation safety behaviors in maintaining anxiety and negative beliefs. *Behavior Therapy*, **26**, 153–161.

Wells, A. & Papageorgiou, C. (1995). Worry and the incubation of intrusive images following stress. *Behaviour Research and Therapy*, **33**, 579–583.

Wells, A. & Butler, G. (1997). Generalized anxiety disorder. In D. M. Clark & C. G. Fairburn (eds), *Science and Practice of Cognitive Behavior Therapy*. Oxford: Oxford University Press, pp. 155–178.

Williams, S. L. (1996). Therapeutic changes in phobic behavior are mediated by changes in perceived self-efficacy. In R. Rapee (ed.), *Current Controversies in the Anxiety Disorders*. New York: Guilford, pp. 344–368.

Williams, J. L. & Maier, S. (1977). Trans-situational immunization and therapy of learned helplessness in the rat. *Journal of Experimental Psychology: Animal Behavior Processes*, **3**, 240–252.

Williams, S. L. & Zane, G. (1989). Guided mastery and stimulus exposure treatments for severe performance anxiety in agoraphobics. *Behaviour Research and Therapy*, **27**, 237–247.

Zajonc, R. B. & Markus, H. (1984). Affect and cognition: the hard interface. In C. Izard, J. Kagan & R. B. Zajonc (eds), *Emotion, Cognition, and Behavior*. Cambridge: Cambridge University Press, pp. 73–102.

Chapter 36

Creativity in the Domain of Emotion

James R. Averill
University of Massachusetts, Amherst, MA, USA

On the border between cognition and emotion lies creativity. On the cognitive side of the border, creativity is often grouped among the highest of the "higher" thought processes; on the emotional side, creativity is the occasion for some of life's most intense affective experiences, from the depths of despair to the heights of ecstasy. But the relation between cognition, creativity and emotion is even closer than this border-hopping analogy might suggest. In ordinary language, *cognition* refers to the process of gaining knowledge; *emotion* refers to the way we evaluate and act upon events of personal relevance. As with all terms taken from ordinary language, "cognition" and "emotion" are ultimately based on observable behavior as interpreted within a social context; they do not refer to underlying neurological or psychological mechanisms. A basic assumption of this chapter is that cognitive and emotional behaviors do not differ fundamentally in terms of underlying mechanisms; that is, the same mechanisms (e.g. perception, memory, association, judgment, reasoning) that help mediate cognition also help mediate emotion, albeit perhaps in different combination and degree, depending on the circumstances. One implication of this assumption is that creativity, which also involves these same underlying mechanisms, is as relevant to the emotional as to the cognitive domain.

The focus of this chapter is on emotional creativity; therefore, I will have little to say about cognitive creativity. The chapter is divided into four parts: first, I examine various meanings of "emotion", for not all aspects of emotion are equally susceptible to innovation and change; second, I illustrate the criteria for assessing creativity in the domain of emotion; third, I review empirical evidence for emotional creativity; and, finally, I distinguish between emotional creativity and three closely related topics, namely, emotional intelligence, the management of emotion, and the effect of emotions on problem-solving.

Handbook of Cognition and Emotion. Edited by T. Dalgleish and M. Power.
© 1999 John Wiley & Sons Ltd.

MEANINGS OF EMOTION

The concept of emotion is complex and subject to varying interpretation. Two sources of ambiguity exist. First, as a generic term, "emotion" encompasses a variety of specific emotions (such as anger, pride, joy, grief, love and guilt) that are held together only by vague "family resemblances". It should go without saying that creativity does not apply equally to all members of the emotion family—for example, sudden fright is largely reflexive, whereas love is subject to indefinite variation. I will not consider such differences among emotions further, for the relatively inflexible emotions (such as sudden fright) are few and not paradigmatic of emotion in general.

A second source of ambiguity is more relevant to understanding emotional creativity. Regardless of the specific emotion under consideration (e.g. anger as opposed to fright), four logically distinct types of variables can be distinguished, namely, emotional syndromes, emotional schemas emotional states, and emotional responses. To conflate these types of variables (e.g. to assume that what is true of angry responses is also true of anger as a syndrome) is to commit what Ryle (1949) has called a "category mistake". Each type of variable will be explained and then its relevance to emotional creativity discussed.

Emotional Syndromes

Emotional syndromes are what is named in ordinary language by such abstract nouns as anger, fear, grief, love and the like. These terms do not refer to observable objects or events (e.g. neural circuits or patterns of response); rather, they are folk-theoretical constructs, similar in many respects to the "intervening variables" proposed by psychologists to explain behavior.

To be more specific, the meaning of emotion *qua* syndrome depends on a matrix of culturally specific beliefs (implicit theories) about the nature of emotion. Two broad categories of beliefs can be distinguished: existential beliefs and social rules. Existential beliefs concern what *is*, what exists. Some such beliefs may be true in the sense that they are accurate reflections of how people respond when emotional. For example, it is true that when people are in love they generally want to be together. Other existential beliefs are mythical, for example, that love is made in heaven, that there is only one "true" love, and so forth. Needless to say, myths can lend meaning and significance to life, sometimes even more than true beliefs. The important point is that emotional syndromes are constituted, in part, by the existential beliefs we hold about them.

Emotional syndromes are also constituted—not just regulated—by social rules (Averill, 1984; Hochschild, 1983). Succinctly put, our folk theories of emotion not only describe what *is*, whether in fact or myth, they also prescribe what *should be*. Among other things, this means that emotional syndromes are infused with values, a point about which I will have more to say below.

Emotional Schemas

Before a person can experience a particular emotion, he/she must internalize the relevant beliefs and rules regarding that emotion. In other words, the person must have appropriate emotional schemas or internal representations. Internalization is never complete, however. Due to individual differences in temperament, socialization and position in society, only a subset of beliefs and rules may be internalized, and then with varying degrees of accuracy. In this way, emotional syndromes are personalized and made subject to individual innovation and change.

The relation between emotional syndromes and schemas is depicted in the top portion of Figure 36.1. The clear oval within the more encompassing emotional syndrome represents the existential beliefs and social rules internalized by the individual, that is, emotional schemas.

Figure 36.1 necessarily oversimplifies the relation between emotional schemas and emotional syndromes. Emotional schemas are mental phenomena—knowledge structures—that guide the processing of information within the nervous system. Schemas are multifaceted: at the simplest level, they include associative elements (e.g. acquired through conditioning); at a more complex level, they include propositional elements (beliefs and rules expressible in language); and at a more complex level still, they include abstractions that cannot be fully articulated in language—what Polanyi (1964) has called "tacit knowledge" in the case of scientific understanding. In the case of emotion, tacit knowledge may be manifested in art, music, ritual and other expressive forms (for a more detailed discussion of the multifaceted nature of emotional schemas, and some of the complications that may introduce, see Teasdale, this volume).

Emotional States

An emotional state involves the activation of relevant emotional schemas; it is a temporary (episodic) disposition to respond in a manner consistent with an emotional syndrome, as that syndrome is understood by the individual. Some emotional states last only few moments (e.g. sudden fright), others may last for hours (e.g. anger), and still others may last for months or even years (e.g. grief, love). Particularly during the longer episodes, considerable latitude exists for the manner and kind of responses a person might make.

Emotional schemas need not exist fully formed in the mind (or brain) of the individual, just waiting to be activated by appropriate initiating conditions. Like other mental structures, some emotional schemas may be stored and recalled as such. When the situation is unusual and the episode complex, however, emotional schemas may be constructed "on-line", so to speak, as the episode develops. In constructing a schema on-line, the person has recourse to a large database of previous experience stored in memory, as well as general beliefs about the emotion and its consequences. Depending on the situation and the person's

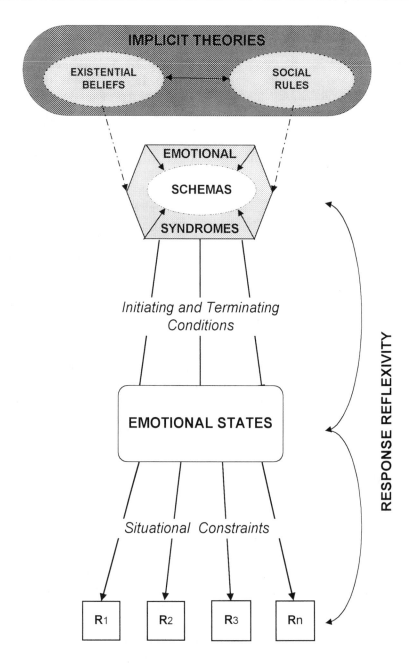

Figure 36.1 Relations among emotional syndromes, schemas, states and responses. Shaded areas at the top of the figure indicate that emotional syndromes, and the implicit theories on which they are based, are intersubjective, that is, external to the individual. By contrast, emotional schemas, states, and responses are subjective or personal variables

motives and goals, only a subset of this stored of information may be accessed in any given episode.

To draw an analogy, we might compare an emotional state or episode to a musical performance. Some performances are based on a pre-established score, whereas others involve a good deal of improvization. Similarly, some emotional "performances" are well-scripted (follow closely pre-established cultural beliefs and rules), whereas other episodes are improvized. It is important to note, however, that "improvizational" does not mean "unruly" or "disordered".

Emotional Responses

Emotional responses are what a person actually does when in an emotional state. A reflexive or bidirectional relation exists among emotional responses, states and syndromes, as illustrated by the curved arrows at the right of Figure 36.1. Looking down the hierarchy depicted in the figure, emotional syndromes literally inform (help organize and direct) the kinds of responses that are exhibited during an emotional state. Conversely, looking upward in the hierarchy, emotional responses lend substance to otherwise "empty" schemas. Even responses that are relatively automatic (such as changes in visceral activity) are experienced as emotional only to the extent that they are interpreted within the framework of an emotional syndrome; it is this reflexivity that transforms mere arousal (e.g. from climbing the stairs) into emotional arousal (an angry episode, say).

One kind of response deserves special mention, namely, feelings. For some theorists, these are the *sine qua non* of emotion. It is therefore important to note that feelings are subject to social and motivational influences, just as are other kinds of response. An analogy may help to clarify this point. In certain respects, emotional feelings can be compared with more elementary perceptual responses, such as hearing voices. A person can hear voices even when no-one is speaking, not hear voices when someone is speaking, misinterpret what is heard, or hear correctly. Feeling an emotion is much more complex that than hearing voices and is even more subject to confounding, based on situational and personal factors. For example, we need not—and often do not—accept at face value a person's assertion, no matter how sincerely expressed at the moment, that he feels angry (sad, in love, etc.); conversely, we may recognize that a person is angry (sad, in love, etc.) even though he sincerely denies having any such feelings. In short, the criteria for *being* emotional and *feeling* emotional are not the same, a fact dramatically illustrated in court cases involving crimes of passion (Averill, 1993).

EMOTIONAL CREATIVITY

Emotional creativity involves innovation primarily at the level of emotional syndromes. As the above discussion suggests, change can proceed in either a top-down or bottom-up direction. In a top-down approach, emphasis is placed on the identification and change in the beliefs and rules that constitute an emotional syndrome, or at least its internal representation, the corresponding emotional schemas. A bottom-up approach begins with the acquisition or training of component responses, which only subsequently are incorporated into broader structures. Sudden religious or political conversions, such as that described by St Augustine in his *Confessions* (397–400/1949, Bk. VIII) provide dramatic examples of a top-down approach. Learning trance in Bali, as described by Bateson (1976), provides a good example of a bottom-up approach. Balinese children first learn the component responses for trance (e.g. automatic body movements), and only later integrate them into a meaningful syndrome. In general, bottom-up approaches predominate during childhood, before well-formed emotional schemas are developed, and top-down approaches are more common during adulthood. (In actual practice, of course, a person seeking emotional change typically will tack back and forth between acquiring new responses and altering previously formed schemas.)

Changes in emotional syndromes can be considered creative (as opposed, for example, to neurotic or merely eccentric) if three criteria are met: first, the emotion should be in some way *novel* or distinct, either in terms of the individual's own past behavior or with reference to broader social expectations; second, the emotion should be *effective* in solving the problems which produce the emotion in the first place, at least in the long run, and if not for the individual, then for the larger group; and, finally, the emotion should be *authentic*, that is, a reflection of the person's own beliefs and values and not a mere copy of others' expectations. Although easily stated, each of these criteria may be quite difficult to assess in practice, for each is relative to the person and the situation. For example, a response can be judged novel only in contrast to what is commonplace, either for the individual or the group (see Averill & Nunley, 1992, for a detailed discussion).

Two Examples

Viktor Frankl (1984) has described the ways prisoners tried to cope with the everyday horrors of life—and death—in Nazi concentration camps. Most ways were relatively unimaginative and ineffective (e.g. despair, dreaming of revenge) but some were highly creative. One particular episode is worth recounting in detail. A semi-starved prisoner had stolen a few pounds of potatoes—a "crime" punishable by death. When the theft was discovered, the authorities demanded that the perpetrator be turned in, or else the entire camp would be deprived of rations for a day. No-one revealed the thief's identity. On the evening of the day of enforced fasting, Frankl describes how the prisoners lay in their huts "in a very low mood"; and when the light suddenly went out, "tempers reached their lowest ebb". At that point, Frankl, himself "cold and hungry, irritable and tired", was asked by the senior block warden (also a prisoner) to speak to the men in an attempt to forestall suicides, which had become frequent of late. Frankl asked his fellow prisoners to remember their pre-war successes and happiness, for as he said, no-one can take from a person his memories. Frankl then spoke of the ways that hardship can make a person stronger:

> I told my comrades (who lay motionless, although occasionally a sigh could be heard) that human life, under any circumstances, never ceases to have a meaning, and that this infinite meaning of life includes suffering and dying, privation and death. I asked the poor creatures who listened to me attentively in the darkness of the hut to face up to the seriousness of our position. They must not lose hope but should keep their courage in the certainty that the hopelessness of our struggle did not detract from its dignity and its meaning. I said that someone looks down on each of us in difficult hours—a friend, a wife, somebody alive or dead, or a God—and he would not expect us to disappoint him. He would hope to find us suffering proudly— not miserably—knowing how to die (Frankl, 1984, p. 104).

This episode (called to my attention by Pano Rodis) illustrates well some of the major features of emotional creativity. Frankl was not engaging in some abstract philosophical discourse, but was attempting to inspire the prisoners, "then and there, in that hut and in that practically hopeless situation". His appeal for emotional transformation was basically a top-down approach. He did not deny the seriousness of the situation; rather, he tried to get the men to reframe their suffering so that they might *feel* differently about it. He did this in two ways: first, by emphasizing the meaning of life even in the face of almost certain death; and, second, by invoking a sense of loyalty or obligation to loved ones, living or dead. Thus, the men were encouraged to take heart despite the hopelessness of their situation, and to "suffer proudly".

Evidently Frankl's appeal was effective, for when the light came on again, he saw "the miserable figures" of his friends limping toward him "with tears in their eyes". More importantly, this ability to find meaning in suffering and to maintain loyalty to departed loved ones (e.g. his wife, who had been killed earlier) was, according to Frankl, one of the main factors that helped him to survive his years in concentration camps—that and considerable good fortune.

Frankl's situation was extreme and, as the saying goes, necessity is the mother of invention. As a second example of emotional creativity, therefore, let us consider Virginia Woolf's (1942) description of her reactions to the death of a moth. Almost everyone has witnessed with interest, or even mild revulsion, the dying of a moth as it flutters against a window pane. Woolf's reaction was different: watching the moth's futile struggle, she was moved "*strangely*" and experienced "a *queer* sense of pity" (emphasis added). There was "something marvelous as well as pathetic" about the moth, as though "the enormous energy of the world had been thrust into his frail and diminutive body". Woolf watched for a time without thinking, but then the moth's helplessness "roused" her. When the moth could no longer raise itself, she stretched out a pencil to help, but then withdrew her hand: "One could only watch the extraordinary efforts made by those tiny legs against an oncoming doom which could, had it chosen, have submerged an entire city, not merely a city, but masses of human beings".

The novelty of Woolf's experience is evident even from this brief description. Moreover, there is no doubt about the authenticity of her reactions: she did not describe this episode to impress an audience; the essay was published posthumously. (In a later section on the management of emotion, I will have more to say about authenticity and its relation to emotional creativity.) The effectiveness of her response was, however, problematic. Not long after this episode, she committed suicide. Woolf—no less than Frankl—had a profound respect for life. But that was not sufficient for her to win her life-long struggle against depression. We can, however, also evaluate effectiveness from the perspective of the group, not just the individual. If we take the frequency with which Woolf's essay has been anthologized as an indication, her experience has moved many others, not only strangely, but perhaps to better effect.

Experiences such as those by Frankl and Woolf illustrate emotional creativity. However, they do not advance our understanding greatly. For that, we must turn to more traditional kinds of research.

A SELECTIVE REVIEW OF RESEARCH

Theoretically, the notion of emotional creativity is a straightforward extension of a social-constructionist view of emotion (Averill, 1980) as applied to individual development and change (Averill, 1984). If the change proves damaging, we may speak of emotional disorders (Averill, 1988), but if it proves valuable, then of emotional creativity (Averill & Thomas-Knowles, 1991; Averill & Nunley, 1992). Social constructionism does not deny the importance of biological pre-determinants of emotion. But just as a log cabin is not a tree masked by housing rules, neither is anger, say, simply aggression masked by display rules. But be that as it may, evidence that supports the social construction of emotion—such as cultural differences in emotional syndromes—is also evidence for emotional creativity.

Cultural Differences

There is no need to review the growing literature on cross-cultural differences in emotion; that such differences exist is not in doubt, although their theoretical significance is subject to dispute (cf. Kitayama & Markus, 1994; Mesquita & Frijda, 1992; Russell, 1991). Here, I will discuss briefly two subsidiary issues, namely, the relation of language to emotion and the role of culture in fostering emotional creativity.

As described earlier, abstract nouns such as "anger", "fear" and "grief" name emotional syndromes. This does not mean that emotion words are simply labels arbitrarily pinned on independently existing entities. Rather, emotional concepts (and the words that represent those concepts) are given meaning by the same implicit theories (existential beliefs and social rules) that help constitute emotional syndromes. One learns the meaning of an emotional concept as one learns how to behave and feel in a manner appropriate to the emotional syndrome.

The relation of language to emotional creativity is thus two-sided. On the one hand, emotion words can serve as catalysts for emotional development—the acquisition of syndromes that are standard (and named) within the culture. On the other hand, language also constrains experience, forcing emotions into preordained conceptual categories. A truly creative emotional experience needs break the bonds of ordinary language.

Large cultural differences exist in the language of emotion. At the high end of the continuum, the English language contains roughly 550–600 words (nouns, verbs, adjectives, adverbs) that have a rather clear-cut emotional connotation (Averill, 1975; Johnson-Laird & Oatley, 1989; Storm & Storm, 1987). Some languages may have an even larger emotion lexicon, although comparisons are made difficult by variations in the inclusiveness of "emotion" as a generic category (Russell, 1991). At the low end of the continuum, some languages have few words for emotion. For example, Lutz (1982) found no general term equivalent to "emotion" among the Ifaluk, a people of Micronesia, and only 58 words that she considered unambiguously emotional in connotation ("about our insides").

As noted above, language can serve as a catalyst for emotional development. Does that mean that the Ifaluk have a less rich emotional life than English-speaking peoples? Not necessarily. Three caveats must be kept in mind. First, language is only one way of conveying concepts; other, non-linguistic symbol systems (e.g. music, dance, painting) can be used to enrich the emotional lives of a people. Second, some words that are very broad in scope can also be very rich in meaning. The English word "love", for example, is not noted for its fine nuances, yet it is clearly very meaningful. Indeed, the very breadth and vagueness of a concept may allow for greater flexibility—and creativity—in the corresponding emotion. Third, behavior that is conceptualized as emotional in one culture may be conceptualized quite differently, but no less meaningfully, in another culture. To illustrate, Tahitians have no terms in their language for emotions that in English would be described as "sadness", "longing", or "loneliness" (although the Tahitians do have terms for severe grief and lamentation). What a Westerner might interpret as sadness, Tahitians might attribute to fatigue or illness (Levy, 1984).

In short, societies help determine the number and kind of emotions available to their members, a fact that is reflected (albeit inexactly) in language. Emotional creativity, however, involves the development of new emotional syndromes, a process that can be hindered as well as facilitated by the availability of conceptually "pre-packaged" emotions. When considering emotional creativity, non-linguistic factors must also be taken into account.

Historically, within Western societies, Simonton (1975) has identified two conditions that have been associated with creativity, namely, cultural diversity and the existence of role-models. When these conditions exist in one generation, creativity evidently increases in the next generation. Simonton's analysis was limited to creativity in the arts and sciences, but there is no reason to believe that his findings are any less important for creativity in the domain of emotion. Whenever people of different backgrounds and values interact on more than a superficial level, the potential for conflict and the need for positive accommodation are heightened. A willingness to be emotionally innovative is essential during such periods, and the presence of role models may point the way.

Simonton also identified one condition, namely, political instability, that tends to inhibit creativity. Political instability is often accompanied by a restriction of freedom and a call for return to "traditional values". As described earlier, emotions are laden with value; a change in emotion implies a change in values. It follows that during times of political unrest or insecurity, emotional innovation would be particularly threatening and subject to condemnation. Bertrand Russell (1930/1958) put the issue well when he observed that: "Caution is enjoined both in the name of morality and in the name of worldly wisdom, with the result that generosity and adventurousness are discouraged where the affections are concerned" (p. 185).

Individual Differences

A culture could not evolve were it not for the creativity of its members. However, not all members of a society are equally creative. This is true in the intellectual and artistic domains, and, if the arguments presented thus far are valid, it is also true in the domain of emotion. One way, then, to explore emotional creativity is, first, by demonstrating the existence of individual differences in the ability to produce innovative yet adaptive emotional responses and, second, by examining the antecedents and correlates of such individual differences.

Wallas (1926) outlined four stages of the creative process: preparation, incubation, illumination and verification. The three criteria for creativity outlined earlier (novelty, effectiveness, authenticity) pertain to Wallas's final stage of verification; that is, they represent standards for evaluating a response as creative. The first or preparatory stage is also important for the assessment of individual differences in creativity. Creativity does not strike suddenly, out of nowhere, with little or no prior effort. Just the opposite is the case (Hayes, 1981; Perkins, 1981; Weisberg, 1986). We would expect, then, that people who know about, think about, and are attentive to their emotions are also emotionally more creative than are people who treat their emotions as uncontrollable "happenings".

Based on individual differences in preparation for—as well as the perceived novelty, effectiveness and authenticity of—one's emotional life, a self-report *Emotional Creativity Inventory* (ECI) has been constructed (Averill, 1994, in press). This inventory, which consists of 30 items (seven for preparation, 14 for novelty, five for effectiveness, and four for authenticity) was designed for research and screening purposes, not for individual assessment. Factor analyses suggest that the preparedness items form one facet; the novelty items, another facet; and the effectiveness and authenticity items, a third facet.

In laboratory studies, participants who score high on the ECI are better able to express their emotions creatively in both written and pictorial form (Gutbezahl & Averill, 1996). For example, high-scoring subjects write more innovative stories combining seemingly incompatible emotions (such as serene, bewildered, and impulsive); they describe more creative resolutions to seemingly irresolvable conflicts; and they draw more creative pictures that depict emotions in abstract form. Persons who score high on the ECI are also judged by acquaintances to be more emotionally creative, presumably on the basis of behavior in everyday situations (Averill, in press).

Scores on the ECI are also associated in a predictable manner with a variety of other personality variables. Among the "Big Five" personality dimensions, for example, the ECI is significantly correlated with Openness to Experience ($r[147] = 0.58$) and Agreeableness ($r[147] = 0.23$), but not with Neuroticism, Extraversion, or Conscientiousness, as measured by the NEO-PI (Costa & McCrae, 1985). People who score high on the ECI are more prone to mystic-like experiences (e.g. transcendence of space and time, the loss of ego boundaries, and a sense that all things are alive), as measured by Hood's (1975) scale ($r[89] = 0.46$). Self-confidence should facilitate receptivity to unusual experiences; not surprisingly, therefore, a modest correlation exists between the ECI and Rosenberg's (1965) self-esteem scale ($r[89] = 0.25$). Finally, a negative relation exists between the ECI and alexithymia ($r[87] = -0.34$), as measured by the TAS-20 (Bagby, Parker & Taylor, 1994). These correlations are for the total scores on the ECI; the pattern of relations differ somewhat when the preparedness, novelty and effectiveness-authenticity facets are considered separately.

The negative correlation between the ECI and alexithymia scales deserves brief elaboration, for unusual emotional experiences are often taken as a sign of psychopathology. As its name implies, alexithymia is a condition that involves an inability to identify and describe one's own emotional experiences. Novel emotions are also difficult to identify and describe, and in this respect, some overlap exists between the constructs of emotional creativity and alexithymia. However, people suffering from alexithymia have an impoverished fantasy life, a reduced ability to experience positive emotions, and susceptibility to poorly differentiated negative affect (Taylor, 1994). Such characteristics are antithetical to emotional creativity. The point that needs emphasis here is that the susceptibility to unusual emotional experiences is not *per se* a sign of psychopathology; rather, depending on the person and the circumstances, it may be a sign of creativity.

In contemporary psychology, emphasis has been placed on the potential detrimental effects of stressful experience, from subsequent constriction of affect to repetition compulsion (as in post-traumatic stress disorder). Without minimizing the incidence or significance of such detrimental effects, we should also recognize that stress, if properly managed, can have beneficial outcomes (e.g.

Aldwin, Sutton & Lachman, 1996). Certainly, that appears true with respect to emotional creativity. People who score high on the ECI report more traumatic experiences during childhood and adolescence (e.g. the death of someone close, divorce of parents, verbal or physical abuse, serious accident or illness) than do people who score low. High scorers also report more minor hassles and disappointments during their formative years.

In short, individual differences in emotional creativity, as measured—however approximately—by the ECI, show theoretically meaningful relations to emotional behavior, to other personality variables and to early experience.

RELATED FORMULATIONS

Emotional creativity overlaps with three other areas of current research, namely, emotional intelligence, the management of emotion, and the effect of emotion on creative problem-solving.

Emotional Intelligence

Salovey & Mayer (1990) define emotional intelligence as "the ability to monitor one's own and others' feelings and emotions, to discriminate among them and to use this information to guide one's thinking and actions" (p. 189). More loosely defined to include almost any adaptive emotional response, the concept of emotional intelligence has also been made the topic of a best-selling book by Goleman (1995). Similar ideas under different names have been formulated by others, for example, "intra- and interpersonal intelligence" (Gardner, 1983) and "constructive thinking" (Epstein, 1992).

Under the general heading of emotional intelligence, Mayer & Salovey (1995, 1997) recognize four more specific abilities: (a) to perceive, appraise and express emotions accurately; (b) to use emotions to facilitate thought; (c) to understand and employ knowledge about emotions (e.g. to name emotions, and to distinguish between closely-related emotions, such as loving and liking); and (d) to regulate emotions to promote growth. Since these abilities are assumed to be semi-independent, patterns of emotional intelligence can presumably vary among individuals; that is, one person might be high on one ability and low on another, whereas another person might show the opposite pattern.

Each of the above four abilities are also assumed to vary in complexity, from a relatively automatic, non-conscious level to a multifaceted, self-reflective level. A person who is emotionally intelligent at one level need not be intelligent at another (either higher or lower) level. For example, an angry person might respond intelligently at the automatic level, but have little explicit knowledge about anger at the meta-level, whereas another person might respond unreasonably at the automatic level, and yet be quite introspective and knowledgeable about anger at the meta-level.

Salovey, Mayer and their colleagues have developed several tests to assess emotional intelligence. The Trait Meta-Mood Scale (Salovey et al., 1995) is a self-report measure composed of three factors: (a) the *attention* people devote to their emotions; (b) the *clarity* of their emotional experiences; and (c) the ability to *repair* negative moods or to prolong positive ones. A second instrument, the Emotional IQ Test (Mayer, Salovey & Caruso, 1977), is a performance-based measure in which persons are presented with miniature "problems", much as on a regular IQ test. For example, persons are asked to identify emotions expressed in faces, musical selections and abstract designs, to indicate the most appropriate or effective ways of responding to a variety of emotional situations, and to demonstrate knowledge of emotional concepts. Each task is accompanied by a set of alternative responses or ratings scales, and scoring is objective in that some answers are considered "right" and others are "wrong".

There is an obvious overlap between the constructs of emotional intelligence and emotional creativity. Both assume an awareness of, and sensitivity to, one's own and others' feelings, and both emphasize the effectiveness of emotional responses. However, the two constructs differ in the emphasis they place on the novelty and authenticity of an emotion. Specifically, emotional intelligence emphasizes the ability to process emotionally relevant information in ways that are standard (and hence presumably effective) within a culture. Emotional creativity, by contrast, emphasizes the novelty or non-conforming aspects of emotional life, and also the degree to which the emotions (whether novel or not) reflect an individual's authentic or "true" feelings—a topic to which I will return shortly.

To conclude this brief discussion of emotional intelligence, we might take a clue from the cognitive domain, where intellectual intelligence (IQ)—beyond the level required for competence within a field—is relatively independent of creativity. Given two people of equal intellectual ability, one may be creative and the other not. There is no reason to believe the situation to be different in the domain of emotion.

The Management of Emotion

The ability to manage or regulate one's emotions to fit the circumstances is a facet of both emotional intelligence and emotional creativity. However, the management of emotion is a much older and broader topic than either of these two constructs. For example, emotional regulation has long been a staple of clinical psychology in general, and of stress management in particular. Recently, industrial psychologists and sociologists have also become interested in the management of emotion on the institutional as well as the individual level. Hochschild (1983), for example, analyzed the "emotional work" expected by some organizations of their employees. She suggests that behind the forced cheerfulness of an airline stewardess, or the anger of a bill collector, there exist feelings that are authentic and from which employees may become estranged in the furtherance of corporate interests, often at considerable expense to themselves (e.g. in the form of stress). Others have expressed similar concerns (e.g. Fineman, 1995).

Of the many issues raised by the management of emotion, I will focus on authenticity, one of the criteria for an emotionally creative response. As the above observations by Hochschild imply, the institutional management of emotions can lead to a lack of authenticity; the same is true on the individual level, as when a person feigns an emotion—love, say, or anger—for ulterior reasons (the "feigning" need not, of course, be conscious). Put bluntly, persons who adroitly express the emotions expected of them are no more creative than the skilled painter who copies the work of another for personal or commercial profit. But what constitutes an authentic emotion or, in colloquial terms, a "true feeling"?

Perhaps the most common way of interpreting authentic emotions is in biological terms. According to this view, some emotions are more "basic" than others in that they serve—or, during earlier periods of human evolution, did serve—an adaptive function. Such basic emotions presumably can be regulated only with difficulty and are relatively impervious to change. We should, however, be wary about making biology the sanctuary for authentic emotions. As noted earlier, emotions are laden with value; to ascribe authentic emotions to biology— or to any other immutable source—is to put those values beyond question. Paradoxically, that is precisely what some socially orientated theorists wish to achieve, even as they look askance at what they consider "biological determinism" in almost every other domain. Activists of diverse persuasion, conservative or radical, secular or religious, urge people to "get in touch with their true feelings", that is, with feelings presumably unsullied by social influence. In most cases, what is considered true is whatever agrees with the activist's own ideology; and whatever disagrees is dismissed as unauthentic, a sign of "bad faith" (Sartre) or "false consciousness" (Marx).

To explore the way ordinary people—as opposed to psychological theorists or social activists—characterize authentic emotions, Morgan & Averill (1992) asked participants in a study to describe an episode that reflected their "true feelings" and to contrast that episode with another, more typical episode of similar intensity. The most frequently mentioned contrast between true and typical feelings (cited by 92% of the participants) was that "the true feelings taught me more about myself". Other frequently mentioned contrasts were, "the true feelings helped more in clarifying my values" (73%), "the true feelings helped more to guide me in my life" (63%), and "the true feelings taught me more about relating to others" (63%).

Without going into further detail, the conditions that led to ostensibly true or authentic emotions typically involved a challenge to a person's fundamental beliefs and values. The primary source of those beliefs and values, needless to say, is social. Under certain circumstances (e.g. falling in love, loss of a relationship, or interpersonal conflict) people may commit themselves to new beliefs and values, or recommit themselves to ones long held. The emotions experienced in those circumstances tend to be complex, nebulous and difficult to describe in ordinary language. Nevertheless, they are assessed as true or authentic.

In short, authenticity in the domain of emotion does not imply immutability, as some discussions of emotional management seem to imply. On the contrary: authenticity is a sign of change, or at least of challenge. This point deserves special emphasis. In the arts and sciences, authenticity is more closely associated with innovation than with received knowledge. The same applies to the emotions.

Emotion and Creative Problem-solving

Most discussions of emotion and creativity focus on the influence of emotional states on creativity in non-emotional domains (cf. Shaw & Runco, 1994). For example, Isen (1993) has shown that the induction of a mild positive mood (e.g. by viewing a short comedy film or receiving a small gift) may facilitate creative problem-solving in both laboratory and applied settings, provided the task is of interest or importance to the individual. When in a positive mood, people enjoy exploring new ideas, are more flexible in their thinking, and are more thoughtful in their relationships with others.

Consistent with the above findings, people who suffer from bipolar affective disorders are more likely to be creative when in a positive (hypomanic) than in a negative (depressed) state (Jamison, 1994). The musician Schumann provides an oft-cited example. In each of 2 years when he was hypomanic, Schumann composed over 25 pieces; in each of 2 years that he was depressed, he produced little (two compositions in one year, none in the other).

When evaluating findings such as the above, three qualifications must be kept in mind. First, most of the research done to date has focused on the influence of positive and negative moods rather than on specific emotions. Little is known about the potential effects of emotions such as love, fear, anger, etc., on the creative process. (An exception to this generalization is grief following bereavement; Marris, 1975; Pollock, 1989.) Second, creativity involves a willingness to take risks; yet mild positive moods tend to make people more cautious or risk-averse, lest they disrupt their pleasant state (Isen, 1993). Third, some people actually cultivate negative experiences as a goad to, or source of, creativity (Parrott, 1993).

Any attempt to unravel the complex interactions between positive and negative emotional states, on the one hand, and creativity, on the other, would require breaking creativity into stages or components, from the initial motivation and formulation of a problem to its final solution and implementation. Emotional states that facilitate one stage of the process may well hinder another stage. But such an analysis is beyond the scope of this chapter (see, Russ, 1993). Our concern in this chapter has not been with the effects of emotion on creativity but, rather, with emotions themselves as creative products. It remains to be seen whether findings on mood and creativity in non-emotional domains can be generalized to creativity in the domain of emotion itself.

CONCLUDING OBSERVATIONS

In ordinary language, "cognition" refers to the process of gaining knowledge, and like knowledge itself, cognition is presumably dispassionate and objective. You can know what I know, for in the final analysis, individual idiosyncrasies are subtracted from the process, like noise from a message. Emotions, on the other hand, individuate. My fears, my hopes, my loves, my hates: these are among my most distinguishing features; they help make me the unique person that I am. But emotions are not like noise in the system, as some traditional theories would have it.

Emotions may be related to cognition—gaining knowledge—in several ways, for example, as antecedents, as accompaniments and as consequences of creative problem-solving. But these ways are background. As in a reversible figure, what is background from one perspective may become focal from another perspective. The construct of emotional creativity makes such a reversal, viewing emotions as creative products in their own right, with cognition providing the background.

Emotional creativity is important for both theoretical and practical reasons. Theoretically, it highlights the commonalities in processes that underlie all human behavior, so that insights gained in one domain (cognition) can fruitfully be applied to the other (emotion) and vice versa. On a more practical level, examples abound of organizations and entire societies that were unable to utilize technological innovations because their members could not adapt emotionally to change. Creativity in the domain of emotion is as important for success as is creativity in the intellectual domain.

REFERENCES

Aldwin, C. M., Sutton, K. J. & Lachman, M. L. (1996). The development of coping resources in adulthood. *Journal of Personality*, **64**, 837–869.

Augustine (397–400/1949). *The Confessions of Saint Augustine* (E. B. Pusey, trans.). New York: Modern Library (original work written 397–400 AD).

Averill, J. R. (1975). A semantic atlas of emotional concepts. *JSAS Catalogue of Selected Documents in Psychology*, **5**, 330 (MS. No. 1103).

Averill, J. R. (1980). A constructivist view of emotion. In R. Plutchik & H. Kellerman (eds), *Theories of Emotion*. New York: Academic Press, pp. 305–340.

Averill, J. R. (1984). The acquisition of emotions during adulthood. In C. Z. Malatesta & C. E. Izard (eds), *Emotion in Adult Development*. Beverly Hills, CA: Sage, pp. 23–43.

Averill, J. R. (1988). Disorders of emotion. *Journal of Social & Clinical Psychology*, **8**, 247–268.

Averill, J. R. (1993). Illusions of anger. In R. B. Felson & J. T. Tedeschi (eds), *Aggression and Violence: Social Interactionist Perspectives*. Washington, DC: American Psychological Association, pp. 171–192.

Averill, J. R. (1994). Emotional creativity inventory: scale construction and validation. Paper presented at International Society for Research on Emotion, Cambridge, July.

Abstract in N. H. Frijda (ed.), *Proceedings of the VIIth Conference of the International Society for Research on Emotions*. Storrs, CT: ISRE, pp. 227–231.

Averill, J. R. (in press). Individual differences in emotional creativity: Structure and correlates. *Journal of Personality*.

Averill, J. R. & Nunley, E. P. (1992). *Voyages of the Heart: Living an Emotionally Creative Life*. New York: Free Press.

Averill, J. R. & Thomas-Knowles, C. (1991). Emotional creativity. In K. T. Strongman (ed.), *International Review of Studies on Emotion*, Vol. 1. London: Wiley, pp. 269–299.

Bagby, R. M., Parker, J. A. D. & Taylor, G. J. (1994). The twenty-item Toronto alexithymia scale—I. Item selection and cross-validation of the factor structure. *Journal of Psychosomatic Research*, **38**, 23–32.

Bateson, G. (1976). Some components of socialization for trance. In T. Schwartz (ed.), *Socialization as Cultural Communication*. Berkeley, CA: University of California Press.

Costa, P. T. Jr & McCrae, R. R. (1985). *The NEO Personality Inventory Manual*. Odessa, FL: Psychological Assessment Resources.

Epstein, S. (1992). Constructive thinking and mental and physical well-being. In L. Montada, S.-H. Filipp & M. J. Lerner (eds), *Life Crises and Experiences of Loss in Adulthood*. Hillsdale, NJ: Erlbaum, pp. 385–409.

Fineman, S. (1995). Stress, emotion and intervention. In T. Newton, J. Handy & S. Fineman, *Managing Stress: Emotion and Power at Work*. London: Sage, pp. 120–135.

Frankl, V. E. (1984). *Man's Search for Meaning, revisd edn*. New York: Washington Square Press.

Gardner, H. (1983). *Frames of Mind: The Theory of Multiple Intelligences*. New York: Basic Books.

Goleman, D. (1995). *Emotional Intelligence*. New York: Bantam Books.

Gutbezahl, J. & Averill, J. R. (1996). Individual differences in emotional creativity as manifested in words and pictures. *Creativity Research Journal*, **9**, 327–337.

Hayes, J. R. (1981). *The Complete Problem Solver*. Philadelphia, PA: Franklin Institute Press.

Hochschild, A. R. (1983). *The Managed Heart*. Berkeley, CA: University of California Press.

Hood, R. W. Jr (1975). The construction and preliminary validation of a measure of reported mystical experience. *Journal for the Scientific Study of Religion*, **14**, 29–41.

Isen, A. M. (1993). Positive affect and decision making. In M. Lewis & J. M. Haviland (eds), *Handbook of Emotions*. New York: Guilford, pp. 261–277.

Jamison, K. R. (1994). *Touched with Fire: Manic-depressive Illness and the Artistic Temperament*. New York: Free Press.

Johnson-Laird, P. N. & Oatley, K. (1989). The language of emotions: an analysis of a semantic field. *Cognition and Emotion*, **3**, 81–123.

Kitayama, S. & Markus, H. R. (eds) (1994). *Emotion and Culture: Empirical Studies of Mutual Influence*. Washington, DC: American Psychological Association.

Levy, R. I. (1984). The emotions in comparative perspective. In K. R. Scherer & P. Elman (eds), *Approaches to Emotion*. Hillsdale, NJ: Erlbaum, pp. 397–412.

Lutz, C. (1982). The domain of emotion words on Ifaluk. *American Ethnologist*, **9**, 113–128.

Marris, P. (1975). *Loss and Change*. Garden City, NY: Anchor Press.

Mayer, J. D. & Salovey, P. (1995). Emotional intelligence and the construction and regulation of feelings. *Applied & Preventive Psychology*, **4**, 197–208.

Mayer, J. D. & Salovey, P. (1997). What is emotional intelligence? In P. Salovey & D. Sluyter (eds), *Emotional Development an Emotional Intelligence: Implications for Educators*. New York: Basic Books, pp. 3–31.

Mayer, J. D., Salovey, P. & Caruso, D. R. (1977). *Emotional IQ Test* (CD-ROM version). Needham, MA: Virtual Knowledge.

Mesquita, B. & Frijda, N. H. (1992).   Cultural variations in emotions: a review. *Psychological Bulletin*, **112**, 179–204.

Morgan, C. & Averill, J. R. (1992).   True feelings, the self, and authenticity: a psychosocial perspective. In D. D. Franks & V. Gauchos (eds), *Social Perspectives on Emotion*, Vol. 1. Greenwich, CT: JAI, pp. 95–124.

Parrott, W. G. (1993).   Beyond hedonism: motives for inhibiting good moods and for maintaining bad moods. In D. M. Wegner & J. W. Pennebaker (eds), *Handbook of Mental Control*. Englewood Cliffs, NJ: Prentice Hall, pp. 278–305.

Perkins, D. N. (1981).   *The Mind's Best Work*. Cambridge, MA: Harvard University Press.

Pollock, G. H. (1989).   The mourning process, the creative process, and the creation. In D. R. Dietrich & P. C. Shabad (eds), *The Problem of Loss and Mourning*. Madison, CT: International Universities Press, pp. 27–59.

Polanyi, M. (1964).   *Personal Knowledge: Towards a Post-critical Knowledge*. New York: Harper Torchbook.

Russ, S. W. (1993).   *Affect and Creativity: The Role of Affect and Play in the Creative Process*. Hillsdale, NJ: Erlbaum.

Russell, B. (1930/1958).   *The Conquest of Happiness*. New York: Liveright (original work published 1930).

Russell, J. A. (1991).   Culture and the categorization of emotions. *Psychological Bulletin*, **110**, 426–450.

Rosenberg, M. (1965).   *Society and the Adolescent Self-image*. Princeton, NJ: Princeton University Press.

Ryle, G. (1949).   *The Concept of Mind*. London: Hutchinson.

Salovey, P. & Mayer, J. D. (1990).   Emotional intelligence. *Imagination, cognition, and personality*, **9**(3), 185–211.

Salovey, P., Mayer, J. D. et al. (1995).   Emotional attention, clarity, and repair: exploring emotional intelligence using the trait meta-mood scale. In J. W. Pennebaker (ed.), *Emotion, Disclosure, and Health*. Washington, DC: American Psychological Association, pp. 125–154.

Shaw, M. P. & Runco, M. A. (eds) (1994).   *Creativity and Affect*. Norwood, NJ: Ablex.

Simonton, D. K. (1975).   Sociocultural context of individual creativity: a trans-historical time-series analysis. *Journal of Personality and Social Psychology*, **32**, 1119–1133.

Storm, C. & Storm, T. (1987).   A taxonomic study of the vocabulary of emotions. *Journal of Personality and Social Psychology*, **53**, 805–816.

Taylor, G. T. (1994).   The alexithymia construct: conceptualization, validation, and relationship with basic dimensions of personality. *New Trends in Experimental and Clinical Psychiatry*, **X**(2), 61–74.

Wallas, G. (1926).   *The Art of Thought*. New York: Harcourt, Brace.

Weisberg, R. W. (1986).   *Creativity: Genius and Other Myths*. New York: W. H. Freeman.

Woolf, V. (1942).   *The Death of the Moth and Other Essays*. New York: Harcourt, Brace.

Chapter 37

Forensic Applications of Theories of Cognition and Emotion

Debra A. Bekerian*
and
Susan J. Goodrich
Department of Psychology, University of East London, UK

Applied psychology involves the extrapolation of basic theory and research to a particular real world situation, or class of situations. Ideally, the relationship between theory and real world application is reciprocal. Theory should dictate what factors in the real situation are likely to be important. On the basis of existing research, the psychologist offers an explanation of the factors contributing to the situation, and suggests what might be done to remedy difficulties that are arising. In turn, the real world situation can identify what factors are in need of greater attention, as perhaps theory has yet to consider them or they require further investigation.

One area of extensive collaboration between psychology and the real world is in the application of theories of memory and emotion to forensic domains. Broadly speaking, forensic domains are those pertaining to the courts of judicature, and those procedures involved in investigations. There is remarkable overlap between those issues that are regarded as basic to the understanding of human memory and emotion, and those that are critical in forensic situations. Because of these common interests, psychologists are regarded as potential experts in many different forensic situations, taking key roles in providing evidence regarding memory and its operations.

---

* All correspondence should be sent to: D.A. Bekerian, Psychology Department, University of East London, Romford Road, London, E15 4LZ.

Handbook of Cognition and Emotion. Edited by T. Dalgleish and M. Power.
© 1999 John Wiley & Sons Ltd.

There is no doubt that the forensic domain is fertile ground for developing theory and research. However, the work is not without its critics (see Banajii & Crowder, 1989; McCloskey & Egeth, 1983). This chapter examines the extent to which advances in basic research have contributed to our understanding of memory in forensic contexts.

PROBLEMS OF MEMORY IN THE FORENSIC CONTEXT

The aim of any investigator is to obtain reliable, consistent and accurate information from witnesses and victims, e.g. description and identification of perpetrator, narrative accounts of the event. How to achieve this is not always obvious, given the complexities of the real world. Two main classes of variables have been identified by researchers that can affect memory, estimator variables and system variables (cf. Wells, 1978). Estimator variables are those variables outside the control of the investigator/experimenter, e.g. the emotional state of the witness at the time of the incident. System variables are those over which the investigator has some control, e.g. general features of the retrieval environment, such as instructions to witnesses. These concepts are commonly employed by researchers in their discussions of eyewitness identification and eyewitness event memory.

EYEWITNESS IDENTIFICATION

Most researchers agree that: (a) memory for faces consists of featural information (e.g. shape of nose) and configural information (relationship of features to each other), with the latter dominating (e.g. Carey & Diamond, 1977; Wells & Hryciw, 1984); (b) information from memory is compared with targets, e.g. members of the line-up (e.g. Tulving, 1981); (c) on the basis of some threshold, the witness decides to select, or reject, all candidates (e.g. Deffenbacher, 1996; Ebbesen & Wixted, 1994). The fundamental principles governing identification appear consistent across developmental ages (see Ceci, Toglia & Ross, 1987), although children may engage in more feature-extraction processes than adults (see Diamond & Carey, 1977).

Effects of Verbal Rehearsal on Eyewitness Identification

In the forensic situation, the witness engages in some form of verbal rehearsal prior to any identification task, e.g. he/she describes the perpetrator. Studies exploring the effects of verbal rehearsal show that verbalization can in fact impair correct recognition when a single target is to be identified (e.g. Schooler, Ryan & Reder, 1996; Fallshore & Schooler, 1995; Dodson, Johnson & Schooler, in press; Read & Schooler, 1994), although some studies fail to find any effects (e.g. Yu & Geiselman, 1993).

One explanation for these "verbal overshadowing" effects is that verbalization inhibits the processing of configural information, which is essential for face recognition (Schooler, Ryan & Reder, 1996; Wells & Hryciw, 1984). Such an explanation is consistent with dual code notions of episodic memory (cf. Paivio, 1986). Another equally plausible explanation is that verbalization introduces a disparity between encoding and retrieval conditions. The inconsistency between "default encoding conditions", which automatically focus on configural information (Schooler, Ryan & Reder, 1996, p. 56), and the retrieval conditions imposed by verbalization results in impaired memory performance. This explanation is essentially an extension of the encoding specificity principle (cf. Tulving & Thomson, 1973; see Fallshore & Schooler, 1995).[1]

In contrast, when multiple rather than single targets are to be identified, prior verbalization has been shown to improve memory of faces. For example, Ryan & Schooler (1994) found that verbalization improved recognition performance, and reduced interference between multiple targets. These results imply that a prior description will protect the witness when subsequently viewing multiple mug-shots, a finding that could have great practical implications (see also Schooler, Ryan & Reder, 1996).

Although this research is highly promising, there are caveats (see Schooler, Ryan & Reder, 1996). The research is far from conclusive regarding the effects of verbalization. Equally problematic, individual differences (i.e. estimator variables) have been shown to mediate any effects of verbalization (e.g. Ryan & Schooler, 1995). The impact of such estimator variables has not been evaluated systematically. As a consequence, practical advice about the effects of verbalization is likely to be speculative and will require revision.

Identification Line-ups

Most theories of episodic memory assume that, in recognition, the relationship between memory and the target is assessed. Tulving (1981) refers to this as ecphoric similarity, where the similarity between information in the memory trace and the physical stimulus determines whether an item is judged as "old" or "new". However, in the case of identification, it is argued that recognition will be based not only on the similarity between what the witness remembers and the face of one of the line-up members (e.g. absolute threshold levels) but also the *relative* similarity of one member compared to the others (e.g. Lindsay & Wells, 1985; Wells, 1984). Wells (1993) suggests that, ". . . as long as one line-up member shows greater ecphoric similarity than do the others, there is a propensity to positively identify that line-up member, even if the absolute level of ecphoric similarity is only modest".

There is considerable evidence to support this relative judgement view, imply-

---

[1] There are other explanation for these results, as discussed by Schooler, Ryan & Reder, 1996, p. 55.

ing that the mere presence of multiple candidates encourages the witness to rely on relative judgements, even when they are wrong (e.g. Malpass & Devine, 1981; Lindsay & Wells, 1980; Shapiro & Penrod, 1986; Wells, 1993; Gonzalez, Ellsworth & Pembroke, 1990). However, other evidence suggests that identification is not simply based on relative judgements, and is highly influenced by absolute threshold (see Malpass & Devine, 1981; Lindsay & Wells, 1980; Wells & Turtle, 1986). Thus, theoretical accounts of eyewitness identification will need to consider how absolute and relative judgements interact to produce an identification response.

Two biases are assumed to be particularly problematic in identification procedures: response demands and characteristics of the line-up. Response demands are biases resulting from the person's belief of what is expected of him/her. For example, witnesses might operate on the incorrect assumption that at least one of the members of the line-up is a suspect, otherwise the police would not have bothered, and consequently that a positive identification is expected of them. In support of this, evidence suggests that informing witnesses that the culprit might be absent can be effective in reducing error rates, without influencing the proportion of hits or correct judgements (e.g. Malpass & Devine, 1981).

The characteristics of the line-up can also introduce biases, e.g. when only one member of the line-up fits the witness's description (Wells, Lindsay & Ferguson, 1979; Loftus, 1979; Lindsay & Wells, 1980; Malpass & Devine, 1981; Wells, Lindsay & Ferguson, 1979; Wells, 1993). There is consensus that all members of a line-up should match the description given by the witness. Additionally, Wells (1993) suggests that there are sound theoretical grounds for avoiding excessive similarity between line-up members. When too much similarity exists, the witness's memory for the perpetrator may be impaired, as in retroactive interference. Because of this, Wells (1993) suggests that investigators should aim for differences in the appearance of members of the line-up, with all members matching the witness' description.

In sum, the applied work on eyewitness identification has drawn heavily on laboratory-derived theories of face recognition and more general theories of recognition memory. However, there are questions about the applicability and appropriateness of such theories. For example, some critics argue that face recognition theories are inapplicable because of the discrepancy between findings from traditional laboratory studies of face recognition and outcomes from simulations of eyewitness identification procedures (e.g. Shapiro & Penrod, 1986; Ellis, 1981). This might suggest that general recognition theories are more appropriate. However, there is strong evidence that face recognition is highly specialized and qualitatively distinct from other types of recognition, e.g. prosopagnosia (see Young, 1996). This must cast doubt on the utility of general recognition theories. Thus, we have no single compelling theoretical analogue for discussing eyewitness identification. While the psychologist can undoubtedly assist in problems of eyewitness identification, the links between theory and practice remain unresolved.

EYEWITNESS EVENT MEMORY

The research falling under this heading focuses on processes involved in event memory, with most attention being given to the fallibility of eyewitness memory. It has long been noted that people's memories for events can be distorted (e.g. Freud, cited in Janet, 1919/1925). Distortions in eyewitness memory can come from two sources, external and internal. External sources include the presentation of post-event information which contradicts a detail originally seen, or introduces a detail which was not present (e.g. Ceci & Bruck, 1993; Loftus & Hoffman, 1989). Distortions introduced by internal sources, e.g. self-generated errors, fall under the heading of autosuggestibility (e.g. Ackerman, 1992; Brainerd & Reyna, 1995). Distinctions have also been drawn between suggestibility for event details, where an event occurred and the person is misled about specific details of that event; and suggestibility for entire events, where the episode did not, in fact, occur (Bekerian & Goodrich, 1995; Reyna, 1995). The latter has been referred to as "implantation" of memory, and will be discussed separately (see Recovered Memories).

There are a number of variables that influence suggestibility: (a) age (see Ceci & Bruck, 1993); (b) delay between the original experience and the subsequent misinformation; (c) the similarity between the original and post-event information; (d) the plausibility of the post-event information; and (e) the extent of rehearsal of the original information (see Belli, 1993). Non-memorial factors also need to be considered. For example, people are more suggestible if they perceive the source of the misleading information to be reliable than when the source is perceived as unreliable (e.g. Loftus, 1979).

A number of theoretical hypotheses have been advanced to account for suggestiblity. Essentially, they fall into two types and reflect the classic arguments that have been used in the literature on forgetting (e.g. Postman & Underwood, 1973): one proposes that suggestibility is due to the removal of the original information from memory; the other that suggestibility is due to interference from the post-event information. The former view has been most strongly advocated by Loftus (e.g. 1995) in her constructivist approach, while source monitoring hypotheses (e.g. Johnson, Hashtroudi & Lindsay, 1993) are modern examples of an interference view (see also Bekerian & Bowers, 1983; Christiansen & Ochalek, 1983; Morton, Hammersley & Bekerian, 1985). More recently, alternative hypotheses have been put forward, for example fuzzy trace theory (see Reyna & Titcomb, 1997), with both decay and interference combining to produce suggestibility.

There is considerable disagreement over which explanation best accounts for the findings. The constructivist approach has been criticized for being vague. For example, Loftus (1995) suggests that, "sometimes memory might be shaped by such constructive, elaborative processes and sometimes not". Similarly, many interference hypotheses (e.g. Bekerian & Bowers, 1983) have been challenged for being ambiguous regarding the precise nature of the interference (see

McCloskey & Zaragoza, 1985). Recent alternatives, like fuzzy trace theory (e.g. Reyna & Titcomb, 1997), integrate the literature, and attempt some specificity in their predictions. However, in the final analysis, they retreat from making definitive statements regarding retrieval operations:

> ... although resistance to misleading details is greatest when verbatim memory remains accessible, the witness cannot be relied on to invariably reject erroneous details, especially if such details are evaluated with respect to memory for gist (Renya & Titcomb, 1997, p. 170).

McCloskey & Zaragoza (1985) have lodged serious criticisms against all theoretical hypotheses put forward to account for suggestibility. They argue that the effects can result from failures to encode the original information, failures to remember the original information, failures to discriminate the source of the information, or perceived response demands. These different conditions are indistinguishable behaviourally on the explicit memory tests used in experimental studies. McCloskey & Zaragoza conclude that most theoretical explanations confound these disparate conditions methodologically, and are therefore flawed.

Other critics have claimed that the theoretical explanations for suggestibility are so poorly specified that they can accommodate most, if not all, possible outcomes (see Morton, Hammersley & Bekerian, 1985). This is unfortunate. Whether information is lost from memory or simply inaccessible has immense practical implications for an investigator.

One solution to the problem may be in the use of converging operations, e.g. combinations of implicit and explicit memory tests (see Schacter, 1990, for the distinction). For example, implicit tests are known to be sensitive to memory even when the person is unable to access the information consciously (Loftus, 1991). This would give information as to whether information was truly lost in memory or merely inaccessible.

Techniques for Interviewing Eyewitnesses

Based on theories of memory, most psychologists suggest that interviewing should follow a phased approach, with care being taken to avoid misleading questions and diminish response demands (e.g. Bekerian & Dennett, 1993). The most comprehensive set of practical suggestions for interviewers has been provided in the Cognitive Interview (CI) technique (e.g. Geiselman & Fisher, 1997). The available evidence suggests that, when used properly, CI can assist the eyewitness in producing more complete and accurate accounts. However, there are important qualifications as to its use (see Bekerian & Dennett, 1993). For example, theory predicts that certain mnemonics used in CI, e.g. context reinstatement and imagery, are likely to have negative effects on memory (see Bartlett, 1932; Bekerian & Dennett, 1993). These negative effects include greater autosuggestibility and inflations in witnesses' confidence about these self-generated errors. Given that much weight is placed on testimony that is highly confident (see Deffenbacher, 1996), this is a serious issue. These, and other issues, have yet to be addressed adequately and caution against the automatic use of CI in all forensic situations.

EFFECTS OF EMOTIONS ON EYEWITNESS MEMORY

It would be negligent to entertain explanations for eyewitness memory without simultaneously considering the effects of emotions on the retrieval of episodic information. As other chapters have considered the general research regarding emotions and memory, we will focus on a few issues that are most pertinent to eyewitness and victim testimony. In general, the findings from both laboratory and field research argue against a simple relationship between emotion and memory.

Part of the difficulty in summarizing research on emotions and eyewitness testimony results from the divergence of approaches taken to study the relationship. For example, definitions of emotional arousal are not uniform in the literature (see Heuer, Reisberg & Rio, 1997). Little attention has been paid to the effects of specific emotional states on memory, e.g. fear vs. anger (see Heuer, Reisberg & Rio, 1997; Bekerian, Goodrich & Dritschel, in preparation), with most attention being given to the effects of generic negative emotional arousal on memory. Equally, different researchers employ different operational definitions to distinguish charactersitics of events, such as central and peripheral details (see Heuer, Reisberg & Rio, 1997). To further complicate matters, some researchers focus on the accuracy of memory reports of emotional events (e.g. Yuille & Cutshall, 1986), while others emphasize errors in memory and its decline with time (e.g. Wagenaar & Groeneweg, 1990).

Christianson (e.g. 1992, 1997; Christianson & Loftus, 1991) has contributed significantly to research on emotion and eyewitness memory, and challenges conclusions that suggest that increases in negative arousal are associated with poorer memory. He concludes that, while the literature is complex, it nonetheless demonstrates that negative emotionally arousing events are relatively well retained: central features of the event will remain highly memorable while peripheral features are less well retained (as compared to their neutral counterparts). This general pattern applies only when certain conditions are met. First, the event itself must be perceived as being personally negative. Second, central features of the event must be viewed as inherently negative and causal to the negative outcome of the event.

Christianson uses Easterbrook's (1959) cue-utilization hypothesis as a point of departure to account for the effects that emotional arousal can have on memory. He argues that superior memory for central details is the result of two factors. One, there is differential attentional processing in response to the negative features of the event. This occurs early on in perceptual processing and results in the preferential processing of information related to the negative arousal. Two, there is increased subsequent post-stimulus elaboration of those features that are central to the emotional content of the event. Christianson also speculates that post-stimulus elaboration is likely to be influenced by the early preferential attention given to emotionally arousing information. Although speculative, it is a reasonable suggestion to make as it links attentional processing to later memory operations.

Thus, emotional arousal directs attentional procesing, or focusing, to those features which are central to the arousal, and this, in turn, results in people engaging in more controlled, or post-stimulus, processing of central features at the expense of peripheral details. Christianson suggests that his explanation can also account for the findings from studies showing that information either preceding or following the emotionally arousing material is suppressed, e.g. "functional" retrograde and anterograde amnesia: increased attention and greater post-stimulus elaboration of the emotionally arousing material will disrupt both attention to and elaboration of those items surrounding the emotional material, due to their proximity. However, other studies have found that these functional amnesic effects are influenced by the nature of the retrieval environment (e.g. Christianson & Nilsson, 1984; Scrivner & Safer, 1988; Wagenaar, 1986) and also the time of testing (e.g. Christianson, 1984). For example, with delayed testing, there appears to be something akin to the recovery of previously suppressed information.

It is important to note that the time of testing is also likely to influence the accessibility of information from the emotionally arousing event. For example, Heuer, Reisberg and Rio (1997) suggest that negative emotions at the time of encoding may initially impair a witness' memory; but some critical detail and some peripheral information may be more resistant to forgetting over time than their neutral counterparts (see also Heuer & Reisberg, 1990). This implies that witnesses/victims who are in high states of emotional arousal at the time of the interview may produce less complete accounts, and that brief delays before the initial interview may actually benefit recall. Heuer et al. also note that emotional reappraisal, which may occur through thinking or talking about the event, particularly with longer retention intervals, will influence the characteristics of information retrieved and the accuracy of the information (e.g. Heuer & Reisberg, 1992; Pillemer, 1992).

The reports from laboratory studies suggest that while emotional events may be better remembered, memory for both central and peripheral information from emotional events changes over time. Recent observational studies analysing victim's accounts of trauma support the conclusions drawn from laboratory work. Victims report new information, both central and peripheral details, as reported anxiety during recall decreases (Bekerian & Foa, 1993; Foa, Molnar & Cashman, 1995).[2] Thus, both field and laboratory studies for negatively arousing materials

---

[2] Central here refers to whether the information was directly thematically related to the trauma, or not.

support the claim that memory for emotional events can change over time (Scrivner & Safer, 1988).

The relationship between emotion and eyewitness memory involves the interaction of a multitude of factors, making general conclusions difficult to draw. Any explanations of the effects will need to include discussions about the type of event, the type of detail, the characteristics of the retrieval environment, and the time of test. Research from both laboratory experiments and field studies suggest that memory is unstable, particularly when the event is emotionally salient (e.g. Reyna & Titcomb, 1997). While changes in memory might not always be cause for concern, the investigator may need to question the authenticity of the information if the victim has been exposed to misleading information. These very questions form the centre of one of the most troubled debates ever considered by applied memory psychologists, the debate over recovered memories of trauma.

Recovered Memories

"Recovered memories" refer to instances where adults claim to remember experiences of sexual abuse that occurred in childhood following periods of amnesia. The pattern of recovery can take several forms (Harvey & Herman, 1994), although the most controversial cases are those where memories of child sexual abuse are recovered following total amnesia. Within forensic contexts, these claims have been used as evidence in civil and criminal litigation. As with any evidence used in litigation, the investigator must be assured that these memories are accurate, or historically true. Because of their expertise in memory, applied psychologists have taken a central role in debates over the authenticity of such memories. Here we will evaluate studies exploring the generation of false memories of childhood events in adults and the effects of trauma on memory.

Neisser (1982) discusses the notion of historical truth in his distinction between the ideal of verity and the ideal of utility. When memory operates under the ideal of verity, the account is a *reproduction* of what happened and is largely unbiased by subjective interpretation. Although there is no suggestion that the ideal of verity will produce accounts that are totally error-free, Neisser argues that under these conditions memory is largely accurate. In contrast, when memory operates under the ideal of utility, the account is an *interpretation* of the past, motivated by objectives at the time of recounting. Under the ideal of utility, Neisser claims that memory is *reconstructive* and will include errors. Importantly, the person may be unaware of his/her motives under these conditions.

Neisser argues that the type of retrieval conditions imposed on the person will determine which idea! will be operating. If the conditions are open, unrestricted and unbiased, the person will be dominated by the ideal of verity and produce an accurate account. If the conditions are constrained or biased, where the person is required to produce specific types of information, then the ideal of utility will dominate and the person will introduce errors into his/her account to comply with the demands. Under these circumstances, the person can be inadvertently directed by misinformation (Bekerian & Dennett, 1995; Loftus, 1979).

Neisser's identification of the effects that retrieval conditions can have on the reconstructive nature of memory is highly pertinent to the recovered memory debate. Some researchers have expressed concern that therapeutic techniques which are orientated towards helping clients recover memories of abuse acutly lead clients to create illusory memories (Loftus & Rosenwald, 1993; Lindsay & Read, 1994; Weiskrantz, 1995), e.g. the therapist tells clients with no memories of abuse that their symptoms are indicative of sexual abuse; the therapist endorses memories relating to abuse as true and discourages doubts over the truth of these memories. In essence, these researchers argue that vulnerable clients are being coerced by therapists to generate false memories. Using Neisser's distinction, we can see that any therapeutic techniques which constrain or bias the client could lead to retrieval conditions that encourage reconstructive memories.

Hyman and colleagues have conducted a series of studies looking at conditions under which false accounts of childhood experiences can be generated in adults (Hyman, Husband & Billings, 1995; Hyman & Billings, 1998; Hyman & Pentland, 1996). In all these studies, people were asked over a series of interviews to describe a number of childhood life events, some true, others falsely generated by the experimenter. Results showed that false memories could consistently be induced in approximately 25% of people. Crucially, the false event had to be consonant with the person's autobiography. When people were encouraged to use imagery, there was an increased probability of generating false memories. Individual differences on some personality tests also correlated with a person's willingness to generate false memories.

Hyman and colleagues note similarities between their laboratory studies and the therapeutic context. For instance, pressure was put on people by an authority figure (the experimenter) to recall alleged childhood events. Therapy, the authors argue, involves repeated sessions under the guidance of a powerful authority figure.

While agreeing with Hyman that there are important similarities, we suggest that laboratory studies differ in significant ways. First, Hyman et al. told people that the events had parental verification. The extent of parental verification in real cases of recovered memories is not known. To address the effects of parental verification, additional control conditions would be required. The most extreme would be where the person was told by the experimenter that the event had occurred, while the parents disputed it—a situation that is not uncommon in cases of recovered memories of abuse. Second, for a person to be misled, the false event had to be compatible with the person's autobiography. Frequently, when recovering memories of abuse, people report loving relationships with the alleged abuser. Hyman, Husband & Billings (1995) note, however, that many people have childhood experiences where they are touched against their will. Such incidents can, they argue, provide the foundation for the construction of false memories.

Perhaps the most important difference is that the false events used in these studies were fairly innocuous and non-traumatic. Intuitively, this appears very different from implanting a memory of what might be severe and protracted abuse. If non-traumatic and traumatic memories are qualitatively distinct, this may restrict the generalization of laboratory studies to the therapeutic context.

The question of whether non-traumatic and traumatic memories are qualitatively distinct has been hotly debated (see Janet's clinical observations, 1919/1925; for a more recent review, Hembrooke & Ceci, 1995; Whitfield, 1995). Janet (1919/1925) held that traumatic memories were qualitatively distinct from non-traumatic memories. Similarly, some modern theorists argue for a distinction, proposing that traumatic memories leave an indelible, invariant trace, while non-traumatic memories are malleable and subject to social demands (van der Kolk & Fisler, 1995).

van der Kolk and Fisler (1995) examined the recovery of formerly forgotten traumatic memories in adults. Their data show that on initial recovery, the memories take the form of visual and auditory images, affectives states and sensations. It is only as time passes that some people come to produce narrative accounts. van der Kolk and Fisler note that these initial non-verbally mediated memories ("images") are invariant and not susceptible to distortions, while the subsequent narrative accounts are susceptible to memory biases, like suggestibility.

van der Kolk and Fisler (1995) provide important evidence about the retrieval of traumatic memories (see also Andrews et al., 1996). However, their study cannot be taken as conclusive evidence that traumatic memories are qualitatively distinct from non-traumatic ones. For example, they fail to include adequate controls for the recovery of non-traumatic memories, so that their data confound the two variables of interest, trauma and recovery. Further, their explanation regarding the retrieval of traumatic memories is remarkably similar to theoretical descriptions advanced to account for the retrieval of non-traumatic, autobiographical memories (e.g. Conway & Bekerian, 1987). The question of whether traumatic memories requires specialized memory mechanisms remains open.

It has been suggested that the debate over recovered memories of abuse is "... the greatest challenge currently facing cognitive psychology" (Recovery of memories of child sexual abuse (special issue), *Applied Cognitive Psychology*, 8(4), 1994). For the investigator, the main issue is whether an account is true, be it from a highly traumatized victim or a non-involved witness. Thus far, there is no systematic way of assessing the authenticity of any account in the absence of corroborating evidence (see Bekerian & Dennett, 1993). However, future research in this area could progress in several ways. First, we agree with Saywitz & Moan-Hardie (1994) when they suggest that:

> ... greater understanding may be achieved by examining factors that raise or lower the potential for distortion, in contrast to focusing exclusively on the veracity of

childhood memories, a strategy that polarizes the debate and fails to address the complexities inherent in the process of reconstructing the past (p. 409).

Second, we endorse the views of others (e.g. Kihlstrom, 1995) who argue that the best way forward is to conduct multidisciplinary research, linking practitioners, clinical investigators and memory researchers. A number of projects are beginning to adopt this approach (e.g. Andrews et al., 1995).

CONCLUDING COMMENTS

Wells (1993) observes that:

> ... players in the legal system (e.g. attorneys, judges, police) are now viewing psychologists as their main resource for help on issues of eyewitness identification from line-ups and photospreads.

Theory has equally benefited from such application. The practical situation consistently forces psychologists to develop theory more fully (e.g. Bekerian & Dennett, 1993). Overall, there is a productive relationship between the domains of forensic investigations and the psychology of memory and emotion. However, there is no room for complacency.

One important question is how future developments of memory theory will effect forensic investigations. Recent exciting advances, such as Koriat and Goldsmith's correspondence metaphor of event memory (1996), focus on memory in the real world with emphasis on the qualitative aspects of remembering, as opposed to more traditional perspectives that emphasize quantitative characteristics. However, although the correspondence metaphor enhances theoretical insights, its potential contribution to forensic settings is unclear (see Fisher, 1996).

Another question is the adequacy of basic theory to explain behaviour in the forensic situation. The forensic setting contains a multiplicity of estimator and system variables: (a) those concerning the individual, such as emotional states, inherent abilities and encoding conditions; (b) those of the retrieval environment, such as the nature of questions asked and the mode of reporting; (c) those of the dialogue between interviewer and victim/witness, including socio-linguistic maxims; (d) those of the relationship between the individuals in the dialogue; and (e) those of the event, including its social and personal significance within familial and cultural mores. Laboratory-derived theories typically isolate single sets of variables in the hope that their data will contribute towards an understanding of the more complex situation. The problem is that the sum of the parts may not equal the whole. Multi-level theories (see Teasdale, this volume) ultimately may be the only way in which to discuss the diversity of factors influencing memory in forensic settings. However, they may fail to generate empirical research, to the extent that they are not testable (Morton & Bekerian, 1986).

Finally, there are glaring omissions in applied research, e.g. attention to individual differences (see Schooler, Ryan & Reder, 1996). There is no doubt that witnesses and victims differ in their abilities and that their inherent abilities determine behaviour. As long as individual differences are ignored, applied research will fail to provide comprehensive explanations of eyewitness behaviour.

REFERENCES

Ackerman, B. (1992).   The sources of childrens' source errors in judging causal inferences. *Journal of Experimental Child Psychology*, **54**, 90–119.

Andrews, B., Morton, J., Bekerian, D., Brewin, C., Davies, G. & Mollon, P. (1995).   The recovery of memories in clinical practice: experiences and beliefs of British Psychological Society Practitioners. *The Psychologist*, **8**, 209–214.

Banajii, M. & Crowder, R. (1989).   The bankruptcy of everyday memory. *American Psychologist*, **44**, 1185–1193.

Bartlett, F. (1932).   *Remembering*. Cambridge: Cambridge University Press.

Bekerian, D. A. & Bowers, J. M. (1983).   Eyewitness testimony: were we misled? *Journal of Experimental Psychology: Learning, Memory & Cognition*, **9**, 139–145.

Bekerian, D. A. & Dennett, J. L. (1993).   The cognitive interview technique: reviving the issues. *Applied Cognitive Psychology*, **7**, 275–297.

Bekerian, D. A. & Foa, E. (1993).   Memory for traumatic events. Paper presented at BPS Cognitive Section, New Hall, Cambridge, September 1993.

Bekerian, D. A. & Goodrich, S. J. (1995).   Telling the truth in the recovered memory debate. *Consciousness and Cognition*, **4**, 120–124.

Bekerian, D. A., Goodrich, S. J. & Dritschel, B.   The effects of violence on basic cognitive processes (in preparation).

Belli, R. (1993).   Failures of interpolated tests in inducing memory impairment with final modifed tests: evidence unfavorable to the blocking hypothesis. *American Journal of Psychology*, **106**, 407–427.

Brainerd, C. & Reyna, V. (1995).   Memory loci of suggestibility development: comment on Ceci, Ross and Toglia. *Journal of Experimental Psychology: General*, **117**, 197–200.

Carey, S. & Diamond, R. (1977).   From piecemeal to configural representations of faces. *Science*, **195**, 312–314.

Ceci, S. J. & Bruck, M. (1993).   The suggestibility of the child witness: a historical review and synthesis. *Psychological Bulletin*, **113**, 403–439.

Ceci, S. J., Toglia, M. & Ross, D. (eds) (1987).   *Children's Eyewitness Memory*. New York: Springer-Verlag.

Christiansen, R. & Ochalek, K. (1983).   Editing misleading information from memory: evidence for the co-existence of original and post-event information. *Memory & Cognition*, **11**, 467–475.

Christianson, S.-Å. (1992).   Emotional stress and eyewitness memory: a critical review. *Psychological Bulletin*, **112**, 284–309.

Christianson, S.-Å. (1997).   On emotional stress and memory: we need to recognize threatening situations and we need to "forget" unpleasant experiences. In D. Payne, & F. Conrad, (eds), *Intersections in Basic and Applied Memory Research*. Mahwah, NJ: Erlbaum.

Christianson, S.-Å. (1984).   The relationship between induced emotinal arousal and amnesia. *Scandinavian Journal of Psychology*, **28**, 147–160.

Christianson, S.-Å. & Loftus, E. (1991).   Remembering emotional events: the fate of detailed information. *Cognition & Emotion*, **5**, 81–108.

Christianson, S.-Å. & Nilsson, L. (1984).   Functional amnesia as induced by a psychologi-
    cal trauma. *Memory & Cognition*, **12**, 142–155.
Conway, M. & Bekerian, D. A. (1987).   Organization in autobiographical memory.
    Memory and Cognition, **15**, 119–132.
Deffenbacher, K. (1996).   Updating the scientific validity of three key estimator variables
    in eyewitness testimony. In D. Hermann, C. McEvoy, C. Hertzog, P. Hertel &
    M. Johnson, (eds), *Basic Applied Memory Research: Theory in Context*, Vol. 2.
    Mahwah, NJ: Erlbaum.
Diamond, R. & Carey, S. (1977).   Developmental changes in the representation of faces.
    Journal of Experimental Child Psychology, **23**, 1–22.
Dodson, C., Johnson, M. & Schooler, J. (in press). Can subjects escape the verbal
    overshadowing effect? *Memory and Cognition*.
Easterbrook, J. A. (1959).   The effect of emotion on cue utilization and the organization
    of behavior. *Psychological Review*, **66**, 183–201.
Ebbesen, E. & Wixted, J. (1994).   A signal detection analysis of the relationship between
    confidence and accuracy in face recognition memory. Unpublished manuscript,
    University of California, San Diego, CA.
Ellis, H. (1981).   Theoretical aspects of face recognition. In G. Davies, H. Ellis &
    J. Shepherd (eds), *Perceiving and Remembering Faces*. London: Academic Press.
Fallshore, M. & Schooler, J. (1995).   The verbal vulnerability of perceptual expertise.
    Journal of Experimental Psychology: Learning, Memory and Cognition, **21**, 1608–1623.
Fisher, R. (1996).   Implications of output-bound measures for laboratory and field
    research in memory. *Behavioural and Brain Science*, **19**, 197–198.
Foa, E., Molnar, C. & Cashman, L. (1995).   Change in rape narratives during exposure
    therapy for posttraumatic stress disorder. *Journal of Traumatic Stress*, **8**, 675–690.
Geiselman, R. E. & Fisher, R. (1997).   Ten years of cognitive interviewing. In D. Payne
    & F. Conrad (eds), *Intersections in Basic and Applied Memory Research*. Mahwah, NJ:
    Erlbaum.
Gonzalez, R., Ellsworth, P. & Pembroke, M. (1990).   Misidentifications and failures to
    identify in line-ups and show-ups. Unpublished manuscript, Stanford University,
    Stanford, CT.
Harvey, M. R. & Herman, J. L. (1994).   Amnesia, partial amnesia and delayed recall
    among adult survivors of childhood trauma. *Consciousness and Cognition*, **3**, 295.
Hembrooke, H. & Ceci, S. J. (1995).   Traumatic memories: do we need to invoke special
    mechanisms. *Consciousness and Cognition*, **4**, 75–82.
Heuer, F. & Reisberg, D. (1992).   Emotion, arousal and memory for detail. In
    S.-Å. Christianson (ed.), *The Handbook of Emotion and Memory*. Hillsdale, NJ:
    Erlbaum.
Heuer, F. & Reisberg, D. (1990).   Vivid memories of emotional events: the accuracy of
    remembered minutiae. *Memory & Cognition*, **18**, 496–506.
Heuer, F., Reisberg, D. & Rio, C. (1997).   The memory effects of thematically induced
    emotion. In D. Payne & F. Conrad (eds), *Intersections in Basic and Applied Memory
    Research*. Mahwah, NJ: Erlbaum.
Hyman, I. E. & Billings, F. J. (1998).   Individual differences and the creation of false
    childhood memories. *Memory*, **6**, 1–20.
Hyman, I. E., Husband, T. H. & Billings, F. J. (1995).   False memories of childhood
    experiences. *Applied Cognitive Psychology*, **9**, 181–197.
Hyman, I. E. & Pentland, J. (1996).   The role of mental imagery in the creation of false
    childhood memories. *Journal of Memory and Language*, **35**, 101–117.
Janet, P. (1919/1925).   *Psychological Healing*. New York: Macmillan (original publica-
    tion, Janet, P., 1919, Les medications psychologiques. Paris: Alcan).
Johnson, M., Hashtroudi, S. & Lindsay, D. (1993).   Source monitoring. *Psychological
    Bulletin*, **114**, 3–28.

Kihlstrom, J. F. (1995). The trauma–memory argument. *Consciousness and Cognition*, **4**, 63–67.

Koriat, A. & Goldsmith, M. (1996). Memory metaphors and the real-life/laboratory controversy. *Behavioural and Brain Science*, **19**, 167–187.

Lindsay, D. S. & Read, J. D. (1994). Psychotherapy and memories of childhood sexual abuse: a cognitive perspective. *Applied Cognitive Psychology*, **8**, 281–338.

Lindsay, R. & Wells, G. (1985). Improving eyewitness identifications from lineups: simultaneous versus sequential lineup presentations. *Journal of Applied Psychology*, **70**, 556–564.

Lindsay, R. & Wells, G. (1980). What price justice? Exploring the relationship of line-up fairness to identification accuracy. *Law and Human Behavior*, **4**, 303–314.

Loftus, E. (1979). *Eyewitness Testimony*. London: Harvard University Press.

Loftus, E. (1991). Made in memory: distortion in recollection after misleading information. In G. Bower (ed.), *The Psychology of Learning and Motivation: Advances in Research and Theory*, Vol. 27. London: Academic Press, pp. 187–213.

Loftus, E. (1995). Memory malleability: constructivist and fuzzy-trace explanations. *Learning and Individual Differences*, **7**, 133–137.

Loftus, E. & Hoffman, H. (1989). Misinformation in memory: the creation of new memories. *Journal of Experimental Psychology: General*, **118**, 100–104.

Loftus, E. & Rosenwald, L. A. (1993). Buried memories, shattered lives. ABA Journal, **November**, 70–73.

Malpass, R. & Devine, P. (1981). Eyewitness identification: line-up instructions and the absence of the offender. *Journal of Applied Psychology*, **66**, 482–489.

McCloskey, M. & Egeth, H. (1983). Eyewitness identification: what can a psychologist tell a jury? *American Psychologist*, **38**, 550–563.

McCloskey, M. & Zaragoza, M. (1985). Misleading postevent information and memory for events: arguments and evidence against memory impairment hypotheses. *Journal of Experimental Psychology: General*, **114**, 1–16.

Morton, J. & Bekerian, D. A. (1986). Three ways of looking at memory. In N. Sharkey (ed.), *Cognitive Science*, Vol. 1. Chicheter: Ellis Horwood, pp. 43–71.

Morton, J. M., Hammersley, R. & Bekerian, D. A. (1985). Headed records: a model of memory and its failures. *Cognition*, **20**, 1–23.

Neisser, U. (1982). Memory: what are the important questions? In U. Neisser (ed.), *Memory Observed: Remembering in Natural Contexts*. San Francisco, CA: Freeman.

Paivio, A. (1986). *Mental Representations: A Dual Coding Approach*. New York: Oxford University Press.

Pillemer, D. (1992). Remembering personal circumstances: a functional analysis. In E. Winograd & U. Neisser (eds), *Affect and Accuracy in Recall: The Problem of "Flashbulb" Memories*. New York: Academic Press.

Postman, L. & Underwood, B. (1973). Critical issues in interference theory. *Memory and Cognition*, **1**, 19–40.

Read, D. & Schooler, J. (1994). Verbalization decrements in long-term person identification. Paper presented at the Third Practical Aspects of Memory Conference, College Park, MD.

Reyna, V. (1995). Interference effects in memory and reasoning: a fuzzy-trace theory analysis. In F. N. Demptster & C. J. Brainerd (eds.), *Interference and Inhibition in Cognition*. San Diego, CA: Springer-Verlag, pp. 29–59.

Reyna, V. & Titcomb, A. (1997). Constraints on the suggestibility of eyewitness testimony: a fuzzy-trace theory analysis. In D. Payne & F. Conrad (eds), *Intersections in Basic and Applied Memory Research*. Mahwah, NJ: Erlbaum.

Recovery of memories of child sexual abuse (special issue). (1994*)*. *Applied Cognitive Psychology*, **8**(4).

Ryan, R. & Schooler, J. (1994). Verbalization can reduce interference. Unpublished manuscript, University of Pittsburgh.

Ryan, R. & Schooler, J. (1995). Describing a Face Impairs the Face Recogntion of Holistic Processors More than Analytic Processors. Poster presented at the annual meeting of the American Psychological Society, New York, June.

Saywitz, K. J. & Moan-Hardie, S. (1994). Reducing the potential for distortion of childhood memories. *Consciousness and Cognition*, **3**, 408–425.

Schacter, D. (1990). Introduction to "implicit memory": multiple perspectives. *Bulletin of the Psychonomic Society*, **28**, 338–340.

Schooler, J., Ryan, R. & Reder, L. (1996). The costs and benefits of verbally rehearsing memory for faces. In D. Hermann, C. McEvoy, C. Hertzog, P. Hertel & M. Johnson (eds), *Basic Applied Memory Research: Theory in Context*, Vol. 1. Mahwah, NJ: Erlbaum.

Scrivner, E. & Safer, M. (1988). Eyewitnesses show hypermnesia for details about a violent event. *Journal of Applied Psychology*, **73**, 371–377.

Shapiro, P. & Penrod, S. (1986). Meta-analysis of facial identification studies. *Psychological Bulletin*, **100**, 139–156.

Tulving, E. (1981). Similarity relations in recognition. *Journal of Verbal Learning & Verbal Behavior*, **20**, 479–496.

Tulving, E. & Thomson, D. (1973). Encoding specificity and retrieval processes in episodic memory. *Psychological Review*, **80**, 352–373.

van der Kolk, B. A. & Fisler R. (1995). Dissociation and the fragmentary nature of traumatic memories. *Journal of Traumatic Stress*, **8**, 505–525.

Wagenaar, W. A. (1986). My memory: a study of autobiographical memory over six years. *Cognitive Psychology*, **18**, 225–252.

Wagenaar, W. A. & Groeneweg, J. (1990). The memory of concentration camp survivors. *Applied Cognitive Psychology*, **4**, 77–87.

Wells, G. (1978). Applied eyewtiness testimony research: system variables and estimator variables. *Journal of Personality and Social Psychology*, **36**, 1546–1557.

Wells, G. (1984). The psychology of line-up identifications. *Journal of Applied Social Psychology*, **14**, 89–103.

Wells, G. (1993). What do we know about eyewitness identification? *American Psychologist*, **32**, 1–36.

Wells, G. & Hryciw, B. (1984). Memory for faces: encoding and retrieval operations. *Memory and Cognition*, **12**, 338–344.

Wells, G., Lindsay, R. & Ferguson, T. (1979). Accuracy, confidence and juror perceptions in eyewitness identification. *Journal of Applied Psychology*, **64**, 440–448.

Wells, G. & Turtle, J. (1986). Eyewitness identification: the importance of lineup models. *Psychological Bulletin*, **99**, 320–329.

Weiskrantz, L. (1995). Comments on the report of the working party of the British Psychological Society on "recovered memories". *The Therapist*, **2**, 4.

Whitfield, C. L. (1995). The forgotten difference: ordinary memory versus traumatic memory. *Consciousness and Cognition*, **4**, 88–94.

Young, A. (1996). Face recognition. In J. G. Beaumont, P. M. Kenely & M. J. Royers (eds), *Blackwell Dictionary of Neuropsychology*. Oxford: Blackwell, pp. 341–345.

Yu, C. & Geiselman, R. E. (1993). Effects of constructing identi-kit composites on photospread identification performance. *Criminal Justice and Behavior*, **20**, 280–292.

Yuille, J. & Cutshall, J. (1986). A case study of eyewitness memory of a crime. *Journal of Applied Psychology*, **71**, 291–301.

Chapter 38

Cognition and Emotion: Future Directions

Tim Dalgleish
MRC Cognition and Brain Sciences Unit, Cambridge, UK
and
Mick J. Power
Department of Psychiatry, University of Edinburgh, UK

In the context of the history of ideas on emotion, the suggestion that there is an important link between the way we cognize about the world and our emotional responses to that same world is by no means new. In *The Art of Rhetoric*, Aristotle (1991) makes an eloquent case for thinking of emotions as a function of appraisals about what events mean. This thread has been unravelled across the centuries by the Stoic philosophers, Thomas Aquinas and Baruch Spinoza among others (see the chapter by Lyons). More recently, the debate about the relationship between cognition and emotion has become more fine-tuned (see the chapter by Lazarus), with many researchers coming full circle and seeing cognition as a fundamental component of emotion.

The main aim of the present *Handbook of Cognition and Emotion* has been to gather together contributions from the leading figures in the field in order to provide an overview of cognition and emotion research over 2000 years after Aristotle's contribution. In this final chapter we shall endeavour to identify the principal emergent themes in the area and make some suggestions about where research in cognition and emotion is currently heading. In order to facilitate this process, the chapter is divided into sections that mirror the parts in the book itself.

GENERAL ASPECTS OF COGNITION AND EMOTION RESEARCH

The contemporary community of cognition–emotion researchers employs a wealth of different methodologies and techniques, within a variety of research designs, in order to understand its subject matter. As Parrott & Hertel conclude in their chapter reviewing these approaches, an appreciation is emerging that a rapprochement is necessary between naturalistic, ecologically valid research on the one hand and tightly controlled laboratory-based studies on the other. Perhaps more importantly, and this is an idea that emerges from all of the Parts of the present volume, there is a need to integrate research across different levels of explanation within psychology. At present, cognition–emotion relations are conceptualized at a number of levels of analysis: the neurobiological, the functional, the social and the cultural. What will become necessary in the short to medium term are theories integrating across these various levels of analysis. This type of approach is exemplified by the provocative ideas presented in Gray's chapter on consciousness.

It is this need for integrative theorizing and research that is likely to extend the range of research methodologies employed in cognition and emotion over the next decade. It is almost certain that there will be a mushrooming of research in neuroimaging using positron emission topography (PET) and magnetic resonance imaging (MRI) (see the chapter by Davidson). The challenge in this field will be to resist the temptation to pursue a modern-day phrenological mapping of the brain but, instead, to try to utilize neuroimaging techniques to refine and develop the functional-level theories about cognition–emotion relations, such as those presented in Part IV of the present book. It seems likely that an intermediate stage of theorizing, in which functional level theories are mapped onto theories in neurobiology, may be necessary before tractable hypotheses can be generated and the potential of neuroimaging work will begin to be realized.

At the other end of the continuum, the development of more sophisticated techniques of qualitative data analysis is likely to provide a window into the complex cognitive dynamics of real-life interactions and dialogues revolving around emotions and emotional issues. These developments are already apparent in the increased interest in narrative, particularly in the trauma literature (see, for example, Pennebaker, 1995). The emphasis on understanding supra-propositional meaning structures that emerge out of verbal protocols echoes the idea of the role for supra-propositional representations, as formulated in the more recent multi-level theories described in the chapter by Teasdale.

Other research methodologies that have gathered momentum in the late 1980s and early 1990s, in terms of their application to cognition and emotion, are social cognitive techniques (see the chapter by Bentall & Kinderman) and, related to this, face processing (see Chapter 16 by Ekman). Researchers are beginning to consider the role of facial processing in emotional disorders and the similarities to the processing of non-facial emotional information (see the chapter by Mogg & Bradley). Faces provide an ecologically valid set of complex emotional stimuli that avoid all of the methodological baggage associated with laboratory studies of word lists and verbal material in general. It seems likely that the use of faces as an heuristic tool in laboratory studies of cognition and emotion in the future will increase.

Finally, it seems clear that the emphasis in cognitive science on computational modelling, both connectionist and symbolic, will spread to the domain of cognition and emotion. At present, it is only relatively low-level aspects of processing, such as attentional bias on the Stroop task, that are seen as tractable in the modelling community (see Williams, Mathews & MacLeod, 1996). However, over the next decade, with increased emphasis on mathematical and attribute space modelling, more high-level aspects of cognition–emotion relations are likely to become the focus for modelling research.

In addition to integration across levels of explanation in cognition and emotion research, there is increasing interest in integration across the life span, as illustrated by the pioneering work in developmental psychology described in the chapters by Michael Lewis, Stein & Levine, and Lewis & Granic. The next stage of this process might usefully see the extension across the age range of the predominantly adult-centred theoretical ideas presented in Part IV. This is particularly important in the area of emotional disorders, given the historically strong emphasis on the developmental origins of many of these states (e.g. Daleiden & Vasey, 1997).

COGNITIVE PROCESSES

Since the mid-1980s there has been a proliferation of research examining the link between emotional states and emotional disorders and the basic cognitive processes of attention and memory (see chapters by Colin MacLeod, Ellis & Moore, Mogg & Bradley and Matthews & Wells for comprehensive reviews). This research endeavour has proved highly successful in mapping out the various cognitive changes that accompany different normal and pathological emotional states.

An underlying theme of this work on basic cognitive processes has been the link between emotion and emotional disorder. Research findings have illustrated, for example, that anxious and depressed moods in the non-clinical population relate to systematic patterns of information processing in ways broadly similar to those in patients with anxiety disorders and clinical depression. One upshot of this aspect of the research had been the hope that greater understanding of basic cognition–emotion relations would lead to refinements in therapeutic interventions. Progress in this area has been disappointing to date; however, the innovative work described by Colin MacLeod on "training" of biases for emotional information opens the door to the possibility of transferring these ideas and methodologies to the clinic, thereby providing a potential non-self-report vehicle for assessing emotion-related processing.

Perhaps one of the greatest influences of this research on cognitive processes has been the way in which it allows us to deconstruct the notion of a single edifice of "cognition". This development is not just apparent in the distinction between research on basic processes, such as attention vs. work on so-called higher-order cognitive procedures, such as appraisal or judgement (see chapters by Scherer and Andrew MacLeod). It is also revealed by the new generation of theories that conceptualize cognitive processes in terms of the dynamic interrelationship between varieties of representational systems within a given cognitive framework (see the chapter by Teasdale).

In addition to the ongoing deconstruction of the basic cognitive processes associated with emotion, the 1990s has seen the research community exhibit a revived interest in the relationship of emotion to consciousness (see the chapter by Öhman); in particular, the intrusion of unwanted emotional material into awareness (see chapters by Tallis and Dalgleish et al.). This interest in inhibition has clear topical relevance with respect to its potential to shed light on the truth or otherwise of so-called recovered memory experiences (see chapter by Bekerian & Goodrich). Related to the interest in consciousness is an emphasis on work into the "self" (see chapters by Michael Lewis, Andrew MacLeod and Healy & Williams). Such complex concepts have traditionally been ducked by cognition and emotion researchers, despite attracting considerable theoretical interest in the clinical domain. Increased attention to consciousness and the self is likely to increase the potential for cross-fertilisation between the clinic and the laboratory in cognition–emotion research.

EMOTIONS

Much of the research that has examined cognition–emotion interactions has concentrated on what might be called "basic emotions" (see Ekman's Chapter 3). Although there is some disagreement as to which emotions might be reasonably construed as basic, there seems little controversy over the inclusion of sadness, anger, disgust, joy and fear on the list. The current research into these emotions is covered thoroughly in the chapters by Power, Berkowitz, Rozin et al., Isen, and Colin MacLeod, respectively. Again, the relationship between the normal experience of these emotions and emotional disorders associated with them is an emergent theme. In particular, the 1990s have been something of a Zeitgeist for research into disgust, with emphasis not just on disgust experiences in normal subjects but also on its potentially pivotal role in clinical states such as obsessive-compulsive disorders, eating disorders, phobias and depression (Power & Dalgleish, 1997). Furthermore, it has been the focus of studies in neuroscience that have linked disgust to the basal ganglia regions of the brain (Phillips et al., 1997; Sprengelmeyer, Lange & Homberg, 1994).

In addition to the concentrated body of research on basic emotions, the focus of new research is expanding to examine what some might call complex emotions, for example, the self-conscious emotions of shame, embarrassment, pride and guilt (see the chapter by Tangney) and of jealousy and envy (see the chapter by East & Watts). A clear direction for the future is to begin to explore the links between the more complex emotions and emotional disorder. This approach is well-exemplified by the work on abuse, depression and shame by Paul Gilbert (e.g. Gilbert, Allan & Goss, 1996).

THEORIES

The current state of theoretical progress within cognition and emotion includes a provocative mixture of the old and the new. Well-established theories are continually being refined and the latest instantiations of appraisal theory (see the chapter by Scherer), associative network theory (see the chapter by Forgas) and attribution theory (see the chapter by Gotlib & Abramson) are eloquently discussed in Part IV.

However, in addition to these historically well-established views, the next generation of functional theoretical models is presented in the chapter by John Teasdale, with discussion of multi-level theories such as interacting cognitive subsystems (ICS; Teasdale & Barnard, 1993) and SPAARS (Power & Dalgleish, 1997). These models, along with the dynamic conceptualization of Marc Lewis, emphasize a systems approach in which it is the integration of multiple representations and multiple processes in particular patterns that defines emotion and, importantly, emotional disorder. Furthermore, these models permit the integration of associative network ideas with the notions of higher-order appraisals in a single approach. It seems likely that such multi-representational architectures will provide a strong challenge in the immediate future to the theories described by Forgas, Scherer and Gotlib & Abramson.

APPLICATIONS

Since the 1970s, research into cognition and emotion has travelled two parallel roads. The road of basic research has generated the data and ideas presented in the first four Parts of the present volume. However, a second road investigating the role of cognitive processes in the applied clinical domain has also proved productive. The central place of cognition in the cognitive therapies has always been a fertile area for ideas (see chapter by Segal & Rokke); however, increasingly clinicians from more diverse traditions, such as behaviour therapy (see chapter by Mineka & Thomas) and psychotherapy (see chapter by Westen), have begun to elucidate the potentially crucial role of cognitive processing within their disciplines. In part, this represents a general move in psychology towards cognitive models of mind; however, more locally, it reflects the powerful impact of cognitive therapies in the field of mental health. Finally, some less immediately obvious applications of cognition and emotion are represented in Part V by the chapters from Bekerian & Goodrich on forensic applications and from Jim Averill on emotional creativity.

SUMMARY AND CONCLUSIONS

Throughout our discussion of the content of the five sections of this book we have sought to identify a number of emergent themes that characterize the current state of cognition and emotion research and thereby provide pointers to the directions in which the area is likely to develop. In summary, the most prominent themes that we identify are:

1. the development of systemic and multi-level theoretical characterizations of the problems space, as illustrated in the reviews by Teasdale and Marc Lewis;
2. the application of neuroscience to understanding cognition–emotion relations, as illustrated in the chapters by Davidson and Gray;
3. the relationship between theory and data concerning normal emotional experiences and emotional disorders;
4. the application of a developmental perspective to cognition–emotion interactions;
5. the expansion of methodology to embrace neuroimaging, computational and quantitative modelling, and qualitative techniques;
6. the increasing application of basic research ideas in the clinic.

When taken together, these developments indicate that cognition–emotion research has a healthy, methodologically sophisticated future, in which the theoretical promise of the early basic research will increasingly be applied to tractable real-life problems. At the same time, however, we should recall Goethe's maxim, "Those who cannot draw on three thousand years are living from hand to mouth". We are certainly not the first to puzzle over the relationship between cognition and emotion, and we shall certainly not be the last.

REFERENCES

Aristotle (1991). *The Art of Rhetoric*. Harmondsworth: Penguin.
Daleiden, E. L. & Vasey, M. W. (1997). An information-processing perspective on childhood anxiety. *Clinical Psychology Review*, **17**, 407–429.
Gilbert, P., Allan, S. & Goss, K. (1996). Parental representations, shame, interpersonal problems, and vulnerability to psychopathology. *Clinical Psychology and Psychotherapy*, **3**, 23–34.
Pennebaker, J. (ed.) (1995). *Emotion, Disclosure and Health*. Washington, DC: American Psychological Association.
Phillips, M. L., Young, A. W., Senior, C., Brammer, M., Andrew, C., Calder, A. J., Bullmore, E. T., Perrett, D. I., Rowland, D., Williams, S. C., Gray, J. A. & David, A. S.

(1997). A specific neural substrate for perceiving facial expressions of disgust. *Nature*, **389**, 495–498.

Power, M. J. & Dalgleish, T. (1997). *Cognition and Emotion: From Order to Disorder*. Hove: Psychology Press.

Sprengelmeyer, R., Lange, H. & Homberg, V. (1994). The pattern of attentional deficits in Huntington's disease. *Brain*, **118**, 145–152.

Teasdale, J. & Barnard, P. (1993). *Affect, Cognition and Change*. Hove: Erlbaum.

Williams, J. M. G., Mathews, A. & MacLeod, C. (1996). The emotional Stroop task and psychopathology. *Psychological Bulletin*, **120**, 3–24.

Author Index

Abelson, R.P.   236, 640, 696
Abercrombie, H.C.   117
Abraham, K.   357
Abrahamsen, A.   690
Abramowitz, J.S.   747
Abramson, L.Y.   268, 360, 361, 372, 512,
   515, 618, 619, 620, 621, 622, 623, 624,
   625, 626, 627, 628, 630, 717, 803
Ackerman, B.   787
Adams, H.E.   572, 577
Adams, P.   543
Ahmad, S.   185
Ahmad, T.   485
Ahn, W.   273
Ainsworth, M.D.S.   505
Alavi, F.N.   95
Albro, E.R.   386, 390, 401
Aldwin, C.M.   776
Alessandri, S.M.   137, 139, 387, 388, 390,
   552, 558
Alexander, J.   489
Allan, S.   548, 552, 803
Allen, J.P.   63
Alloy, L.B.   69, 268, 361, 372, 515, 618,
   622, 623, 624, 625, 626, 627, 629, 632
Allport, A.   160, 172
Allport, F.H.   46
Alvarez, W.   232
Amaral, D.G.   115, 117
Amin, J.   455
Amir, N.   254, 449, 453, 460, 462, 485,
   488, 491
Amsel, A.   86
Amsterdam, B.   542
Amstutz, D.   572
Ancoli, S.   73

Andersen, S.M.   713, 742
Anderson, C.A.   420, 424
Anderson, J.R.   182, 595, 597, 617, 741
Anderson, K.   360
Anderson, K.B.   420, 423
Anderson, M.C.   244, 252, 256
Anderson, R.C.   260, 261
Anderson, S.J.   233
Anderson, S.M.   269, 276
Andrews, B.   212, 252, 629, 793, 794
Angyal, A.   431, 432, 439
Antes, J.R.   712
Antoniou, A.A.   385, 638, 640, 641, 644
Antony, M.M.   489
Appadurai, A.   436, 438
Apter, M.J.   440
Aquinas, Thomas   5, 26, 28, 29, 799
Arcuri, L.   305
Arends, H.   572
Aristotle   5, 6, 21, 22, 23, 26, 27, 37, 282,
   637, 799
Arius Didymus   24
Arndt, J.   251
Arnold, M.B.   12
Arntz, A.   153, 161, 449, 451, 454, 468,
   491, 719
Aronson, E.   572, 578
Asch, S.E.   4
Asendorpf, J.   73, 250
Ashbrook, P.W.   63, 69, 198, 200, 201,
   202, 204, 217, 218, 237, 515, 604, 714
Ashby, F.G.   534, 536
Ashby, W.R.   684
Ashmore, M.   440, 441
Ashworth, C.M.   371
Asmundson, G.J.G.   486

Aspinwall, L.G.   526, 532
Astley, C.A.   108
Augustoni-Ziskind, M.   439
Austin, J.T.   267
Averill, J.R.   412, 415, 418, 419, 766, 769, 770, 772, 773, 774, 775, 778, 804
Ax, A.F.   49

Baars, B.J.   7, 10
Babcock, M.K.   554, 556
Back, M.   221
Bacon   27
Baddeley, A.D.   231, 237, 326, 447, 667, 713
Bagby, R.M.   775
Bailey, S.   360
Bakan, P.   176
Baker, L.   730
Baker, S.   599, 601
Baldwin, D.A.   388
Baldwin, M.W.   696, 739
Ball, S.   292
Balota, D.A.   331
Banajii, M.R.   76, 784
Bandura, A.   8, 705, 749, 754, 757, 758, 759
Banse, R.   645, 650
Baptista, A.   481
Bargh, J.A.   178, 247, 269, 276, 281, 287, 326, 327, 343, 491, 674, 713, 715, 720, 730, 741, 750
Barlow, D.H.   146, 268, 285, 291, 345, 547, 615, 712, 747, 748, 749, 750, 752, 753, 755, 757, 758, 759
Barnard, P.J.   198, 205, 230, 283, 289, 294, 448, 465, 574, 669, 670, 671, 678, 679, 680, 803
Barndollar, K.   730, 741
Barnett, P.A.   624, 626
Barnhardt, T.M.   330, 331
Baron, R.   606
Baron, R.A.   526
Baron-Cohen, S.   366
Barrett, K.C.   134, 403, 542, 543, 550, 552, 553, 558
Barrett, L.F.   72
Barsade, S.G.   535
Barsalou, L.W.   233
Bartlett, F.C.   220, 788
Baruch, I.   89
Basoglu, M.   753
Bateson, G.   770
Bauer, P.   388
Bauer, R.M.   327, 368

Baumeister, R.F.   6, 546, 547, 549, 553
Baumeister, R.G.   543
Baxter L.R.   285, 287
Baylis, G.C.   243
Beach, S.R.H.   630
Bearison, D.J.   7, 12
Beauregard, K.   63
Bechara, A.   135, 733
Bechtel, W   690
Beck, A.T.   69, 70, 84, 139, 146, 161, 174, 179, 236, 248, 268, 282, 283, 288, 289, 290, 448, 464, 489, 490, 512, 513, 514, 613, 616, 617, 621, 622, 625, 626, 627, 629, 654, 708, 710, 713, 715, 716, 717, 719, 720, 751
Beck, J.G.   486, 487
Beck, R.C.   199
Becker, E.   435, 460, 462, 487, 508
Behar, D.   287
Beidel, D.C.   283
Bekerian, D.B.   233, 252, 269, 275, 276, 641, 787, 788, 789, 790, 792, 793, 794, 802, 804
Belli, R.   787
Belsher, G.   615
Bender, D.B.   129
Benedict, R.   544
Bentall, R.P.   355, 358, 359, 360, 361, 362, 363, 364, 365, 367, 369, 370, 371, 372, 373, 374, 508, 800
Bentley, A.F.   11
Berkowitz, L.   65, 395, 416, 419, 420, 422, 424, 425, 583, 593, 601, 606, 645, 646, 802
Bernas, R.   386
Berner, P.   358
Bernet, C.Z.   201
Bernston, G.G.   74, 109
Berrios, G.   358
Bers, S.A.   584
Bertenthal, B.L.   542
Bibring, E.   511, 512
Bierbrauer, G.   553
Biddle, S.J.   656
Biferno, M.A.   325
Billings, F.J.   220, 792
Billings, R.S.   529, 535
Birchwood, M.   354
Birdwhistell, R.   303, 308
Birnbaum, D.   602
Bischof-Kohler, D.   137
Bisiach, E.   335
Bjork, R.A.   243, 244, 252, 256
Black, J.B.   236

Blackburn, I.M.   371
Blanchard, D.C.   98
Blanchard, E.   284
Blanchard, R.J.   98
Blaney, P.H.   65, 147, 195, 197, 200, 526, 598
Blashfield, K.   355
Blatt, S.J.   548
Blaxton, T.A.   463
Blehar, M.C.   615
Bless, H.   526, 535, 604
Bleuler, E.   357
Block, N.   84
Bluck, S.   386
Bobrow, D.G.   236
Boden, J.M.   6
Bodenhausen, G.V.   525, 535, 603
Bohr, N.   282
Boice, R.   758
Boiten, F.   49
Bolles, R.C.   4
Bolton, D.   294
Bonano, G.A.   250
Boon, C.   286
Booth, R.J.   249
Borg, I.   556, 641
Boring, E.G.   323
Borkovec, T.D.   269, 284, 285, 292, 711, 751, 756
Borod, J.C.   116
Boucher, J.D.   53, 54, 305, 307
Bourque, P.   754
Bouton, M.E.   754
Bowen-Jones, K.   360
Bower, G.H.   12, 63, 146, 161, 174, 193, 195, 196, 198, 199, 201, 204, 217, 218, 220, 230, 290, 375, 422, 464, 514, 591, 592, 593, 594, 595, 596, 597, 598, 599, 602, 604, 605, 613, 617, 666, 714
Bowers, J.M.   787
Bowers, K.S.   328, 329, 330, 331, 333
Bowlby, J.   268, 503, 504, 505, 507, 729, 730, 731
Boyce, W.T.   386
Brainerd, C.   787
Bradley, B.P.   146, 147, 149, 151, 152, 155, 157, 158, 159, 160, 161, 162, 165, 177, 195, 253, 254, 341, 595, 801
Bradley, M.   105, 113, 160, 163, 339
Brand, N.   175
Brant, M.E.   53, 54
Brawman-Mintzer, O.   615
Bremer, D.   73

Brenner   729
Breuer, J.   294, 322
Breuer, P.   489
Brewer, M.   599, 601, 603
Brewin, C.R.   212, 217, 232, 234, 235, 250, 252, 257, 258, 259, 260, 323, 357, 360, 502, 629, 667
Briere, J.   252
Briggs, J.L.   243
Bringle, R.G.   569, 572, 575, 576, 577, 578, 580
Brittlebank, A.D.   231, 234
Broadbent, D.E.   172, 178, 287, 447
Broadbent, K.   231
Broadbent, M.H.P.   178, 447
Brockington, I.F.   355
Brodie, P.   548
Brooks, J.   136
Brooks-Gunn, J.   125, 128, 136
Brosschot, J.F.   161, 449
Brown, A.L.   235
Brown, D.E.   306
Brown, G.   236, 268
Brown, J.D.   621
Brown, R.   66
Brown, T.   712
Bruch, H.   510
Bruck, M.   787
Bruder, G.E.   116
Bruner, J.   11, 12, 13, 324
Bruyer   734
Bryson, J.B.   578
Bucci   730
Buck, R.   51, 687
Buddin, B.   505
Buehler, R.   275, 277
Bullington, J.C.   195
Bunce, S.   734
Bunyan, J.   286
Burgess, A.W.   215
Burgess, I.S.   483
Burgess, S.L.   386
Burggraf, S.A.   548, 550, 551, 559
Burke, A.   214
Burke, M.   195, 199, 458, 594, 595
Burt, D.B.   70, 714
Burton, A.   235
Bush, M.   548
Buss, A.H.   183, 556, 731
Buswell, B.N.   545, 555
Butler, G.   146, 269, 290, 294, 455, 481, 756
Butterfield, W.C.   281, 325
Buttolph, L.   284

Buunk, B.P.   570, 571, 572, 576, 577, 578, 579, 585
Bygrave, H.M.   176, 184
Byrne, A.   68, 158, 270, 272, 463

Cacioppo, J.T.   73, 74, 109
Calhoun, K.   748
Calicchia, D.   386
Caltagirone, C.   217
Calvo, M.G.   177, 178, 447, 457, 458, 713
Campbell, D.T.   67
Campbell, H.   136
Campbell, L.   274, 470
Campbell, P.   292
Campbell, W.K.   195
Campos, J.J.   386, 387, 388, 390, 543
Camras, L.A.   54, 313, 402, 692, 693
Candido, C.L.   361
Cane, D.B.   162, 615
Cannon, W.B.   32, 128
Cantor, N.   330, 529, 530, 532
Cantril, H.   288
Capuzzo, N.   285
Carey, J.   282
Carey, S.   784
Carlson, G.A.   368
Carlson, G.E.   305, 306
Carlsson, A.   89
Carnap, R.   33, 34
Carnevale, P.J.D.   526, 530, 532
Carnochan, P.   513, 687
Carter, K.   187
Carver, C.S.   110, 175, 176, 179, 267, 268, 291
Caruso, D.R.   777
Case, R.   696
Cashman, L.   790
Cassiday, K.L.   454
Castillo, D.   458
Castillo, M.D.   177, 178, 457
Ceci, S.J.   784, 787, 793
Ceschi, G.   641, 656
Chaiken, S.   599, 601
Challman, A.   290
Chalmers, D.J.   84, 92, 94, 97
Chamberlain, K.   236
Chambless, D.L.   580, 748
Champion, L.A.   278, 499, 508, 510, 515
Champoux, M.   753, 754
Chandler, C.   641
Chapman, J.P.   98, 116, 358
Chapman, L.J.   358, 369
Chapman, L.P.   116
Charcot, J.M.   136

Charney, D.S.   221
Chartier, G.M.   63
Cheesman, J.   152, 331, 332
Chen, E.   254, 485
Chevalier-Skolnikoff, S.   54, 315
Chiang, T.   553
Chiu, C.   137
Chorpita, B.F.   753
Christiansen, R.   787
Christianson, S.-Å.   158, 194, 204, 213, 214, 215, 216, 217, 218, 219, 221, 789, 790
Chrousos, G.P.   114
Chrysippus   24
Churchill, L.   107
Chwelos, G.   655
Cialdini, R.B.   524, 527
Cicchetti, D.   696
Ciompi, L.   355
Cisamolo, D.   412, 413, 414, 417
Clanton, G.   570
Claparede, E.   215
Claridge, G.C.   235
Clark, A.M.   595
Clark, D.A.   708
Clark, D.M.   63, 73, 178, 184, 185, 195, 230, 236, 292, 345, 355, 454, 455, 464, 481, 482, 489, 490, 491, 751
Clark, L.A.   69, 72, 110, 270
Clark, M.S.   198, 199, 203, 204, 591, 601, 604
Clarkson, M.G.   388
Claudio, V.   244
Clayton, P.J.   507
Clifton, R.K.   388
Cloitre, M.   257, 258, 459, 460, 487, 488
Clore, G.L.   85, 198, 276, 277, 334, 336, 345, 415, 416, 418, 422, 424, 556, 591, 592, 599, 601, 603, 605, 640, 641
Cochran, S.   420, 425
Cochrane, R.   508
Coe, C.L.   363
Cohen, B.D.   362
Cohen, I.   457
Cohen, I.L.   483
Cohen, J.D.   148, 174, 178, 179, 335
Cohen, N.J.   98
Cohen, P.R.   12, 591, 592, 597, 666
Colby, C.A.   628
Colby, K.M.   357, 362
Cole, P.   552
Collins, A.   85, 230, 286, 336, 345, 415, 416, 556, 592, 640, 641
Collins, P.F.   107

Conklin, A.   739
Conway, M.A.   68, 217, 233, 238, 334, 336, 591, 599, 601, 603, 605, 641, 793
Cook, D.R.   548
Cook, M.   455, 753, 755
Cook, T.D.   67
Cools, J.   235
Corcoran, R.   367
Corteen, R.S.   333
Cosmides, L.   46, 52, 337
Costa, P.T. Jr   775
Costello, C.G.   355, 615
Courage, M.   212, 213
Coyle, K.   487
Coyne, J.C.   11, 181, 622
Craik, F.I.M.   718
Cramer, P.   525, 527, 528
Craske, M.G.   254, 460, 485, 759
Crick, F.   93, 94
Crits-Christoph, P.   740, 742
Cronbach, L.J.   479
Cropley, M.L.   269, 272
Crow, T.J.   88, 355
Crowder, R.G.   76, 784
Crowne, D.P.   250
Cupach, W.R.   554, 557
Cupchik, G.C.   218
Cuthbert, B.   105, 113, 160, 163, 339, 756
Cutler, L.   548
Cutshall, J.L.   213, 789

D'Afflitti, J.P.   548
Daleiden, E.L.   492, 801
Dalgleish, T.   68, 75, 195, 199, 201, 217, 231, 244, 246, 247, 260, 287, 288, 294, 341, 441, 453, 454, 460, 480, 497, 498, 499, 500, 502, 505, 506, 507, 511, 512, 514, 515, 595, 673, 674, 675, 696, 719, 734, 802, 803
Daly, J.A.   553
Damasio, A.R.   249, 283, 327, 339, 343, 692
Damasio, H.   249, 327
Damon, W.   543
Damhuis, I.   546
Darby, B.   524, 527
Darke, S.   448
Darley, J.   527
Darwin, C.   24, 45, 54, 125, 128, 132, 133, 302, 303, 314, 429, 430, 431, 554
Dashiell, J.F.   308
Daubman, K.A.   230, 530, 531, 532
Davey, G.C.L.   285, 441
Davidson, B.J.   147

Davidson, R.J.   48, 49, 50, 72, 74, 103, 104, 107, 108, 109, 110, 111, 113, 114, 116, 117, 118, 250, 315, 631, 645, 800, 804
Davies, D.R.   175
Davies, R.M.   572, 577
Davis, M.   117, 335, 339, 748
Davis, P.J.   257
Davitz, J.R.   412
Davison, K.P.   249
Dawkins, R.   282
Dawkins, K.   253, 450
Dawson, M.E.   325, 333
de Bono, J.   161
de-Jong, P.   455
de Ruiter, C.   449
De Schuyter, J.   68
de Silva, P.   289
de Sousa, R.   41
De Vita, J.L.   108
Deardorff, W.W.   69
Deary, I.J.   183
Deffenbacher, J.L.   447
Deffenbacher, K.   784, 789
DeFrancisco, V.L.   68
Delespaul, P.A.E.   543
Dember, W.   616
DeNeve, K.M.   420, 423
DeNisi, A.   180
Dennett, J.L.   788, 792, 793, 794
Depue, R.A.   107, 625
Derakshan, N.   342
DeRivera, J.   546, 638, 640
Derry, P.A.   195, 513, 716
Derryberry, D.   104, 535
DeRubeis, R.   757
Descartes, R.   27, 28, 29, 30, 31, 637
Detweiler, M.   174
Deuser, W.E.   420, 423
Devine, P.   731, 786
Dewey, J.   11, 13
Dewick H.   294
Diamond, R.   784
Dias, M.G.   438, 651
Dickerson M.   282, 291
Dickman, S.   325, 332
Diener, V.E.   109
Dienstbier,   552
Dimberg, U.   316, 337, 338, 339, 340
Distel, N.   69
Dixon, N.F.   287, 325
Dobson, K.S.   717
Doctoroff, G.   441
Dodge, K.A.   139, 696

Dodgson, G.   359
Dodson, C.   784
Dollard, J.   732
Domesick, V.B.   89
Donnell, C.D.   459, 486, 487, 490
Donnellan, A.M.   448
Donnelly, E.F.   371
Dorn, L.   179
Dovidio, J.F.   533
Dozier, M.   734
Drevets, W.C.   74, 108
Dritschel, B.   233, 235, 237, 789
Drobes, D.J.   750, 752
Druschel, B.   441
Ducci, L.   305
Duchenne, B.   303
DuClos, S.E.   422
Dudley, R.E.J.   359
Dumais, S.T.   174, 175, 325, 326
Dunbar, K.   148, 174, 178, 179
Dunbar, R.I.M.   367
Duncan, E.   68, 497, 504
Duncan, S.   387, 388
Duncan, T.E.   656
Duncker, K.   531
Dunlop, L.   440, 441
Dunn, J.   11, 12, 440
Dunning, D.   269, 270
Duval, S.   291
Dweck, C.S.   134, 137, 623
Dyck, M.J.   513, 708
Dykman, B.M.   620, 622
Dyregrov, A.   221

Eagle, M.   734
East, M.P.   803
Easterbrook J.A.   291, 789
Eastman, C.   510
Ebbesen, E.   784
Ebert, R.   430
Ebsworthy, G.   470
Eckblad, M.   369
Edelman, G.M.   692, 695
Edelmann, R.   455
Edelmann, R.J.   554, 557
Edwards, K.   423
Edwards, P.   645
Edwards, S.   282, 291
Egeth, H.   784
Ehlers, A.   449, 484, 487, 489, 719
Ehrlichman, H.   63
Eibl-Eibesfeldt, I.   129
Eich, E.   72, 194, 196, 197, 198, 199, 204,
   218, 594, 596

Eichenbaum, H.   98
Eisenberg, N.   547
Ekman, P.   45, 46, 47, 48, 49, 50, 51, 53,
   55, 72, 73, 128, 129, 303, 304, 305, 307,
   308, 310, 312, 315, 316, 317, 400, 412,
   413, 429, 430, 645, 650, 689, 690, 691,
   750, 800, 802
Elias, N.   434, 437
Elhag, N.   492
Elliot, D.M.   252
Ellis, A.   7, 282, 513, 548
Ellis, H.C.   63, 64, 69, 194, 198, 200, 201,
   202, 203, 204, 217, 218, 237, 359, 515,
   604, 621, 714, 786, 801
Ellory   161
Ellsworth, P.C.   52, 128, 345, 416,
   419, 423, 592, 606, 637, 638, 641,
   642, 643, 645, 646, 649, 652, 656, 687,
   786
Embree, M.   420, 425
Emde, R.   390, 697
Emery, G.   146, 288, 289, 448, 464, 489,
   490, 715, 718, 751
Emmelkamp, P.   747
Emmons, R.A.   109, 267
Engelberg, E.   217, 218, 219
Engen, T.   218
English, G.E.   454
Epicurus   25
Epstein, S.   730, 733, 776
Erber, M.W.   515, 598, 601, 603
Erber, R.   198, 515, 598, 601, 603
Erdelyi, M.H.   247, 252, 325, 730, 740
Eriksen, C.W.   324, 325, 328, 330, 331,
   332
Erikson, E.H.   133
Ernst, D.   513, 708
Esses, V.M.   63
Estevaz, A.   457
Esteves, F.   327, 340
Estrada, C.A.   531, 532, 533, 535
Etienne, M.A.   116
Evans, J.   235, 709
Evans, M.D.   757
Evdokas, A.   644
Evenbeck, S.E.   578
Everhart, D.   733
Eysenck, H.J.   163
Eysenck, M.W.   68, 145, 147, 146, 150,
   153, 154, 158, 163, 165, 172, 175, 176,
   178, 179, 180, 285, 290, 291, 342, 447,
   448, 450, 456, 457, 463, 467, 480, 492,
   596, 713
Eysenck, S.G.   163

Fürniss, T.   221
Fallon, A.E.   431, 432, 433, 434, 439, 513
Falls, W.A.   117
Fallshore, M.   784, 785
Faneslow, M.S.   338, 339
Farde, L.   118
Farley, A.   388
Faught, W.S.   357, 362
Fazio, R.H.   253, 731
Fear, C.F.   359, 361, 367
Fehr, B.   414, 418, 419, 422
Feiring, C.   139
Feist, G.J.   66
Feldman-Summers, S.   252
Feldon, J.   89
Fenigstein, A.   183, 291
Ferguson, T.J.   543, 546, 550, 551, 552, 786
Fernald, A.   387
Fernandez, E.   420, 656
Feske, U.   748
Festinger, L.   582
Fiedler, K.   195, 199, 204, 591, 594, 596, 598, 599, 602, 603, 604, 605
Fineman, S.   778
Fischer, K.W.   403, 512, 542, 543, 558, 687
Fischer, R.P.   219
Fisher, R.   788, 794
Fishman, D.L.   244, 256
Fisler, R.   793
Fitness, J.   641
Fletcher, G.J.O.   641
Flett, G.L.   69, 179
Flowers, D.L.   116
Flykt, A.   339, 340
Foa, E.B.   139, 153, 284, 291, 293, 294, 449, 451, 454, 455, 459, 460, 468, 482, 486, 487, 489, 490, 491, 712, 719, 747, 749, 750, 751, 752, 753, 754, 755, 756, 757, 758, 759, 760, 790
Fodor, J.A.   286
Fogarty, S.J.   195, 229, 524, 525, 594, 715
Fogel, A.   685, 692, 693, 694, 698
Foley, J.P. Jr   314, 315
Folkman, S.   11, 180, 181, 384, 385, 386, 573, 641, 643, 648, 656
Forbes, J.L.   128
Forgas, J.P.   67, 193, 195, 197, 198, 199, 204, 375, 525, 591, 592, 593, 594, 595, 596, 596, 597, 598, 599, 601, 602, 603, 604, 605, 606, 803
Forrester, E.
Foulds, G.A.   176

Fowler, C.A.   331
Fowles, D.C.   163
Fox, E.   63, 68, 159, 178, 250, 253, 254, 255, 447
Fox, N.A.   109
Frame, C.L.   139
Frankl, V.E.   770, 771, 772
Fransson, A.   447
Frazer, J.G.   433
Freedman, R.   356
Frege   33
French, C.C.   177, 178, 369, 457, 458, 461, 462
Frenkel, E.   366, 375
Frese, M.   14
Freud   4, 22, 30, 98, 131, 133, 135, 136, 217, 229, 248, 257, 289, 290, 291, 294, 322, 323, 356, 357, 511, 548, 620, 728, 729, 730, 739, 787
Frey, K.   63
Fridlund, A.J.   73, 312, 313
Friedman, W.J.   219
Friesen, W.V.   47, 48, 49, 50, 53, 73, 128, 304, 305, 307, 308, 312, 315, 316, 412, 430, 750
Frijda, N.H.   71, 385, 415, 418, 419, 424, 604, 638, 641, 643, 647, 648, 649, 650, 652, 687, 688, 689, 691, 698, 772
Friswell, R.   63
Frith, C.D.   97, 287, 367
Frith, U.   355, 366
Fulcher, E.   254, 255
Funabiki, D.   69
Furnham, A.   253, 450

Gaffan, D.   98
Gaensbauer, T.   697
Gainotti, G.   217
Galanter, E.H.   267
Galileo   27
Gallagher-Thompson, D.   624
Gallistel, C.R.   14
Gara, M.A.   362
Garber, J.   622, 628, 707
Gardner, H.   776
Garety, P.A.   359
Gavanski, I.   546
Gazzaniga, M.S.   135
Geen, R.G.   175
Gehm, T.L.   545, 641, 651
Geiselman, R.E.   219, 244, 256, 784, 788
Gelder, M.G.   345
Gemar, M.   717
Gendlin, E.   670

George, M.S. 106
Georgis, T. 305
Gergely, G. 390
Gergen, K.J. 412
Geva, N. 530
Gewirtz, J.C. 117
Giacchino, J. 108
Gilbert, P. 548, 550, 551, 552, 555, 805
Gilboa, E. 69, 198, 199, 617, 628, 629
Gillespie, R.D. 357
Gilligan, S.G. 194, 195, 196, 198, 201, 594, 595
Giovannini, D. 412, 413, 414
Gittleson, N. 290
Giuliano, T. 291
Glaser, R. 114
Glass, D.C. 619
Glazer, W. 358
Gleicher, F. 599, 601
Glenn, C.G. 394
Glick, M. 355, 356, 362, 372
Globisch, J. 336, 339
Glowalia, U. 194, 196
Goddard, L. 235
Goethe, J.W. von 804
Goffman, E. 554
Gold, P.W. 114
Goldberg, D. 355
Goldberg, S 136
Goldman, S.L. 72
Goldman-Rakic, P.S. 114
Goldsmith, M. 794
Goleman, D. 776
Golin, S. 622
Gollwitzer, P.M. 674
Gonzalez, P. 194, 198, 199, 594
Gonzalez, R. 786
Good, B. 499
Good, B.J. 508
Goodall, G. 510
Goodman, C.C. 324
Goodman, G.S. 212, 213, 221, 286
Goodman, S.H. 615
Goodrich, S. 252, 787, 789, 802, 804
Goodwin, A.M. 63
Goodwin, F.K. 114, 356, 368, 369
Gordon, R.M. 41
Goss, K. 548, 552, 803
Gotlib, I.H. 69, 162, 195, 198, 199, 204, 212, 369, 372, 514, 515, 615, 616, 617, 621, 622, 624, 626, 628, 629, 630, 631, 712, 713, 715, 803
Gottman, J.M. 317
Grace, A.A. 95

Graf, P. 148, 211, 326, 465
Graham, D.T. 49
Graham, S. 641
Gralinski, J.H. 542
Gramzow, R. 546, 548, 549
Granic, I. 801
Gray, J.A. 40, 83, 84, 85, 87, 88, 89, 90, 91, 92, 93, 94, 95, 96, 97, 98, 110, 163, 164, 172, 175, 270, 330, 338, 739, 752, 800, 804
Gray, K. 578
Greaves, G. 271
Green, D.P. 72
Green, M.F. 367
Greenberg, J. 269, 729, 751
Greenberg, R.C. 146, 448, 464
Greenberg, R.L. 288, 289, 489, 490
Greenberger, D. 721
Greene, T.R. 531, 532
Greenspan, P. 41
Greenwald, A.G. 325, 327, 333
Griffin, D. 275, 276
Griffin, S. 543
Griffitt, W. 601
Grill, H.J. 432, 432
Groeneweg, J. 789
Gross, C.J. 129
Gross, E. 554
Gross, J.J. 63, 103, 248
Groves, P.M. 748
Gruba, F.P. 362
Gudjonsson, G.H. 250
Guidano, V.L. 283
Guiliano, T. 291
Gunnar, M. 753, 754
Gurnee, H. 570
Gustavsson, J.P. 118
Gutbezahl, J. 775

Haack, L.J. 622, 625
Haaga, D.A.F. 69, 197, 513, 708
Hagan, R. 153, 468, 469, 618
Haidt, J. 429, 430, 431, 433, 434, 435, 437, 438, 440, 441, 557, 651, 652
Haith, M.M. 387, 388, 390
Halberstadt, L.J. 625, 626
Hall, R. 221
Hallowell, N. 151, 159, 253, 254
Halpern, J.N. 63
Hamilton, E.W. 717
Hamm, A.O. 336, 339
Hammen, C.L. 369, 372, 621, 624
Hammer, L. 439
Hammersley, R. 787, 788

Hampshire, S. 29
Hampson, R.J. 554
Hansen, C.H. 158
Hansen, G.L. 577
Hansen, R.D. 158
Hansson, R.O. 504
Happé, F. 366
Harder, D.W. 548, 550, 551
Hardin, T.S. 237, 515, 714
Hare, R.D. 249
Harley, T.A. 173, 178, 180, 184, 449
Harlow, H.F. 4
Harmon, R. 697
Harrington, R. 508
Harris, T.O. 268
Harrison, J. 289
Harrow, M. 369
Hart, D. 543
Hart, J.D. 750
Harter, S. 505
Hartlage, S. 172, 175, 176, 714
Hartman, C.R. 215
Hartmann, E. 548
Hartmann, H. 728
Harvey, J.M. 481
Harvey, M.R. 791
Harvey, N.S. 287
Hasher, L. 515, 714
Hashimoto, E. 557
Hashtroudi, S. 787
Haviland, J.M. 694, 698
Havner, P.H. 362
Hayes, A.H. 361, 372, 375
Hayes, S.C. 259
Hayes, J.R. 774
Haynes, K.N. 653
Hayward, P. 485
Healy, D. 359, 361, 367
Healy, H. 802
Heatherton, T.F. 544, 546, 549, 553
Hebb, D.O. 695
Heckhausen, H. 543, 558
Hedlund, S. 200
Hegley, D. 54
Heider, F. 4, 582, 595
Heider, K.G. 310, 316
Heimberg, R.G. 153, 449, 451, 468, 485, 491
Hejmadi, A. 429
Heller, W. 116
Hellstrom, K. 754
Hembrooke, H. 793
Hemsbree, E.A. 387
Hemsley, D.R. 88, 89, 91, 98, 359, 712

Hendersen, R. 753
Henderson, D.K. 357
Henriksen, S.J. 108
Henriques, J.B. 74, 116
Hepps, D.H. 212
Herman, C.P. 291
Herman, J.L. 243, 246, 252, 791
Hermann, D.J. 233
Hermans, H.J.M. 696
Herrmann, D. 76
Hertel, G. 604
Hertel, P.T. 64, 65, 69, 75, 194, 198, 201, 202, 203, 204, 237, 515, 713, 714, 800
Herz, R. 218
Herzenberger, S. 361
Heuer, F. 75, 213, 215, 790
Hewitt, P.L. 179
Higgins, E.T. 179, 285, 288, 362, 363, 372, 720, 738
Hilgard, E.R. 135, 136, 591, 605
Hill, A.B. 168, 656
Hirsch, C. 457
Hirst, W. 466
Hoblitzelle, W. 548
Hoch, S.J. 276
Hochschild, A.R. 129, 766, 777, 778
Hockey, G.R.J. 172
Hodde-Vargas, J. 506
Hodgson, R. 291
Hodgson, R.I. 246
Hoehn-Saric, R. 287
Hofmann, T. 640, 641, 643
Hoffman, H. 787
Hoffman, M.L. 547, 549, 552, 731
Hokker, L. 470
Holender, D. 151, 328, 330, 331
Hollan, J.D. 236
Holland, A. 284
Holle, C. 485
Hollon, S.D. 622, 628, 706, 707, 757
Holmes, D.S. 245, 253, 255, 256, 258, 259
Holt, K. 269
Holtgraves, T. 221
Homberg, V. 802
Hong, Y. 137
Hood, R.W. Jr. 775
Hooven, C. 317
Hope, D.A. 153, 449, 451, 468, 484, 485, 491, 712, 719
Horder, P. 492
Horowitz, M.J. 221, 232, 250, 286, 294, 730, 739
Horowitz, T. 439
Howe, M.L. 212, 213

Howes, D.H.   324
Hryciw, B.   784, 785
Hu, S.   756
Huebner, R.R.   387
Hume, D.   637
Humphrey, N.   282
Humphreys, M.S.   175, 176, 713
Hunter, R.   356
Hupka, R.P.   572, 578, 579
Huq, S.F.   359
Husband, T.H.   220, 792
Huxley, P.   355
Hyman, I.E.   220, 792

Ibelle, B.P.   362
Ickes, W.   551, 620
Idzihowski, C.   447
Imada, S.   434
Imahori, T.T.   557
Ingram, I.M.   290
Ingram, R.E.   70, 174, 176, 201, 288, 707,
   709, 710, 751
Insel, T.R.   285
Inz, J.   756
Irani, K.D.   42
Irwin, W.   108
Isen, A.   63, 198, 199, 202, 230, 502, 524,
   525, 526, 527, 528, 529, 530, 531, 532,
   533, 534, 535, 536, 591, 593, 601, 604,
   779, 802
Ishida, N.   307
Iwawaki, S.   557
Izard, C.E.   12, 54, 55, 72, 128, 305, 307,
   317, 335, 362, 387, 414, 419, 420, 423,
   424, 430, 499, 556, 645, 689, 690, 691,
   694, 695, 696

Jönsson, E.   118
Jackson, H.F.   355
Jackson, R.L.   492
Jacoby, L.L.   329, 330, 333, 334, 488
Jaeger, J.   116
Jaffe, Y.   622, 628
James, W.   31, 33, 40, 128, 132, 281, 321,
   324, 325, 326, 330, 334, 343, 414, 637,
   654, 686
Jamison, K.R.   356, 368, 369, 779
Janet, P.   135, 136, 248, 787, 793
Janis, I.L.   285, 286, 291
Janoff-Bulman, R.   623
Jaspers, K.   358
Jastrow, J.   331
Jaynes, J.   127
Jeffrey, R.W.   754

Jenkins, J.H.   508
Jenkins, J.M.   21
Jennings, J.M.   329, 330, 333, 334
Jerusalem, M.   656
Jian, M.   96
John, C.H.   359
John, O.P.   253
Johnson, B.   622
Johnson, E.   534
Johnson, J.E.   362
Johnson, M.H.   176, 714, 784, 787
Johnson, M.K.   211, 216, 218, 466, 671,
   672, 673, 733
Johnson, N.   385, 392, 393
Johnson, R.C.   553
Johnson-Laird, P.N.   46, 53, 56, 84, 132,
   145, 179, 343, 345, 385, 414, 416, 418,
   419, 423, 431, 437, 465, 498, 502, 510,
   638, 640, 642, 689, 773
Johnston, D.W.   345
Johnstone, E.C.   355
Johnstone, T.   645
Joiner, T.E.   621, 630
Jolles, J.   175
Jones, E.E.   619
Jones, E.G.   95
Jones, F.N.   128
Jones, G.V.   492
Jones, J.L.   447
Jones, M.H.   128
Jones, S.H.   89
Jones, W.H.   543
Jose, P.E.   385, 415, 416, 638, 640, 641,
   643, 644
Joseph, S.   217, 232, 248
Joyce, J.   282
Junyk, N.   689

Kagan, J.   103, 133, 492, 542, 686
Kahn, B.   529, 530
Kahneman, D.   233, 270, 273, 275, 283,
   290, 325, 329, 713, 717
Kaiser, S.   645, 653
Kalbaugh, P.   694
Kalin, N.H.   103, 114
Kalivas, P.W.   107
Kamieniecki, G.W.   482
Kamin, L.J.   89
Kaney, S.   359, 360, 361, 362, 363, 364,
   370, 372, 373
Kang, D.H.   114
Kaplan, B.L.   199
Kaplan, H.B.   362
Kappas, A.   643, 645, 650, 653, 655

Karasawa, K.   640, 643
Kasimatis, M.   63
Kaspi, S.P.   449
Kass, L.   434
Katschnig, H.   358
Katz, A.N.   515, 622, 713, 715
Katz, L.F.   317
Kaufman,   556
Kaufman, G.   551
Kaufman, L.   221
Kauffman, S.A.   685
Kazdin, A.E.   755
Keane, T.   748
Keating, J.P.   73
Keir, R.   759
Kekes, J.   436
Kekule, F.   282
Keller, M.B.   615
Kelley, H.H.   619, 624, 755
Kelly, A.E.   89, 282
Kelly, G.A.   4
Kelly, H.H.   576
Kelly, K.A.   750, 753
Keltner, D.   73, 316, 423, 430, 545, 550, 555, 557
Kemp-Wheeler, S.M.   168
Kemper, T.D.   49
Kendall, P.C.   69
Kendell, R.E.   355
Kendler, K.S.   358
Kenealy, P.   64
Kenny, A.   26
Kentish, J.   151
Kernberg, O.   730
Kessler, R.C.   505, 615
Ketcham, K.   252
Ketelaar, T.V.   103
Khanna, S.   284
Kiecolt-Glaser, J.K.   114
Kihlstrom, J.F.   76, 194, 197, 199, 201, 202, 216, 218, 325, 327, 330, 331, 595, 730, 794
Killeen, P.R.   685
Kim, E.   484
Kim, J.K.   216, 733
Kim, S.H.   584
Kindt, M.   161
Kinderman, P.   359, 362, 363, 364, 365, 367, 371, 372, 373, 374, 508, 800
Kirby, L.D.   645, 650, 653
Kitayama, S.   173, 553, 650, 772
Klass, E.T.   551, 556
Kleinginna, A.M.   7, 10
Kleinginna, P.A.   7, 10

Kleinman, A.   499, 508
Klerman, G.L.   508
Kline, J.P.   248
Klineberg, O.   302, 314
Kling, K.C.   511
Klinger, E.   268
Klinger, M.R.   325, 327, 333
Klitenick, M.A.   107
Klug, F.   454
Kluger, A.N.   180
Knight, R.A.   97
Knight, R.T.   115
Kobak, R.   734
Koch, C.   93
Kochanska   552
Koehler, D.J.   276
Koestner, R.   730
Kolb, B,   387
Koller, S.H.   438, 651
Kolodner, J.L.   236
Koob, G.F.   95
Kopelman, M.D.   231
Kopp, C.B.   542
Koriat, A.   794
Korsakoff, S.S.   218
Kosins, D.J.   570
Kotin, J.   369
Kovacs, M.   616
Kovecses   412
Kozak, M.H.   284, 293, 294
Kozak, M.J.   489, 490, 749, 751, 752, 754, 755, 756, 757, 758, 759, 760
Kraepelin, E.   354
Kraiger, K.   529, 535
Kramer, G.P.   525, 535
Krames, L.   69
Krantz, S.   596, 597, 598
Krantz, S.E.   624
Krasner, L.   359
Kretschmer, E.   357
Kretzmann, N.   26
Kriss, M.R.   707
Kruglanski, A.W.   599, 622, 628
Krystal, J.H.   221
Kugler, K.   543
Kuiken, D.   204
Kuiper, N.A.   195, 513, 716, 718
Kuipers, P.   418, 419, 424, 641, 643, 649
Kulik, J.A.   66
Kunda, Z.   601
Kunst-Wilson, W.R.   327, 646
Kuyken, W.   231, 232, 234
Kuykendall, D.   73

LaBerge, D.   145, 160
Lacey, J.L.   325
Lachman, J.L.   281, 325
Lachman, M.L.   776
Lachman, R.   281, 325
Lader, M.H.   748
Ladouceur, R.   754
Laing, R.D.   137
Laird, J.D.   63
Laird, J.E.   173
Lakatos, I.   622
Lakoff   412, 414
Lam, D.H.   508, 511
Lam, Y.-W.   88
Lamon, M.   63
Landel, J.L.   550, 555
Lang, A.J.   460
Lang, P.J.   71, 105, 107, 113, 113, 160,
   163, 246, 258, 294, 324, 335, 339, 748,
   749, 750, 751, 752, 756
Lange-Gunn, L.   623
Lange   412
Lange, C.   31
Lange, H.   802
Lanterman, E.D.   64, 71
LaPointe, K.   580
Larsen, R.J.   63, 219
Larson, J.   710
Latané, B.   527
Laungani, P.   497
Laurence, J.-R.   323
Lavin, A.   95
Lavy, E.   153, 161, 288, 292, 449, 450,
   451, 454, 468, 491, 719
Lawless, H.   218
Lawrence, D.H.   281, 282
Layden, M.A.   620
Lazarus, R.S.   3, 6, 7, 8, 9, 10, 11, 15, 16,
   46, 51, 52, 53, 72, 107, 180, 181, 203,
   282, 283, 313, 324, 385, 395, 416, 498,
   573, 574, 592, 637, 640, 641, 642, 643,
   644, 645, 647, 648, 654, 656, 665, 686,
   687, 689, 799
Lea, M.F.   641
Leafhead, K.M.   359
Leary, M.R.   554, 555, 557
Lebra, T.S.   553
LeDoux, J.E.   7, 51, 98, 106, 108, 117,
   118, 156, 163, 164, 175, 217, 326, 327,
   335, 337, 338, 339, 340, 343, 344, 345,
   386, 387, 645, 676, 677, 678, 679, 680
Lee, D.J.   221
Lee, I.   489
Lee, S.   161, 162

Lees, J.L.   175
Leff, J.P.   511
Leggett, E.L.   134, 137
Leight, K.A.   194
Leith, K.P.   547
Lemieux, A.M.   363
Leon, M.R.   448
Leonard, J.M.   238
Leonhard, K.   354
Lerew, D.R.   492
Lerman, D.   641
Lesch, K.-P.   173
Leslie, A.M.   366
Levenson, R.W.   48, 49, 50, 63, 248, 315,
   412, 430, 750
Leventhal, H.   7, 10, 14, 51, 71, 216, 218,
   645, 646, 654, 665, 667, 668, 669, 670,
   733
Levi, A.   3, 275
Levin, P.F.   527
Levine, L.J.   68, 71, 356, 384, 385, 386,
   391, 392, 393, 395, 403, 416, 417, 419,
   420, 638, 640, 801
Levinger, G.   605
Levinson, B.W.   215
Levy, R.I.   773
Lewicki, P.   327
Lewin, B.D.   511
Lewin, K.A.   4, 740
Lewin, M.R.   254, 485
Lewine, R.R.J.   356
Lewinsohn, P.M.   594, 626, 710, 716, 717
Lewis, A.   290
Lewis, H.B.   139, 543, 544, 545, 546, 547,
   550, 551, 556, 557
Lewis, M.   125, 128, 129, 131, 132, 134,
   136, 137, 138, 139, 387, 388, 390, 403,
   513, 542, 543, 552, 555, 556, 558, 559,
   649, 687, 688, 689, 691, 692, 694, 697,
   801, 802, 803, 804
Lewis, S.J.   548, 550, 551
Li, K.   641
Libet, B.   330
Licht, B.   623
Liebowitz, M.R.   459, 487
Liker, R.   69
Linderman, E.   291
Lindsay, D.S.   252, 792
Lindsay, R.   785, 786
Lindsay-Hartz, J.   543, 546
Linton, M.   233
Liotto, G.   283
Lipke, H.J.   454, 491
Lipman, A.J.   626

Lishman, W.A.   229, 594
Litman-Adizes, T.   623
Litz, B.T.   249
Liwag, M.   219, 384, 385, 386, 391, 392,
   393, 394, 395, 397, 403, 416
Llinas, R.   93
Lloyd, G.G.   229, 594
Lochrie, B.   183
Loehlin, J.C.   173
Loewenstein, R.   548
Loftus, D.A.   198, 203, 221
Loftus, E.F.   252, 286, 327, 786, 787, 788,
   789, 792
Logan, G.D.   247, 674
Loosen, P.T.   706
Lorenz, M.   492
Lorig, T.S.   221
Lortie, C.   243
Lovibond, P.F.   455
Lowery, L.   430
Loye, F.   506
Lubin, B.   72
Luborsky, L.   739, 742
Lubow, R.E.   89
Lucretius 25
Lundh, L.-G.   330, 459, 487
Lundqvist, D.   339
Lutz, C.A.   499, 773
Lydiard, R.B.   615
Lyon, H.   361, 364, 369, 370, 371, 372,
   373
Lyonfields, J.D.   292
Lyons, W.   38, 654, 799
Lyubomirsky, S.   710

Macalpine, I.   356
Macaulay, E.   197, 198, 596
MacDonald, M.R.   718
MacDowell, K.A.   645
Mackie, D.M.   526, 535, 604
MacKintosh, B.   254, 255
Mackintosh, N.   748
MacLeod, A.   145, 268, 269, 270, 271,
   272, 274, 275, 276, 283, 341, 802
MacLeod, C.   86, 146, 147, 149, 151, 152,
   153, 154, 155, 159, 160, 162, 165, 172,
   177, 195, 198, 199, 205, 253, 254, 288,
   341, 342, 359, 360, 448, 449, 450, 451,
   452, 453, 454, 456, 457, 459, 460, 461,
   462, 468, 469, 470, 479, 480, 483, 484,
   485, 486, 492, 595, 596, 617, 618, 712,
   713, 714, 718, 801, 802
MacMillan, F.   354
MacNamara, J.   160, 165

Maddison, S.   107
Magai, C.   69, 691, 692, 694, 697, 698
Magaro, P.A.   176, 714
Mahapatra, M.   438
Maher, B.A.   359
Mahoney, M.J.   706
Maidenberg, E.   484, 485
Maier, S.F.   618, 754
Main, M.   504
Mairet, A.   581
Malatesta, C.Z.   687, 689, 691, 694, 696
Malla, A.K.   354
Malpass, R.   786
Mandler, G.   5, 32, 148, 343, 385, 388,
   412, 414, 465, 623, 645
Mandler, J.M.   385
Manis, M.   734
Mann, R.L.E.   177
Manson, K.   371, 372
Manstead, A.S.R.   71, 72, 73, 554, 555,
   556, 640, 641, 643, 687
Mantovani, G.   15
Manzella, L.   742
Mao Tse Tung   22
Marcel, A.   327, 331, 335, 336
Margalit, B.   147
Margraf, J.   460, 462, 487, 747
Marks, I.   291, 339
Markus, H.   195, 269, 288, 362, 553, 645,
   650, 750, 772
Markwith, M.   434, 435, 439
Marlowe, D.   250
Marmar, C.R.   249
Marmara, V.   439
Marris, P.   779
Marschall, D.E.   547
Martin, L.L.   525
Martin, M.   178, 454, 492
Marx, E.M.   235
Marx, K.   778
Mascolo, M.F.   543, 546, 558
Masson, J.L.   429
Matchett, G.   441
Mathes, E.W.   572, 574, 575, 577, 578,
   579, 580
Mathews, A.   86, 145, 146, 147, 149, 150,
   151, 152, 153, 154, 159, 160, 162, 165,
   166, 172, 175, 177, 194, 195, 198, 199,
   204, 205, 253, 254, 255, 268, 269, 288,
   341, 342, 345, 359, 360, 448, 450, 451,
   452, 453, 454, 455, 456, 458, 459, 460,
   461, 462, 463, 467, 468, 481, 484, 485,
   486, 492, 594, 595, 596, 687, 712, 713,
   714, 718, 734, 801

Matsumoto, D.R. 316, 649, 651
Matsumoto, H. 553
Matt, G.E. 195
Matthews, G. 166, 171, 173, 174, 175, 176, 177, 178, 179, 180, 181, 183, 184, 185, 187, 286, 292, 449, 480, 490, 491, 712, 800
Mattia, J.I. 153, 449, 451, 468, 491
Mattick, R. 345
Maughan, B. 510
Mauro, R. 641, 643, 651, 652
Mauss, M. 433
Mayer, J.D. 63, 73, 194, 196, 199, 594, 596, 597, 603, 606, 776, 777
Mayer-Gross, W. 357
Mayman, M. 734
Mayo, P.R. 183, 458
Mayr, E. 337, 431
McAndrew, F.T. 305
McAuley, E. 641, 656
McBee, W. 199
McCabe, S.B. 198, 622
McCann, C.D. 195, 712
McCauley, C. 331, 429, 431, 433, 434, 435, 440, 441
McCleary, R.A. 324
McClelland, D.C. 4, 730
McClelland, J.L. 148, 174, 178, 179, 243
McClintic, S. 125, 133, 542, 558
McCloskey, M. 784, 788
McConkey, K.M. 63
McCrae, R.R. 775
McCrone, J. 93
McCulloch, W. 684
McCusker, G. 557
McDonough 388
McDougall 267
McFadden, S.H. 694
McFarlane, A.C. 232
McGinnies, E. 324
McGlaughlin, K. 460, 462
McGraw, K.M. 641
McGuire, P.K. 287
McIntosh, D.N. 129
McLachlan, A.L. 515, 622, 713, 715
McLaughlin, S.C. 201
McLelland, J. 467
McNally, R.J. 65, 86, 151, 153, 177, 181, 232, 234, 253, 292, 449, 450, 451, 453, 454, 455, 459, 460, 462, 468, 479, 480, 481, 482, 484, 485, 486, 487, 490, 491, 492, 712, 749, 750, 751, 752, 754, 759
McNaughton, N. 85, 98, 752
McNeil, D.W. 485

McPherson, F.M. 371
Mead, M. 310
Meadows, S. 555, 557
Means, B. 532, 533, 535
Mednick, E.V. 531
Mednick, M.T. 531
Mednick, S.A. 531
Meehl, P.E. 103
Mees, U. 652
Meichenbaum, D. 282
Melamed, B.J. 750
Melchert, T.P. 247, 252
Melges, F.T. 268, 271
Mercer, G. 367
Merikle, P.M. 152, 329, 331, 332, 333
Merkelbach, H. 292, 455
Mervielde, I. 68
Mesquita, B. 650, 652, 772
Metalsky, G.I. 268, 361, 372, 618, 622, 623, 624, 625, 626, 630
Metcalfe, J. 197
Metts, S. 554, 557
Metzger, R.L. 285
Meyer, T.J. 268
Michalson, L. 125, 128, 129, 131, 136
Milan, S. 75
Milberg, S. 198
Mill, J.S. 510
Millar, G.A. 63
Millar, N. 157, 158, 160, 162
Miller, D.T. 621
Miller, G.A. 116, 267
Miller, H. 196
Miller, N. 732
Miller, R.S. 554, 555, 556, 557
Miller, S.M. 139
Miller, W.I. 434, 437, 438, 440, 441
Millman, L. 433
Mineka, S. 53, 166, 199, 270, 338, 455, 462, 750, 753, 754, 755, 759, 803
Miranda, J. 717
Mirsky, J. 579
Mischel, W. 691
Mitchell, S. 729
Miyake, K. 552
Moan-Hardie, S. 793
Modigliani, A. 554, 556
Moffitt, T. 557
Mogg, K. 75, 146, 147, 149, 151, 152, 153, 154, 15, 157, 158, 159, 160, 161, 162, 177, 253, 254, 341, 449, 450, 451, 452, 454, 456, 459, 460, 467, 468, 491, 715, 801
Mohamed, A. 183
Molenaar, P.C.M. 697

Molina, S. 269
Molnar, C. 790
Monahan, J.L. 10, 646, 734
Monteiro, K.P. 194, 195, 196, 198, 201, 594
Moore 34
Moore, B.A. 714, 801
Moore, R.G. 231
Morgan, C. 778
Morgan, I.A. 183
Morgan, M.A. 117
Morgan, R.D. 543, 546, 547
Morgenson, G.J. 90, 95
Morgenstern, H. 358
Morris, W.N. 596
Morrow, J. 66, 68, 710
Morton, J. 787, 788, 794
Moses, L.J. 388
Mosher, D.L. 556
Mowrer, O.H. 752
Moylan, S. 67, 375, 594, 597, 605, 606
Mueller, T.I. 615, 619
Mullen, P.E. 570, 571, 572, 575, 577, 578, 580, 581
Multhaup, K.S. 211, 216, 218, 671, 673
Munakata, Y. 594
Munn, N.L. 32
Muran, J.C. 717, 718
Murdock, T.B. 460
Muris, P. 292
Murphy, D.L. 196, 371
Murphy, E. 510
Murphy, G. 4, 13
Murphy, S.T. 10, 129, 646, 734
Murray, H.A. 4
Murray, N. 530
Murrell, E. 345
Musalek, M. 358
Myers, G.E. 42
Myers, L.B. 250, 257, 259, 260, 502
Myers, N.A. 388

Nadel, L. 98
Nader, K. 221
Nagel, L. 54
Najavits, L. 706
Narrow, W.E. 615
Nasby, W. 195
Nathanson, D.L. 550
Navon, D. 147
Naylor, C.E. 116
Neale, J.M 357, 361, 368, 370, 371, 373, 511
Neely, J.H. 177, 332, 458, 485

Neisser, U. 14, 174, 181, 205, 212, 335, 596, 603, 791, 792
Nelson, H.F. 361
Nelson, K. 695
Nemeroff, C. 433, 434
Neu, J. 31, 582
Newell, A. 173
Newman, J. 93
Newport, E.L. 402
Ng, V. 469
Niedenthal, P. 529, 546, 595, 596
Niederehe, G. 70, 714
Nielsen, M. 90, 95
Nigg, J. 730, 733
Niit, T. 305
Nilsson, L.-G. 214, 215, 790
Nisbett, R.E. 345, 641
Noice, H. 531, 532
Nolen-Hoeksema, S. 66, 68, 162, 508, 710, 712
Norgren, R. 432
Norman, D.A. 174, 236, 286, 290
Norman, R.M.G. 354
Nowak, A. 685
Nowicki, G.P. 230, 531, 532
Nugent, K. 462
Nulty, D.D. 712
Nunley, E.P. 770, 772
Nunn, J.D. 459
Nurcombe, B. 371
Nurmi, J. 278
Nusbaum, B. 692, 694, 697
Nygren, T.E. 534

O'Connor, 729
O'Hara, M.W. 363
O'Heeron, R. 221
O'Keefe, J. 98
O'Leary, T. 712
Oatley, K. 21, 46, 53, 56, 68, 84, 132, 145, 150, 174, 179, 277, 343, 345, 385, 414, 416, 418, 419, 423, 431, 437, 465, 497, 498, 502, 503, 504, 510, 638, 640, 642, 655, 689, 773
Ochalek, K. 787
Öhman, A. 50, 51, 52, 53, 145, 150, 156, 316, 325, 327, 328, 329, 336, 337, 338, 339, 340, 344, 734, 802
Olasov-Rothbaum, B. 753
Olds, M.E. 128
Omdahl, B.L. 656
Oppliger, P.A. 440, 441
Oren, D.A. 615
Ornstein, P.A. 212

Orr, S.P.   249
Ortony, A.   45, 85, 132, 336, 345, 415, 416, 556, 592, 640, 641, 649
Osberg, T.M.   273, 274
Öst, L.-G.   337, 338, 459, 468, 481, 487, 491, 754
Oster, H.   54, 313, 432, 439
Otto, J.H.   64, 71
Otto, M.W.   487, 488
Otto, T.   98
Overmier, J.B.   618
Overwalle, F. Van   68
Owen, S.E.   371
Ozyurek, A.   386

Padesky, C.   720, 721
Paez, D.   248
Painter, M.   161
Paivio, A.   785
Panksepp, J.   98, 419, 423
Papageorgiou, C.   185, 186, 756
Pape D.   292
Paradiso, S.   106
Pardo, J.V.   116
Parker, J.A.   775
Parker, L.   710
Parkes, C.M.   286, 497
Parkinson, B.   71, 72, 641, 643, 649, 655, 687
Parkinson, R.C.   357, 362
Parra, C.   334, 340
Parrott, W.G.   65, 71, 72, 76, 195, 258, 502, 554, 555, 571, 572, 581, 582, 583, 584, 585, 597, 598, 779, 800
Parsons, O.A.   74
Pashler, H.   172
Patrick, R.E.   530, 538
Patton, K.M.   550, 555
Patwardhan, M.V.   429
Pauli, P.   489
Paulus, D.   580
Pavlov, I.P.   323
Payne, G.C.   543, 546, 547
Payvar, S.   235
Pecchinenda, A.   73, 645, 650
Pembroke, M.   786
Penrod, S.   786
Pennebaker, J.W.   221, 246, 247, 251, 291, 711, 800
Pentland, J.   792
Perkins, D.N.   774
Perrig, P.   64, 65, 195
Perrig, W.J.   64, 65, 195
Perring, C.   277

Perry, C.   323
Persons, J.B.   355, 717
Peselow, E.   116
Petersen, S.E.   116, 160, 365
Peterson, C.   212, 213, 361, 621
Petrie, K.   236, 249
Petty, R.E.   73, 199, 599, 601, 603
Philippot, P.   63, 412, 413, 414, 417
Phillips, M.L.   802
Piaget   13, 128, 685, 692
Pichert, J.W.   260, 261
Pickles, A.J.   459
Pierce, C.S.   331
Pierce, G.R.   198
Pietromonaco, P.R.   195, 269, 327
Pilgrim, D.   355
Pillemer, D.B.   219, 220, 790
Pinborg, J.   26
Pines, A.   572, 578
Pitcaithly, D.   177
Pitman, R.K.   249, 752
Pittman, N.L.   620
Pittman, T.S.   620
Pitts, W.   684
Planalp, S.   68
Plato   5, 22, 23, 26, 39
Platt, S.   235
Pliner, P.   433, 439
Plutchik, R.   10, 47, 54, 132, 731
Polanyi, M.   767
Polivy, J.   291
Pollock, G.H.   779
Pope, K.S.   252, 645
Pope, L.K.   653, 655
Popper, K.R.   622
Port, R.F.   683, 685, 686
Porter, C.A.   621
Posidonius   24
Posner, M.I.   116, 147, 160, 171, 281, 325, 332
Postman, L.   787
Potter-Efron, R.T.   552
Powell, M.   712
Power, M.J.   244, 246, 247, 256, 257, 258, 259, 260, 278, 294, 323, 357, 441, 480, 497, 498, 499, 500, 502, 505, 506, 507, 508, 510, 511, 512, 513, 514, 515, 673, 674, 675, 696, 802, 803
Powys, M.   160, 165
Pratto, F.   153, 253
Pribram, K.   267, 706
Price, V.   759
Prigogine, I.   685, 686
Pruitt, D.G.   532

Pruzinsky, T. 285
Pryor, J.B. 275 .
Puffet, A. 231
Putnam, F.W. 220
Pylyshyn, H. 173
Pynoos, R.S. 221
Pysczcynski, T. 269, 751

Quigley, B.M. 423
Quigley, J.F. 441
Quillian, M.R. 230
Quinlin, D.M. 548
Quinn, M.J. 249

Rachman, S. 161, 246, 283, 289, 291, 293, 294, 711, 748, 749, 758
Rado, S. 357
Rae, D.S. 615
Raichle, M.E. 74
Ramsey, D.S. 137
Randall, F. 178
Ranganath, C 631
Ranieri, D.J. 63
Rapaport, D. 217, 728
Rapoport, J. 440
Rapee, R.M. 146, 345, 459, 487, 489, 753, 759
Rawlins, J.N.P. 89
Rawlinson, H. 159
Rawls, J. 582, 583
Razran, G. 323
Read, J.D. 252, 792
Recchia, S. 125, 133, 542, 558
Reder, L. 784, 785
Redican, W.K. 54, 315
Reed, M.A. 104, 212
Reeve, J. 55
Rehm, L.P. 716
Reidbord, S.P. 221
Reiger, D.A. 615
Reim, B. 619
Reiman, E.M. 108
Reingold, E.M. 329, 332, 333
Reis, H.T. 543
Reisberg, D. 213, 214, 789, 790
Reisberg, G. 75
Reisenzein, R. 637, 640, 641, 643, 750
Reiser, B.J. 236
Reiss, S. 460, 479
Reivich, K. 365
Resick, P. 748
Retzinger, S.R. 547
Revelle, W. 172, 175, 176, 198, 203, 448, 713

Reyna, V. 787, 788, 791
Reynolds, S. 355
Reznick, I. 742
Reznick, J.S. 103, 387, 390
Rhodewalt, F. 601, 603
Ricciardi, J.N. 181, 292
Richards, A. 177, 178, 369, 454, 456, 457, 458, 461, 462
Ridgeway, V. 151, 162
Riemann, B.C. 253, 453, 484, 485
Riggs, D.S. 747
Rimé, B. 68, 412, 413, 414, 417
Rinck, M. 194, 196, 460, 462, 487
Rio, C. 789, 790
Riskind, J.H. 201, 203, 204
Risse, G. 216, 733
Roberts, J.E. 69, 198, 617
Roberts, R.J. 49
Robertson, G.C. 6, 654
Robertson, G.S. 96
Robey, K.L. 362
Robins, C.J. 177, 361, 372, 375
Robins, L.N. 615
Robinson, J. 547, 550, 552
Rocha-Miranda, C.E. 129
Rockart, L. 548
Rodin, J. 66, 548, 572, 582, 584
Rodis, P. 771
Rodriguez, I.A. 201, 714
Roediger, H.L. 463
Roemer, L. 711
Rogers, A.H. 362
Rogers, G.M. 116
Rohde, P. 626
Rokke, P. 716, 803
Rolls, E. 107
Romanski, L. 117, 677
Romney, D.M. 361
Rorty, A. 42
Rosch, E. 310, 683
Rose, D.T. 629, 630
Rose, G.S. 268, 271, 277
Roseman, I.J. 385, 395, 415, 416, 425, 592, 638, 640, 641, 642, 643, 644, 649, 652, 655
Rosen, V. 220
Rosenbaum, M. 594
Rosenblatt, B. 729
Rosenberg, K.L. 552
Rosenberg, E.L. 55, 307, 315
Rosenberg, M. 775
Rosenblum, L. 128
Rosenblume, P.S. 173
Rosenfeld, J.P. 631

Rosenstein, D.   314, 432
Rosenwald, L.A.   792
Rosenzweig, A.S.   532, 533, 535
Roskos-Ewoldsen, D.R.   253
Rosmarin, D.M.   580
Ross, D.   784
Ross, E.D.   47
Ross, J.   204
Ross, M.   275, 357
Rothbaum, B.O.   139
Rothkopf, J.S.   195
Rothman, A.   582
Rotter, J.B.   4
Rozin, P.   429, 430, 431, 432, 433, 434,
   435, 438, 439, 440, 441, 513, 802
Rubin, D.C.   233
Ruch, W.   315
Rude, S.R.   65, 69
Rude, S.S.   198, 200, 201, 202, 203, 713,
   714
Rudnick, J.R.   553
Rudy, L.   213
Ruiz-Caballero, J.A.   194, 198, 199, 594
Rumelhart, D.E.   220, 243
Runco, M.A.   779
Russ, S.W.   779
Russell, B.   33, 774
Russell, D.   641
Russell, J.A.   109, 305, 306, 307, 310, 314,
   414, 418, 419, 422, 650, 772, 773
Russell, M.L.   195, 198, 594
Russell, P.A.   338
Rutherford, D.   68
Rutherford, E.M.   151, 155, 253, 341, 342,
   451, 452, 435, 454, 460, 470
Rutter, M.   278, 510
Ryan, J.M.   579
Ryan, L.   197, 198, 596
Ryan, R.   784, 785
Rychlak, J.F.   8
Ryff, C.D.   106
Ryle, G.   34, 35, 36, 766

Säisä, J.   216
Sabini, J.   14, 195, 258, 502, 554, 555, 556,
   597, 598
Sabini, S.F.   65, 76
St Augustine,   770
Safer, M.   790, 791
Saisa, J.   158
Salkovskis, P.   289, 290, 292, 339, 451,
   479, 754
Salovey, P.   66, 72, 194, 200, 250, 572,
   582, 584, 591, 596, 602, 603, 606, 731,

776, 777
Salter, D.   235
Salthouse, T.A.   713
Sanderson, W.C.   345
Sandler, J.   729, 730, 739
Sanftner, J.L.   548
Santostefano, S.   12, 13, 14
Sanz, J.   460
Saporta, J.   222
Sarason, B.R.   198
Sarason, I.G.   175, 180, 198, 713
Saron, C.   116, 315
Sarter, M.   74
Sartre, J-P.   778
Sato, K.   641, 643, 651, 652
Sattler, J.M.   554
Saywitz, K.J.   793
Schab, F.R.   218
Schacter, D.L.   211, 216, 218, 326, 343,
   460, 488, 595, 788
Schachter, S.   5, 194, 197, 199, 412
Schaffer, C.E.   116
Scheff, T.J.   7, 8, 11, 547
Scheier, M.F.   175, 179, 183, 267, 268
Schell, A.M.   333
Scherer, K.R.   7, 10, 14, 51, 52, 54, 71,
   250, 345, 412, 413, 414, 415, 416, 417,
   430, 553, 542, 545, 546, 637, 638, 640,
   641, 642, 643, 644, 645, 646, 648, 649,
   650, 651, 652, 653, 654, 655, 656, 665,
   668, 670, 667, 687, 688, 690, 698, 802,
   803
Schiff, B.B.   63
Schiffenbauer, A.I.   596
Schmajuk, N.A.   88
Schmaltz, C.M.   579
Schmedel, K.   578
Schmidt, N.B.   492
Schmidt, S.   645
Schmitt, B.H.   579
Schneider, S.   747
Schneider, W.   84, 97, 174, 175, 194, 196,
   245, 246, 325, 326, 332, 491, 674
Schoeman, F.   42
Scholfield, E.J.C.   369
Schonpflug, W.   637
Schooler, J.W.   233, 335, 784, 785
Schore, A.N.   550
Schotte, D.E.   235
Schreber, D.   356, 357
Schuh, E.S.   325, 333
Schultz, W.   107
Schumann, R.   779
Schutzelaars, A.J.H.   641

Schwab, P.J.   356
Schwartz, C.E.   492
Schwartz, G.E.   48, 248, 250, 257, 334, 336
Schwartz, J.C.   412, 414, 418
Schwarz, N.   198, 276, 277, 526, 591, 597, 599, 601, 602, 603, 604, 605
Scott, J.   231, 233, 363
Scrivner, E.   790, 791
Searle, J.R.   84
Sebastian, S.   254, 453, 485
Sedikides, C.   596, 597, 598, 606
Seeley, J.R.   626
Segal, Z.V.   162, 177, 613, 707, 716, 717, 718, 719, 720, 803
Seibert, P.S.   64, 198, 201, 202, 714
Seiffer, A.   159
Seligman, M.E.P.   338, 360, 365, 366, 372, 510, 512, 618, 619, 620, 621, 629, 753
Semin, G.R.   554, 555
Seneca   5, 6
Setterlund, M.B.   595, 596
Severa, N.   578
Shaffer, D.R.   535
Shafran, R.   287
Shalev, A.   232, 249
Shalker, T.E.   528
Shallice, T.   84, 174, 175, 286, 290, 667
Shank, R.C.   696
Shapiro, P.   786
Shapiro, R.W.   615
Share, D.L.   439
Sharkey, W.F.   557
Sharp, H.M.   359, 361, 367
Sharpsteen, D.J.   577, 579
Shaver, P.   403, 412, 414, 417, 418, 513, 553, 687
Shaw, B.F.   717
Shaw, M.P.   779
Shedler, J.   734
Sheingold, K.   212
Shelton, R.C.   706
Shelton, S.E.   103, 114
Sherman, M.F.   441
Sherman, S.J.   276
Shettel-Neuber, J.   578
Shevrin, H.   325, 332
Shields, S.A.   412
Shiffrin, R.M.   84, 97, 174, 175, 245, 246, 325, 326, 491, 674
Shimizu, T.   557
Shore, C.M.   388
Shott, S.   556
Showers, C.J.   511, 530, 532

Shrauger, J.S.   273, 274
Shuchter, S.R.   249, 507
Shweder, R.A.   16, 429, 437, 438, 650
Sides, J.K.   751
Siegal, M.S.   439
Sigel, I.E.   12, 13
Silbertstein, L.   549
Silfvenius, H.   158, 216
Silver, M.   554, 555
Silver, R.C.   505
Silver, R.L.   286
Silverman, L.H.   325
Silverstone, P.H.   362
Simmonds, S.F.   527, 534
Simons, A.D.   146
Simonton, D.K.   773, 774
Sineshaw, T.   305
Singer, B.   106, 249
Singer, J.A.   49, 200, 591, 730, 742
Singer, J.E.   343, 412, 619
Singer, J.L.   2, 250, 260
Sinha, R.   74
Skinner, B.F.   33, 323, 324
Skowronski, J.J.   220
Slater, E.   357
Slife, B.D.   7, 8
Slovic, P.   717
Slyker, J.P.   65
Small, S.A.   177
Smart, L.   6
Smith, C.A.   73, 345, 385, 395, 416, 419, 592, 606, 638, 640, 641, 642, 643, 644, 645, 646, 649, 650, 652, 653, 655, 656, 687
Smith, J.   354
Smith, L.B.   685, 686, 692, 695
Smith, O.A.   108
Smith, R.H.   581, 583, 584
Smith, R.L.   325
Smith, S.F.   71, 72, 554, 555
Smith, S.M.   199, 535, 601, 603
Smith, T.W.   709
Smolenaars, A.J.   641
Snidman, N.   103, 492
Snyder, M.   65, 69, 147, 199, 268, 281, 525, 594
Soares, J.J.F.   150, 328, 329, 336, 339, 340
Soloman, R.   41, 324, 415, 638, 640
Solomon, A.   69
Sommerfeld, B.K.   629
Sonnemans, J.   71
Sorenson, E.R.   304, 305, 307, 310
Southall, A.   177
Southwick, S.M.   221

Sparkes, T.J. 176, 184
Spelke, E.S. 402
Spellman, B.A. 244, 256
Spezzano, C. 728
Spiegel, D. 221
Spielberger, C.D. 72, 424, 468
Spielhofer, C. 641, 643
Spielman, L.A. 269, 276, 713
Spindel, M.S. 415, 416, 640, 641, 643
Spinoza, B. 29, 30, 31, 637, 799
Spitz, R. 697
Sprengelmeyer, R. 439, 440, 804
Spring, B.J. 625
Squire, L. 216, 222
Sroufe, A. 384, 386, 388
Srull, T.K. 602
Srull, T.R. 247
Stafford, L. 557
Stanley, M.A. 283
Starr, M.D. 753
Startup, M. 369, 370, 371, 372, 373
Staufenbiel, Th. 641
Staw, B.M. 535
Stearns, C.S. 497, 499
Steele, C. 738
Steer, R.A. 236
Stegge, H. 543, 546, 550, 552
Stein, M.B. 486
Stein, N.L. 46, 51, 56, 107, 219, 384, 385,
  386, 390, 391, 392, 393, 394, 395, 397,
  401, 402, 403, 416, 417, 419, 420, 638,
  640, 642, 689, 801
Stein, N.L. 53
Steiner, J.E. 432
Steketee, G.S. 479
Stemmler, G. 49
Stenberg, C.R. 386, 387, 388, 390
Stengers, I. 685, 686
Stern, D. 386
Stevens, A. 282
Stevenson, R. 459
Stillwell, A.M. 544, 546, 549, 553
Stipek, D. 126, 133, 137, 542, 558, 641
Stoess, C. 439
Stoler, L.S. 482, 491
Stone, G.P. 554
Stones, M.H. 286
Storm, C. 773
Storm, T. 773
Story, A.L. 269, 270
Stouffer, S. 759
Stouthamer-Loeber, M. 557
Strathman, A. 268
Stratton, P. 365

Strauman, T.J. 363, 372
Strauss, J.S. 358
Striegel-Moore, R. 549
Stroebe, M.S. 504
Stroehm, W. 195, 504
Stroop, J.R. 287, 449, 719
Strube, M.J. 601
Sueda, K. 557
Sullivan, H.S. 580, 696
Sullivan, M. 137, 387, 388, 390
Sullivan, M.W. 558
Summerfield, A.B. 412, 414, 651
Summerfield, W.B. 54
Susser, K. 525, 535
Sutton, K.J. 776
Sutton, S.K. 103, 107, 108, 110, 111, 113,
  118, 455
Suzuki, N. 307
Svedin, S. 221
Swann, W.B. 742
Swartz, T.S. 425
Sweeney, P. 360
Swerdlow, N.R. 95
Szulecka, T.K. 359

Talland, G.A. 202
Tallis, F. 250, 251, 284, 285, 286, 287,
  289, 290, 292, 802
Tangney, J.P. 134, 403, 542, 543, 545,
  546, 547, 548, 549, 550, 551, 552, 553,
  554, 556, 559, 802
Tannenbaum, P.H. 412, 648
Tarbuck, A. 276
Tarrier, N. 581
Taska, L. 139
Tata, P. 147, 162, 165, 341, 342, 450, 492
Tataryn, D.J. 330, 331
Tayloe, D.R. 220
Taylor, G. 249, 582, 775
Taylor, J.G. 95
Taylor, L. 387
Taylor, R. 525, 715
Taylor, S.E. 526, 532, 621
Teasdale, J.D. 195, 198, 205, 229, 230,
  237, 283, 289, 294, 360, 372, 448, 465,
  499, 512, 524, 525, 574, 594, 617, 619,
  620, 654, 666, 669, 670, 671, 678, 679,
  680, 678, 714, 715, 733, 767, 794, 800,
  802, 803, 804
Tedeschi, J.T. 423
Telch, M. 747
Tellegen, A. 72, 109, 110, 163, 270
Tennen, H. 361
Tenney, Y.J. 212

ter Schure, E. 418, 419, 424, 641, 643, 649
Terr, L. 213, 222
Terrell, F. 622
Tesser, A. 580, 641
Tetlock, P.E. 3, 640, 643
Thelen, E. 685, 686, 692, 695
Thibaut, J.W. 576
Thoits, P.A. 508
Thomas, C. 803
Thomas, R.I.L. 201
Thomas, R.L. 714
Thomas-Knowles, C. 772
Thompson, C.P. 219, 220
Thompson, E. 683
Thompson, R.A. 104
Thompson, R.F. 748
Thomson, D.M. 219, 238, 751, 785
Thornton, J.C. 89
Thorpe, S. 107, 339, 451
Thorpe, S.J. 479
Thrasher, S.M. 288, 719
Thut, G. 107
Thynn, L. 292
Tipper, S.P. 243, 244, 255
Titcomb, A. 787, 788, 791
Toates, F. 286
Tobena, A. 291
Tobias, B.A. 194, 197, 199, 216, 218, 595
Toch, H. 6
Toglia, M. 784
Tollestrup, P.A. 76, 213
Tolman, E.C. 4, 267
Tomarken, A.J. 104, 109, 110, 111, 114, 455
Tomkins, S.S. 45, 55, 128, 305, 550, 687, 730, 739
Tooby, J. 46, 52, 337
Tooke, W.S. 551
Tota, M.E. 715
Trabasso, T. 46, 51, 56, 107, 384, 385, 386, 390, 391, 392, 393, 402, 416, 642, 689
Tranel, D. 249, 327
Traue, H.C. 246, 247
Treisman, A. 329
Trinder, H. 292
Tróccoli, T. 65
Troccoli, B.T. 601
Trumble, D. 753
Tsourtos, G. 482
Tucker, A. 536
Tucker, D.M. 692
Tucker, J. 641, 643, 651, 652

Tulving, E. 211, 219, 238, 594, 718, 751, 784, 785
Turk, D.C. 420, 656
Turken, A. 531, 536
Turner, S.M. 283
Turner, T.J. 45, 132, 649
Turovsky, J. 753
Turtle, J. 786
Turvey, C. 250
Turvey, M. 450
Tversky, A. 233, 270, 273, 275, 283, 534, 171
Tylor, E.B. 433
Tyrer, P. 355, 489

Ucros, C.G. 197
Uleman J.S. 281, 287
Ullmann, L.P. 359
Ulrich, B.D. 692, 695
Underwood, B. 787
Usher, J.A. 212

Valentine, E.R. 267
Valentine, J.D. 270
Vallaches, R.R. 685
Valsiner, J. 305
Van Aken, C. 204
van den Broeck, M.D. 459
van den Hout, M. 153, 161, 288, 292, 449, 450, 451, 454, 468, 469, 491, 719
Van der Heijden, A.H.C. 172
Van der Kolk, B.A. 222, 793
van der Maas, H.J.L. 697
van Geert, P. 375, 685, 692
van Gelder, T. 683, 685, 686
Van Oppen, P. 288, 449
van Reekum, C.M. 646, 653, 655
Van Sommers, P. 569, 571, 576, 585
Vancouver, J.B. 267
Vangelisti, A.L. 553
Varela, F.J. 683
Vargas, L.A. 506
Varner, L.J. 201, 202, 204
Vasey, M.W. 492, 801
Vaughn, C.E. 511
Vazquez, C. 195, 515
Veale, D. 287
Vella, D.D. 177
Velmans, M. 93, 94
Velten, E. 63, 64, 497
Venables, P.H. 97
Vermilyea, J.A. 758
Vincent, J. 524, 527
Volans, P.J. 447

Volanth, A.J.   596
von Hofsten, C.   14, 387, 390
von Neumann, J.   684
Vrana, S.R.   756
Vrendenburg, K.   69

Wachtel, P.   732, 733, 742
Waddell, B.A.   595
Wade, E.   384, 386
Wade, T.   482
Wagaman, J.   73
Wagenaar, W.A.   789, 790
Wagner, H.L.   73
Wagner, K.D.   621
Wagner, P.E.   546, 547, 548, 549, 550
Walker, C.   358
Wallas, G.   774
Wallbott, H.G.   54, 412, 413, 414, 430,
    542, 546, 553, 651
Wardle, J.   485
Ware, J.   439, 441
Warrington, E.K.   326
Watkins, T.   199, 595
Watson, D.   69, 72, 109, 110, 157, 159,
    163, 270, 355
Watson, J.B.   32, 33, 34
Watts, F.N.   149, 172, 195, 199, 231, 341,
    449, 459, 460, 484, 487, 490, 491, 595,
    654, 748, 803
Webb, K.   441
Weerts, T.C.   49
Wegern, M.A.   128
Wegner, D.M.   251, 286, 291, 292, 711,
    734
Wehrle, T.   645, 655
Weinberger, D.A.   49, 250, 325, 734
Weinberger, J.   730
Weiner, B.   3, 133, 134, 360, 619, 623,
    638, 641, 643
Weiner, I.   91
Weingartner, H.   196
Weinman, J.   147, 152, 160, 449, 459, 460
Weinstein, N.D.   621
Weisberg, R.W.   774
Weiskrantz, L.   326, 330, 792
Weiss, J.   549, 551
Weiss, P.A.   13
Weissman, A.   717
Weissman, M.M.   508, 615
Weisz, A.E.   271
Wells, A.   166, 171, 174, 180, 181, 183,
    184, 185, 186, 187, 286, 288, 290, 292,
    294, 480, 490, 491, 492, 756, 801

Wells, G.   784, 785, 786
Wessely, S.   359
Westen, D.   729, 730, 731, 732, 733, 737,
    739, 742, 803
Westerman, S.J.   176
Westling, B.E.   468, 481, 491
Wetzel, R.D.   235
Whalan, G.   459
Wheeler, R.E.   104, 111
Whiffen, V.E.   630
White, B.B.   556
White, G.L.   570, 572, 573, 574, 575, 577,
    578, 579, 580, 581
White, E.   525
White, J.   187
White, P.   594
White, P.A.   16, 65, 69, 199, 365
White, R.W.   4
White, S.H.   219
White, T.L.   110
Whitfield, C.L.   793
Whitten, W.B.   238
Wickens, C.D.   176
Wicker, F.W.   543, 546, 547
Wicklund R.A.   291
Wiest, C.   425
Wilhelm, S.   231, 257, 258
Willats, P.   388, 390
Williams, D.M.   236
Williams, J.L.   754
Williams, J.M.G.   63, 70, 76, 147, 148,
    149, 150, 151, 152, 153, 154, 159, 162,
    164, 173, 178, 205, 230, 231, 233, 234,
    235, 237, 248, 254, 269, 271, 272, 274,
    275, 276, 341, 342, 359, 360, 448, 449,
    460, 466, 467, 479, 484, 485, 489, 490,
    514, 597, 709, 712, 716, 721, 801, 802
Williams, L.M.   214, 252
Williams, R.M.   454
Williams, S.   717, 749, 757
Williamson, D.A.   151, 162
Wilner, N.   232
Wilson, A.   687, 691, 694, 696
Wilson, B.A.   231
Wilson, T.D.   345, 641
Wilson, W.R.   734
Wine, J.D.   176
Wing, L.   748
Winograd, E.   205
Winslow, J.T.   285
Winters, K.C.   357, 361, 370, 371, 373,
    511
Winton, E.   292, 455

Winton, M.   183
Wiseman, R.L.   557
Wittchen, H.   615
Wittgenstein   33, 34
Wixted, J.   784
Wood, B.   333
Wood, F.B.   116
Wood, J.   734
Woolf, V.   771, 772
Worth, L.T.   526, 535, 604
Wortman, C.B.   505
Wright, C.L.   754
Wright, J.C.   691
Wu, S.   412, 414, 418
Wurf, E.   362
Wysocki, J.   601
Wylie, R.C.   362

Xagoraris, A.   677

Yamada, Y.   434
Yamazaki, K.   552
Yee, B.   89
Yonellinas, A.P.   329, 330, 333, 334
Young, A.W.   367, 786
Young, B.   497
Young, C.E.   578

Young, M.J.   531, 532, 533, 535
Young, J.E.   289, 359
Yu, C.   784
Yufit, R.I.   271
Yuille, J.C.   76, 213, 789
Yule, W.   288, 719

Zacks, R.T.   515, 714
Zahn-Waxler, C.   134, 547, 549, 550, 552
Zajonc, R.B.   7, 8, 10, 12, 51, 125, 129,
    132, 203, 282, 326, 327, 419, 423, 645,
    646, 665, 734, 750
Zaragoza, M.   788
Zeitlin, S.B.   454
Zeller, A.   256
Zembar, M.J.   70, 714
Zeno of Citium   24
Zigler, E.   355, 356, 362, 372
Zillmann, D.   440, 441
Zimiles, H.   7, 12
Zinbarg, R.   139, 615, 753, 754
Zinberg, R   166
Zisook, S.   249, 507
Zoccolotti, P.   217
Zubin, J.   625
Zuckerman, M.   72
Zullow, H.M.   360

Subject Index

Abuse, 139, 214–15, 218, 221, 243, 247, 257, 629–30, 791–3, 803
Action tendency, 546, 649, 655
Activation, 199, 233, 244, 246, 254, 286, 293, 329, 338, 342, 344–5, 501–2, 591, 593, 596–7, 617, 666, 668, 684, 689, 752, 756, 767
Addiction, 522, 526, 535
Affect infusion, *see also* Affect Infusion Model, 598–602, 605–6
Affect Infusion Model (AIM), 592, 597–606
Affective chronometry, 106, 118
Affective decision mechanism (ADM), *see also* Interaction hypothesis, 148, 467
Affective style, *see also* Disposition, 103–4, 106, 109, 118
Agency, 395, 639–40, 643
Alexithymia, 249–250, 775
Ambiguity, 165, 177–8, 199, 528, 455–8, 465, 468, 481–2, 595–6
Ambiguous sentence task, *see* Ambiguity
Ambivalence, 440, 505, 511
Amnesia, 326, 790–1
Amphetamine, 89, 94–5
Amygdala, 108–9, 115, 117–18, 135–6, 163–4, 335, 338–9, 343, 387, 676–9, 733, 738
Analogical level, *see also* Multi-level theories, 673, 675
Analytic reduction, 13–14
Anger, 5–6, 23, 30, 36, 66, 243, 305, 308–9, 316, 318, 336, 369, 395–6, 398, 400–1, 403, Chapter 20, 525, 503–7, 516, 547, 550–1, 572, 577, 639, 696

behaviour, 424–5
Cognitive-Neoassociationist model of (CNA), 420–3
sources of, 420
Annoyance, 415–16, 418
Anorexia, *see also* Eating disorders, 510
Anthropology, 544, 651
Anticipation, *see* Judgement
Anticipatory behaviour, 387
Anxiety, *see also under specific disorders*, 85–8, 94, 97–99, Chapter 8, 175–80, 183–4, 195, 203, 230, 238, 250, 254–5, 257, 268–72, 274, 276–7, 341–2, 343–4, 346, 354–5, 362–3, 369, 503, 514, 548, Chapter 22, 571–2, 594–7, 614–18, 707–9, 711–13, 715, 719, 728, Chapter 35, 801
cognitive theories of, 616–18
epidemiology, 615
signal anxiety, 728
social anxiety, 343
state anxiety, *see also* Arousal; Mood induction, 145, 148–50, 154–9, 161, 452–4, 456–7
symptoms, 447, 615
trait anxiety, 146, 148–50, 154–61, 163–5, 452–4, 456–8, 471, 480, 492
Anxiety Sensitivity Index (ASI), 479–80
Appraisal, *see also* Evaluation, 9, 15, 37, 67, 71, 150, 163–5, 174, 181–2, 217, 334, 336, 344, 346, 383–4, 386, 390, 392–400, 402, 415–16, 418–25, 429, 498, 500, 505–7, 558, 572–4, 579–80, 585, 606, 665, 679, 686–9, 691, 799, 802
during anger, 415–16, 418–25

automatic, 51–53, 642
criteria, 638–9, 642–3
definition of, 647
deliberate, 51–53
mechanisms of, 648–9
role in pathology, 653–4
primary/secondary, 416, 572, 585, 637,
    686–7
reappraisal, 790
themes, 640
theories, Chapter 30, 803
    hypothesis testing, 644–5
Architecture, *see* Cognitive architecture
Arousal, 203–4, 205, 291, 293, 344, 485–7,
    580, 591, 751, 758, 769, 789–90
physiological, 31–33
theories, 203–4
Asperger's syndrome, 366
Assimilation, 294
Associationism, 737–9
Associative learning, 89, 767
Associative level, *see also* Multi-level
    theories, 502
Associative networks, *see also* Affect
    Infusion Model, 199–200, 220–2,
    230–1, 233, 422–3, Chapter 28, 666,
    732, 739–42, 803
fan effect, 597
problems with, 596–8
Attachment theory (Bowlby), 503–5
Attention, 104, 118, Chapter 9, 200–3, 205,
    213, 288–9, 291, 325–6, 329–30, 333,
    341–2, 367, 369, 387–8, 535, 447,
    465, 597, 789–90, 801–2
bias, *see* Bias
divided, 131, 135–9
inhibition of, 252–5
neuropsychology of, 95, 116–17
orienting, 157, 160–2
in schizophrenia, 88–9
selective, Chapter 8, 172, 177, 187, 243,
    329, 359–60, 467, 595
self focused, 176
to threat, 86
training, 187, 470–1, 801
Attitudes, 247, 253, 268, 317, 336, 358,
    511, 716, 731
Attitudes to Emotional Expression
    Questionnaire (AEQ), 248
Attribution theories, *see also* Learned
    helplessness, Chapter 29, 803
Attributional style, 134–5, 139, 361, 366–7,
    372–3, 620–1, 624, 629–31
Attributional style questionnaire (ASQ),

361, 365, 370
Attributions, 273, 275, 277, 343–5, 359–64,
    367–8, 370–4, 556, 638–40, 653
Autism, 366
Automatic processing, *see also*
    Preattentive processing;
    Unconscious processing, 97, 104,
    166, 174–5, 177–8, 182–3, 217, 276,
    286–9, 325–6, 332, 338, 340, 342,
    423, 500, 450–3, 458, 465, 471, 483,
    490–1, 617, 645, 647, 674, 696, 707–
    9, 714–15, 721–2, 776
in inhibition, *see* Inhibition
Availability, 220
Availability heuristic, *see also* Simulation
    heuristic, 233, 273–4, 277, 290
Avoidance, 148–9, 154–7, 159–61, 165,
    186, 232, 234, 237, 247, 251, 253,
    295, 335, 337, 341–2, 450, 453, 466,
    470–1, 480, 574, 740, 747–50, 753–6,
    759
Awareness thresholds, *see also*
    Consciousness, 152, 328–9, 330–3

Basal ganglia, 90, 95, 97, 107–8, 287, 439,
    802
Basic emotions, *see* Emotion
Beck Hopelessness Scale, 268
Behaviour, 36
action readiness, 424
in anger, 424–5
in disgust, 430
impulses, 424–5
peripheralist and centralist accounts, 36
in positive affect, 521
Behavioural Inhibition System (BIS), 85–
    87, 110–12, 270
comparator, 86–7, 89–90, 93–4, 96–8
Behaviourism, 4, 15, 27, 32–6, 39, 323–4
linguistic analysis, 34–5
and physics, 33
physiology of, 33
Beliefs, *see also* Spinoza, 23, 37, 41, 175,
    289, 358, 384–5, 396–401, 433, 479–
    80, 583–4, 666, 706, 716, 720–1, 729,
    749, 751–3, 757, 759–60, 766–7, 770,
    778
functions of, 399–400
in Epicurean philosophy, 25
Bereavement, 249, 284, 503, 505–7, 710,
    779
Bias, 270, 277, 282, 360–1, 366, 370, 373,
    448, 467–71, 501, 513–15, 489–91,
    585, 614, 617, 621–2, 632, 653–5,

670, 696, 706, 715, 717–20, 751, 786,
791–3, 801
attentional, 117, Chapter 8, 171–4, 176–
81, 184, 253–5, 287–8, 341–2, 367,
372, 516, 448–55, 470–1, 480, 483–6,
492, 712–13, 801
interoceptive, 480, 488–9
interpretative, 200, 455–8, 468, 480–3,
491, 710
judgemental, 269–72, 455
mnemonic, 360, 365, 458–64, 480, 486–8,
491, 713–16, 793
positive, 528–30
response, 332, 529, 456, 459, 483, 577,
786, 788
"Big Five" personality traits, 775
Binding problem, 92–3, 96
Bioinformational theory (Lang), 749–51
Bipolar affective disorder, *see also* Mania;
Psychoses, 354–7, 368, 779
Blame, 415–16, 423
Blindsight, 330
Blushing, 73
Bodily events, 30
Bodily feelings, 23, 481, 486, 488–90
Bodily sensations, *see* Bodily feelings
Brain stem, 748
Bulimia, *see* Eating disorders

Candle Problem (Dunker's), 531
Capacity, *see* Resources
Capgras delusion, 359–60, 367
Cartesianism, 25–32, 34–5
Catastrophic misinterpretation, 483, 490,
708, 751
Categories (of cognition and emotion), 13
Categorization, 521, 528–9, 533
Category mistakes, 34
Causal belonging hypothesis, 596
Causality, *see also* Design issues, 375, 467,
469–71, 514, 618, 623–5, 752
analytic, 16
reciprocal, 8, 688–9
synthetic, 16
Children, *see also* Emotions-at birth;
Development, 109, 137–9, 212–3,
219, 221–2, 237, 313–14, 366, 417,
433, 439, Chapter 19, 492, 504–5,
542, 547, 552, 558, 792
Church (the), 5, 27, 29
Class differences, 441
Cognition, 37, 39, 41
cognition–emotion debate, *see also*
Zajonc–Lazarus debate, 3–16

definition of, 10, 646, 765, 780
during positive affect, 521, Chapter 25
relation to emotion, 3–16, Chapter 7,
524, 591–3, 597, 605–6, 680, Part
IV, Chapter 38
relation to motivation, 3–6, 10–13, 16
Cognitions
prospective, Chapter 14
cued, 272, 274
over-general, 272
unconscious, *see also* Preattentive
processing, Chapter 17
Cognitive architecture, 173–4, 176, 179–
82, 187, 289
Cognitive impenetrability, 666–7, 674, 679
Cognitive initiative theory, 202–3
Cognitive interference, 200–1, 205
Cognitive Interview (CI), 788
Cognitive relativism, 650–3
Cognitive restructuring: historical
perspective, 6
Cognitive science, 37
Cognitive theories of emotion, *see*
Emotion theories
Cognitive therapy, *see also* Treatment,
exposure therapy, 84–5, 99, 146,
148, 153–4, 185–6, 229, 248, 451,
513, 628–9, 654, Chapter 33, 747,
80
Schema-Focused Cognitive Therapy,
289
Cognitive triad, 616
Cognitivism, 4–6, 41, 645, 654, 688
Comorbidity (of anxiety and depression),
69–70, 270, 355, 615
Comparator, *see* Behavioural Inhibition
System
Complex systems, *see also* Self-
organization, 688, 692–4
Component process theory (Scherer),
648–9
Computational approach, 684, 697, 801,
804
Computer analogies, 37, 655
Conatus, 29
Conceptual level, *see also* Multi-level
theories, 668–9
Conceptual processing, *see* Perceptual vs
conceptual processing
Conditioning, 89, 316, 323–5, 327, 339–40,
344, 593, 677, 733–4, 748, 753
classical (Pavlovian), 85, 88, 95–6, 344,
748, 754
Conflict, *see also* Psychoanalysis-

compromise formation, 401, 526, 729–30, 740, 774
origins in Greek philosophy, 5
Confounds, *see under* Design issues
Connectionism, 739, 741, 801
Connectionist networks, 95, 148, 174, 178, 180, 220, 243, 335, 345, 467, 683–4, 689
Consciousness, 28, 31–32, 83–5, 91–9, 281–2, 287, 292, Chapter 17, 800, 802
in anxiety, 87–8
and cognitive psychology, 84–5
criteria for, 328–9, 331–2
and emotion, 84–5, 97–9, Chapter 7
inhibition of, 246, Chapter 13
location of, 94–7
phenomenology of, 329–30
in schizophrenia, 91–2
Consideration of Future Consequences Scale, 268
Construct accessibility theory, 720–1
Constructivism, *see also* Social constructivism, 324, 787
Consumer preferences, 529–30, 606
Contagion, 433–4, 439
Contempt, 316, 418, 549
Content specificity, 152, 449, 451, 454, 484–6, 708–9
Control (perceptions of), 749–50, 752–9
Controlled processing, *see also* Consciousness, 174–80, 182–3, 202–3, 205, 213, 234, 281–2, 286–7, 291–2, 295, 325–6, 332, 514, 453, 458, 465–6, 490–1, 598–9, 645, 674
Conventionalization, 45
Conversion experiences, 770
Coping, *see also* Repressive coping style, 5, 181–4, 222, 282, 291–3, 342, 384, 504–7, 522, 526, 482, 573–4, 577, 579–80, 639, 653, 710, 732, 754–5, 757–8, 770
Core relational theme, *see also* Appraisal theories, 15, 53, 640, 647
Corpus callosum, 135
Correspondence metaphor, 794
Cortex, 676
association, 677
neocortex, 423
prefrontal, 107–19
visual, 327, 330
Cortisol, 114
Cotard delusion, 359, 367
Counterfactual thinking, 546
Courage, 758

Creativity, 530–1, Chapter 36
Crying, 385
Cultural issues, 49, 53–4, 301–14, 316–18, 412–14, 425, 499, 505, 508, 553, 557, 578–9, 650–3, 772–4
disgust, 430, 433, 437–8, 442
jealousy, 578–9
preliterate cultures, 308–10, 316
subcultural differences, 652

Death, 435, 441
Decision making, 521, 527–8, 530, 533, 535
Delusional disorder, 354, 358
Delusions, 353–6, 358–60, 362–3, 367–8, 581, 585
Dementia praecox, 354
Depression, 116, 139, 146–8, 150, 157, 162–3, 165, 175–6, 179, 181, 183, 195, 200–3, 205, 229–32, 234–8, 268–72, 274, 276–7, 290–1, 353–6, 360–4, 366–9, 371–2, 375, 497, 507–14, 525, 548, 572, 594, 595, 597, 613–32, 666, 669, 671, 687, 707–10, 712–19, 748, 751, 772, 779, 801–3
attributional theories, 618–28
cognitive theories, 616–18
depressive realism, 513, 515, 621–2, 629
epidemiology, 615
hopelessness depression, 618, 623, 625–8
postnatal depression, 510
symptoms, 614–15, 623
vulnerability to, 616, 620, 624–32
Design issues, 62–7, 74–7
behavioural high-risk design, 625
blocking, 485
causality, 67
confounds, 63–4, 75–6
demand, 64–6, 310, 456, 523
emotional control conditions, 74–6
ethics, 66
generalisability, 69, 104–6
specificity, 69–70
subject compliance hypothesis, 65
triangulation, 523
validity, 523–4
Desire, 37–8, 41
Determinism, 29
Development, 212, 234, 801, 804
of disgust, 439
of emotions, *see also* Emotions, at birth, 125–7, 131, 133, 136–7, 139, Chapter 19
of emotional understanding, Chapter 19

emergence, 386–91
emotion evoking events, 391–2
goal appraisals, 392–400
verbal, 388–91
wishes, 400–2
of personality, 694–7
of pride, 558–9
of self-conscious emotions, 542–3
self-organizational perspective, 692–7
of shame and guilt, 550–3
of vulnerability to depression, 629–31
Dichotic listening tasks, 151, 450, 483, 734
Directed forgetting task, *see* Forgetting
Disclosure, 251
Disgust, 108, 305, 308, 312, 315–16, 318,
Chapter 21, 503–4, 507, 509, 511–
13, 516, 549, 581, 802
animal-nature, 434–5
behaviour, 430
core disgust, 431–4, 437
development, 439
elicitors, 433–5
evolution of, 431–2, 436
interpersonal, 435
neurobiology, 439–40
physiology, 430
socio-moral, 436–7
of surfeit, 437
Display rules, *see* Facial expression
Disposition, *see also* Emotional traits, 38,
103, 110, 114
Dissociation, 130–1, 220, 223, 245, 248,
259–60, 332, 336, 344, 574, 665–6,
748, 752, 759
peri-traumatic, 249
Distaste, 432
Distortion, 513, 730, 787
Dopamine, 89, 95–6, 531, 536
hypothesis, *see* Psychoses
Dot probe task, 147, 151–2, 154, 158–62,
253, 341–2, 450, 452, 470–1, 486,
492
Drive, 5, 26, 27
Dualism, 22, 27, 31, 34, 36–7
Duchenne smile, *see* Smiling
Dynamic systems, *see also* Self-
organization, 685, 692, 694, 805
Dysfunctional Attitude Scale, 364, 511,
717
Dysphoria, 69, 157, 162, 470

Eating disorder, 548, 706, 802
Ecphoric similarity, 785
EEG measures, 50, 74, 116–17, 250, 315

Effort, *see* Resources
Ego psychology, 728–9
Elaboration, 236, 465–7, 528, 530, 595,
721, 790
Embarrassment, 137–9, 316, 541–4, 554–7,
803
functions of, 555–6
Embryological experiments, 13–14
EMG (electromyograph), 73–4, 113, 649
Emotion
antecedents of, 53–4
authenticity, 770, 772, 775, 777–9
basic emotions, 27, Chapter 3, 125, 132,
345–6, 383–4, 393, 396, 402, 403–4,
429, 437, 497–8, 500, 502–13, 672,
688–90, 693, 778, 802
common characteristics, 55–6
in ancient philosophy, 29
list of, 55
at birth, 54, 386–7, 402, 432, 513, 668
Cartesian view of, 29, 31
complex emotions, 46, 132–3, 437, 502–
3, Chapter 26, Chapter 27, 802
coupling, 502–4, 506–7, 512, 516
definition of, 10, 21, 35, 98, 128, 193,
689, 765–6
Epicureans view of, 25
evolutionary view, *see also* Evolution,
45–6, 48–9
families, 55
"hot" and "cold", 12, 327, 412–13, 666,
669, 739
independence from motivation and
cognition, 10–13
intense, 522
location of, 26, 128
measurement, 71–4
behavioural, 73
biological, 114
cognitive, 73
physiological, 73, 109–10, 112–13,
116–17
self-report, 113
neurobiology of, *see also under
individual emotions*, 676–80, 800
novelty of, 770, 772, 774, 777
philosophy of, *see* Philosophy
physiology of, *see also under*
Physiology, 48–51, 220, 390, 501
priming task, *see* Priming
re-experiencing, 71
regulation, *see* Mood regulation
relation to cognition and motivation, *see
also* Zajonc–Lazarus debate, 3–16

relation to cognition, *see* Cognition
self-conscious emotions, Chapter 7, 403,
    Chapter 26
specificity, 104
Stoics view of, 24–5, 799
time course of, 54
universal, 47–8, 413
Emotion theories, *see also* Attribution
    theories; Associative networks;
    Appraisal theories; Multi-level
    theories, 411
  Beck's cognitive theory, 146–7, 180, 200,
    268, 288, 464, 490, 512, 514, 616,
    622, 716
  Bower's Associative network theory,
    see also Associative networks, 146–
    7, 173, 199–200, 230, 422–3, 464,
    490, 514, 605, 617
  causal-evaluative, 21, 38
  Clark's cognitive theory of panic, 481
  cognitive, 30–1, 35, 38–42, 294, 336
  Cognitive-motivational view (Mogg &
    Bradley), 149, 160, 163–6
  Cognitive-transactional theory
    (Lazarus), 573
  history of, 22
  hypervigilance theory, 150, 291
  Interacting Cognitive Subsystems (ICS),
    283, 669–72, 677–80, 823
  of jealousy, 573–7
  Klinger's incentive-disengagement
    theory, 268
  neoassociationist model of anger, *see*
    Anger
  network theories, *see* Associative
    networks
  Oatley & Johnson Laird, 345–6, 437
  prototype models, 417–19
  Schematic Propositional Associative
    Analogical Representation Systems
    (SPAARS), 499–502, 506–7, 515,
    673–5, 803
  Self-Regulatory Executive Function
    (SREF), 171, 181–4, 187
  Williams et al., 148–9, 154–6, 159–60,
    164, 173, 465–7, 597
Emotional Creativity Inventory (ECI),
    774
Emotional events, 391–2
Emotional intelligence, 776–7
Emotional interpretation, *see under* Self-
    organization
Emotional IQ Test, 777
Emotional processing, 293–5

Emotional responses, 768–9
Emotional schemas, 767–8
Emotional states, *see also* Feelings;
    Anxiety-state; Mood states, 38, 375,
    553, 691, 750–1, 767–8, 779, 793,
    801
  antecedents, 67
  as dependent variable, 61–2, 66–7
  as independent variable, 61–6
  naturalistic, 67–8
  remembered, 70–1
Emotional syndromes, 766, 768
Emotional traits, *see also* Anxiety-trait,
    63, 68–70, 248–9, 253, 255, 375,
    546–7, 559, 574–5, 580–1, 653, 691,
    694, 696
Empathy, 137, 546–7, 551
Encoding Specificity Principle, 594, 785
Enjoyment, 49, 50
Enriched task, 529
Envy, *see also* Jealousy, 66, 569–70, 581–
    85, 803
Epicureans, 23–5
Epidemiology, 507
Epilepsy, 216
Estimator variables, 784–5, 794
Ethics, *see* Design issues
Evaluation, *see also* Appraisal, 9, 37, 38–
    41, 528
Evolution, 37, 48, 49, 53, 55, 99, 128, 150,
    159, 164, 166, 211, 216–17, 282, 314,
    316, 318, 337–9, 340–1, 344, 346,
    604, 685, 692, 778
  disgust, 431–2, 436
Exchange theories, 576–7
Expectancies, *see* Judgement
Experimental design, *see* Design issues
Experimenter demand, *see* Design issues
Expertise, 453, 454
Expressed Emotion (EE), 401, 511
Expression
  emotional, 47–8
  facial, *see* Facial expression
Extinction, 748–9, 752, 754
Eye movements, *see also* Gaze, 713
Eyewitness memory, 784–91
  event memory, 787–9
  identification, 784–6

Face processing, 359, 800
Face recognition, *see also* Eyewitness
    identification, 440, 785–6
Facial Action Coding System, 313
Facial expression, 47–8, 73, 125, 128–9,

156–8, Chapter 16, 338, 343, 422, 432, 649–50, 750
in children, 313–14
display rules, 312–13, 317–18
facial movements, 312–14
physiology of, 315
posed, 310–11
spontaneous, 311–14, 316
universality, Chapter 16
Facial muscles, 339, 430, 750
Facilitation, 217, 234, 525–6, 535, 500–1
Fan effect, see Associative networks
Fantasies, 325, 729, 775
Fear, see also Anxiety, 27, 28, 30, 50, 108, 130, 145, 293, 305, 308–10, 316, 335–41, 343–6, 395–6, 398, 400, 403, 413, 421, 441, 525, 639, 671, 676, 748, 751–6, 766
fight or flight, 421–2
Feedback loops, 501–2, 684–7, 689, 692
Feelings, see also Emotional states, 40, 55, 127–33, 214, 246–50, 257–9, 313, 317, 334–5, 336–7, 343, 414, 425, 418, 425, 669, 731, 733, 739–40, 759, 769, 777–8
Flashbulb memory, 67
Flexibility, 530–3
Forced choice tasks, 328–32, 339, 455
Forensic psychology, Chapter 37
Forgetting, 211, 243–4, 334, 787, 790
directed forgetting task, 244, 256–9
Fright, see Fear
Frontal lobes, 287, 343
Fusion
cognition and emotion, 10–13
thought–action, 289
Fuzzy trace theory, 787–8

GABA, 95–6, 117
Gaze, see also Eye movements, 157–8, 162
Gaze aversion, 73
Gender differences, 441, 508
Generalised Anxiety Disorder (GAD), 146–7, 150–4, 158, 162, 180, 251, 254, 283–6, 289–90, 295, 449–51, 454–6, 458–63, 467–8, 481, 492, 615, 719, 747, 750
Genetic factors, 552
Germ theory of disease, 15
Goals, 4–5, 8, 9, 12, 46, 107–8, 145, 149, 163–5, 173–6, 179–85, 187, 267, 336, 345–6, 383–6, 388, 390–7, 400–2, 416–17, 419, 424–5, 536, 498–500, 505, 507–10, 515–16, 555, 558–9,

601–3, 639–40, 650, 653, 674, 689, 739–40
Gratitude, 336
Gray's Neuropsychological Theory, Chapter 5, 110–12
anxiety, 85–8, 173
schizophrenia, 88–91
Grief, 779
Guilt, 133–4, 139, 511, 541–53, 556, 652, 729, 734, 752, 803
Guilt induction, 553

Habituation, 285, 291, 293, 387, 711–12, 748–9, 751–2, 754, 760
Hallucinations, 354
Happiness, see also Positive affect, 201–2, 205, 305, 308–9, 316, 336, 394–8, 400, 403, 498, 503, 510, 513, 668
Hate, 55, 336
in ancient philosophy, 30
Hellenistic Buddhism, 25
Hellenistic period, 23
Hemispheric asymmetry, 107–19, 158, 216, 315, 487, 631–2
Hindu caste system, 436
Hippocampus, 86–7, 89–91, 97–8, 135, 164, 222, 344, 423, 677, 733
Holistism, 13–16
Homographs, see Ambiguity
Hope, 37, 336
Hope Scale, 268
Hopelessness, see also under Depression, 234–6, 239, 268, 271, 507
Hubris, 559, 738
Humour, see Laughter
Huntington's Disease, 439
Hyperfrontality, 285
Hypervigilance Theory, see Emotion theories
Hypnosis, 323
Hypomania, see also Mania, 779
Hypothalamus, 86, 108, 339, 738
Hysteria, 322–3

Imagery, 237–8, 294, 788, 792–3
Imaging, 74, 106–8, 110, 116–19, 287, 800, 804
Immune system, 249
Implicational code, see also Multi-level theories, 669–70
In vitro, 13–14
In vivo, 13–14, 218
Individual differences, 103–6, 108–14, 117–18, 245, 273, 317–18, 386, 425,

440–1, 468–9, 487, 551–3, 557, 559–
   60, 580–1, 601, 603, 619–20, 624–5,
   653–5, 694, 774–6, 785, 792, 795
Industrial psychology, 777
Infants, 33
Information processing, 84–7, 90, 94, 97,
   145–6, 150, 152, 187, 230, 325, 335,
   338, 357, 359–60, 369, 448, 468,
   470–1, 479–80, 490, 598–9, 601–2,
   604, 647, 669–71, 706, 801
Inhibition, 109, 115–18, 211, 214, 217, 222,
   234–6, Chapter 13, 287, 316, 500–2,
   507, 447, 453, 711–12, 734, 756, 802
   automatic, 245–7, 249–57, 258–60
   controlled, 245–51, 258–9
   of feelings, 245–50, 257–61
   of information, 245–7, 250–61
   strong theory, 244–5, 248, 253, 256,
      257–9
   weak theory, 244–5, 248, 253, 255–8
Insight, 732–3, 758, 760
Insomnia, 285
Integration, see also Emotion theories,
   Williams et al., 465–7
Intellect, 34
Interacting Cognitive Subsystems (ICS),
   see Emotion theories
Interaction hypothesis, see Emotion
   theories, Williams et al.
Interdependence
   neurophysiological, 14
   of cognition and emotion, 10–13
Internal representation, see
   Representation
Internal, Personal and Situational
   Attributions Questionnaire
   (IPASQ), 365, 374
International Affective Picture System
   (IAPS), see Materials
Interoception, see Bias
Interpersonal relationships, 569–81, 584–5,
   692, 729–30, 779, 792
Interpretation, see also Bias, 465, 595, 708
Interviewing, 788–9
Intrapsychic censorship, 131
Introspection, 32, 35, 288, 322–3, 329–30,
   479–80, 585, 776
Intrusive thoughts, 186, 205, 213, 232,
   237–8, 251, Chapter 15, 486, 711–
   12, 802
Irritation, 418

Jealousy, 30, 569–81, 584–5, 803
   cross cultural issues, 578–9

pathological, 581
   theories of, 573–7
   types of, 571, 585
Joy, 107, 525
Judgement, see also Bias, 37, 515, 785–6,
   802
   anticipation, 272, 274
   expectancies, 270, 272, 275, 277, 340
   of facial expressions, 303–9, 311–12,
      316–17
   subjective probability, 269–72, 273–4,
      276, 534

Kamin blocking effect, 89
Kinesics, 303
Knowledge, 217, 219, 288, 384, 389–90,
   394, 402–3, 416–17, 602, 717, 765,
   767, 780
   autobiographical, 233
   situationally accessible, 217
   verbally accessible, 217
Korsakoff's syndrome, 216, 673, 733

Language, 317, 337, 369, 389, 431, 436,
   772–3
Latent Inhibition, 88–9, 94–6, 95–6
Lateralization, see Hemipsheric
   asymmetry
Laughter, 385, 440
Learned helplessness, 360–1, 510, 512,
   614, 618–19, 629
   hopelessness version, 268, 361, 365,
      622–9
   treatment implications, 628–9
   reformulated, 619–22
Lexical decision task, 177–8, 230, 327, 457
Libido, 30
Life events, 284, 469, 617, 623, 626, 792
Life Orientation Test, 268
Likert scales, 72
Limbic system, 646, 692
Logical behaviourism, 33
Logical positivism, see Positivism
Love, 30, 32, 55, 336, 574–5, 578, 580, 766,
   773

Mania, see also Psychoses, 511, 516, 522,
   535, 779
Manic defence hypothesis, 368–9, 371, 511
Manic depression, see Bipolar affective
   disorder
Manipulation checks, 62–4
Masking, 151–5, 158, 162, 178, 254, 312–
   13, 316, 327, 329, 339–42, 450–3,

468–9, 471

Materialism, 29

Materials, 75, 105, 113, 197, 219
   International Affective Picture System
     (IAPS), 160
   materials effects, 75

Meaning, 15

Means-Ends Problem Solving Task, 235

Measurement, *see* Emotion

Medication, neuroleptic, 89

Memory, *see also* Eyewitness memory,
     Chapters 10 and 11, 293–4, 326,
     333–4, 344, 367, 369, 386, 388,
     524–5, 527–8, 531, 447, 448, 593–7,
     602, 668–73, 767, 783–94, 801
   and judgement, 273–5
   autobiographical, 76, 195, 197, 216, 219,
     Chapter 12, 255, 257–8, 272, 274,
     277, 363, 458, 709, 793
   bias, *see* Bias
   episodic, 219
   explicit, 147, 205, 212, 222–3, 334, 460–
     4, 466, 488, 514
   implantation, *see also* Memory-
     recovered, 787
   implicit, 199, 205, 213, 216, 223, 326,
     334, 460–6, 488, 514, 594–5
   inhibition of, 255–7
   multiple-entry memory (MEM), *see also*
     Multi-level theories, 466, 671–3
   over-general, 231–6, 274, 709
   recovered, 252, 791–4, 802
   shared, 221
   state dependent, *see* Mood dependent
     memory
   tunnel, 213–14

Mental codes, *see* Interacting Cognitive
     Subsystems

Mental load, 251

Mere exposure effect, 327, 734

Metatheory, 10, 13, 15, 317

Mind, in Greek philosophy, 23–4, 28

Mnemonic interlock, 236

Mobius syndrome, 47

Modularity, 172, 500
   of brain function, 135–6

Monism, 29

Mood, Chapter 10
   congruence, 65, 146–7, 177, 231, 592,
     594–5, 597–9, 602–6, 719
   congruent memory, 193–6, 290, 594–5
   congruent retrieval, *see* Mood
     congruent memory
   dependent memory, 193–4, 196–8, 594,

596
   diurnal variation, 230
   effect on judgement, 276–7
   incongruence, 65, 195–6, 230, 502, 515,
     603
   induction, *see also* Stressors; Arousal,
     62–7, 194, 197, 229, 311, 497, 502,
     523–4, 585, 593, 596–7, 714, 756
     validity of, 523–4
   mood state dependent retrieval, *see also*
     Mood-dependent memory
   regulation, 104, 117, 165, 734–5, 739–42,
     777–9
   repair, 258, 601, 603–4, 777
   states, 198, 592, 594, 714–15, 722

Morality, 438–9
   Three Ethics of Morality theory, 437–8

Morbid jealousy, *see* Jealousy

Motivation, 202, 205, 270, 324, 521, 526,
     534–5, 555, 601, 603–4, 606, 728–9,
     739–42, 752, 755
   in ancient philosophy, 29
   relation to cognition and emotion, 4, 6,
     8, 9, 10, 16

Motivational theory, 202

Motives, *see also* Motivation, 40, 791

Multi-level theories, *see also under*
     Emotion theories, 171, 181, 500–2,
     646–7, 654, Chapter 31, 733, 794,
     800, 803
   Brewin, 667
   evaluation of, 675
   Perceptual Motor Processing model
     (Leventhal), 667–9

Multiple personality disorder, 213

Multiple-entry memory (MEM), *see*
     Memory

Myths, 766

Naturalistic approaches, 76–7, 197, 254,
     258, 342–3, 453, 596, 735, 800

Nausea, 432

Negative affect, 108–10, 114, 117–18, 157,
     173, 230, 270–1, 311, 421–2, 424,
     524–5, 557, 775

Negative priming, 244, 254–5

Neural networks, *see* Connectionist
     networks

Neural pathways, 90, 95–7
   auditory, 340
   fronto-striatal, 285
   monoaminergic, 86
   nigrostriatal, 89

Neuroimaging, *see* Imaging

Neuropsychological models, 83
Neuroticism, 183, 557, 580, 585
Nostalgia, 498, 503
Novelty, *see also* Task familiarity, 387–8, 673
Nucleus accumbens, 89–92, 95–7, 107–8
Nucleus reticularis thalami (NRT), *see* Thalamus

Object relations theories, 729–30
Obsessive-Compulsive Disorders (OCD), 153, 181, 231, 257, 283–92, 295, 439–40, 449–51, 468, 747, 751–2, 802
Odors, 218, 435
Overvalued ideation, 751
Ownership, 133

Pain, 420, 646, 731
  in ancient philosophy, 30
Panic, 181, 184, 344, 369, 449, 459–62, 468, Chapter 23, 706, 708, 747, 753
Parallel Distributed Processing (PDP), *see* Connectionist models
Paranoia, *see* Psychoses
Parasuicide, *see also* Suicide, 231, 235–6, 271–2, 276
Parkinson's disease, 531
Penn State Worry Questionnaire (PSWQ), 268–9
Perception, 4, 329–30
  in ancient philosophy, 28
Perceptual defence, 252–3, 324
Perceptual vs conceptual processing, 463, 488
Perfectionism, 179, 364, 720–1
Personality disorders, 720, 730, 733
Philosophy
  ancient, Chapters 1 and 2
  emotion, 4–5, 22–9
  of meta-emotion, 317
Phobias, 150, 161, 254, 339, 342, 345, 441, 458, 468, Chapter 23, 737, 747–8, 750, 754–5, 757, 802
  agoraphobia, 345, 459, 480–3, 485, 489
  social phobia, 153, 185–6, 254, 363, 449, 451, 453, 459–60, 480–1, 483–7, 491, 747, 756
  spider phobia, 153, 173, 339, 451, 460, 484, 487, 491
Physics and psychology, 33
Physiology, *see also under* Emotion; Emotional states, 38, 250, 259, 250, 259, 291, 293–4, 315, 327, 335, 337,

339, 343, 363, 649–50, 655, 748, 756, 758
  of anger, 411–14
  of disgust, 430
Pineal gland, 28
Planning fallacy, 275
Plans, *see also* Emotion theories, Self-Regulatory Executive Function, 267, 278, 343, 346, 346, 384–8, 390, 397, 400–2, 505, 507, 683, 685
Platonic Form, 26
Pleasure, 731
  in ancient philosophy, 30
  principle, 323
Pons, 339
Popout tasks, 158
Positive affect, 107–10, 112, 118, 230, 270–1, Chapter 25, 779
  and cognition, 525–7
  memory, 524, 527–8, 531
  mild, 522–3, 536
Positivism, 33, 34
Post-traumatic stress disorder (PTSD), 139, 183, 231–2, 234, 250–1, 283–6, 288–9, 293, 295, 344, 449, 454, 462, 709, 747, 752, 775
Posture, 422
Pragmatic Inference Task, 361, 370
Preattentive processing, *see also* Automatic processing, 147–8, 150–6, 158, 160–3, 165–6, 173, 177, 215, 514
Preconscious processing, *see* Preattentive processing
Pride, 133–4, 139, 336, 541–4, 557–60, 740, 803
Primates, 54, 114, 129, 302, 314–15, 550, 555
Priming, 177, 199, 201, 204–5, 258, 327, 331–2, 336, 457–8, 464, 485, 488, 529, 595–8, 601–6, 617, 646, 734
Problem solving, 235–6, 337, 390, 521–2, 526, 528, 531–3, 535, 709–10, 716, 770, 779–80
Processing efficiency, 713
Production systems, 592
Propositional level, *see also* Multi-level theories, 669–70, 672–3, 675, 767
Propositions, 500–2, 640, 666
Prosopagnosia, 327, 733, 786
Prototype models of emotion, *see* Emotion theories
Psyche, 22
Psychoanalysis, *see also* Psychotherapy;

Treatment, 4, 133, 247, 325, 356–7, 431, 435, 437, 511, 620, Chapter 34
  classical, 729
  compromise formation, 729
  relation to cognition and emotion, 728–30
Psychobiological principle, 51
Psychogenic amnesia, 211, 213–14, 220, 222, 245–7, 252
Psychogenic fugue, 213, 245
Psychomotor retardation, 73
Psychopath, 214, 249
Psychoses, Chapter 18
  mania, 353–8, 368–74
  paranoia, 353, 355–67, 372–4
  schizo-affective disorder, 354
  schizophrenia, 83, 88–91, 94, 97, 231–2, 287, 354–5, 358, 511, 581
    dopamine hypothesis, 89–90
  symptoms, 88, 91, 95, 97–8, 354
Psychotherapy, *see also* Psychoanalysis; Cognitive therapy; Treatment, 229, 252, 282, 290, 551, 705–6, 803
Punishment, 575

Qualia, 84, 430

Rashomon effect, 513
Ratings, 219, 260, 329
Reasoning, inductive, 447
Rebound effect, 292
Recovered memories, *see* Memory-recovered
Reduction, *see* Analytic reduction
Reduction of emotions, 27
Reflexes, 386–7
Relativism, *see* Cognitive relativism
Remote Associates Test (Mednicks'), 531
Representations, 244, 254–5, 294, 330, 387, 465–6, 501, 593, 666, 675, 729–31, 737–9, 749, 751–2, 767, 770, 800
  of anger, 411–15, 417
  dual, 216–17
  interconnected, 217–20
  of self, *see also* Self concept, 359, 362–5, 371–3, 375
Repression, *see also* Repressive coping style, 131, 221, 229, 245, 247–8, 250, 252–3, 256–60, 322, 334, 342, 435
  return of the repressed, 255–6
Repressive coping style, 249–50, 734
Repressors, 450, 502
Research methods, Chapter 4
Resentment, 416

Resource allocation mechanism (RAM), *see also* Interaction hypothesis, 148
Resource allocation model (Ellis & Ashbrook), 200–1, 237, 714
Resources, 172, 175–7, 180, 184, 200–3, 205, 235–7, 254–5, 287, 325–6, 346, 367, 447–8, 490–1, 515, 526, 535, 601–4, 653, 713–14, 758
Response bias, *see* Bias
Retrieval, mood congruent, *see* Mood congruent memory
Retrieval induced inhibition, 244, 256
Retroactive interference, 786–7
Reward, 575–6
Risk, 521, 530, 534, 751, 779
Ritualization, 46, 290
Rumination, 237, 276, 283, 285, 287–8, 466, 549, 709–12

Sadness, 31, 305, 308, 312, 316, 336, 395–6, 398, 400–1, 403, Chapter 24, 524–5, 639, 773
  definition of, 498
  function of, 499
Safety behaviours, 756
Schadenfreude, 317
Schemata, 146, 174, 200, 205, 217, 221, 260, 276, 288–90, 293, 363, 413, 422, 500–2, 613, 616, 622, 668, 696, 716, 720–2, 729, 738
Schematic level, *see also* Multi-level theories, 668–70, 673, 675
Schizo-affective disorder, *see* Psychoses
Schizophrenia, *see* Psychoses
Scientific method, 27
Self concept, Chapter 7, 212–13, 222, 330, 334, 353, 356, 362–5, 367, 371–4, 507, 511–13, 515, 542, 582, 624, 693, 696, 718, 721, 737–8, 802
Self-conscious Affect and Attribution Inventory (SCAAI), 559
Self-discrepancy theory, 362, 371
Self efficacy theory (Bandura), 749, 757–9
Self-organization, Chapter 32
Self referent encoding task (SRET), *see* Self referent processing
Self referent processing, 195, 230, 258, 260, 269, 288, 291, 361, 364–5, 371, 514–15, 632, 718–19
Self-Regulatory Executive Function (SREF), *see* Emotion theories
Self report, 72, 248, 268–9, 315, 345, 514, 523–4, 468, 479–81, 641
Self-scenarios, 717–18

Serotonin, 173
Shadowing task, 333
Shame, 133–4, 139, 511, 541–53, 556, 579, 652, 803
   functions of, 550–1
Signal detection, 461, 488
Simulation heuristic, 273, 277
Situated actions, 15
Skill theory (Anderson's), 182
Skin conductance response (SCR), 327, 329, 333, 339–40
Smiling, 303, 315
   Duchenne smile, 303, 315
Social constructionism, 45–6, 49, 412–13, 415, 772
Social desirability, 250, 342, 371, 577
Social interaction, *see also* Interpersonal relationships, 526–7, 532, 543–4, 550, 733
Social learning, 52, 53
Social referencing, 558
Social rules, 766–7, 770
Somatic marker hypothesis, 283, 343
Soul, 28
Specificity (of memories), 231–3, 234–6, 238
Spinoza, 30
Spreading activation, *see* Activation
SRGs (standards, rules and goals), 133–4
Stance, 12
Startle, 113, 117, 336, 339, 385
Stimuli, *see also* Materials
   biologically prepared, 338, 344
Stoics, 23–5
Strange Situation Test, 505
Strategic processing, *see* Controlled processing
Stress, *see also* Stressors
   transactional model, 180–1
Stressors, *see also* Mood induction, 154–6, 172, 200, 255–6, 284, 453, 455, 468–70, 756, 775
Stroop task, 146–8, 151–5, 162, 174, 177–9, 184, 253, 287, 327, 332, 341, 359–60, 364, 369, 449, 458, 484–5, 491–2, 712, 719–20, 801
Subception, 324
Subject compliance hypothesis, *see* Design issues
Subjective probabilities, *see* Judgement
Subliminal processing, *see* Preattentive processing
Suggestibility, 787–9, 793
Suicide, *see also* Parasuicide, 234–8, 271,

274, 709
Suppression, *see* Inhibition; Repression
Surprise, 49, 50, 127, 302, 305, 308, 310, 316
Synthesis, 13, 16
Synthetic apperception, 648
System variables, 784, 794

Task complexity, 602–3, 713
Task demand, 179
Task familiarity, 602
Task performance, 172, 176, 181, 256, 447, 448, 593–4, 713–14
Taste aversion, 674
Teleology, 267
Temperament, *see* Disposition
Test of Self-conscious Affect (TOSCA), 559
Thalamus, 86, 163, 330, 338, 340, 387, 677, 692
   nucleus reticularis thalami (NRT), 95–6
Thematic Apperception Test, 595, 733
Theology, Christian, 26
Theory of Mind, 365–7
Therapy, *see* Treatment; Psychotherapy; Cognitive therapy
Thought monitoring, 709, 715
Thought sampling, 275
Thought suppression, 251, 259, 291–3
Threat monitoring, *see* Emotion theories, Self-Regulatory Executive Function (SREF)
Threat superiority effect, 158
Threat value, 159–60, 165
Tip of the tongue phenomenon, 218
Trait, *see* Emotional traits
Trait Meta-Mood Scale, 777
Transference, 357, 741–2
Trauma, 211, 214, 216–17, 220–2, 229, 232, 238, 248–52, 259, 283–6, 289, 294–5, 711, 776, 790–1, 793, 800
Treatment, *see also* Cognitive therapy; Psychoanalysis; Psychotherapy, 153–4, 175, 184–7, 222, 229, 232, 238, 229, 239, 452, 454, 467–71, 482, 491, 551, 614, 628, 666, 801
   activity scheduling, 711, 715
   consequential analysis, 716
   cost–benefit analysis, 716, 721
   exposure therapy, 246, 732, 737, Chapter 35
   graded task assignment, 711
   rule breaking, 720
   systematic desensitization, 748

Tripartite model
Twin studies, 552
Two-factor theory, 5

Unconscious processing, *see also*
     Preattentive processing, Chapter
     17, 730, 733–4, 740–1
  criteria for, 328–9, 331–2
  fear, 339–41
  history of, 321–8
Unintended thoughts, *see* Intrusive
     thoughts
Universal signal, *see* Emotion-universal
Universalism, *see also* Facial expression,
     650

Validity-ecological, 76
Values, 766
Velten Mood Induction Procedure, *see
     also* Mood induction, 63, 65
Verbal fluency paradigm, 271–2, 274
Verbal rehearsal, 784–5
Virtual reality, 15

Visual cortex, *see* Cortex
Vulnerability, *see also under* Depression,
     103, 106, 108, 112, 147–8, 150–1,
     154, 156, 164–5, 284, 357, 366, 375,
     448, 451–2, 455, 458, 461, 464–71,
     492, 505, 508–9, 511, 514, 516, 548–
     9, 616, 620, 624–32
  biological, 631–2

White noise, *see* Signal detection
Wisconsin Card Sorting Task, 531
Word stem completion task, 326, 460–3,
     488
Worry, *see also* Anxiety, 283, 285, 290,
     294, 447, 467, 711–12, 756

Zajonc–Lazarus debate, 7–10
  consciousness, 10
  contributors to, 7
  independence of cognition, emotion
     and motivation, 10–13
  primacy, 8, 203–4, 282, 326, 645–7, 665
  relation to neural processes, 9